T0331690

Applied Natural Language Processing:

Identification, Investigation, and Resolution

Philip M. McCarthy
The University of Memphis, USA

Chutima Boonthum–Denecke
Hampton University, USA

Managing Director:	Lindsay Johnston
Senior Editorial Director:	Heather Probst
Book Production Manager:	Sean Woznicki
Development Manager:	Joel Gamon
Development Editor:	Joel Gamon
Acquisitions Editor:	Erika Gallagher
Typesetter:	Christopher Shearer
Print Coordinator:	Jamie Snavely
Cover Design:	Nick Newcomer, Greg Snader

Published in the United States of America by
Information Science Reference (an imprint of IGI Global)
701 E. Chocolate Avenue
Hershey PA 17033
Tel: 717-533-8845
Fax: 717-533-8661
E-mail: cust@igi-global.com
Web site: http://www.igi-global.com

Library of Congress Cataloging-in-Publication Data

Applied natural language processing: identification, investigation, and resolution / Philip M. McCarthy and Chutima Boonthum-Denecke, editors.
    p. cm.
  Includes bibliographical references and index.
  Summary: "This book offers a description of ANLP: what it is, what it does; and where it's going, including defining the role of ANLP within NLP, and alongside other disciplines such as linguistics, computer science, and cognitive science"-- Provided by publisher.
  ISBN 978-1-60960-741-8 (hardcover) -- ISBN 978-1-60960-742-5 (ebook) -- ISBN 978-1-60960-743-2 (print & perpetual access) 1. Natural language processing (Computer science) I. McCarthy, Philip M., 1967- II. Boonthum-Denecke, Chutima, 1976-
  QA76.9.N38A68 2012
  006.3'5--dc23
                                2011031141

British Cataloguing in Publication Data
A Cataloguing in Publication record for this book is available from the British Library.

All work contributed to this book is new, previously-unpublished material. The views expressed in this book are those of the authors, but not necessarily of the publisher.

Editorial Advisory Board

Table of Contents

Section 1
Foundations: The Role of NLP

Chapter 1
Arthur C. Graesser, The University of Memphis, USA
Vasile Rus, The University of Memphis, USA
Zhiqiang Cai, The University of Memphis, USA
Xiangen Hu, The University of Memphis, USA

Chapter 2
Martin Hassel, Stockholm University, Sweden
Hercules Dalianis, Stockholm University, Sweden

Chapter 3
Alexandra Kent, Loughborough University, UK
Philip M. McCarthy, The University of Memphis, USA & Decooda.com

Chapter 4
Christian F. Hempelmann, Purdue University, USA

Section 3
New Research in ANLP

Danielle S. McNamara, Arizona State University, USA
Roxanne Raine, The University of Memphis, USA
Rod Roscoe, Arizona State University, USA
Scott A. Crossley, Georgia State University, USA
G. Tanner Jackson, Arizona State University, USA
Jianmin Dai, Arizona State University, USA
Zhiqiang Cai, The University of Memphis, USA
Adam Renner, The University of Memphis, USA
Russell Brandon, Arizona State University, USA
Jennifer Weston, Arizona State University, USA
Kyle Dempsey, Mississippi University for Women, USA
Diana Carney, The University of Memphis, USA
Susan Sullivan, The University of Memphis, USA
Loel Kim, The University of Memphis, USA
Vasile Rus, The University of Memphis, USA
Randy Floyd, The University of Memphis, USA
Philip M. McCarthy, The University of Memphis, USA & Decooda.com
Arthur C. Graesser, The University of Memphis, USA

Philip M. McCarthy, The University of Memphis, USA & Decooda.com
Shinobu Watanabe, The University of Memphis, USA
Travis A. Lamkin, The University of Memphis, USA

Bryan Rink, University of Texas at Dallas, USA
Cosmin Adrian Bejan, University of Southern California, USA
Sanda Harabagiu, University of Texas at Dallas, USA

Detailed Table of Contents

Section 1
Foundations: The Role of NLP

Chapter 1

Arthur C. Graesser, The University of Memphis, USA
Vasile Rus, The University of Memphis, USA
Zhiqiang Cai, The University of Memphis, USA
Xiangen Hu, The University of Memphis, USA

Automated Question Answering and Asking are two active areas of Natural Language Processing with the former dominating the past decade and the latter most likely to dominate the next one. Due to the vast amounts of information available electronically in the Internet era, automated Question Answering is needed to fulfill information needs in an efficient and effective manner. Automated Question Answering is the task of providing answers automatically to questions asked in natural language. Typically, the answers are retrieved from large collections of documents. While answering any question is difficult, successful automated solutions to answer some type of questions, so-called factoid questions, have been developed recently, culminating with the just announced Watson Question Answering system developed by I.B.M. to compete in Jeopardy-like games. The flip process, automated Question Asking or Generation, is about generating questions from some form of input such as a text, meaning representation, or database. Question Asking/Generation is an important component in the full gamut of learning technologies, from conventional computer-based training to tutoring systems. Advances in Question Asking/Generation are projected to revolutionize learning and dialogue systems. This chapter presents an overview of recent developments in Question Answering and Generation starting with the landscape of questions that people ask.

Chapter 2

Martin Hassel, Stockholm University, Sweden

Hercules Dalianis, Stockholm University, Sweden

Today, with digitally stored information available in abundance, even for many minor languages, this information must by some means be filtered and extracted in order to avoid drowning in it. Automatic summarization is one such technique, where a computer summarizes a longer text to a shorter non-redundant form. The development of advanced summarization systems also for smaller languages may unfortunately prove too costly. Nevertheless, there will still be a need for summarization tools for these languages in order to curb the immense flow of digital information. This chapter sets the focus on automatic summarization of text using as few direct human resources as possible, resulting in what can be perceived as an intermediary system. Furthermore, it presents the notion of taking a holistic view of the generation of summaries.

Chapter 3

Alexandra Kent, Loughborough University, UK

Philip M. McCarthy, The University of Memphis, USA & Decooda.com

The goal of this chapter is to outline a (primarily) qualitative and (secondarily) quantitative approach to the analysis of discourse. Discourse Analysis thrives on the variation and inconsistencies in our everyday language. Rather than focusing on *what* is said and seeking to reduce and homogenise accounts to find a central meaning, discourse analysis is interested in the consequences of "saying it that particular way at that particular time." Put another way, it is interested in "what was said that didn't have to be, and why?" and "what wasn't said that could have been, and why not?" The chapter outlines the basic theoretical assumptions that underpin the many different methodological approaches within Discourse Analysis. It then considers these approaches in terms of the major themes of their research, the ongoing and future directions for study, and the scope of contribution to scientific knowledge that discourse analytic research can make. At the beginning and end of the chapter, we attempt to outline a role for Applied Natural Language Processing (ANLP) in Discourse Analysis. We discuss possible reasons for a lack of computational tools and techniques in traditional Discourse Analysis but we also offer suggestions as to the application of computational resources so that researchers in both disciplines might have an avenue of interest that assists their work, without directing it.

Chapter 4

Christian F. Hempelmann, RiverGlass Inc., USA & Purdue University, USA

This chapter presents an account of key NLP issues in search, sketches current solutions, and then outlines in detail an approach for deep-meaning representation, ontological semantic technology (OST), for a specific, complex NLP application: a meaning-based search engine. The aim is to provide a general overview on NLP and search, ignoring non-NLP issues and solutions, and to show how OST, as an example of a semantic approach, is implemented for search. OST parses natural language text and transposes it into a representation of its meaning, structured around events and their participants as mentioned in the text and as known from the OST resources. Queries can then be matched to this meaning representation in anticipation of any of the permutations in which they can surface in text. These permutations centrally include overspecification (e.g., not listing all synonyms, which non-semantic search engines require their users to do) and, more importantly, underspecification (as language does in principle). For the latter case, ambiguity can only be reduced by giving the search engine what humans use for disambiguation, namely knowledge of the world as represented in an ontology.

Data Mining provides approaches for the identification and discovery of non-trivial patterns and models hidden in large collections of data. In the applied natural language processing domain, data mining usually requires preprocessed data that has been extracted from textual documents. Additionally, this data is often integrated with other data sources. This chapter provides an overview on data mining focusing on approaches for pattern mining, cluster analysis, and predictive model construction. For those, we discuss exemplary techniques that are especially useful in the applied natural language processing context. Additionally, we describe how the presented data mining approaches are connected to text mining, text classification, and clustering, and discuss interesting problems and future research directions.

This chapter discusses historical and recent work in dialogue act tagging and dialogue structure inference. Dialogue act tagging is a classification task in which utterances in dialogue are marked with the intentions of the speaker. It is possible to classify utterances using only features relating to the utterance itself (for example, words and prosodic features), but much work has also utilized dialogue-level features such as previous speaker and previous dialogue acts. The structure of dialogue can be represented by dialogue grammar, segmentation, or with a hierarchical structure.

Assessing the semantic similarity between two texts is a central task in many applications, including summarization, intelligent tutoring systems, and software testing. Similarity of texts is typically explored at the level of word, sentence, paragraph, and document. The similarity can be defined quantitatively (e.g. in the form of a normalized value between 0 and 1) and qualitatively in the form of semantic relations such as elaboration, entailment, or paraphrase. In this chapter, we focus first on measuring quantitatively and then on detecting qualitatively sentence-level text-to-text semantic relations. A generic approach that relies on word-to-word similarity measures is presented as well as experiments and results obtained with various instantiations of the approach. In addition, we provide results of a study on the role of weighting in Latent Semantic Analysis, a statistical technique to assess similarity of texts. The results were obtained on two data sets: a standard data set on sentence-level paraphrase detection and a data set from an intelligent tutoring system.

This chapter is aimed at students and researchers who are eager to learn about practical programmatic solutions to natural language processing (NLP) problems. In addition to introducing the readers to programming basics, programming tools, and complete programs, we also hope to pique their interest to actively explore the broad and fascinating field of automatic natural language processing. Part I introduces programming basics and the Python programming language. Part II takes a step by step approach in illustrating the development of a program to solve a NLP problem. Part III provides some hints to help readers initiate their own NLP programming projects.

Section 2

Successful ANLP Applications or Systems

LSA is a machine learning method that constructs a map of meaning that permits one to calculate the semantic similarity between words and texts. We describe an educational application of LSA that provides immediate, individualized content feedback to middle school students writing summaries.

AutoTutor is an intelligent tutoring system that helps students learn science, technology, and other technical subject matters by holding conversations with the student in natural language. AutoTutor's dialogues are organized around difficult questions and problems that require reasoning and explanations in the answers. The major components of AutoTutor include an animated conversational agent, dialogue management, speech act classification, a curriculum script, semantic evaluation of student contributions, and electronic documents (e.g., textbook and glossary). This chapter describes the computational components of AutoTutor, the similarity of these components to human tutors, and some challenges in handling smooth dialogue. We describe some ways that AutoTutor has been evaluated with respect to learning gains, conversation quality, and learner impressions. AutoTutor is sufficiently modular that the content and dialogue mechanisms can be modified with authoring tools. AutoTutor has spawned a number of other agent-based learning environments, such as AutoTutor-lite, Operation Aries!, and Guru.

Chapter 11
Danielle S. McNamara, Arizona State University, USA
Arthur C. Graesser, The University of Memphis, USA

Coh-Metrix provides indices for the characteristics of texts on multiple levels of analysis, including word characteristics, sentence characteristics, and the discourse relationships between ideas in text. Coh-Metrix was developed to provide a wide range of indices within one tool. This chapter describes Coh-Metrix and studies that have been conducted validating the Coh-Metrix indices. Coh-Metrix can be used to better understand differences between texts and to explore the extent to which linguistic and discourse features successfully distinguish between text types. Coh-Metrix can also be used to develop and improve natural language processing approaches. We also describe the Coh-Metrix Text Easability Component Scores, which provide a picture of text ease (and hence potential challenges). The Text Easability components provided by Coh-Metrix go beyond traditional readability measures by providing metrics of text characteristics on multiple levels of language and discourse.

Chapter 12
Cindy K. Chung, The University of Texas at Austin, USA
James W. Pennebaker, The University of Texas at Austin, USA

Linguistic Inquiry and Word Count (LIWC; Pennebaker, Booth, & Francis, 2007) is a word counting software program that references a dictionary of grammatical, psychological, and content word categories. LIWC has been used to efficiently classify texts along psychological dimensions and to predict behavioral outcomes, making it a text analysis tool widely used in the social sciences. LIWC can be considered to be a tool for applied natural language processing since, beyond classification, the relative uses of various LIWC categories can reflect the underlying psychology of demographic characteristics, honesty, health, status, relationship quality, group dynamics, or social context. By using a comparison group or longitudinal information, or validation with other psychological measures, LIWC analyses can be informative of a variety of psychological states and behaviors. Combining LIWC categories using new algorithms or using the processor to assess new categories and languages further extend the potential applications of LIWC.

HAL (Hyperspace Analog to Language) is a high-dimensional model of semantic space that uses the global co-occurrence frequency of words in a large corpus of text as the basis for a representation of semantic memory. In the original HAL model, many parameters were set without any *a priori* rationale. In this chapter we describe a new computer application called the High Dimensional Explorer (HiDEx) that makes it possible to systematically alter the values of the model's parameters and thereby to examine their effect on the co-occurrence matrix that instantiates the model. New parameter sets give us measures of semantic density that improve the model's ability to predict behavioral measures. Implications for such models are discussed.

We present in this chapter the architecture of the intelligent tutoring system MetaTutor that trains students to use metacognitive strategies while learning about complex science topics. The emphasis of this chapter is on the natural language components. In particular, we present in detail the natural language input assessment component used to detect students' mental models during prior knowledge activation, a metacognitive strategy, and the micro-dialogue component used during sub-goal generation, another metacognitive strategy in MetaTutor. Sub-goal generation involves sub-goal assessment and feedback provided by the system. For mental model detection from prior knowledge activation paragraphs, we have experimented with three benchmark methods and six machine learning algorithms. Bayes Nets, in combination with a word-weighting method, provided the best accuracy (76.31%) and best human-computer agreement scores (kappa=0.63). For sub-goal assessment and feedback, a taxonomy-driven micro-dialogue mechanism yields very good to excellent human-computer agreement scores for sub-goal assessment (average kappa=0.77).

Intelligent Tutoring Systems (ITSs) are becoming an increasingly common method for students to engage with and learn course material. ITSs are designed to provide students with one-on-one learning that is tailored to their own pace and needs. These systems can adapt to each users' individual knowledge and ability level to provide the most pedagogically effective learning environment. Tutoring systems have been designed that cover a variety of topics, including both well-defined and ill-defined domains. ITSs have seen great success within well-defined domains, where the topic itself provides only a limited set of responses. For example, in the domain of algebra, there is a limited set of possible actions that can be performed to solve for an unknown variable. Knowing this complete set of actions allows the tutoring system to predict all possible responses from the user. In contrast, ill-defined domains are more abstract and open ended. Reading comprehension is an ill-defined, open ended domain that can incorporate text from any subject, and involve numerous processes and problems for the learner. The number of associations that learners can make with a given text (e.g., based on personal memories, previous courses, ideas within different parts of the same text, etc.) is virtually infinite. These associations make it almost impossible to predict how a user will respond to a text. In addition to working with more abstract concepts, ITSs within ill-defined domains often have the added challenge of interpreting natural language user input. Incorporating natural language allows learners to use their own words and ideas as they interact with the content; however, this also increases the ambiguity of the interaction and decreases the system's ability to build a precise model of the learner. Building an accurate learner model is essential for the system to adapt the interaction in a pedagogically appropriate manner.

Chapter 16

Suguru Ishizaki, Carnegie Mellon University, USA
David Kaufer, Carnegie Mellon University, USA

This chapter presents a corpus-based text analysis tool along with a research approach to conducting a rhetorical analysis of individual text as well as text collections. The motivation for our computational approach, the system development, evaluation, and research and educational applications are discussed. The tool, called DocuScope, supports both quantitative and quantitatively-informed qualitative analyses of rhetorical strategies found in a broad range of textual artifacts, using a standard home-grown dictionary consisting of more than 40 million unique patterns of English that are classified into over 100 rhetorical functions. DocuScope also provides an authoring environment allowing investigators to build their own customized dictionaries according to their own language theories. Research published with both the standard and customized dictionaries is discussed, as well as tradeoffs, limitations, and directions for the future.

> Danielle S. McNamara, Arizona State University, USA
> Roxanne Raine, The University of Memphis, USA
> Rod Roscoe, Arizona State University, USA
> Scott A. Crossley, Georgia State University, USA
> G. Tanner Jackson, Arizona State University, USA
> Jianmin Dai, Arizona State University, USA
> Zhiqiang Cai, The University of Memphis, USA
> Adam Renner, The University of Memphis, USA
> Russell Brandon, Arizona State University, USA
> Jennifer L. Weston, Arizona State University, USA
> Kyle Dempsey, Mississippi University for Women, USA
> Diana Carney, The University of Memphis, USA
> Susan Sullivan, The University of Memphis, USA
> Loel Kim, The University of Memphis, USA
> Vasile Rus, The University of Memphis, USA
> Randy Floyd, The University of Memphis, USA
> Philip M. McCarthy, The University of Memphis, USA & Decooda.com
> Arthur C. Graesser, The University of Memphis, USA

The Writing-Pal (W-Pal) is an intelligent tutoring system (ITS) that provides writing strategy instruction to high school students and entering college students. One unique quality of W-Pal is that it provides feedback to students' natural language input. Thus, much of our focus during the W-Pal project has been on Applied Natural Language Processing (ANLP). This chapter describes W-Pal and various NLP projects geared toward providing automated feedback to students' writing during writing strategy training and practice.

> Philip M. McCarthy, The University of Memphis, USA & Decooda.com
> Shinobu Watanabe, The University of Memphis, USA
> Travis A. Lamkin, The University of Memphis, USA

Natural language processing tools, such as Coh-Metrix (see Chapter 11, this volume) and LIWC (see Chapter 12, this volume), have been tremendously successful in offering insight into quantifiable differences between text types. Such quantitative assessments have certainly been highly informative in terms of evaluating theoretical linguistic and psychological categories that distinguish text types (e.g., referential overlap, lexical diversity, positive emotion words, and so forth). Although these identifications are extremely important in revealing ability deficiencies, knowledge gaps, comprehension failures, and underlying psychological phenomena, such assessments can be difficult to interpret because they do not explicitly inform readers and researchers as to which specific linguistic features are driving the text type identification (i.e., the *words* and *word clusters* of the text). For example, a tool such as Coh-Metrix informs us that expository texts are more cohesive than narrative texts in terms of sentential referential overlap (McNamara, Louwerse, & Graesser, in press; McCarthy, 2010), but it does not tell us which words (or word clusters) are driving that cohesion. That is, we do not learn which actual words tend to be indicative of the text type differences. These actual words may tend to cluster around certain psychological, cultural, or generic differences, and, as a result, researchers and materials designers who might wish to create or modify text, so as to better meet the needs of readers, are left somewhat in the dark as to which specific language to use. What is needed is a textual analysis tool that offers *qualitative* output (in addition to quantitative output) that researchers and materials designers might use as a guide to the lexical characteristics of the texts under analysis. The Gramulator is such a tool.

Chapter 19

Bryan Rink, University of Texas at Dallas, USA
Cosmin Adrian Bejan, University of Southern California, USA
Sanda Harabagiu, University of Texas at Dallas, USA

We present a novel method for discovering causal relations between events encoded in text. In order to determine if two events from the same sentence are in a causal relation or not, we first build a graph representation of the sentence that encodes lexical, syntactic, and semantic information. From such graph representations we automatically extract multiple graph patterns (or subgraphs). The patterns are sorted according to their contribution to the expression of intra-sentential causality between events. To decide whether a pair of events is in a causal relation, we employ a binary classifier that uses the graph patterns. Our experimental results indicate that capturing causal event relations using graph patterns outperforms existing methods.

Chapter 20

Nate Blaylock, Florida Institute for Human and Machine Cognition, USA
William de Beaumont, Florida Institute for Human and Machine Cognition, USA
Lucian Galescu, Florida Institute for Human and Machine Cognition, USA
Hyuckchul Jung, Florida Institute for Human and Machine Cognition, USA
James Allen, University of Rochester, USA
George Ferguson, University of Rochester, USA
Mary Swift, University of Rochester, USA

This chapter describes a dialog system for task learning and its application to textual user interfaces. Our system, PLOW, uses observation of user demonstration, together with the user's play-by-play description of that demonstration, to learn complex tasks. We describe some preliminary experiments which show that this technique may make it possible for users without any programming experience to create tasks via natural language.

Chapter 21

Jennifer L. Weston, Arizona State University, USA
Scott A. Crossley, Georgia State University, USA
Danielle S. McNamara, Arizona State University, USA

This study examines the relationship between the linguistic features of freewrites and human assessments of freewrite quality. Freewriting is a prewriting strategy that has received little experimental attention, particularly in terms of linguistic differences between high and low quality freewrites. This study builds upon the authors' previous study, in which linguistic features of freewrites written by 9th and 11th grade students were included in a model of the freewrites' quality (Weston, Crossley, & McNamara; 2010). The current study reexamines this model using a larger data set of freewrites. The results show that similar linguistic features reported in the Weston et al. model positively correlate with expert ratings in the new data set. Significant predictors in the current model of freewrite quality were total number of words and stem overlap. In addition, analyses suggest that 11th graders, as compared to 9th graders, wrote higher quality and longer freewrites. Overall, the results of this study support the conclusion that better freewrites are longer and more cohesive than poor freewrites.

Chapter 22

Khaled Shaalan, The British University in Dubai, UAE
Marwa Magdy, Cairo University, Egypt
Aly Fahmy, Cairo University, Egypt

Arabic is a language of rich and complex morphology. The nature and peculiarity of Arabic make its morphological and phonological rules confusing for second language learners (SLLs). The conjugation of Arabic verbs is central to the formulation of an Arabic sentence because of its richness of form and meaning. In this research, we address issues related to the morphological analysis of ill-formed Arabic verbs in order to identify the source of errors and provide an informative feedback to SLLs of Arabic. The edit distance and constraint relaxation techniques are used to demonstrate the capability of the proposed system in generating all possible analyses of erroneous Arabic verbs written by SLLs. Filtering mechanisms are applied to exclude the irrelevant constructions and determine the target stem which is used as the base for constructing the feedback to the learner. The proposed system has been developed and effectively evaluated using real test data. It achieved satisfactory results in terms of the recall rate.

Chapter 23

Kyoko Baba, Kinjo Gakuin University, Japan
Ryo Nitta, Nagoya Gakuin University, Japan

The longitudinal effects of repeating a timed writing activity on English as a Foreign Language (EFL) students' second language (L2) writing development were investigated. Data for 46 students in two university classes (23 in each class), each with a different course objective, were collected 30 times in the same way over one year. The students' compositions were analyzed for fluency, grammatical complexity, and lexical complexity. Text analysis using *Coh-Metrix* showed that task repetition had an overall effect on L2 writing development. The text analysis was supplemented with a visual analysis using moving min-max graphs. Grammatical complexity developed more prominently than the other aspects of writing in both classes. This counter-predictive result points to the significance of the writers' reflective consciousness towards their own writing. This study also emphasizes that it is important to study the dynamics in L2 writing development with multi-wave data.

Chapter 24

Wei Xiong, New Jersey Institute of Technology, USA
Min Song, New Jersey Institute of Technology, USA
Lori Watrous deVersterre, New Jersey Institute of Technology, USA

Word sense disambiguation is the problem of selecting a sense for a word from a set of predefined possibilities. This is a significant problem in the biomedical domain where a single word may be used to describe a gene, protein, or abbreviation. In this paper, we evaluate SENSATIONAL, a novel unsupervised WSD technique, in comparison with two popular learning algorithms: support vector machines (SVM) and K-means. Based on the accuracy measure, our results show that SENSATIONAL outperforms SVM and K-means by 2% and 17%, respectively. In addition, we develop a polysemy-based search engine and an experimental visualization application that utilizes SENSATIONAL's clustering technique.

Chapter 25

Scott A. Crossley, Georgia State University, USA
Danielle S. McNamara, Arizona State University, USA

This study investigates the production of and exposure to lexical features when non-native speakers (NNS) converse with each other (NNS-NNS) engaging in interlanguage talk, as compared to when they engage in naturalistic speech with a native speaker (NS). The authors focus on lexical features that are associated with *breadth* of lexical knowledge including lexical diversity and lexical frequency. Spoken corpora from three types of dyads (NS-NNS, NNS-NS, NNS-NNS) are analyzed using the computational tool, Coh-Metrix. The results indicate that NNSs produce language with significantly greater lexical diversity and higher word frequency (i.e., more common words) when speaking to another NNS than when speaking to a NS. Hence, there is greater breadth of lexical knowledge apparent within interlanguage dyads (i.e., NNS-NNS) than within NNS-NS dyads in the variety of words produced, but not the frequency of the words. There were no significant differences in NNS exposure to breadth of lexical knowledge features as a function of whether the speaker was a NS or NNS. Hence, NNSs were exposed to similar levels of lexically comprehensible input regardless of interlocutor. These findings have important implications for the developmental role of interlanguage talk in reference to lexical production and exposure.

Chapter 26

Adam M. Renner, The University of Memphis, USA
Philip M. McCarthy, The University of Memphis, USA & Decooda.com
Chutima Boonthum, Hampton University, USA
Danielle S. McNamara, Arizona State University, USA

A continuing problem for ANLP (compared with NLP) is that language tends to be more *natural* in ANLP than that examined in more controlled natural language processing (NLP) studies. Specifically, ineffective or misleading feedback can result from faulty assessment of misspelled words. This chapter describes the *Harmonizer* system for addressing the problem of user input irregularities (e.g., typos). The Harmonizer is specifically designed for Intelligence Tutoring Systems (ITSs) that use NLP to provide assessment and feedback based on the typed input of the user. Our approach is to "harmonize" similar words to the same form in the benchmark, rather than correcting them to dictionary entries. This chapter describes the Harmonizer, and evaluates its performance using various computational approaches on *un*edited input from high school students in the context of an ITS (i.e., iSTART). Our results indicate that various metric approaches to NLP (such as word-overlap cohesion scores) are moderately affected when student errors are filtered by the Harmonizer. Given the prevalence of typing errors in the sample, the study substantiates the need to "clean" typed input in comparable NLP-based learning systems. The Harmonizer provides such ability and is easy to implement with light processing requirements.

The identification of new versus given information within a text has been frequently investigated by researchers of language and discourse. Despite theoretical advances, an accurate computational method for assessing the degree to which a text contains new versus given information has not previously been implemented. This study discusses a variety of computational new/given systems and analyzes four typical expository and narrative texts against a widely accepted theory of new/given proposed by Prince (1981). Our findings suggest that a latent semantic analysis (LSA) based measure called *span* outperforms standard LSA in detecting both new and given information in text. Further, span outperforms standard LSA for distinguishing low versus high cohesion versions of text. Our results suggest that span may be a useful variable in a wide array of discourse analyses.

The problem of recognizing textual entailment (RTE) has been recently addressed using syntactic and lexical models with some success. Here, a new approach is taken to apply world knowledge in much the same way as humans, but captured in large semantic graphs such as WordNet. We show that semantic graphs made of synsets and selected relationships between them enable fairly simple methods that provide very competitive performance. First, assuming a solution to word sense disambiguation, we report on the performance of these methods in four basic areas: information retrieval (IR), information extraction (IE), question answering (QA), and multi-document summarization (SUM), as described using benchmark datasets designed to test the entailment problem in the 2006 Recognizing Textual Entailment (RTE-2) challenge. We then show how the same methods yield a *solution to word sense disambiguation,* which combined with the previous solution, yields a *fully automated* solution with about the same performance. We then evaluate this solution on two subsequent RTE Challenge datasets. Finally, we evaluate the contribution of WordNet to provide world knowledge. We conclude that the protocol itself works well at solving entailment given a quality source of world knowledge, but WordNet is not able to provide enough information to resolve entailment with this inclusion protocol.

Chapter 29

Aqil Azmi, King Saud University, Saudi Arabia
Nawaf Al Badia, General Organization for Social Insurance, Saudi Arabia

Hadiths are narrations originating from the words and deeds of Prophet Muhammad. Each hadith starts with a list of narrators involved in transmitting it. A hadith scholar judges a hadith based on the narration chain along with the individual narrators in the chain. In this chapter, we report on a method that automatically extracts the transmission chains from the hadith text and graphically displays it. Computationally, this is a challenging problem. Foremost each hadith has its own peculiar way of listing narrators; and the text of hadith is in Arabic, a language rich in morphology. Our proposed solution involves parsing and annotating the hadith text and recognizing the narrators' names. We use shallow parsing along with a domain specific grammar to parse the hadith content. Experiments on sample hadiths show our approach to have a very good success rate.

Chapter 30

Kirk Roberts, University of Texas at Dallas, USA
Cosmin Adrian Bejan, University of Southern California, USA
Sanda Harabagiu, University of Texas at Dallas, USA

This chapter discusses a method for improving the disambiguation of location names using limited event semantics. Location names are often ambiguous, as the same name may refer to locations in different states, countries, or continents. Ambiguous location names, also known as toponyms, need to be disambiguated (or grounded) when resolving many spatial relations expressed in textual documents. Previous methods for disambiguating toponyms have utilized simple heuristics, statistical ranking, and ontological methods in order to resolve a location reference. However, since toponyms are used in documents that refer to events, semantic knowledge characterizing events can be used to ground location names. We propose an ontology-based method with a technique that considers the participants in events such as people, organizations, and other locations. Event semantics are integrated into an ontology that is used to distinguish geographical names through a probabilistic approach based on logistic regression. Our experimental results on the SpatialML corpus (Mani et al., 2008) indicate that using event structures improves the quality of disambiguated toponyms.

In this chapter I approach three automatic methods for the evaluation of summaries from narrative and expository texts in Spanish. The task consisted of correlating the evaluation made by three raters for 373 summaries with results provided by latent semantic analysis. Scores assigned by latent semantic analysis were obtained by means of the following three methods: 1) Comparison of summaries with the source text, 2) Comparison of summaries with a summary approved by consensus, and 3) Comparison of summaries with three summaries constructed by three language teachers. The most relevant results are a) a high positive correlation between the evaluation made by the raters (r= 0.642); b) a high positive correlation between the computer methods (r= 0.810); and c) a moderate-high positive correlation between the evaluations of raters and the second and third LSA methods (r= 0.585 and 0,604), in summaries from narrative texts. Both methods did not differ significantly in statistical terms from the correlation among raters when the texts evaluated were predominantly narrative. These results allow us to assert that at least two holistic LSA-based methods are useful for assessing reading comprehension of narrative texts written in Spanish.

We use computational linguistic tools to investigate gender differences in language use within the context of marital conflict. Using the Language Inquiry and Word Count tool (LIWC), differences between genders were significant for the use of *self references,* but not for the use of *social words* and *positive* and *negative emotion words*. Using Coh-Metrix, differences were significant for the use of *syntactic complexity, global argument overlap,* and *density of logical connectors* but not for the use of word *frequency, frequency of causal verbs and particles, global Latent Semantic Analysis (LSA), local argument overlap,* and *local LSA*. These results confirmed some expectations but failed to confirm the majority of the expectations based on the biological theory of gender, which defines gender in terms of biological sex resulting in polarized and static language differences based on the speaker's gender.

Foreword

Artificial Intelligence (AI) is the branch of Computer Science that builds computing artifacts that display intelligence. This intelligence is often defined as displaying the types of behavior that humans display, and computationally, that typically means solving exponentially hard problems using only polynomial resources. The application of AI to real-world problems is a driving force that underlies AI research, and applied AI systems must succeed within the resource constraints. It is in this setting that Applied Natural Language Processing (ANLP) exists. Natural Language Processing (NLP) is one of the oldest fields of AI, generally considered to have started in the 1950s alongside AI itself. Early efforts to apply NLP revealed the complexity and difficulty of the general task of processing natural language, in terms of input processing, capturing meaning, linking to other AI components, and producing satisfactory natural language output. Much progress has been made, and today we are commonly expected to "converse" with computing systems using (limited) natural language. This progress in the application of NLP has led to the identification of ANLP as a distinct sub-field, with a focus on the identification, investigation, and solution to real-life language-related issues.

This volume serves to provide an overview and a survey of the state-of-the-art in ANLP. This is achieved through an examination of the foundations of NLP that have contributed to ANLP, a review of several successful ANLP applications, and a selection of work describing new research results in ANLP. The foundations include question answering, text summarization, information extraction, dialogue, and programming practices for ANLP. The applications (i.e., ANLP) refer to educational systems, text assessment tools, and various approaches to measuring psychological features. New results include work on intelligent tutoring systems, user interfaces, quality analysis, extraction of semantics, and identification of linguistic styles. The contributions to the volume come from established and recognized ANLP researchers and practitioners, with a wide range of viewpoints and skill-sets. As a result, this volume is truly comprehensive, and will be a starting point for much further work.

The future will place increasing demands on ANLP, as an increasingly savvy public demand increasingly natural (language) interfaces to computing devices and online data sources. Intelligent processing of user input and requests, effective querying of textual databases, and the generation of results in a natural (language) form, will necessarily become common-place. Research and development of such capabilities fall into the purview of ANLP. The principles and practices described in this volume will provide starting points and inspiration. As such, this volume can be used for a graduate class in the area, for independent study by research students and faculty, and by a more general AI audience as an introduction to the field. Because ANLP is inherently inter-disciplinary, the book is sufficiently diverse to accommodate departments of Computer Science, Cognitive Science, and Linguistics, and yet at the same time to be cohesive enough to bring researchers and students from these departments together.

It is interesting to note the history that led to this volume. ANLP conferences were originally linked to the Association for Computational Linguistics (ACL) Conference and the International Conference on Computational Linguistics (COLING), in the years 1983 to 2000. After a hiatus, the conference in 2006 re-emerged as a track of the International FLAIRS (Florida Artificial Intelligence Research Society) Conference, where it flourished. The success of the ANLP track at FLAIRS led directly to this book, and the FLAIRS setting provided a source for contributions that straddle the boundaries of conventional fields. This is therefore, in some sense, a unique opportunity to get to grips with the exciting field of Applied Natural Language Processing, in one collected set of readings.

Geoff Sutcliffe
University of Miami, USA

Geoff Sutcliffe *is an Associate Professor in the Department of Computer Science at the University of Miami, USA. He is currently Vice President of the Florida Artificial Intelligence Research Society (FLAIRS).*

Preface

APPLIED NATURAL LANGUAGE PROCESSING

Applied Natural Language Processing (ANLP) is an emerging field of study concerned with how computational approaches can assist with the identification, investigation, and resolution of real-life language-related issues. The NLP part of ANLP is predominantly (but not exclusively) the domain of computer scientists. It is they who are responsible for most (but not all) of the advancements in textual analysis tools and approaches. The A part of ANLP is predominantly (but not exclusively) the domain of cognitive psychologists and linguists. It is they who predominantly (but not exclusively) apply NLP to linguistic data with the goal of increasing our knowledge of how the mind represents and retrieves knowledge, increasing our ability to mimic human intelligence, and/or increasing our ability to assess and describe how language impacts the world and the individuals and groups within it.

We label ANLP an "emerging" field because it is not yet clear whether it is sufficiently focused to draw in researchers under its own gravity. Thus, ANLP could be described as a "field" because, like other fields, it produces knowledge and establishes practices that can be taught and researched. But at the same time, ANLP may equally be described as simply a convenient bucket into which many pieces of otherwise homeless research are dropped. That is, a great many studies simply *end up* as ANLP, while the studies' researchers would not label themselves as members of the field of ANLP. Perhaps this scenario is to be expected from interdisciplinary studies of real world problems, and therefore ANLP will always be (largely) a field in which we graze rather than sow.

ANLP may well be an emerging field, but if it is to lose its modifier, it has to begin forming a recognized identity. With this in mind, we can admit that there is clearly much to be done: There is terminology to be agreed; there are prototypical topics to be established; there are seminal works to be sanctified, and there is a form, a voice, and discourse move that need to coalesce. Of course, all these aspects of any field come largely as a result of convention, and conventions take time. We hope that this book represents a suitable point of departure for such conventions, and that it at least provides current researchers with some guidelines from which to begin, some framework within which to work, and some goals for which to strive.

NLP AND ANLP

The amount of information that humans have gathered and made available to other humans is, of course, phenomenal. And however large this repository of knowledge is, we know that by this time tomorrow, it will be larger still. But perhaps what is most relevant to us about this information is that most of it appears in textual form, and that if we are ever to manage it, understand it, assess it, evaluate it, summarize it, or even find it, then a broad range of natural language processing tools, systems, algorithms, models, theories, and techniques will be needed. The fields of Natural Language Processing (NLP) and Applied Natural Language Processing (ANLP) are both dedicated to this venture. But while their goals are highly overlapping (as is much of their research), their contribution to those goals is quite distinguishable.

The field of NLP is concerned with the development of natural language processing approaches (i.e., tools, systems, algorithms, models, theories, and techniques). More specifically, it is concerned with how these approaches are applied to a fairly well established set of tasks (e.g., summarization, part-of-speech tagging, named entity recognition, co-reference resolution, natural language understanding, text-type disambiguation, and so forth) that have fairly well established methods of appraisal (e.g., compare recall, precision, F1 to previously tested systems) and fairly well established sets of data (e.g., corpora such as the Wall Street Journal or the Microsoft Paraphrase Corpus). This having been said, we should not think of such tasks as trivial or esoteric. Instead, NLP might be thought of as the laboratory, the prototypes, and the testing ground.

NLP can be said to have become ANLP when the focus of the research shifts away from honing the accuracy and validity of the NLP approach to adapting the technology wholesale to a real world situation. Thus, a prototypical example of NLP might be described as Vasile Rus' development of a lexico-syntactic approach to entailment assessment (Rus et al., 2008); whereas a prototypical example of ANLP might be described as Vasile Rus' using that approach to assess paraphrase evaluation in an Intelligent Tutoring System (Rus et al., in press).

But of course, research is more than simply *using* something. ANLP is concerned with how those approaches stack up against new problems, issues, identified knowledge gaps, or real world based data sets. In many ways then, ANLP can be distinguished from NLP not so much by its content, form, or span, but by its focus. This change in focus results in research where less time and attention is spent concerned with the approach, which has presumably been described elsewhere, as it is spent concerned with the issue, the investigation, and the resolution. This is not to say that the mechanics of the approach can be ignored (they cannot), but it is to say that the mechanics are relegated to being, as it were, a guest at the party, as opposed to the host.

Given the nature of ANLP, it is often an *X-solution* applied to a *Y-problem*. As such, ANLP can often be a quick and "sufficient" answer, even while it may be a far from perfect one. For example, latent semantic analysis (see Kintsch and Kintsch, this volume) was not designed to assess feedback for paraphrase evaluations anymore than it was designed to be the foundation stone of dialogue management in intelligent tutoring systems. Yet McCarthy, Guess, and McNamara (2009) identified feedback for paraphrase evaluation problems and successfully used latent semantic analysis (LSA) to resolve them. Similarly, researchers of intelligent systems (see AutoTutor: this volume; iSTART: this volume) have also implemented LSA to verify dialogue. To be sure, LSA results have ranged from extremely encouraging (McNamara et al. 2007) to quite problematic (McCarthy et al., 2007, 2008). Thus, one key element of ANLP research is establishing the degree to which an approach works, and the identification of which elements in that research need to be addressed to make the approach more than merely "sufficient." This identification of a partial solution along with its limitations may often result in the later development of hybrid approaches, as with paraphrase evaluation through a combination of LSA and syntactic assessment (McCarthy et al., 2009) or as with introducing *entailment evaluations* to dialogue assessment in combination with LSA (Rus et al., 2008). Thus, ANLP research does not *have to* be viewed as solely a solution; it is often a journey, often a treatment, often a diagnostic, often a finger in the damn till help arrives.

Although the focus of ANLP might contrast with NLP, the areas of interest do not: anywhere NLP goes, *A*NLP must surely follow (and often arrive first). Thus, the topics of interest for ANLP include (but, by definition, are not limited to) summarization, text mining, categorization, authorship recognition, genre recognition, word sense disambiguation, first/second language acquisition, text and discourse analysis, paraphrasing, entailment, anaphora resolution, co-reference resolution, text cohesion and coherence, dialogue management and systems, language generation, language models, human computer interfaces, multilingual processing, standardization issues, language resources, corpora, learning environments, semantics, ontologies, machine translation, intelligent tutoring, question answering, parsing, tagging, annotating, tokenization, morphology, stemming, information extraction, syntax, English for specific purposes, humor analysis, user language understanding and assessment, web assessment, blog analysis, grammar checking, speech recognition, speech production, data mining, and any and all other areas that involve computation and text.

A BRIEF HISTORY OF ANLP

If ANLP is an emerging field, then we must describe from where it has emerged, and from where it continues to be emerging. Not surprisingly, we find that the history of ANLP is closely tied to NLP and, more specifically, at various times, in various ways, to offshoots from NLP into real world issues. These offshoots have met with varying degrees of success (in some ways, perhaps too much success), but as we will see from the history described below, it is hard to ignore the fact that there is no shortage of interest in the activities of ANLP.

In 1983, a series of ANLP conferences began and continued until 2000. The ANLP series grew out of the Association for Computational Linguistics (ACL) conference. More specifically, the series was an outgrowth of a 1981 ACL workshop. The ACL conference at that time was small, met yearly, and was somewhat similar to the International Conference on Computational Linguistics (COLING), which met bi-yearly. An ANLP conference was proposed as an alternate venue for papers where there could be discussions of the role of natural language processing in solving real world problems.

The first ANLP conference was held in Santa Monica in 1983. It featured 26 papers across six tracks: 1) domain-independent natural language interfaces, 2) knowledge-based approaches, 3) handling ill-formed input, 4) text analysis, 5) machine translation, and 6) speech interfaces. The third conference went international, being held in Trento, Italy. Although the conferences would never grow much larger than their initial numbers, they did expand each meeting so that for the sixth and final conference in 2000, the program committee chose from 131 submissions received from 24 different countries.

The proceedings from these conferences display an increasing focus on the interaction of technology and the market. As technology advanced, business and government enterprises were better able to use NLP techniques to resolve, or at least investigate, their problems. The advent of digital communication expanded both NLP technologies and the ability of the conference organizers to get submissions and attendees. By 2000, nearly a third of the submissions represented business, private interests, or government, rather than academic sources. This success would prove problematic, however, with increasing amounts of ANLP research and tools becoming proprietary.

The conferences' success, in terms of interest, would eventually lead to its early retirement. Research that had been brought to light from the previous six ANLP conferences now meant that more established conferences were welcoming, and even expecting papers with direct applications to real world problems.

With ACL and COLING conferences being held regularly, and ANLP conferences with gaps as long as four years, researchers could hardly be blamed for looking elsewhere for venues. But in order to accommodate the requirements of these NLP conferences, ANLP research needed to become more empirical, which ultimately led to ANLP blurring back into NLP.

Although the ANLP conferences were now a thing of the past, interest in ANLP certainly was not. In 2006, Vasile Rus introduced a track to the International Florida Artificial Intelligence Research Society (FLAIRS) focused on research and tools concerned with the understanding, organizing, and mining of text based information. Despite being a new track, it received a lot of attention, gaining 19 submissions (about 10% of the over-all track submissions), 8 of which were accepted as papers. Vasile had correctly detected a revived interest in ANLP. He also saw that this interest was in step with new developments in intelligent tutoring systems, such as AutoTutor and iSTART (see Chapters 11 and 16 this book). These systems require the development of specialized algorithms and assessment approaches in order that they can provide suitable feedback to users. In other words, NLP was needed to solve real world problems. In yet other words, *A*NLP was needed.

In 2007, Christian Hempelman and Phil McCarthy took over Vasile's track and renamed it Applied Natural Language Processing (ANLP), the name it still has today. The interest from 2006 was maintained in 2007, and grew steadily through 2008 and 2009 under the direction of Phil McCarthy and Scott Crossly. In 2010, Phil McCarthy was joined by Chutima Boonthum-Denecke. By this time, Phil McCarthy was chairing the FLAIRS program itself, and Chutima Boonthum-Denecke was the special tracks chair of FLAIRS, so Vasile Rus stepped back into the leadership role of the ANLP track together with Mihai Lintean. Their promotion of the track led to the most successful year for ANLP to date: 19 accepted papers, a workshop, a demonstration session, and a special track invited guest. In fact, by this time, ANLP was receiving more submissions and producing more talks than the conference main track.

The role of FLAIRS as the stage for the emerging field of ANLP is undeniable. But if it could be said that there was any single person or place that was the driving force being the products that FLAIRS put on show, then that person would be Danielle McNamara, and that place would be the Institute for Intelligent Systems (IIS) at the University of Memphis. All of the researchers that chaired the ANLP track at FLAIRS passed through the IIS at some stage of their careers, and each of them have also worked with Danielle McNamara on at least one of her projects. As of 2011, Danielle (now director of the IIS) had co-authored 27 FLAIRS publications, and in 2007, she was the first invited speaker of the track. Her main contribution to the field was the Coh-Metrix text analysis tool (see Chapter 11). Coh-Metrix was the first free, widely available software of its kind, allowing researchers to process large numbers of text to assess such metrics as cohesion, readability, lexical diversity, frequency, semantic overlap, and numerous others. In short, Coh-Metrix was (and arguably still is) the ultimate ANLP tool. Danielle would also contribute to FLAIRS and science in general (especially cognitive science) with her intelligent tutoring systems (iSTART and Wpal: see chapters 15 and 17). She also plays a part in the development of other systems such as AutoTutor (see Chapter 10) and other assessment approaches (see entailment in Chapter 7). Each of these projects has also appeared at FLAIRS. In sum, the field of ANLP owes a great debt of gratitude to Danielle McNamara and the Institute of Intelligent Systems.

The burgeoning interest in ANLP led directly to this book. The design of the book was such that the leading names and most notable achievements in ANLP could be brought together so that the *emerging* field might sooner become *emerged*. But the book's purview was not simply to compile what existed; it was also to draw in new researchers, especially those whose work had often been seen as merely straddling the boundaries of conventional fields. The book was also designed with students in mind. Thus, it had to be accessible enough to be integrated into courses as a main or supplemental course book, relevant to graduate students and advanced under-graduates. Because ANLP is inherently inter-disciplinary, the book also had to be sufficiently diverse to accommodate departments of Computer Science, Cognitive Science, and Linguistics, and yet at the same time to be cohesive enough to bring researchers and students from these departments together.

To what degree this book has successfully achieved its goals will be determined further along the road. However, that its goals are realistic is evidenced by the breadth of researchers who have made contributions to it. Indeed, one of the editors is a linguist, the other is a computer scientist, and the researcher whose name appears most often in this book (Danielle McNamara) is a cognitive scientist. As for the book being embraced in the classroom, we point to Hearst (2005), who argued that there is much that can and needs to be taught in ANLP, but that there is no suitable text for such a course. This problem, at least, we hope we have addressed here.

ORGANIZATION OF THE BOOK

Although NLP might seem to be able to get along without ANLP, the reverse is a more difficult case to make. For this reason, Section 1 of this book focuses on foundational sub-fields of NLP. Of course, it is impossible to cover all sub-fields of NLP (even if such a list were possible), therefore, we offer in Section 1 seven chapters that perhaps speak most closely to issues that arise in ANLP. An eighth chapter in Section 1 directly addresses an issue highlighted by Hearst (2005) in her paper on teaching ANLP: the need for a guide to practical programming.

Section 2 focuses on successful systems and approach in ANLP. By successful, we mean that the systems and approaches have become established, generated a large amount of research, and/or become seminal works in ANLP. The eight chapters range from multiple text processing tools (e.g., Coh-Metrix, LIWC, DocuScope) through semantic assessment tools (e.g., LSA), to intelligent tutoring systems (e.g., AutoTutor, Summary Street) that incorporate numerous NLP approaches.

For any field to fully emerge, it has to be constantly and consistently producing high quality research. Section 3 features 16 such examples. The studies cover all aspects of ANLP including developing intelligent tutoring systems, text processing tools, algorithms, methods, techniques, and approaches.

Section 1

Following this introduction, Chapter 1 features Arthur C. Graesser, Vasile Rus, Zhiqiang Cai, and Xiangen Hu, who provide an overview of recent developments in question answering and generation. They define automated question answering as the task of providing answers automatically to questions asked in natural language, and they explain the flip process of question asking, which is automated question asking or generation, as the task of supplying answers automatically to questions by the use of various forms of input (e.g., text, meaning representation, databases). The authors also speculate on the future of these pursuits, arguing that question asking/generation will revolutionize learning and dialogue systems.

In Chapter 2, Martin Hassel and Hercules Dalianis discuss the development of automatic summarization systems. The authors' focus is on systems that use methods that are more or less directly transferable from one language to another.

In Chapter 3, Alexandra Kent and Philip McCarthey outline the basic theoretical assumptions that underpin the many different methodological approaches within Discourse Analysis. The chapter then considers these approaches in terms of the major themes of their research, the ongoing and future directions for study, and the scope of contribution to scientific knowledge that discourse analytic research can make.

In Chapter 4, Christian Hempelmann presents an account of key NLP issues in *search*. More specifically, he gives a general overview on NLP and *search* to show the advantages of ontological semantic technology (OST) and ways in which it can be implemented.

In Chapter 5, Martin Atzmueller gives an overview on data mining, focusing on approaches for pattern mining, cluster analysis, and predictive model construction. For each of these approaches, the author describes exemplary techniques that are especially useful in the context of applied natural language processing.

In Chapter 6, T. Daniel Midgley discusses historical and recent work in dialogue act tagging and dialogue structure inference. He explains that dialogue act tagging is a classification task in which utterances in dialogue are marked with the intentions of the speaker. The chapter argues that the structure of dialogue can be represented by dialogue grammar, segmentation, or with a hierarchical structure.

In Chapter 7, Vasile Rus, Mihai Lintean, Arthur C. Graesser, and Danielle S. McNamara discuss measuring semantic similarity between texts. According to the authors, semantic similarity can be defined quantitatively, e.g. in the form of a normalized value between 0 and 1, and qualitatively in the form of semantic relations such as elaboration, entailment, or paraphrase. The authors present a generic approach that relies on word-to-word similarity measures as well as experiments and results obtained with various instantiations of the approach.

In Chapter 8, Patrick Jeuniaux, Andrew M. Olney, and Sidney D'Mello address students and researchers who are eager to learn about practical programmatic solutions to natural language processing (NLP) problems. They discuss the role of programming and specifically the Python programming language. They then give a step by step approach in illustrating the development of a program to solve a NLP problem. The authors also provide some hints to help readers initiate their own NLP programming projects.

Section 2

In Chapter 9, Walter and Eileen Kintsch describe an educational application of latent semantic analysis (LSA) that provides immediate, individualized content feedback to middle school students writing summaries. The authors describe LSA as a machine learning method that constructs a map of meaning that permits researchers to calculate the semantic similarity between words and texts.

In Chapter 10, Arthur C. Graesser, Sidney D'Mello, Xiangen Hu, Zhiqiang Cai, Andrew Olney, and Brent Morgan describe AutoTutor, an intelligent tutoring system that helps students learn science, technology, and other technical subject matters. The authors also describe some ways that AutoTutor has been evaluated with respect to learning gains, conversation quality, and learner impressions.

In Chapter 11, Danielle S. McNamara and Arthur C. Graesser describe Coh-Metrix and studies that have been conducted validating the Coh-Metrix indices. Coh-Metrix provides indices for the characteristics of texts on multiple levels of analysis, including word characteristics, sentence characteristics, and the discourse relationships between ideas in text. They also describe the Coh-Metrix text easability component scores, which provide a picture of text ease (and hence potential challenges).

In Chapter 12, Cindy K. Chung and James W. Pennebaker examine the ANLP role of the linguistic inquiry and word count (LIWC) program. The authors explain that LIWC is a word counting software program that references a dictionary of grammatical, psychological, and content word categories. They go on to show that LIWC has been used to efficiently classify texts along psychological dimensions and to predict behavioral outcomes in a wide variety of studies in social sciences.

In Chapter 13, Cyrus Shaoul and Chris Westbury present the *High Dimensional Explorer* (HiDEx). HiDEx is a tool for exploring a class of models of lexical semantics derived from the Hyperspace Analog to Language (HAL). The authors describe HAL as a high-dimensional model of semantic space that uses the global co-occurrence frequency of words in a large corpus of text as the basis for a representation of semantic memory.

In Chapter 14, Mihai Lintean, Vasile Rus, Zhiqiang Cai, Amy Witherspoon, Arthur C. Graesser, and Roger Azevedo present the architecture of the intelligent tutoring system MetaTutor. The system trains students to use metacognitive strategies while learning about complex science topics. The authors particularly focus on MetaTutor's natural language components.

In Chapter 15, G. Tanner Jackson and Danielle S. McNamara discuss the intelligent tutoring system Interactive Strategy Training for Active Reading and Thinking (iSTART). iSTART utilizes a complex set of algorithms to evaluate student input and subsequently select real-time appropriate responses.

In Chapter 16, Suguru Ishizaki and David Kaufer present a corpus-based text analysis tool along with a research approach to conducting a rhetorical analysis of individual text and text collections. The tool, DocuScope, supports both quantitative and quantitatively-informed qualitative analyses of rhetorical strategies found in a broad range of textual artifacts.

Section 3

In Chapter 17, Danielle S. McNamara, Roxanne Raine, Rod Roscoe, Scott Crossley, G. Tanner Jackson, Jianmin Dai, Zhiqiang Cai, Adam Renner, Russell Brandon, Jennifer L. Weston, Kyle Dempsey, Diana Lam, Susan Sullivan, Loel Kim, Vasile Rus, Randy Floyd, Philip M. McCarthy, and Arthur C. Graesser present Writing-Pal (W-Pal), an intelligent tutoring system that provides writing strategy instruction to high school students and students entering college. The chapter describes the W-Pal system itself, as well as various NLP projects geared toward providing automated feedback to students using the system.

In Chapter 18, Philip McCarthy, Shinobu Watanabe, and Travis Lamkin present the Gramulator, a freely available tool for qualitative and quantitative computational textual analysis. The Gramulator is designed to allow researchers and materials designers to identify indicative lexical features of texts and text types. It also offers a wide range of text assessment metrics, and useful analysis tools such a concordancer, a lemmatizer, and a parser

In Chapter 19, Bryan Rink, Cosmin Adrian Bejan, and Sanda Harabagiu present a novel method for discovering causal relations between events encoded in text. In order to determine if two events from the same sentence are in a causal relation or not, they first build a graph representation of the sentence that encodes lexical, syntactic, and semantic information. From such graph representations, the authors automatically extract multiple graph patterns (or *subgraphs*). The authors sort the patterns according to their contribution to the expression of intra-sentential causality between events.

In Chapter 20, Nate Blaylock, William de Beaumont, Lucian Galescu, and Hyuckchul Jung describe a system for task learning and its application to textual user interfaces. The system, PLOW, uses observation of user demonstration, together with the user's play-by-play description of that demonstration, to learn complex tasks. The authors suggest that PLOW may make it possible for users without any programming experience to create tasks via natural language.

In Chapter 21, Jennifer L. Weston, Scott A. Crossley, and Danielle S. McNamara examine the relation between the linguistic features of freewrites and human assessments of freewrite quality. This classical example of ANLP shows how one system (Coh-Metrix) can be used to address issues in development with another system (W-Pal).

In Chapter 22, Khaled Shalaan, Marwa Magdy, and Aly Fahmy address issues related to the morphological analysis of ill-formed Arabic verbs. Edit distance and constraint relaxation techniques are used to demonstrate the capability of the proposed system in generating all possible analyses of erroneous Arabic verbs written by language learners.

In Chapter 23, Kyokoa Baba and Ryo Nitta investigate the longitudinal effects of repeating a timed writing activity on English language learners. The authors analyze the texts using a variety of *Coh-Metrix* indices.

In Chapter 24, Wei Xiong, Min Song, and Lori Watrous-deVersterre evaluate SENSATIONAL, a novel unsupervised word sense disambiguation technique. The authors define word sense disambiguation as the problem of selecting a sense for a word from a set of predefined possibilities.

In Chapter 25, Scott A. Crossley and Danielle S. McNamara investigate the production *of* and exposure *to* lexical features when non-native speakers (NNS) converse with each other. The authors focus on lexical features that are associated with *breadth* of lexical knowledge including lexical diversity and lexical frequency.

In Chapter 26, Adam M. Renner, Philip M. McCarthy, Chutima Boonthum-Denecke, and Danielle S. McNamara describe the Harmonizer, a system that addresses the problem of user input irregularities (e.g., typos). The Harmonizer is specifically designed for intelligent tutoring systems (ITSs) that use NLP to provide assessment and feedback based on the typed input of the user. The performance of the tool is evaluated using various computational approaches on *un*edited input from high school students in the context of an ITS (i.e., iSTART).

In Chapter 27, Philip M. McCarthy, David Dufty, Christian Hempelman, Zhiqiang Cai, Danielle S. McNamara, and Arthur C. Graesser address the problem of identifying *new* versus *given* information within a text. The authors discuss a variety of computational new/given systems and analyze four typical expository and narrative texts.

In Chapter 28, Andrew J. Neel and Max H. Garzon take a new approach to the problem of recognizing textual entailment (RTE). They show that semantic graphs can provide a very competitive performance. The semantic graphs are made of synonym sets (*synsets*) and selected relationships between those synsets.

In Chapter 29, Aqil Azmi and Suha Al-Thanyyan present *Ikhtasir*, an automatic extractive Arabic text summarization system. The system integrates a Rhetorical Structure Theory (RST) based system with a sentence scoring system, where individual sentences are scored.

In Chapter 30, Kirk Roberts, Cosmin Adrian Bejan, and Sanda Harabagiu discuss an ontology-based method for improving the disambiguation of ambiguous location names (or toponyms) using limited event semantics. Location names are often ambiguous, as the same name may refer to locations in different states, countries, or continents.

In Chapter 31, René Venegas approaches three automatic methods for the evaluation of summaries from narrative and expository texts in Spanish. This task consists of correlating the evaluation made by human raters with results provided by latent semantic analysis.

In Chapter 32, Courtney M. Bell, Philip M. McCarthy, and Danielle S. McNamara use Coh-Metrix and LIWC to investigate gender differences in language use within the context of marital conflict.

THE FUTURE OF ANLP

The future of ANLP is bright. It is inconceivable that the coming years will see anything less than a continuing rise in the number, availability, and scope of computational systems that address real world issues through the medium of language. These systems will develop the ever growing need of users to request and retrieve information quickly, easily, and accurately. Each avenue of daily life will increase its dependency on language related applications: governmental, commercial, educational, recreational; system designers will seek out new approaches, methods, and techniques that address issues such as speech recognition, question answering, information extraction, and all such computationally linguistic tasks that are discussed in this book. Soon enough, other researchers will collect the algorithms that make these approaches, methods, and techniques possible, and with them, they will create newer, faster, and more accessible analysis systems, which, in turn, will find yet newer researchers who use these algorithms in novel applications. In short, the *identification* of computationally solvable language issues will be addressed by a broad *investigation* of developing textual analysis systems, which will lead to a *resolution* through *applied natural language processing*.

REFERENCES

Graesser, A. C., Lu, S., Jackson, G. T., Mitchell, H., Ventura, M., Olney, A., & Louwerse, M. M. (2004). AutoTutor: A tutor with dialogue in natural language. *Behavior Research Methods, Instruments, & Computers, 136*, 180–193. doi:10.3758/BF03195563

Hearst, M. (2005). *Teaching applied natural language processing: Triumphs and tribulations*. The Second ACL Workshop on Effective Tools and Methodologies for Teaching Natural Language Processing And Computational Linguistics, Ann Arbor, MI, June 2005.

Kintsch, W., & Kintsch, E. (in press). LSA in the classroom. In McCarthy, P. M., & Boonthum-Denecke, C. (Eds.), *Applied Natural language processing and content analysis: Identification, investigation, and resolution*. Hershey, PA: IGI Global.

Landauer, T. K., McNamara, D. S., Dennis, S., & Kintsch, W. (Eds.). (2007). *Handbook of latent semantic analysis*. Mahwah, NJ: Erlbaum.

McCarthy, P. M., Guess, R., & McNamara, D. S. (2009). The components of paraphrase evaluations. *Behavior Research Methods, 41*, 682–690. doi:10.3758/BRM.41.3.682

McCarthy, P. M., Rus, V., Crossley, S. A., Bigham, S. C., Graesser, A. C., & McNamara, D. S. (2007). Assessing entailer with a corpus of natural language from an intelligent tutoring system. In D. Wilson & G. Sutcliffe (Eds.), *Proceedings of the 20th International Florida Artificial Intelligence Research Society Conference* (pp. 247-252). Menlo Park, CA: The AAAI Press.

McCarthy, P. M., Rus, V., Crossley, S. A., Graesser, A. C., & McNamara, D. S. (2008). Assessing forward-, reverse-, and average-entailment indices on natural language input from the intelligent tutoring system, iSTART. In D. Wilson & G. Sutcliffe (Eds.), *Proceedings of the 21st International Florida Artificial Intelligence Research Society Conference* (pp. 165-170). Menlo Park, CA: The AAAI Press.

McNamara, D. S., Boonthum, C., Levinstein, I. B., & Millis, K. (2007). Evaluating self-explanations in iSTART: Comparing word-based and LSA systems. In Landauer, T. K., McNamara, D. S., Dennis, S., & Kintsch, W. (Eds.), *Handbook of latent semantic analysis* (pp. 227–241). Mahwah, NJ: Erlbaum.

McNamara, D. S., Levinstein, I. B., & Boonthum, C. (2004). iSTART: Interactive strategy training for active reading and thinking. *Behavior Research Methods, Instruments, & Computers, 36,* 222–233. doi:10.3758/BF03195567

Rus, V., Feng, S., Brandon, R., Crossley, S. A., & McNamara, D. S. (in press). A linguistic analysis of student-generated paraphrases. In C. Murray & P. M. McCarthy (Eds.), *Proceedings of the 24th International Florida Artificial Intelligence Research Society Conference* (pp. 293-298). Menlo Park, CA: The AAAI Press.

Rus, V., McCarthy, P. M., McNamara, D. S., & Graesser, A. C. (2008). A study of textual entailment. *International Journal of Artificial Intelligence Tools, 17,* 659–685. doi:10.1142/S0218213008004096

Acknowledgment

We would like to thank all the authors for their contributions to this project, and also to thank them for their patience and trust during the process. We would like to thank all the reviewers for their hard work, diligence, and time, and for lending us their expertise. We would also be remiss if we failed to extend our gratitude to Danielle S. McNamara, Arthur C. Graesser, and the FLAIRS organization for their key roles in the emergence and growth of ANLP as an independent field of research.

Philip M. McCarthy
The University of Memphis, USA

Chutima Boonthum-Denecke
Hampton University, USA

Section 1
Foundations:
The Role of NLP

Chapter 1
Question Answering and Generation

Arthur C. Graesser
The University of Memphis, USA

Vasile Rus
The University of Memphis, USA

Zhiqiang Cai
The University of Memphis, USA

Xiangen Hu
The University of Memphis, USA

ABSTRACT

Automated Question Answering and Asking are two active areas of Natural Language Processing with the former dominating the past decade and the latter most likely to dominate the next one. Due to the vast amounts of information available electronically in the Internet era, automated Question Answering is needed to fulfill information needs in an efficient and effective manner. Automated Question Answering is the task of providing answers automatically to questions asked in natural language. Typically, the answers are retrieved from large collections of documents. While answering any question is difficult, successful automated solutions to answer some type of questions, so-called factoid questions, have been developed recently, culminating with the just announced Watson Question Answering system developed by I.B.M. to compete in Jeopardy-like games. The flip process, automated Question Asking or Generation, is about generating questions from some form of input such as a text, meaning representation, or database. Question Asking/Generation is an important component in the full gamut of learning technologies, from conventional computer-based training to tutoring systems. Advances in Question Asking/Generation are projected to revolutionize learning and dialogue systems. This chapter presents an overview of recent developments in Question Answering and Generation starting with the landscape of questions that people ask.

DOI: 10.4018/978-1-60960-741-8.ch001

INTRODUCTION

For the first time in history, a person can ask a question on the web and receive answers in a few seconds. Twenty years ago, it would take hours or weeks to receive answers to the same questions as a person hunted through documents in a library. In the future, electronic textbooks and information sources will be mainstream and they will be accompanied by sophisticated question answering and generation facilities. As a result, we believe that the Google generation is destined to have a much more inquisitive mind than the generations who relied on passive reading and libraries. The new technologies will radically transform how we think and behave.

BACKGROUND

Automatic Question Answering is the task of providing meaningful answers to questions in natural language. There are two features that make automatic Question Answering attractive: (1) it keeps the user-system interface natural because users can ask questions the way they ask other humans, thereby eliminating the need to train users on specific query languages and (2) it can provide effective access for everyone to the huge online repository of knowledge stored on the Internet. Advanced online Question Answering services can provide effective access to information to everyone, computer-savvy or not, as interface barriers are eliminated.

Early explorations of automated Question Answering have been attempted since the beginning of the computing era, but the advent of the Internet in the 1990s greatly stimulated research on Question Answering in order to provide effective access to the vast repositories of information available on the web. In particular, research during the last decade has focused on building Question Answering technologies that can successfully answer one type of questions, namely factoid questions, which have well-defined, relatively short answers. This chapter emphasizes these recent developments on factoid Question Answering.

The reverse process of Question Generation (QG) or asking is a fundamental human capacity that is present in childhood as a primary form of learning, curiosity, and discovery. Students in K12, college, and adult populations are known to improve their learning after they learn how to acquire improved skills of QG. QG is an essential component of learning environments, help systems, information seeking systems, and a myriad of other applications. Mechanisms of QG have been less explored in the Computational Linguistics and Text Retrieval community, the two communities that led the recent efforts on Question Answering processes. We know that language generation is a very difficult task to take on, as all natural language generation tasks are, but do not believe that the inherent difficulty should prevent the exploration of automated QG. Recent efforts by Rus and colleagues (2007, 2009a, 2009b) launched the creation of a coherent and strong QG research community that has grand research plans for the next decade.

QUESTION QUALITY, COMPLEXITY, AND TAXONOMIES

An important initial step in a Question Answering or Generation project is to take stock of the landscape of question categories so that researchers can specify what types of questions they have in mind, as well as the educational context (Rus, Cai, & Graesser, 2007). This section identifies some QG categories, taxonomies, and dimensions that might be considered. The complexity and quality of the questions systematically vary across the broad landscape of questions. Finding the relevant criteria of question quality is a key requirement for good performance of QG systems. What we present in this section is merely the tip of the iceberg.

Question taxonomies have been proposed by researchers who have developed models of Question Answering and Generation in the fields of artificial intelligence, computational linguistics (Voorhees, 2001), discourse processing, education and a number of other fields in the cognitive sciences (for a review, see Graesser, Ozuru, & Sullins, 2009).

Sincere-Information Seeking (SIS) vs. Other Types of Questions

Questions are often generated by a person's knowledge deficits and cognitive disequilibrium, which occurs when there are obstacles to goals, contradictions, impasses during problem solving, anomalous information, and uncertainty. Whereas SIS questions are bona fide *knowledge deficit* questions, other types of questions address communication and social interaction processes. *Common ground* questions are asked when the questioner wants to establish or confirm whether knowledge is shared between participants in the conversation ("Did you say/mean oxygen?," "Are you understanding this?"). *Social coordination* questions are indirect requests for the addressee to perform an action or for the questioner to have permission to perform an action in a collaborative activity (e.g., "Could you graph these numbers?," "Can we take a break now?"). *Conversation-control* questions are asked to manipulate the flow of conversation or the attention of the speech participants (e.g., "Can I ask you a question?").

Assumptions behind Questions

Most questions posed by students and teachers are not SIS questions. Van der Meij (1987) identified 11 assumptions that need to be in place in order for a question to qualify as a SIS question.

1. The questioner does not know the information he asks for with the question.

2. The question specifies the information sought after.

3. The questioner believes that the presuppositions to the question are true.

4. The questioner believes that an answer exists.

5. The questioner wants to know the answer.

6. The questioner can assess whether a reply constitutes an answer.

7. The questioner poses the question only if the benefits exceed the costs.

8. The questioner believes that the respondent knows the answer.

9. The questioner believes that the respondent will not give the answer in absence of a question.

10. The questioner believes that the respondent will supply the answer.

11. A question solicits a reply.

A question is a non-SIS question if one or more of these assumptions are not met. For example, when a physics teacher grills students with a series of questions in a classroom (e.g., *What forces are acting on the vehicle in the collision?, What are the directions of the forces?, What is the mass of the vehicle?*), they are not SIS questions because they violate assumptions 1, 5, 8, and 10. Teachers know the answers to most questions they ask during these grilling sessions, so they are not modeling bona fide inquiry. Similarly, assumptions are violated when there are rhetorical questions (*When does a person know when he or she is happy?*), gripes (*When is it going to stop raining?*), greetings (*How are you?*), and attempts to redirect the flow of conversation in a group (a hostess asks a silent guest: *So when is your next vacation?*). In contrast, a question is a SIS question when a person's computer is malfunctioning and the person asks a technical assistant the following questions: *What's wrong with my computer? How can I get it fixed? How much will it cost?*

Question Categories

The following 16 question categories were either proposed by Lehnert (1978) in their computer program called QUALM or by Graesser and Person (1994) in their analysis of tutoring. It should be noted that sometimes a question can be a hybrid between two categories.

1. **Verification:** invites a yes or no answer.
2. **Disjunctive:** Is X, Y, or Z the case?
3. **Concept completion:** Who? What? When? Where?
4. **Example:** What is an example of X?
5. **Feature specification:** What are the properties of X?
6. **Quantification:** How much? How many?
7. **Definition:** What does X mean?
8. **Comparison:** How is X similar to Y?
9. **Interpretation:** What is the significance of X?
10. **Causal antecedent:** Why/how did X occur?
11. **Causal consequence:** What next? What if?
12. **Goal orientation:** Why did an agent do X?
13. **Instrumental/procedural:** How did an agent do X?
14. **Enablement:** What enabled X to occur?
15. **Expectation:** Why didn't X occur?
16. **Judgmental:** What do you think of X?

Categories 1-4 were classified as simple/shallow, 5-8 as intermediate, and 9-16 as complex/deep questions in Graesser and Person's empirical analyses of questions in educational settings. This scale of depth was validated to the extent that it correlated significantly ($r = .60 \pm .05$) with both Mosenthal's (1996) scale of question depth and the original Bloom's taxonomy of cognitive difficulty (1956). Although the Graesser-Person scheme has some degree of validity, it is an imperfect scale for depth and quality. For example, one can readily identify *disjunctive* questions that require considerable thought and reasoning,

as in the case of the difficult physics question: *When the passenger is rear-ended, does the head initially (a) go forward, (b) go backwards, or (c) stay the same?* Generating an answer to this question requires a causal analysis, which corresponds to question categories 10 and 11, so this question may functionally be a hybrid question. But hybrid questions present a problem if we are trying to create a unidimensional scale of depth. One task for researchers is to formulate and test a categorization scheme that scales questions on depth as well as other dimensions of quality.

Other Dimensions of Questions

Some other dimensions of questions are frequently addressed in classification schemes (Graesser, Ozuru, & Sullins, 2009).

1. **Information sources:** Does the answer come from a text, world knowledge, both, elsewhere?
2. **Length of answer:** Is the answer a single word, a phrase, a sentence, or a paragraph?
3. **Type of knowledge:** Is the knowledge organized as a semantic network, plan, causal structure, spatial layout, rule set, list of facts, etc.?
4. **Cognitive process:** What cognitive processes are involved with asking and answering the question? For example, using Bloom's taxonomy, do the cognitive processes involve recognition memory, recall of information, deep comprehension, inference, application of ideas, synthesis of information from multiple sources, comparison, or evaluation?

Given the diversity of questions that can be asked, building systems that can automatically answer them can be challenging. We present next an overview of automated approaches to the task of Question Answering.

QUESTION ANSWERING

Building computer systems that could answer natural language questions has been puzzling the research community since the early days of computing. Early automated Question Answering systems have focused on providing quick and natural access to expert knowledge stored in some computational form (formal knowledge bases, structured databases, etc.). A good example is Woods and colleagues' LUNAR system (Woods, Kaplan, & Webber, 1972). LUNAR was created to answer questions about the Apollo 11 moon rocks for the NASA Manned Spacecraft Center. In particular, the goal was to built a system "sufficiently natural and complete" that the wording of a question would require negligible effort for the user. An example of questions that the LUNAR system was supposed to answer is "What is the average concentration of aluminum in high-alkali rocks?"

The PLANES (Waltz, 1978) Question Answering System was intended to offer a natural language interface to access information in a structured database (aircraft maintenance domain). The basic idea was to allow a non-programmer to retrieve information from a structured database with minimal prior training. One interesting feature of the system was educating the user in formulating questions that the system could understand.

As we already pointed out, answering any type of question is very challenging because it requires knowledge about the world, the users' task, inference capabilities, user modeling, linguistics knowledge, and knowledge about the pragmatics of discourse and dialogue. To make the task more palatable given the current technological advancements, in the late 1990s the research community decided to focus on one type of question, called *factoid questions,* whose answers are relatively short and well-defined. The National Institute for Standards and Technology (NIST) initiated in 1999 the Question Answering challenge, the first large-scale evaluation of domain-independent Question Answering systems (Voorhees & Tice, 2000). The Question Answering challenge was one of the many challenges NIST proposed as part of its Text Retrieval Conference (TREC; trec.nist.gov), which promotes advances in text retrieval technologies.

Probably the most important factor that prompted the NIST's Question Answering challenge was the advent of the Internet and the World Wide Web in the 1990s. There was an explosion of textual information available online, but the information was not represented as formal knowledge or structured databases. As a first response to the information retrieval challenge posed by the Internet, commercial services in the form of search engines were created to provide information search functions to users looking for information on the web. Nevertheless, the traditional search engines of that era were classical information retrieval systems that lacked two important features that were needed by the community of Internet users, most of them mundane users. The two missing features were: (1) the user queries were not natural language questions but rather sets of keywords and (2) the output of these systems was a ranked list of documents (web pages); users had to look up the answer in the list of documents in order to fulfill their particular information needs, which is a time-consuming task. NIST's Question Answering challenge fostered the development of large-scale Question Answering systems that could retrieve short answers to users' factual questions from large collections of documents (millions or billions of documents). NIST provided the framework to evaluate and monitor progress of developed large-scale, open-domain Question Answering systems. The open-domain label referred to the generality of the topics covered by the collections of documents. These were topics of general interest, such as news articles or government documents. The open-domain label did not refer to the ability of QA systems to answer any questions in any domain.

The Question Answering track focused solely on factual questions of the form *Who is the voice of Miss Piggy?* (Answer: Frank Oz) or *How much could you rent a Volkswagen bug for in 1966?* (for the curious reader the answer is $1 per day). Participants in the QA track were given a set of test questions (200 at TREC-8 in 1999) and a large collection of documents (~5 GB of text). They were supposed to provide a ranked list of 5 answers in the form of generated answers or of excerpts from documents where the answers are located. Answers were of two types: short (up to 50 characters) and long (up to 250 characters). An answer was considered correct if a person reading it would consider it so. The output of all participants was automatically compared to a gold standard of correct answers (collected and/or checked manually by human judges) using regular-expressions in the matching algorithms. The scoring rubric was designed to reward the system's ability to provide correct answers in the first positions of the ranked list of answers. The score assigned to each test question was the reciprocal of the rank of the first correct answer in the list of 5 answers. For instance, a correct answer at the top of the list was given a perfect score of 1 while a correct answer in the second position would be assigned a score of 0.5, in the third person a score of 0.33, and so on. An overall mean reciprocal rank (MRR) score was computed for the set of test questions by averaging the ranking scores of the individual questions. In the first TREC Question Answering challenge, the best systems obtained MRR scores ~0.5-0.6 for the short answer category (50 bytes at most per answer), meaning they provided the first correct answer, on average, in the second position in the list of 5 ranked answers.

Since the first Question Answering challenge was offered in 1999 at TREC-8, many systems have been developed and substantial research has been conducted that explore various steps in the QA process, such as question classification or answer justification. The major approaches to answering factual questions range from shallow (Moldovan et al., 1999) to deep (Rus, 2002). Shallow approaches use shallow linguistic methods that are combined with heuristic-based scoring techniques to locate and rank answers. Deep approaches rely on world knowledge and inference mechanisms to retrieve correct answers. Deep approaches can justify the correctness of the answers using logical explanations (Rus, 2002).

There are several important outcomes resulting from NIST's decade-long QA track. First, there is a better understanding of factoid questions and factoid Question Answering processes. Second, many successful Question Answering systems were developed and are now available in many languages. Third, Question Answering research led to better search engines, which now can take queries in the form of natural language questions and provide a ranked list of short answers instead of just documents. Fourth, high-performance Question Answering systems are being built, culminating with the recent announcement by I.B.M. of its Deep QA system, codename Watson. Watson is intended to be precise and fast enough to compete in real-time with top human contestants of the game of Jeopardy.

Considerable progress has been made in the area of automated Question Answering on variants of factoid questions, including simple factoid questions, list factoid questions where the answer is a list of items such as names, multilingual Question Answering, and so on. However, there is a long road ahead to develop Question Answering systems that can answer any type of question in any domain for any user. In particular, there is need to develop methods to automatically handle deep questions and to provide answers tailored to a particular user's background. Answers delivered to an expert should be at a fine-grain level of detail with domain-specific language whereas answers to a novice should be more course-grain with plain language.

QUESTION ASKING

As research on Question Answering was flourishing over the last decade, there was less attention paid to automatic Question Asking/Generation. This was clearly an oversight because applications of automated QG facilities will be far reaching. Sample applications of automated QG facilities include the following:

1. Suggested good questions that learners might ask while reading documents and other media.
2. Questions that human and computer tutors might ask to promote and assess deeper learning.
3. Suggested questions for patients and caretakers in medicine.
4. Suggested questions that might be asked in legal contexts by litigants or in security contexts by interrogators.
5. Questions automatically generated from information repositories as candidates for Frequently Asked Question (FAQ) facilities.

To enable such applications, QG technologies must be developed in a more systematic and large-scale manner. The development of these systems need to build on the disciplinary and interdisciplinary work on QG that has been evolving in the fields of education, the social sciences (psychology, linguistics, anthropology, sociology), and computer science (computational linguistics, artificial intelligence, human-computer interaction, information retrieval).

Early Question Generation and Question Asking Research

Early explorations of QG were sporadic and less systematic. Cognitive science and education researchers paid more attention to Question Generation, which they called *Question Asking*, than other communities because Question Asking

has frequently been considered a fundamental cognitive process. The ideal learner is an active, self-motivated, creative, and inquisitive person who asks deep questions and searches for answers to such thought-provoking questions. There is a long history of researchers who have advocated learning environments that support inquiry learning and question asking (Craig, Sullins, Witherspoon, & Gholson, 2006; Rosenshine, Meister, & Chapman, 1996; Van der Meij, 1994). Question Asking is one of the processing components that underlies higher level cognitive activities, such as comprehension, problem solving, and reasoning.

Existing research on Question Asking has sometimes embraced the notion that clashes between stimulus input and world knowledge are very much at the essence of Question Asking/Generation (Dillon, 1988; Graesser & Olde, 2003; Otero & Graesser, 2001). Thus, questions are asked when there are contradictions, anomalous information, obstacles to goals, uncertainty, and obvious gaps in knowledge. Although it is widely acknowledged that discrepancies between input and knowledge trigger questions, the precise mechanisms need to be specified in more detail than has been achieved in psychology and education.

The field of Artificial Intelligence (AI) has offered computational models that make some attempt to specify the knowledge representations and knowledge discrepancies that underlie Question Asking/Generation. According to Schank's SWALE model (Schank, 1986), for example, questions are asked when we observe anomalous events and request explanations for such events (e.g., *Why did the event occur?*). Long-term memory is viewed as a large inventory of cases that record anomalous events and their associated explanations, which are driven by *why, what-if,* and other deep questions.

Models of Question Asking/Generation in AI have excelled in analytical detail and computational precision, but the models have not been adequately tested on Question Asking in humans.

In contrast, the fields of psychology and education have empirically tested general theoretical claims about Question Asking, but they have underachieved in formulating the precise conditions, knowledge representations, and computational mechanisms that generate the questions.

The PREG model of Question Asking (Otero & Graesser, 2001) reduced this gap between the two enterprises. PREG is a comprehensive analytical model of Question Asking/Generation that incorporates the mechanisms that have been identified in education, psychology, discourse processing, and artificial intelligence. The model was used to predict the particular questions that children and adults would ask when they read expository texts on scientific phenomena. The predicted questions are sensitive to four information sources or processing components: (1) the explicit text, (2) the reader's world knowledge about the topics in the text, (3) the reader's metacognitive skills, and (4) the reader's knowledge about the pragmatics of communication. The PREG model has received some support in psychological investigations, but more research is needed to determine the precise conditions under which particular questions are generated. This step can only be achieved by interdisciplinary efforts that embrace artificial intelligence and computational linguistics.

Attempts at QG in Natural Language Processing/Computational Linguistics can be categorized into three groups: *Query/Question Reformulation, pseudo Question Generation,* and *simple Question Generation.* The task in *Query/Question Reformulation* is to generate queries/questions after being given a question as input. The goal is to improve the question in order to refine the search for a good set of answers. A representative system for Query/Question Reformulation is the CO-OP system (McKeown, 1983), which implements question reformulation through paraphrasing in the context of database access. CO-OP's goal was to allow non-experts to send queries to a database management system using natural language–based questions. Regarding *pseudo Question Genera-*

tion, Hoshino and Hiroshi (2005) used the term Question Generation to refer to sentences with gaps in multiple-choice language tests. In these tests the student is asked to choose, from a list of options, the word that best fills the gap in a given sentence so that the most appropriate sentence is formed. Since the generated output is not a question, we consider this work to be *pseudo* Question Generation rather than true Question Generation. Regarding *simple Question Generation*, Mitkov and Ha (2003) developed a computer-aided procedure for generating multiple-choice questions, given a set of documents on a topic. The procedure first identifies candidate concepts and sentences in which they appear. Given the sentence, it uses a shallow syntactic parser, transformational rules, and WordNet (G.A. Miller, Beckwith, Fellbaum, Gross, & K. Miller, 1990) to map the sentence into its interrogative form. If the sentence is "the lawyers won the lawsuit," then the questions might be: "Who won the lawsuit?" or "What did the lawyers win?" The system can only handle sentences whose structure is SVO or SV (S-Subject; V-Verb; O-Object). For example, an SVO sentence is transformed into *Which HVO? question,* where H is a *hypernym* (a more general term) of the S term (e.g., *vehicle* is a hypernym of *car*). Due to its limited scope, we call Mitkov and Ha's work *simple Question Generation.*

For many years there was relative isolation of the researchers from the various communities working on Question Generation/Asking. Therefore in 2007 Rus, Cai, and Graesser (2007) launched a series of workshops with the goal to assemble Question Generation/Asking researchers and to form a community that coordinates research efforts in a coherent and systematic way.

Assembling the Question Generation Research Community

With NSF support, the 1st Workshop on Question Generation took place in September 2008 in Arlington, VA. The workshop was attended by 29 participants from all over the world, from both academia and industry (e.g., Microsoft, Yahoo). Since then, two other workshops were organized in 2009 and 2010 with an ever-growing number of participants (33 participants in 2009 and 35 participants in 2010). In 2010 the first Question Generation Shared Task Evaluation Campaign (QG-STEC) was organized by The University of Memphis and Open University of the United Kingdom. Two tasks were offered: Question Generation from Paragraphs (Task A) and Question Generation from Sentences (Task B). These tasks evolved naturally from the 1st Workshop on Question Generation that identified four categories of QG tasks (Rus & Graesser, 2009): Text-to-Question, Tutorial Dialogue, Assessment, and Query-to-Question. Tasks A and B in the first QG-STEC are part of the more general Text-to-Text category of Natural Language Generation tasks identified by the NLG community (Rus et al., 2007).

Current Question Generation Research

Automated QG is currently seen as a discourse task (Rus & Graesser, 2009) that is beyond a traditional natural language generation task. Automated QG consists of three major steps: (1) target concept identification, (2) question type selection, and (3) question construction. It is still an open question whether the three main steps in the QG processing pipeline are independent and follow each other sequentially, or are executed in parallel. It may be the case that they can be executed both sequentially and in parallel, in which case the exact conditions under which one type of execution is more appropriate are yet to be identified. A computational QG model can be informed by studies on human question asking processes in order to refine these research issues. For example, in the case of humans reading text, the identification of target content and the subsequent decision on question type do not appear to be separate modular processes that

are executed in an independent, sequential manner. Rather, they seem to be directly dependent on cognitive disequilibrium (Graesser & McMahen, 1993; Otero, 2009; Otero & Graesser, 2001). The generation of deep questions in human readers is essentially triggered by the existence of an obstacle that prevents a reader with particular domain knowledge from achieving a discourse representation goal. Therefore, reading goals and the obstacles found by a reader in achieving them play a primary role in the definition of target content and type of questions asked.

The Question Generation Shared Task Evaluation Campaign

An important activity of the QG research community was the organization during Spring 2010 of the first Question Generation Shared Task Evaluation Challenge (QG-STEC). The QG-STEC followed a long tradition of STECs in Natural Language Processing; this includes the various tracks at the Text REtrieval Conference (TREC; trec.nist.gov) and the Question Answering track mentioned earlier. The QG-STEC was inspired by the Natural Language Generation (NLG) community's goal to offer shared task evaluation campaigns as a potential avenue to encourage focused research efforts (White & Dale, 2008).

The two tasks offered in the first QG-STEC were selected by the members of the QG community among five candidate tasks. A consensus-reaching process was implemented to decide the two tasks. Community members were invited to proposed tasks, and then a preference poll was conducted to select the two most preferred tasks. Question Generation from Paragraphs (Task A) and Question Generation from Sentences (Task B) were selected to be offered in the first QG-STEC. The other three candidate tasks were (a) ranking automatically generated questions, (b) concept identification and ordering, and (c) question type identification. Regarding input representation, both Tasks A and B used raw text to avoid representational commitments. The alternative would have annotated texts so that participants would focus on the fundamental targeted task of QG and not get bogged down with extra work on understanding text input. However, arriving at an acceptable annotation scheme for the entire community to use would be challenge so it was postponed for future QG-STEC efforts.

There was some overlap between Tasks A and B in the first QG-STEC. The overlap was intentional, with the aim of encouraging people preferring one task to participate in the other too. The overlap consisted of types of questions in Task A, namely the *specific questions*, being somewhat similar to the types of questions targeted by Task B. In task B, participants were asked to generate specific questions of a certain type (e.g., *Who)* whereas in Task A there was no such constraint.

Six research centers emerged as major contributors in the evolution of the QG-STEC campaign. A brief description of the directions of each center is provided in order to show how question generation is an important mechanism to understand.

Research Center 1: University of Memphis

The University of Memphis has been involved in QG research for two decades (Graesser, Person, & Huber, 1992; Graesser & Person, 1994; Otero & Graesser, 2001; Rus et al., 2007; Rus & Graesser, 2009; Rus et al., 2010). Graesser and his colleagues have developed a cognitive model of question asking called PREG (Graesser & Olde, 2003; Otero & Graesser, 2001; Graesser, Lu, Olde, Cooper-Pye, & Whitten, 2005) that embraces cognitive disequilibrium in its foundation, as described earlier.

More recently, the Memphis team developed an automated QG system that was originally motivated by work in building AutoTutor (Graesser et al., 2004, see Chapter 10), an intelligent tutoring system that helps students learn by holding a conversation in natural language. The core pedagogical strategy of AutoTutor is called *Expectation and Misconception Tailored* dialogue. The dialogue manager tries to get the learner to articulate a number of sentence-like answers (called expectations). AutoTutor gets the student to do the talking by giving generic pumps ("tell me more"), hints (e.g., "What about X?," "What is the relation between X and Y?"), and question prompts ("After release, the horizontal force on the packet is what?") for the student to fill in specific words. A QG Mark-up Language (QGML) was developed to automatically generate questions from sentence-like expectations (Cai et al., 2006; Rus, Cai, & Graesser, 2007). This was considered a very useful facility because it is very difficult to train human authors (instructors, lesson planners) to generate these dialogue moves that have subtle linguistic constraints.

Vasile Rus and Art Graesser at the University of Memphis led the initial building of the QG research community (Rus et al., 2007; Rus & Graesser, 2009; Rus & Lester, 2009) and organized the first QG-STEC (Rus et al., 2010). The University of Memphis ran Task A, Question Generation from Paragraphs, as part of the first QG-STEC.

Research Center 2: Open University

Research on QG at the Open University (OU) is conducted in the Natural Language Generation Group of the Centre for Research in Computing. Paul Piwek pioneered research on Text-to-Dialogue (T2D) generation based on discourse relations (Piwek et al., 2007). His CODA project (Piwek & Stoyanchev, 2010; Stoyanchev & Piwek 2010) investigates the automatic generation of dialogue text (akin to FAQs) from monologue. This includes the automatic generation of questions from text in monologue form. This effort includes collaboration with the National Institute of Informatics in Tokyo, which focuses on creating computer-animated movies from dialogue text.

The DataMIX project brings together UK researchers from seven different disciplines (computational linguistics, design, theoretical physics, chemistry, and music computing) to investigate more inclusive ways of presenting data and information. The OU contribution investigates the utility of presenting data in question-answer form to different users. The users include lay persons, experts, individuals with visual impairments, and those affected by the digital divide.

Members of the OU team have participated and presented work at all QG workshops to date, including a paper on an open-source QG system (Wyse & Piwek, 2009). In 2010, the OU team was involved in the organization of Task B in the first QG-STEC and co-chaired the Third Workshop on QG.

Research Center 3: North Carolina State University

Kristy Boyer and James Lester investigate automatic QG in task-oriented dialogue. Their JAVATUTOR project (Boyer, Vouk, & Lester, 2007; Boyer et al., 2009) develops adaptive task-oriented dialogue systems by using data-driven approaches that learn dialogue policies from corpora. Research has shown that the effectiveness of human tutorial dialogue is facilitated by rich tutor-student interactions, students' self-explanations, and tutors' targeted, adaptive feedback (see Chapters 15 and 17). Tutorial dialogue systems must be able to generate questions in order to support these activities. In a mixed-initiative dialogue with a student, a tutoring system must be able to answer student questions and also to pose questions. Supporting students' self-explanations also involves asking questions that elicit those explanations, especially deep questions (Craig et al., 2006; Graesser & Person, 1994).

Most tutorial dialogue systems handle QG with a set of hand-authored questions or question templates that offer limited flexibility and content coverage. An automated data-driven approach to

QG would help correct these limitations. Automatic QG therefore holds significant promise for increasing the effectiveness of tutorial dialogue systems, including the task-oriented tutorial dialogue systems such as JAVATUTOR (Boyer et al., 2009).

To facilitate research on automatic QG within task-oriented tutorial dialogue, additional annotated corpora are needed, ideally in multiple domains. These corpora would consist of successful human-human textual or spoken dialogues that are annotated with dialogue act tags that capture cognitive and affective aspects of each utterance. Task structure would also be tagged, as would the correctness of students' task actions (Boyer et al., 2010; Fossati et al., 2010; Lane, 2004). With such annotated corpora, it would be possible to explore several important research questions: (1) When should the tutor ask questions? (2) What should the question topics be? (3) What are potential surface realizations of the question? The answers to these questions will contribute to creating the next generation of tutorial dialogue systems that are more flexible and effective than their predecessors.

Research Center 4: Carnegie Mellon University

Heilman and Smith (2009, 2010) investigate QG for the creation of educational materials to improve reading practice and assessment. Their goal is to create an automated system that can take as input a text (e.g., an article that a student might read for homework or during class) and produce as output a ranked list of questions for assessing students' knowledge of information in the text. Their QG system leverages existing NLP tools and formalisms to solve various linguistic challenges. Manually written rules encode linguistic knowledge about question formation and generate a large set of candidate questions. These candidate questions are then ranked by a statistical model of question quality to address semantic and pragmatic issues that are not easily captured with rules. A large annotated corpus allows the development of machine-learning-based QG models that induce question formation rules. This eliminates the need to manually create such rules, a task that is both time-consuming and error-prone. Heilman and Smith proposed one of the five initial tasks for the first QG-STEC: ranking automatically generated questions.

Research Center 5:
University of Colorado

Rodney Nielsen and colleagues at The University of Colorado investigate QG in a variety of contexts, including intelligent tutoring systems, other educational settings, clinical informatics, and personal dialogue. They have been active contributors to the recent QG research efforts in the QG workshops (Becker et al., 2009; Becker et al., 2010; Nielsen, 2008; Nielsen et al., 2008). Nielsen led the evaluation methods and metrics team at the first QG workshop and proposed one of the five initial tasks for the QG-STEC, namely the concept identification and ordering task.

The University of Colorado's research on QG covers several basic questions, but particularly targets the first step in the QG processing pipeline: Target Concept Identification (TCI) (Nielsen, 2008; Vanderwende, 2008). If the concept is not important, is the question really worth asking? TCI requires deciding which concepts in general are worth discussing, what their relative merit is, how they depend on one another, how to elicit them from the student, or how to help the student discover and comprehend them given the current dialogue context.

TCI is performed during the dialogue and is a context-sensitive task. It is important to identify *a priori* the set of key question-worthy concepts in the knowledge source. Given the application domain, the objective of Key Concept Identification is to identify the most important content in the text that should launch questions. This task is

hopefully less sensitive to the application domain and should therefore appeal to a broad research community. Related issues are Concept Sequencing (defining a logical sequence of concepts) and Concept Relation Identification and Classification (the detection and labeling of inter-concept relationships).

Research Center 6: The
University of Pennsylvania

Rashmi Prasad and Aravind Joshi participated in all three QG workshops and also in Task A of the first QG-STEC. Their research focus includes the generation of higher-order questions, similar to the medium/discourse-level questions in QG-STEC's Task A. Unlike questions generated from the content of a single clause, higher-order questions are derived from discourse relations that connect clausal and sentential arguments.

Discourse relations in a given input have been pre-specified in a QG-STEC so that participants can focus on the higher-order QG challenges rather than on developing the discourse-level resources needed to identify the discourse relations. Therefore, the first QG-STEC provided the discourse relation annotations using an existing automatic discourse parser (HILDA, duVerle & Prendinger, 2009) that was based on Rhetorical Structure Theory (Mann and Thompson, 1988). Mannem et al (2010) have argued that an exhaustive set of discourse relations is not required as the input knowledge for QG and that the complete discourse structure of a text need not be specified. Much of the recent research on shallow discourse parsing (Prasad et al., 2010) exploits the Penn Discourse Treebank (PDTB) corpus (Prasad et al., 2008), which contains low-level annotations of discourse relations. Rashmi Prasad and Aravind Joshi at UPenn have led the development of the PDTB and are exploring a semi-automatic annotation approach towards developing the discourse-level infrastructure for QG.

Research by Other Team Members

Calvo and colleagues have explored the role of QG in supporting writing activities (Liu & Calvo, 2009; Liu, Calvo, & Rus, 2010). Hirashima (2009) automatically generates physics problems and studies their impact on students' problem solving skills. Automated QG is being used to scaffold self-questioning strategies automatically to help children in grades 1-3 understand informational text (Chen, Aist, & Mostow, 2009).

CONCLUSION AND FUTURE RESEARCH DIRECTIONS

Question Answering and Generation are two important challenges for the Google generation. Since the advent of the Internet, the information focus shifted from access to information to information overload so natural retrieval methods with natural language have been explored and developed. We can now effectively provide answers to factoid questions that seek specific nuggets of information that are well-defined. Providing user-tailored answers to deep questions is still an open problem that waits to be explored at some point in the future. Asking factoid questions presupposes knowing what you are looking for. When you do not know what to ask for, as in learning, the reverse process of asking questions takes central stage. Question Asking or Generation has been explored sporadically in education and psychology but a few years ago the challenge was taken up by the field of computer science. The recently created Question Generation community provides a coherent and systematic framework for advancing the field and influencing other fields, particularly the learning sciences.

Question Answering and Generation will ultimately work in tandem in future learning and information delivery environments. The citizens of the Google generation know that they can ask questions and receive reasonable answers within seconds and minutes. This is very different from 20 years ago when it would take hours, days, or months to get answers to the same questions. We live in an era when the gap between curiosity and answers is vanishing. The younger generation is impatient or angry when answers are not quickly available to their Internet fingertips. The information world has changed. Hence our thinking styles are changing. We are convinced that changes in inquiry strategies constitute the most fundamental change in the new millennium.

One promising approach is to automate Question Answering and Generation processes in a fashion that mimics the typical human processes of inquiry. More specifically, questions are asked in natural language and answered by a large array of question answering procedures. However, we know that it is also important to investigate ideal intelligent question asking and answering mechanisms. We also know that questions can be asked through human-computer interfaces other than natural language. That is, questions can be asked by consulting Frequently Asked Questions list, by creating questions via primitives available as Graphical User Interface elements, by Point & Query facilities where the users point to (or clicks on) a hot spot on the display and then a menu of contextually-relevant questions appears (see Graesser et al., 2002 for an example), by questions that are asked by a combination of speech, gesture, and gaze, and by questions inferred from the user's actions. It was beyond the scope of this chapter to provide an overview of all these forms of inquiry so we focused on those with natural language interaction.

The seeds of learning start with curiosity about intrinsically interesting topics and strange events that occur in the world. These states and events spawn questions. However, it has always been difficult for people to express their questions and to quickly retrieve relevant answers. For the first time in the history of humankind, technology will help us conquer these barriers.

REFERENCES

Bloom, B. S. (1956). *Taxonomy of educational objectives: The classification of educational goals. Handbook I: Cognitive Domain*. New York, NY: McKay.

Craig, S. D., Sullins, J., Witherspoon, A., & Gholson, B. (2006). Deep-level reasoning questions effect: The role of dialog and deep-level reasoning questions during vicarious learning. *Cognition and Instruction, 24*(4), 563–589. doi:10.1207/s1532690xci2404_4

Dillon, J. (1988). *Questioning and teaching: A manual of practice*. New York, NY: Teachers College Press.

Graesser, A., Ozuru, Y., & Sullins, J. (2009). What is a good question? In McKeown, M. G., & Kucan, L. (Eds.), *Threads of coherence in research on the development of reading ability* (pp. 112–141). New York, NY: Guilford.

Graesser, A. C., & McMahen, C. L. (1993). Anomalous information triggers questions when adults solve problems and comprehend stories. *Journal of Educational Psychology, 85*, 136–151. doi:10.1037/0022-0663.85.1.136

Graesser, A. C., & Olde, B. A. (2003). How does one know whether a person understands a device? The quality of the questions the person asks when the device breaks down. *Journal of Educational Psychology, 95*, 524–536. doi:10.1037/0022-0663.95.3.524

Graesser, A. C., & Person, N. K. (1994). Question asking during tutoring. *American Educational Research Journal, 31*, 104–137.

Lehnert, W. G. (1978). *The process of question answering: A computer simulation of cognition*. Hillsdale, NJ: Erlbaum.

Miller, G. A., Beckwith, R., Fellbaum, C. D., Gross, D., & Miller, K. (1990). WordNet: An online lexical database. *International Journal of Lexicography, 3-4*, 235–244. doi:10.1093/ijl/3.4.235

Moldovan, D., Harabagiu, S., Pasca, M., Mihalcea, R., Goodrum, R., Girju, R., & Rus, V. (1999). LASSO: A tool for surfing the answer net. In *Proceedings of the Text Retrieval Conference* (TREC-8), November, 1999.

Mosenthal, P. (1996). Understanding the strategies of document literacy and their conditions of use. *Journal of Educational Psychology, 88*, 314–332. doi:10.1037/0022-0663.88.2.314

Otero, J. (2009). Question generation and anomaly detection in texts. In Hacker, D., Dunlosky, J., & Graesser, A. (Eds.), *Handbook of metacognition in education*. New York, NY: Routledge.

Otero, J., & Graesser, A. C. (2001). PREG: Elements of a model of question asking. *Cognition and Instruction, 19*, 143–175. doi:10.1207/S1532690XCI1902_01

Rosenshine, B., Meister, C., & Chapman, S. (1996). Teaching students to generate questions: A review of the intervention studies. *Review of Educational Research, 66*, 181–221.

Rus, V. (2002). *Logic form for WordNet glosses and application to question answering*. Computer Science Department, School of Engineering, Southern Methodist University, PhD Thesis, May 2002, Dallas, Texas.

Rus, V., Cai, Z., & Graesser, A. C. (2007). *Evaluation in natural language generation: The question generation task*. Workshop on Shared Tasks and Comparative Evaluation in Natural Language Generation, Arlington, VA, April 20-21, 2007.

Rus, V., & Graesser, A. C. (Eds.). (2009a). *The question generation shared task and evaluation challenge*.

Rus, V., & Lester, J. (Eds.). (2009b). *Proceedings of the 2nd Workshop on Question Generation*, July 6, 2009, Brighton, UK.

Schank, R. C. (1986). *Explanation patterns: Understanding mechanically and creatively*. Hillsdale, NJ: Erlbaum.

Van der Meij, H. (1994). Student questioning: A componential analysis. *Learning and Individual Differences*, *6*, 137–161. doi:10.1016/1041-6080(94)90007-8

Voorhees, E. M., & Tice, D. M. (2000). The TREC-8 question answering track evaluation. In E.M. Voorhees & D. K. Harman, (Eds.), *Proceedings of the Eighth Text REtrieval Conference* (TREC-8). Retrieved from http://trec.nist.gov/pubs.htrul.

Waltz, D. L. (1978). An English language question answering system for a large relational database. *Communications of the ACM*, *21*(7), 526–539. doi:10.1145/359545.359550

Woods, W. A., Kaplan, R. M., & Webber, B. N. (1972). *The lunar sciences natural language Information System: Final report. BBN Report 2378*. Cambridge, MA: Bolt Beranek and Newman, Inc.

ADDITIONAL READING

Beck, I. L., McKeown, M. G., Hamilton, R. L., & Kucan, L. (1997). *Questioning the Author: An approach for enhancing student engagement with text*. Delaware: International Reading Association.

Ciardiello, A. V. (1998). Did you ask a good question today? Alternative cognitive and metacognitive strategies. *Journal of Adolescent & Adult Literacy*, *42*, 210–219.

Collins, A. (1988). Different goals of inquiry teaching. *Questioning Exchange*, *2*, 39–45.

Davey, B., & McBride, S. (1986). Effects of question generation on reading comprehension. *Journal of Educational Psychology*, *78*, 256–262. doi:10.1037/0022-0663.78.4.256

Dillon, J. (1988). *Questioning and teaching: A manual of practice*. New York: Teachers College Press.

Flammer, A. (1981). Towards a theory of question asking. *Psychological Research*, *43*, 407–420. doi:10.1007/BF00309225

Gavelek, J. R., & Raphael, T. E. (1985). Metacognition, instruction, and the role of questioning activities. In Forrest-Pressley, D. L., MacKinnon, G. E., & Waller, G. T. (Eds.), *Metacognition, cognition, & human performance: Instructional practices* (*Vol. 2*, pp. 103–136). Orlando, FL: Academic Press.

Good, T. L., Slavings, R. L., Harel, K. H., & Emerson, M. (1987). Students" passivity: A study of question asking in K-12 classrooms. *Sociology of Education*, *60*, 181–199. doi:10.2307/2112275

Graesser, A., Ozuru, Y., & Sullins, J. (2009). What is a good question? In McKeown, M. G., & Kucan, L. (Eds.), *Threads of coherence in research on the development of reading ability* (pp. 112–141). New York, NY: Guilford.

King, A. (1989). Effects of self-questioning training on college students' comprehension of lectures. *Contemporary Educational Psychology*, *14*, 366–381. doi:10.1016/0361-476X(89)90022-2

King, A. (1992). Comparison of self-questioning, summarizing, and notetaking-review as strategies for learning from lectures. *American Educational Research Journal*, *29*, 303–323.

Lehnert, W. G. (1978). *The Process of Question Answering: a computer simulation of cognition*. Lawrence Erlbaum Associates.

Otero, J., & Graesser, A. C. (2001). PREG: Elements of a model of question asking. *Cognition and Instruction*, *19*, 143–175. doi:10.1207/S1532690XCI1902_01

Reder, L. (1987). Strategy selection in question answering. *Cognitive Psychology*, *19*, 90–138. doi:10.1016/0010-0285(87)90005-3

Reeves, B., & Nass, C. (1996). *The media equation: How people treat computers, televisions, and new media like real people and places*. Cambridge, U.K.: Cambridge University Press.

Singer, M. (2003). Processes of question answering. In Rickheit, G., Hermann, T., & Deutsch, W. (Eds.), *Psycholinguistics* (pp. 422–431). Berlin: Walter de Gruyter.

Van der Meij, H. (1987). Assumptions if information-seeking questions. *Questioning Exchange*, *1*, 111–118.

Wong, B. Y. L. (1985). Self-questioning instructional research: A review. *Review of Educational Research*, *55*, 227–268.

KEY TERMS AND DEFINITIONS

Cognitive Disequilibrium: This occurs when the person experiences obstacles to goals, contradictions, anomalous information, uncertainty, and obvious gaps in knowledge.

Common Ground: The shared knowledge between participants in a communicative exchange, such as questioner and answerer.

Frequently Asked Questions (FAQ): A compute facility that presents likely questions that users would ask along with their answers.

Question Answering: The task of providing answers from large collection of documents to naturally asked questions.

Question Generation: The task of generating questions from various inputs such as raw text, semantic representations, or databases.

Shallow vs. Deep Questions: Shallow questions invite short answers that may or may not require reasoning. Deep questions (such as why, how, what-if) require lengthier answers and reasoning.

Sincere Information Seeking Questions: Questions that people genuinely want to ask to fill knowledge gaps, as opposed to questions that fulfill pragmatic goals of keeping the conversation flowing.

Chapter 2
Portable Text Summarization

Martin Hassel
Stockholm University, Sweden

Hercules Dalianis
Stockholm University, Sweden

ABSTRACT

Today, with digitally stored information available in abundance, even for many minor languages, this information must by some means be filtered and extracted in order to avoid drowning in it. Automatic summarization is one such technique, where a computer summarizes a longer text to a shorter non-redundant form. The development of advanced summarization systems also for smaller languages may unfortunately prove too costly. Nevertheless, there will still be a need for summarization tools for these languages in order to curb the immense flow of digital information. This chapter sets the focus on automatic summarization of text using as few direct human resources as possible, resulting in what can be perceived as an intermediary system. Furthermore, it presents the notion of taking a holistic view of the generation of summaries.

INTRODUCTION

Text summarization is the process of creating a summary of one or more texts. This summary may serve several purposes. One might, for example, want to get an overview of a document set in order to choose what documents one needs to read in full. Another plausible scenario would be getting the gist of a constant news flow, without having to wade through inherently redundant articles run by several news agencies, in order to find what might differ in reports from different parties. With digitally stored information available in abundance and in a myriad of forms, even for many minor languages, it has now become near impossible to manually search, sift and choose which information one should incorporate. Instead this information must by some means be filtered and extracted in order to avoid drowning in it. Automatic summarization is one such technique.

The title of this chapter sets the focus on summarization of text, automatically carried out by a computer program using methods more or less directly transferable from one language to an-

DOI: 10.4018/978-1-60960-741-8.ch002

other. This accomplished by using as few human resources as possible. The resources that are used should to as high extent as possible be already existing, not specifically aimed at summarization and, preferably, created as part of natural literary processes. Moreover, the summarization system should be able to be easily assembled using only a small set of basic language processing tools, again, not specifically aimed at summarization. The summarization system should thus be near language independent as to be quickly ported between different natural languages. The motivation for this is as simple as intuitive. Apart from the major languages of the world, there simply are a lot of languages for which large bodies of data aimed at language technology research, let alone research in automatic text summarization, are lacking. There might also not be resources available to develop such bodies of data, since it is usually time-consuming and hence expensive. Nevertheless, there will still be a need for sufficiently efficacious automatic text summarization for these languages, acting as intermediate states, in order to subdue this constantly increasing amount of electronically produced text.

The application areas for automatic text summarization are extensive. As the amount of information on the Internet grows abundantly, it is difficult to select relevant information. Information is published simultaneously on many media channels in different versions, for instance, a paper newspaper, web newspaper, SMS news flash, mobile radio newscast, and a spoken newspaper for the visually impaired. Also, these may today be accessed by a myriad of display devices, sporting a wide range of presentation capacity. Customization of information for different channels and formats is an immense editing job that notably involves shortening of original texts. Automatic text summarization can automate this work completely, or at least assist in the process by producing a draft summary. Also, documents can be made accessible in other languages by first summarizing them before translation, which in

many cases would be sufficient to establish the relevance of a foreign language document, and hence save human translators work since they need not translate every document manually. Automatic text summarization can also be used to summarize a text before an automatic speech synthesizer reads it, thus reducing the time needed to absorb the key facts in a document. In particular, automatic text summarization can be used to prepare information for use in small mobile devices, such as a PDA, which may need considerable reduction of content.

BACKGROUND

Summarization approaches are often divided into two main groups, *text extraction* and *text abstraction*. Text abstraction is in many aspects similar to what humans abstractors do when writing an abstract, even though professional abstractors often utilize surface-level information such as headings, key phrases and position in the text as well as the overall organization of the text into more or less genre specific sections (Liddy 1991, Endres-Niggemeyer et al. 1995, Cremmins 1996). The parsing and interpretation of text is a venerable research area that has been investigated for many years. In this area we have a wide spectrum of techniques and methods ranging from word by word parsing to rhetorical discourse parsing as well as more statistical methods, or a mixture of all. Also the generation of text is a vigorous research field with techniques ranging from canned text and template filling to more advanced systems with discourse planners and surface realizers.

Text extraction, on the other hand, simply reuses a subset of the original text, thus preserving the original wording and structure of the source text. Sometimes the extracted fragments are post-edited, for example by deleting subordinate clauses or joining incomplete clauses to form complete clauses (Jing and McKeown 2000, Jing 2000). Most of the research in the field of automatic text summarization has to the nature been that of text extraction. If the aim is a portable system that can with as little friction as possible travel between languages, then semantic parsing into a formal description as well as the use of handcrafted semantic resources certainly is out of the question.

Language Independence

A distinction most pertinent to this chapter is that of *language dependent* and *language independent* natural language processing (NLP). A language dependent system would be a system geared at a specific language, or a set of languages. It might perhaps utilize manually built lexical resources such as ontologies, thesauri or other language or domain specific knowledge bases. Other dependencies constraining a system to a specific language may be the employment of advanced tools as, for example, full parsers, semantic role assigners or named entity tagging, or the use of techniques such as template filling. The term "language independent," on the other hand, usually denotes a NLP system that is easily transferred between languages or domains. The system is thereby independent of the target language. In this chapter we will mainly investigate two research topics in the context of automatic text summarization. These two desired properties are *resource lean* and *portable*.

LANGUAGE DEPENDENT PROCESSING

A *true* language independent NLP system should be directly transferable to new domains or a completely different natural language. As will be discussed in this chapter, there are many steps to cover on the way to a portable summarization system. No matter to what extent an extractive summarization system is, or claims to be, language independent it still has to do some more or less language dependent preprocessing before it can be applied to the task in question. At the very least

some basic knowledge about natural languages in general must be made available to the system in order to facilitate segmentation of the text into desirable units of extraction.

Preprocessing

Prior to any deeper linguistic treatment of a text the units of that text must be demarcated and possibly classified. The text can initially be viewed as a mere sequence of characters within which we must define these units (Grefenstette & Tapanainen 1994). First after having defined and isolated the units we are interested in we can begin to operate on them. This stage of isolation occurs on many levels (e.g. tokenization divides the character sequence into words, sentence splitting further divides sequences of words into sentences, and so on). These preprocessing steps are often more or less language dependent, and thus deserve a brief discussion.

Segmentation

In order to perform extractive summarization we must first decide on what granularity our extraction segments will have (i.e. the "size" of the textual units that we copy from the original text and paste into our summary). This could be a paragraph, a sentence, a phrase or even a clause, although the most common probably is extraction performed on sentence level. Often it is necessary to first split the text into words (tokens) in order to correctly identify these boundaries between clauses, phrases or sentences. Sentence splitting as such is often considered as a non-trivial task, considering the irregularities of natural languages. However, at least for many Germanic and Romance languages a small set of regular expressions, perhaps accompanied by a list of abbreviations commonly including a punctuation mark, usually produces an acceptable result. Using a list of abbreviations of course makes the tokenization inherently language dependent as an abbreviation list usually is handcrafted. There are, though, languages lacking word-boundary markers, such as Chinese and Japanese, which certainly provide a more challenging task (Crystal 1987), but much statistical work has been carried out also for these languages (e.g. Chinese word segmentation) (Luk 1994).

Term Normalization

In running text the same word unit in many languages can occur in several different morphological variants. These inflected forms are governed by the context (i.e. if the text is presented in singular or plural form, present or past tense, etc.). In most cases these different lexical forms have similar semantic interpretations and can consequently often be considered as equivalent for the purpose of many Information Management applications. In order for an information management system to be able to treat these inflected forms as one concept, often referred to as a lexeme, it is common to use a so-called stemming algorithm. Efforts towards statistical language independent stemming have been taken, so this step can possibly be automated in a truly language independent system. A promising such approach, where stem classes are built using co-occurrence statistics, has been proposed by Xu & Croft (1998). They have demonstrated an improvement in information retrieval after clustering stem classes for English and Spanish, but for more morphologically complex languages the challenge of language independence still awaits. Another such approach by Bacchin et al. (2002) treats prefixes and suffixes as a community of sub-strings. They attempt to discover these communities by means of searching for the best word splits, which in turn give the best word stems.

Most statistical language models are more or less susceptible to sparse-data issues. In reality this means that the presence of very rare words, or patterns, adds noise to the model since the statistical grounds for modeling a representation

of these are too weak. One such phenomenon is compounding. Agglutinative languages, which are languages in which most words are formed by joining morphemes together, tend to be very productive in creating compound words (Crystal 1987). Theoretically the length of a compound word is unlimited, however longer compounds tend to become unwieldy and are infrequent in actual discourse. For example, the fully valid Swedish compound noun *strålbehandlingsplaneringsdatortomografi* would translate into English, being a mostly analytic language, as "radiation treatment planning computer tomography." This 40-letter word of course makes for a very rare occurrence even in a gigaword corpus. It should thus be perfectly clear that the representation of a document's content would benefit highly from having each constituting lexeme represented separately, thereby consolidating frequencies. Consequently, related to the task of stemming is that of compound splitting. Several statistical approaches to identifying lexeme boundaries in compounds exist, and may be used in different combinations, where one for instance can take advantage of co-occurrence statistics letting words that occur more often in the same text be the preferred split (Sjöbergh & Kann 2004).

Also, it is common to remove so-called stop words prior to the construction of these document descriptions, leaving only the content bearing words in the text during processing. Often a predefined, handcrafted stop list containing common words is used for removal of words known to be function words, which although far more high frequent than content words are far fewer in number. This does, however, make the creation of document content representations language dependent. Instead, one could, for example, apply term frequency thresholds, where both terms (words) that have a very high and possibly those that have a very low frequency are removed, thereby reducing noise in the model.

LANGUAGE INDEPENDENT PROCESSING

The approach to language independent summarization presented in this chapter heavily relies on the notion that documents, or rather a source document and a set of proposed summaries, can be compared for similarity. This notion is well established in, for example, Information Retrieval, where user queries act as fuzzy "descriptions" that are matched to a set of documents in order to find the document most similar to that description. When comparing documents for content similarity it is common practice to produce some form of document signatures. These signatures represent the content in some way, often as a vector of features, which are used as basis for such comparison. This comparison can be attempted on several levels (e.g. on lexical, syntactic, or semantic grounds).

The Vector Space Model

The Vector Space model is a document similarity model commonly used in Information Retrieval (Salton 1971). In this model the document signatures are represented as feature vectors consisting of the words that occur within the documents, with weights attached to each word denoting its importance for the document. We can, for example, for each term (word) record the number of times it occurs in each document. This gives us what is commonly called a document-term matrix, where the rows represent the documents in the document collection and the columns each represent a specific term existing in any of the documents (a weight can thus be zero).

If we, using this matrix, view the feature vectors as projections in a multi- dimensional space, where the dimensionality is given by the number of documents and the number of index terms (the vocabulary, if you will). We can then measure the lexical similarity between two documents simply by calculating the in information retrieval commonly used *cosine* angle between these vectors. For our purposes, the two documents being compared for similarity might as well be a document being summarized coupled with a summary of said document, as we shall see further on.

Term Weighting

When constructing document signatures it also common to modify word frequency counts in the hope of promoting semantically salient words. There are many theories on how to model salience, where the most common probably is the *tf·idf* model. In this model *tf* represents the term frequency, and corresponds to the number of times a certain content word, represented by its stem or lemma, occurs within a specific document. However, much as with the much more frequent function words adding noise when attempting to identify content words describing the content of a document, in the same manner can very common content words "drown" content words describing a specific document (e.g. within a specific domain). One example of this would be that if we have set of documents discussing the medical treatment of cancer, then certain domain specific content words would to a high extent exist with a high frequency in each of the documents. In order to counter this phenomenon of domain specificity it is common weigh the term frequency by in how many documents the term occurs (Spärck-Jones 1972). This notion of document specificity is often referred to as the inverse document frequency, or simply *idf*.

As defining salience as frequency fluctuations between documents, the *tf·idf* model requires a set of documents as well as the necessity of examining all of them noting in which documents a specific term occurs in order to calculate the weight of each term. To overcome this several other approaches to capturing salience have been put forth. One such, proposed by Ortuño et al. (2002), models salience by tracking the distributional pattern of terms within a document. They

21

show that the spatial information of a word is reliable in predicting the relevance of that word to the text being processed, independently of its relative frequency. The base of this observation is that words relevant to a text will normally appear in a very specific context, concentrated in a region of the text, presenting large frequency fluctuations (i.e. keywords come in bursts). The burstiness of a word is here calculated using the standard deviation of the distance between different occurrences of the same word in the text. However, words that occur only with large distances between occurrences usually have a high standard deviation by chance, so the standard deviation is divided by the mean distance between occurrences. This way the salience model only relies on the document currently under consideration.

The problem with counting terms on a lexical level is that the relation between the terms is not always what they seem to be, at least not by only looking at the constituting characters. Rather, the relation between words and concepts is many-to-many. For example, we have synonymy, where a number of words with same "meaning" have very different lexical appearances. In this case lexical term matching misses relevant frequency conflations thus impacting recall negatively. A hypothetical example would that we have document *D* such as *D = {kitten, dog, pussy, cat, mouser, doggie, feline}*. It is quite obvious, given that you know the meanings of the words occurring in the document, that the document is mainly about cats.

The Meaning of Words

Modeling of the meaning of words has always been an elusive task in natural language processing. Words are nothing more than sounds or a sequence of graphemes until they become associated with an object, an action or some characteristic. Words therefore not only come to denote objects, phenomena or ideas in the physical world, but also gain a connotative substance based on how and when they are used (Mill 1843). In the Sau-

ssurean tradition this connotation, or meaning, is seen as to arise from the relative difference between words in a linguistic system. According to Saussure this constantly restructured system of differences is negotiated through social activity in a community of users (Saussure 1916). Two types of relations constitute the base of this difference, where syntagmatic relations concern positioning and paradigmatic relations act as functional contrasts (substitution). The meaning of a word is thus defined by the company it keeps.

Semantic Vector Space Models

Until the early nineties most of the work in statistical language learning was concentrated on syntax (Charniak 1993). However, with the induction of Latent Semantic Analysis (Dumais et al. 1988) a whole new field of lexical statistical semantics sprang into existence and today enjoys considerable attention in current research on computational semantics.

The general idea behind semantic vector space models, or word space models, is to use statistics on word distributions in order to generate a high-dimensional vector space – a concept space. In this vector space the words are represented by context vectors whose relative directions are assumed to indicate semantic similarity. The basis of this assumption is the distributional hypothesis (Harris 1954), according to which words that occur in similar contexts also tend to have similar properties (meanings/functions). From this follows that if we repeatedly observe two words in the same (or very similar) contexts, then it is not too far fetched to assume that they also mean similar things, or at the very least to some extent share properties. Furthermore, depending on how we model these contexts we should be able to capture different traits. We should for instance be able to populate the word space model with syntagmatic relations if we collect information about which words that tend to co-occur, and with paradigmatic relations if we collect information about which words that tend to share neighbors (Sahlgren 2006).

This approach is often seen as a solution to semantic difficulties in NLP like synonymy and hyperonymy, which are not captured by the traditional vector space model. It should however be noted that semantic vector space methods still are oblivious to the nature of the lexical strings they are tracking. Therefore, given a definition of what constitutes a meaning bearing token in a particular language, it usually is advantageous to perform stemming and/or stop word removal, depending on the level of morphology of the language in question. Such considerations taken into account a word space model can be applied to basically any language. For instance, word space models have been applied to, among many other languages; English, German, Spanish, Swedish as well as Japanese (Hassel 2005, Sahlgren & Karlgren 2005, Sahlgren 2006).

Holistic Summarization

The traditional way to perform extractive summarization is to rank the sentences in a source document for their respective appropriateness for inclusion in a summary of this document. These sentences are then concatenated into a summary, which is delivered to the user. This conjugate is seen as containing the sentences most central to the topic of the input text, thus being a representative summary. As contrast, the idea behind a holistic view on summarization is that summaries should be weighed for fitness as a whole, already in the production step. This means that no prejudice is exercised on individual sentences – all sentences are treated as equal. Instead it is their ability to co-operate in forming an overview of the source text that is judged upon.

In order to evaluate this fitness we need to have some way of comparing a source document with one or more summary candidates for content similarity. This is accomplished by letting the concepts we have accumulated by tracking co-

occurrences of words in contexts (i.e. by use of Latent Semantic Analysis [Landauer et al. 1998] or Random Indexing Random Indexing Random Indexing [Kanerva et al. 2000]) form document signatures. Analogously to how we projected the words' semantic representations into a concept space we can now, by letting the document/summary descriptions be weighted the aggregate of the concept vectors of the words contained in that document/summary, project the documents into a multi-dimensional document space.

As with the concepts we can now measure the semantic similarity between the document being summarized and a proposed summary by taking the cosine angle between the content vectors of the two. Here it might well be noted that this optimization of semantic similarity between the source document and the considered summary is not in any way constrained to computationally generated summaries. The summaries being evaluated and selected from could in practice be produced by any means, even being man-made.

The HolSum Summarizer

We will now exemplify this what we have discussed so far with a summarization system that embodies both the notion of near language independent, portable summarization and that of taking a holistic view of the summary under consideration. HolSum (Hassel 2007) is a text summarizer that aims at providing overview summaries by generating a set of summary candidates, from which it presents the summary most similar to the source to the user. In practice this means that HolSum tries to represent the various (sub) topics of the source text in the summary to the same extent as they occur in the source text.

HolSum is trainable for most languages provided a tokenizer that can segment the text into the desired extraction units (e.g. sentences) and tokens suitable for co-occurrence statistics (e.g. words), as defined by that language. Apart from the obligatory sentence and word splitter, and the optional stop word filter and stemmer/ compound splitter, there are three main areas of interest in the HolSum system. These three areas, marked with the numbers one through three in the HolSum system layout (see Figure 1), are the acquisition semantic knowledge, the application of the acquired semantic knowledge and, lastly, the semantic navigation of the space of possible summaries.

1. The acquisition of semantic knowledge is carried out by using Random Indexing to build concept representations – context vec-

tors – for a very large vocabulary. Even though we have chosen to use RI as means for acquiring the co-occurrence statistics on words, you could basically use any sufficient model for acquiring such semantic knowledge. It should not, at least in theory, make any difference whether you use for instance RI, LSA or HAL. These models are equally language independent given a definition of what constitutes a meaning bearing token (i.e. a "content word") in a specific language, and do all use vectors as their representation for concepts.

Figure 1. A detailed schematic overview of the HolSum system, with its core language independent properties numbered. (1) being the acquisition of semantic knowledge, (2) the application of the acquired semantic knowledge, and (3) the semantic navigation of the space of possible summaries.

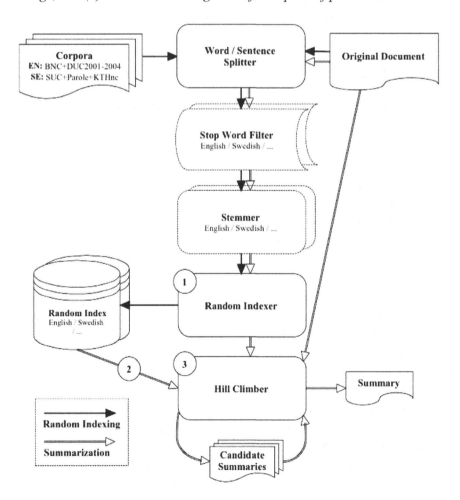

2. In this model document signatures are formed by aggregating context vectors (i.e. the constituting words' co-occurrence vectors). This is not an approach specific to our model; rather it is common practice when using word space models as means for document representation. Nevertheless, it is not, from a linguistic point of view, a particularly appetizing approach to the encapsulation of a documents semantic content, albeit one that clearly improves on the traditional vector space model (Hassel & Sjöbergh 2006). The Achilles' heal of this approach, theory-wise, is that while the formation of concept representations, in Random Indexing, shies away from the bag-of-words approach in that it has the ability to capture syntactically governed semantic relations between words, the document representations regress into a bag-of-concepts model. Even so, relenting to the model we have there is still room for different models of salience weights when producing these document signatures. In the context of HolSum two such models have been evaluated; the traditional tf·idf model and the standard deviation of word occurrences (Hassel 2007).

3. As mentioned, the document signatures crafted in (2), being vectors as they are, can be positioned in a high-dimensional space where they can be compared for content similarity. Lacking a set of man-made summaries to compare and choose from, a suitable set of summaries must be computationally generated. In the current architecture this is performed by using a greedy search algorithm starting in some initial summary (e.g. the leading sentences of the text being summarized) and iteratively reshaping the summary by swapping sentences from the source text in and out of the summary, until no better summary is found (according to some criteria). Using this approach it is obvious that we risk getting stranded in a

local optimum, however, it is not feasible to exhaustively explore the entire document space in the search of the globally best summary. Furthermore, we do not even know how many "best" summaries there are for the current text, which would be interesting in itself perhaps being a measure of the text's "summaribility," which leaves us with little information on whether we should restart the search or not. Despite these objections the approach has performed reasonably well in standard evaluations.

Evaluation of the Portable Holistic Approach

The HolSum approach has mainly been evaluated along the lines of the evaluation setup for task 2 in the Document Understanding Conferences 2004 (Over & Yen, 2004), providing both a well known evaluation data set and metrics, as well as both a human ceiling and a score of other summarization systems as reference. The system has also been evaluated for Swedish. The data used for building the conceptual representations for English was comprised of over 100 million words, while the Swedish representations were built on merely 34 million words.

The impact of the dimensionality chosen for the Random Indexing step has been evaluated by running the experiments several times, building semantic representations using a variation of dimensionalities. The results show little variation over different dimensionalities. This means that as long as one does not choose too few dimensions, the dimensionality is not a parameter that needs considerable attention. For each dimensionality the mean performance using four different random seeds was also calculated, since there is a slight variation in how well the method works with different random projections. The dimensionality showing the most variation in the experiments spanned 33.8-34.4% ROUGE-1 (Hassel & Sjöbergh 2006). Variations for the other dimensions were slightly less. The best systems in DUC 2004 scored roughly 39% (Over and Yen, 2004), with many of the participating systems scoring below 34%. This shows that by applying a set of basic text processing tools with latent semantic analysis one can device a highly portable extraction-based summarization method that, in contrast to most extraction- based systems, does not rank the individual extract segments contributing to the summary. Instead it compares complete summaries to the original text, and chooses the best summary candidate it can find by a simple search strategy.

APPLICATIONS OF AUTOMATIC TEXT SUMMARIZATION

The very first application area for automatic text summarization was to create abstracts/extracts from articles without abstracts to be stored in library systems together with the title and author name, (Luhn 1959). At that time one could not store the whole article digitally in the library system due to storage constraints.

Today there is a wide range of application areas for automatic text summarization, the most common and obvious one is in information retrieval. We can already observe it in the result list of search engines where a summarized part of each retrieved document is presented interweaved together with the search terms of the user, the so-called snippets. We can consider these snippets to be a crude form of user adapted text summaries. Another possible application is in the mass media area. Today a news article is written by a journalist, but when typesetting the newspaper the article is cut down manually to the correct size so that it can fit in the layout, in between the ads. In parallel the same article is also typeset for the web, WAP or SMS text messages. An experiment is described in Dalianis et al (2004) where both manual editors and the SweSum text summarizer (Dalianis 2000) where given the task to summarize 334 news texts written in Swedish to the appropriate

format for the newspaper Sydsvenska Dagbladet. The manually cut down texts were compared with the automatically summarized texts and it was found that the texts where almost identical. Both the editors and the SweSum text summarizer cut down and summarized the texts mainly from the end. The same experiment was carried out for SMS format (maximum 160 characters) and the results from SweSum was considered suitable to be used directly in news paper production.

Business Intelligence systems or news monitoring systems are today very common where one surveys a large flow of news media, this news flow can be summarized so the user can obtain an overview of the stream before deciding if she should click on the news summary and read the complete news article. One nice live application is the Columbia News Blaster, which takes several news articles describing the same topic and summarizes it to one single news flash (McKeown & Radev 1999, McKeown et al. 2003).

If we go to the area of medicine and biomedicine we find several attempts to use automatic text summarization and also the closely related area natural language generation to adapt both text and data to different user groups such as patients, physicians, nurses and scientists. In Hirst et al. (1997) a system is presented that from medical digital libraries produces user adapted information towards individual patients' specific needs, summarized from information on surgery of breast cancer to living with diabetes but also general health education. If we look at generation of text from source data Portet et al. (2007) describe a system that takes survey data from a baby at a neonatal clinic and generates a textual description for several different user groups such as the clinicians, the parents or even the relatives and friends of the patient. The textual description contains information that is adapted to the interest and needs of each user group.

Another system is PERSIVAL, which is described in McKeown et al. (2001). PERSIVAL generates user-adapted information both for patients and physicians, and uses as input the patient record of the patient to find what topics the generated text should contain. PERSIVAL then searches for the relevant information in external resources and summarizes it to the relevant level of the user. The text that is constructed for patients origins from several consumer health texts, while the text constructed for physicians is collected from medical journal articles.

FUTURE RESEARCH DIRECTIONS

We can envision a truly self regulating system that learns more and more about a given domain or language the more the system processes texts and therefore can create progressively more fine tuned text summaries. The HolSum application shows promising results in this direction.

In the future specialist books will be ordered on demand. A specialist book will be user adapted and customized according to who orders the book, delivering content at an appropriate complexity level. The book will contain different parts from other books, pictures, sound samples, videos and maybe even material from other languages that are translated automatically to the target language. An extension to this application could be to in a coherent way incorporate diagrams and tables into the summary, such that the quality of the summary further increases. We already see some advancement in multi-media summarization. In the wake of this development we also believe that more research should be put into the presentation of summarized material, perhaps incorporating the temporal factor. This could, for instance, be done by presenting a steady flow of news on different topics as constantly reshaping documents, much in the manner of Google Wave, where contents could be adapted, evolved and honed as the news story progresses. This would also suit the medical domain, by providing snap-shots of a patient's health status and progression.

Another possible near-future application is that newspapers will be produced completely automatically. The articles will of course be written by journalists, but all typesetting including layout of advertisements will be performed by systems that have embedded text summarization both for the news article and for the advertisement texts.

CONCLUSION

As we have seen in this chapter there are several linguistically motivated text processing tasks that need to be addressed from a language independence point of view. Among these are such tasks as *tokenization* and *sentence segmentation*. Furthermore, we have discussed the impact of these tasks on the representation of the contents of documents (i.e. *document signatures*). The impact of *stemming* and *compound splitting* on document signatures is also discussed. These document signatures can then be compared for similarity using the *vector space model*. Related to this discussion is the notion of *salience* and how one can promote topically relevant words and *concept representations* in the document signatures. These concept representations are crafted by gathering *word co-occurrence statistics* used for grouping semantically related words in a *word space model*. This model is based on the *distributional hypothesis* according to which words occurring in similar contexts tend to have similar *meaning* or *function*.

Lastly, we have presented the notion of *holistic summarization* were a set of summaries are internally ranked and the "best" summary presented to the user, rather than the traditional conjugate of individually ranked sentences. This notion has been exemplified with the *HolSum summarizer*, which employs the *Random Indexing* word space model for crafting concept representations. These concept representations are used to form document signatures for both the *input text* as well as *generated summaries*, which are compared for *semantic similarity* in a *document space*. The discussion up to this point supports the portability of the approach, as it requires no sophisticated tools, although stop word filtering and simple stemming clearly improves the results. Even though access to large amounts of raw (unannotated) text is needed for good performance, this is for many languages readily available, for instance on the World Wide Web.

REFERENCES

Bacchin, M., Ferro, N., & Melucci, M. (2002). The effectiveness of a graph-based algorithm for stemming. In *Proceedings of the 5th International Conference on Asian Digital Libraries* (pp. 117–128). London, UK: Springer-Verlag.

Charniak, E. (1993). *Statistical language learning*. Cambridge, MA: MIT Press.

Cremmins, E. T. (1996). *The art of abstracting* (2nd ed.). Arlington, VA: Information Resources Press.

Crystal, D. (1987). *The Cambridge encyclopedia of language*. Cambridge University Press.

Dalianis, H. (2000). *SweSum - A text summarizer for Swedish*. Technical report TRITA-NA-P0015, IPLab-174, NADA, KTH, October 2000.

Dalianis, H., Hassel, M., de Smedt, K., Liseth, A., Lech, T. C., & Wedekind, J. (2004). Porting and evaluation of automatic summarization. In Holmboe, H. (Ed.), *Nordisk Sprogteknologi 2003. Årbog for Nordisk Språkteknologisk Forskningsprogram 2000-2004* (pp. 107–121). Museum Tusculanums Forlag.

de Saussure, F. (1916). *Course in general linguistics (trans. Roy Harris, 1983)*. London: Duckworth.

Dumais, S. T., Furnas, G. W., Landauer, T. K., & Deerwester, S. C. (1988). Using latent semantic analysis to improve information retrieval. In *Proceedings of CHI'88: Conference on Human Factors in Computing* (pp. 281–285), Washington DC, USA. May 15-19 1988.

Endres-Niggemeyer, B., Maier, E., & Sigel, A. (1995). How to implement a naturalistic model of abstracting: Four core working steps of an expert abstractor. *Information Processing & Management, 31*(5), 631–674. doi:10.1016/0306-4573(95)00028-F

Grefenstette, G., & Tapanainen, P. (1994). What is a word, what is a sentence? Problems of tokenization. In *Proceedings of the 3rd International Conference on Computational Lexicography* (pp. 79–87), Budapest, Hungary.

Harris, Z. S. (1954). Distributional structure. *Word, 10*(23), 146–162.

Hassel, M. (2005). Word sense disambiguation using co-occurrence statistics on random labels. In *Proceedings of Recent Advances in Natural Language Processing 2005*. Borovets, Bulgaria.

Hassel, M. (2007). *Resource lean and portable automatic text summarization*. Doctoral thesis, School of Computer Science and Communication, Royal Institute of Technology. Stockholm, Sweden.

Hassel, M., & Sjöbergh, J. (2006). Towards holistic summarization: Selecting summaries, not sentences. In *Proceedings of Language Resources and Evaluation 2006*. Genoa, Italy.

Hirst, G., DiMarco, C., Hovy, E., & Parsons, K. (1997). Authoring and generating health-education documents that are tailored to the needs of the individual patient. In *Proceedings of the Sixth International Conference on User Modeling* (pp. 107-118). New York, NY: Springer.

Jing, H. (2000). Sentence reduction for automatic text summarization. In *Proceedings of the 6th Applied Natural Language Processing Conference* (pp. 310–315). Seattle, Washington. April 29–May 4, 2000.

Jing, H., & McKeown, K. R. (2000). Cut and paste-based text summarization. In *Proceedings of the 6th Applied Natural Language Processing Conference and the 1st Meeting of the North American Chapter of the Association for Computational Linguistics* (pp. 178–185), Seattle, Washington. April 29–May 4, 2000.

Kanerva, P., Kristoferson, J., & Holst, A. (2000). Random Indexing of text samples for latent semantic analysis. In *Proceedings 22nd Annual Conference of the Cognitive Science Society*, Pennsylvania, USA.

Landauer, T. K., Foltz, P. W., & Laham, D. (1998). Introduction to latent semantic analysis. *Discourse Processes, 25*, 259–284. doi:10.1080/01638539809545028

Liddy, E. D. (1991). Discourse-level structure of empirical abstracts: An exploratory study. *Information Processing & Management, 27*(1), 550–581. doi:10.1016/0306-4573(91)90031-G

Luhn, H. P. (1959). The automatic creation of literature abstracts. *IBM Journal of Research and Development*, 159–165.

Luk, R. W. P. (1994). An IBM-PC environment for Chinese corpus analysis. In *Proceedings of the 15th Conference on Computational Linguistics* (pp. 584–587). Morristown, New Jersey, USA.

McKeown, K. R., Barzilay, R., Chen, J., Elson, D., Evans, D., & Klavans, J. … Sigelman, S. (2003). Columbia's Newsblaster: New features and future directions. In *Proceedings of the Human Language Technology Conference*, vol. II. Edmonton, Canada.

McKeown, K. R., Chang, S.-F., Cimino, J., Feiner, S. K., Friedman, C., & Gravano, L. … Teufel, S. (2001). PERSIVAL, a system for personalized search and summarization over multimedia healthcare information. In *Proceedings of the Joint ACM/IEEE Conference on Digital Libraries (JCDL-01)*, (pp. 331–340). Roanoke, Virginia, June 2001.

McKeown, K. R., & Radev, D. R. (1999). Generating summaries of multiple news articles. In Mani, I., & Maybury, M. T. (Eds.), *Advances in automatic text summarization* (pp. 381–389). Cambridge, MA: The MIT Press.

Mill, J. S. (1843). *A system of logic, raciocinative and inductive*. London.

Ortuño, M., Carpena, P., Bernaola-Galvan, P., Munoz, E., & Somoza, A. (2002). Keyword detection in natural languages and DNA. *Europhysics Letters, 57*, 759–764. doi:10.1209/epl/i2002-00528-3

Over, P., & Yen, J. (2004). *An introduction to DUC 2004 intrinsic evaluation of generic new text summarization systems*. Retrieved from http://www-nlpir.nist.gov/projects/duc/pubs/2004slides/duc2004.intro.pdf.

Portet, F., Reiter, E., Gatt, A., Hunter, J., Sripada, S., Freer, Y., & Sykes, C. (2009). Automatic generation of textual summaries from neonatal intensive care data. *Artificial Intelligence, 173*(7-8), 789–816. Essex, UK: Elsevier Science Publishers Ltd. doi:10.1016/j.artint.2008.12.002.

Sahlgren, M. (2006). *The word-space model: Using distributional analysis to represent syntagmatic and paradigmatic relations between words in high-dimensional vector spaces*. Doctoral thesis, Department of Linguistics, Stockholm University. Stockholm, Sweden.

Sahlgren, M., & Karlgren, J. (2005). Automatic bilingual lexicon acquisition using random indexing of parallel corpora. *Journal of Natural Language Engineering, Special Issue on Parallel Texts, 11*(3).

Salton, G. (1971). *The SMART retrieval system – Experiments in automatic document processing.* Upper Saddle River, NJ: Prentice-Hall, Inc.

Sjöbergh, J., & Kann, V. (2004). Finding the correct interpretation of Swedish compounds a statistical approach. In *Proceedings of Language Resources and Evaluation, 2004*, 899–902. Lisbon, Portugal.

Spärck-Jones, K. (1972). A statistical interpretation of term specificity and its application in retrieval. *The Journal of Documentation, 28*, 11–21. doi:10.1108/eb026526

Xu, J., & Croft, B. (1998). Corpus-based stemming using co-occurrence of word variants. *ACM Transactions on Information Systems, 16*(1), 61–81. doi:10.1145/267954.267957

ADDITIONAL READING

Dalianis, H., Hassel, M., Wedekind, J., Haltrup, D., de Smedt, K., & Christopher, T. L. (2003). From SweSum to ScandSum: Automatic text summarization for the Scandinavian languages. In Holmboe, H. (Ed.), *Nordisk Sprogteknologi 2002: Årbog for Nordisk Språkteknologisk Forskningsprogram 2000-2004* (pp. 153–163). Copenhagen: Museum Tusculanums Forlag.

Hassel, M. (2003). Exploitation of Named Entities in Automatic Text Summarization for Swedish. In the *Proceedings of NODALIDA '03 - 14th Nordic Conference on Computational Linguistics.* Reykjavik, Iceland. May 30-31, 2003.

Hassel, M., & Dalianis, H. (2005). Generation of Reference Summaries. In *Proceedings of 2nd Language & Technology Conference: Human Language Technologies as a Challenge for Computer Science and Linguistics.* Poznan, Poland. April 21-23, 2005.

Hassel, M., & Mazdak, N. (2004). FarsiSum - A Persian text summarizer. In *Proceedings of Computational Approaches to Arabic Script-based Languages workshop at COLING '04.* Geneva, Switzerland. August 28, 2004.

Hovy, E. H., & Lin, C.-Y. (1998). Automating Text Summarization in SUMMARIST. In Mani, I., & Maybury, M. (Eds.), *Advances in Automated Text Summarization.* Cambridge, Massachusetts: MIT Press.

Jing, H., & McKeown, K. R. (1999). The Decomposition of Human-Written Summary Sentences. In M. Hearst, G. F., & Tong, R. (editors), In *Proceedings of the 22nd Annual International ACM SIGIR Conference on Research and Development in Information Retrieval* (pp. 129–136). University of California, Berkeley.

Lin, C.-Y. (2004). ROUGE: A Package for Automatic Evaluation of Summaries. In *Proceedings of the Workshop on Text Summarization Branches Out (WAS 2004).* Barcelona, Spain. July 25 - 26, 2004.

Lin, C.-Y. (2005). ROUGE: Recall-oriented understudy for gisting evaluation. http://berouge.com/.

Mani, I. (1999). *Advances in Automatic Text Summarization.* Cambridge, Massachusetts: MIT Press.

Marcu, D. (1999). The automatic construction of large-scale corpora for summarization research. In *Proceedings of 22nd International ACM SIGIR Conference on Research and Development in Information Retrieval (SIGIR '99)* (pp. 137-144). Berkeley, California.

Nenkova, A., Passonneau, R. & McKeown, K.R. (2007). The Pyramid Method: Incorporating Human Content Selection Variation in Summarization Evaluation. *ACM Transactions on Speech and Language Processing (TSLP)*, Volume 4, Issue 2. May 2007.

Radev, D. R., Blair-Goldensohn, S., Zhang, Z., & Raghavan, R. S. (2001). Newsinessence: A System for Domain-Independent, Real-Time News Clustering and Multi-Document Summarization. In *Proceedings of Human Language Technology Conference (HLT 2001)* San Diego, California.

Radev, D. R., Jing, H., & Budzikowska, M. (2000). Centroid-Based Summarization of Multiple Documents: Sentence Extraction, Utility-Based Evaluation, and User Studies. In Udo Hahn. Chin-Yew Lin, Inderjeet Mani, and Dragomir R. Radev (editors), *Proceedings of the Workshop on Automatic Summarization at the 6th Applied Natural Language Processing Conference and NAACL 2000*, Seattle, Washington.

Sahlgren, M. (2005). An Introduction to Random Indexing. In *Methods and Applications of Semantic Indexing Workshop at the 7th International Conference on Terminology and Knowledge Engineering*. Copenhagen, Denmark. August 16, 2005.

Sjöbergh, J. (2007). Older versions of the ROUGEeval summarization evaluation system were easier to fool. *Journal of Information Processing and Management, Special Issue on Summarization* (pp. 1500-1505), Volume 43, Issue 6, November, ISSN:0306-4573.

Spärk-Jones, K., & Galliers, K. R. (1995). *Evaluating Natural Language Processing Systems: An Analysis and Review. Lecture Notes in Artificial Intelligence, number 1083*. Springer.

Winkel, A., & Radev, D. R. (2002). MEADeval: An evaluation framework for extractive summarization. http://tangra.si.umich.edu/clair/meadeval/meadeval.pdf.

KEY TERMS AND DEFINITIONS

Corpus: A large collection of writings of a specific kind or on a specific subject. A corpus should be balanced so that it is representative for the language or domain that covers. Corpora are often used in statistical language technology for both training of machine learning approaches and evaluation of the end result.

Holistic: The philosophical view that all the properties of a given system (may it be physical, biological, chemical, social, economic, mental or linguistic) cannot be determined by its component parts alone. Instead, the system as a whole governs in an important way how the parts behave within the system. In the context of summarization this view stands in contrast of the customary ranking of individual sentences within a text being summarized.

Intermediary: Components that are intended to be consumed or converted into another component, and therefore not destined to appear in the final production system. These system or component states need to be sufficiently efficacious when initially moving a language technology system to new domain or language. Given the availability of necessary resources these intermediates are often honed in later stages of research.

Language Independent: The ability to seamlessly move from one language or domain to another. This transfer should be facilitated by the systems' ability to adapt to the irregularities natural languages exhibit (e.g., by learning new instances of language use, without the use of hard-coded language specific knowledge or need of specifically annotated or structured data).

Portable: The portability of a system or method is most often an issue of cost. When lacking the necessary resources to build advanced systems the ability to transfer an intermediary system to other languages or domains, with as little effort as possible, becomes crucial. This applies both to the system itself as to the evaluation of the system in its new context.

Resource Lean: Resources can be many things (e.g., human resources, economic resources, spatial or temporal resources, data resources, etc.). The research on summarization in focus in this chapter is in some sense lean on human resources since while it demands large bodies of data for training, this data does, however, not need to be annotated nor structured in any way, and can be collected "in the wild" (e.g. it can be text already in existence, produced for entirely different purposes). Thus it most certainly is resource lean regarding the other identified resource types, since (1) structuring and annotation of data takes time and requires quite a bit of human effort; (2) human labor (usually) is more time consuming than the computerized counterpart; (3) humans desire more space than (most) computers require; (4) time, space and human labor most definitely cost money.

ROUGE Scores: Automatic summarization evaluation using unigram co-occurrences between summary pairs. Has in studies been shown to correlate surprising well with human evaluations, but has also met critique for not performing well on longer word chains as well as in earlier versions being quite easy to fool. Inspired by BLEU scores, a similar metric used in machine translation.

Text Abstraction: The production of text that is a shorter non-redundant rendition of the source text. This is accomplished by parsing the original text in a deep linguistic way, interpreting the text semantically into a formal representation, finding new more concise concepts to describe the information carried by the source text and then re-generated in a new shorter form. An abstract may thus contain words and expressions not used in the original text, while still conveying the same basic information as the source text.

Text Extraction: Generation of a shorter content representation by reusing a subset of the original text. This relies on the identification of the most relevant passages in one or more documents, often using standard statistically based information retrieval techniques augmented with more or less shallow natural language processing and genre or language specific heuristics. These passages, often sentences or phrases, are then extracted and pasted together to form a non-redundant summary that is shorter than the original document with as little information loss as possible.

Chapter 3
Discourse Analysis and ANLP

Alexandra Kent
Loughborough University, UK

Philip M. McCarthy
The University of Memphis, USA

ABSTRACT

The goal of this chapter is to outline a (primarily) qualitative and (secondarily) quantitative approach to the analysis of discourse. Discourse Analysis thrives on the variation and inconsistencies in our everyday language. Rather than focusing on what is said and seeking to reduce and homogenise accounts to find a central meaning, discourse analysis is interested in the consequences of "saying it that particular way at that particular time." Put another way, it is interested in "what was said that didn't have to be, and why?" and "what wasn't said that could have been, and why not?" The chapter outlines the basic theoretical assumptions that underpin the many different methodological approaches within Discourse Analysis. It then considers these approaches in terms of the major themes of their research, the ongoing and future directions for study, and the scope of contribution to scientific knowledge that discourse analytic research can make. At the beginning and end of the chapter, we attempt to outline a role for Applied Natural Language Processing (ANLP) in Discourse Analysis. We discuss possible reasons for a lack of computational tools and techniques in traditional Discourse Analysis but we also offer suggestions as to the application of computational resources so that researchers in both disciplines might have an avenue of interest that assists their work, without directing it.

INTRODUCTION

Discourse Analysis is a big tent. Various people, who each would describe themselves as discourse analysts, employ a wide range of different methods and may make very different sets of assump-

tions (Phillips & Jorgensen, 2002). That having been said, and at a very basic level, we can assume that Discourse Analysis is the analysis of data involving words (either spoken or written). Generally, this analysis is part of talk in a social interaction (Howitt, 2010), although sometimes the analysis can reach the level of an entire text (Trappes-Lomax, & Hughs, 2004); at which

DOI: 10.4018/978-1-60960-741-8.ch003

point, Discourse Analysis might be said to merge somewhat with field of Text Analysis. Discourse Analysis is most often a qualitative methodology, although post-positivistic discourse analysts often accept the assistance of (low level) computational and statistical approaches so as to gain a broader perspective of the subject of interest (Denzin & Lincoln, 2005; Gee, 2005). In such a big tent, it is perhaps not surprising that few researchers agree on how Discourse Analysis should be conducted. For example, some researchers advocate that only naturally occurring data should be used, whereas others feel discourse analysis can be fruitfully applied to researcher generated data such as interviews or focus groups (McKinlay & McVittie, 2008). To this end, Howitt (2010) offers a neat map of several different varieties of Discourse Analysis, showing how they relate to each other (2010: 217).

On the face of it, the field of Discourse Analysis would seem like an obvious complement to the theme of this book: Applied Natural Language Processing (ANLP). After all, the word *discourse* in Discourse Analysis clearly relates closely to the words *natural language* in A*N*LP; and the word *analysis* in Discourse Analysis relates closely to the word *processing* in ANLP. However, the reality is that the field of Discourse Analysis lies far from more prototypical ANLP pursuits such as Natural Language Understanding and Processing (see Rus, this volume), Corpus Linguistics (see Hall this volume), Data Mining, (see Atzmueller this volume) and so forth. This distance between Discourse Analysis and the more prototypical fields results from the focus of studies that are of typical interest to Discourse Analysts. These interests do not easily or obviously lend themselves to computational approaches. Such an issue may reasonably lead readers to ask why a chapter on Discourse Analysis is even necessary in this book. Our response to such a question is to argue that while computationally addressing areas of interest to Discourse Analysis are, undoubtedly, challenging, they are, nevertheless, opportunities

for resourceful researchers who wish to apply developments in textual technology. As such, we view studies in Discourse Analysis as a largely untapped reservoir of ANLP research.

In this chapter, we begin with a brief discussion as to why computational (quantitative) approaches have been relatively rare in Discourse Analysis. We then discuss the basic assumptions of Discourse Analysis before outlining some of the major fields of interest in Discourse Analysis. We end with our thoughts on where and how ANLP research might be employed so as to enhance Discourse Analysis research.

DISCOURSE ANALYSIS AND ANLP (OR LACK THEREOF)

Discourse Analysis does not have a strong tradition in ANLP. Three major issues help to explain this observation. First, although studies in Discourse Analysis can focus on spoken or written text, it is probably fair to argue that the majority of studies (and the best known studies) are on the computationally less favourable spoken form. Second, Discourse Analysts are frequently interested in what was not said, that could have been said. From a computational point of view, it is difficult enough to evaluate with any accuracy what the text actually is, let alone what it could have been. The third point relates closely to the second. For Discourse Analysts, it is not just *what* was not said, but *why* it was not said, and what might this "choice" tell us about our world, our societies, and ourselves. Clearly, such interests are predominantly qualitative pursuits that seem far from the quantifications that are more popular with computational approaches.

TALK AS TOPIC

Discourse Analysts are interested in what talk does, not what it is about (Wood & Kroger, 2000). This feature is key in distinguishing Discourse Analysis from other types of research that focus on the information delivered, ostensibly accurately, through the medium of language (e.g. protocol analysis or Interpretive Phenomenological Analysis). Consider a set of recorded consultations from an ante-natal clinic where an expectant mother and the physician are discussing home birth options. Discourse Analysts might look at the strategies used by the expectant mother to secure the physician's agreement for a home birth (e.g., drawing on anecdotal evidence from her personal family history to position herself as expert in her family's birth history without challenging the physician's medical expertise). They would not look at what motivations the expectant mother had for wanting to give birth at home, or what medial reasons the physician may have for advocating a hospital birth. Crucially, discourse is not taken to be a medium through which researchers can access the mental lives of their participants. Discourse is treated as a phenomenon of its own, meriting study in its own right (McKinlay & McVittie, 2008). This is not to say that discourse analysts are not at all interested in the wider world, simply that they study talk for *how* it is used and what it is used for (be that for example, to accomplish an action like getting someone to bring you a cup of tea, or to maintain a social assumption that women are inferior to men).

The use of talk as a topic for research is not just a methodological feature of Discourse Analysis. It brings with it a fundamental theoretical shift away from more cognitive understandings of the world. With talk as the topic, the study of social interaction becomes an exploration into how events or ideas come to be; be that how a group of friends successfully arrange to meet up, or how the British and American governments worked to present a legitimate case for war in Iraq following the 9/11 attacks. We will now briefly elaborate on some of the key theoretical assumptions that lie behind the decision to treat talk as the topic of research.

Key Theoretical Assumptions

Talk is Action: Our Words do Things

The idea of talk-as-action can be understood in a very literal sense, as with defined 'speech acts.' For example, in the sentence 'I now pronounce you man and wife,' the words themselves perform actual action, in this case the legal act of marrying two people (Austin, 1962; Searle, 1969). However, all discourse has functions (e.g., greeting, requesting, explaining, complaining [Potter & Wetherell, 1987]) so talk can be studied in terms of what speakers are doing with their words rather than what their words reveal about their inner thoughts. Thus, the Discourse Analyst is interested in the role language plays in the performance of social activities and social identities (Gee, 2005).

Language is Constructive and Constructed

One of the things that people do with their talk is build meanings and understandings about objects or events in the world that can be shared and understood by everyone else. For example, although "odd, discrepant or deviant behaviour" has persisted throughout human history, the same behaviour has been described at various points in time as 'schizophrenia,' 'witchcraft' or 'adolescent delinquency' (Wetherell 2001 p16). What "odd, discrepant, or deviant behaviour" are understood to be and to mean is constructed through the words used to describe them. Thus, someone who is schizophrenic cannot at the same time be a witch because the use of one word denies other possible meanings for the behaviour. In this sense, how we understand, react to, and judge events or behaviours is based on the words we have available to describe them. Discourse Analysts therefore argue that discourse produces and maintains the social reality in which we live (Phillips & Hardy, 2002).

If we consider the speech of individuals, we can still see the constructive nature of language at work. Take for example a criminal court case: the defence and the prosecution lawyers work with the same evidence presented to the jury but use it to build two different accounts of events, one which condemns defendants and one which exonerates them. Thus, language is used to build different versions of reality. Through this understanding, we can see that speakers *design* their talk in order to accomplish specific goals in interaction (e.g. securing a conviction, or persuading market traders to lower prices). So the second theoretical assumption of Discourse Analysis is that language is both constructive and constructed (Potter, 1996).

The notion of construction is key to Discourse Analysis. It relates both to the fact that talk builds versions of realities (is constructive), but also that it is constrained by the situation in which it is delivered and in a sense constructed by the world around it.

Gill (2000) helpfully expands on the metaphor of construction for discourse. She explains that the language we use is replete with conventions that are widely, although often unconsciously followed. For example, we can think about how telephone conversations begin not just with "hello" "how are you?" sequences, but even before that with the convention that the person answering speaks first (Schegloff, 1968). Although our language is constrained by conventions and practices, Gill points out that we still have options, many of which can reveal much about our worldview. For example, there is a town in Northern Ireland that is referred to as Londonderry by unionists and Derry by nationalists. The word choice positions the speakers as a member of one of other of Northern Ireland's main communities, thereby associating them with a particular political stance especially during the height of the Irish "troubles." In America, a similar political word choice is played out with the terms *undocumented workers* and *illegal aliens*: the former suggesting a liberal affiliation, the latter a conservative. Finally, Gill argues that if the language we use is constructed, so in using it do we affirm its construction. However, because no two experiences can be wholly identical, our use of language to some degree modifies the construction. Therefore, our every talk is an interaction between the constructed and constructive facets of our language and the world.

Language is Situated

All talk occurs in a specific environment. This refers in part to the institutional location such as a classroom or doctor's surgery where there are particular expectations about likely formats of conversations. However, talk is also located within the structure of a conversation: invitations get acceptances or refusals, complaints get apologies or counter complaints (Howitt, 2010; Potter, 2009). Also, what is said and what those words mean may vary depending on the situation. Consider the two statements 'the coffee has spilled, get a broom' and 'the coffee has spilled get a mop.' In the first statement, the word 'broom' leads us to infer that 'coffee' would describe beans or grains, and in the second the use of 'mop' suggests that 'coffee' now refers to a liquid (Gee, 2005). The situation can also depend on who's doing the talking: the sentence "I hate women" probably means something very different depending on whether Jack or Jane said it; and the possible consequences of saying it are also likely to depend on the gender of the speaker. It is through variations in situations like these that the constructive and constructed nature of language becomes visible.

Whereas we could argue that psychology has traditionally treated variation as a problem and sought to eliminate it to produce consistent homogenous results (as with Latent Semantic Analysis, see Kintsch & Kintsch, this volume), Discourse Analysts study variation and use it as a central part of analysis to help reveal how talk is constructed and what function it is performing in that specific situation (Wood & Kroger, 2000). Such explanations form part of the reason why some discourse analysts say they are studying talk-in-interaction; talk in the context in which it was delivered.

Treating talk as the topic of research in its own right marks Discourse Analysis as a radical development in social science research (Woofitt, 2005). Discourse Analysis does not look through language to study the motivations or thought processes of the speakers. For example it would not be able to offer a coherent answer to the question 'what are the factors that led to non-compliance with physiotherapists exercise instructions?.' It would, however, be able to offer insight into how patients accounted for their failure to follow medical advice during future consultations. Discourse Analysis provides a means to consider how psychological matters (such as beliefs and memories) become live in interaction and what participants use them for (Edwards, 2006a). For example 'I thought it would get better if I just rested' as an account for failing to do physiotherapy exercises invokes the notion of reasoning, displaying the patient as someone actively concerned with recovery. It also bases the account in the past tense therefore not displaying present or future reluctance to comply with medical orders. As a rhetorical formulation to support the patient's position, the talk does the work regardless of whether or not the patient did or didn't think resting would help.

This section aimed to offer an outline of some of the theoretical underpinnings to Discourse Analysis. By treating talk as the topic of research, Discourse Analysis challenges the basic assumptions of research that looks through language, treating it as a neutral reflection of the beliefs and attitudes it describes (Potter, 1996). In so doing, Discourse Analysis has the potential to reveal the ontological and epistemological assumptions behind projects, methods, or even systems of classification (Gee, 2005). This very "potential" is what we aim to highlight in this chapter, because at some stage, and in some important ways, applications in natural language processing are likely to be critical to the development of Discourse Analysis.

BACKGROUND

Many different types of research have been called Discourse Analysis. This section will focus on some of the branches of Discourse Analysis that have developed from the social constructionist work exemplified by Wetherell & Potter's (1987) book *Discourse and social psychology: Beyond behaviour and attitudes.*

Discursive Psychology

Early Discourse Analysis work includes Gilbert and Mulkay (1984) who assessed scientists' accounts of their work. They highlighted the variability and flexibility of the language used and pointed out that language was put to use in service to a particular goal such as defending findings rather than neutrally reporting what happened during an experiment. This work was developed within psychology by Edwards and Middleton (1986; 1987; 1988) who began to look critically at cognitive psychological explanations of social interaction (e.g., stereotypes, or memory). Wetherell and Potter (1987) offered a similar criticism of traditional attitudinal research that ignored the situational factors that influenced what and how something was said.

The type of work just described, and subsequent work now called Discursive Psychology, involves re-specifying traditional psychological notions in relation to the function they perform in discourse (Potter, 2009). Instead of trying to get at the internal states of participants, discursive psychologists look at how participants draw on notions of psychological phenomena such as emotion in order to accomplish an interactional goal. An often cited example is Edwards (1995; 1997) analysis of "Connie and Jimmy." Within their ostensibly factual descriptions of events during a counselling session, Connie and Jimmy depict each other as "endemically jealous" and "flirtatious" respectively (Edwards & Potter, 2005, p245). By constructing each other as jealous or flirtatious the speakers simultaneously both provide conceptual support for their own account and discredit alternative understandings; If Jimmy is always jealous then he is overreacting to Connie's behaviour, or if Connie is being provocative towards other men then Jimmy is justified in being unhappy with her behaviour (Edwards, 1995). The example allows us to understand how Connie uses a psychological concept like 'jealousy' not necessarily because that is how it 'really' happened (that is not of relevance here), but because it is *interactionally* useful for her to employ that concept at that time to support her argument.

Conversation Analysis

Some of earliest work that treated talk as the topic of research was conducted by ethnomethodologists such as Harold Garfinkel (Heritage, 1984). Garfinkel was interested in how discourse was used by people to reach a shared understanding of the world around them. Researchers such as Goffman (1959) highlighted a structure and orderliness to everyday life and talk. This work led Harvey Sacks to study that order and structure in more detail. It was from this early work that Conversation Analysis developed.

Conversation Analysis represents a very specific methodological approach to discourse analysis that looks at the organisation and structure of conversations (e.g., how speakers negotiate taking turns at talking (Sacks, Schegloff et al., 1974). Because of its focus on conversations, Conversation Analysis uses naturally occurring data rather than researcher generated data (such as interviews). It is a specialized form of Discourse Analysis that focuses on talk-in-interaction; it seeks to understand how we do conversation (Liddicoat, 2007). Conversation Analysis pays very close attention to the specific piece of interaction under study (Psathas, 1995; ten Have, 2007). It is not that wider culture is ignored, but rather that analysis is based solely on what the participants orient to as relevant, not what the analyst may seek

to impose from the wider culture. For example, when studying a family meal time conversation the familial relationships (e.g., husband, wife, mother, father, son, brother, sister, daughter) may be being drawn on at different points in time but only when it can be shown that the participant is using that relationship to accomplish something within in the interaction is the analysis considered sound. For example a wife who says to her husband "*Daddy*, can you pull Lucy's chair in" may be invoking his status as father to draw attention to his parental rights and obligations.

Critical Discourse Analysis

A third variant of Discourse Analysis is Critical Discourse Analysis. This approach was influenced by the early work of Michel Foucault on power, knowledge, and subject positions (Foucault, 1972; Hall, 2001). Foucault introduced the idea that individuals, just like activities or events, cannot be thought of as immune from the constructive effects of language (Phillips & Jorgensen, 2002). People are constructed (and therefore constrained and shaped) by discourse. Norman Fairclough (Fairclough, 1989) developed a framework for analysing discourse based on the premise that language and power are closely linked. From this, Critical Discourse Analysis developed as a form of social science research.

Critical Discourse Analysis often tends to adopt an expressed political stance, seeking to highlight how discourse can be used to oppress a social group (Woofitt, 2005). This is one of the areas that highlights how very different types of research can be conducted under the banner of Discourse Analysis. The same data analysed using different branches of Discourse Analysis would focus on different aspects and make different contributions to research. Using data from police interviews, a Discursive Psychologist may be interested in how language could be used by the suspect to counter claims that they could have committed the crime. For example, Edwards (2006b) found that suspects used 'would' to claim a personality trait inconsistent with the crime "I wouldn't hurt an old lady" (2006b: 497). Here the focus is on how language is used *in situ* to perform a specific rhetorical function. In contrast, the Critical Discourse Analyst may look at much the same data but examine it in terms of how the talk enabled entrenched social practices to be carried out. Haworth (2006) used recordings of early police interviews with the later convicted serial killer Dr. Harold Shipman to show how the interview process and subsequent treatment of the transcript during the trial enhanced the institutional power of the police.

Theory and Method

Despite the difference between the branches of Discourse Analysis outlined above, what unites them is a commitment to treat talk as the topic of research. Discourse Analysis does not treat language as a mirror, faithfully reflecting an objective reality; it views language as a construction site, where it plays an active role in creating and changing how people view the world (Potter & Wetherell, 1987; Potter, 1996). Despite differences in data collection (naturally occurring versus researcher generated), analytic focus (interaction, using psychological phenomena as rhetorical devices, power struggles) and outcome of the research (how is conversation achieved, what do people do with their talk, how does talk oppress social groups), the various forms of Discourse Analysis are united by their approach to language. Thus, Discourse Analysis is a range of methods collected around a theoretical position.

Discourse Analysis, although arguably able to work with both talk and texts tends to focus mainly on talk in interaction. This tendency is because talk in interaction is (a) the primordial site of human sociality (Schegloff, 1987) and (b) situated, embodied, inflected and unfolds sequentially in real time. Conversations are rich with context and have an ever-changing and negotiated meaning for the participants in the conversation. Thus the challenge posed by the 'meaning making' that happens in real time within interaction often offers a more direct route to look at what people do with their words than is possible with the permanence of the written word.

THEMES IN DISCOURSE RESEARCH

Discourse Analysis research output is a large, diverse and constantly growing body of work. We will thus focus on a few key themes in Discourse Analysis research: (1) reality construction through discourse, (2) discursive practices in service to interactional goals, and (3) representations of social groups in discourse.

Social Construction

People communicate through discourse; it is the only means they have of making shared sense of anything. By talking to people we transmit ideas, beliefs, understandings, and ways of thinking about the world. In this sense, it is through interaction that identities can be affirmed or denied and culture can be transmitted and adapted (Goodwin & Heritage, 1990).

When approached through Discourse Analysis, traditional topics of psychological inquiry are re-specified and examined from a fresh perspective. For example measuring attitudes on scales would be re-worked as a study of how and when people make evaluative statements in practice (Edwards, 2005). In their influential study, Potter and Wetherell (1987) demonstrated the diversity of evaluative constructions of the same object (in this case New Zealand Maori and Polynesian Islanders) to be found within a single respondent's talk. The empirical variability and inconsistency in the expression of evaluative statements argued against the existence of a fixed, stable attitude that informs behaviour. They suggested instead that the expression of attitudes did not relate to an "abstract and idealized object" but to a specifically designed description in service to building a particular account (Potter & Wetherell, 1987, p54). For Discourse Analysts what is relevant is not that a person has an underlying orientation towards, for example, Maoris, but rather, that they have chosen to build a particular evaluation at that specific point in the discourse. The question is then to work out what interactional goal that expression is in service to or what the consequences of that expression might be.

Instead of dealing with how people understand the reality around them, Discourse Analysts look at how people construct the reality around them and what purpose there is in constructing it in that particular way at that particular time. Potter and Edwards (1990) criticised experimental work on attributional theory for the assumption, embedded in its use of vignettes or short descriptions as stimulus materials, that the descriptions provided were somehow neutral, representations of the world (Edwards & Potter, 1993; Potter & Edwards, 1990). They demonstrated that attributions, like attitudes, were in practice oriented to "a wider web of social and discursive activities, such as blaming, accusations, and rebuttals" (Woofitt, 2005, p54). What is relevant here is that any description of an object or event represents just one possible way of describing it to the exclusion of all others. Recall the case of "Connie and Jimmy" (see earlier section on Discursive Psychology), the married couple in a relationship counselling session. Edwards (1997) showed how both parties worked to construct a version of events that presented the breakdown of their marriage as the responsibility of the other party rather than a consequence of their own actions. Note that what is not an issue here is the 'truth' of the situation. It is not for the discourse analyst to pass judgement on which version is correct. Instead, Discourse Analysis reveals the work done by participants in order to present their version of reality.

Discursive Practices

Early work within Discourse Analysis has highlighted just how much discursive effort people routinely employ both to design their own talk as objective or factual, and to undermine the factual basis of other accounts as subjective or partial (Potter, 2009). Discourse Analysis has identified repeatable and recognisable practices of 'fact construction' that pervade even ostensibly simple descriptions.

One of the ways in which people build accounts as factual is through the use of stake management (Potter, 1996). Participants are not naïve; they know that descriptions are used to 'do things,' and that talk can be designed to offer support for a personal desire, motivation or allegiance. Because of this concern, participants design their talk in such a way as to counter or pre-empt the claim of 'oh you would say that, wouldn't you?' so as to 'inoculate' themselves so to speak (Edwards & Potter, 1992).

The claim, 'Oh you would say that, wouldn't you?' treats the speaker as having a vested interest based on some aspect of their identity (e.g., background, interests, and attitudes; Potter, 1996). Discourse produces versions of people as well as version of events. For example, the same person could be accurately described as female, single, mother, interior designer, university graduate, or any other of a number of such terms. But each description brings with it a different set of assumptions about stake, interest, and motivation – the single mother who works a 70-hour week is neglecting her child, but the interior designer who works a 70-hour week is committed to developing her career. Descriptions draw on categories and use the assumptions tied to those categories to reference particular versions of the world. Key work on categories within discourse comes from Sacks' early work on membership categorisation in Conversational Analysis.

Representation

We cannot get away from the implications of vested interest or assumptions of how 'someone like us' should feel, act, or describe. In this sense, the speaker is also the subject of language. That is to say if one accepts the premise that discourse is constructive then discourse must represent and construct all aspects the social world, including its actors (Wetherell, 2001).

The foundation for looking at speakers as subjects constrained by their discourse can be found in Foucault (1972) where he argues that language users cannot stand outside the discourse they use (see also Hall, 2001). We are all bound up by the discourses that represent our social world. Our understanding of that social world is based on our being a part of it, and, as such, represented through its discourses. The forms of Discourse Analysis, like Critical Discourse Analysis, that include an orientation to the wider social context look not only at how people use language, but also how they are used in language (Woofitt, 2005). Jorgensen and Phillips (2002) offer a neat example of this:

"If a child says 'mum' and the adult responds, then the adult has become interpellated with [or placed in] a particular identity – a 'mother' – to which particular expectations about her behaviour are attached" (2002: 40)

When considering social groups, the interest for the Discourse Analyst is in how social groups are reflected (or represented) in talk (McKinlay & McVittie, 2008). A key contribution of Discourse Analysis to understandings of social representation is that language cannot be wholly equivalent to a material object in the world. It can only represent selected pertinent aspects of it (Wetherell, 2001). Because representations are necessarily selective they can be constructed through discourse to support particular arguments or refute others. For example, a group of teenagers gathering on a street corner at night can be represented in discourse as an example of the local authority's failure to provide appropriate youth facilities or as an example of how local shops are being driven out of business through the intimidation of customers by gangs of out of control "yobs."

Contested representations mean that there is a political dimension to consider. Social groups of people do not exist until they are constructed in discourse. For example, it wasn't until 'the new man' was introduced as a discourse of masculinity that the traditional discourse contrasting 'man' and 'feeling' was challenged as a way of representing masculinity (Phillips & Jorgensen, 2002). The role of Discourse Analysis can be seen as investigating how the available discursive resources are used to legitimise one way of viewing the world or suppressing another (Potter, 2009).

FUTURE RESEARCH DIRECTIONS

A key methodological feature of Discourse Analysis is that it does not have to start with a specific research question or hypothesis to be tested (although, note that "does not have to" does not mean "must not"). A recurrent technique within Discourse Analysis is to begin with a social setting – a courtroom, classroom, radio talk show etc. – and investigate the discursive practices within that setting. Starting from the data and exploring the actions within its discourse can reveal ways in which people's ability to contribute to discussion or to represent their position are restricted or restrained. For example, during a court case the interaction is structured such that lawyers ask questions and defendants and witnesses answer. The structure of the interaction is designed so as to restrict defendants and witnesses ability to introduce new information or shape the flow of the conversation (Atkinson & Drew, 1979).

Early setting-based work often contrasted the notion of 'institutional' talk with ordinary, everyday talk. Institutional talk refers to situations where participants have specific and limited goals, potentially restricted means of contributing, and activity specific inferential frameworks (e.g., medical consultations, television interviews, classrooms; Drew & Heritage, 1992). More recent work has begun to unpick this polarity and study each setting in terms of the discursive practices and resources that participants use rather than treating all talk as a product of its location. This is an exciting and diverse field of research that has real-world implications for how we understand our interactions with others. For example, Goodwin & Goodwin have shown how even speakers with extremely limited ability to communicate verbally can be considered full and active participants in conversations when their physical conduct and gestures are analysed alongside talk (Goodwin & Goodwin, 2004; Goodwin & Goodwin, 2000).

Recently there has been an increased body of work looking at calls to various telephone helplines. For example, researchers in both the UK and Australia have considered the challenges faced by child callers to various helplines (Danby & Emmison, in press; Emmison & Danby, 2007; Hepburn, 2005). Calls to home birth helplines have been analysed in terms of how they both offer advice (Kitzinger, 2007; Shaw & Kitzinger, 2007) and empower women (Shaw & Kitzinger, 2005). Work such as this has the potential for real change in phone operator practices that can improve the effectiveness of the interaction for the participants involved.

Another interesting new line of work involves police interrogations, in particular on the discursive practices used by police interviewers to elicit confessions of intentions to commit crimes. Such work has shown how police interviewers routinely draw on modal constructions such as 'would' and on notions of intentionality to lead suspects towards formulations of their actions that could constitute a crime (Edwards, 2006b; Edwards, 2008; Stokoe & Edwards, 2008).

A final example is the growing body of work concentrating on family mealtimes. This work has contributed to our understanding of how food at-

titudes and evaluations are worked up to manage other interactional business (Wiggins & Potter, 2003; Wiggins, 2004b), and how advice about diet and health are both given and received in real-life situations (Wiggins, 2004a). By studying how food and eating are constituted amongst family members there is the potential to develop more effective dietary health communication strategies.

Contributions to Knowledge

To match the plurality of approaches within Discourse Analysis, there are, unsurprisingly, a variety of contributions that the different types of Discourse Analysis can make to knowledge. It can point to the ways in which certain practices might perpetuate prejudiced assumptions. For example Wood and Kroger (2000) use the example of how *nurse* is used without modification for a female nurse, but is often changed to *male nurse* when referring to a man. They argue this propagates an assumption that nurses should be women. By highlighting the unspoken assumptions present in our everyday language, Discourse Analysis can work to bring about a change in language use that is, because of the constructive nature of language, a change in practice, and ultimately in social reality (Wood & Kroger, 2000). The kind of research that embodies a specific political stance and emancipatory goals such as championing a group that appears oppressed tends to make use of Critical Discourse Analysis and other 'context-inclusive' modes of analysis. Typically this approach has less of a prescribed, standard methodological process (Woofitt, 2005).

Discourse Analysis research within Discursive Psychology asks important questions about 'taken-for-granted' assumptions within conventional research. It challenges researchers to question the link between discourse and cognition. Particularly it advocates against assuming that the expression of an evaluative statement (e.g., *John said this fish is delicious*) necessarily relates to an enduring and fixed mental state (e.g., *John likes fish*) when the evidence may not support their existence outside of the discourse (e.g., the speaker was complimenting a nervous cook (Potter & Wetherell, 1987). The job of the analyst is therefore to unpick the function of the participant's talk rather than to assume it is a neutral reflection of either the social or cognitive world of the speaker. Increasingly this kind of research is moving towards making use of the methodological rigour of Conversation Analysis CA to ground its claims in empirical data (Edwards, 2005).

The approaches within Discourse Analysis, although diverse, do not have to be oppositional and conflicting. As the historical body of Discourse Analysis research increases, the growing base of knowledge about how language is used and what it is used for can complement each other. Let us take for example the various discursive practices that participants can use to construct their version of events as factual. Fact construction is a means of privileging one's own account above those of others to ensure that a version of reality that casts oneself in a positive light becomes the dominant discourse. Thus, we can argue that in everyday discourse one can see the micro-level functioning of discourse as it operates within broad social themes of discrimination and oppression.

At a societal level, what is taken to be factual and true has profound implications for the people it represents. For example, a 'social fact' that absent mothers cause delinquent or affectionless children impacts on opportunities for women in the workplace. Through Critical Discourse Analysis, representations of working women as negligent mothers can be identified and brought to public awareness. On an interpersonal level, the precise discursive practices through which individuals can 'work-up' the idea that 'children need their mothers' can be revealed and explicated through the close analysis of Discursive Psychology. Finally, Conversation Analysis can provide the mechanics of exactly how fact construction is achieved within everyday real-life interaction, and consequently how practices can be changed.

Some Discourse Analysis Issues for ANLP Consideration

So far in this chapter, we have broadly discussed a wide variety of assumptions and practices concerning Discourse Analysis. At this point, we turn our attention to a brief analysis of how ANLP tools and techniques may have relevance to these assumptions and practices, and consequently, how ANLP and Discourse Analysis may have a future.

To begin, we need to outline some of the tools and approaches that are most likely to address issues in Discourse Analysis. We will restrict ourselves to tools and approaches that are discussed in detail elsewhere in this book, so that the interested reader can easily learn more. The tools in question are Coh-Metrix (this volume), LIWC (this volume), and the Gramulator (this volume). And the primary approaches are Latent Semantic Analysis (this volume) and entailment analysis (this volume). Although the aforementioned tools and techniques are sufficient for the analysis presented here, we do not claim that they are the only approaches available to researchers in Discourse Analysis. Indeed, the interested reader is also advised to see chapters in this volume such as Docuscope (this volume) and Hidex (this volume) among others.

Coh-Metrix, LIWC, and the Gramulator are textual analysis tools (and therefore they are Discourse Analysis tools). Coh-Metrix was primarily designed to assess text for cohesion so that readers could be better matched to reading material. However, in practice, the dozens of measures that Coh-Metrix makes available (e.g. LSA, lexical diversity, word frequency) have been used more often in classification analyses (see McNamara and Graesser, this volume). Somewhat similar to Coh-Metrix, LIWC was designed to facilitate the identification of psychological phenomena by analyzing word choice across groups of texts. Like Coh-Metrix, LIWC features dozens of measures and consequently, it too has featured in numerous text disambiguation studies. And finally, the

Gramulator is designed to identify differential linguistic features of correlative text types. The correlative texts can be a corpus of English language abstracts written by Americans and a corpus of English language abstracts written by Koreans (see Min & McCarthy 2010); or a corpus of fairy tales and a corpus of texts for English language learners (see Rufenacht, McCarthy, & Lamkin in press). The correlative corpora are analyzed relative to each other, so that the output is language that is characteristic of one set of texts, while being uncharacteristic of the contrasting set of texts. Thus, by its very nature, the Gramulator is also a disambiguation tool.

Tools such as Coh-Metrix, LIWC, and the Gramulator typically use *measures* to assess text. Often, the measures are groups of associated words such as *connectives*, *positive emotion words*, or *indicative narrative features*. However, tools can also employ more sophisticated measures like LSA or entailment assessment. LSA assesses the similarity between words (or groups of words). This assessment is grounded on the assumption that words that occur together are more semantically similar to each other than words that seldom (or never) appear together. Thus, *swamp* is similar to *alligator* because they often (but not always) appear in the same text. In contrast, *blueberry* and *alligator* are dissimilar because they are highly unlikely to occur in the same text. While LSA typically measures the similarity between texts, entailment approaches assess the degree to which one text can be logically inferred from another (Dagan, Glickman, & Magnini, 2005). For example, "Jane went to the store to buy some food" may *imply* that Jane *drove* to store, and/or that Jane *likes* bread, and/or that Jane *was hungry*, but *entailment* only applies to statements such as *Food is sold at the store Jane went to.*

The remainder of this section offers a brief assessment of how the tools and approaches described above might apply in Discourse Analysis. Because of space restrictions, the discussion is restricted to just three of the issues that we

have argued are central to Discourse Analysis. Although such a list is far from exhaustive, we argue that these points are, at least, a useful point of departure for discussing the role of ANLP in Discourse Analysis.

The Function of the Language

The function of the language can be understood as an emphasis towards what language does rather than what language means. This functioning may be unconscious, as when we allow the person answering the phone to speak first; conscious, as when opposing lawyers construct their contrasting cases from the same evidence; or somewhere between, perhaps as when individuals are treated as if they were representatives of a group. In ANLP terms, the function of a text is likely to need some kind of qualitative interpretation, as with factor analyses; however, as an assist to this interpretation, the function of text might be assessed relative to *move analysis* (Swales 1990), *text segmentation* (Salton, Allan, & Buckley 1993), and *entailment* (Rus this volume).

Moves are sections of text (usually sentences) that can be identified as fulfilling an identifiable role (i.e., function). Computationally, Lamkin and McCarthy (in press) use the Gramulator to identify moves in detective novels such as *introducing a character*, *setting a scene*, and *providing background*. In their study, the Gramulator highlights indicative features of *whodunit* and *hard boiled* detection fiction, and demonstrates how functionally similar procedures are constructed differently in each genre.

Text segmentation is the process of dividing texts into thematically distinct parts. More than just identifying headers and paragraph breaks, text segmentation seeks to identify within a text common threads or topics (e.g., functions). One popular approach to segmentation is to use LSA (e.g., Choi, Wiemer-Hastings, & Moore, 2001). Because LSA can assess the similarity between sentences, common themes can be identified through clustering. Such techniques also allow for summarization (Kintsch and Kintsch), and more advanced LSA approaches such as the topics model (Griffiths & Steyvers, 2002) offer the opportunity of condensing entire corpora into thematic dimensions.

On occasions when the function of language contrasts discourse with cognition, we might turn to an entailment approach. For example, and as we have seen above, a statement such as "John said the fish is delicious" does not entail "John likes fish." In entailment terms, we might take the statement and investigate the word *said*, and conclude that had it been replaced with the word *thought* then entailment would have been much more likely.

The Choice of Words Used

The choice of words used is an issue best expressed by two related questions: *What words were used, that didn't have to be, and why*? And, *What words weren't used, that could have been, and why not*? In ANLP terms, we can say that in the choice of any given word (W0), we are excluding other possible words (e.g., W1, W2, ... Wn). The choice of W0 over W1, W2 ... Wn is crucial to Discourse Analysts. However, computational approaches, such as LSA, can only inform us that W0 is similar to W1, W2 ... Wn. For Discourse analysts, it is less important to find the similarity between differences as it is to find the differences between similarities. More specifically, W0 cannot mean W1, W2 ... Wn, because W1, W2 ... Wn were not chosen. Indeed, if W1, W2 ... Wn literally meant W0 then both words would likely not exist. As such, choice is everything. And understanding that choice tells us more about the speaker/writer or the context within which the text was created.

The issue of distinguishing similarities is probably best addressed by the Gramulator because identifying differences between commonalities is its primary purpose. To give an example, Lamkin and McCarthy (in press) took a large corpus

of "detective texts" and divided them into the sub-corpora of *whodunit* detective fiction and *hardboiled* detective fiction. The Gramulator identified the most common features of both sub-corpora and then removed all such features that were shared by both. What remain are the features that are indicative of each corpus (i.e., typical of one but not typical of the other). These indicative features are then used, both quantitatively and qualitatively, to identify how (and also why) semantically similar lexical items are formally different in correlative texts. In the Lamkin and McCarthy study, one example included *a/the guy* in hardboiled detective fiction vs *the young man* in whodunit fiction. The authors explained that hardboiled fiction is designed to be more reflective of a believable world, meaning that terms such as "a guy" or "the guy" are likely to be used rather than the somewhat lofty "the young man." In contrast, whodunit texts are more precise (hence the adjective in "the young man") because of the need to provide useful (or obfuscating) information to the reader.

Turning to LSA, we have noted that finding similarities between different words is a more common computational practice than finding differences between similar words. However, this ability for LSA to assess similarity can be useful to researchers in Discourse Analysis. LSA is able to identify semantically similar words for any given word (or words); these similar words are referred to as *nearest neighbours*. Thus, a word such as *guy* may return a list of semantically similar terms such as *kid*, *man*, and *youth*. These alternative terms may be associated with similarity values, and may also be different depending on the semantic space (i.e. *context*) in which they appear. Thus, *kid* may be the most similar term to *guy* in hardboiled fiction but *man* may be more similar in whodunit fiction. Using this kind of LSA approach, it is easy to imagine a Discourse Analysis tool that analyzes a discourse for non-present but highly related terms. Although such a tool could not easily explain *why* these thematically similar terms were *not* mentioned in the discourse, they would at least provide researchers with data to scrutinize.

The Issue of Context

We have discussed previously the role of context in Discourse Analysis. That is, *who* says *whatever* can be just as important as *whatever* is said. Indeed, *when*, *how*, and *where* are also factors that are important to Discourse Analysts; and it is certainly a fair argument that computational approaches to textual analysis have overwhelmingly focused more on the explicit *what* of the language in text rather than the implicit anything else.

Although the actual words in any text are generally the foremost concern of most computational analyses, the *who*, *where*, and *when* can also be (and have also been) analyzed. Granted, the ANLP studies mentioned below are hardly likely to be seminal literature in most Discourse Analysis courses; however, their goals and findings may offer Discourse analysts some avenues of interest for extending their research. For example, in Coh-Metrix studies, McCarthy, Lewis, Dufty, and McNamara (2006) consider the factor of *who* and *when* in Victorian literature. They demonstrate that although the writing style of authors varies over their careers, the language of each author remains distinctive. The factor of *who* and *where*, is considered in McCarthy et al. (2009); and Hall et al.,, (2007). These studies show that the seemingly neutral studies of science and law, respectively, differ considerably depending on whether the writers are British or American. Additionally, Bruss et al., (2004) considers *when* is their study of developing scientific articles; Bell and McCarthy (2007) consider the *who* of gender in their study on help groups; and Duran et al. (2007) consider temporality in their investigation of genre. LIWC studies offer a similar amount of *who*, *when*, and *where* research. For example, Chung and Pennebaker (this volume) describe studies on the different choices of words made by men and women (i.e., *who*); studies on how word

choice varies with age (i.e., *when*), and studies on word choice in deceptive speech encompassing colleges, courtrooms, prisons, and even the White House (i.e., *where*). And although the Gramulator is relatively young in textual studies, it can still boast studies that raise important questions as to *where* (Haertl & McCarthy in press, Lamkin & McCarthy in press) and *how* (Terwilleger and McCarthy in press).

Coh-Metrix, LIWC, and the Gramulator are able to distinguish non-trivial text by applying varying computational measures (e.g., lexical diversity). However, these measures, in and of themselves are also reflective of Discourse Analysis issues. For example, LIWC makes use of "dictionaries," which are collections of thematically related words (such as *anxiety words* or *positive emotion words*). These sets of words remind us that the choice of words used in a text constructs meaning; and by the same token, the meaning of these words is constructed, deconstructed, modified, and/or reinforced by their implementation in the text. In other words, computational tools that rely on word lists (especially non-flexible lists), can be as useful to understanding text and they can be in defining it.

And finally on the issue of context, some approach to textual analysis rely not so much on word lists as they do on word spaces. For example, LSA approaches typically use very large collections of text relevant to a specific theme (e.g., science, literature, and medical journals.) These spaces allow us to compare word(s) as they are used in different situations; thus, we might find that the meaning of *patient* is closely associated with *nurses* and *doctors* in 3rd grade reading texts, whereas it is more closely associated with *surgery* and *medication* in college level reading texts.

CONCLUSION

Discourse Analysis is an umbrella term that encompasses a range of approaches to research. Despite their differences, all the approaches share basic assumptions about the functional, constructed, constructive, and variable properties of language. It is through language and interaction that people come to have a shared understanding of the social world around them. The social world is built and sustained through the discourse of its members. By studying the real-life practices of discourse, we can begin to understand how particular social encounters (e.g., medical consultations, family mealtimes, political conferences) are organised, how contributions to the interaction can be managed, and what ideas or positions are privileged or inhibited by the shape of the interaction.

Discourse Analysis has developed within multiple fields; most notably linguistics, sociology, and psychology. It stands at a crossroads between these three disciplines and offers a vibrant and challenging field of study for the researcher. Researchers from the various backgrounds bring different traditions, interests and understandings to their work. This background may help to account for why there are so many different approaches all calling themselves part of Discourse Analysis. Nevertheless, each approach offers a different angle on a situation, a different insight, all working to build up our understanding of how discourse works and what people do with it. Crucially, just as a single Discourse Analysis study 'thrives on variation' in the accounts it studies, so too does Discourse Analysis as a discipline thrive on the variation in how its researchers approach their work.

Just as Discourse Analysis has a history and a tradition, so too does it have a future and challenges. Technological advancements offer a brand new set of tools for the analysis of discourse and the potential for exciting collaborations between computational scientists and Discourse Analysts. To be sure, discourse analysts and computer scientists have different interests and different goals. But as we have seen here, tools of the computational trade could be applied to the goals of Discourse Analysis; and the goals of Discourse Analysis may offer the kinds of challenges upon

which computational scientists thrive. In short, we suggest that the time is ripe for a bridge between ANLP and Discourse Analysis.

REFERENCES

Atkinson, J. M., & Drew, P. (1979). *Order in court: Verbal interaction in judicial settings*. London, UK: Macmillan.

Atzuella, M. (in press). Data mining. In McCarthy, P. M., & Boonthum, C. (Eds.), *Applied natural language processing: Identification, investigation, and resolution*. Hershey, PA: IGI Global.

Austin, J. L. (1962). *How to do things with words*. Oxford, UK: Clarendon Press.

Bell, C., Mccarthy, P. M., & Mcnamara, D. S. (in press). Gender and language. In McCarthy, P. M., & Boonthum, C. (Eds.), *Applied natural language processing: Identification, investigation, and resolution*. Hershey, PA: IGI Global.

Brunelle, J. F., Jackson, G. T., Dempsey, K., Boonthum, C., Levenstein, I. B., & McNamara, D. S. (2010). Game-based iSTART practice: From MiBoard to self-explanation showdown. In H.W. Guesgen & C. Murray (Eds.), *Proceedings of the 23rd International Florida Artificial Intelligence Research Society (FLAIRS) Conference* (pp. 480-485). Menlo Park, CA: The AAAI Press. [PDF]

Bruss, M., Albers, M. J., & Mcnamara, D. S. (2004). Changes in scientific articles over two hundred years: A Coh-Metrix analysis. In S. Tilley & S. Huang (Eds.), *Proceedings of the 22nd Annual International Conference on Design of Communication: the Engineering of Quality Documentation* (pp. 104-109). New York, NY: ACM Press.

Choi, F. Y. Y., Wiemer-Hastings, P., & Moore, J. (2001). Latent semantic analysis for text segmentation. In *Proceedings of the 2001 Conference on Empirical Methods in Natural Language Processing*, (pp. 109–117).

Danby, S., & Emmison, M. (in press). Kids, counsellors and troubles-telling: morality-in-action in talk on an Australian children's helpline. In J. Cromdal & M. Tholander, Eds., *Children, morality and interaction.* New York, NY: Nova Science.

Denzin, N. K., & Lincoln, Y. S. (Eds.). (2009). *The Sage handbook of qualitative research* (3rd ed.). Newbury Park, CA: Sage.

Drew, P., & Heritage, J. (1992). Analysing talk at work: An introduction. In Drew, P., & Heritage, J. (Eds.), *Talk at work* (pp. 3–65). Cambridge, UK: Cambridge University Press.

Duran, N. D., Mccarthy, P. M., Graesser, A. C., & Mcnamara, D. S. (2007). Using temporal cohesion to predict temporal coherence in narrative and expository texts. *Behavior Research Methods, 39,* 212–223. doi:10.3758/BF03193150

Edwards, D. (1995). Two to tango: Script formulations, disposition, and rhetorical symmetry in relationship troubles talk. *Research on Language and Social Interaction, 28*(4), 319–350. doi:10.1207/s15327973rlsi2804_1

Edwards, D. (1997). *Discourse and cognition.* London, UK: Sage.

Edwards, D. (2005). Discursive psychology. In Fitch, K. L., & Sanders, R. E. (Eds.), *Handbook of language and social interaction* (pp. 257–273). New Jersey: Lawrence Erlbaum.

Edwards, D. (2006a). Discourse, cognition and social practices: The rich surface of language and social interaction. *Discourse Studies, 8,* 41–49. doi:10.1177/1461445606059551

Edwards, D. (2006b). Facts, norms, and dispositions: Practical uses of the modal would in police interrogations. *Discourse Studies, 8*(4), 1–23. doi:10.1177/1461445606064830

Edwards, D. (2008). Intentionality and *mens rea* in police interrogations: The production of actions as crimes. *Intercultural Pragmatics, 5*(2), 177–199. doi:10.1515/IP.2008.010

Edwards, D., & Middleton, D. (1986). Joint remembering: Constructing and account of shared experience through conversational discourse. *Discourse Processes, 9,* 423–459. doi:10.1080/01638538609544651

Edwards, D., & Middleton, D. (1987). Conversation and remembering: Bartlett revisited. *Applied Cognitive Psychology, 1,* 77–92. doi:10.1002/acp.2350010202

Edwards, D., & Middleton, D. (1988). Conversational remembering and family relationships: How children learn to remember. *Journal of Social and Personal Relationships, 5*(3), 25.

Edwards, D., & Potter, J. (1992). *Discursive psychology.* London, UK: Sage.

Edwards, D., & Potter, J. (1993). Language and causation: A discursive action model of description and attribution. *Psychological Review, 100*(1), 23–41. doi:10.1037/0033-295X.100.1.23

Edwards, D., & Potter, J. (2005). Discursive psychology, mental states, and descriptions. In Molder, H. T. E., & Potter, J. (Eds.), *Conversation and cognition* (pp. 241–259). Cambridge, UK: Cambridge University Press. doi:10.1017/CBO9780511489990.012

Emmison, M., & Danby, S. (2007). Troubles announcements and reasons for calling: Initial actions in opening sequences in calls to a national children's helpline. *Research on Language and Social Interaction, 40*(1), 63–87. doi:10.1080/08351810701331273

Fairclough, N. (1989). *Language and power.* London, UK: Longman.

Foucault, M. (1972). *The archaeology of knowledge.* London, UK: Routledge.

Gee, J. P. (2005). *An introduction to discourse analysis* (2nd ed.). New York, NY: Routledge.

Gilbert, G. N., & Mulkay, M. J. (1984). *Opening Pandora's box: A sociological analysis of scientists' discourse*. Cambridge, UK: Cambridge University Press.

Gill, R. (2000). Discourse analysis. In Bauer, M., & Gaskell, G. (Eds.), *Qualitative researching with text, image and sound* (pp. 172–190). London, UK: Sage.

Goffman, E. (1959). *The presentation of self in everyday life*. New York, NY: Doubleday.

Goodwin, C., & Goodwin, M. H. (2004). Participation. In Duranti, A. (Ed.), *A companion to linguistic anthropology* (pp. 222–243). Oxford, UK: Basil Blackwell.

Goodwin, C., & Heritage, J. (1990). Conversation analysis. *Annual Review of Anthropology, 19*, 283–307. doi:10.1146/annurev.an.19.100190.001435

Goodwin, M. H., & Goodwin, C. (2000). Emotion within situated activity. In Duranti, A. (Ed.), *Linguistic anthropology: A reader* (pp. 239–255). Oxford, UK: Blackwell.

Griffiths, T. L., & Steyvers, M. (2002). A probabilistic approach to semantic representation. In W. D. Gray & C. D. Schunn (Eds.), *Proceedings of the Twenty-fourth Annual Meeting of the Cognitive Science Society* (pp. 244-249). Mawah, NJ: Erlbaum.

Haertl, B., & McCarthy, P. M. (in press). Differential linguistic features in U.S. immigration newspaper articles: A contrastive corpus analysis using the Gramulator. In C. Murray & P. M. McCarthy (Eds.), *Proceedings of the 24rd International Florida Artificial Intelligence Research Society Conference* (p. xx). Menlo Park, CA: The AAAI Press.

Hall, C. (in press). Corpora and Concordancers. In McCarthy, P. M., & Boonthum, C. (Eds.), *Applied natural language processing: Identification, investigation, and resolution*. Hershcy, PA: IGI Global.

Hall, C., McCarthy, P. M., Lewis, G. A., Lee, D. S., & McNamara, D. S. (2007). A Coh-Metrix assessment of American and English/Welsh Legal English. *Coyote Papers: Psycholinguistic and Computational Perspectives. University of Arizona Working Papers in Linguistics, 15*, 40-54.

Hall, S. (2001). Foucault: Power, Knowledge and Discourse. In Wetherell, M., Taylor, S., & Yates, S. J. (Eds.), *Discourse theory and practice: A reader* (pp. 72–81). London, UK: Sage.

Haworth, K. (2006). The dynamics of power and resistance in police interview discourse. *Discourse & Society, 17*(6), 739–759. doi:10.1177/0957926506068430

Hepburn, A. (2005). "You're not takin me seriously": Ethics and asymmetry in calls to a child protection helpline. *Journal of Constructivist Psychology, 18*, 255–276. doi:10.1080/10720530590948836

Heritage, J. (1984). *Garfinkel and ethnomethodology*. Cambridge, UK: Polity Press.

Howitt, D. (2010). *Introduction to qualitative methods in psychology*. Harlow, England: Prentice Hall.

Ishizaki, S., & Kaufer, D. (in press). Computer-aided rhetorical analysis. In McCarthy, P. M., & Boonthum, C. (Eds.), *Applied natural language processing: Identification, investigation, and resolution*. Hershey, PA: IGI Global.

Kintsch, W., & Kintsch, E. (in press). LSA in the classroom. In McCarthy, P. M., & Boonthum, C. (Eds.), *Applied natural language processing: Identification, investigation, and resolution*. Hershey, PA: IGI Global.

Kitzinger, C. (2007). Birth trauma: Talking with women and the value of conversation analysis. *British Journal of Midwifery, 15*(5), 256–264.

Lamkin, T. A., & Mccarthy, P. M. (in press). The hierarchy of detective fiction. In C. Murray & P. M. McCarthy (Eds.), *Proceedings of the 24rd International Florida Artificial Intelligence Research Society Conference* (p. xx). Menlo Park, CA: The AAAI Press.

Liddicoat, A. J. (2007). *An introduction to conversation analysis*. London, UK: Continuum.

Mccarthy, P. M., Hall, C., Duran, N. D., Doiuchi, M., Duncan, B., Fujiwara, Y., & Mcnamara, D. D. (2009). A computational analysis of journal abstracts written by Japanese, American, and British scientists. *The ESPecialist, 30,* 141–173.

Mccarthy, P. M., Lewis, G. A., Dufty, D. F., & Mcnamara, D. S. (2006). Analyzing writing styles with Coh-Metrix. In *Proceedings of the Florida Artificial Intelligence Research Society International Conference (FLAIRS)* (pp. 764-770).

McCarthy, P. M., Myers, J. C., Briner, S. W., Graesser, A. C., & McNamara, D. S. (2009). A psychological and computational study of sub-sentential genre recognition. [PDF]. *Journal for Language Technology and Computational Linguistics, 24,* 23–55.

Mckinlay, A., & McVittie, C. (2008). *Social psychology and discourse*. Chichester, UK: Wiley-Blackwell. doi:10.1002/9781444303094

McNamara, D. S. (2009). The importance of teaching reading strategies. [PDF]. *Perspectives on Language and Literacy, 35,* 34–40.

McNamara, D. S., Boonthum, C., Kurby, C. A., Magliano, J., Pillarisetti, S., & Bellissens, C. (2009). Interactive paraphrasing training: The development and testing of an iSTART module. In Dimitrova, V., Mizoguchi, R., du Boulay, B., & Graesser, A. C. (Eds.), *Artificial intelligence in education; Building learning systems that care; From knowledge representation to affective modeling* (pp. 181–188). Amsterdam, The Netherlands: IOS Press. [PDF]

Mcnamara, D. S., & Graesser, A. C. (in press). Coh-Metrix: An automated tool for theoretical and applied natural language processing. In McCarthy, P. M., & Boonthum, C. (Eds.), *Applied natural language processing: Identification, investigation, and resolution*. Hershey, PA: IGI Global.

McNamara, D. S., Jackson, G. T., & Graesser, A. C. (2009). Intelligent tutoring and games (iTaG). In H.C. Lane, A. Ogan, & V. Shute (Eds.), *Proceedings of the Workshop on Intelligent Educational Games at the 14th Annual Conference on Artificial Intelligence in Education* (pp. 1-10). Brighton, UK: AIED. [PDF]

McNamara, D. S., & Magliano, J. P. (2009). Self-explanation and metacognition: The dynamics of reading. In Hacker, J. D., Dunlosky, J., & Graesser, A. C. (Eds.), *Handbook of Metacognition in Education* (pp. 60–81). Mahwah, NJ: Erlbaum. [PDF]

McNamara, D. S., & Magliano, J. P. (2009). Towards a comprehensive model of comprehension. In Ross, B. (Ed.), *The psychology of learning and motivation*. New York, NY: Elsevier Science. [PDF] doi:10.1016/S0079-7421(09)51009-2

McNamara, D. S., & O'Reilly, T. (2009). Theories of comprehension skill: Knowledge and strategies versus capacity and suppression. In Columbus, A. M. (Ed.), *Advances in Psychology Research, 62, (pp.)*. Hauppauge, NY: Nova Science Publishers, Inc.[PDF]

Min, H. C., & Mccarthy, P. M. (2010). Identifying varietals in the discourse of American and Korean scientists: A contrastive corpus analysis using the Gramulator. In H. W. Guesgen & C. Murray (Eds.), *Proceedings of the 23rd International Florida Artificial Intelligence Research Society Conference* (pp. 247-252). Menlo Park, CA: The AAAI Press.

Ozuru, Y., Dempsey, K., & McNamara, D. S. (2009). Prior knowledge, reading skill, and text cohesion in the comprehension of science texts. [PDF]. *Learning and Instruction, 19,* 228–242. doi:10.1016/j.learninstruc.2008.04.003

Phillips, L., & Jorgensen, M. W. (2002). *Discourse analysis as theory and method*. London, UK: Sage.

Phillips, N., & Hardy, C. (2002). *Discourse analysis: Investigating processing of social construction*. London, UK: Sage.

Potter, J. (1996). *Representing Reality: Discourse Rhetoric and Social Construction*. London: Sage.

Potter, J. (2009). Discourse analysis. In Bryman, A., & Hardy, M. A. (Eds.), *Handbook of data analysis* (pp. 607–624). London, UK: Sage.

Potter, J., & Edwards, D. (1990). Nigel Lawson's tent: discourse analysis, attribution theory and the social psychology of fact. *European Journal of Phycology, 20*, 405–424.

Potter, J., & Hepburn, A. (2008). Discursive constructionism. In Holstein, J. A., & Gubrium, J. F. (Eds.), *Handbook of constructionist research* (pp. 275–293). New York, NY: Guildford.

Potter, J., & Wetherell, M. (1987). *Discourse and social psychology: Beyond behaviour and attitudes*. London, UK: Sage.

Psathas, G. (1995). *Conversation analysis: The study of talk-in interaction*. London, UK: Sage.

Renner, A. M., McCarthy, P. M., Boonthum, C., & McNamara, D. S. (2009). Speling mistacks and typeos: Can your ITS handle them? In P. Dessus, S. Trausan-Matu, P. van Rosmalen, & F. Wild (Eds.), *Proceedings of the Workshop on Natural Language Processing in Support of Learning; Metrics, Feedback, & Connectivity at the 14th International Conference on Artificial Intelligence in Education* (pp. 26-33). Brighton, UK: AIED. [PDF]

Renner, A. M., McCarthy, P. M., & McNamara, D. S. (2009). Computational considerations in correcting user-language. In C.H. Lane & H.W. Guesgen (Eds.), *Proceedings of the 22ⁿᵈ International Florida Artificial Intelligence Research Society (FLAIRS) Conference* (pp. 278-283). Menlo Park, CA: The AAAI Press. [PDF]

Rufenacht, R. M., Mccarthy, P. M., & Lamkin, T. A. (in press). Fairy tales and ESL texts: An analysis of linguistic features using the Gramulator. In C. Murray & P. M. McCarthy (Eds.), *Proceedings of the 24rd International Florida Artificial Intelligence Research Society Conference* (p. xx). Menlo Park, CA: The AAAI Press.

Rus, V., Lintean, M., Graesser, A. C., & McNamara, D. S. (2009). Assessing student paraphrases using lexical semantics and word weighting. In Dimitrova, V., Mizoguchi, R., du Boulay, B., & Graesser, A. C. (Eds.), *Artificial intelligence in education; Building learning systems that care; From knowledge representation to affective modeling* (pp. 165–172). Amsterdam, The Netherlands: IOS Press. [PDF]

Rus, V., Lintean, M., Graesser, A. C., & Mcnamara, D. S. (in press). Text-to-text similarity of sentences. In McCarthy, P. M., & Boonthum, C. (Eds.), *Applied natural language processing: Identification, investigation, and resolution*. Hershey, PA: IGI Global.

Rus, V., McCarthy, P. M., Graesser, A. C., & McNamara, D. S. (2009). Identification of sentence-to-sentence relations using a textual entailer. [PDF]. *Research on Language and Computation, 7*, 1–21. doi:10.1007/s11168-009-9065-y

Rus, V., Mccarthy, P. M., Mcnamara, D. S., & Graesser, A. C. (2008). A study of textual entailment. *International Journal of Artificial Intelligence Tools, 17*, 659–685. doi:10.1142/S0218213008004096

Sacks, H., Schegloff, E. A., & Jefferson, G. (1974). A simplest systematics for the organisation of turn-taking for conversation. *Language, 50*(4), 696–735. doi:10.2307/412243

Salton, G., Allan, J., & Buckley, C. (1993). Approaches to passage retrieval in full text information systems. In *SIGIR-93* (pp 49-58). Pittsburgh, PA: ACM.

Schegloff, E. A. (1968). Sequencing in conversational openings. *American Anthropologist, 70*(6), 1075–1095. doi:10.1525/aa.1968.70.6.02a00030

Schegloff, E. A. (1987). Analyzing single episodes of interaction: An exercise in conversation analysis. *Social Psychology Quarterly, 50*(2), 101–114. doi:10.2307/2786745

Searle, J. R. (1969). *Speech acts: An essay in the philosophy of language.* Cambridge, UK: Cambridge University Press.

Shaoul, C., & Westbury, C. (in press). HiDEx: The high dimensional explorer. In McCarthy, P. M., & Boonthum, C. (Eds.), *Applied natural language processing: Identification, investigation, and resolution.* Hershey, PA: IGI Global.

Shaw, R., & Kitzinger, C. (2005). Calls to a home birth helpline: Empowerment in childbirth. *Social Science & Medicine, 61*(11), 2374–2383. doi:10.1016/j.socscimed.2005.04.029

Shaw, R., & Kitzinger, C. (2007). Problem presentation and advice-giving on a home birth helpline: A feminist conversation analytic study. *Feminism & Psychology, 17*, 203–213. doi:10.1177/0959353507076553

Stokoe, E., & Edwards, D. (2008). Did you have permission to smash your neighbour's door? Silly questions and their answers in police suspect interrogations. *Discourse Studies, 10*(1), 89–111. doi:10.1177/1461445607085592

Swales, J. M. (1990). *Genre analysis: English in academic and research settings.* Cambridge, UK: Cambridge University Press.

Ten Have, P. (2007). *Doing conversation analysis: A practical guide* (2nd ed.). London, UK: Sage.

Terwilleger, B., & McCarthy, P. M. (in press). Bias in hard news articles from Fox News and MSNBC: An empirical assessment using the Gramulator. In C. Murray & P. M. McCarthy (Eds.), *Proceedings of the 24rd International Florida Artificial Intelligence Research Society Conference* (p. xx). Menlo Park, CA: The AAAI Press.

Trappes-Lomax, H. (2004). Discourse analysis. In Davies & C. Elder (Eds.), *The handbook of applied linguistics*, (pp. 133–164). Oxford, UK: Blackwell.

Van Dijk, T. A. (2001). Critical discourse analysis. In Tannen, D., Schiffrin, D., & Hamilton, H. E. (Eds.), *The handbook of discourse analysis* (pp. 352–371). Oxford, UK: Blackwell.

Wetherell, M. (2001). Themes in discourse research: The case of Diana. In Wetherell, M., Taylor, S., & Yates, S. J. (Eds.), *Discourse theory and practice: A reader* (pp. 14–28). London, UK: Sage.

Wiggins, S. (2004a). Good for you: Generic and individual healthy eating advice in family mealtimes. *Journal of Health Psychology, 9*(4), 535–548. doi:10.1177/1359105304044037

Wiggins, S. (2004b). Talking about taste: Using a discursive psychological approach to examine challenges to food evaluation. *Appetite, 43*, 29–38. doi:10.1016/j.appet.2004.01.007

Wiggins, S., & Potter, J. (2003). Attitudes and evaluative practices: Category vs. item and subjective vs. objective construction in everyday food assessments. *The British Journal of Social Psychology, 513*, 531.

Wodak, R. (2006). Mediation between discourse and society: Assessing cognitive approaches in CDA. *Discourse Studies, 8*, 179–190. doi:10.1177/1461445606059566

Wood, L. A., & Kroger, R. O. (2000). *Doing discourse analysis: Methods for studying action in talk and text.* London, UK: Sage.

Woofitt, R. (2005). *Conversation analysis and discourse analysis: A comparative and critical introduction.* London, UK: Sage.

Chapter 4
NLP for Search

Christian F. Hempelmann
Purdue University, USA

ABSTRACT

This chapter presents an account of key NLP issues in search, sketches current solutions, and then outlines in detail an approach for deep-meaning representation, ontological semantic technology (OST), for a specific, complex NLP application: a meaning-based search engine. The aim is to provide a general overview on NLP and search, ignoring non-NLP issues and solutions, and to show how OST, as an example of a semantic approach, is implemented for search. OST parses natural language text and transposes it into a representation of its meaning, structured around events and their participants as mentioned in the text and as known from the OST resources. Queries can then be matched to this meaning representation in anticipation of any of the permutations in which they can surface in text. These permutations centrally include overspecification (e.g., not listing all synonyms, which non-semantic search engines require their users to do) and, more importantly, underspecification (as language does in principle). For the latter case, ambiguity can only be reduced by giving the search engine what humans use for disambiguation, namely knowledge of the world as represented in an ontology.

INTRODUCTION

This chapter could have been written as an intro to applying standard Information Retrieval (IR) techniques to internet search as these techniques are the basis for most approaches to search today ("have method, looking for application"). In a nutshell, IR techniques operate by identifying desired keywords or their clusters in a collection of texts and retrieving document, for example www pages, that match the keywords. But such introductions have been done elsewhere and better than this author could. This chapter could also have been written as a theoretical comparison of IR and Information Extraction (IE) techniques, based on the tenets of research in Artificial Intel-

DOI: 10.4018/978-1-60960-741-8.ch004

ligence (AI), which is where NLP contributions to search seem to be headed, as I will argue. To put it simply, IE techniques aim to 'understand' text to varying degrees and extract the relevant small bits in relation to the information needs of users (for a generic system, see Hobbs 1993). But such introductions have also been done elsewhere and better than this author could. Instead this chapter is going to sketch these issues in its introduction, before focusing on one application in this new direction, based on the experience of its author, namely in building and improving a search engine that is based on representation of meaning with the help of linguistic AI and facilitating IE-style search. As such, this chapter will largely ignore non-linguistic problems and solutions in search.

As for the majority of areas in NLP, text search is largely dominated by statistical approaches. The basic issue for any ANLP is that the complexity, some call it mess, of natural language needs to be made palatable to the computer, to discover in or impose on the unstructured mess of language some formal structure. This formal representation of language, and hopefully some aspect of its meaning gleaned from its surface structure, can then be used by the computer with any formal algorithm, hopefully suggested by a theory for a given application, but often just the favored algorithm of a research group in search for new applications.

Such non-linguistic approaches choose to ignore that language is language and operate under the assumption that its surface manifestation, in particular co-occurrence in its surface representation, are a sufficient window on the underlying meaning. After all, meaning is what all approaches are after, because it is the level at which humans interface with each other through language, and the meaning of language does indeed correlate with its surface manifestation, the text, to a large degree. But the degree to which meaning doesn't surface repeatedly and regularly in natural language text is inaccessible to statistical methods and responsible for there being an ultimate limit

to what these methods can achieve. Furthermore, "language events" are very sparse, which can be gleaned from the famous observation that in a large corpus, trigrams are 85% unique (which can be alleviated to some degree through smoothing and extraction). In other words, of the sequences of three words in a text, the large majority does not recur.

Another approach, actually the rationale of IR in contrast to IE, is to assume that ultimately humans will be the consumers of the application's output. Under this assumption, human searchers are sufficiently served by documents to his or her query that are deemed relevant by the computer because of overlap to the query and other relatively easily formalized ranking factors. The humans can then extract the information from those documents that fill their information needs on their own, that is, the machine doesn't have to do semantics, since the human is at the end of the processing chain. In contrast to this, the assumption in the main part of this chapter is that giving the machine semantics to use in matching and ranking will improve its performance and decrease human work load, both common main motivations in automation. In sum, on the basis of the unit concept, the computer represents the meaning of documents and fills the information need of the human from a knowledge base, not a document base (cf. Spärck Jones 1990).

ADDING NLP TO SEARCH

To Know or to Guess

In the field of language and computers, the fashion changes back and forth between representational and statistical dominance, under different names and with different 'applications' on the banners of the proponents of either side. As mentioned, NLP for Internet search is largely identical with the methods traditionally described under the term Information Retrieval (IR). Recently, and not for the first time in NLP, Information Extraction (IE) techniques, for which the system needs to understand the language it processes, have been emphasized more strongly: "Some people have speculated that information extraction techniques could eventually transform text search into a database problem by extracting all of the important information from text and storing it in structured form ..." (Croft et al. 2010: 113). But suggestions to add (representational) linguistics into non-representational, statistical IR-type search can be traced back at least to the 1960s (e.g., Wilks 1964; Hutchins 1970). This current swing towards representational methods in search can be seen in the light of general resurgence of knowledge-based methods, to be used in conjunction with statistical methods or instead of them. The reason for this shift is statistical methods seem to have reached their ceiling of performance, with reported improvements commonly only in the range of fractions of percents.

World Wide Web search is currently the most common field of real applications in NLP, having started in the late 1990s. This section will focus on what makes web search specific. Furthermore the focus will be specifically on new solutions to search that aim at processing the meaning of language and not its surface manifestations, and to extract that meaningful information, not just to retrieve documents (possibly) containing the information. For general IR/IE issues, like error correction, building, weighting/scoring, the reader is referred to standard text books like Croft et al. (2010) or Manning et al. (2008). Non-linguistic or marginally linguistic issues like crawling, indexing, or database structures will not be addressed either, as won't general preprocessing tasks like conversion from (proprietary) formats, tokenization, tagging, stemming. What should be noted from among the non-linguistic issues in search is that indexing is a key issue in search engine design, with linearly or even exponentially growing indices being not usable for search engines that have to operate on corpora the size of the Internet.

The author of this chapter has been involved in creating knowledge-based NLP solutions for over ten years, the last four of which focusing on search. As we're coming out of the "statistical winter," NLP for search, dominated by statistical/machine learning (SML, Raskin 2010) approaches, had to paid lip service to knowledge-based solutions under the labels of "Web 2.0" and "semantic web." The reality is still different with most approaches largely or exclusively relying on keywords and statistics.

Finally, it needs to be noted that much of the information on the actual workings of existing search engines, the majority of which are commercial, is proprietary, including that of the main section of this chapter. They can be fairly well guessed at from presentations at SemTech and similar industry forums, white papers, or press releases on company websites, and from actually using the search engines. But for obvious reasons much remains unquotable, unless it comes from academic test tube versions.

After having introduced its rationale and scope, the objectives of this chapter are to outline the role of NLP in current approaches to search, argue for the resurgence knowledge-based approaches, and lastly to introduce one such approach in as much detail as is possible to provide without revealing proprietary methods developed by the research teams working on these approaches, mainly at RiverGlass, Inc.

Search in Transition

The typical "search engineer" according to Croft et. al. (2010: 9) is usually "trained in computer science, although information science, mathematics, and occasionally, social science and computational linguistics are also represented." Linguistic training is indeed usually not listed among the main requirements in job ads for search engineers, but it is mentioned among additional desirable qualifications. And as we know computational linguists commonly are statisticians who have linguistic training only in cases where that couldn't be prevented in time, a sentiment reflected in the famous apocryphal quip by Jelinek that anytime a linguist leaves the group, the recognition rate goes up (Hirschberg 1998). In general, as Croft et al. (2010: 74) observe, "Search engines work because much of the meaning of text is captured by counts of word occurrences and co-occurrences" (Croft et al. 2010: 74). The obvious question is, if indeed (enough) meaning is captured in this way.

There are good reason the big search engines like Google have until recently used almost no linguistic NLP, except in mild preprocessing and query expansion, where permutations of the keywords entered by the user, like stemmed forms or even synonyms, are searched for as well. For one, they don't have to, because there is no competition that would offer a fully NLP-powered search engine with relevant coverage yet. For another, users are happy with what they get without linguistic NLP, and have adapted their language behavior to the limited capabilities of the search engines: users now speak "keywordese" rather than search engines speaking natural language, despite attempts at making users use more than just two to three keywords, but ask natural language questions. Such questions would provide the search engine with important additional clues as to the information needs of the user, not least the interrogative pronouns themselves: a 'how' search is very different from a 'who' search. Query-type identification and other question-answering techniques should be considered attainable semantic techniques that mark the early transition to semantic search engines. But in general, linguistic NLP as commonly practiced today doesn't do much, or too much dangerous stuff, for real applications, according to those who make the decisions at search engine companies. Notably, linguistics plays no role in one of the most foundational algorithms in Google's search technology, PageRank (Brin and Page 1998), which ranks page according to the number and quality of links pointing to that page.

Conversely, "keywordese" queries are a hard challenge for meaning-based systems is that they have a representation of the meaning of document text, like the one described below. Thus the meaning of such sparse queries can't be processed and matched to document meanings. But describing the search engines that are designed to process "artificialized" language, as this section does, is of course actually not describing natural language processing, but accordingly "arificialized language processing."

As mentioned above, search is traditionally considered to be an IR task, largely blind to the peculiarities of natural language, but more and more 'real' NLP, first by trying to revive syntax and for a while now by paying lip service to some often un- or ill-defined notion of 'semantics,' not delivering and disappointing, for example, the efforts under the "Web 2.0" headline, and recently by actually trying to develop semantic systems. This gap between "semantic" marketing and non-semantic, often still outright anti-semantic, technological reality can be illustrated by the different construal of "ontology" in the various schools of NLP and their approach to search. The task of search engines based on extremely sparse query input, commonly between 2 to 3 words, 2.6 on average per web query (Herder 2007), clearly too short to be self-disambiguating, thus highly ambiguous, so world knowledge needs to come to the rescue of search engines. And ontologies are the repositories of this knowledge.

Ontologies are sexy, but building them is hard, both in the sense of arduousness as well as complexity. Some so-called ontologies are merely controlled vocabularies, where words are restricted to a single sense, a behavior that words almost never exhibit in the free-range corpora that search engines have to handle. This is common in warehouse or sales environments, where the behavior of the users involved can be controlled and adapted to the limited capabilities of the search engine. An engineer at a car maker looking to optimize a manufacturing process can be trained to call certain subroutines with single technical terms rather than using any of the terms used on the factory floor. Members of a car enthusiasts web forum are unlikely to being amenable to that. So searching the wealth of information found in many such forums can't be powered by controlled-vocabulary ontologies. If a word is ambiguous and can refer to several items, as most words in natural language are and do, other senses of it are marked with additional text, for example, by adding adjectives or creating compounds: to distinguish the metaphorical use of "desktop" in the user interface context from the literal one that refers to the upper surface of a piece of furniture, you can refer to the former as "computer desktop."

Other so-called ontologies have only one or a few semantic dimensions. A typical example is WordNet, which started out with the most common ontological relation of subsumption, usually labeled "is-a," and illustrated by the relation of TABLE1 is-a FURNITURE, where in an ontology rich with properties, the concept TABLE would *inherit* all properties of the concept FURNITURE, but have additional ones that other child concepts of FURNITURE, like CHAIR, might not share. Such richer, yet still overall shallow ontologies, already play a role in limited search solutions, like those internally used at a single company or at least limited to a certain "vertical" domain, like medicine or law. With its purchase of Metaweb, Google might have made a move towards using ontology-based methods in general Internet search. Metaweb's Freebase is basically a named-entity dictionary based on a shallow ontology. In contrast to such ontologies, the main section of this chapter will describe a rich ontology for natural language meaning processing and how it powers natural language search.

The promise of the World Wide Web includes the Semantic Web (Berners-Lee et al. 2001), which necessarily incorporates the research agenda of AI-like, IE-style NLP (Halpin 2005; Wilks and Brewster 2006) (i.e., an NLP that understands the meaning of text). In this connection it is important to see that the main task of NLP is *not* the formal (logical or statistical) manipulation of symbols. That kind of manipulation is merely, well, logic or statistics. The main task of NLP, and one that is messy and hard and thus often ignored, taken as solved, or understood to be solved by someone else in the future, is the translation of natural language text into such symbols in an artificial, formal language. These symbols can then be manipulated with the neat methods known to operate on artificial languages. Thus, much of NLP today, and definitely the Semantic Web, presupposes as accomplished that which actually is its task. It enjoys to play before having done its work. Logic can't inform the task of understanding of NL, statistics even less so, rather, linguistics is required. This leads us to ontological-semantic technology, of which, again, more below.

Tasks, Linguistic, and Other

Let us briefly look at the processing tasks of a search engine. While details of the solutions of extant engines vary, the general pipeline of tasks is the same between them, and largely overlapping with any NLP pipeline. The corpus of text needs to be gathered, which includes crawling for Internet search, and preprocessed. This preprocessing includes the conversion of proprietary document formats to enable text extraction, the selection of which text parts of documents or pages to use gather text from. Next the text is tokenized, and the tokens are processed before they are indexed. This processing commonly involves stop-word removal, marking the position in the text from which the tokens were (e.g., headline vs. body) and stemming either by algorithm alone (e.g., Porter 1980) or with a hybrid stemmer using both an algorithm and an exception list (e.g., Krovetz 1993).

In addition to stemming, many search engines also use a part of speech tagger in order to identify phrases and compound nouns, which to index may make more sense than the individual tokens (e.g., "germ warfare"). As in all NLP pipelines stemmers and taggers introduce information, both right and wrong, and the errors can become compounded between the two (e.g., the past participle "wound" being stemmed to "wind" and then mistagged as a noun). But there "can be no doubt that even very low-level representations, however obtained, when added to the words can produce results that would be hard to imagine without them." (Wilks 2005: 262). Finally, search engines then index pages and usually compress the index as well, neither of which task involves linguistics in an interesting form.

For ranking results, search of text that is marked up, can make use of additional information for indexing (e.g., if the keyword is boldface, in a hyperlink, a URL, a headline, a list, or, importantly anchor text that links to the page being indexed). A hyperlink on page A with the anchor text "marketing techniques" is likely to link to a page B that has pertinent information on such techniques, even if the words "marketing" and "technique" do not (co-)occur significantly on page B. Again, the 'cleverer' these methods get in terms of making assumptions that are based on frequent usage of the authors of text rather than on actual text understanding, the more dangerous they also become, which is why they need to be used very judiciously.

Another NLP task involved in search technology is spelling correction, for which edit distances like Damerau-Levenshtein distance are the lay of the land. Phonetics is often allowed to play a role, as are keyboard layouts. Apart from observed mistakes in query logs in relation to pages actually retrieved results, classic solutions are descendants of Soundex, patented in 1918, such as Metaphone (Philips 1990), Aspell.net.

Further tasks in search where linguistics or NLP can be helpful are query expansion where results include terms that are assumed to be synonymous to varying degrees to those found in the query. Obviously, such terms will, again, need to be successfully disambiguated, because, for example, not all senses of "bump" are synonymous with "crash." One common solution is to offer various senses to the users to let them disambiguate, a user interface decision not preferred in general search applications because it complicates the process, but often used in enterprise search.

As an example of the move towards more linguistically-informed search, Penev and Wong (2006) sketch how even shallow linguistic techniques can improve current statistical and bag-of-words approaches, which merely use word lists for various filtering and ranking purposes, in search engines. Their approach is a basically just a ranking wrapper over Google results using part-of-speech tagging and an inverse document frequency (IDF) table.

Another hybrid system is presented by Wilks and Brewster (2009) who assume that "IR is described as MT since it involves the retrieval of one string by means of another. IR classically meant the retrieval of documents by queries, but the string-to-string version notion has now been extended by IR researchers who have moved on to QA work where they describe an answer as a 'translation' of its question." (28). Similarly, the former Internet search engine hakia tried to anticipate what are the most likely queries given a certain text and to build their index from these queries. In addition, their assumption was not to turn it into a common inverted index that would grow exponentially, but that this index of "anticipated queries" would have less redundancy and grow less than linearly after a certain number of queries has been reached. Today hakia is focused on the enterprise search market and away from linguistic technologies for which it was once the groundbreaker.

SEMANTIC SEARCH[2]

Formality and Formalism

Without experience in linguistic description, it's easy to confuse a formalism with what it is supposed to formalize. It is one thing to develop a formal environment for accommodating certain types of information. It is an entirely different task to make that information flow into this environment. Along these lines, the Semantic Web is currently running, or might already have run, its course. Web Ontology Language (OWL) is an elaborate knowledge representation environment that comes without methodology, concern, or understanding of how the information will automatically flow from natural language into OWL.

Besides the above-mentioned attempts to simulate meaning analysis with statistics and/or using the ineffective WordNet (Fellbaum 1998) resource for the same purpose, an increasing number of search engine companies have been trying to make semantic claims. Further scrutiny of these claims discovers the absence of the necessary complexity for natural-language-meaning representation, and the claim is reduced at best to the use of a taxonomy or a quasi-ontology, with habitual references to the Semantic Web (Berners-Lee et al. 2001). Ontological-semantic resources and technology are essential for search. The Semantic Web has not made any real progress towards its vague goal of making the semantic content of the websites available to all because they have focused exclusively on the development of a complex formalism, OWL (700 pages worth of rules) for expressing the content rather than on the methodology of automatic flow of text and data information into that formalism. The various ontological products, especially, the government-supported ones, are old taxonomies under a new name.

In a comment on NLP-based search technology, Sullivan (2005), the owner of the influential site SearchEngineWatch.com, correctly criticized a number of companies making NLP claims for not delivering much by way of real quality. He proceeded to dismiss any NLP technology, saying, correctly, that to be effective, the system must know every word in the lexicon, and that, he added incorrectly, is decades down the line. Knowing every word in the lexicon is just one part of the ontological-semantic approach, along with much more to make real meaning analysis in the search a commercial reality.

The different uses of ontology in semantic and non-semantic NLP briefly mentioned above illustrate the distinction between form(alism) and content well. At closer inspection, the word "ontology" is currently used to denote at least three distinctly different kinds of resources that have distinctly different kinds of uses, not all within the realm of NLP and text processing. Obrst (2007) includes a graph of the "ontology spectrum," which relates the different kinds of databases to each other. A large percentage of ontologies are controlled vocabularies, organized as taxonomies or thesauri. These are not really "ontologies" in any sense of the word because they contain no or very little relational information between concepts. They are useful for establishing standard usage of vocabularies and other pieces of information, and organizing, sorting, and modifying databases. These ontologies can grow to enormous sizes of hundreds of thousands or even millions of pieces of data, because they have no mechanism for cross-categorizing and specifying within each datum. In this way, they stand in contrast to the true ontologies, which contain conceptual information, meaning that each individual entry is no longer a single datum, but rather a compilation of data about a thing. Ontologies of this sort are able to relate entries to each other in a variety of ways and to make cross-comparisons of the properties of their entries. Because entries are more complex, or in current measures, aren't just one triple, but several triples of information, they are likely to contain far fewer entries, probably on the order of singles or tens of thousands.

Ontological-semantic technology (OST) leverages this kind of "weak ontology" for NLP by linking it to a controlled vocabulary (a lexicon) for each language that the system is competent to deal with. Though the ontology in OST needs to be very small, possibly fewer than 10,000 concepts, the lexicon for each language is as expansive as one would expect a controlled vocabulary to be, with the English lexicon currently well over 50,000 senses, and not having moved extensively into special domain coverage, except for several proprietary applications.

The final stage of evolution in ontologies is the "strong ontology" in which entries contain information that allows for inline computation, usually first order logic or mathematical equations. Because OST appreciates flexibility and because it is geared towards NLP, in which any given rule is found to have exceptions, it has chosen to place calculations and logic into the software components may use the ontology and lexicon, rather than into the ontology itself.

The following bullets and related brief comments below capture the major differences between the ontological semantics ontology-cum-lexicon and a typical controlled-vocabulary type:

- **full meaning representation:** in ontological terms, of each lexical entry;
- **nodes with interrelated properties:** as shown below, each concept is a set of ontological properties;
- **properties as essential part of ontology;**
- **non-monotonic inheritance;**
- **domain extension capability;**
- **fully automatic applications:** going far beyond the task of terminology unification into a large set of meaning processing applications (see the last section) and on to non-natural-language ontological support for specific domains;
- **focus on content, not formalism:** results in compatibility with any reasonable formalism.

The last bullet point is of crucial importance here. There is a strong tendency, in the formalism-oriented communities, in view of the already-mentioned tendency to confuse the knowledge representation formalism, which provides the means to capture some information, with the final results of NL or data information having been actually transposed into that format. Most of the work stops at the formalism. There is nothing revealing about our formalism, based on LISP format. The OST formalism stands for content, not form. It stands for natural language meaning as understood by humans, and it comes with the technology for automatically transposing NL text or data into the ontology-based formalism.

Semantics can be done semantically or with the method *du jour* in order to avoid having to do it semantically. These methods, largely statistical and formal-logical, tend to hide the lacking motivation for their application to an issue that requires access to meaning beyond neat formalism. Jackendoff specifically addresses this problem with respect to Latent Semantic Analysis (LSA; Deerwester et al. 2000), a prominent algorithm to avoid semantics: "We cannot afford the strategy that regrettably seems endemic in the cognitive sciences: one discovers a new tool, decides it is the only tool needed, and, in an act of academic (and funding) territoriality, loudly proclaims the superiority of this tool over all others" (2002: xiii). Doing semantics semantically, on the other hand, means being aware of the importance of meaning determination for the processed text. This awareness is universally shared since funding for non-semantic projects evaporated in the mid-1990s. OST is part of a growing minority who "does it semantically" while the vast majority "does it non-semantically."

Practically, doing semantics semantically means to emulate human processing. This entails to acquire large human-like knowledge resources, in particular the language-independent ontology (conceptual hierarchy) and a language-specific lexicon (anchored in the ontology). It also means to acknowledge the compositional basis of sentence meaning and an aspiration to more than 95% accuracy, because less is not acceptable to human users. Ultimately, it means the implementation of systems based on these resources as the only valid evaluation criterion.

If one does not want to do semantics semantically, for reasons briefly speculated about below, one would usually use syntactic/statistical/annotating methods in order to not have to acquire any semantic resources. In other words, the aim is to guess meaning from non-meaning phenomena, like co-occurrence and other surface structure properties of language and their quantification. Such attempts to get to meaning are often hailed as non-aprioristic and empirical, whereas they should rather be mistrusted as not disclosing their theoretical assumptions, which entails non-scalability and usually non-implementability: "[D] o the data of performance exhaust the domain of interest to the linguist, or is he also concerned with other facts, in particular those pertaining to the deeper systems that underlie behavior? [This] behaviorist position is not an arguable matter. It is simply an expression of lack of interest in theory and explanation. [...] Characteristically, this lack of interest in linguistic theory expresses itself in the proposals to limit the term 'theory' to 'summary of data [...]" (Chomsky 1965: 193f).

Statisticians in computational linguistics or psychology or any other task where quantification is assumed to be a heuristic method, often cite this quote by Kelvin (1889): "When you can measure what you are speaking about, and express it in numbers, you know something about it; but when you cannot measure it, when you cannot express it in numbers, your knowledge is of a meager and unsatisfactory kind: it may be the beginning of knowledge, but you have scarcely, in your thoughts, advanced to the stage of science." Kelvin mistook quantifiable method for science, as Nietzsche observed: "It is not the victory of science that characterizes our 19th century, but the victory of the scientific method over science" (my

translation; Nietzsche 1901: 466). For semantics, Lyons commented on this line of reasoning: "Not all that is measurable is meaning!" (1963: 13). But meaning is what linguistics is about.

Implementation

A second dimension of difference of the OST approach to search, theoretically orthogonal to the degree to which linguistics informs computational linguistics, but correlating to it because of similar psychological and disciplinary-philosophical issues, is the degree to which an NLP system is really (intended to be) doing something useful. Because statistical systems usually hit a ceiling of performance below levels of user acceptability, they can rarely employed for a real task other than comparing them to other such systems. Seemingly easy, they are stop-gap measures that don't scale up and the non-scalability is usually overlooked, because the systems are not implemented. In academic contexts, they are models of systems that would not be feasible to be built at a real scale, because the feeble materials they are built from could not bear the necessary loads. From this stems the prevalent culture in NLP of creating proofs-of-concept and toy applications in limited domains, as well as comparing these proofs-of-concept and toy applications to each other. While they are indeed comparable to each other, the performance data derived in that way have no meaning, because they don't reflect performance in relation to an implementation.

Actually using software provides criteria for its design and a metric for its success or failure. Implementedness puts the following main demands on a system (cf. Hempelmann 2007):

- **Knowing on what input you can and can't fail:** non-critical gaps, allowing for low-penalty errors.
- **Being able to handle unattested input:** robustness.

- **Operating fast enough for users to accept the implementation:** speed.
- **Having a theory how this method can in principle be improved:** scalability.

ONTOLOGICAL-SEMANTIC SEARCH

Overview

Ontological semantic technology developed from early work in computational semantics, in the late 1960s to early 1970s. on meaning-based NLP systems for limited domains/sublanguages for science and technology (Raskin 1971), development of script-based semantics in the early 1980s (Raskin 1986), and concurrent work on the semantic interlingua (e.g., Nirenburg, Raskin, and Tucker 1987). After a joint NSF grant, shared by the Purdue NLP Lab and the Center for Machine Translation at Carnegie Mellon University, the initial set of ontological semantics resources was created (see Nirenburg and Raskin 2004), primarily in the MikroKosmos MT project, largely at the Computing Research Laboratory (CRL) at New Mexico State University in Las Cruces, NM, in 1994-2000. Since 2004, there has been an initial ontological and lexical acquisition effort guided by the intended application to Internet search, followed since 2008 by a focused effort towards enterprise search more strongly supported and funded than previous commercial efforts.

An OST system represents input text as a complex text-meaning representation (TMR)—initially, one for each clause. For this it has developed the ability to represent the meaning of text automatically, emulating the mental processes of a human who reads a text. Very simplistically, the Semantic Text Analyzer (STAn) reads every sentence linearly, looks up every word in it, and for each lexical token retrieves to the underlying concept(s) in the semantic structure (sem-struc) of each lexical entry. The STAn output is stored in InfoStore, the indexed database component of the system. Because the first example, like most

sentences in NL, does not match all the numerous properties of the event concept, other sentences of the same text, as well as other texts already processed, upon successful co-reference resolution, may provide additional information that will fill the slots in those additional properties.

In actual processing, things are much more complex, as they always get when dealing with natural-language representation of reality and NL more or less loosely reflecting and usually underdetermining it. The identification of the main event of a clause is often hard as there may be competition for the essential slots. There may be no filler for an essential slot, such as agent or theme. Some techniques to resolve these and many other issues are dealt with in Nirenburg and Raskin (2004, Ch. 8); many more have been developed for the proprietary STAn.

The success of semantic search closely correlates to the state of The STAn implementation and resource acquisition and cleaning and thus improving constantly. Fewer problems occur because of unattested input (e.g., the occurrence of a word which is not in the lexicon) because the system is robust in guessing and automatically creating a partial lexical entry for such a word, but they can never be excluded entirely. A subsection below will sketch how unattested named entities are handled by OST. Functions like these ensure that, while the OST system is, in all senses, a work in progress, the current stage in the development can already support a useful system.

Figure 1. The top-level of the ontology

Figure 2. Top-level of the EVENT-branch of the ontology

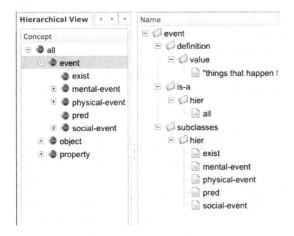

Figure 3. Top-level of the OBJECT-branch of the ontology

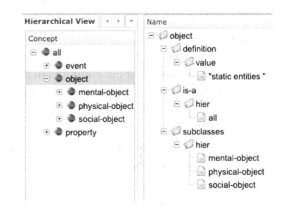

Figures 1 to 4 illustrate the overall structure of the OST ontology, ROOT and first branches in Figure 1; EVENT in Figure 2; OBJECT as in Figure 3; PROPERTY as in Figure 4.

Formally, the ontology is a tangled hierarchy of conceptual nodes, each of which can be represented as:

- concept-name
- (property-slot property-value)+

In other words, a concept has one or (usually) more properties. Every concept but the root ALL has the property IS-A, and the value of the property is the parent of this concept, the higher node—so the concept MENTAL-PROCESS, a child of PROCESS, is, on partial view, as follows:

- mental-process
- is-aprocess
- (property-slot property-value)+

Equipped with this capacity of representing the meaning of input text as TMRs, the approach has been successfully implemented in a couple of dozen applications, ranging from the highly accurate MT to IR, IE, DM, and QA. It has also developed a new toolbox for homogeneous semi-automatic

acquisition (Taylor et al. 2010) of ontological concepts and lexical entries, an improvement on the slow and defunct KBAE (2002).

Disambiguation in OST

This subsection discusses the basic process of semantic disambiguation, as one of three examples where OST contributes improved solutions to tasks in search. Based on the sentence *the dog ate a mouse* and provides more detail on how the main resources of OST contribute to its processing capabilities (cf. Hempelmann et al. 2010). The sentence appears to be simple on the surface, but it can help to show the challenges of disambigua-

Figure 4. Top-level of the PROPERTY-branch of the ontology

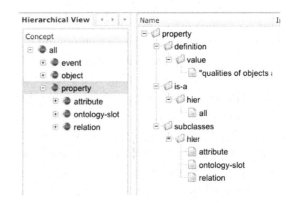

tion and the problems that result from discarding all but the most obvious interpretation. In order for the STAn to create TMRs of the sentence, all possible interpretations of it have to be created, as suggested and permitted by the knowledge contained in the lexicon and the ontology. In the following description we will skip preprocessing steps and focus on the operation of the STAn.

Our lexicon contains Exhibit 1's senses of the polysemous words *eat* and *mouse*. The entries for *dog*, *a*, *the* have only one sense each and are not shown.

For a human processor it is easy to understand from their definitions that only the senses eat-v1 and eat-v4 should be used: a dog can swallow a mouse (possibly by mistake) or attempt to eat it for its nourishment value. When the STAn reads the lexicon, it looks for clues in the senses' syntax (syn-struc) as well as semantics (sem-struc and ontology) in order to find entries that can be discarded right away. For example, eat-v2 will be discarded because according to its syn-struc, it needs the word *out* to be next too the word *eat*. Similarly, eat-v3 is discarded. We are thus left with senses eat-v1, eat-v4, and eat-v5.

Using the combination of syn-struc and sem-struc, the OST resources allow for Exhibit 2's hypotheses as representations of the sentence's meaning, given here in simplified form (actual STAn output will be given in the next subsection).

The next processing step, the STAn accesses knowledge in the ontology. The definitions of concepts EAT and SWALLOW are shown In Exibit 3. The concept FEAR is omitted as, according to the ontology, DOG is not an acceptable PRECONDITION of FEAR, and thus the actual STAn output did not include TMRs using FEAR as the core event around which TMRs are build, leading to the rejection of the fifth and the sixth hypotheses. Note that the concept EAT lacks an AGENT in its definition, as it is inherited from its parent, SURVIVAL-EVENT.

To test the first hypothesis, the STAn checks if RODENTIA is allowed as a THEME of EAT and if DOG is allowed as an AGENT of EAT. It can be seen from the definition of the concept EAT, that ANIMAL is a legitimate THEME, and since RODENTIA is a child of ANIMAL, it is also a legitimate THEME. ANIMAL is inherited as an AGENT, and DOG as a child of animal meets this constraint. Thus, the first hypothesis can't be rejected. To test the fourth hypothesis, the STAn checks if COMPUTER-MOUSE is allowed as a THEME of EAT and if DOG is allowed as an AGENT of EAT. According to the definition of EAT, only FOOD, ANIMAL, and PLANT can be its themes. COMPUTER-MOUSE is none of those. Thus, the fourth hypothesis is discarded. The second and third hypotheses are found to hold using the same principles, leaving only three interpretations out of six to be considered.

Exhibit 4 is the actual output of the STAn. The difference to the hypotheses described above is that the analyzer creates numbered instances of concepts for later coreference resolution processing. For example, instead of DOG, we see dog1.

In sum, in the course of the general processing procedures for any sentence words are looked up in the lexicon, and possible interpretations of word combinations are checked with the lexical and ontological constraints.

Query Expansion in OST

Like other search applications, one powered by OST can attempt to optimize search results be expanding on the query. But in contrast to other applications it can do so based on the meaning of the query. This subsection will describe this approach in a generalized way covering techniques simple enough to be partially emulated by non-semantic engines as well. For example, suppose that a user with a headache wants to know what remedies for his condition are available. A bag-of-word, keywordese search for this information might be "aspirin headache," or "cure headache," and neither would produce all of the desired results.

An OST search engine, on the other hand, takes the natural language query "does aspirin cure headaches?" and automatically expands upon

Exhibit 1. Polysemous words eat and mouse

```
(eat
        (eat-v1
                (cat(v))
                (anno(def "to ingest for nourishment through digestion")
                (ex "he ate the apple"))
                (synonyms "consume-v1, feed-v2")
                (syn-struc(
                        (subject((root($var1))(cat(np))))
                        (root($var0))(cat(v))
                        (directobject((root($var2))
                                    (opt(+))(cat(np))))))
                (sem-struc(eat
                        (agent(value(^$var1)))
                        (theme(value(^$var2)))))
        )
        (eat-v2
                (cat(v))
                (anno(def "eat outside the home")
                (ex "they eat out once a week."))
                (synonyms "")
                (syn-struc(
                        (subject((root($var1))(cat(np))))
                        (root($var0))(cat(v))
                        (phr((root(out))(cat(phr))))))
                (sem-struc(meal
                        (agent(value(^$var1)))
                        (location(sem(restaurant))))))
        )
        (eat-v3
                (cat(v))
                (anno(def "gradually destroy, erode")
                (ex "the heavy rains ate away at the cliffs."))
                (synonyms "")
                (syn-struc(
                        (subject((root($var1))(cat(np))))
                        (root($var0))(cat(v))
                        (phr((opt(+))(root(away))(cat(phr))))
                        (phr((root(at))(cat(phr)))
                        (obj((root($var2))(cat(np)))))))
                (sem-struc(dissolve
                        (precondition(value(^$var1)))
                        (theme(value(^$var2)))))
```

continued on following page

Exhibit 1. Continued

```
            )
        (eat-v4
                (cat(v))
                (anno(def "to swallow other than for nourishment")(ex "he ate
the pill"))
                (synonyms "chug-v2, devour-v1, down-v1,
                        gobble-v1, gulp-v1, imbibe-v1,
                        ingest-v1, quaff-v1, sip-v1")
                (syn-struc(
                        (subject((root($var1))(cat(np))))
                        (root($var0))(cat(v))
                        (directobject((root($var2))
                                (opt(+))(cat(np))))))
                (sem-struc(swallow
                        (agent(value(^$var1)))
                        (theme(value(^$var2)))))
        )
        (eat-v5
                (anno(ex "what's eating Gilbert?"))
                (synonyms "")
                (cat(v))
                (syn-struc(
                        (subject((root($var1))(cat(np))))
                        (root($var0))(cat(v))
                        (directobject((root($var2))(cat(np))))))
                (sem-struc(fear
                        (precondition(value(^$var1)))
                        (experiencer(value(^$var2)))))
        )
)
  (mouse
        (mouse-n1
                (cat(n))
                (anno(def "a computer mouse")
                (ex "he bought a new mouse"))
                (synonyms "")
                (syn-struc((root($var0))(cat(n))))
                (sem-struc(computer-mouse))
        )
        (mouse-n2
                (cat(n))
                (synonyms "")
```

continued on following page

Exhibit 1. Continued

```
                (anno(def "")(comments "")(ex ""))
                (syn-struc((root($var0))(cat(n))))
                (sem-struc(rodentia))
        )
)
```

Exhibit 2. Hypotheses

- eat
  ```
        (agent(dog))
        (theme(rodentia))
  ```
- swallow
  ```
        (agent(dog))
        (theme(rodentia))
  ```
- swallow
  ```
        (agent(dog))
        (theme(computer-mouse))
  ```
- eat
  ```
        (agent(dog))
        (theme(computer-mouse)
  ```
- fear
  ```
        (precondition(dog))
        (experiencer(rodentia))
  ```
- fear
  ```
        (precondition(dog))
        (experiencer(computer-mouse))
  ```

the query's meaning to produce a more thorough search. "Aspirin" would trigger a search not just for the word aspirin, but rather for all words linked to its ontology concept, and words linked to that concept's parent and child concepts—not only "aspirin" but "acetylsalicylic acid" and all of its known brand names, as well as generic words and brand names of conceptually similar drugs—other painkillers in the same family as aspirin. The same would be done for "cure," bringing up search results for other similar words such as "treat" and "relieve," and for "headache," looking up results for specific types of headaches (child concepts of HEADACHE), as well as other similar painful

conditions (parent concepts of HEADACHE, or PAIN in the same area).

The implementation to web search determines the design of the OST resources ontology and lexicon. Relevant questions include how many concepts should be created as separate children under PAIN and CURE, and how to distribute meaning between the ontological concept and the lexicon sense for the task at hand, as well as future use. This becomes particularly important for expanding queries in the way described above. For the example, the goal is to take a word-concept pair like (TREAT, TREAT-ILLNESS) and get lexicon entries like "care for." An earlier simplified method for

Exhibit 3. Definitions of concepts EAT and SWALLOW

```
(eat
        (definition(value("to eat and drink")))
        (is-a(hier(survival-event)))
        (effect(sem(defecate)))
        (theme(default(food))(sem(animal plant)))
        (has-event-as-part(sem(bite chew digest swallow)))
)
 (swallow
        (definition(value("to swallow")))
        (is-a(hier(immerse)))
        (end-location(sem(stomach)))
        (path(sem(esophagus)))
        (part-of-event(sem(eat)))
        (agent(sem(animal)))
        (start-location(sem(mouth)))
)
```

Exhibit 4. STAn output

```
DEBUG 09 May 2010 16:54:36 [main.SemTextAnalyzer] the dog ate a mouse .
List of TMRs:
TMR 1:Weight(TMR): 4.84
Event: eat-v3, eat
        agent(value (dog-n1, dog))
        theme(value (mouse-n2, rodentia))
TMR 2:Weight(TMR): 3.8200002
Event: eat-v6, swallow
        agent(value (dog-n1, dog))
        theme(value (mouse-n2, rodentia))
TMR 3:Weight(TMR): 3.8200002
Event: eat-v6, swallow
        agent(value (dog-n1, dog))
        theme(value (mouse-n1, computer-mouse))
```

this used all other lexical entries that use the same ontological concept as the basis of their meaning. More intelligent and proprietary algorithms based on OST have since been implemented.

This simple assumption is sufficient if the OST resources are geared towards it, namely, lexical entries that are mapped onto the same concept are indeed sufficiently "parallel," "similar," of the right degree of "synonymy." Here, again the implementation guides us to decide what "synonymy" means. For internet search, "synonymy" can be operationalized as the relation between two lexicon entries a and b, where entry b should also be considered a correct search result, when entry a is found in the search query. With the simplified assumption, expanding from "aspirin" will yield all senses mapped onto the concept DRUG. If a daughter concept PAINKILLER for "aspirin" and other painkillers is created, the current algorithm won't equate "aspirin" and "lysinopril" anymore, as these are grounded in different concepts. Instead, the algorithm be improved to take full sem-strucs into account or only consider fully identical sem-strucs. In addition, we are currently making the algorithm more discerning by enabling it to read sem-strucs in more detail (e.g., allowing for identical constraints in the agent/theme/instrument case roles to be criteria for query expansion).

Unattested Named-Entity Processing in OST

Another basic, but crucial module in OST processing for search is handling named entities, both as covered by the OST resourced as well as unattested, the more frequent and harder case (see also Hempelmann et al. 2010). Named entities, such as products, places, and persons are key items to be searched for, so covering and handling them is crucial for good search systems. As is common, named entity understanding (NEU) is triggered by capitalized tokens, as it is assumed that non-capitalized tokens are not named entities in English, and therefore are not part of our lexicon-like Proper Name Dictionary (PND), which contains commonly-known named entities or those acquired for a specific application. Whenever the STAn sees a capitalized token or sequence or group of tokens, it assumes that these tokens are fillers for the value of the property indicating the name of the concept denoted by the token(s). Thus, only those concepts that can have a name are considered.

In contrast to existing systems for recognition and classification of named entities (for a survey, see Nadeau and Sekine 2009) the STAn doesn't have a limited set of semi-supervised co-occurrence, morphological, etc. rules or rules

"machine-learned" from a tagged training corpus. Such rules selectively highlight only parts of the text assumed to help in NE-related tasks. The OST rules, on the other hand, attempt NEU on the basis of the understanding of the entire text and using all the semantic information available. In the simplest case, the unknown capitalized tokens are near the EVENT, and they are needed to fill the syn/sem-struc of this event by the TMRbuilder module, as in *Police arrested Elliot Madison in a hotel room in Pittsburgh, Pennsylvania.*

The syn-struc of arrest-v1 requires a directobject, here filled by *Elliot Madison*, who is not found in the OST resources. In the sem-struc, the STAn finds the variable $^\wedge$var3 corresponding to that of the directobject of the syn-struc and restricted to HUMAN. We will thus assume that the unknown named-entity is HUMAN.

Whenever a sequence of capitalized tokens is not interrupted by a preposition or punctuation, the STAn assumes that it represents the same concept, as defined by the sem-struc. In this case, both words are the name of a single HUMAN. Assuming this, the STAn needs to find the properties to fill with the two tokens *Elliot* and *Madison*. There are five properties that are children of PND-NAME-ATTRIBUTE, and the domain of these attributes constitutes the candidate set for unknown capitalized tokens (see Figure 5). Note that the children of PNP-NAME-ATTRIBUTE cover the "enamex" group of person/location/organization (Grisham and Sundheim 1996) at a finer grain size.

At this point, the STAn needs to choose the properties of HUMAN that correspond to the two capitalized tokens. For this purpose, it ignores the children of PND-NAME-ATTRIBUTE whose range cannot be a string and whose domain is not HUMAN or one of its descendants (and SOCIAL-ROLE, such as FOOTBALL-PLAYER, because social roles that can metonymically stand for HUMAN). With these properties discarded, the STAn selects those with the closest-fitting domain to the concept HUMAN that also contains HUMAN itself. For example, HAS-GIVEN-NAME and HAS-FAMILY-NAME both have HUMAN

Exhibit 5. Sync-struc of arrest-v1

```
(arrest-v1
        (cat(v))
        (anno(def "to seize a person by legal authority or warrant")(ex "the
police arrested the arsonist")
                (synonyms "")
                (syn-struc...)
                (sem-struc(arrest
                            (agent(value(^$var2)))
                            (beneficiary(value(^$var3(
                                    should-be-a(sem(human))))))))))
)
```

Figure 5. Partial list of children of PND-NAME-
ATTRIBUTE

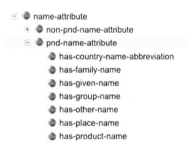

in their domain, whereas, for example, HAS-PLACE-
NAME and HAS-PRODUCT-NAME do not. Since we
only need two properties, STAn chooses HAS-
GIVEN-NAME and HAS-FAMILY-NAME, as their domains
fits most closely.

For the choice of which property to use for
which token in the case of HUMAN, excluding titles,
ranks, offices, etc., the following is our current
approximation, with similar ones existing for other
named entities, that will undergo revision as we
process more documents.

- **1 token:** fill HAS-FAMILY-NAME (unless
  found in our list of common first names, or
  unless coreferential with a token previously identified as a first name, when a 2-to-

ken version was parsed in the same text,
then fill HAS-GIVEN-NAME)
- **2 tokens:** fill HAS-GIVEN-NAME, HAS-FAMILY-
  NAME (in that order), unless a comma separates the entries, in which case the roles are
  reversed.
- **3 tokens:** the two first tokens to be used as
  HAS-GIVEN-NAME fillers, the last one as HAS-
  FAMILY-NAME filler, with a correction for
  comma, as above.

DEBUG 13 Feb 2010 13:21:41 [main.Sem-
TextAnalyzer] Police arrested Elliot Madison in a
hotel room in Pittsburgh, Pennsylvania (Exhibit 6).

Because the same unknown names can occur
in the same text more than once, the resolved
names are stored in memory for the duration of
the processing of a document. Once another unknown entity is found in a sentence, STAn looks
at those that have already been resolved to see if
a match is found. All of the unattested PND tokens
whose senses that are guessed by this module are
quarantined new entries for the PND, flagged for
approval and marked as provisional in InfoStore.
After approval in the PND, the InfoStore of the
TMRs that contain them is updated.

Exhibit 6. Police arrested Elliot Madison in a hotel room

```
List of TMRs:
TMR 1:
Event: arrest-v1, arrest1
        agent(value (police-n2, police-officer1))
        beneficiary(value (Elliot-Madison-n1,
                human1
                            (has-family-name(value(Madison)))
                            (has-given-name(value(Elliot))) ))
            location(value (hotel-room-n1, hotel-room1))
                    location(value (Pittsburgh-n1, city
                                    has-locale(value (Pennsylvania-n1, state))))
TMR 2:
Event: arrest-v1, arrest1
        agent(value (police-n2, police-officer1))
        beneficiary(value (Elliot-Madison-n1,
                human1
                        (has-family-name(value(Madison)))
                        (has-given-name(value(Elliot)))
                            inside-of(value (hotel-room-n1, hotel-
room1))))
                                location(value (Pittsburgh-n1, city
                                        has-locale(value (Pennsylva-
nia-n1, state))))
```

CONCLUSION

This chapter hopes to have highlighted where NLP already contributes to search, as well as introduce a comprehensive, linguistic approach to meaning-based search. Other important NLP tasks crucial for search that couldn't be described in more detail in this short overview include MWE processing for which OST provides unique new solutions as well (Taylor et al. 2010). What the chapter hopes to have achieved is showing that a system exist that derives 'agent-action-object' triples, proto-facts, robustly in very large numbers (cf. Bhagat et al. 2005).

Besides developing what is hoped to be a successful meaning-processing system, the search engine based on it is epxeted to raise the users' expectations beyond popularity algorithms (Brin and Page 1998) that are combined with results coming from language being treated largely like non-symbolic, normally distributed, countable, unambiguous, and sufficiently mutually exclusive items, the ontological semantic approach to NLP brings forth an essentially new discipline of natural language meaning processing, as opposed to BOW-and-statistics natural language surface text processing. The current NLP approaches, on the other hand, are still trying to get at the meaning without directly addressing the semantic substance of language, while trying to use ready-made (and, rarely, to create) word and frequency lists, Word-Nets, OWL formalisms, and other resources that are simple to acquire and used for that very reason. It must be noted, however, that OST comes from a representationalist, AI-type position.

REFERENCES

Berners-Lee, T., Hendler, J., & Lassila, O. (2001). The Semantic Web: A new form of Web content that is meaningful to computers will unleash a revolution of new possibilities. *Scientific American, 284,* 34–43. doi:10.1038/scientificamerican0501-34

Bhagat, R., Leuski, A., & Hovy, E. (2005). Statistical shallow semantic parsing despite little training data. In Association for Computational Linguistics (Ed.), *Proceedings of the Ninth International Workshop on Parsing Technology* (pp. 186-187). Vancouver, British Columbia, Canada.

Brin, S., & Page, L. (1998). The anatomy of a large-scale hypertextual Web search engine. *Computer Networks and ISDN Systems, 30,* 107–117. doi:10.1016/S0169-7552(98)00110-X

Chomsky, N. (1965). *Aspects of the theory of syntax.* Cambridge, MA: MIT Press.

Croft, B., Metzler, D., & Strohman, T. (2010). *Search engines. Information retrieval in practice.* Boston, MA: Addison Wesley.

Deerwester, S., Dumais, S., Furnas, G. W., Landauer, T. K., & Harshman, R. (1990). Indexing by latent semantic analysis. *Journal of the American Society for Information Science American Society for Information Science, 41,* 391–407. doi:10.1002/(SICI)1097-4571(199009)41:6<391::AID-ASI1>3.0.CO;2-9

Fellbaum, C. (1998). *WordNet. An electronic lexical database.* Cambridge, MA: MIT Press.

Grisham, R., & Sundheim, B. (1996). Message understanding conference-6: A brief history. In *Proceedings of the 16th Conference on Computational Linguistics, vol. 1.* (pp. 466-471). Morristown, NJ: ACM.

Hempelmann, C. F. (2007). Beyond proof-of-concept: Implementing ontological semantics as a commercial product. In V. Raskin & J. Spartz (Eds.), *Proceedings of the 4th Midwest Computational Linguistics Colloquium 2007.* Purdue University, West Lafayette, Indiana.

Hempelmann, C. F., Taylor, J. M., & Raskin, V. (2010). Application-guided ontological engineering. In H. A. Arabnia, D. de la Fuente, E. B. Kozerenko, & J. A. Olivas (Eds.), *Proceedings of International Conference on Artificial Intelligence.* Las Vegas, NV.

Herder, E. (2007). *An analysis of user behavior on the web.* Saarbrücken, Germany: VDM Verlag.

Hirschberg, J. (1998). *"Every time I fire a linguist, my performance goes up," and other myths of the statistical natural language processing revolution.* Paper presented at the Fifteenth National Conference on Artificial Intelligence (AAAI-98).

Hobbs, J. R. (1993). The generic information extraction system. In *Proceeding of the 5th Message Understanding Conference (MUC)* (pp. 87-91). Morristown, NJ: ACM.

Jackendoff, R. (2002). *Foundations of language.* Oxford, UK: Oxford University Press. doi:10.1093/acprof:oso/9780198270126.001.0001

KBAE. (2002). *Knowledge-based acquisition editor,* Purdue version 2.1. [Computer software]. W. Lafayette, IN: NLP Lab and CERIAS, Purdue University. Retrieved from http://kbae.cerias.purdue.edu:443/.

Kelvin, W. T. (1889). *Popular lectures and addresses.* London, UK: Macmillan.

Krovetz, R. (1993). Viewing morphology as an inference process. In R. Korfhage et al. (Eds.), *Proceedings of the 16th ACM SIGIR Conference* (pp. 191-202). New York, NY: ACM.

Lyons, J. (1963). *Structural semantics: An analysis of part of the vocabulary of Plato*. Oxford, UK: Blackwell.

Manning, C. D., Raghavan, P., & Schütze, H. (2008). *Introduction to information retrieval*. Cambridge, UK: CUP.

Manning, C. D., & Schütze, H. (1999). *Foundations of statistical natural language processing*. Cambridge, MA: MIT Press.

Nadeau, D., & Sekine, S. (2009). A survey of named entity recognition and classification. In Sekine, S., & Ranchhod, E. (Eds.), *Named entities: Recognition, classification and use* (pp. 3–25). Amsterdam, The Netherlands: John Benjamins.

Navigli, R., & Velardi, P. (2003). An analysis of ontology-based query expansion strategies. In *Proceedings of the Workshop on Adaptive Text Extraction and Mining (ATEM 2003) at the 14th European Conference on Machine Learning (ECML 2003)* (pp. 42-49). Cavtat-Dubrovnik, Croatia.

Nietzsche, F. (1901). *Der Wille zur Macht* [Will to power]. Leipzig, Germany: Naumann.

Nirenburg, S., & Raskin, V. (2004). *Ontological semantics*. Cambridge, MA: MIT Press.

Nirenburg, S., Raskin, V., & Tucker, A. (1987). The structure of interlingua in TRANSLATOR. In Nirenburg, S. (Ed.), *Machine translation: Theoretical and methodological issues* (pp. 90–113). New York, NY: Cambridge University Press.

Obrst, L. (2007). Ontology and ontologies: Why it and they matter to the intelligence community. In *ACM International Conference Proceeding Series; Vol. 171 archive. Proceedings of the Second International Ontology for the Intelligence Community Conference. OIC-2007*. Columbia, MD.

Penev, A., & Wong, R. (2006). Shallow NLP techniques for internet search. In *Proceedings of the 29th Australasian Computer Science Conference*, vol. 48 (pp. 167–176). Hobart, Australia.

Philips, L. (1990). Hanging on the metaphone. *Computer Language, 7-12*, 39-43.

Porter, M. F. (1980). An algorithm for suffix stripping. *Program, 14*, 130–137.

Raskin, V. (1971). *K teorii yazykovykh podsistem* [Towards a theory of language subsystems]. Moscow, Russia: Moscow State University Press.

Raskin, V. (1986). Script-based semantic theory. In Ellis, D. G., & Donahue, W. A. (Eds.), *Contemporary issues in language and discourse processes* (pp. 23–61). Hillsdale, NJ: Erlbaum.

Raskin, V., Hempelmann, C. F., & Triezenberg, K. E. (2008). Ontological semantic forensics: Meaning-based deception detection. Paper presented at the *23rd International Information Security Conference (SEC 2008)*. Milan, Italy - September 8-10, 2008.

Spärck-Jones, K. (1990). *Retrieving information or answering questions? British library annual research lecture*. London, UK: British Library.

Taylor, J. M., Hempelmann, C. F., & Raskin, V. (2010). On an automatic acquisition toolbox for ontologies and lexicons. In *Proceeding of ICAI'10*, Las Vegas, USA, July 2010.

Taylor, J. M., Raskin, V., Petrenko, M. S., & Hempelmann, C. F. (2010). *Multiple noun expression analysis. An implementation of ontological semantic theory*. Paper accepted at Computational Linguistics - Applications Workshop of the International Multiconference on Computer Science and Information Technology in Wisła, Poland, October 18-20, 2010.

Wilks, Y. (1965). *The application of CRLU's method of semantic analysis to information retrieval*. Cambridge Research Unit Memo ML 173.

Wilks, Y. (2005). Unhappy bedfellows: The relationship of AI and IR. In Tait, J. I. (Ed.), *Charting a new course: Natural language processing and information retrieval. Essays in honour of Karen Spärck Jones* (pp. 255–282). Berlin, Germany: Springer. doi:10.1007/1-4020-3467-9_14

Wilks, Y., & Brewster, C. (2006). Natural language processing as a foundation of the Semantic Web. *Foundations in Web Science, 1*(3-4), 199–327.

ADDITIONAL READING

Croft, B., Metzler, D., & Strohman, T. (2010). *Search Engines. Information Retrieval in Practice.* Boston, MA: Addison Wesley.

Levene, M. (2010). *An introduction to search engines and web navigation* (2nd ed.). Hoboken: John Wiley & Sons. doi:10.1002/9780470874233

Manning, C. D., Raghavan, P., & Schütze, H. (2008). *Introduction to information retrieval.* Cambridge: CUP.

Nirenburg, S., & Raskin, V. (2004). *Ontological semantics.* Cambridge, MA: MIT Press.

Tait, J. I. (Ed.). (2005). *Charting a new course: Natural language processing and information retrieval. Essays in honour of Karen Spärck Jones.* Berlin: Springer. doi:10.1007/1-4020-3467-9

Wilks, Y. & Brewster, C. (2006). Natural language processing as a foundation of the semantic web. *Foundations in Web Science, 1/3-4,* 199-327.

KEY TERMS AND DEFINITIONS

Information Extraction: Extracting from information from documents in accordance with an information need of a user as captured by the meaning of the information.

Information Retrieval: Retrieving documents in accordance with an information need of a user as captured in keywords for the user to gather the pertinent information from the document.

Ontological Semantics: Representing the meaning of a text by processing the text in relation to an ontology of concepts that is used to represent the lexical items of the language of the text.

ENDNOTES

[1] As is common, ONTOLOGICAL CONCEPTS are formatted in small caps to distinguish them from lexical items. The difference between the concept TABLE and the English word "table" from which the concept derives its name, is that the English word has meanings that use other concepts, like the one paraphrasable as "text element with rows and columns," while the concept TABLE can also be used for lexical items of other language, like German "Tisch," as well as other lexical items in English, like "desk."

[2] Parts of this section are based on earlier conference presentations of the material cited in the references and describe research and development work at RiverGlass, Inc., in close cooperation with Victor Raskin and Julia M. Taylor, as well as developer support by Vikas Mehra.

Chapter 5
Data Mining

Martin Atzmueller
University of Kassel, Germany

ABSTRACT

Data Mining provides approaches for the identification and discovery of non-trivial patterns and models hidden in large collections of data. In the applied natural language processing domain, data mining usually requires preprocessed data that has been extracted from textual documents. Additionally, this data is often integrated with other data sources. This chapter provides an overview on data mining focusing on approaches for pattern mining, cluster analysis, and predictive model construction. For those, we discuss exemplary techniques that are especially useful in the applied natural language processing context. Additionally, we describe how the presented data mining approaches are connected to text mining, text classification, and clustering, and discuss interesting problems and future research directions.

INTRODUCTION

In the context of applied natural language processing, data mining provides for powerful approaches for the mining and discovery of regularities, or patterns, in structured data. In the text and language processing context, the input data, that is, structured data is often acquired in a preprocessing and data integration phase. The original sources are usually textual documents that are first preprocessed and integrated with other data sources. Text mining, information extraction, and data integration methods provide powerful tools for these steps.

This chapter focuses on data mining in the applied natural language processing context. Data mining is used for mining patterns or models from data. A closely related topic is text mining, which partly overlaps with data mining: While data mining considers structured data as input, text mining directly works on unstructured or semi-structured documents. In that sense, several text

DOI: 10.4018/978-1-60960-741-8.ch005

mining methods can be regarded as preprocessing steps for data mining, while data mining can be interpreted as the last step in the text mining process. The specific mining methods applied for both topics are usually quite similar, and have their origin in the data mining and knowledge discovery context.

In the following, we first describe the background of data mining and outline the general data mining process according to the CRISP-DM process model. After that, the remaining chapter is split into three parts: First, we consider *pattern mining*, including frequent pattern mining, association rule mining and subgroup mining. Next, we focus on *cluster analysis* including partitioning and hierarchical approaches. Finally, we discuss *predictive model* construction, discussing decision trees, naïve Bayes, k-nearest neighbor and rule-based (associative) classification. Since the latter two sections concerning prediction, classification and clustering are also covered in specialized chapters on text classification and text clustering, we outline the basics of the approach, put them into context and refer to the respective chapters for more details.

Considering the CRISP-DM process model, we especially concentrate on pattern mining (i.e., the knowledge discovery step in this chapter) in order to show how data mining can be applied for knowledge discovery, extraction or rapid knowledge capture using automated mining methods. Then, the extracted patterns can be applied for further analysis, knowledge engineering, and knowledge capture.

The objectives of the chapter are to provide an overview on the data mining field and to introduce prominent exemplary techniques in the context of applied natural language processing. Since data mining is closely related to text mining, we include a discussion of issues that are present in the intersection of both topics, and refer to the respective text mining chapter for more details. Furthermore, we discuss open issues, and interesting directions for future research.

BACKGROUND

Data mining, also popularly referred to as knowledge discovery in databases (KDD) is concerned with the automatic or semi-automatic extraction of patterns. These patterns represent knowledge implicitly stored in large databases, data warehouses, the Web, other massive information repositories, and data streams. Informally, data mining is used for obtaining patterns and summaries of new and nontrivial information based on the available data (*description*), alternatively for the creation of predictive models of a certain system or phenomena (*prediction*).

The literature mentions several definitions of data mining, also in relation to knowledge discovery in databases. Fayyad et al. (1996), for example, define KDD as: "the process of discovering valid, novel, interesting, and potential useful knowledge," data mining is considered as the core step of the whole KDD process, that is, the concrete knowledge discovery method. Other definitions regard data mining as the "process of discovering various models, summaries, and derived values from a given collection of data" – see Kantardzic (2002). Han and Kamber (2006) also consider data mining a step in the knowledge discovery process (i.e., as an "essential process where intelligent methods are applied in order to extract data patterns"), but choose to use the term "data mining" in favor of "knowledge discovery in databases," subsuming the older term. They therefore take a broad view of data mining functionality, and consider data mining as the general process of discovering interesting knowledge from large amounts of data stored in databases, data warehouses, or other information repositories.

To sum up, data mining has been considered as an approach and a collection of methods, as a process, or a step in the general knowledge discovery process. In the following, we will take a broader view, similar to Han and Kamber (2008) and consider data mining as a comprehensive approach that can be mapped to a concrete process, that is, the CRISP-DM process, cf. Chapman et al. (2000), Wirth and Hipp (2000), and aims to discover regularities, patterns and ultimately knowledge in (large) data sets. Within the process, concrete data mining *methods* are applied for the respective mining step.

As sketched above, data mining methods can be roughly divided into descriptive and predictive methods: While *descriptive* methods are used for summarizing and/or identifying hidden information in the form of *patterns* contained in the data, *predictive* methods are used for constructing predictive (classification) *models*. However, these can also be constructed using the discovered regularities, for example, as in methods for associative classification.

Patterns can be represented by association patterns and can be shown as clusters for the analysis of groups of objects that are determined based on the similarity of the respective objects. There are various types of predictive models (e.g., decision trees, simple Bayesian models, and more complex models such as support-vector machines). Data mining works on a collection of data usually organized in data bases and data warehouses. In contrast to text mining, that considers collections of textual documents (i.e., unstructured or semi-structured texts), data mining is mainly utilized for knowledge extraction and discovery from structured data.

Data mining is an iterative and often incremental process such that a partial solution is often refined in order to arrive at the final solution, especially in semi-automatic approaches. There exist several process models for data mining, see (Kurgan & Musilek 2006). The most prominent of which is given by the CRISP-DM process. Figure 1 shows the data mining process structured according to the CRISP-DM process. It can be roughly divided into three sub-processes: Domain focusing (understanding and data preparation), pattern modeling (the mining step), and model implementation (evaluation and deployment). CRISP-DM consists of 6 phases in total and is

thus split into 5 iterative phases: business understanding, data understanding, data preparation, modeling, and evaluation, followed by the final deployment phase. The arrows in Figure 1 show the incremental approach such that data and information can be transferred back to an earlier step in order to improve the quality of the result.

1. **Business Understanding:** Clearly defines the goal of data mining (i.e., to make it actionable and measurable) and propagates the general understanding to all participants
2. **Data Understanding:** Checks if the data is sufficient and applicable for reaching the defined goals. It considers the concepts, attributes and their properties, in order to clarify their semantics.
3. **Data Preparation:** Usually needs about 80% of the total effort of the process. The data is put into a format suitable for the later modeling step (e.g., by transforming and cleaning the data).
4. **Modeling:** The modeling phase applies a specific data mining method. In this phase, regularities and patterns are extracted from the data for constructing the data mining model.
5. **Evaluation:** The quality of the mined model needs to be assessed. Additionally, the goals and measurable criteria defined during the business understanding phase need to be checked here.
6. **Deployment:** The model is applied for the planned task, for example, pattern understanding, analysis prediction, classification, or clustering.

From a text mining perspective, data mining is mainly concerned with mining structured data, while text mining is usually applied on semi-structured or unstructured data. Therefore, one central step for text mining and data mining from texts is a preprocessing phase for transforming the data into a more structured format. There are

Figure 1. CRISP data mining process

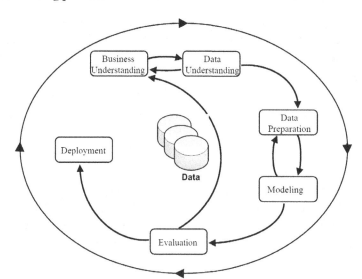

several techniques for structuring the data. As a prominent method, information extraction techniques, for example, can be used for obtaining structure from the data. In the context of applied natural language processing, the data mining process therefore usually includes a large fraction of the text mining process in its preprocessing phase (i.e., in data understanding and data preparation steps). Then, the applied data mining method itself is concluded by the modeling step of the data mining process, before the mined models are evaluated and finally deployed.

In general, text mining applies several data mining techniques in its final step, while several text mining tasks can be applied for preprocessing and data preparation. In the following, we discuss the pattern modeling step of the CRISP-DM process since this is the central contribution of data mining in the applied natural language processing context. We discuss pattern mining and clustering as descriptive approaches, and predictive modeling for classification and prediction. We especially focus on methods and techniques that are suitable for the application for natural language processing and text mining.

DATA MINING IN THE APPLIED NATURAL LANGUAGE PROCESSING CONTEXT

As noted above, data mining can be divided into descriptive and predictive approaches. Orthogonal to that, there is also a distinction between supervised and unsupervised methods. The latter do not need a class labeling of the applied data set, while the former require a class label for each training instance. For the descriptive methods, we discuss pattern mining and clustering. While pattern mining covers both supervised and unsupervised methods, clustering is purely unsupervised. Pattern mining and clustering are prominent approaches in the context of applied natural language processing and text mining (e.g., for discovering concept sets and associations). Concerning predictive approaches, we consider methods for classification and categorization.

We discuss exemplary methods for the approaches and discuss their application in the context of applied natural language processing. After that, we discuss open problems and issues for future research. Finally, we discuss the relation to text mining, text clustering, and text classification.

Pattern Mining

The focus of pattern mining methods are mainly descriptive approaches (e.g., for characterizing a set of data, for concept description, and for providing regularities and associations between elements). However, the resulting patterns can in principle also be applied for prediction. We consider associative classification as a predictive approach in the next section below, applying association rules for rule-based classification.

In the following, we turn to unsupervised (frequent pattern mining) and supervised approaches (association rules, subgroup mining) for pattern mining. The unsupervised frequent pattern mining approach can be considered as the basis for association rules, while association rules are similar to subgroup patterns. However, the latter patterns focus on a user-definable concept of interest and can be applied for a wide range of analytical questions, since their quality criteria can be determined as needed.

Frequent pattern mining (e.g., Han et al. [2007]) for a survey) aims to detect patterns which are frequent according to a certain minimal support threshold. Association rule mining, (see Hipp et al. [2000] for an overview) builds on frequent pattern mining to generate implication rules. Subgroup mining (e.g., Atzmueller & Puppe [2006]) aims

to discover subgroups that are distributionally most unusual according to a specific concept of interest. In the following, we will summarize these techniques and provide illustrative examples of their application. Table 1 depicts the characteristics of the pattern types.

For some basic notation, we consider a structured dataset D containing a set of instances (data tuples) with attributes a_i, $i = 1 \ldots n$. Each nominal attribute has a finite set of values v_{ij}, and a continuous value domain for continuous attributes.

Frequent Pattern Mining

The notion of frequent patterns is based on the co-occurrence of attribute values in a data set. Frequent pattern approaches have first been applied in market-basket scenarios for analyzing the purchase patterns of customers in stores. In those, the input data is given by market basket-type data, corresponding to binary feature vectors. A frequent item set for a buying pattern could be the set *bread $\wedge$ butter $\wedge$ milk*.

In general, we can consider items as selectors or selection expressions ($a_i = v_{ij}$) on values v_{ij} of attributes a_i. Then, a frequent pattern is given by the conjunction of a set of selectors ($a_1 = v_{1i}$) $\wedge$ ($a_2 = v_{2j}$) $\wedge \ldots \wedge$ ($a_l = v_{lk}$). For binary data, the above simplifies to $a_1 \wedge a_2 \wedge \ldots \wedge a_l$, since the attributes can be regarded as items (with the default value if present). Measures of the quality of the frequent

Table 1. Summary of pattern form, criteria, and exemplary applications in the ANLP context. a, b, c, d, e denote (symbolic) attribute-value assignments, for example, word instances or items in market-basket data.

Pattern type	Form	Criteria	ANLP Applications
Frequent patterns	$a \wedge b \wedge c$	support of conjunctive pattern	frequent terms/concepts (in document)
Association rules	$a \wedge b \wedge c \rightarrow d \wedge e$	support and confidence of conjunctive pattern	ontology learning, relation extraction
Subgroup patterns	$a \wedge b \wedge c \rightarrow d$ (fixed target concept d)	arbitrary quality function (axioms) (e.g., Lift, WRACC, Piatetsky-Shapiro)	ontology learning, relation extraction, concept description, text classification

patterns are usually the support of the patterns, relating to their frequency in the given dataset.

Since the problem of finding all frequent sets above a minimal support threshold is computationally rather expensive, efficient solutions are necessary. Most approaches are based on the A-priori principle (anti-monotone property), that the subset of a frequent pattern must also be frequent according to the minimal support threshold. In this way, levelwise approaches can be implemented, and whole leaves of the search tree can be simply pruned according to the minimal support (i.e., if the subset is not frequent then no superset can be frequent). For the basic *a priori* algorithm first all frequent sets for a specific search depth are generated, then all of these are pruned for which there are no frequent subsets. Next, the frequencies of the remaining sets are updated, and these are utilized in the next iteration. There are various variants, adaptations, and extensions of the basic *a priori* principle (e.g., the FP-Growth method using prefix-trees for efficiently pre-computing frequent patterns) and for efficient pruning.

In the context of applied natural language processing, support is the number (or percentage) of documents containing the given pattern (i.e., the co-occurrence frequency). A pattern could, for example, be given by the conjunction of a set of terms or concepts extracted from a set of documents. Therefore, application examples in applied natural language processing include the mining of frequent concept sets, and, as a prerequisite, for the mining of associations between concepts.

As we will see below, finding frequent sets can be regarded as an intermediate step in finding association rules. However, discovering frequent sets alone also provides a lot of information for data mining in general. It is both useful for searching for patterns in its own right (consider it as a query on the conjunction of the contained concepts or features) and also as a preparatory step in the discovery of associations (cf. association rules below).

Association Rules

Association rules were first mentioned in research on "market basket" mining problems that also led to the identification of frequent sets in data mining. Since then, association rules have been widely discussed in literature on data mining and knowledge discovery targeted at both structured and unstructured data.

In the terminology introduced above, association rules indicate (directed) relations between selectors or sets of selectors. An association rule is generally an expression of the form $B \rightarrow H$, where B and H are disjoint sets of selectors. An association rule $B \rightarrow H$ indicates that instances of the dataset that involve B also tend to involve H.

For the quality measures, *support* of association rules measures the number (or percentage) of instances containing the given rule. *Confidence* considers the percentage of the time that the rule is true (i.e., its accuracy). For instance, for the association rule $B \rightarrow H$, confidence is the percentage of documents that include all the concepts in H within the subset of those documents that include all the concepts in B. Support is the percentage (or number) of documents that include all the concepts in B and H.

In the market-basket and shopping domain, for example, an association rule might be "42 percent of the instances contained in the dataset that contain beer also contain diapers; 23 percent of all transactions contain both items." In this example, 42 percent refers to the confidence level of the association rule, and 23 percent refers to the level of support of the rule.

Association rule mining considers the problem of finding all the association rules with and minimal support value *minsup* and a minimal confidence *minconf*. The basic approach to discovering associations is a generally straightforward two-step process that can be summarized as follows:

1. Find all frequent sets B (i.e., all combinations of concepts with a support greater than the minimal support *minsup*).
2. Test whether B\H → H holds (for all subsets H of the set B) with the required minimal confidence threshold *minconf*.

Given these steps, if there are *m* selectors in a dataset, then, in a single pass all possible 2^m subsets for that dataset need to be checked. In extremely large, feature-rich datasets, this is often a nontrivial task. Moreover, because of the implications of generating an overabundance of association rules, additional procedures, such as structural or statistical pruning, redundancy elimination, etc., can be used to supplement the main association rule extraction procedure in order to limit the number of generated associations. For example, there are approaches for reducing the number of association rules by considering certain "reductions" of association rules that convey the same information as a complete set of association rules, but drastically reduce the size of the result set of association rules.

Applications of association rules are rather broad: They can be applied for gaining an initial understanding of the relations of a dataset. In applied natural language processing contexts they are often applied for ontology learning and relation extraction. Usually, all association rules above minimal support and confidence thresholds are considered, or a selection of the top-k association rules is returned. The application is thus similar to the use of subgroup patterns; however, the latter focus on a specific target concept and feature more flexible quality functions, as discussed below.

Subgroup Mining

Subgroup mining is a flexible approach that is usually applied for descriptive data mining but can also be utilized for predictive mining using associative classification techniques.

Subgroup mining aims at identifying groups of individuals that deviate from the norm considering a certain property of interest (i.e., a target concept). In the following, we consider a standard descriptive scenario, and will shortly discuss associative classification for prediction in the next section.

Subgroup mining provides a broad range of applications in business, medical and technical areas. For example, subgroup mining is often applied for user targeting in marketing, the discovery of risk factors in the medical domain, or for the analysis of industrial processes for optimization. We can investigate, for example, whether certain combinations of factors cause an increased repair and/or scrap rate in a manufacturing scenario, e.g., that the combination *(humidity=high) AND (dayOfWeek=Monday)* causes an increase of the *repair rate* from 20% to 80%. Furthermore, we can identify risk factors (and combinations) for certain diseases, e.g., that *(smoking=yes) AND (familyHistory=positive)* causes a 90% risk of *coronary heart disease*, compared to 10% in the total population. In the applied natural language domain, we can mine for (sets of) concepts that are significantly associated with a certain target concept, e.g., the concept set *{Java, Thread}* with the concept *Multi-threading*.

Subgroup patterns can be formalized as rules as shown in Table 1. For example, for the fixed target concept e, a rule of the form a ∧ b ∧ c → d indicates, that the individuals described by the conjunction of the selection expressions a, b, and c are associated with the target concept d with certain additional quality parameters. In comparison to association rules, subgroup patterns can be regarded as rules with a fixed one-element rule-head (or consequent). The rule body is given by the subgroup description that specifies the individuals covered by the description belonging to the subgroup.

Efficient and effective subgroup mining algorithms combine exhaustive search with pruning features that make the mining step still tractable. Typical algorithms (e.g., the SD-Map* algorithm) perform a top-k search for the k-best patterns according to the given quality function.

In contrast to association rule mining that only utilizes support and confidence for ranking the association rules, subgroup mining features a flexible, user-definable quality function that can incorporate application dependent criteria, see Figure 2 for examples. Usually, quality functions from certain common families of functions are selected. Then, the *generality* of the subgroup given by its size n, is an important factor. Additionally, for binary targets the target shares p and p_0 in the subgroup and the total population (the whole dataset), respectively, are important parameters; for numeric target concepts this relates to the target means in the subgroup m and the total population m_0 accordingly. These are then usually related $(p-p_0)$, and $(m-m_0)$ measuring the (distributional) difference in the subgroup vs. the total population.

Different quality functions give different weights to these components of the quality function. The Piatetsky-Shapiro considers an equal weight $n*(p-p_0)$, while the so-called weighted relative accuracy (WRACC) gives more weight to the target share differences $\sqrt{n}*(p-p_0)$. Finally, the so-called relative gain (RG) quality function does not consider the generality at all and considers the difference in the target share $(p-p_0)$. Therefore, a minimal subgroup size (generality) is required for a reasonable application.

In the domain of text mining and applied natural language processing, subgroup mining can be applied for ontology learning and relation discovery. Concepts that are significantly associated with a certain target concept can be identified for a first sketch towards building an ontology.

Clustering/Cluster Analysis

Cluster analysis and clustering deal with the problem of partitioning a dataset into subsets (clusters) such that the instances in a cluster are similar, and that each cluster is dissimilar to the other clusters. Clustering approaches for obtaining a disjoint set of clusters, or overlapping clusters, can be applied. While the former alternative provides a comprehensive segmentation of the instances contained in the dataset, the latter allows a more flexible assignment of the cluster objects. If an instance

Figure 2. Exemplary subgroup patterns for the dataset on the left with respect to the target concept (Income=high)

	Income	Sex	Age	Education level	Married	Has Chidren
	High	M	>50	High	Y	Y
	High	M	>50	Medium	Y	Y
	High	F	40-50	Medium	Y	Y
	High	M	40-50	Low	N	Y
	Medium	M	30-40	Medium	Y	Y
	Medium	M	>50	High	Y	N
	Low	M	<30	High	Y	N
	Medium	F	<30	Medium	Y	N
	Low	F	40-50	Low	Y	N
	Low	M	40-50	Medium	N	N
	Medium	F	>50	Medium	N	N
	Low	F	<30	Low	N	N
	Low	F	30-40	Medium	N	N
	Low	F	40-50	Low	N	N
	Low	M	<30	Low	N	N
	Medium	F	30-40	Medium	N	N

Target concept: ,Income' = ,high'
Quality function: $q = n/N * (p - p_0)$
$N = 16$; $p_0 = 0.25$

SG 1: ,Sex' = ,M'$\land$ Age = , < 30'
$n = 2$; $p = 0$ → $q = -0.03125$

SG 2: ,Married' = ,Y'
$n = 8$; $p = 0.375$ → $q = 0.0625$

SG 3: ,HasChildren' = ,Y'
$n = 5$; $p = 0.8$ → $q = 0.172...$

is conceptually a member of two groups, then this can only be modeled using overlapping clusters.

Clustering can be regarded as a data modeling technique for providing a rough overview and summary of the data. Clustering therefore plays an important role in a broad range of applications, and can be applied in various scenarios as a basic analytical strategy. Clusters basically correspond to hidden patterns. From a data perspective, the application of clustering is often cost-effective, since the search for clusters is regarded as unsupervised learning, and therefore does not require any (acquisition of) class-labels for the instances.

Algorithms for clustering can be roughly divided into two families, (see Jain & Marty & Flynn (1999) and Berkhin (2002) for a survey on clustering approaches). Partitioning approaches work by completely dividing the dataset into a set of (disjoint) clusters, while hierarchical approaches build a tree-structure (dendrogram) of clusters, either top-down or bottom up. Individual instances are the leaves of the tree, and the interior nodes are given by nonempty clusters. Sibling nodes partition the clusters given by their parents. Top-down divisive approaches split larger clusters – starting with a single cluster containing the whole dataset – into smaller ones until a stopping criterion is reached. Bottom-up agglomerative methods build the clusters such that cluster objects – starting with single instances – are merged into larger clusters until a stopping criterion is reached (e.g., the requested number k of clusters) (see Figure 3).

The advantages of hierarchical clustering include significant flexibility regarding the level of the granularity of the clusters, the possibility to integrate virtually any form of similarity or distance measure, and the broad applicability to any given attribute type. One disadvantage of hierarchical clustering is the difficulty of choosing the right criterion to stop building clusters. Additionally, most hierarchical algorithms do not revisit (intermediate) clusters once they are constructed,

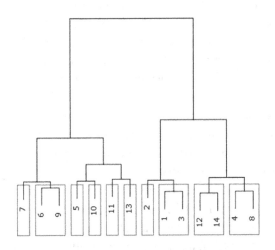

Figure 3. Cluster-dendrogram for an example dataset containing 14 instances. The leaves of the dendrogram "tree" denote the single instances, and are agglomerated from bottom to top based on their similarity.

for tuning and adapting the overall cluster structure.

Partitioning methods construct clusters directly. They aim at discovering clusters either by iteratively redistributing instances between clusters or by identifying areas that are "dense" in that sense that they are heavily populated with data. Prominent examples of the former techniques include the EM algorithm, AUTOCLASS, the k-medoids algorithm, or the popular k-mean-based methods. These methods estimate how well instances "fit" into their clusters and tend to build clusters of proper convex shapes. The latter density-based methods enable clusters of arbitrary shape.

The k-means algorithm is an especially popular partitioning method since it is rather easy to implement and often provides good results. K-Means takes the input parameter k, corresponding to the number of clusters, and partitions the n instances in the dataset into k clusters so that the resulting intra-cluster similarity is high but the inter-cluster similarity is low. The cluster similarity is measured using the mean value of the objects in a cluster, that is, the *centroid* or the *center of gravity* of the cluster. K-means first randomly selects k instances representing a cluster mean. Then, the algorithm iterates over the remaining instances, assigning each instance to the cluster that it is most similar to. Then, the new means of the clusters are computed, until a criterion function converges. Typically, the squared-error criterion is used, that sums over all squared differences between instances and mean for each cluster. This criterion aims at making the k clusters as compact and as separate as possible. For estimating the distances, an instance-based distance measure (e.g., Euclidean, Manhattan, or the Minkowski distance between the attribute-value vectors are considered).

A general challenge for clustering is given by high dimensional datasets. For data mining, usually large databases with many attributes (dimensions) are applied. In such contexts, standard algorithms such as k-means are not very successful due to unclear similarity assessment in the high-dimensional space. There are several strategies for handling high-dimensional data (e.g., using dimensionality methods as a preprocessing step or special algorithms). Another way to address the problem is through special algorithms (e.g., subspace or projected clustering, and co-clustering). Projected clustering only considers a subset of the data attributes each forming subspaces for clusters, while co-clustering clusters attributes and instances simultaneously.

Predictive Model Construction

Predictive data mining is concerned with the construction of models that are used for prediction and classification. In contrast to descriptive approaches, the output of the methods is not a set of patterns that reveals regularities or information hidden within the data, but models that are "distilled" from the data. The output of these models is often a single class, while multiple classes are also possible, especially for text mining and ap-

plied natural language processing. The input to these models is then a feature vector, the output is another class vector, either single or multi-class.

Another distinction from descriptive approaches is the fact that predictive models do not need to be understandable to humans necessarily, since the interpretation is not as important as the classification power or accuracy of the model. For surveys on prominent algorithms for predictive data mining consider (e.g., Murthy [2004] and Apte & Weiss [1997] for decision trees, Rennie et al. [2003] for naïve Bayes, Eui-Hong & Han & Kumar [2001] for k-nearest neighbor, Thabtah [2007] for rule-based classification, and Joachims [1998], Joachims [1999] for support-vector machines). Although the latter method is a black-box method (the interpretability of the learned model for humans is rather limited), the other approaches are transparent and can thus be assessed by the user.

Decision Trees and Decision Rules

A decision tree is a flowchart-like tree structure, where each internal node (non-leaf node) denotes a test on an attribute (value), each branch represents an outcome of the test, and each leaf node (or terminal node) holds a class label. The topmost node in a tree is the root node (see Figure 4).

For classification of an instance, the tree is traversed according to the tests on the branches: Consequently, a path is traced from the root to a leaf node that holds the class prediction for the instance. By traversing the paths to the leaves and simultaneously collecting the tests along a path, a tree can also be simply turned into a set of classification rules corresponding to the traversed paths.

There are several algorithms for decision tree learning. The key decision is the selection of the "best" test at the respective position in the tree. One strategy used in the prominent C4.5 algorithm uses the notion of information entropy. At each node of the tree (starting at the root node),

Figure 4. An exemplary decision tree for the class "play," and the attributes "outlook," "humidity," "windy"

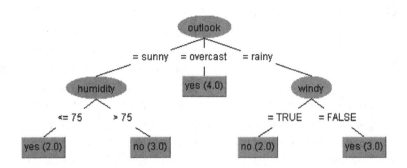

the algorithm chooses the attribute that most effectively splits the set of instances present at the current node into subsets specific for one class or the other. In this way, homogenous splits for one class are favored, and the number of tests going from root to the leaves is minimized. The criterion for choosing an attribute is the normalized information gain (i.e., the difference in impurity considering the attribute partitions, when splitting on the attribute as a test). After selecting an attribute test and splitting on the respective attribute, the algorithm recurses on the smaller subsets. The recursion steps, when all instances for a node belong to the same class, or when no further information gain can be obtained. Then, the expected class value is assigned.

Naïve Bayes

Classification using naïve Bayes is a statistical approach based on Bayes' theorem, described below. While naïve Bayes is a rather simple approach, studies comparing classification algorithms have shown that the naïve Bayes classifier is often comparable in performance with decision trees, while achieving high accuracy and speed being applied to large databases.

Naïve Bayes tries to estimate the conditional probability of the class alternatives given the available evidence (i.e., the attribute values contained in the test instance). Then, the class maximizing the probability is chosen.

For the naïve Bayes classifier, the contribution or the effect of an attribute is considered independently from the other attributes. This "naïve" class conditional independence assumption is the basis of the algorithm, and simplifies the computations involved.

The basis of the algorithm is provided by the theorem of Bayes. In essence, Bayes theorem can be formulated as follows: Let E denote an instance from the database (i.e., the "evidence"). We want to test a hypothesis (e.g., that instance E belongs to class C). Then, the desired probability for classification of instance E, is given by $P(C|E) = P(E|C)*P(C)/P(E)$.

The probabilities $P(E|C)$, i.e., the posterior probability of E conditioned on class C, $P(C)$ and $P(E)$ can be estimated from the given data, while the formula directly outputs an estimate how probable the classification of instance E for the class C is.

The naïve Bayesian classifier then just needs to test the hypothesis for all classes and select the class for which the probability is maximized. The unique assumption of the naïve classifier simplifies the computation, since the class independence assumption enables a simple computation of $P(E|C)$.

$P(E|C) = \prod P(e_i|C)$, for all attribute values e_i contained in the instance E. The probabilities $P(e_i|C)$ can be simply estimated using the number of instances having class C and value e_i for the given dataset.

K-Nearest Neighbor

Nearest-neighbor classifiers are based on the principle of learning by analogy, that is, they compare a given test instance that needs to be classified to a set of pre-classified training instances. Then, the "nearest" neighbors are retrieved, and finally a class is selected from these by a voting mechanism.

K-nearest neighbor algorithms are also called lazy-learners, because they do not need to learn a special model for classification, but they just store their training examples, and postpone the generalization until the classification decision is actually needed. The "k-nearest" neighbors are obtained based on the closeness to the test instance. The "closeness" is defined in terms of the similarity or, equivalently, the distance to the test instance. Distance metrics, for example, the Euclidean distance, Manhattan distance, Hamming distance, or equivalently similarity metrics such as the Cosine similarity can be applied. The Euclidean distance, for example, is defined by the square root of the sum of the individual instance values between two instances.

One drawback of nearest-neighbor classifier is their performance, if very many training instances in the dataset are used. In this case, index structures can significantly speed up the computation. Additionally, methods for the maintenance of the classifier dataset (i.e., for updates and cleanup of instances and considering the training instances for updates can provide potential for quality improvements).

Rule-Based and Associative Classification

Using the results of descriptive pattern mining, the complete set and an optimized subset of the discovered patterns can also be considered as a predictive data mining model. Similar to rule-based classification, associative classification methods are applied for combining local predictions of the individual patterns into a global classification method.

Approaches for rule-based and associative classification consider sets of rules and/or patterns for classification. Associative rules show strong associations between attribute-value pairs (selectors) that occur frequently in a given dataset. The general idea is to combine the predictions of single (local) patterns into a global model. Simple IF-THEN rules can be combined by different firing strategies (i.e., using ordered and unordered strategies). In the ordered case, the rules are applied in a certain precedence order (e.g., based on their accuracy [confidence] and/or support). The first rule that matches then determines the predicted class.

In the unordered case, all applicable rules are tried in arbitrary order, and the final prediction is usually decided by accumulating the votes of all applied rules, and applying the majority vote (i.e., selecting the class with the highest score). Furthermore, more elaborate combination strategies can also be applied (e.g., using Bayesian- or regression-based approaches for the combination of the predictions).

Rule-based and associative classification approaches can in principle both apply single- and multi-class approaches for classification. In the former case, a single class needs to be determined by voting, in the latter case a threshold-based selection from the result set needs to be employed.

Support-Vector Machines

Approaches using support vector machines are popular data mining methods for high-dimensional data (e.g., using preprocessed textual data such as word vectors [in a bag of words representation]). The origin of support vector machines lies in computational learning theory and considers a partition of the classification in the multidimensional data space. The goal is to identify a specific separating hyper-plane in the attribute hyperspace by separating positive from negative examples. New examples are then classified depending on their position regarding the detected hyperplane. Support vector machines have the advantage that they integrate attribute subset selection by automatically assigning weights to the attributes, thus filtering irrelevant attributes.

Support vector machines apply a (non-)linear mapping of the training data into a higher dimensional space. Within this space, the machine searches for a "decision boundary" (i.e., a hyperplane separating one class from the other [for binary classification problems]). Using an appropriate non-linear mapping with a sufficiently high-dimensional feature space, data from two classes can always be separated by a hyperplane. The support vector machine finds this separating hyperplane using the *support-vectors* (which are "essential" instances for setting up the boundary) and special *margins* (that are defined using the support vectors). The construction itself is implemented by solving a quadratic optimization problem for finding the maximum-margin hyperplane (i.e., the hyperplane that maximizes the distance from it to the nearest instance on each side).

Support vector machines are typically applied for binary class problems. The construction algorithm builds a model that decides to which class a new test instance belongs. Therefore, multi-class problems need to be mapped to binary class problems first. This can be achieved either by turning the problem into multiple one-vs-all class or one-vs-one class problems. Then, the class with the highest rating is selected. Support vector machines show good performance in practice; however, their explanation capabilities and the introspection options are very limited, due to the black-box classification approach.

OPEN PROBLEMS AND FUTURE RESEARCH DIRECTIONS

As more and more data are collected and integrated, the datasets are often too large to fit into the main memory. Thus, efficient and effective distributed and parallel methods are necessary; the search spaces are often too large to get a solution efficiently without parallelization. An emerging trend is the distribution of the data mining algorithms into the cloud (e.g., using the Map/Reduce framework).

Another issue concerns the increasing number of dimensions together with the large amount of data that is being collected. The "curse of dimensionality," cf. Bellman (1961) (i.e., the large feature space and its related efficiency and effectiveness problems) is a problem for many data mining algorithms. Therefore, feature subset selection is very important for identifying the relevant set of.

User interaction and involvement in assessing the results is especially helpful in descriptive scenarios, since the user ultimately needs to check whether the discovered patterns are useful, interesting, or valid to domain criteria.

A further issue is given by explanation capabilities for data mining. In the CRISP-DM model, we can distinguish two roles: The data mining engineer, and the user. These roles can be applied, for example, for explaining steps in the process or the results of data mining to the user. For descriptive approaches, for example, we can explain specific patterns to the user (e.g., how and why they were derived, or why they are interesting). For predictive approaches, we can explain the result (i.e., the application of the model to the user). This is often simpler for white-box models (e.g., trees, rules, association patterns) than for black-box approaches (e.g., support-vector machines).

The inclusion of background knowledge into the mining process can significantly increase the interestingness, relevance and accuracy of the results. Prominent approaches of helpful background knowledge include ontologies and taxonomies (e.g., concept hierarchies in text mining, topics for grouping sets of concepts, or linguistic resources such as Wordnet).

Relation to Text Mining, Text Clustering, and Text Classification

While both approaches share similarities, the focus of data mining and text mining are different. On the one hand text mining applies data mining methods, on the other hand several text mining tasks can be considered as a necessary preprocessing step for data mining. Therefore, both approaches have a significant overlap, while the input data is different. Data mining works with structured data while text mining can be applied for structuring the input documents and deriving patterns afterwards.

Text Mining Tasks

Typical text mining tasks include information extraction concerning concept and entity extraction as a step towards entity relation modeling, and construction of (granular) taxonomies, text extraction, document summarization, text clustering, text classification, text categorization, and sentiment analysis, and. For these applications, predictive models for text mining also often consider multi-class classification. Additionally, text mining usually has to cope with very high-dimensional data. By construction, texts feature a very high number of features and sparse structures.

Information Extraction

Techniques for information extraction methods can be split in automatic and semi-automatic approaches (e.g., Sarawagi [2008] for a survey). Furthermore, knowledge-based (e.g., rule-based methods incorporating background knowledge) can also be applied, as utilized in the TextMarker system, cf. Atzmueller et al. (2008). Information extraction is used for concept and entity extraction and aims to identify facts from texts; the methods are usually included in the text mining preprocessing chain. Extensions consider the extraction of relations between concepts, and the construction of taxonomies between concepts.

Text Extraction and Document Summarization

Methods for text extraction summarize texts and construct a condensed form of the content, cf. Afantenos et al. (2005) for a survey. A document is analyzed using linguistic methods in order to identify relevant sections, sentences or phrases. After that, these *key phrases* are applied for generating a summary of the text. In contrast to data mining, no other (implicit or) discovered information is added to the document in addition to the explicit information contained in the texts. Techniques for (multi-)document summarization work on a collection of textual documents and aim at the summarization of the collection as a whole. The task is therefore more complex than just summarizing a single document, due to the possible thematic diversity in the document collection. Then, the main topics should be extracted and summarized in a readable, concise, and complete way.

Text Clustering

As an unsupervised approach, text clustering (e.g., Hotho et al. [2002]) assigns documents to clusters based on the contained textual content. The applied similarity measure is usually word-vector based. Therefore, usually a large set of dimensions is generated. Then, either the clustering methods need to be suitable for the large set of dimensions, or appropriate dimensionality reduction methods need to be applied. Either features are removed if they are determined to be unimportant, or a global dimensionality reduction method (e.g., latent semantic indexing (LSI) is applied).

Text Classification and Categorization

Text classification and categorization methods, cf. Sebastiani (2002), are prominent applications for assigning labels to documents. For this task, we can distinguish single label vs. multiple label approaches, for which multiple label classification can often be generalized from single label classification. Similar to the clustering task, the number of dimensions is usually high, therefore feature reduction techniques (e.g., removal of stop words), or latent semantic indexing are prominent approaches for preprocessing of documents.

Sentiment Analysis

Sentiment analysis is concerned with identifying the polarity of a text (i.e., whether it is positive, negative, or neutral). For this purpose various techniques from machine learning and natural language processing can be applied, cf., Liu (2010) for an overview.

CONCLUSION

Data mining provides powerful means for discovering hidden patterns and relations in structured data. In this chapter, we have provided an overview on data mining in the context of applied natural language processing. After presenting the data mining process, we focused on approaches for pattern mining, cluster analysis, and predictive model construction, and discussed exemplary

techniques for those areas. Additionally, we discussed interesting problems and future research directions. Finally, we described how the presented data mining approaches are connected to text mining, text classification and clustering. For more details, we refer to the respective chapters for an in-depth discussion.

REFERENCES

Afantenos, S., Karkaletsis, V., & Stamatopoulos, P. (2005). Summarization from medical documents: A survey. *Artificial Intelligence in Medicine, 33*(2), 157–177. doi:10.1016/j.artmed.2004.07.017

Apte, C., & Weiss, S. M. (1997). Data mining with decision trees and decision rules. *Computer Systems, 13*, 197–210.

Atzmueller, M., Kluegl, P., & Puppe, F. (2008). Rule-based information extraction for structured data acquisition using TextMarker. In *Proceedings LWA-2008, Special Track on Knowledge Discovery and Machine Learning*. Wuerzburg, Germany: University of Wuerzburg.

Atzmueller, M., & Puppe, F. (2006). SD-map - A fast algorithm for exhaustive subgroup discovery. In *Proceedings of the 10th European Conference on Principles and Practice of Knowledge Discovery in Databases (PKDD 2006)*, (pp. 6-17). Berlin, Germany: Springer.

Bellman, R. (1961). *Adaptive control processes: A guided tour*. Princeton, NJ: Princeton Univ. Press.

Berkhin, P. (2002). Survey of clustering data mining techniques. In Kogan, J., Nicholas, C., & Teboulle, M. (Eds.), *Grouping multidimensional data* (pp. 25–72). Berlin, Germany: Springer.

Chapman, P., Clinton, J., Kerber, R., Khabaza, T., Reinartz, T., Shearer, C., & Wirth, R. (2000). *CRISP-DM 1.0 Step-by-step data mining guide*. Retrieved from http://www.crisp-dm.org/CRISP-WP-0800.pdf.

Eui-Hong, S., Han, G., & Kumar, V. (2001). Text categorization using weight adjusted k-nearest neighbor classification. In *Proceedings 5th Pacific-Asia Conference on Knowledge Discovery and Data Mining* (PAKDD), (pp. 53-65). Springer.

Fayyad, U. M., Piatetsky-Shapiro, G., Smyth, P., & Uthurusamy, R. (1996). From data mining to knowledge discovery: An overview. In Fayyad, U. M., Piatetsky-Shapiro, G., & Smyth, P. (Eds.), *Advances in Knowledge Discovery and Data Mining* (pp. 1–34). Cambridge, MA: AAAI Press.

Goethals, B. (2000). *Survey on frequent pattern mining*. Technical Report. Retrieved from http://www.cs.helsinki.fi/u/goethals/publications/survey.ps.

Han, J., Cheng, H., Xin, D., & Yan, X. (2007). Frequent pattern mining: Current status and future directions. *Data Mining and Knowledge Discovery*, *15*, 55–86. doi:10.1007/s10618-006-0059-1

Han, J., & Kamber, M. (2006). *Data mining – Concepts and techniques* (2nd ed.). San Francisco, CA: Morgan Kaufman.

Hipp, J., Güntzer, U., & Nakhaeizadeh, G. (2000). Algorithms for association rule mining-A general survey and comparison. *SIGKDD Explorations*, *2*(1), 58–64. doi:10.1145/360402.360421

Hotho, A., Maedche, A., & Staab, S. (2002). Text clustering based on good aggregations. *Kuenstliche Intelligenz KI, 16*(4).

Jain, A. K., Murty, M. N., & Flynn, P. J. (1999). Data clustering: A review. [New York, NY, USA.]. *ACM Computing Surveys*, *31*(3), 264–323. doi:10.1145/331499.331504

Joachims, T. (1998). Text categorization with support vector machines: Learning with many relevant features. In C. Nedellec & C. Rouveirol (Eds.), *In Proceedings of the 10th European Conference on Machine Learning*, (pp. 137-142). Berlin, Germany: Springer.

Joachims, T. (1999). Transductive inference for text classification using support vector machines. In *Proceedings of ICML-99, 16th International Conference on Machine Learning*, (pp. 143-151). San Francisco, CA: Morgan Kaufmann.

Kantaardzic, M. (2002). *Data mining – Concepts, models, methods, and algorithms*. John Wiley & Sons. Kurgan, L., & Musilek, P. (2006). A survey of knowledge discovery and data mining process models. *The Knowledge Engineering Review*, *21*(1), 1–24. Cambridge University Press.

Liu, B. (2010). Sentiment analysis and subjectivity. In Indurkhya, N., & Damerau, F. J. (Eds.), *Handbook of natural language processing. CRC Press*. Taylor and Francis.

Murthy, S. (2004). Automatic construction of decision trees from data: A multi-disciplinary survey. *Data Mining and Knowledge Discovery*, *2*(4), 345–389. Berlin, Germany: Springer. doi:10.1023/A:1009744630224

Rennie, J., Shih, L., Teevan, J., & Karger, D. (2003). Tackling the poor assumptions of naive Bayes text classifiers. In *Proceedings of the Twentieth International Conference on Machine Learning*, (pp. 616-623). Menlo Park, CA: AAAI Press.

Sarawagi, S. (2008). Information extraction. *Foundations and Trends in Databases*, *1*(3), 261–377. doi:10.1561/1900000003

Sebastiani, F. (2002). Machine learning in automated text categorization. *ACM Computing Surveys*, *34*(1), 1–47. doi:10.1145/505282.505283

Thabtah, F. A. (2007). A review of association classification mining. *The Knowledge Engineering Review*, *22*(1), 37–65. doi:10.1017/S0269888907001026

Wirth, R., & Hipp, J. (2000). CRISP-DM: Towards a standard process model for data mining. In *Proceedings of the 4th International Conference on the Practical Application of Knowledge Discovery and Data Mining* (pp. 29-39). Morgan Kaufmann.

ADDITIONAL READING

Atzmueller, M., & Beer, S. (2010). *Validation of Mixed-Structured Data Using Pattern Mining and Information Extraction*. In Proceedings 55th International Scientific Colloquium, International Workshop on Design, Evaluation and Refinement of Intelligent Systems, Technical University of Ilmenau, Germany.

Atzmueller, M., Kluegl, P., & Puppe, F. (2008). Rule-Based Information Extraction for Structured Data Acquisition using TextMarker. In *Proceedings LWA-2008, Special Track on Knowledge Discovery and Machine Learning*. Wuerzburg, Germany: University of Wuerzburg.

Atzmueller, M., & Nalepa, G. (2009). A Textual Subgroup Mining Approach for Rapid ARD+ Model Capture. In *Proceedings of the Twenty-Second International Florida Artificial Intelligence Research Society Conference*, pp. 414-415, AAAI Press.

Atzmueller, M., & Puppe, F. (2008). Semi-Automatic Refinement and Assessment of Subgroup Patterns. In *Proceedings of the 21th International Florida Artificial Intelligence Research Society Conference*, pp. 323-328. AAAI Press.

Atzmueller, M., Puppe, F., & Buscher, H.-P. (2005). Exploiting Background Knowledge for nowledge-Intensive Subgroup Discovery. In *Proceedings of the 19th International Joint Conference on Artificial Intelligence (IJCAI-05)*, pp. 647-652.

Atzmueller, M., & Roth-Berghofer, T. (2010): *The Mining and Analysis Continuum of Explaining Uncovered*. In Proceedings 30th SGAI International Conference on Artificial Intelligence AI-2010, Springer, Berlin.

Baeza-Yates, R. A., & Riberio-Neta, B. A. (1999). *Modern Information Retrieval*. New York/Reading, MA: ACM Press/Addison-Wesley.

Bradley, P., Fayyad, U., & Reina, C. (1998). Scaling Clustering Algorithms to Large Databases. In *Proceedings of the 4th International Conference on Knowledge Discovery and Data Mining*. AAAI Press.

Breiman, L., Friedman, J. H., Olshen, R. A., & Stone, C. J. (1984). *Classification and regression trees*. Monterey, CA: Wadsworth & Brooks/Cole.

Daniel, C., & Wood, F. C. (1980). *Fitting Equations to Data: Computer Analysis of Multifactor Data*. New York, NY, USA: Wiley.

Dean, J., & Ghemawat, S. (2008). MapReduce: Simplified Data Processing on Large Clusters. *Communications of the ACM, 51*(1).

Deerwester, S., Dumais, S., Furnas, G. W., Landauer, T. K., & Harshman, R. (1990). Indexing by Latent Semantic Analysis. *Journal of the American Society for Information Science American Society for Information Science, 41*(6), 391–407. doi:10.1002/(SICI)1097-4571(199009)41:6<391::AID-ASI1>3.0.CO;2-9

Dhillon, I. S., Fan, J., & Guan, Y. (2001). Efficient Clustering of Very Large Document Collections. In Grossman, R., Kamath, C., Kegelmeyer, P., Kumar, V., & Namburu, R. (Eds.), *Data Mining for Scientific and Engineering Applications* (pp. 357–391). Dordrecht: Klüwer.

Dubes, R. C. (1993). *Cluster Analysis and Related Issues. Handbook of Pattern Recognition and Computer Vision*. World Scientific.

Eberle, W., & Holder, L. (2007). Anomaly Detection in Data Represented as Graphs. *Intelligent Data Analysis: An International Journal, 11*(6), 663–689.

Everitt, B. (1993). *Cluster Analysis*. New York, NY, USA: Wiley.

Faloutsos, C., & Lin, K. (1995). Fastmap: A Fast Algorithm for Indexing, Data mining and Visualization of Traditional and Multimedia Datasets. In *Proceedings of the ACM SIGMOD International Conference on Management of Data*, pp. 163-174. New York, NY, USA: ACM.

Feldman, R., & Sanger, J. (2007). *The Text Mining Handbook: Advanced Approaches in Analyzing Unstructured Data*. New York, NY, USA: Cambridge University Press.

Ghosh, J., & Strehl, A. (2006). Similarity-Based Text Clustering: A Comparative Study. In *Grouping Multidimensional Data* (pp. 73–97). Berlin, Heidelberg: Springer. doi:10.1007/3-540-28349-8_3

Gibson, D., Kleinberg, J., & Raghavan, P. (1998). Clustering Categorical Data: An Approach Based on Dynamic Systems. In *Proceedings of the 24th International Conference on Very Large Databases*, pp. 311-323, New York, NY, USA, 1998.

Han, J., Pei, J., Yiwen, Y., & Mao, R. (2004). Frequent Patterns without Candidate Generation: A Frequent-Pattern Tree Approach. *Data Mining and Knowledge Discovery*, 8(1), 35–87. doi:10.1023/B:DAMI.0000005258.31418.83

Hotho, A., Staab, S., & Maedche, A. (2001). *Ontology-Based Text Clustering*. In Proceedings of the IJCAI-2001 Workshop on Text Learning Beyond Supervision. Seattle.

Hotho, A., Staab, S., & Stumme, G. (2003). *Text Clustering Based on Background Knowledge* (pp. 1–35). Germany: Institute of Applied Informatics and Formal Descriptive Methods, University of Karlsruhe.

Kloesgen, W. (1996). Explora: A Multipattern and Multistrategy Discovery Assistant. In Fayyad, U. M., Piatetsky-Shapiro, G., & Smyth, P. (Eds.), *Advances in Knowledge Discovery and Data Mining*. USA: Cambridge/Massachussetts.

Knobbe, A., Fürnkranz, J., Cremilleux, B., & Scholz, M. (2008). From Local Patterns to Global Models: The LeGo Approach to Data Mining. In *Proceedings of the ECML/PKDD 2008 Workshop: From Local Patterns to Global Models*.

Landauer, T. K., Foltz, P. W., & Laham, D. (1998). Introduction to Latent Semantic Analysis. *Discourse Processes*, *25*, 259–284. doi:10.1080/01638539809545028

Lavrac, N., Kavsek, B., Flach, P., & Todorovski, L. (2004). Subgroup Discovery with CN2-SD. *Journal of Machine Learning Research*, *5*, 153–188. MIT-Press.

Maedche, A., & Staab, S. (2000). *Mining Ontologies from Text. Knowledge Engineering and Knowledge Management Methods, Models, and Tools*. Berlin, Heidelberg: Springer.

Matsuo, Y., & Ishizuka, M. (2004). Keyword Extraction from a Single Document using Word Co-occurence Statistical Information. *International Journal of Artificial Intelligence Tools*, *13*(1), 157–169. doi:10.1142/S0218213004001466

Mooney, R. J., & Roy, L. (1999). Content-Based Book Recommending using Learning for Text Categorization. In *Proceedings of the SIGIR-99 Workshop on Recommender Systems: Algorithms and Evaluation*, pp. 195-204, 1999.

Nigam, K., McCallum, A., Thrun, S., & Mitchell, T. (1998). Learning to Classify Text from Labeled and Unlabeled Documents. In *Proceedings of the 15th National Conference on Artificial Intelligence*, pp. 792-799. AAAI Press.

Pasquier, N., Bastide, Y., Taouil, R., & Lakhal, L. (1999). Efficient Mining of Association Rules using Closed Itemset Lattices. *Information Systems*, *24*(1), 25–46. Elsevier Science. doi:10.1016/S0306-4379(99)00003-4

Quinlan, J. R. (1986). Induction of Decision Trees. *Machine Learning*, *1*(1), 81–106. doi:10.1007/BF00116251

Roth-Berghofer, T., & Cassens, J. (2005). Mapping Goals and Kinds of Explanations to the Knowledge Containers of Case-Based Reasoning Systems. In Munoz-Avila, H. & Ricci, F. (Eds.): *Case-Based Reasoning Research and Development, 6th International Conference on Case-Based Reasoning, ICCBR 2005*, pp. 451-464. Berlin/ Heidelberg: Springer.

Salton, G. (1989). *Automatic Text Processing: The Transformation, Analysis and Retrieval of Information by Computers*. Reading, MA: Addison-Wesley.

Yutaka, M., & Mitsuru, I. (2004). Keyword Extraction from a Single Document using Word Co-ocurrence Statistical Information. *International Journal of Artificial Intelligence Tools, 13*(1), 157–169. doi:10.1142/S0218213004001466

KEY TERMS AND DEFINITIONS

Association Rule: First applied for discovering associations between item sets (binary features), the association is usually measured using metrics like confidence and support (i.e., comparing the frequency of items in the rule head relative to the body) and items in the body relative to the database, respectively.

Associative Classification: Aims at the classification of new data using a set of association rules that each indicate a certain class. These rules are applied on the input data such that the matching rules are utilized for obtaining the class (e.g., by majority voting).

Clustering: Assigns objects to a set of clusters according to a similarity measure between the objects, with the goal of optimizing intra-cluster similarity and maximizing inter-cluster similarities (i.e., grouping related or similar objects in one cluster).

CRISP-DM: An industry standard process model for data mining. CRISP-DM (*CR*oss *In*-dustry *S*tandard *P*rocess for *D*ata *M*ining) specifies the complete data mining cycle, including business understanding, data understanding, data preparation, modeling, evaluation, and the final deployment.

Data Mining: The term data mining is either used as a synonym for the knowledge discovery process as a whole, or as the core step of this process, that is, employing data mining methods for the modeling step for obtaining descriptive patterns or predictive models.

Decision Tree: A decision tree is used for classification: Its nodes contain tests on the attribute values, for example, Age < 23. The leaves of the tree denote a class assignment. For the classification of new data, the tree is traversed from the root to a leaf, according to the tests on the nodes that match the data.

Frequent Pattern Mining: Frequent Pattern Mining is concerned with the identification of patterns that occur with a minimal frequency (support) of data tuples (instances) of a database. After that, they can be utilized, for example, for association rule mining.

K-Nearest Neighbor: K-Nearest Neighbor is a classification approach that compares a tuple (instance) to the tuples contained in a database and identifies the k closest tuples using a similarity measure. Using the k-nearest neighbors, a class is then determined, for example, by majority voting strategy.

Knowledge Discovery in Databases: Defined as the process of identifying novel, potentially, useful, and valid knowledge using data mining techniques.

Naïve Bayes: Naïve Bayes is a classification approach using simple conditional probabilities of a feature and a class that are combined using Bayes formula. The method relies on an independence assumption between classes and works relatively well in practical applications.

Pattern Mining: Aims at the discovery of interesting patterns in the data according to a given quality measure. Pattern mining can be applied both for descriptive and predictive approaches.

Predictive Modeling: Aims at generating a predictive model that can be applied for future classification of novel input data.

Subgroup Mining: As a method for local pattern detection, subgroup mining or subgroup discovery aims to detect statistically interesting subgroups with respect to a certain property of interest, for example, comparing shares or means of a specific target variable in a subgroup and the general database.

Chapter 6
Dialogue Acts and Dialogue Structure

T. Daniel Midgley
University of Western Australia, Australia

ABSTRACT

This chapter discusses historical and recent work in dialogue act tagging and dialogue structure infer-ence. Dialogue act tagging is a classification task in which utterances in dialogue are marked with the intentions of the speaker. It is possible to classify utterances using only features relating to the utterance itself (for example, words and prosodic features), but much work has also utilized dialogue-level features such as previous speaker and previous dialogue acts. The structure of dialogue can be represented by dialogue grammar, segmentation, or with a hierarchical structure.

INTRODUCTION

When human speakers engage in dialogue, they construct their utterances to accomplish some joint action, whether exchanging information, or requesting or offering assistance. They arrange these utterances according to well-recognized patterns that help make the flow of dialogue easier to follow. Dialogue researchers are interested in understanding and modeling both the purpose of human utterances and the structure of human

dialogue. In a practical sense, both of these are important in the creation of a conversational agent, or a dialogue manager, used in spoken language systems to track the state of the dialogue and de-cide what kind of speech acts the system should generate next. Classifying dialogue acts correctly can have a salubrious effect on other aspects of natural language processing, such as automatic speech recognition (Taylor *et al.*1998). Also, understanding dialogue acts and dialogue struc-ture is a key to understanding what a dialogue is about, an important part of true natural language understanding.

DOI: 10.4018/978-1-60960-741-8.ch006

This chapter gives a brief outline of two important aspects of dialogue modeling: *dialogue act tagging*, which involves interpreting the intentions of a speaker's utterance, and *dialogue structure inference*.

BACKGROUND

Dialogue act tagging (or DA tagging) is a classification task in which utterances in a dialogue are labeled automatically according to the intentions of the speaker. More formally, for each utterance, given the available evidence e, the tagger will try to select the dialogue act d that has the highest posterior probability $P(d|e)$. Then, by Bayes' well-known equation:

$$d = \arg\max_d P(d \mid e)$$
$$= \arg\max_d \frac{P(d)P(d \mid e)}{P(e)}$$
$$= \arg\max_d P(d)P(e \mid d)$$

DA tagging involves using data from a dialogue corpus, which has been marked with DA tags by human annotators. Features and machine learning techniques are selected which will maximize the likelihood of obtaining correct classifications.

Table 1 shows an example of text from VERBMOBIL-2 (Alexandersson 1997), a corpus of appointment scheduling dialogues. Note that each utterance has information about the speaker, the words in the utterance, and annotators' opinion as to the dialogue act. Other information is available, including phonetic transcriptions and part-of-speech tags.

Dialogue act tagging is difficult for a number of reasons.

- The same kind of dialogue act can be worded in many different ways. Looking for syntactic cues (e.g. question syntax) will only be of partial help, since requests can appear in statement syntax or question syntax. For example, a SUGGEST dialogue act could appear variously:
  - *Let's go on Thursday.*
  - *How is Thursday for you?*
  - *Is March all right?*
  - *Do you have any time in March?*
  - *Next week would be good.*
  - *Why don't we try next week?*
  - *If it were a little earlier, it would be fine.*

These utterances do have elements in common. They include time words (names of days,

Table 1. An example of dialogue from the VERBMOBIL-2 corpus

Speaker	Words	DA tag
DNC	I have nothing in November	INFORM
DNC	pretty much unless you can do that Wednesday Thursday and Friday	SUGGEST
RGM	no that is bad for me unfortunately	REJECT
RGM	I am <uh> I have got to set up chairs at the county fair <uh>	GIVE_REASON
DNC	all right	FEEDBACK_POSITIVE
DNC	okay	FEEDBACK_POSITIVE
DNC	how about <uh> nothing in October	REQUEST_SUGGEST
RGM	in October let us see	DELIBERATE
RGM	I have got <uh> the second through the sixth	SUGGEST
DNC	no	REJECT

months, or phrases like 'next week'), and certain verbs (go, leave). However, these items also appear in other DAs besides SUGGEST. The wide lexical and syntactic variability poses challenges for a DA tagger.

- Conversely, the same utterance can encode different DA's. Short utterances that appear frequently are often ambiguous. For example, in the VERBMOBIL corpus, the one-word utterance "okay" is marked at different times as ACCEPT, FEED-BACK_POSITIVE, BACKCHANNEL, and REQUEST_COMMENT.

- In any dialogue, most utterances will be unique, made especially for that conversation. Compare this to a similar task, *part-of-speech tagging*, where individual words are marked for their syntactic role in a sentence. In a worst-case scenario, it would be possible to simply look up the most likely part-of-speech tag for a word in a corpus. But in dialogue, most utterances are one-off constructions that will never appear again, so they cannot be looked up. For utterances, it can be helpful to perform some kind of semantic clustering. We use the machine learning package WEKA (Hall 2009) to sort utterances into an arbitrarily large number of clusters (say, 200) based on the strings of words (known as *n*-grams) in the utterance. This brings the search space down to a manageable level.

- A speaker may accomplish several different intentions in the same utterance. In saying 'okay,' a speaker may be acknowledging the previous speaker's utterance and agreeing with it all at once. The difficulty of settling on just one dialogue act per utterance is a shortcoming of dialogue act tagging.

Jurafsky (2003) describes two broad approaches which are commonly used in DA tagging. One is the *plan-based* approach, also called

a *BDI* approach because it attempts to model the beliefs, desires, and intentions of the speaker, as well as propositions that have been introduced. A representative implementation of this approach can be seen in James Allen's TRAINS project (Allen 1994).

The other, more common approach to dialogue act tagging is a *statistical* approach, which uses available evidence to classify the dialogue act according to machine learning techniques. Statistical methods are less thoroughgoing than BDI methods, but they are still able to get excellent results, without the computational overhead that speakers' modeling requires. This chapter will mainly consider statistical approaches to DA tagging.

UNITS OF DIALOGUE

So far, we've discussed *utterances*, normally the level of analysis that DA tagging is concerned with. We're defining an utterance here as a group of words from one speaker that instantiate one speech act (insofar as this is possible to determine). There may be more than one utterance in a speaker's *turn*.

But dialogue can be profitably analyzed from other perspectives than the utterance level. We will see that going beyond the utterance level to higher orders of dialogue structure can reveal insights about dialogue, as well as helping to improve the accuracy of a DA tagger.

Transactions

At the highest level, dialogue can be segmented into what Sinclair and Coulthard (1975) call *transactions* (see also Carletta *et al.* 1997). These are sections that accomplish major goals in the dialogue.

Alexandersson (1997) describes five major phases:

- **Hello:** where dialogue participants greet each other and exchange pleasantries
- **Opening:** where the purpose of the dialogue is stated
- **Negotiation:** in which the topics of the dialogue are sorted out, one by one
- **Closing:** all topics have been negotiated, and participants agree that it is time to finish the dialogue
- **Goodbye:** the participants say goodbye to each other and the dialogue finishes.

Boundaries for these segments are not difficult to place. The Hello and Goodbye segments are typically comprised of formulaic utterances. Openings and Closings are less lexically uniform, and therefore more difficult to detect automatically. For task-oriented dialogues, the Negotiation phase can be divided further into sub-dialogues by topic. For example, in Verbmobil dialogues the participants discuss meeting dates, flight times, choice of hotel rooms, and other topics, each of which must be negotiated. A lexical approach, such as a variation on the TextTiling algorithm (Hearst 1997) would be able track differences in the kinds of vocabulary used.

Conversational Games

Within these transactions, there appear *conversational games* (to use Carletta's terminology). A conversational game could be thought of a series of utterances that accomplish a subgoal of the dialogue.

Midgley (2003) used dialogue segmentation as a way of improving DA tagging. This work split up dialogues into segments based on *propositionality*; utterances that introduced a new proposition signaled the beginning of a new segment. In addition, a new feature was used: distance from top of segment. By including this extra feature, accuracy on the Verbmobil-2 corpus (with its 32 tags) improved from a 52% baseline to 65%, indicating that certain DAs tend to be

seen closer to the top of a segment. For example, the utterance 'okay' near the top of a segment tends to be tagged as ACCEPT, whereas later on in the segment, an 'okay' is more likely to be a FEEDBACK_POSITIVE.

Figure 1 shows an example of the Map Task corpus (Bard *et al.* 1995), which is annotated with information about conversational games. This sample shows them as Games 6–8.

Moves

Conversational games are themselves made up of *moves*, or individual dialogue acts where the speaker intends to accomplish something. The boundaries of these moves need to be identified, as there may be more than one move in a speaker's turn. Identifying move boundaries is non-trivial. Some researchers (e.g. Warnke *et al.* 1997, Purver *et al.* 2006) attempt to perform dialogue act segmentation and classification at the same time. The job is easier when using corpora like VERBMOBIL and Map Task because the utterances have already been segmented into moves.

RELATED WORK

Dialogue act tagging has its philosophical foundations in work by John Austin, who used the term *illocutionary force* to describe speaker intention. Austin (1962) noted that certain utterances (which he labeled '*performatives*') have the effect of performing some action in the world, rather than just describing some state of affairs. For example, the utterance *I now pronounce you husband and wife* causes a change in the state of the world, if the officiant has the authority to marry, if the participants intend to get married, and if other extra-linguistic factors are in place.

Dialogue act tagging continues this practice of labeling utterances based on the intention of the speaker, although instead of the five categories devised by Austin — and later, John Searle

Figure 1. An example of the Map Task corpus

Game 6 giver query-yn	
Move 12 query-yn » see the old mill ... can you find the old mill on your map ?	
	Game 7 follower check
	Move 13 check » the mill wheel ?
Move 14 reply-w » it's an old mill	
	Game 8 follower explain
	Move 15 explain » i don't have an old mill ... it says mill wheel ... must be the same thing
Move 16 acknowledge » okay right	

(1976) — dialogue act *tagsets* are customarily more fine-grained, with 30 or more tags. Currently, there is no consensus on tagsets across different corpora, but the DAMSL (Dialogue Act Markup in Several Layers) scheme has been especially influential (Core and Allen 1997). It classifies utterances along four different dimensions, including communicative status, information level, and forward- and backward-looking functions. There are about 4 million possible combinations of tags using the DAMSL system, but in tagging the Switchboard corpus Jurafsky *et al.* (1997) found that only 220 of those combinations occurred. These were reduced to 42 tags.

The field of Conversation Analysis has contributed to dialogue work. Harvey Sacks and Emanuel Schegloff (Schegloff & Sacks, 1973) recognized that dialogue participants organize their conversation in terms of *adjacency pairs*, or pairs of utterances that appear in close proximity and match each other; for example, *question/answer*, *suggest/accept*, or *inform/feedback*.

Adjacency pairs are often used in DA tagging because they give a quite reliable indication as to what is coming next. Dialogue participants use adjacency pairs remarkably consistently and

somewhat unconsciously. People could potentially say anything they like following the emergence of an adjacency pair, but major deviations are rare in practice. If someone asks a speaker: *"Do you know what time it is?"* the speaker is very likely to respond with one of these speech acts:

- *"It's ten past five."* (fulfillment of request)
- *"I haven't got a watch."* (explanation for failure to fulfill request)
- *"The time?"* (clarification question)

arguably less likely to respond with the following:

- *"Get lost!"* (refusal to cooperate)

and not all likely to respond with one of these speech acts:

- *"Bananas are yellow."* (non sequitur information)
- *walks away* (close conversation)

Because of their reliability, adjacency pairs are often used as a simple source of information about dialogue structure. The ISCI meeting corpus

(Shriberg *et al.* 2004) is annotated with information for adjacency pairs, as well as dialogue acts and turn management.

Other structures have been suggested which are somewhat similar to adjacency pairs. Clark and Schaefer (1989) introduce the notion of *contributions*. When someone introduces a suggest or comment, it creates an expectation for the other party to acknowledge it. These acknowledgements need to be themselves acknowledged. Accordingly, Clark and Schaefer divide utterances in dialogue into *contribution trees*, consisting of *presentation phases* and *acceptance phases*. Another suggestion is Jöhnsson's *initiative/response* units (Jöhnsson 1991).

Corpora

In the 1990s, the task of classifying dialogue acts automatically became more feasible due to faster and more powerful computers and the increasing availability of electronic dialogue corpora and machine learning techniques.

A dialogue corpus can be *task-oriented* or *non-task-oriented*. The Switchboard corpus and the CALLHOME corpus are in this latter category. They consist of telephone conversations with a suggested topic, but no particular goal. On the other hand, task-oriented corpora may include such scenarios as

- appointment scheduling (VERBMOBIL),
- giving directions on maps (Map Task),
- arranging air travel (ATIS),
- scheduling business meetings (ISCI) or
- moving goods from place to place (TRAINS).

These corpora offer sound files (and in many cases transcriptions of the text), along with different layers of annotation, including part-of-speech (POS) tags, DA tags, information about pauses, and more. Many are available from the Linguistic Data Consortium (www.ldc.upenn.edu).

Most DA tagging projects have opted for a supervised approach (in which annotators have marked the corpus with 'correct' answers), but Venkataraman *et al.* (2003) uses unlabeled data on the SPINE corpus (Speech In Noisy Environments) (Navy Research Laboratory 2001).

Features

DA taggers are typically designed to use a combination of local and dialogue-level features. The local features of an utterance are those features, which concern that utterance itself, including its words or *n*-grams (strings of words), or its prosodic features.

Some words are more important for classification than others. The field of linguistics known as Discourse Analysis has helped to focus attention on *cue phrases* — words and phrases that appear in an utterance (particularly the beginning of the utterance) that mark how the information in the utterance relates to preceding utterances (Hirschberg and Litman 1993). Cue phrases could be simple connectives ('so,' 'but'), discourse markers ('well'), or longer strings of words ('on the other hand,' 'having said that').

Prosodic features can be helpful in classifying certain kinds of dialogue acts. Upward intonation is indicative of questions, intonational lowering is typical of information-giving. Refusals are usually given with downward intonation. Short utterances are particularly difficult to disambiguate in the absence of prosodic information (see Kowtko 1994).

Speaker information is another dialogue-level feature. Is the speaker of this utterance the same as the speaker of the last utterance? This matters because if Speaker A asks a question, we should expect an answer from Speaker B, but a clarification if Speaker A continues. Accordingly, a 'speaker change' feature is sometimes used in DA tagging (see Table 2).

Taylor *et al.* (1998) used a simple dialogue act model that examined the likelihood of DAs lo-

Table 2. Selected work in DA tagging

Source	Corpus	Tags	Features	ML technique	Accuracy
Woszczyna and Waibel (1994)	Spontaneous Scheduling Task (ESST)	6	*n*-grams, dialogue history	Hidden Markov models (HMM)	74.10%
Reithinger and Klesen (1997)	VERBMOBIL	18	*n*-grams, dialogue history	HMM	74.70%
Warnke *et al.* (1997)	VERBMOBIL	18	*n*-grams, dialogue history	HMM, A* (for segmentation)	53.40%
Chu-Carroll (1998)	SRI airline dialogues	15	Speaker change, syntactic form of utterance, push/pop dialogue model	HMM	49.71%
Taylor (1998)	Map Task	12	DA bi-grams, previous move, previous speaker's last move	HMM	47%
Samuel (1998)	VERBMOBIL	18	*n*-grams, cue phrases, speaker change, DA bi- & tri-grams	Transformation-based learning (Brill 1995)	75.12%
Stolcke *et al.* (2000)	Switchboard	42	*n*-grams, prosody, DA bi- & tri-grams	Classification and regression trees, neural networks	65%
Venkataraman *et al.* (2003)	SPINE	6	*n*-grams, DA bi- & tri-grams	HMM (unsupervised)	83.98%
Serafin *et al.* (2003)	DIAG, CALLHOME Spanish	37	words, DA *n*-grams	Latent Semantic Analysis (LSA)	74.26%62.59%
Webb *et al.* (2005)	Switchboard, VERB-MOBIL, Map Task	141812	*n*-grams, utterance length, cue phrases, interruptions	Probabilistic tagging, plus cross-validation	69.09%

cally from intonation and automatically recognized words, but included a novel dialogue-level feature: whereas other work has used the previous DA (no matter which speaker said it), this work used the last DA from the end of the previous speaker's turn. This is likely to be a discriminating feature; Sacks, Schegloff, and Jefferson (1974) point out that the last DA in a speaker's turn is likely to be the first part of an adjacency pair, and therefore a good indicator of what will happen next.

Hidden Markov models were extremely popular in early work, but later work has included a range of machine learning techniques, including classification and regression trees (Stolcke *et al.* 2000), transformation-based learning (Samuel 1998), Bayesian networks, (Kaizer & op den Akker 2007), and support vector machines (Lampert *et al.* 2009).

Table 2 shows a broad cross-section of work in DA tagging, with some elements of their features

and performance. Caution should be exercised when comparing work in DA tagging, since these were run on different corpora with different tagsets and different parameters (e.g. with or without automatic speech recognition, automatic segmentation and classification, and so on). It should also be noted that human taggers do not always agree with each other — for Stolcke *et al.* (2000), the rate of agreement was 84%, which suggests an upper boundary for a project of that tagset size.

INFERRING DIALOGUE STRUCTURE

One of the weaknesses of much DA tagging work is the tendency to treat strings of dialogue acts as linear sequences. Adjacency pairs, useful as they are, are not always observed by speakers. At times, a question is followed not by a corresponding answer, but by a clarification question, a hesitation noise, an incomplete utterance, or even a change in topic as participants compete for initiative over the sub-dialogue. Yet many systems seem to expect the parts of adjacency pairs to follow each other automatically. The commonly used DA bi-gram feature ensures that if the first half of an adjacency pair is not met with its second half immediately, it will be forgotten by the classifier. Chu-Carroll (1998) was an early proponent of the view that a knowledge of dialogue structure could be used to help a dialogue act tagger. This part of the chapter discusses attempts to infer dialogue structure

The work of inferring dialogue structure has typically taken three forms: what could be termed 'simple dialogue grammars,' dialogue segmentation (or *chunking*), and hierarchical structure.

Dialogue Grammars

DA bi-grams (in which the previous tag is considered) and even tri-grams (in which the two previous tags are considered) are often used in DA tagging because adjacency pairs provide strong expectations for future DAs. DA *n*-grams higher than $n = 3$ are not commonly used because of the sparseness of longer sequences — as *n* increases, individual sequences become less and less likely. Stolcke *et al*. (2000) and Venkataraman, Stolcke, and Shriberg (2002) found no benefit from using higher-order grammars.

We found some interesting results when examining pairs of DAs in the VERBMOBIL-2 corpus (Midgley *et al*. 2006). For each utterance in the corpus, we noted frequently occurring previous DAs, as well as the last DA from the previous speaker's turn (borrowing the feature from Taylor 1988, mentioned earlier.) We tested each of the resulting pairs for statistical significance using a X^2 test. Placing the significant pairs into a directed graph shows some revealing things about dialogue sequences. For example, when speakers ACCEPT a suggestion, they usually do so right away, with no intervening DA's. However, as shown in Figure 2, DELIBERATE speech acts tend not to be followed by ACCEPTs, but by other dispreferred responses

like REJECT and FEEDBACK_NEGATIVE. In other words, speakers use DELIBERATE as a hedge for dispreferred responses.

Dialogue Segmentation

The process of dialogue segmentation is similar to another NLP task: phrase segmentation. Much work has been done on recognizing phrasal units, especially noun phrases, and this work can inform dialogue segmentation. A brief discussion of this is in order.

Part of speech tagging (also known as *POS tagging*, or simply *tagging*) refers to the process of labeling words in a sentence with an appropriate syntactic tag (e.g. noun, verb, etc., though most tagsets are much more fine-grained than this). POS taggers are able to mark English words (including made-up words) to an accuracy of more than 97% (e.g. Shen *et al*. 2007). POS chunking (or simply *chunking*) was conceived as a simple way of parsing a sentence. POS tags are used to group words into likely syntactic constituents, for example, noun phrases like 'the big red dog.'

In like manner, dialogue segmentation could be seen as a way of 'parsing' a conversation, and getting a view to its structure. We can also use some of the same techniques that have been used in POS chunking. For example, we are currently investigating a kind of prototype-driven

Figure 2. Dialogue acts (from VERBMOBIL-2) likely to appear from the same speaker after DELIBERATE

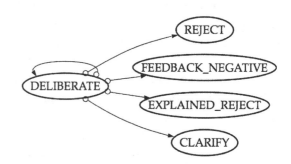

segmentation that has been used successfully in POS chunking (Haghighi and Klein 2006). A small number of prototypical segments are defined by hand, and the dialogue is divided in ways that create segments with the least amount of deviation from the prototypes.

Topic segmentation has a long history in discourse, especially for segmenting news stories (see for example Beeferman, Berger, & Lafferty 1997), but topic segmentation in dialogue is a relatively new concern. Most work in this area centers on multi-party topic segmentation using the ISCI Meeting Corpus (e.g. Galley *et al.* 2003, Hsueh & Moore 2006, Purver *et al.* 2006).

Segmenting a dialogue entails finding the boundaries of its segments, however those are defined. One approach to syntactic segmentation (as in Ramshaw & Marcus 1995, Osbourne 2000) is a supervised method: mark the first element of each segment with a 'B' (for 'beginning'), and every other segment with an 'I' (for 'intermediate'). The task thus becomes a two-class problem. Ends of segments are not always marked explicitly because they are very hard to detect and seem to have little to distinguish them from other elements of the segment. The end of a dialogue segment often seems to be marked, not by an explicit ending, but by the appearance of a new segment.

One difficulty with the 'B-I' approach is that there are typically many fewer 'B's than 'I's. Some machine learning algorithms do not perform well on two-class problems when one class is over-represented, and tend to mark everything as 'I.' You may have to implement a cost matrix in which the classifier is penalized for certain kinds of wrong answers. A software package like WEKA (Hall 2009) makes it easy to implement such a scheme.

Another approach to text segmentation involves identifying likely boundaries. The TextTiling algorithm (Hearst 1997) does this by looking for lexical cohesion. When the vocabulary used in a stream of text begins to differ from previous text, a boundary has likely been found. This method is also used by Latent Semantic Analysis, or LSA (Choi 2001). This method is more commonly used for single-party discourse, but the methods can be adapted for use in dialogue.

Our recent experiments have focused on producing reliable annotations for dialogue segments. Dialogue annotation can be expensive; it requires training and time. It is possible to use volunteer annotators from the Internet, but this comes with its own risks. Training will be minimal, restricted to only what an average web surfer is willing to read. The task must not be too difficult, or annotators will give up. There may also be perverse or uncomprehending annotators who may skew the data. We found that individual users performed reasonably well (with an average WindowDiff score of 0.225), but when the results of all volunteers were aggregated according to a method described in (Midgley 2009), agreement compares favorably to expert annotators, with average WD scores of .108.

Segmentation is a simple way of uncovering the basics of dialogue structure without a lot of computational overhead.

Hierarchical Structure

Representing dialogue in a hierarchical way overcomes some of the limitations of using dialogue segmentation to infer dialogue structure. Because segmentation infers a flat structure, it is not good at recognizing clarification subdialogues and other nested parts of a conversation. It is also difficult to tell what will happen at the beginning of the next segment, unless one resorts to higher order structural information (Poesio & Mikheev 1998). Unfortunately, no agreement exists as to how this structure should be represented, or what features are important.

Alexandersson and Reithinger (1997) represented the intentional structure of a dialogue as a tree. VERBMOBIL dialogues were marked with states corresponding to transactions, turns, and dialogue acts. Stochastic processes were used to discover likely combinations of dialogue acts as with adjacency pairs, but with the important difference of allowing a speaker's turn to include more than one DA. This allowed combinations of *greet/ greet+initiative* for an opening, or *response+bye/ confirm+bye* for a closing.

Poesio and Mikheev (1998) noted that using hierarchical dialogue information, as well as information about speaker change, improved tagger performance beyond simply using DA bi-grams. They used the Map Task corpus (which is divided into moves and games), and gave their tagger information identifying the current game, and where within the game the current utterance lay.

Chu-Carroll (1998) used a stack to model dialogue structure. If a nested sub-dialogue is recognized, then the current state of the dialogue is pushed onto a stack until the sub-dialogue is resolved. Using this structure improved the DA tagger. However, the difficulty is recognizing when a change in the dialogue level has occurred.

Bangalore & Stent (2009) also uses a stack, treating the structure of dialogue as a tree that can be parsed. The system has information about what kind of events need to happen for the goals of a dialogue to be met (say, in which someone wishes to order an item from a catalogue). As one conversational game is concluded, the system moves on to others in turn. This approach works well for constrained dialogues between a person and a computer; it may be less well-suited to understanding human-human communication.

EVALUATION OF DIALOGUE SEGMENTATION

Segment evaluation means checking whether your boundaries correspond well with the boundaries in a reference copy of your corpus. Cohen's kappa (κ) was for a time the standard for segment evaluation (Carletta 1996). For this method, a reference copy (the 'gold standard') is compared to a hypothesis copy of the corpus. If a boundary in the hypothesis copy matches a corresponding boundary in the reference copy, then there has been agreement; otherwise not. κ measures the observed agreement (A_O) against the agreement we should expect by chance (A_E), as follows:

$$K = \frac{A_O - A_E}{1 - A_E}$$

A score of 1 would indicate perfect agreement, but $\kappa \geq 0.8$ is considered very strong agreement for most disciplines. However, in the NLP community, $\kappa \geq 0.66$ is generally considered strong agreement (see Di Eugenio & Glass 2004).

It has since become clear that κ is a very stringent metric, only considering whether the boundaries are detected. This means that it treats all misses the same, whether they're close or not. Lately, other metrics have come into use that do a better job of taking near-misses into account. These are P_k (Beeferman, Berger, and Lafferty 1999) and WindowDiff, or WD (Pevzner and Hearst 2001). These work by using a sliding window over the dialogue. The window is set to half the average true segment size. Both algorithms check for discrepancies between the reference and the hypothesis. P_k checks to see if the first and last elements in the window are in the same or in different segments. WD checks for the number of segment boundaries within the window. If there is a discrepancy, a counter is incremented by one. For either algorithm, the score is the number of discrepancies, divided by the number of measurements taken.

The disadvantage of using P_k and WD is that there is no widespread agreement in the NLP community as to what constitutes a 'good WD score,' except that lower numbers are better.

FUTURE RESEARCH DIRECTIONS

Work on dialogue act tagging and dialogue structure has heretofore focused on spoken dialogue corpora. The current wave of research is using electronic media. Emails, instant messages, blog comments, Facebook posts, and 'tweets' all resemble a kind of dialogue, insofar as they raise topics or respond to earlier comments from others.

Andrew Lampert is working on email segmentation (see for example, Lampert *et al.* 2009), using the Enron corpus (Klimt and Yang, 2004). This involves segmenting emails into 'zones,' such as the new content in a email, replies, signatures, and greetings and signoffs.

Edward Ivanovich (2005) has done work on dialogue act recognition in instant messaging (IM) chat sessions. This is more challenging than spoken human dialogue because it involves simultaneous segmentation and classification. In addition, the usual adjacency pairs do not necessarily apply, since chat participants can become desynchronized when their messages accidentally overrun each other.

Future dialogue work will see a continuation of this expansion into electronic communication, as well as the construction of more accurate dialogue managers.

As the accuracy of dialogue act taggers continues to improve, we should expect to see it moving into other fields. Kumar *et al.* (2008) have shown improvement in machine translation with the use of dialogue level information, including prosody and discourse function.

CONCLUSION

Dialogue act classification has attracted continuing interest since its conception as an NLP task. Nevertheless, it remains an unsolved problem. Little agreement exists as to the best methods to use, and current work uses the same word- and dialogue-level features that appear in early projects. However, the field has advanced in application as it expands to electronic communication, multi-party communication, and areas beyond dialogue.

REFERENCES

Alexandersson, J., Buschbeck-Wolf, B., Fujinami, T., Maier, E., Reithinger, N., Schmitz, B., & Siegel, M. (1997). *Dialogue acts in VERBMOBIL-2*, vol. 4, (pp. 2231-2235). Verbmobil Report 204, DFKI, University of Saarbruecken. Greece.

Alexandersson, J., & Reithinger, N. (1997). Learning dialogue structure from a corpus. In *Proceedings of Eurospeech '97 (5th European Conference on Speech Communication and Technology)*, Rhodes.

Allen, J. F., Schubert, L. K., Ferguson, G., Heeman, P., Hwang, C. H., & Kato, T. (1994). The TRAINS Project: A case study in building a conversational planning agent. *Journal of Experimental and Theoretical AI, 7*, 7–48. doi:10.1080/09528139508953799

Austin, J. L. (1962). *How to do things with words*. Cambridge, MA: Harvard University Press.

Bangalore, S., & Stent, A. J. (2009). Incremental parsing models for dialog task structure. In *Proceedings of the 12th Conference of the European Chapter of the ACL*, (pp. 94–102). 30 March – 3 April. Athens, Greece.

Bard, E. G., Sotillo, C., Anderson, A. H., & Taylor, M. M. (1995). The DCIEM map task corpus: Spontaneous dialogues under sleep deprivation and drug treatment. In *Proc. of the ESCA-NATO Tutorial and Workshop on Speech under Stress*, Lisbon.

Beeferman, D., Berger, A., & Lafferty, J. (1997). Text segmentation using exponential models. In *Proceedings of the 2nd Conference on Empirical Methods in Natural Language Processing* (pp. 35–46). Providence, RI.

Beeferman, D., Berger, A., & Lafferty, J. (1999, February). Statistical models of text segmentation. *Machine Learning, 34*(1–3).

Brill, E. (1995). Transformation-based error-driven learning and natural language processing: A case study in part of speech tagging. *Computational Linguistics*, *21*(4), 543–565.

Carletta, J. (1996). Assessing agreement on classification tasks: The Kappa statistic. *Computational Linguistics*, *22*(2), 249–254.

Carletta, J., Isard, A., Isard, S., Kowtko, J., Newlands, A., Doherty-Sneddon, G., & Anderson, A. (1997). The reliability of a dialogue structure coding scheme. *Computational Linguistics*, *23*(1), 13–31.

Choi, F. Y. Y., Wiemer-Hastings, P., & Moore, J. (2001). Semantic analysis for text segmentation. In *Proceedings of 2001 Conference on Empirical Methods in Natural Language Processing (EMNLP-2001)*. (pp. 109–117). 3-4 June, Pittsburgh, Pennsylvania.

Chu-Carroll, J. (1998). A statistical model for discourse act recognition in dialogue interactions. In J. Chu-Carroll & N. Green (Eds.), *Working Notes of AAAI Spring Symposium on Applying Machine Learning to Discourse Processing*, (pp. 12–17). AAAI Press.

Clark, H. H., & Schaefer, E. F. (1989). Contributing to discourse. *Cognitive Science*, *13*, 259–294. doi:10.1207/s15516709cog1302_7

Core, M., & Allen, J. (1997). Coding dialogs with the DAMSL annotation scheme. In *Working Notes of the AAAI Fall Symposium on Communicative Action in Humans and Machines*, (pp. 28–35). Cambridge, MA, November.

Di Eugenio, B., & Glass, M. (2004). The Kappa statistic: A second look. *Computational Linguistics*, *30*(1), 95–101. doi:10.1162/089120104773633402

Galley, M., McKeown, K., Fosler-Lussier, E., & Jing, H. (2003). Discourse segmentation of multiparty conversation. In *Proceedings of the 41st Annual Meeting of the Association for Computational Linguistics*, (pp. 562–569).

Haghighi, A., & Klein, D. (2006). Prototype-driven grammar induction. In *Proceedings of the 21st International Conference on Computational Linguistics and the 44th Annual Meeting of the Association for Computational Linguistics*. 17–21 July. Sydney, Australia.

Hall, M., Frank, E., Holmes, G., Pfahringer, B., Reutemann, P., & Witten, I. H. (2009). The WEKA data mining software: An update. *SIGKDD Explorations*, *11*(1). doi:10.1145/1656274.1656278

Hearst, M. A. (1997). TextTiling: Segmenting text into multi-paragraph subtopic passages. *Computational Linguistics*, *23*(1), 33–64.

Hirschberg, J., & Litman, D. (1993). Empirical studies on the disambiguation of cue phrases. *Computational Linguistics*, *19*(3), 501–530.

Hsueh, P., Moore, J., & Renals, S. (2006). Automatic segmentation of multiparty dialogue. In *Proceedings of the EACL 2006*, (pp. 273–280).

Ivanovic, E. (2005). Dialogue act tagging for instant messaging chat sessions. In *Proceedings of the ACL Student Research Workshop*, (pp. 79–84). 27 June, Ann Arbor, Michigan.

Jönsson, A. (1991). A dialogue manager using initiative-response units and distributed control. In *Proceedings of the Fifth Conference of the European Association for Computational Linguistics*, (pp. 233–238).

Jurafsky, D. (2003). Pragmatics and computational linguistics. In Horn, L. R., & Ward, G. (Eds.), *Handbook of pragmatics*. Oxford, UK: Blackwell.

Jurafsky, D., Bates, R., Coccaro, N., Martin, R., Meteer, M., & Ries, K. … Van Ess-Dykema, C. (1997). Automatic detection of discourse structure for speech recognition and understanding. In *Proceedings of the 1997 IEEE Workshop on Speech Recognition and Understanding*, (pp. 88–95). 14–17 December, Santa Barbara, CA.

Keizer, S., & op den Akker, R. (2005). Dialogue act recognition under uncertainty using Bayesian networks. *Natural Language Engineering, 1*, 1–30.

Klimt, B., & Yang, Y. (2004). Introducing the Enron corpus. In *Proceedings of the Conference on Email and Anti-Spam (CEAS)*. Mountain View, CA.

Kowtko, J. (1994). On the function of intonation in wee utterances. In *Proceedings of the Edinburgh Linguistics Department Conference, 94*, 77–85.

Kumar, V., Sridhar, R., Narayanan, S., & Bangalore, S. (2008). Enriching spoken language translation with dialog acts. In *Proceedings of the 46th Annual Meeting of the Association for Computational Linguistics on Human Language Technologies*. June 19–20, Columbus, Ohio.

Lampert, A., Dale, R., & Paris, C. (2009). Segmenting email message text into zones, In *Proceedings of Empirical Methods in Natural Language Processing (EMNLP 2009)*, (pp. 919–928). August 6–7, Singapore.

Midgley, T. D. (2003). Discourse chunking: A tool in dialogue act tagging. In *Proceedings of the 41st Annual Meeting on Association for Computational Linguistics*, (pp. 58–63). 7–12 July, Sapporo, Japan.

Midgley, T. D. (2009). Dialogue segmentation with large numbers of volunteer Internet annotators. In *Proceedings of the 47th Annual Meeting of the ACL and the 4th IJCNLP of the AFNLP* (pp. 897–904). 2–7 August, Singapore.

Midgley, T. D., Harrison, S. P., & MacNish, C. (2006). Empirical verification of adjacency pairs using dialogue segmentation. In *Proceedings of the 7th SIGdial Workshop on Discourse and Dialogue* (pp. 104–108). 15–16 July, Sydney, Australia.

Navy Research Laboratory. (2001). *Speech in noisy environments*. Retrieved from http://www.ldc.upenn.edu/Catalog/CatalogEntry.jsp?catalogId=LDC2000S87.

Osborne, M. (2000). Shallow parsing as part-of-speech tagging. In *Proceedings of the 2nd Workshop on Learning Language in Logic and the 4th Conference on Computational Natural Language Learning*. September 13–14, Lisbon, Portugal.

Pevzner, L., & Hearst, M. A. (2002). A critique and improvement of an evaluation metric for text segmentation. *Computational Linguistics, 28*(1), 19–36. doi:10.1162/089120102317341756

Poesio, M., & Mikheev, A. (1998). The predictive power of game structure in dialogue act recognition: Experimental results using maximum entropy estimation. In *Proceedings of ICSLP-98*, Sydney, 1998.

Purver, M., Körding, K. P., Griffiths, T. L., & Tenenbaumm, J. B. (2006). Unsupervised topic modelling for multi-party spoken discourse. In *Proceedings of the 21st International Conference on Computational Linguistics and 44th Annual Meeting of the ACL*, (pp. 17–24).

Ramshaw, L. A., & Marcus, M. P. (1995). Text chunking using transformation-based learning, In *Proceedings of the Third Workshop on Very Large Corpora*. Cambridge, MA, USA.

Reithinger, N., & Klesen, M. (1997). Dialogue act classification using language models. In G. Kokkinakis, N. Fakotakis, & E. Dermatas (Eds.), *Proceedings of the 5th European Conference on Speech Communication and Technology*, volume 4, (pp. 2235–2238). Rhodes, Greece, September.

Sacks, H., Schegloff, E. A., & Jefferson, G. (1974). A simplest systematics for the organization of turn-taking for conversation. *Language, 50*, 696–735. doi:10.2307/412243

Samuel, K., Carberry, S., & Vijay-Shanker, K. (1998). Dialogue act tagging with transformation-based learning. In *Proceedings of COLING/ACL'98*, (pp. 1150–1156).

Schegloff, E. A., & Sacks, H. (1973). Opening up closings. *Semiotica, 7*(4), 289–327. doi:10.1515/semi.1973.8.4.289

Searle, J. R. (1979). A taxonomy of illocutionary acts. In Searle, J. R. (Ed.), *Expression and meaning: Studies in the theory of speech acts* (pp. 1–29). Cambridge, MA: Cambridge University Press.

Serafin, R., Di Eugenio, B., & Glass, M. (2003). Latent semantic analysis for dialogue act classification. In *Proceedings of the HLT-NAACL, 2003*, 28–30. May, Edmonton, Alberta, Canada.

Shen, L., Satta, G., & Joshi, A. (2007). Guided learning for bidirectional sequence classification. In *Proceedings of the 45th Annual Meeting of the Association of Computational Linguistics (ACL 2007)*, (pp. 760–767).

Shriberg, E., Dhillon, R., Bhagat, S., Ang, J., & Carvey, H. (2004). The ICSI Meeting Recorder Dialog Act (MRDA) corpus. In *Proceedings of the 5th SIGdial Workshop on Discourse and Dialogue at HLT-NAACL 2004* (pp. 97–100). April 30 – May 1, Cambridge, MA.

Sinclair, J., & Coulthard, M. (1975). *Toward an analysis of discourse: The English used by teachers and pupils*. Oxford, UK: Oxford University Press.

Stolcke, A., Coccaro, N., Bates, R., Taylor, P., Ess-Dykema, C. V., & Ries, K. (2000). Dialogue act modeling for automatic tagging and recognition of conversational speech. *Computational Linguistics, 26*(3), 339–373. doi:10.1162/089120100561737

Taylor, P., King, S., Isard, S., & Wright, H. (1998). Intonation and dialogue context as constraints for speech recognition. *Language and Speech, 41*, 489–508.

Venkataraman, A., Ferrer, L., Stolcke, A., & Shriberg, E. (2003). Training a prosody-based dialog act tagger from unlabeled data. In *Proceedings of the IEEE International Conference on Acoustics, Speech, and Signal Processing (ICASSP '03)*, vol. 1, (pp. 272–275).

Venkataraman, A., Stolcke, A., & Shriberg, E. (2002). Automatic dialog act labeling with minimal supervision. In *Proceedings of the 9th Australian International Conference on Speech Science & Technology*. 2–5 December, Melbourne, Australia.

Warnke, V., Kompe, R., Niemann, H., & Nöth, E. (1997). Integrated dialog act segmentation and classification using prosodic features and language models. In G. Kokkinakis, N. Fakotakis, & E. Dermatas, (Eds.), *Proceedings of the 5th European Conference on Speech Communication and Technology*, volume 1, (pp. 207–210). Rhodes, Greece, September.

Webb, N., Hepple, M., & Wilks, Y. (2005). Dialogue act classification based on intra-utterance features. In *Proceedings of the AAAI Workshop on Spoken Language Understanding*, 9–10 July, Pittsburgh, PA.

Woszczyna, M., & Waibel, A. (1994). Inferring linguistic structure in spoken language. In *Proceedings of the International Conference on Spoken Language Processing,* volume 2, (pp. 847–850). 18–22 September, Yokohama.

ADDITIONAL READING

Forbes, K., Miltsakaki, E., Prasad, R., Sarkar, A., Joshi, A., & Webber, B. (2001). D-LTAG System: Discourse Parsing with a Lexicalized Tree Adjoining Grammar. In *Proceedings of ESSLLI 2001 Workshop on Information Structure, Discourse Structure and Discourse Semantics*.

Traum, D. (2000). 20 questions on dialogue act taxonomies. *Journal of Semantics*, *17*(1), 7–30. doi:10.1093/jos/17.1.7

KEY TERMS AND DEFINITIONS

Adjacency Pair: Two utterances from different speakers that are contiguous, and appropriately matched (e.g. *question/answer*).

Contribution Tree: In Clark and Schaefer's work, a structure that shows how utterances relate to each other. Contribution trees have a presentation phase and an acceptance phase.

Conversational Game: A unit of dialogue that accomplishes a subtask in a dialogue. Conversational games contain a number of moves.

Dialogue Act: A simplified representation of a speaker's intention in making an utterance.

Dialogue Grammar: A formalism that describes how utterances follow on from each other, for the purpose of predicting or recognizing dialogue acts.

Illocutionary Force: The intention a speaker has when making an utterance.

Move / Utterance: A unit of speech that comprises one dialogue act.

Segment: A number of units of dialogue which, taken together, perform a coherent function.

Transaction: A major part of a dialogue, such as opening, closing, or negotiation.

Turn: An instance of speaking. A speaker's turn contains one or more moves.

Chapter 7
Text–to–Text Similarity of Sentences

Vasile Rus
The University of Memphis, USA

Mihai Lintean
The University of Memphis, USA

Arthur C. Graesser
The University of Memphis, USA

Danielle S. McNamara
Arizona State University, USA

ABSTRACT

Assessing the semantic similarity between two texts is a central task in many applications, including summarization, intelligent tutoring systems, and software testing. Similarity of texts is typically explored at the level of word, sentence, paragraph, and document. The similarity can be defined quantitatively (e.g. in the form of a normalized value between 0 and 1) and qualitatively in the form of semantic relations such as elaboration, entailment, or paraphrase. In this chapter, we focus first on measuring quantitatively and then on detecting qualitatively sentence-level text-to-text semantic relations. A generic approach that relies on word-to-word similarity measures is presented as well as experiments and results obtained with various instantiations of the approach. In addition, we provide results of a study on the role of weighting in Latent Semantic Analysis, a statistical technique to assess similarity of texts. The results were obtained on two data sets: a standard data set on sentence-level paraphrase detection and a data set from an intelligent tutoring system.

INTRODUCTION

Computational approaches to language understanding can be classified into two major categories: *true-understanding* and *text-to-text similarity*. In true understanding, the goal is to map language

statements onto a deep semantic representation that relate language constructs to world and domain knowledge. Current state-of-the-art approaches that fall into this true-understanding category offer adequate solutions only in very limited contexts (i.e. toy-domains) lacking scalability and thus having limited use in real world applications such as summarization or intelligent tutoring systems.

DOI: 10.4018/978-1-60960-741-8.ch007

Text-to-text similarity approaches (T2T) to text semantic analysis avoid the hard task of true understanding by defining the meaning of a text based on its similarity to other texts, whose meaning is assumed to be known. Such methods are called benchmarking methods as they rely on a benchmark text, analyzed by experts, to indentify the meaning of new, unseen texts. We adopt in this chapter a T2T approach to semantic text analysis.

In particular, we focus on the task of quantifying how similar two texts are, and based on this, we then decide whether they are similar enough to be considered a paraphrase or not. An example of two texts, a textbase (T) and student paraphrase (SP; reproduced as typed by the student in iSTART, an intelligent tutoring system; McNamara, Levinstein, & Boonthum, 2004), is provided below (from the User Language Paraphrase Challenge; McCarthy & McNamara, 2008):

- **T**: *During vigorous exercise, the heat generated by working muscles can increase total heat production in the body markedly.*
- **SP**: *alot of excercise can make your body warmer.*

Human judges deemed the T and SP in this example to be similar (i.e. in a paraphrase relationship).

We present in this chapter two categories of approaches to the task of sentence-level paraphrase identification: knowledge-based and statistical-based. A generic approach that relies on knowledge-based word-to-word similarity measures is discussed. In addition, we present a generic approach based on Latent Semantic Analysis (LSA; Landauer et al., 2007), a statistical technique to assess similarity of texts, which is used in combination with several weighting schemes to address the task of paraphrase identification. These approaches were tested on two data sets: the Microsoft Research Paraphrase corpus (MSRP; Dolan, Quirk, & Brockett, 2004), a standard data set on sentence-level paraphrase detection, and a data set from the intelligent tutoring system iSTART (McCarthy & McNamara, 2008).

BACKGROUND

In this section, we present background information related to word-level similarity measures, as they form the foundation of methods we propose.

There are two main groups of word-level similarity techniques: knowledge-based and statistical. In the knowledge-based category, the lexical database WordNet is used as a knowledge base (Miller, 1995). WordNet groups words with same meaning into *synsets* (i.e. synonymous sets). Each synset defines a concept (i.e. a uniquely identified meaning). A word can belong to more than one synset in cases where the word is polysemous (i.e. it has many senses). WordNet contains only content words: nouns, verbs, adjectives, and adverbs. It should be noted that WordNet simply offers a glossary of possible senses for words. Identifying the exact meaning (out of many) of a word according to WordNet is equivalent to identifying the synset that best captures the meaning of the word given its context in a particular text fragment. That is, the meaning of the word is entailed by the company it keeps in a text fragment. The task of identifying the correct sense given the context is called word sense disambiguation, one of the most difficult tasks in natural language processing. Text-to-text similarity methods that rely on WordNet-based word-to-word similarity measures need word sense disambiguation in order to be used.

There are nearly a dozen WordNet-based similarity measures available (Pedersen, Patwardhan, & Michelizzi, 2004). These measures are further divided into two groups: similarity measures and relatedness measures. The similarity measures are limited to within-category concepts (noun-noun or verb-verb) and usually they work only for nouns and verbs. The text relatedness measures on the other hand can be used to compute similarity among words belonging to different categories (e.g. between a noun and an adjective). The cross-category applicability is very important to us because, for instance, the semantic similarity between the adjective *warmer* in the student paraphrase and the noun *heat* in the textbase of the example given above can be computed with relatedness measures but not with similarity measures. Therefore, we focus in this chapter on the relatedness measures.

Word relatedness measures use lexico-semantic information in WordNet to decide semantic similarity between words. As already mentioned, WordNet groups words that have the same meaning (i.e. synonyms) into synsets. For instance, the synset of *{affectionate, fond, lovesome, tender, warm}* corresponds to the concept of *(having or displaying warmth or affection)*, which is the definition of the concept in WordNet. Each concept has attached to it a gloss, which contains its definition and several usage examples. Words can belong to more than one synset/concept in WordNet, in case they have more than one meaning. Concepts are linked via lexico-semantic relations such as *hypernymy (is-a)*, *hyponymy (reverse is-a)*, and *meronymy (part-of)*. The nouns and verbs are organized into a hierarchy using the hypernymy relation. An example of a hypernymy relation is shown in Figure 1 between the concept of *organ* and that of *body-part*. The interpretation is that *organ* is a subconcept, or a specialization of *body-part* or simply "*organ is a type of body-part.*" A snapshot of the WordNet hierarchy is shown in Figure 1.

In general, two concepts are semantically more related if they are closer to each other in the WordNet web of concepts. In Figure 1, the concept of *{muscle, musculus}* is more related to the concept of *{contractile organ, contractor}* than to *{body}*. The rationale is that the former two concepts are one *hypernymy* link away whereas the latter two are four links away (including one change of direction while following the *hyper-*

Figure 1. Snapshot of WordNet hierarchy

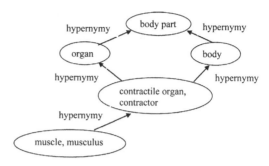

nymy link between *{ body part}* and *{body}*). Various WordNet relatedness measures compute the distance in different ways. We experimented with several measures, described later.

Latent Semantic Analysis (LSA; Landauer et al., 2007) is a statistical approach to both representing the semantic of texts in the form of a vector representation and computing similarity between texts. It can be used to assess word-to-word, sentence-to-sentence, and paragraph-to-paragraph semantic similarities.

LSA defines the meaning of words through a co-occurrence analysis of words in large collections of texts (called *documents*). The idea is that two words are related if they co-occur frequently in the same contexts. The co-occurrence statistics are first stored in a term-by-document matrix in which each cell represents the weight of the term in the corresponding document. The weight can be binary, raw or normalized frequency, or any other weighting such as the well-established term-frequency/inverted-document-frequency weight (tf-idf) used in information retrieval. The term-by-document frequency is then passed as input to a mathematical procedure, Singular Value Decomposition (SVD), with the ultimate goal to find an approximation of the initial term-by-document matrix based on the largest k singular values obtained with SVD. Usually, k is somewhere between 300 and 500 resulting in a representation for individual words in the form of a 300-500-dimension vector. Each dimension in this representation is a so-called latent concept. The similarity of two words can be quantitatively characterized by computing the cosine of the two words' LSA vectors (i.e. the normalized dot-product of the vectors). If binary weighting is used then the dot-product is identical to computing a word overlap score (i.e. the number of common words). Normalization discounts the effect of document lengths on the value of the dot-product.

In a way, the meaning of a word is defined by the words it co-occurs with (i.e. the company it keeps). In contrast to WordNet, according to LSA each word has a unique meaning. Polysemy is not possible in LSA-based representations. A consequence of this latter fact is that there is no need for word sense disambiguation in text-to-text similarity approaches that rely on LSA-based representations. One advantage of the LSA representation is its scalability beyond individual words to sentences and paragraphs. The LSA representation of a sentence can be obtained by adding up the LSA vectors corresponding to the individual words in the sentence. Similarly, for paragraphs one can simply add the LSA vectors of the corresponding words. The sum of vectors can be weighted, meaning the vectors of some words in the sentence or paragraph can be given more, or less, importance. In McNamara, Cai, and Louwerse (2007), we evaluated variations of the LSA algorithm to examine whether the performance of LSA could be improved by varying two factors: emphasis on high versus low frequency words, and similarity strictness. In the first study, a variation of LSA in which the weight of rare words was emphasized enhanced the algorithm's ability to detect differences in relatedness between three types of sentence pairs. This variation also better detected differences between high and low cohesion texts. By contrast, performance in terms of making fine grained distinctions between paraphrases was enhanced when the algorithm emphasized more frequent words. Overall, the study indicated that different algorithms may be more apt to detect differences in meaning depending on the level

of analysis. Thus, different algorithms may be more or less appropriate and effective depending on the cognitive processes that are targeted in the particular study.

Another type of weighting has been explored by Hu and colleagues (2003) in which they considered dimensionality weighting based on the observation that the first dimension in LSA vectors is always larger than the remaining dimensions. To summarize, there are three types of weighting in LSA: pre-weighting in the term-by-document matrix, post-weighting when summing up the vectors of individual words to obtain LSA-based representations of longer texts, and dimensionality weighting that can be applied during cosine computation. Post-weighting is an important aspect of extending word-to-word similarity methods beyond the word-level in our text-to-text similarity methods presented later.

PARAPHRASE: A TEXT-TO-TEXT SEMANTIC RELATION

A major issue in paraphrase identification is that the exact definition of a paraphrase at sentence level is yet to be discovered. A quick search with the query *What is a paraphrase?* on a major search engine reveals many definitions for the concept of paraphrase. Table 1 presents a small sample of such definitions. From the table, we notice that the most common feature in all these definitions is different/own words. That is, a sentence is a paraphrase of another sentence if it conveys the same meaning using different words. While these definitions seem to be quite clear, when it comes to sentence-level paraphrases (i.e. among texts the size of a sentence) there seems to be some issues that apparently are in contradiction with the above definitions.

For sentential paraphrases, the feature of *different words* seems to be too restrictive, although not impossible. Instances in both the iSTART and MSRP corpora support this latter claim as the

Table 1. Definitions of paraphrases from various sources

Source	Definition (A paraphrase is...)
Wikipedia	a restatement of a text or passage *using different words.*
WordNet	express the same message in *different words*; *rewording* for the purpose of clarification.
Purdue's Online Writing Lab	*your own rendition* of essential information and ideas expressed by someone else, presented in a new form.
Pearson's Glossary	to record someone else's words in the writer's *own words.*

paraphrases in the these corpora tend to have many words in common: 67.98% average word overlap in the MSRP corpus and 57.65% average word overlap in the iSTART corpus; when lemmatizing the words the overlaps are 69.5% and 57.65%, respectively). Although the high lexical overlap of the paraphrases in the MSRP corpus can be explained by the protocol used to create the corpus (keywords were used to retrieve the same stories from different sources on the web), in general, we can argue that avoiding the high word overlap issue in sentential paraphrasing would be difficult. Given an isolated sentence, it would be quite challenging to omit/replace some core concepts when trying to paraphrase it. Here is an example of a sentence, *Junya Tanase is a forex strategist at JP Morgan Chase.*, which would be hard to paraphrase with many new/different words due to the large number of named entities in it (this is from instance 962 in the MSRP corpus). In the iSTART corpus, the cause of high-lexical overlap may be students' modest background on the topic at hand (i.e. biology). If given a biology sentence and asked to paraphrase, students tend to re-use many of the words in the original sentence as their knowledge is limited. It is beyond the scope of this chapter to provide a final answer with respect to whether high lexical overlap should be acceptable or not in sentential paraphrases. Further research will resolve this issue.

Another interesting aspect of sentential paraphrases is the fact that there seem to be two different ways to judge sentential paraphrases. On the one hand, two sentences are considered paraphrases of each other if and only if they are semantically equivalent (i.e. they both convey the same message with no additional information present in one of the sentences). An example of two sentences in a semantic equivalence is given below. The example is from the MSRP corpus.

- **Text A:** *York had no problem with MTA's insisting the decision to shift funds had been within its legal rights.*
- **Text B:** *York had no problem with MTA's saying the decision to shift funds was within its powers.*

In this case, to detect whether two sentences are paraphrases of each other, we only need to find one concept which is present in one sentence but not in the other to make a non-paraphrase decision.

On the other hand, two sentences are in a paraphrase relation if they convey roughly the same message with some minor details being different. In this case, the paraphrase relation can be looked at as a bidirectional entailment relation (Rus et al., 2009). To exemplify such loose paraphrases, we show below a pair of sentences that has been tagged as a paraphrase in the MSRP corpus:

- **Text A:** *Ricky Clemons' brief, troubled Missouri basketball career is over.*
- **Text B:** *Missouri kicked Ricky Clemons off its team, ending his troubled career there.*

In this example, the first sentence specifies that the career of Mr. Clemons was brief, while the second sentence specifies the reason why Mr. Clemons' career is over. The MSRP corpus, one of our experimental data sets, contains both types of sentential paraphrases (i.e. precise and loose paraphrases). This characteristic of the MSRP corpus impacts the performance of general approaches to paraphrase identification, such as ours, that are not tailored towards judges' biases.

Solutions and Recommendations

As already mentioned, we focus in this chapter on text-to-text similarity approaches that rely on word-to-word similarity measures to compute similarity between two longer texts.

Knowledge-Based Text-to-Text Similarity

These approaches combine word-level similarities between pairs of words in the two texts. For instance, Rus and Graesser (2006) used a lexical overlap component combined with syntactic overlap and negation components to compute a unidirectional subsumption score, proposed for the task of entailment, between two sentences T (Text) and H (Hypothesis). The subsumption score reflects how much a text is subsumed or contained by another. Equation 1 provides the overall subsumption score, which can be averaged both ways to compute a similarity score, as opposed to just the subsumption score, between the two texts as shown in Equation 2. The lexical component can be used by itself (given a weight of 1 with the syntactic component given a weight of 0) in which case the similarity between the two texts is just an extension of word-to-word similarity measures. The *match* function in Equation 1 can be any word-to-word similarity measure including simple word match, WordNet similarity measures, or LSA-based similarity.

Equation 1. Entailment score between a Text and a Hypothesis. Max represents the maximum function while match is a matching operation of words V_h and V_t, one in the Hypothesis and one in Text, respectively.

$$entscore(T,H) = \alpha \times \frac{\sum_{V_k \in H_v} \max_{V_l \in T_v} match(V_h, V_t)}{|V_h|} +$$
$$\beta \times \frac{\sum_{E_k \in H_e} \max_{E_l T_e} match(E_h, E_t)}{|E_h|} + \gamma) \times \left(\frac{1 + (-1)^{\#neg\_rel}}{2} \right)$$

Equation 2. Paraphrase score between texts T1 and T2 based on an Entailment score (entscore). Entscore (T1, T2) is the entailment score between T1 and T2 obtained using Equation 1.

$$paraphrase(T1, T2) = \frac{entscore(T1, T2) + entscore(T2, T1)}{2}$$

A similar approach has been proposed by Rus et al. (2009), who weighted each word by its importance using an inverted-document-frequency weight. They only used lexical similarities (no syntactic similarities) to assess the degree of semantic relatedness between two sentences. Lexical similarities between words were assessed using various WordNet-based word-to-word similarity functions. Equation 3 illustrates the weighted sum of word-level similarities. This score can be generalized as shown in Equation 4 where we use generic *weight* and *word-sim* functions. We will use this generic approach and instantiate it by replacing the generic weight and word-sim functions with specific weights and word-to-word similarity measures. If the weight for each word is set to 1 then the similarity score in Equation 3 is equivalent to the lexical component in Equation 1. Likewise, Mihalcea, Corley, and Strapparava (2006) used a similarity technique based on word-to-word similarity measures for identifying paraphrase relations between sentences in a pair. Fernando and Stevenson (2008) also relied on word-level similarities to compute similarities of sentences. Instead of relying on the maximum similarity score between a word in one text and the words in the other text, which is what we do, they used average similarities between one word in the first text and all the words in the other. Taking the average scores gives credit to words in one sentence that are relatively similar but not very closely related to words in the other sentence.

Equation 3. Semantic similarity score between texts T1 and T2 using WordNet-based word-to-word similarity measures.

$$score(T1, T2) =$$

$$\frac{\sum_{v \in T1} idf(v) * \max_{w \in T2} WordNet - sim(v, w)}{\sum_{v \in T1} idf(v)}$$

Equation 4. Generic semantic similarity score between texts T1 and T2.

$$score(T1, T2) =$$

$$\frac{\sum_{v \in T1} weight(v) * \max_{w \in T2} word - sim(v, w)}{\sum_{v \in T1} idf(v)}$$

Text-to-Text Similarity Based on Latent Semantic Analysis

The use of LSA to compute similarity of texts beyond word-level relies mainly on combining the vector representation of individual words. Specifically, the vector representation of a text containing two or more words is the weighted sum of the LSA vectors of the individual words. If we denote $weight_w$ as the weight of a word w given by some scheme, local or global, then the vector of a text T (sentence or paragraph) is given by Equation 5. In Equation 5, w takes value from the set of unique words in a text T (i.e. from the set of word types of T). If a word type occurs several times in the document that will be captured by the local weight ($loc - weight$). *Glob − weight* in Equation 5 represents the global weight associated with type w, as derived from a large corpus of documents, which is Wikipedia in our case.

Equation 5. Formula to generate an LSA-based vector for a text T based in the individual LSA vectors of the words it contains.

$$V(T) = \sum_{w \in T} loc - weight_w * glob - weight_w V_w$$

To find the LSA similarity score between two texts T1 and T2 (i.e. LSA[T1, T2]) we first represent each sentence as vectors in the LSA space, V (T1) and V (T2), and then compute the cosine between the two vectors. Cosine is the normalized dot-product of the corresponding vectors.

There are several ways to compute local and global weights. For local weighting, the most common schemes are *binary, type frequency*, and *log-type frequency. Binary* weighting refers to the use of 1 if the word type occurs at least once in the document and 0 if it does not occur at all. *Type frequency* weight is defined as the number of times a word type appears in a text, sentence, or paragraph. *Log-type frequency* weight is defined as log(1 + *type frequency*). Dumais (1991) argued that type frequency gives too much weight/importance to very common (i.e. frequent) words. A frequent word such as *the*, which does not carry much meaning, will have a big impact although its entropy (described next) is low, which is counterintuitive. To diminish the frequency factor for such words, but not eliminate it entirely, the log-type weighting scheme was proposed.

As global weight, we started with a binary weight: 1 if the word exists in the text, 0 otherwise. The most commonly used global weight is entropy-based. It is defined as

$$1 + \sum_j \frac{p_{ij} * \log_2 p_{ij}}{\log_2 n}$$

where $p_{ij} = tf_{ij}/gf_i$, tf_{ij} is type of frequency of type i in document j, and gf_i is the total number of times that type i appears in the entire collection of n documents. We also used IDF (Inverted Document

Frequency), as a global weight. IDF was derived from the English section of Wikipedia (details provided later).

Experiments and Results

We present experiments and results with the generic approach in Equation 4 as well as with the LSA-based approach in Equation 5.

Two sentence-level data sets were used in our experiments: the Microsoft Research Paraphrase Corpus (Dolan et al., 2004) and the intelligent tutoring systems ULPC/iSTART corpus (McCarthy & McNamara, 2008). We report results using the performance measures of accuracy and kappa. *Accuracy* is the percentage of correct predictions out of all predictions. *Kappa* coefficient measures the level of agreement between predicted categories and expert-assigned categories while also accounting for chance agreement. Results were obtained using 10-fold cross-validation, except for the MSR dataset, which contains an explicit test subset. In k-fold cross validation the available data is divided into k equal folds. Then, k trials are run, one for each fold. In each trial one fold is set aside for testing and the other $(k - 1)$ are used for training. The average of the accuracies for the k trials is reported. When $k = 10$, we have 10-fold cross validation.

Given the need for word distributional information for our weighting schemes (i.e. inverted document frequency [idf]) it is important to derive as accurate estimates of word statistics as possible. Accurate word statistics means being representative of overall word usage (by all people at all times). The accuracy of the estimates is largely influenced by the collection of texts from which the statistics are derived. Various collections have been used to derive word statistics. For instance, Corley and Mihalcea (2005) used the British National Corpus as a source for their idf values. We chose Wikipedia instead because it encompasses texts related to both general knowledge and specialized domains and it has been edited by many

individuals, thus capturing diversity of language expression across individuals. Furthermore, Wikipedia is one of the largest publicly available collections of English texts. Extracting df values and word statistics from very large collections of text, such as Wikipedia, is a non-trivial task. Due to space limitations we do not present the details of this step. We just mention that the number of distinct words chosen after many processing steps was *2,118,550*. We have collected distributional information for this set of words and used it in our experiments.

Sentence-Level Similarity in iSTART

In this section, we focus on evaluating student input in iSTART (Interactive Strategy Training for Active Reading and Thinking; McNamara et al., 2004), an ITS that provides students with reading strategy training. One of the modules in iSTART focuses on training students to paraphrase science sentences, called *textbases* (T). Assessing the student paraphrases (SP) is a critical step in iSTART because this assessment detects possible student misunderstandings and provides the necessary corrective feedback.

The User Language Paraphrase Corpus (ULPC; McCarthy & McNamara, 2008) is a compiled data set of 1998 pairs of Textbase-SP in iSTART. There are 10 dimensions of analysis available in the ULPC including elaboration, semantic completeness, entailment, lexical similarity, and paraphrase quality. It should be noted that some of these dimensions have meanings in the ULPC that need be specified as they are not obvious or differ from definitions used by others. In the ULPC, elaboration refers to student paraphrases regarding the theme of the textbase rather than a restatement of it. Semantic completeness refers to a SP having the same meaning as the textbase, regardless of word- or structural-overlap. This dimension is of most interest to us because it best matches our goal of detecting semantic similarities among texts. Paraphrase quality takes into account semantic-overlap, syntactical variation, and writing quality. Given these definitions, the semantic completeness dimension in ULPC is equivalent to the paraphrase evaluation in the MSRP corpus (Dolan, Quirk, & Brockett, 2004).

An example of a textbase and student paraphrase in iSTART was provided in the *Introduction* section. We present next several instantiations of the generic approach to Text-to-Text similarity presented earlier for the problem of assessing student paraphrases in iSTART. The instantiations were obtained by replacing the WordNet-sim function in the formula in Equation 4 with several knowledge-based word-to-word similarity measures.

WordNet-Based Similarity

We first discuss how to instantiate the generic approach using WordNet-based similarity measures. We used the following word relatedness measures (implemented in the WordNet::Similarity package; Pedersen, Patwardhan, & Michelizzi, 2004): HSO (Hirst & St-Onge, 1998), LESK (Banerjee & Pedersen, 2003), and VECTOR (Patwardhan, 2003). Given two WordNet concepts, these measures provide a real value indicating how semantically related the two concepts are.

The HSO measure is path based (i.e., it uses the relations between concepts) and assigns direction to relations in WordNet. For example, the *is-a* relation is upwards, while the *has-part* relation is horizontal. The LESK and VECTOR measures are gloss-based. That is, they use the text of the gloss as the source of meaning for the underlying concept.

One challenge with these measures is that natural language texts use words and not concepts which are needed as input by these measures. To be able to use the measures we must map words to concepts in WordNet (i.e. we must do word sense disambiguation [WSD]). It is beyond the scope of our investigation to fully solve the WSD problem, one of the hardest in the area of Natural Language Processing. Instead, we address the issue in two

ways: (1) map words in the textbase T and SP onto the concept corresponding to their most frequent sense, which is sense #1 in WordNet, and (2) map words onto all the concepts corresponding to all the senses and take the maximum of the relatedness scores for each pair of senses. We label the former method as ONE (sense one), whereas the latter is labeled as ALL (all senses).

In our evaluation, we have explored a space of 3x2x2=12 solutions/instantiations as a result of combining three relatedness measures (HSO, LESK, and VECTOR), two word sense disambiguation methods (ONE and ALL), and the two weighting schemes (with and without IDF weighting). The labels of each instantiation have a specific meaning. For instance, the label ALL_IDF_LESK means the instantiation that uses ALL the senses of words to compute word-to-word relatedness, weights words using IDF values, and applies the LESK relatedness measure. If no IDF is mentioned in the name of a solution but rather a dash (-) (e.g. ONE-LESK) it means no word weighting was used. In order to measure accuracy, we used the binary values for human judgments in the iSTART/ULPC corpus (1.00-3.49 = 0 [low]; 3.50-6.00 = 1 [high]).

Each method goes through a training phase. The training consists of finding a threshold value for a particular solution (e.g. ONE-LESK) above which a prediction is considered high, and low otherwise. These predictions are then compared with the binary human judgments in order to compute the accuracy.

An analysis of the results indicated that the LESK measure provides best results across weighting schemes and word sense disambiguation methods (accuracy=79.47%). Using idf seems to help in combination with the LESK measure. Picking the first sense in WordNet as the disambiguation method is sufficient for the LESK method. Actually, LESK with no weighting and ALL disambiguation yields slightly worse results than with the ONE disambiguation method.

Regarding weighting, using idf helps all the related measures regardless of the disambiguation method while the disambiguation method does not seem to make a difference. Actually, when no weighting is used the ALL method seems to hurt some the accuracy results.

For the more balanced dimension of paraphrase quality, kappa varies from 0.335 to 0.449 (for ONE_IDF_LESK). LSA yields a kappa of 0.361 and the best kappa is 0.434 (for R-Ent).

Latent Semantic Analysis

We investigated the impact of several local and global weighting schemes for the ability of Latent Semantic Analysis' (LSA) to capture semantic similarity between two texts. We show results with two local and two global weighting schemes. For local weighting, we used binary weighting and raw term-frequency. For global weighting, we relied on binary and inverted document frequencies (idf) collected from the English Wikipedia. The results are shown in Table 2. Best overall accuracy (78.13) is obtained for a combination of raw frequency local weighting and idf global weighting.

The Microsoft Research Paraphrase Corpus

As already mentioned, the Microsoft Research Paraphrase (MSRP) corpus (Dolan, Quirk, & Brockett 2004) is a standardized data set for paraphrase identification. Although it has limitations (see Zhang & Patrick, 2005; Lintean & Rus, 2011), the MSR Paraphrase Corpus is the largest publicly available annotated paraphrase corpus. It has been frequently used in many recent studies that address the problem of paraphrase identification. The corpus consists of 5801 sentence pairs collected from newswire articles, 3900 of which were labeled as paraphrases by human annotators. The whole set is divided into a training subset (4076 sentences of which 2753, or 67%, are true paraphrases), and a test subset (1725 pairs of which 1147, or 66%, are true paraphrases). The MSRP corpus uses a loose definition of a paraphrase. Two sentences were judged as forming a paraphrase if they conveyed roughly the same message (minor details being different is acceptable). Examples were provided earlier in the section *Paraphrase: A Text-to-Text Semantic Relation*. The obtained results are shown in Table 3. In terms of accuracy,

Table 2. Results obtained with various combinations of local and global weighting in LSA on the ULPCS/ iSTART corpus

Global\Local Weighting	Binary		Raw	
	Accuracy	Kappa	Accuracy	Kappa
Binary	76.88	.368	76.88	.364
Idf	77.83	.409	78.13	.417

Table 3. Results obtained with various combinations of local and global weighting in LSA for the MSRP corpus

Global\Local Weighting	Binary		Raw frequency	
	Accuracy	Kappa	Accuracy	Kappa
Binary	70.38	.247	70.55	.244
Idf	69.85	.231	69.74	.228

the results seem to be very close to each other for the four combinations of local and global weighting schemes.

FUTURE RESEARCH DIRECTIONS

There are many possible avenues for continuing the quest for the best way solve the problem of text-to-text similarity in general and of paraphrase identification in particular. First, we plan to integrate more types of knowledge in our basic approaches to text-to-text similarity (e.g. semantic information from semantic parsers). Second, we plan to explore further the impact of the various parameters of the proposed methods such as various weighting schemes as well as using averages of word-to-word measures instead of taking the maximum of the similarity scores between pairs of words, one word in one text and the other word from the other text. Third, we plan to explore how well the knowledge-based measures work on the MSRP corpus.

CONCLUSION

We presented in this paper several methods to address the task of text-to-text similarity of texts the size of a sentence. The methods fall into the two major categories of general Natural Language Processing approaches: knowledge-based and statistical. A comparison between knowledge-based and statistical on the iSTART corpus gave a slight advantage to the knowledge-based methods as the best accuracy results with the knowledge-based methods was 79.47% versus 78.13% for best Latent Semantic Analysis method which used raw frequency for local weighting and inverted-document-frequency for global weighting. The advantage of the knowledge-based approaches is their interpretability, which means decisions can be justified based on the explicit paths and semantic relations in the knowledge-based that were used

to compute the similarity between words. On the other hand, Latent Semantic Analysis has a scalability advantage. It would be interesting to see how a combination of these two approaches would perform, a possible item in our plans for the future.

REFERENCES

Banerjee, S., & Pedersen, T. (2003). Extended gloss overlaps as a measure of semantic relatedness. In *Proceedings of the Eighteenth International Joint Conference on Artificial Intelligence,* (pp. 805-810).

Corley, C., & Mihalcea, R. (2005). Measuring the semantic similarity of texts. In *Proceedings of the ACL Workshop on Empirical Modeling of Semantic Equivalence and Entailment,* Ann Arbor, MI.

Dolan, B., Quirk, C., & Brockett, C. (2004). Unsupervised construction of large paraphrase corpora: Exploiting massively parallel news sources. In *Proceedings of COLING,* Geneva, Switzerland.

Fernando, S., & Stevenson, M. (2008). A semantic approach to paraphrase identification. In *Proceedings of the 11th Annual Research Colloquium of the UK Special-interest group for Computational Lingusitics,* Oxford, England, 2008.

Hirst, G., & St-Onge, D. (1998). Lexical chains as representations of context for the detection and correction of malapropisms. In Fellbaum, C. (Ed.), *WordNet: An electronic lexical database.* MIT Press.

Landauer, T., McNamara, D. S., Dennis, S., & Kintsch, W. (Eds.). (2007). *Latent semantic analysis: A road to meaning.* Mahwah, NJ: Erlbaum.

Lintean, M., & Rus, V. (2011). Dissimilarity kernels for paraphrase identification. *In Proceedings of the Twenty-Fourth International FLAIRS Conference,* Palm Beach, FL, May 2011.

McNamara, D. S., Cai, Z., & Louwerse, M. M. (2007). Comparing latent and non-latent measures of cohesion. In Landauer, T., McNamara, D. S., Dennis, S., & Kintsch, W. (Eds.), *Handbook of latent semantic analysis* (pp. 379–400). Mahwah, NJ: Erlbaum.

McNamara, D. S., Levinstein, I., & Boonthum, C. (2004). iSTART: Interactive strategy trainer for active reading and thinking. *Behavior Research Methods, Instruments, & Computers*, *36*(2), 222–233. doi:10.3758/BF03195567

Mihalcea, R., Corley, C., & Strapparava, C. (2006). Corpus-based and knowledge-based measures of text semantic similarity. In *Proc. of the 21st Conference of American Association for Artificial Intelligence (AAAI-06)*, Boston, Massachusetts, July 16-20 2006.

Patwardhan, S. (2003). *Incorporating dictionary and corpus information into a context vector measure of semantic relatedness*. Master's thesis, Univ. of Minnesota, Duluth.

Pedersen, T., Patwardhan, S., & Michelizzi, J. (2004). WordNet: Similarity - Measuring the relatedness of concepts. In the *Proceedings of the Nineteenth National Conference on Artificial Intelligence* (AAAI-04), (pp. 1024-1025). July 25-29, 2004, San Jose, CA (Intelligent Systems Demonstration) McCarthy, P. M., & McNamara, D. S. (2008). *User-language paraphrase corpus challenge*.

Rus, V., & Graesser, A. C. (2006). *Deeper Natural Language Processing for Evaluating Student Answers in Intelligent Tutoring Systems*, Proceedings of the Twenty-First National Conference on Artificial Intelligence (AAAI-06).

Rus, V., Lintean, M., Shiva, S., & Marinov, D. (submitted). *Automated identification of duplicate defect reports using word semantics*. Submitted to the Workshop on Mining Software Repositories.

Rus, V., McCarthy, P. M., Graesser, A. C., & McNamara, D. S. (2009). Identification of sentence-to-sentence relations using a textual entailer. *The International Journal on Research in Language and Computation*, *7*(2-4).

Zhang, Y., & Patrick, J. (2005). Paraphrase identification by text canonicalization. *In Proceedings of the Australasian Language Technology Workshop*.

KEY TERMS AND DEFINITIONS

Intelligent Tutoring Systems: Systems that mimic human tutors in their attempt to provide high-quality instruction to students on topics varying from biology to physics to financial literacy.

Knowledge-Based Similarity Measures: Similarity measures that rely on knowledge resources that explicitly encode semantic relations among words. WordNet is an example of such a resource that specifies semantic relations among the words.

Latent Semantic Analysis: Statistical method for semantic representation of language constructs such as words, sentences, and paragraphs.

Paraphrase: Semantic relation between two texts having the same meaning. While the texts have the same meaning, it is widely accepted they should express it in different ways.

Text-to-Text Similarity Measures: Methods to quantify how semantically similar two texts are. The two texts should contain two or more words (i.e. being phrases, sentences, paragraphs, or even documents).

Word-to-Word Similarity Measures: Methods to quantify how semantically similar two words are.

Word Weighting: Technique to assign more importance to some words when composing the meaning of larger chunks of texts from the meaning of individual words.

Chapter 8
Practical Programming for NLP

Patrick Jeuniaux
Université Laval, Canada

Andrew Olney
The University of Memphis, USA

Sidney D'Mello
The University of Memphis, USA

ABSTRACT

This chapter is aimed at students and researchers who are eager to learn about practical programmatic solutions to natural language processing (NLP) problems. In addition to introducing the readers to programming basics, programming tools, and complete programs, we also hope to pique their interest to actively explore the broad and fascinating field of automatic natural language processing. Part I introduces programming basics and the Python programming language. Part II takes a step by step approach in illustrating the development of a program to solve a NLP problem. Part III provides some hints to help readers initiate their own NLP programming projects.

INTRODUCTION

Natural language processing (NLP) attempts to automatically analyze the languages spoken by humans (i.e., natural languages). For instance, you can program a computer to automatically identify the language of a text, extract the grammatical structure of sentences, categorize texts by genre (e.g., decide whether a text is a scientific or a narrative text), summarize a text, etc. This chapter is aimed at teaching specialized, yet introductory, programming skills that are required to use avail-

able NLP tools. We hope that this chapter serves as a catalyst to launch NLP projects by motivating novice programmers to learn more about programming and encouraging more advanced programmers to develop NLP programs. The chapter is aimed at readers from the interdisciplinary arena that encompasses computer science, cognitive psychology, and linguistics. It is geared for individuals who have a practical NLP problem and for curious readers who are eager to learn about practical solutions for such problems.

Fortifying students with the requisite programming skills to tackle an NLP problem in a single chapter is a daunting task for two primary

DOI: 10.4018/978-1-60960-741-8.ch008

reasons. First, along with advanced statistics, programming is probably the most intimidating task that practitioners in disciplines like linguistics or cognitive psychology can undertake. The typical student or researcher in these fields has little formal training in mathematics, logic, and computer science, hence, their first foray into programming can be a bit challenging. Second, although computer scientists have considerable experience with programming and have mastered many computer technologies, they might not be privy to the libraries or packages that are readily and freely available for NLP projects. In other words, there is a lot to cover if we attempt to address both these audiences, and it seems like an impossible challenge to design a chapter extending from the basics of programming to the specifics of NLP. Fortunately, for the reader and us, the availability of state-of-the-art NLP technologies and the enhanced usability available through easy-to-use interfaces alleviates some of these challenges.

Because of space limitations, we could not achieve the coverage depth we had hoped for. We originally had planned to include programming projects in several languages such as Python, Perl, Java and PHP, along with numerous screen captures of captivating programming demonstrations. The chapter is now more focused on examples in Python. Fortunately, the materials that could not be included in the chapter (e.g., scripts, examples, screen captures), are available for your convenience on the companion website at http://patrickjeuniaux.info/NLPchapter. It also provides a series of links to NLP resources, as well as detailed instructions about how to execute the programs that are needed for the exercises. A great advantage of having a website is that it can be updated with current content, so do not hesitate to contact us if you wish to give us feedback.

This chapter has three parts. Part I offers an introduction to programming. Part II gives a concrete example of programming for a specific NLP project. Part III provides general hints about starting your own NLP programming project.

Readers who do not have programming experience or who do not know Python should definitely start with Part I. Individuals who have a working knowledge of Python can skip most of Part I. Among these people, the ones who do not know about NLTK could limit their reading of Part I to the section on functions and onwards. Although Part I covers a lot of material, the topic coverage is far from exhaustive. When you are done with this chapter, we encourage you to read a more complete introduction. We particularly recommend Elkner, Downey, and Meyers (2009). The same can be said of Part II. We also recommend reading Bird, Klein and Loper (2009), who give a thorough treatment of NLP programming with Python's Natural Language Processing Toolkit (NLTK).

PROGRAMMING BASICS

Computers are controlled by sets of instructions called programs. Because they are somewhat simple machines, computers can only follow the most unambiguous instructions. To achieve this ideal of precision, a program is written in a restricted language. Programming languages use a specific vocabulary (i.e. a set of words), a syntax (i.e., a set of rules defining how to use these words), and semantics (i.e., the meaning of the words and rules from a programming point of view). Learning the basic rules of a language is the first step towards writing meaningful and useful programs. But prior to learning a language, it might be good to learn about the history of computer programming. Knowing the historical motivation behind programming will help you grasp what programming is all about.

Programming in Context

Today we usually think of a computer as a general purpose device. However, this was not always the case. Whether you consider Babbage's Difference

Engine (Swade, 2002), which solved polynomial functions, or Colossus, which helped decipher the Enigma codes during World War II (Hodges, 2000) to be computers, the fact remains that a "computer" is simply something that performs calculations. In fact, before the 20th century people whose jobs were to perform complex calculations for various purposes were called 'computers' (Anderson, 2009).

As the science and technology of computing advanced, man-made computers became more complex and were able to perform more complex calculations. However, the process for doing so was extremely tedious and error prone. Computers were massive beasts of machines in those days, often taking up entire rooms. Programming sometimes meant re-patching cables on a switchboard (Petzold, 2000), a far cry from the text editors and visual interfaces that we are familiar with today.

At this time it became clear to the scientists involved with creating and using these machines that the difficulty of using computers was an obstruction to their widespread use and acceptance. Their solution to this problem was to create layers of abstraction between the user and the computer. This process of increasing abstraction has continued to the present day and shows no signs of stopping in the foreseeable future. For example, consider your computer's desktop. "Desktop" is just an abstraction and analogy for a physical desktop for pens and paper. Similarly, the folders on your desktop are analogous to physical file cabinets used to store paper documents.

Programming languages are just another kind of abstraction over the underlying computer instructions ("machine code"). The machine code is simply a very detailed and hard to use programming language. For most applications, programmers do not use machine code but use instead modern programming languages which are designed to simplify the programmer's life (by reducing the size of the program, reducing the likelihood of programming error, etc.). Programming languages have evolved in such a way that

programming is no longer restricted to the purview of professional computer scientists. So-called high level languages allow practitioners of other fields (like psychology, and linguistics) to enjoy the power and flexibility of programming. One of the goals of this chapter is to show how this is feasible. Like in all fields, it is not possible to immediately benefit from practical applications without knowing the fundamental principles underlying them. Hence, the next section is aimed at bringing you up to speed with such principles.

Fundamental Concepts of Computer Programming

Fundamental programming concepts include (a) values and types, (b) syntax and semantics, (c) operations, (d) variables, constants, and assignments, (e) data structures, (f) conditionals, (g) iterations, and (h) functions. We start by presenting these concepts with step-by-step examples of programs written in the Python language – a language whose simplicity seduces the most unwilling learners. While reviewing these basic ideas we also present some programming constructs that are especially relevant for NLP; these include strings, corpora, text files, input-output (I/O), etc. Before we begin, it is important to consider the two steps involved in writing a program: *pseudo-code* (planning) and *implementation* (executing). Finally, we will describe one important aspect of efficient code implementation: *incremental programming*.

Pseudo-Code

As you will see in the subsequent examples, Python has a quite intuitive syntax. In some respects, Python syntax looks like pseudo-code. Pseudo-code is a high-level description of a program that makes no reference to a particular language. For instance, Exhibit 1 presents pseudo-code for a program that translates sentences in a document. Each line is an instruction. The first line opens an input file and the last line closes it. The lines

Exhibit 1. Pseudo-code for translating a document

```
Open the file.
For each line in the file,

        Translate the line.
Close the file.
```

in between translate each line in the file. Pseudo-code is important because it provides a conceptual representation of what you intend to program, before you do any real programming. Planning by using some kind of pseudo-code (whether purely textual or even graphical) is an important part of conducting a successful programming project, because it very frequently unveils obstacles that you did not originally foresee when you started to think about the problem. Once you have figured out what to program (i.e., with a pseudo-code description), most of the remaining difficulties are mainly technical in nature (i.e., how to program).

Implementation

Learning to program is analogous to learning a new skill. It would be impossible to learn to ride a bicycle by reading about bicycles. Reading programming books will not suffice. You need to get your hands dirty and actually program things in conjunction with reading about them. Learning a programming language is also similar to learning a real language. You learn a real language by placing yourself in new situations where you have to communicate. Likewise you learn programming by putting yourself in new situations where you have to solve new problems. This involves downloading resources, installing the required software, setting up your working environment (e.g., a text editor or an Integrated Development Environment), writing code, and executing it. The greater the variety of the problems you solve, the more experienced of a programmer you will become.

Therefore, we cannot encourage you enough to download Python and reproduce all the examples which are explained below. These examples all assume that you are using Python IDLE – the interactive console and development environment provided with Python. Complete instructions are available on the companion website. They tell you where to find Python, how to install it, and how to use the software that can run your code. Get ready to see how user friendly Python is!

During this journey, if you are serious about implementing code, you will likely accumulate a substantial amount of files containing either code or data (i.e., material generated or used by your programs). Similar to how it is easier to find a document on a well ordered desktop than in a pile of random papers, it will be useful for you to organize the files on your computer in an orderly manner. If you are not familiar with the file system on your machine (i.e., how files and folders are organized, how to create them, move them, etc.), you should consult the links available on the companion website. When you are ready, create one folder on your machine. Let's call it the test folder. This is where you are going to put all your files. Because you wish to provide a structure to your files, within the test folder, create two other folders: the data and scripts folders, where you will place your data and your code, respectively.

Incremental Programming

Most problems will require programmers to implement their solutions step-by-step (i.e., increment by increment), leaving some parts of the program untouched until they feel it is time to tackle them. Making errors is a natural outcome of any programming activity, and it is best to work on a program one piece at a time, so that one knows where the errors come from, rather than programming all aspects simultaneously. In general, such a divide-and-conquer approach to programming is very efficient. Exhibit 2 exemplifies the order in which a programmer could have implemented the Pseudo-code exhibited in Exhibit 1.

Exhibit 2. The incremental approach to programming

```
(a)
Open the file.
(b)
Open the file.
Close the file.
(c)
Open the file.
For each line in the file,
        print the line.
Close the file.
(d)
Open the file.
For each line in the file,
        translate the line.
Close the file.
```

Part (a) in Exhibit 2 shows that the programmer first attempts to open the file. To implement this idea, several lines might have to be written. The programmer works on that part until the result is satisfactory. In part (b), one more component is added: closing the file. It is generally important to free a resource that was mobilized when "opening" a file. Once this is working, it is typically a good idea to inspect the content of the file, line by line, by printing each line on the screen, as shown in part (c). If one can realize such a simple step, then one can address the more involved operation of translating the line, as shown in part (d). Whereas part (a) focused on the input to the program, part (c) added a way of producing some output. In general, it is useful to implement simple operations for introducing some information from the external environment into your program (i.e., the input), and saving information from your program in the external environment (i.e., the output), before addressing more sophisticated parts of the program, like the translation step of part (d). The next sections illustrate programming basics with simple Python commands.

Try them out by typing them or copying them from the website.

Values and Data Types

Programs contain instructions that tell the computer how to use values. Values can be of different types (or "data types"). Exhibit 3 provides examples. The prompt of Python IDLE (i.e., the signal that Python expects an instruction) is represented by >>>. The commands follow that sign. To execute a command, type it and then press the Enter key. The output resulting from the execution of the command is displayed in bold characters. The first command in Part (a) of Exhibit 3 requires the computer to print a value of the *string* type, and whose content is "Hello World!" A string is a sequence of characters (letters, numbers, punctuation marks, and other special characters), usually surrounded by single quotes (' ') or double quotes (""). To check that "Hello World!" is a string, use the second command in Part (a). Python IDLE prints a message indicating the type (i.e., str for *string*). Another type is the *integer*, which corresponds to natural numbers like 1, 2, 3, etc. The first command in Part (b) shows how to print the integer 123. To check that it is indeed an integer, use the type command on the number, as illustrated in Part (b). If you surround the number by quotes it will be interpreted as a string.

Syntax and Semantics

As shown in Exhibit 3, quotes are important to recognize strings. This simple example illustrates that a programmer must respect the syntax of a language (i.e., rules) in order to express ideas in a program (also called "code"). These ideas correspond to the semantics of the program (i.e., what it is supposed to do). In other words, when we need to use natural numbers (i.e., a semantic constraint) we do not use quotes (i.e., a syntactical constraint). The syntactical aspect of a language is where beginners first stumble. Luckily for them,

Exhibit 3. Examples of commands and outputs to understand values and types in Python.

```
(a)
>>> print "Hello World!"
Hello World!
>>> type("Hello World!")
<type 'str'>
(b)
>>> print 123
123
>>> type(123)
<type 'int'>
>>> type('123')
<type 'str'>
```

a language like Python has a very gentle syntax, and this allows a beginner to readily focus on the more interesting aspect of the language, namely its semantics and what it can do for the programmer.

Operations

Why are there several data types like strings and integers? It is because these values have different properties, and allow the computer to perform different kinds of operations. Operations in a programming language can modify values. For instance, strings can have an arbitrary content (e.g., on the screen you could have printed "Hello World!" or the entire works of Shakespeare) but they do not support conventional numerical operations (e.g., adding Othello to Hamlet does not result in a number). Contrary to strings, integers must be natural numbers (e.g., 1, 2, 3, 4.5, 2.78) and you can perform conventional numerical operations with them (e.g., addition, multiplication). Exhibit 4 presents examples of operations in Python.

Part (a) requests Python to add 1 and 2 to obtain 3. The second command in Part (a) shows how to multiply 3 by 4 to obtain 12. Despite the fact that we did not use the print command, 12 is printed because the Python interactive software prints values by default. In the context of numbers, the signs + and * behave like arithmetical operators.

When a string is involved, their meaning is different. For instance, Part (b) shows how to *concatenate* the strings "pine" and "apple." This

Exhibit 4. Examples of operations in Python

```
(a)
>>> print 1 + 2
3
>>> 3 * 4
12
(b)
>>> "pine" + "apple"
'pineapple'
>>> 3 * "pine"
'pinepinepine'
>>> 1 + "pine"
Traceback (most recent call last):
  File "<pyshell#12>", line 1, in <module>
    1 + "pine"
TypeError: unsupported operand type(s) for +: 'int' and 'str'
```

operation pastes the two strings to create a new string – the string "pineapple." We then create a new string – the string "pinepinepine" – by repeating "pine" three times. Finally we attempted to perform an invalid operation based on an erroneous use of syntax, since it is not possible to add a string to an integer or concatenate a string with an integer (i.e., 1 + "pine" is meaningless). Read the error message which is generated: it is very instructive, because it mentions the key notions of operators, types, integer and string.

Variables, Constants, and Assignment

What happened to all the values we have created? As soon as "Hello Word!" is printed, or that 1 + 2 is computed, these values disappear, in the sense that if you want to reproduce these events again, you need to repeat the commands used to create them. In order to maintain access to values in a program, you need to give them a name. Names, like all kinds of words, are symbols which stand for (or represent) values. For instance, the word *car* represents a four-wheel vehicle used by humans. It is mainly a matter of convention. It could have been called something else, like *platypus* or *bora-bora*. The only thing which matters is that the users of the word agree upon the convention. In programming terms, these names are called *variables*.

Similarly to what happens in real life, the computer program will agree to identify variables by respecting the labels you have adopted (i.e., that is by following your convention). To assign a label to values, you use the equal sign (=). Exhibit 5 gives some examples. Part (a) in Exhibit 5 shows how to assign the value 3 to the variable X. If you then type X, the value 3 is displayed (i.e., the content referred to by X is displayed).

What are variables useful for? Like we said, they represent the real value. That very simple fact helps us to save lots of time. In the same way that in reality we do not need to have a cat, a mammoth, or a unicorn in front of us to speak

about them, in programming we simply use variables to realize operations on the values the names refer to. For instance, in Part (b), we multiply 3 by 4 by using the variables X and Y instead of directly using the integers 3 and 4.

In Python, names whose values *will change* during the course of the program execution are called *variables*; otherwise they are said to be *constant*. For instance, the value of X in Parts (a) and (b) never changes, and so X is a constant. However, it changes in part (c), and therefore, in that example it is a variable. In other programming languages, you must specify from the start if a label is a variable or a constant by using a particular syntax; there is no such rule in Python.

Python is also *dynamically typed*, in the sense that you decide at any time, what the data type of a value is (i.e., you do not have to decide it from the start like in C or Java). For instance, Part (c) shows that X is assigned an integer, and then assigned a string. When this occurs, X represents the string "Hello World!" and not the integer 1. This is because the string assignment statement followed the integer assignment statement.

Finally, although the choice of labels is mostly a question of personal convention, there are few rules you need to respect. First, you cannot use empty spaces in your variable names, you cannot start the variable name with a number, and you cannot use certain keywords like if, and, def, return, which are part of the Python syntax as variable names (see a Python introduction for details). Violating these rules will result in a *syntax error*. Second, because programming is about saving time, you want your labels to be meaningful. Part (d) shows such labels for referring to our names (Name1, Name2, Name3, Authors). For the program itself it does not matter (a computer is after all just a symbol crunching machine, which does not understand symbols in the human sense), but it would save lots of trouble to any programmer who tries to understand your program (including yourself at a later date).

Exhibit 5. Examples of assignments in Python

```
(a)
>>> X = 3
>>> X
3
(b)
>>> X = 1 + 2
>>> Y = 4
>>> X * Y
12
(c)
>>> X = 1
>>> X
1
>>> X = "Hello World!"
>>> X
'Hello World!'
(d)
>>> Name1 = "Patrick"
>>> Name2 = "Andrew"
>>> Name3 = "Sidney"
>>> S = ", "
>>> Authors = Name1 + S + Name2 + S + Name3
>>> Authors
'Patrick, Andrew, Sidney'
```

Data Structures

The assignment of values to labels is only one step towards the power of abstraction behind a programming language. Data structures are one step further. A data structures is basically a collection of data that is organized for efficient and quick access. Instead of having a name referring to a simple value (like a digit) we now refer to a collection of values. Just as some data types are better for some operations than others, data structures have their own specializations. Exhibit 6 provides examples of basic data structures that are part of Python: strings, tuples, lists and dictionary.

The operations illustrated in these examples offer only a glimpse of the myriad of possibilities. You can consult a programming reference to learn

more about them. Moreover, external packages, or libraries (often available on the internet) provide other specialized data structures. Finally you can build your own data structures (for instance, a data structure to represent syntactical trees).

Let's return to the string type. Unlike the integer type, the string type is made up of other types – *characters* – which you can selectively access. Strings can be thought of as sequences of characters. For instance, Part (a) in Exhibit 6 shows a string of three characters ("abc"). You can assign such a string to a variable X. Type X and press the Enter key to make sure the string has been assigned to X. If you multiply the string by 2, it will create a new string in which the initial string is repeated twice.

Exhibit 6. Examples of data structures in Python: String, tuple, list and dictionary

```
(a)
>>> X = "abc"
>>> X
'abc'
>>> X * 2
'abcabc'
>>> X[0]
'a'
>>> X[1]
'b'
>>> X[0] = "z"
Traceback (most recent call last):
  File "<pyshell#34>", line 1, in <module>X[0] = "z"
TypeError: 'str' object does not support item assignment
>>> X = "zbc"
(b)
>>> X = (1,2,"abc")
>>> X
(1, 2, 'abc')
>>> X * 2
(1, 2, 'abc', 1, 2, 'abc')
>>> X[0]
1
>>> X[0] = "z"
Traceback (most recent call last):
  File "<pyshell#41>", line 1, in <module>
    X[0] = "z"
TypeError: 'tuple' object does not support item assignment
>>> X = X + (7,8,9)
>>> X
 (1, 2, 'abc', 7, 8, 9)
(c)
>>> X = [1,2,"abc"]
>>> X
[1, 2, 'abc']
>>> X * 2
[1, 2, 'abc', 1, 2, 'abc']
>>> X[0]
1
>>> X[0] = "z"
>>> X[3]
Traceback (most recent call last):
```

continued on following page

Exhibit 6. Continued

```
  File "<pyshell#50>", line 1, in <module>
    X[3]
IndexError: list index out of range
>>> X = X + [7,8,9]
>>> X
 [1, 2, 'abc', 7, 8, 9]
(d)
>>> X = {'dog':'chien',
'mouse':'souris'}
>>> X['cat'] = 'chat'
>>> X
{'mouse': 'souris', 'dog': 'chien', 'cat': 'chat'}
>>> X['dog']
'chien'
>>> X['cat']='z'
```

You can access the individual characters of a string by using an *index* surrounded by brackets. The first character has the index 0, the second character the index 1, etc. Pay close attention to the fact that the first element is indexed by the digit 0, and not by the digit 1! Indexing in Python starts at zero. This is a common source of confusion for novice programmers. The last character corresponds to X[2]. Beyond index 2, there is nothing, so you would get an error message by typing, say, X[3]. Moreover, strings are *immutable*, which means that you cannot decide to selectively change one of its characters. For instance, if you want to set the first element (i.e., the element whose index is 0) to "z," you get an error message. To have a "z" instead of "a" you would need to reconstruct a string from scratch (i.e., "zbc") and reassign it to the variable which pointed to your initial string (i.e., "abc").

Part (b) shows a *tuple* made of three elements. A tuple represents a sequence of values (i.e., values following each other in a strict order). Contrary to strings which only contain characters, tuples can contain any type of values. In Part (b), the first two elements of X are integers (1 and 2) and the last element is a string ("abc"). Besides this exception,

tuples are very much like strings. Similar to strings, you can access the element of tuples with indices starting at 0. You will also get an error message if you go beyond the range of available elements or attempt to change an element (i.e., tuples are immutable too). As with strings you can repeat tuples (i.e., by using the multiplication operator) and use the concatenation operator (i.e., "+") to make bigger tuples.

Part (c) illustrates the use of a *list* also made of two integers and a string. Note the change in syntax (i.e., use of square brackets instead of parentheses). Lists are like tuples (e.g., you can multiply the list by a number and obtain another list) except that lists are *mutable*. This means that you can selectively change elements of a list. For instance, you can set the first element to "z." Lists are therefore more flexible than tuples.

Dictionaries are a very powerful and frequently used data type. Part (d) shows how to use the dictionary data structure to map English words onto French words. You access the French words by using the corresponding English words. X is first initialized to a dictionary whose *key* is dog and *value* chien, etc (note the use of curly brackets and simple quotes). Note that the command is extended to more than one line because it is too large for the column in Exhibit 6. A third element is then added (with cat as a key and chat as a value). Contrary to strings, tuples and lists which are ordered sets of elements, dictionaries are not inherently ordered. Instead of using indices to access elements of a dictionary, you access elements with the keys of any type (e.g., integers, strings, tuples). Similar to lists, you can reassign new values to the elements of a dictionary (e.g., you can assign 'z' to the entry *cat*). In other words, like lists, dictionaries are mutable.

The essential characteristics of the string, tuple, list and dictionary are summarized in Table 1.

In essence, (1) dictionaries and lists are mutable, but tuples and strings are not; (2) lists, tuples and strings are sequences, but dictionaries are not; (3) dictionaries, lists, and tuples can contain different types of elements, whereas strings only contain characters.

Conditionals

The preceding examples have portrayed programming as the execution of lines of code, one after the other in a linear fashion. Although some simple programs might be organized this way, most programs contain instructions to be executed in some circumstances, and avoided in others, depending on a test. If the test is passed, then the corresponding lines of code can be executed. For instance, you could design rules to determine the gender of Spanish names: *if* the name ends with

Table 1. Comparing four data types in Python: string, tuple, list and dictionary

Data type	Is mutable	Is a sequence	Restrictions on values
String	No	Yes	Characters only
Tuple	No	Yes	None
List	Yes	Yes	None
Dictionary	Yes	No	None

the letter *o* (like in *Mario*), *then* the person is a male, but *if* the name ends with the letter *a* (like in *Maria*), *then* the person is a female, etc. Such *if-then* sequences are called *conditionals* (see the examples in Exhibit 7).

Part (a) shows a sequence of tests for the value of X. First X is assigned the value 2. The first conditional assigns the value 0 to X if X is equal to 1 (note the use of the equality operator = =, different from the assignment operator). The two other conditionals test whether X is smaller, or greater than 1. Part (b) shows the same program but where X is initialized to 1, instead of 2. Part (c) uses the *logical operators* (and, or, not). The first conditional checks whether X is equal to 1 and Y is greater than 3. The second conditional checks whether X is equal to 1 or Y is greater than 3. The third conditional checks whether it is true that Y is not greater than 3.

Iterations

Programs are especially helpful when they repeat operations a great number of times. For instance, imagine that you have to count the number of persons who have a disyllabic name in the telephone directory. One could easily write a program that reads the directory one entry at a time, checks whether the name is disyllabic and increments a counter if that is the case. *Iterations* are one way to repeat lines of code in a program. Recall that Exhibit 1 involved pseudo-code that iterated through the lines of a document and translated each line. Part (a) in Exhibit 8 first shows how to iterate through the characters of a string. Note the use of a for ... in ...: syntax.

We can also iterate through the elements of a list, using the same syntax. Part (b) shows how to iterate through a dictionary. The first two for ... in ...: statements return the keys of the dictionary (i.e., *dog* and *cat*), whereas the third statement returns the values (i.e., *chien* and *chat*). The last statement returns tuples with both keys and values.

Exhibit 7. Examples of conditionals in Python

```
(a)
>>> X = 2
>>> if X == 1: X = 0
>>> X
2
>>> if X < 1: X = 3
>>> X
2
>>> if X > 1: X = 4
>>> X
4
(b)
>>> X = 1
>>> if X == 1: X = 0
>>> X
0
>>> if X < 1: X = 3
>>> X
3
>>> if X > 1: X = 4
>>> X
4
(c)
>>> X = 1
>>> Y = 2
>>> if X == 1 and Y > 3: print 'a'
>>> if X == 1 or Y > 3: print 'b'
'b'
>>> if not Y > 3: print 'c'
'c'
```

Part (c) uses a while loop to iterate through the elements of a list. The index i is initialized to 0. Then, while i is less than 3, we keep printing the ith element of X and then increment i by one. The while statement actually contains two commands, separated by a semicolon (;). Semicolons are used when several commands are on the same line. The while statement has been repeated in Part (c), this time with one command per line. In that case, it is not necessary to use the semicolon. However,

it is now necessary to use some indentation in order to tell Python that these commands are to be executed "inside that while loop." This is called a nested structure. You can indent your code with the Tab key on your keyboard.

Functions

Functions are key components of programming abstraction. A function is like a mini-program which you can invoke at any time in your program. For example, you might need to compute the average daily balance of a million customers. This can be easily achieved by using a function for calculating the average for one customer. This function can then be used a million times; once for each customer. In another example, the rule for determining the gender of Spanish name could be placed in a function called gender(). When you needed to apply the rules to a name, you would call this function and retrieve the gender of a person. All the details associated with the rules to determine a person's gender would be conveniently hidden from you. The organization of your code would be improved, thereby allowing you to navigate through it with ease. Functions makes it easier to engage in the incremental programming approach described earlier (see Exhibit 2). For instance, one could implement the example in Exhibit 2, by writing all the code except for a translate() function which would be fleshed out last. This approach is illustrated in the implementation section of the NLP project in Part II.

Another advantage of functions is that you reuse functions programmed by other people or write your own if you cannot find one to fit your needs. For instance, the type() command used Exhibit 3 is a function already defined in Python (i.e., you do not have to program it yourself). In further section, we will explain how you can build your own functions.

Functions have *parameters* and *return values*. Return values are the values that functions generates and can which can be reused inside the

Exhibit 8. Examples of iterations in Python

```
(a)
>>> X = "abc"
>>> for z in X: print z
a
b
c
>>> X = [1,2,3]
>>> for z in X: print z
1
2
3
(b)
>>> X = {}
>>> X['dog'] = 'chien'
>>> X['cat'] = 'chat'
>>> for z in X: print z
dog
cat
>>> for z in X.keys(): print z
dog
cat
>>> for z in X.values(): print z
chien
chat
>>> for z in X.items(): print z
('dog', 'chien')
('cat', 'chat')
(c)
>>> X = [1,2,3]
>>> i = 0
>>> while(i < 3): print X[i]; i=i+1
1
2
3
>>> i = 0
>>> while(i < 3):
        print X[i]
        i = i + 1
1
2
3
```

program. For instance, type(123) returns the string <type 'int'>. You could capture that string by assigning it to a variable: x = type(123). Parameters specify how you can use a function. The type() function has an "object" parameter. One could formulate this by writing type(object). In our previous example, we decided to inquiry about the type of the number 123, by calling the function type() with 123 as an *argument*: type(123). We call 123 an argument because it is the specific values that we decide to assign to the "object" parameter of the function.

Exhibit 9 illustrates the notion of functions that are available in an external library (i.e., outside of your code). Defining your own functions is sometimes tricky, and it is often a significant time-saver to reuse functions developed by other programmers who gave them careful thought. The library we are using in this example is NLTK. The example was inspired by the second chapter of Bird et al (2009). It illustrates how to load a sample of the Gutenberg corpus (http://www.gutenberg.org). The Gutenberg project makes available over 30,000 free electronic books (eBooks). It was started in the 1970s by Michael Hart and includes books like Alice in Wonderland (by Lewis Carroll), Moby Dick (by Herman Melville), Roget's Thesaurus, the Devil's dictionary (by Ambrose Bierce), and the Bible. The example has also been built step by step – from Part (a) to Part (h) – in order to illustrate the incremental approach to programming, hereby stimulating you to adopt a similar attitude when you repeat the examples, play with the code, or work on a programming project of your own. Part (i) shows the final result. In Part (i), comments (in italics) have been added to the program to help you understand what the code is doing. Comments must start with a # sign (called a hash, pound, or number sign). This sign tells Python not to execute the statement that follows. It is a good practice to put a reasonable amount of comments in your code in order to facilitate its readability and maintenance.

NLTK is designed as a Python module – a resource which is not inherently provided with Python but can be imported at will. To import the NLTK module, we use the import statement at the beginning of the code. But before being able to import the module you need to download and install it on your machine (see the companion website for instructions). In Part (a), there is an import statement to load the real division function (pay attention to the use of double underscores). Depending on the version of Python you use you may not need that statement. In some versions of Python, the division sign (/) does not behave like the conventional division operator, and that statement is therefore necessary. A second import statement loads NLTK. Finally a third import statement refers to the NLTK sample of Gutenberg corpus.

In Part (b), to make sure that NLTK knows where to find the corpus, we set a path variable, and we add it to the list of paths called nltk.data. path which is provided by NLTK (Part b). To add a new path to the list, we turn the path (a string data type) into a list, by surrounding it with brackets ([ ]). The + operator becomes in this context a concatenation operator and adds the two lists together to form a larger list. The specific path you will use will depend on where you decided to install the NLTK corpora. Please see the website for further instruction regarding the confusing topic of system path. It is not particularly complicated to understand, but it might be intimidating for the novice.

In Part (c), we iterate through all files of the corpus, retrieving the name of each file (e.g., carroll-alice.txt, Shakespeare-hamlet.txt) in a list with the fileids() function. That code is interesting because, if it executes properly, not only can we see all the files in the corpus, but we also know that we have access to the corpus through the NLTK module! Once again, this illustrates the incremental approach to programming. When you develop your code for the first time, it is preferable to ensure that the basic elements of your code function properly before engaging in

more sophisticated operations. Pay close attention to the fact that we did not have to define the fileids() function; it is provided by NLTK, and we are happy to use it! Finally, note that all of this is done on one line. This is not practical in more complex situations, so a more readable version of the code is presented in Part (d).

As you may have noticed, the filename being printed is contained in a variable called id. We could have called it filename, like in Part (e). The choice does not really matter so far as we are consistent with ourselves (see a Python introduction for more coverage on that topic). However, the name fileids() is fixed, and we must use it if we want to invoke that function.

Inside the loop presented in Parts (c)-(e), more interesting operations than printing can occur. In part (f), we use the raw() function of the Gutenberg corpus to retrieve all the characters of the file in a string. We provide the result of that function to another function which, this time, is built into Python (i.e., is not part of NLTK): the len() function (short for *length*). In this context, len() counts the number of characters (i.e., the length of the string in characters). That count is then assigned to the NC variable, whose content is finally printed. The len() function is very useful and flexible function which will adapt its behavior to different data types. For instance, for a list A, len(A) will count the number of elements in A.

Parts (g) and (h) represent two more steps in our incremental programming journey. In (g) we retrieve the words through the words() function. After counting the number of words, and dividing the number of characters by the number of words, you get the average size of words in terms of characters. In Part (h) we retrieve the number of sentences through the sents() function, and compute the average size of sentence in terms of words. Three values are then printed. Pay attention to the commas in the print statement. These commas serve to separate the three values within a tuple. What is therefore being printed is a tuple. Again, play around with the code (e.g., compute

Exhibit 9. Use of external functions present in the NLTK module

```
(a)
from __future__ import division
import nltk
from nltk.corpus import gutenberg
(b)
path = "C:/test/data/nltk"
nltk.data.path = [path] + nltk.data.path
(c)
for id in gutenberg.fileids(): print id
(d)
 for id in gutenberg.fileids():
       print id
(e)
for filename in gutenberg.fileids():
       print filename
(f)
for id in gutenberg.fileids():
        NC = len(gutenberg.raw(id))
        print NC
(g)
for id in gutenberg.fileids():
        NC = len(gutenberg.raw(id))
        NW = len(gutenberg.words(id))
        print NC / NW
(h)
for id in gutenberg.fileids():
        NC = len(gutenberg.raw(id))
        NW = len(gutenberg.words(id))
        NS = len(gutenberg.sents(id))
        AWL = NC / NW
        ASL = NW / NS
       print AWL, ASL, id
(i)
# import
from __future__ import division
import nltk
from nltk.corpus import gutenberg
# path
path = "C:/test/data/nltk"
nltk.data.path = [path] + nltk.data.path
# for each file in the corpus, get its id
for id in gutenberg.fileids():
```

continued on following page

Exhibit 9. Continued

```
# get number of characters
NC = len(gutenberg.raw(id))

# get number of words
NW = len(gutenberg.words(id))

# get number of sentences
NS = len(gutenberg.sents(id))

# average word length (in characters)
AWL = NC / NW

# average sentence length (in words)
ASL = NW / NS
# print on the screen
print AWL, ASL, id
```

the average size of sentence in terms of characters) to gain further insight.

Imagine the time you are saving by using functions to access text files and information without having to deal with the difficult aspects of file manipulation, tokenization (i.e., character and word recognition), and sentence splitting. As is apparent in Chapter XXX of this book, such operations are time consuming. Part (i) shows the final code.

What would you do if you had to repeat the same operations for other corpora? For instance, you may want to repeat the exercise for the book of Genesis, translated in several languages, also available through NLTK. Would it not be annoying to rewrite the same lines of code? The good news is that you can embed any part of your program in a function and make it generic enough so that you can reuse it in multiple contexts (i.e., Gutenberg, the book of Genesis, etc.). Part (a) in Exhibit 10 shows precisely how to do that by creating a getCorpusInfo() function.

A function definition starts with a def keyword, then the name of the function (getCorpusInfo), followed by parentheses and, possibly one or more

parameters. In the case of getCorpusInfo() there is only one parameter (corpus) which stands for the name of the corpus (whatever it is) that is going to be used when the function is invoked. The def statement ends with a colon (:), and the rest of the program is similar to Exhibit 9 with the exception that, first, there is another layer of indentation; second, we removed the comments; and, third, we replaced the name gutenberg, by the more generic name corpus. When the function has been defined, you simply need to import the corpora, and then use the getCorpusInfo() function with the name of your corpora passed as an argument to the function (e.g., getCorpusInfo(Genesis)).

An excerpt of the result of applying the function is displayed in Exhibit 11. On Exhibit 11, you can see there that the average word length of the texts from the Gutenberg corpus does not vary very much (i.e., between 4 and 5 for every line), as explained in Bird et al (2009) because they all are English texts and the English language exhibits this property. When you explore the Genesis corpus, you realize that the variability increases, probably because the corpus contains texts written in different languages.

Exhibit 10. Defining your own functions

```
(a)
# import
from __future__ import division
import nltk
from nltk.corpus import (gutenberg, genesis)
# path
path = "C:/test/data/nltk"
nltk.data.path = [path] + nltk.data.path
# my function
def getCorpusInfo(corpus):
        for id in corpus.fileids():
                NC = len(corpus.raw(id))
                NW = len(corpus.words(id))
                NS = len(corpus.sents(id))
                AWL = NC / NW
                ASL = NW / NS
                print AWL, ASL, id
# get information about each corpus
getCorpusInfo(gutenberg)
getCorpusInfo(genesis)
(b)
# import
from __future__ import division
import nltk
from nltk.corpus import (gutenberg, genesis)
# path
path = "C:/test/data/nltk"
nltk.data.path = [path] + nltk.data.path
# my functions
def getCorpusInfo(corpus):
        for id in corpus.fileids():
                getTextInfo(id, corpus)
def getTextInfo(id, corpus):
        NC = len(corpus.raw(id))
        NW = len(corpus.words(id))
        NS = len(corpus.sents(id))
        AWL = NC / NW
        ASL = NW / NS
        print AWL, ASL, id
# get information about each corpus
getCorpusInfo(gutenberg)
getCorpusInfo(genesis)
getTextInfo("austen-emma.txt", gutenberg)
getTextInfo("french.txt", genesis)
```

Exhibit 11. Using functions and NLTK to analyze different corpora

```
>>> getCorpusInfo(Gutenberg)
4.60990921232 18.3701193317 austen-emma.txt
4.74979372727 23.6841978287 austen-persuasion.txt
4.75378595242 21.8144838213 austen-sense.txt
4.28688156382 33.5843551657 bible-kjv.txt
 (...)
>>> getCorpusInfo(genesis)
4.3676838531 30.6183310534 english-kjv.txt
4.28260770872 19.7374551971 english-web.txt
5.94474169742 15.0834879406 finnish.txt
3.44761394102 40.367965368 swedish.txt
```

The main difference between Part (a) and Part (b) is that we made a subpart of the original getCorpusInfo() function, a function in its own right, and called it getTextInfo(). By doing so, we modularized our code and increased its flexibility. For instance, by separating a getCorpusInfo() function and a getTextInfo() function, we can call getTextInfo() and therefore obtain information on only one text (instead of information on all texts). Moreover, when we are working on the code, we may modify one function without having to alter the other one.

Text File Input/Output

After going through all the examples presented so far, you most likely have learned important concepts but all the output which has been produced on the screen is now gone, or waiting for you to be manually copied in a text file, etc. Would it not be simpler if you could save the output information

Table 2. A sample from the Devil's Dictionary

BEG, v.	To ask for something with an earnestness proportioned to the belief that it will not be given.
DENTIST, n.	A prestidigitator who, putting metal into your mouth, pulls coins out of your pocket.
LANGUAGE, n.	The music with which we charm the serpents guarding another's treasure.
LIBERTY, n.	On of Imagination's most precious possessions.
MEDAL, n.	A small metal disk given as a reward for virtues, attainments, or services more or less authentic.
NEPOTISM, n.	Appointing your grandmother to office for the good of the party.
PAINTING, n.	The art of protecting flat surfaces from the weather and exposing them to the critic.
PLAN, v.t.	To bother about the best method of accomplishing an accidental result.
SCRIBBLER, n.	A professional writer whose views are antagonistic to one's own.
TRUTHFUL, adj.	Dumb and illiterate.

directly to a file? Similarly, what would you do if you wanted to open a text file, read it, process its contents, and save it under another name? These steps are the landmarks of many NLP programs which primarily handle text files. To illustrate these operations, you may for instance use the text displayed in Table 2.

The text presented in Table 2 is composed of ten entries extracted from the Devil's Dictionary by Ambrose Bierce. Type each entry on a separate line in a text file and save the file as dictionary. txt in the data folder. Or simply, copy and paste these lines from the companion website into a text file.

Part (a) in Exhibit 12 shows how to print the objects in your data directory (i.e., files and folders). There is an import statement for the os (i.e., operating system) module. The listdir() function returns a list of objects found in the path (p) passed as an argument. After executing that code, you should at least see dictionary.txt in the list displayed on the screen. In part (b) we then add the filename dictionary.txt to the path. We import the fileinput module (a module to read and save files). Then, for each line in the file, we print the length of the line (in number of characters). Finally the input file is closed with the close() function. In Part (c), two paths are set, one for the input (dictionary.txt) and one for the output (dictionary. out.txt). The built-in open() function specifies that a file must get ready to receive information in appending mode (i.e., the file will add text incrementally). For each line, we compute the length (in characters), print the length of the line and the line itself to the output file. The length of the line and the line are separated by a tabulation (represented by a tab sign \t). Finally we close the input and the output.

This short example of file operations concludes Part I. Although Part I was about programming basics, we have already laid a foundation for solving NLP problems. Part II builds on this foundation by concretely showing how to conduct an NLP project.

Exhibit 12. Processing text files in Python

```
(a)
# set path
p = "C:/test/data"
# import
import os
# for each object
for x in os.listdir(p):
        print x
(b)
# set path
p = "C:/test/data"
p = p + '/dictionary.txt'
# import
import fileinput
# for each line
for li in fileinput.input(p):
        L = str(len(li))
        print L + ":: " + li
# close
fileinput.close()
(c)
# set path
p = "C:/test/data"
p_in = p + '/dictionary.txt'
p_out = p + '/dictionary.out.txt'
# import
import fileinput
# open file for saving
out = open(p_out, 'a')
# for each line
for line in fileinput.input(p_in):
        L = str(len(line))
        print line
        info = L + "\t" + line
        out.write(info)
# close
fileinput.close()
out.close()
```

A STEP-BY-STEP EXAMPLE

The chapter so far has been focused on programming basics. The section on Functions in Part I included an example of reuse of resources (NLTK) within a Python program (see Exhibits 9 and 10). That application was however not motivated by any specific NLP requirements. In other words, we were not in a situation in which we had to solve a particular problem. In this section, we describe an actual NLP problem and a possible solution. This problem and its solution have been chosen to offer a reasonable degree of complexity to both the novice and the more advanced programmer. The companion website includes other problems and solutions with various degrees of complexity and implemented in different programming languages (e.g., Python, Perl, and Java).

The Problem of Predicting the Speed of Lexical Access

The problem we will tackle in this section is fairly complicated, and we will only propose one possible – and easy to understand – solution. Humans have the remarkable ability to learn and use language. When they read a text they need to access the meaning of words in order to construct the meaning of sentences. Contrary to programming languages, with unambiguous semantics, natural languages contain numerous semantic ambiguities. For instance, a word like *page* is ambiguous in that it can refer to the side of a sheet of paper, as well as to a young person employed to do errands. Humans are usually very good at determining which meaning of a word is intended in a given text by examining the context surrounding the words.

Although humans seamlessly perform semantic disambiguation activities, the underlying cognitive processes employed for this task are not fully understood. Actually, even a seemingly simple step such as recognizing that a word is known (i.e., to access it in the mental lexicon) is

still the topic of much research. Psycholinguistic experiments have demonstrated that it takes some time (several hundred milliseconds) to decide whether written words are known or not, and that response time is influenced by the different meanings of the words. In such experiments, words are presented on a computer screen, one at a time. In typical experiments, the participant has to decide whether a stimulus word is an existing word (e.g., *page*) or if it is a non-word (e.g., *gepa*), by pressing one of two keys on the keyboard. The number of milliseconds elapsed between the time the word (or non-word) is displayed and the time the key is pressed is called the response time, and is our primary measure of interest.

Many useful insights have been gleaned with this rather simple experimental protocol. For instance, Rodd, Gaskell and Marslen-Wilson (2002) found out that it takes on average longer to recognize ambiguous words (i.e., to establish that they are existing words) like *page* than unambiguous words like *load*. In one of their experiments, they operationalized ambiguous words as ones that had more than one entry in the Wordsmyth Dictionary (Parks et al., 1998). For instance, the word *page* has two different entries whereas the word *load* has only one entry.

Moreover, Rodd et al (2002) demonstrated that the number of senses of the words also had an impact on the speed of lexical access. By senses they referred to all the meanings that a word could have, whether these meanings were semantically related or not. For instance, in the Wordsmyth Dictionary, the first entry of the word *page* (the "sheet of paper") corresponds to a variety of senses including the content of the paper, an instance from the past (like in "a page of history"), the act of turning pages, etc. Similarly, the second entry of the word *page* (the "young person") has several senses including a young person who attends to a king or the act of calling someone via electronic communication (i.e., with a pager). Most interestingly, they found out that the number of senses has a reverse effect on lexical access time: while more ambiguity slowed down response time, more senses sped it up.

Several psychological accounts attempt to explain the impact of ambiguity and number of senses on response times (see Rodd et al, 2002). What matters for our limited NLP exercise, however, is the information about ambiguity and number of senses can be used to automatically predict response time. Such an automated application could be used to design experimental material, develop more efficient advertising campaigns. It can even find use in applications aimed at assessing text difficulty (e.g., Graesser, McNamara, Louwerse, & Cai, 2004). Although many more factors could potentially influence the ease of lexical access (Rayner, 1998; Rodd et al, 2002), semantic ambiguity and number of senses seem to be two important factors to take into account. For the sake of this example we define our NLP problem as follows: given any word, estimate its ambiguity, number of senses, and response time. The next section offers a simple solution to this problem.

Designing a Solution

The first question of course is *what knowledge and what computations shall we use to do the job?* Our problem actually involves three sub problems. The first one pertains to determining the ambiguity of a word. The second one concerns counting the number of senses of the word. The third one deals with determining the response time, on the basis of ambiguity and number of senses. For the first sub-problem, we know from the previous description of Rodd et al's (2002) experiment that they have used the online Wordsmyth dictionary to retrieve the number of entries associated with a given word; this is their measure of ambiguity. So we need some way to extract information from the online Wordsmyth dictionary. Although one could imagine accessing the online Wordsmyth dictionary from within the program, it is not convenient (e.g., when an internet connection is not available). Moreover, accessing online resources through artificial means (i.e., web crawlers etc) is usually discouraged by developers of online services. Hence, we decided to download a freely accessible dictionary which had a similar structure to the Wordsmyth dictionary. The dictionary we chose to use is the GNU version of the collaborative international dictionary of English, presented in the Extensible Markup Language (GCIDE_XML; Dyck, 2002).

For the second sub-problem, among other things, Rodd et al (2002) relied on WordNet (Miller, 1995). WordNet is a widely used online resource and was designed to serve as a lexical resource that was organized according to the principles underlying human semantic memory (the organization of words in terms of meaning). Moreover, WordNet is organized in terms of senses – whether they are semantically related or not – and contains information that is not readily available in conventional dictionaries such as the Wordsmyth dictionary or the GCIDE. Finally, it is also accessible in Python through the NLTK module (Bird et al, 2009). These advantages make WordNet look like an ideal candidate for a solution written in Python. A broad overview of our problem and its solution is depicted in Figure 1.

Pseudo-code for the general procedure used in the program to produce the number of entries, the number of senses, and the predicted response time is presented in Exhibit 13.

To test our program we plan to read a text file containing the words from Rodd et al's (2002) Experiment 2. For evaluation purposes, the text file will also indicate whether the words are ambiguous or not, and whether they have many senses or not, as indicated in Rodd et al's (2002) Appendix B. Table 3 displays the first five lines of this file. This information is loaded in a dictionary W. For each word w in W, the number of entries of w is first determined by consulting the GCIDE. Based on the number of entries in the GCIDE and a preset "ambiguity threshold" we decided if w is ambiguous or not. The number of

Figure 1. General representation of the problem and its solution

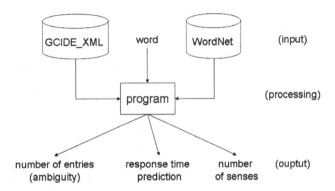

senses is then retrieved from WordNet. This information, coupled with a preset "sense threshold" is used to decide if w has few or many senses. These two pieces of information are used to predict the mean response time for w. These findings are saved in the main dictionary W. When all words have been processed, W is saved to a file, and the quality of the obtained classification (ambiguous vs. unambiguous; few senses vs. many senses) is evaluated by comparing it to results reported in Rodd et al (2002).

The pseudo-code of Exhibit 13 left out some essential information such as the threshold values and how to compute the mean response time from ambiguity and number of senses. We turn to Rodd et al's (2002) experiment for this data. The authors defined ambiguous words as ones with two or more entries in the Wordsmyth dictionary. Unfortunately, the GCIDE has more entries than the Wordsmyth dictionary, which will likely lead to an overestimation of the number of ambiguous words when applying Rodd et al's (2002) rule.

Exhibit 13. Pseudo-code describing the general procedure of the program

```
Load all the words into a dictionary W.
For each word w in W,
          # Pseudo-code to obtain ambiguity
          Open the page of GCIDE where you can find the word w.
          Count the number of entries for the word w.
          If that number is greater or equal to an "ambiguity threshold",
                    the word w is ambiguous; otherwise it is unambiguous.

          Close the page of the GCIDE.
          # Pseudo-code to get number of senses
          Retrieve the number of senses in WordNet for the word w.
          If that number is greater or equal to a "sense threshold",
                    the word w has many senses; otherwise it has few senses.
          Predict the mean response time of the word w.
          Add the new information about the word w to the dictionary W.
Evaluate the quality of the classification.
Write the information stored in W to a file.
```

Table 3. Five first lines of input to the program; data is from Rodd et al's (2002) Experiment 2

Word	Ambiguous (1 = yes ; 0 = no)	Has many senses (1 = yes ; 0 = no)
ash	1	0
duck	1	1
heap	0	0
roll	0	1

For this reason, the optimal value for our threshold will have to be estimated from the data. This task will be tackled in the *Implementing the Solution* section.

Similarly, Rodd et al (2002) used a procedure to determine whether a word has many senses or only a few. That rule however was not made fully explicit, and relied on both the Wordsmyth dictionary and WordNet. For the sake of simplicity we decided to use a simple threshold based on the number of senses extracted from WordNet, and estimated this threshold from the data similar to the ambiguity threshold.

The predicted response times correspond to the mean response times of Rodd et al's (2002) Experiment 2. The "prediction" is simply the assignment of one of five mean response times, depending on the nature of the word: 587 ms for ambiguous words with few senses, 578 ms for ambiguous words with many senses, 586 ms for unambiguous words with few senses, 567 ms for unambiguous words with many senses and 659 ms for non-words.

Implementing the Solution

The following description is a step-by-step implementation of the program. That description involves nine steps. You will find the corresponding nine versions of the script on the companion website. This step-by-step implementation follows the incremental approach to programming which has been advocated at the beginning of

this chapter. You should be able to execute each step of the program in the Python interface and analyze its behavior.

Step 1 lays down the general structure of the program (see Exhibit 14). Let's read it from bottom to top. The main program is located at the bottom of the code. It calls four functions (load_words(), process_words(), evaluate_results(), and save_results()) that we need to be defined. The load_words() function will load the input material in the format specified in Table 3. The process_words() function will generate the results we attempt to achieve. The evaluate_results() function will evaluate those results, and the save_results() function will save them to a file. Above the main program, a *functions definitions* section contains place holders for these definitions, using the pass keyword to tell Python to ignore these incomplete definitions. We will implement these functions one by one, following the natural progression from the input to the output. A *parameter* section will contain data which the user of the program will be able to change at will (e.g., specifying other values for the path to the input data file). The words_input_path variable contains the path to the input material, it is used as an argument of the load_words() function to load the desired material. The *import* section is still empty but will contain import statements as needed.

Step 2 consists of implementing the load_words() function (see Exhibit 15). Since it uses the fileinput Python module, we need to add an import statement accordingly. This function initializes a dictionary called W, and stores information about each word, using the word as a key in the dictionary W. More detailed comments about this function are available in the function itself (Exhibit 15).

In step 3, we implement the process_words() function (see Exhibit 16). It will apply five other functions (for which we create place holders), for each word in W. We will now implement each of them, one at a time.

Exhibit 14. The general structure of the program

```
# import
# parameters
words_input_path = "C:/test/data/Rodd_et_al_2002_experiment_2.txt"
# functions definitions
def load_words(input_path): pass
def process_words(): pass
def evaluate_results(): pass
def save_results(output_path): pass
# main program
print "--- START"
words = load_words(words_input_path)
process_words()
evaluate_results()
save_results(output_path)
print "--- END"
```

Exhibit 15. The load_words() function

```
# import
import fileinput
# parameters
(...)
def load_words(input_path):
    W = {} # initialization of the dictionary
    i = 0 # counter used to skip the first line of the file because it is a
header
    for line in fileinput.input(input_path):
        i = i + 1
        if i == 1: continue # if this is the first line, skip it (i.e., con-
tinue to the next line)
        line = line.strip() # remove the white character at the beginning and
end of the line
        information = line.split("\t") # split the file, using the tab as a
separator
        (word, ambiguous, many_senses) = information # assign its elements to
distinct variables
        W[word] = {} # initialize a dictionary in the dictionary with that
word as a key
        W[word]["ambiguous"] = int(ambiguous) # we record the value, convert-
ing it to an integer
        W[word]["many_senses"] = int(many_senses)
    fileinput.close()
    return W # we return the dictionary
```

Exhibit 16. The process_words() function

```
def process_words():
    for word in W:
        print word
        retrieve_number_of_entries(word)
        determine_word_ambiguity(word)
        retrieve_number_of_senses(word)
        determine_if_word_has_many_senses(word)
        predict_mean_response_time(word)
def retrieve_number_of_entries(word): pass
def determine_word_ambiguity(word): pass
def retrieve_number_of_senses(word): pass
def determine_if_word_has_many_senses(word): pass
def predict_mean_response_time(word): pass
```

Exhibit 17. The retrieve_number_of_entries() function

```
# parameters
GCIDE_xml_path = "C:/Resources/Various/P/Programming/NLP/chapter/data/gcide_
xml"
(...)
def retrieve_number_of_entries(word):
    target = "<hw>"+word+"</hw>" # the target is the word with HTML tags
    target = target.upper() # we convert to upper case letters for normaliza-
tion purposes
    first_letter = word[0] # we extract the first letter of the word
    path = GCIDE_xml_path + "/gcide_" + first_letter + ".xml" # define the
file to the page
    entries = 0 # we initialize the counter for number of entries
    for line in fileinput.input(path):
        line = line.upper() # to upper case letter, again for normalization
purposes
        line = line.replace('`', '') # ` characters are removed
        line = line.replace('"', '') # " characters are removed
        line = line.replace('*', '') # * characters are removed
        if target in line: entries = entries + 1 # if we find an entry, we
count it
    fileinput.close()
    W[word]["number_of_entries"] = entries # record the number of entries
```

In step 4, the retrieve_number_of_entries() function is implemented (see Exhibit 17). The path to the folder containing the GCIDE is defined in the *parameters* section. The parentheses *(...)* are not part of the program but indicate that a portion of code has been skipped. The function will be looking for the word surrounded by two HTML tags (<hw>, </hw>), which is the way separate entries are distinguished in the GCIDE. Since the dictionary is distributed on separate files (one for each letter of the alphabet), the first letter of the word is extracted in order to identify the file in which the word must be searched. The file is then opened and read line by line, while counting the number of times the word is encountered.

One will note that this is a time consuming operation, which will be unduly repeated for each word. For instance, a same dictionary page will be read twice for two words with the same first letter. Our function is more straightforward from an instructional point of view and could be replaced by a more computationally efficient one. A standard approach would be to read all words into a dictionary similar to W and store it for later reuse.

In step 5, the determine_word_ambiguity() function is developed (see Exhibit 18). It stores

Exhibit 18. The determine_word_ambiguity() function

```
# parameters
ambiguity_threshold = 4
(...)
def determine_word_ambiguity(word):
    if W[word]["number_of_entries"] >= ambiguity_threshold:
        W[word]["predicted_ambiguity"] = 1
    else:
        W[word]["predicted_ambiguity"] = 0
```

Exhibit 19. The retrieve_number_of_senses() and determine_if_word_has_many_senses() functions

```
# import
import fileinput, nltk
# parameters
NLTKp = "C:/test/data/nltk"
nltk.data.path = [NLTKp] + nltk.data.path
senses_threshold = 9
(...)
def retrieve_number_of_senses(word):
    number_of_senses = len(nltk.corpus.wordnet.synsets(word))
    W[word]["number_of_senses"] = number_of_senses
def determine_if_word_has_many_senses(word):
    if W[word]["number_of_senses"] >= senses_threshold:
        W[word]["predicted_many_senses"] = 1
    else:
        W[word]["predicted_many_senses"] = 0
```

a value of 1 for words whose number of entries are greater than or equal to a specified threshold.

In step 6, the retrieve_number_of_senses() and determine_if_word_has_many_senses() functions are implemented. The *import* section is modified to import the NLTK module. The *parameters* section is modified to include the path to the NLTK resources. The retrieve_number_of_senses() function simply counts the number of senses retrieved from WordNet. The senses for any given word are accessed by NLTK through the synsets() function which returns a list of senses. The size of that list is then calculated by the len() function (See Exhibit 19).

In step 7, the predict_mean_response_time() function is implemented. It simply assigns the values (in milliseconds) which are defined in the RT dictionary in the *parameters* section. The values of RT come from Rodd et al's (2002) Exhibit 7. A word which has a number of senses

equal to zero is considered as a non-word and therefore assigned the response time associated to non-words (See Exhibit 20).

In step 8, we implement the evaluate_results() function (see Exhibit 21). It starts by building six lists, A, B, A1, A2, B1, and B2 with the codes corresponding to our classification as well as to the data of Rodd et al (2002). The lists A and B are made of tuples – one tuple per word – where each tuple consists of two integers (0 or 1). Each tuple is therefore either (0,0), (1,0), (0,1) or (1,1). The first integer specifies whether the word was classified as ambiguous (1) or not (0), whereas the second integer represents whether the word was classified has having many (1) or few (0) senses. The procedure we have decided to use to build these lists of tuples employs the *list comprehension* feature of Python. It is essentially a device to build lists in a more concise way. Basically, we iterate through W for each word w, and

Exhibit 20. The predict_mean_response_time() function

```
# parameters
RT = {}
RT["ambiguous_few_senses"] = 587
RT["ambiguous_many_senses"] = 578
RT["unambiguous_few_senses"] = 586
RT["unambiguous_many_senses"] = 567
RT["nonwords"] = 659
(...)
def predict_mean_response_time(word):
    if W[word]["number_of_senses"] == 0:
        W[word]["predicted_response_time"] = RT["nonwords"]
    else:
        ambiguity = "unambiguous"
        senses = "few_senses"
        if W[word]["predicted_ambiguity"] == 1:
            ambiguity = "ambiguous"

        if W[word]["predicted_many_senses"] == 1:
            senses = "many_senses"
        W[word]["predicted_response_time"] = RT[ambiguity + "_" + senses]
```

build a tuple with the ambiguity value and the sense value for w. All these tuples are then put in a list.

The list A corresponds to the classification made by our program whereas the list B corresponds to the classification of Rodd et al (2002). We then compare these two classifications through a confusion_matrix() function. That function builds a confusion matrix through a function provided by NLTK (similar to the one displayed on Table 5). The percentage of correct responses is then computed. Finally, the matrix and the percentage are displayed on the screen. Note that at the time of the writing the operator division truncated the result of the division to an integer in the presence of integer operands (e.g., 7/2 would give 3 instead of the expected 2.5). In order to change that behavior it was necessary to add the from __future__ import division statement at the top of your file.

In order to evaluate the ambiguity classification separately from the sense classification we build four more lists: A1 and B1 for ambiguity classification and A2 and B2 for sense classification. These new lists are obtained by transferring the corresponding members of each tuple to separate lists, through the zip() function. The asterisk preceding the argument in that function (e.g., zip(*A)), is a way of telling Python to "unzip" the members of the tuples to separate lists. Confusions matrices are finally constructed for these two groups.

The two thresholds used in our program have been estimated by running the program with different values, and keeping the values corresponding to the best performance. Table 4 displays the proportion of correct classifications for ambiguity and senses for different values of the thresholds.

The best results were obtained with an ambiguity threshold of 4 and a sense threshold of 9. The combined classification in terms of ambiguity and sense resulting from using these two threshold values has a 69% accuracy. The confu-

Exhibit 21. The evaluate_results() and confusion_matrix() functions

```
# import
from __future__ import division
import fileinput, nltk
(...)
def evaluate_results():
    A = [(W[w]["predicted_ambiguity"],W[w]["predicted_many_senses"]) for w in
W]
    B = [(W[w]["ambiguous"],W[w]["many_senses"]) for w in W]
    confusion_matrix(A, B) # analyze our joint classification in terms of am-
biguity and senses

    A1, A2 = zip(*A)
    B1, B2 = zip(*B)
    confusion_matrix(A1, B1) # analyze our ambiguity classification
    confusion_matrix(A2, B2) # analyze our senses classification
def confusion matrix(reference, test):
    CM = nltk.ConfusionMatrix(reference, test) # build the confusion matrix
    percent_correct = CM._correct / len(reference)
    print CM
    print "correct = " + str(round(percent_correct, 2)) + " % "
```

Table 4. Proportions of correct classifications for ambiguity and senses depending on the threshold

Ambiguity		Senses	
Threshold	**Proportion of correct classifications**	**Threshold**	**Proportion of correct classifications**
2	0.55	6	0.77
3	0.61	7	0.86
4	**0.77**	8	0.88
5	0.68	**9**	**0.89**
6	0.6	10	0.84
7	0.54	11	0.75

sion matrix for this classification is displayed in Table 5. The rows contain the reference classifications (i.e., the ground truth) (Rodd et al, 2002). The columns contain classifications from our program. The cells in the diagonal correspond to correct classifications ($n = 88$), whereas the cells off the diagonal correspond to incorrect classification ($n = 40$).

It is important to note that this validation process is only a first step towards ensuring the quality of our program. If we were confident that the principles behind our program were worth pursuing, we could cross-validate it or validate it using another data set (see Manning & Schütze, 1999). However, an analysis of the classification errors made by our program might motivate us to try improving the resources or mechanisms that we use in order to reproduce Rodd et al's (2002) classification. Indeed, 75% of the errors were cases in which our program overestimated the number of entries or the number of senses compared to the reference. More precisely, about half of the errors were unambiguous words (as per the reference) classified as ambiguous words by our program.

Reusing a local copy of the Wordsmyth dictionary (instead of the GCIDE) would improve the results. Another method would be to filter out the senses which are too strongly related (and which might be counted as separate entries in the GCIDE). Finally, about a quarter of the errors were words with few senses (as per the reference) classified as having many senses by our program. Here again, it would be helpful to detect the senses which are too strongly related, in order to decrease the number of senses considered as distinct.

At step 9, the classification is saved to a file (see Exhibit 22). The os module is imported. The path to the output file is specified. A list with column names is specified. It contains the name of key variables in the W dictionary. In the save_results() function, the presence of the output is first

Table 5. Confusion matrix with ambiguity threshold = 4 and sense threshold = 9

			Our classification			
			Unambiguous		Ambiguous	
			Few-senses	**Many-senses**	**Few-senses**	**Many-senses**
Reference (Rodd et al, 2002)	**Unambiguous**	**Few-senses**	29	4	13	2
		Many-senses	1	23	1	6
	Ambiguous	**Few-senses**	2	0	16	4
		Many-senses	0	5	2	20

detected. The file is removed if it already exists. The column names are then added, separated by tabs (\t). Finally, the data in W is written to the file, one word per line.

Discussing the Example

What general lessons can we learn from this example? What general programming principles can we distinguish? We have tried to synthesize some of the lessons and principles:

1. Our program required us to transfer information from one structure to another (e.g., integer, string, list, tuple). We used variables to refer to these structures.
2. Programming is about saving some of your time, notably by reusing code written by other programmers. Hence our example was reusing features of the NLTK module (which was itself reusing the WordNet dictionary), and other modules related to the operating system (os) and the file system (fileinput).
3. There was a certain degree of organization in our program. Our examples isolated parts of the code in functions. Organization helps program maintenance, particularly for longer programs. The better your organization, the easiest the maintenance.
4. If you are novice at programming, the program might appear overwhelming to you. Although our example was developed step by step, and its development has been made apparent to facilitate its understanding, it will only make sense if you also examine it, step by step, actually try to reproduce the program, and attempt to see the connection between the code and its output. Understanding

Exhibit 22. The save_results() function

```
# import
from __future__ import division
import fileinput, nltk, os
(...)
# parameters
output_path = "C:/test/data/Rodd_et_al_2002_experiment_2_output.txt"
column_names = ["number_of_entries", "number_of_senses"]
column_names.append("predicted_ambiguity")
column_names.append("predicted_many_senses")
column_names.append("predicted_response_time")
(...)
def save_results(output_path):
    if os.path.exists(output_path): os.remove(output_path)
    out = open(output_path, 'a')
    out.write("word" + "\t" +  "\t".join(column_names))
    for word in W:
        data = "\n" + word
        for variable in column_names:
            data += "\t" + str(W[word][variable])
        out.write(data)
    out.close()
```

this connection will be greatly facilitated if you devote some of your time to learning the underlying programming language.

The program developed in this example was only one example of a possible solution to this problem. For the sake of achieving certain pedagogical goals, we chose quite a naive approach to a quite complex problem. One could have imagined other solutions (different algorithms), possibly using other packages, and with other languages. A good NLP project will be based on a clear understanding of the problem and knowledge of what tools can be employed for what purposes. It is therefore important to invest in understanding the theoretical aspects of programming and NLP, and their practical aspects (i.e., libraries, and other resources). These topics are briefly discussed in Part III.

HOW TO CONDUCT AN NLP PROGRAMMING PROJECT

Part I informed the novice programmers and programmers unfamiliar with Python to basic programming in Python. Part II illustrated how to solve a practical NLP problem with a Python program. Now you might be motivated to undertake a project on your own. This section aims at delivering helpful hints to start such an adventure.

So Which Language is Right for Me?

The choice of a programming language depends on the nature of the problem as well as on available resources like the programmer's experience, the time devoted to solve the problem and the access to software, documentation, corpora, etc. There are a multitude of programming languages to choose from. Programming languages vary in terms of vocabulary, syntax, availability of libraries, ease of learning, vitality of the supporting communities, etc. Choosing a language involves striking a

delicate balance between its advantages and disadvantages. For instance, computationally efficient (i.e., fast) languages like C++ might be particularly appropriate to solve certain NLP problems which require speed, but they might be more difficult to learn. Alternatively, you might not have much time to implement a solution so you use an available library, but that library does not include the most efficient program for your problem. Should you use the slower but ready-made existing program or write your own faster program from scratch? In other words, a programmer faces a problem of limited computational and human resources which must be allocated wisely.

The Right Tool for the Job at Hand

The programming languages option space might appear to be quite large. However, the option space is somewhat restricted by the fact that some languages were designed for specific kinds of problems (e.g., Matlab for numerical computing; R for statistical analysis; PHP for web applications; SQL for interfacing with databases, LaTeX as a document markup). In other words, one language might be more appropriate for a particular problem than another language, thereby reducing the option space. Thus perhaps the best and most useful analogy is to consider each language itself to be a kind of tool. A computing professional will know a dozen languages or more, and like a master craftsman will select the right tool for the job at hand.

In general, however, when considering a language to learn and use there are many issues to consider. These questions, in one way or another, all tie back into the question of time and efficiency. A language that is hard to learn and useful for only one project may not be the best choice, especially for a first language. But a professional who already knows several languages might make a different choice.

Questions to ask oneself before choosing a language for a particular task:

- What kind of user community exists for this language (books/forums/friends)?
- What libraries exist for this language that I can use in my work?
- What kinds of development tools are available for this language?
- How well does this language address the problems I am working on now or in the future?
- How easy is it to learn the language and the various other resources I need?

When learning anything, it is important to think about the resources available. Typically, more popular languages have better resources, but not always. Very specific languages might have virtually no user base, no recent books, and essentially no future. A major issue to consider, especially for first time language learners, is whether the language you are learning has useful libraries for the problems you are working on. As a first time language learner, it will take some time before you can create sophisticated libraries of your own. However, even a novice can use a library written by someone else (which you have already started to do by using NLTK in Parts I and II). Fortunately, there exist a broad set of tools/packages which can be used and re-used for a variety of NLP objectives. See the companion website for a table with pointers to these resources.

Finally, a point that is often overlooked by even professional programmers is the development tools available for a language. Many programmers start out using a text editor (e.g., notepad) and a compiler, and many stay with those tools their whole careers. However, as anyone who has ever used a well constructed IDE (integrated development environment) can tell you, an IDE with an integrated editor, compiler, debugger, support for refactoring, and built-in documentation can save tremendous amounts of time. The Python IDLE that you might have used while working out the examples of Parts I and II is just an example. Have you noticed that it kindly used a special color coding scheme to highlight the structure of your programs? A simple text editor would not do that. On the other hand, it should be noted that an IDE by itself can have an initial learning curve.

A Word of Advice

If you are new at programming, you are likely to be new to NLP as well, and you will benefit from a friendly language like Python. You can learn both programming and NLP techniques simultaneously through NLTK, which was explicitly designed for educational purposes (Bird et al, 2008). But even if you are not new to programming or to NLP, NLTK offers the advantage of an integrated set of routines, lexicons, and corpora which allows you to easily prototype your ideas. If you are familiar with Java or C++, you will likely prefer using toolboxes like LingPipe or GATE, amongst others (see the companion website for the relevant links).

Of course, you might not need an entire NLP toolbox to carry the operations you wish to accomplish. If, for instance, you are merely concerned with parsing a group of texts, you may want to use a tool tailored for that goal, like the Stanford or Charniak parsers. In general, although at first glance it might appear tempting to conduct a whole project within the same programming environment, you might consider picking and choosing from a variety of languages and packages for different parts of your project – hereby considering the set of available toolboxes as one giant toolbox. Actually, many NLP pipelines operate on text and return text (which is why Part I contained a section about text input-output). Therefore you can easily use different programming languages or tools.

For example, let's say that you want to parse a text. You might first use a tagger. This would output a list of tagged words. Then you can run a parser over it using these tagged words as input, and outputting a parse in a Penn Treebank style. You could then use that parse and add semantic information to it, and use that information to answer some questions about the text. This demonstrates the basic idea of an *NLP pipeline* where each operation produces a new file of text, which the succeeding state operates upon. At every step you could use a different tool or programming language. Overall, the nature of your project will dictate much of the technology you have to use.

For complete beginners, it is important to first gain grasp of simple programming operations and learn as many fundamentals of programming as possible. If you do not do that, you run the risk of wasting your time reinventing the wheel, creating inefficient solutions to very well known problems, or making certain mistakes which will vitiate your project at its core. Implementing the program is likely to be the most difficult part for a beginner. Towards this end, readers are encouraged to consult some of the many excellent tutorials and books on programming (e.g., Sande & Sande, 2009).

For more advanced users, we advise starting with the how-to tutorials that come with the various NLP tools listed on the companion website. Both beginners and advanced users will gain from reusing small pieces of code and incrementally building from there, similar to what we have done in Parts I and II.

CONCLUSION

Engaging in the practical task of programming NLP applications is not beyond the reach of novice programmers with an eye for solving NLP problems. A multitude of resources have been developed by a very vivid community of researchers, computer scientists, and coders. The reader should be now familiar with basic notions of programming (in particular, data is acquired, transformed, and released), and the notion that a variety of tools and languages exist in order to program NLP operations. Before beginning a project it is important to choose wisely because the choice of a tool/language depends on a variety of factors (nature of the task, power of the tool, learning curve, documentation, etc.). It is also important to reflect on the problem before starting programming and to proceed incrementally. Overall, programming can be useful and even fun. In some case, it can even produce a flow-like experience (Csikszentmihalyi, 1990) when the programmer is so absorbed in the task that time and fatigue disappear. We hope that this will be your experience with programming.

ACKNOWLEDGMENT

We want to thank Laurence Dumont, Katherine Guérard, Bernard Jeuniaux, Michaël Jeuniaux, William Jeuniaux, and Bernard Lebel for commenting on various versions of this chapter. Their help was crucial in improving the readability of the chapter. We also thank two reviewers, for their extremely helpful comments and corrections. The first author is also grateful to the Linguistic Society of America for providing funds to attend the 2007 Linguistic Institute, where Steven Bird, Ewan Klein, and Edward Loper gave a fantastic course involving Python and NLTK. This research was also supported by the National Science Foundation (REC 0106965, ITR 0325428, HCC 0834847) and Institute of Education Sciences, U.S. Department of Education (R305A080594). Any opinions, findings and conclusions, or recommendations expressed in this paper are those of the authors and do not necessarily reflect the views of the NSF and DoE.

REFERENCES

Anderson, D. P. (2009). An interview with Maurice Wilkes. *Communications of the ACM, 52*(9), 39–42. doi:10.1145/1562164.1562180

Bird, S., Klein, E., & Loper, E. (2009). *Natural language processing with Python*. O'Reilly Media.

Bird, S., Klein, E., Loper, E., & Baldridge, J. (2008). Multidisciplinary instruction with the natural language toolkit. In *Proceedings of the Third Workshop on Issues in Teaching Computational Linguistics*, Columbus, Ohio.

Csikszentmihalyi, M. (1990). *Flow: The psychology of optimal experience*. New York, NY: Harper and Row.

Dyck, M. (2002). *The GNU version of the collaborative international dictionary of English, presented in the Extensible Markup Language*. Retrieved May 20, 2010, from http://www.ibiblio.org/webster/.

Elkner, J., Downey, A. B., & Meyers, C. (2009). *How to think like a computer scientist. Learning with Python* (2nd ed.). Retrieved December 27, 2009, from http://www.openbookproject.net/thinkCSpy.

Graesser, A. C., McNamara, D. S., Louwerse, M. M., & Cai, Z. (2004). Coh-Metrix: Analysis of text on cohesion and language. *Behavior Research Methods, Instruments, & Computers, 36*(2), 193–202. doi:10.3758/BF03195564

Hodges, A. (2000). *Alan Turing: The enigma*. Walker & Company.

Manning, C. D., & Schütze, H. (1999). *Foundations of statistical natural language processing*. The MIT Press.

Miller, G. A. (1995). WordNet: A lexical database for English. *Communications of the ACM, 38*(11), 39–41. doi:10.1145/219717.219748

Parks, R., Ray, J., & Bland, S. (1998).*Wordsmyth English dictionary – Thesaurus*. University of Chicago. [Online]. Retrieved from http://www.wordsmyth.net/.

Petzold, C. (2000). *Code: The hidden language of computer hardware and software*. Microsoft Press.

Rodd, J., Gaskell, G., & Marslen-Wilson, W. (2002). Making sense of semantic ambiguity: Semantic competition in lexical access.*Journal of Memory and Language, 46*, 245–266. doi:10.1006/jmla.2001.2810

Sande, W., & Sande, C. (2009). *Hello world! Computer programming for kids and other beginners*. Manning Publications.

Swade, D. (2002). *The difference engine: Charles Babbage and the quest to build the first computer*. Penguin.

ADDITIONAL READING

Blackburn, P., & Bos, J. (2005). *Representation and Inference for Natural Language: A First Course in Computational Semantics*. Stanford, CA: CSLI Publications.

Feldman, R., & Sanger, J. (2006). *The Text Mining Handbook: Advanced Approaches in Analyzing Unstructured Data*. Cambridge University Press. doi:10.1017/CBO9780511546914

Gries, S. T. (2009). *Quantitative Corpus Linguistics with R: A Practical introduction*. Routledge.

Guzdial, M. (2005). *Introduction to Computing and Programming in Python: A Multimedia Approach*. Prentice Hall.

Jurafsky, D., & Martin, J. H. (2009). *Speech and language processing. An Introduction to Natural Language Processing* (2nd ed.). Computational Linguistics, and Speech Recognition.

Konchady, M. (2006). *Text Mining Application Programming*. Charles River Media.

LingPipe's Competition. (2009). Retrieved December 27, 2009, from http://alias-i.com/lingpipe/web/competition.html.

Marcus, M. P., Santorini, B., & Marcinkiewicz, M. A. (1993). Building a large annotated corpus of English: the Penn Treebank. *Computational Linguistics, 19*(2), 313–330.

McConnell, S. (2004). *Code Complete: A Practical Handbook of Software Construction*. Microsoft Press.

Mertz, D. (2003). *Text Processing in Python*. Boston: Addison-Wesley.

Meyer, C. (2002). *English Corpus Linguistics: An Introduction*. Cambridge University Press. doi:10.1017/CBO9780511606311

Mitkov, R. (2005). *The Oxford Handbook of Computational Linguistics*. USA: Oxford University Press.

Nugues, P. M. (2006). *An introduction to language processing with Perl and Prolog: An Outline of Theories, Implementation, and Application with Special Consideration of English, French, and German (Cognitive Technologies)*. Springer.

OpenNLP. (2009). Retrieved December 27, 2009, from http://opennlp.sourceforge.net.

KEY TERMS AND DEFINITIONS

Artificial Intelligence: Study of how to design intelligent creatures.

Computational Linguistics: Study of the computational properties of language.

Computer Science: Study of how to make computers and programs.

Corpus: Organized set of documents.

Linguistics: Study of human languages.

Natural Language Processing: Using computers to automatically deal with human languages.

Programming: Giving instructions to computer to perform certain tasks.

Section 2
Successful ANLP Applications or Systems

Chapter 9
LSA in the Classroom

Walter Kintsch
University of Colorado, USA

Eileen Kintsch
University of Colorado, USA

ABSTRACT

LSA is a machine learning method that constructs a map of meaning that permits one to calculate the semantic similarity between words and texts. We describe an educational application of LSA that provides immediate, individualized content feedback to middle school students writing summaries.

INTRODUCTION

The development of ever more efficient machine learning systems during the past decades has the potential to revolutionize computer applications in education. These systems are capable of learning, without supervision, the meaning of words from a large linguistic corpus, as well as the meaning of sentences and texts composed with these words. As we shall show, certain restrictions apply, but this work has already reached a sufficient level of maturity with several educational applications currently in use. Examples of the kind of systems we have in mind are Latent Semantic Analysis (LSA) (Landauer, McNamara, Dennis, & Kintsch, 2007), the topics model (Griffiths, Steyvers, &

Tenenbaum, 2007), and the holograph model (Jones & Mewhort, 2007). We shall limit our discussion here to LSA, the method most widely used in education. The following section briefly summarizes the LSA method, but an example of an educational application of LSA will be the main focus of this chapter, concluding with a brief discussion of the limitations of this approach.

LSA was introduced by Landauer and Dumais in a seminal paper in 1997 (Landauer & Dumais, 1997). LSA was originally developed in the context of information retrieval, but Landauer and Dumais realized the potential of the method for modeling a wide variety of semantic phenomena. LSA infers word meanings from analyzing a large linguistic corpus. An example of a widely used corpus is the TASA corpus that consists of 44k documents a high-school graduate might have

DOI: 10.4018/978-1-60960-741-8.ch009

been exposed to during his or her lifetime. The total corpus comprises 11M word tokens, about 90k different words. This is a rich corpus, but the only information LSA actually uses consists of which words co-occurred which other words in each document. Sentence structure, syntax, discourse structure and so on are all neglected. Nevertheless, there is a great deal of information remaining, which LSA makes good use of.

The input to LSA consists of a huge matrix, listing the frequencies with which each word occurs in each document. This is an extremely sparse matrix, with most cells filled with 0's, because most words co-occur with only relatively few other words. The problem with such a matrix is that words whose meanings are quite unrelated do co-occur in the same document. Thus, although the raw word vector has all the right information in it, it is drowned in a sea of irrelevancies. What we want is the latent structure underlying the co-occurrence data, disregarding the noise inherent in the data. This latent structure is what LSA computes. LSA first uses a weighting scheme that de-emphasizes semantically uninformative words. For instance function words like "the," "of," or "but" play a very important role in comprehension in that they allow us to construct the syntactic structure of a sentence, specifying which role each word plays in a sentence. But since these high-frequency function words occur with many different words, they carry little weight semantically. LSA then uses a well-known mathematical technique called singular-value decomposition to reduce the dimensionality of the original matrix to about 300 dimensions. Dimensionality reduction achieves a two-fold purpose: It gets rid of much of the irrelevant noise in the corpus data, revealing its latent structure, and it fills in the original, sparse matrix, relating the main meaning-bearing words to each other, whether they had co-occurred in the corpus or not. As a result, in LSA each word in the corpus and each document is represented by a vector of 300 numbers. These numbers have no meaning by themselves, but together they define a semantic space – a high-dimensional map of meanings. Just as in a familiar two-dimensional map we can locate any two points with respect to each other and measure the distance between them, we can locate word meanings and document meanings in this 300-dimensional space and measure their distance. A useful measure of the similarity of two words, or of a word and a document, is the cosine between their vectors. Words that are unrelated have a cosine of 0 (or even a small negative value), and the more similar they are, the higher their cosine; identical words have a cosine of 1. Introductions to how LSA actually works can be found in Landauer and Dumais (1997) and Landauer et al. (2007).

What makes this semantic map so useful is the ability to calculate similarity measures (cosines) between any two points in the space, even though they may have never co-occurred in the corpus from which the space has been derived. Most importantly, we can represent the meaning of new documents in this space. A basic assumption upon which LSA is built is that the meaning of a document is the sum of the meaning of the words in that document. Thus, for any new, arbitrary document we can just add up all the word vectors to obtain the LSA vector for that document. Obviously, the assumption that the meaning of a document is the sum of the word meanings cannot be strictly true. "The hunter killed the deer" and "The deer killed the hunter" have the same words but have very different meanings. Nevertheless, for many purposes this simplifying assumption provides a very good approximation. The neglect of syntax limits the usefulness of LSA, as we shall see below, but there are many cases, both of theoretical and practical interest, where LSA has proven to be a powerful tool for the analysis of semantic phenomena.

We shall not discuss here the uses of LSA for the purpose of modeling human language understanding. The interested reader will find discussions of that approach in Landauer et al. (2007). Instead, we will describe an educational application of

LSA, specifically *Summary Street*, a computer tutor that helps middle-school students learn how to write summaries. Other applications, such as the *Intelligent Essay Assessor* are discussed in Landauer et al. (2007), or are available from the *WriteToLearn* program of Pearson Knowledge Technologies, http://www.pearsonkt.com.

The usefulness of LSA for educational purposes arises from the fact that it allows us to compute a vector representation for a new text, thus allowing us to compute the semantic similarity between any words and any texts. Specifically, given a text written by a student, we can evaluate it in comparison with some standard and assign it a grade, or we can indicate what content is missing that should be included. There are two ways of doing that with LSA: a good way and a better way.

The good way consists in comparing what the student wrote with some gold standard: Both texts are turned into LSA vectors, their cosine is computed, and depending on how high the cosine is, the student's writing is considered acceptable or not. Thus, we could use the teacher's essay to grade a student's essay and if the cosine is high enough, praise it; if it is low reject it; and if it is intermediate give some appropriate intermediate response (e.g., 'nice try," but needs more work"). In the case of *Summary Street*, as we show below, we compare the student's summary with the various sections of the to-be-summarized text passage and tell the student which sections, that is, which topics are adequately covered in his summary and which are not.

A better method can be used if we have available a set of essays on the topic in question that have already been graded by human experts. LSA converts each of these essays into a vector in the semantic space, which makes it possible to determine the closest neighbors of a new essay. We can then assign a grade to the new essay that is the weighted average of its nearest neighbors in the semantic space. The *Intelligent Essay Assessor* uses this technique. The nearest-neighbor algorithm gives better results than the

gold standard approach because it compares the student's writing with what other students have written rather than what the teacher has written in her own language, which is not quite the same as how students express themselves. Of course, there is a cost associated with this: namely, we need to have a large enough set of pre-graded essays, whereas for *Summary Street* the student's summary can simply be compared to the text that is being summarized.

Note that what LSA does is to check whether the student has written about the right information. The student does not have to use the same words as the teacher or the text passage; she can use her own words, but she needs to somehow convey the same semantic content. LSA by itself cannot indicate how well an essay or summary is written, whether it is full of syntax errors and badly organized. This limitation of LSA must be taken into account in educational applications. For example, the *Intelligent Essay Assessor* includes syntax checks, while *Summary Street* expects the student to hand in his final summary to the teacher for her evaluation. Note, however, that in practice, content and style are correlated in writing: It is very hard to describe the appropriate content in a disorganized way, with garbled syntax. Indeed, we have observed that as students learn to summarize content properly, their writing style improves even though *Summary Street* gives them no feedback on that (Franzke, Kintsch, E., Caccamise, Johnson, & Dooley, 2005).

SUMMARY STREET: A COMPUTER-BASED LEARNING TOOL

Several years ago our research team at the University of Colorado's Institute for Cognitive Science began developing *Summary Street*, one of the first educational applications of LSA. LSA provides similarity judgments between two texts as accurately as and much more quickly than well-trained human scorers do (Landauer, Laham, & Foltz,

2003; Landauer et al., 2007). Hence, we believed that an educational tool based on this capability could become a valuable asset to overburdened classroom teachers.

Summarization is a key process in text comprehension and a strategy that is now emphasized in many instructional programs and standards-based assessment as well (e.g., National Reading Panel, 2000; Palinscar & Brown, 1984). Summarizing difficult-to-understand informational texts helps readers to form an accurate and coherent memory representation of the content and to pinpoint what they do and do not understand (e.g., Brown & Day, 1984; Kintsch & Kintsch, 2005). By summarizing, students deepen and consolidate their memory of the content, much more than is achieved by rereading it, or even by answering questions. Writing a summary requires distilling the essential text meaning by working and reworking with the ideas, reconstructing the meaning by selecting which content to include and generalizing across the details in order to convey the content in a briefer form. These activities serve not only to expose gaps in one's understanding, but also to reinforce the memory representation of the content and to integrate it into one's personal knowledge. A coherent representation of the text meaning that is closely linked to existing knowledge is essential for being able to later access and use the content in multiple ways.

However, summarizing is not an easy skill for middle school students to acquire without extensive practice and direction, much more than can be provided by a classroom teacher. We therefore envisioned using the LSA technology in a computer tutor that would guide students through the process of writing a summary by means of multiple cycles of individualized feedback and revision. Moreover, such a tool would provide an ideal test bed for evaluating and extending the LSA methodology and theory of meaning.

Summary Street was originally developed by David Wade-Stein as his dissertation project (Steinhart, 2001; Wade-Stein & E. Kintsch, 2004)

in cooperation with W. Kintsch, Tom Landauer, E. Kintsch, and others. As detailed descriptions and the initial empirical tests of *Summary Street* are available in other publications (e.g., E. Kintsch et al., 2000; E. Kintsch, Caccamise, Franzke, Johnson, & Dooley, 2007; and Wade-Stein & E. Kintsch, 2004), we limit this description to its main features. Our focus here is on the large-scale evaluation of the tool during its use over a two-year period in a wide variety of Colorado classrooms.

A Look at Summary Street

Summary Street is a computer tutor that offers a supportive context for students to learn about and practice summarizing. Students are guided through successive drafts of a summary with feedback on the content of their writing. Students send their written drafts via the Internet for evaluation by LSA, which compares the similarity in meaning between the input summary and the source text from which it was derived. A graphic interface displays the feedback in an easy-to-grasp form that a student can use to revise his/her summary until it reaches the criterion for content coverage and appropriate length. Figure 1 shows an example of the feedback page: horizontal bars correspond to the section headings of the text to be summarized. The vertical bar on the right provides a length guideline. For each topic section, LSA computes a cosine as a measure of similarity between the information in the summary about that topic and the source text.

Students see improvement in content coverage in terms of how closely each horizontal bar approaches the vertical black threshold line. Color provides an additional cue: Initially red, each bar turns yellow, then green when each topic has been adequately described. The length indicator uses color in a similar manner: Red and yellow indicate that that the summary is much or somewhat too short or too long, green that the length is in the appropriate range. Students may request additional checks to help correct spelling errors and

Figure 1. Screenshot of a Summary Street feedback page

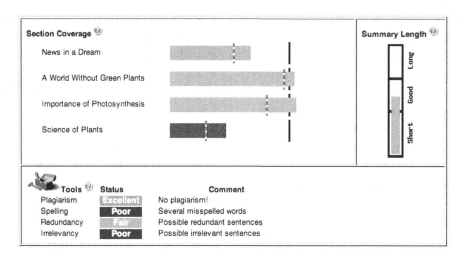

to deal with problem sentences: When requested, sentences that are overly redundant with other sentences in the summary or that are not relevant to the topic are marked by highlighting. Plagiarized sentences are similarly flagged to prevent students from simply cutting and pasting sentences into their summary, forcing them to re-state ideas in their own words. Feedback from *Summary Street* is directed at the content of the writing and does not directly evaluate organization, writing style or mechanics (e.g., grammar and punctuation). *Summary Street* is designed to help students make sure the content of their summary is adequate – that all the main topics are covered in a concise manner – before handling it to their teacher for final evaluation.

Preliminary Classroom Evaluations of Summary Street

Summary Street was initially tested in two studies, conducted in middle school classrooms (Wade-Stein & E. Kintsch, 2005; Franzke, E. Kintsch, Caccamise, Johnson, & Dooley, 2005). Both studies showed improved summary writing by students who used the system as compared to control students who wrote summaries without this support.

When writing a summary, middle school students will typically cover content in the early parts of the source text, neglecting further information once the required word count has been fulfilled. Feedback from *Summary Street*, however, helped the students realize that they needed to describe all the important content, for example, all the main subtopics shown in Figure 1, and to avoid overloading their summaries with lesser details. Moreover, compared to the summaries of the control group students, *Summary Street* summaries in the Franzke et al. (2005) study were also rated superior on measures that the program does not directly support, such as organization and writing style. Apparently, getting the right content also benefited the overall writing quality of the summaries. This study further suggested that the guided practice in summarizing provided by this tool may also benefit students' comprehension in general. The effect was apparent on items of a comprehension test that tapped gist-level processing. Thus, it appears that summary practice with feedback that directs students to attend to relevant content can transfer to reading outside the summary writing context. However, simply practicing summary writing in the absence of such feedback, as the control group in this study did, is not beneficial. Without corrective feedback, students persist with the same bad habits.

LARGE-SCALE EVALUATION STUDY

Between 2001 and 2006, classroom use of *Summary Street* was evaluated in middle-school classes in Colorado. The several thousand students who used *Summary Street* represent a broad sample of urban, suburban and rural populations with diverse ethnicity and SES backgrounds. NSF-IERI provided funding for this study, which will be described in detail in Caccamise et al. (in preparation).

Altogether, 4,166 students from Grades 5 to 9 in 120 classrooms used *Summary Street* during the two-year evaluation period. Our data are based on 2,847 students from whom we obtained consent forms. The largest group was from 7th Grade, reflecting the instructional emphasis by many middle schools on learning summarization strategies. The number of texts summarized with *Summary Street* varied a great deal, and teachers were free to implement the program in their instruction as they saw fit. In general, number of texts corresponded to the number of times the tool was used, which ranged from 0 to 12 times on average, with 3 to 7 texts the norm. Thus, most students got a reasonable amount of practice with the tool.

A pre-post experimental – control group design was employed to evaluate the effectiveness of the program. The students in *Summary Street* classrooms were matched in terms of age and demographic background with students in control classrooms whom their teachers taught to summarize in their usual manner. The pre- and posttests consisted of two parts: pre- and post-intervention summaries and a comprehension test. First, at the beginning and at the end of the year students composed handwritten summaries without support of the software. The informational pre- and post texts they summarized were matched in length, complexity, and lexile level, and were chosen to be

in the normal reading range of the students' grade level. Second, students were given two subtests of the TORC comprehension test. In addition we had available the results of standardized reading comprehension tests administered by individual schools and students' scores on the Colorado mandated assessment test (CSAP), which allowed us to control for the effects of general performance levels in our analyses. The CSAP scores show a normal distribution pattern for students who participated in the study.

The quality of the summaries written on the pre- and posttest texts was measured in terms of the proportion of sections that passed the LSA-based thresholds, termed the "pass-ratio." This metric is the same metric as that used to give feedback during the intervention. The scores were adjusted for text difficulty by subtracting the mean scores for the texts on the pretest from the pre- and posttest scores. On average the post-intervention summary scores of the *Summary Street* participants were significantly higher than those of the control group participants. However, average results are misleading, since many students in the experimental group used *Summary Street* only a few times or not at all. Hence a better impression of the effectiveness of *Summary Street* is obtained if we look at Figure 2, where improvement in summarization is plotted as a function of the number of texts that a student summarized using the system. (As the results are very similar, the data are collapsed across the two years of the study.) The dosage effect data shown in Figure 2 indicate that all students benefited from using *Summary Street* and the more they practiced with the system, the better their summaries became. These middle school students were able to fulfill the basic requirements of summary writing – making sure their summaries succinctly covered the important content – in only six-to-eight sessions of guided practice with *Summary Street*. Note that the data in Figure 2 are based on summaries written without the help of the system. Thus, they show that the students were able to apply the lessons learned when the supportive feedback was not available. Also note that Figure 2 represents not just a selection artifact – (better students using *Summary Street* more and writing better summaries) because ability (CSAP scores) were partialled out.

Practice with *Summary Street* appears to have more general effects on students' comprehension as well. This transfer effect is seen in Figure 3, which shows a dosage effect on the pre- post- comprehension test quite similar to the summary scores in Figure 2: Once again, the more texts students summarized, the better their TORC scores became. Apparently, the guided summarization practice improved the students' ability to differentiate between important and less important, detailed content, not only in their summaries but as they were reading as well.

. Figure 3. Performance on two subtests of the TORC as a function of the number of texts summarized with *Summary Street* during the school year. The pre-test scores for the same test were included in the analysis to control for student ability differences (from Caccamise et al., in prep.).

Figure 2. Proportion of sections passed on summary posttest as a function of the number of texts summarized with Summary Street during the school year, using CSAP scores to control for differences in ability (from Caccamise et al., in prep)

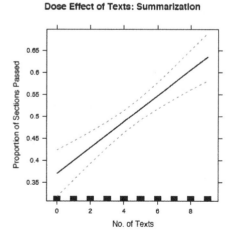

Lessons Learned: Use of Summary Street in the Classroom

Support

The amount of human/researcher support needed for successful implementation was fairly minimal: A single 15-minute introduction was sufficient to explain and demonstrate how to use the basic features of *Summary Street*, followed by guidance for individual students' problems during the first classroom session. Thereafter, students could easily use the tool on their own. Most of the problems we encountered in the classroom were not related to use of the program, but rather to difficulties with the cognitive task of summarizing – identifying the important ideas, stating them in their own words in order to avoid plagiarizing and composing overly long summaries.

Technical support for teachers, however, was essential. In collaboration with Pearson Knowledge Technologies (PKT) several useful tools were developed, including: (1) a record keeping capability to track individual students' and entire classroom's progress over time; (2) a library of texts on topics that fit the regular teaching curriculum, mainly on physical, biological and social science topics; and (3) an editing tool to allow teachers and researchers to insert new texts, modify them if needed (e.g., shorten them), and to adjust thresholds for the individual sections of a text and for the additional toolbox functions (evaluation of redundancy, relevance and plagiarism).

Summary Street, now sporting a new look and additional features, has since become a component of PKT's commercially successful educational tool, called *WriteToLearn* (see http://www.Write-ToLearn.net for more information).

Limitations

Our research across all three studies has shown that *Summary Street* is an effective way to teach middle school students how to summarize. Students need about four to six practice sessions to learn what the system has to offer, which can easily be accommodated in classroom schedules. So far, so good, but *Summary Street* only addresses part of the comprehension problem – forming a gist representation of a text. In our controlled study, for example, we found no improvement in students' ability to answer inference questions. Clearly, more is needed to get students working with difficult text at a deeper level. This limitation of the tool is inherent in LSA, which deals best with text-based meaning evaluation, not with the interpretation of text content, which requires inferring beyond the text meaning.

A second limitation of LSA has to do with the evaluation of short answer responses constructed in students' own words. Such questions, tedious to score by hand, are a valuable tool for assessing what a student has really learned from reading or instruction in new topic areas. Unfortunately, LSA provides no solution, as it requires extended text samples (ideally, about 200 words) for accurate evaluation. LSA by itself is therefore not suited to evaluating the accuracy of short constructed responses to questions. However, acceptable accuracy in scoring short answers can be achieved by supplementing LSA with a number of text coherence and other language metrics (see the Coh-Metrix approach developed by Graesser and his colleaguesGraesser and his colleagues-2004Graesser and his colleaguesGraesser and his colleagues: e.g., Graesser, McNamara, Louwerse, & Cai, 2004!).

Teacher Factors

In our classroom studies of *Summary Street*, we witnessed over and over how much successful learning with the tool depended on a teachers' commitment. Our results indicate that students can learn the essentials of how to summarize in just a few sessions (using different texts) with *Summary Street* and that they continue to use the skill in the absence of support. Still, like many other computer-assisted learning tools, it is possible to use *Summary Street* in a superficial manner, more as an add-on or supplemental summary writing aid. We have argued that in order to fully exploit its usefulness, computer guided summary writing needs to be embedded in curricular content. Teachers of language arts classes enthusiastically embraced *Summary Street*, as a way to provide students with individualized feedback on their efforts to get the content right, an important aspect of learning to summarize. However, it proved harder to convince content area teachers of *Summary Street's* potential to deepen their students' understanding of the informational texts being used to teach a particular unit. Content area teachers often regarded the ability to summarize as an issue for literacy instruction in language arts classes and failed to see that summarization is an important subskill of text comprehension. Text comprehension, in turn, is an important factor in content learning, as content learning often involves learning from texts, a crucial skill for academic success in the higher grades.

FUTURE DIRECTIONS

Summary Street works because it provides guided practice. Most teachers in our study gave only minimal or no instruction in how to summarize. Whether more systematic instruction would have been useful remains to be determined. The important thing for students is to receive individualized, prompt, and useable guidance. Practice alone does no good. In one study (Franzke et al., 2005) students who practiced summary writing without immediate feedback actually got worse by repeating their initial mistakes[1]. The advantage of computer tutors like *Summary Street* is the ability to provide the kind of just-in-time and individually targeted guidance needed to optimize students' own efforts to complete a complex task. Effective tutors work best not by giving students the correct answer, but rather by making it possible for them to debug their own thinking and writing. Of course, a teacher can always give better feedback than *Summary Street*, but she cannot supervise dozens of individuals writing multiple drafts.

Summary Street is effective in teaching summarization to middle-school students. In its current form it does little for the average high-school student, who knows how to summarize and can write a reasonable summary of a text that is not too difficult and unfamiliar. Summarization is certainly an important, indeed crucial subskill of text comprehension, but there is more to comprehension than that. The time is ripe for a comprehensive tutor that teaches students, all the way up to college students, effective strategies beyond summarization for comprehending difficult, dense texts, the kind they need to deal with in content areas, including literature. We fully expect such computer tutors to be developed in the near future.

LSA will play a role in such developments, but not an exclusive one. LSA works well with text that is long enough, but in tutoring situations short answer questions are often the method of choice (e.g., Graesser & Person, 1994). When LSA can average word vectors over 150-200 words, it arrives at quite accurate representations of the gist of the text. However, the averaging method does not work as well when the texts are too short – just a sentence or two long. In that case, the neglect of syntax becomes problematic. However, new LSA-like systems that are syntax sensitive are being developed, such as Kintsch and Mangalath (2011), that will make it possible to deal with short-answers as well as LSA does with longer texts.

Computerized comprehension tutors will play an important role in the future. Although the guidance they can provide is much cruder than what a teacher could do, they can do it on an individualized basis for all the students in a classroom; they are readily available, prompt, and cheap. The feedback is nothing fancy, but

provides the guidance necessary to ensure that practice is indeed effective.

REFERENCES

Brown, A. L., & Day, J. D. (1984). Macrorules for summarizing texts: The development of expertise. *Journal of Verbal Learning and Verbal Behavior, 22*, 1–14. doi:10.1016/S0022-5371(83)80002-4

Caccamise, D. J., Snyder, L., Allen, C., Oliver, W., DeHart, M., Kintsch, E., & Kintsch, W. (in preparation). *Teaching comprehension via technology-driven tools: A large scale scale-up of Summary Street.*

Ericsson, K. A., Charness, N., Hoffman, R. R., & Feltovich, P. J. (2006). *The Cambridge handbook of expertise and expert performance.* New York, NY: Cambridge University Press.

Franzke, M., Kintsch, E., Caccamise, D., Johnson, N., & Dooley, S. (2005). Summary Street®: Computer support for comprehension and writing. *Journal of Educational Computing Research, 33*, 53–80. doi:10.2190/DH8F-QJWM-J457-FQVB

Graesser, A. C., McNamara, D. S., & Louwerse, M, M., & Cai, Z. (2004). Coh-Metrix: Analysis of text on cohesion and language. *Behavior Research Methods, Instruments, & Computers, 36*, 193–202. doi:10.3758/BF03195564

Graesser, A. C., & Person, N. K. (1994). Question asking during tutoring. *American Educational Research Journal, 31*, 104–137.

Griffiths, T. L., Steyvers, M., & Tenenbaum, J. B. (2007). Topics in semantic representation. *Psychological Review, 114*, 211–244. doi:10.1037/0033-295X.114.2.211

Jones, M. N., & Mewhort, D. (2007). Representing word meaning and order information in a composite holographic lexicon. *Psychological Review, 114*, 1–37. doi:10.1037/0033-295X.114.1.1

Kintsch, E., Caccamise, D., Franzke, M., Johnson, N., & Dooley, S. (2007). Summary Street: Computer-guided summary writing. In Landauer, T. K., McNamara, D., Dennis, S., & Kintsch, W. (Eds.), *Handbook of latent semantic analysis* (pp. 263–278). Mahwah, NJ: Erlbaum.

Kintsch, E., Steinhart, D., Stahl, G., Matthews, C., Lamb, R., & Group, L. R. (2000). Developing summarization skills through the use of LSA-backed feedback. *Interactive Learning Environments*, 8, 87–109. doi:10.1076/1049-4820(200008)8:2;1-B;FT087

Kintsch, W., & Kintsch, E. (2005). Comprehension. In Paris, S. G., & Stahl, S. A. (Eds.), *Children's reading comprehension and assessment* (pp. 71–92). Mahwah, NJ: Erlbaum.

Kintsch, W., & Mangalath, P. (2011). The construction of meaning. *TopiCS in Cognitive Science*, 3, 346–370. doi:10.1111/j.1756-8765.2010.01107.x

Landauer, T. K., & Dumais, S. T. (1997). A solution to Plato's problem: The latent semantic analysis theory of acquisition, induction and representation of knowledge. *Psychological Review*, 104, 211–240. doi:10.1037/0033-295X.104.2.211

Landauer, T. K., Laham, D., & Foltz, P. (2003). Automatic essay assessment. *Assessment in Education*, 10, 295–308. doi:10.1080/0969594032000148154

Landauer, T. K., McNamara, D., Dennis, S., & Kintsch, W. (Eds.). (2007). *Latent semantic analysis*. Mahwah, NJ: Erlbaum.

National Reading Panel. (2000). *Teaching children to read: An evidence-based assessment of the scientific research literature on reading and its implications for reading instruction (NIH Pub. No. 00-4769)* (pp. 4-2–4-131). Jessup, MD: National Institute for Literacy.

Palincsar, A. S., & Brown, A. L. (1984). Reciprocal teaching of comprehension-fostering and monitoring activities. *Cognition and Instruction*, 12, 117–175.

Wade-Stein, D., & Kintsch, E. (2004). Summary Street: Computer support for writing. *Cognition and Instruction*, 22(3), 333–362. doi:10.1207/s1532690xci2203_3

ADDITIONAL READING

Bransford, J. D., Brown, A. L., & Cocking, R. R. (Eds.). (2000). *How people learn: Brain, mind, experience, and school*. Washington, DC: National Academy Press.

Hampton, S., & Resnick, L. B. (2008). *Reading and writing with understanding. University of Pittsburg and The National Center on Education and the Economy*. Washington, DC: International Reading Association.

Kintsch, W., & Kintsch, E. (2005). Comprehension. In Paris, S. G., & Stahl, D. S. (Eds.), *Children's reading comprehension and assessment* (pp. 71–92). Mahwah, NJ: Erlbaum.

Landauer, T. K., McNamara, D. S., Dennis, S., & Kintsch, W. (20070. *Handbook of Latent Semantic Analysis*. Mahwah, NJ: Erlbaum.

KEY TERMS AND DEFINITIONS

CSAP: Colorado Student Assessment Program, state mandated assessment of students' level of mastery of the Colorado Model Content Standards in reading, writing, mathematics, and science.

Dimension: The number of coordinates in a geometric space; e.g,. Euclidean space has three dimensions; the LSA semantic space has 300 dimensions.

Dose Effect: A graph showing the effectiveness of different dose sizes (e.g., amounts of training).

Guided Practice: Practice that is supervised by a mentor or coach providing feedback.

Latent Semantic Analysis (LSA): An unsupervised machine learning method that infers the meaning of words and texts.

Linguistic Corpus: A collection of texts.

Pass-Ratio: The proportion of sections passed.

Semantic Space: a multi-dimensional map of meaning.

TORC-3: Test of Reading Comprehension, third edition, a normed test of silent reading comprehension.

Vector: A sequence of numbers that specify a value along a dimension in a space; e.g. (x,y,z) is a vector specifying the coordinates of a point in Euclidean space; $(x_1, x_2, \ldots x_{300})$ is an LSA vector.

ENDNOTE

[1] This is true for the acquisition of expertise in any field (Ericsson et al., 2006): Practice alone without careful mentoring or coaching is ineffective.

Chapter 10
AutoTutor

Arthur C. Graesser
The University of Memphis, USA

Sidney D'Mello
The University of Memphis, USA

Xiangen Hu
The University of Memphis, USA

Zhiqiang Cai
The University of Memphis, USA

Andrew Olney
The University of Memphis, USA

Brent Morgan
The University of Memphis, USA

ABSTRACT

AutoTutor is an intelligent tutoring system that helps students learn science, technology, and other technical subject matters by holding conversations with the student in natural language. AutoTutor's dialogues are organized around difficult questions and problems that require reasoning and explanations in the answers. The major components of AutoTutor include an animated conversational agent, dialogue management, speech act classification, a curriculum script, semantic evaluation of student contributions, and electronic documents (e.g., textbook and glossary). This chapter describes the computational components of AutoTutor, the similarity of these components to human tutors, and some challenges in handling smooth dialogue. We describe some ways that AutoTutor has been evaluated with respect to learning gains, conversation quality, and learner impressions. AutoTutor is sufficiently modular that the content and dialogue mechanisms can be modified with authoring tools. AutoTutor has spawned a number of other agent-based learning environments, such as AutoTutor-lite, Operation Aries!, and Guru.

INTRODUCTION AND BACKGROUND

Intelligent Tutoring Systems (ITS) are computerized learning environments that incorporate computational models in the cognitive sciences, learning sciences, artificial intelligence, computational linguistics, and other fields that develop intelligent systems (Sleeman & Brown, 1982; Woolf, 2009). In a process called student modelling, the ITS tracks the psychological states of learners, such as subject matter knowledge, cognitive skills, strategies, motivation, and emotions. An ITS adaptively responds with activities that are sensitive to these psychological states, the history of the student-tutor interaction, and the instructional agenda. An ITS is very different from more rigid, insensitive, and inflexible learning environments such as reading a book or listening to a lecture.

DOI: 10.4018/978-1-60960-741-8.ch010

ITS environments were originally developed for mathematically well-formed subject matters. Impressive systems have been developed and tested for algebra, geometry, and programming languages (the *Cognitive Tutors*: Anderson et al., 1995; Koedinger et al., 1997; Ritter et al., 2007, *ALEKS*: Doignon & Falmagne, 1999), for physics (*Andes, Atlas*: VanLehn et al., 2002), for electronics (*SHERLOCK*: Lesgold, Lajoie, Bunzo, & Eggan, 1992), and for information technology (*KERMIT*: Mitrovic, Martin, & Suraweera, 2007). More recently the ITS enterprise has evolved to handle conversational interaction in natural language on verbal topics that require conceptual reasoning. This chapter focuses on *AutoTutor* (Graesser, Lu et al., 2004), but other systems have been developed with similar goals: *ITSPOKE* (Litman et al., 2006), *Spoken Conversational Computer* (Pon-Barry, Clark, Schultz, Bratt, Peters, & Haley, 2005), *Tactical Language and Culture Training System* (Johnson & Valente, 2008), *Why-Atlas* (VanLehn et al., 2007), and iSTART (McNamara, Levinstein, & Boonthum, 2004). These systems automatically analyze language and discourse by incorporating recent advances in computational linguistics (Jurafsky & Martin, 2008) and statistical representations of world knowledge (Landauer, McNamara, Dennis, & Kintsch, 2007).

Most ITSs fit within VanLehn's (2006) analyses of the outer loop and the inner loop when characterizing the scaffolding of solutions to problems, answers to questions, or completion of complex tasks. The outer loop involves the selection of topics and problems to cover, assessments of the student's topic knowledge and general cognitive abilities, and global aspects of the tutorial interaction. The inner loop consists of covering individual steps within a problem at a micro-level. Adaptivity and intelligence are necessary at both the outer loop and the inner loop in a bona fide ITS.

This chapter describes the computational components of AutoTutor and some of the challenges faced when simulating smooth and pedagogically effective dialogue. AutoTutor's architecture incorporates dialogue mechanisms of human tutors in addition to ideal tutoring strategies. We describe evaluations of AutoTutor with respect to learning gains, conversation quality, and learner impressions. The modular architecture of AutoTutor allows developers to develop new content and dialogue strategies with authoring tools. We end the chapter by identifying some of AutoTutor's progeny that also have conversational agents, such as AutoTutor-lite, Guru, and Operation Aries!.

AUTOTUTOR MECHANISMS

AutoTutor simulates a tutor by holding a conversation in natural language (Graesser, Chipman, Haynes, & Olney, 2005; Graesser, Jeon, & Dufty, 2008; Graesser, Graesser, Lu et al., 2004; Graesser, Person, & Harter, 2001). Students type in their contributions through a keyboard in most applications. However, we have developed a version that handles spoken input from the student through the Dragon Naturally Speaking ™ (version 6) speech recognition system (D'Mello, King, Chipman, & Graesser, in press). AutoTutor communicates through an animated conversational agent with speech, facial expressions, and some rudimentary gestures.

Figure 1 shows a screen shot of AutoTutor on the topic of computer literacy. Most versions of AutoTutor have the three major areas shown in Figure 1. Area 1 (top of screen) is the main question (or problem) that stays on the computer screen throughout the conversation that collaboratively constructs an answer to the question. Area 2 (left middle) is the animated conversational agent that speaks the content of AutoTutor's turns. Area 3 (right middle) is either blank or has auxiliary diagrams on the subject matter. When the students type in their contributions, there is an area at the bottom that displays what the student types in. In versions with speech recognition, there are two buttons on the keyboard that the learner presses to start speaking and stop speaking. The interface can also include a dialogue area that presents the history of the turn-by-turn tutorial dialogue; students can scroll back as far as they want in this dialogue history.

The outer loop of AutoTutor consists of a serious of didactic lessons and challenging problems or questions (such as *why, how, what-if*). The example main question in Figure 1 is "When you turn on the computer, how is the operating system first activated and loaded into RAM?" The order of lessons, problems, and questions can be dynamically selected based on the profile of student abilities, but the order is fixed in most versions of AutoTutor we have developed. The interactive dialogue occurs during the problems/questions but not the didactic delivery of information (e.g., reading text, viewing a diagram). The answer to a question (or solution to a problem) requires several sentences of information in an ideal answer. AutoTutor assists the learners in constructing their answers after they enter their initial response. The inner loop of AutoTutor consists of this collaborative interaction while answering a question (or solving a problem). It is this inner loop that is the distinctive hallmark of AutoTutor. The tutor draws out more of the student's knowledge (through hints and prompts), helps fill in missing information, repairs misconceptions, and answers student questions. The inner loop dialogue between AutoTutor and the student takes approximately 100

dialogue turns to answer a single challenging question, approximately the length of a conversation with a human tutor.

There are augmented versions of AutoTutor with special features that are designed to enhance the learning experience. Several versions of AutoTutor have been developed since 1997, when the system was created. One version of AutoTutor, called *AutoTutor-3D,* guides learners on using interactive simulations of physics microworlds (Graesser, Chipman et al., 2005; Jackson et al., 2006). For each of the physics problems, there is an interactive simulation world with people, objects, and the spatial setting associated with the problem. The student manipulates parameters of the situation (e.g., mass of objects, speed of objects, distance between objects), asks the system to simulate what will happen, and then gets prompted by the tutor to describe what the student sees. AutoTutor manages the dialogue with hints and suggestions that scaffold the learning process with dialogue. Another version is sensitive to the student's emotions, which are tracked automatically by detecting particular dialogue patterns, facial expressions, and body motions (D'Mello & Graesser, in press; chapter XX in this volume). Yet another version adds game features with feedback and points that are contingent on the student's performance (Jackson & Graesser, 2007). However, it is the conversational interaction of AutoTutor's inner loop that is the signature contribution of AutoTutor.

What Does AutoTutor Do?

Perhaps the best way to convey what AutoTutor does in the inner loop is through an example conversational dialogue. The excerpts below were extracted from an actual conversation with a student on the topic of conceptual physics. The conversation begins with a main question selected by AutoTutor.

Figure 1. A screen shot of AutoTutor

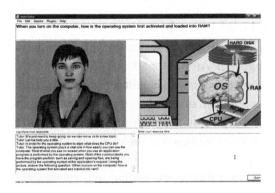

- **AutoTutor:** *When a car without headrests on the seats is struck from behind, the passengers often suffer neck injuries? Explain why.* (MAIN QUESTION)
- **Student:** *I don't know.* (This expression by the student is classified as a Metacognitive speech act because it conveys what the student knows about his/her own knowledge.)
- **AutoTutor:** *Could you at least try to give me an answer? That way, we'll have something as a starting place to work from.* (PUMP. This dialogue move encourages the student to say more, but does not direct the student to express particular information.)

As the dialogue continues, AutoTutor detects that an important expected piece of information is missing (i.e., the impact of the collision on the neck).

- **AutoTutor:** *Let's try this together.* (DISCOURSE MARKER. This is a discourse marker that introduces or connects dialogue moves within a turn.) *When the collision provides a large force to accelerate the head, what could happen to the neck?* (HINT. This dialogue move leads the student to articulate a particular sentence, clause, or proposition.)

At one point in the dialogue, the student asks a question, so AutoTutor needs to provide an answer. AutoTutor can answer some classes of questions (such as definitional questions), but not all questions, so AutoTutor needs to productively manage the dialogue surrounding student question asking.

- **Student:** *What is a force?*
- **AutoTutor:** *I'll take a crack at answering your question.* (DISCOURSE MARKER) *Force is any influence that tends to accelerate an object; a push or pull; measured in newtons. Force is a vector quantity.*

(ANSWER. AutoTutor answers the student's direct question. Answers are either accessed from electronic glossaries or a paragraph is dynamically selected from a textbook.) *Was that what you were looking for?* (QUESTION SOLICITATION. AutoTutor allows the student the opportunity to rephrase his question.)

As the dialogue continues AutoTutor believes it has detected a misconception.

- **AutoTutor:** *See if you know the answer to this.* (DISCOURSE MARKER. AutoTutor prepares the student for a direct question.) *When the head and body are moving at the same acceleration, they are moving at the same _____?* (PROMPT. This dialogue move encourages the student to fill in a particular word or phrase of information, in this case the word "rate." Prompts are frequently needed for students who have low verbal fluency in order to elicit a particular noun, verb, or adjective that is missing in an answer.)
- **Student:** *distance*
- **AutoTutor:** *Moving at the same rate.* (PROMPT COMPLETION. AutoTutor splices in the correct information if the student provides an incorrect answer to its prompt.)

At this point, the dialogue continues until all of the relevant expected answers are covered in the conversation. The conversation then ends with a summary answer by the tutor.

The example illustrates the mixed-initiative dialogue of AutoTutor. AutoTutor attempts to interpret or otherwise handle any question, assertion, comment, or extraneous speech acts that the student expresses. Each turn of AutoTutor requires the generation of one or more dialogue moves that adaptively respond to what the student expresses, that advance the conversation in a constructive manner, that covers good answer information, or that corrects misconceptions. The tutor's dialogue moves within a turn are connected by discourse markers, as illustrated in the example. Some dialogue moves are responsive to the student's preceding turn, such as short feedback (positive, neutral, versus negative), answers to student questions, and corrections of student misconceptions. Other dialogue moves push the dialogue forward in an attempt to cover the expected answers to the main question.

Dialogue Structure

The dialogue structure of AutoTutor is similar to the dialogue patterns of human tutors. Graesser and Person analyzed dialogue patterns of typical human tutors in middle school and in college (Graesser & Person, 1994; Graesser, Person, & Magliano, 1995). Similar analyses have been conducted by other researchers on naturalistic tutoring corpora (Chi et al., 2004; Evens & Michael, 2006; Litman et al., 2006). The following dialogue structures are implemented in AutoTutor and are prominent in human tutors: (a) a curriculum script with didactic content and problems (i.e., difficult tasks or questions), (b) a 5-step Tutoring Frame, (c) Expectation and Misconception Tailored (EMT) dialogue, and (d) Conversational Turn Management.

Curriculum Script

The tutor covers a curriculum with didactic content and a set of questions or problems that address the content. Didactic content can be presented in a mini-lecture, hopefully at the appropriate time for each individual learner. The questions/problems require the student to actively apply their knowledge. The curriculum script includes expected answers, misconceptions, hints, prompt questions, and other inner loop information.

5-Step Tutoring Frame

When a challenging main question (or problem) is selected to work on, the question is answered through an interaction that is structured by a 5-Step Tutoring Frame. The 5 steps are: (1) Tutor presents a main question, (2) Student gives an initial answer, (3) Tutor gives short feedback on the quality of the Student's initial answer, (4) the Tutor and Student collaboratively improve on the answer in a turn-by-turn dialogue that may be lengthy, and (5) the Tutor evaluates whether the Student understands (e.g., asking "Do you understand?" or testing with a follow-up task). This 5-step tutoring frame involves collaborative discussion, joint action, and encouragement for the student to construct knowledge rather than merely receiving knowledge.

Expectation and Misconception Tailored (EMT) Dialogue

Human tutors typically have a list of *expectations* (i.e. anticipated good answers or steps in a procedure) and a list of anticipated *misconceptions* (incorrect information) associated with each main question. They want the expectation content covered in order to handle the main question that is selected. The tutor guides the student in articulating the expectations through a number of dialogue moves, namely *pumps* ("What else?"), *hints*, *prompt questions* to extract specific information from students, *assertions* that capture particular expectations, and *answers* to students' questions. As the dialogue progresses, tutors tend to lead more while trying to get the student to articulate an expectation. They start with a pump and then move to a hint if the pump fails, followed by a prompt question and an assertion if students fail to articulate the expectation. The pump → hint → prompt → assertion cycle is implemented by AutoTutor to encourage the student to articulate the answer and cover expectations. The correct answers are eventually covered and the misconceptions are hopefully corrected.

Conversational Turn Management

Human tutors structure their conversational turns systematically. Nearly every turn of the tutor has three information slots. The first slot of most turns is feedback on the quality of the learner's last turn. This feedback is either positive (*very good, yeah*), neutral (*uh huh, I see*), or negative (*not quite, not really*). The second slot advances the interaction with a prompt for specific information, a hint, an assertion with correct information, a correction of misconceptions, or an answer to the student's question. The third slot is a cue for the floor to shift from the tutor as the speaker to the learner. For example, the human ends each turn with a question or a gesture to cue the learner to do the talking. Otherwise the student and AutoTutor are at a standstill waiting for the other to take the next turn.

Student Modeling

One of the central questions is how well the tutor can track the psychological states of the student as the tutor implements tutoring strategies. Available evidence suggests that human tutors are not able to conduct student modeling at a fine-grained level (Chi, Siler, & Jeong, 2004; Graesser, D'Mello, & Person 2009). They are limited to performing approximate assessments rather than fine-grain assessments. Computers can potentially show advantages over humans to the extent that artificial intelligence can accurately conduct student modeling and generate intelligent responses.

Student modeling in the inner loop consists of comparing what the student express in language with the list of expectations and misconceptions associated with a main question. For example, supposed that expectations E1 and E2 and misconceptions M1 and M2 are relevant to a particular

physics question that involves a head-on collision between a large and small vehicle.

- **E1.** The magnitudes of the forces exerted by A and B on each other are equal.
- **E2.** If A exerts a force on B, then B exerts a force on A in the opposite direction.
- **M1:** A lighter/smaller object exerts no force on a heavier/larger object.
- **M2:** Heavier objects accelerate faster for the same force than lighter objects

AutoTutor guides the student in articulating the expectations through pumps, hints, and prompts. Hints and prompts are carefully selected by AutoTutor to produce content in the answers that fills in missing content words, phrases, and propositions. For example, a hint to get the student to articulate expectation E1 might be "What about the forces exerted by the vehicles on each other?"; this hint would ideally elicit the answer "The magnitudes of the forces are equal." A prompt to get the student to say "equal" would be "What are the magnitudes of the forces of the two vehicles on each other?" If the student fails to articulate E1 after many attempts, then AutoTutor asserts the expectation at the end of the pump → hint → prompt → assertion cycle. However, there is an early exit from the cycle when the student articulates the information in E1. As the learner expresses information over many turns, the list of expectations is eventually covered and the main question is scored as answered.

Complete coverage of the answer requires AutoTutor to have a pool of hints and prompts in the curriculum script that are available to extract all of the content words, phrases, and propositions in each expectation. AutoTutor adaptively selects those hints and prompts that fill missing constituents and thereby achieves *pattern completion*. For example, the following family of candidate prompts is available for selection by AutoTutor to encourage the student to articulate words in expectation E1.

a. The magnitudes of the forces exerted by two objects on each other are ____.
b. The magnitudes of forces are equal for the two _____.
c. The two vehicles exert on each other an equal magnitude of ____.
d. The force of the two vehicles on each other are equal in ____.

If the student has failed to articulate one of the four content words (*equal, objects, force, magnitude*), then AutoTutor selects the corresponding prompt (a, b, c, and d, respectively).

Student modelling is executed after every student turn by comparing the verbal contributions of the student with the list of expectations and misconceptions. This requires *semantic matching* algorithms that compare the student input with AutoTutor's Es and Ms. However, it is widely acknowledged that natural language is imprecise, fragmentary, vague, ungrammatical, and elliptical, so it would not be prudent to rely entirely on semantically well-formed semantic matches. AutoTutor therefore incorporates several semantic evaluation algorithms when performing these matches, most notably Latent Semantic Analysis (Landauer et al., 2007), regular expressions (Jurafsky & Martin, 2008), content word overlap metrics (that have higher weight for low frequency words than high frequency words), and occasionally logical entailment (Rus & Graesser, 2006).

As an example, early versions of AutoTutor relied exclusively on LSA in its semantic evaluation of student input. The LSA algorithm computed the extent to which the information within the student turns (i.e., an individual turn, a combination of turns, or collective sequence of turns) matches each expectation in the ideal answer. Expectation E_i is considered covered if the content of the learner's cumulative set of turns meets or exceeds a threshold T in its LSA cosine value (which varies from near 0 to 1). That is, E_i is covered if the cosine match between E_i and the student input I (includ-ing turns 1 though N) is high enough: cosine (E_i, I) $\geq$ T. The threshold has varied between .40 and .75 in previous instantiations of AutoTutor. Each expectation E_i has an associated family of prompts and hints to get the student to fill in most or all of the content words and propositions in E_i. Prompts and hints are selected to maximize an increase in the LSA cosine match score (hereafter called the *match score*) when answered successfully. Stated differently, hints and prompts are selected to maximize pattern completion. Sometimes the student expresses misconceptions during the dialogue. This happens when the student input I matches a misconception M with a sufficiently high match score. At that point AutoTutor corrects the misconception and goes on.

During the course of the dialogue and student modeling, the system periodically identifies a missing expectation and posts the goal of covering the expectation. When expectation E_i is missed (and therefore posted), AutoTutor attempts to get the student to articulate it by generating hints and prompts affiliated with E_i to encourage the student to fill in missing words and propositions. The selection of the next E_i to cover follows the principle of the *zone of proximal development* or what some call frontier learning: AutoTutor builds on what the student has managed to articulate. More formally, AutoTutor selects the next E_i from the set of expectations that (a) has the highest match score and (b) has a subthreshold match score. This *subthreshold expectation selection* algorithm assumes that the expectations should not be covered in a prescribed sequential order. However, ordering constraints may also be considered in a *sequential expectation selection* algorithm. Some subject matters have ordering constraints but others do not.

Sometimes there are errors in AutoTutor's semantic matching. This can be disconcerting to the student when the students believe they have provided good, relevant contributions, yet it seems AutoTutor is not listening, or the short feedback is negative. The AutoTutor research teams have spent considerable efforts in improving the semantic match algorithms with techniques that go beyond LSA (see Graesser, Penumatsa, Ventura, Cai, & Hu, 2007; Rus & Graesser, 2006), but it is beyond the scope of this chapter to describe these improvements. AutoTutor's feedback and dialogue move generator also face limitations when the curriculum script does not have a full family of hints and prompts to cover all of the content words in each expectation E_i. A lazy lesson planner or knowledge engineer may cut corners and fail to specify prompts for important content words. When this happens, there is the risk of the threshold T never being met in the semantic match computations, which spawns two unfortunate consequences: AutoTutor generates irrelevant or redundant prompts and hints, or AutoTutor generates assertions that echo what the student has already expressed (which seems like AutoTutor is not listening). AutoTutor works quite well, however, when the curriculum script is adequately constructed and the semantic matching algorithms are on the mark.

AutoTutor computes a number of metrics of psychological characteristics during the course of student modeling. These metrics are collected from information in a log file that records a rich amount of information about the AutoTutor-student interaction after each conversational turn. This chapter concentrates on the cognitive metrics whereas the chapter by D'Mello and Graesser (Chapter xx) covers metrics of emotions and motivation. The cognitive metrics vary in grain size and apply to either the inner loop, the outer loop, or both.

The quality of student contributions is computed at all levels of grain size: each turn, each expectation, each main question/problem, and the set of main questions in the curriculum script. The student modeling, therefore, is assessed from inner to outer loop, or local to global spans. The metric is similar at all levels. Specifically, the semantic match score computes what the student contributes compared with the expectations. Stated differently, does the student or AutoTutor

have to articulate the content when answering the question? At the level of the turn, the match score is computed between the student's contribution and the expectation, with values varying from 0 to 1. A large number of scores are computed, including highest match score for all of the turns that address an expectation $E_{i, and}$ the mean match score over all the expectations for a main question. Global student knowledge for the subject matter is the mean match score when averaging over all of the previous questions/problems the student has worked on. Alternatively, relatively high match scores to misconceptions reflect low knowledge. Besides match scores, AutoTutor computes the volume of the student's contributions, which is called *verbosity*. A high-verbosity student expresses a large amount of information (measured in words or alphanumeric characters) compared with fellow students.

The accuracy of the student model algorithms have been evaluated over the years. In one analysis of conceptual physics, we collected pretest scores on a psychometrically validated test by Hestenes, Wells, and Swackhamer (1992), called the Force Concept Inventory. If AutoTutor is performing effective user modeling, then the dialogue moves selected by AutoTutor should be correlated with the students' prior knowledge of physics. Such predictions held up when we analyzed the dialogue moves of AutoTutor as a function of students of varying ability (Jackson & Graesser, 2006). For example, the short feedback that AutoTutor provides after the student's turns is either positive, neutral, or negative. The students' physics knowledge had a significant positive correlation with proportion of short feedbacks that were positive ($r = .38$) and a negative correlation with negative feedback ($r = -.37$). Another example applies to the corrections that AutoTutor made when identifying student errors and misconceptions. The correlation was negative ($r = -.24$), and marginally significant when compared with the corrections by AutoTutor. Yet another example considers the four dialogue move categories that attempt to cover the content of the expectations in the curriculum script: Pumps, hints, prompts, and assertions. The proportion of dialogue moves in these categories should be sensitive to the student's knowledge of physics. There is a continuum from the student-provided information to tutor-provided information as we move from pumps, to hints, to prompts, to assertions. The correlations with student knowledge reflected this continuum perfectly, with values of .49, .24, -.19, and -.40, respectively. Thus, for students with more knowledge of physics, all AutoTutor needs to do is primarily pump and hint, thereby encouraging or nudging the student to supply the answer to the question and articulate the expectations. For students with less knowledge of physics, AutoTutor needs to generate prompts for specific words or to assert the correct information, thereby extracting knowledge piecemeal or telling the student the correct information. These results support the claim that AutoTutor performs user modeling with some degree of accuracy and adaptively responds to the student's level of knowledge.

AUTOTUTOR ARCHITECTURE

Figure 2 presents the major components of Auto-Tutor's architecture. The bottom left depicts the student entering information via the user interface. The information in each student turn is segmented into speech acts, based on punctuation and (in some systems) a syntactic parser. Each speech act is assigned to one of approximately 20 speech act categories. These categories include assertions, 16 different categories of questions, short responses (yeah, right), meta-cognitive expressions (I don't understand, I see), and meta-communicative expressions (What did you say?). The accuracy of classifying the student speech acts into categories varies from .87-.96 (Olney et al., 2003), which is almost, but not quite, perfect. The dialogue coherence breaks down when some misclassification errors occur, which ends up confusing students.

However, these problems are rare because the vast majority of student contributions are statement contributions or short responses, as opposed to questions. Students rarely take control in tutoring environments by asking questions, recommending problems to work on, or changing topics (Graesser, Person, & Magliano, 1995; Graesser, McNamara, & VanLehn, 2005). Instead, it is the tutor who controls the agenda.

The speech acts expressed by the student on any given turn N constrain AutoTutor's conversation management of turn N+1. If the student asks a question, AutoTutor needs to answer it if it has an answer, or otherwise (a) generate dialogue moves to put the onus on the student to find an answer ("Good question. How would you answer it?") or (b) generate dialogue moves that evade getting an answer ("Good question, but I cannot answer it now. Let's move on."). If the student asks a metacognitive question ("I'm lost, I don't know"), which are normally frozen expressions, then AutoTutor acknowledges this and presents a hint to advance the dialogue in productive avenues. Student statement contributions are evaluated on quality, which drives the pump → hint → prompt → assertion cycles. The conversation dynamically flows from the student turns on the basis of the Conversation Manager module that is sensitive to the student's speech acts. The Conversation Manager module consists of a set of IF<state>THEN <action> production rules (Anderson & Gluck, 2001) or of a finite-state transition network (see Graesser, Person, & Harter, 2001). However, it is beyond the scope of this chapter to describe the computational mechanism of the Conversation Manager in more detail (see chapter xx by Olney & Graesser). The Conversation Manager subsequently passes information to the Response Generator, which is a sequence of dialogue moves and discourse markers. This content is expressed either in text or by an animated conversational agent that is displayed on the interface.

Figure 2. Architecture of AutoTutor

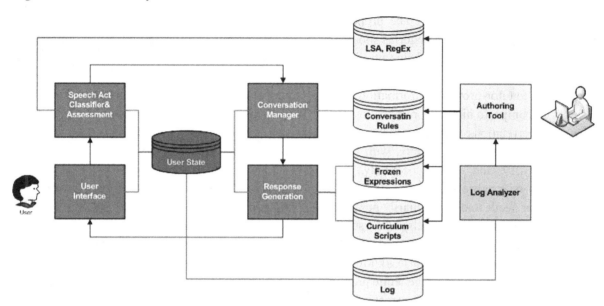

Animated conversational agents have become ubiquitous in recent advanced learning environments (Baylor & Kim, 2005; Gholson et al., 2009; McNamara, Levinstein, & Boonthum, 2004; Moreno & Mayer, 2007). The agents express themselves with speech, facial expression, gesture, posture, and other embodied actions. AutoTutor has used a wide array of agents that vary in quality of the speech and visual display. However, the learning gains of AutoTutor are not affected much by these agent characteristics (Graesser et al., 2003), whereas the impact of the dialogue content is extremely robust. Therefore, most of the AutoTutor team's efforts have concentrated on the content and conversation rather than the aesthetics of the talking head. We anticipate that the flashy dimensions of the animated agents will be developed by other research teams and eventually integrated with AutoTutor.

As depicted in Figure 2, AutoTutor has a repository of different static data structures that can be created and updated with authoring tools. First, all versions of AutoTutor represent world knowledge as *LSA* spaces (see Chapter xx by Kintsch & Kintsch), but some versions of Au-

toTutor or its progeny have incorporated other forms of world knowledge representation, such as textbooks, glossaries, and conceptual graph structures. Second, there are *Conversation Rules* that are represented as production rules, finite-state transition networks, or recursive augmented state transition networks (see chapter by Olney, Graesser & Person, chapter xx). Third, there are different categories of *Frozen Expressions* that have different discourse functions. For example, there are different ways for AutoTutor to express positive feedback (yes, yeah, good, great, fantastic, right on) and different ways that the student can express Metacommunicative speech acts (What did you say? Please repeat. I did not hear that.) Fourth, there is the *Curriculum Script*, as described earlier.

All of the information collected during the AutoTutor-student interaction is stored in the *Log* files. These files are fed into the *Log Analyzer* that can be inspected by the researcher and can inform the lesson planner or knowledge engineer who uses the *Authoring Tools*. These modules are, of course, standard for all learning management systems.

EVALUATION OF AUTOTUTOR

AutoTutor has been evaluated on its psychological impact on the student. Perhaps the most important question is whether AutoTutor helps students learn. The learning gains of AutoTutor have been evaluated in over 20 experiments since its inception in 1997. Assessments of AutoTutor on learning gains have shown effect sizes of approximately 0.8 standard deviation units in the areas of computer literacy (Graesser et al., 2004) and Newtonian physics (VanLehn, Graesser et al., 2007). These effect sizes place AutoTutor somewhere between an untrained human tutor (Cohen, Kulik, & Kulik, 1982) and an intelligent tutoring system with ideal tutoring strategies (Corbett, 2001). AutoTutor improves learning between 0 and 2.1 sigma (a mean of 0.8), depending on the learning performance measure, the comparison condition, the subject matter, and the version of AutoTutor. Measures of learning have included: (1) multiple choice questions on shallow knowledge that tap definitions, facts and properties of concepts, (2) multiple choice questions on deep knowledge that taps causal reasoning, justifications of claims, and functional underpinnings of procedures, (3) essay quality when students attempt to answer challenging problems, (4) a cloze task that has students fill in missing words of texts that articulate explanatory reasoning on the subject matter, and (5) performance on problems that require problem-solving.

Assessments of learning gains obviously depend on the comparison conditions. The learning gains are approximately .8 for AutoTutor compared to a pretest and a condition of reading from a textbook on the same topics for an equivalent amount of time. The learning gains are approximately the same for AutoTutor and an expert human tutor who interacts with the student by computer-mediated communication (as opposed to face-to-face). The largest learning gains from AutoTutor have been on deep-reasoning measures rather than measures of shallow knowledge. AutoTutor is most effective when there is an intermediate gap between the student's prior knowledge and the ideal answers of AutoTutor; AutoTutor is not particularly effective in facilitating learning in students with high domain knowledge, nor when the material is too much over the student's head. It should be noted that the effectiveness of AutoTutor is less prominent in comparison conditions that attempt to control for the content that students are exposed to. The conversational AutoTutor has (a) a 0.22 sigma compared with reading textbook segments directly relevant to the AutoTutor's main questions/problems, (b) a 0.07 sigma compared with reading a script that succinctly answers the questions posed by AutoTutor, and (c) a 0.13 sigma compared with AutoTutor presenting speech acts in print instead of the talking head. The interactive AutoTutor-3D version has a .22 effect size over the normal conversational AutoTutor.

The conversations managed by AutoTutor are not perfect, but they are adequate for guiding students through the sessions with minimal difficulties. In fact, the dialogue is sufficiently tuned so that a bystander who observes tutorial dialogue in print cannot tell whether a particular turn was generated by AutoTutor or by an expert human tutor of computer literacy (Person & Graesser, 2002). A series of studies were conducted that randomly sampled AutoTutor's turns. Half of the turns were generated by AutoTutor and half were substituted by a human expert tutor on the basis of the dialogue history. Bystander participants were presented these tutoring moves in a written transcript and asked to decide whether each was generated by a computer or a human. The bystanders were unable correctly identify which moves were generated by the human tutor versus AutoTutor. Thus, AutoTutor successfully passed the *bystander Turing test* for individual tutoring turns. However, a bystander can eventually tell whether a sequence of turns was part of a dialogue with AutoTutor versus a human tutor. In conclusion, AutoTutor is close enough to human tutorial dialogue to keep the conversation going and also to promote learning.

Student ratings of AutoTutor have also been collected in order to get their impressions of the tutoring environment. The ratings lean toward the positive side, but there have been no systematic comparisons with human tutors or alternative learning environments. We have compared different versions of AutoTutor, but a provocative finding has made us somewhat skeptical about relying on ratings of student impressions. Specifically, Jackson and Graesser (2007) documented that there was a negative relationship between deep learning and enjoyment: students least preferred those versions from which they learned most. Students' metacognition of learning is limited (Graesser, D'Mello, & Person, 2009), so it is perhaps not surprising that their ratings of liking were not positively correlated with learning. Deep learning is challenging and sometimes painful, which may clash with an enjoyable experience for some groups of students.

These assessments point to the successes of AutoTutor, but it is important also to acknowledge some of its limitations. One limitation is that the conversational dialogue may have minimal incremental gains on learning when the exchange is time-consuming and the knowledge covered is shallow rather than deep. The conversational interaction is tedious for some students and even irritating far a small percentage. A second limitation is that students lose patience with AutoTutor when the conversation breaks down. As mentioned throughout this chapter, such breakdowns occur when the student modeling is imperfect, the curriculum script is incomplete, student speech acts are misclassified, and AutoTutor is viewed as being unresponsive to what the student is saying. A third limitation is that AutoTutor can correctly answer only a modest proportion of student questions (Graesser, McNamara, & VanLehn, 2005) so students eventually stop asking them. This puts a damper on self-regulated learning and also mixed-initiative dialogue.

FUTURE RESEARCH DIRECTIONS AND AUTOTUTOR EXTENSIONS

One important future direction is to improve the student modeling and conversational facilities of AutoTutor in order to minimize some of its persistent blemishes. This can be accomplished in a number of ways. There can be checks in the authoring tools to make sure that the content is complete when it is prepared by the author of the curriculum scripts. We have tried to correct this by developing facilities to improve the ease and quality of authoring the curriculum scripts, but this has not been an easy road. The best authors of content have some nontrivial expertise in information technologies, language, and discourse rather than being an instructor without such expertise. There needs to be a more intense research effort on understanding the process of authoring content in AutoTutor as well as other advanced learning environments.

A second direction is to develop systems that analyze language and discourse at deeper levels. Researchers can move beyond LSA and regular expressions and into more structure-sensitive processing and semantic decomposition (Olney, 2009; Olney, Graesser, & Person, 2010; Rus, McCarthy, McNamara, & Graesser, 2008). The dialogue manager module can move beyond lists of production rules and finite-state grammars and into the realm of recursive, complex planning and multiple-goal agendas. This approach of deeper natural language processing and discourse management is currently being pursued by Adrew Olney's Guru (see chapter XX by Olney, Person, & Graesser, 2010) in the area of biology and by Vasile Rus's DeepTutor in the area of physics. These extensions of AutoTutor are currently under development in the Institute for Intelligent Systems at the University of Memphis.

A third direction is to develop more sophisticated question answering facilities so that AutoTutor can answer a broad diversity of questions. This would contribute to mixed-initiative dialogue and put more control in the hands of the learner. There currently is a community of researchers who are exploring and testing computational models of question generation in learning environments (Rus & Graesser, 2009; see chapter xx). These efforts should contribute significantly to this direction.

A fourth direction is to build a version of AutoTutor that is sensitive to the learner's emotions and motivational states. D'Mello and Graesser (in press, chapoter xx) discusses this exciting extension. Related approaches to address motivation include: improvements in the agents speech and visual displays, implementing dimensions of personality in the agents, and integrating game-based facilities.

A fifth direction is to build a system that enhances AutoTutor's scalability. Xiangen Hu's AutoTutor-Lite is a minimalistic version of AutoTutor that includes the AutoTutor-style interface and interaction (animated agent and natural language conversation), but with a lightweight language analyzer and dialogue manager. AutoTutor-Lite has excellent authoring tools that lesson planners and instructors can use, even when they have minimal computer skills. Moreover, AutoTutor-Lite can be applied to powerpoint content on any verbal subject matter, is easily customizable, and can be integrated into e-learning environments on the web as well as the desktop. One can imagine an industry that "autotutorizes" the conventional eLearning content that is widely available.

Finally, AutoTutor has been a component in more comprehensive advanced learning environments. The Human Use Regulatory Affairs Advisor (HURAA) trains military personnel on research ethics in a web facility that has a full suite of learning modules, including an AutoTutor-like navigational guide (Hu & Graesser, 1994). Operation ARIES! (Millis, Cai, Graesser, Halpern, & Wallace, 2009) helps students learn about scientific methods in a game environment that includes an eBook with 22 chapters and case studies that are critiqued by students regarding scientific flaws. This system is guided by multiple animated agents, including a tutor agent and a peer agent; the human student is both tutored by the human agent and actively tutors the student agent. Danielle McNamara also has developed trainers with multiple interactive agents, as in the case of iSTART for teaching self explanations during reading (McNamara et al., 2004, 2007, see chapter xx) and of W-Pal for teaching writing (McNamara et al., chapter xx).

We believe that researchers have only begun to scratch the surface of using animated pedagogical agents with natural language interaction. Agents can have an endless number of dialogue styles, strategies, personalities, and physical features. We have developed one AutoTutor version that is emotionally supportive and another version that tries to shake up the emotions of the student by being rude and pretentiously telling the student what emotion the student is having. The rude AutoTutor is very engaging for some students whereas others would rather interact with the polite tutor. Student motivation may improve when the agents are matched to the cognitive, personality, emotional, and social profiles of individual students. The world of pedagogical agents is indeed on par with communication with other humans.

REFERENCES

Anderson, J. R., & Gluck, K. (2001). What role do cognitive architectures play in intelligent tutoring systems? In Klahr, D., & Carver, S. M. (Eds.), *Cognition & instruction: Twenty-five years of progress* (pp. 227–262). Hillsdale, NJ: Erlbaum.

Baylor, A. L., & Kim, Y. (2005). Simulating instructional roles through pedagogical agents. *International Journal of Artificial Intelligence in Education, 15*, 5–115.

Chi, M. T. H., Siler, S. A., & Jeong, H. (2004). Can tutors monitor students' understanding accurately? *Cognition and Instruction, 22*(3), 363–387. doi:10.1207/s1532690xci2203_4

Cohen, P. A., Kulik, J. A., & Kulik, C. C. (1982). Educational outcomes of tutoring: A meta-analysis of findings. *American Educational Research Journal, 19,* 237–248.

Corbett, A. T. (2001). Cognitive computer tutors: Solving the two-sigma problem. *User Modeling: Proceedings of the Eighth International Conference, UM 2001,* (pp. 137-147).

D'Mello, S., & Graesser, A. C. (in press). Multimodal semi-automated affect detection from conversational cues, gross body language, and facial features. *User Modeling and User-Adapted Interaction.*

D'Mello, S., King, B., Chipman, P., & Graesser, A. C. (in press). Towards spoken human-computer tutorial dialogues. *Human-Computer Interaction.*

D'Mello, S., Olney, A. M., & Person, N. (in press). Mining collaborative patterns in tutorial dialogues. *Journal of Educational Data Mining.*

Doignon, J. P., & Falmagne, J. C. (1999). *Knowledge spaces.* Berlin, Germany: Springer. doi:10.1007/978-3-642-58625-5

Evens, M., & Michael, J. (2006). *One-on-one tutoring by humans and machines.* Mahwah, NJ: Erlbaum.

Gholson, B., Witherspoon, A., Morgan, B., Brittingham, J. K., Coles, R., & Graesser, A. C. (2009). Exploring the deep-level reasoning questions effect during vicarious learning among eighth to eleventh graders in the domains of computer literacy and Newtonian physics. *Instructional Science, 37,* 487–493. doi:10.1007/s11251-008-9069-2

Graesser, A. C., Chipman, P., Haynes, B. C., & Olney, A. (2005). AutoTutor: An intelligent tutoring system with mixed-initiative dialogue. *IEEE Transactions on Education, 48,* 612–618. doi:10.1109/TE.2005.856149

Graesser, A. C., D'Mello, S., & Person, N. K. (2009). Metaknowledge in tutoring. In Hacker, D., Donlosky, J., & Graesser, A. C. (Eds.), *Handbook of metacognition in education* (pp. 361–382). New York, NY: Taylor & Francis.

Graesser, A. C., Jeon, M., & Dufty, D. (2008). Agent technologies designed to facilitate interactive knowledge construction. *Discourse Processes, 45,* 298–322. doi:10.1080/01638530802145395

Graesser, A. C., Lu, S., Jackson, G. T., Mitchell, H., Ventura, M., Olney, A., & Louwerse, M. M. (2004). AutoTutor: A tutor with dialogue in natural language. *Behavior Research Methods, Instruments, & Computers, 36,* 180–193. doi:10.3758/BF03195563

Graesser, A. C., Lu, S., Jackson, G. T., Mitchell, H., Ventura, M., Olney, A., & Louwerse, M. M. (2004). AutoTutor: A tutor with dialogue in natural language. *Behavior Research Methods, Instruments, & Computers, 36,* 180–193. doi:10.3758/BF03195563

Graesser, A. C., McNamara, D. S., & VanLehn, K. (2005). Scaffolding deep comprehension strategies through Point&Query, AutoTutor, and iSTART. *Educational Psychologist, 40,* 225–234. doi:10.1207/s15326985ep4004_4

Graesser, A. C., Moreno, K., Marineau, J., Adcock, A., Olney, A., & Person, N. (2003). AutoTutor improves deep learning of computer literacy: Is it the dialog or the talking head? In Hoppe, U., Verdejo, F., & Kay, J. (Eds.), *Proceedings of artificial intelligence in education (pp, 47-.54).* Amsterdam, The Netherlands: IOS Press.

Graesser, A. C., Penumatsa, P., Ventura, M., Cai, Z., & Hu, X. (2007). Using LSA in AutoTutor: Learning through mixed initiative dialogue in natural language. In Landauer, T., McNamara, D., Dennis, S., & Kintsch, W. (Eds.), *Handbook of latent semantic analysis* (pp. 243–262). Mahwah, NJ: Erlbaum.

Graesser, A. C., Person, N., & Harter, D. Tutoring Research Group. (2001). Teaching tactics and dialog in AutoTutor. *International Journal of Artificial Intelligence in Education, 12*, 257–279.

Graesser, A. C., & Person, N. K. (1994). Question asking during tutoring. *American Educational Research Journal, 31*, 104–137.

Graesser, A. C., Person, N. K., & Magliano, J. P. (1995). Collaborative dialogue patterns in naturalistic one-to-one tutoring. *Applied Cognitive Psychology, 9*, 495–522. doi:10.1002/acp.2350090604

Hestenes, D., Wells, M., & Swackhamer, G. (1992). Force concept inventory. *The Physics Teacher, 30*, 141–158. doi:10.1119/1.2343497

Hu, X., & Graesser, A. C. (2004). Human use regulatory affairs advisor (HURAA): Learning about research ethics with intelligent learning modules. *Behavior Research Methods, Instruments, & Computers, 36*, 241–249. doi:10.3758/BF03195569

Jackson, G. T., & Graesser, A. C. (2006). Applications of human tutorial dialog in AutoTutor: An intelligent tutoring system. *Revista Signos, 39*, 31–48.

Jackson, G. T., & Graesser, A. C. (2007). Content matters: An investigation of feedback categories within an ITS. In Luckin, R., Koedinger, K., & Greer, J. (Eds.), *Artificial intelligence in education: Building technology rich learning contexts that work* (pp. 127–134). Amsterdam, The Netherlands: IOS Press.

Jackson, G. T., Olney, A., Graesser, A. C., & Kim, H. J. (2006). AutoTutor 3-D simulations: Analyzing user's actions and learning trends. In R. Son (Ed.), *Proceedings of the 28th Annual Meeting of the Cognitive Science Society* (pp. 1557–1562). Mahwah, NJ: Erlbaum.

Johnson, W. L., & Valente, A. (2008). Tactical language and culture training systems: Using artificial intelligence to teach foreign languages and cultures. In *Proceedings of the 20th Innovative Applications of Artificial Intelligence (IAAI) Conference.*

Jurafsky, D., & Martin, J. H. (2008). *Speech and language processing: An introduction to natural language processing, computational linguistics, and speech recognition.* Upper Saddle River, NJ: Prentice-Hall.

Koedinger, K. R., Anderson, J. R., Hadley, W. H., & Mark, M. (1997). Intelligent tutoring goes to school in the big city. *International Journal of Artificial Intelligence in Education, 8*, 30–43.

Landauer, T., McNamara, D. S., Dennis, S., & Kintsch, W. (Eds.). (2007). *Handbook of latent semantic analysis.* Mahwah, NJ: Erlbaum.

Lesgold, A., Lajoie, S. P., Bunzo, M., & Eggan, G. (1992). SHERLOCK: A coached practice environment for an electronics trouble-shooting job. In Larkin, J. H., & Chabay, R. W. (Eds.), *Computer assisted instruction and intelligent tutoring systems: Shared goals and complementary approaches* (pp. 201–238). Hillsdale, NJ: Erlbaum.

Litman, D. J., Rose, C. P., Forbes-Riley, K., VanLehn, K., Bhembe, D., & Silliman, S. (2006). Spoken versus typed human and computer dialogue tutoring. *International Journal of Artificial Intelligence in Education, 16*, 145–170.

McNamara, D. S., Levinstein, I. B., & Boonthum, C. (2004). iSTART: Interactive strategy training for active reading and thinking. *Behavior Research Methods, Instruments, & Computers, 36*, 222–233. doi:10.3758/BF03195567

McNamara, D. S., O'Reilly, T., Rowe, M., Boonthum, C., & Levinstein, I. B. (2007). iSTART: A web-based tutor that teaches self-explanation and metacognitive reading strategies. In D. S. McNamara (Ed.), *Reading comprehension strategies: Theories, interventions, and technologies.* Mahwah, NJ: Erlbaum.

Millis, K., Cai, Z., Graesser, A., Halpern, D., & Wallace, P. (2009). Learning scientific inquiry by asking questions in an educational game. In T. Bastiaens, et al. (Eds.), *Proceedings of World Conference on E-Learning in Corporate, Government, Healthcare, and Higher Education* (pp. 2951-2956). Chesapeake, VA: AACE.

Mitrovic, A., Martin, B., & Suraweera, P. (2007). Intelligent tutors for all: The constraint-based approach. *IEEE Intelligent Systems, 22*(4), 38–45. doi:10.1109/MIS.2007.74

Moreno, R., & Mayer, R. E. (2007). Interactive multimodal learning environments. *Educational Psychology Review, 19*, 309–326. doi:10.1007/s10648-007-9047-2

Olney, A., Louwerse, M., Mathews, E., Marineau, J., Hite-Mitchell, H., & Graesser, A. (2003). Utterance classification in AutoTutor. In J. Burstein & C. Leacock (Eds.), *Proceedings of the HLT-NAACL 03 Workshop on Building Educational Applications Using Natural Language Processing*. Philadelphia, PA: Association for Computational Linguistics.

Olney, A. M. (2009). GnuTutor: An open source intelligent tutoring system based on AutoTutor. In *Proceedings of the 2009 AAAI Fall Symposium on Cognitive and Metacognitive Educational Systems* (pp. 70-75). Washington, DC: AAAI Press.

Olney, A. M., Graesser, A. C., & Person, N. K. (2010). Tutorial dialog in natural language. In Nkambou, R., Mizoguchi, R., & Bourdeau, J. (Eds.), *Advances in intelligent tutoring systems* (p. xx). New York, NY: Springer. doi:10.1007/978-3-642-14363-2_9

Olney, A. M., Person, N. K., & Graesser, A. C. (2011). Guru: Designing a conversational expert intelligent tutoring system. In McCarthy, P. M., & Boonthum-Denecke, C. (Eds.), *Applied natural language processing and content analysis: Identification, investigation, and resolution*. Hershey, PA: IGI Global.

Person, N. K., & Graesser, A. C., & the Tutoring Research Group. (2002, June). *Human or computer? AutoTutor in a bystander Turing test*. Paper presented at the Intelligent Tutoring Systems 2002 Conference, Biarritz, France.

Pon-Barry, H., Clark, B., Schultz, K., Bratt, E. O., Peters, S., & Haley, D. (2005). Contextualizing reflective dialogue in a spoken conversational tutor. *Journal of Educational Technology & Society, 8*, 42–51.

Ritter, S., Anderson, J. R., Koedinger, K. R., & Corbett, A. (2007). Cognitive tutor: Applied research in mathematics education. *Psychonomic Bulletin & Review, 14*, 249–255. doi:10.3758/BF03194060

Rus, V., & Graesser, A. C. (2006). Deeper natural language processing for evaluating student answers in intelligent tutoring systems. *Proceedings of the American Association of Artificial Intelligence*. Menlo Park, CA: AAAI.

Rus, V., & Graesser, A. C. (Eds.). (2009). *The question generation shared task and evaluation challenge*.

Rus, V., McCarthy, P. M., McNamara, D. S., & Graesser, A. C. (2008). A study of textual entailment. *International Journal of Artificial Intelligence Tools, 17*, 659–685. doi:10.1142/S0218213008004096

Sleeman, D., & Brown, J. S. (Eds.). (1982). *Intelligent tutoring systems*. Orlando, FL: Academic Press, Inc.

VanLehn, K. (2006). The behavior of tutoring systems. *International Journal of Artificial Intelligence in Education, 16*(3), 227–265.

VanLehn, K., Graesser, A. C., Jackson, G. T., Jordan, P., Olney, A., & Rose, C. P. (2007). When are tutorial dialogues more effective than reading? *Cognitive Science, 31*, 3–62. doi:10.1080/03640210709336984

VanLehn, K., Jordan, P., Rosé, C. P., et al. (2002). The architecture of Why2-Atlas: A coach for qualitative physics essay writing. In S. A. Cerri, G. Gouarderes, & F. Paraguacu (Eds.), *Intelligent Tutoring Systems: 6th International Conference* (pp. 158-167). Berlin, Germany: Springer.

Woolf, B. (2009). *Building intelligent interactive tutors: Student-centered strategies for revolutionizing e-learning*. San Francisco, CA: Elsevier Inc., Morgan Kauffman.

ADDITIONAL READING

Anderson, J. R., Corbett, A. T., Koedinger, K. R., & Pelletier, R. (1995). Cognitive tutors: Lessons learned. *Journal of the Learning Sciences*, *4*, 167–207. doi:10.1207/s15327809jls0402_2

Baker, R. S., Corbett, A. T., Koedinger, K. R., & Wagner, A. Z. (2004). Off-task behavior in the cognitive tutor classroom: When students "Game the System". *Proceedings of ACM CHI 2004: Computer-Human Interaction*, 383-390.

Biswas, G., Leelawong, K., Schwartz, D., & Vye, N.The Teachable Agents Group at Vanderbilt. (2005). Learning by teaching: A new agent paradigm for educational software. *Applied Artificial Intelligence*, *19*, 363–392. doi:10.1080/08839510590910200

Bloom, B. S. (1984). The 2 sigma problem: The search for methods of group instruction as effective as one-to-one tutoring. *Educational Researcher*, *13*, 4–16.

Bull, S., & Kay, J. (2007). Student models that invite the learner in: The SMILI open learner modeling framework. *International Journal of Artificial Intelligence in Education*, *17*, 89–120.

Chi, M. T. H., Roy, M., & Hausmann, R. G. M. (2008). Observing tutorial dialogues collaboratively: Insights about human tutoring effectiveness from vicarious learning. *Cognitive Science*, *32*(2), 301–341. doi:10.1080/03640210701863396

Chi, M. T. H., Siler, S., Yamauchi, T., Jeong, H., & Hausmann, R. (2001). Learning from human tutoring. *Cognitive Science*, *25*, 471–534. doi:10.1207/s15516709cog2504_1

Cole, R., van Vuuren, S., Pellom, B., Hacioglu, K., Ma, J., & Movellan, J. (2003). Perceptive animated interfaces: First steps toward a new paradigm for human computer interaction. *Proceedings of the IEEE*, *91*, 1391–1405. doi:10.1109/JPROC.2003.817143

Collins, A., & Halverson, R. (2009). *Rethinking education in the age of technology: The digital revolution and schooling in America*. New York: Teacher College Press.

Corbett, A. T., & Anderson, J. R. (1995). Knowledge tracing: Modeling the acquisition of procedural knowledge. *User Modeling and User-Adapted Interaction*, *4*, 253–278. doi:10.1007/BF01099821

Craig, S. D., Sullins, J., Witherspoon, A., & Gholson, B. (2006). Deep-level reasoning questions effect: The role of dialog and deep-level reasoning questions during vicarious learning. *Cognition and Instruction*, *24*(4), 563–589. doi:10.1207/s1532690xci2404_4

D'Mello, S. K., Picard, R., & Graesser, A. C. (2007). Toward an affect-sensitive AutoTutor. *IEEE Intelligent Systems*, *22*, 53–61. doi:10.1109/MIS.2007.79

Fuchs, L., Fuchs, D., Bentz, J., Phillips, N., & Hamlett, C. (1994). The nature of students' interactions during peer tutoring with and without prior training and experience. *American Educational Research Journal*, *31*, 75–103.

Gholson, B., Witherspoon, A., Morgan, B., Brittingham, J. K., Coles, R., & Graesser, A. C. (2009). Exploring the deep-level reasoning questions effect during vicarious learning among eighth to eleventh graders in the domains of computer literacy and Newtonian physics. *Instructional Science, 37*, 487–493. doi:10.1007/s11251-008-9069-2

Graesser, A. C., Conley, M. W., & Olney, A. (in preparation). Intelligent tutoring systems. In Graham, S., & Harris, K. (Eds.), *APA Handbook of Educational Psychology*. Washington, DC: American Psychological Association.

Gratch, J., Rickel, J., Andre, E., Cassell, J., Petajan, E., & Badler, N. (2002). Creating interactive virtual humans: Some assembly required. *IEEE Intelligent Systems, 17*, 54–63. doi:10.1109/MIS.2002.1024753

Kolodner, J., Cox, M., & Gonzalez-Calero, P. (2005). Case-based reasoning-inspired approaches to education. *The Knowledge Engineering Review, 20*(3), 299–303. doi:10.1017/S0269888906000634

Lepper, M. R., & Woolverton, M. (2002). The wisdom of practice: Lessons learned from the study of highly effective tutors. In Aronson, J. (Ed.), *Improving academic achievement: Impact of psychological factors on education* (pp. 135–158). Orlando, FL: Academic Press. doi:10.1016/B978-012064455-1/50010-5

McQuiggan, S., & Lester, J. (2007). Modeling and evaluating empathy in embodied companion agents. *International Journal of Human-Computer Studies, 65*, 348–360. doi:10.1016/j.ijhcs.2006.11.015

Moreno, R., & Mayer, R. E. (2004). Personalized messages that promote science learning in virtual environments. *Journal of Educational Psychology, 96*, 165–173. doi:10.1037/0022-0663.96.1.165

Palincsar, A. S., & Brown, A. L. (1984). Reciprocal teaching of comprehension- fostering and monitoring activities. *Cognition and Instruction, 1*, 117–175. doi:10.1207/s1532690xci0102_1

Person, N. K., Kreuz, R. J., Zwaan, R., & Graesser, A. C. (1995). Pragmatics and pedagogy: Conversational rules and politeness strategies may inhibit effective tutoring. *Cognition and Instruction, 13*, 161–188. doi:10.1207/s1532690xci1302_1

Reeves, B., & Nass, C. (1996). *The Media Equasion: how people treat computers, televisions, and new media like real people and places*. Stanford, California: University Press.

Roscoe, R. D., & Chi, M. T. H. (2007). Understanding tutor learning: Knowledge-building and knowledge-telling in peer tutors' explanations and questions. *Review of Educational Research, 77*, 534–574. doi:10.3102/0034654307309920

Schwartz, D. L., & Bransford, J. D. (1998). A time for telling. *Cognition and Instruction, 16*(4), 475–522. doi:10.1207/s1532690xci1604_4

KEY TERMS AND DEFINITIONS

Agent: A computer module that intelligently interacts with a human by detecting states of the human and system and by responding to the human in a fashion that achieves specific goals.

Authoring Tool: A computer facility for creating and modifying content in a computerized learning environment.

Curriculum Script: The subject matter knowledge that is stored in the computer on the topic being tutored. The learning management system accesses and uses this content during the course of producing responses to the student.

Dialogue Management: The algorithms that the system uses to track the student's knowledge, the dialogue history, and the state of the system, and to respond in a fashion that achieves conversational goals in a coherent manner.

Latent Semantic Analysis (LSA): A statistical representation of words and world knowledge that is based on the words that are used in a large corpus of documents.

Metacognition: Knowledge about nature of cognitive states and processes.

Pattern Matching and Pattern Completion: Pattern matching is an algorithm that computes the extent to which student contributions match expectations. Pattern completion is the generation of actions that attempt to achieve high pattern matches.

Semantic Matching: A comparison between two texts on the degree to which they have similar meaning. For example, student expressions are compared with expectations of the tutor.

Speech Act: A statement or utterance in a conversational turn that has a particular discourse function, such as a question, command, assertion, promise, or feedback expression.

Student Modeling: The computer algorithms for tracking what the student knows about subject matter knowledge.

Chapter 11

Coh-Metrix:
An Automated Tool for Theoretical and Applied Natural Language Processing

Danielle S. McNamara
Arizona State University, USA

Arthur C. Graesser
The University of Memphis, USA

ABSTRACT

Coh-Metrix provides indices for the characteristics of texts on multiple levels of analysis, including word characteristics, sentence characteristics, and the discourse relationships between ideas in text. Coh-Metrix was developed to provide a wide range of indices within one tool. This chapter describes Coh-Metrix and studies that have been conducted validating the Coh-Metrix indices. Coh-Metrix can be used to better understand differences between texts and to explore the extent to which linguistic and discourse features successfully distinguish between text types. Coh-Metrix can also be used to develop and improve natural language processing approaches. We also describe the Coh-Metrix Text Easability Component Scores, which provide a picture of text ease (and hence potential challenges). The Text Easability components provided by Coh-Metrix go beyond traditional readability measures by providing metrics of text characteristics on multiple levels of language and discourse.

INTRODUCTION

Coh-Metrix is an automated tool that provides linguistic indices for text and discourse (Graesser, McNamara, Louwerse, & Cai, 2004). Coh-Metrix was developed to meet three practical needs. First,

at the time that the Coh-Metrix research project began in 2002, there were no readily available tools that provided an array of indices on words or texts. For example, if a researcher needed the word frequency values for words or sentences in a text, one tool might be available (though challenging to find). But another tool would have to be used for measures of word concreteness,

DOI: 10.4018/978-1-60960-741-8.ch011

familiarity, imagery, syntactic complexity, and so on. In other words, there existed no linguistic workbench capable of providing a wide array of measures on language and discourse. Second, traditional measures of text difficulty, referred to as *readability*, were outdated given the maturation of our understanding of text and discourse (Clark, 1996; Graesser, Gernsbacher, & Goldman, 2003; Kintsch, 1998). There was a growing recognition of a number of factors contributing to text difficulty that are not considered within traditional measures of text readability. Third, there existed no automated measures of text cohesion. Whereas recognition of the importance of cohesion had flourished in the 80s and 90s (Gernsbacher, 1990; Goldman, Graesser, & Van den Broek, 1999; Louwerse, 2001; McNamara & Kintsch, 1996; Sanders & Noordman, 2000), there were no objective, implemented measures of cohesion available. Thus, with the overarching goal of providing more informative measures of text complexity, particularly considering text cohesion, we embarked in 2002 on a mission to develop Coh-Metrix (initially funded by an Institute of Education Sciences). This chapter describes some motivating factors that led to Coh-Metrix, an overview of the measures provided by Coh-Metrix, some of the many NLP studies that have been completed over the last eight years, and the ultimate outcome of our endeavors: Coh-Metrix *Text Complexity* Components.

READABILITY VS. COHESION: WHY COH-METRIX WAS DEVELOPED

Readability measures are the most common approach to estimating the difficulty of a text and hundreds have been developed over the past century. Readability formulas became popular in the 1950s and by the 1980s over 200 readability algorithms had been developed, with over a 1000 supporting studies (Chall & Dale, 1995; Dubay, 2004). The most well known readability measures include Flesch-Kincaid Grade Level (Klare, 1974-5), Degrees of Reading Power (DRP; Koslin, Zeno, & Koslin, 1987), and Lexile scores (Stenner, 2006). Measures of readability are highly correlated because they are based on the same constructs: the difficulty of the individual words and the complexity of the separate sentences in the text. However, the way in which these constructs are operationalized and the underlying statistical assumptions vary somewhat across readability measures. The Flesch-Kincaid Grade Level metric is based on the length of words (i.e., number of letters or syllables) and length of sentences (i.e., number of words). DRP and Lexile scores relate these characteristics of the texts to readers' performance on cloze tasks. In a cloze task, the reader reads a text with some words left blank; the reader is asked to fill in the words by generating them or by selecting a word from a set of options (usually the latter). Using this methodology, the appropriateness of a text for a particular reader can be calculated based on the characteristics of the texts and the reader's performance on cloze tasks. A particular text would be predicated to be at the reader's level of proficiency if the reader can perform the cloze task at a threshold of performance (75%) for texts with similar characteristics (i.e., with the same word and sentence level difficulties). A text can be defined as too easy if performance is higher than 75% and too difficult to the extent it is lower than 75%.

Readability measures based on word and sentence characteristics (i.e., usually length) have validity as indices of text difficulty. When words contain more letters or syllables, they tend to be less frequently used in a language. Readers need to have greater exposure to language and text in order to encounter less frequent words and to know what they mean. Clearly, a requisite to comprehension is knowing the meaning of the words in a text. In turn, to the extent that a sentence contains more words, there is a greater likelihood that the sentence is more complex syntactically. Readers who have had less exposure to language and text (i.e., younger and less skilled readers) face greater challenges in parsing syntactically complex sentences.

In sum, word and sentence factors go a long way in accounting for sources of text difficulty. However, these factors alone explain only a part of text comprehension, and ignore many language and discourse features that are theoretically influential at estimating comprehension difficulty. At the heart of Coh-Metrix is the assumption that *cohesion* is one of the most important aspects of language that is ignored by readability measures. Cohesion is the linguistic glue that holds together the events and concepts conveyed within a text. Beyond the words and separate sentences in the text, are the relationships between the sentences and larger units of text. Explicit cues in the text help the reader to process, understand, or infer those relationships. A simple but powerful source of cohesion is referential and semantic overlap of adjacent sentences, pairs of sentences in a paragraph, and adjacent paragraphs. Simply put, when words, concepts, or ideas overlap between sentences, that content forms a link between the sentences. Another source of cohesion is connecting words (or *connectives*) such as *because* and *however*. Connectives tell the reader that there is a relationship between two ideas, and help the reader to understand the direction of the relationship.

Cohesive cues help the reader to understand connections among sentences and paragraphs. This, in turn, facilitates understanding of the words and sentences, and enhances the reader' global understanding of the text. Many studies, across a variety of paradigms and dependent measures, have shown that cohesive cues in text facilitate reading comprehension and help readers construct more coherent mental representations of text content (Britton & Gulgoz, 1991; McNamara, 2001; Zwaan & Radvanksy, 1998). For this reason, the primary bank of indices provided by Coh-Metrix assesses the cohesion of the text.

COH-METRIX MEASURES OF LANGUAGE AND COHESION

The number and particular measures that are provided by Coh-Metrix depends on the version and the type of tool. We have developed public versions of the tool that analyze individual texts and have provided between 40 and 80 validated indices. We have also developed internal versions of Coh-Metrix that analyze texts in batches and that include 600-1000 indices, many of which are redundant and many of which have not been validated (and thus we don't release them to the public). Although the specific Coh-Metrix measures vary somewhat across versions and tools, the banks of measures are quite similar.

Descriptive

Coh-Metrix provides descriptive indices such as the number and length of words, sentences, and paragraphs. These indices help the user to check the Coh-Metrix output (e.g., to make sure that the numbers make sense) and also to interpret patterns of data.

Co-Referential Cohesion

Co-referential cohesion refers to overlap in content words between local sentences. For example, this sentence overlaps with the previous sentence by means of the singular form of the word *sentence*. The sentences below provide another example from Chapter 2 of the novel, Jane Eyre:

"I resisted all the way: a new thing for me." Jane says this as Bessie is taking her to be locked in the red-room after she had fought back when John Reed struck her. For the first time Jane is asserting her rights, and this action leads to her eventually being sent to Lowood School.

In this excerpt, the explicit referential cohesion is provided only by the overlap in the subject, Jane. While there is some semantic overlap, much of this must be inferred by the reader.

Coh-Metrix indices of co-referential cohesion vary along two dimensions. First, the indices vary in terms of locality, from local to more global indices. Local indices include overlap between consecutive, adjacent sentences. Indices become increasingly global to the extent that they consider overlap among 2, 3, 4, or all of the sentences in a paragraph or text. Second, the indices vary in terms of the explicitness of the overlap. Noun overlap measures the proportion of sentences in a text for which there are overlapping nouns. Argument overlap relaxes the noun constraint by also considering nouns that have the same stems (e.g., baby, babies; mouse, mice) and also considers overlap between pronouns. It should be noted, however, that Coh-Metrix does not attempt to determine the referents of pronouns (e.g., *they* refers to Sally and John). Stem overlap includes overlap between nouns in one sentence with words that share a common stem in another, including nouns as well as other types of content words (i.e., verbs, adjectives, adverbs). Whereas the latter three indices are binary (i.e., there either *is* or *is not* any overlap between a pair of sentences), content word overlap refers to the proportion of content words that are shared between sentences.

Latent Semantic Analysis (LSA; Landauer, McNamara, Dennis, & Kintsch, 2007; also see Kintsch & Kintsch, this volume) provides measures of semantic overlap between sentences or between paragraphs. LSA considers meaning overlap between explicit words and also words that are implicitly similar or related in meaning. For example, *home* in one sentence will have a relatively high degree of semantic overlap with *house* and *table* in another sentence. LSA uses a statistical technique called singular value decomposition to condense a large corpus of texts to 100-500 statistical dimensions. The conceptual similarity between any two text excerpts (e.g.,

word, clause, sentence, text) is computed as the geometric cosine between the values and weighted dimensions of the two text excerpts. The value of the cosine typically varies from 0 to 1. Coh-Metrix measures LSA-based cohesion in several ways, such as LSA similarity between adjacent sentences, LSA similarity between all possible pairs of sentences in a paragraph, and LSA similarity between adjacent paragraphs.

Situation Model

Referential cohesion is one linguistic feature that can influence a reader's deeper understanding of text. However, there are deeper levels of meaning that go beyond the words. The expression *situation model* has been used by researchers in discourse processing and cognitive science to refer to the deeper meaning representations that involve much more than the explicit words (van Dijk & Kintsch, 1983; Graesser & McNamara, in press; Graesser, Singer, & Trabasso, 1994; Kintsch, 1998; Zwaan & Radvansky, 1998). For example, with episodes in narrative text, the situation model would include *the plot*; and, in an informational text about the circulatory system, the situation model might include *the flow of the blood*. The situation model comprises a mental representation of the deeper meaning of the text (Kintsch, 1998). And, some researchers have described the situational model in terms of the features that are present in the comprehender's mental representation when a given context is activated (e.g., Singer & Leon, 2007).

The content words and connective words systematically constrain and are aligned with aspects of these inferred meaning representations, but the explicit words do not go the full distance in specifying the deep meanings. Coh-Metrix provides indices for a number of measures that are potentially related the reader's situation model understanding. These include measures of causality, such as incidence scores for causal verbs, intentional verbs, and causal particles (e.g., connectives like *because, in order to*), and ratios of causal particles to causal verbs. There are measures of verb overlap. These indices are indicative of the extent to which verbs (which have salient links to actions, events, and states) are repeated across the text. There are measures of temporal cohesion and logical cohesion as well. These and other measures are reflective of elements of a text that are more or less likely to support a reader's construction of a coherent situation model.

Lexical Diversity

Lexical diversity refers to the variety of words (*types*) that occur in a text in relation to the number of words (*tokens*). When the number of word types is equal to the total number of words (tokens), then all of the words are different. In that case, lexical diversity is at a maximum, and the text is either very low in cohesion or very short. Lexical diversity is lower (and cohesion is higher) when more words are used multiple times across the text. Coh-Metrix includes three indices of lexical diversity: type-token ratio (TTR), *vocd*, and the Measure of Textual Lexical Diversity (MTLD). TTR is simply the number of unique words divided by the number of tokens of the words. The index produced by *vocd* is calculated through a computational procedure that fits TTR random samples with ideal TTR curves. MTLD is calculated as the mean length of sequential word strings in a text that maintain a given TTR value. TTR is correlated with text length because as the number of word tokens increases, there is a lower likelihood of those words being unique. Measures such as *vocd* and MTLD overcome that confound by using sampling methods (McCarthy & Jarvis, 2010).

Connectives

Coh-Metrix provides an incidence score (occurrence per 1000 words) for all connectives as well as different types of connectives. Indices are provided on five general types of connectives:

causal (*because, so*), additive *(and, moreover)*, temporal *(first, until)*, logical *(and, or)*, and adversative/contrastive *(although, whereas)*. In addition, there is a distinction between positive connectives (*also, moreover*) and negative connectives (*however, but*).

Words and Sentences

Coh-Metrix also assesses text difficulty at the word and sentence level, but in comparison to readability measures, does so in ways that are driven by theories of reading comprehension. For example, in addition to word frequency, Coh-Metrix assesses the degree to which the text contains abstract versus concrete words. When a text contains more abstract ideas, it is more difficult to process. Coh-Metrix assesses words on abstractness, parts of speech, familiarity, multiple senses of a word, age of acquisition, and many other features. At the sentence level, Coh-Metrix directly analyzes syntactic complexity, such as the number of modifiers in noun-phrases and the number of words before the main verb in a sentence.

APPLIED NATURAL LANGUAGE PROCESSING STUDIES USING COH-METRIX

Well over 70 studies have been conducted in our laboratory using Coh-Metrix, and the number grows steadily each year. Indeed, there are nine studies reported in this volume that have made use of Coh-Metrix tools (Adam, McCarthy, Boonthum, & McNamara, this volume; Baba & Nitta, this volume; Bell, McCarthy, & McNamara, this volume; Crossley & McNamara, this volume; Jackson & McNamara, this volume; McCarthy, Dufty, Hempelman, Cai, McNamara & Graesser, this volume; McCarthy & McNamara, this volume; McNamara et al., this volume; Weston, Crossley, & McNamara, this volume). In addition, a growing number of researchers are using Coh-Metrix to investigate differences among texts, to develop stimuli, and to describe characteristics of texts. In sum, it is a very useful tool, particularly in the context of ANLP.

In our laboratory, Coh-Metrix is often used to understand the features of texts that are used in the context of experimental studies of text comprehension. For example, Ozuru, Dempsey, and McNamara (2009) and Ozuru, Briner, Best, and McNamara (in press) used Coh-Metrix indices to guide cohesion modifications to high and low cohesion texts and to validate their overall cohesiveness. Coh-Metrix has also been used in the context of three main types of corpus studies. These include validation studies, exploratory studies, and natural language studies. In this section of the chapter, we provide a few examples of each type of study.

Validation Studies

One important part of the Coh-Metrix project is the validation of the indices. It is necessary to verify that the indices measure what we think they are measuring and that they are theoretically compatible with patterns of data corresponding to types of texts or human performance. We have conducted many studies of this nature. One example of a validation study in this volume is McCarthy, Dufty, Hempelman, Cai, McNamara, and Graesser who examined the validity of our LSA Given/New measure.

Another example of a validation study is McNamara, Louwerse, McCarthy, and Graesser (2010). This study investigated the validity of Coh-Metrix as a measure of cohesion differences in text. We reviewed studies that had empirically investigated text cohesion. We collected 19 pairs of high and low cohesion texts from 12 of these studies. The results of this study indicated that commonly used readability indices (e.g., Flesch-Kincaid) inappropriately distinguished between low and high cohesion texts. Specifically, according to readability estimates, the low cohesion texts should

have been easier to read and understand than the high cohesion texts, which is not the case. Using Coh-Metrix, we confirmed that the co-reference indices provided by Coh-Metrix revealed significant differences between the high and low cohesion texts, showing higher cohesion scores for the high-cohesion texts than the low-cohesion texts. We also used discriminant analysis to examine which of the indices provided a greater distinction between the high and low cohesion texts. These analyses indicated that a combination of two indices, noun co-reference and causal cohesion, best discriminated between high and low cohesion texts. Notably, the researchers who had modified the texts had done so with co-reference and causal cohesion in mind; thus, it not surprising that these measures rose to the surface. Nonetheless, given the empirical results of the studies indicating that these cohesion modifications do indeed affect comprehension, the results of this corpus study provide additional evidence that referential and causal relationships play important roles in the difficulty of texts. And, at a practical level, this study validated the ability of Coh-Metrix indices to provide measures of text cohesion.

A third example of a validation study comes from Duran, McCarthy, Graesser, and McNamara (2007). This study validated temporal cohesion measures using a corpus of high school texts from the domains of science, history, and narrative. Assessing temporality in text is important because of its ubiquitous presence in organizing language and discourse. Indeed, situation model theories of text comprehension consider temporality to be one of the critical dimensions for building a coherent mental representation of described events, particularly in narrative texts (Zwaan & Radvansky, 1998). Temporality is partially represented through inflected tense morphemes (e.g., *-ed, is, has*) in every sentence of the English language. The temporal dimension also depicts unique internal event timeframes, such as an event that is complete or ongoing, by incorporating a diverse tense-aspect system (ter Meulen, 1995). The occurrence of events at a point in time can also be established by a large repertoire of adverbial cues, such as *before, after, then* (Klein, 1994). These temporal features provide several different indices of the temporal cohesion of a text.

To validate Coh-Metrix measures of temporality in Duran et al. (2007), experts in discourse processing rated the 150 texts in terms of temporal coherence on three continuous scale measures designed to capture unique representations of time. These evaluations established a gold standard of temporality. A multiple regression analysis using Coh-Metrix temporal indices significantly predicted human ratings. The predictors included in the model were a subset of five temporal cohesion features generated by Coh-Metrix: incidence of temporal expression words, incidence of positive temporal connectives, incidence of past tense, incidence of present tense, and temporal adverbial phrases. Collectively, all but one of the predictors (i.e., the incidence of positive connectives) significantly predicted the expert ratings. The indices accounted for 40 to 64 percent of the variance in the experts' ratings (depending on the type of rating). The study thus demonstrated that the Coh-Metrix indices of local, temporal cohesion significantly predicted human interpretations of temporal coherence. A discriminant analysis further indicated that these indices were highly predictive of text genres (i.e., science, history, and narrative), and were able to classify texts as belonging to a particular genre with very good reliability (i.e., recall and precision ranged from .47 to .92, with an average F-measure of .68). This study validated the temporal indices both in terms of human ratings of temporal cohesion and their ability to distinguish between text types.

Exploratory Studies

Another type of study can be characterized as exploratory. One such study appears in this volume (Bell, McCarthy, & McNamara, this volume). In this type of study, we and others have examined

how far linguistic features can go towards characterizing and identifying different types of texts. To some extent, these studies serve as validation studies because they provide additional evidence that certain text features play important roles in characterizing text and discourse. Indeed, the distinction between these two types of studies may be hazy. One difference is that exploratory studies are not focusing on validating any particular measures or indices, but instead serve to validate the general utility of Coh-Metrix. In sum, they explore the extent to which linguistic and discourse features alone successfully characterize essential differences between texts and among corpora.

We have conducted many exploratory studies. One such study was conducted by Hall, McCarthy, Lewis, Lee, and McNamara (2007). In this study, Coh-Metrix indices were used to examine variations in American and British English, specifically in texts regarding the topic of Law. Their corpus included 400 American and English/Welsh legal cases. The results suggested that there were substantial differences between the two, casting doubt on generalizations about British and American writing. In addition, a discriminant function analysis including five indices of cohesion (referential, causal, syntactic, semantic, and lexical diversity) was able to correctly classify an impressive 85% of the texts in the test set. Thus, cohesion was found to be an important and highly significant predictor of differences between American and British English.

Another example of an exploratory study using Coh-Metrix was conducted by McCarthy, Renner, Duncan, Duran, Lightman, and McNamara (2008). In this study, a combination of 12 Coh-Metrix indices was used to form a measure of topic sentencehood. Four experiments were conducted to assess two models of topic sentencehood identification: the Derived Model and the Free Model. According to the Derived Model, topic sentences are identified in the context of the paragraph and in terms of how well each sentence in the paragraph captures the paragraph's theme.

In contrast, according to the Free Model, topic sentences can be identified based on sentential features without reference to other sentences in the paragraph (i.e., without context). The results of the experiments suggested that human raters were able to identify topic sentences both with and without the context of the other sentences in the paragraph. The authors also developed computational implementations for each of the theoretical models using Coh-Metrix indices. When computational versions were assessed, the results for the Free Model were promising; however, the Derived Model results were poor. These results collectively implied that humans' identification of topic sentences in context may rely more heavily on sentential features than on the relationships between sentences in a paragraph. The authors' overall conclusion was that there are (at least) two types of topic sentences. One type is *ideal* and can be represented by the computational implementation of the Free Model (i.e., out of context). These types of topic sentences are often used as examples in textbooks and they are computationally identifiable with a high degree of accuracy. The other type of topic sentence is more *naturalistic*. Without the context of surrounding text, these sentences are more difficult and perhaps impossible to recognize as topic sentences.

Natural Language Studies

By far, most of the studies we have conducted in the context of the Coh-Metrix project focus on natural language. These include studies examining a wide range of topics and tasks such as deception, paraphrasing, explaining, answering questions, and writing essays. Indeed, there are seven chapters within this volume that describe such studies with Coh-Metrix (see in this volume: Adam, McCarthy, Boonthum, & McNamara, this volume; Bell, McCarthy, & McNamara, this volume; Crossley & McNamara; Jackson, Boonthum, & McNamara, this volume; McCarthy & McNamara, this volume;

McNamara et al., this volume; Weston, Crossley, & McNamara, this volume).

Studies of natural language using Coh-Metrix afford analyses of discourse under a wide variety of circumstances, and thus have the potential to improve our understanding of multiple aspects of language processing (e.g., Crossley, Salsbury, & McNamara, in press; Duran, Hall, McCarthy, & McNamara, 2010; Hancock et al., 2010). Studies of natural language using Coh-Metrix are also motivated by our interests in dialogue management in the context of intelligent tutoring systems. Coh-Metrix and Coh-Metrix tools have played important roles in the context of AutoTutor (D'Mello & Graesser, this volume; Graesser et al., this volume; Graesser, Person, Lu, Jeon, & McDaniel, 2005), iSTART (Jackson et al., this volume), question asking and answering (Graesser, Rus, Cai, & Hu, this volume), and W-Pal (McNamara et al., this volume).

One example of such a study was conducted by Graesser, Jeon, Yang, and Cai (2007). In this study, tutorial dialogues in the context of Auto-Tutor were analyzed using Coh-Metrix to investigate the effect of college students' background knowledge on various cohesion relations in the dialogue. Coh-Metrix was used in this study to compare the tutorial dialogues of high-knowledge students who had already taken the relevant topics in a college physics class as compared to novice students who had not taken college physics. AutoTutor is an animated pedagogical agent that scaffolds students to learn about conceptual physics and other topics by holding conversations in natural language (Graesser, this volume; Graesser, Jackson, & McDaniel, 2007; Van Lehn, Graesser, et al., 2007). AutoTutor scaffolds students to generate ideal answers to difficult questions requiring deep reasoning by using a variety of dialogue moves (e.g., hints, prompts, assertions, corrections, answers to student questions). The findings of the study conducted by Graesser, Jeon, et al. (2007) showed that the tutorial dialogues of high-knowledge students shared substantially similar linguistic features with the dialogue of novice students in co-reference, syntax, connectives, causal cohesion, logical operators, and other measures. However, there were significant differences in the dialogue with high-knowledge students versus novice students in semantic or conceptual overlap. This result supported the notion that background knowledge on subject matter promotes deeper levels of comprehension (i.e., the mental models) of conceptual physics while interacting with AutoTutor (see also, Graesser, Jeon, Cai, & McNamara, 2008; Jeon, 2008).

Another example of a study of natural language was conducted by McCarthy, Guess, and McNamara (2009). This study examined the nature of paraphrases in the context of iSTART (see Jackson, Boonthum, & McNamara, this volume) and developed a computational model to predict the quality of the paraphrases. Two sentences can be considered to be paraphrases of one another if their meanings are equivalent but their words and syntax are different. Understanding paraphrasing is important in a number of contexts because paraphrasing can be used to aid comprehension, stimulate prior knowledge, and assist in writing-skills development. However, computational studies of paraphrasing have been primarily conducted using artificial, edited paraphrases and has most often examined only binary dimensions (i.e., *is* or *is not* a paraphrase). By contrast, McCarthy et al. examined a large database ($N = 1,998$) of natural paraphrases generated by high school students that was collected in the context of the reading strategy tutoring system, iSTART. The paraphrases were assessed by expert raters along 10 dimensions (see McCarthy & McNamara, this volume). A model including LSA (semantics), minimal edit distances (syntax), and the difference in length between the text and the paraphrase correlated .51 with the human evaluations of the paraphrases. These results suggested that semantic completeness and syntactical similarity were the primary components of paraphrase quality.

A third example of a natural language study is in the realm of writing. We are currently developing a writing strategy tutoring system called the Writing-Pal that will provide high school students with instruction and practice on writing prompt-based essays (see McNamara et al., this volume). One part of the W-Pal project has involved collecting essays written by students so that we can better understand the linguistic features of essays and how those features relate to their quality. One such study was conducted by McNamara, Crossley, and McCarthy (2010). Coh-Metrix was used to examine the degree to which high and low proficiency essays could be identified using linguistic indices of cohesion (i.e., co-reference and connectives), syntactic complexity (e.g., number of words before the main verb, sentence structure overlap), lexical diversity, and the characteristics of words (e.g., frequency, concreteness, imagability). Contrary to expectations, the three most predictive indices of essay quality in this study were syntactic complexity (as measured by number of words before the main verb), lexical diversity (as measured by MTLD), and word frequency (as measured by CELEX, logarithm for all words). Using 26 validated indices of referential and semantic cohesion from Coh-Metrix, none showed differences between high and low proficiency essays and no indices of cohesion correlated with essay ratings. Although lexical diversity might be associated with cohesion, the lexical diversity measure indicated that the higher quality essays were *higher* in diversity and thus *lower* in cohesion. Otherwise, cohesion as measured by Coh-Metrix played no role in predicting the quality of the essays. These results indicate that the textual features that characterize good student writing are not aligned with those features that facilitate reading comprehension such as text cohesion. Rather, higher quality essays were more likely to contain linguistic features associated with text difficulty and sophisticated language.

COH-METRIX TEXT EASABILITY COMPONENTS

One motivation for the development of Coh-Metrix was to provide better measures of text difficulty (see e.g., Duran, Bellissens, Taylor, & McNamara, 2007), and particularly the specific sources of potential challenges or scaffolds within texts. One limitation of traditional readability measures is that they consider only the superficial features of text, which in turn tend to be predictive of readers' surface understanding: their understanding of the words and separate sentences. In turn, aassessments that are used to validate or provide readability scores most often use a cloze task. Cloze tasks (i.e., filling in missing words in text) assesses comprehension only within sentences based on word associations (Shanahan, Kamil, & Tobin, 1982) and depends primarily on decoding rather than language comprehension skills (Keenan, Betjemann, & Olson, 2008). However, many comprehension models (Graesser & McNamara, in press; Kintsch, 1998; McNamara & Magliano, 2010; Van Dijk & Kintsch, 1983) propose that there are multidimensional levels of understanding that emerge during the comprehension process, including (at least) surface, textbase, and situation model levels. Readability formulas by contrast assume a uni-dimensional representation.

Uni-dimensional representations of comprehension ignore the importance of readers' deeper levels of understanding. Another limitation is that uni-dimensional metrics of text difficulty are not particularly helpful to educators when specific guidance is needed for diagnosing what is wrong and planning remediation for students. Readability formulas do not identify the particular characteristic of the text that may be challenging or *helpful* to a student. One major advantage of Coh-Metrix is that it provides metrics on multiple levels of language and discourse.

One reason that the difficulty or ease of a text should not be assessed at only one level of language is because multiple levels often work to compensate for one another (McNamara, Louwerse, & Graesser, in press). For example, in a recent analysis we found that narrative texts (stories, novels) tend to have low co-referential cohesion and low verb cohesion (McNamara, Graesser, & Louwerse, in press). By themselves, these indices may imply that narratives are difficult to read. However, narratives also tend to be composed of more frequent words and they often have high causal cohesion and temporal cohesion, allowing the reader to form a coherent mental model of the contents of the text. There are times when language in narrative texts at the situation model levels compensates for more challenging sentences and low overlap in words and concepts. By contrast, science texts are composed of rare words, making it challenging for students to understand the concepts in the text. These challenges are sometimes offset by reducing the syntactic complexity of the text and increasing the overlap in words and concepts (i.e., co-referential cohesion).

Thus, Coh-Metrix, in contrast to traditional measures of text readability, has the potential to offer a more complete picture of the potential challenges that may be faced by a reader as well as the potential scaffolds that may be offered by the text. Coh-Metrix is motivated by theories of discourse and text comprehension. Such theories describe comprehension at multiple levels, from shallow, text-based comprehension to deeper levels of comprehension that integrates multiple ideas in the text and brings to bear information that elaborates the ideas in the text using world and domain knowledge (Graesser & McNamara, in press). Coh-Metrix assesses challenges that may occur at the word and sentence levels. In addition, it is able to assess deeper levels of language in terms of cohesion and the situation model. By doing so, it comes closer to having the capability to estimate how well a reader will comprehend a text at deeper levels of cognition.

In a recent study (Graesser, McNamara, & Kulikowich, in prepartion), we have developed

Coh-Metrix Text Easability Components to describe the multiple levels of text ease and potential challenges that arise from textual features. To do so, we examined 54 Coh-Metrix indices calculated on 37,651 texts from the Touchstone Applied Science Associates (TASA) corpus. This corpus comprises excerpts (M=287 words) from texts (without paragraph break markers) that a typical senior in high school might have encountered throughout schooling in kindergarten through 12th grade. The text genres primarily comprise language arts, science, and social studies/history texts, but also included text in the domains of business, health, home economics, and industrial arts. The TASA corpus is the most comprehension collection of K-12 texts currently available for research. A principal components analysis of the corpus revealed that the following 8 dimensions (in order of robustness) accounted for 67% of the variability among texts. We consider the first five of these components to be most highly associated with text ease (and they were the most robust components, accounting for 54% of the variance).

1. **Narrativity.** Narrative text tells a story, with characters, events, places, and things that are familiar to the reader. Narrative is closely affiliated with everyday oral conversation. This robust component is highly affiliated with word familiarity, world knowledge, and oral language. Non-narrative texts on less familiar topics would lie at the opposite end of the continuum.

2. **Referential cohesion.** This component includes Coh-Metrix indices that assess referential cohesion. High cohesion text contains words and ideas that overlap across sentences and the entire text, forming explicit threads that connect the text for the reader. Low cohesion text is typically more difficult to process because there are fewer threads that tie the ideas together for the reader.

3. **Syntactic Simplicity.** This component reflects the degree to which the sentences in the text contain fewer words and use more simple, familiar syntactic structures, which are less challenging to process. At the opposite end of the continuum are texts that contain sentences with more words and use complex, unfamiliar syntactic structures.

4. **Word Concreteness.** Texts that contain content words that are concrete, meaningful, and evoke mental images are easier to process and understand. Abstract words represent concepts that are difficult to represent visually. Texts that contain more abstract words are more challenging to understand.

5. **Deep cohesion.** This dimension reflects the degree to which the text contains causal, intentional, and temporal connectives. These connectives help the reader to form a more coherent and deeper understanding of the causal events, processes, and actions in the text.

6. **Verb cohesion.** This component reflects the degree to which there are overlapping verbs in the text. When there are repeated verbs, the text likely includes a more coherent event structure that will facilitate and enhance situation model understanding.

7. **Logical cohesion.** This component reflects the degree to which the text contains explicit adversative, additive, and comparative connectives to express relations in the text. This component reflects the number of logical relations in the text that are explicitly conveyed. This component is related to the reader's deeper understanding of the relations in the text.

8. **Temporal cohesion.** Texts that contain more cues about temporality and that have more consistent temporality (i.e., tense, aspect) are easier to process and understand. In addition, temporal cohesion contributes to the reader's situation model level understanding of the events in the text.

Using the results of the analysis, we can compute percentile scores for the eight components. A percentile score varies from 0 to 100%, with higher scores meaning the text is likely to be more difficult to read than other texts in the corpus. For example, a percentile score of 80% means that 80% of the texts are easier and 20% are more difficult. Four such texts are presented below in Figure 1, including two narrative texts and two science texts. We have only graphed the first five components because they account for the most variance in the characteristics of the texts (and for ease of processing of the graphs).

As would be predicted, the novel and drama texts are substantially more narrative than the two science texts. It is well documented that narrative is easier to read than informational texts (Bruner, 1986; Haberlandt & Graesser, 1985; Graesser, Olde, & Klettke, 2002), a fact that should be incorporated in assessments of text ease and complexity. However, it is possible for narratives to have informational content that explains the setting or context, and it is possible for science texts to have story-like language (e.g., the journey of a water molecule through the water system). In either case, the move toward increased narrativity will generally make the text easier to understand.

The two example narrative texts (Jane Eyre and Glass Menagerie) are declared to be at a 9-10 grade band. However, they have very different profiles on the various dimensions. Jane Eyre is more difficult when inspecting syntax (as well as verb cohesion, logical cohesion, and temporal cohesion, which are not presented on the graph), but it is less difficult with respect to word abstractness and deep cohesion; the two narratives have about the same referential cohesion demands. These are very different profiles of text

Figure 1. Percentile scores for ease of reading in four selected texts

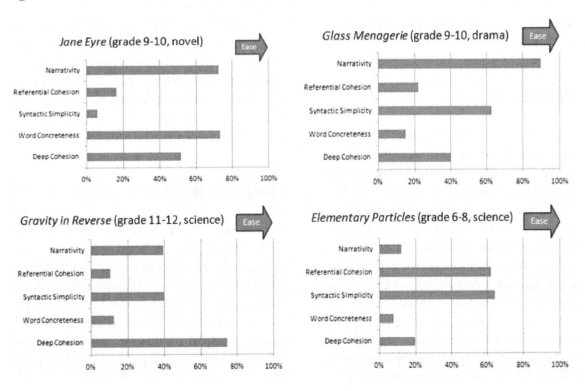

ease even though both texts were declared to be in the Grade 9-10 band.

The two science texts have very different grade bands declared. Elementary Particles is grade 6-8 whereas Gravity Reversed is grade 11-12. However, Gravity Reversed is not uniformly more difficult on all Coh-Metrix dimensions. Gravity Reversed is more difficult with respect to referential cohesion, syntax, and verb cohesions, but the opposite is the case with respect to narrativity and deep cohesion, (as well as logical and temporal cohesion); it's a draw with respect to word concreteness. Therefore, these comparative profiles should raise questions about the grade levels of these texts.

Such a *picture* of texts is hoped to provide teachers with more information about text ease, and by consequence, their ease of processing and at the lower end of the spectrum, their potential challenges. This information can in turn inform their pedagogical practice. One goal is to bring to fruition the Coh-Metrix project so that educators can more fully understand the complexity and nature of the texts that they use in the classroom, particularly in concert with their pedagogical goals and the individual abilities of their students.

CONCLUSION

Our goal in the Coh-Metrix project has been to provide indices for the characteristics of texts on multiple levels of analysis, including word characteristics, sentence characteristics, and the discourse relationships between ideas in text, within one tool. Our objective has been to go beyond traditional measures of readability that focus on surface characteristics of texts, which in turn tend to principally affect surface comprehension. Indeed, the validation of traditional readability algorithms using word and sentence characteristics (e.g., number of letters or number of words) has been almost exclusively done using assessments that primarily tap surface comprehension (e.g.,

cloze tests). Coh-Metrix can be used to better understand differences between texts and to explore the extent to which linguistic and discourse features successfully distinguish between text types. Coh-Metrix can also be used to develop and improve natural language processing approaches.

In the course of using Coh-Metrix and validating its measures, we have come to better understand differences between texts and which indices are most reliable in detecting differences between texts at meaningful, consequential levels. This work has culminated most recently in the development of the Coh-Metrix Easability Components. These components provide a more complete picture of text ease (and hence potential challenges) that may emerge from the linguistic characteristics of texts. The Text Easability components provided by Coh-Metrix go beyond traditional readability measures by providing metrics of text characteristics on multiple levels of language and discourse. Moreover, they are well aligned with theories of text and discourse comprehension (e.g., Graesser et al., 1994; Kintsch, 1998).

Coh-Metrix offers numerous opportunities to researchers, teachers, and students across a variety of fields. With the unlimited wealth and diversity of texts that technology such as the internet brings, computer assessment of text stands to increase dramatically in the next few years, and Coh-Metrix offers what may be the best approach for such assessments to be conducted.

ACKNOWLEDGMENT

We are grateful to numerous people who have contributed to the Coh-Metrix project over the past decade and who have provided feedback and help in writing this chapter. Without these collaborations, this project would not have been possible. Many of the projects reported in this chapter were partially funded by the Institute for Education Sciences (IES R305G020018-02). The development of the Coh-Metrix Text Easability Components was funded by the Gates Foundation.

REFERENCES

Baba, K., & Nitta, R. (in press). Dynamic effects of task type practice on the Japanese EFL university student's writing: Text analysis with Coh-Metrix. In McCarthy, P. M., & Boonthum, C. (Eds.), *Applied natural language processing: Identification, investigation, and resolution*. Hershey, PA: IGI Global.

Bell, C., McCarthy, P. M., & McNamara, D. S. (in press). Gender and language. In McCarthy, P. M., & Boonthum, C. (Eds.), *Applied natural language processing: Identification, investigation, and resolution*. Hershey, PA: IGI Global.

Britton, B. K., & Gulgoz, S. (1991). Using Kintsch's computational model to improve instructional text: Effects of repairing inference calls on recall and cognitive structures. *Journal of Educational Psychology, 83*, 329–345. doi:10.1037/0022-0663.83.3.329

Bruner, J. (1986). *Actual minds, possible worlds*. New York, NY: Plenum Press.

Chall, J. S., & Dale, E. (1995). *Readability revisited, the new Dale-Chall readability formula*. Cambridge, MA: Brookline Books.

Clark, H. H. (1996). *Using language*. Cambridge, UK: Cambridge University Press.

Crossley, S., & McNamara, D. S. (in press). Interlanguage talk: What can breadth of knowledge features tell us about input and output differences? In McCarthy, P. M., & Boonthum, C. (Eds.), *Applied natural language processing: Identification, investigation, and resolution*. Hershey, PA: IGI Global.

Crossley, S. A., Salsbury, T., & McNamara, D. S. (in press). The role of lexical cohesive devices in triggering negotiations for meaning. *Issues in Applied Linguistics*.

D'Mello, S. K., & Graesser, A. C. (in press). Automated detection of cognitive-affective states from text dialogues. In McCarthy, P. M., & Boonthum, C. (Eds.), *Applied natural language processing: Identification, investigation, and resolution*. Hershey, PA: IGI Global.

DuBay, W. (2004). *The principles of readability*. Costa Mesa, CA: Impact Information.

Duran, N., Bellissens, C., Taylor, R., & McNamara, D. (2007). Qualifying text difficulty with automated indices of cohesion and semantics. In D.S. McNamara & G. Trafton (Eds.), *Proceedings of the 29th Annual Meeting of the Cognitive Science Society* (pp. 233-238). Austin, TX: Cognitive Science Society.

Duran, N. D., Hall, C., McCarthy, P. M., & McNamara, D. S. (2010). The linguistic correlates of conversational deception: Comparing natural language processing technologies. *Applied Psycholinguistics*.

Duran, N. D., McCarthy, P. M., Graesser, A. C., & McNamara, D. S. (2007). Using temporal cohesion to predict temporal coherence in narrative and expository texts. *Behavior Research Methods, 39*, 212–223. doi:10.3758/BF03193150

Gernsbacher, M. A. (1990). *Language comprehension as structure building*. Hillsdale, NJ: Erlbaum.

Goldman, S., Graesser, A. C., & van den Broek, P. (1999). *Narrative comprehension, causality, and coherence*. Mahwah, NJ: Erlbaum.

Graesser, A. C. (in press). AutoTutor. In McCarthy, P. M., & Boonthum, C. (Eds.), *Applied natural language processing: Identification, investigation, and resolution*. Hershey, PA: IGI Global.

Graesser, A. C., D'Mello, S. K., Hu, X., Cai, Z., Olney, A., & Morgam, B. (in press). AutoTutor. In McCarthy, P. M., & Boonthum, C. (Eds.), *Applied natural language processing: Identification, investigation, and resolution*. Hershey, PA: IGI Global.

Graesser, A. C., Gernsbacher, M. A., & Goldman, S. (Eds.). (2003). *Handbook of discourse processes*. Mahwah, NJ: Erlbaum.

Graesser, A. C., Jackson, G. T., & McDaniel, B. (2007). AutoTutor holds conversations with learners that are responsive to their cognitive and emotional states. *Educational Technology, 47*, 19–22.

Graesser, A. C., Jeon, M., Cai, Z., & McNamara, D. S. (2008). Automatic analyses of language, discourse, and situation models. In Auracher, J., & van Peer, W. (Eds.), *New beginnings in literary studies* (pp. 72–88). Cambridge, UK: Cambridge Scholars Publishing.

Graesser, A. C., Jeon, M., Yang, Y., & Cai, Z. (2007). Discourse cohesion in text and tutorial dialogue. *Information Design Journal, 15*, 199–213.

Graesser, A. C., & McNamara, D. S. (in press). Computational analyses of multilevel discourse comprehension. *Topics in Cognitive Science.*

Graesser, A. C., McNamara, D. S., & Kulikowich, J. (in preparation). *Theoretical and automated dimensions of text difficulty: How easy are the texts we read?*

Graesser, A. C., McNamara, D. S., Louwerse, M., & Cai, Z. (2004). Coh-Metrix: Analysis of text on cohesion and language. *Behavior Research Methods, Instruments, & Computers, 36*, 193–202. doi:10.3758/BF03195564

Graesser, A. C., Olde, B., & Klettke, B. (2002). How does the mind construct and represent stories? In Green, M. C., Strange, J. J., & Brock, T. C. (Eds.), *Narrative impact: Social and cognitive foundations* (pp. 231–263). Mahwah, NJ: Erlbaum.

Graesser, A. C., Person, N., Lu, Z., Jeon, M. G., & McDaniel, B. (2005). Learning while holding a conversation with a computer. In Pytlik Zillig, L., Bodvarsson, M., & Bruning, R. (Eds.), *Technology-based education: Bringing researchers and practitioners together* (pp. 143–167). Greenwich, CT: Information Age Publishing.

Graesser, A. C., Rus, V., Cai, Z., & Hu, X. (in press). Question answering and asking. In McCarthy, P. M., & Boonthum, C. (Eds.), *Applied natural language processing: Identification, investigation, and resolution*. Hershey, PA: IGI Global.

Graesser, A. C., Singer, M., & Trabasso, T. (1994). Constructing inferences during narrative text comprehension. *Psychological Review, 101*, 371–395. doi:10.1037/0033-295X.101.3.371

Haberlandt, K. F., & Graesser, A. C. (1985). Component processes in text comprehension. *Journal of Experimental Psychology. General, 114*, 357–374. doi:10.1037/0096-3445.114.3.357

Hall, C., McCarthy, P. M., Lewis, G. A., Lee, D. S., & McNamara, D. S. (2007). A Coh-Metrix assessment of American and English/Welsh legal English. *Coyote Papers: Psycholinguistic and Computational Perspectives. University of Arizona Working Papers in Linguistics, 15*, 40-54.

Hancock, J. T., Beaver, D. I., Chung, C. K., Frazee, J., Pennebaker, J. W., Graesser, A., & Cai, Z. (2010). Social language processing: A framework for analyzing the communication of terrorists and authoritarian regimes. *Behavioral Science of Terrorism and Political Aggression, 2*, 108–132. doi:10.1080/19434471003597415

Jackson, G. T., & McNamara, D. S. (in press). Applying NLP metrics to students' self explanations. In McCarthy, P. M., & Boonthum, C. (Eds.), *Applied natural language processing: Identification, investigation, and resolution*. Hershey, PA: IGI Global.

Jeon, M. (2008). *Automated analyses of cohesion and coherence in tutorial dialogue*. Unpublished doctoral dissertation. University of Memphis.

Keenan, J. M., Betjemann, R. B., & Olson, R. K. (2008). Reading comprehension tests vary in the skills they assess: Differential dependence on decoding and oral comprehension. *Scientific Studies of Reading*, *12*, 281–300. doi:10.1080/10888430802132279

Kintsch, W. (1998). *Comprehension: A paradigm for cognition*. Cambridge, MA: Cambridge University Press.

Kintsch, W., & Kintsch, E. (in press). *Applied natural language processing: Identification, investigation, and resolution* (McCarthy, P. M., & Boonthum, C., Eds.). Hershey, PA: IGI Global.

Klare, G. R. (1974–1975). Assessing readability. *Reading Research Quarterly*, *10*, 62–102. doi:10.2307/747086

Klein, W. (1994). *Time in language*. London, UK: Routledge.

Koslin, B. L., Zeno, S., & Koslin, S. (1987). *The DRP: An effectiveness measure in reading*. New York, NY: College Entrance Examination Board.

Landauer, T., McNamara, D. S., Dennis, S., & Kintsch, W. (Eds.). (2007). *Handbook of latent semantic analysis*. Mahwah, NJ: Erlbaum.

Louwerse, M. M. (2001). An analytic and cognitive parameterization of coherence relations. *Cognitive Linguistics*, *12*, 291–315. doi:10.1515/cogl.2002.005

McCarthy, P. M., Dufty, D., & Hempelman, C. Cai., Z., Graesser, A. C., & McNamara, D. S. (in press). Evaluating givenness/newness. In P. M. McCarthy & C. Boonthum (Eds.), *Applied natural language processing: Identification, investigation, and resolution*. Hershey, PA: IGI Global.

McCarthy, P. M., Guess, R. H., & McNamara, D. S. (2009). The components of paraphrase evaluations. *Behavior Research Methods*, *41*, 682–690. doi:10.3758/BRM.41.3.682

McCarthy, P. M., & Jarvis, S. (2010). MTLD, vocd-D, and HD-D: A validation study of sophisticated approaches to lexical diversity assessment. *Behavior Research Methods*, *42*(2), 381–392. doi:10.3758/BRM.42.2.381

McCarthy, P. M., & McNamara, D. S. (in press). User language paraphrase corpus. In McCarthy, P. M., & Boonthum, C. (Eds.), *Applied natural language processing: Identification, investigation, and resolution*. Hershey, PA: IGI Global.

McCarthy, P. M., Renner, A. M., Duncan, M. G., Duran, N. D., Lightman, E. J., & McNamara, D. S. (2008). Identifying topic sentencehood. *Behavior Research Methods*, *40*, 647–664. doi:10.3758/BRM.40.3.647

McNamara, D. S. (2001). Reading both high-coherence and low-coherence texts: Effects of text sequence and prior knowledge. *Canadian Journal of Experimental Psychology*, *55*, 51–62. doi:10.1037/h0087352

McNamara, D. S. (in press). Computational methods to extract meaning from text and advance theories of human cognition. *Topics in Cognitive Science*.

McNamara, D. S., Crossley, S. A., & McCarthy, P. M. (2010). Linguistic features of writing quality. *Written Communication*, *27*, 57–86. doi:10.1177/0741088309351547

McNamara, D. S., Graesser, A. C., & Louwerse, M. M. (in press). Sources of text difficulty: Across the ages and genres. In Sabatini, J. P., & Albro, E. (Eds.), *Assessing reading in the 21st century: Aligning and applying advances in the reading and measurement sciences*. Lanham, MD: R&L Education.

McNamara, D. S., & Kintsch, W. (1996). Learning from text: Effects of prior knowledge and text coherence. *Discourse Processes*, *22*, 247–287. doi:10.1080/01638539609544975

McNamara, D. S., Louwerse, M. M., McCarthy, P. M., & Graesser, A. C. (2010). Coh-Metrix: Capturing linguistic features of cohesion. *Discourse Processes*, *47*, 292–330. doi:10.1080/01638530902959943

McNamara, D. S., & Magliano, J. P. (2009). Towards a comprehensive model of comprehension. In Ross, B. (Ed.), *The psychology of learning and motivation*. New York, NY: Elsevier Science. doi:10.1016/S0079-7421(09)51009-2

McNamara, D. S., Raine, R., Roscoe, R., Crossley, S., Jackson, G. T., & Dai, J. (in press). The Writing-Pal: Natural language algorithms to support intelligent tutoring on writing strategies. In McCarthy, P. M., & Boonthum, C. (Eds.), *Applied natural language processing: Identification, investigation, and resolution*. Hershey, PA: IGI Global.

Ozuru, Y., Briner, S., Best, R., & McNamara, D. S. (2010). Contributions of self-explanation to comprehension of high and low cohesion texts. *Discourse Processes*, *47*, 641–667. doi:10.1080/01638531003628809

Ozuru, Y., Dempsey, K., & McNamara, D. S. (2009). Prior knowledge, reading skill, and text cohesion in the comprehension of science texts. *Learning and Instruction*, *19*, 228–242. doi:10.1016/j.learninstruc.2008.04.003

Renner, A., McCarthy, P., Boonthum, C., & McNamara, D. S. (in press). Maximizing ANLP evaluation: Harmonizing flawed input. In McCarthy, P. M., & Boonthum, C. (Eds.), *Applied natural language processing: Identification, investigation, and resolution*. Hershey, PA: IGI Global.

Sanders, T. J. M., & Noordman, L. G. M. (2000). The role of coherence relations and their linguistic markers in text processing. *Discourse Processes*, *29*, 37–60. doi:10.1207/S15326950dp2901_3

Shanahan, T., Kamil, M. L., & Tobin, A. W. (1982). Cloze as a measure of intersentential comprehension. *Reading Research Quarterly*, *17*, 229–255. doi:10.2307/747485

Singer, M., & Leon, J. (2007). Psychological studies of higher language processes: Behavioral and empirical approaches. In Schmalhofer, F., & Perfetti, C. (Eds.), *Higher level language processes in the brain: Inference and comprehension processes*. Mahwah, NJ.

Stenner, A. J., Burdick, H., Sanford, E. E., & Burdick, D. S. (2006). How accurate are Lexile text measures? *Journal of Applied Measurement*, *7*(3), 307–322.

Ter Meulen, A. G. B. (1995). *Representing time in natural language: The dynamic interpretation of tense and aspect*. Cambridge, MA: MIT Press.

van Dijk, T. A., & Kintsch, W. (1983). *Strategies of discourse comprehension*. New York, NY: Academic.

VanLehn, K., Graesser, A. C., Jackson, G. T., Jordan, P., Olney, A., & Rose, C. P. (2007). When are tutorial dialogues more effective than reading? *Cognitive Science*, *31*, 3–62. doi:10.1080/03640210709336984

Weston, J., Crossley, S., & McNamara, D. S. (in press). Computationally assessing human judgments of freewriting quality. In McCarthy, P. M., & Boonthum, C. (Eds.), *Applied natural language processing: Identification, investigation, and resolution*. Hershey, PA: IGI Global.

Zwaan, R. A., & Radvansky, G. A. (1998). Situation models in language comprehension and memory. *Psychological Bulletin*, *123*, 162–185. doi:10.1037/0033-2909.123.2.162

ADDITIONAL READING

Graesser, A. C., Singer, M., & Trabasso, T. (1994). Constructing inferences during narrative text comprehension. *Psychological Review*, *101*, 371–395. doi:10.1037/0033-295X.101.3.371

Kintsch, W. (1998). *Comprehension: A paradigm for cognition*. Cambridge, MA: Cambridge University Press.

Chapter 12

Linguistic Inquiry and Word Count (LIWC):
Pronounced "Luke,". .. and Other Useful Facts

Cindy K. Chung
The University of Texas at Austin, USA

James W. Pennebaker
The University of Texas at Austin, USA

ABSTRACT

Linguistic Inquiry and Word Count (LIWC; Pennebaker, Booth, & Francis, 2007) is a word counting software program that references a dictionary of grammatical, psychological, and content word categories. LIWC has been used to efficiently classify texts along psychological dimensions and to predict behavioral outcomes, making it a text analysis tool widely used in the social sciences. LIWC can be considered to be a tool for applied natural language processing since, beyond classification, the relative uses of various LIWC categories can reflect the underlying psychology of demographic characteristics, honesty, health, status, relationship quality, group dynamics, or social context. By using a comparison group or longitudinal information, or validation with other psychological measures, LIWC analyses can be informative of a variety of psychological states and behaviors. Combining LIWC categories using new algorithms or using the processor to assess new categories and languages further extend the potential applications of LIWC.

INTRODUCTION

Linguistic Inquiry and Word Count (LIWC; Pennebaker et al., 2007) is a word counting software tool widely used for quantitative text analysis in the social sciences. Although LIWC is able to

quantify features in text that allow for text classification and predictions for a variety of behavioral outcomes, it has primarily been used to identify word features that are informative of the underlying psychological states of an author or speaker or groups. LIWC was originally developed to address content analytic issues in experimental psychology. Today, there are an increasing number

DOI: 10.4018/978-1-60960-741-8.ch012

of applications across fields such as computational linguistics, forensics, marketing, and social computing. Together, the widespread applications to various fields, along with the psychological information that can be gleaned about an author or speaker, place LIWC in the realm of applied natural language processing (ANLP) approaches.

In this chapter, we describe the rationale of the LIWC approach, and highlight several applications of LIWC – for example, as a lie detector, a status decoder, or a social barometer. The main issues of a LIWC approach relative to other natural language processing (NLP) approaches are discussed, along with several solutions and recommendations. Finally, we present novel ways in which LIWC is being applied, and how it might be used in future research. (Note: LIWC is pronounced "Luke"; LIWC may be used as a noun, adjective [e.g., the LIWCed data], and verb [e.g., "Please LIWC the speech"]; adverb usage is under development.).

BACKGROUND

The story of the origin and development of LIWC is instructive for how the use of LIWC has evolved and expanded. In the nineteen-eighties, the second author conducted a series of studies examining health improvements after writing about one's deepest thoughts and feelings regarding a traumatic or stressful event for 15 minutes a day over three to four days (e.g., Pennebaker & Beall, 1986). As more studies confirmed the health effects of expressive writing, multiple labs started to test what factors could account for the health and psychological changes associated with putting emotional upheavals into words.

In an attempt to determine if some features of the ways people wrote could shed light on the expressive writing phenomenon, Pennebaker initially had large groups of research assistants conduct qualitative content analysis on the essays. The task proved to be too complex, unreliable, and

subjective, leading him to seek a computer-based approach to analyzing text (Graybeal, Seagal, & Pennebaker, 2002). With the help of his graduate student Martha E. Francis, he developed a relatively simple precursor of LIWC that counted a small group of emotion-related words. The initial success of the program led to a more concerted effort to capture a wider range of categories that ultimately resulted in the first commercial version of the LIWC program (e.g., Pennebaker & Francis, 1996).

It is important to acknowledge that a small number of computer-based word counting programs preceded LIWC in the social sciences. The most impressive, *General Inquirer*, had been created in the 1960s (Stone, Dunphy, Smith, & Ogilvie, 1966) for use on a mainframe computer. A handful of word counting approaches soon followed but, like *General Inquirer*, were not transparent in their operation, unavailable for desktop computers, and were heavily theoretical in their orientation, making them less broadly applicable. Whereas *General Inquirer* was developed to test need-based motivational theories, others were influenced by Freud and the psychoanalytic movement (Gottschalk, 2000; Martindale, 1990; Mergenthaler, 1996; Weintraub, 1989). All of the computer-based word counting systems at the time, including more recent programs such as Hart's (2000) DICTION program, relied on dictionaries and complex algorithms not accessible to the users.

THE LIWC DICTIONARY

The heart of the LIWC program is its dictionary system. The current version of LIWC relies on approximately 80 default dictionaries made up of a total of about 4,000 words and word stems. The default dictionaries generally fall into one of four broader language dimensions that are grammatical (e.g. articles, numbers, pronouns), psychological, (e.g., social, emotions, cognitive mechanisms), and content (e.g. achievement, death, religion) categories.

The LIWC dictionary took several years to develop and relied on the help of dozens of undergraduates and graduate students starting in the early 1990s. The initial idea was to identify categories that were commonly used in psychology including basic emotional and cognitive dimensions often studied in social, health, and personality psychology. With time, the domain of word categories expanded considerably. In the first phases of development, candidate words were generated by referring to thesauruses, dictionaries, questionnaires, and by the students themselves. A second phase then relied on 3-4 human judges who independently decided if a given word was appropriate to a given category (Pennebaker, Francis, & Booth, 2001; Pennebaker, Chung, Ireland, Gonzales, & Booth, 2007). The second rating process was initiated to ensure high inter-judge reliability.

Each word or word stem defines one or more word categories or subdictionaries. For example, the word *cried* is part of five word categories: sadness, negative emotion, overall affect, verb, and past tense verb. Hence, if it is found in the target text, each of these five subdictionary scale scores is incremented. As in this example, many of the LIWC categories are arranged hierarchically. All sadness words, by definition, will be categorized as negative emotion and overall emotion words.

Finally, the LIWC dictionary system was upgraded in 1997, 2001, and 2007. Although users can see the words that are part of each LIWC category, the default internal dictionary cannot be modified. The purpose of this is to allow for direct comparison of results from one user to another. Although the default internal dictionary cannot be modified, LIWC allows users to use custom dictionaries to process text.

THE LIWC PROCESSOR

The central LIWC processing program was developed by Martha Francis and then was refined over the years by Roger J. Booth, an immunologist at the University of Auckland Medical School. The software program searches words in text files, and if there is match in the text and the dictionary that the software references, a particular word category (or categories) is incremented. The output is a matrix of text files (rows) and each of the LIWC dictionary word categories (columns). The percentage of total words in a file belonging to a particular category appears in each of the cells. The output also includes basic information about each text, such as the word count, the percentage of words that the dictionary captured within the text, as well as the percentage of words with six-letters or more, and punctuation characters appearing in the text. The official software was formally published and released in 2001 (LIWC2001; Pennebaker et al., 2001). In 2007, an updated version was released (LIWC2007; Pennebaker et al., 2007) with several word categories culled, created, or expanded, along with various text highlighting features, the ability to count phrases and to process Unicode text for cross language investigations.

The window display of the software program has few options and buttons, and is easy to use. The options enable users to analyze text in segments, to display only specified word categories in the output, and to upload a user-defined dictionary to reference in addition to the default dictionary previously described. For example, a list of words could be typed into a text file (e.g, *beavertail*; canad*; eh; gretzky*; inukshuk*; maple; mountie*; poutine; toque*; toronto*; zamboni**, etc.,). This dictionary could be uploaded in the LIWC processor, and the degree to which any writer or speaker is au courant with fine Canadian culture could be assessed. Although the user manual specifies several handy tips for cleaning the text prior to processing, the results for large numbers of text are relatively unaffected by a few spelling errors (Pennebaker et al., 2001).

LIWC AS AN ANLP TOOL

The first ANLP application of LIWC was used to evaluate if certain word dimensions could be used to predict who would benefit from expressive writing. That is, could certain ways of using words when writing about emotional upheavals enhance people's physical health, immune system activity, and health behaviors? Analyzing writing samples from seven expressive writing studies, Pennebaker, Mayne, and Francis (1997) found that a moderate rate of negative emotion words (e.g., *anxious, depressed, hate*), a high rate of positive emotion words (e.g., *awesome, love, yay*), and an increasing use of cognitive mechanism words (e.g., *accept, realize, understand*) over the three to four days of expressive writing were predictive of improved health (as measured by fewer visits to a doctor for illness) in the weeks after expressive writing. Confronting negative emotions and expressing positive emotions had salutary effects. A high rate of positive emotion words suggested that participants were finding benefits that had come from their experience. More important, an increased use of cognitive mechanism words suggested that participants were making meaning and gaining insight from their traumatic or stressful event.

The LIWC analyses of the expressive writing work showed that simple word counts in the essays could predict important outcomes. More importantly, the findings showed that psychological information could be gained about the essay authors and about the salutary coping processes in trauma narratives. In other words, beyond prediction and classification, a LIWC approach allows for a reliable and efficient measure of psychologically and theoretically meaningful features (Pen-

nebaker, Mehl, & Niederhoffer, 2003), making it a widely used tool for ANLP tasks.

WORD FEATURES

Hundreds of studies have used LIWC (see Tausczik & Pennebaker, 2010) to assess the psychology of individuals (e.g., literary writers, political figures, college students, psychotics, terrorists, etc.), and the psychology of groups (e.g., bloggers, work, clinical, political, and cultural groups, etc.). LIWC can be used to track individuals over time, or within and between groups. The word categories that are reliably used by people of various groups can tell us how speakers or authors are attending to their topics and social worlds (Pennebaker, 2011). A consistent finding is that many of the word categories that are used to reliably classify psychological states can be considered to be a part of *language style* as opposed to *language content*. That is, how people say things are oftentimes more revealing that what they are saying. Language style can be detected through the use of function words (also known as closed-class words or junk words), whereas language content is largely made up of content words (also known as open-class words).

Among LIWC's content categories, which are largely made up of nouns, regular verbs, adverbs, and adjectives, the most commonly studied category has been emotion words. While the taxonomy of emotions is debatable, a commonly accepted distinction in many theories of emotions is in the valence of emotions (Fontaine, Scherer, Roesch, & Ellsworth, 2007). That is, people generally distinguish between positive and negative emotions, and this distinction appears in most word counting tools developed by psychologists (e.g. Stone et al., 1966; Pennebaker et al., 2007). Other content categories are associated with social words (e.g., *communication, family, friends*) which tap the degree to which people are attending to their social worlds. Cognitive mechanism categories (e.g. causal word categories, insight categories, tentativeness) tap the degree to which people are thinking about causes, consequences, or conflicts about a particular topic. Note that certain function words are also grouped with cognitive mechanism word categories. For example, LIWC's discrepancy category includes modal verbs such as *should*, *ought*, and *must*, along with content words such as *hope*, *mistake* and *regret*.

Function words include pronouns, prepositions, articles, conjunctions, and auxiliary verbs, and account for over half of the words we use in daily speech (Rochon, Saffran, Berndt, & Schwartz, 2000). Function words are generally very short (usually 1-4 letters), are spoken quickly and read quickly (van Petten & Kutas, 1991). Given that the use of function words is so difficult to control, examining the use of these words in natural language samples has provided a nonreactive way to explore social and personality processes (Chung & Pennebaker, 2007; Pennebaker, 2011). Much like other implicit measures used in experimental lab studies in psychology, the authors or speakers that are examined often aren't aware of the dependent variable under investigation (Fazio & Olson, 2003). In fact, most of the language samples that have been analyzed using LIWC come from sources in which natural language is recorded for purposes other than linguistic analyses, and therefore have the advantage of being more externally valid than the majority of studies involving implicit measures.

Since rates of function word use cannot be readily manipulated or computed by listeners of a conversation or readers of text, the computerized assessment of language style can be considered to be a novel form of remote sensing. That is, the computerized measurement of function words provides an assessment of psychological states when they are difficult or impossible to assess through traditional self-report methods in psychology due to, for example, social desirability, reactivity, (lack of) self-awareness, or even simply access to participants' reports.

APPLICATIONS

Today, there are an increasing number of applications of LIWC analyses in personality, forensic, clinical, relationship, and cultural assessments. Below, we review various applications of LIWC as a metric of demographics, lies, health, status, relationships, and social climate.

Author Identification

LIWC has been used to assess how men and women use words differently, and how word use changes with age. Many researchers have been able to apply these language markers to author identification or to the automatic detection of personality in their own natural language processing tasks (e.g., Argamon, Dawhle, Koppel, & Pennebaker, 2005; Argamon, Koppel, Pennebaker, & Schler, 2007; Mairesse, Walker, Mehl, & Moore, 2007). That is, the word categories in LIWC found to be used differently between males and females, and by extraverts and neurotics have been used in addition to word features typically used in author identification tasks (e.g., syntactic features, word length, syllables, etc.) to increase the accuracy of classifying texts according to gender or personality. Furthermore, the word categories themselves are particularly revealing of underlying individual differences in psychology.

Demographics

In a study examining over 14,000 text files of speeches, natural conversations, published literature, essays, lyrics, blogs, personal ads, and poems, a LIWC analysis revealed differences in rates of particular words use by men and women (Newman, Groom, Handelman, & Pennebaker, 2008). For example, men tend to use bigger words, articles (i.e., *a, an, the*), and prepositions, whereas women tend to use more personal pronouns, social words, and verbs. These findings are consistent with previous research showing that men are more object-oriented and females engage in more relational thinking, especially about people. Another LIWC study found that men and women talk approximately the same number of words in a given day, debunking the myth of female talkativeness (Mehl, Vazire, Ramirez-Esparza, Slatcher, & Pennebaker, 2007). Likewise, an analysis of published literature and blogs revealed that self-references decrease with age, while positive emotion word use, and the use of future tense words increase with age (Pennebaker & Stone, 2003), contradicting stereotypes of the elderly as lonely, crabby, and living in the past.

Personality

LIWC has been used to characterize the personality traits of political figures (e.g., Pennebaker, Slatcher, & Chung, 2005; Slatcher, Chung, Pennebaker, & Handelman, 2006) and college freshman (e.g., Mehl, Gosling, & Pennebaker, 2006; Pennebaker & King, 1999). Larger correlations have been found for word use and specific directly observable behaviors than with self-ratings on broad personality traits. For example, Fast and Funder (2008) found that the use of LIWC's certainty category (e.g., *absolutely, definitely, sure*) was highly correlated with behavior ratings of speaking fluently and loudly. The use of LIWC's sexual category (e.g., *ass, porn, sex*) was highly correlated with behavior ratings of being talkative and dominant, which reflect a high need for attention. Overall, these studies suggest that word counts provide meaningful measures for a variety of thoughts and behaviors. Note that LIWC assessments of personality from Twitter tweets (www.analyzewords.com), or from typed self-descriptions or Thematic Apperception Tests (www.Utpsyc.org) are publicly and freely available online (see also www.liwc.net).

Another example of LIWC as a remote sensor of personality comes from tracking the public statements of two of al-Qaeda's top leaders Bin Ladin and al-Zawahiri over time (Pennebaker &

Chung, 2008). Bin Ladin evidenced an increase in the rate of positive emotion words as well as negative emotion words – especially anger words (e.g., *furious, kill, punish*) – over time. He also showed higher rates of exclusive words (e.g., *but, except, without*) over the last decade, which often marks cognitive complexity in thinking. On the other hand, al-Zawahiri tended to be slightly more positive and significantly less negative and less cognitively complex than bin Ladin in his statements. He evidenced a surprising shift in his use of first person singular pronouns (hereon referenced as *I*) over the last two years. This was interpreted as indicating greater insecurity, feelings of threat, and, perhaps, a shift in his relationship with bin Ladin. Luckily, an analysis of pronouns over time provided a look at how these political leaders were attending and responding to events and their social worlds without having to (first find and then) ask bin Ladin and al-Zawahiri directly.

Lie Detection

Across several experiments with college students, researchers have accurately classified deceptive communications at a rate of approximately 67% (Hancock, Curry, Goorha, & Woodworth, 2008; Newman, Pennebaker, Berry, & Richards, 2003; Zhou, Burgoon, Twitchell, Qin, & Nunamaker, 2004). Similar rates have been found for classifying truthful and deceptive statements in experimental tests among prison inmates (Bond & Lee, 2005). The most consistent language dimensions in detecting deception include lower rates of *I*, exclusive words, positive emotion words and higher rates of negative emotion words. Note that the patterns of effects vary somewhat depending on the experimental paradigm (for a review, see Hancock et al., 2008).

Correlational real world studies have found similar patterns. In an analysis of courtroom testimony of over 40 people convicted of felonies, those who were later exonerated (approximately half of the sample) showed similar patterns of honest language, such as much higher rates of *I* (Pennebaker & Huddle, 2009). A more controversial real world example of classifying false and true statements is in the investigation of the claims produced by Bush administration officials as justification for the Iraq war. Specifically, Hancock and his colleagues (2009) examined false (e.g., claims that Iraq had WMD or direct links to al-Qaeda) and non-false statements (e.g., that Hussein had gassed his citizens) for words previously found to be associated with deceptive statements. Their LIWC analysis revealed that the statements that had been classified as false contained significantly less *I*, fewer exclusive words, more negative emotion words, and more action verbs (e.g., *lift, push, run*).

Beyond classification, the use of various word categories associated with lies have been used to infer the underlying psychology of deception. Deception involves less ownership of a story (i.e., fewer *I*), less complexity (i.e., fewer exclusive words), more emotional leakage (i.e., more negative emotion words), and greater focus on actions as opposed to intent (i.e., more action verbs). Based on the use of these words, approximately 77% of the statements made by the Bush administration were correctly classified as either false or not false. Note that these numbers are likely inflated since estimates of the veracity of statements is dependent on the selection of statements themselves – as opposed to a broader analysis of all statements made by the Bush administration.

It is important to note that the strength of the language model in predicting deception is that it has been applied to a wide variety of natural language samples from low to high stakes situations. Being able to classify the veracity of communications could lead to efficient allocation of resources for forensic investigations. Beyond simple classification, the word features are also telling of the underlying psychology of the author or speaker.

Health Diagnostics

The advantage of all word count tools for the analysis of therapeutic text is that word counts tend to be a less biased measure of therapeutic improvements than clinician's self-reports (Bucci & Maskit, 2005). In addition, word counts can be assessed at the turn level, by sessions over time, and for the overall treatment. In sum, word count tools have the potential to provide an objective evaluation of psychological disorders and therapeutic improvements (Bucci & Maskit, 2007; Wolf, Chung, & Kordy, 2010a, 2010b).

Mood Disorders

The high use of *I* has been linked to self-focus. High degrees of self-focus, in turn, have been found to be aversive and lead to negative affect even in healthy college student populations (Duval & Wicklund, 1972). Accordingly, the use of *I* has been found to be a better marker of depression, characterized by a high degree of self-focus and rumination, than the use of negative emotion words (Mehl, 2006; Rude, Gortner, & Pennebaker, 2004; Weintraub, 1989). Similar word patterns have been found in Spanish speaking online bulletin boards for depression (Ramirez-Esparza, Chung, Kacewicz, & Pennebaker, 2008). The greater use of *I* and negative emotion words has also been found to be correlated with the use of words describing bipolar disorder (e.g., *bipolar, dysphoria, psychosis, stabilizer*) in a bipolar disorder support chatroom (Kramer, Fussell, & Setlock, 2004).

Furthermore, Stirman and Pennebaker (2001) found that poets who eventually committed suicide used *I* at higher rates in their published poetry throughout their careers, and less *we* later in their career than those who did not commit suicide. The suicidal poets' language use suggested that they were focused more on the self, and less socially integrated in later life than non-suicidal poets. Surprisingly, there were no significant differences in the use of positive and negative emotion words between the two groups, and only a marginal effect of greater death related words (e.g., *die, funeral, grave*) used by the poets who committed suicide. Similar effects were found in later case studies of suicide blogs, letters, and notes (Hui, Tang, Wu, & Lam, 2009; Stone & Pennebaker, 2004). These results highlight the importance of linguistic style markers (assessed by word count tools) as potentially more psychologically revealing than content words (which would more likely be the focus of judge-based thematic coding).

Psychotic Disorders

There is also evidence that word counts are diagnostic of various psychiatric disorders, and can reflect psychopathological symptoms. For example, Junghaenel, Smyth, and Santner (2008) found that a sample of psychiatric patients (largely made up of individuals with a diagnosis of some type of schizophrenia or other psychotic disorder) tended to use fewer cognitive mechanism words and especially exclusive prepositions, as well as fewer communication words (e.g., *discuss, share, talk*) than do people who are not mentally ill, reflecting patients' tendencies to avoid in-depth processing and their general disconnect from social bonds.

Self-Regulation

Another study looked at word use and social networks in an online blog community devoted to weight loss (Chung, 2009). Having larger weight loss goals and blogging about personal events (i.e. using more *I*) was a more effective weight loss strategy than using the blog as a food intake diary (i.e. using more ingestion words). The degree to which bloggers were socially integrated with the blog community (i.e. commented to many other bloggers and received many comments) was found to be a potent predictor of weight loss. In sum, pronouns and the size of one's social network

were significant predictors of weight loss within the online diet community.

Self-focus and pathological eating styles have been found in Internet language use by pro-anorexics (i.e. anorexics who espouse a lifestyle of starvation). Lyons, Mehl, and Pennebaker (2006) found that pro-anorexia online message boards contained fewer *I*, fewer cognitive mechanism words, and more positive emotion words than online message boards for recovering anorexics. The authors suggested that attention away from the self allowed pro-anorexics to stabilize emotionally, and to sustain their immunity to psychological treatment. Together, the diet blog findings and the research on pro-anorexics suggest that a moderate degree of self-focus may be required for successful self-change. Indeed, most psychotherapies are based on the idea that self-reflection is important in the self-change process.

Status Decoder

Across multiple lab studies, higher status participants tend to use more words, fewer *I's*, and more first person plural pronouns (hereon referenced as *we*) than lower status participants (Kacewicz, Pennebaker, Davis, Jeon, & Graesser, 2009). Similar pronoun findings have been found in naturalistic data, for example, in e-mails between professors, graduate students, and undergraduate students (Kacewicz et al., 2009), in instant messaging (IM) chats within employees of a research and development firm (Scholand, Tausczik, & Pennebaker, 2010; Tausczik, 2009), in the Watergate tapes between Nixon and his aides (see Chung & Pennebaker, 2007), and in translations of memos between members of Saddam Hussain's administration (Hancock, Beaver, Chung, Frazee, Pennebaker, Graesser, & Cai, 2010). The greater use of *I* by lower status individuals likely reflects the self-focus required by lower status individuals to accommodate how they are being viewed by their higher status counterpart, while *we* use is presumed to reflect the authority to speak for the group, or to politely order minions around (e.g., "Don't you think we should take out the trash?").

Relationship Whisperer

Although the topics that people discuss are important clues to what they are attending to, a number of research studies using LIWC show that oftentimes 'invisible' features of language style and especially pronouns reveal important information about one's relationship orientation, quality, and longevity. A LIWC analysis, then, can provide diagnostic and prognostic information about a relationship that may not be obvious by the content of conversations alone.

Individual Outlook on Relationships

Word use has shown to be reflective of underlying psychological, and even physiological changes. For example, one study examined 1 to 2 years of personal journals and outgoing emails of two adults (one biological male and one biological female) who were undergoing testosterone therapy for different reasons (Pennebaker, Groom, Loew, & Dabbs, 2003). Overall, testosterone had the effect of suppressing the participants' use of pronouns referring to others. As testosterone levels dropped in the weeks after the hormone injections, the participants began making more references to other people. There were no statistically significant changes in the rate of self references. Furthermore, no consistent mood or other language correlates of testosterone emerged. The LIWC findings suggested that one function of testosterone, then, may be to steer people's interests away from other people as social beings.

Another example is in the examination of the press conferences of New York City's former Mayor, Rudolph Giuliani (Pennebaker & Lay, 2002). Upon being diagnosed with prostate cancer, and the publicizing of his divorce, people in his office and the general public perceived Giuliani

to be warmer, more sensitive to others, and more genuine. Giuliani's apparent personality shift was associated with large increases in *I*, drops in *we*, and modest increases in positive emotion words, relative to his first four years in office. After 9/11, his language shifted again, with an increase in *we*, and increases in both positive emotion and negative emotion words, reflecting an even more pronounced communal orientation.

Romantic Relationship Quality and Longevity

As found in the above studies, the use of *we* can indicate relationship closeness. Indeed, previous studies have shown that using *we* at high rates in interactive tasks in the lab predict relationship functioning and marital satisfaction (Gottman and Levenson, 2000; Sillars, Shellen, McIntosh, & Pomegranate, 1997; Simmons, Gordon, and Chambless, 2005). Another study found that *we* use, reflecting a communal orientation to coping by spouses in interviews about a patient's heart failure condition was predictive of improvements in heart failure symptoms of the patient in the months following the interview (Rohrbaugh, Mehl, Shoham, Reilly, & Ewy, 2008). However, a study of over 80 couples interacting outside of the lab with each other via IM over 10 days failed to show a relationship with *we*. Rather, the more participants used emotion words in talking with each other – both positive and negative emotion words – the more likely their relationship was to survive over a 3 to 6 month interval (Slatcher & Pennebaker, 2006). The research suggests that although brief speech samples can be reliably related to the functioning and quality of a relationship, natural language outside of the lab can provide a different picture of what types of communication patterns are associated with long-term relationship stability

Group Closeness

One example of word use reflecting group processes is in Sexton and Helmreich's (2000) analysis of the cockpit communication of dozens of flight teams that took part in a NASA B727 simulator study. They found that pronouns varied as a function of how long the crew had worked together; the longer the group had worked together, the less people used *I* and the more they used *we*. The dropping-*I*, increasing-*we* phenomenon is a reliable effect apparent in the transcripts from a large therapy group (N=22) that met for a week every 6 months for three years (Odom, 2006), in the lyrics written by the Beatles over their 10-year collaboration (Petrie, Pennebaker, & Sivertson, 2008), and in an analysis of the Watergate tapes (Mullen, Chapman, & Peaugh, 2001). Again, these analyses demonstrate the ability of LIWC analyses to act as a remote sensor for group dynamics.

Social Barometer

Natural language use on the Internet can be downloaded and assessed as a phenomenon unfolds, in addition to baseline information archived before the event occurred. Using LIWC, researchers have been able to track the lifespan of a topic, tap the virtual social worlds of thousands of participants, and provide validation for models of shared upheavals.

Reactions to September 11, 2001 Attacks

Cohn, Mehl, and Pennebaker (2001) assessed 1,100 blogs from livejournal.com, a site for public online journals. The researchers downloaded blog entries for 2 months prior to and after 9/11 to examine baseline behavior, as well as immediate and long term reactions to the event. Word usage followed a social coping model (Pennebaker & Harber, 1993), wherein the words people used reflected an increase in positive emotion words, and references to others following the event (e.g., *she, they, family, friends*), without fully returning to baseline levels within 2 months of the event. An elevated use of negative emotion words after 9/11 returned to baseline within a few days. Taken together, these suggested that the terrorist attacks had the effect of bringing people together, and that people were more focused on positive than negative experiences. This pattern of effects was also found in American Online (AOL) real-time chat room transcripts in the four weeks following the death of Princess Diana (Stone & Pennebaker, 2002).

Reactions to the 2009 Swine Flu Epidemic

To track public reactions, 9,508 blogs that mentioned H1N1 or swine flu were downloaded during the period from when the World Health Organization had publicly announced the appearance of swine flu, April 24, 2009 to May 7, 2009 (Tausczik, Faase, Pennebaker, & Petrie, in press). The number of blog entries mentioning swine flu was highest during the period of April 29 to May 1st, and dropped rapidly thereafter. Despite the risk of infection being greater in later weeks, a LIWC analysis showed that perceived anxiety levels (e.g., *anxious, nervous, worry*) were highest immediately after the WHO announcement. The initial jump in anxiety may have been warded off by publicized (low) morbidity rates, and replaced by anger (e.g., *furious, hate, kill*), which is consistent with research that has reported increases in hostility when an infectious disease originates in a foreign country. By applying text analysis to the archives of natural language text on the Internet, near real-time measurements of shared upheavals and larger social processes were possible. In addition, examining language use in blogs presented a non-reactive and unobtrusive way to bypass some of the problems that arise when online users are invited to participate in a research survey, such as selection biases, response rates, along with memory biases and distortions.

DISCUSSION

Despite the vast number of studies demonstrating the utility of LIWC in identifying psychological features through word counts, there are several issues that researchers should consider when LIWC is used as an ANLP tool (i.e. deriving psychological information about an author or speaker) beyond simple classification tasks.

Issues, Controversies, Problems

Word Features

LIWC analyses, like most NLP approaches, are task-driven in that they aim to classify texts using word features, and each of these approaches can incorporate top-down (theoretical) or bottom-up (exploratory) strategies. Compared to other NLP approaches that use any simple (individual) word features, LIWC uses handcrafted categories grouped by grammar or by judges' ratings of semantic meaning. Accordingly, the number of word features considered in other NLP approaches can be much greater (e.g., parts of speech, unique words), while the number of LIWC categories is fixed at a maximum of approximately 80 categories; LIWC users typically tend to refer to its default, validated categories as opposed to creating new categories validated by independent judges. Together, these suggest that the accuracy by which other NLP approaches can classify texts will tend to be better than a simple LIWC approach.

NLP approaches typically include a stopword list to exclude function words in analyses, whereas function words are typically the main categories of interest in LIWC analyses. That is, rather than being an unwanted guest at most NLP parties, function words are typically the host at most LIWC parties. Similarly, most NLP approaches

don't care whether or not a word feature was an invited guest or a party crasher as long as they could accurately predict how successful their party would be. On the other hand, LIWC approaches care about each word feature that showed up and make sure that they find out what it means to the word feature to have attended the party, and what other parties the word feature might attend, even if there was only a single guest to a marginally successful party. In other words, developing a theoretical understanding of a word category is important to LIWC approaches in order to develop hypotheses and to evaluate its generalizability to other psychological contexts.

Statistics. NLP approaches typically use very large corpora, in the scale of thousands or millions of texts, whereas LIWC approaches have typically examined corpora of smaller sizes, in the scale of tens to thousands. Some reasons for this are due to psychological annotations being more difficult to acquire (i.e. from the authors or speakers themselves, or requiring some experimental or clinical tasks, judges' ratings, or previously validated questionnaires). These have led to smaller sample size issues within LIWC approaches, such as decreased statistical power, and decreased reliability. With such large sample sizes, NLP tasks are able to incorporate a great deal of statistics, sometimes iteratively, within the task to achieve their aim. On the other hand, most applications of LIWC have typically included inferential statistics only at the end of text processing.

Solutions and Recommendations

Word Features

Although NLP approaches will outperform LIWC on many classification tasks, there can be advantages to using LIWC to classify texts, people, or even groups. The first reason is that the LIWC dimensions aggregate multiple words into single groups, making each dimension more stable than single word entries. Second, LIWC is a window based program, meaning little programming knowledge is required for its use, and possibly a reason why it has gained such popularity in the traditionally programming-lite fields, such as the social sciences, more so than in programming-heavy fields, such as computer and information sciences. However, even with the small set of word features in LIWC, LIWC researchers have found reliable correlates of psychological states.

LIWC researchers have found that the use of function words are markers of psychological states across a wide variety of texts, and that reliable changes in function word use can signal changes in psychological states (Chung & Pennebaker, 2007; Pennebaker, 2011). This would have been extremely difficult to discover using manual coding, since function words are often "invisible" to readers of natural language, and impossible to discover using NLP methods that include stoplists consisting of function words. On the other hand, there are many word features used by NLP approaches that LIWC does not consider. Future research directions for LIWC may be to incorporate predictive word features from NLP tasks, such as different parts of speech or single words (as discussed in the Future Directions section below).

Statistics

High accuracy rates for classification are a necessary condition to make inferences about psychological states. But LIWC only provides a probability of classification using a known comparison group or similar texts, rather than being a precise diagnostic tool. Although it would be great for LIWC to act as a black box for accurately predicting, say, whether or not a potential mate is a compulsive liar, the discriminating word categories should be correlated with other psychological measures to further validate the meaning that the word categories might convey. The potential information gained about the author or speaker from this validation process can add much more

value to the probability associated with a given text when making any clinical, forensic, or political decisions based on the results of a text analysis.

LIWC tasks must consider limitations of large sample size data, typically from an online sample, such as the self-selection and anonymity of participants, lack of verifiable personal information, and an uneven number of contributions by each participant (see Stone & Pennebaker, 2002). The tradeoffs of the psychological information gleaned must be weighed against the statistical power, reliability, and ecological validity afforded by Internet natural language samples. LIWC analyses from experimental lab studies with much smaller sample sizes, and naturalistic data from Internet archives should both be encouraged in order to better understand how word features reflect various psychological states.

FUTURE RESEARCH DIRECTIONS

The LIWC dictionary and the LIWC processor have been applied to understand interaction dynamics, other languages, and topic analyses. These approaches include the novel application of statistical techniques and algorithms with either the existing or user-defined dictionaries.

Future Directions Using the LIWC Dictionary

Below, we describe ways in which the LIWC dictionary has been used to start studying communication dynamics and different cultures using algorithms and translations. We discuss research under development as well as further work that is needed along these research directions.

Language Style Matching (LSM)

One measure of verbal synchrony, language style matching (LSM; Ireland & Pennebaker, 2009; Niederhoffer & Pennebaker, 2002) is a measure of the degree to which any two text samples match in their rates of function word use. LSM can be compared across individual speaking turns or segments of writing, between individuals, between pairs, or between groups. Note that a language style approach goes beyond obvious key terms (specialized topics, slang) and common syntactic constructions that characterize group membership and that are readily manipulated, making LSM a remote sensor of relationships and group dynamics.

Previous lab work showed that while verbal synchrony is related to attraction in dyads and small work groups, it does not necessarily indicate that groups are working more effectively in a cooperative task (Gonzales, Hancock, & Pennebaker, 2010). Rather, LSM is a measure of when people are trying harder to "get on the same page," or to establish common ground (Clark, 1996). To assess the ability of LSM to reflect engagement within relationships over time, archives of written letters and professional work between well-known pairs of spouses and friends over the course of their relationship were assessed using LIWC (Ireland & Pennebaker, 2010). The pairs included Sigmund Freud and Carl Jung, Robert and Elizabeth Barrett Browning, and Sylvia Plath and Ted Hughes. LSM was highest during times of relationship harmony and lowest during times of illness and relationship disharmony. Importantly, these studies showed that LSM changes reliably in response to relationship functioning over time in naturalistic contexts.

In the study of IMs exchanged between 22 employees of a real research and development firm, individuals who were rated by the employees as having higher status tended to style match less with their interaction partners on average, (i.e. they had lower average LSM scores; Tausczik, 2009). This might reflect lower status individuals' attempts to work harder to get on the same page as their higher status counterparts. In addition, LSM tends to be higher when interactants are more equal in status. That is, the more similar the ways people

use function words, the smaller the difference in status between them (Kacewicz, Pennebaker, Davis, Jeon, & Graesser, unpublished data).

A more recent set of lab studies using simulated negotiations provide further evidence that LSM is a marker of engagement and shared attention (Ireland & Henderson, 2009). LSM was highest in competitive negotiations between dyads that did not reach an agreement. Furthermore, LSM was associated with less efficiency (i.e., higher word count and longer negotiation times) in dyads that reached an agreement. The effects of LSM and the likelihood of reaching an agreement were fully mediated by ratings of contentiousness by the participants. These studies showed that rather than only reflecting positive engagement, LSM reflects engagement or shared attention more generally. In the case of competitive interactions, then, LSM can indicate conflict or negative outcomes.

LIWC in Other Languages

The LIWC software comes with the default dictionary, along with access to several translations of the LIWC dictionary in other languages upon their validation. Currently, this set includes Spanish (Ramirez-Esparza, Pennebaker, Garcia, & Suria, 2007), and German (Wolf, Horn, Mehl, Haug, Pennebaker, & Kordy, 2008). Translated versions of either the LIWC2001 or the LIWC2007 dictionary into Italian, Dutch, Norwegian, Arabic, Turkish, Chinese, French, Hungarian, Korean, Portuguese, and Russian are completed or in various stages of development (see www.liwc.net).

An intriguing problem is that most languages have function words that may not translate readily into other languages. For example, German and most Romance languages have a formal and informal second person *you* form. Japanese, Korean, and other languages do not have articles. Turkish includes a verb form that identifies if a statement of fact was directly experienced or gleaned from another source. Programs such as LIWC can easily capture these dimensions in other languages and create relevant categories for the English speaker. In other words, an English speaker could LIWC Spanish dialogue and determine the degree to which the speakers used formal or informal second person pronouns. Following this logic, an Arabic LIWC of function words based on an Arabic grammatical scheme and its translation into English have been developed (Hayeri, Chung, & Pennebaker, 2009). The set of Arabic LIWC dictionaries will enable one to assess the language style features that are lost or gained in a corpus of translations.

We are now testing the viability of an English-based LIWC on automatic translations of non-English text. For example, it is possible to use Google Translate (translate.google.com) to translate Spanish or Chinese text into English. To a native English speaker or a professional translator, the translations are often quite crude and may not make sense. Nevertheless, when the translations are LIWCed, the quality of the LIWC output is comparable to professional translations or LIWC analyses done using the Spanish or Chinese LIWC versions. In other words, the central features of a language that are captured by LIWC appear to be translated quite efficiently by automated translation systems.

Expansion of word features. With the increase in the use of the Internet, and with instant messaging (IM) chats as the preferred method of communication for undergraduates (Shiu & Lenhart, 2004), there is an increase in the use of SMS language or textese. The LIWC2007 dictionary includes some textese (e.g., *u* is categorized in the second person pronouns category; *LOL, ROFL,* and *LMAO* are all categorized in the positive emotion words category). However, further work is clearly needed, as *WTF* is not yet an entry in the swear words category, nor does *IMNSHO* appear in the categories for prepositions, first person singular pronouns, negations, quantifiers, or cognitive mechanisms category. Future versions of LIWC may also consider different emoticons as part of its categories. Future categories may include different parts of speech (e.g., modal verbs, pronominal adverbs, etc.), especially if NLP investigations suggest that they are "purer" categories of psychological relevance (note that many of the psychological categories in LIWC include any words from any part of speech as long as the word has been judged to fit the category).

Future Directions using the LIWC Processor

LIWC2007 for Mac came with additional features to count the occurrences of n-grams in a text, to highlight words in a given text that were captured by the dictionary that it references, and the ability to process Unicode text. Accordingly, future research using LIWC may include, for example, phrase level analyses, or cross-language work. The simple window-based processing capabilities of the LIWC processor make it an accessible tool to many researchers who are not proficient in programming to conduct, for example, an analysis of single word features as in NLP tasks that require more programming than in the social sciences.

Meaning Extraction Method (MEM)

LIWC has been used as a processor for dictionaries consisting of single word categories to assess the occurrence of the word and its forms in a given text. For example, in the Meaning Extraction Method (Chung & Pennebaker, 2008), the co-occurrences of high frequency words in a corpus are assessed by first finding the most frequently occurring content words in a corpus, for example, using WordSmith (Scott, 2004). A LIWC dictionary is then made of all root forms of the most frequently occurring words. Next, the same corpus is processed using the resultant LIWC dictionary and LIWC's processor. The output is then subject to a factor analysis in SPSS. All of these allow a windows-based user, with little to no programming language to be able to semi-automatically extract themes from any large corpus.

The MEM is capable of producing inductive, content valid themes. For example, Chung and Pennebaker (2008) showed that their MEM-derived factors from self-descriptions were correlated with self-ratings on the Big Five Inventory (BFI; John & Srivastava, 1999) of personality in some expected ways (e.g. neurotic people talked more about negative emotions; introverts talked about socializing or not; extroverts talked about ways of relating to others; conscientious people talked more about school/work). Pennebaker and Chung's (2008) MEM-derived word factors of al-Qaeda statements and interviews across time differentially peaked during the times when those factors/topics were most salient to al-Qaeda's missions. Finally, in an unpublished data set, Chung, Rentfrow & Pennebaker (2009) found that MEM-derived word factor scores from "This I Believe" essays (i.e. open-ended essays written to address one's personal beliefs) were strongly associated with Census Bureau data and state-level personality traits in expected ways. For example, an Achievement factor (e.g. achieve, succeed, dream, hard, work) was positively correlated with state levels of Conscientiousness. The Marriage factor (e.g. husband, wife, marry, wedding) was negatively related to the percentage of the population in a state that is married, but positively related to the percentage of state residents who were separated or widowed. The Illness factor (e.g. death, health, sick, illness, care) was consistently positively related to deaths due to heart disease and cancer, and negatively related to life expectancy. In sum, MEM-derived factors have been shown to have content validity across multiple domains.

Cross-Language Comparisons

Since the method only depends on characters separated by spaces, the MEM is particularly well-suited to less biased cross-language investigations. That is, inductive categories can be derived within each culture, and translations would only occur at the end of all analyses. A MEM analysis in Spanish and in English depression chat forums have been conducted, showing similarities and differences in the construal of depression across cultures (Ramirez-Esparza et al., 2008), in personality descriptions across cultures without imported and translated questionnaires and associated response biases (Ramirez-Esparza, Chung, Sierra-Otero, & Pennebaker, in press). Finally, the MEM has been adapted to examine e-mails between outpatients and their psychotherapists in German (Wolf, Chung, & Kordy, 2010a, 2010b). For German, the MEM dictionary included only nouns, since German verbs and adjectives tend to require too many conjugations to make a manageable dictionary for analysis. The MEM themes from this corpus were correlated with improvement from inpatient treatments, showing that those patients who experienced the least treatment gains during their inpatient stay tended to perseverate on discussing their symptoms in their emails during outpatient aftercare. In brief, MEM-derived factors in other languages have also been shown to be important predictors in behavioral outcomes.

CONCLUSION

Beyond classification, LIWC analyses can be informative of the psychological states underlying word use by an author or speaker. With the growing number of genres that archive text on the Internet, the corpora for psychological analyses have become larger and more complex. Accordingly, research in the psychological analysis of natural language texts has been extended to interactions with more speakers with larger audiences, across languages, cultures, and time. The examination of larger groups has helped psychologists to identify and understand patterns in how relationships form, how group identity and commitment develop, and how emotional reactions and information spread in a network. Future research should incorporate further validations of word use with psychological measures or qualitative analyses. In addition, future research should sample baseline language for comparisons, or compare groups across time in order to assess what relative rates of word use are signaling. LIWC is just one tool in a researcher's toolkit that can lead to cheap, fast, and easy assessments of linguistic style, and a deeper understanding of the psychological processes in communication.

ACKNOWLEDGMENT

Department of Psychology A8000, University of Texas at Austin, Austin, Texas 78712. Emails: CindyK.Chung@mail.utexas.edu and Pennebaker@mail.utexas.edu. Preparation of this manuscript was aided by funding from the Army Research Institute (W91WAW-07-C-0029), National Science Foundation (NSCC-0904913), Department of Defense (HHM402-10-C-0100), and Department of Homeland Security, National Consortium for the Study of Terrorism and Responses to Terrorism (START Z934002). The authors would like to thank David I. Beaver, Joey Frazee, Dan Velleman, Dylan Bumford, George Bronnikov, Molly E. Ireland, and Yla R. Tausczik for their helpful comments in the preparation of the manuscript.

Financial and Disclosure Issues: The LIWC2007 program, which is co-owned by Pennebaker, is commercially available for $89 USD (for the full package), $29 USD (student version), with discounts for bulk purchases on www.liwc.net. LIWC2007 demos, downloads, and products can be found on www.liwc.net. Text data for research purposes will be analyzed by Pennebaker free of charge. All profits that go to Pennebaker from LIWC2007 sales are donated to the University of Texas at Austin Psychology Department.

REFERENCES

Argamon, S., Dawhle, S., Koppel, M., & Pennebaker, J. W. (2005). Lexical predictors of personality type. *Proceedings of Classification Society of North America,* St. Louis MI, June 2005.

Argamon, S., Koppel, M., Pennebaker, J. W., & Schler, J. (2007). Mining the Blogosphere: Age, gender and the varieties of self–expression. *First Monday*, 12.

Bond, G. D., & Lee, A. Y. (2005). Language of lies in prison: Linguistic classification of prisoners' truthful and deceptive natural language. *Applied Cognitive Psychology, 19,* 313–329. doi:10.1002/acp.1087

Bucci, W., & Maskit, B. (2005). Building a weighted dictionary for referential activity. In Qu, Y., Shanahan, J. G., & Wiebe, J. (Eds.), *Computing attitude and affect in text* (pp. 49–60). Dordrecht, The Netherlands: Springer.

Bucci, W., & Maskit, B. (2007). Beneath the surface of the therapeutic interaction: The psychoanalytic method in modern dress. *Journal of the American Psychoanalytic Association, 44,* 1355–1397. doi:10.1177/000306510705500412

Chung, C. K. (2009). *Predicting weight loss in blogs using computerized text analysis.* Unpublished dissertation. Austin, TX: The University of Texas at Austin.

Chung, C. K., & Pennebaker, J. W. (2007). The psychological function of function words. In Fiedler, K. (Ed.), *Social communication: Frontiers of social psychology* (pp. 343–359). New York, NY: Psychology Press.

Chung, C. K., & Pennebaker, J. W. (2008). Revealing dimensions of thinking in open-ended self-descriptions: An automated meaning extraction method for natural language. *Journal of Research in Personality, 42,* 96–132. doi:10.1016/j.jrp.2007.04.006

Chung, C. K., Rentfrow, P. J., & Pennebaker, J. W. (2009). *This I believe: Validity of themes mapped across America using text analysis*. Unpublished data.

Clark, H. H. (1996). *Using language*. Cambridge, UK: Cambridge University Press.

Cohn, M. A., Mehl, M. R., & Pennebaker, J. W. (2004). Linguistic markers of psychological change surrounding September 11, 2001. *Psychological Science, 15*, 687–693. doi:10.1111/j.0956-7976.2004.00741.x

Duval, S., & Wicklund, R. A. (1972). *A theory of objective self-awareness*. Oxford, UK: Academic Press.

Fast, L. A., & Funder, D. C. (2008). Personality as manifest in word use: Correlations with self-report, acquaintance report, and behavior. *Journal of Personality and Social Psychology, 94*, 334–346. doi:10.1037/0022-3514.94.2.334

Fazio, R. H., & Olson, M. A. (2003). Implicit measures in social cognition research: Their meaning and use. *Annual Review of Psychology, 54*, 297–327. doi:10.1146/annurev.psych.54.101601.145225

Fontaine, R. J., Scherer, K. R., Roesch, E. B., & Ellsworth, C. (2007). The world of emotions is not two-dimensional. *Psychological Science, 18*, 1050–1057. doi:10.1111/j.1467-9280.2007.02024.x

Gonzales, A. L., Pennebaker, J. W., & Hancock, J. T. (2010). Linguistic indicators of social dynamics in small groups. *Communication Research, 37*, 3–19. doi:10.1177/0093650209351468

Gottman, J. R., & Levenson, R. W. (2000). The timing of divorce: Predicting when a couple will divorce over a 14-year period. *Journal of Marriage and the Family, 62*, 737–745. doi:10.1111/j.1741-3737.2000.00737.x

Gottschalk, L. A. (2000). The application of computerized content analysis of natural language in psychotherapy research now and in the future. *American Journal of Psychotherapy, 54*, 305–311.

Graybeal, A., Seagal, J. D., & Pennebaker, J. W. (2002). The role of story-making in disclosure writing: The psychometrics of narrative. *Psychology & Health, 17*, 571–581. doi:10.1080/08870440290025786

Hancock, J. T., Bazarova, N. N., & Markowitz, D. (2009). *A linguistic analysis of Bush administration statements on Iraq*. Manuscript submitted for publication.

Hancock, J. T., Beaver, D. I., Chung, C. K., Frazee, J., Pennebaker, J. W., Graesser, A. C., & Cai, Z. (2010). Social language processing: A framework for analyzing the communication of terrorists and authoritarian regimes. *Behavioral Sciences in Terrorism and Political Aggression. Special Issue: Memory and Terrorism, 2*, 108–132.

Hancock, J. T., Curry, L., Goorha, S., & Woodworth, M. T. (2008). On lying and being lied to: A linguistic analysis of deception. *Discourse Processes, 45*, 1–23. doi:10.1080/01638530701739181

Hart, R. P. (2000). *DICTION 5.0: The text analysis program*. Thousand Oaks, CA: Sage-Scolari.

Hayeri, N., Chung, C. K., & Pennebaker, J. W. (2009). *Arabic linguistic inquiry and word count: Viewing the world through English and Arabic eyes*. Manuscript in preparation.

Hui, N. H. H., Tang, V. W. K., Wu, G. H. H., & Lam, B. C. P. (June, 2009). *ON-line to OFF-life? Linguistic comparison of suicide completer and attempter's online diaries*. Paper presented at the International Conference on Psychology in Modern Cities, Hong Kong.

Ireland, M. E., & Henderson, M. D. (2009). *Verbal mimicry in negotiation: The language of the deal*. Manuscript submitted for publication.

Ireland, M. E., & Pennebaker, J. W. (2010). Language style matching in reading and writing: Synchrony in essays, correspondence, and poetry. *Journal of Personality and Social Psychology, 99*, 549–571. doi:10.1037/a0020386

John, O. P., & Srivastava, S. (1999). The Big Five Trait taxonomy: History, measurement, and theoretical perspectives. In Pervin, L. A., & John, O. P. (Eds.), *Handbook of personality: Theory and research* (2nd ed., pp. 102–138). New York, NY: Guilford Press.

Junghaenel, D. U., Smyth, J. M., & Santner, L. (2008). Linguistic dimensions of psychopathology: A quantitative analysis. *Journal of Social and Clinical Psychology, 27*, 36–55. doi:10.1521/jscp.2008.27.1.36

Kacewicz, E., Pennebaker, J. W., Davis, D., Jeon, M., & Graesser, A. C. (2009). *Pronoun use reflects standings in social heirarchies*. Manuscript submitted for publication.

Kacewicz, E., Pennebaker, J. W., Davis, D., Jeon, M., & Graesser, A. C. (2009). *LSM as a function of status discrepancy*. Unpublished data.

Kramer, A. D. I., Fussell, S. R., & Setlock, L. D. (2004). Text analysis as a tool for analyzing conversation in online support groups. *Extended Abstracts of the 2004 Conference on Human Factors and Computing Systems,* (pp. 1485-1488).

Lyons, E. J., Mehl, M. R., & Pennebaker, J. W. (2006). Pro-anorexics and recovering anorexics differ in their linguistic Internet self-presentation. *Journal of Psychosomatic Research, 60*, 253–256. doi:10.1016/j.jpsychores.2005.07.017

Mairesse, F., Walker, M. A., Mehl, M. R., & Moore, R. K. (2007). Using linguistic cues for the automatic recognition of personality in conversation and text. *Journal of Artificial Intelligence Research, 30*, 457–500.

Martindale, C. (1990). *The clockwork muse: The predictability of artistic change*. New York, NY: Basic Books.

Mehl, M. R. (2006). The lay assessment of subclinical depression in daily life. *Psychological Assessment, 18*, 340–345. doi:10.1037/1040-3590.18.3.340

Mehl, M. R., Gosling, S. D., & Pennebaker, J. W. (2006). Personality in its natural habitat: Manifestations and implicit folk theories of personality in daily life. *Journal of Personality and Social Psychology, 90*, 862–877. doi:10.1037/0022-3514.90.5.862

Mehl, M. R., Vazire, S., Ramirez-Esparza, N., Slatcher, R. B., & Pennebaker, J. W. (2007). Are women really more talkative than men? *Science, 317*, 82. doi:10.1126/science.1139940

Mergenthaler, E. (1996). Emotion-abstraction patterns in verbatim protocols: A new way of describing psychotherapeutic processes. *Journal of Consulting and Clinical Psychology, 64*, 1306–1315. doi:10.1037/0022-006X.64.6.1306

Mullen, B., Chapman, J. G., & Peaugh, S. (1989). Focus of attention in groups: A self-attention perspective. *The Journal of Social Psychology, 129*, 807–817. doi:10.1080/00224545.1989.9712089

Newman, M. L., Groom, C. J., Handelman, L. D., & Pennebaker, J. W. (2008). Gender differences in language use: An analysis of 14,000 text samples. *Discourse Processes, 45*, 211–246. doi:10.1080/01638530802073712

Newman, M. L., Pennebaker, J. W., Berry, D. S., & Richards, J. M. (2003). Lying words: Predicting deception from linguistic style. *Personality and Social Psychology Bulletin, 29*, 665–675. doi:10.1177/0146167203029005010

Niederhoffer, K. G., & Pennebaker, J. W. (2002). Linguistic style matching in social interaction. *Journal of Language and Social Psychology, 21,* 337–360. doi:10.1177/026192702237953

Odom, S. D. (2006). *A qualitative and linguistic analysis of an authority issues training group.* Unpublished doctoral dissertation, The University of Texas at Austin, Austin, TX.

Pennebaker, J. W. (2011). *The secret life of pronouns: What our words say about us.* New York: Bloomsbury Press.

Pennebaker, J. W., & Beall, S. (1986). Confronting a traumatic event: Toward an understanding of inhibition and disease. *Journal of Abnormal Psychology, 95,* 274–281. doi:10.1037/0021-843X.95.3.274

Pennebaker, J. W., Booth, R. J., & Francis, M. E. (2007). *Linguistic inquiry and word count (LIWC2007): A text analysis program.* Austin, TX: LIWC.net.

Pennebaker, J. W., & Chung, C. K. (2008). Computerized text analysis of al-Qaeda statements. In Krippendorff, K., & Bock, M. (Eds.), *A content analysis reader* (pp. 453–466). Thousand Oaks, CA: Sage.

Pennebaker, J. W., Chung, C. K., Ireland, M. I., Gonzales, A. L., & Booth, R. J. (2007). *The development and psychometric properties of LIWC2007.* Austin, TX: LIWC.net.

Pennebaker, J. W., & Francis, M. E. (1996). Cognitive, emotional, and language processes in disclosure. *Cognition and Emotion, 10,* 601–626. doi:10.1080/026999396380079

Pennebaker, J. W., Francis, M. E., & Booth, R. J. (2001). *Linguistic inquiry and word count (LIWC) (Version LIWC2001)* [Computer software]. Mahwah, NJ: Erlbaum.

Pennebaker, J. W., Groom, C. J., Loew, D., & Dabbs, J. (2004). Testosterone as a social inhibitor: Two case studies of the effect of testosterone treatment on language. *Journal of Abnormal Psychology, 113,* 172–175. doi:10.1037/0021-843X.113.1.172

Pennebaker, J. W., & Harber, K. D. (1993). A social stage model of collective coping: The Loma Prieta Earthquake and the Persian Gulf War. *The Journal of Social Issues, 49,* 125–145. doi:10.1111/j.1540-4560.1993.tb01184.x

Pennebaker, J. W., & Huddle, D. (2009). *Detecting deception with courtroom transcripts.* Manuscript in preparation.

Pennebaker, J. W., & King, L. A. (1999). Linguistic styles: Language use as an individual difference. *Journal of Personality and Social Psychology, 77,* 1296–1312. doi:10.1037/0022-3514.77.6.1296

Pennebaker, J. W., & Lay, T. C. (2002). Language use and personality during crisis: Analyses of Mayor Rudolph Giuliani's press conferences. *Journal of Research in Personality, 36,* 271–282. doi:10.1006/jrpe.2002.2349

Pennebaker, J. W., Mayne, T. J., & Francis, M. E. (1997). Linguistic predictors of adaptive bereavement. *Journal of Personality and Social Psychology, 72,* 166–183. doi:10.1037/0022-3514.72.4.863

Pennebaker, J. W., Mehl, M. R., & Niederhoffer, K. G. (2003). Psychological aspects of natural language use: Our words, our selves. *Annual Review of Psychology, 54,* 547–577. doi:10.1146/annurev.psych.54.101601.145041

Pennebaker, J. W., Slatcher, R. B., & Chung, C. K. (2005). Linguistic markers of psychological state through media interviews: John Kerry and John Edwards in 2004, Al Gore in 2000. *Analyses of Social Issues and Public Policy, Special Issue: The Social Psychology of the 2004 US Presidential Elections, 5,* 1-9.

Pennebaker, J. W., & Stone, L. D. (2003). Words of wisdom: Language use over the lifespan. *Journal of Personality and Social Psychology, 85*, 291–301. doi:10.1037/0022-3514.85.2.291

Petrie, K. J., Pennebaker, J. W., & Sivertsen, B. (2008). Things we said today: A linguistic analysis of the Beatles. *Psychology of Aesthetics, Creativity, and the Arts, 2*, 197–202. doi:10.1037/a0013117

Ramirez-Esparza, N., Chung, C. K., Kacewicz, E., & Pennebaker, J. W. (2008). The psychology of word use in depression forums in English and in Spanish. Testing two text analytic approaches. *Proceedings of the 2008 International Conference on Weblogs and Social Media,* (pp. 102-108).

Ramirez-Esparza, N., Chung, C. K., Sierra-Otero, G., & Pennebaker, J. W. (in press). Cross-constructions of self-schemas: American and Mexican college students. *Journal of Cross-Cultural Psychology.*

Ramirez-Esparza, N., Pennebaker, J. W., Garcia, F. A., & Suria, R. (2007). La psicología del uso de las palabras: Un programa de comutadora que analiza textos en Español (The psychology of word use: A computer program that analyzes texts in Spanish). *Revista Mexicana de Psicología, 24*, 85–99.

Rochon, E., Saffran, E. M., Berndt, R. S., & Schwartz, M. F. (2000). Quantitative analysis of aphasic sentence production: Further development and new data. *Brain and Language, 72*, 193–218. doi:10.1006/brln.1999.2285

Rohrbaugh, M. J., Mehl, M. R., Shoham, V., Reilly, E. S., & Ewy, G. A. (2008). Prognostic significance of spouse we talk in couples coping with heart failure. *Journal of Consulting and Clinical Psychology, 76*, 781–789. doi:10.1037/a0013238

Rude, S. S., Gortner, E. M., & Pennebaker, J. W. (2004). Language use of depressed and depression-vulnerable college students. *Cognition and Emotion, 18*, 1121–1133. doi:10.1080/02699930441000030

Scholand, A. J., Tausczik, Y. R., & Pennebaker, J. W. (2010). Social language network analysis. *Proceedings of Computer Supported Cooperative Work, 2010*, 23–26.

Scott, M. (2004). *WordSmith tools 4.0.* Oxford, UK: Oxford University Press.

Sexton, J. B., & Helmreich, R. L. (2000). Analyzing cockpit communications: The links between language, performance, error, and workload. *Human Performance in Extreme Environments, 5*, 63–68.

Shiu, E., & Lenhart, A. (2004). How Americans use instant messaging. Retrieved October 14, 2005, from http://www.pewinternet.org/pdfs/PIP_Instantmessage_Report.pdf.

Sillars, A., Shellen, W., McIntosh, A., & Pomegranate, M. (1997). Relational characteristics of language: Elaboration and differentiation in marital conversations. *Western Journal of Communication, 61*, 403–422. doi:10.1080/10570319709374587

Simmons, R. A., Gordon, P. C., & Chambless, D. L. (2005). Pronouns in marital interaction: What do you and I say about marital health? *Psychological Science, 16*, 932–936. doi:10.1111/j.1467-9280.2005.01639.x

Slatcher, R. B., Chung, C. K., Pennebaker, J. W., & Handelman, L. D. (2007). Winning words: Individual differences in linguistic style among U.S. presidential and vice presidential candidates. *Journal of Research in Personality, 41*, 63–75. doi:10.1016/j.jrp.2006.01.006

Slatcher, R. B., & Pennebaker, J. W. (2006). How do I love thee? Let me count the words: The social effects of expressive writing. *Psychological Science, 17,* 660–664. doi:10.1111/j.1467-9280.2006.01762.x

Stirman, S. W., & Pennebaker, J. W. (2001). Word use in the poetry of suicidal and non-suicidal poets. *Psychosomatic Medicine, 63,* 517–522.

Stone, L. D., & Pennebaker, J. W. (2002). Trauma in real time: Talking and avoiding online conversations about the death of Princess Diana. *Basic and Applied Social Psychology, 24,* 172–182.

Stone, L. D., & Pennebaker, J. W. (2004). What was she trying to say? A linguistic analysis of Katie's diaries. In Lester, D. (Ed.), *Katie's diary: Unlocking the mystery of a suicide.* London, UK: Taylor & Francis.

Stone, P. J., Dunphy, D. C., Smith, M. S., & Ogilvie, D. M. (1966). *The general inquirer: A computer approach to content analysis.* Cambridge, MA: MIT Press.

Tausczik, Y. R. (2009). *Linguistic analysis of workplace computer-mediated communication.* Unpublished Master's thesis. Austin, TX: The University of Texas at Austin.

Tausczik, Y. R., Faase, K., Pennebaker, J. W., & Petrie, K. J. (in press). Public anxiety and information seeking following H1N1 outbreak: Weblogs, newspaper articles and Wikipedia visits. *Health Communication.*

Tausczik, Y. R., & Pennebaker, J. W. (2010). The psychological meaning of words: LIWC and computerized text analysis methods. *Journal of Language and Social Psychology, 29,* 24–54. doi:10.1177/0261927X09351676

van Petten, C., & Kutas, M. (1991). Influences of semantic and syntactic context on open- and closed-class words. *Memory & Cognition, 19,* 95–112. doi:10.3758/BF03198500

Weintraub, W. (1989). *Verbal behavior in everyday life.* New York, NY: Springer.

Wolf, M., Chung, C. K., & Kordy, H. (2010a). Inpatient treatment to online aftercare: E-mailing themes as a function of therapeutic outcomes. *Psychotherapy Research, 20,* 71–85. doi:10.1080/10503300903179799

Wolf, M., Chung, C. K., & Kordy, H. (2010b). MEM's search for meaning: A rejoinder. *Psychotherapy Research, 20,* 93–99. doi:10.1080/10503300903527393

Wolf, M., Horn, A. B., Mehl, M. R., Haug, S., Pennebaker, J. W., & Kordy, H. (2008). Computergestützte quantitative Textanalyse: Äquivalenz und Robustheit der deutschen Version des Linguistic Inquiry and Word Count [Computer-aided quantitative text analysis: Equivalence and robustness of the German adaption of the Linguistic Inquiry and Word Count]. *Diagnostica, 54,* 85–98. doi:10.1026/0012-1924.54.2.85

Zhou, L., Burgoon, J. K., Twitchell, D., Qin, T., & Nunamaker, J. F. (2004). A comparison of classification methods for predicting deception in computer-mediated communication. *Journal of Management Information Systems, 20,* 139–165.

ADDITIONAL READING

Alexander-Emery, S., Cohen, L. M., & Prensky, E. H. (2005). Linguistic analysis of college aged smokers and never smokers. *Journal of Psychopathology and Behavioral Assessment, 27,* 11–16. doi:10.1007/s10862-005-3260-4

Alvarez-Conrad, J., Zoellner, L. A., & Foa, E. B. (2001). Linguistic predictors of trauma pathology and physical health. *Applied Cognitive Psychology, 15,* 159–170. doi:10.1002/acp.839

Bantum, E. O., & Owen, J. E. (2009). Evaluating the validity of computerized content analysis programs for identification of emotional expression in cancer narratives. *Psychological Assessment, 21*, 79–88. doi:10.1037/a0014643

Boals, A., & Klein, K. (2005). Word use in emotional narratives about failed romantic relationships and subsequent mental health. *Journal of Language and Social Psychology, 24*, 252–268. doi:10.1177/0261927X05278386

Cohen, A. S., Minor, K. S., Baillie, L. E., & Dahir, A. M. (2008). Clarifying the linguistic signature: Measuring personality from natural speech. *Journal of Personality Assessment, 90*, 559–563. doi:10.1080/00223890802388459

Davis, D., & Brock, T. C. (1975). Use of first person pronouns as a function of increased objective self-awareness and performance feedback. *Journal of Experimental Social Psychology, 11*, 381–388. doi:10.1016/0022-1031(75)90017-7

Dino, A., Reysen, S., & Branscombe, N. R. (2009). Online interactions between group members who differ in status. *Journal of Language and Social Psychology, 28*, 85–94. doi:10.1177/0261927X08325916

Gill, A. J., French, R. M., Gergle, D., & Oberlander, J. (2008). The language of emotion in short blog texts. In Proceedings of the CSCW'08 Computer Supported Cooperative Work (pp. 209-332). New York: Association for Computing Machinery Press.

Gottschalk, L. A., & Bechtel, R. (1993). *Computerized content analysis of natural language or verbal texts*. Palo Alto: Mind garden.

Gottschalk, L. A., & Gleser, G. C. (1969). *The measurement of psychological states through the content analysis of verbal behavior*. Berkeley, CA: The University of California Press.

Gottschalk, L. A., Gleser, G. C., Daniels, R., & Block, S. (1958). The speech patterns of schizophrenic patients: a method of assessing relative degree of personal disorganization and social alienation. *The Journal of Nervous and Mental Disease, 127*, 153–166. doi:10.1097/00005053-195808000-00008

Groom, C. J., & Pennebaker, J. W. (2005). The language of love: Sex, sexual orientation and language use in online personal advertisements. *Sex Roles, 52*, 447–461. doi:10.1007/s11199-005-3711-0

Handelman, L. D., & Lester, D. (2007). The content of suicide notes from attempters and completers. *Crisis, 28*, 102–104. doi:10.1027/0227-5910.28.2.102

Hartley, J., Pennebaker, J. W., & Fox, C. (2003). Abstracts, introductions and discussions: How far do they differ in style? *Scientometrics, 57*, 389–398. doi:10.1023/A:1025008802657

Ireland, M. E., Slatcher, R. B., Eastwick, P. W., Scissors, L. E., Finkel, E. J., & Pennebaker, J. W. (2011). Language style matching predicts relationship formation and stability. *Psychological Science, 22*, 39–44. doi:10.1177/0956797610392928

Kahn, J. H., Tobin, R. M., Massey, A. E., & Anderson, J. A. (2007). Measuring emotional expression with the Linguistic Inquiry and Word Count. *The American Journal of Psychology, 120*, 268–286.

Kramer, A. D. I., & Chung, C. K. (2011). Dimensions of self-expression in Facebook status updates. *Proceedings of the International Conference on Weblogs and Social Media,* (pp. 169-176).

Kramer, A. D. I., Oh, L. M., & Fussell, S. R. (2006). Using linguistic features to measure presence in computer-mediated communication. In *Proceedings of the CHI'06 Conference on Human Factors in Computing Systems* (pp.913-916). New York: Association for Computing Machinery Press.

Lee, C. H., Kim, K., Seo, Y. S., & Chung, C. K. (2007). The relations between personality and language use. *The Journal of General Psychology*, *134*, 405–413. doi:10.3200/GENP.134.4.405-414

Leshed, G., Cosley, D., Hancock, J. T., & Gay, G. (2010). Visualizing language use in team conversations: designing through theory, experiments, and iterations. *CHI Extended Abstracts*, *2010*, 4567–4582.

Lightman, E. J., McCarthy, P. M., Dufty, D. F., & McNamara, D. S. (2007). Using computational text analysis tools to compare the lyrics of suicidal and non-suicidal songwriters. In D. S. McNamara and G. Trafton (Eds.), *Proceedings of the 29th Annual Cognitive Science Society.* Hillsdale, NJ: Erlbaum.

Mehl, M. R. (2006). Quantitative text analysis. In Eid, M., & Diener, E. (Eds.), *Handbook of multimethod measurement in psychology* (pp. 141–156). Washington, DC, USA: American Psychological Association. doi:10.1037/11383-011

Mehl, M. R., & Pennebaker, J. W. (2003). The sounds of social life: A psychometric analysis of students' daily social environments and natural conversations. *Journal of Personality and Social Psychology*, *84*, 857–870. doi:10.1037/0022-3514.84.4.857

Miller, G. (1995). *The science of words*. New York: Scientific American Library.

Oxman, T. E., Rosenberg, S. D., Schnurr, P. P., & Tucker, G. J. (1982). Diagnostic classification through content analysis of patients' speech. *The American Journal of Psychiatry*, *145*, 464–468.

Pasupathi, M. (2007). Telling and the remembered self: Linguistic differences in memories for previously disclosed and previously undisclosed events. *Memory (Hove, England)*, *15*, 258–270. doi:10.1080/09658210701256456

Pennebaker, J. W., & Chung, C. K. (2005). Tracking the social dynamics of responses to terrorism: Language, behavior, and the Internet. In Wessely, S., & Krasnov, V. N. (Eds.), *Psychological responses to the new terrorism: A NATO Russia dialogue* (pp. 159–170). Amsterdam, The Netherlands: IOS Press.

Pennebaker, J. W., & Chung, C. K. (2011). Expressive writing and its links to mental and physical health. In Friedman, H. S. (Ed.), *Oxford handbook of health psychology* (pp. 417–437). New York, NY: Oxford University Press.

Piolat, A., Booth, R. J., Chung, C. K., Davids, M., & Pennebaker, J. W. (2011). La version française du LIWC: modalités de construction et exemples d'application [The French version of LIWC: Modalities of construction and examples of use.]. *Psychologie Française*, *56*, 145–159. doi:10.1016/j.psfr.2011.07.002

Pressman, S. D., & Cohen, S. (2007). Use of social words in autobiographies and longevity. *Psychosomatic Medicine*, *69*, 262–269. doi:10.1097/PSY.0b013e31803cb919

Rellini, A. H., & Meston, C. M. (2007). Sexual desire and linguistic analysis: A comparison of sexually-abused and non-abused women. *Archives of Sexual Behavior*, *36*, 67–77. doi:10.1007/s10508-006-9076-9

Scherwitz, L., & Canick, J. (1988). Self reference and coronary heart disease risk. In Houston, K., & Snyder, C. R. (Eds.), *Type A behavior pattern: Research, theory, and intervention* (pp. 146–167). New York: Wiley.

Sharp, W. G., & Hargrove, D. S. (2004). Emotional expression and modality: An analysis of affective arousal and linguistic output in a computer versus paper paradigm. *Computers in Human Behavior*, *20*, 461–475. doi:10.1016/j.chb.2003.10.007

Slatcher, R. B., Vazire, S., & Pennebaker, J. W. (2008). Am "I" more important than "we"? Couples' word use in instant messages. *Personal Relationships*, *15*, 407–424. doi:10.1111/j.1475-6811.2008.00207.x

Stephenson, G. M., Laszlo, J., Ehmann, B., Lefever, R. M. H., & Lefever, R. (1997). Diaries of significant events: Socio-linguistic correlates of therapeutic outcomes in patients with addiction problems. *Journal of Community & Applied Social Psychology*, *7*, 389–411. doi:10.1002/(SICI)1099-1298(199712)7:5<389::AID-CASP434>3.0.CO;2-R

Taylor, P. J., & Thomas, S. (2008). Linguistic style matching and negotiation outcome. *Negotiation and Conflict Management Research*, *1*, 263–281. doi:10.1111/j.1750-4716.2008.00016.x

Tsai, J. L., Simeonova, D. I., & Watanabe, J. T. (2004). Somatic and social: Chinese Americans talk about emotion. *Personality and Social Psychology Bulletin*, *30*, 1226–1238. doi:10.1177/0146167204264014

KEY TERMS AND DEFINITIONS

Content Words: Words that hold meaning on their own (e.g., some adjectives, some adverbs, nouns, regular verbs, etc.); also known as open-class words.

Function Words: Words that support content words in a sentence for comprehension but do not hold meaning on their own; also known as closed-class words or junk words (e.g., some adjectives, some adverbs, articles, auxiliary verbs, conjunctions, modals, negations, prepositions, pronouns, etc.)

Language Style Matching (LSM): A measure of verbal synchrony that represents shared attention and engagement in an interaction; measured by the degree to which groups of texts contain similar rates of function words.

Linguistic Inquiry and Word Count (LIWC): An automated word counting software whose default dictionary includes grammatical, psychological, and content word categories.

Meaning Extraction Method (MEM): A semi-automated method to extract common themes from a text; computed by a factor analysis of high frequency words in a corpus.

Qualitative Text Analysis: A broad type of content analysis that uses subjective interpretations and systematic judge-based coding to characterize text.

Quantitative Text Analysis: A broad type of content analysis that uses objective numbers (counts or algorithms) to characterize text.

Chapter 13
HiDEx:
The High Dimensional Explorer

Cyrus Shaoul
University of Alberta, Canada

Chris Westbury
University of Alberta, Canada

ABSTRACT

HAL (Hyperspace Analog to Language) is a high-dimensional model of semantic space that uses the global co-occurrence frequency of words in a large corpus of text as the basis for a representation of semantic memory. In the original HAL model, many parameters were set without any a priori rationale. In this chapter we describe a new computer application called the High Dimensional Explorer (HiDEx) that makes it possible to systematically alter the values of the model's parameters and thereby to examine their effect on the co-occurrence matrix that instantiates the model. New parameter sets give us measures of semantic density that improve the model's ability to predict behavioral measures. Implications for such models are discussed.

INTRODUCTION

In this chapter we present a new tool for exploring a class of models of lexical semantics derived from HAL (Hyperspace Analog to Language; Burgess, 1998; Burgess & Lund, 2000), a computational model of word meaning that derives semantic relationships from lexical co-occurrence. Although the original HAL model was well specified, it contains

several parameters whose values were set without formal or empirical justification. Our freely available implementation of the class of HAL-derived models is called the High Dimensional Explorer (HiDEx). HiDEx allows users to systematically vary its defining parameters, creating models that are algorithmically identical, but parameterized differently. In this paper we will explain how HiDEx works, and how we have been able to use it to explore HAL's parameter space.

DOI: 10.4018/978-1-60960-741-8.ch013

INTRODUCTION TO HAL

We begin with a brief overview of the original HAL model (Burgess, 1998; Burgess & Lund, 2000).

HAL uses word co-occurrence to build an abstract data representation called *a vector space* that contains contextual information for every word in a specified dictionary. A vector space is a geometric representation of data that has an ordered set of N numbers associated with each point in an N-dimensional space. For example, any location on the earth's surface can be specified by an ordered set of two numbers (a vector of length two), consisting of the location's latitude and longitude. If we wanted to specify a point off the earth's surface, we would need to add a third number specifying height above or below the surface, requiring us to specify each point with an ordered set of three numbers (a vector of length three). Just as in these examples, in higher dimensions each ordered set of numbers, or vector, defines a point's location in a space.

Conceptually, a vector space can have dimensionality of any size. Each number in a vector simply specifies one quantitative attribute or characteristic of the point in its space. While locations on earth can be fully described with a set of three values, many things require more than three values to define them. We might imagine that instead of simply specifying a point on earth, we wanted to also specify the point's color, temperature, and noise level, so that we would now need a six dimensional space, and therefore vectors of length six to describe every point. The vector space of HAL is made up of vectors for each word in the language. Because HAL includes information about every word's co-occurrence relation to every word in the language (including itself), each vector in HAL has an entry for every word in the language. In the original HAL model, these vectors had more than 100,000 dimensions. Each entry in a HAL vector is a count of the number of times another word co-occurred with the vector's word in a large text corpus, weighted by a factor

that specifies how distant the two words were. Words can co-occur when they are adjacent, or when they are separated by a number of intervening words. The maximum distance between words considered to co-occur is called the *window size*. Window size is one of the free parameters in the HAL model. In the original model, words were considered to have co-occurred if they occurred within ten words of each other, in either direction.

The words in a target word's co-occurrence window are weighted according to their proximity to that target word using a *weighting function*. The original HAL model used a linear weighting function, called *a linear ramp*, as a multiplier to give more weight to the words that co-occurred closer to the center of the window. Words that occurred on either side of the center word of the window were assigned ten co-occurrence points. The center word's next neighbors were assigned nine co-occurrence points, and so on, down a single point for a word that occurred ten words away from the center word (see Figure 1, for an explanatory example with a window size of five).

Lexical memories in the HAL model are built by making the model read words in a text one window at a time, and then sliding the window forward one word, as in Figure 1. After reading a whole corpus and summing the weighted local co-occurrences, the data is stored in a raw co-occurrence matrix containing the frequencies of co-occurrence for all possible combinations of words in all possible positions in the window, similar to the simple, mostly empty matrices shown at the bottom of Figure 1. When the moving window slides across a large corpus instead of the two sentences shown in Figure 1, this matrix can become very large. For example, with a 100,000 word lexicon and HAL's ten-word window in each direction, the number of data points in the matrix would be 100,000 target words x 100,000 co-ocurrence words x 20 positions = 200 billion entries. However, though it is large, the raw co-occurrence matrix is very sparse (containing mostly zeros) because most words never

Figure 1. A visualization of a sliding window five words ahead and five words behind the target word (which we call a 5A5B window), with linear ramp weighting, as it moves over a corpus- in this case, consisting of just two sentences. In this example, the first target word is the word 'lazy' and the second is the word 'dog.' The tables below show the before and after vectors for the target words that the co-occurrence matrix would contain after weighting the counts from the sliding window (but before normalizing the rows). Not shown are all the other words in the language, which will have a zero weighting since they don't appear with any words in this tiny corpus.

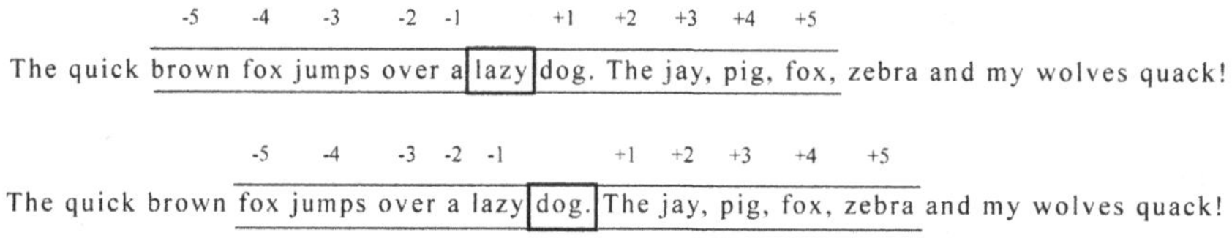

```
        -5   -4   -3   -2  -1        +1  +2  +3  +4  +5
The quick brown fox jumps over a| lazy |dog. The jay, pig, fox, zebra and my wolves quack!
```

```
           -5   -4  -3  -2  -1      +1  +2  +3  +4  +5
The quick brown fox jumps over a lazy | dog. |The jay, pig, fox, zebra and my wolves quack!
```

AHEAD	brown	fox	jumps	over	a	lazy	dog	the	jay	pig	zebra
lazy	0	1	0	0	0	0	5	4	3	2	0
dog	0	2	0	0	0	0	0	5	4	3	1

BEHIND	brown	fox	jumps	over	a	lazy	dog	the	jay	pig	zebra
lazy	1	2	3	4	5	0	0	0	0	0	0
dog	0	1	2	3	4	5	0	0	0	0	0

co-occur with each other. To do any meaningful work with the data, the raw co-occurrence matrix must be condensed into a more compact form in the consolidation phase of the HAL model. One step in this consolidation, or aggregation, is done by simply summing the word frequencies in the window. With a ten-word window size, this aggregation reduces the data set to $1/10^{th}$ of its former size, since a co-occurrence count that needed 20 cells (10 forward and 10 backward) before summing is represented by just two cells (one forward and one backward) after summing (see Figure 2).

These vectors are not yet usable due to the influence of orthographic frequency. A small number of words have much higher orthographic frequencies than the majority of words (Baayen, 2001; Zipf, 1935, 1949), and consequently those words will have very high co-occurrence frequencies. Due to this bias, high frequency words will have vectors that are very dense with large values,

and therefore they will be much closer in context space to all words than low frequency words will be. The original HAL model dealt with this frequency issue by normalizing each vector, by dividing each element in the vector by the vector's length (that is, by the number of co-occurring words).

The final stage in preparing the vectors for distance calculations is the elimination of the sparser, less informative parts of the matrix. In the HAL model this was done by retaining only vectors for the words with the greatest row variances (e.g. eliminating words that co-occur very often or very rarely with the target word). If only the rows with the top 10,000 most variant words are used, the forward and backward aggregates create rows of 20,000 elements instead of 200,000 elements. This matrix is smaller and denser than previous matrices, and is small enough to fit into the memory of modern computers, making the calculations tractable.

Figure 2. Schematic illustration of how HAL word vectors are aggregated (by summing weighted backwards and forwards co-occurrence schemes into a single value each) and inserted in the global matrix. In this example, the target word is 'run' and the co-occurring word is 'bank.' Values are normalized for frequency after all vectors have been inserted in the global co-occurrence matrix (this normalization step is not shown here).

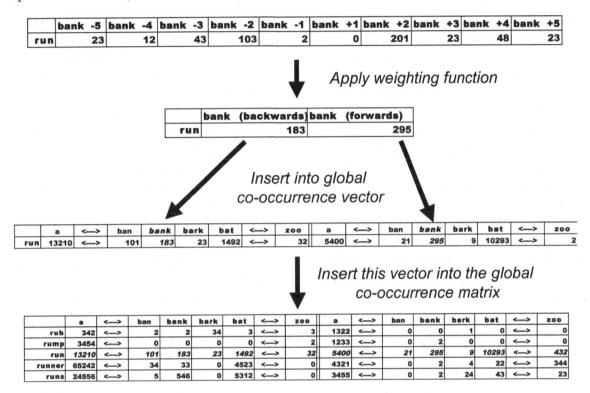

The HAL model used the Euclidean distance metric to calculate the distance between any two words in the space. This distance expresses how similar the *contexts* of usage of the two words are. If the words have similar values in the same dimensions, they will be closer together in the space.

Along with choosing a window size, weighting scheme, distance measure, matrix compression technique, vector size and vector normalization algorithm, two other main decisions had to be made when HAL was originally implemented. One of these was the choice of a lexicon, which defines what will count as a word and thereby defines the dimensionality of the model, since every word vector will have a length equal to the lexicon size. Lund and Burgess (1996) chose a lexicon consisting of approximately 70,000 words.

The second important decision they had to make was a choice of which corpus was to be used to compute co-occurrence. Lund & Burgess used a 160 million word corpus derived from USENET text (Fristrup, 1994).

BACKGROUND: ASSESSMENT OF HAL AND RELATED MODELS

HAL was originally put forth as a model of semantic memory and was soon subjected to scrutiny to see how it performed as a model. In this section we briefly review some of the empirical work suggesting that HAL and related models may serve as models of human behavior or processes.

Buchanan, Burgess, and Lund (1996) used HAL to model deep dyslexia. They found that words with denser neighborhoods produced more errors in deep dyslexics than words with sparser neighborhoods. Buchanan et al. (2001) look at HAL neighborhood effects on lexical decisions and showed that the HAL neighborhood size was a reliable predictor of lexical decision reaction time. Even after removing the contributions of orthographic variables and imageability, there was significant explanatory power from HAL neighborhood size. Siakaluk, Buchanan, and Westbury (2003) investigated the ability of HAL to predict performance in a categorization task. They found that HAL semantic density influenced the decision time on a go/no go semantic decision task. Words with denser co-occurrence neighborhoods were processed faster. Yates, Locker, and Simpson (2003) found a similar facilitatory effect of high-density neighborhoods in a lexical decision task that included pseudohomophone foils.

Song and Bruza (2001), Song, Bruza, Huang, and Lau (2003), and Song, Bruza, and Cole (2004) have applied the HAL model to problems of concept learning, inference, and information flow. They were able to use HAL vectors as part of an intelligent software agent that makes "about-ness" judgments such as judging that the sentence "Welcome to the City of Red Deer, Alberta" has nothing to do with the antlered mammal known scientifically as *Cervus elaphus*. They do this by combining the vectors for all the words in the sentence and then comparing it to the vector for the concept in question (in this case, "deer").

The performance on language tasks of models closely-related to HAL has also been studied. Rohde, Gonnerman, and Plaut (2007) created the COALS (Correlated Occurrence Analogue to Lexical Semantic) model. It is identical in design to HAL except in the following respects: it uses a correlation operation for both vector normalization and similarity measures, it removes closed class words from the model, and uses *singular value decomposition* (SVD) to reduce the dimensionality

of the co-occurrence matrix. SVD is a factorization technique that can be used to calculate a lower-dimensionality approximation of the original, larger matrix. Rohde et al. (2007) show that HAL performs very well on word similarity tasks such as those in the TOEFL exam and other similar tests when SVD is applied to the model.

Bullinaria and Levy (2007) analyzed different influences of excluded closed class words, corpus size, window size and distance metrics. They proposed using an information-theoretic metric, pointwise mutual information (PMI) instead of Euclidean distance, and found that PMI improved the accuracy of their model in their semantic task simulations. PMI is a measure of association that is calculated as the ratio between the probability of two words co-occurring given their joint distribution versus the probability of their co-occurrence given only their individual distributions and assuming independence.

Durda and Buchanan (2008) have created a HAL-type model called WINDSORS (Windsor Improved Norms of Distance and Similarity Of Representations of Semantics). In their model, the influence of word frequency on the model's output is mitigated through the use of various statistical and mathematical methods. Despite the removal of any real correlation with orthographic frequency, the vectors produced by WINDSORS are capable of modeling semantic priming experiments and word similarity norms. Using WINDSORS as a starting point, Durda, Buchanan, and Caron (2009) have taken a first step toward grounding their models in perceptual and motor features. They used a feed-forward neural network to provide a mapping from co-occurrence vectors of concepts (such as BIRD) to feature norms (such as HAS-WINGS). They then generalized this mapping and produced a list of features from the co-occurrence vector of a novel concept. This result supports the claim that co-occurrence vectors contain an enormous amount of information about the words they represent, including perceptually grounded information.

Jones and Mewhort (2007) and Jones, Kintsch, and Mewhort (2006) have built a holographic model of lexical memory, more complex than HAL, that they call BEAGLE (Bound Encoding of the Aggregate Language Environment). BEAGLE encodes the co-occurrence and word order information into vectors using a *convolution* function as a way to model verbal associative memory (Murdock, 1982). Convolution is a mathematical operation that can be applied to any type vector to encode it into a memory trace vector. Later, the information can be extracted from the memory trace by calculating the correlation between a probe item and the combined memory trace. In BEAGLE, this function is applied to language in such a way that word order information and global co-occurrence information are simultaneously encoded into each vector. BEAGLE has been able to account for many different types of semantic priming effects when the prime-target pairs are related by both pure semantic relationships and associations (Jones et al., 2006). It has also been used to model sentence completion and semantic categorization (Jones & Mewhort, 2007).

HiDEx: PARAMETERS, ALGORITHMS, AND RESOURCES

The work reviewed above suggests that HAL and related models have the potential to serve as fruitful models of human processes or behavior. One problem in undertaking new modeling work or assessing previous modeling work with HAL is that the original HAL model had a large number of free parameters and required resources, the values of which were not always supported by any *a priori* rationale. By changing those parameters or resources, it is possible to change HAL, thereby creating a family of HAL models united by a common underlying basic algorithm but differing in the parametric details. Little is known about the effects of varying those parameters, and in particular about which parameter

settings are optimal for what purposes and why. We created HiDEx (High Dimensional Explorer) largely to facilitate systematic exploration of HAL's parameter space by providing an open source implementation of the HAL family of models that has been specifically designed to allow changes to the parameter settings, even by non-programmers. We have also identified or produced freely-available external resources so that the model can be used, without cost, in a standard way between studies. We released this software as an open-source project (which means that the C++ source code is freely available) in December 2008 under the GNU General Public License (Stallman, 2009). The program and some associated resources are available at: http://www.psych.ualberta.ca/~westburylab/downloads.html.

In the following subsection, we describe the parameters, algorithms, and external resources that must be selected or set by users of HiDEx. We focus on the settings and resources that we have used. In the subsection after that, we briefly describe what kind of input HiDEx can use, and explain what kinds of processing it can do and what kinds of output it can produce.

Lexicon Choice

The lexicon that we originally chose to use was derived from the CELEX database (Baayen, Piepenbrock, & Gulikers, 1995) by choosing all the words that had an orthographic frequency of two occurrences per million or greater. This lexicon contains approximately 45,000 words, which is less that the 70,000 word lexicon used by Lund and Burgess (1996). The choice to reduce the lexicon size was made for two reasons: 1) the amount of information contained in the contexts of low frequency words is small, and does not have much influence on the distances between most words in the space, and 2) the computational complexity of the model increases greatly with the size of the lexicon.

The CELEX database is a commercial database that must be purchased. We have released orthographic frequency counts derived from our corpus (described below) that have been released for public use, and which could be used to make a substitute lexicon for the CELEX lexicon. Our lexicon is available from the website referenced above.

Corpus Choice

Another decision that has to be made by users of co-occurrence models is the decision about which corpus to use for computing co-occurrence measures. It is well known that the balance of registers and genres in a corpus has a strong effect on the HAL vectors produced (Shaoul & Westbury, 2006; Bullinaria & Levy, 2007; Rohde et al., 2007). In order to make our results comparable to the majority of studies done on the HAL model, we chose to replicate as closely as possible the USENET corpora used by Lund and Burgess (1996), Burgess and Lund (1997), Burgess (1998), Burgess and Livesay (1998), Burgess, Livesay, and Lund (1998) and Burgess and Lund (2000). We collected 12 billion words of USENET text from 2005 to 2007 (Shaoul & Westbury, 2009), and used a one billion word subset of this corpus to build our models. The same benefits that were described by Lund and Burgess (1996) are true for this corpus: USENET text contains a very broad variety of genres and topics, and most of the text is in a very conversational style, similar in some ways to spoken language. We chose not to use a corpus of 160 million words in size because we found that there were many words in our lexicon that had one or fewer occurrence in a corpus of that size. To obtain observations of multiple occurrences of all the words in our lexicon, it was necessary to use a larger corpus. In addition, Bullinaria and Levy (2007) did a very thorough analysis of the impact of corpus size on HAL. They found that their measures of performance increased as corpus size increased, though the amount of improvement was mostly at ceiling for corpora of 90 million words or greater.

Frequency Normalization

Shaoul and Westbury (2006) demonstrated that the normalization procedure used in the original HAL, dividing each vector by its variance, did not eliminate frequency effects. If HAL neighborhood density is used to predict psycholinguistic phenomena, it would be unfortunate if HAL density measures co-varied with orthographic frequency, one of the most powerful predictors of lexical access (Balota, Black, & Cheney, 1992). Buchanan et al. (2001) proposed dividing the entries in each target word's vector by the orthographic frequency of that target word. This has the effect of normalizing the vectors and removing the effect of the target word's frequency. Concretely, if one target word occurred ten times and co-occurred once with word X and another target word occurred 100 times and co-occurred ten times with word X (at the same distances from the target word, for the sake of keeping the example simple), this division will give the same value for the entry for word X in each of the two target words' vectors. Shaoul and Westbury (2006) showed that the neighborhood densities made with this normalization technique were no longer correlated with orthographic frequency. This is the default normalization procedure used by HiDEx.

Window Size and Co-Occurrence Weighting

As mentioned above, Lund and Burgess (1996) assigned weights to the co-occurrence counts by weighting them in a symmetric ten-word window (in front and behind the target word) with a linear ramp, which multiplied values by their distance from the end of the window. This meant that the count for the word appearing directly adjacent would be multiplied by ten, then the next one out by nine, and so on. There was no *a priori* justification for the window size, its symmetry, or the linear ramp weighting scheme.

In HiDEx we chose to introduce alternative weighting schemes that would reflect the variety of weighting schemes being used by other investigators who have worked with HAL models, as well as introducing new weighting schemes for possible investigation. The built-in weighting schemes are listed in Table 1. It is not difficult to specify additional weighting schemes in HiDEx, although some programming ability is required.

Context Size

One key aspect of implementing HAL-family models is the reduction of the size of the global co-occurrence matrix after the weighting scheme has been applied and the windows have been summed. Because low frequency words co-occur with few words and thereby contribute less co-occurrence information than more frequent words (that is, have more empty cells in their vectors), HiDEx uses the N most frequent words' vectors rather than the most variant vectors as in the original HAL model. 'N' is a free parameter that may be set by the user. By default it is set to 14,000.

Neighborhood Size and Membership Threshold

One extension to HAL proposed by Shaoul and Westbury (2006) was a re-definition to the concept of neighborhood membership and density. Early work with HAL co-occurrence neighborhood density (e.g. Buchanan et al., 2001) used an arbitrarily chosen fixed number (ten) of the closest neighbors as the neighborhood, taking the average distance of these neighbors from the target word as a measure of neighborhood density. The use of a fixed number of neighbors for calculating density is not ideal for two related reasons. One reason is that, if the density distribution of neighbors around a given word is not uniform (and there are many reasons to believe it will not be), then averaging a uniform number of neighbors is not equivalent in different words. A word with many neighbors will probably have more neighbors that are close to it than a word with few neighbors, but may nevertheless have a larger average neighborhood size. By analogy, a person with many friends is more likely to have a few extremely short friends than a person with fewer friends, since extremely short people are

Table 1. List of weighting functions implemented in HiDEx

Function Name	Function: w = window size, p = position (1 to w)	Sample Vector of Weights (symmetric 4-word windows)
Flat Weights	x = 1	[1 1 1 1 1 1 1 1]
Linear Ramp	x = (w - p + 1)	[1 2 3 4 4 3 2 1]
Exponential Ramp	x = (w - p + 1)^2	[1 4 9 16 16 9 4 1]
Forward Linear Ramp, Backward Flat Ramp	x = 1, x = (w - p + 1)	[1 1 1 1 4 3 2 1]
Forward Flat Weights, Backward Linear Ramp	x = (w - p + 1), x = 1	[1 2 3 4 1 1 1 1]
Inverse Linear Ramp	x = p	[4 3 2 1 1 2 3 4]
Inverse Exponential Ramp	x = p^2	[16 9 4 1 1 4 9 16]
Second Word Weighting	if p = 2, x = 10, else x = 1	[1 1 10 1 1 10 1 1]
Third Word Weighting	if p = 3, x = 10, else x = 1	[1 10 1 1 1 1 10 1]
Fourth Word Weighting	if p = 4, x = 10, else x = 1	[10 1 1 1 1 1 1 10]

uncommon. However, the person with many friends may nevertheless have a larger average friend size that the person with fewer friends (see Figure 3). A second problem with using a radius of ten words is that this cut-off point is arbitrary. No one knows if the average distance of a word's closest ten neighbors is a better measure of co-occurrence density than the average distance of its closest 12 or 18 or 56 neighbors. As implicit in Figure 3, it is likely the density measure may be sensitive to number of closest neighbors that are averaged together.

Instead of using a fixed set of neighbors, we calculated a distance in co-occurrence space, called the *neighborhood membership threshold*, which was used as the criterion for neighborhood membership. This threshold is calculated by randomly sampling a user-defined subset of word pairs and calculating their inter-word distances to find the mean and standard deviation of this distance distribution. By default the *sample size* in HiDEx is 5% of all possible pairs of words that have co-occurred at least once in the corpus, a sample that usually consists of billions of word pairs and the neighborhood membership threshold in HiDEx is set to 1.5 *SD*s below the mean distance between words from this sample, which includes about 6.7% of the average distance between any two words in that sample. Most word pairs have only a weak or no relationship. Setting the cut-off point to cover this small fraction of the average distance between words will ensure that words only count as neighbors if they are at least as close as the closest 6.7% of the large set of sampled pairs. A consequence of using this definition of neighborhood membership is that some words

Figure 3. An illustration in two dimensions of the problem with using a set number of neighbors to calculate the density of a target word's co-occurrence neighbors. The data shown here were randomly generated so that the 80 black dots have an average distance from the center (marked with an X) that is 1.5 times further than the average distance of the 20 white squares. However, the smallest circle encompassing the ten black circles closest to the center is much smaller than the smallest circle encompassing the ten closest white squares. This occurs because of the disparity in the number of squares and circles. Taking the average distance of the ten closest neighbors would incorrectly lead to the conclusion that the white squares were more distant from the 'target' (here, the center point) than the black circles. The same reasoning holds in higher dimensional spaces such as co-occurrence space.

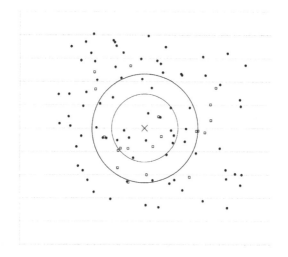

may have more neighbors than others, and some words may have no neighbors at all. (Note that this threshold has to be re-calculated every time any other parameter in the model is changed because the average distance between words will be affected by any parameter change.)

As a consequence of their definition of neighborhood, Shaoul and Westbury (2006) defined two new measures of semantic density. The first measure, *Average Radius of Co-Occurrence* (ARC) is defined as the mean of the distances between the target word and all the neighbors that fell within its threshold. The second measure, *Neighbor Count* (NCOUNT) is the number of neighbor words within that threshold. In practice we have often found it more useful to use a transformation of NCOUNT that we call NCOUNT-INV, which is defined as the reciprocal of (NCOUNT + 1), with the 1 being added to allow the measure to be well defined for words that have zero neighbors. NCOUNT-INV has a value of one for words with no neighbors, and smaller values for words with more neighbors.

HiDEx: USE AND METHODS

HiDEx is a command-line program written in C++ that is configured using a text file containing the user-configurable settings used by the program. The format of this configuration file is described in the HiDEx User Manual that is distributed with the software, and we will not describe it further here.

There are three main stages of processing for users of HiDEx:

- **Stage 1:** Obtain and prepare the corpus for use, then process the corpus with HiDEx to create the global co-occurrence matrix.
- **Stage 2:** Configure the desired settings for all the available parameters. Process the global matrix with HiDEx to create word vectors.

- **Stage 3:** Use HiDEx to measure the contextual similarity between words and then save the output.

In this section we described the operations that are completed in each of these stages in more detail.

Stage 1: Corpus Preparation

During Stage 1, HiDEx performs the initial preprocessing of the corpus. HiDEx will accept corpora in any UTF-8 encoded language. The corpus should be in the form of one large file that includes user-defined document separators. HiDEx will automatically capitalize lower-case letters in the corpus and remove any punctuation (preserving the English apostrophe). Once the corpus is processed, HiDEx stores a large sparse matrix that contains all co-occurrence information for every word in the lexicon and its 10 (default, up to 30 possible) neighbors on either side. No compression is done on this matrix because this process of building a local co-occurrence data set is computationally expensive. Since it is much faster to use this full matrix to collapse across a specified window size than it would be to re-build the entire matrix every time the window size was changed, this sparse matrix is saved to disk for use in Stage 2. It currently takes approximately four days of continuous processing on a personal computer with 4 CPUs and 8 Gb RAM to process our USENET corpus of a billion words. Because this step cannot be easily parallelized and is not limited by RAM, it will not run appreciably faster with more CPUs or more RAM. The actual calculations involve counting the words that co-occur within the window size for every word in the corpus, and incrementing the corresponding values in the co-occurrence matrix. For a matrix the size of ours, this will create a dataset of approximately 63 Gb. This dataset is the raw co-occurrence dataset from which a HAL matrix of word vectors can be computed for a given HAL parameter set.

Stage 2: Processing the Sparse Matrix

During Stage 2, the large sparse matrix is processed into a denser matrix constructed according to a given set of model parameters. HiDEx can be configured to use any of the following settings during Stage 2:

- The sizes of the windows ahead and behind the target word are set independently.
- The weighting scheme can be set to any of the nine weighting functions described in Table 1.
- The number of dimensions to retain (the context size) can be specified. When set to a value N, only the N most frequent word's co-occurrence data are included in the final calculations in Stage 3.
- The Vector Normalization Method can be set to any of the following: (a) Default: Ratio (co-occurrence divided by target word frequency, Shaoul & Westbury, 2006) (b) PPMI (Positive Pointwise Mutual Information, Bullinaria & Levy, 2007) (c) Correlation (Rohde et al., 2007 use correlation for computing the distances between vectors and thereby eliminate the need for explicit normalization prior to computing those distances).

Stage 2 is also computationally expensive. First HiDEx applies the window size and weighting scheme to the raw co-occurrence dataset, consolidating it and creating the global co-occurrence vectors. Then the dimensionality of this matrix is reduced by retaining only the vectors that meet the criterion for inclusion, the N vectors for words with the highest orthographic frequency. These vectors are then frequency-normalized if necessary.

Stage 3: Computing Context Similarity

In Stage 3, the word vectors are used to calculate context similarity. The similarity metrics that are available for use are as follows: (a) Default: (inverse) Euclidean distance (Lund & Burgess, 1996), (b) Cosine (Bullinaria & Levy, 2007), (c) City Block (Rohde et al., 2007) and (d) Correlation (Rohde et al., 2007)

Two main types of context similarity computations can be made with HiDEx: Users can either compute the co-occurrence neighbors of a word (i.e. find the most similar words using the similarity metric specified) or they can measure the contextual similarity between word pairs given as input. As noted above, the neighborhood membership threshold is calculated from a sample of a small percentage of all possible pair-wise distances, usually around two billion distances. To measure how many words fall inside a word's membership threshold, it is necessary to compute the distance between that target word and every

Table 2. 12 closest neighbors to the word LETTUCE and the HiDEx calculated similarity measure

Word	Similarity to LETTUCE
SALAD	0.985
CABBAGE	0.982
TOMATO	0.981
SAUSAGE	0.98
AVOCADO	0.979
PASTA	0.9788
BAKED	0.9782
CHEESE	0.977
MANGO	0.9764
BROCCOLI	0.9761
SPICY	0.975
FRIED	0.975

other word in the lexicon. The process of calculating neighborhoods takes approximately two hours per parameter set for a word list of about 500 words on a 4-core high-performance computer with 8 gigabytes of RAM.

As an example, in Table 2 the nearest neighbors for the word LETTUCE are shown. This neighborhood was created using a USENET corpus (Shaoul & Westbury 2009), a window size of 10 ahead and 10 behind, PPMI normalization, Cosine similarity, 8000 vector context size and the "Inverse Ramp" weighting function.

PARAMETER OPTIMIZATION AND FUTURE RESEARCH DIRECTIONS

As noted above, one of our motivations for developing HiDEx is that the parameters used in the original HAL work were chosen with little or no empirical or theoretical justification. Many questions are left open: Is the model sensitive to these parameters, with respect to its ability to predict human performance on psycholinguistic tasks? Is there a new set of parameters that will create a better model of word meaning? Will this new parameter set give HAL-type models more explanatory power?

Some work comparing different model parameters sets has been done by Bullinaria and Levy (2007) and Lifchitz, Jhean-Larose, and Denhière (2009). Bullinaria and Levy (2007) used four measures to compare the fitness of their models: the score on the TOEFL test (using HAL to choose the one word as the correct answer in a multiple choice exam), a Distance Comparison test (comparing inter-word distances between known semantically related pairs and random pairs), a Semantic Category test (testing if words are closer to the name of their category than to the names of other categories) and a Syntactic Categorization test (testing if a word was closer to its syntactic category center than to other syntactic category centers). These tests provide some information about how the model performs in capturing the structure of the human semantic space. These tests depend on handpicked word lists, and for that reason, they might not generalize beyond the test stimuli.

Bullinaria and Levy (2007) varied many different parameters to their HAL-like model to see which parameter settings performed the best on each of their four tests of fitness. Their search of parameter space was fairly exhaustive, varying each parameter alone or in combination with another parameter. The first parameter varied was the type of co-occurrence frequency measure. They found that the best measure was the Positive Pointwise Mutual Information measure (PPMI), which performed better than all the other measures they tested. The second parameter they looked at was the similarity metric, and they found that the Cosine measure (the cosine of the two vectors) performed better than the Euclidean distance metric, the City Block metric and all other metrics they compared. The third parameter that they looked at was window size, and they found that a symmetrical window of one word ahead and behind produced the highest accuracy. Based on these results, Bullinaria and Levy (2007) propose that the optimum parameters of the HAL model to be: Window size = 1, Weighting scheme = Flat, Similarity Measure=Cosine, Co-occurrence measure = PPMI. This is very different from the original HAL parameters used by Burgess (Window size = 10, Weighting Scheme = Linear Ramp, Similarity Measure=Euclidean Distance, Co-occurrence measure=Raw Frequency).

More recently Lifchitz et al. (2009) explored the parameter space of LSA (Landauer & Dumais, 1997) to find the optimal dimensionality of their model across various corpora of different sizes. They found that their optimal tuning of lemmatization, stop-word lists, term weighting, pseudo-documents, and normalization of document vectors in LSA allowed their model to outperform seventh and eighth grade students on a multiple choice biology test. Both of the Lifchitz et al.

(2009) study and the Bullinaria & Levy (2007) study show how exploring the parameter space of a high-dimensional model can lead to new insights and unexpected optimal parameter sets.

Shaoul & Westbury (in press) undertook a coarse-grained analysis of HiDEx parameter space, focused on the HAL parameters that have the most relevance to our theoretical interests: the window size and the window weighting. To explore the influence of these parameters, we created a list of all the possible combinations of forward and backward window sizes (zero, five or ten) and all the weighting functions listed in Table 1. This list contained 73 sets of parameter combinations. We looked at how varying these four parameters influenced the model's ability to predict mean lexical decision and semantic decision RTs for a large set of randomly chosen words. We showed the prediction of these behavioral measures was highly sensitive to changes in HiDEx parameters, with squared correlations between behavioral measures and predictors derived from HiDEx (ARC and NCOUNT-INV, described above) ranging over six-fold, between 0.04 and 0.25. We also found that the original HAL parameters were not optimal for predicting human behavioral data. Our results suggested that the optimal window weighting was INVERSE RAMP (see Table 1) and the optimal window sizes were those that contained 10 words behind and 0 or 5 words ahead.

Drawing universal conclusions from these studies on parameter optimization is difficult because of the great variability in how the models are built and used. Although new and more complex models that are descendants of HAL continue to be developed (WINDSORS, BEAGLES), we believe that some basic questions of parameterization and algorithm optimization in co-occurrence models will be best answered using standardized models and corpora. We hope that having an open model such as HiDEx may facilitate further research in this field.

CONCLUSION

In this chapter we have introduced an open-source tool for calculating lexical level co-occurrence measures while facilitating parametric exploration. HiDEx is a powerful tool for investigators who need to measure the contextual similarity of words. It allows the user the flexibility to choose any corpus in any language as the input to the model. Many different variants of the HAL model are available, and each model can be configured to so that all permutations of parameters can be tested. The output is also flexible enough to accommodate the needs of the investigator. By comparing the similarity measures produced by HiDEx with behavioral data, experimentalists can better understand the influence of co-occurrence measures on performance. Experiment designers can also use HiDEx to create stimulus sets with particular co-occurrence neighborhood properties. Finally, our software, HiDEx, can be used as a reference implementation for other researchers seeking to compare results produced from identical corpora using different HAL implementations.

ACKNOWLEDGMENT

This research was supported by grants to the authors from the Natural Sciences and Engineering Research Council of Canada (CS & CW) and the Alberta Heritage Foundation for Medical Research (CW). The material in this chapter draws from Shaoul & Westbury (submitted).

REFERENCES

Baayen, H., Piepenbrock, R., & Gulikers, L. (1995). *The CELEX lexical database [CD-ROM]*. Philadelphia, PA: Linguistic Data Consortium.

Baayen, R. H. (2001). *Word frequency distributions*. Boston, MA: Kluwer Academic.

Balota, D., Black, D., & Cheney, M. (1992, May). Automatic and attentional priming in young and older adults: Reevaluation of the two-process model. *Journal of Experimental Psychology. Human Perception and Performance, 18*(2), 485–502. doi:10.1037/0096-1523.18.2.485

Buchanan, L., Burgess, C., & Lund, K. (1996). Overcrowding in semantic neighborhoods: Modeling deep dyslexia. *Brain and Cognition, 32,* 111–114.

Buchanan, L., Westbury, C., & Burgess, C. (2001). Characterizing semantic space: Neighborhood effects in word recognition. *Psychonomic Bulletin & Review, 8,* 531–544. doi:10.3758/BF03196189

Bullinaria, J., & Levy, J. (2007). Extracting semantic representations from word co-occurrence statistics: A computational study. *Behavior Research Methods, 39,* 510–526. doi:10.3758/BF03193020

Burgess, C. (1998). From simple associations to the building blocks of language: Modeling meaning in memory with the HAL model. *Behavior Research Methods, Instruments, & Computers, 30,* 188–198. doi:10.3758/BF03200643

Burgess, C., & Livesay, K. (1998). The effect of corpus size in predicting reaction time in a basic word recognition task: Moving on from Kucera and Francis. *Behavior Research Methods, Instruments, & Computers, 30,* 272–277. doi:10.3758/BF03200655

Burgess, C., Livesay, K., & Lund, K. (1998). Explorations in context space: Words, sentences, discourse. *Discourse Processes, 25,* 211–257. doi:10.1080/01638539809545027

Burgess, C., & Lund, K. (1997). Modelling parsing constraints with high-dimensional context space. *Language and Cognitive Processes, 12,* 177–210. doi:10.1080/016909697386844

Burgess, C., & Lund, K. (2000). The dynamics of meaning in memory. In Dietrich, E., & Markman, A. B. (Eds.), *Cognitive dynamics: Conceptual and representational change in humans and machines* (pp. 117–156). Mahwah, NJ: Lawrence Erlbaum Associates.

Durda, K., & Buchanan, L. (2008). Windsors: Windsor improved norms of distance and similarity of representations of semantics. *Behavior Research Methods, 40*(3), 705–712. doi:10.3758/BRM.40.3.705

Durda, K., Buchanan, L., & Caron, R. (2009). Grounding co-occurrence: Identifying features in a lexical co-occurrence model of semantic memory. *Behavior Research Methods, 41*(4), 1210–1223. doi:10.3758/BRM.41.4.1210

Fristrup, J. A. (1994). *USENET: Netnews for everyone.* Englewood Cliffs, NJ: Prentice Hall.

Jones, M. N., Kintsch, W., & Mewhort, D. J. K. (2006). High-dimensional semantic space accounts of priming. *Journal of Memory and Language, 55,* 534–552. doi:10.1016/j.jml.2006.07.003

Jones, M. N., & Mewhort, D. J. K. (2007). Representing word meaning and order information in a composite holographic lexicon. *Psychological Review, 114,* 1–37. doi:10.1037/0033-295X.114.1.1

Landauer, T. K., & Dumais, S. T. (1997). A solution to Plato's problem: The latent semantic analysis theory of acquisition, induction, and representation of knowledge. *Psychological Review, 104,* 211–240. doi:10.1037/0033-295X.104.2.211

Lifchitz, A., Jhean-Larose, S., & Denhière, G. (2009). Effect of tuned parameters on an LSA multiple choice questions answering model. *Behavior Research Methods, 41*(4), 1201–1209. doi:10.3758/BRM.41.4.1201

Lund, K., & Burgess, C. (1996). Producing high-dimensional semantic spaces from lexical co-occurrence. *Behavior Research Methods, Instruments, & Computers, 28,* 203–208. doi:10.3758/BF03204766

Murdock, B. (1982). A theory for the storage and retrieval of item and associative information. *Psychological Review, 89*, 609–626. doi:10.1037/0033-295X.89.6.609

Rohde, D. L. T., Gonnerman, L. M., & Plaut, D. C. (2007). *An improved method for deriving word meaning from lexical co-occurrence.* Unpublished manuscript. Cambridge, MA: Massachusetts Institute of Technology. Retrieved April 20th, 2007, from http://tedlab.mit.edu/~dr/.

Shaoul, C., & Westbury, C. (2006). Word frequency effects in high-dimensional co-occurrence models: A new approach. *Behavior Research Methods, 38*, 190–195. doi:10.3758/BF03192768

Shaoul, C., & Westbury, C. (2007). *Usenet orthographic frequencies for the 40,481 words in the English lexicon project* (Tech. Rep.). Edmonton, Canada: University of Alberta. Retrieved from http://www.psych.ualberta.ca/~westburylab/downloads.html.

Shaoul, C., & Westbury, C. (2008). *HiDEx: The high dimensional explorer.* Edmonton, AB. Retrieved from http://www.psych.ualberta.ca/~westburylab/downloads.html.

Shaoul, C., & Westbury, C. (2009). *A Usenet corpus (2005-2009)* (Tech. Rep.). Edmonton, Canada: University of Alberta. Retrieved from http://www.psych.ualberta.ca/~westburylab/downloads.html.

Shaoul, C., & Westbury, C. (in press). Exploring lexical co-occurrence space using HiDEx. Accepted for publication in. *Behavior Research Methods.*

Siakaluk, P. D., Buchanan, L., & Westbury, C. (2003). The effect of semantic distance in yes/no and go/no-go semantic categorization tasks. *Memory & Cognition, 31*, 100–113. doi:10.3758/BF03196086

Song, D., Bruza, P., & Cole, R. (2004). *Concept learning and information inferencing on a high-dimensional semantic space.* ACM SIGIR 2004 Workshop on Mathematical/Formal Methods in Information Retrieval (MF/IR'2004), 30 July 2004, Sheffield UK.

Song, D., Bruza, P., Huang, Z., & Lau, R. Y. (2003). Classifying document titles based on information inference. In Carbonell, J. G., & Siekmann, J. (Eds.), *Foundations of intelligent systems* (pp. 297–306). Berlin, Germany: Springer. doi:10.1007/978-3-540-39592-8_41

Song, D., & Bruza, P. D. (2001). *Discovering information flow using a high dimensional conceptual space.* The 24th Annual International ACM SIGIR Conference on Research and Development in Information Retrieval (New Orleans, LA).

Stallman, R. (2009). *GNU general public license.* Cambridge, MA. Retrieved from http://www.fsf.org/licensing/.

Yates, M., Locker, L., & Simpson, G. B. (2003). Semantic and phonological influences on the processing of words and pseudohomophones. *Memory & Cognition, 31*, 856–866. doi:10.3758/BF03196440

Zipf, G. K. (1935). *The psychobiology of language.* New York, NY: Houghton-Mifflin.

Zipf, G. K. (1949). *Human behaviour and the principle of least-effort.* New York, NY: Addison-Wesley.

ADDITIONAL READING

Binder, J. R., Westbury, C. F., McKiernan, K. A., Possing, E. T., & Medler, D. A. (2005). Distinct brain systems for processing concrete and abstract concepts. *Journal of Cognitive Neuroscience, 17*, 905–917. doi:10.1162/0898929054021102

Bruza, P. D., Kitto, K., Nelson, D., & McEvoy, C. L. (2009). Is there something quantum-like about the human mental lexicon? *Journal of Mathematical Psychology, 53,* 362–377. doi:10.1016/j.jmp.2009.04.004

Burgess, C. (2001). Representing and resolving semantic ambiguity: A contribution from high-dimensional memory modeling. In Gorfein, D. S. (Ed.), *On the consequences of meaning selection: Perspectives on resolving lexical ambiguity* (pp. 233–260). Washington, DC: American Psychological Association. doi:10.1037/10459-013

Churchland, P. (1989). *A neurocomputational perspective: the nature of mind and the structure of science.* Cambridge, MA: MIT Press.

Churchland, P., & Sejnowski, T. (1992). *The Computational Brain.* Cambridge, MA: MIT Press.

Collins, A., & Loftus, E. (1975). A spreading-activation theory of semantic processing. *Psychological Review, 82,* 407–428. doi:10.1037/0033-295X.82.6.407

Cree, G. S., McNorgan, C., & McRae, K. (2006). Distinctive features hold a privileged status in the computation of word meaning: Implications for theories of semantic memory. *Journal of Experimental Psychology. Learning, Memory, and Cognition, 32,* 643–658. doi:10.1037/0278-7393.32.4.643

Durda, K., Buchanan, L., & Caron, R. (2009). Grounding co-occurrence: Identifying features in a lexical co-occurrence model of semantic memory. *Behavior Research Methods, 41,* 1210–1223. doi:10.3758/BRM.41.4.1210

Edelman, S. (2008). *Computing The Mind.* Oxford: Oxford University Press.

Elman, J. (2004). An alternative view of the mental lexicon. *Trends in Cognitive Sciences, 8,* 301–330. doi:10.1016/j.tics.2004.05.003

Elman, J. (2009). On the Meaning of Words and Dinosaur Bones: Lexical Knowledge Without a Lexicon. *Cognitive Science, 33,* 1–36. doi:10.1111/j.1551-6709.2009.01023.x

Griffiths, T., Steyvers, M., & Tenenbaum, J. (2007). Topics in semantic representation. *Psychological Review, 114,* 211–244. doi:10.1037/0033-295X.114.2.211

Hinton, G., McClelland, J., & Rumelhart, D. (1986). Distributed representations. In Rumelhart D. E., McClelland J. L., the PDP Research Group (Eds.), *Parallel distributed processing: Explorations in the microstructure of cognition: Vol. 1. Foundations* (pp. 77-109). Cambridge, MA: MIT Press.

Kwantes, P. J. (2005). Using context to build semantics. *Psychonomic Bulletin & Review, 12,* 703–710. doi:10.3758/BF03196761

Martin, A., & Chao, L. (2001). Semantic memory and the brain: Structure and processes. *Current Opinion in Neurobiology, 11,* 194–201. doi:10.1016/S0959-4388(00)00196-3

Mirman, D., & Magnuson, J. S. (2008). Attractor dynamics and semantic neighborhood density: Processing is slowed by near neighbors attractor dynamics and semantic neighborhood density: Processing is slowed by near neighbors and speeded by distant neighbors. *Journal of Experimental Psychology. Learning, Memory, and Cognition, 34,* 65–79. doi:10.1037/0278-7393.34.1.65

Pado, S., & Lapata, M. (2007). Dependency-based construction of semantic space models. *Computational Linguistics, 33,* 161–199. doi:10.1162/coli.2007.33.2.161

Perfetti, C. A. (1998). The limits of co-occurrence: Tools and theories in language research. *Discourse Processes, 25,* 363–377. doi:10.1080/01638539809545033

Pexman, P. M., Hino, Y., & Lupker, S. J. (2004). Semantic ambiguity and the process of generating meaning from print. *Journal of Experimental Psychology. Learning, Memory, and Cognition, 30,* 1252–1270. doi:10.1037/0278-7393.30.6.1252

Steyvers, M., & Tenenbaum, J. (2005). The large-scale structure of semantic networks: Statistical analyses and a model of semantic growth. *Cognitive Science, 29,* 41–78. doi:10.1207/s15516709cog2901_3

KEY TERMS AND DEFINITIONS

Co-Occurrence: First-order co-occurrence refers to whether or not words occur in close proximity. Co-occurrence models such as HAL and HiDEx measure second-order co-occurrence, which refers to whether or not words occur in similar contexts, irrespective of whether they occur in proximity to one another.

Euclidean Distance: A measure of vector similarity that is a generalization of 'ruler distance' in a two- or three-dimensional space. It is defined as the square root of the summed squared differences between entries in each vector location.

HAL: HAL (Hyperspace Analogue to Language) was one of the first high-dimensional models of global co-occurrence, developed by Lund and Burgess (1996).

HiDEx: HiDEx (High Dimensional Explorer) is an open-source high-dimensional program, written in C++, for calculating lexical global co-occurrence, developed by Shaoul and Westbury (2008).

Neighborhood Density: A measure of how near a target word's neighbors are in co-occurrence space. Early co-occurrence models defined density as the average distance of the closest N neighbours. In HiDEx, neighbourhood density is defined as the average distance and/or number of words that fall within a specified threshold distance from the target word.

Pointwise Mutual Information: An information-theoretic (probability-based) metric for measuring similarity between vectors, that compares the probability of the two vectors overlap under the assumption they are independent to the probability of their overlap under the assumption they are not independent.

Semantic Memory: Memory for knowledge of concrete and abstract entities acquired through experience.

Singular Value Decomposition: A method for decreasing the dimensionality of a high-dimensional matrix by decomposing it into its orthogonal components.

Weighting Function: The function that determines to what degree a target word's first-order co-occurrence neighbours are weighted by their proximity to that target word.

Chapter 14

Computational Aspects of the Intelligent Tutoring System MetaTutor

Mihai Lintean
The University of Memphis, USA

Amy Witherspoon-Johnson
Arizona State University, USA

Vasile Rus
The University of Memphis, USA

Arthur C. Graesser
The University of Memphis, USA

Zhiqiang Cai
The University of Memphis, USA

Roger Azevedo
McGill University, Canada

ABSTRACT

We present in this chapter the architecture of the intelligent tutoring system MetaTutor that trains students to use metacognitive strategies while learning about complex science topics. The emphasis of this chapter is on the natural language components. In particular, we present in detail the natural language input assessment component used to detect students' mental models during prior knowledge activation, a metacognitive strategy, and the micro-dialogue component used during sub-goal generation, another metacognitive strategy in MetaTutor. Sub-goal generation involves sub-goal assessment and feedback provided by the system. For mental model detection from prior knowledge activation paragraphs, we have experimented with three benchmark methods and six machine learning algorithms. Bayes Nets, in combination with a word-weighting method, provided the best accuracy (76.31%) and best human-computer agreement scores (kappa=0.63). For sub-goal assessment and feedback, a taxonomy-driven micro-dialogue mechanism yields very good to excellent human-computer agreement scores for sub-goal assessment (average kappa=0.77).

DOI: 10.4018/978-1-60960-741-8.ch014

INTRODUCTION

We describe in this chapter the architecture of the intelligent tutoring system MetaTutor with an emphasis on two components that rely on natural language processing (NLP) techniques: (1) *detection of students' mental models* during prior knowledge activation (PKA), a metacognitive strategy, based on student-generated PKA paragraphs, and (2) the micro-dialogue component which handles *sub-goal assessment and feedback generation* during sub-goal generation (SG), another metacognitive strategy in MetaTutor.

The current MetaTutor is a complex system that consists of nine major logical components: pre-planning, planning, student model, multi-modal interface (includes agents), feedback, scaffolding, assessment, authoring, and a system manager that coordinates the activity of all components. We present details about the role of each of these components and how they are implemented with various underlying technologies including dialogue processing, machine learning methods, and animated agents technology. We will describe in-depth the two NLP-based tasks of mental model detection and sub-goal generation which are part of the mental model and planning modules, respectively.

During prior knowledge activation, which occurs at the beginning of a student-system session, students are asked to write a paragraph describing their prior knowledge with respect to the learning goal. The task is to infer from these PKA paragraphs the students' initial *mental model* that best characterizes their level of understanding of the subject matter. We regard this problem as a text categorization problem. The general approach is to combine textual features with supervised machine learning algorithms to automatically derive classifiers from expert-annotated data. The parameters of the classifiers were derived using six different algorithms: naive Bayes (NB), Bayes Nets (BNets), Support Vector Machines (SVM),

Logistic Regression (LR), and two variants of Decision Trees (J48 and J48graft, an improved version of J48). These algorithms were chosen because of their diversity in terms of patterns in the data they are most suited for. For instance, naive Bayes are best for problems where independent assumptions can be made among the features describing the data. The diversity of the selected learning algorithms allows us to cover a wide range of patterns that may be hidden in the data.

The role of the sub-goal generation strategy in MetaTutor is to have students split the overall learning goal (e.g. *learn about the human circulatory system*) into smaller learning units called *sub-goals*. The sub-goals must be specified at the ideal level of specification (i.e. not too broad/general or too narrow/specific). If student-generated sub-goals are too specific or too general the system must provide appropriate feedback in natural language such that students will be able to re-state the sub-goal in a form closer, if not identical, to the ideal form. The system uses a set of ideal sub-goals, generated by subject matter experts, to assess the student-generated sub-goals. In our work reported here, we have seven ideal sub-goals associated with the general goal of learning about the human circulatory system. The sub-goals can be seen in the second level of nodes in Figure 1. A taxonomy of goals/sub-goals and concepts related to the sub-goals was chosen as the underlying scaffold for the sub-goal assessment and feedback mechanism (see Figure 1). This taxonomy captures general/specific relations among concepts and thus can help us drive the feedback mechanism. For instance, a student-generated sub-goal can be deemed too general if the sub-goal contains concepts above the ideal level in the taxonomy. Similarly, a sub-goal can be deemed too specific if it contains concepts below the ideal level in the taxonomy. We present the details of our taxonomy-driven sub-goal assessment and feedback model and report results on how well the system can assess student-articulated sub-goals.

Figure 1. Partial taxonomy of topics in circulatory system

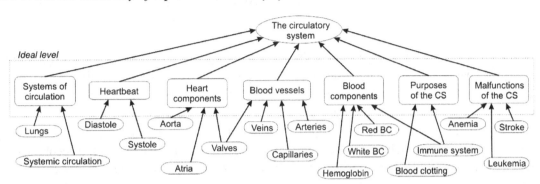

The rest of the chapter is structured as follows. *Previous Work* presents prior research on intelligent tutoring systems with natural language interaction focusing on student input assessment and dialogue management. Next, the architecture of the MetaTutor system is presented. The subsequent section, *Prior Knowledge Activation*, presents our methods to address the task of detecting mental models during prior knowledge activation whereas the *Sub-goal Generation* section describes in detail our taxonomy-based sub-goal assessment and feedback generation method as well as the experiments and results obtained. The *Conclusions* section ends the chapter.

PREVIOUS WORK ON INTELLIGENT TUTORING SYSTEMS WITH NATURAL LANGUAGE

Intelligent tutoring systems with natural language input have been developed at a fast pace recently (VanLehn et al. 2007; Woolf, 2009). We discuss prior research on assessment of natural language student input and on dialogue management in intelligent tutoring systems because these two topics are most related to our work presented here.

Researchers working on intelligent tutoring systems with natural language input explored the accuracy of matching students' written input to a pre-selected stored answer: a question, solution to

a problem, misconception, or other form of benchmark response. Examples of these systems are AutoTutor and Why-Atlas, which tutor students on Newtonian physics (Graesser et al. 2005; VanLehn et al. 2007), and the iSTART system, which helps students read text at deeper levels (McNamara et al. 2007). Systems such as these have typically relied on statistical representations, such as latent semantic analysis (LSA; Landauer et al. 2005) and content word overlap metrics (McNamara et al. 2007). LSA has the advantage of representing the meaning of texts based on latent concepts (the LSA space dimensions, usually 300-500) which are automatically derived from large collection of texts using singular value decomposition (SVD), a technique for dimensionality reduction. However, LSA cannot tell us whether a concept or a text fragment is more specific or more general than the other, which is what we need to handle student input and provide feedback during subgoal generation in MetaTutor. In our approach, we rely on a taxonomy of concepts which explicitly embeds specific/general relations among concepts or phrases. More recently, a lexico-syntactic approach, entailment evaluation (Rus et al., 2007), has been successfully used to meet the challenge of natural language understanding and assessment in intelligent tutoring systems. The entailment approach has been primarily tested on short student inputs, namely individual sentences. It could be extended to handle paragraph-size texts but not in a straightforward manner as it requires the use of a syntactic parser which operates on one sentence at a time. As both LSA and the entailment approach have some challenges with handling longer texts, such as the PKA paragraphs, we opted instead for a set of methods that combine textual features with machine learning algorithms to automatically infer student mental models. Another reason we opted for machine learning based methods is due to the importance of goals and sub-goals in MetaTutor. As we will see later, we choose features for our machine learning models which are tied to the set of sub-goals in MetaTutor.

Dialogue is a major component of natural language intelligent tutoring systems. Various dialogue management models have been proposed in intelligent tutoring systems. These models are usually built around instruction and human tutoring models. The dialogue models can be described at various levels. For example, at one level the AutoTutor dialogue management model (Graesser et al. 2005) can be described as a misconception-expectation model. That is, AutoTutor (and human tutors for that matter) typically has a list of anticipated expectations (good answers) and a list of anticipated misconceptions associated with each challenging question or problem in the curriculum script for a subject matter. Our micro-dialogue management model for providing feedback during sub-goal generation resembles at some extent the misconception-expectation model in AutoTutor in that we do have a set of ideal/expected sub-goals. However, our dialogue management method relies on a taxonomy of concepts to manage the dialogue turns as opposed to a flat set of expectations or misconceptions. There is need for a taxonomy because we must identify general/specific relations in the student input with respect to the ideal sub-goals, as already mentioned.

Figure 2. Overview of MetaTutor's architecture

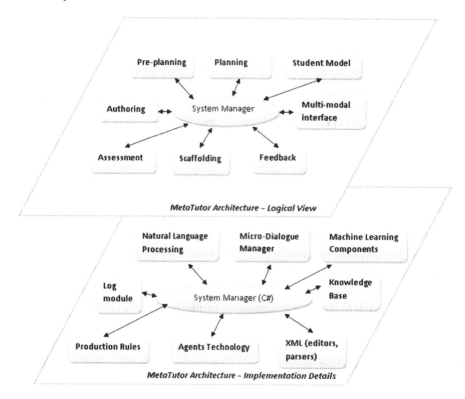

MetaTutor Architecture – Logical View

MetaTutor Architecture – Implementation Details

THE ARCHITECTURE OF METATUTOR

The current MetaTutor is a complex system that consists of nine major logical components (see top part of Figure 2). The implementation details of the system in terms of major technologies used are shown at the bottom of the figure. A screenshot of the main view of the system is shown in Figure 3.

The architecture of the MetaTutor system is open; new modules can be easily accommodated, and major changes can be made to any of the existing modules without redesigning the system from scratch. For instance, if a more advanced micro-dialogue manager is developed in the future then the current micro-dialogue manager component can be replaced (in a plug-and-play manner) without affecting the functionality of the overall system, as long as the interface with the other modules is maintained. If changes to the interface with other modules are needed then such changes must be propagated throughout the system to the connected modules. This is still less cumber-some than redesigning the system from scratch. One other advantage of the current architecture is the decoupling of processing and data. This feature allows easy transfer of MetaTutor from one domain to another without changes in the processing part. All the domain-specific information as well as other configurable information (e.g., the verbal feedback the agents provide) is maintained in external, separate files that can be easily edited by domain experts, dialogue experts, or cognitive scientists. The architecture is also reconfigurable in that some modules can be turned on and off. To run a version of MetaTutor without pedagogical agents (PAs) for comparison purposes and in order to evaluate the role of PAs in self-regulated learning (SRL) modeling and scaffolding, the Scaffolding module can turn off (not call) the Agents Technology implementation module and rely only on the other modules for scaffolding purposes. For instance, it can simply call the Multi-modal Interface module to display the feedback the agents were supposed to utter.

Figure 3. Sample screenshot of MetaTutor

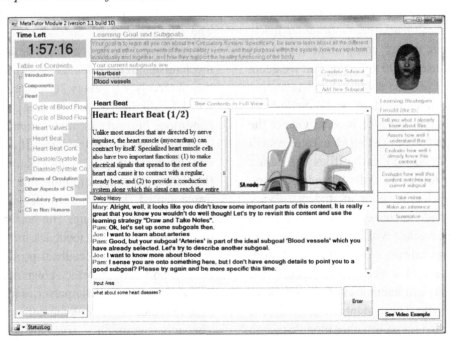

We present next detailed descriptions of MetaTutors' components. The pre-planning component collects student demographic information, delivers a short quiz, and prompts students to activate prior knowledge in the form of a paragraph summarizing their knowledge on the topic to be studied (e.g., the circulatory system). In addition, pre-planning calls other modules, such as the assessment module, to evaluate the quiz responses and the student-generated paragraph (i.e., the prior-knowledge activation [PKA] paragraph). The student model module is also called to update the model based on the results of the quiz and evaluation of the PKA paragraph. The planning module handles the multi-step, mixed-initiative process of breaking the overall learning goal into more manageable sub-goals. It relies on the micro-dialogue manager module (see bottom part of Figure 2, Implementation Details), which handles the multi-turn interaction between the system and the student. The purpose of this call is to determine a set of accurate sub-goals. The planning module calls other modules, such as the student model module, to update variables related to sub-goal generation that are part of the student model. It calls the assessment module to assess each student-articulated sub-goal and then the feedback module to generate appropriate feedback.

The student model component maintains and updates close to 100 variables that we deem important to assess the students' understanding of the subject matter (student mental model) and SRL processes (student SRL model). One of the design principles of the existing MetaTutor system was to collect and store in log files everything that might be related to shifts in understanding and metacognitive behavior in students. Every attempt was made to create an exhaustive set of variables to be tracked within the log files.

Variables include the scores on quizzes given throughout a session as well as assessment of the PKA paragraphs and summaries of content pages that students write. The student model module is called onis called on on by other modules when they need to retrieve or update information regarding students' level of understanding of the subject matter and SRL behavior. The assessment module evaluates various student inputs (textual, actions on the interface, time-related behavior) and sends evaluation results to other components that need these results. It uses information provided by the knowledge base module and various functions provided by the natural language processing and machine learning modules (see Figure 2). For instance, to assess a student-generated sub-goal, the natural language processing module is called onis called on on with the sub-goal taxonomy, which is retrieved from the knowledge base, and the student-articulated sub-goal as input parameters. The output from the natural language processing module is a vector of feature-values that quantifies the similarity between the student sub-goal and each of the ideal sub-goals in the taxonomy. The vector is then passed to a classifier in the machine learning module that classifies the student-articulated sub-goal into one of the following categories: too general, too specific, or ideal.

The scaffolding module handles the implementation of pedagogical strategies. It relies on the knowledge base, XML parser, and production rules modules of the implementation architecture. The production rules encode conditions which are monitored by the system. Through a polling mechanism, all the rules are checked at specified time intervals (e.g., every 30 seconds) (this value will be calibrated based on data), to see if the conditions of a rule are met. When they are, the corresponding rule is triggered. If multiple rules fire simultaneously, a random or uniform policy (implemented using a round-robin algorithm) is implemented. The default policy in the current system is uniform firing. The best policy is yet to be determined. The feedback module handles the type and timing of feedback provided through the PAs and other interface elements. It uses the knowledge base, XML parser, and production rules modules in the implementation of feedback. The authoring module serves the designer of the system, the subject-matter experts, and the cognitive scientists that use the system. It relies on XML editors and text editors to make changes to various configurable items in the knowledge base. The multi-modal interface module handles the complex interface between the student/experimenter/developer and MetaTutor.

The system manager controls the operation of the entire system, assuring proper communication and sequencing among all components. The Log module in the implementation view records every single action by the user and the system such that post-experiment analyses can be performed. The knowledge base module includes the content pages and other knowledge items needed throughout the system, such as the sub-goal taxonomy used during sub-goal generation in the planning module. The agents' technology module handles the four agents used in MetaTutor: Gavin the Guide, Mary the Monitoring agent, Pam the Planner, and Sam the Strategizer.

MENTAL MODEL DETECTION

Self-regulation is most important when students engage in tasks that challenge them. Research has shown that complex science topics, such as the circulatory system, are difficult for students to understand (Azevedo et al., 2008; Chi et al., 2001). Often, students acquire declarative knowledge of these topics, but lack the conceptual understanding, or mental model, necessary to be successful (Azevedo, 2005; Chi, Siler, & Jeong, 2004). Mental models are cognitive representations that include the declarative, procedural, and inferential knowledge necessary to understand how a complex system functions. Mental models go beyond definitions and rote learning to include a deep understanding of the component processes of the system and the ability to make inferences about changes to the system. One way the acquisition of mental models of complex systems can be facilitated is through presenting multiple represen-

tations of information such as text, pictures, and video in a multimedia and hypermedia learning environment (Greene & Azevedo, 2009; Mayer, 2005). Therefore, hypermedia environments, such as MetaTutor, with their flexibility in presenting multiple representations, have been suggested as ideal learning tools for fostering sophisticated mental models of complex systems (Azevedo et al. in press; Goldman, 2003; Kozma, 2003).

Detecting mental model shifts during learning is an important step in diagnosing ineffective learning processes and intervening by providing appropriate feedback. One method to detect students' initial mental model of a topic is to have them write a paragraph. Cognitively, this activity allows the learner to activate their prior knowledge of the topic (e.g., declarative, procedural, and inferential knowledge) and express it in writing so that it can be externalized and amenable to computational methods of analysis. The mental model can be categorized qualitatively, and depending on the current state (e.g., simple model vs. sophisticated model), is then used by the system to provide the necessary instructional content and learning strategies (e.g., prompt to summarize, coordinate informational sources) to facilitate the student's conceptual jump to the next qualitative level of understanding. Along the way, students can be prompted to modify their initial paragraph and thereby demonstrate any subsequent qualitative changes to their initial understanding of the content. This qualitative augmentation is a key to an intelligent, adaptive hypermedia learning environment's ability to accurately foster cognitive growth in learners. This process continues periodically throughout the learning session to examine qualitative shifts during learning.

Mental Model Coding

Due to their qualitative nature, most researchers develop complex coding schemes to represent the underlying knowledge and most commonly used categorical classification systems to denote and represent students' mental models. For example, Chi and colleagues' early work (Chi et al., 2001) focused on 7 mental models of the circulatory system. Azevedo and colleagues (Azevedo, 2005; Azevedo et al., 2008) extended their mental models classification to 12 to accommodate the multiple representations embedded in their hypermedia learning environments. We have re-categorized our existing 12 mental models of the circulatory system into 3 categories of low-, intermediate-, and high-mental models of the circulatory system. The rationale for choosing the 3-category mental models approach was to enhance the ability of determining students' mental models shifts during learning with MetaTutor and because the 12 mental models approach would have been too detailed of a grain size to yield reliable classifications and thus to accurately assess "smaller" qualitative shifts in students' models. Furthermore, with more mental models we would have needed substantially more instances to train our classifiers.

Experiments and Results

We have experimented with an existing dataset consisting of 309 mental model essays collected from previous experiments by Azevedo and colleagues (based on Azevedo, Cromley, & Seibert, 2004; Azevedo, 2005; Azevedo et al., 2007, 2008). These mental model essays were classified by two experts with extensive experience coding mental models. Each expert independently re-coded each mental model essay into one of the three categories and achieved an inter-rater reliability of .92 (i.e., 284/309 agreements) yielding the following new dataset: 139 low mental models, 70 intermediate mental models, and 100 high mental models.

Each item in the dataset is mapped onto a set of 8 features. There is one feature corresponding to each of the seven sub-goals and one feature corresponding to all sub-goals. Each feature represents the semantic overlap between the student-generated PKA and a benchmark. The benchmark can be the nodes in a taxonomy corresponding to a

sub-goal (feature 1-7) or all sub-goals (feature 8), ideal PKA paragraphs generated by experts (there is an ideal PKA paragraph for each of the 7 sub-goals; their union represents the benchmark for feature 8), or content pages corresponding to pages relevant to each of the sub-goals. The relevance of each page to a sub-goal has been identified by human experts. Each of the benchmarking methods (taxonomy, ideal paragraphs, content pages) can be used in combination with several semantic similarity methods. In our case, we used a cosine similarity measure based on tf-idf (term frequency-inverted document frequency) vector representations of student PKA paragraphs and the benchmarks or simple normalized overlap measures based on unigrams or bigrams.

We report results, as accuracy and kappa values, for the best combinations of methods and learning algorithms mentioned above. In Table 1, rows correspond to methods and columns to learning algorithms. A quick look at the results revealed that a tf-idf method combined with Bayes Nets leads to best overall results in terms of both accuracy and kappa values. The second best results were obtained using a combination of unigrams and/or bigrams with SVM or LR. Both SVM and LR are called function-based classifiers as they are both trying to identify a function that would best separate the data into appropriate classes (i.e. mental model types in our case). For the random baseline we obtained (accuracy=0.31, kappa=-0.06 – a kappa close to 0 means chance) based on averaging over 10 random runs while for the uniform baseline (i.e. predicting all the time the dominant class, which is the Low mental model class) we obtained (accuracy=0.45, kappa=0).

SUB-GOAL GENERATION

Sub-goal generation is a critical step in complex learning and problem solving (Anderson & Labiere, 1998; Newell, 1994). Multi-phase models of self-regulated learning (SRL; Azevedo & With-

Table 1. Performance results as accuracy/kappa values

Dataset	NaïveBayes	BayesNet	SVM	LR	J48	J48graft
tf-idf	57.70/0.35	**76.31•/0.63•**	64.12/0.42	54.21•/0.28	68.22•/0.50•	71.19•/0.55•
Tax	61.44/0.39	61.93/0.37	67.18•/0.44	**69.61•/0.50•**	62.23/0.40	62.65/0.40
Ip-uni	66.39/0.48	66.14/**0.48**	67.83/0.45	65.62/0.44	65.85/0.47	65.88/0.47
Ip-bi	61.42/0.38	65.18•/0.43	**67.21•/0.44**	67.05•/0.45•	62.14/0.40	62.37/0.40

•statistically significant improvement compared to NaïveBayes

erspoon, 2009; Pintrich, 2000; Winne & Hadwin, 2008; Zimmerman, 2006) include sub-goal generation as a key element of planning. According to time-dependent SRL models, self-regulatory processes begin with the forethought, planning, and activation phase. During this initial phase of learning, learners create sub-goals for their learning session and activate relevant prior knowledge of the content (stored in long-term memory) and perceptions about the specific learning task and the context in which they will be learning. Sub-goal generation is an important phase in learning about complex science topics with non-linear, multi-representational hypermedia environments whereby the learner may be asked to spend a substantial amount of time creating a deep conceptual understanding of the topic (as measured by a sophisticated mental model). As such, asking learners to create sub-goals forces them to partition an overall learning goal set by the experimenter, or tutor (human or computerized), or teacher into meaningful sub-goals that can be accomplished by integration multiple representations of information in a relatively short period of time. For example, the overall learning goal of *you have two hours to learn about the parts of the human circulatory system, how they work together, and how they support the human body* can be used to create the following sub-goals – *learn about the parts, learn about how the systemic and pulmonary systems work together, learn about the functions of the circulatory system*, etc.

An intelligent tutoring system whose goal is to model and scaffold sub-goal generation should include a component able of first assessing student generated sub-goals and then provide appropriate feedback to help the student set an ideal set of sub-goals.

In MetaTutor, a taxonomy-driven dialogue management mechanism has been implemented to handle sub-goal assessment and feedback generation (see Figure 4). We organized hierarchically the overall learning goal, its seven ideal sub-goals as identified by human experts, and relevant keywords associated with each sub-goal in a taxonomy. In this *sub-goal taxonomy* (see Figure 3), the top node is the most general while the leaves (lowest level nodes) are the most specific. The taxonomy was semi-automatically generated from the set of seven ideal sub-goals and other sources such as WordNet (Miller, 1995). A student sub-goal is assessed by extracting and comparing its key concepts (i.e. words or sequences of words) with entries in the taxonomy. The assessment is performed using the following dimensions:

- **Full or partial match.** If all the key words that describe a sub-goal in the taxonomy are present in the student sub-goal then we have a full match. Otherwise, if only some of the sub-goal's key words are present in the student's input, a partial match occurs.
- **Single or multiple matches.** When a student sub-goal is associated with more than one sub-goal we have multiple matches. That is, the student input points to two or more different sub-goals. An example of a multiple-matches student sub-goal is *I*

Figure 4. Overview of the sub-goal generation process in MetaTutor

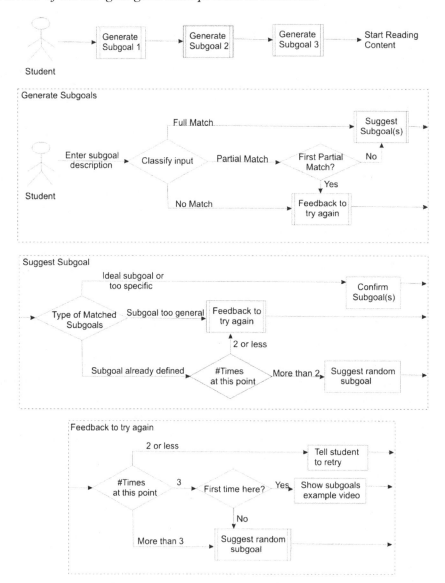

would learn about heart valves. The concept of *valves* is associated with the subgoals of *heart components* and *blood vessels* (see Figure 1).

- **Specific, general, or perfect match.** An example of a perfect match is when the exact concept in the taxonomy is found in the student sub-goal as in *I want to know more about blood vessels (major ones)*. This student sub-goal matches the ideal sub-goal *blood vessels*. In other words, the student sub-goal is not too general, not too specific, and it contains all and only the words of the sub-goal concept in the taxonomy. When a student sub-goal only mentions concepts below the ideal level (see Figure 1) in the taxonomy, the sub-goal is deemed too specific. An example of a specific student sub-goal is *I need to learn more about veins*. It is too specific because *veins* is below *blood vessels*, the ideal level, in the taxonomy.

- **Relevant or Irrelevant.** When a student sub-goal does not match any concept in the taxonomy we have an irrelevant sub-goal. Otherwise, we have a relevant sub-goal.

Based on student sub-goal assessment, a particular type of feedback will be generated. The feedback is specific to each combination of values for the above dimensions of assessment (i.e. a full or partial match, single or multiple matches, specific or general or perfect match, and relevant or irrelevant). For instance, when a student-articulated sub-goal is deemed *full match, too general, single match, relevant*, then the following multi-turn dialog will take place:

- **Student:** I want to learn about the circulatory system
- **System:** *Alright, can you be a little more specific about what you would like to learn about the circulatory system?*
- **Student:** learn about the valves of the heart
- **System:** *That's good, but it's a little too specific level for our objectives today. Let's consider a broader sub-goal. Did you want to learn about 'Heart components' or 'Blood vessels'?*
- **Student:** Heart components
- **System:** *Wonderful! We've just setup a good sub-goal. Please choose another sub-goal.*

For each system turn we have a list of generic templates with placeholders for important items such as sub-goals as in the following example: *Very good! Let's try to set a sub-goal that covers 'Y.' How about we try to learn about 'X.'* which is used when a student-articulated sub-goal *(Y)* is assessed as full match, relevant, too specific, and single match.

To evaluate our sub-goal assessment method, we have experimented with a set of 258 student-generated sub-goals collected from a classroom experiment in which students were asked to generate 3 sub-goals for the overall learning goal of *learning about the circulatory system*. The generated sub-goals were then rated by an expert with respect to which ideal sub-goals students specified. The expert used the following three scores to rate each student-generated sub-goal 0 – sub-goal not specified, 1 – sub-goal partially specified, 2 – sub-goal fully specified. We compared the human judgments with computer judgments and report the results, in terms of kappa scores, in Table 2. The results are reported for each individual sub-goal and also as an average over the seven sub-goals.

FUTURE RESEARCH DIRECTIONS

There are several plans for the future regarding mental model detection and sub-goal generation. First, we would like to further evaluate the proposed methods for mental model detection on larger data sets. Larger data sets will give us more confidence in the conclusions we draw. Second, we intend to explore finer-grain mental models (1-12 instead of just low, medium, and high) which would allow us to detect small shifts in students' mental model during learning with MetaTutor which in turn would enable more accurate feedback provided to students. More accurate feedback

Table 2. Kappa scores for the automated method for assessing student-generated sub-goals

Sub-Goal	Kappa
Bloodflow	0.76
Heartbeat	0.75
Heart components	0.76
Blood vessels	0.95
Blood components	0.77
Purposes of CS	0.69
Malfunctions	0.75
Average	0.77

means better learning gains. Third, we plan to fully automate the sub-goal generation component by adopting machine learning approaches that are able to learn classifiers which are needed for categorizing student utterances along each of the dimensioned used for feedback during sub-goal generation. Fourth, we plan to assess the impact of the proposed methods for mental model detection on the quality of feedback provided during learning with MetaTutor and also of the sub-goal generation method on the efficacy of sub-goal generation.

CONCLUSION

We presented and evaluated two components, mental model detection and sub-goal generation, of the intelligent tutoring system MetaTutor. We have found that a tf-idf method combined with the Bayes Nets algorithm provides best accuracy and kappa results on the task of mental model detection. A taxonomy-driven method to handle sub-goal generation yielded very good human-computer agreement scores for sub-goal assessment. We plan to further validate the proposed methods using larger data sets and also experiment with finer-grained mental models that would allow more accurate feedback during learning with MetaTutor. We also intend to assess the impact of the proposed methods on the quality of feedback and efficacy of sub-goal generation.

ACKNOWLEDGMENT

The research presented in this paper has been supported by funding from the National Science Foundation (Early Career Grant 0133346, 0633918, and 0731828) awarded to Dr. Azevedo and (RI 0836259, RI 0938239) awarded to Dr. Vasile Rus. We thank Jennifer Cromley, Daniel Moos, and Jeffrey Greene for data collection and analysis. We also thank Michael Cox and Ashley Fike for data preparation.

REFERENCES

Anderson, J. R., & Lebiere, C. (1998). *The atomic components of thought*. Mahwah, NJ: Erlbaum.

Azevedo, R. (2005). Computer environments as metacognitive tools for enhancing learning. *Educational Psychologist, 40*, 193–197. doi:10.1207/s15326985ep4004_1

Azevedo, R. (in press). The role of self-regulation in learning about science with hypermedia. In Robinson, D., & Schraw, G. (Eds.), *Current perspectives on cognition, learning, and instruction*.

Azevedo, R., Cromley, J. G., & Seibert, D. (2004). Does adaptive scaffolding facilitate students' ability to regulate their learning with hypermedia? *Contemporary Educational Psychology, 29*, 344–370. doi:10.1016/j.cedpsych.2003.09.002

Azevedo, R., Witherspoon, A., Graesser, A. C., McNamara, D. S., Rus, V., Cai, Z., & Lintean, M. (2008). *MetaTutor: An adaptive hypermedia system for training and fostering self-regulated learning about complex science topics*. Annual Meeting of Society for Computers in Psychology, Chicago, IL.

Azevedo, R., & Witherspoon, A. M. (2009). Self-regulated use of hypermedia. In Hacker, D. J., Dunlosky, J., & Graesser, A. C. (Eds.), *Handbook of metacognition in education*. Mahwah, NJ: Erlbaum.

Chi, M. T. H., Siler, S., & Jeong, H. (2004). Can tutors monitor students' understanding accurately? *Cognition and Instruction, 22*, 363–387. doi:10.1207/s1532690xci2203_4

Chi, M. T. H., Siler, S. A., Jeong, H., Yamauchi, T., & Hausmann, R. G. (2001). Learning from human tutoring. *Cognitive Science, 25*, 471–533. doi:10.1207/s15516709cog2504_1

Goldman, S. (2003). Learning in complex domains: When and why do multiple representations help? *Learning and Instruction, 13*, 239–244. doi:10.1016/S0959-4752(02)00023-3

Graesser, A. C., Hu, X., & McNamara, D. S. (2005). Computerized learning environments that incorporate research in discourse psychology, cognitive science, and computational linguistics. In Healy, A. (Ed.), *Experimental cognitive psychology and its applications* (pp. 59–72). Washington, DC: APA. doi:10.1037/10895-014

Greene, J. A., & Azevedo, R. (2009). A macro-level analysis of SRL processes and their relations to the acquisition of a sophisticated mental model of a complex system. *Contemporary Educational Psychology, 34*, 18–29. doi:10.1016/j.cedpsych.2008.05.006

Kozma, R. (2003). The material features of multiple representations and their cognitive and social affordances for science understanding. *Learning and Instruction, 13*(2), 205–226. doi:10.1016/S0959-4752(02)00021-X

Landauer, T., McNamara, D. S., Dennis, S., & Kintsch, W. (Eds.). (2005). *Latent semantic analysis: A road to meaning.* Mahwah, NJ: Erlbaum.

Mayer, R. (2005). *The Cambridge handbook of multimedia learning.* New York, NY: Cambridge University Press.

McNamara, D. S., Boonthum, C., Levinstein, I. B., & Millis, K. (2007). Evaluating selfexplanations in iSTART: Comparing word-based and LSA algorithms. In Landauer, T., McNamara, D. S., Dennis, S., & Kintsch, W. (Eds.), *Handbook of LSA* (pp. 227–241). NJ: Erlbaum.

Miller, G. (1995). Wordnet: A lexical database for English. *Communications of the ACM, 38*(11), 3941. doi:10.1145/219717.219748

Newell, A. (1994). *Unified theories of cognition.* Harvard University Press.

Pintrich, P. R. (2000). The role of goal orientation in self-regulated learning. In Boekaerts, M., Pintrich, P., & Zeidner, M. (Eds.), *Handbook of self-regulation* (pp. 451–502). San Diego, CA: Academic Press.

Rus, V., McCarthy, P. M., Lintean, M., Graesser, A. C., & McNamara, D. S. (2007). Assessing student selfexplanations in an intelligent tutoring system. In D. S. McNamara & G. Trafton (Eds.), *Proceedings of the 29th Annual Conference of the Cognitive Science Society.*

VanLehn, K., Graesser, A. C., Jackson, T., Jordan, P., Olney, A., & Rose, C. (2007). When are tutorial dialogues more effective than reading? *Cognitive Science, 31*(1), 3–62. doi:10.1080/03640210709336984

Winne, P., & Hadwin, A. (2008). The weave of motivation and self-regulated learning. In Schunk, D., & Zimmerman, B. (Eds.), *Motivation and self-regulated learning: Theory, research, and applications* (pp. 297–314). Mahwah, NJ: Erlbaum.

Woolf, B. P. (2009). *Building intelligent interactive tutors.* Burlington, MA: Elsevier.

Zimmerman, B. (2006). Development and adaptation of expertise: The role of self-regulatory processes and beliefs. In Ericsson, K., Charness, N., Feltovich, P., & Hoffman, R. (Eds.), *The Cambridge handbook of expertise and expert performance* (pp. 705–722). New York, NY: Cambridge University Press.

KEY TERMS AND DEFINITIONS

Feedback: It refers to the form of scaffolding that a tutor, computer or human, provides to a tutee during tutoring.

Intelligent Tutoring System: A computer system that can teach students various subjects by mimicking a human-tutor.

Machine Learning: A domain of study that focuses on developing methods that learn from experience.

Mental Model: A concept describing students' level of understanding with respect to a topic.

MetaTutor: An intelligent tutoring system that trains students to use meta-cognitive strategies while learning about complex science topics.

Sub-Goal: A smaller unit of learning part of an overall learning goal.

Tf-idf: Term-frequency, Inverted-Document-Frequency is a popular word-weighting scheme used in vector space model.

Chapter 15
Applying NLP Metrics to Students' Self-Explanations

G. Tanner Jackson
Arizona State University, USA

Danielle S. McNamara
Arizona State University, USA

ABSTRACT

Intelligent Tutoring Systems (ITSs) are becoming an increasingly common method for students to engage with and learn course material. ITSs are designed to provide students with one-on-one learning that is tailored to their own pace and needs. These systems can adapt to each users' individual knowledge and ability level to provide the most pedagogically effective learning environment. Tutoring systems have been designed that cover a variety of topics, including both well-defined and ill-defined domains. ITSs have seen great success within well-defined domains, where the topic itself provides only a limited set of responses. For example, in the domain of algebra, there is a limited set of possible actions that can be performed to solve for an unknown variable. Knowing this complete set of actions allows the tutoring system to predict all possible responses from the user. In contrast, ill-defined domains are more abstract and open ended. Reading comprehension is an ill-defined, open ended domain that can incorporate text from any subject, and involve numerous processes and problems for the learner. The number of associations that learners can make with a given text (e.g., based on personal memories, previous courses, ideas within different parts of the same text, etc.) is virtually infinite. These associations make it almost impossible to predict how a user will respond to a text. In addition to working with more abstract concepts, ITSs within ill-defined domains often have the added challenge of interpreting natural language user input. Incorporating natural language allows learners to use their own words and ideas as they interact with the content; however, this also increases the ambiguity of the interaction and decreases the system's ability to build a precise model of the learner. Building an accurate learner model is essential for the system to adapt the interaction in a pedagogically appropriate manner.

DOI: 10.4018/978-1-60960-741-8.ch015

INTRODUCTION

Recent advances in Natural Language Processing (NLP) have dramatically increased the ability to interpret user language input. These advances have made it possible to develop ITSs that rely heavily on natural language input to drive the interaction with the system (Graesser, Lu, Jackson, Mitchell, Ventura, Olney, & Louwerse, 2004; McNamara, Boonthum, Levinstein, & Millis, 2007; VanLehn, Graesser, Jackson, Jordan, Olney, & Rose, 2007). An ITS called Interactive Strategy Training for Active Reading and Thinking (iSTART) is one of these systems that relies on users' natural language. iSTART utilizes a complex NLP algorithm to evaluate student contributions and select an appropriate system response. Previous evaluations of the algorithm have provided strong evidence that it produces an adequate representation of student input (Jackson, Guess, McNamara, 2010; McNamara, Boonthum, Levinstein, & Millis, 2007). Nonetheless, there are still potential improvements that could increase the assessment accuracy. The aim of the current chapter is to assess the viability of including new linguistic measures from Coh-Metrix (Graesser, McNamara, Louwerse, & Cai, 2004) to the existing iSTART assessment algorithm.

iSTART

iSTART is a web-based tutoring system designed to improve high school and college students' reading comprehension by providing instruction and practice using self-explanation and reading strategies. The iSTART system was originally modeled after a human-based intervention called Self-Explanation Reading Training, or SERT (McNamara, 2004; McNamara & Scott, 1999; O'Reilly, Best, & McNamara, 2004). The automated iSTART system has consistently produced gains equivalent to the human-based SERT program (Magliano et al., 2004; O'Reilly,

Sinclair, & McNamara, 2004; O'Reilly, Best, & McNamara, 2004). Unlike SERT, iSTART is web-based, and can potentially provide training to schools or individuals with internet access. Furthermore, because it is automated, it can work with students on an individual level and provide self-paced instruction. iSTART also maintains a record of student performance and can use this information to adapt its feedback and instruction for each student. Lastly, iSTART combines pedagogical agents and automated linguistic analysis to engage the student in an interactive dialogue and create an active learning environment (e.g., Bransford, Brown, & Cocking, 2000; Graesser, Hu, & Person, 2001; Graesser, Hu, & McNamara, 2005; Louwerse, Graesser, & Olney, 2002).

iSTART Modules

iSTART incorporates pedagogical agents that engage users with the system and tutor them on how to correctly apply various reading strategies. The agents were designed to introduce students to the concept of self-explanation and to demonstrate specific strategies that could potentially enhance their ability to self-explain and in turn, their reading comprehension. The iSTART program consists of three system modules that implement the pedagogical principle of modeling-scaffolding-fading: introduction, demonstration, and practice.

The introduction module uses a classroom-like discussion format between three animated agents (a teacher, Dr. Julie, and two student agents, Sheila and Mike) to present the relevant reading strategies within iSTART. These agents interact with each other, providing students with information, posing questions to each other, and providing example self-explanations to illustrate appropriate strategy use (including counterexamples). These interactions exemplify the active processing that students should use when generating their own self-explanations. For each strategy, the students also answer multiple-choice questions that gauge their understanding of the recently covered concepts.

After all strategies are introduced, students progress to the demonstration module. In the demonstration module, new animated characters interact (Merlin and Genie) and guide the students as they attempt to analyze example self-explanations provided by the Genie agent. In this capacity, Genie acts as another example student, reads text aloud, and provides a self-explanation for each sentence. Meanwhile, Merlin instructs the learner to identify the strategies used within each of Genie's self-explanations. Merlin provides feedback to Genie on his self-explanations and to the students on the accuracy of their strategy identifications. For example, Merlin will tell Genie that his self-explanation is too short and ask him to add more information, or he will applaud when a student makes a correct identification. The feedback provided to Genie is similar to the feedback that Merlin will give to the students when they finish that section and move on to the practice module.

Once the students have reached the practice module, Merlin serves as their self-explanation coach (See Figure 1 for screenshot). He provides feedback on their self-explanations and prompts them to generate new self-explanations using their newly acquired repertoire of strategies. The main focus of this module is to provide the students with an opportunity to apply the reading strategies to new texts and to integrate their knowledge from different sources in order to understand a challenging text. Their self-explanation may include knowledge from prior text, or come from world and domain knowledge. Merlin provides feedback for each self-explanation generated by the students. For example, he may prompt them to expand the self-explanation, ask the students to incorporate more information, or suggest that they make a connection in the self-explanation back to other parts of the text. Merlin sometimes takes the practice one step further and has students identify which strategies they used and where they

were used. Throughout this interaction, Merlin's responses are adapted to the quality of each student's self-explanation. For example, longer and more relevant self-explanations are given more enthusiastic expressions, while short and irrelevant self-explanations prompt Merlin to provide more scaffolding and support.

There are two types of practice modules. The first practice module is situated within the context of the initial 2-hour training. That is, initially, the student goes through the introduction, demonstration, and practice in about 2 hours. The initial practice includes the self-explanation of two brief science texts.

The second phase of practice, extended practice, begins subsequently. Extended practice can be used in situations where the classroom or a student has committed to using the system over time, such as over the course of a year. During this practice phase, the student is assigned to read texts that are usually chosen by the teacher. These are texts that may be entered into the system with little notice. Because of the need to provide texts *on the fly*, the iSTART feedback algorithms must provide appropriate feedback, not only for the texts during initial practice (for which the iSTART algorithms are highly tuned), but also for new texts. For this reason, the iSTART evaluation algorithms must be highly flexible and must be able to generalize to virtually any text.

iSTART Algorithm

Determining the appropriate feedback for each explanation depends on the evaluation algorithm implemented within iSTART. Obviously the feedback has the potential to be more appropriate when the evaluation algorithm more accurately depicts explanation quality and related characteristics. In order to accomplish this task and interact with students in a meaningful way, the system must be able to adequately interpret natural language text explanations.

Figure 1. iSTART practice module

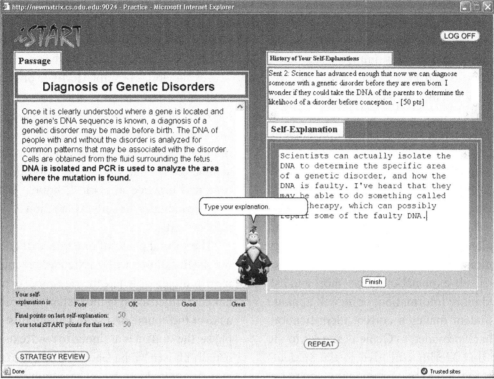

Algorithm Development

Several versions of the iSTART evaluation algorithm have been tested and validated with human performance (Jackson, Guess, & McNamara, 2010; McNamara, Boonthum, Levinstein, & Millis, 2007). Previous versions have utilized various combinations of NLP measures including word-matching, LSA, and topic models. Most of the earlier iterations required hand-coded texts that were tailored to the tutoring system. Subsequent advancements not only improved the accuracy of the algorithm, but also made it possible to completely automatize the entire process so that no hand-coding was necessary (McNamara, Boonthum, Levinstein, & Millis, 2007). McNamara et al., (2007) found a reliable interaction between the NLP techniques and the strategies being identified. They found that a combined measure (both statistical and word-based indices) best

accomplished the goal of differentiating between different strategies because it produced the largest difference in scores between each the levels of strategy use.

Based on these findings, the current algorithm that is used in iSTART incorporates a combination of both word-based and latent semantic analysis (LSA) based approaches. The word-based approaches provide a more accurate picture of the lower level explanations (ones that are irrelevant, or simply repeat the target sentence). They are able to provide a finer distinction between these groups than does LSA. In contrast, the LSA-based algorithm provides a better measure for the higher level and more complex aspects of the explanations. Therefore a combination of these approaches is used to calculate the final system evaluation of a self-explanation.

The word based approach originally required a significant amount of hand-coding, but now uses automatic methods when new texts are added. The original measure required experts to create a list of "important" words for each text as well as a list of associated words for each "important" word. This methodology was replaced, and now the word-based component relies on a list of "content" words (nouns, verbs, adjectives, adverbs) that are automatically pulled from the text via Coh-Metrix (Graesser, McNamara, Louwerse, & Cai, 2004; McNamara & Graesser, this volume). The word-based assessment also includes length criteria wherein the student's explanation must exceed a certain number of words (calculated as the product of the number of words in the target sentence and some coefficient).

The LSA-based approach utilizes a set of benchmarks to compare student explanations to various text features. These LSA benchmarks include: 1) the title of the passage, 2) the words in the target sentence, and 3) the words in the previous two sentences. The third benchmark originally involved only words from causally related sentences, but this required more hand-coding, and thus was replaced by the words from recent sentences. Within the science genre, this replacement was expected to do well, due to the linear argumentation most often employed in science textbooks. However, it is unclear how successful this approach will fare in other domains such as literature.

iSTART currently situates the instruction of self-explanation in the context of science text; however the concepts and strategies of self-explanation extend to a wide range of texts and genres. Therefore, the iSTART algorithm should be capable of accommodating a comparable range of explanations. In the event that new texts are added, this evaluation system was designed to be automated so that the text repository could be expanded without consequence to system performance (i.e., so that the evaluation algorithm should perform equally well across newly encountered texts).

Algorithm Scoring

The iSTART assessment algorithm evaluates every student self-explanation. This assessment is coded as a 0, 1, 2, or 3. An assessment of "0" relates to self-explanations that are either too short or contain mostly irrelevant information. An iSTART score of "1" is associated with a self-explanation that primarily relates only to the target sentence itself (sentence-based). A "2" means that the student's self-explanation incorporated some aspect of the text beyond the target sentence (text-based). If a self-explanation earns a "3," then it is interpreted to have incorporated information at a global level, and may include outside information or refer to an overall theme across the whole text (global-based). Examples of these four types of self-explanation are provided in Table 1.

The iSTART algorithm currently includes only semantic and word-based indices. The algorithm is based on semantic overlap with the target sentence and surrounding text, as well as its length. The algorithm does not consider linguistic indices reflective of the types of words used within the self-explanation. One goal of this study is to examine whether linguistic features reveal differences between types of self-explanations. For example, students may use linguistic tricks to game the algorithm. Or, certain strategies may be associated with the use of particular types of words. If this is the case, then there should be a relation between the human ratings of the self-explanations and the associated linguistic measures. This study examines this potential relation by evaluating the presence of linguistic features and how they are related to self-explanation quality.

Coh-Metrix

Coh-Metrix is a tool that provides a wide range of computational linguistic indices to meet the growing need for comprehensive and automatic text analyses. Coh-Metrix uses lexicons, a syn-

Table 1. Examples of self-explanation categories

iSTART Score	Category	Example
	Target Sentence	"The goldfish may depend on other living things for food, or it may be food for other life."
0	Irrelevant	"No I will not you crazy magic man haha. the dog id blue and wishes he could run really fast like!!"
1	Sentence-based	"Sometimes animals will eat food and sometimes they'll be food."
2	Text-based	"In the living environment, living factors are called biotic factors. A goldfish's relationship w/ other organisms is an example of a biotic factor."
3	Global-based	"If the goldfish populations were to decrease, the animals that depend on them to survive would have to find another source of food or they would die out over a short period of time."

tactic parser, latent semantic analysis (LSA), and several other components that are widely used in computational linguistics (Graesser, McNamara, Louwerse, & Cai, 2004; McNamara & Graesser, this volume). For example, the MRC database is used for psycholinguistic information about words (Coltheart, 1981). Syntax and parts-of-speech are analyzed using Charniak's syntactic parser (Charniak, 2000) and WordNet provides linguistic and semantic features of words and relations between them (Fellbaum, 1998; Miller, Beckwith, Fellbaum, Gross, & Miller, 1990). LSA is used to compute the semantic similarities between words, sentences, and paragraphs by applying statistical computations, including Singular Value Decomposition, to a large corpus of text (Landauer & Dumais, 1997; Landauer, McNamara, Dennis, & Kintsch, 2007).

Coh-Metrix thus seems to fulfill the need of discourse psychologists and other researchers to have access to one computational linguistic tool that analyzes texts on various linguistic features. Indeed, Coh-Metrix has been used to detect a wide variety of differences in text and discourse. For instance, several studies have identified differences between spoken discourse and written text (Graesser, Jeon, Yang, & Cai, 2007; Louwerse, McCarthy, McNamara, & Graesser, 2004), as well as differences between different sources, purposes, and even the specific writers of written text (Crossley, Louwerse, McCarthy, & McNa-

mara, 2007; Graesser, Jeon, Cai, & McNamara, 2008; McCarthy, Briner, Rus, & McNamara, 2007; McCarthy, Lewis, Dufty, & McNamara, 2006). Collectively, these studies demonstrate that Coh-Metrix provides a powerful text analysis tool, capable of assessing and differentiating a wide variety of text types from the chapter level to the word level.

CURRENT STUDY

In the current study, 549 high school students interacted with iSTART throughout the course of an academic year. Students spent time each week reading and self-explaining science texts, which were selected and assigned by their teachers. This long-term interaction between students and iSTART provided a large corpus of student self-explanations (approximately 40,000). A subset of 5,400 self-explanations was coded by human raters.

All students interacted with the same version of iSTART (as described above). After training was complete (introduction module, demonstration module, and practice module), students used an iSTART extended practice module to self-explain texts assigned by their teachers. This extended practice module functioned just like the practice module within iSTART (including feedback). As students interacted with the texts during extended practice, their self-explanations were evaluated by iSTART, feedback was provided, and the explanations were logged for future use. The only difference between the practice module and the extended practice module was the text being read and explained. The practice module used the same set of two texts for every student, whereas the texts in the extended practice module were added based on the teachers' requests. Hence, the accuracy of the iSTART algorithm for these new texts was unknown.

Human Ratings

Three experts independently rated the subset of 5,400 student self-explanations collected during extended practice. These experts were extensively trained on self-explanation strategies but had little or no knowledge in how LSA works, and the ratings were provided independently of the iSTART algorithm scores (i.e., raters never saw the output from iSTART). The expert raters provided scores for each self-explanation on seven categories: garbage, vague/irrelevant, repetition, paraphrase, elaboration, local bridging, and global bridging. An explanation contained garbage if any words or entries were not coherent. Vague and irrelevant explanations consisted of information out of context that does not pertain to and would not contribute to comprehension of the text. The student explanations that simply repeated the words from the target sentence were classified as repetition. When students used their own words to restate the ideas from the target sentence an explanation was categorized as a paraphrase. An elaboration required that students expand on the information from the text and incorporate some of their personal knowledge. Local bridging occurred when students self-explained by using information from previous sentences within the text. Lastly, the raters considered global bridging to be present when a student explanation attempted to draw together a main idea or theme from the

text (this could possibly be a combination of both local bridging and elaboration together).

Ratings were provided on all seven categories for each student self-explanation. The ratings ranged from 1 (definitely not present) to 6 (definitely present). Raters were told to consider the difference between each rating level to be equal, such that the distance between 1 and 2 was equal to the distance between 2 and 3, and so forth. Inter-rater reliability on a training set of data (including all 3 raters) resulted in an average correlation of .70 across all seven categories. The ratings for some of these categories were combined to form composite scores that represent scores analogous to those provided by the iSTART algorithm. In essence, the human ratings were combined to provide a similar score of 0, 1, 2, or 3 that represented nonsense/irrelevant explanations, sentence-based explanations, text-based explanations, and global-based explanations, respectively. The original seven categories provide a fine grained account of the student explanations, but these composite scores provide a more continuous measure of the cognitive processing that is most likely to contribute to each self-explanation.

The composite ratings provide a general indicator for the amount of cognitive complexity involved in generating each self-explanation. The nonsense/irrelevant explanations obviously lack appropriate effort and/or focus and require no processing of the text. The nonsense/irrelevant explanations receive a score of "0" because they represent the least amount of cognitive effort (which is none at all). Generating a sentence-based explanation requires only minimal processing of the target text, and does not demonstrate any inference making or knowledge activation. These explanations are a step up from the previous category and involve minimal processing, and thus receive a score of "1." Creating text-based explanations requires integration between the target sentence and prior sentences, at least to the extent of connecting two ideas explicitly present in different parts of the text. Text-based explanations receive a score of "2" because drawing a connection between the current sentence and a sentence/idea previously covered is more complex than addressing a single sentence alone. Going beyond the text-based local connections, a global-based explanation requires the activation of outside knowledge and/or making generalizations across multiple points within the text. The global-based explanations include the activation and integration of knowledge, as well as using it appropriately (i.e., not including irrelevant information), and therefore represent the highest category of explanation here (a score of "3"). Together these scores provide a direct analog between the human scores and the iSTART scores. Previous analyses indicate that there is a positive relation between the scores from the composite human ratings and those generated by the iSTART algorithm, kappa = .646 (see Jackson, Guess, & McNamara, 2010 for further analyses and discussion). This result indicates that the current algorithm is an adequate predictor of self-explanation quality, but there is room for improvement.

Coh-Metrix Analyses

Correlational analyses were performed to investigate the strength of the relations between the Coh-Metrix indices and the expert ratings (garbage, vague/irrelevant, repeat, paraphrase, elaboration, local bridging, global bridging). The resulting correlations revealed several different types of linguistic measures that were associated with the expert ratings. The linguistic indices with the strongest relationships to self-explanation ratings included measures of word frequency, semantic diversity, hypernymy, and syntactic complexity.

A higher word frequency measure is indicative of the use of more common words. Semantic diversity represents the number of different ideas present in the self-explanation. Hypernymy is based on hierarchical associations between superordinate (e.g., animal) and subordinate words (e.g., dog). Hypernymy values are indicative of the

word's abstractness (e.g., animal is more abstract than dog and has a lower hypernymy value). A high syntactic complexity value means that the textual input is more structurally diverse. The strongest positive and negative correlations for these linguistic measures are presented in Table 2.

The correlations indicate the students' responses that were rated as containing more garbage tend to include less frequent words (- word frequency) that are more concrete (- hypernymy), and are more likely to include a variety of different ideas (+ semantic diversity) and a greater incidence of noun phrases. Similarly, those explanations rated as including more irrelevant information also tended to contain more concrete words (- hypernymy), a variety of ideas (+ semantic diversity), and a high ratio of pronouns to noun phrases. These low quality self-explanations with garbage and/or irrelevant material often include little of the target text (often quoting or badly paraphrasing the terminology), tend not to use punctuation, and usually ramble about the immediate environment, include song lyrics, or discuss completely unrelated topics. Example 1 displays a self-explanation that received a high garbage and irrelevant score by the expert raters. It had a semantic diversity score of .76, a log word frequency score of 3.49, a noun hypernymy score of 3.51, and a noun incidence score of 333.

*   **Example Self-Explanation 1.** herrrrrrr-rrrrrrrrrrrrbivore. vegan is hottt. animals heterotroph www.peta2.com trollsens rotfl feeds directly on autotohps mmhm seed eating grazing algae eaing yuck lol okay whatever

The trends for the irrelevant responses contrasted neatly with those that were simple repeats or paraphrases of the target sentence. Those responses tend to include more frequent words (+ word frequency), a variety of words (standard deviation of word frequency) that are more abstract (+ hypernymy), and are less likely

Table 2. Strongest correlations between Coh-Metrix and human ratings (all correlations p<.001)

Human Rating Category	Coh-Metrix Measure	Pearson r
Garbage		
Positively Related	Semantic diversity	+.45
	Noun phrase incidence*	+.36
Negatively Related	Log of word frequency for all words	-.78
	Log of word frequency for content words	-.72
	Mean hypernym values for nouns	-.43
	Mean hypernym values for verbs	-.37
Vague/Irrelevant		
Positively Related	Ratio: pronoun to noun phrases*	+.32
	Semantic diversity	+.17
Negatively Related	Mean hypernym values for nouns	-.16
Repeat		
Positively Related	Standard deviation of log word frequency	+.47
	Log of word frequency for all words	+.36
	Mean hypernym values for nouns	+.26
Negatively Related	Semantic diversity	-.28
	Ratio: pronoun to noun phrases*	-.26
Paraphrase		
Positively Related	Log of word frequency for all words	+.38
	Mean hypernym values for nouns	+.27
Negatively Related	Semantic diversity	-.25
	Noun phrase incidence*	-.21
Elaboration		
Positively Related	Log of word frequency for content words	+.23
Local Bridging		
Positively Related	Log of word frequency for all words	+.27
	Mean hypernym values for all nouns	+.16
Negatively Related	Semantic diversity	-.24
Global Bridging		
Positively Related	Log of word frequency for all words	+.43
	Log of word frequency for content words	+.40
	Mean hypernym values for nouns	+.28
	Mean hypernym values for verbs	+.21
Negatively Related	Semantic diversity	-.27
	Noun phrase incidence*	-.24

*denotes a syntactic complexity measure

to include a variety of different ideas (- semantic diversity), fewer noun phrases, and a lower ratio of pronouns to noun phrases. These trends indicate that the responses are more similar in nature to the science texts that they are explaining than are responses that are off topic.

The elaboration scores correlated with few variables. There was one significant but weak trend for those self-explanations rated high in elaboration to also include more frequent words. This indicates that elaborations can take form linguistically in a variety of ways using a variety of different types of words, which is quite characteristic of elaborations that by their very definition go beyond the text.

The features correlated with the presence of local bridging and global bridging were quite similar to one another. Word frequency is positively correlated with the global and local bridging scores, suggesting that self-explanations with higher local and global bridging ratings tend to incorporate more common words (+ log word frequency). Bridging self-explanations also use more abstract words (+ hypernymy), and stay more focused by including fewer ideas (- semantic diversity) and less complex syntax (- noun phrase incidence). Thus, it seems that higher quality self-explanations with more bridging will tend to stay on topic and discuss concepts related to the text as they connect the different ideas together by using their own words (which tend to be more colloquial). Example 2 illustrates these trends with a self-explanation that received a high global bridging score. It had a semantic diversity score of .55, word frequency of 4.67, noun hypernymy of 5.47, and a noun phrase incidence of 375.

- **Example Self-Explanation 2.** the about of precipitation determines how each biome will form. for example if there is little rain there might be a desert there or if there is alot of rain the might be a rain forest.

Based on these correlations, the strongest measure for each of the four linguistic categories were included as predictors for the fine-grained human ratings. Specifically, the measures with the highest predictive values and lowest collinearity included log word frequency, semantic diversity, noun hypernymy, and noun phrase incidence. If these measures can reliably predict the degree of presence/absence within these expert rated categories, then the measures could potentially provide a substantial improvement to the current iSTART algorithm.

Regression Analyses

A series of regressions were performed to predict the human ratings within each of the seven coding categories. The predictors consisted of the iSTART algorithm score for each self-explanation as well as the strongest measure from each of the four predominant linguistic categories (see Table 3 for results).

Based on the results in Table 3, it appears that the four Coh-Metrix measures can account for a significant amount of variance within several of the human coding categories. Most notably, the Coh-Metrix measures explain 63 percent of the variance for the garbage category and almost 20 percent of the variance for the global bridging category. This finding suggests that these linguistic measures may provide an additional benefit above and beyond the current iSTART algorithm. Therefore these linguistic measures were included within a series of subsequent analyses that aim to predict the composite human scores.

Composite Score Classification

The measures used within the regression analyses were also used within a series of discriminant function analyses that attempted to predict the composite human ratings. A discriminant analysis is a statistical procedure that is able to predict group membership (in this case composite hu-

Table 3. R^2 for regressions to predict human ratings within each category (all p<.001)

Human Rating Category	Variables used to predict human ratings:		
	4 Coh-Metrix Measures*	iSTART Algorithm Score	4 Coh-Metrix Measures + iSTART Score
Garbage	.629	.095	.632
Vague/Irrelevant	.031	.041	.053
Repeat	.156	.056	.317
Paraphrase	.159	.057	.170
Elaboration	.018	.025	.038
Local Bridging	.083	.392	.395
Global Bridging	.190	.129	.239

* measures included: log word frequency, noun hypernymy, semantic diversity, and syntactic complexity.

man ratings of 0, 1, 2, or 3) using a series of independent variables (in this case the selected Coh-Metrix variables and iSTART algorithm). The first discriminant function analysis included only the four Coh-Metrix measures to try and predict the composite expert ratings (0, 1, 2, or 3). The results of this classification analysis are illustrated in Figure 2.

Unfortunately, the four Coh-Metrix measures used in the function presented in Figure 2 yielded only a 38.2% accuracy for classification categories, kappa = .151, *p*<.001. While this kappa is technically significant, due to the high number of observations, it is low and indicates that the algorithm is not sufficiently accurate for classifica-

tion or evaluation purposes. This performance was compared to a function that used only the iSTART algorithm score and attempted to predict the same composite human codings. Figure 3 shows that the iSTART algorithm alone can accurately classify 79.1% of the human categories, kappa = .634, *p*<.001.

A final analysis was conducted to determine if the Coh-Metrix measures could provide any benefit above and beyond the iSTART algorithm. The accuracy of the combined algorithms illustrated in Figure 4, was 71.6% correct, kappa = .528, *p*<.001. Thus, the combination of the iSTART algorithm and the four Coh-Metrix measures causes a slight reduction in the classification accuracy compared to iSTART alone.

Figure 2. Predicting original human ratings using only 4 Coh-Metrix measures

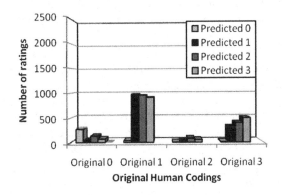

Figure 3. Predicting original human ratings using only the iSTART algorithm

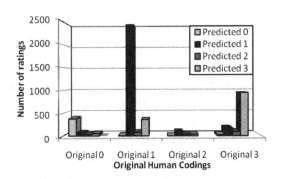

Figure 4. Predicting original human ratings using only both the iSTART algorithm and Coh-Metrix measures

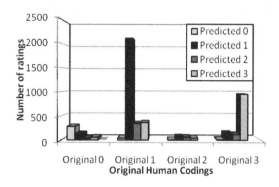

The discriminant function analyses for overall quality suggest that the linguistic measures do not provide any benefit beyond the current iSTART algorithm. In fact, the measures slightly reduce the performance of the iSTART algorithm.

CONCLUSION AND DISCUSSION

Applying natural language processing efforts within a system is always a difficult task. The results discussed here help to illustrate the complex nature of finding the right NLP techniques that match the goal of the application. The current findings here suggest that while some specific strategies for self-explanation can be partially characterized by linguistic properties, the overall quality of a self-explanation cannot necessarily be predicted by the specific linguistic properties.

The correlations indicate that better self-explanations (those that include more bridging and elaboration) tend to remain focused on the topic and use more abstract common words. In contrast, the poorer self-explanations (those that include nonsense or irrelevant information) tend to include many ideas and use less common concrete words. While these trends are significant, further analyses demonstrate that they are an inadequate means of classifying the overall quality of a student's self-explanation. Thus, it appears that

students are not employing any linguistic-based tricks to try and circumvent the existing algorithm.

One of the most interesting findings here is that the linguistic measures can reliably predict the ratings within a given category, but they cannot accurately predict the composite ratings across categories. The fine-grained analyses on the human coding categories revealed that the linguistic measures in Coh-Metrix provide a significant method for predicting the human ratings within a specific category. Being able to determine to amount of garbage, or the amount of bridging within a self-explanation may provide very useful information to the system if it needs to know which specific strategy is being employed within a given self-explanation. These linguistic features may be helpful in determining the most relevant constructive feedback to help the students improve upon a given self-explanation. However they are an insufficient means of gauging students' overall self-explanation quality.

REFERENCES

Bransford, J., Brown, A., & Cocking, R. (Eds.). (2000). *How people learn: Brain, mind, experience, and school.* Washington, DC: National Academy Press. Retrieved from http://www.nap. edu/html/howpeople1/.

Charniak, E. (2000). A maximum-entropy-inspired parser. *Proceedings of the First Conference on North American Chapter of the Association for Computational Linguistics* (pp. 132-139). San Francisco, CA: Morgan Kaufmann Publishers.

Coltheart, M. (1981). The MRC psycholinguistic database. *Quarterly Journal of Experimental Psychology, 33A,* 497–505.

Crossley, S. A., Louwerse, M., McCarthy, P. M., & McNamara, D. S. (2007). A linguistic analysis of simplified and authentic texts. *Modern Language Journal, 91,* 15–30. doi:10.1111/j.1540-4781.2007.00507.x

Fellbaum, C. (Ed.). (1998). *WordNet: An electronic lexical database*. Cambridge, MA: MIT Press.

Graesser, A. C., Hu, X., & McNamara, D. S. (2005). Computerized learning environments that incorporate research in discourse psychology, cognitive science, and computational linguistics. In Healy, A. F. (Ed.), *Experimental cognitive psychology and its applications: Festschrift in honor of Lyle Bourne* (pp. 183–194). Walter Kintsch, and Thomas Landauer. doi:10.1037/10895-014

Graesser, A. C., Hu, X., & Person, N. (2001). Teaching with the help of talking heads. In T. Okamoto, R. Hartley, Kinshuk, & J. P. Klus (Eds.), *Proceedings IEEE International Conference on Advanced Learning Technology: Issues, Achievements and Challenges* (pp. 460-461).

Graesser, A. C., Jeon, M., Cai, Z., & McNamara, D. S. (2008). Automatic analyses of language, discourse, and situation models. In Auracher, J., & van Peer, W. (Eds.), *New beginnings in literary studies* (pp. 72–88). Cambridge, UK: Cambridge Scholars Publishing.

Graesser, A. C., Jeon, M., Yang, Y., & Cai, Z. (2007). Discourse cohesion in text and tutorial dialogue. *Information Design Journal, 15*, 199-213.

Graesser, A. C., Lu, S., Jackson, G. T., Mitchell, H., Ventura, M., Olney, A., & Louwerse, M. M. (2004). AutoTutor: A tutor with dialogue in natural language. *Behavior Research Methods, Instruments, & Computers, 36*, 180–193. doi:10.3758/BF03195563

Graesser, A. C., McNamara, D. S., Louwerse, M. M., & Cai, Z. (2004). Coh-Metrix: Analysis of text on cohesion and language. *Behavior Research Methods, Instruments, & Computers, 36*, 193–202. doi:10.3758/BF03195564

Jackson, G. T., Guess, R. H., & McNamara, D. S. (2010). Assessing cognitively complex strategy use in an untrained domain. *Topics in Cognitive Science, 2*, 127–137. doi:10.1111/j.1756-8765.2009.01068.x

Landauer, T. K., & Dumais, S. T. (1997). A solution to Plato's problem: The latent semantic analysis theory of the acquisition, induction, and representation of knowledge. *Psychological Review, 104*, 211–240. doi:10.1037/0033-295X.104.2.211

Landauer, T. K., McNamara, D. S., Dennis, S., & Kintsch, W. (Eds.). (2007). *LSA: A road to meaning*. Mahwah, NJ: Erlbaum.

Louwerse, M. M., Graesser, A. C., & Olney, A., & the Tutoring Research Group. (2002). Good computational manners: Mixed-initiative dialog in conversational agents. In C. Miller (Ed.), *Etiquette for Human-Computer Work, Papers from the 2002 Fall Symposium, Technical Report FS-02-02*, (pp. 71-76).

Louwerse, M. M., McCarthy, P. M., McNamara, D. S., & Graesser, A. C. (2004). Variation in language and cohesion across written and spoken registers. In K. Forbus, D. Gentner, & T. Regier (Eds.), *Proceedings of the Twenty-Sixth Annual Conference of the Cognitive Science Society* (pp. 843–848). Mahwah, NJ: Erlbaum.

Magliano, J. P., Todaro, S., Millis, K. K., Wiemer-Hastings, K., Kim, H. J., & McNamara, D. S. (2004). Changes in reading strategies as a function of reading training: A comparison of live and computerized training. *Journal of Educational Computing Research, 32*, 185–208. doi:10.2190/1LN8-7BQE-8TN0-M91L

McCarthy, P. M., Briner, S. W., Rus, V., & McNamara, D. S. (2007). Textual signatures: Identifying text-types using latent semantic analysis to measure the cohesion of text structures. In Kao, A., & Poteet, S. (Eds.), *Natural language processing and text mining* (pp. 107–122). London, UK: Springer-Verlag UK. doi:10.1007/978-1-84628-754-1_7

McCarthy, P. M., Lewis, G. A., Dufty, D. F., & McNamara, D. S. (2006). Analyzing writing styles with Coh-Metrix. In G. C. J. Sutcliffe & R. G. Goebel (Eds.), *Proceedings of the 19th Annual Florida Artificial Intelligence Research Society International Conference (FLAIRS)* (pp. 764–770). Melbourne Beach, FL: AAAI Press.

McNamara, D. S. (2004). SERT: Self-explanation reading training. *Discourse Processes, 38,* 1–30. doi:10.1207/s15326950dp3801_1

McNamara, D. S., Boonthum, C., Levinstein, I. B., & Millis, K. (2007). Evaluating self-explanations in iSTART: Comparing word-based and LSA algorithms. In Landauer, T., McNamara, D. S., Dennis, S., & Kintsch, W. (Eds.), *Handbook of latent semantic analysis* (pp. 227–241). Mahwah, NJ: Erlbaum.

McNamara, D. S., Louwerse, M. M., & Graesser, A. C. (2002). *Coh-Metrix: Automated cohesion and coherence scores to predict text readability and facilitate comprehension. Technical report.* Memphis, TN: Institute for Intelligent Systems, University of Memphis.

McNamara, D. S., & Scott, J. L. (1999). Training reading strategies. In M. Hahn & S. C. Stoness (Eds.), *Proceedings of the Twenty-first Annual Meeting of the Cognitive Science Society* (pp. 387-392). Hillsdale, NJ: Erlbaum.

Miller, G. A., Beckwith, R., Fellbaum, C., Gross, D., & Miller, K. (1990). *Five papers on WordNet.* Princeton, NJ: Princeton University Press.

O'Reilly, T., Best, R., & McNamara, D. S. (2004). Self-Explanation reading training: Effects for low-knowledge readers. In K. Forbus, D. Gentner, T. Regier (Eds.), *Proceedings of the Twenty-Sixth Annual Meeting of the Cognitive Science Society* (pp. 1053-1058). Mahwah, NJ: Erlbaum.

O'Reilly, T., Sinclair, G. P., & McNamara, D. S. (2004). Reading strategy training: Automated verses live. In K. Forbus, D. Gentner, T. Regier (Eds.), *Proceedings of the Twenty-Sixth Annual Meeting of the Cognitive Science Society* (pp. 1059-1064). Mahwah, NJ: Erlbaum.

VanLehn, K., Graesser, A. C., Jackson, G. T., Jordan, P., Olney, A., & Rose, C. P. (2007). When are tutorial dialogues more effective than reading? *Cognitive Science, 31,* 3–62. doi:10.1080/03640210709336984

ADDITIONAL READING

Jackson, G. T., Dempsey, K. B., & McNamara, D. S. (2010). The evolution of an automated reading strategy tutor: From classroom to a game-enhanced automated system. In Khine, M. S., & Saleh, I. M. (Eds.), *New Science of learning: Cognition, computers and collaboration in education* (pp. 283–306). New York, NY: Springer.

Landauer, T., McNamara, D. S., Dennis, S., & Kintsch, W. (Eds.). (2007). *Handbook of Latent Semantic Analysis.* Mahwah, NJ: Erlbaum.

McNamara, D. S. (Ed.). (2007). *Reading comprehension strategies: Theory, interventions, and technologies.* Mahwah, NJ: Erlbaum.

McNamara, D. S. (2010). Computational methods to extract meaning from text and advance theories of human cognition. *Topics in Cognitive Science, 2,* 1–15.

McNamara, D. S., Boonthum, C., Levinstein, I. B., & Millis, K. (2007). Evaluating self-explanations in iSTART: comparing word-based and LSA algorithms. In Landauer, T., McNamara, D. S., Dennis, S., & Kintsch, W. (Eds.), *Handbook of Latent Semantic Analysis* (pp. 227–241). Mahwah, NJ: Erlbaum.

McNamara, D. S., Louwerse, M. M., McCarthy, P. M., & Graesser, A. C. (2010). Coh-Metrix: Capturing linguistic features of cohesion. *Discourse Processes, 47,* 292–330. doi:10.1080/01638530902959943

Chapter 16
Computer–Aided Rhetorical Analysis

Suguru Ishizaki
Carnegie Mellon University, USA

David Kaufer[1]
Carnegie Mellon University, USA

ABSTRACT

This chapter presents a corpus-based text analysis tool along with a research approach to conducting a rhetorical analysis of individual text as well as text collections. The motivation for our computational approach, the system development, evaluation, and research and educational applications are discussed. The tool, called DocuScope, supports both quantitative and quantitatively-informed qualitative analyses of rhetorical strategies found in a broad range of textual artifacts, using a standard home-grown dictionary consisting of more than 40 million unique patterns of English that are classified into over 100 rhetorical functions. DocuScope also provides an authoring environment allowing investigators to build their own customized dictionaries according to their own language theories. Research published with both the standard and customized dictionaries is discussed, as well as tradeoffs, limitations, and directions for the future.

INTRODUCTION

Our research seeks to account for the wide variation in the experiences texts afford. In particular, we are interested in uncovering how the writer's small and recurring linguistic choices contribute to the whole text experience of the reader. Answering

DOI: 10.4018/978-1-60960-741-8.ch016

this question is important to rhetorical analysts who wish to understand how the plasticity of language choice affects the plasticity of responses to rhetorical situations. Answers to these questions are also important to writing instructors who wish to understand the wide palette to which students must be exposed in order to master writing across a range of genres and situations. Our research is concerned with the kernel of rhetorical theory by exploring the relationship between micro (surface) linguistic choices versus a holistic rhetorical effect in language design. We have sought to explore the extent to which local language decisions traditionally associated with "style" aggregate to inform global linguistic organization associated with "invention" and "genre" (Bawarshi, 2003).

In what sense can micro-selections of textual expressions contribute compositionally to a text's overall genre features? Research on first and second-language learning has independently converged with and benefited our efforts, particularly the cognitive work of Ellis (Ellis & Ferreira-Junior, 2009), and the linguistic work of Hoey (2005). From different disciplines, both researchers have demonstrated that language learners do not learn a single word at a time, but they acquire strings of words as units over time through a process which Ellis refers to as a "statistical ensemble." A conventional dictionary enumerates the various meanings and parts of speech (e.g., noun, verb, adjective) a word may reference, but language users learn words by understanding the various streams of discourse to which individual words contribute in a culturally and socially meaningful

context. Take the single word "smear." Language users learn that the expression to "smear a politician" contributes to a negative expression while "smearing soap in the shower" contributes to an expression of everyday motion. Hundreds of millions of everyday strings like these enter a cultural repository of meaning-making potential. Speakers and writers exploit the cultural repository to be understood. Listeners and readers exploit it to understand. Through rhetorical strategies, speakers and writers may invent new expressions, which become candidates for entering and extending the cultural repository. The picture looks something like Figure 1 with respect to writers, readers, and texts.

These language patterns with "smear" and others alone have small but real effects. Taken as an aggregate, they exert great influence on the experience of the reader. At the whole text level, language patterns can determine a number of holistic effects about the overall shape of a text. In other words, what we call types or genres of writing are created by the small and often implicit design decisions writers make along these and many other choices. Our research has sought

Figure 1. A picture of literate language learning. Writers rely on previous shared experience with language patterns to be understood. Readers rely on this same repository to understand. Writers, through rhetorical strategies that may be site specific, can invent new expressions that may or may not add to the shared cultural inventory.

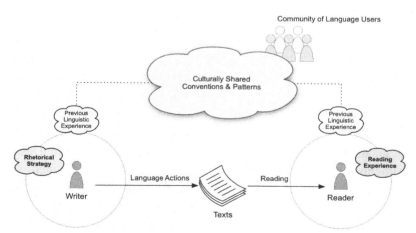

to uncover what these implicit choices are, and the various ranges of reader response they afford.

On the one hand, readers' elaboration of a particular text as a whole depends upon their own socio-cultural positioning and historical experience and cannot be reproduced by other readers. On the other hand, readers' experience of specific textual patterns is often reproducible because it derives from a shared cultural repository. For example, two readers may read a political text in entirely different ways. But their different interpretations will still be launched from many points of agreement about what the text is saying. We assume they both will agree that "smearing the politician" is a negative expression, even if that agreement is overwhelmed by larger disagreements. Our research was meant to capture these "interpretation-light" points of agreement in the stream of text. We call these points of agreement in textual interpretation a *primitive reading experience* authorized by conventional understanding within the community of language users. And, we postulate that a primitive reading experience is implemented through a series of language actions. For example, the language action "smearing the politician" contributes to the creation of negative expression. A type of language actions that creates

a specific primitive experience is called Language Action Type (LAT). The term "primitive reading experience" (or simply reading experience) and the term "language action type" seem to be used interchangeably; but the former is used to refer to the experience of the reader/audience; and the latter is used to refer to a collection of language actions (i.e., English strings) that are defined in our software. The theoretical framework is illustrated in Figure 2. We relied on this framework to begin the process of identifying primitive reading experiences in English, and identifying actual language patterns that implement each primitive experience.

OUR APPROACH

In order to identify Language Action Types, and fill them with specific language actions, we developed a custom software tool, called DocuScope, which is similar to typical dictionary-based text analysis tools. The key difference between Docu-Scope and existing dictionary-based text analysis programs is the purpose of the program. While most dictionary-based programs aim to characterize the theme of a given text (i.e., thematic

Figure 2. We assume that there are "interpretation-light" experiences (e), which represent the smallest units of interpreted agreement in the discourse stream. e is implemented by the author through language actions, which are actual strings of English (e.g., "smear soap in the shower"). A group of language actions that create a specific primitive experience, e, is called Language Action Type, or LAT.

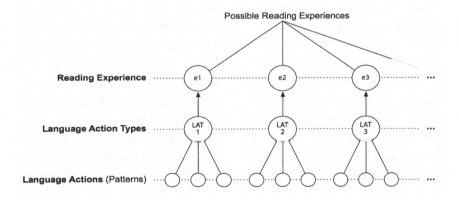

analysis), our goal is to help text analysts uncover the recurrent rhetorical strategies (i.e., Language Action Types) found in a text collection. For us, it is also important to help analysts examine the micro linguistic patterns that are manifest in an individual textural surface.

Most dictionary-based tools were not designed for the open development of dictionaries and especially across variable-length strings. One of our goals was to create a tool that overcame these limitations. We wanted to help text analysts identity and test emergent concepts in the discourse stream iteratively in order to build dictionaries with a large number of linguistic patterns consistently classified. We wanted to support the development of robust dictionaries with an inventory of strings that ran into the millions. The size of our dictionary is significantly larger than typical dictionary-based tools, many of which use less than 10,000 patterns (Klein, 2002-2005). While typical thematic analysis might be possible with a relatively small number of language patterns, we realized in our early experiments that a much wider coverage of language strings beyond individual words was critical in order for us to examine micro-macro connections in language design. Programs handling only single words tend to be highly unstable and ambiguous for matching on recurrent meaning. Hart's DICTION program, covering some 10,000 single words, proves a very accurate tool for measuring the placement of a single text's rhetorical features within a cloud of 20,000 reference texts. But it is not highly informative about a single text's rhetorical properties taken on its own terms. Pennebaker's *Linguistic Inquiry and Word Count: LIWC* program, measuring the interface of writing, mental health and personality, is also based on single words. What makes single word tagging programs robust is the ability of the investigator to supplement the language analysis with focused theory, in Hart's case, political communication, in Pennebaker's case, the psychology of personality. While these dictionary-based approaches use essentially the

same computational method—i.e., counting of patterns, these tools serve fundamentally different purposes from DocuScope.

DocuScope is often used for genre analysis. However, it should be distinguished from genre classification and analysis tools, which are primarily designed to automate genre analysis (e.g., McCarthy et al. 2006; Stein & Eissen, 2008; Argamon et al. 2007). Since the goal of these tools is to automate the process, the reasoning behind the analysis does not have to be made available. In other words, the primary goal of these tools is to classify or retrieve text, rather than to uncover the rhetorical strategies employed by the authors. Therefore, providing a human-readable description of computational analysis at the surface textual level is not important. Our goal, on the other hand, was to deepen the understanding of how genre is strategically enacted on the textural surface through micro language actions. Hence, it was critical for us to develop a system where the analytical procedure is highly transparent, both to authors or analysts.

Our current phrase-based dictionaries, which exclude proper names and place names, have been shown to cover approximately 70-75% of contemporary American English. The coverage of our dictionaries is extensive enough to have supported peer-reviewed publication on Shakespeare's English by leading experts in Shakespeare's language (Witmore & Hope, 2007). As suggested above, we also wanted to make the DocuScope environment a good mix of the conventional strengths of quantitative and qualitative coding. We sought to accomplish this by allowing for complete flexibility in a coding unit (offered by qualitative methods) along with the capacity to statistically tabulate and aggregate units (offered by a quantitative methods). Reliable segmentation of the textual stream typically requires coders to make hard decisions on the units of language to be coded: words, t-units, clauses, nominals, verbals, indexicals, pronouns, modals, and the like[47]. As Geisler (2003) notes (pg 29), it is nearly impossible for coders to achieve reliability at counting patterns in the discourse stream without first fixing on the units to be counted. Yet this commitment to fixed coding units runs counter to the fact that many of the most important and intriguing elements of discourse can span unpredictably in range in the discourse stream. For instance, coding units for a "point," "theme," "story" or "argument"—just to mention four common coding categories—typically span single words to propositions to segments of paragraphs. This flexibility of coding units is certainly one of many reasons behind the trend of discourse analysts turning away from quantitative methods in favor of qualitative ones. Quantitative analysis is sometimes stereotyped by discourse analysts as inheriting fixed-length coding units, while qualitative analysis promises flexibility. By using a multi-word string matching with the flexible coding units, we hoped to integrate some of the reliability and precision of quantitative coding with the richness and flexibility of qualitative coding.

DEVELOPING THE STANDARD DICTIONARY

How many LATs does English contain and how could we go about finding and filling them with English strings? The vastness of studying English across so many different text types meant we needed automatic methods. That decision left us with a further decision to make about how to write a computer program that can perform automatic coding: the dictionary-based approach or the machine learning approach. Most theory-driven text analysis software employs the dictionary-based approach, where search patterns are manually entered by human experts. One potential problem of this approach is that the bigger the dictionary becomes, the longer it takes to complete the dictionary and the more potential for inconsistency and incompleteness. Thus, as we anticipated the

need for an extremely large dictionary, we considered an alternative approach—machine learning.

Text analysis tools that use machine learning techniques "learn" to perform coding automatically without a dictionary manually created by the researcher. Typically, the program "learns" by examining coding samples generated by human experts (Anthony & Lashkia, 2003; Burstein, Marcu, & Knight, 2003). The advantage of the machine learning approach is to save on human dictionary building time. The disadvantage is that it is extremely difficult to create a program that can penetrate the profound interaction of language and cultural practice. Some of the successful application of machine learning approaches seem to work effectively only when the phenomenon being captured is well-defined, such as research paper introductions (Anthony & Lashkia, 2003) and thesis statements in five paragraph essays (Burstein, Marcu, & Knight, 2003).

This initial analysis of methods led us to finally adopt a dictionary-based approach. Rather than train a computer to tag English, a manual approach relies on human experts to build a large library of contiguous strings classified by rhetorical effect. In this approach, human experts sensitive to language-culture interactions explore and build the coding scheme and the dictionary. The pronoun "I" is tagged as a "first person" effect. The word "if" is associated with a "contingency" effect. These are simple examples using one word coding. However, our approach also allows for coding that can be built up over longer strings (e.g., a five-word string like "in this paper, I will" to reflect metadiscourse at the beginning of an essay). With this approach, a wide range of patterns are harvested, classified, and stored within a database. Nonetheless, adopting a dictionary-based approach also meant that we had to address its inherent problems.

Whereas a dictionary-based approach avoids the (machine learning) problem of a high noise ratio in coding, it poses a different challenge—how to bound the coding project that both gives some procedural meaning to "covering" the language while staying within the very limited capacities of human labor. Because of the rich combinations of word strings, it seems impossible for a human expert to enumerate all possible patterns of English that are potentially relevant to a rhetorical theory of text. Our way of meeting this challenge was to imagine an expert "covering" the rhetorical patterns of English at the grain of contiguous word strings in five phrases. In the first phase, we focused on achieving what we deemed to be a "complete" category system for strings. Completeness of the category system was not the same as completeness of the category members (the actual strings). This first phase needed to continue for as long as our human dictionary building effort uncovered new major categories for new strings. The phase would be concluded when we found we no longer had to invent new categories for new string input. In other words, all new tokens found in the input stream of English were covered by our existing category types. The success of this first phase depended upon our inspecting as broad a range of English prose texts as we could find. We found our coding categories (and initial bank of rhetorical strings) from the Lincoln/Douglas debates, from student writings in a multi genre course (written journals, profiles, scenic field-guides, historical narratives, exposition, popular explanation, instructions, and argument), from a 120 text digital archive of introspective fiction, character based short stories, and essays of reminiscence, reflection, and social criticism. We took a second archive from a course on information systems. This archive contained 45 electronic documents including client proposals, design specifications, meeting minutes, documentation, focus group reports, public relation announcements, and interviews. We took a third oral-written archive from the Federalist papers, the Presidential Inaugurals, the journals of Lewis and Clark, talk radio, song lyrics, newspaper columnists, fables of Aesop and the Brother's Grimm, the writings of Malcolm X, the 100 great speeches of the 20th century, 10

years of newspaper reporting on the Exxon Valdez disaster, and The New Yorker.

We divided the texts compiled into training and test samples. We coded strings from the training sample and then tested the codings on the test samples. Although we could not visually inspect every one of the strings that our string matcher matched, we built an interface that allowed us to visually inspect any of the matches made during test and improvement cycles. A "collision detector" in the software we built pointed out strings that were inadvertently included under multiple categories, making it easy for us to keep the coding decisions mutually exclusive and providing an additional logical check on the development of our categories. We also recruited students in writing courses as a user community providing formative feedback. We asked students to run their assignments through our software and evaluate how their prose had been tagged. We asked them to evaluate the meaningfulness, completeness, usefulness, and accuracy of our categories. Were the category names understandable? Were the category names exhaustive, or were there categories that would be useful to add? Were the categories useful to you in helping to explain how you had planned your text? Were the categories accurately applied, or were their inaccuracies in matching categories to actual strings in the input text? The first phase of dictionary building took three years to complete. Phase 1 had focused on completeness in the coding categories rather than "completeness" filling the categories with strings. By the end of the first phase, we had catalogued over a one million unique strings of English (a fact less impressive than it seems, as it owes to the combinatorics of strings more than to our special coding prowess) but only 19,000 single words of English. Our categories were robust, but our system covered random texts of English very sparsely.

Phase 2 assured that our coding would systematically penetrate the most frequently occurring English words. In the second phase, we applied our coding categories to the 100,000 most

Figure 3. The dictionary-building effort for the standard dictionary

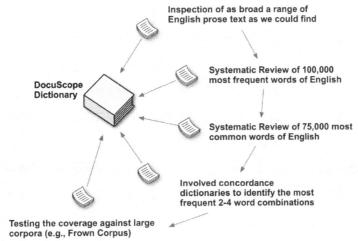

frequent words of English. By the end of Phase 2, which required one-person year of effort, we had bumped our single word entries to 130,000 single words. In Phase 3, we then turned our attention to the 75,000 most "common" words of American English. Common words range in their frequency but are typically lower in frequency than the 100,000 most frequent English words. Nonetheless, common words are words considered important enough for lexicographers to include in their dictionary entries. Over a 9 months period, we expanded our string libraries to include words and phrases involving all of the 75,000 common words. Subsequently, in Phase 4, we used concordance dictionaries to identify the most frequent 2-4 word combinations from the 10,000 or so most frequent words of English. Finally, in Phase 5, we compared the dictionary against Brown and Frown corpus using DocuScope, and identified language patterns that are not included in our dictionary. All the missing patterns are added to the dictionary, excluding proper names and non-standard hyphenated expressions. Figure 3 illustrates our dictionary-building effort.

We completed the initial dictionary development effort in 2005, but we have continued to add new strings as we encounter them in our analysis

of other text collections. Although did not have to create new major LATs, we also have increased the number of LATs by sub-dividing them into a finer categories. We found that finer LATs were sometimes necessary in order to increase the sensitivity of the dictionary. For example, initially we had an LAT for creating an experience of Negativity. This LAT was later sub-divided into Negativity (general negative emotion), Anger, Sadness, and Fear. Because of the need to refine the granularity of LATs, DocuScope organizes LATs in a hierarchical fashion. Figure 4 shows the current hierarchy of LATs.

The current dictionary includes roughly 45.5 million patterns of English categorized into 112 Language Action Types (LATs) at the lowest level of hierarchy. The largest and the smallest LATs include 40.7 million patterns (89%) and 8 patterns respectively. The median LAT includes 3,996 patterns. The largest LAT is Time Duration, which creates an experience of temporal intervals (e.g., "for two years," "extend over 90 days"), contains 89% of all the patterns. This exceptionally large LAT is created because it includes significant number of patterns that include multiple numbers (e.g., "from 90 to 180 days") are algorithmically enumerated. Although the large

Figure 4. The hierarchy of Language Action Types (LATs)

Subjective Register	First Person	
	First Person Personal	Self Disclosure
		Self Reluctance
		Autobiography
	Personal Register	Private Thinking
		Disclosure
		Intensity
		Immediacy
		Subjective Time
		Subjective Perception
	Dialog Orality	Dialog Cues
		Oral Cues
	Confidence	
	Uncertainty	
Emotion	Positive Emotion	
	Negative Emotion	Negativity
		Anger
		Fear
		Sadness
		Reluctance
		Apology
Description	Sensory Language	Sense Property
		Sense Object
	Space Movement	Space Relation
		Scene Shift
		Motions
Institutional Register	Public Sources	In Media
		Common Authorities
	Public Responsibility	
	Positive Values	Positive Values
		Innovations
	Negative Values	
Academic Register	Abstract Thought	Abstract Concepts
		Communicator Role
		Language Reference
	Citing Others	Precedent Defending
		Received Point of View
		Confirmed Thought
		Citations
		Negative Citation
		Repair Citation
		Speculative Citation
		Authoritative Citation
		Contested Citation
		Attack Citation
		Quotation
	Metadiscourse	
Future	Future	Project Ahead
		Predicted Future
Past	Past	Project Back
		Future in Past
Personal Relations	Positive Relations	Promise
		Self Promise
		Reassure
		Reinforce
		Acknowledge
	Inclusive Relations	
	Negative Relations	

Reasoning	Constructive Reasoning	Reason Forward
		Reason Backward
		Direct Reasoning
		Support
	Contingent Reasoning	
	Oppositional Reasoning	Deny Disclaim
		Concessive
		Resistance
Interactive	Inquiry	Curiosity
		Question
		Future Question
		Open Query
	AddressingOther	Direct Address
		Request
		Follow Up
		Feedback
		Positive Feedback
		Negative Feedback
		Prior Knowledge
Information	GeneralExampleExcept	Generalization
		Example
		Exceptions
	Comparison	Comparison
		Resemblances
	Defining Specifying	Specifiers
		Definition
Reporting	Reporting States	
	Reporting Events	
	Reporting Process	Recurring Events
		Generic Events
		Sequence
		Mature Process
		Cause
	Reporting Change	Transformation
		Substitution
		Updates
		Precedent Setting
Directing	Directives	Imperative
		Procedures
		Move Body
		Confirm Experience
		Error Recovery
	Insistence	
Narrative	Narrative Verbs	
	Time Expressions	Time Shift
		Time Duration
		Biographical Time
		Time Date
	Personal Attribution	Person Pronoun
		Positive Attribution
		Negative Attribution
		Neutral Attribution
		Person Property
	Narrative Background	

size of our dictionary represents the extensive coverage of English language, these numbers must be understood as a rough reference. Since some of the patterns are generated with simple algorithms without considering English grammar (e.g., verb agreement) or cultural knowledge, the dictionary includes patterns that may never be used. We decided not to exclude those unused patterns in favor of increasing the coverage since having unused patterns has no effect on the analysis.

Table 1 shows the distribution of pattern according to their length (# of words). The third column shows the numbers excluding the Time Duration LAT. Figure 5 is a visual representation of the third column.

Testing the Standard Dictionary against Independent Corpora

How well do our LATs and strings classify texts and genres in ways that human classifiers differentiate

Table 1. Count of patterns per size (# of words)

# words	with Time Duration	without Time Duration
1	220,197	218,439
2	482,380	469,460
3	860,478	558,941
4	3,954,225	2,010,651
5	3,724,296	756,095
6	35,767,792	395,304
7	409,535	377,375
8	47,366	41,966
9	6,997	6,997
10	993	993
11	63,803	299
12	50	50
13	45	45
14	39	39
15	3	3
16	6	6
17	37	37

them? Collins (2003) investigated this question in his dissertation even before our dictionary building efforts were completed. Using DocuScope, he analyzed the first half (250) of the texts from the 500 text Brown Corpus, which compiled American English of the 1960s into 15 genres. He ran a statistical procedure (exploratory factor analysis) to identify the major groupings of LATs (i.e., factors) that are salient within this sample of texts. He then analyzed the remaining half (250) of the Brown Corpus as well 500 texts from the Freiburg-Brown Corpus (an update of the Brown Corpus using English of the 1990s) using confirmatory factor analysis to find out whether the original factors found in the first half could explain text/genre differences in the remaining half (250). In this study, Collins found that the original factors uncovered by our dictionary for the first half of the Brown Corpus (1960s English) successfully accounted for the genre variation in the second half of the Brown Corpus and the Freiburg-Brown Corpus (1990s English). These results provided direct evidence that our dictionary of LATs and strings were separating written English into genre families and subfamilies across a 30 year period robustly, consistently, and in ways consistent with human classifiers. It further provided support for our theoretical hypotheses about the deep connection between style (micro-choices of individual strings of language) and invention (macro-choices about recurring constellations of text).

THE DOCUSCOPE ENVIRONMENT AS A SYSTEM

As a system DocuScope consists of the following processes illustrated in Figure 6. Incoming text collections are parsed and annotated according to a dictionary of LATs, which consists of strings of English. This creates a set of annotated texts that are then routed to an analysis module. The analysis module first generate a two dimensional matrix that presents the frequencies of each LAT in individual

Figure 5. A histogram showing the distribution of English patterns according to their length (# of words), excluding the Time Duration LAT

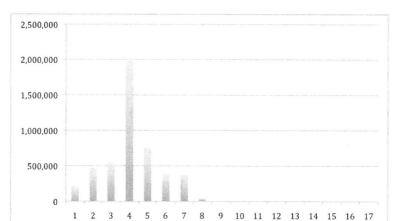

texts; then passes the matrix to a server running the statistical package R. The R server then runs a suite of multivariate statistical analyses, such as factor analysis, ANOVA, on the matrix. If the analyst is interested in comparing two or more text collections, factor analysis will identify a set of factors (i.e., groups of LATs) that differentiate the groups. If the analyst is interested in profiling

Figure 6. The DocuScope system

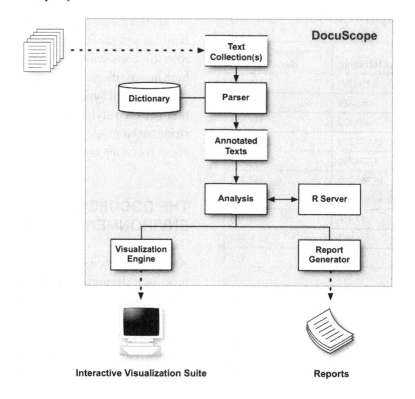

a single text collection, descriptive statistics can be used to examine the salient LATs present in the text collection. The analyst may also compare a single text collection against a know reference corpus, such as the Brown Corpus. The analysis module then uses a visualization engine and a report generator to create printable PDF reports of the statistical analyses. There is also a stand-alone interactive visualization suite that allows the investigator to visually inspect single and multiple annotated-documents using descriptive statistics (see Figure 7 for the multiple text visualization interface and Figure 9 for the single-text visualization interface). This interactive visualization suite proved crucial during the dictionary development process. The multi-text visualizations allowed us to quickly find specific text files that are high or low on a specific LAT, helping us examine the validity of the LAT. The single-text visualization allowed us to examine specific language actions found in a text file, allowing us to find erroneous classifications, or missing language actions that have not been included in the dictionaries.

APPLICATIONS

As we mentioned in the previous sections, DocuScope can be used with the large standard dictionary or a custom-built dictionary. In this section, we first introduce a series of applications best suited for this large knowledge source. We then present example research projects that are enabled by custom dictionaries.

Applications Using the Standard Dictionary

The pre-defined dictionary works reasonably well when the investigator is working with mature, established, or more or less uncontroversial textual groupings and seeks to understand the linguistic foundations underlying the different groups. What follows is a small inventory of research that fits this vein.

Figure 7. A multiple-text visualization of the self-representations of the English and Mechanical Engineering Faculties at Carnegie Mellon available on their homepages

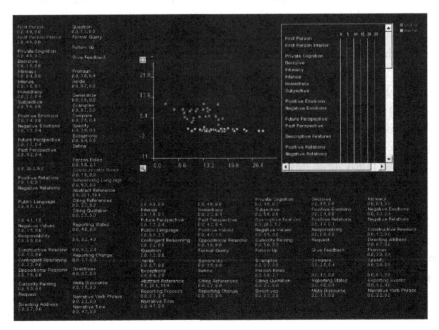

Comparing Self-Presentations of Faculty Members across Disciplines

Let us start with a simple and whimsical example. Faculty from different disciplines tend to create different self-representations of a career. A professor of English will tend to talk about her career in ways different from a professor of mechanical engineering. To explore this idea, we analyzed the language of the homepages of the faculties of English and computer science at Carnegie Mellon. The typical English professor described her career in terms of a first person autobiographical and narrative journey of questions and books written to explore these questions. Canonical language of the English professor is "In 1990, I published my first novel…I then wrote some essays about…" The typical professor of mechanical engineering marks her career through inventions made and patents given. The language is much more object-oriented description and information-dense reportage than first-person agent oriented and narrative. Figure 7 shows a multiple text visualization of the different faculty's homepages where they describe their careers. This visualization collapses an n-dimensional space onto two dimensions. On both the horizontal (X) and vertical (Y) axes, the investigator can activate LATs. When an LAT is activated, the texts containing strings within that LAT move right (on the X axis) or up (on the Y axis) to indicate their involvement in that language action type. In Figure 7, LATs associated with English professors (first person, first person autobiography, narrative) have been activated on the Y axis. LATs associated with the mechanical engineering professors (innovation, description, reportage) have been activated on the X axis. These settings create a 100% separation between the homepages, meaning that a discriminant line can be mathematically formulated that puts all the English homepages on one side of the line and all the homepages of mechanical engineers on the other. Although this example compares only

two text collections, DocuScope allows analysts to compare up to eight text collections.

Investigators may need to use trial and error to find the settings on the X and Y axis that give the best separation. However, Docuscope's automatic report function can help find these settings automatically by applying an inferential statistical technique, such as factor analysis, ANOVA, and Kolmogorov-Smirnov Test. For the study of English vs. Mechanical Professors' profiles, a bootstrapped version of the two sample Kolmogorov-Smirnov Test or KS test (Sekhon n.d.) was used. The two sample KS Test is a non parametric method for comparing the distributions of two data sets, and it allows us to find if one distribution is the same as, greater than, or lower than the other data set. In our system, this test allowed us to find the LATs that are significantly more frequent among the English professors' profiles compared to the Brown/Frown corpus, as well as the LATs that are significantly more frequent among the Mechanical Engineering Professors' profiles compared to the Brown/Frown corpus. By comparing the two results, we then find the LATs that are commonly frequent in both English and Mechanical Engineering professors' profiles.

Although this is a relatively simple example, Atkinson, Kaufer, and Ishizaki (2008) presented more serious research how comparing different modes of self-presentation can usefully extend Perelman's theory (Perelman & Olbrechts-Tyteca, 1969) of authorial presence in texts.

Studies of Arab American Press Coverage of "Arab Terrorism" Pre and Post-9/11

9/11 was a watershed event that made coverage of terrorism in the Arab American press likely to change. But did in fact the Arab American Press change its coverage of "Arab terrorism" before and after 9/11 and, if so, how were these changes reflected in the language of the coverage? Kaufer and Al-Malki (2007) used DocuScope's standard

Table 2. DocuScope's Tabular report on the Language of the professors of English and mechanical engineering. The LATs listed under the "English" column indicate LATs significantly more frequent in the language of the English professors than in the language of the mechanical engineers or the Brown/Frown Corpus. The LATs listed under the "Mechanical Engineering" column indicate LATs significantly more frequent in the language of the mechanical engineering professors than in the language of the English professors or in The Brown/Frown Corpus. The LATs listed under the "Common" column indicate LATs shared by both faculties that are significantly higher in frequency than in the Brown/Frown corpus.

English	Common	Mechanical Engineering
First Person Self-Disclosure Autobiography Communicator Role Language Reference	Commonplace Authority Abstract Concepts	Sense Objects Innovation Report Events Generic Events

dictionary to analyze a corpus of 113 news articles from the Detroit Arab press on terrorism, 56 prior to 9/11 and 57 afterward. They discovered that pre 9/11 texts were significantly more negative than post 9/11 texts. This finding at first seemed counterintuitive. However Kaufer and Al-Malki reported that pre 9/11, Arab American news stories took a skeptical attitude toward "Arab terrorism" and in these articles bitterly criticized American official's treatment of suspected terrorists. Post 9/11, however, Arab Americans faced extreme anti-Arab attitudes and featured many more stories touting Arab American patriotism and loyalty to the Bush administration.

Discovering the Linguistic Determinants of Well-Established Theories of Text Types

In 1995 Robert Hariman published a highly regarded theory of political styles that differentiated four specific styles and text types that exemplified them: Machiavellian, courtly, republican, and bureaucratic. While Hariman had some prototypical examples to illustrate these styles and conjectured several hypotheses about the language of these styles, he had yet to empirically test whether the language of these styles could be differentiated by compiling a corpus of texts representing these

styles. To see if Hariman's theoretical statements about his style could be sustained across a large corpus, Kaufer and Hariman (2008) compiled a corpus of 52 CEO profiles and corporate planning reports to represent the Machiavellian style; they compiled a corpus of 51 celebrity gossip articles to represent the courtly style; they compiled a corpus of 63 tax, regulatory and other government documents seeking compliance to represent bureaucratic writing; they compiled a corpus of 65 bipartisan and foundation reports to represent the republican style. Using the standard dictionary on the 231 total documents, Kaufer and Hariman (2007) were able to confirm many of Hariman's theoretical statements about his styles and even extend Hariman's theory with theoretical predictions that were consistent with but not articulated as part of his original theory.

Understanding Latent Rhetorical Strategies Being Sold When Commercial Publishers Sell Strategic Advice about Textual Strategies through Self-Help Writing Books

One interesting marketing phenomenon are the rise of commercial "how to" books that promise purchasers they will learn to write letters for "all occasions." Books of this kind provide templates for a variety of real world writing situations: making complaints, fielding complaints, offering congratulations, extending sympathy, resigning from a job, responding to a resignation, firing someone, giving thanks, fundraising, collecting money, making requests, and more. Kaufer and Ishizaki (2007) digitized 936 template letters across 15 categories in one best-selling book. Using the standard dictionary, they tagged and factor analyzed the book's writing templates and looked for the largest latent factors underlying the letters. They reasoned that these latent factors represented the hidden rhetorical strategies that were most consequential in the book's presentation. Indirectly, they were also the hidden strategies that were most likely available to and consequential to the book purchaser. Kaufer and Ishizaki found that, despite the book's touting it taught letters "for all occasions," the strategies taught were deeply weighted to support templates in two genres: collecting and fundraising. The books were essentially teaching letters that collected money or raised it. Further cultural research revealed that in a tight economy, the industries of collection and fundraising remain growth industries and so can help explain part of the market appeal of these self-help writing books.

Understanding Ethnic Differences within the Same Genre

Sometimes interesting comparisons can be made within a written genre. The Asian community in America is sometimes plagued by the "Model Minority" stereotype. Asians often feel plagued by the stereotype because it masks poverty, dropout rates, underemployment and unemployment in Asian communities. This is the stereotype that minorities can thrive without government help or support. While Asian-Americans are at the top of this stereotype, whether there might be some relationship between this stereotype and the way Indian Americans and African Americans portray themselves in "personal profiles," a genre inde-

pendently indexed by the database. Selecting 68 profiles from the Indian American community and 67 from the African American community (n = 135 profiles), Kaufer hypothesized that personal profiles emphasizing the model minority stereotype would focus on achievement and life inside the resume. Profiles at the other end of this stereotype would be more descriptive and create a balance between life outside as well as life inside the resume. Using the standard dictionary, Kaufer was able to confirm these hypotheses and then was able to set out to find why editors of the Indian magazines would perpetuate the model minority stereotype.

Auditing Writing Assignments in Writing Curricula to Make Sure That the Assignments Offer Non-Redundant Challenges

The archival dictionaries can be used to investigate student writing to make sure the learning goals promised in the syllabus show up in the actions-on-the-ground that students in fact take. Kaufer, Ishizaki, Collins, Vlachos (2004) showed how this method could be used to audit writing assignments in an advanced writing course for masters students. Kaufer, Geisler, Vlachos, and Ishizaki (2006) used the same technique to audit the major assignments of a freshman writing program at Carnegie Mellon.

Applications with Custom-Built Dictionaries

In many instances, investigators do not start with stable textual groupings. In these contexts, investigators have used DocuScope as a qualitative exploratory tool to discover concepts of interest and then to build custom dictionaries based on these concepts. Building customized dictionaries follows a systematic iterative process. Close reading of the texts leads to an initial categorization of LATs and strings. These categorizations and

Figure 8. The iterative process by which dictionaries are built

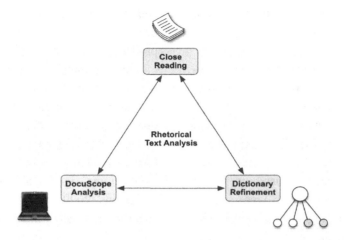

strings are then subjected to testing on unread texts using DocuScope's parser. The results are then inspected and evaluated through close reading and DocuScope's single text visualization environment and the process continues for as many

generations needed until the categories stabilize. The process is illustrated in Figure 8. DocuScope's single text visualization environment is illustrated in Figure 9.

Figure 9. An illustration of single-text visualization within DocuScope. LATs appear on the left hand panel and can be turned on or off, which causes the matching strings in the text (right hand panel) to appear or disappear. In this diagram, all the LATs are turned on and so the text on the right appears as a dense map of underlined strings.

Let us briefly consider some research projects that relied on customized dictionaries built from the DocuScope environment.

- **Dimensionalizing unidimensional stereotypical binaries about an ethnic group from textual data.** Although Western social science has demonstrated that Western journalism has traditionally portrayed Arab women as "passive," most of these studies have focused on image bites of veiled women who were spoken for rather than playing speaking roles. The active-passive dichotomy is not well-developed for textual data. Using a database of 22 months of stories about Arab women from the Arab press in translation, Al-Malki, Kaufer, Ishizaki, and Dreher (2010) have used DocuScope's environment to dimensionalize what it means for Arab women to act actively or passively in reported news. Kaufer and Al-Malki (2009) were able to show that the western press broke stereotypical coverage of Saudi women when the women being covered were influential trend-setters.
- **Developing verbal profiles of parents and teens in medical focus group transcripts.** Using a corpus of parent and teen focus group data on sexually transmitted disease, Akers, Kaufer, Ishizaki, Seltman, Greenhouse (in progress) used the DocuScope environment to create a typology of fathers toward daughters, dating behavior, and disease. They were not only able to distinguish nostalgic, prescriptive, and nurturing fathers, but also the different recurrent patterns associated with each type.

CONCLUSION

In this chapter, we have presented an overview of the DocuScope environment, including our moti-

vations, design rationales, theoretical foundation, and applications. The project has covered much ground so far, but remains a developing work in progress.

One ongoing issue stems from the tradeoff we made to build a system based on dictionaries that must be manually developed. We relied on human-crafted dictionaries to capture the interface between language and culture. It has been estimated that over 70% of language stems from idioms, figures, and other formulas (Wray & Perkins, 2000). Most if not all are culturally specific, and based in history within a specific community of language users. This makes any dictionary system, even if maintained in an orderly database, a work of. Thus, it is challenging to conduct empirical tests directly on the validity of our dictionary classifications without entering the can of worms that linguists enter when they seek empirical tests of native speaker intuitions of grammaticality. We currently deal with this issue by taking a statistical approach that relies on the accuracy of large numbers. Our dictionaries may contain certain amount of noise on various local matches, yet they tend to uncover the overall impression of reader experience rather accurately at the granularity of the whole text, and even more so when describing a text collection.

Another approach to manage the issue associated with hand-crafted dictionaries is to build social organizations around the development of dictionaries. Such would be a rhetorical cousin of what George Miller and the WordNet group at Princeton (Miller, 1995) did for organizing lexicographers to build purely semantic dictionaries. The development of such social organization for refining the classification of language patterns will eventually lead to the development of more accurate and stable dictionary.

Finally, because dictionaries in our environment capture the deep intuitions of the native speaker, transferring our dictionaries to other languages is a particularly time-consuming process. While translating our dictionaries into other languages is time-consuming, we are working with native speakers of Arabic to create Arabic and version of the environment. Our preliminary studies suggest that that most of our rhetorical categories for English transfer into Arabic language. Having different language versions of DocuScope available will also allows us to investigate how well the tool supports the analysis of non-English languages as well as translations.

REFERENCES

Akers, A., Kaufer, D., Ishizaki, S., Seltman, H., & Greenhouse, J. (2009). *Computer-based methods for analyzing the language of medical focus groups. Technical report.* University of Pittsburgh Medical School.

Al-Malki, A., Kaufer, D., Ishizaki, S., & Kira Dreher. (manuscript). *Old stereotypes in new media: Active/passive images of Arab women in translated news.*

Anthony, L., & Lashkia, G. (2003). Mover: A machine learning tool to assist in the reading and writing of technical papers. *IEEE Transactions on Professional Communication, 46*, 185–193. doi:10.1109/TPC.2003.816789

Argamon, S., Whitelaw, C., Chase, P., & Hota, S. R. (2007). Stylistic text classification using functional lexical features. *Journal of the American Society for Information Science and Technology, 58*(6). doi:10.1002/asi.20553

Atlas.Ti. (2007). *Computer program*, version 5.2. Berlin, Germany.

Burstein, J., Marcu, D., & Knight, K. (2003). Finding the WRITE stuff: Automatic identification of discourse structure in student essays. *IEEE Intelligent Systems: Special Issue on Advances in Natural Language Processing, 18*(1), 32–39.

Collins, J. (2003). *Variations in written English: Characterizing the authors' rhetorical language choices across corpora of published texts.* PhD thesis, Carnegie Mellon University.

Ellis, N. C., & Ferreira-Junior, F. (2009). Construction learning as a function of frequency, frequency distribution, and function. *Modern Language Journal, 93*, 370–385. doi:10.1111/j.1540-4781.2009.00896.x

Geisler, C. (2003). *Analyzing streams of language: Twelve steps to the systematic coding of text, talk, and other verbal data.* New York, NY: Longman.

Hart, R. P. (2001). *Diction 5.0 (computer software)*. Thousand Oaks, CA: Sage.

Hoey, M. (2005). *Lexical priming: A new theory of words and language.* London, UK: Routledge.

Ishizaki, S. (2009). *Toward a unified theory of verbal-visual strategies in communication design.* Best Paper. IEEE International Professional Communication Conference. Hawaii, July 19-22.

Kaufer, D. 2000. *Flaming: A white paper.* Retrieved from www.eudora.com.

Kaufer, D. (2006). Genre variation and minority ethnic identity: Exploring the personal profile in Indian American community publications. *Discourse & Society, 17*(6), 761–784. doi:10.1177/0957926506068432

Kaufer, D., & Al-Malki, A. (2009). A first for women in the kingdom: Arab/west representations of female trendsetters in Saudi Arabia. *Journal of Arab and Muslim Media Research, 2*(2), 113–133. doi:10.1386/jammr.2.1and2.113/1

Kaufer, D., & Al-Malki, A. M. (2009). The war on terror through Arab-American eyes: The Arab-American press as a rhetorical counterpublic. *Rhetoric Review, 28*(1), 47–65. doi:10.1080/07350190802540724

Kaufer, D., & Butler, B. (1996). *Rhetoric and the arts of design.* Mahwah, NJ: Lawrence Erlbaum and Associates.

Kaufer, D., & Butler, B. (2000). *Designing interactive worlds with words: Principles of writing as representational composition*. Mahwah, NJ: Lawrence Erlbaum and Associates.

Kaufer, D., Geisler, C., Ishizaki, S., & Vlachos, P. (2005). Computer-support for genre analysis and discovery in ambient intelligence for scientific discovery. In Cai, Y. (Ed.), *Ambient intelligence for scientific discovery* (pp. 129–151). New York, NY: Springer. doi:10.1007/978-3-540-32263-4_7

Kaufer, D., & Hariman, R. (2008). A corpus analysis evaluating Hariman's theory of political style. *Text & Talk*, *28*(4), 475–500.

Kaufer, D., & Ishizaki, S. (2006). A corpus study of canned letters: Mining the latent rhetorical proficiencies marketed to writers in a hurry and non-writers. *IEEE Transactions on Professional Communication*, *40*(3), 254–266. doi:10.1109/TPC.2006.880743

Kaufer, D., Ishizaki, S., Butler, B., & Collins, J. (2004). *The power of words: Unveiling the speaker and writer's hidden craft*. Mahwah, NJ: Lawrence Erlbaum and Associates.

Kaufer, D., Ishizaki, S., Collins, J., & Vlachos, P. (2004). Teaching language awareness in rhetorical choice using IText and visualization in classroom genre assignments. *Journal for Business and Technical Communication*, *18*(3), 361–402. doi:10.1177/1050651904263980

Klein, H. Klein H. (2009). *Text analysis info: Category systems*. Retrieved August 18, 2009, from http://www.textanalysis.info.

McCarthy, P. M., Graesser, A. C., & McNamara, D. S. (2006, July). *Distinguishing genre using Coh-Metrix indices of cohesion*. Paper presented at the Society for Text and Discourse Conference, Minneapolis, MN.

Miller, G. A. (1995). WordNet: A lexical database for English. *Communications of the ACM*, *38*(11), 39–41. doi:10.1145/219717.219748

Ong, W. (2004). *Ramus, method, and the decay of dialogue: From the art of discourse to the art of reason*. Chicago, IL: University of Chicago Press. (Original work published 1958)

Pennebaker, J. W., Booth, R. J., & Francis, M. E. (2007). *Linguistic inquiry and word count: LIWC*. Austin, TX: LIWC. Retrieved August 18, 2009 from www.liwc.net.

Perelman, C., & Olbrechts-Tyteca, L. (1969). *The new rhetoric: A treatise on argumentation*. South Bend, IN: Notre Dame Press.

Popping, R. (2000). *Computer-assisted text analysis*. Thousand Oaks, CA: Sage.

Richards, L. (1999). *Using NVivo in qualitative research*. London, UK: Sage.

Sekhon, J. (n.d.). *Bootstrap Kolmogorov-Smirnov*. Retrieved on March 28, 2010, from http://sekhon.berkeley.edu/matching/ks.boot.html.

Stein, B., & Eissen, M. (2008). Retrieval models for genre classification. *Scandinavian Journal of Information Systems*, *20*(1).

Witmore, M., & Hope, J. (2007). Shakespeare by the numbers: On the linguistic texture of the late plays. In Mukherji, S., & Lyne, R. (Eds.), *Early modern tragicomedy* (pp. 133–153). Cambridge, UK: D.S. Brewer.

Wray, A., & Perkins, M. (2000). The functions of formulaic language: An integrated model. *Language & Communication*, *20*, 1–28. doi:10.1016/S0271-5309(99)00015-4

ADDITIONAL READING

Altenberg, B. (1990). Speech as linear composition. In G. Caie, K. Haastrup, A. L. Jakobsen, A. L. Nielsen, J. Sevaldsen, H. Specht, & A. Zettersten (Eds.), Proceedings from the Fourth Nordic Conference for English Studies, Vol 1. (pp. 133-143). Copenhagen: University of Copenhagen.

Bainton, G. (1890). (Ed.), The art of authorship: Literary reminiscences, methods of work, and advice to young beginners, personally contributed by leading authors of the day. New York: D. Appleton and Company, 1890.

Bazerman, C. (1994). Systems of genres and the enactment of social intentions. In Freedman, A., & Medway, P. (Eds.), *Genre and the New Rhetoric* (pp. 79–101). London, UK: Taylor & Francis.

Bell, M. S. (1997). *Narrative design: A writer's guide to structure.* New York, NY: Norton.

Berkenkotter, C., & Huckin, T. (1995). *Genre knowledge in disciplinary communication: cognition/culture/power.* Mahwah, NJ: Lawrence Erlbaum & Associates.

Biber, D. (1988). *Variation across speech and writing.* Cambridge, UK: Cambridge University Press.

Biber, D., & Conrad, S. (2004). Cortes. V. *If you look at ...:* lexical bundles in University teaching and textbooks. *Applied Linguistics, 25*(3), 371–405. doi:10.1093/applin/25.3.371

Biber, D., Conrad, S., & Reppen, R. (1998). *Corpus linguistics: Investigating language structure and use.* Cambridge, UK: Cambridge University Press.

Burke, K. (1969). *Rhetoric of motives. Berkeley, CA: University of California Press.* Cambridge, MA: Harvard University Press.

Chafe, W. (1994). *Discourse, consciousness, and time: The flow and displacement of conscious experience in speaking and writing.* Chicago, IL: University of Chicago Press.

Channell, J. (2000). Corpus-based analysis of evaluative lexis. In Hunston & Thompson (Eds.), Evaluation in text: Authorial stance and the construction of discourse (pp. 38-55). Oxford, UK: Oxford University Press.

Clark, H. (1996). *Using language.* Cambridge, UK: Cambridge University Press.

Collins, J., Kaufer, D., Vlachos, P., Butler, B., & Ishizaki, S. (2004). Detecting collaborations in text. Comparing the authors' rhetorical language choices in the federalist papers. *Computers and the Humanities, 15*(1), 15–36. doi:10.1023/B:CHUM.0000009291.06947.52

Coulson, R., & Oakley, A. (2000). Blending basics. *Cognitive Linguistics, 11*, 175–196. doi:10.1515/cogl.2001.014

Crismore, A. (1989). *Talking with readers: Metadiscourse as rhetorical act.* New York, NY: Peter Lang Publishing.

Ellis, N. C. (2007). Implicit and explicit knowledge about language. In J. Cenoz & N. H. Hornberger (Eds.) *Encyclopedia of Language and Education, Second Edition, Volume 6: Knowledge about Language* (pp. 119-132). Springer.

Ellis, N. C. (2008). Phraseology: The periphery and the heart of language. Preface to F. Meunier and S. Granger (Eds.), *Phraseology in language learning and teaching, pp. 1-13.* Amsterdam: John Benjamins.

Ellis, N. C. (in press). Construction learning as category learning. In Pütz, M., & Sicola, L. (Eds.), *Inside the Learner's Mind: Cognitive Processing and Second Language Acquisition.* Amsterdam: John Benjamins.

Ellis, N. C., & Frey, E. (2009). The Psycholinguistic Reality of Collocation and Semantic Prosody (2): Affective Priming. In R. Corrigan, E. Moravcsik, H. Ouali & K. Wheatley (Eds.) *Formulaic Language* (pp. 473-497). Typological Studies in Language. Amsterdam: John Benjamins.

Ellis, N. C., Frey, E., & Jalkanen, I. (2009). The Psycholinguistic Reality of Collocation and Semantic Prosody (1): Lexical Access. In U. Römer & R. Schulze, (Eds.) *Exploring the Lexis-Grammar Interface* (pp. 89-114). Studies in Corpus Linguistics. Amsterdam: John Benjamins.

Ellis, N. C., & Simpson-Vlach, R. (2009). Formulaic language in native speakers: Triangulating psycholinguistics, corpus linguistics, and education. *Corpus Linguistics and Linguistic Theory, 5,* 61–78. doi:10.1515/CLLT.2009.003

Fairclough, N. (1989). *Language and power.* London, UK: Longman.

Fauconnier, G. (1994). *Mental Spaces: Aspects of Meaning Construction in Natural Language.* New York, NY: Cambridge University Press. doi:10.1017/CBO9780511624582

Fauconnier, G. (1997). *Mappings in Thought and Language.* New York, NY: Cambridge University Press.

Fauconnier, G., & Turner, M. (1998). Conceptual Integration Networks. *Cognitive Science, 22,* 133–187. doi:10.1207/s15516709cog2202_1

Freedman, A., & Medway, P. (1994). Locating genre studies: Antecedents and prospects. In Freedman, A., & Medway, P. (Eds.), *Genre and the new rhetoric* (pp. 1–22). London, UK: Taylor & Francis.

Halliday, M. A. K. (1994). *An Introduction to functional grammar* (2nd ed.). London, UK: Edward Arnold.

Halliday, M. A. K., & Hasan, R. (1976). *Cohesion in English.* London, UK: Longman.

Halliday, M. A. K., & Matthieson, C. (1999). *Construing experience through meaning.* New York, NY: Cassell.

Hart, R. (2000). *Campaign talk: Why elections are good for us.* Princeton, NJ: Princeton University Press.

Hopper, P., & Thompson, S. (1980). Transitivity in grammar and discourse. *Language, 56*(2), 251–299. doi:10.2307/413757

Hopper, P., & Traugott, E. (1993). *Grammaticalization (Cambridge Textbooks in Linguistics).* Cambridge, UK: Cambridge University Press.

Hunston, S., & Thompson, (Eds.). (2000). Evaluation in text: Authorial stance and the construction of discourse. New York, NY: Oxford University Press.

Hyland, K. (2000). *Disciplinary discourses: Social interactions in academic writing.* New York, NY: Longman.

Hyland, K. (2001). Bringing in the reader: Addressee features in academic article. *Written Communication, 18,* 549–574. doi:10.1177/0741088301018004005

Jackendoff, R. (1999). The representational structures of the language faculty and their interactions. In Brown, C. M., & Hagoort, P. (Eds.), *The neurocognition of language* (pp. 37–71). Oxford, UK: Oxford University Press.

Johnstone, B. (2002). *Discourse analysis.* London, UK: Blackwell.

Kucera, H., & Francis, W. (1967). *Computational analysis of present-day American English.* Providence, RI: Brown University Press.

Langacker, R. (1987). Foundations of Cognitive Grammar: *Vol. 1. Theoretical Prerequisites.* Stanford, CA: Stanford University Press.

Manning, C. D., & Schutze, H. (2001). *Foundations of statistical natural language processing.* Cambridge, MA: MIT Press.

Olson, D. (1994). *The world on paper.* New York: Cambridge University Press.

Parsons, T. (1990). *Events in the semantics of English: A study in subatomic semantics.* Cambridge, MA: MIT Press.

Perelman, C., & Olbrechts-Tyteca, L. (1969). *The new rhetoric: A treatise on argumentation* (Wilkinson, J., & Weaver, P., Trans.). South Bend: Notre Dame Press.

Roberts, C. (1997). A theoretical map for selecting among text analysis methods. In Roberts, C. (Ed.), *Text Analysis for the social sciences* (pp. 275–283). Mahwah, NJ: Lawrence Erlbaum Associates.

Scott, M. (1998). *The WordSmith Program*. Oxford, UK: Oxford University Press.

Sinclair, J. M. (1991). *Corpus, concordance, collocation*. New York, NY: Oxford University Press.

Sinclair, J. M. (Ed.). (1995). *Collins COBUILD English dictionary*. London, UK: HarperCollins.

Swales, J. (1990). *Genre analysis. Analysing academic and research texts*. Cambridge, UK: Cambridge University Press.

KEY TERMS AND DEFINITIONS

Custom-Built Dictionaries: Compilations of language categories and words and phrases filling them that investigators select to meet the demands of their own theoretical focus and inquiry.

Dictionary-Based Text Analysis/Coding: Systems that incorporate human selected words and phrases for use in the statistical analysis of tests.

Machine-Learning Based Text Coding: Systems that learn to extend the annotations started by human selection.

Pattern-Based Language Learning: The idea that language is not learned one word or at a time or as full sentence grammar. Rather language learners are exposed to millions of 2-5 word patterns (word sequences) and these become a cultural repository of meaning making. The meanings of individual words on this theory (e.g., smear) fall out from the various contributions the word makes to the expressions in which it participates (e.g., smear a politician, smear soap).

Rhetorical Language Theory: In the context of this chapter, it is a view of language that associates language categories with audience experience and effect. Coupled with pattern-based language learning, this view accounts for the fact that greater control and fluency of the patterns of a language coincide with the ability of the language user to shape the experience of listeners/readers in purposeful ways. The standard dictionaries of the DocuScope environment are based in rhetorical language theory.

Standard Dictionary: Words and phrases that follow a certain theory or orientation to language that users inherit when they use a system and its archive.

Visualizations: Visualizations provides the equivalent of a jeweler's "loupe" so that the investigator can understand and evaluate the results of DocuScope analyses. In the context of user-defined custom dictionaries, visualizations help the investigator construct the theory of language, the categories of the theory, and the strings that fill in the categories.

ENDNOTE

[1] Both authors contributed equally to this manuscript. The order of authorship is alphabetical.

Section 3
New Research in ANLP

Chapter 17
The Writing-Pal:
Natural Language Algorithms to Support Intelligent Tutoring on Writing Strategies

Danielle S. McNamara
Arizona State University, USA

Roxanne Raine
The University of Memphis, USA

Rod Roscoe
Arizona State University, USA

Scott A. Crossley
Georgia State University, USA

G. Tanner Jackson
Arizona State University, USA

Jianmin Dai
Arizona State University, USA

Zhiqiang Cai
The University of Memphis, USA

Adam Renner
The University of Memphis, USA

Russell Brandon
Arizona State University, USA

Jennifer L. Weston
Arizona State University, USA

Kyle Dempsey
Mississippi University for Women, USA

Diana Carney
The University of Memphis, USA

Susan Sullivan
The University of Memphis, USA

Loel Kim
The University of Memphis, USA

Vasile Rus
The University of Memphis, USA

Randy Floyd
The University of Memphis, USA

Philip M. McCarthy
The University of Memphis, USA

Arthur C. Graesser
The University of Memphis, USA

ABSTRACT

The Writing-Pal (W-Pal) is an intelligent tutoring system (ITS) that provides writing strategy instruction to high school students and entering college students. One unique quality of W-Pal is that it provides feedback to students' natural language input. Thus, much of our focus during the W-Pal project has

DOI: 10.4018/978-1-60960-741-8.ch017

been on Applied Natural Language Processing (ANLP). This chapter describes W-Pal and various NLP projects geared toward providing automated feedback to students' writing during writing strategy training and practice.

INTRODUCTION

Our motivation to develop W-Pal rests on two underlying assumptions. First, we assume that writing well is important to academic as well as professional success (Geiser & Studley, 2001; Light, 2001; Sharp, 2007). Writing skills allow individuals to articulate ideas, argue opinions, and synthesize multiple perspectives. Effective writing is essential to communicating persuasively with others, including teachers, peers, colleagues, co-workers, and the community at large (Connor, 1987; Crowhurst, 1990; National Commission on Writing, 2004).

Second, we assume that strategies facilitate performance on tasks, and that teaching students to use strategies can hasten the acquisition of skills (McNamara, 2009). Strategies have been found to facilitate and enhance performance on a variety of learning-related tasks, which leads to the expectation that the same might be found for writing. Many students lack the skills necessary to successfully communicate in writing. For example, the 2002 NAEP report (Institute of Education Sciences, 2003) indicated that more than two thirds of American students scored *below* their proficiency levels in writing assignments (4th graders: 72%; 8th graders: 69%; 12th graders: 79% below proficiency appropriate for their grade level). In addition, only 2% of the students in these three sample grades wrote at advanced levels. We believe that the solution lies not in continuing to correct their grammar and spelling (Shaughnessy, 1977), but rather in teaching students powerful writing strategies that scaffold them toward more effective written communication, meeting a wide array of writing needs applicable to many writing genres.

The difference between skills and strategies is central to understanding the purpose and intent of W-Pal. Skills are acquired through *deliberate* practice over long periods of time (Ericsson, 2006). For example, reading skills are acquired from very early childhood to young adulthood (Ericsson & Kintsch, 1995). Like reading skills, writing skills also take time to acquire. Skilled writers have likely engaged in extensive deliberate practice, received feedback on their work, and have likely written for a wide variety of genres (e.g., essays, letters, summaries, short responses, etc.). Through these experiences, children slowly acquire the necessary skills to be successful writers. For example, the use of correct grammar is gained through extensive instruction, practice, and feedback. Likewise, correct spelling is based on a relatively stable body of knowledge, constructed over time, again with extensive instruction, exposure, practice, and feedback. Correct grammar and spelling cannot come from a simple mnemonic or a couple of hours of practice. Hence, grammar and spelling are considered skills, and are, by consequence, not a focus of W-Pal. By contrast, *freewriting* is a strategy that can be taught and practiced relatively quickly (and refined over time through practice). Similarly, there are strategies to help students plan, construct, assess, and revise their writings. These strategies are rules of thumb, short-cuts, and mnemonics that can help less skilled students to compensate for their weaknesses in the short term and become skilled writers in the long term.

AN OVERVIEW OF W-PAL

W-Pal consists of two principle components: *Strategy Training* and *Essay Writing*. The Strategy

Training Component includes lessons that correspond to the three phases of the writing process: *Prewriting*, *Drafting*, and *Revising*. Training modules are provided for strategies that facilitate each phase of writing. Prewriting modules include (a) Freewriting, and (b) Planning. Drafting strategies include (a) Introduction Building (b) Body Building, and (c) Conclusion Building. The revising strategies include (a) Paraphrasing, (b) Cohesion Building, and (e) overall Revising of the text. Thus, there are eight strategy training modules, in addition to a Prologue Module that introduces the students to the program. W-Pal lessons are presented by three pedagogical agents, Dr. Julie, a teacher agent, and Sheila and Mike, two student agents. The student agents learn the strategies from Dr. Julie, engage in discussions and ask questions about the strategies. For example, in Figure 1, Dr. Julie (on the left) is explaining the importance of writing skills to Sheila and Mike. Each module consists of an introductory lesson and several guided practice activities.

The second component of W-Pal is the Essay Writing module. In this module, students write complete essays and are provided with feedback on the essay and suggestions to use particular strategies to improve the essay. The students can view particular modules and choose to write complete essays at any time. Although there is an implicit, recommended sequence for these modules, the students are not obligated to complete the modules in any particular order.

Essay Genre

W-Pal targets the needs of high school students, who are often required to write short prompt-based essays as a means toward the fulfillment of college and university entrance requirements. The following are examples of prompts used for these types of essays:

- **Example Prompt 1.** Many people believe that to move up the ladder of success and achievement, they must forget their past, repress it, and let it go. But others have just the opposite view. They see their old memories as a chance to reckon with their past

Figure 1. The Prologue discusses how writing skills are beneficial within the classroom and beyond

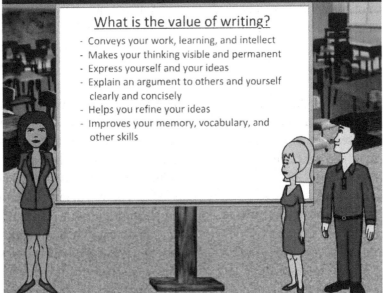

and integrate past and present. Do personal memories hinder or help people in their effort to learn from their past and succeed in the present?

- **Example Prompt 2.** The arts—literature, music, painting, and other creative activities—are considered important by some but not by others. Many people consider the arts unnecessary because they provide us with nothing more than entertainment. Yet, others believe that the arts are extremely valuable because they teach us about the world around us and help people find meaning in life. What is the main value of the arts in society today?

Typically, prompt-based essays are *persuasive* (argue for one side of an issue), relatively short (they must be written under time constraints of 20-25 minutes), and source-independent (students are not allowed access to external references). These essays have an archetypal structure of an introduction paragraph, approximately three body paragraphs, and a conclusion paragraph (Albertson, 2007; Myers, McCarthy, Duran, & McNamara, in press). W-Pal focuses on this genre of essay for a number of reasons: secondary school educators tend to cover this kind of essay in their curriculum, college entrance exams such as the SAT usually require this type of essay, and professionals benefit from skills with writing these persuasive essays. In addition, strategies for this genre of essay are basic: they are applicable to virtually all genres of essays. Although W-Pal is intended for high school students, the writing strategies that W-Pal teaches are sufficiently general to be applicable and effective for a wide range of audiences.

Underlying Principles and Structure

W-Pal was founded on the successful implementation of the intelligent tutoring system, iSTART, which was developed to teach *reading* strategies

to high school students (McNamara, Levinstein, & Boonthum, 2004). Like iSTART, W-Pal focuses on a set of well documented strategies that are taught by pedagogical agents who guide the student through presentation and practice sessions. W-Pal modules follow the three heuristics that are used in iSTART (McNamara, O'Reilly, Rowe, Boonthum, & Levinstein, 2007). The first is that to-be-learned information needs to be presented, modeled, and practiced following a *faded scaffolding model* (Collins, Brown, & Newman, 1989; McNamara et al., 2007; Rogoff, 1990). The second is that of vicarious learning (Bandura, 1997; Craig, Graesser, Sullins, & Gholson, 2004; Zimmerman & Risemberg, 1997), whereby the learning process is modeled by animated pedagogical agents. The third is that the modules are interactive, eliciting responses from and holding interactive dialogues with the student. As such, computational linguistic algorithms are needed to guide the interactions with the students and to provide adaptive feedback. These heuristics help to ensure that the system induces self-reflective, generative, and metacognitive learning on the part of the students.

Lesson content within W-Pal is based on English Composition curricula and is designed to provide the users with strategies that will help students to compose a persuasive essay. The scripts for the interactions were developed through a collaborative process between ITS experts and composition experts. The lessons average about 20-30 minutes in length, and are accompanied by an introductory text and a summary text that compliment the videos in two ways: They allow teachers to have paper copies of the lessons, and they also allow the students to review the lessons without necessarily re-watching the interactive videos. The W-Pal interface also contains a notepad feature that allows students to digitally record information within the program. The lessons are presented in the contexts of a virtual classroom. This classroom features a whiteboard to present information as the students and teacher describe it during discussion. The lessons are created through a combination of Media Semantics Character Builder and Loquendo Text-to-Speech Engine. The whiteboard information is created within the Character Builder software or inserted from slides designed in Microsoft PowerPoint.

Lessons are interspersed with brief *checkpoints*. Throughout the lessons, students practice the strategies by completing brief exercises (i.e., *checkpoints*) and completing practice modules (i.e., *challenges*). Checkpoints are brief probes, multiple choice questions, tasks, or mini-games inserted into the lessons that help to maintain student engagement, discourage passive viewing, and provide reinforcement of learning through multiple testing opportunities. Challenges are longer than checkpoints and are intended to be accessed after the corresponding lesson has been completed. To potentially enhance student engagement, all of the challenges are designed as games (McNamara, Jackson, & Graesser, 2010). Many of the challenge practices parallel the structure of one or more of a lesson's corresponding checkpoints. The following are brief descriptions of the W-Pal modules. In the section following, we describe our work to develop the NLP algorithms to support these modules.

W-PAL MODULES

Module 1: Prologue

The prologue module provides the context and purpose of the W-Pal training. During this module, the student agents express a general discontent with their writing grades and are concerned because they do not understand how to fix their problems. The teacher explains to them that she can help with their essays. She also explains how the ability to write well will help them in their lives in general (see Figure 1). The teacher explains the structure and purpose of a persuasive essay and then presents the strategies that the student will learn throughout the W-Pal program. These presentations are brief and merely offer an exposure to the strategies. Because the prologue module is intended to prepare the students for the content-based modules that follow, it does not contain any checkpoints or challenges. The remaining modules all contain checkpoints and challenges that allow the students to practice using the strategies.

Module 2: Freewriting

The Freewriting module provides strategies for establishing ideas before planning the essay. During freewriting, the student writes, without stopping, as much as possible in a given period of time (e.g., 5 minutes). Students are taught the mnemonic FAST PACE to facilitate the freewriting and idea generation process. The letters in FAST PACE stand for techniques that students can use to generate ideas: Find evidence, Ask and answer questions, Spell out your argument, Think about the other side, Re-read the Prompt, Add details, Connect ideas, and Provide more Examples. Freewriting helps writers generate ideas. Then, with a little organization after the freewrite, writers have a better idea of what they can write about, what they would need to learn more about, and what they should include in their essay.

Module 3: Planning

After freewriting, the student needs to plan the essay and choose the ideas that are most relevant to a chosen position. The planning module is designed to help the student visually: (1) establish a *position*, (2) establish *arguments* for that position, (3) establish *support* for the arguments, and (4) *integrate* these components into an organized structure. Students are exposed to a variety of ways to organize an essay and learn strategies that facilitate that process.

Module 4: Introduction Building

The goals of an essay introduction are to clearly state the position on the topic, provide a preview of the remainder of the essay, and to engage the reader's interest. The Introduction Building module includes the TAG strategy as a mnemonic device for required elements of a good introduction: a clear *Thesis* statement, a succinct preview of the main *Arguments* that will be explained in the body, and a stylistic technique that *Grabs* the reader's attention. The students also learn more specifically about *attention-grabbing* techniques to make their introduction more engaging, including: ask-a-question, historical review, set a scene, personal anecdote, and controversy.

Module 5: Body Building

Body paragraphs have two main features: A *topic sentence* and *evidence sentences*. The Body Building lesson teaches the mnemonic *Keep Initial Sentence Short (KISS) and tell*. Students should have a short topic sentence (KISS) that is explained further in their evidence sentences (tell). Evidence sentences are crucial to body paragraphs because they support the topic sentence. They are usually longer than topic sentences because it takes more words to explain than to state a claim. During this module, students learn how to build evidence sentences from outlined concepts. In this way, the student is scaffolded towards composing a body paragraph from outlines.

Module 6: Conclusion Building

Conclusions summarize and reiterate the author's position and major arguments, wrap up the essay, and do so in an engaging manner. The *RECAP* mnemonic helps students to keep track of these requirements: Good conclusions need to *Restate* the thesis of the essay, *Explain* how the arguments supported the thesis, *Close* the essay using a clos-

ing phrase (e.g., In conclusion), *Avoid* adding new arguments and information, and *Present* the conclusion in an interesting way. This module also describes four stylistic techniques that can be used to hold the reader's attention and conclude essays in a memorable way (i.e., personal anecdotes, further research, importance, and make a recommendation). These techniques are also intended to reduce writing anxiety, and help students wrap up an essay more easily.

Module 7: Paraphrasing

Paraphrasing is revision at the sentence level. Its primary purpose in the context of W-Pal is to improve writing. The central purpose of the lesson is for students to learn that a sentence can be written in many different ways. The lesson progresses through several paraphrasing techniques (e.g., changing words, changing structure, changing words and structure, and condensing sentences). Checkpoints prompt students to reflect on the many different ways a sentence can be reworded. During this lesson, students generate several paraphrases using different techniques, and afterwards they are shown expert paraphrases to reinforce the notion that there are multiple ways to word a sentence. This feedback also helps to demonstrate how the meaning of a sentence can be preserved despite changes in structure or wording.

Module 8: Cohesion Building

This module targets revision at the inter-sentential level. Coherence refers to the overall sense of unity in a text, which is achieved by clearly expressing the relationships between ideas in the text using cohesive devices. W-Pal provides instruction on three cohesion strategies for linking ideas across two or more adjacent sentences: Threading, This-and-That, and Connectives. *Threading* is the term used for linking sentences with common words or phrases; *This-and-That* refers to resolving ambiguity when using demonstratives (words that depend on an external frame of reference); and *Connectives* refers to the use of words that make explicit the logical relations between two clauses or sentences (e.g., *therefore*, *nevertheless*, *meanwhile*, etc.).

Module 9: Revising

The revising module targets revision at the global level. Students often see revision not as a chance to develop and improve a piece of writing, but merely to hastily correct any typos or cosmetic errors. Revision, however, is the very essence of the writing process. The primary purpose of this lesson is for students to learn the importance of getting a "big picture" view of the whole draft and to revise the entire draft to ensure the coherence of the essay. The ARMS mnemonic suggests courses of action students could take when revising an essay, including Adding, Removing, Moving, or Substituting ideas and text. The TETRIS mnemonic focuses on specific elements of the essay to assess: Thesis and conclusion, Evidence, Transitions and organization, Relevance, Interest, and Spelling and grammar. This helps students think critically about particular sections or qualities of the essay, and how each piece contributes to the essay.

Essay-Writing Component

The Essay Writing Component scaffolds the writing of complete compositions by providing feedback on a complete essay and suggestions on strategies that might help to improve the essay. The student is provided with an essay prompt (see Examples 1 and 2 earlier) and instructions to write a persuasive essay. After freewriting and planning, and writing an initial version of the essay, the student is provided with feedback coupled with suggestions to use corresponding strategies that they learned during the lessons.

NATURAL LANGUAGE PROCESSING IN W-PAL

The foundation of much of the NLP in W-Pal comes from Coh-Metrix. Coh-Metrix is an automated tool that provides indices on multiple linguistic features of language. This tool is described more fully in several other chapters within this volume (e.g., McNamara & Graesser, in press). It, as well as other similar tools developed in our laboratory, allow us to fully explore the linguistic features of writing.

Predicting the Quality of Essays

One of our goals in the W-Pal project has been to explore the extent to which linguistic features are predictive of the quality of essays. In the context of W-Pal, our overarching goal is to provide feedback to the students on their essays, particularly within the Essay Writing Component. Hence, a good deal of effort has been devoted toward the collection and NLP analyses of sample essays.

We have been particularly interested in the role of cohesion in the quality of essays. This interest is partially motivated by Coh-Metrix, which was developed expressly for that purpose: to provide indices on linguistic features associated with and indicative of text cohesion. Cohesion refers to the presence or absence of cues in the text that help the reader to infer relationships between ideas expressed in the text. These cues include referential overlap (words or ideas that are repeated across sentences or larger sections of text) and connectives (words such as *because*, *however*, and *therefore*, that express relationships between ideas). When there are more explicit cues, the text is considered higher in cohesion and is more easily understood by the reader (McNamara, 2001; McNamara, Louwerse, McCarthy, & Graesser, 2010). Likewise, many have assumed that cohesion plays an important role in writing (e.g., Collins, 1998; Connor, 1990; DeVillez, 2003; Witte

& Faigley, 1981). Better writing is assumed to be more cohesive and cohesive devices are assumed to be necessary elements of a text that afford effective communication and facilitate the goal of conveying a writer's arguments.

To explore these assumptions, McNamara, Crossley, and McCarthy (2010) analyzed a corpus of 120 argumentative essays written by college undergraduates and scored by expert raters. The essays were scored on a 1-6 scaled SAT rubric and then categorized as high or low quality essays. The results indicated that no indices of cohesion (e.g., word overlap, causality, connectives) were associated with differences between higher and lower quality essays. More specifically, the results indicated that high quality essays can be high or low in cohesion, and that low quality essays can be high or low in cohesion. In contrast, the indices that were found to be related to essay quality were those that render comprehension more, rather than less, challenging. These indices included lexical diversity, word frequency, and syntactic complexity. The essays were rated as being higher in quality when they had a greater variety of words, the words were less frequent in language (i.e., less familiar), and the syntax was more complex. These three indices accounted for 22 percent of the variance and within a discriminant analysis correctly classified 67 percent of the texts.

The results of the McNamara et al. (2010) study provided initial evidence that text cohesion may not be indicative of essay quality. That is, expert raters in the McNamara et al. study appear to judge texts that are more difficult to process as more proficient. This trend has also been found among second language (L2) writers. Crossley and McNamara (in press) examined the extent to which linguistic features predicted essays scores for 1200 L2 college level essays. The results, similar to those reported for L1 essays by McNamara et al., indicated that higher quality essays were more lexically diverse, composed of less familiar words, and were more syntactically complex. Indeed, indices of cohesion were negatively cor-

related with essay quality. The results indicated that higher proficiency L2 writers do not produce essays that are more cohesive and readable, but instead produce texts that are more linguistically complex.

These results prompted the question of whether providing training in W-Pal to be more cohesive might actually be detrimental to students' writing quality. Specifically, will recommendations to use connectives and to increase referential overlap actually decrease scores? We have explored this issue from two angles. The first was to verify that human ratings of essay coherence and continuity were positively related to essay quality. Indeed, Crossley and McNamara (2010) found that expert ratings of coherence and cohesion correlated .80 and .65 respectively with overall ratings of the essay quality. Interestingly, Coh-Metrix indices of cohesion were negatively related to expert's ratings of coherence. Thus, the absence of cohesive devices resulted in a more coherent mental representation of the text in the minds of the expert raters.

Our second approach was to examine the issue experimentally. The goal of the study (unpublished; see McNamara & CSEP Lab, 2010, project report) was to examine whether essays scores were positively influenced by two factors, cohesion and elaboration. These factors were manipulated experimentally, in contrast to the correlational approach used within the corpus studies. The 35 participants wrote two essays and were then asked to spend 15 minutes elaborating on the ideas in the essay. These four essays (2 original, 2 elaborated) were then modified by an experimenter in terms of cohesion by adding lexical coreference and conceptual overlap. Coh-Metrix scores confirmed that the cohesion manipulations were associated with increased scores on the indices related to cohesion. This produced a total of eight essays on two topics, with four versions per topic. Twelve trained raters evaluated the essays using a standardized rubric, with three raters assigned to each essay. The results of the study indicated that both manipulations improved essays scores. Having students elaborate their essays resulted in higher scores, and increasing the cohesion of students' essays resulted in higher essay scores. These results indicate that encouraging students to add to their essays will have positive benefits and also, providing instruction about cohesion and how to increase cohesion should have positive benefits.

In sum, Coh-Metrix cohesion scores are not related to essay quality but increasing cohesion is positively related to essay quality, and expert raters of essays consider higher quality essays to be more coherent and more cohesive. Our analyses indicating that the absence of cohesion potentially resulted in a more coherent representation for the expert raters might be interpreted within the *Reverse Cohesion* account of reading comprehension (e.g., O'Reilly & McNamara, 2007), according to which readers with more knowledge tend to make more inferences when reading text with cohesion gaps. However, this *Rater Inference account* could not at the same time explain the results of our experimental study in which manipulations of cohesion in the essays led to higher scores. Thus, it seems more likely that *cohesion* and *coherence* in essays emerge from different linguistic and semantic features. Our current focus in the W-Pal project is in solving this puzzle computationally. We expect that the solution lies in computational assessments of both the structure of the essay and semantic aspects of the essays, in conjunction with the linguistic features.

Predicting the Quality of Freewrites

While much of our effort has been devoted to computational analyses of essays, another focus has been on collecting and analyzing freewrites. One strategy to prepare to write an essay is to generate ideas using freewriting. Within the Freewriting module (see Figure 2), students practice freewriting in the context of a game called Freewrite Feud. The goal of the Freewrite Feud game is to type as much as possible and to include as many keywords as possible that overlap with the game's randomly chosen nine keywords. Points are awarded for the number of matching keywords and bonus points are awarded based on an NLP algorithm that assesses the quality of the freewrite.

The algorithm that assesses the freewrite within this module is based on a three large corpora of of freewrites assessed by expert raters (using a rubric specifically designed for freewrites). These corpora provide numerous examples of freewrites of differing quality that students can study as part of the lessons and practice activities. Analyses of these freewrites also contribute to indices and algorithms for assessing freewrite quality, length, and content diversity

Figure 2. In the final freewriting checkpoint, students generate freewrites for two minutes

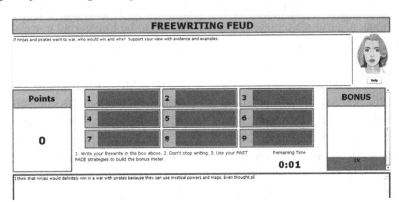

(Weston, Crossley & McNamara, 2010; Weston, Crossley, & McNamara, in press). A chapter in this volume describes one such study (Weston et al., in press). The results showed that many linguistic features positively correlated with the expert ratings of the freewrite, including referential cohesion, syntactic complexity, and lexical difficulty. However, within a regression analysis, the only significant predictors were the number of words and stem overlap. Based on this study, better freewrites seem to be characterized as being more cohesive and containing more words. Thus, whereas linguistic features associated with cohesion have not been found to be related to essay quality, this is not the case with regard to freewrite quality. Our future analyses will examine the relationships between freewrites and essays, and in particular whether certain features or qualities of freewrites are related to subsequent essay quality.

Predicting the Parts of Essays

A second goal in the W-Pal project has been to explore the extent to which linguistic features can differentiate between the parts of essays (i.e., introduction, body, conclusion) and are predictive of the quality of these parts. There are two aspects of W-Pal driving this work. First, the three drafting modules (Introduction Building, Body Building, and Conclusion Building) include challenges in which the students write parts of the essays. Second, during the Essay Writing Component of W-Pal, the students write complete essays. We need computational algorithms to assess the presence of these essay sections and their quality. The majority of this work is in progress; however, several studies have been completed that explore the ability of linguistic features in distinguishing between the parts of the essay (Dempsey, McCarthy, Myers, Weston, & McNamara, 2009; Crossley, Dempsey, & McNamara, submitted).

In the study reported by Crossley et al. (under review), 182 initial, middle, and final paragraphs

from student, argumentative essays were analyzed using Coh-Metrix. The paragraphs were classified by human raters based on paragraph type (introduction, body, conclusion). The eight indices found to significantly discriminate between the parts of the essays included measures of length, cohesion, and word difficulty. The performance of the reported model was well above chance and reported an accuracy of classification that was similar to human judgments of paragraph type (66% accuracy for human versus 65% accuracy for our model). The model's accuracy increased in analyses restricted to those paragraphs that were longer and provided more linguistic coverage and those paragraphs judged by human raters to be of higher quality. As the quality and length of the paragraph increased, the linguistic differences among paragraph types became more acute.

The results reported by Crossley et al. (under review) indicated that introductory paragraphs are shorter, include few cohesion cues, and include words that are more specific, meaningful, and imageable as compared to body and conclusion paragraphs. In comparison to conclusion paragraphs, the words in introductions are also less familiar. This combination of linguistic features results in a rhetorical structure that is less embedded syntactically than other paragraphs allowing for the production of a clear, direct main idea. Because the goal of an introduction paragraph is merely to state the main idea and the themes of the supporting arguments, the introduction does not depend on cohesion to produce a coherent structure. In contrast, body paragraphs were found to be longer and more cohesive compared to introductory and conclusion paragraphs. They also tended to include less imageable (abstract) words compared to introductions, but more imageable (concrete) words compared to conclusions. These linguistic features can be associated with the rhetorical purpose of body paragraphs (Grady, 1971). For instance, more words and higher cohesion support the assumption that body paragraphs feature a tighter coupling of ideas that expand on the supporting arguments introduced within the first paragraph. Unlike an introduction paragraph, body paragraphs elaborate ideas and thus likely do not rely on highly imageable words. The features of conclusion paragraphs also corresponded to the rhetorical purpose of final paragraphs to summarize the information in the essay without presenting new information (Grady, 1971). The process of summarization produces shorter paragraphs containing more connectives. The words used in the summarization are found to be less specific in nature, but also more familiar.

Our results thus far support the assumption that paragraph types contain specific linguistic features that allow them to be distinguished from one another. In addition, the corpora also provide stimuli for the modules in which the students distinguish between good and poor introductions and conclusions. Our current work is focused on expanding the linguistic and semantic features that are considered in order to predict the quality of the paragraphs. In sum, the research outlined in this chapter shows promise of being building blocks for the construction of a successful algorithm capable of assessing the quality of essay parts.

Anticipated Computational Approach within Essay Writing Component

Within the Essay Writing Component of W-Pal, the student writes a complete essay and receives feedback that scaffolds the use of W-Pal strategies to improve the essay. We are currently building this system. We anticipate that our approach to this computational challenge will be to use layered algorithms. First, the system will assess whether the essay is long enough. The first step to improving short essays is to write more. The strategies for writing more were covered within the Freewriting module (i.e., FAST PACE).

The second step will be to assess whether the essay contains enough paragraphs. First, the archetypical essay contains five paragraphs, and at the least contains an introduction, body, and

conclusion. Hence, if the student has not included enough paragraphs, a reminder can be provided to use strategies provided within the Planning Module, which covers the structure of the essay and how to organize the essay.

Once the essay is long enough and contains enough paragraphs, then the quality of the entire essay and the parts of the essay can be assessed. This assessment can be done in parallel. If the separate parts are not distinguishable in terms of their features or are low in quality, then the student will be advised to use strategies associated with the drafting modules. For example if the first paragraph does not have features associated with Introductions (as compared to Bodies and Conclusions) and does not have features associated with high quality introductions, the student would be reminded of the TAG strategy. If the algorithms indicated that the final paragraph did not contain features characteristic of good conclusions, then the student would be reminded of the RECAP strategy. At the same time, certain features may indicate that the essay is low in quality overall. If that were the case, the student might be reminded of strategies to revise the essay at the sentence (i.e., paraphrasing), paragraph (i.e., cohesion strategies), and global levels (e.g., the ARMS and TETRIS strategies). Of course, it is important not to overwhelm the student with suggestions and frustrate the student with too much negative feedback. Hence, after a few revisions, the student's essay would be considered complete and the student will be given an essay score. Across multiple essays, with greater practice in using the strategies, we expect the overall score for students' essays to increase. In time, no prompting to use the strategies should be necessary because the student would use them on the first attempt.

CONCLUSION

Our work on W-Pal has been primarily devoted to its design and the development of the architecture, the pedagogical content, and the NLP algorithms. The purpose of this chapter was to provide a brief overview of the system and to describe some of our ANLP efforts towards building an interactive ITS. We are currently conducting pilot tests and evaluations of the separate modules, which will prepare us for the overall empirical evaluation of the tutoring system in its entirety. This evaluation will comprise a year-long study of high-schools students who will work through the modules. We will observe the students' performance and compare their performance to students who do not receive writing tutoring. In order to optimize the efficacy and utility of this program, it is necessary to empirically examine a number of factors related to the lessons, interface and pedagogical material; and how those factors influence students' engagement in the tutoring system and their improvements in writing. Such studies will also allow us to refine our NLP algorithms. We expect to engage in numerous iterations to improve and refine our algorithms as well as how they are implemented in terms of feedback to the student writer.

The objectives of W-Pal are to improve high school students' writing abilities and reduce demands on teachers. The former objective should provide students with some of the tools necessary to become successful writers, whereas the latter will allow teachers more focused time with students. Both of these objectives contribute to a foundation for a better-prepared youth, because more adept writers have increased aptitude in career and personal success. It is also worth noting that the development of W-Pal's components will certainly have secondary benefits to a number of other professionals, including teachers, human-computer interaction researchers, gaming designers, education researchers, linguistics scientists, computer scientists, interface designers, as well as researchers working within the general framework of Applied Natural Language Processing.

REFERENCES

Albertson, B. R. (2007). Organization and development features of grade 8 and grade 10 writers: A descriptive study of Delaware Student Testing Program (DSTP) essays. *Research in the Teaching of English, 41*, 435–464.

Bandura, A. (1997). *Self-efficacy: The exercise of control*. New York, NY: Freeman.

Collins, A., Brown, J. S., & Newman, S. E. (1989). Cognitive apprenticeship: Teaching the craft of reading, writing, and mathematics. In Resnick, L. B. (Ed.), *Knowing, learning, and instruction: Essays in honor of Robert Glaser* (pp. 453–494). Hillsdale, NJ: Lawrence Erlbaum.

Collins, J. L. (1998). *Strategies for struggling writers*. New York, NY: Guilford Publications.

Connor, U. (1987). Research frontiers in writing analysis. *TESOL Quarterly, 21*, 677–696. doi:10.2307/3586989

Connor, U. (1990). Linguistic/rhetorical measures for international student persuasive writing. *Research in the Teaching of English, 24*, 67–87.

Craig, S. D., Graesser, A. C., Sullins, J., & Gholson, B. (2004). Affect and learning: An exploratory look into the role of affect in learning with AutoTutor. *Journal of Educational Media, 29*, 241–250. doi:10.1080/1358165042000283101

Crossley, S. A., Dempsey, K. B., & McNamara, D. S. (Manuscript submitted for publication). Classifying paragraph types using linguistic features: Is paragraph positioning important? *Research in the Teaching of English*.

Crossley, S. A., & McNamara, D. S. (2010). Cohesion, coherence, and expert evaluations of writing proficiency. In R. Catrambone & S. Ohlsson (Eds.), *Proceedings of the 32nd Annual Conference of the Cognitive Science Society*.

Crossley, S. A., & McNamara, D. S. (in press). Predicting second language writing proficiency: The role of cohesion, readability, and lexical difficulty. *Journal of Research in Reading*.

Crowhurst, M. (1990). Reading/writing relationships: An intervention study. *Canadian Journal of Education, 15*, 155–172. doi:10.2307/1495373

Dempsey, K. B., McCarthy, P. M., Myers, J. C., Weston, J., & McNamara, D. S. (2009). Determining paragraph type from paragraph position. In C. H. Lane & H. W. Guesgen (Eds.), *Proceedings of the 22nd International Florida Artificial Intelligence Research Society (FLAIRS) Conference* (pp. 33-38). Menlo Park, CA: The AAAI Press.

DeVillez, R. (2003). *Writing: Step by step*. Dubuque, IA: Kendall/Hunt Publishing Company.

Ericsson, K. A. (2006). The influence of experience and deliberate practice on the development of superior expert performance. In Ericsson, K. A., Charness, N., Feltovich, P., & Hoffman, R. R. (Eds.), *Cambridge handbook of expertise and expert performance* (pp. 685–706). Cambridge, UK: Cambridge University Press.

Ericsson, K. A., & Kintsch, W. (1995). Long-term working memory. *Psychological Review, 102*, 211–245. doi:10.1037/0033-295X.102.2.211

Geiser, S., & Studley, R. (2001, October). *UC and the SAT: Predictive validity and differential impact of the SAT I and SAT II at the University of California*. Paper presented at the Meeting of the Board of Admissions and Relations with Schools of the University of California.

Grady, M. (1971). A conceptual rhetoric of the composition. *College Composition and Communication, 22*, 348–354. doi:10.2307/356208

Institute of Education Sciences. (2003). *The nation's report card: Writing 2002*. NCES 2003-529. Retrieved from http://nces.ed.gov/nationsreportcard/pubs/main2002/2003529.asp.

Light, R. (2001). *Making the most of college*. Cambridge, MA: Harvard University Press.

McNamara, D. S. (2001). Reading both high and low coherence texts: Effects of text sequence and prior knowledge. *Canadian Journal of Experimental Psychology, 55*, 51–62. doi:10.1037/h0087352

McNamara, D. S. (2009). The importance of teaching reading strategies. *Perspectives on Language and Literacy, Spring*, 34-40.

McNamara, D. S., & CSEP Lab. (2010). *W-Pal: Writing Pal*. Annual project report submitted to the Institute of Education Sciences (IES).

McNamara, D. S., Crossley, S. A., & McCarthy, P. M. (2010). The linguistic features of quality writing. *Written Communication, 27*, 57–86. doi:10.1177/0741088309351547

McNamara, D. S., Jackson, G. T., & Graesser, A. C. (2009). Intelligent tutoring and games (iTaG). In H. C. Lane, A. Ogen, & V. Shute (Eds.), *Proceedings of the Workshop on Intelligent Educational Games at the 14th Annual Conference on Artificial Intelligence in Education* (pp. 1-10). Brighton, UK: AIED.

McNamara, D. S., Jackson, G. T., & Graesser, A. C. (in press). Intelligent tutoring and games (ITaG). In Baek, Y. K. (Ed.), *Gaming for classroom-based learning: Digital role-playing as a motivator of study*. Hershey, PA: IGI Global.

McNamara, D. S., Levinstein, I. B., & Boonthum, C. (2004). iSTART: Interactive strategy trainer for active reading and thinking. *Behavior Research Methods, Instruments, & Computers, 36*, 222–233. doi:10.3758/BF03195567

McNamara, D. S., Louwerse, M. M., McCarthy, P. M., & Graesser, A. C. (2010). Coh-Metrix: Capturing linguistic features of cohesion. *Discourse Processes, 47*, 292–330. doi:10.1080/01638530902959943

McNamara, D. S., O'Reilly, T., Rowe, M., Boonthum, C., & Levinstein, I. B. (2007). iSTART: A web-based tutor that teaches self-explanation and metacognitive reading strategies. In D. S. McNamara (Ed.), *Reading comprehension strategies: Theories, interventions, and technologies* (pp. 397-421). Mahwah, NJ: Erlbaum.

Myers, J. C., McCarthy, P. M., Duran, N. D., & McNamara, D. S. (in press). The bit in the middle and why it's important: A computational analysis of the linguistic features of body paragraphs. *Behavior Research Methods*.

National Commission on Writing. (2004). *Writing: A ticket to work... Or a ticket out, a survey of business leaders*. Retrieved from http://www.host-collegeboard.com/advocacy/writing/publications.html.

O'Reilly, T., & McNamara, D. S. (2007). Reversing the reverse cohesion effect: Good texts can be better for strategic, high-knowledge readers. *Discourse Processes, 43*, 121–152.

Rogoff, B. (1990). *Apprenticeship in thinking*. New York, NY: Oxford University Press.

Sharp, D. B. (2007). *Learn to write*. ISA Career website. Retrieved from http://www.isa.org/Template.cfm?Section=Careers&Template=/ContentManagement/ContentDisplay.cfm&ContentID=5328.

Shaughnessy, M. P. (1977). *Errors and expectations: A guide for the teacher of basic writing*. New York, NY: Oxford University Press.

Weston, J., Crossley, S. A., & McNamara, D. S. (2010). Towards a computational assessment of freewriting quality. In H. W. Guesgen & C. Murray (Eds.), *Proceedings of the 23rd International Florida Artificial Intelligence Research Society (FLAIRS)*. Menlo Park, CA: The AAAI Press.

Weston, J., Crossley, S. A., & McNamara, D. S. (in press). Differences in freewriting quality: Perspectives, approaches, and applications. In McCarthy, P. M., & Boonthum, C. (Eds.), *Applied natural language processing and content analysis: Identification, investigation, and resolution*. Hershey, PA: IGI Global.

Witte, S., & Faigley, L. (1981). Coherence, cohesion, and writing quality. *College Composition and Communication, 32*, 189–204. doi:10.2307/356693

Zimmerman, B. J., & Risemberg, R. (1997). Self-regulatory dimensions of academic learning and motivation. In Phye, G. D. (Ed.), *Handbook of academic learning: Construction of knowledge* (pp. 105–125). New York, NY: Academic Press. doi:10.1016/B978-012554255-5/50005-3

Chapter 18
The Gramulator:
A Tool to Identify Differential Linguistic Features of Correlative Text Types

Philip M. McCarthy
The University of Memphis, USA

Shinobu Watanabe
The University of Memphis, USA

Travis A. Lamkin
The University of Memphis, USA

ABSTRACT

Natural language processing tools, such as Coh-Metrix (see Chapter 11, this volume) and LIWC (see Chapter 12, this volume), have been tremendously successful in offering insight into quantifiable differences between text types. Such quantitative assessments have certainly been highly informative in terms of evaluating theoretical linguistic and psychological categories that distinguish text types (e.g., referential overlap, lexical diversity, positive emotion words, and so forth). Although these identifications are extremely important in revealing ability deficiencies, knowledge gaps, comprehension failures, and underlying psychological phenomena, such assessments can be difficult to interpret because they do not explicitly inform readers and researchers as to which specific linguistic features are driving the text type identification (i.e., the words and word clusters of the text). For example, a tool such as Coh-Metrix informs us that expository texts are more cohesive than narrative texts in terms of sentential referential overlap (McNamara, Louwerse, & Graesser, in press; McCarthy, 2010), but it does not tell us which words (or word clusters) are driving that cohesion. That is, we do not learn which actual words tend to be indicative of the text type differences. These actual words may tend to cluster around certain psychological, cultural, or generic differences, and, as a result, researchers and materials designers who might wish to create or modify text, so as to better meet the needs of readers, are left somewhat in the dark as to which specific language to use. What is needed is a textual analysis tool that offers qualitative output (in addition to quantitative output) that researchers and materials designers might use as a guide to the lexical characteristics of the texts under analysis. The Gramulator is such a tool.

DOI: 10.4018/978-1-60960-741-8.ch018

WHAT IS THE GRAMULATOR?

The *Gramulator* is a freely available qualitative and quantitative computational textual analysis tool. It is designed to allow researchers and materials designers to identify indicative lexical features of texts and text types. More formally, the Gramulator is designed to *identify differential linguistic features of correlative text types*.

The Gramulator primarily functions by analyzing two *sister corpora*. Sister corpora are two highly related, yet theoretically distinguishable, sets of data. The Gramulator analyzes these two sister corpora relative to each other, and identifies the lexical features (called *differentials*) that are indicative of one sister corpus while being antithetical of the other sister corpus. Thus, the Gramulator always produces two sets of output (i.e., differentials), and these sets of differentials are always relative to the two sets of data analyzed.

As examples of suitable sister corpora for the Gramulator to process, *science fiction literature* could be compared to *romantic literature*, *modernist poetry* could be compared to *post-modern poetry*, *Shakespearean drama* could be compared to *Greek tragedy*, or *introduction sections* from scholarly articles could be compared to *discussion sections*. The object of such analyses is to *shake out* from the two sister corpora (i.e., the *correlative corpora*) the lexical features that differentiate, distinguish, and identify the respective text type (i.e., produce the differentials).

THE RELEVANCE OF THE GRAMULATOR

Identifying indicative features of text types is important to language learners, educators, material designers, and a wide range of researchers from fields such as cognitive science, linguistics, and second language learning. Explicit knowledge of these indicative lexical features helps in several ways. For example, 1) a better understanding of

language conventions and practices can be attained, especially when and where two closely related registers meet (e.g., reviewing and summarizing); 2) materials to meet the needs of students can be better prepared, especially where focused practice is called for (e.g., for language learners); 3) a better understanding of register hierarchies to distinguish cases of different practices from cases of advanced practices can be achieved; 4) the characteristics of the moves that constitute the functionality of registers can be identified; and 5) differences between similar texts (e.g., a manipulated text) can be accessed more easily so that potential learning gains can be better established.

Looking at these issues in more detail, we begin with language conventions. The use of indicative lexical features that constitute a genre, register, or variety (or broadly speaking a *text type*) are typically unconsciously agreed upon conventions (Downs 1998; Hymes 1972). Having knowledge of these conventions is beneficial to those who need or want to diversify their discourse communities because such knowledge provides a greater likelihood of the employment of appropriate comprehension strategies and production formats. At a finer level, awareness of discourse specific language features is facilitative for memory activations, expectations, inferences, depth of comprehension, evaluation of truth and relevance, pragmatic ground-rules, and other psychological mechanisms that depend upon discourse interpretation (Bhatia 1997; Graesser et al. 2002; van Dijk & Kintsch 1983; Zwaan 1993).

Turning to pragmatic issues, teachers' and materials designers' understanding of indicative features of text types offers the possibility of better preparing texts that are appropriate for the designated audience. For example, in language learning situations, care must be taken to ensure that key words and phrases of the target genre are present in the reading assignment, and, furthermore, that they are highlighted in pre-reading activities. However, it is not simply high frequency words that need to be considered. Of possibly more importance for language learners is awareness of the lexical features that uniquely identify the text type. For Bhatia (1997), this awareness is the most important of all communication skills. Similarly, Flowerdew (1999, 2000, 2004) shows that a lack of text-type specific knowledge is a major hindrance for language learners' progress. And by the same token, Bazerman (1988) and Halliday and Hasan (1989) suggest that those who have learned the expected linguistic and rhetorical conventions of the text type are more likely to progress in their desired field. Obviously, the kind of knowledge outlined here also applies to first language learning situations. If learning optimally takes place in a zone of proximal development (Vygotsky, 1978), it is reasonable to assume that a better understanding of the language used in that proximity (see also Krashen, 1988) will lead to better matching of text to reader, and therefore to learning.

Lexical features are clearly important; however, lexical features themselves may be evidence of larger and more functional discourse components such as *moves*. Moves are textual features that define a text type (Bunton, 1998; Hopkins & Dudley-Evans 1988, Henry & Roseberry, 2001, Upton & Conner, 2001). For example, as McNamara, Graesser, McCarthy, and Cai (in press) explain, a research paper is composed of approximately 11 major moves, many with several minor moves within. These moves include *presenting the research question, situating the research within the literature,* and *demonstrating the relevance of the study*. Because moves serve functions, those functions are reflected in the common lexical constructions used to make the moves. McNamara and colleagues refer to these constructions as *frozen expressions*. The frozen expressions include *The goal/purpose of this study is to* [+ explicit statement of the goal], which heads the goal-of-the-study move; *This study is important to* [+ field or practice for which it is important], which heads the relevance-of-the-study move; and *This study fills a gap in the literature by* [+ how it fills that identified gap],

which heads the motivation-of-the- study move. These expressions signal the experienced reader to the function of the forthcoming discourse, and, arguably more importantly, signal knowledge of membership by the writer in that particular discourse community's practices.

Because the Gramulator analyzes sister corpora (one relative to the other), it is able to identify differentials that are characteristic of the moves of the text. An identification of moves offers researchers and educators the opportunity to better understand and explain the framework around which discourse is constituted. Furthermore, it offers the potential to reveal whether text types are hierarchical members of a genre or distinct genres that merely have a passing resemblance to another text type. Thus, we may ask *is western fiction a member of adventure fiction?* And *is modern art criticism as a text form distinct from the earlier forms of photography criticism?*

In terms of research, making subtle changes in discourse contexts helps cognitive scientists better evaluate learning gains. McNamara, Louwerse, McCarthy and Graesser (2010) review 19 such studies, all of which feature minor textual modifications resulting in learning gains. In other studies, modification is merely a suggestion. McCarthy et al. (2009) suggest that increasing narrative structures in expository texts might facilitate lesser skilled/knowledge readers because of presumably increased familiarity with the lexical features. The greater familiarity may reduce the cognitive burden, freeing up resources for processing more content relevant information. Given this supposition, knowledge of what linguistic features are familiar to (or indicative of) the text type is presumably paramount. Indeed, if indicative features of text types are not identified and evaluated then numerous psychological studies face the danger of assuming (but not knowing) that they have used text types that are homogenous (see, for example, Trabassao & Batolone 2003; Radvansky et al. 2001; and Zwaan, Magliano, & Graesser 1995). Such a homogeneity assumption runs counter to many findings on textual heterogeneity (2009Mc-Carthy and colleagues, 2009!, McCarthy, 2010, Rouet et al., 1996, and Hendersen & Clark, 2007). In sum then, the analysis of text types for indicative linguistic features offers valuable insight for a broad array of interests.

THE GRAMULATOR APPROACH

The textual analysis approach of the Gramulator operates broadly within a hybrid of two methods: *Contrastive Corpus Analysis* (CCA) and *Machine Differential Diagnosis* (MDD). CCA can be considered the framework of the Gramulator approach, whereas MDD is the operationalization of the approach. Used in conjunction, these two methods result in the primary output of the Gramulator: two sets of mutually exclusive n-grams that we refer to as the *differentials*.

Contrastive Corpus Analysis

Contrastive Corpus Analysis (CCA) is the name we attribute to the method through which the meaningfulness of lexical features is generated as a process of relativity. The principle of CCA is that any discourse unit (e.g., text-type, register, genre, variety, or section of text) is best understood, and perhaps only understandable, within the context of its contrast to some other discourse unit.

In textual analysis, CCA can perhaps date its origins to the landmark Brown Corpus (Kučera & Nelson, 1967). The Brown Corpus was important because it was the first large collection of texts (500) that had been collected and divided into 15 comparable categories. This breadth and categorization allowed numerous studies, arguably most famously Biber (1989), to better understand text types as much by where they overlapped as where they did not.

From the 1990s onward, the steady growth in computationally readable corpora, the development of personal computing, and the increasing

ease of applying statistical procedures provided an environment for contrastive approaches to flourish. Probably the best example of this development was the Coh-Metrix project (see Chapter X), wherein numerous studies were conducted on contrasting corpora using the 100s of textual analysis variables that Coh-Metrix provides. Once analyzed, the corpora in the Coh-Metrix study were invariably distinguished using statistical procedures such as discriminant analysis, logistic regression, and factor analysis (see for examples Louwerse et al., 2004, McCarthy et al. 2006, and Crossley et al., 2007).

A second branch of CCA can be attributed to the field of second language learning (SLL), and more particularly to Cobb (2003). Cobb is the earliest example we know of that uses the term *contrastive corpus analysis*; however, having done so, Cobb attributes the method itself to Granger (1998). Cobb describes CCA as the comparison of two corpora, through which, what is present and what is not present can be derived. Meanwhile, Granger's work does not refer to CCA by name, but does highlight how language learners can benefit from contrasting learner corpora to native-speaker corpora. Arguably a better example of CCA, although again the term is not used, stems from Scott and Tribble (2006). They collect "micro corpora" (not unlike the corpora that is typical in Gramulator studies) and reveal lexico-grammatical features of these corpora in the form of *key words*. These key words are words of unusual (typically high) frequency relative to general and much larger corpora. Although the identification of key words by Scott and Tribble is different from the Gramulator, as is their much more limited automation, the goal of their work is clearly similar to this project.

Machine Differential Diagnosis

Although Contrastive Corpus Analysis (CCA) provides a general framework *by which* to identify endemic features of text types, it does not offer a

314

method *through which* the identification of these features are filtered from more general features. The identification of endemic features is paramount because any feature that is symptomatic of two corpora is diagnostic of neither. Thus, to operationalize CCA, we turn to the dynamic method of Differential Diagnosis, and more specifically to Machine Differential Diagnosis.

Differential Diagnosis is a medical method used to identify the most probable cause of the *presenting problem*. For example, although symptom S1, S2, and S3 may be common to condition C1, C2, and C3, the presence of symptom S4 is only common to condition C2. As such, we can deduce that C2 is a more likely cause of all four symptoms.

Machine Differential Diagnosis (MDD) is simply an automation of the Differential Diagnosis method. MDD is relevant in studies such as Garg et al. (2005) and Rahati and Kabanza (2010), but arguably the clearest example of MDD is Shortliffe (1987), which describes a wide variety of programs used by doctors to support diagnoses. Among these are tools that provide information that is based on comparing, assessing, and incorporating or rejecting sets of data about a patient.

Obviously, the Gramulator is not a medical tool; however, the principal of the Gramulator is very similar. That is, the system first collects the symptoms (i.e., all the frequent n-grams), and then systematically eliminates those features that are not unique identifiers. The remaining features at the end of this process are the lexical features, i.e., differentials, that are indicative of one text type relative to the other. The researcher is then required to link these features to the theoretical linguistic or psychological constructs that were hypothesized to underlie the text types. Thus, in a sense, the identified construct is the *condition*; the initial collection of all n-grams corresponds to the initial list of symptoms; and the differentials are the symptoms identified as the probable cause of the condition.

THE UNIT OF ANALYSIS: N-GRAMS

N-Grams

The primary unit of analysis in the Gramulator is the n-gram. N-grams are strings of adjacently positioned lexical items. A string of two lexical items is called a bigram, a string of three is called a trigram, etc. For example, the first three bigrams of this paragraph are *the primary*, *primary unit*, and *unit of*. The first three trigrams are *the primary unit*, *primary unit of*, and *unit of analysis*.

As reported by Jurafsky and Martin (2008), n-grams are widely used in computational linguistics technologies such as speech recognition, hand writing recognition, parsers, augmentative communication systems for the disabled, spelling error detection, as well as any other development where the probability of one word can be calculated by the presence of adjacent words (e.g., optical character recognition, machine translation, and information retrieval).

In general, n-grams are considered useful analytical units because they help to detect patterns (or *signals*) within data. For instance, in everyday conversation, background noise means that many words are missed, and so we generally "fill in" those gaps by using some form of probability that is based on what we *do* actually know from the text (i.e., words that surround the missing items). A second reason for the usefulness of n-grams is that they can function across syntactic boundaries. This characteristic can often offer rare insight into language production. For example, Min and McCarthy (2010) discovered that native English speaking scientists from America were more likely to use the structure "patients with" than their Korean counterparts. This finding suggested that native English speaking scientists were more likely to modify noun phrases with prepositional phrases, whereas non-native English speakers might prefer the simpler structure of noun modifying noun (e.g., compare *patients with HIV* to *HIV patients*). Such findings are useful because they help non-native English speakers (of which there are many) to produce more prototypical textual features when writing in the dominant language of academia.

N-gram analysis is fairly consistent in its conceptualization and calculation (see examples from Jurafsky & Martin, 2008). Thus, in most applied natural language processing (ANLP) developments, n-grams are calculated from very large data bases (over a million words), carefully "trained" on representative and balanced corpora so as to maximize generalizability, and calculated in terms of probabilities so as to offer a limited choice of possible forthcoming alternatives. Moreover, longer n-grams are presumed to be more accurate than shorter ones; and therefore more useful for many applications because the more that precedes a missing word, the fewer are the possibilities of what that missing word is. For example, we might not be too sure what word would follow *your…* or even *for your…*, but we would surely be confident of the following word of *penny for your…* (i.e., *penny for your thoughts*).

The Gramulator utilizes the n-gram conventions outlined above, but implements them by turning general weaknesses into four specific strengths. First, a context sensitive corpus is problematic for traditional n-gram analysis because it is unlikely that derived n-grams can be generalized to other contexts. However, for the Gramulator, it is this very issue of context sensitivity that we want to identify, and it is the generalizability to other text types that we want to suppress. That is, we want to identify the lexical features that are indicative of sensitive contexts. Second, a large data base is required for traditional n-gram analysis, because accurate examples of low frequency possibilities need to be calculated. However, for the Gramulator, it is only the most common n-grams that are used for calculations; thus, the corpus size can be relatively small, because often as few as two examples of an n-gram are sufficiently informative. Third, in traditional analysis, longer n-grams provide greater accuracy and therefore larger corpora

are needed to produce them; however, Gramulator studies are largely interested in simple bigrams (which require far less training data) because the prediction of the following word is not the goal, the bigram, in and of itself, is the informative unit. Finally, traditional n-gram analysis tends to produce multiple selections of possible next words based on a series of probabilities; however, although the Gramulator can produce probabilities, its function is to produce lexical *themes* (such as family membership, locations, grammatical choices, and other features associated with discourse analysis). As such, the probabilities of forthcoming words are not of primary interest, whereas the associations between the n-gram examples are.

The Gramulator's Use of N-Grams

The Gramulator processes text using n-grams. Bigrams are generally the primary level of analysis, although other forms such as trigrams and quadgrams can be requested. Typically, the most frequent n-grams do not differ greatly from corpus to corpus (e.g., *of the* is either the highest or near highest bigram in most analyses). As such, highly frequent n-grams are seldom diagnostic in a contrastive corpus analysis because they are highly common to both corpora. Despite their lack of diagnostic ability, the most frequent n-grams of any analysis (called *typicals*) are tagged and stored by the system in case the researcher finds a need for their analysis.

For the Gramulator, the most important aspect of the typicals is that the all-important differentials are derived from them. Differential n-grams are those n-grams that are among the most commonly occurring in one corpus (i.e., among the 50% most frequent n-grams) but are uncommon to the contrasting corpus (i.e., *not* among the 50% most frequent n-grams). The differentials are derived from the typicals by following the principals of machine differential diagnostics: namely, all typicals that are common to both corpora (called *shared n-grams*) are diagnostic of neither corpus, and therefore they are removed. The remaining n-grams are the most frequently occurring n-grams that are present in just one of the two corpora. To take an example, Min and McCarthy (2010) reported that a differential trigram in the writing of Korean scientists was *in order to*. Although this trigram was also present in American scientists' writing, it did not occur with above average frequency, and therefore was not a *typical*. Consequently, *in order to* is termed a *differential trigram* of Korean scientist writing relative to American scientist writing. It is important to note that differentials are always relative to their sister corpus, whereas typicals are never relative to anything.

THE ASSUMPTIONS OF THE GRAMULATOR

Gramulator analyses assume two closely related text types (i.e., *sister corpora*). The critical assumption of the corpora is that they are the same only where they are not theorized to be different. Thus, the number of texts in each corpus is assumed to be the same, the length of the texts is assumed to be the same, the time when the texts were written is assumed to be the same, the purpose for which the texts were written is assumed to be the same, and so on and so forth (see also Altenberg & Granger, 2002; McEnery et al., 2006; McEnery & Wilson, 1996). At some critical point, the corpora are theorized to be different, and it is only at that point that we can have cause to describe the corpora as *two* text types rather than *one*. It is this critical point of *differences within similarity* that the Gramulator aims to reveal in the form of differentials.

In an important sense then, the Gramulator approach can be viewed as a cognitive tool that is an application of *alignable differences theory* (Gentner & Markman, 1997). The theory holds that identification of *differences* is a cognitive process best achieved by first identifying similarities (or

commonalities as they are termed). For example, to better understand the differences between high school narrative texts and high school expository texts their point of similarity first of all needs to be established (e.g., *they are similar in that they both have the goal of describing and explaining events*). Once their common ground has been established, we can better understand that narratives describe and explain a series of events in terms of the author's understanding of the nature of the individual's role in the world, whereas expository texts describe and explain a series of events in terms of an (attempted) objective account of processes, causes and effects, comparison and contrast, problem presentation and proposed solution, or categorization of facts or events (Reutzel & Cooter, 2007). The Gramulator process adheres to alignable difference theory in that it first establishes similarities (the typicals), and from these it derives the differences (the differentials).

Ideally, the analysis conducted by the Gramulator reveals lexical features that are evidence of the proposed theoretical difference. To take a hypothetical example, sister corpora could be formed from a series of dialogues. The dialogue turns (or utterances) are likely to be highly similar with the possible exception that one person is the conversational *initiator* and the second person is the conversational *patient*. Thus, the sister corpora could be established as dialogue-initiator and dialogue-patient. The researchers might hypothesize that the initiators are more likely to have question forms in their data (perhaps because the initiator is more likely to be requesting), and the researchers may also hypothesize that initiators use more hedges (perhaps to guard against encroachments of negative face). Gramulator output is used to confirm, disconfirm, and/or elaborate upon such hypotheses.

Obviously, no sister corpora are ever likely to be perfectly matched (whether in Gramulator studies, Coh-Metrix studies, LIWC studies, or any psychological or linguistic study). However, it is important to appreciate that whereof the Gramulator's assumptions are not met, thereof the materials are likely to be limiting. And although these limitations do not render the analysis meaningless, anymore than any other analysis of any two groups, these limitations nonetheless need to be considered and reported (i.e., report the corpora descriptives carefully). In sum then, if corpora differ in terms of a few texts or a few words, it is likely to have a correspondingly small effect on the output; and if they differ by a large number of texts, or a large number of words, then a correspondingly larger effect is likely.

Future research involving the Gramulator needs to provide researchers with useful parameters with regard to corpora sizes, variations, and all processing assumptions. Indeed, such studies are under way. But that having been acknowledged,

it is important to acknowledge that computational textual analysis tools must first of all establish their usefulness and their place in the discourse community's tool box of analysis; only then can their limitations be fully established. Until that point, we urge users to err on the side of caution with analysis, and keep their corpora (wherever possible) relatively large (between 50 and 500 texts per corpus), and relatively long (between 100 and 1000 words per text), and also to keep their conclusions from the data relatively conservative. Current studies within the Gramulator project are working within these broad assumptions, which are basically drawn from similar assumption used by comparable tools such as Coh-Metrix. As testing takes place, more detailed guidelines will be established.

Figure 1. The architecture of the Gramulator

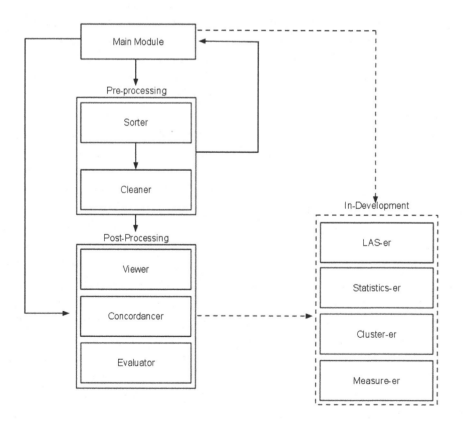

THE ARCHITECTURE OF THE GRAMULATOR

The Gramulator features five central modules with several other in-house modules that are planned for release on the public tool (see Figure 1). The modules released at the time of this publication are the pre-processing modules the *Cleanser* and the *Sorter*, and the post-processing modules the *Viewer,* the *Concordancer* and the *Evaluator*. Each of these five modules is a satellite to the main processing module, referred to as the *Main Module* or simply as the *Gramulator*. In this section, we give a brief overview of each of these modules.

The Main Module

The Gramulator opens with the main module. It is here that the researcher specifies the sister corpora to be analyzed. A key feature at this stage of the analysis is the choice of *weighting*. Through the file menu, the researcher can select *Parameters→*

Weighting and then choose between *term frequency* (TF) and *term frequency: document frequency* (TF: DF). TF bases analysis on a simple count of the frequencies of all n-grams. TF: DF, the default selection, first counts the frequencies (as with TF) but then values that count as a percentage of the number of documents in which the n-gram occurs. Thus, if the n-gram *patients with* appears 12 times in the corpus, and it appears in 10% of the documents then its final value will be 10% of $12 = 1.2$. Once the parameters have been selected and sister corpora are loaded, the researcher will typically choose to process the corpora for differentials. This operation is achieved by selecting *Analyze → Process → D-grams*. The Gramulator then automatically guides the researcher through various operation choices (e.g., unigram, bigram analysis, trigram, or cluster-gram analysis). In addition, the Gramulator offers conventionalized naming options for the output data although the researcher is free to name data as desired. The main module processes the two sister corpora

Figure 2. The main module of the Gramulator

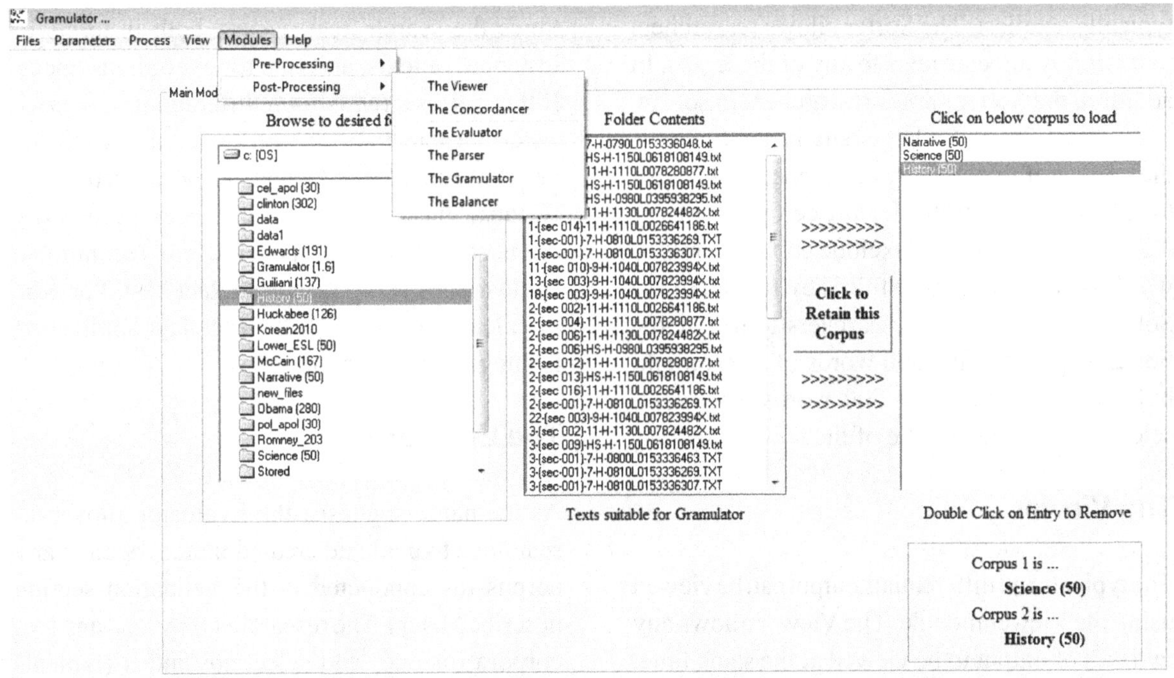

and automatically saves four outputs: the two sets of *typicals* for each corpora, and the two sets of *differentials* for each corpora (Figure 2).

The Cleanser

Before any processing can be conducted in any textual analysis tool, the texts must be "cleaned." Cleaning is a process whereby the texts that comprise the corpus are made *consistent*. This process may include lemmatizing, spell checking, or removing/modifying/supplementing certain parts of the text. In addition, the researcher may need to consider whether elements of the text will be considered as one word or multiple words. For example, features such as *didn't* and *people's* can be interpreted as one word or two words. The Cleanser module allows these and many other functions to be performed.

The Sorter

In many corpus studies, there is a need to divide the data into *training*, *validation*, and *testing* sets. These sets may be of various sizes although training sets are typically largest and validation sets typically smallest. The Sorter allows researchers to randomly allocate texts to any of these sets. In addition, the Sorter allows researchers to sort by key words. Thus, if a large data base of texts is the source of documents, researchers may wish to only include texts that feature certain words, or word combinations, (or exclude certain words or word combinations). The third key feature of the Sorter is that it allows researchers to trim texts. For example, the first 500 words of a text might be selected, or the final 500 words, or even a selection from the middle of the text.

The Viewer

The typicals and differentials output can be viewed using the Viewer module. The Viewer allows any two sets of output to be viewed at the same time.

The Viewer also features a corpus comparison option. This option converts the n-grams from each output into parallel vectors from which their similarity value is assessed as a cosine. The process begins by aligning the n-grams from each output. The value assigned to each n-gram is the weighted or unweighted frequency. If an n-gram appears in one vector but not in the other vector, that n-gram is added and assigned a value of zero. The two sets of differentials produced from sister corpora will always produce a cosine of zero; because, by definition, they have no overlap. The corpora similarity value can be useful when comparing differentials or typicals across studies because it provides a quick and easily interpretable evaluation of similarity.

The Concordancer

Researchers can view in context any n-gram results using the Concordancer module. The Concordancer, like any concordance, allows researchers to enter any word or n-gram (typical, differential, or any lexical item whatsoever) and view all examples of the selection within a requested frame of words. Researchers can also learn how many times the search item occurs, both in terms of instances of texts, and also for over-all instances. If the word search is for a differential of the two sister corpora then one of those values will be very low (otherwise it would not be a differential). Because these counts of instances necessarily often reflect low frequencies, we recommend comparisons using Fisher's Exact Test. For ease of calculation, a Fisher's Exact Test application is integrated into the tool.

The Evaluator

As the name suggests, the Evaluator allows researchers to evaluate created indices against any corpus (as conducted in the Validation section described later). The researcher may load any two corpora (or one) and select any index (typicals or differentials) to assess the corpus. Indices can be modified by the user (added to, changed, or deleted), and indices can also be combined. If the researcher so wishes, the changed indices can be saved and later re-used. Indices can also be made up on the spot or borrowed from other studies. Indices can be of any length and any frequency. In short, the indices are very flexible. Having selected a corpus and an index, the researcher simply chooses *Analysis → Process* in the file menu and the Evaluator processes the texts and outputs the results. Two outputs are created. The first output is a worksheet that is designed to be copied and pasted to Excel. The primary value of the output is a variable calculated as *tokens / words / searches* * 1000. *Searches* refers to the number of n-grams in the index. *Words* refers to the number of words in the evaluated text. And *tokens* refers to the number of instances per text for the sum of all searches. For example, if the current paragraph were a text it would include 332 words. If the index of interest contained the following three n-grams (*it would*, *of the*, and *to integrate*) then we would have 7 tokens, 332 words, and 3 searches, which, multiplied by 1000 equals 7.028. Researchers are free to use any values of the output; however, the primary value produced in the output is normalized based on length of text and breadth of search; it is therefore useful because it provides researchers with a way of comparing any two analyses. For ease of calculation, an Excel worksheet featuring within and between t-tests is packaged with the tool. As with Fisher's Exact, the plan is to integrate the tests directly into the tool.

Although the Gramulator clearly features a wealth of analysis tools, more are already in development and are planned to be released. The new modules have been given working names that reflect their function and their similarity to other modules[1]. In brief, the *Measure-er* will provide a host of other indices including co-reference overlap, lexical diversity, function word density, and many others. The *LSA-er* will provide similarity values for n-grams, indices, and corpora.

The *Cluster-er* will group n-grams of potential similarity so that researchers can more easily assess thematic traces. And the *Statistics-er* will provide various statistical analyses of the results produced by the Evaluator. Although currently envisioned as new modules, these developments may become part of existing modules as the needs and requests of users become apparent.

STUDIES USING THE GRAMULATOR

Although a relatively new tool at the time of this publication, the Gramulator has already featured in several studies, and is currently the central tool in many new projects and dissertations. We briefly summarize here the published studies in order to provide a clearer idea of the range and depth of analysis that the Gramulator is able to produce.

The first Gramulator study was McCarthy et al. (2009). Although the study was conducted with a very early version of the tool, the authors were still able to present a revealing analysis of writing styles as used by American, British, and Japanese scientists writing in English.

Min and McCarthy (2010) built on the McCarthy et al. (2009) study, revealing several systematic discourse distinctions between the writing styles of American and Korean scientists, most prevalent of which was the American preference for noun phrase + preposition phrase in descriptions such as ...*patient with HIV*, and the Korean preference for noun phrase + noun Phrase in similar descriptions ...*HIV patient*. The study concluded that the Korean scientists' English was perfectly grammatical but often non-prototypical in terms of lexical forms and features.

Duran and McCarthy (2009) analyzed the phrases and thematic content that comprise the truthful and deceptive discourse of general conversations and persuasive argumentation. More specifically, the study revealed a number of differences between how poeple lie and how they tell the truth. For example, the study reports that deceivers tend to lie about boyfriends (but not girlfriends), and that the lying event tends to be situated in places of lower personal affiliation (e.g., we seem happier lying about high school than we do lying about our homes and family). The study was of particular importance to the development of the Gramulator because it made necessary numerous additional features (e.g., the Evaluator module) so as to provide a greater range of quantitative analysis.

Hullender and McCarthy (2010) conducted an analysis of modern art criticism and photography criticism. The study suggested that differences in linguistic features of the two forms of criticism made them distinct genres rather than one hierarchically composed genre. Most salient of the linguistic differences was the modern art critics tendency to hedge claims with features such as *in a way*, *in terms of*, and *is a kind of*.

Finally, the Gramulator has already spawned its own child: GPAT (McCarthy, 2010). GPAT (the Genre Purity Assessment Tool) calculates *genre purity* for narrative and expository texts, and produces results that are at least as accurate as a combination of 30 complex textual analysis indices produced by Coh-Metrix. Like the Gramulator, GPAT is based on n-gram differentials; however, GPAT's analysis is at the level of the graph (e.g., a, b, c, 1, 2, 3, !, @, #, etc.). GPAT is an important development for the Gramulator because it demonstrates that the produced differentials can easily be automated into a standalone tool. Note also that GPAT featured in the Hullender and McCarthy (2010) study where results suggested that the photography criticism was more expository and the modern art criticism was more narrative.

VALIDATION STUDY

It is common practice in ANLP for the value of the application to be demonstrated long before the tool itself is validated. After all, ANLP is as often about getting a job done as it is in advancing a theoretical position. To be sure, in some ways, this *getting a job done* can be described as a form of *face validity*, which, although there is almost universal agreement that it is the weakest form of validity, and therefore not worth reporting, it is nonetheless, almost always the first form of validity used. Although demonstration typically precedes validation, validation is nonetheless necessary. The usefulness of the Gramulator having been shown in the studies mentioned previously, a validation procedure now needs to be put in place.

Perhaps the major problem in validation studies is the formidable number of *validity types* that contribute to the overall construct validity (for a broader discussion see American Education Research Association; McCarthy and Jarvis, 2010; and Ong & Van Dulman, 2006). In the case of the Gramulator, the most appropriate and demonstrable validity type is *external validity*, or, as described here, the Proximal Similarity Model (PSMPSMPSM: Campbell, 1986). In computational discourse analysis studies, external validity refers to the attribute of generalizability in a given process. In other words, external validity refers to how well a given process "works" when applied to different data sets. Thus, if process X works for data set D1, and data sets D2, D3, and D4 are theorized to be highly similar data sets to D1, then X is predicted to work for D2, D3, and D4 equally as well as it works for D1. A more conservative form of external validity is PSM. PSM goes beyond D1 = D2 = D3 = D4 and asks us to theorize the order of similarity in the generalized data sets. Thus, if D4 is a weaker example than D3, and D3 is a weaker example than D2, and D2 is a weaker example than D1, then the argument becomes: if X works for D1, then it is predicted to work quite well for D2, moderately well for D3, and marginally for D4. It is this form of validity testing, PSM, that we apply to the Gramulator.

The Corpora

For our validation study, we used one corpus of expository texts (represented by the subject of "science") and one corpus of narrative texts (represented by the subject of "literature"). The use of expository and narrative may seem less "highly related" corpora than other Gramulator studies; however, we argue that the choice of expository and narrative corpora is a reasonable point of departure for the following five reasons:

1. Expository and narrative corpora provide a very large selection of texts, which is necessary in a validation study. Previous Gramulator studies of sister corpora (e.g., *dialogue lies/truth, American English/ Korean English scientific abstracts*, and *art/ photography criticism*) are probably much more highly related; however, they cannot provide the frequency, consistency, and representation necessary to generalize findings for a sufficiently compelling proximal similarity model.

2. Expository and narrative corpora are probably the mostly widely examined text types (e.g., Albrecht, O'Brien, Kendeou & van den Broek 2005; Linderholm & van den Broek 2002; Mason, & Myers 1995; Kaup & Zwaan 2003; Trabassao & Batolone 2003). Thus, the ubiquity of interest makes such a genre choice a relatively uncontroversial point of departure.

3. The corpora of expository and narrative texts used in this study have been widely used in numerous other projects. As such, their inclusion and examination increases confidence in the validation claims.

4. The corpora of expository and narrative texts are highly consistent in terms of number of texts, length of texts, transcribers of texts, source of texts, and audience for texts. As such, their frequency, consistency, and representation are well suited to the general-ization of findings necessary for a proximal similarity model.

5. The selection of expository and narrative texts is pragmatic. As McCarthy et al. (2006) argued, these text types are particularly well suited for initial investigations because the corpora provide enough diversity in terms of structure, style, and purpose to be distinguishable, while at the same time, the corpora provide enough overlap that the task of distinguishing indicative features of each is not trivial.

All texts were selected from the Touchstone Applied Science Associates (TASA) corpus. The "Degrees of Reading Power" reading comprehension index (provided by TASA) was used to sub-select only texts considered as appropriate for readers at or above the 4th grade level. The 4th grade level was selected because of common consensus that the first three grades constitute *learning to read*, whereas subsequent grades constitute *reading to learn* (Chall, 1983). Thus the selection of grades provided greater confidence in the consistency of the corpus. From these grade levels 900 narrative texts (N) and 900 expository texts (E) were randomly selected. These texts, in turn, were randomly distributed as six sub-corpora (three narrative sub-corpora: N1, N2, and N3 and three expository sub-corpora: E1, E2, and E3). The sub-samples of 300 were necessary to demonstrate generalization patterns; that is, we can theorize that (N1 = N2 = N3) = Nx and that (E1 = E2 = E3) = Ex and that Nx ≠ Ex. As such, the sub-corpora allow us to analyze one corpus and then generalize those results to other related corpora.

Nomenclature for Gramulator Studies

As discussed, the Gramulator functions by contrasting two sister corpora. For example, if corpus N3 and E2 are processed, the two resultant sets of differentials are N3(E2) and E2(N3). The first corpus in such a *pairing* is referred to as the *dominant corpus*, and the second corpus is referred to as the *recessive corpus*. In the case of N3(E2), N3 is dominant and E2 is recessive. In the case of E2(N3), E2 is dominant and N3 is recessive. Note that Gramulator processing entails that all differentials stem from the dominant corpus only; the recessive corpus is only able to subtract from the n-grams produced by the dominant corpus: The recessive corpus can never add to the set of n-grams or differentials. As a result, both sets of differentials are mutually exclusive. For example, no differential that occurs in N3(E2) is the same as any differential that occurs in E2(N3). This point is of particular importance because it must *not* be assumed that N3(E2) = E2(N3); indeed, their overlap is precisely zero.

Given that there are three narrative sub-corpora (N1, N2, and N3) and three expository sub-corpora (E1, E2, E3), a total of 30 *dominant(recessive)* combinations is possible (see Table 1).

The dominant(recessive) combinations are comprised of differentials; these sets of differentials (considered as a single group) are referred to as *indices* (*indices* is the plural form of *index*). Thus, E2(E3) is an index and E3(E2) is an index. These indices can be processed by the Evaluator module of the Gramulator to assess values of the individual texts of any corpus. The value of any text is the degree to which the text is composed of the index selected. For example, if we process the texts of sub-corpus E1 with the index E2(N3) we find the degree to which E1 texts are composed of E2 differentials that are relative to N3. We

would expect the values in this example to be high because E2 and E1 are theoretically equal (the same genre), and the recessive corpus that subtracted some of the potential n-grams is from a different genre (narrative), meaning that few potentially informative differentials have been removed.

In this study, the texts against which all of the indices are processed are the six sub-corpora (i.e., Nx and Ex), meaning that there is a total of 180 (i.e. 6 * 30) *derived variables*. A derived variable refers to the 300 items (i.e., texts) that comprise each of the sub-corpora along with its corresponding value as generated by one of the 30 indices.

To take an example, let us say that we have processed through the Gramulator the pairing of the sub-corpora N1 with N2. The result of this processing is two sets of differentials, which are the indices of N1(N2) and N2(N1). These two indices can be used in the Evaluator module to assess values for any corpus of texts. So, let us say that we use the Evaluator module to assess the corpus E2. We may use any of the 30 indices (e.g., N1[N2]) to assess this corpus. So, if the texts of sub-corpus E2 are evaluated using the index N1(N2) then we write E2 → N1(N2). And by the same token, if the sub-corpus of E2 is evaluated using the index N2(N1) then we write E2 → N2(N1). Because there are six sub-corpora, N1, N2, N3, E1, E2, and E3, and there are 30 indices N1(N2), N2(N1) etc. there is a total of 180 possible evaluations in all. For this study, we randomly selected one corpus from each genre (N1 and E2) to process against each of the 30 indices. Thus, we produced 30 derived variables for N1 (e.g.,

Table 1. The 30 dominant (recessive) combinations for the narrative and expository corpora

N1 (N2)	N2 (N1)	N3 (N1)	E1 (N1)	E2 (N1)	E3 (N1)
N1 (N3)	N2 (N3)	N3 (N2)	E1 (N2)	E2 (N2)	E3 (N2)
N1 (E1)	N2 (E1)	N3 (E1)	E1 (N3)	E2 (N3)	E3 (N3)
N1 (E2)	N2 (E2)	N3 (E2)	E1 (E2)	E2 (E1)	E3 (E1)
N1 (E3)	N2 (E3)	N3 (E3)	E1 (E3)	E2 (E3)	E3 (E2)

$N1 \rightarrow N1(N2)$, $N1 \rightarrow N1(N2)$, $N1 \rightarrow N1(N2)$, $N1 \rightarrow N1(N2)$, $N1 \rightarrow N1(N2)$, etc.), and we also produced 30 derived variables for E2 (e.g., $E2 \rightarrow N1(N2)$, $E2 \rightarrow N1(N2)$, $E2 \rightarrow N1(N2)$, $E2 \rightarrow N1(N2)$, $E2 \rightarrow N1(N2)$, etc.).

Predictions

Our predictions are based on three levels of analysis. These levels correspond to the evaluated texts (N1 and E2), to the dominant texts (N1, N2, N3, E1, E2, E3), and to the recessive texts (N1, N2, N3, E1, E2, E3). The following three rules need to be applied in order: First, values will be higher if the dominant text is the same genre as the evaluated text. Second, values will be higher if the recessive text is a different genre from the evaluated text. And third, higher values will result if the recessive text is a different text from the evaluated text (see Table 2).

The asterisk for the rankings of 5 and 6 in Table 2 refers to two possible outcomes. If there is no significant difference in terms of lexical diversity between the narrative and expository texts then we can expect the outcomes shown in Table 2. However, if narratives are more diverse than expository texts (see McNamara, et al in press; McCarthy Jarvis 2007), we can expect examples such as $N1 \rightarrow N2(N1)$ to be higher than $N1 \rightarrow E1(E2)$ and also for examples such as $E2 \rightarrow N1(N2)$ to be higher than $E2 \rightarrow E1(E2)$. Higher relative lexical diversity is important because the greater the diversity of the dominant corpus the lower is the likelihood of the recessive corpus substantially subtracting from it.

RESULTS

To assess our predictions, we processed all combinations of corpora to create 30 indices (e.g., N1(N2), N1(N3) etc.). Second, we evaluated the two randomly selected genres (N1 and E2) using all 30 indices. Third, we calculated the mean of each of the 60 derived variables (30 for N1 and 30 for E2). Fourth, we separated the two sets of derived variables (i.e., the observed results) and aligned them with the predicted order (i.e.,

Table 2. Prediction expected rankings (Exp) for combinations (Com)

Exp	N-Com	E-Com	Exp	E-Com	N-Com
1	$N1 \rightarrow N1(E1)$	$E2 \rightarrow E2(N1)$	6*	$N1 \rightarrow E1(E2)$	$E2 \rightarrow N1(N2)$
1	$N1 \rightarrow N1(E2)$	$E2 \rightarrow E2(N2)$	6*	$N1 \rightarrow E1(E3)$	$E2 \rightarrow N1(N3)$
1	$N1 \rightarrow N1(E3)$	$E2 \rightarrow E2(N3)$	6*	$N1 \rightarrow E2(E1)$	$E2 \rightarrow N2(N1)$
2	$N1 \rightarrow N2(E1)$	$E2 \rightarrow E3(N1)$	6*	$N1 \rightarrow E2(E3)$	$E2 \rightarrow N2(N3)$
2	$N1 \rightarrow N2(E2)$	$E2 \rightarrow E3(N2)$	6*	$N1 \rightarrow E3(E1)$	$E2 \rightarrow N3(N1)$
2	$N1 \rightarrow N2(E3)$	$E2 \rightarrow E3(N3)$	6*	$N1 \rightarrow E3(E2)$	$E2 \rightarrow N3(N2)$
2	$N1 \rightarrow N3(E1)$	$E2 \rightarrow E1(N1)$	7	$N1 \rightarrow E1(N2)$	$E2 \rightarrow N1(E1)$
2	$N1 \rightarrow N3(E2)$	$E2 \rightarrow E1(N2)$	7	$N1 \rightarrow E1(N3)$	$E2 \rightarrow N1(E3)$
2	$N1 \rightarrow N3(E3)$	$E2 \rightarrow E1(N3)$	7	$N1 \rightarrow E2(N2)$	$E2 \rightarrow N2(E1)$
3	$N1 \rightarrow N1(N2)$	$E2 \rightarrow E2(E1)$	7	$N1 \rightarrow E2(N3)$	$E2 \rightarrow N2(E3)$
3	$N1 \rightarrow N1(N3)$	$E2 \rightarrow E2(E3)$	7	$N1 \rightarrow E3(N2)$	$E2 \rightarrow N3(E1)$
4	$N1 \rightarrow N3(N2)$	$E2 \rightarrow E3(E1)$	7	$N1 \rightarrow E3(N3)$	$E2 \rightarrow N3(E3)$
4	$N1 \rightarrow N2(N3)$	$E2 \rightarrow E1(E3)$	8	$N1 \rightarrow E1(N1)$	$E2 \rightarrow N3(E2)$
5*	$N1 \rightarrow N2(N1)$	$E2 \rightarrow E1(E2)$	8	$N1 \rightarrow E2(N1)$	$E2 \rightarrow N1(E2)$
5*	$N1 \rightarrow N3(N1)$	$E2 \rightarrow E3(E2)$	8	$N1 \rightarrow E3(N1)$	$E2 \rightarrow N2(E2)$

Table 3. Expected (Exp) and observed (Obs) ranks and means for N1

Exp	Obs	Mean	Combinations	Exp	Obs	Mean	Combinations
1	1	0.210	N1 → N1(E1)	6	6	0.089	N1 → E1(E2)
1	1	0.224	N1 → N1(E2)	6	5	0.072	N1 → E1(E3)
1	2	0.214	N1 → N1(E3)	6	5	0.056	N1 → E2(E1)
2	1	0.196	N1 → N2(E1)	6	6	0.057	N1 → E2(E3)
2	2	0.209	N1 → N2(E2)	6	6	0.088	N1 → E3(E1)
2	2	0.199	N1 → N2(E3)	6	6	0.108	N1 → E3(E2)
2	2	0.198	N1 → N3(E1)	7	7	0.046	N1 → E1(N2)
2	2	0.213	N1 → N3(E2)	7	7	0.048	N1 → E1(N3)
2	2	0.202	N1 → N3(E3)	7	7	0.046	N1 → E2(N2)
3	3	0.156	N1 → N1(N2)	7	7	0.047	N1 → E2(N3)
3	3	0.153	N1 → N1(N3)	7	8	0.051	N1 → E3(N2)
4	4	0.119	N1 → N3(N2)	7	7	0.051	N1 → E3(N3)
4	4	0.112	N1 → N2(N3)	8	7	0.042	N1 → E1(N1)
5	6	0.087	N1 → N2(N1)	8	8	0.042	N1 → E2(N1)
5	6	0.090	N1 → N3(N1)	8	8	0.046	N1 → E3(N1)

expected results). Finally, we conducted Spearman correlations using the expected order and the observed order as the two variables. The results were as predicted, there was a significant correlation between the empirically derived order of the variables and the theoretically based order of the variables (N1 correlations: $rho = .974$, $p < 0.001$; E2 correlations: $rho = 0.963$, $p < 0.001$; See Table 3 and Table 4).

The analysis was repeated by replacing the empirically derived observed order of the variables with their respective mean value. Again, the results were as predicted, there was a significant correlation between the means and the theoretically based order of the variables (N1 correlations: $rho = -0.976$, $p < 0.001$; E2 correlations: $rho = -0.969$, $p < 0.001$).

The results for all levels (1 through 8) were in line with our predictions for the narrative sub-corpora; however, for the expository sub-corpora, levels 5 and 6 were reversed. The result can be explained by greater levels of diversity in narratives (see Predictions section above). To confirm this hypothesis, we conducted a between

texts t-test to assess the effect of lexical diversity on the combined corpora of narrative ($n = 900$) and expository ($n = 900$). For an assessment of lexical diversity, we used the MTLD assessment tool described in McCarthy and Jarvis (in press). The result confirmed that narrative texts are more lexically diverse than expository texts: $t(1,1798) = 27.988$, $p < 0.001$, $d = 1.319$.

Taken as a whole, the results are evidence that the Gramulator's derived indices generalize to other sets of data. Thus, N1 predicted N2 and N3, even though all three sub-corpora were composed of different texts. Similarly, E2 predicted E1 and E3, even though, again, all three sub-corpora were composed of different texts. In other words, the Evaluator process appears to be able to create an index from a given corpus and subsequently evaluate accurately the composition of a different set of texts of the same genre.

Although the correlations described above are encouraging, we not only predicted the order of the values of the derived variables, we also predicted that there would be significant differences between each of the eight prediction levels. Thus,

Table 4. Expected (Exp) and observed (Obs) ranks and means for E2

Exp	Obs	Mean	Combinations	Exp	Obs	Mean	Combinations
1	1	0.234	E2 →E2(N1)	6	7	0.078	E2 →N1(N2)
1	1	0.227	E2 →E2(N2)	6	6	0.081	E2 →N1(N3)
1	1	0.228	E2 →E2(N3)	6	5	0.114	E2 →N2(N1)
2	2	0.231	E2 →E3(N1)	6	6	0.095	E2 →N2(N3)
2	2	0.206	E2 →E3(N2)	6	5	0.111	E2 →N3(N1)
2	2	0.206	E2 →E3(N3)	6	6	0.085	E2 →N3(N2)
2	2	0.197	E2 →E1(N1)	7	6	0.046	E2 →N1(E1)
2	2	0.192	E2 →E1(N2)	7	7	0.045	E2 →N1(E3)
2	2	0.192	E2 →E1(N3)	7	7	0.044	E2 →N2(E1)
3	3	0.169	E2 →E2(E1)	7	7	0.100	E2 →N2(E3)
3	3	0.171	E2 →E2(E3)	7	7	0.046	E2 →N3(E1)
4	4	0.118	E2 →E3(E1)	7	7	0.044	E2 →N3(E3)
4	6	0.112	E2 →E1(E3)	8	8	0.042	E2 →N3(E2)
5	4	0.083	E2 →E1(E2)	8	8	0.042	E2 →N1(E2)
5	6	0.087	E2 →E3(E2)	8	8	0.040	E2 →N2(E2)

to supplement the correlational evidence, we conducted a second analysis using a repeated design. However, a problem with the repeated design of this study is that although we predicted differences between some of the levels, we predicted no differences between the derived variables that comprised each level. As such, before conducting the analysis, it was necessary to merge the derived variables predicted to be not significantly different into a single variable. Thus, the 30 derived variables were reduced to eight variables. For example, the following six derived variables were all predicted to rank second in order of magnitude of values: N1 → N2(E1), N1 → N2(E2), N1 → N2(E3), N1 → N3(E1), N1 → N3(E2), N1 → N3(E3), a prediction supported by the correlations reported above. To reduce the theoretically identical variables into one variable, we simply averaged across all the derived values for each of the eight predicted levels. Naturally, this process included all 300 texts in all sub-corpora.

Two repeated measures tests were conducted to determine the effect of the genre indices (30 merged into 8) on each of the two testing genres

(N1 and E2). As predicted, the trend analysis suggested a significant linear relationship between the predicted group orders and the eight genre indices (N1 trend analysis: $F(1, 299) = 711.031$, $p < 0.001$; E2 trend analysis: $F(1, 299) = 734.503$, $p < 0.001$; see Figure 3). The result is further evidence of support for the claim that Gramulator derived indices generalize to other sets of data.

The result of the trend analysis supports the results of the Spearman Correlations reported earlier in this section; however, the trend analysis results do not confirm significant differences between the eight predicted levels. Thus, to assess our prediction, we followed Field (2005) and modified our statistical test by changing the default polynomial contrast to a simple contrast and then comparing each of the levels (e.g., level 1 to level 8, level 2 to level 8, level 3 to level 8 and so forth.) By removing each level in turn, we were able to assess differences between every level of prediction. The results were as predicted. All predicted levels for all combinations of both N1 and E2 were significantly different at the $p < 0.001$

Figure 3. Trend analysis between predicted order and the mean value

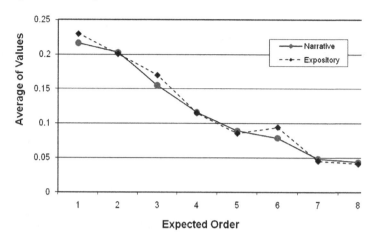

level. The one reversed level for the E2 text was also significant ($p = 0.006$).

The results of these analyses offer compelling evidence that the Gramulator is able to satisfy the conditions of a proximal similarity model (Campbell, 1986). Specifically, it is not only able to produce results for externally similar data, but it is also able to produce results that rank those external data in terms of similarity.

In addition, to validating the derived indices of the Gramulator, the data also validates the size of the corpora used. That is, if the size of the corpus (300 texts each of about 300 words each) produced the predicted results then the size of the corpus is presumably sufficient for the task. The result lends some support to Granger, et al. (2002) and other members of the second language learning field who have long held that small corpora are sufficiently informative.

CONCLUSION

In this chapter we discussed the theoretical underpinnings of the Gramulator and its architecture. We also presented results of a validation study. In terms of the ANLP motif: Identification, Investigation, and Resolution, we can describe the Gramulator

as follows. The *identified* issue was that existing computational discourse tools are not sufficiently equipped to provide researchers with explicit examples of construct evaluations at the lexical feature level. That is, although we can learn that a text is "high" in terms of a psychological or linguistic phenomenon (e.g., cohesion), it is difficult to know which examples of that phenomenon of the text are driving (and which are not driving) such effects. Our *investigation* of this issue led us to linguistic and psychological methods and theories that would guide a new application. The methods and theories included contrastive corpus analysis, machine differential diagnosis, and alignable differences theory. The *resolution* of the issue was the development of the Gramulator, together with production evidence from several studies and a validation study presented here.

The Gramulator supplies researchers with arrays of linguistic features that can facilitate the identification of explicit and implicit genre specific features. However, we must readily accept that there is any number of features to a text, and we can make no claim that the Gramulator reveals all the important features. We also would like to make clear that we make no claim that the Gramulator's contribution to textual analysis is superior to that of other tools such as Coh-Metrix,

LIWC, or others. Instead, our position is that the Gramulator offers an original approach to extracting potentially diagnostic content of groups of texts, and that the features currently offered by the tool are an important step towards a greater qualitative and quantitative understanding of the linguistic and psychological phenomena of recognition, differentiation, and categorization.

REFERENCES

Altenberg, B., & Granger, S. (2002). *Lexis in contrast: Corpus-based approaches.* Amsterdam, The Netherlands: Benjamins.

Bazerman, C. (1988). *Shaping written knowledge: The genre and activity of the experimental article in science.* Madison, WI: University of Wisconsin Press.

Bhatia, V. (1997). Applied genre analysis and ESP. In Miller, T. (Ed.), *Functional approaches to written text: Classroom applications.* Washington, DC: USIA.

Biber, D. (1989). A typology of English texts. *Linguistics, 27,* 3–43. doi:10.1515/ling.1989.27.1.3

Biber, D. (1993). Representativeness in corpus design. *Literary and Linguistic Computing, 8*(4), 243–257. doi:10.1093/llc/8.4.243

Bunton, D. (1998). *Linguistic and textual problems in PhD and MPhil thesis: An analysis of genre moves and metatext.* Unpublished doctoral dissertation, The University of Hong Kong.

Campbell, D. T. (1986). Relabeling internal and external validity for applied social scientists. In Trochim, W. M. K. (Ed.), *Advances in quasi-experimental design and analysis. New directions for program evaluation, no. 31.* San Francisco, CA: Jossey-Bass.

Chall, J. S. (1983). *Stages of reading development.* New York, NY: McGraw-Hill.

Cobb, T. 2003. Analyzing late interlanguage with learner corpora: Québec replications of three European studies. *The Canadian Modern Language Review/La Revue canadienne des langues vivantes, 59*(3), 393-423.

Crossley, S. A., McCarthy, P. M., & McNamara, D. S. (2007). Discriminating between second language learning text-types. In D. Wilson & G. Sutcliffe (Eds.), *Proceedings of the Twentieth International Florida Artificial Intelligence Research Society Conference* (pp. 205-210). Menlo Park, CA: The AAAI Press.

Downs, W. (1998). *Language and society.* Cambridge University Press.

Duran, N. D., & McCarthy, P. M. (November, 2010). *Using statistically improbable n-gram features to reveal the thematic content of deception.* Paper presented at the Society for Computers in Psychology (SCiP), Houston, Texas.

Field, A. (2005). *Discovering statistics using SPSS* (2nd ed.). London, UK: Sage.

Flowerdew, L. (1999). Corpus linguistics in ESP: A genre-based perspective. Penetrating discourse: Integrating theory with practice in second language teaching. *9th International Conference, Language Centre,* HKUST, Hong Kong (22-23 June, 1999), (pp. 21-35).

Flowerdew, L. (2000). Using a genre-based framework to teach organizational structure in academic writing. *ELT Journal, 54*(4), 369–378. doi:10.1093/elt/54.4.369

Flowerdew, L. (2004in press). The argument for using English specialized corpora to understand academic and professional language. In Connor, U., & Upton, T. (Eds.), *Discourse in the professions: Perspectives from corpus linguistics.* Amsterdam, The Netherlands: John Benjamins.

Garg, A. X., Adhikari, N. K., McDonald, H., Rosas-Arellano, M. P., Devereaux, P. J., & Beyene, J. (2005). Effects of computerized clinical decision support systems on practitioner performance and patient outcomes: A systematic review. *Journal of the American Medical Association*, *293*, 1223–1238. doi:10.1001/jama.293.10.1223

Graesser, A. C., Olde, B. A., & Klettke, B. (2002). How does the mind construct and represent stories? In Green, M., Strange, J., & Brock, T. (Eds.), *Narrative impact: Social and cognitive foundations*. Mahwah, NJ: Erlbaum.

Granger, S. (Ed.). (1998). *Learner English on computer*. London, UK: Longman.

Granger, S., Hung, J., & Petch-Tyson, S. (Eds.). (2002). *Computer learner corpora, second language acquisition and foreign language teaching*. Amsterdam, The Netherlands: Benjamins.

Halliday, M. A. K., & Hasan, R. (1989). *Language, context, and text: Aspects of language in a social-semiotic perspective*. Oxford, UK: Oxford University Press.

Hendersen, D. J. O., & Clark, H. (2007). Retelling narratives as fiction or nonfiction. In D. S. McNamara & G. Trafton (Eds.), *Proceedings of the 29th Annual Conference of the Cognitive Science Society* (pp. 353-358). Cognitive Science Society.

Henry, A., & Roseberry, R. (2001). A narrow-angled corpus analysis of moves and strategies of the genre: Letter of application. *English for Specific Purposes*, *20*, 153–167. doi:10.1016/S0889-4906(99)00037-X

Hopkins, A., & Dudley-Evans, T. (1988). A genre-based investigation of the discussion sections in articles and dissertations. *English for Specific Purposes*, *7*, 113–121. doi:10.1016/0889-4906(88)90029-4

Hullender, A., & McCarthy, P. M. (2011). *Analyses of modern art criticism and photography criticism as separate genres*. Paper presented at the Southeastern Conference on Linguistics (SECOL).

Hymes, D. (1972). Models of interaction of language and social life. In Gumperz, J. J., & Hymes, D. (Eds.), *Directions of sociolinguistics: The ethnography of communication*. New York, NY: Holt, Rinehart and Winston.

Jurafsky, D., & Martin, H. (2009). *Speech and language processing: An introduction to natural language processing, speech recognition, and computational linguistics* (2nd ed.). Prentice-Hall.

Krashen, S. D. (1988). *Second language acquisition and second language learning*. Prentice-Hall International.

Kučera, H., & Nelson, F. (1967). *Computational analysis of present-day American English*. Brown University Press.

Louwerse, M. M., McCarthy, P. M., McNamara, D. S., & Graesser, A. C. (2004). Variation in language and cohesion across written and spoken registers. In K. Forbus, D. Gentner & T. Regier (Eds.), *Proceedings of the 26th Annual Cognitive Science Society* (pp. 843-848). Mahwah, NJ: Erlbaum.

McCarthy, P. M. (April, 2010). *Special presentation of the Gramulator*. Presented at the Southeastern Conference on Linguistics (*SECOL*).

McCarthy, P. M. (2010). GPAT paper: A genre purity assessment tool. In H. W. Guesgen & C. Murray (Eds.), *Proceedings of the 23rd International Florida Artificial Intelligence Research Society Conference* (pp. 241-246). Menlo Park, CA: The AAAI Press.

McCarthy, P. M., Hall, C., Duran, N. D., Doiuchi, M., Duncan, B., Fujiwara, Y., & McNamara, D. S. (in press). A computational analysis of journal abstracts written by Japanese, American, and British scientists. *The ESPecialist*.

McCarthy, P. M., & Jarvis, S. (2007). A theoretical and empirical evaluation of *vocd*. *Language Testing*, *24*, 459–488. doi:10.1177/0265532207080767

McCarthy, P. M., Lewis, G. A., Dufty, D. F., & McNamara, D. S. (2006). Analyzing writing styles with Coh-Metrix. In *Proceedings of the Florida Artificial Intelligence Research Society International Conference (FLAIRS)* (pp. 764-770).

McCarthy, P. M., Lightman, E. J., Dufty, D. F., & McNamara, D. S. (2006). Using Coh-Metrix to assess distributions of cohesion and difficulty: An investigation of the structure of highschool textbooks. *Proceedings of the 28th Annual Conference of the Cognitive Science Society.*

McEnery, T., & Wilson, A. (1996). *Corpus linguistics.* Edinburgh, UK: Edinburgh University Press.

McEnery, T., Xiao, R., & Tono, Y. (2006). *Corpus-based language studies: An advanced resource book.* London, UK: Routledge.

McNamara, D. S., Graesser, A. C., & Louwerse, M. M. (in press). Sources of text difficulty: Across the ages and genres. In Sabatini, J. P., & Albro, E. (Eds.), *Assessing reading in the 21st century: Aligning and applying advances in the reading and measurment sciences.* Lanham, MD: R&L Education.

McNamara, D. S., Graesser, A. C., McCarthy, P. M., & Cai Z. (in press). *Coh-Metrix: Automated evaluation of text and discourse.* Cambridge University Press.

McNamara, D. S., Louwerse, M. M., McCarthy, P. M., & Graesser, A. C. (2010). Coh-Metrix: Capturing linguistic features of cohesion. *Discourse Processes*, *47*, 292–330. doi:10.1080/01638530902959943

Min, H. C., & McCarthy, P. M. (April, 2010). *Identifying variations in the discourse of American and Korean scientists. A contrastive corpus analysis using the Gramulator and Coh-Metrix.* Paper presented at the South-eastern Conference on Linguistics (*SECOL*).

Min, H. C., & McCarthy, P. M. (2010). Identifying varietals in the discourse of American and Korean scientists: A contrastive corpus analysis using the Gramulator. In H. W. Guesgen & C. Murray (Eds.), *Proceedings of the 23rd International Florida Artificial Intelligence Research Society Conference* (pp. 247-252). Menlo Park, CA: The AAAI Press.

Radvansky, G. A., Zwaan, R. A., Curiel, J. M., & Copeland, D. E. (2001). Situation models and aging. *Psychology and Aging*, *16*, 145–160. doi:10.1037/0882-7974.16.1.145

Rahati, A., & Kabanza, F. (2010). Persuasive dialogues in an intelligent tutoring system for medical diagnosis. In *Proceedings of the 10th Annual Intelligent Tutoring Systems International Conference* (pp. 51-61), Berlin, Germany: Springer.

Reutzel, D. R., & Cooter, R. B. Jr. (2007). *Strategies for reading assessment and instruction: Helping every child succeed* (3rd ed.). Upper Saddle River, NJ: Merrill Prentice Hall.

Rouet, J. F., Levonen, J., Dillon, A. P., & Spiro, R. J. (Eds.). (1996). *Hypertext and cognition.* Mahwah, NJ: Lawrence Erlbaum Associates.

Scott, M., & Tribble, C. (2006). *Textual patterns: Key words and corpus analysis in language education.* Amsterdam, The Netherlands: John Benjamins.

Shortliffe, E. H. (1987). Computer programs to support clinical decision making. *Journal of the American Medical Association*, *258*, 61–66. doi:10.1001/jama.258.1.61

Trabasso, T., & Bartolone, J. (2003). Story understanding and counterfactual reasoning. *Journal of Experimental Psychology. Learning, Memory, and Cognition*, *29*, 904–923. doi:10.1037/0278-7393.29.5.904

Upton, T., & Connor, U. (2001). Using computerised corpus analysis to investigate the text linguistic discourse moves of a genre. *English for Specific Purposes*, *20*(4), 313–329. doi:10.1016/S0889-4906(00)00022-3

Van Dijk, T. A., & Kintsch, W. (1983). *Strategies of discourse comprehension*. New York, NY: Academic Press.

Vygotsky, L. S. (1978). Interaction between learning and development. In Cole, M., John-Steiner, V., Scribner, S., & Souberman, E. (Eds.), *Mind in society: The development of higher psychological processes* (pp. 79–91). (Lopez-Morillas, M., Trans.). Cambridge, MA: Harvard University Press.

Zwaan, R. A. (1993). *Aspects of literary comprehension*. Amsterdam, The Netherlands: John Benjamins.

Zwaan, R. A., Magliano, J. P., & Graesser, A. C. (1995). Dimensions of situations model construction in narrative comprehension. *Journal of Experimental Psychology. Learning, Memory, and Cognition*, *21*, 386–397. doi:10.1037/0278-7393.21.2.386

ENDNOTE

[1]   And we also like to think the names reflect the relaxed atmosphere of our laboritory and the people in it.

Chapter 19
The Role of Textual Graph Patterns in Discovering Event Causality

Bryan Rink
University of Texas at Dallas, USA

Cosmin Adrian Bejan
University of Southern California, USA

Sanda Harabagiu
University of Texas at Dallas, USA

ABSTRACT

We present a novel method for discovering causal relations between events encoded in text. In order to determine if two events from the same sentence are in a causal relation or not, we first build a graph representation of the sentence that encodes lexical, syntactic, and semantic information. From such graph representations we automatically extract multiple graph patterns (or subgraphs). The patterns are sorted according to their contribution to the expression of intra-sentential causality between events. To decide whether a pair of events is in a causal relation, we employ a binary classifier that uses the graph patterns. Our experimental results indicate that capturing causal event relations using graph patterns outperforms existing methods.

INTRODUCTION

Automatic discovery of causal relations between textual events is a central task for various applications in Natural Language Processing (NLP). Specifically, tasks that require some form of reasoning such as probabilistic reasoning (Narayanan, 1997), common sense reasoning (Mueller,

2007), and question answering (Girju, 2003). An example of a causal relation between two events is presented in the following sentence:

- **S1:** *He wound up and let loose a fastball.*

This example encodes a special type of causal relation called ENABLEMENT, in which the event *wound* enables the event *let loose* to happen. In this case, the event *let loose* will take place only

DOI: 10.4018/978-1-60960-741-8.ch019

if the event *wound* occurs. Moreover, causal relations are closely related with temporal relations that hold between two events. For example, the ENABLEMENT relation from sentence S1 corresponds to a BEFORE temporal relation established between the *wound* event and the *let loose* event.

We cast causal relation detection as a classification task. Most existing approaches for discovering causal relations use machine learning classifiers based on unstructured linguistic features. In this chapter, we describe a method that captures the contextual information of the two events. Contextual information is captured by lexical, syntactic, and semantic features as well as dependencies that exist between these features. Features are structured into graphs, enabling us to discover graph patterns that account for causality between pairs of intra-sentential events.

The remainder of the chapter is organized as follows. We first describe the related work. Next we detail the graph representation that captures the structural dependencies of lexical, syntactic, and semantic features characterizing pairs of events that belong to a causal relation. In that section we detail each type of feature as well. The following section discusses the method of discovering syntactic and lexico-semantic graph patterns that characterize causality. Patterns are used for training a binary classifier which decides whether there exists a causal relation between pairs of intra-sentential events. In a separate section we discuss the experimental results and the error analysis. We also discuss the future research directions before summarizing the conclusions of the chapter.

RELATED WORK

Causality can be expressed in texts in many ways. Moreover, linguists and researchers have established that there are several forms of causality, including PURPOSE, REASON, and ENABLEMENT (Bejan & Harabagiu, 2008a). Traditionally, causality in

text has been viewed as a discourse phenomenon or as a semantic-specific function. Methods that have focused on the discourse-level information attempted to recognized causal relations between discourse units in the same way as they would recognize other discourse relations (e.g. ELABORATION, PARALLEL, and VIOLATED-EXPECTATIONS). For example, Marcu & Echihabi (2002) have used a naïve Bayes classifier trained on pairs of words from discourse segments separated by cue phrases such as *thus* and *because*. Their approach achieved very high scores when evaluated on CAUSE-EXPLANATION-EVIDENCE relations.

The previous techniques that focused on the semantic aspects of causality have relied on a combination of syntactic and lexico-semantic knowledge. For example, Girju and Moldovan (2002) have studied causal relations between nominals. They were able to obtain promising results by focusing on patterns of the form [NOUN—VERB—NOUN] and using semantic knowledge encoded in WordNet (Fellbaum et al., 1998). WordNet is a large lexico-semantic knowledge base that encodes the vast majority of English nouns, verbs, adjectives, and adverbs. Word senses and hypernym information available from WordNet were used to detect causal relations in the approach reported in (Girju and Moldovan 2002). The results were promising, and thus they have prompted a task dedicated to the recognition of nominal causal relations in SemEval 2007. SemEval (formerly Senseval) is a series of evaluations of semantic analysis systems. The task for classification of semantic relations between nominals asked participants to identify whether a given semantic relation (e.g., PRODUCT-PRODUCER, PART-WHOLE, CAUSE-EFFECT, etc.) exists between two nouns from a sentence. The approach reported in (Beamer et al., 2007) uses several lexico-syntactic features, including the word stems and sequences of part of speech between the nominals. They used some general features including whether the nouns encode a time or location. They also used features based on the context of the nouns such as grammatical role, semantic role, and the sequence of stemmed words between the nouns.

Causal relations were also discovered by the method reported in (Khoo, Chan, & Niu, 2000). The method used manually constructed dependency tree patterns to detect causal relations in a specific subset of medical domain documents. This method not only detects whether causality is expressed in the medical articles, but they also detect the characteristics of the causal relations (e.g. enabling conditions), size of the effect, and size of the cause (e.g. dosage in their domain). Their approach obtains remarkably accurate results, which are justified by the manual effort used for identifying causal patterns.

In a separate effort, Bethard and Martin (2008) have studied the interaction between causal and temporal relations in texts. They train a classifier using surface features, WordNet hypernym and lexical files, as well as syntactic paths, and a scoring feature for the events based on web counts.

The method described in this chapter discovers causal relations in a novel way by automatically detecting patterns which can simultaneously incorporate lexical, syntactic, and semantic information. The patterns we presented are more expressive than most existing pattern-based approaches for causality recognition. This allows us to achieve a higher score than existing systems, while using fewer features. We performed our evaluation on the same corpus used by Bethard and Martin (2008) to compare our structured feature approach against their approach.

TEXTUAL GRAPH REPRESENTATIONS

Our approach to detecting causality is based on building graph representations of input sentences and using those graphs to detect textual patterns in the form of subgraphs. The graphs contain lexical, syntactic, and semantic properties of the text, enabling the recognition of these pieces of linguistic information.

Textual content, when viewed at the surface level, is simply a sequence of words, or tokens. Each word is a token, and certain punctuation marks are treated as tokens as well. Because tokens are the basic unit in text, they also form the core of the graphs we build. For each token in the text, we create a *tok* node, as in Figure 1(a). The other nodes from the graph correspond to: (1) The word (e.g. *He*); (2) The syntactic parse nodes (e.g. *parse:NP*); (3) Lexical information (e.g. *pos:PRP);* or (4) nodes indicating events (e.g. *Event1)*. The edges from the graph illustrated in Figure 1(a) represent: (a) syntactic links determined by the parser, (b) lexical information corresponding to each token node, and (c) event information from the corpus.

Each token is associated with a node that corresponds to that token's part of speech (POS). Part of speech determines whether a word is a noun, verb, preposition, and so forth. Part of speech is an important property of tokens because it helps to disambiguate the meaning of a word in text. For instance, in Figure 1(a) the word "wound" is tagged with a VBD part of speech, or past tense verb. This informs us that the word "wound" in this sentence should not be interpreted as the noun form of *wound* (an injury). In Figure 1(a) we have used the Penn Treebank (Marcus et al., 1994) tags with *pos:* nodes that are connected to the *tok* nodes. The pos: prefix is used to differentiate these nodes from other nodes such as the word nodes mentioned before. In Figure 1(a) we have connected the *pos:* nodes together according to the sequence of their tokens in the text. This structure allows us to create patterns that capture sequences of POS tags.

We can add many other linguistic properties to these graphs to capture additional features of the text. Another example of a textual feature is the lemma of a token, which is an unconjugated, non-plural version of the word. This allows us to capture a more general meaning independent of the

Figure 1. (a) An example text graph encoding lexical and syntactic information. (b) A basic pattern, matching the highlighted portion of (a). (c) WordNet hypernyms used in the graph structure.

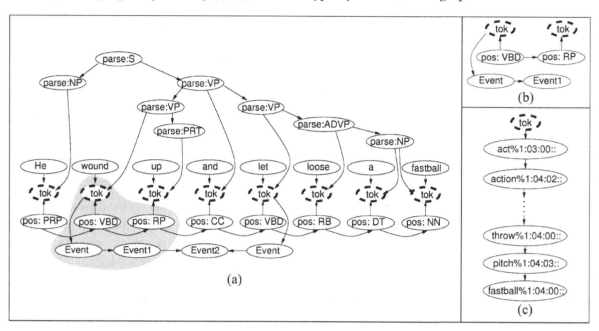

specific form of the word chosen by the speaker. For example, "winds," "wound," and "wind" all have the lemma "wind," allowing a pattern to use *lemma:wind* to match any of these variations.

In addition to single token properties of the text we can also capture syntactic and semantic relations that exist between the tokens. A familiar syntactic relationship is the syntax parse tree. An example can be seen in Figure 1 by observing the *parse:* nodes. These nodes, along with the *tok* nodes form a tree that describes the syntax of this sentence. The sentence root, represented by *parse:S* decomposes into a noun phrase (*parse:NP*) and a verb phrase (*parse:VP*) which decompose further, until the leaf *tok* nodes are reached.

For the task of detecting causality between two events encoded as single words, we attach an *Event* node to each event's token node. It is to be noted that the graph contains four event nodes: two that indicate that a token corresponds to an event, and two others which indicate which one is the first event and which one is the second event. The *Event1* node is linked to the *Event2* node to

enable the recognition of patterns that consider only the context of the events without regard to the intervening tokens. The general-to-specific structure of the event nodes allows more flexibility in the potential patterns that can be extracted from these graphs. The presence of the general *Event* nodes allows for a pattern that matches either event, rather than a specific one. However, the presence of the *EventX* nodes allows for that specificity if necessary.

Semantic relationships, such as hypernymy, can be added to the graphs as well. A hypernym of a word is another word which is more general. For example, "pitch" is a hypernym of "fastball," and "throw" is a hypernym of "pitch." The lexical resource WordNet (Fellbaum et al., 1998) contains a hypernym hierarchy for most English words. We used this hierarchy to add hypernym information to the graphs. Each *tok* node is connected first to the *highest* hypernym. An example can be seen in Figure 1(c), which uses WordNet sense keys to unambiguously identify a specific word sense. The highest hypernym is then connected to the next highest, and so on, until the specific synset for the token is added. Synsets are the units used by WordNet to represent hypernyms. This structure allows for patterns that match on tokens at a high hypernym level, or by including intermediate hypernyms, down to the most specific sense level, again using a general-to-specific structure like the event nodes.

Semantic parses, such as those based on Propbank (Kingsbury & Palmer, 2002) and FrameNet (Baker et al., 1998) can be incorporated into the graphs as well. For example, in Figure 1(a) a semantic role AGENT can be added between the *tok* nodes for *He* and *wound* because *He* acts as the agent of the predicate *wound*.

Although this work describes the automatic detection of patterns, it is informative to examine the power of potential patterns on these graphs. The graph structure allows for patterns that act as conjunctions on the features of a token. For example, we could construct a pattern such as [*word:cause → :tok: → pos:VBP*] to recognize the verb form of the word *cause* rather than the noun form. This pattern fragment could then be joined with others to form an even more restrictive pattern. Looking at the patterns in this way (i.e., as conjunctions of feature restrictions) is reminiscent of rule learning such as that in (Cohen, 1996). One difference is that the patterns we propose can capture textual dependencies (such as chains of POS) and also the structure of syntactic trees.

The structure we chose for the graphs is influenced by the patterns it enables, and also by the limitations of our pattern finding approach. For example, to allow for more generic and hence more powerful patterns, we could connect the *next* edges between *tok* nodes rather than *POS* nodes. However, increasing the power of the patterns in this way significantly increases the search space of patterns, beyond the memory capacity of the machine we ran the discovery algorithm on. Therefore, connecting the POS nodes with *next* edges is a compromise that still allows some

generality to be captured without generating too many candidate patterns.

EXTRACTING PATTERNS FROM TEXTUAL GRAPHS

The graph representation of text illustrated in Figure 1(a) allows for representing and matching patterns in the form of connected subgraphs. Consider Figure 1(b), where we show a very simple pattern. The *tok* node of this pattern will match against the second *tok* node in Figure 1(a), and the other nodes will match against corresponding nodes from Figure 1(a). This pattern will match in sentences whose first event mention and the next token correspond to VBD (past tense) and RP (particle) parts-of-speech respectively. So, patterns are represented as connected graphs. Furthermore, a pattern matches a sentence if the pattern is a subgraph of that sentence's textual graph. Patterns are considered to match a target graph if all nodes and edges in the pattern correspond to equivalent nodes and edges in the target graph. The knowledge of whether or not a pattern matches a graph could be a useful indicator of whether the event might be causal. We explain later how to use the presence of patterns within sentences as features for a classifier to detect causally related events.

The graph patterns described above could be derived in two ways, either manually constructed or automatically discovered. Many existing approaches, such as (Hearst, 1998) and (Khoo, Chan, & Niu, 2000) use manually constructed patterns. The textual graphs we describe can encompass the patterns from these existing approaches. For example, patterns consisting of sequences of words between named entities could be created by adding directed links between the *word* nodes in the graph, and by adding named entity nodes connected to the token nodes for the entities. Other works have achieved automatic discovery of patterns, but are generally limited to sequence patterns, such as sequences of words or paths within syntax or dependency trees. We consider our approach a generalization of such methods, including (Ravichandran & Hovy, 2002). In that work, they have two entities and discover lexical patterns between the two entities by running a suffix tree algorithm over the tokens in the documents. This is very similar to the approach we take here, with the difference that we can discover full graphical patterns rather than simply sequences. Other works (Chang & Choi, 2006) have discovered patterns on dependency trees, but they are generally limited to only matching on the dependency tree and do not incorporate other properties of the text.

By transforming sentences into graphs of textual features and relations, we can cast the task of finding textual patterns as a task of finding graph patterns. For our purposes we would like to find any connected subgraph that occurs more than a certain number of times in the training examples and call those patterns. A subgraph which occurs infrequently in the dataset will not have enough support to determine whether it is a good indicator for causality or not, so we restrict our consideration to frequent subgraphs. An infrequent subgraph may be a good pattern, but if it only occurs in one example in our training set we cannot say with any conviction whether its presence in a sentence indicates causality or not. Moreover, we will consider all frequent patterns, even if they do not contain an event node. Such patterns can still provide useful clues that the sentence overall is structured as a causal sentence, independent of the specific events being considered.

Therefore, we build on top of existing research in the area of finding frequent subgraphs from a set of graphs (Yan & Han, 2002; Nijssen & Kok, 2005; Kuramochi & Karypis, 2001). Enumerating all possible subgraphs is problematic because the number of subgraphs is exponential in the size of the graph. This problem arises because of the large number of possible choices that can be made about which nodes and edges go into a subgraph. However, since we are only interested in the fre-

quent subgraphs, and not all possible subgraphs, we can make use of a key insight in frequent subgraph discovery that makes it a feasible problem. The insight is that any frequent subgraph must consist of smaller subgraphs which occur at least as frequently. Following this insight recursively to its end, we can first find all nodes that occur frequently, because we know any subgraph occurring frequently must consist entirely of such nodes. Thus, all nodes that occur less than some threshold, called the minimum support, are filtered out. Next, the remaining nodes are extended into two-node subgraphs which occur in the collection. Those with a frequency below the threshold are filtered out. This process is continued until all frequent subgraphs have been found.

The process outlined above is an overview of the gSpan algorithm (Yan & Han, 2002). We used an implementation of the algorithm[1] to find all subgraphs from our set of text graphs which occur in at least 5% of the causal examples. This provides a good balance between generating too many possible patterns and missing good, but less frequent patterns. We also used the CloseGraph algorithm (Yan & Han, 2003) to further reduce the number of patterns generated. CloseGraph filters out smaller frequent subgraphs that also appear within a larger frequent subgraph.

Therefore, our approach for discovering patterns for matching causal event relations consists of: (i) building graph representations for all the sentences that contain causal examples in the training set; and (ii) using gSpan to detect the frequent patterns.

PATTERN MATCHING

Once the patterns have been discovered from the training set, we need a method for determining when a sentence contains a pattern. This information will be used to determine when patterns match in the non-causal training examples (since patterns are generated only from the causal examples), and to detect pattern matches within the test set. Since the patterns are simply subgraphs, pattern matching reduces to the problem of determining whether a subgraph is contained in another graph. That is, we want to find a homomorphism from the pattern to a target graph. A graph homomorphism is a mapping of the nodes and edges of a query graph (the pattern) onto the nodes and edges of a target graph, such that adjacent nodes in the query graph map to adjacent nodes in the target graph. We actually want a specific kind of homomorphism known as a monomorphism. A monomorphism is a homomorphism in which unique nodes from the query graph map to unique nodes in the target graph (forming an injective, or one-to-one, mapping). So, to test whether a pattern matches in a graph, we test that each node in the pattern has a corresponding node in the graph, and each edge between nodes in the pattern has a corresponding edge between the mapped nodes in the graph. The idea is laid out formally below.

A homomorphism is a mapping $\pi(x)$ which, given a graph $T = (V_t, E_t)$ and a graph $S = (V_s, E_s)$ meets the following constraints:

1. $\forall v \in V_s : \pi(v) \varepsilon V_t \wedge \text{label}(v) = \text{label}(\pi(v))$
2. $\forall e \in E_s : \pi(e) \in E_t \wedge \text{label}(e) = \text{label}(\pi(e))$
3. $\forall (v_1, v_2) \in E_s : \pi((v_1, v_2)) = (\pi(v_1), \pi(v_2))$

Monomorphism has the additional constraints that $\pi(v_1) \neq \pi(v_2) \forall v_1 \in V_s$ where $v_1 \neq v_2$.

Graph monomorphism is an NP-complete problem. However, graphs built from individual sentences are small enough that the time taken to determine a mapping is manageable. To solve the matching problem we cast it as a constraint satisfaction problem (CSP) following the constraints specified above. Then, using a CSP solver[2] we determine the satisfiability of the match. The CSP is satisfiable if and only if there is a match. As an optimization we pre-filter any graphs that do not contain any possible matches for the nodes and edges from the pattern.

GRAPH CLASSIFICATION

The pattern discovery process determines which subgraphs occur frequently in the causal examples from the training set. Some of those patterns will be good indicators for a causal relation, but many will not be. We use the pattern matching technique to determine which causal and non-causal examples a pattern matches. A good discriminative pattern will match primarily on causal examples, and on very few non-causal examples. Table 1 shows an example hit count for a good causal pattern. The training set is dominated by non-causal examples, so even though this pattern matches some non-causal examples, the fact that it matches so many more causal examples shows that it is a good indicator for causality. This example pattern matched causal examples 18 times, but non-causal examples only 5 times. Therefore this pattern is a strong indicator for causality. In this section we describe how we determine the strength of a pattern as an indicator for causality, and then how the evidence provided by multiple pattern matches can be combined together to come to a decision on causality.

The strength of a pattern is calculated by computing Fisher's exact test on the contingency table for the pattern. The contingency table is constructed as in the example shown in Table 1, where cells count training examples, columns indicate whether an example was matched or not matched by the pattern, and rows indicate whether the example was causal or non-causal. We use Fisher's exact test because it indicates how likely a pattern's hit counts are to be seen, assuming independence between the event of a pattern

Table 1. Contingency table example for a pattern

	Match	No Match
Causal	18	189
Non-Causal	5	485

matching an example and whether the example contains a CAUSE relation. Using these scores, we perform an initial ranking of all discovered patterns, from lower Fisher probability to higher. The probability assigned to a contingency table whose first row is $<a, b>$, whose second row is $<c, d>$, and where $n=a+b+c+d$, is calculated as follows:

$$p = \frac{(a+b)!(c+d)!(a+c)!(b+d)!}{n!\,a!\,b!\,c!\,d!}$$

This initial ranking is done because our experiments show that using all of the discovered patterns produces inferior results to choosing only the best patterns and then using those to train a classifier (Shown later in Figure 2 and Table 2).

We further refine the ranking to remove near-duplicates. Since the pattern discovery process discovers *all* patterns that occur above some frequency, it has a tendency to find patterns that match on exactly the same set of sentences, or

almost exactly the same set. One example of such a near-duplicate pair is given below:

- **P1:** *word:someone→:tok: → pos:NN*
- **P2:** *word:someone→:tok: → lemma:someone*

Both P1 and P2 will match on all of the same sentences because the word "someone" should always be tagged with part of speech NN (singular noun), and it will always have a lemma of "someone." However, these are two distinct patterns. To overcome the situation where we provide the classifier with many similar patterns we adapted Thoma et al. (2009)'s Sequential Cover algorithm into our Pattern Ranking algorithm (Algorithm 1).

The input of this algorithm is a set of patterns ranked by Fisher's exact test as described above. For each pattern the algorithm decides to either keep it or discard it. The algorithm filters patterns that only match examples that have already been

Figure 2. F1 scores corresponding to Table 3

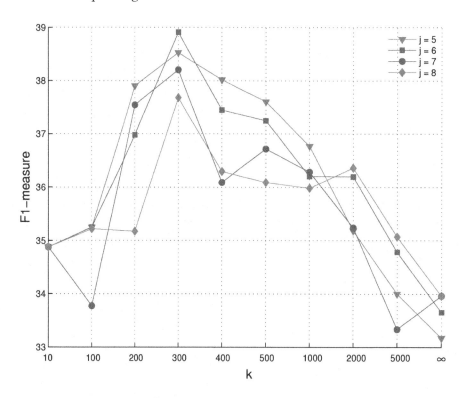

Table 2. Values of F1 on the test set for various values j and k on the Word+POS+Parse configuration

	10k	100k	200k	300k	400k	500k	1000k	2000k	5000k	∞k
1j	18.0	13.7	15.2	5.2	152	150	15.7	20.0	14.1	5.6
1.5j	175	17.3	18.5	20.6	20.3	21.0	8.0	29.6	25.4	19.8
2j	17.5	19.1	27.5	28.3	29.9	31.5	32.0	33.1	29.1	29.8
3j	17.5	35.1	35.0	36.7	34.1	34.2	34.5	34.3	33.1	36.6
4j	34.8	34.8	36.5	36.6	38.0	35.2	33.9	333	34.7	33.8
5j	34.8	35.2	37.9	38.5	38.0	37.6	36.7	35.1	34.0	33.1
6j	34.8	35.2	36.9	38.9	37.4	37.2	36.2	36.1	34.7	33.6
7j	34.8	33.7	37.5	38.2	36.0	36.7	36.2	35.2	33.3	33.9
8j	34.8	35.2	35.1	37.6	36.2	36.0	35.9	36.3	35.0	33.9
10j	34.8	34.3	33.5	36.2	34.0	35.6	36.0	33.8	34.5	33.9
50j	34.8	34.8	35.3	35.6	34.3	35.1	32.3	34.1	34.2	33.9
100j	34.8	34.8	35.3	35.6	34.3	35.1	32.3	34.1	34.2	33.9

matched by a previously kept pattern. Previous matches are only counted when a causal pattern matches a causal (positive) example, or a non-causal pattern matches a non-causal (negative) example. A pattern is considered causal if more than 30% of the sentences it matches in the training set are causal. This threshold was chosen because roughly 30% of the examples in the training set have a causal relation. After Algorithm 1 is run once, it is run again on the discarded patterns to provide a ranking to those patterns and

they are ranked behind the patterns chosen in the first pass. This is repeated until all patterns have been ranked.

The purpose of ordering the patterns is to take the k highest ranking ones and pass them to a classifier for learning the causality relation between events. The representation of each sentence given to the classifier is a binary vector indicating which patterns fired. For instance, if we use k patterns then a sentence will be represented as a binary vector with k elements where the ith element is 1

Algorithm 1. Pattern ranking

```
Let R = ∅
while |Tp| ≥ 0 ∧ |Tn| ≥ 0 ∧ |P| > 0 do
        Let p0 = first pattern in P
        ifp0 is causal and matches at least on graph in Tpthen
                Tp = Tp \ {g | g∈Tp is matched by p0}
                R = R ∪ {p0}
        elseifp0 is non-causal and matches at least one graph in Tnthen
                Tn = Tn \ {g | g∈Tn is matched by p0}
                R = R ∪ {p0}
        end if
        P = P \ {p0}
end while
```

if the ith pattern matches that sentence, and 0 if it does not match. All of the training examples are converted to binary vectors and then passed along with their causal/non-causal label to an SVM classifier[3]. Following Bethard and Martin (2008), we optimized for the F1 measure rather than accuracy. This was accomplished by adjusting the cost factor *j* for the SVM to give more weight to positive instances.

EXPERIMENTAL RESULTS

We evaluated our system using different configurations of textual features on a corpus of 1,000 causal and non-causal examples (Bethard et al., 2008). Three of our configurations correspond to configurations used by a previous system, (Bethard and Martin, 2008), to compare the performance of our system.

Dataset

The dataset consists of 1,000 sentences containing a pair of events which are joined by a conjunction. For example, from S1: "*He wound up and let loose a fastball.*" The event *wound* and the event *let loose* are syntactically joined by the conjunction *and*. The corpus consists only of events in this form because such event pairs are often either causally or temporally related. We split the corpus into a training set and test set, using the same split as Bethard and Martin (2008), containing 697 training examples, and 303 testing examples.

Setup

We build graphs from the sentences using sets of the following textual features:

- **Word:** The surface word (e.g., *ran*);
- **POS:** The part of speech (e.g., *VBD*);
- **Parse:** *A syntactic parse tree as in* Figure 1;
- **Stem:** The WordNet lemma (e.g., *run*);

- **VerbOcean:** Semantic links between verbs taken from VerbOcean (Chklovski & Pantel, 2004), without weights;
- **Dep (Dependency parse)[4]:** Each dependency link is represented by one node in the graph, with a directed edge coming in to it from the source of the dependency, and a directed edge leaving the node to the *tok* node for the destination of the dependency. An example can be seen from the pattern in Figure 4;
- **WSD:** The hypernym chain for the senses from word sense disambiguation (Mihalcea & Csomai, 2005);
- **FNType:** Using the UTD-SRL semantic parser (Bejan & Hathaway, 2007), we extract for each event the semantic frame it evokes;
- **Tmp:** Manually annotated temporal links from the corpus (BEFORE, AFTER, NO-REL).

Table 3 lists different sets of textual features used to build the graphs, discover patterns, and train a classifier, along with the results obtained with that set of features. We list the number of patterns discovered, along with the number of top patterns used, *k*; the SVM cost factor, *j*, which gives higher weight to positive instances; the precision and recall; and the F1 measure.

Discussion of Results

Table 3 shows that our system was able to achieve higher F1-measures than the existing system for comparable sets of features. We compute F1 measure as $F1 = 2 \times p \times r/(p+r)$. The precision, *p*, is the number of correct causal classifications divided by the number of events the system says are causal. The recall, *r*, is the number of number of correctly classified causal relations divided by the number of manually annotated causal relations. A higher F1 corresponds to a system that performs better, at least in terms of trade off between precision and recall.

Table 3. Comparison using different sets of annotations. k is the number of top patterns passed to the classifier, and j is the cost ratio used for the SVM. The patterns column shows the total number of patterns discovered under each configuration.

Configuration	Patterns	k	j	P	R	F1
Bethard & Martin Syntactic	-	-	-	24	80	37.4
Bethard & Martin Semantic	-	-	-	27	64	38.1
Word+POS+Parse	16377	1000	1.5	26	78	38.9
Word+POS+Parse+Stem	16415	1000	1.5	27	70	39.1
Word+POS+Dep	14800	200	5.0	26	70	38.3
Word+POS+Dep+VerbOcean	14811	200	3.0	29	59	38.8
Word+POS+Dep+FNType	14984	200	3.0	31	63	41.7
Word+POS+Dep+WSD	39341	400	3.0	33	61	42.9
Bethard & Martin All+Tmp	-	-	-	47	59	52.4
Word+POS+Parse+Tmp	18464	10	1.5	51	66	57.5
Word+POS+Dep+WSD+Tmp	43275	10	1.5	52	66	57.9

The parameters to the system are the number of patterns k, and the SVM cost ratio, j. Ideally these parameters would be learned by cross-validation on the training set, however differences between the training set and the test set inhibited this process. The training set has a different distribution of causal versus non-causal examples, as a result of Bethard and Martin's decision to split documents before a specific date into training, and all the rest into test. The training set is 29.7% causal examples, while the test set is only 21.5% causal examples. We attempted to evaluate our system using cross validation on the entire dataset instead, but this resulted in considerably higher scores than those reported above. This is because random splits on the entire dataset result in easier learning problems. Therefore, to form a fair comparison, we use Bethard and Martin's training and test sets. We present the scores for the best choice of parameters in Table 3 and scores for a full range of parameter choices for the Word+POS+Parse model in Table 2.

We created a set of graphs using the Word, POS, and Parse features to use as a comparison against Bethard & Martin's Syntactic model (2008). The Word+POS+Parse model outperformed their sys-tem, achieving an F-measure of 38.9, versus the existing system's F-measure of 37.4. Similarly, Bethard & Martin's Semantic model achieved a score of 38.1, while our model was boosted to 39.1 by adding word stems from WordNet. Table 3 shows the results for additional sets of features as well. The best result without temporal information was obtained by using a dependency parse and word sense disambiguation hypernym chains. The three systems listed at the bottom of the table make use of a hand annotated temporal relation between the events such as BEFORE, AFTER, or DURING. With that additional information the system was able to perform 15% better than without it, showing the importance of temporal relations in detecting causality.

The patterns chosen by the system as discriminative causal patterns are complex and not ones that a human would necessarily choose a priori. Figure 3 and Figure 4 show two of the top discovered patterns. Figure 3 shows a pattern detected in the Word+POS+Parse graphs. This pattern was a very good indicator for causality on the training set. It matches in 14 casual examples and zero non-causal examples, so it was ranked very high. Most patterns match at least some non-causal examples, motivating the use of a classifier to learn causality given evidence provided by the pattern matches. The pattern in Figure 3 is detecting a generalization of passive voice structure. The pattern will match in a sentence where a token with part of speech VBD (past tense) is followed by a token with POS VBN (past participle). The other nodes of the pattern match against the syntax tree of the sentence, and require that the match take place under three levels of verb phrase nesting.

An example of a sentence from the corpus matched by this pattern is given in S2:

- **S2:** *Hells Angels was**formed**in 1948 and**incorporated**in 1966.*

For this sentence, the pattern captures the passive voice verbal phrase, *"was formed,"* which is matched by VBD → VBN.

Figure 4 shows a pattern that was discovered in the graphs created using the

Figure 3. A highly ranked causal pattern that detects passive voice constructions

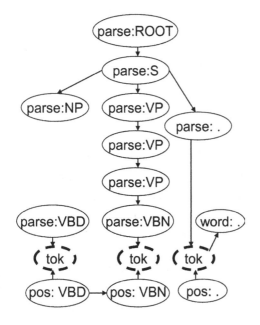

Word+POS+Dep+WSD configuration. The following sentence is one of the training examples matched by this pattern:

- **S3:** *Under the agreement, Westinghouse will be able to**purchase**smaller combustion turbines from its Japanese partner, and**package**and sell them with its own generators and other equipment.*

This is an example of an ENABLEMENT causal relation, because purchasing the turbines enables Westinghouse to package them. The pattern from Figure 4 will match on a three word prepositional phrase involving some form of communication. The first two tokens are a preposition (IN) and a determiner (DT), followed by a word which is a hyponym of *communication* in WordNet. In the example, the pattern matches the expression *"Under the agreement."* Examples of other textual expressions this pattern matched in the training set are: *"[out] of the question," "In that decision," "In the affidavits,"* and *"that the offer."* These phrases might be indications that the sentence is referring to a chain of events, which would imply a causal relation.

Error Analysis

We observed that a disproportionate number of system errors come in the form of *saying* events. For instance, this sentence was incorrectly marked as causal during the best run of the system: *"Delmed**said**yesterday that Fresenius USA would*

Figure 4. A semantic pattern detected by the system that looks for a phrase involving some form of communication

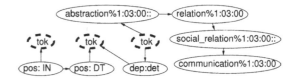

begin *distributing the product and that the company is***investigating***other possible distribution channels.*" The investigation is not caused by the fact that Delmed makes a statement, so no causal relation is present. A very similar, but crucially different sentence is the following: "*People have been***seeing***headline after headline after headline and***saying*:*. . .*" Here the event *saying* is caused by the event *seeing*. The order of the *saying* events in these two examples is different and is probably an important clue for causality detection. We also hypothesize that there simply weren't enough examples in the training set to learn this order clue for *saying* events.

Another type of error which could be alleviated with additional data is the use of cue phrases. As an example, the following sentence was incorrectly marked non-causal: "*... they were not necessary to prove historical points,* **failed** *the fair-use test and therefore* **infringed** *copyright.*" In this example, the cue phrase *therefore* provides evidence that the events are causally related. Such cue phrases could either be learned with additional training data or a list of cue phrases could be compiled and implemented as an additional feature in the graph structure to reduce the learning burden and amount of training data needed. This could be accomplished by linking the *tok* nodes for the words of a cue phrase to a *cue:* node. In this way, patterns could incorporate information about the presence of a cue phrase.

FUTURE RESEARCH DIRECTIONS

The process of understanding natural language is based on the assumption that documents are written with a model representation in mind that underlies a causal structure of the real-world events involved in a specific situation. We define an event scenario encoded in a document collection as the set of textual events participating in a specific situation (Bejan, 2008). Therefore, a natural extension of the work presented in this

chapter is to discover the event causal relations that capture the interactions between events in event scenarios. For instance, the events emphasized in the document example listed below is relevant in an event scenario describing a natural disaster. Furthermore, these events do not occur and operate independently, but rather each event is interrelated with other events and entities that participate in this scenario. As shown in this example, the event *earthquake* causes the event *tsunami* to happen, which consequently produces a series of effects: death of many people, destruction of multiple regions, rescue operations, etc. The entire causal structure corresponding to the events emphasized in this example is illustrated in Figure 5.

Excerpt from a News Article Describing a Natural Disaster

Tremors were **felt** *instantly in Malaysia and southern Thailand and as far off as southern India, but it was* **tidal waves** *or* **tsunamis** *caused by the* **earthquake** *that inflicted most of the* **death** *and* **destruction** *in the region. In India, at least 3,000 people* **died**, *most in the state of Tamil Nadu, Reuters news agency reported. It said the worst affected area in Indonesia was Banda Aceh, capital of Aceh province, where 3,000 had been* **killed**.

Helicopters in India **rushed** *medicine to stricken areas, while warships in Thailand* **steamed** *to island resorts to* **rescue** *survivors. In Thailand,*

Figure 5. The causal structure of the event scenario describing a natural disaster

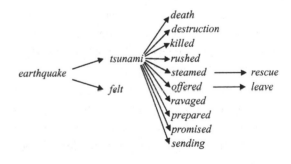

*the government **offered** free flights for thousands of Western tourists desperate to **leave** the southern resorts **ravaged** by the **tsunami**. The United States **dispatched** disaster teams and **prepared** a $15 million aid package to the Asian countries, and the 25-nation European Union **promised** to quickly **deliver** $4 million. Japan, China and Russia were **sending** teams of experts.*

For discovering the causal structure of event scenarios, we first propose to extract the event scenarios from a document collection by employing the unsupervised model described in (Bejan, 2008; Bejan & Harabagiu, 2008b). This model is based on the Latent Dirichlet Allocation (Blei, Ng, & Jordan, 2003) in order to express the documents as probabilistic mixtures of event scenarios as well as to compute for each event scenario a probabilistic distribution over the entire set of events from the document collection. Next, for every pair of events from an event scenario, we propose to adapt the method described in this chapter in order to decide whether there is a causal relation between the events or not. We consider the extension feasible since, in case the events belong to different sentences, we can combine the textual graphs associated with the two sentences.

CONCLUSION

This chapter outlined a new approach for discovering causal relations between events in text using graph patterns as features for a classifier. Unlike previous approaches, feature combinations and textual structure are automatically discovered rather than manually determined. As a consequence, adding a new feature to the textual graphs could be equivalent to trying many feature combinations in a traditional machine learning approach, reducing the manual effort required to explore various combinations. Using a graph representation to capture the dependencies be-

tween features allowed this approach to achieve better results when compared with a method that uses an unstructured representation on the same set of features.

REFERENCES

Baker, C. F., Fillmore, C. J., & Lowe, J. B. (1998). The Berkeley FrameNet project. In *Proceedings of the 17th International Conference on Computational Linguistics,* volume 1 (pp. 86-90). Morristown, NJ: Association for Computational Linguistics.

Beamer, B., Bhat, S., Chee, B., Fister, A., Rozovskaya, A., & Girju, R. (2007). UIUC: A knowledge-rich approach to identifying semantic relations between nominals. In *Proceedings of the 4th International Workshop on Semantic Evaluations* (pp. 386-389).

Bejan, C. A. (2008). Unsupervised discovery of event scenarios from texts. In *Proceedings of the Twenty-First International Florida Artificial Intelligence Research Society Conference* (pp. 124-129). Menlo Park, CA: AAAI Press.

Bejan, C. A., & Harabagiu, S. (2008a). A linguistic resource for discovering event structures and resolving event co-reference. In *Proceedings of the Sixth International Language Resources and Evaluation (LREC'08)*. Marrakech, Morocco: European Language Resources Association (ELRA).

Bejan, C. A., & Harabagiu, S. (2008b). Using clustering methods for discovering event structures. In *Proceedings of the 23rd National Conference on Artificial Intelligence,* volume 3 (pp. 1776-1777). Chicago, IL: AAAI Press.

Bejan, C. A., & Hathaway, C. (2007). UTD-SRL: A pipeline architecture for extracting frame semantic structures. In *Proceedings of the 4th International Workshop on Semantic Evaluations,* (pp. 460–463).

Bethard, S., Corvey, W., Klingenstein, S., & Martin, J. H. (2008). *Building a corpus of temporal-causal structure*. In Language Resources and Evaluation Conference (LREC).

Bethard, S., & Martin, J. H. (2008). Learning semantic links from a corpus of parallel temporal and causal relations. In *Proceedings of the 46th Annual Meeting of the Association for Computational Linguistics on Human Language Technologies: Short Papers* (pp. 662-678). Association for Computational Linguistics.

Chang, D. S., & Choi, K. S. (2006). Incremental cue phrase learning and bootstrapping method for causality extraction using cue phrase and word pair probabilities. *Information Processing & Management, 42*(3), 662–678. doi:10.1016/j.ipm.2005.04.004

Chklovski, T., & Pantel, P. (2004). Verbocean: Mining the web for fine-grained semantic verb relations. In *Proceedings of EMNLP, 4*, 33–40.

Cohen, W. (1996). Learning trees and rules with set-valued features. In *The 1996 13th National Conference on Artificial Intelligence, AAAI 96*, part 1(of 2) (pp. 709-716).

Fellbaum, C. (1998). *WordNet: An electronic lexical database*. Cambridge, MA: MIT Press.

Girju, R. (2003). Automatic detection of causal relations for question answering. In *ACL 2003 Workshop on Multilingual Summarization and Question Answering - Machine Learning and Beyond (p. 83)*. Association for Computational Linguistics.

Girju, R., & Moldovan, D. (2002). Mining answers for causation questions. In *Proc. The AAAI Spring Symposium on Mining Answers from Texts and Knowledge Bases*.

Girju, R., Nakov, P., Nastase, V., Szpakowicz, S., Turney, P., & Yuret, D. (2007). SemEval-2007 task 04: Classification of semantic relations between nominals. In *Proceedings of the 4th International Workshop on Semantic Evaluations* (pp. 13-18). Association for Computational Linguistics.

Hearst, M. A. (1998). Automated discovery of wordnet relations. In Fellbaum, C. (Ed.), *WordNet: An electronic lexical database* (pp. 131–151).

Khoo, C. S. G., Chan, S., & Niu, Y. (2000). Extracting causal knowledge from a medical database using graphical patterns. In *Annual Meeting-Association for Computational Linguistics, 38*(1), 336–343.

Kingsbury, P., & Palmer, M. (2002). From treebank to propbank. In *Proceedings of the 3rd International Conference on Language Resources and Evaluation* (LREC-2002) (pp. 1989-1993).

Kuramochi, M., & Karypis, G. (2001). Frequent subgraph discovery. In *Proceedings of the 2001 IEEE International Conference on Data Mining*, (pp. 313-320).

Marcu, D., & Echihabi, A. (2002). An unsupervised approach to recognizing discourse relations. In *Proceedings of the 40th Annual Meeting on Association for Computational Linguistics* (pp. 368-375). Morristown, NJ: Association for Computational Linguistics.

Marcus, M. P., Santorini, B., & Marcinkiewicz, M. A. (1994). Building a large annotated corpus of English: The Penn Treebank. *Computational Linguistics, 19*(2), 313–330.

Mihalcea, R., & Csomai, A. (2005). SenseLearner: Word sense disambiguation for all words in unrestricted text. In *Proceedings of the ACL 2005 on Interactive Poster and Demonstration Sessions* (pp. 53-56). Morristown, NJ: Association for Computational Linguistics.

Mueller, E. T. (2007). Modelling space and time in narratives about restaurants. *Literary and Linguistic Computing, 22*(1), 67. doi:10.1093/llc/fql014

Narayanan, S. (1997). *KARMA: Knowledge-based action representations for metaphor and aspect.* Ph.D. Dissertation, University of California, Berkeley.

Nijssen, S., & Kok, J. N. (2005). The Gaston tool for frequent subgraph mining. *Electronic Notes in Theoretical Computer Science, 127*(1), 77–87. doi:10.1016/j.entcs.2004.12.039

Ravichandran, D., & Hovy, E. (2002). Learning surface text patterns for a question answering system. In *Proceedings of ACL, 2,* 41-47.

Thoma, M., Cheng, H., Gretton, A., Han, J., Kriegel, H. P., & Smola, A. … Borgwardt, K. (2009). *Near-optimal supervised feature selection among frequent subgraphs.* In SIAM Intl Conf. on Data Mining.

Yan, X., & Han, J. (2002). gSpan: Graph-based substructure pattern mining. In *Proceedings of the 2002 IEEE International Conference on Data Mining (ICDM'02),* (p. 721).

Yan, X., & Han, J. (2003). CloseGraph: Mining closed frequent graph patterns. In *Proceedings of the Ninth ACM SIGKDD International Conference on Knowledge Discovery and Data Mining,* (pp. 286–295).

ADDITIONAL READING

Beamer, B., & Girju, R. (2009). Using a Bigram Event Model to Predict Causal Potential. In *Proceedings of the 10th International Conference on Computational Linguistics and Intelligent Text Processing.* (pp. 430-441). Springer Berlin / Heidelberg.

Blanco, E., Castell, N., & Moldovan, D. (2008). Causal Relation Extraction. In *Proceedings of the Sixth International Language Resources and Evaluation (LREC'08).* Marrakech, Morocco: European Language Resources Association (ELRA).

Comrie, B. (1981). Causative constructions. In *Language Universals and Linguistic Typology.* Chicago, IL: University of Chicago Press.

Davidson, D. (1967). Causal relations. *The Journal of Philosophy,* 691–703. doi:10.2307/2023853

Garcia, D. (2006). COATIS, an NLP system to locate expressions of actions connected by causality. In *Knowledge Acquisition, Modeling and Management.* (pp. 347-352). Springer Berlin / Heidelberg.

Garvey & Caramazza. (1974). Implicit causality in verbs. *Linguistic Inquiry, 5,* 549–564.

Higashinaka, R. & Isozaki, H. (2008). Automatically Acquiring Causal Expression Patterns from Relation-annotated Corpora to Improve Question Answering for why-Questions. *ACM Transactions on Asian Language Information Processing (TALIP), 7*(2), article 6.

Hobbs, J. (2005). Toward a useful concept of causality for lexical semantics. *Journal of Semantics, 22*(2), 181. doi:10.1093/jos/ffh024

Inui, T., Inui, K., & Matsumoto, Y. (2003). What Kinds and Amounts of Causal Knowledge Can Be Acquired from Text by Using Connective Markers as Clues? In *Lecture notes in computer science.* (pp. 180-103). Springer.

Inui, T., Inui, K., & Matsumoto, Y. (2005). Acquiring causal knowledge from text using the connective marker *tame.* [TALIP]. *ACM Transactions on Asian Language Information Processing, 4*(4), 435–474. doi:10.1145/1113308.1113313

Kaplan, R., & Berry-Rogghe, G. (1991). Knowledge-based acquisition of causal relationships in text. *Knowledge Acquisition*, *3*(3), 317–337. doi:10.1016/1042-8143(91)90009-C

Kim, J. (1971). Causes and events: Mackie on causation. *The Journal of Philosophy*, *68*(14), 426–441. doi:10.2307/2025175

Lewis, D. (2001). *Counterfactuals*. Wiley-Blackwell.

Lin, D., & Pantel, P. (2001). Discovery of inference rules for question-answering. *Natural Language Engineering*, *7*(4), 343–360.doi:10.1017/S1351324901002765

Pechsiri, C., & Kawtrakul, A. (2007). Mining Causality from Texts for Question Answering System. *IEICE Transactions on Information and Systems*, *90*(10), 1523–1533. doi:10.1093/ietisy/e90-d.10.1523

Suppes, P. (1970). A probabilistic theory of causation. *Acta Philosophica Fennica*, XXIV.

Talmy, L. (2000). Toward a cognitive semantics (Volume 1 & 2). Cambridge, MA: MIT Press.

Tsuda, K. (2007). Entire regularization paths for graph data. In *Proceedings of the 24th international conference on Machine learning*. (pp. 919-926). New York, NY: ACM.

Vendler, Z. (1967). Causal relations. *The Journal of Philosophy*, 704–713. doi:10.2307/2023854

White, P. (1990). Ideas about causation in philosophy and psychology. *Psychological Bulletin*, *108*(1), 3–18. doi:10.1037/0033-2909.108.1.3

KEY TERMS AND DEFINITIONS

Causal Example: A sentence from the data set that is marked as having a CAUSE relation.

Causal Pattern: A pattern whose matches contain a CAUSE relation at least 30% of the time.

Causal Relation: Two events are said to be have a causal relation between them if one event can be seen as a cause of the other. One test that can be performed is to see whether one can insert the phrase "and, as a consequence," or "and, as a result" between the events. If so, then the events are probably in a causal relation.

Event: This chapter uses actions encoded as verbs in text as events.

Match: A pattern matches within a graph if a monomorphism exists from the pattern to the graph.

Monomorphism: A mapping from a one graph to a subgraph of another, where unique nodes and edges of the pattern map to unique nodes and edges in the other graph.

Pattern: For the purposes of this chapter a pattern is a connected subgraph of a textual graph. When viewed alone they can be seen as complete graphs themselves.

Subgraph: A graph which is entirely contained within another graph.

ENDNOTES

[1]   http://www2.informatik.uni-erlangen.de/EN/research/ParSeMiS/index.html.
[2]   http://bach.istc.kobe-u.ac.jp/cream/.
[3]   SVM[light] from http://svmlight.joachims.org/.
[4]   We use the Stanford dependency parser http://nlp.stanford.edu/software/lex-parser.shtml.

Chapter 20
Play-by-Play Learning for Textual User Interfaces

Nate Blaylock
Florida Institute for Human and Machine Cognition, USA

William de Beaumont
Florida Institute for Human and Machine Cognition, USA

Lucian Galescu
Florida Institute for Human and Machine Cognition, USA

Hyuckchul Jung
Florida Institute for Human and Machine Cognition, USA

James Allen
University of Rochester, USA

George Ferguson
University of Rochester, USA

Mary Swift
University of Rochester, USA

ABSTRACT

This chapter describes a dialog system for task learning and its application to textual user interfaces. Our system, PLOW, uses observation of user demonstration, together with the user's play-by-play description of that demonstration, to learn complex tasks. We describe some preliminary experiments which show that this technique may make it possible for users without any programming experience to create tasks via natural language.

INTRODUCTION

Our daily activities typically involve the execution of a series of tasks, and we envision personal assistant agents that can help by performing many of these tasks on our behalf. However, for computers to perform tasks for us, they must be "taught" how to do those tasks. One way to do this is traditional programming: an experienced programmer speci-

fies the task in a computer language. This is the current method for teaching computers how to do things for us, and there are a lot of useful programs out there. Unfortunately, several factors severely limit the effectiveness of this traditional method: first, the ability to program resides with a very small portion of the population; second, creating a program can be expensive (in both money and time); and lastly, there are a great number of tasks that are specific to an individual or a small group. The combination of these factors means that a

DOI: 10.4018/978-1-60960-741-8.ch020

great number of tasks do not get implemented, not because they would not be useful, but because most people cannot program their own tasks and the economics makes it prohibitive for individuals or small groups to get tasks written for them.

Another possible method for learning tasks is by observation. Researchers have attempted to learn these models by having the computer observe the user's actions when performing a task (Angros et al. 2002; Lau and Weld 1999; van Lent and Laird 2001; Faaborg and Lieberman 2006). However, these techniques require multiple examples of the same task, and the number of required training examples increases with the complexity of the task.

Previously, we presented work on the PLOW system (Jung et al. 2008; 2010), which is able to learn tasks on the web from only a handful of examples (often even with a single example) through observation accompanied by a natural language (NL) "play-by-play" description from the user. The play-by-play approach in NL enables our task learning system to build a task with high-level constructs that are not inferable from observed actions alone. The synergy between the information encoded in the user's NL description and observed actions makes it possible to learn, from a simple sequence of actions, a complex task structure that reflects the user's underlying intentions in the demonstration.

Intuitively, the approach taken by PLOW is that the user "shows" the computer how to do a task, much in the same way he would show another person. In this sense, when the user is teaching, PLOW is looking over the user's shoulder, watching what is done on the screen, and also listening to the user's description and explanation of the actions performed. As most humans have the capability to show other humans how to do something, our hope is that this type of interaction will allow any person, including those with little or no programming experience, to be able to easily and quickly teach the computer a task.

The Application Domain

The Composite Health Computer System (CHCS) is a textual user interface system used throughout the US Military Health System for booking patient appointments and other tasks. In CHCS, the keyboard is used to navigate through a complex web of menus and screens in order to book and cancel appointments, look up patient information, and perform other administrative tasks. A typical screenshot of the system is shown in Figure 1. In the top part of the figure, spacing is used to make visual tables. The bottom shows a mnemonics-based menu and the cursor awaiting user keyboard input.

In this chapter, we discuss the application of the PLOW system to textual user interfaces, specifically the CHCS system. In developing and evaluating the system, we were given access to the actual CHCS server in use at Naval Hospital Pensacola, although, to protect live data, testing was done on a fictitious database used for training staff on CHCS use. As part of the development process, we conducted interviews and observation sessions with several types of diverse system users including nurses, clerks in specialist departments, and operators in the hospital call center. The call center was chosen as the focal point for our evaluations, as the high volume of calls and tasks performed lent themselves to testing.

Challenges

In this paper, we discuss our work on porting the PLOW system to the appointment booking domain in CHCS. In moving to this domain, we addressed the following challenges:

- **Learning Collaborative Tasks:** While the PLOW system has been successfully applied to various tasks on the Web (e.g., finding restaurants/flights/etc.), the tasks performed by the system were mostly performed in a batch style in that, given a task

Figure 1. A screenshot of the CHCS system[1]

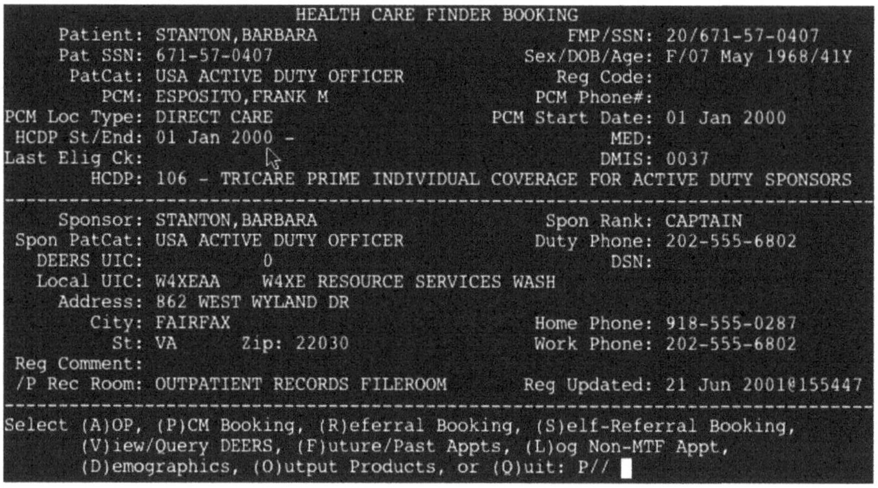

```
                        HEALTH CARE FINDER BOOKING
       Patient: STANTON,BARBARA                   FMP/SSN: 20/671-57-0407
       Pat SSN: 671-57-0407                     Sex/DOB/Age: F/07 May 1968/41Y
       PatCat: USA ACTIVE DUTY OFFICER             Reg Code:
          PCM: ESPOSITO,FRANK M                   PCM Phone#:
PCM Loc Type: DIRECT CARE                     PCM Start Date: 01 Jan 2000
 HCDP St/End: 01 Jan 2000 -                          MED:
Last Elig Ck:           ⌐                           DMIS: 0037
         HCDP: 106 - TRICARE PRIME INDIVIDUAL COVERAGE FOR ACTIVE DUTY SPONSORS
------------------------------------------------------------------------------
      Sponsor: STANTON,BARBARA                   Spon Rank: CAPTAIN
 Spon PatCat: USA ACTIVE DUTY OFFICER           Duty Phone: 202-555-6802
   DEERS UIC:           0                              DSN:
   Local UIC: W4XEAA    W4XE RESOURCE SERVICES WASH
     Address: 862 WEST WYLAND DR
        City: FAIRFAX                          Home Phone: 918-555-0287
          St: VA      Zip: 22030               Work Phone: 202-555-6802
 Reg Comment:
 /P Rec Room: OUTPATIENT RECORDS FILEROOM      Reg Updated: 21 Jun 2001@155447
------------------------------------------------------------------------------
Select (A)OP, (P)CM Booking, (R)eferral Booking, (S)elf-Referral Booking,
       (V)iew/Query DEERS, (F)uture/Past Appts, (L)og Non-MTF Appt,
       (D)emographics, (O)utput Products, or (Q)uit: P// █
```

invocation request, the system asks for some inputs and then the system executes the task until it gets the final results to present or hits problems (that can be corrected by a user in a debugging session). The model does not work for some tasks in the appointment booking domain. We extended PLOW to learn and execute collaborative tasks, where certain actions are assigned to the user.

- **Learning in an Unstructured Application Environment:** CHCS uses a terminal-based textual user interface, as opposed to the Web interface used by PLOW. We extended the system to interface with textual user interface systems, including work on understanding screens that are presented as text, not backed by a structured model such as the Document Object Model (DOM) of a webpage.

Moving to a new domain also provided an opportunity to test the robustness and applicability of the PLOW system across different domains by checking *which parts of the system we were able to reuse in the new domain*. In this paper, we first describe the original PLOW system. We then present our approach for the above-mentioned challenges and finally the results of an evaluation of the system with end-users with no programming experience.

THE PLOW SYSTEM

The PLOW system is an extension to TRIPS: our collaborative problem solving-based dialog system (Allen et al. 2000). The system's core components include speech recognition, a robust semantic parsing system, an interpretation manager, an ontology manager, and generation. Figure 2 shows a high-level view of the PLOW system. At the center lies a collaborative problem solving agent (CPS) that computes the most likely communicative intention in the given problem-solving context. CPS also coordinates and drives other parts of the system to learn what a user intends to build as a task and invoke execution when needed.

While the system's core reasoning modules are designed to learn tasks in any domain (e.g., office applications, robots, etc.), it focused on tasks on the web, which involve actions such as web navigation, information extraction, and form-filling with an extended ontology to cover web

Figure 2. Information flow in the PLOW system

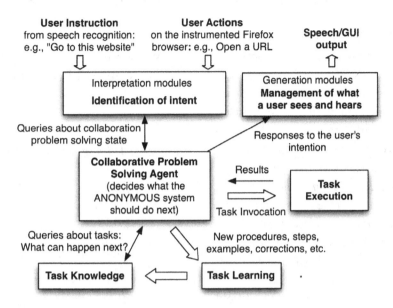

browsing actions. Figure 3 shows a screenshot of the original system. The main window on the left is the Firefox browser which has been instrumented with an extension that allows the system to monitor user actions and execute actions for learned tasks. This instrumentation provides the system with a high-level model of browser interaction, allowing the system to access and ma-

Figure 3. A screenshot of the original web-based PLOW system

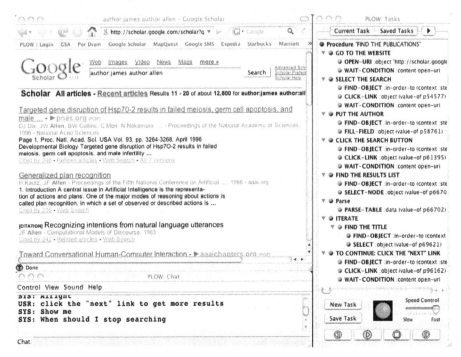

nipulate the browser through the tree-like DOM of the webpage. On the right is a window that summarizes a task under construction, highlights steps in execution for verification, and provides tools to manage learned tasks. A chat window at the bottom shows language interaction and allows both speech and typed interaction from the user.

NL provides rich information about the structure and elements of a task to learn. For instance, a single user utterance such as "*let me show you how to find publications for an author*" tells the system (i) the task goal, (ii) the final results (a set of publications), and (iii) a required input parameter (i.e., an author). For a step, the user's play-by-play description of a browsing action provides semantics for the action. Saying "*put the author's name here*" before inputting text into a text field helps the system figure out that the field requires a name role of an author.

Furthermore, NL provides key information for iterative structures that normally require numerous examples for a system to infer from pure observation. Figure 4 shows a sample dialogue from the system. Utterances such as "*this is a list of articles*" and "*select next to get more results*" indicate the boundary of a loop as well as the context for an action for a next round. The semantic information encoded in NL also enables the system to reliably identify objects in non-static web pages. For instance, for the action to select a link labeled as "advanced scholar search," if a user describes the action by saying, "*select the advanced search link*," the system can learn the relation between the semantic concept with its linguistic forms and the link's attributes in the DOM. Linguistic variation and similar ontological concepts are also considered in finding such a relation.

In Figure 4, user actions (italic texts) are accompanied by user's natural language description (normal texts labeled with "User"). While most of the actions in the figure are normal browsing actions, with PLOW, a user may need to perform some easy-to-perform special actions such as highlighting a text or an area of the screen by

clicking and dragging to directly tell PLOW which information the user is interested in (underlined texts in the figure).

While user actions in a browser provide useful information, it is very difficult for a system

Figure 4. A dialogue to find hotels near an address

1. User: Let me teach you how to find hotels
near an address
2. User: Go to this website
*Types a URL, http://www.mapquest.com, in the
browser's navigation box and hits Enter*
3. User: Put hotels here
Types "hotels" in the business type field
4. User: You need to know the address
5. PLOW: **What is the address?**
6. User: *Types an address, "40 South Alcaniz Street,
Pensacola, FL", in a special GUI for inputs*
7. User: Put the street address here
*Types the street address, "40 South Alcaniz
Street", in the street field*
8. User: Put the city here
Types "Pensacola" in the city field
9. User: Put the state here
Types "FL" in the state field
10. User: Click the search button
Presses a button with a label "Search"
11. User: Here is the list of hotels
<u>*Highlights an area with a list of hotels*</u>
12. PLOW: **Can you check if I understand the list?**
< Displays a special GUI that shows
the contents of the hotel list >
13. User: This is the hotel name
<u>*Highlights the hotel name in the special GUI*</u>
14. PLOW: < Identifies hotel names for the other hotels
and display the names >
15. User: This is the hotel address
<u>*Highlights the address of a hotel*</u>
16. PLOW: < Identifies hotel addresses for the other
hotels and display them >
17. User: This is the hotel distance
<u>*Highlights the distance for a hotel*</u>
18. PLOW: < Identifies distances for the other hotels
and display them >
19. User: Click the next link to get more results
Click the link labeled "next"
20. PLOW: **When should I stop searching?**
21. User: When the distance is greater than two miles
22. PLOW: **I will try that**
< Visits multiple pages and extracts
information (i.e., hotel name, address, and
distance) until the iteration termination
condition is satisfied and displays the results
in the special GUI >
23. PLOW: **I am finished.**
24. User: I am done

to identify key high-level task information from the demonstration alone, for example:

- **Identifying a task goal:** What is the final goal of the current task? What are the input and the output?
- **Identifying correct parameterization:** What values are required to perform the task? Is a value a constant or a variable? For variables, what is the relation among them?
- **Identifying iteration control structures:** What is the boundary of iteration? What actions should be repeated? Under which conditions should the iteration stop?
- **Identifying task hierarchy:** When does a new (sub)task start or end?

With approaches based on only observation such as Angros et al. (2002), Van Kleek et al. (2008) and van Lent and Laird (2001), in order to identify the above key aspects of a task, multiple examples are required to generalize learned knowledge. However, PLOW is able to build a task from a single demonstration by inferring the key task information described above from the natural language description provided by a user in the play-by-play demonstration.

The TRIPS system provides the architecture and the domain-independent capabilities for supporting mixed-initiative dialogues in various applications and domains. Its central components are based on a domain independent representation, including a linguistically based semantic form, illocutionary acts, and a collaborative problem-solving model. The system can be tailored to individual domains through an ontology mapping system that maps domain-independent representations into domain-specific representations (Dzikovska et al. 2008).

Figure 5 shows the core components and architecture of TRIPS, including: (1) a toolkit for rapid development of language models for the Sphinx-III speech recognition system; (2) a

robust parsing system that uses a broad-coverage grammar and lexicon of spoken language; (3) an interpretation manager (IM) that provides contextual interpretation based on the current discourse context, including reference resolution, ellipsis processing and the generation of intended speech act hypotheses; (4) an ontology manager (OM) that translates between representations; and (5) a generation manager (GM) and surface generator that generate system utterances from the domain-independent logical form.

The IM coordinates the interpretation of utterances and observed cyber actions. It draws from the Discourse Context module as well to help resolve ambiguities in the input, and coordinates the synchronization of the user's utterances and observed actions. Then IM interacts with a behavioral agent (BA) to identify the most likely intended interpretations in terms of collaborative problem solving acts (e.g., propose an action, accept a problem solving act or ignore it, work on something more pressing, etc.) The BA gets support from additional reasoning modules specialized for each application domain and reports its status to the GM, which plans a linguistic act to communicate the BA's intentions to the user.

TRIPS components interact with each other by exchanging messages through a facilitator module. Therefore, they can be distributed among networked computers. For further information about TRIPS, refer to (Ferguson and Allen 1998; Allen et al. 2002).

System Reusability

For the new CHCS domain, most of the PLOW system components were reused, with minor additions to the lexicon and the ontology for the new domain, as well as additions for handling collaborative behavior; the one extension requiring significant effort was the switch from the DOM-backed instrumentation of the browser interface to the instrumentation of the text-based terminal

Figure 5. Architecture of the TRIPS dialog system

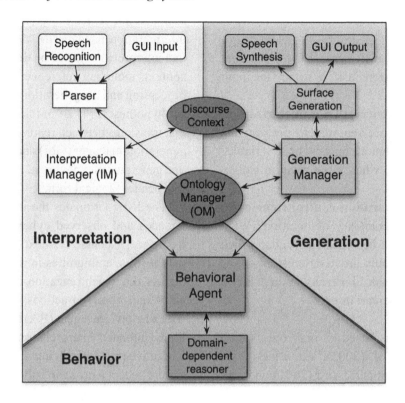

interface. Retaining most NLP and task learning components with little or very minor updates, the system enabled intuitive and natural dialogs in the new domain at the level of complexity shown in the sample dialog shown in Figure 6.

ADDING SUPPORT FOR TEXTUAL USER INTERFACES

The first challenge of moving to the CHCS domain was moving from a Web environment to a terminal-based textual user interface. As with the web-based PLOW system, we found that, in textual user interfaces, the level of interaction between the terminal and the system needed to be at a sufficiently high-level so that observed actions roughly corresponded to what was being talked about in the user's utterances. Additionally, the system needed a higher-level representation

of displayed text on the screen in order to support information extraction for task execution.

Terminal Instrumentation

To access the CHCS system, we instrumented an open-source terminal emulator, JCTerm, to allow PLOW to observe user actions and screen updates and report them at a high level and to allow it to control the interface.

Action Observation and Control

At a low level, all user commands in a terminal system are of the form of keystrokes, or rather, ASCII characters sent to the system. For better understanding, the instrumented JCTerm models commands at a higher-level, including string input (cf. form filling), sending of control codes, and

Figure 6. A portion of a dialog for teaching a task to select a patient's record

---

1. User: Let me teach you how to find patient
   records

....

2. User: Put the patient search info here
   Types the last name and hits ENTER
3. User: This is a list of patients
   *Highlights a patient list by drawing
   a rectangle around it*
4. User: This is the selection number
   *Highlights the number in front of
   one of the rows*
5. User: This is the patient name
   *Highlights the patient's name from
   one of the rows*
6. User: This is the social security number
   *Highlights the social security
   number on the row*
7. User: Hit enter to get more results
   Hits the ENTER key
8. **PLOW: When should I stop searching?**
9. User: Get all of them

....

---

screen navigation (using *RETURN*, arrow keys, *PAGE UP/DOWN*, etc.)

Screen Update Modeling

In the web version of PLOW, a browsing action may cause one or more page loading events (e.g., some websites show multiple intermediate pages before presenting search results). In such a case, explicit wait conditions are included into a task model based on the number of observed page loadings so that the following action would not be performed on an intermediate or a partially loaded page. Task learning in a textual user interface encounters the same type of problem—knowing when a screen update is done. However, terminal interfaces receive a continuous stream of commands to update parts of the screen (without explicit ending signals). We addressed this screen update issue by distinguishing major (new screen

or partial scrolling) from minor (key echo) screen updates.

In our task model, each action that causes a major update results in a wait condition for the final resulting screen state (represented by the position of the cursor and its surrounding text). During execution, for each wait condition, the system checks if the current screen state matches the state identified in learning whenever it observes a burst of screen update activities followed by a silent period (e.g., 250ms). While the wait conditions in the Web system worked very well, identifying terminal screen states was not robust. Failures or false-positives on recognizing screen states caused problems, making the system wait unnecessarily long or proceed prematurely. (This problem was exacerbated by a slow network environment, putting our system at a significant disadvantage as described below.)

Screen Understanding

Useful tasks are able to not only echo commands (such as macros), but also understand and extract screen content, either for providing results to the user, or for recognizing values needed for conditional statements in the task. The Web PLOW system contained a module that used semantic information from both the page and the user's description, along with the DOM structure of the page to learn patterns for extracting and parsing parts of the webpage as part of the learned task (Chambers et al. 2006).

We implemented a similar capability in the terminal PLOW system. We extended JCTerm to allow the user to use the mouse to highlight rectangular regions of interest on the screen. The system was extended to use information from the screen, paired with the language description to learn a pattern for extracting and parsing the same region of interest during execution. Figure 7 shows a screenshot of the terminal PLOW system with highlighting on the terminal screen and the resultant table (in the GUI window to the right) the system extracted during execution.

It is important to note that finding these regions in CHCS is not as trivial as just extracting a rectangle with the same screen coordinates as were used in learning. The terminal screen in Figure 7 shows the CHCS patient-finding subsystem. Here, matching patients from the search screen are displayed in groups of five, and the user can either choose one of the listed numbers by typing in the number, or can hit *RETURN* to get the next five search results. The screen in the figure shows parts of the first four lists of results, which are successively extracted by the system in the middle of a loop. Because this list scrolls up, instead of loading a new page and displaying in the exact same region, a more complex algorithm was necessary.

The system learns and executes extraction patterns by first processing the screen in order to find important regions within it, and the relationships among their boundaries. It recognizes runs of characters with the same color and style attributes, and runs of singly-spaced words. Then it composes these runs into columns, if they are vertically adjacent and aligned on the left side. Other important regions include the entire screen, the cursor, and the area of the screen that has been updated since the last keyboard events.

The system then learns patterns for finding regions by building a graph of the relationships among the natural language representation, the neighboring important regions in the screen state, and the region to find. To do this, the system performs a best-first search over alignments between this graph and that of the current screen state and then extracts the analogous region in the current screen graph.

COLLABORATIVE TASKS

In the initial version of PLOW, the system learned tasks that it itself executed. The model was that, when given an execution request, the system queried the user for any task parameters. Once the parameters were known, the system went off and executed the task, reporting the results to the user when execution was complete.

Figure 7. A screenshot of the PLOW system on a terminal running CHCS

An important improvement made to the PLOW system is support for learning and executing *collaborative* tasks, where both the system and the user are assigned actions. Collaborative tasks allow a much wider range of behavior to be learned by the system. This was necessary in the appointment booking domain for two reasons: first, collaborative tasks allow the user and system to work together in execution more *efficiently and intuitively*. As an example, at the start of a booking task, the database entry for the patient needs to be identified from a patient's last name and his/her last four SSN digits.

A collaborative task (shown in execution in Figure 7) will let the system ask for the last name, gather up search results that it learned to extract, and present them to the user for selection. Once selection is done, the selected patient's number will be automatically input and the patient's information will be accessed and further processed by the system as taught before. This results in a more efficient interaction where the user needs only to provide the last name and then clicks on the matching patient from the result list in a clear view, with repetitive navigation and information-extraction steps performed by the system.

The second reason that collaborative tasks were necessary for this domain was that certain knowledge needed by the system to make decisions is sometimes only available after partial task execution and can be very difficult for the system to access/query. The example here is which timeslot should be chosen for the appointment. In non-collaborative tasks, where the user specifies parameters beforehand, this is not possible. The available dates and times for appointments are dependent upon several factors such as the patient's primary care physician, the appointment type (e.g., initial visit, wellness, sick visit), and the availability/preference of the caller (the patient). Because these factors are not initially available/accessible and may need to be negotiated with the caller, it is impossible to build a workable task in a batch style. With collaborative tasks, the system can be taught a task where execution proceeds to the point where the list of available appointment dates and times becomes available. At this point, the user is assigned an action of choosing the desired appointment time, and then the system can finish the remaining steps of the booking task.

Note that NL and the system's contextual understanding play a key role for the system to learn collaborative tasks. For the above appointment selection example, during the teaching session, a user can (1) indicate when the user plans to take an initiative by saying, "*Let me choose an appointment*," and (2) let the system know when his/her actions are completed by saying, "*I'm done*." During execution, at a step assigned to a user, the system would signal that it is the user's turn by saying something like "*I am waiting*." After the user's turn is complete, he/she would say, "I'm finished" so the system could resume the task execution. A user does not necessarily have to always make such a closing remark for every user initiative step. If the system learned that a step was to simply select a row (like the case in Figure 7) from user's NL description (e.g., "*Let me select a row for the patient*") and related mouse/keystroke action(s), the system can figure out when the user is done by comparing observed actions in learning with the current user actions in execution.

EVALUATION

In 2006 and 2007, Web PLOW was evaluated along with three other task learning systems by an independent agency as a part of DARPA CALO project. Sixteen human subjects received training on each system and they were given ten problems that can be performed on various web sites. PLOW receiving a grade of 2.82 (2006) and 3.47 (2007) out of 4 (The test score was given by human evaluators based on a complex scheme that took into account the completeness and the correctness of the results.)

In a separate test in 2006, test subjects were given a set of new 10 "surprise" problems (unknown to the researchers), some of which were substantially different from the original ten problems. They were free to choose from different systems. However, PLOW was the system of choice among the subjects. In the testing, 55 task models out of possible 160 individual models were constructed by 16 users. PLOW was used to create 30 out of the 55 completed task models, and 13 out of 16 users used PLOW at least once (the next most used system was used by 8 users). PLOW also received the highest average score (2.2 out of 4) in the test.

In our empirical evaluation of PLOW on CHCS, we were interested in two issues: (1) are people who have no programming experience able to successfully teach tasks to the system? and, (2) can the executing of taught tasks improve the average call time for appointment booking? To test both of these, we conducted an experiment with two Navy Corpsmen from Naval Hospital Pensacola, who were regular users of CHCS but had no previous programming experience. Although the system does support speech input, in order to more closely control the system robustness, the Corpsmen were taught to interact with the system solely through the typed text interface. The following sections describe the experiment and then discuss the results.

Teaching Evaluation

The Corpsmen were each trained for four hours on the system. They were then each given three tasks to teach the system and four hours to complete them. The three evaluation tasks were (1) *Find a patient's phone number*, (2) *Start booking an appointment*, and (3) *Book a primary care appointment*. The separation of the last two tasks is partly an artifact of the way the CHCS booking process works. All appointment booking shares a common set of preliminary tasks of navigating to the booking subsystem, searching for and select-ing the correct patient, and then navigating to the appointment booking screen (which is shown in Figure 7). This task is the second task listed above.

Once that is done, there are several distinct ways an appointment is booked, depending mostly on the type of appointment to be booked. The third task listed above is for booking a patient an appointment with their primary care provider. Other appointment types (such as with a specialist) are done through other subsystems and require different tasks to be taught. The Corpsmen were given a written description of the tasks to teach and were allowed to ask any clarification questions about the tasks. They were then given four hours to teach the tasks in any order they wished. Both Corpsmen finished teaching the three tasks in less than two hours. After the teaching session, the tasks taught by the Corpsmen were evaluated for correctness. All three tasks were successfully taught by both Corpsmen.

Execution Evaluation

After the teaching evaluation, a separate evaluation was performed to measure the impact of task use on the time spent on booking phone calls. Two confederates (who were not involved in the project) took turns making simulated phone calls to the Corpsmen in order to either book appointments as fictitious patients or as fictitious doctors wanting to look up a patient phone number. Three sets of 25 calls were made to each Corpsman. The first five calls of each set were used as a warm-up, and were not counted in the overall evaluation. In one set of calls, the Corpsmen used only the CHCS system to accomplish the tasks as they would normally do. In another set, the Corpsmen used PLOW with the tasks that they themselves taught in the task teaching phase. In the final set, they used tasks taught by researchers (who we are terming as "experts" in system use).

Table 1 shows the average time of calls for each of the three sets performed with remote access to the actual CHCS system in use. The average time

Table 1. Average call times for execution evaluation

	Without System (Baseline)	Own Taught Task	Difference from Baseline	Expert Taught Task	Difference from Baseline
Actual Ave. Call Time	55.7s	64.4s	+8.7s	61.7s	+6.0s
Adjusted Ave. Call Time	55.7s	49.4s	-6.3s	46.7s	-9.0s

for calls with the Corpsman-defined tasks was 8.7 seconds longer than without PLOW. Calls using expert-defined tasks were marginally faster than the calls with the Corpsman tasks, but still 6.0 seconds slower than calls without PLOW. Our analysis showed that the reason for this slowdown was primarily three factors. First was the system's timeout-based method for recognizing when the screen has finished updating (described above). Almost every step had a major screen update to be checked and the system waited 250ms before it started checking if the current screen matched the expected state, causing significant delay.

The second factor was frequent network slowdowns that caused long pauses (some where over 1 second long) in the middle of a screen update. When the Corpsmen used the CHCS system alone, they often proceeded to the next step as soon as they had enough information, even if the screen was not fully loaded. In contrast, the system had to wait for the update to finish before moving on. Furthermore, the intermittent screen updates increased the chance of false positives that made the system prematurely move ahead and have a failure in the next step. A failure recovery mechanism ensured the system would be able to re-synchronize the state of the task's execution with the state of the application; thus, the system was able to complete the tasks, but at additional time expense. In addition, only government-furnished computers were able to access to CHCS network. The computers used for the evaluation had 2.0GHz Intel Core Duo processors with only 1GB RAM and were measurably slower than our own off-the-shelf development machines.

We performed a post-evaluation analysis of the timing in log data from the evaluations. Based on the analysis, we (conservatively) re-estimated the time of each call assuming correct screen state recognition was implemented as well as assuming the system was running on our own test computers. The resulting adjusted average call times are shown in the second line of Table 1 and result in significant improvements over the previous calls. Our estimated adjusted call times were 6.3 seconds faster than just CHCS for Corpsman tasks and 9.0 seconds faster for expert tasks.

Discussion

Due to the small size of the evaluation (the number of subjects, tasks, and calls), and system slowdown problems, it is impossible to make definite statements about the system and its usability. However, the evaluation does show that it is possible for at least some non-programmers to effectively teach tasks to the system. It also seems to show that it may be possible to speed up appointment booking phone calls using tasks that are taught by the users themselves.

RELATED WORK

A major technique in task learning is an observation-based approach in which agents learn task models through observation of the actions performed by an expert (Angros et al. 2002; Lau and Weld 1999; van Lent and Laird 2001; Faaborg and Lieberman 2006). However, a significant drawback of these approaches is that they require multiple examples, making them infeasible for one-shot learning.

Researchers have also investigated techniques that do not require observation. For instance, (Garland, Ryall, and Rich 2001) proposed techniques to encode experts' knowledge with annotation. A scripting system with pseudo natural language was also developed to automate online tasks (Leshed et al. 2008). While these approaches are useful, without the help of demonstration observation, the task learning can be difficult for complex control constructs such as iteration and dynamic web object identification. Furthermore, the coverage of the pseudo languages used in these approaches is limited to handle complex control structures.

Note that task learning approaches described above are not designed to learn collaborative tasks and their application domain is either Web or special simulators. In contrast, our system works together with a user to learn collaborative tasks and the understanding of the terminal interface can be applied to other systems with similar textual interfaces.

CONCLUSION

Collaborative tasks allow a wide range of behavior to be learned and performed by a system. This chapter has presented a system (PLOW) that shows the possibility for non-programmer users to teach collaborative tasks with relatively little training. NL plays a critical role in making the interaction between a user and a learning system intuitive and non-intrusive. Although the evaluation was done on a small scale, it revealed problems (to be fixed with better engineering) as well as great potential of this NL-based collaborative task learning.

ACKNOWLEDGMENT

We would like to thank the personnel of Naval Hospital Pensacola for their assistance with this project. This work was supported in part by DARPA grant NBCH-D-03-0010 under a subcontract from SRI International.

REFERENCES

Allen, J., Blaylock, N., & Ferguson, G. (2002). A problem solving model for collaborative agents. *Proceedings of the International Joint Conference on Autonomous Agents and Multi-Agent Systems*.

Allen, J., Byron, D., Dzikovska, M., Ferguson, G., Galescu, L., & Stent, A. (2000). An architecture for a generic dialogue shell. *Journal of Natural Language Engineering*, *6*(3), 1–16. doi:10.1017/S135132490000245X

Angros, R., Jr., Johnson, W. L., Rickel, J., & Scholer, A. (2002). Learning domain knowledge for teaching procedural skills. In *Proceedings of the International Joint Conference on Autonomous Agents and Multiagent Systems*.

Chambers, N., Allen, J., Galescu, L., Jung, H., & Taysom, W. (2006). Using semantics to identify web objects. In *Proceedings of the Twenty-First National Conference on Artificial Intelligence (AAAI-06)*.

Dzikovska, M., Allen, J., & Swift, M. (2008). Linking semantic and knowledge representations in a multi-domain dialogue system. *Journal of Logic and Computation*, *18*(3), 405–430. doi:10.1093/logcom/exm067

Faaborg, A., & Lieberman, H. (2006). A goal-oriented web browser. In *Proceedings of the SIGCHI Conference on Human Factors in Computing Systems*.

Ferguson, G., & Allen, J. (1998). TRIPS: An integrated intelligent problem-solving assistant. In *Proceedings of the National Conference on Artificial Intelligence (AAAI)*.

Garland, A., Ryall, K., & Rich, C. (2001). *Learning hierarchical task models by defining and refining examples*. In International Conference on Knowledge Capture.

Jung, H., Allen, J., de Beaumont, W., Blaylock, N., Ferguson, G., Galescu, L., & Swift, M. (2010). Going beyond PBD: A play-by-play and mixed-initiative approach. In Cypher, A., Dontcheva, L. M., Lau, T., & Nichols, J. (Eds.), *No code required: Giving users tools to transform the Web*. Morgan Kaufmann Publishers.

Jung, H., Allen, J., Galescu, L., Chambers, N., Swift, M., & Taysom, W. (2008). Using natural language for one-shot task learning. *Journal of Logic and Computation, 18*(3), 475–493. doi:10.1093/logcom/exm071

Lau, T., & Weld, D. (1999). *Programming by demonstration: An inductive learning formulation*. In International Conference on Intelligent User Interfaces.

Leshed, G., Haber, E., Matthews, T., & Lau, T. (2008). Coscripter: Automating and sharing how-to knowledge in the enterprise. In *Proceedings of the SIGCHI Conference on Human Factors in Computing Systems*.

Van Kleek, M., André, P., Perttunen, M., Bernstein, M., Karger, D., Miller, R., & Schraefel, M. C. (2008). Personal reactive automation for the Web, In *Proceedings of the Annual ACM Symposium on User Interface Software and Technology*.

van Lent, M., & Laird, J. (2001). *Learning procedural knowledge through observation*. In International Conference on Knowledge Capture.

ENDNOTE

[1] The patient information shown here and in other figures is part of a training database and is fictitious.

Chapter 21
Computationally Assessing Expert Judgments of Freewriting Quality

Jennifer L. Weston
Arizona State University, USA

Scott A. Crossley
Georgia State University, USA

Danielle S. McNamara
Arizona State University, USA

ABSTRACT

This study examines the relationship between the linguistic features of freewrites and human assessments of freewrite quality. Freewriting is a prewriting strategy that has received little experimental attention, particularly in terms of linguistic differences between high and low quality freewrites. This study builds upon the authors' previous study, in which linguistic features of freewrites written by 9th and 11th grade students were included in a model of the freewrites' quality (Weston, Crossley, & McNamara; 2010). The current study reexamines this model using a larger data set of freewrites. The results show that similar linguistic features reported in the Weston et al. model positively correlate with expert ratings in the new data set. Significant predictors in the current model of freewrite quality were total number of words and stem overlap. In addition, analyses suggest that 11th graders, as compared to 9th graders, wrote higher quality and longer freewrites. Overall, the results of this study support the conclusion that better freewrites are longer and more cohesive than poor freewrites.

INTRODUCTION

Arguably the most important skill a student learns is how to write effectively. This notion is supported by a 2001 survey by Light wherein over 90% of professionals responded that writing was essential to their job. Nonetheless, there are many students who leave high school without the necessary proficiency in writing needed to procure a job or to be successful in higher education. One means of increasing writing proficiency is through the instruction and use of writing strategies. The use of strategies can help to activate prior knowledge

DOI: 10.4018/978-1-60960-741-8.ch021

and lessen the demands on working memory. In addition, the use of writing strategies helps to focus the writer on the steps needed to produce a successful written product. The present study focuses specifically on one common writing strategy: freewriting. Freewriting is a timed writing exercise during which the writer produces as many ideas as possible as quickly as possible with little regard to the rules of structure, grammar, and punctuation (Elbow, 1979). It can take different forms including *focused* freewriting where a person writes with a topic or prompt in mind (Hinkle & Hinkle, 1990). Freewriting is generally a prewriting task and is often part of planning (Renyolds, 1984). Planning is the first step in many writing tasks and can take many forms, including freewriting, outlining, concept maps, and lists (Loader, 1989; Brondey et al., 1999; Reese & Cumming, 1996; Vinson, 1980).

Our goal in this study is to better understand which linguistic features of a freewrite are related to freewrite quality. Identifying these features is necessary in order to build automated NLP assessments of freewrite quality. Automated freewrite assessment will allow educators and intelligent tutoring systems to provide targeted feedback to writers engaging in freewriting. Better understanding the nature and features of freewrites will also afford future investigations of the relationship between freewrite quality and essay quality. Assuming there is a link between freewrite quality and essay quality, feedback can be designed to help students produce higher quality essays. As such, this study serves as one step toward the overarching goal of providing effective tools that use artificial intelligence to help students learn how to improve their writing and help researchers and educators understand the nature of writing.

Although much has been written on the topic of freewriting, most published research has been anecdotal (Belanoff, 1991; Fontaine, 1991; Haswell, 1991; Sweedler-Brown, 1984). That is to say, the claims made in many freewriting studies are based on little to no experimental data. In ad-

dition what little research has been conducted on freewriting has been limited to qualitative research on samples of convenience. In addition, the few experimental studies conducted on freewriting were not investigating the product of freewriting (Hinkle & Hinkle, 1990; Knudson, 1989). Rather, these studies examined freewriting as a comprehension strategy to be used immediately following classroom lectures and thus focused on the effects of freewriting on comprehension scores, not the written products. Thus, these researchers never examined the freewrites that students wrote.

Most studies that have been concerned with the product of freewriting have lacked the necessary experimental conditions for generalizable inferences to be made. For instance, Belanoff (1991) examined differences in freewrites as a function of skill level. Based on a semester's worth of written assignments, Belanoff sorted his students into five skill categories. Only the freewrites from the students in the highest (n=5) and lowest writing skill groups (n=4) were analyzed in this study. Belanoff's qualitative analysis identified five qualities of skilled writers' freewrites, and one principal difference between their freewriting and the freewriting of less skilled writers. He deduced that skilled writers tended not to use logical connections and did not come to closure within the freewrite. Belanoff characterized skilled writers' freewrites as more chaotic and less focused than those of the less skilled writers. However, the skilled writers were also more likely to include discernable passages with well-formed, eloquent language, as well as meta-comments and questions alluding to their knowledge of the task and why they were performing it. He also found that the style of skilled writers' freewrites and essays differed in terms of structure and use of language. By contrast, Belanoff noted that unskilled writers' freewrites bore a great resemblance to the finished pieces of writing they had turned in throughout the semester. Less skilled writers also tended to write about what they knew with few deviations into the unknown or speculation. In sum, Belanoff's observations suggest that the indicators of quality freewrites may deviate from the normal hallmarks of good writing (e.g., grammar, paragraph structure, logical flow of ideas, etc.).

A recent study by Weston, Crossley, and McNamara (2010) also considered differences in freewrites. Their study used expert ratings of freewrite quality, rather than post-hoc judgments of a writer's overall skill level as in the Belanoff (1991) study. Weston et al. identified which linguistic features of freewrites were predictive of expert ratings of freewrite quality in a corpus of 96 focused (prompt-based) freewrites generated by 9th and 11th grade high school students. The freewrites were assessed by expert raters using a holistic scale and analyzed using the computational tool Coh-Metrix (Graesser, McNamara, Louwerse, & Cai, 2004; McNamara & Graesser, in press). Weston et al. selected linguistic indices from Coh-Metrix based on the strength of the correlations between the indices and the holistic freewrite score and the absence of multicollinearity among indices. Four indices (number of words, LSA given information, noun overlap, and mean number of words before the main verb) were regressed onto the expert ratings using a stepwise regression. This model yielded two significant predictors: number of words and noun overlap.

The Weston et al. (2010) results thus indicated that higher quality freewrites are longer and contain overlap in ideas between consecutive sentences. Thus, writers of freewrites that were rated as higher in quality wrote more and tended to stay more on topic. These results make sense intuitively, but do not align well with Belanoff's findings. The difference in findings between the two studies may be due any number of factors, including the population, the kinds of freewrites being assessed, and the methodologies employed. In particular, Belanoff's student freewrites were not focused onto any particular prompt or topic and thus may have lacked some of the cohesion that can be expected in a focused freewrite. Focused freewrites may tend to be less chaotic

(i.e., remaining on topic) and contain more word overlap between sentences due to their focus on the prompt at hand. In addition, some proponents of traditional freewrites consider it a daily writing strategy, not one focused on the end goal of writing a specific paper (Elbow, 1973). Thus, the differing goals of traditional and focused freewrites may lead to different linguistic characteristics of the different types of freewrite.

Although Belanoff (1991) and Weston et al. (2010) are to our knowledge the only studies that have examined the differences in freewrites as a function of the human judgments of writing quality, other studies have examined freewriting in a general sense (Haswell, 1991; Fontaine, 1991; Sweedler-Brown, 1984). Many of the characteristics of freewrites reported in these studies are similar to those noted by Belanoff. For instance, Haswell (1991) and Fontaine (1991) both noted the presence of eloquent language and the chaotic nature of freewrites, which is somewhat aligned with Belanoff's findings. In addition, Sweedler-Brown (1984) analyzed her student freewrites in relation to the essays the students wrote. Sweedler-Brown found that students who had access to their freewrites tended to use many of the ideas in the freewrite in their final essay even when advised not to include the ideas, whereas students who were not allowed to keep their freewrites wrote better final papers. This finding is congruous with Belanoff's deduction that better writers in his class produced essays that were qualitatively different from their freewrites.

The literature on freewriting has pinpointed several features considered important to higher quality freewrites and freewriting in general. Although studies on freewrites have been informative, more work needs to be completed. The lack of control in most of these studies limits our ability to draw broader inferences outside of the situations in which the observations were made. Another limitation revolves around the types of freewrites written and the freewriting goals. Because our eventual objective is to understand the effect of freewrites on essays, the assessment of freewrites that are written with a focus towards an essay prompt are of prime importance to us. Although not all of the previous literature is entirely relevant to our overarching goals, it provides a starting point. The present study builds upon these previous studies in the hopes of improving upon their methods with a focus on our end goal of providing feedback to students who are using focused freewriting as a writing strategy.

METHODS

The primary goal of this study is to identify linguistic features that are predictive of human assessments of quality freewrites by expanding on the previous study by Weston et al. (2010) with a larger, expanded corpus of freewrites. This study includes the same freewrites as in the previous Weston et al. study, as well as an additional set which had not been scored at the time that the previous dataset was analyzed. Scoring freewrites is somewhat costly and thus for the Weston et al. (2010) study, only a subset of the freewrites were scored. However, the results pointed to the need for a larger data set and increased power. Additionally, the expanded data set allows us to examine how the linguistic features of freewrites vary by grade level, which may be correlated with writing ability. In order to obtain measures of linguistic features and lexical indices, the computational tool Coh-Metrix (Graesser et al., 2004) was used to analyze the corpus of freewrites. The freewrites were also scored by expert raters trained to use a holistic rubric similar to the one used by the College Board to evaluate SAT essays.

Corpus Collection

Prompt-based freewrites were collected from high school students at a suburban public high school in upstate New York. The enrollment of the high schools was 1600 students for the 2008-2009 school year. The high school maintains an average class size of 23 students and a graduation rate of 99% (Carmody, 2009).

The 105 students who participated and wrote freewrites were enrolled in either an 11th grade advanced placement English class or in a 9th grade Regents level (basic state level) English class (64 9th graders and 41 11th graders). These students ranged in age from 14 to 18. Consent forms were sent home to parents informing them of the study and allowing them to opt their child out of the in-class activities. The students came from five classes that were all taught by one teacher who volunteered her classes to participate in this study. The advanced placement students represent the highest level of student in that grade, while the 9th graders can be considered to be "typical" students. All students received the same instructions and materials.

The data used in the present study is part of a larger data set that also includes paired student essays. In addition to the writing samples, participants also completed a set of questionnaires which were given to students the class prior and returned during the experiment. Experimental packets were distributed that included all of the writing tasks in a preselected order. The order of tasks contained in the packet were as follows: The freewriting instructions (adapted from Elbow, 1973), a 5-minute freewrite, a 25-minute essay, a 5-minute freewrite, and a final 5-minute freewrite (only for the 11th grade students). Each written task had a unique prompt with the only exception being that the prompt for the first freewrite was matched with an essay prompt. The experimenter read aloud the freewriting and essay instructions, timed the tasks, and informed students when to move onto the next task in their packets. The students in different grades completed a different number of freewrites depending on time constraints due to the time that was required to distribute experimental materials and explain the tasks. The junior advanced placement classes were more cooperative and were thus able to finish three freewrites, whereas the freshman classes completed only two freewrites.

Students completed a paired freewrite and essay on one of two essays prompts. The prompts were counter-balanced with the freewriting prompt always appearing as a prewriting task. The students also freewrote on either one or two other prompts. There were four possible prompts from which the additional two prompts were assigned. The prompts were assigned in all possible combinations and orders. The prompts used for this study were adapted from past SAT prompts obtained from www.onlinemathlearning.com/sat-test-prep.html. The essay instructions presented to students were adapted from the SAT writing section instructions (The College Board, 2009) and were modified as little as possible. The only instruction removed concerned the lack of additional paper that would be provided because we supplied the students with as much paper as they needed. In addition, a reminder was added to the instructions that the experimenter could not clarify the prompt. The students' freewrites were transcribed as written, with the spelling and grammar errors retained. The 105 students produced 247 freewrites that were transcribed and analyzed for this study. The freewrite prompts included the following:

a.   Many persons believe that to move up the ladder of success and achievement, they must forget the past, repress it, and relinquish it. But others have just the opposite view. They see old memories as a chance to reckon with the past and integrate past and present. Do personal memories hinder or help people in their effort to learn from their past and succeed in the present? (n=51);

b.   People today have so many choices. For instance, thirty years ago most television viewers could choose from only a few channels; today there are more than a hundred channels available. And choices do not just abound when it comes to the media. People have more options in almost every area of life. With so much to choose from, how can we not be happy? Does having a large number of options to choose from increase or decrease satisfaction with the choices people make? (n=38);

c.   Being loyal—faithful or dedicated to someone or something—is not always easy. People often have conflicting loyalties, and there are no guidelines that help them decide to what or whom they should be loyal. Moreover, people are often loyal to something bad. Still, loyalty is one of the essential attributes a person must have and must demand of others. Should people always be loyal? (n=34);

d.   In many circumstances, optimism—the expectation that one's ideas and plans will always turn out for the best—is unwarranted. In these situations what is needed is not an upbeat view but a realistic one. There are times when people need to take a tough-minded view of the possibilities of success, give up, and invest their energies elsewhere rather than find reasons to continue to pursue the original project or idea. Is it better for people to be realistic or optimistic? (n=56);

e.   Many people believe that our government should do more to solve our problems. People think that individuals do not have the ability to create jobs, build roads, improve schools, or help to provide the many other benefits that we have come to enjoy. However, expecting the government to come up with the solutions to society's problems may have made us less self-reliant and undermined our independence and self-sufficiency. Should individuals or the government be responsible for solving problems that affect our communities and the nation in general? (n=33);

f.   Many people lead careful and sensible lives. They watch their diet, exercise regularly, and check the weather report before leaving the house. They carefully control many aspects of their lives. Others believe that life should be more carefree and reckless, and people should not try to control what can't be fully controlled. They also take more chances, even against their better judgments. Is it sometimes better to take risks than to follow a more reasonable course of action? (n=35).

The distribution of freewrites across the sessions was 104 1st freewrites, 104 2nd freewrites, and 39 3rd freewrites. One student's data was not included because the assignment was completed in Spanish instead of English.

Survey Instrument

The holistic grading rubric used in this study (see Appendix A) was created and used by Weston et al. (2010). It was modeled on the standardized grading rubric used by the College Board to score SAT essays. Belanoff's (1991) report, along with other anecdotal reports, and our own expectations were used to design the rubric. The holistic rubric focuses on those things we believe to be important to freewrite quality, including the development of ideas, the use of appropriate examples, organization, sections with some local coherence, lexical variety, and syntactic variety. We defined a quality freewrite as one that developed a variety of ideas, used appropriate examples, and contained a variety of lexical and syntactic structures. In contrast to an essay rubric, it was specified that for a freewrite to be judged of high quality, it did not need to be well organized, fully coherent, or grammatical.

RESULTS

Expert Ratings

To assess the 247 writing samples that comprised our written corpus, two composition instructors from Mississippi State University, who were native speakers of English, were trained as expert raters. Both raters had Master's degrees and three years of experience teaching English. The raters were trained on an initial selection of freewrites. The ratings ranged between 1 (minimum) and 6 (maximum). Pearson correlations were calculated to assess inter-rater reliability. The Pearson correlations on the training set from the first study exceeded .70 ($p < .001$). The average correlation between the two raters on the freewrites was .77 ($p < .001$), and the weighted Kappa was .56, suggesting an acceptable level of agreement. Over 56% of the freewrites were scored the same by both raters, 40% difference of 1, and 3% having a difference of 2. If the scores varied, the final freewrite score was computed as an average of the two given scores.

Variable Selection

Coh-Metrix provided linguistic indices for each of the freewrites (Graesser et al., 2004; McNamara & Graesser, this volume). Coh-Metrix is a computational tool used to assess texts that reports over 600 linguistic indices. These indices are related to conceptual knowledge, cohesion, lexical difficulty, syntactic complexity, and simple incidence scores. Due to length and structure many of the freewrites, not all indices could be investigated. For example, many of the freewrites consisted of a single paragraph, making paragraph to paragraph comparisons impossible. In addition many freewrites were fewer than 100 words, which is the minimum threshold recommended for lexical diversity measures (McCarthy & Jarvis, 2007).

The corpus was split into training ($n = 164$) and test set ($n = 83$) using a 67/33 split. We used Pearson correlations to assess which variables were predictive of freewrite quality in the corpus. The training set was used to identify which of the Coh-Metrix variables correlated highly to the expert ratings assigned to each freewrite. The variables identified in the training set were selected and used to predict the expert ratings in the training set, using a linear regression model.

The same regression equation was used to evaluate the freewrites in the test set in order to test the accuracy of this model (Witten & Frank, 2005).

To allow for a reliable interpretation of the multiple regression, we ensured that we had an appropriate case to variable ratio. According to Field (2005), a 15 to 1 ratio of cases to variable allows for the interpretation of each variable's unique contribution to the regression model. With 164 cases in the training set, we were able to include up to 11 variables. Pearson correlations were used to select variables from each bank of measures to be used in the multiple regression. After eliminating those variables that exhibited multicollinearity ($r > .70$) with variables that were more highly correlated with freewrite quality, five variables remained that correlated significantly with the outcome variable (freewrite quality). The measures and their respective indices are discussed below in reference to their importance to lexical proficiency.

Measures

Number of Words

A freewrite that contains more words indicates that the writer was able to write more on the topic. In addition, the number of words present in a text may also be related to the number of ideas present.

Syntactic Complexity

Coh-Metrix measures syntactic complexity in a variety of ways, three of these principal ways were of interest to this study. The first measure calculates the mean number of words before the main verb. The second and third metrics used by *Coh-Metrix* to measure syntactic complexity assess the mean number of high level constituents (sentences and embedded sentence constituents) per word and per noun phrase. Sentences with difficult syntactic constructions include the use of embedded constituents and are often structurally dense, syntactically ambiguous, or ungrammatical (Graesser et al., 2004). Consequently, more complex structures are more difficult to process and comprehend (Perfetti et al., 2005).

Connectives and Logical Operators

The density of connectives is measured in Coh-Metrix using two dimensions. The first dimension contrasts positive versus negative connectives, whereas the second dimension is associated with particular classes of cohesion identified by Halliday and Hasan (1976) and Louwerse (2001). These connectives are associated with positive additive (*also, moreover*), negative additive (*however, but*), positive temporal (*after, before*), negative temporal (*until*), and causal (*because, so*) measures. The logical operators measured in *Coh-Metrix* include variants of *or*, *and*, *not*, and *if-then* combinations. Connectives and logical operators play an important role in the creation of cohesive links between ideas and clauses (Crismore, Markkanenen, & Steffensen, 1993; Longo, 1994).

Causality

Coh-Metrix measures causal cohesion by calculating the ratio of causal verbs to causal particles (Graesser et al., 2004). The occurrence of causal verbs and causal particles in a text relates to the conveyance of causal content and causal cohesion. The causal verb count is based on the number of main causal verbs identified through WordNet (Fellbaum, 1998; Miller et al., 1990). Causal verbs and particles help the reader infer the causal relations in the text (Kintsch & van Dijk, 1978). A measure of causal verbs is investigated here to assess causal cohesion in freewrites.

Lexical Overlap

Coh-Metrix considers four forms of lexical overlap between sentences: noun overlap, argument overlap, stem overlap, and content word overlap. Noun overlap measures how often a common noun of the same form is shared between two sentences. Argument overlap measures how often two sentences share nouns with common stems (including pronouns), while stem overlap measures how often a noun in one sentence shares a common stem with other word types in another sentence (not including pronouns). Content word overlap refers to how often content words are shared between sentences at proportional intervals (including pronouns). Lexical overlap has been shown to aid in text comprehension and reading speed (Douglas, 1981; Kintsch & van Dijk, 1978; Rashotte & Torgesen, 1985).

Semantic Coreferentiality

Coh-Metrix measures semantic coreferentiality using Latent Semantic Analysis (LSA; Landauer, McNamara, Dennis, & Kintsch, 2007), a mathematical technique for representing deeper world knowledge based on large corpora of texts. LSA uses a general form of factor analysis to condense a very large corpus of texts to approximately 300 dimensions. These dimensions represent how often a word occurs within a document (defined at the sentence level, the paragraph level, or in larger sections of texts) and each word, sentence, or text becomes a weighted vector (Landauer & Dumais, 1997; Landauer, Foltz, & Laham, 1998). Unlike lexical overlap indices of co-referentiality, LSA measures associations between words based on semantic similarity, which can be used to assess the amount of semantic coreferentiality in a text (Crossley, Louwerse, McCarthy, & McNamara, 2007). Coh-Metrix also assesses given/newness through LSA by measuring the proportion of new information each sentence provides (Hempelmann et al., 2005). The given information is thought to be recoverable from the preceding discourse (Halliday, 1967) and does not require activation (Chafe, 1975).

Word Characteristics

Coh-Metrix reports on a variety of lexical indices taken from WordNet (Fellbaum, 1998; Miller, G., Beckwith, Fellbaum, Gross & Miller, K., 1990) and MRC Psycholinguistic Database (Wilson, 1988). Coh-Metrix derives hypernymy and polysemy indices from WordNet. Hypernymy indices relate to the specificity of words (*cat* vs. *animal*). A lower hypernymy score equates to less specific word choices. Polysemy indices relate to how many senses a word contains. Some words have more senses (e.g., *class*) while others have fewer (e.g., *apricot*). The more senses a word has, the more ambiguous it is. From the MRC Psycholinguistic Database, Coh-Metrix derives indices of word familiarity, word concreteness, and word imagability. All of these indices relate to the accessibility of core lexical items. Core items are closer to prototypical items so higher scores equate to words that are more concrete or more familiar and imageable. The MRC indices are based on the works of Paivio (1965), Toglia and Battig (1978), and Gilhooly and Logie (1980), who used human subjects to rate large collections of words for psychological properties.

Word Frequency

A measure of word frequency indicates how often particular words occur in the English language. This frequency is derived by Coh-Metrix utilizing frequency counts from CELEX (Baayen, Piepenbrock, & Gulikers, 1995) CELEX is a database from the Centre for Lexical Information that uses frequency counts based on the words in representative text corpora. This database consists of frequencies from the early 1991 version of the COBUILD corpus, a 17.9 million word corpus.

Pearson Correlations Training Set

Pearson correlations from the training set demonstrated that indices from 14 measures correlated significantly with the expert ratings. To select the variables for the final analysis, we assessed multicollinearity between the variables and the variable's susceptibility to spelling errors. Multicollinearity between variables was considered problematic when two variables correlated with each other above .70. Susceptibility to spelling errors was assessed via comparing Coh-Metrix indices of lemmatized and original freewrites. The lemmatization process corrected for spelling mistakes and transformed each word into its root. If the target index from the normal and the lemmatized freewrite did not correlate to at least a .85 level the index was considered to be susceptible to spelling errors. After assessing multicollinearity and susceptibility to spelling errors, five variables were selected. These five variables along with their r and p values, are presented in Table 1 sorted by the strength of the correlation. Nine variables were not retained in the analysis because they demonstrated multicollinearity with other variables. These nine variables measured syntactic similarity, locational cohesion, motional cohesion, argument overlap (two variables), noun overlap (two variables), and word frequency (two variables).

Multiple Regression Training Set

A stepwise linear regression was conducted that regressed the five variables (number of words, LSA given information, spatial cohesion, stem overlap, word familiarity) onto raters' score for the 164 freewrites in the training set. The stepwise method was used to determine which indices were most predictive of expert ratings of freewrite quality so that we can build a model that is both parsimonious and predictive in implementation.

The stepwise linear regression using the five variables yielded a significant model, $F(2, 161) = 94.635, p < .001$; adj. $r^2 = .535$. However, the only significant predictors were number of words ($B = .024, t(161) = 12.94, p < .001$) and stem overlap ($B = .559, t(161) = 3.30, p = .001$). The results

Table 1. Selected variables based on person correlations

Variable	r value
Number of Words	0.714**
LSA Given/New Information	0.330**
Spatial Cohesion	0.300**
Stem overlap	0.250*
Word Familiarity	-0.180*
*$p < .05$; ** $p < .001$	

from the stepwise linear regression demonstrate that these two variables account for 54% of the variance in the expert evaluations of freewriting quality for the 164 essays examined in the training set. These results suggest that not only are the writers generating ideas, but that these ideas are related to each other (locally) by explicit means of a repetition of nouns or word stems across consecutive sentences. The results further show that some of the features that were identified as important markers both by previous qualitative research and by our intuitive notions of the function of freewrites can be computationally identified using computational tools such as Coh-Metrix.

Test Set Model

In order to test this model, the multiple regression conducted on the training set was used to predict the scores from the test set. The B weights and the constant from regression equation derived from the training set multiple regression analysis were used to obtain the predicted values on the 83 freewrites from the test set; Predicted score = .961 + .024(number of words) + .559(stem overlap). A Pearson correlation between the predicted score and the actual score was conducted to assess the model. We used this correlation along with the adjusted r^2 obtained from running the linear regression on the test data to demonstrate the strength of the model on an independent data set. Predicted scores for the test set significantly correlated with the actual scores, $r = .469$, $p < .001$. The model for the test set yielded an adj. $r^2 = .201$, $p < .001$. The results from the test set model demonstrate that the combination of these variables accounted for 20% of the variance in the evaluation of the 83 freewriting samples comprising the test set.

Post-Hoc Analyses

To support the findings of our multiple regression analysis, we conducted a post-hoc analysis to assess if the lexical diversity scores for the freewrites in the entire corpus correlated to the assigned freewrite scores. For this analysis, we selected the Measure of Textual Lexical Diversity (MTLD). While primarily an index of lexical diversity, MTLD can also be used to assess word overlap (McCarthy & Jarvis, 2010). Thus, MTLD can provide supportive validity for our earlier findings. Although MTLD was not a significant correlate with freewrite score in the training set, our post-hoc analysis demonstrated that it was a significant correlate with freewrite score in the corpus as a whole, ($r = .168$, $p = .008$), lending credence to our claim that highly scored freewrites contain many related ideas.

Differences between 9th and 11th Grade Student Freewrites

Students in this study generated either two or three freewrites, the first two of which were used to compare freewriting across grade levels. These first two freewrites were written with approximately 30 minutes between each one, during which the students wrote an essay. Table 2 presents the means for freewrite scores, number of words, and stem overlap as a function of grade level and attempt.

A 2 x 2 repeated-measures ANOVA (Grade level x Freewrite attempt) was conducted to assess differences between the freewrite scores for 9th and 11th grade students (see Table 2). There was a main effect of grade level, $F(1,102) = 28.83$, $p < .001$) with 11th grade students scoring on aver-

age 0.73 points higher than 9th grade students. The main effect of freewrite attempt was not significant, but there was a marginally significant interaction, $F(1,102) = 3.68$, $p = .056$. This interaction reflected the finding that 11th grade students' freewrite scores did not significantly change from the first to the second freewrite attempt, $t(39) = -.116$, $p = .896$, $d = -.02$, whereas 9th grade students' second freewrite received lower scores than did the first freewrite, $t(63) = -3.05$, $p = .003$, $d = -.417$.

Analyses were also conducted to examine the effects of grade level and freewrite attempt for the Coh-Metrix indices (i.e., number of words and stem overlap) calculated for each of the freewrites. For each index, a 2 x 2 repeated measures ANOVAs (Grade level x Attempt) was conducted. There were no differences in stem overlap as a function of grade level or attempt (both $F < 1$), and the interaction was not significant $F(1,102) = 1.52$, $p = .220$).

There was a main effect for grade level in number of words in the freewrites, $F(1,102) = 45.044$, $p < .001$), with 11th grade students writ-

Table 2. Means for freewrite scores, number of words, and stem overlap as a function of grade level and attempt

		Grade Level		
	9th Grade		11th Grade	
	Mean	SD	Mean	SD
Overall Means				
Freewrite Scores	2.88	0.762	3.61	0.897
Number Words	73.92	22.84	101.29	25.6
Stem Overlap	0.402	0.311	0.381	0.255
Freewrite 1				
Freewrite Scores	3.04	0.763	3.6	0.864
Number Words	78.27	23.92	104.43	30.06
Stem Overlap	0.373	0.27	0.39	0.221
Freewrite 2				
Freewrite Scores	2.72	0.734	3.63	0.904
Number Words	69.58	21	98.15	20.08
Stem Overlap	0.412	0.346	0.348	0.259

ing on average 27 more words per freewrite than did 9th grade students (see Table 2). There was also a main effect of attempt, $F (1,102) = 8.94$, $p = .003$, reflecting the finding students' wrote 7.5 more words on their first freewrite (M=88.3, SD =29.1) than their second freewrite (M=80.6, SD= 24.7). The interaction between grade level and attempt in terms of number of words was not significant ($F < 1$).

DISCUSSION

Based on previous qualitative research along with our intuitive notions of the function of freewriting, we developed a rubric to assess freewrites that emphasized the number of ideas generated, the appropriateness of examples, and syntactic and lexical variety. A regression of linguistic features onto expert ratings of the freewrites showed that the only significant predictors of freewriting quality were the mean number of words and lexical overlap (i.e., stem overlap). The previous study by Weston et al. (2010) found noun overlap to be a significant predictor of freewrite quality ratings, but it did not correlate strongly enough with freewrite scores to be included in the present study. However, stem overlap, which is a close cousin to noun overlap, was a significant correlate and predictor. When examining the results of both studies in conjunction with the holistic freewriting rubric, we can begin to draw some interesting inferences on what drives human assessments of freewriting quality (when using this particular rubric).

The purpose of focused freewriting is to brainstorm ideas quickly by producing a large number of ideas within a set period of time. Considering the goal of freewriting, it makes sense that number of words is the most significant predictor of expert ratings of freewrite quality. In addition, those students who wrote more words were likely produced more ideas, which resulted in more highly rated freewrites. Notably, of course, the rubric focused on the number of ideas generated, and so this result is somewhat circular in nature.

The significance of stem overlap in predicting expert freewrite scores is consistent with the notion that a better freewrite will have a large number of overlapping ideas. This can be shown qualitatively in the two freewrites presented below.

Freewrite 1:Score 5, Stem Overlap .69

Optimism is everything. If people are not optimistic about what they are doing, then they will never be able to complete anything. Think of an istance where somebody seems to do the impossible; this can only be accomplished as a result of optimism.

Optimism is always having a bright outlook on the future. Optimistic people do not let past failures detur them, and they never give up on what they set out to do. How would our world be a better place if these type of people were not around? The optimism given off by a single person can spread to others as well. Many people may become focused and determined about a certain idea if they suddenly have the optimist to do it.

Many noble feats were accomplished as a resulf of the optimism of courages individuals. Take, for instance, Christopher Columbus, who . . .

Freewrite 2: Score 2, Stem Overlap .03

*OBVIOUSLY THE ENJOYMENT LEVEL THAT GOES WITH MORE CHOICES IS HIGHER! who wouldn't want hundreds of millions of choices each and everyday! When a person can choose which colour to make their room the end result is bloody brilliant! I WISH I HAD WAYYYY MORE CHOICES WHEN I AM DOING EVERYDAY THINGS! Omg my like FAV. channel ever is MTV! Its like totallyyy awesome. Isn't eminem just the hottest guy ever? My favorite tv station is sci-fi. I had a ball looking out the old Land of the Lost show. Those graphics were so crappy *SNORT**

Freewrite one shows repetition of the words *optimism, optimistic, person* and *people* as a means to build upon the topic of optimism. This freewrite not only stays on topic but also begins to build ideas on which an essay could be written. In contrast freewrite two only repeats one pertinent word, *choices* and yields few ideas from which one could write a detailed essay. The differences in overlap of word stems in these freewrites manifestes itself on how well the freewrites stay on topic and addresses the prompt. While not measured by stem overlap it can be seen that even though the same word is being repeated multiple time in the higher quality freewrite the person is building upon their ideas and not simply repeating the prompt or key words.

The significance of stem overlap in predicting expert freewrite scores is consistent with the notion that a better freewrite will have a large number of overlapping ideas. These results suggest that not only are the writers generating ideas, but that these ideas are related to each other (locally) by explicit means of a repetition of nouns or word stems across consecutive sentences. Furthermore the significant correlation between MTLD and freewrite score within the full corpus also provides evidence that those freewrites that received higher scores contained related ideas. The results further show that some of the features that were identified as important markers both by previous qualitative research and by our intuitive notions of the function of freewrites can be computationally identified using computational tools such as Coh-Metrix.

We also found that more skilled 11th grade writers (from the Advanced Placement program) wrote longer freewrites, and received higher scores than did the less skilled 9th grade students. The interaction between freewrite order and score, along with the finding that students wrote fewer words on their second freewrite, suggests that there may have been a fatigue effect, but that fatigue or reduction in number of words seemed to only affect the 9th grade students.

The larger, expanded data set in this study allowed us the opportunity to more thoroughly analyze the features considered important to freewrite quality (word characteristics, causality, connectives and logical operators, etc.) and to demonstrate that salient features exist (number of words and stem overlap) that contribute to expert ratings of freewrite quality. The regression equation derived from the training set explained only 21% of the variance in the test set suggesting that there may be other pertinent linguistic features that play a role in expert judgments of freewrite quality. The significance of the correlations between multiple measures related to cohesion, including LSA given/new, spatial cohesion and MTLD suggest that a composite index of cohesion (see McNamara & Graesser, this volume), taking into account these multiple ways in which cohesion can manifested itself in text would be highly useful in predicting freewrite quality. A composite index of cohesion would prevent variables having to be eliminated from analyses because of high multicollinearity between the measures. The relationship between score and multiple measures related to cohesion suggests that quality prompt-based freewrites are not only longer but may be more focused than the freewrites that receive lower quality scores.

Notably, other variables also significantly correlated with freewrite quality, such as the familiarity of the words and the repetition of syntactic structures. As we have found previously, more skilled writers tend to use less familiar words and more complex, varied syntax (McNamara, Crossley, & McCarthy, 2010). We are constrained here by our statistical approach of using regression to produce a model, which is in turn constrained by sample size. If we look at this through the lens of artificial intelligence and cognitive science, we should keep in mind that these variables might still be quite useful (despite their lack of significance in the regression model) in predicting the quality of the freewrites, and writing quality in general.

Another very important constraint in the current study is that we are using our rubric and the expert evaluations of the freewrites (based on that rubric) as our gold standard. We do not know yet whether the freewrite scores are related to the quality of the essays written by the students. For example, perhaps lower quality freewrites lead to better essays, although such an outcome is highly unlikely. However, without having established the construct validity of the freewrite quality scores, these results need to be interpreted with caution. Nonetheless, this is an important step because no previous researchers have attempted to score freewrites and thus, in some sense, it needs to be recognized that to conduct Applied NLP *you have to start somewhere*. In future work, we will relate the freewrite scores to the scores for the essays they preceded to explore the ways in which the features of freewrites are predictive of better essays. Additionally we will analyze idea units as a variable that may lead to essay quality. The analysis of these paired freewrites and essays will allow us the ability to develop more effective training and feedback for students learning to freewrite. In addition these analyses allow for the development of a quantitative assessment for freewrites using computational tools, like Coh-Metrix, to provide real time feedback to students training to freewrite. Through the teaching of writing strategies such as freewriting, we hope to be able to scaffold students toward building better writing skills.

ACKNOWLEDGMENT

This research was supported by the Institute for Education Sciences (IES R305G020018-02; IES R305A080589). Any opinions, findings, and conclusions or recommendations expressed in this material are those of the authors and do not necessarily reflect the views of the IES. We would also like to thank our expert raters, Kristen Dechert and Joshua Thompson, for their help in evaluating the quality of the freewrites and Karen Savella for allowing us to come into her classroom.

REFERENCES

Baayen, R. H., Piepenbrock, R., & Gulikers, L. (1995). *The CELEX lexical database (Release 2)* [CDROM]. Philadelphia, PA: Linguistic Data Consortium, University of Pennsylvania.

Belanoff, P. (1991). Freewriting: An aid to rereading theorists. In Belanoff, P., Elbow, P., & Fontaine, S. I. (Eds.), *Nothing begins with N* (pp. 16–32). Carbondale, IL: Southern Illinois University Press.

Carmody, A. (2009). *Vote May 19, 2009-2010 budget proposal*. Retrieved from http://www.websterschools.org/files/filesystem/200910%20Budget%20Newsletter.pdf.

Chafe, W. L. (1975). Givenness, contrastiveness, definiteness, subjects, topics, and point of view. In Li, C. N. (Ed.), *Subject and topic* (pp. 26–55). New York, NY: Academic.

Crismore, A., Markkanen, R., & Steffensen, M. S. (1993). Metadiscourse in persuasive writing: A study of texts written by American and Finnish university students. *Written Communication*, *10*, 39–71. doi:10.1177/0741088393010001002

Crossley, S. A., Louwerse, M. M., McCarthy, P. M., & McNamara, D. S. (2007). A linguistic analysis of simplified and authentic texts. *Modern Language Journal*, *91*, 15–30. doi:10.1111/j.1540-4781.2007.00507.x

Douglas, D. (1981). An exploratory study of bilingual reading proficiency. In Hudelson, S. (Ed.), *Learning to read in different languages* (pp. 33–102). Washington, DC: Center for Applied Linguistics.

Elbow, P. (1973). *Writing without teachers*. New York, NY: Oxford University Press.

Fellbaum, C. (1998). *WordNet: An electronic lexical database*. Cambridge, MA: MIT Press.

Field, A. (2005). *Discovering statistics using SPSS*. London, UK: Sage Publications, Ltd.

Fontaine, S. I. (1991). Recording and transforming: the mystery of the ten-minute freewrite. In Belanoff, P., Elbow, P., & Fontaine, S. I. (Eds.), *Nothing begins with N* (pp. 3–16). Carbondale, IL: Southern Illinois University Press.

Gilhooly, K. J., & Logie, R. H. (1980). Age of acquisition, imagery, concreteness, familiarity and ambiguity measures for 1944 words. *Behavior Research Methods and Instrumentation, 12*, 395–427. doi:10.3758/BF03201693

Graesser, A. C., McNamara, D. S., Louwerse, M. M., & Cai, Z. (2004). Coh-Metrix: Analysis of text on cohesion and language. *Behavior Research Methods, Instruments, & Computers, 36*, 193–202. doi:10.3758/BF03195564

Halliday, M. A. K. (1967). Notes on transitivity and theme in English. *Journal of Linguistics, 3*, 199–244. doi:10.1017/S0022226700016613

Halliday, M. A. K., & Hasan, R. (1976). *Cohesion in English*. London, UK: Longman.

Haswell, R. H. (1991). Bound forms in freewriting: The issue of organization. In Belanoff, P., Elbow, P., & Fontaine, S. I. (Eds.), *Nothing begins with N* (pp. 32–71). Carbondale, IL: Southern Illinois University Press.

Hempelmann, C. F., Dufty, D., McCarthy, P. M., Graesser, A. C., Cai, Z., & McNamara, D. S. (2005). Using LSA to automatically identify givenness and newness of noun phrases in written discourse. In B. G. Bara, L. Barsalou, & M. Bucciarelli (Eds.), *Proceedings of the 27th Annual Conference of the Cognitive Science Society* (pp. 941-946). Mahwah, NJ: Erlbaum.

Hinkle, S., & Hinkle, A. (1990). An experimental comparison of the effects of focused freewriting and other study strategies on lecture comprehension. *Teaching of Psychology, 17*, 31–35. doi:10.1207/s15328023top1701_7

Kintsch, W., & van Dijk, T. A. (1978). Toward a model of text comprehension and production. *Psychological Review, 85*, 363–394. doi:10.1037/0033-295X.85.5.363

Knudson, R. E. (1989). Effect of instructional strategies on children's informational writing. *The Journal of Educational Research, 83*, 91–96.

Landauer, T., McNamara, D. S., Dennis, S., & Kintsch, W. (Eds.). (2007). *Handbook of latent semantic analysis*. Mahwah, NJ: Erlbaum.

Landauer, T. K., & Dumais, S. T. (1997). A solution to Plato's problem: The latent semantic analysis theory of the acquisition, induction, and representation of knowledge. *Psychological Review, 104*, 211–240. doi:10.1037/0033-295X.104.2.211

Landauer, T. K., Foltz, P. W., & Laham, D. (1998). Introduction to latent semantic analysis. *Discourse Processes, 25*, 259–284. doi:10.1080/01638539809545028

Light, R. J. (2001). *Making the most of college: Students speaking their minds*. Cambridge, MA: Harvard University Press.

Longo, B. (1994). Current research in technical communication: The role of metadiscourse in persuasion. *Technical Communication, 41*, 348–352.

Louwerse, M. M. (2001). An analytic and cognitive parameterization of coherence relations. *Cognitive Linguistics, 12*, 291–315. doi:10.1515/cogl.2002.005

Malvern, D. D., Richards, B. J., Chipere, N., & Durán, P. (2004). *Lexical diversity and language development: Quantification and assessment*. Houndmills, UK: Palgrave Macmillan. doi:10.1057/9780230511804

McCarthy, P. M., & Jarvis, S. (2007). A theoretical and empirical evaluation of vocd. *Language Testing, 24*, 459–488. doi:10.1177/0265532207080767

McCarthy, P. M., & Jarvis, S. (2010). MTLD, vocd-D, and HD-D: A validation study of sophisticated approaches to lexical diversity assessment. *Behavior Research Methods, 42,* 381–392. doi:10.3758/BRM.42.2.381

McNamara, D. S., Crossley, S. A., & McCarthy, P. M. (2010). Linguistic features of writing quality. *Written Communication, 27,* 57–86. doi:10.1177/0741088309351547

McNamara, D. S., & Scott, J. L. (2001). Working memory capacity and strategy use. *Memory & Cognition, 29,* 10–17. doi:10.3758/BF03195736

Miller, G. A., Beckwith, R., Fellbaum, C., Gross, D., & Miller, K. (1990). *Five papers on Word-Net. Cognitive Science Laboratory.* Princeton University.

Paivio, A. (1965). Abstractness, imagery, and meaningfulness in paired-associate learning. *Journal of Verbal Learning and Verbal Behavior, 4,* 32–38. doi:10.1016/S0022-5371(65)80064-0

Perfetti, C. A., Landi, N., & Oakhill, J. (2005). The acquisition of reading comprehension skill. In Snowling, M. J., & Hulme, C. (Eds.), *The science of reading: A handbook* (pp. 227–247). Oxford, UK: Blackwell. doi:10.1002/9780470757642.ch13

Rashotte, C. A., & Torgesen, J. K. (1985). Repeated reading and reading fluency in learning disabled children. *Reading Research Quarterly, 20,* 180–188. doi:10.1598/RRQ.20.2.4

Renyolds, M. (1984). Freewritings origin. *English Journal, 73,* 81–82. doi:10.2307/817229

The College Board. (2005-2008). *SAT essay prompts.* Retrieved from http://www.onlinemathlearning.com/sat-test-prep.html.

Toglia, M. P., & Battig, W. F. (1978). *Handbook of semantic word norms.* New York, NY: Lawrence Erlbaum Associates.

Weston, J. L., Crossley, S. A., & McNamara, D. S. (2010). Towards a computational assessment of freewriting quality. In H. W. Guesgen & C. Murray (Eds.), *Proceedings of the 23rd International Florida Artificial Intelligence Research Society.* Menlo Park, CA: The AAAI Press.

Whitten, I. A., & Frank, E. (2005). *Data mining.* San Francisco, CA: Elsevier.

Wilson, M. D. (1988). The MRC psycholinguistic database: Machine readable dictionary, version 2. *Behavior Research Methods, Instruments, & Computers, 201,* 6–11. doi:10.3758/BF03202594

ADDITIONAL READING

Belanoff, P. (1991). Freewriting: an aid to re-reading theorists. In P. Belanoff, P. Elbow & S. I. Fontaine (Eds.). *Nothing begins with N* (pp. 16-32). Carbondale and Edwardsville: Southern Illinois University Press.

Fontaine, S. I. (1991). Recording and transforming: the mystery of the ten-minute freewrite. In P. Belanoff, P. Elbow & S. I. Fontaine (Eds.). *Nothing begins with N* (pp. 3-16). Carbondale and Edwardsville: Southern Illinois University Press.

Hinkle, S., & Hinkle, A. (1990). An experimental comparison of the effects of focused freewriting and other study strategies on lecture comprehension. *Teaching of Psychology, 17,* 31–35. doi:10.1207/s15328023top1701_7

Renyolds, M. (1984). Freewritings origin. *The English Journal, 73,* 81–82. doi:10.2307/817229

Weston, J. L., Crossley, S. A., & McNamara, D. S. (2010). Towards a computational assessment of freewriting quality. In H. W. Guesgen & C. Murray (Eds.), *Proceedings of the 23rd International Florida Artificial Intelligence Research Society.* Menlo Park, CA: The AAAI Press.

KEY TERMS AND DEFINITIONS

Focused Freewriting: Freewriting that is completed based on a specified topic or domain area.

Freewriting: A five minute exercise in which a writer writes as much as they can as fast as they can without worrying about grammar or punctuation.

Prewriting: Activities engaged in prior to beginning writing, includes but is not limited to freewriting, outlining and concept maps.

APPENDIX A: HOLISTIC FREEWRITING RUBRIC

SCORE OF 6

A freewrite in this category demonstrates *clear and consistent mastery of freewriting*, although it may occasionally resemble an essay.
  • Effectively and insightfully develops ideas on an issue with few unnecessary tangents.
  • demonstrates outstanding critical thinking, using appropriate examples, reasons, and other evidence to support ideas
  • is not well organized or clearly focused, occasionally demonstrating clear coherence, rarely demonstrating a smooth progression of ideas
  • parts of free write exhibit skillful use of language, using a varied vocabulary
  • demonstrates meaningful variety in sentence structure
  • has errors in grammar, usage, and mechanics without attempts to correct them

---

SCORE OF 5

A freewrite in this category demonstrates *reasonably consistent mastery of freewriting*, although it will have occasional lapses in structure and resemble an essay.
  • effectively develops ideas on the issue with some unnecessary tangents
  • demonstrates strong critical thinking, generally using appropriate examples, reasons, and other evidence to support ideas
  • is somewhat organized and focused, demonstrating more frequent coherence and some progression of ideas
  • lacks most punctuation and connectives, using appropriate vocabulary
  • demonstrates variety in sentence structure when sentences are used
  • has many errors in grammar, usage, and mechanics with only a few attempts to correct them.

SCORE OF 4

A freewrite in this category demonstrates *adequate mastery freewriting*, although it will have lapses in quality and will have sections that resemble an essay
  • develops ideas on the issue and demonstrates competent critical thinking, using adequate examples, reasons, and other evidence as support for ideas
  • has sections that are generally organized and focused,
  • demonstrating some coherence and progression of ideas
  • general knowledge vocabulary used, very little variation.
  • demonstrates some variety in sentence structure
  • has some errors in grammar, usage, and mechanics with a moderate number of corrections

---

SCORE OF 3

A freewrite in this category demonstrates *developing mastery.* These freewrites are characterized by ONE OR MORE of the following weaknesses:
  • develops a point of view on the issue, demonstrating some critical thinking, but may do so inconsistently or use inadequate examples, reasons, or other evidence to support ideas.
  • uses some organization and there is some focus on writing in an essay format. There are some lapses in coherence or progression of ideas freely
  • sometimes uses weak vocabulary or inappropriate word choice
  • lacks variety in sentence structure when sentences are used
  • contains an accumulation of errors in grammar, usage, and mechanics with attempts to correct them.

SCORE OF 2

A freewrite in this category demonstrates *little mastery of freewriting.* Characterized by ONE OR MORE of the following weaknesses:
  • develops a point of view on the issue that is vague or seriously limited, and demonstrates weak critical thinking, providing inappropriate or insufficient examples, reasons, or other evidence to support ideas
  • is organized and/or focused like an essay
  • very limited vocabulary or incorrect word choice
  • contains errors in grammar, usage, and mechanics so serious that meaning is somewhat obscured with attempts to change the errors that are noticed by the writer

---

SCORE OF 1

A freewrite of this score resembles a poor quality finished essay.
  • develops no viable point of view on the issue, or provides little or no evidence to support its ideas
  • Structured into a basic essay format.
  • is disorganized or unfocused, but resulting in a disjointed or incoherent essay
  • Ideas are fully formed and no loose ends are left.
  • little variation in sentence structure
  • Contains pervasive errors in grammar, usage, or mechanics that persistently interfere with meaning within a normal essay format.
  • Whenever a known error is made a correction is made

Freewrites not written on the prompt or that continually repeat I don't know what to say or have excessive strings of profanity will receive a score of zero.

APPENDIX B

Sample Freewrites with Scores

Overlapping Words Italicized/ Bolded

Freewrite A: Score 5

A person may have *loyalties* only to one group, person, etc. If this is the case, then people should always be *loyal*. For example, in the institution of marriage, the **spouses** should be *loyal* to only each other—that is, a **spouse** should not have *loyalties* to any other people aside for his **spouse**. The same holds true for national *loyalty*. A person should be *loyal* only to the country in which he is a citizen, except if the country is a repressive one. Finally, this especially holds true for religion. A single person cannot practice Christianity, Buddmism, and Hinduism.

Freewrite B: Score 4

Personal memories are key to success in the future. If one has no *past*, they have no guidelines to where they want to go or what they want to do. From *past* **experience** is how a **person** realizes their interests and also how they learn what may be a good or bad idea. If a **person** is choosing a career path, they will look back on *past* **experiences** to see if a *past* event interests them. For example, if a child grows up liking and working with clothing, she may look back at her life, realize that she loved it, and pursue a career of design.

    Past memories or **experiences** allows a . . .

Freewrite C: Score 3

It is sometimes better for people to take *risks*. Like the game of *Risk*, the Green **army**had controll of only a small part of Europe with little troops while the black **army** had control of everything else and wiped out every **army** but the green **army**. The only chance Green had at winning was going straight for the HQ of Black **army**. They took the chance lost a little amount of **men**, Black lost hundreds of **men** on they way and green ended up conquering, Japan and winning. If risks aren't taken nothing can get done.

Freewrite D: Score 2

If the **people**complain a lot about the *problems*, then the government should step in to do something. If only a few **people** complain about the *problem*, then they should do something about it. There is no government OR individuals. It is both. It all depends on the situation. As explained above, if matters are that bad, **people** should do stuff about it.

Freewrite E: Score 1

It is better to be *realistic* because being *realistic* allows people to understand more clearly. It shows that it is more explanitory and . . .

Chapter 22
Morphological Analysis of Ill-Formed Arabic Verbs for Second Language Learners

Khaled Shaalan
The British University in Dubai, UAE

Marwa Magdy
Cairo University, Egypt

Aly Fahmy
Cairo University, Egypt

ABSTRACT

Arabic is a language of rich and complex morphology. The nature and peculiarity of Arabic make its morphological and phonological rules confusing for second language learners (SLLs). The conjugation of Arabic verbs is central to the formulation of an Arabic sentence because of its richness of form and meaning. In this research, we address issues related to the morphological analysis of ill-formed Arabic verbs in order to identify the source of errors and provide an informative feedback to SLLs of Arabic. The edit distance and constraint relaxation techniques are used to demonstrate the capability of the proposed system in generating all possible analyses of erroneous Arabic verbs written by SLLs. Filtering mechanisms are applied to exclude the irrelevant constructions and determine the target stem which is used as the base for constructing the feedback to the learner. The proposed system has been developed and effectively evaluated using real test data. It achieved satisfactory results in terms of the recall rate.

INTRODUCTION

Language is a way of communicating ideas and feelings among people by the use of conventional symbols. People need to learn second languages to be able to communicate with other non-native speakers. Second language acquisition is a difficult task, especially for adults. There are various methods to acquire a new language and all of them require some form of feedback, which can be described as a reaction to what has been said or written. This feedback most often comes from other human beings with whom the language

DOI: 10.4018/978-1-60960-741-8.ch022

learner is interacting. There are, however, other means to receive automated feedback. One is the use of intelligent language tutoring system (ILTS) software. This software contains exercises for language learners. Their response to these exercises is analyzed by the system which provides some form of feedback that could identify the exact source of error a learner has made.

There are some types of exercises that are easy to be error diagnosed, such as multiple choice questions and gap filling exercises, because the number of possible answers is very limited. Simple methods can then be employed to provide a feedback to learners. Whenever the range of possible answers is large or even infinite, specialized intelligent tools are needed. For instance, in the case of exercises requiring learners to produce sentences in the language they are learning, Natural Language Processing (NLP) tools and techniques are necessary to analyze the learner's answer and produce intelligent feedback. In a morphological rich language such Arabic, an inflected verb can form a complete sentence (e.g. the verb سمعتك /samiEtuka/[1] [heard-I-you]) contains a complete syntactic structure in just a one-word sentence. In this case the NLP tools and techniques are also required to analyze the learner's answer and produce intelligent feedback.

The work presented in this chapter addresses issues related to the morphological analysis of ill-formed Arabic verbs written by beginner to intermediate SLLs. The proposed system is an integral part of an ILTS for Arabic. SLLs of Arabic, however, face a lot of morphological and syntactic difficulties during their language learning tasks, such as *word formation*, *word recognition*, *sentence construction*, and *disambiguation*. This complexity in learning Arabic makes addressing the diagnosis of *Arabic lexical errors* a challenge. This has motivated us to develop a tool that addresses the *word formation* problem that is usually faced by SLLs of Arabic. This is achieved by making the proposed tool analyzes the learner's

answer which is used to provide learner with some form of feedback that identifies the exact source of the error s/he might made.

The edit distance and constraint relaxation techniques are used to generate all possible analyses of erroneous Arabic verbs. Filtering mechanisms are applied after the extraction of affixes and stems to exclude the irrelevant constructions and determine the target stem. For each case, a morphological gloss is incrementally formulated which is to be used as a base for constructing the feedback to the learner.

Many research, however, have attacked the problem of Arabic morphological analysis (Ahmed 2000; Beesley 2001; Buckwalter 2002; Darwish 2002; Al-Sughaiyer and Al-Kharashi 2004; Attia 2006). But to the best of our knowledge few research have addressed the problem of analysis of ill-formed Arabic words (e.g., Bowden and Kiraz 1995; Ahmed 2000; Buckwalter 2002). Bowden and Kiraz (1995) investigated the problem of correcting words in Semitic languages including Arabic language. Their approach integrated with morphological analysis using a multi-tape formalism. The model had two-level error rules that handle the following error types: vowel shift, deleted consonant, deleted long vowels, and substituted consonant. Moreover, Ahmed (2000) and Buckwalter (2002) applied some spelling relaxation rules (to deal with orthographic variations like the use of the final letter ه /h/ instead of the letter ة /p/) to get all possible analyses of an erroneous word. However, these systems only handle performance errors made by native speakers of the language. In contrast to the proposed system that handles competence errors made by nonnative speakers of Arabic. It does so by incorporating morphological knowledge and non-native intuitions into its algorithm. It does not depend on simple string matching between correct and erroneous words

The rest of this paper is structured as follows. Section 2 discusses lexical error analysis problem. Section 3 presents a background on Arabic morphology. Section 4 introduces an analysis of common Arabic lexical errors. Section 5 describes the proposed model. Section 6 discusses the results from an experiment. Finally, in Section 7 we give some concluding remarks.

LEXICAL ERROR ANALYSIS

Lexical (word) analysis is the first step for tools and applications that concerns recognizing the detailed structure of the inflected word. It is also necessary at this step to verify that the input word is linguistically correct (i.e. belongs to the respective language and conforms to its morphological rules). This is the basic level of checking and was included quite early in text processing software to ensure that the next levels of analysis are based on linguistically correct input words. Lexical errors can be classified into three classes (Tschichold 2003):

- **Errors in word formation.** These errors are related to the correct application of morphological and phonological rules. For example, it is incorrect to conjugate weak (irregular) verbs with regular verb morphological rules such as generating the imperfect form of نوصل /na-**wo**Sil/ instead of نصل /na-Sil/ (we arrive), which incorrectly leaves the weak letter (و) /w/ of the assimilated (first weak) verb in the imperfect form.
- **Errors in semantic or word choice.** These errors are to some extent related to ambiguity in word senses and phonetics. For example, it is incorrect to conjugate verbs that belong to the same root but differ in their patterns by mixing up one pattern with another such as incorrectly generating the perfect tense form of the verb ابتاع / {ibotAEa/ (purchased) according to the pattern افتعل /{ifotaEala/ and root ع-ي-ب

/b-y-E/ instead of generating it as باع / bAEa/ (sold), which has the intended pattern فعل /faEala/ and root ع-ي-ب /b-y-E/.
- **Errors at the interface of lexical and grammar.** These errors are related to the morpho-syntactic features of words. For example, it is incorrect to negate a verb in its perfect form with the negative particle لم /Lam/ (*not*) unless this verb is in jussive imperfect form such as لم وجد [2]* /lam wajada/ (did-not find) instead of لم يجد /lam ya-jid/ (does-not find).

Existing studies of lexical error analysis fall into two main closely related systems: *Spelling Checkers* and *Intelligent Language Tutoring Systems*. The purpose of most spelling checkers is neither teaching nor learning as they are only designed for detecting spelling errors and suggesting possibly correct spelling (Hsieh et al., 2002). SLLs not only ask for correcting their errors, by just choosing the right word from a list of alternatives, but they also want to improve their language skills in order not to do same errors over and over again. Moreover, most of checkers are inappropriate for nonnative speakers because they are mainly designed for native speakers and as such they are not suitable for detecting and correcting competence errors made by nonnative speakers. For example, recent Microsoft office's Arabic spell checker© detects the word يقالن * / ya-qAlo-na/ as an error but it doesn't suggest the correct form يقلن /ya-qulo-na/ (they-(f) said). On the contrary, ILTS try to overcome these problems and be more useful to SLLs by making true diagnosis[3] of errors. Consequently, they point the learner to the right direction on how to correct their errors rather than providing the correct version directly (Faltin, 2003). However, most ILTS developed until now try to overcome shortcomings of general spell checkers. They do so by incorporating morphological knowledge and non-native intuitions into their algorithms in order to be able to handle competence errors made by nonnative writers. Therefore, the basic step in any ILTS is to morphologically analyze learner's answer and uses this analysis to make a true diagnosis of the learner's answer.

THE ARABIC MORPHOLOGY SYSTEM

Arabic language is one of the Semitic languages that is defined as a *diacritized* language where the pronunciation of its words cannot be fully determined by their spelling characters only. It depends also on some special marks put above or below the spelling characters to determine the correct pronunciation; these marks are called diacritics, so-called "Tashkil" in Arabic.

Unfortunately, in nowadays Arabic writing, people do not explicitly mention diacritics. They depend on their knowledge of the language and the context to understand none or partial diacritized text. Due to the optional diacritization, two or more words in Arabic are homographic: they have the same orthographic form, though the pronunciation and meaning is totally different (Ahmed 2000; Attia 2006). Table 1 lists some homographic examples.

Arabic language has very rich derivational and inflectional morphology. Al-Sughaiyer et al. (2004) defined derivational morphology as the process of concatenating a set of morphemes to a given word that may affect the syntactic category of the word. While inflectional morphology is the process of creating the various forms of

Table 1. An Arabic word that is homographic

Word	Lemma	Different Interpretations
يعد / yEd/	أعاد />aEAd/	يعِد /yuEid/ (bring back)
	عاد /EAd/	يعُد /yaEud/ (return)
	وعد /waEid/	يعِد /yaEid/ (promise)
	عد /Ead~/	يعُدّ /yaEud~/ (count)
	أعد />aEd~/	يعُدّ /yuEid~/ (prepare)

each word. It doesn't affect the word syntactic category such as verb, noun …etc. Features such as case, gender, number, tense, person, mood and voice are some examples that may be affected by the inflectional morphology. The next two subsections present Arabic derivational and inflectional morphology. The last subsection presents an introduction to Arabic verbal system.

Arabic Derivational Morphology

The Arabic derivational morphology has some challenging feature: morphotactic (rules governing which morphemes may come with each other). Whereas most languages construct words out of morphemes which are just concatenated one after another, as in *un-fail + ing – ly* (بدقة دائمة), Arabic words are derived using three concepts: root, pattern and form. Generally, each pattern carries a meaning which, when combined with the meaning inherent in the root, gives the goal meaning of the inflected form. Although Arabic roots and patterns carry one or more specific meaning, they cannot be an Arabic word on its own. Table 2 illustrates some examples of the derivation process of some Arabic words.

The derivation process in Arabic makes it has the richest vocabulary ever found among all important natural languages although it has a relatively small number of derivative *patterns* (Ahmed 2000). Each pattern is a string of two types of characters: *fixed*, possibly none, and three or four *generic* characters. For example, the pattern تفعيل /tafoEiyl/ has two fixed characters: (ت) /t/ and (ي) /y/ and three generic characters: ف- ع - ل /f-E-l/. Arabic has also a limited number of derivative *roots*. Each root is a set of three or four fixed characters.

Arabic Inflectional Morphology

The Arabic inflectional morphology changes the morpho-syntactic features of the word. It defines the number (singular, plural, and dual), gender

Table 2. The derivation process of some Arabic words

Pattern	Root	Form	Derived Word	Description
فاعل /fAEil/	كـ-تـ-ب /k-t-b/	The active participle noun (اسم الفاعل) "the doer of the action"	كاتب /kAtib/ (writer)	Both the word form and the root meaning (to write) form together a word that indicates the doer of the action of writing (writer).
مفعول /mafoEuwl/	و-لـ-د /w-l-d/	The passive participle noun (اسم المفعول) "the object upon which the action is done"	مولود /mawoluwd/ (new born person)	Both the word form and the root meaning (to give birth) form together a word that indicates being born action (a new born person).
تفعيل /tafoEiyl/	د-ر-س /d-r-s/	The verbal noun (المصدر) "the action of doing something"	تدريس /tadoriys/ (teaching- instruction)	both the word form and the root meaning (to study) form together a word that indicates the action of teaching (teaching or instructing)

(feminine, masculine, and neutral), definiteness (definite, indefinite) and case (nominative, accusative, genitive) features for nouns. While it defines the following features for verbs: tense (prefect, imperfect, imperative), voice (active, passive), mood (indicative, subjunctive, jussive), subject and object (person, number, gender). It does so by adding more affixes to the stem[4] to form a well-formed Arabic word.

Arabic affixes can be prefixes such as ي /ya/ (imperfective subject 3rd person singular), suffixes such as تُ /tu/ (perfective subject 1st person singular) or circumfixes such as تـ + + ان /t + + An/ (imperfective subject 2nd person dual). Multiple affixes can appear in a word. For example, the word وسيكتبونها /wasayaktubuwnahA/ (and-they-will-write-it) has two prefixes; one circumfix and one suffix (Habash and Rambow 2006):

- وسيكتبونها /wasayaktubuwnahA/
- و /wa/ + س /sa/ + ي /ya/ + بـتـك /ktub/ + نو /uwna/ + اه /hA/
- And + will + 3rd person + write + masculine-plural + it

In general, the following can be inferred as a simple structure of the Arabic words (Darwish 2002; Ahmed 2000):

- The main part, a noun or verb, of the word occurs in the middle. Let us call this part as word *stem*.
- The stem may be prefixed by something like the definitive article, a preposition, a tense determiner... etc. or some combination of them. The prefix itself cannot be a standalone word. It may be absent and in this case, we can assume it as a null. When a prefix precedes a stem, it may modify its string and also be modified. For example, the deletion of the letter (و) /w/ from the stem وعد /waEada/ (promised) can be explained by taking the imperfect tense of this stem. The resulting word is يعد /yaEid/ (he promises). Also, the deletion of the letter (ا) /A/ from the prefix ال /Al/ (the) can be explained by adding the preposition ل /l/ (for) to this prefix. The resulting prefix will be لل /lial/ (for-the).
- The stem may be suffixed by something like a pronoun, a gender determiner... etc. or some combination of them. The suffix itself cannot be a standalone word. It may be absent and in this case, we can assume it as a null. When a suffix succeeds a stem, it may modify its string and also be modified. For example, the conversion of letter (ء) /'/ into (و) /w/ in the stem صحراء /SaHorA'/

(desert) can be explained by taking the dual form of this noun. The resulting word is صحراوان /SaHorAwAn/ (two deserts).

Introduction to Arabic Verbal System

One of the most puzzling problems in the study of Arabic is its verbal system which is very rich in forms and meaning (Soudi, Cavalli, and Jamari 2001). Arabic verbs can be conjugated from either trilateral or quadrilateral roots according to one of the traditionally recognized patterns (or forms). There are 15 trilateral forms[5] and 4 quadrilateral ones. Examples of all Arabic forms are shown in Table 3 (Bowden and Kiraz 1995; Wright 1967).

The conjugation of verbs in different tenses, voices and mood is achieved using well behaved morphological rules. The irregularities are due to

the phonological constraints of certain root consonants. The important irregularity issues are related to Arabic weak verbs that include one or more weak letter. Weak letters can be deleted or substituted by other letters because of Arabic phonological constraints (El-Sadany and Hashish 1989). For example, the replacement of the letter (و) /w/ by (ا) in taking the past (perfect) tense of the trilateral root ق-و-ل /q-w-l/, using regular rules would generate قَوَلَ* /qawala/ but as it is a hollow (middle weak) verb it should be generated according to special weak rules and thus it is written as قَالَ /qAla/ (said).

To sum up, in this section, we demonstrated the difficulties that can make the process of learning Arabic verbs a difficult one. This has motivated us to address the challenges in developing a morphological analyzer that can handle ill-formed Arabic

Table 3. Arabic verbal forms

Form Number	Pattern	Active Voice Example
1	فعل /faEala/	شرب /$ariba/ (drank)
(a) Trilateral verbs		
2	فعّل /faE~ala/	كسّر /kas~ara/ (shattered)
3	فاعل /fAEala/	ضاعف /DAEafa/ (doubled)
4	أفعل />afEal /	أراح /<arAHa/ (brought relief)
5	تفعّل /tafaE~ala/	تعلّم /taEal~ama/ (studied)
6	تفاعل /tafAEala/	تساقط /tasAqaTa/ (collapsed - fall piece by piece)
7	انفعل /{inofaEala/	انكسر /{inokasara/ (broke)
8	افتعل /{ifotaEala/	اقتفى /{iqotafaY/ (follow)
9	استفعل /{isotafaEala/	استغاث /{isotagAva/ (asked for help)
10	افعلّ /{ifoEal~a/	احمرّ /{iHomar~a/ (turned red)
11	افعالّ /{ifoEaAl~/	ازراقّ /{izoraAq~/ (became blue)
12	افعوعل /{ifoEawoEala/	اغرورق /{igoraworaqa/ (immersed)
13	افعوّل /{ifoEaw~la/	اجلوّز /{ijolaw~za/ (lasted long)
14	افعنلل /{ifoEanolala/	احلنكك /{iHolanokaka/ (turned jet black)
15	افعنلى /{ifoEanolay/	احبنطى /{iHobanoTay/ (caused swollen)
(b) Quadrilateral verbs		
1	فعلل /faEolala/	دحرج /daHoraja/ (rolled)
2	تفعلل /tafaEolala/	تزلزل /tazalozala/ (quaked)
3	افعنلل /{ifoEanolala/	افرنقع /{iforanoqaEa/ (dismissed)
4	افعللّ /{ifoEalal~a/	اضمحلّ /{iDomaHal~a/ (faded away)

verbs which will be used as a tool in intelligent language tutoring framework to diagnose errors made by SLLs of Arabic.

ARABIC LEXICAL ERROR TYPOLOGY

An important step in the implementation of an error analysis system is to decide which type of errors to be analyzed. Realistically, not every imaginable error type can be analyzed within a single system (Faltin 2003). There are two main criteria to select errors. On the one hand, errors which are easy to implement given the linguistic resources at hand and the diagnosis techniques available. On the other hand, there are the needs of the end-user population which makes specific kinds of errors.

To decide on the set of errors handled by our system, the Arabic SLLs needs were investigated by examining a set of linguistic studies which indicates the most frequent types of errors made by SLLs (cf. Ali 1998; Abd Alghaniy 1998; Jassem 2000). Tables 4 through 5 provide details of possible errors which are commonly made by SLLs of Arabic. These errors are classified as *word formation errors* due to improper application of *morphology* and *phonology.*

However, the proposed system focuses on word formation errors. Other errors (i.e. semantic errors and errors at the interface of lexical and grammar) are out of this paper scope.

THE PROPOSED MODEL

The proposed model takes into consideration a set of linguistic studies which follow error analysis approach in identifying most frequent errors made by SLLs. This approach, however, follows some steps to identify and classify errors: data collection, error identification, error classification, error description, error explanation and pedagogical application (Jassem 2000). These studies have acquired real materials written by SLLs in a typical teaching/learning environment; these learners have different backgrounds (i.e., differ in their first language). Consequently, the extracted errors are generally not aimed to a specific sort of learners. Therefore, the proposed model is general enough to be used by different sort of learners.

However, the proposed model generates *all* possible word analyses for each ill-formed learner answer. It uses *constraint relaxation* and *edit-distance* techniques to split each erroneous word into three segments: *prefix+ stem+ suffix.* In any language model, the partial structures can combine only if some constraints or conditions are met. When these constraints are relaxed, an

Table 4. Word formation errors due to morphology

Error Type	Source of Error
Connected pronouns Acronym: CP	Incorrect usage of pronouns with respect to verb tense **Example:** Wrong: يجئت *[6] /ya-ji}o-tu/ (I-he-came) Correct: جئت /ji}o-tu/ (I-came)
Verb conjugation Acronym: VC	Incorrect conjugation of Arabic weak verbs **Example:** wrong: نجو* /najaw/ correct: نجا /najA/ (he escaped)

Table 5. Word formation errors due to phonology

Error Type	Source of Error
Consonant letters Acronym: CL	Incorrect usage of letters with a closely related pronunciation **Example:** Wrong: أصطيع*/ />a-SotaTiyE/ Correct: أستطيع />a-sotaTiyE / (I-am-able).
Vowel letters Acronym: VL	Making short vowel a long one **Example:** Wrong: أصباحت*/ />aSobAH-at/. Correct: أصبحت />aSobaH-at / (became)
	Making long vowel a short one **Example:** Wrong: تزرين* /ta-zuri-yna/. Correct: تزورين /ta-zwri-yna/ (you-visit)

attachment is allowed even if the constraint is not satisfied (Faltin 2003).

In Arabic, various constraints should be met to formulate a well-formed word such as *usage of certain connected pronouns with respect to a verb tense* and *the usage of certain affixes or clitics with conjugated verbs*. In the proposed model, these two example constraints can be relaxed to allow for error diagnosis.

In general, the proposed model takes every erroneous input word and proceeds with the following steps to perform its functionality:

1. Extract a list of all possible suffixes.
2. Filter the suffixes list.
3. Extract a list of all possible prefixes.
4. Filter the prefixes list.
5. Construct all possible correct stems.
6. Form groups of similar stems.
7. Get the base word forms[7] from stem strings.
8. Match the correct answer base word form with the learner answer base word forms and determine the analyses of the ill-formed input.

These steps are necessary as the conjugated verb might be made ill-*formed* due to either ill-formed generation of a stem as a result of applying an incorrect pattern to a root or ill-formed inflection of a stem with affixes. The following shows the application of these steps on Example 1.

Example 1. Write a Sentence Using the Following Arabic Roots.

- ق-و-ل، ح-ق، د-و-م /q-w-l, H-q, d-w-m/.

Assume the following two answers; where (a) includes a wrong conjugation of a *Hollow* (middle weak) verb, and (b) is the correct answer.

a. ‏*قالتو الحق دائما/qAlo-tw AlHaq~ dA}imAF/ (I always told the-truth).

b. ‏أقول الحق دائما /a-quwl AlHaq~ dA}imAF/ (I always tell the-truth).

The proposed model first matches the correct answer with the learner answer and filters out the matched words. This leaves the correct answer with the word أقول/>a-quwl/ (I-tell) while it leaves the learner answer with the word قالتو /qAlo-tw/ (told-I). Then the model applies all the previous steps on the word قالتو*.

Step 1: Extract a List of All Possible Suffixes

The model uses regular expressions for representing the list of affixes to be extracted. The regular expressions are implemented using the deterministic finite-state automata (FSA) approach. For more information about FSA, see (Jurafsky and Martin 2008). The suffix list is represented in the deterministic FSA in reverse order to facilitate left to right matches. Figure 1 illustrates a FSA representation of the suffixes: ت, ا, ات, وا /Waw-Alef, Alef-Teh, Alef, Teh/.

To extract the suffix list, the system matches the input word against the suffix automata. The match begins at the *end* of the word (Position 1) and works *backwards*. The system relaxes the *usage of certain affixes* constraint by using a *three-way-match* technique (Elmi and Evens 1998) to compare two strings: a suffix of the learner input with a legal suffix. This method assumes

Figure 1. A finite-state automata for four suffixes

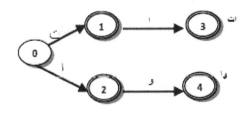

that when a character at location *n* of the first string does not match a character at location *m* of second string, there exist an error and two other comparisons are made (character at position *n* with character at position *m+1* and character at position *n+1* with character at position *m*); Initially, *n=1* to point to the last letter of the input string and *m=0* to point to a letter at the initial state in the FSA. The three-way-match comparison and the order of the comparisons are shown in Figure 2.

Given the FSA at Figure 1 and a learner response with the word وتلاق* /qAlo-tw/ (told-I), the system tries to: 1) match the last letter (*n=1*) و /w/ of the input word with the Arabic suffix ت (Teh) that occurs at the end (*m=1*) of Arabic verbs. The match fails. So, it tries to match again with the one but last letter (*n+1=2*) of the input word ت /t/ which succeeds. This process interprets the letter ت /t/ as a possible suffix and the letter و /w/ as an extra letter occurring at the end of the input word. Similarly, the match exhaustively proceeds with other Arabic suffixes yielding the following 10 possible solutions along with their error indications, respectively:

1. [""]. NULL suffix.

Figure 2. The three-way-match comparison and the order of the comparison

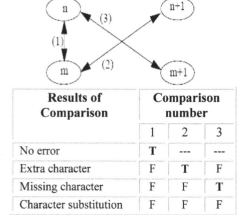

Results of Comparison	Comparison number		
	1	2	3
No error	T	---	---
Extra character	F	T	F
Missing character	F	F	T
Character substitution	F	F	F

2. ["ات"]. Feminine plural noun suffix with extra Waw and missing Alef.
3. ["ت"]. Third person singular feminine perfect verb suffix with extra Waw.
4. ["ت"]. First person singular perfect verb suffix with extra Waw.
5. ["ت"]. Second person singular feminine perfect verb suffix with extra Waw.
6. ["ت"]. Second person singular masculine perfect verb suffix with extra Waw.
7. ["و"]. Masculine plural noun suffix.
8. ["او"]. Second person masculine plural imperative verb suffix with missing Alef.
9. ["او"]. Masculine plural imperfect verb suffix with missing Alef.
10. ["او"]. Third person masculine plural perfect verb suffix with missing Alef.

Practically, however, the use of constraint relaxation in analyzing Arabic verbs leads to over-generation. In order to resolve this issue, we introduced *heuristic rules* that eliminate highly implausible analyses made by Arabic SLLs. For example, SLLs of Arabic might find it difficult to choose among a vowel sign such as (الضمة) /u/ and a genuine character, such as letter و /w/. So, one set of the heuristic rules restricts itself to handle the extra or missing weak letters. Another set of rules restricts itself to recognize a letter substituted by another letter that is similar in pronunciation. We categorized the closely related pronunciation letters into 7 groups: 1) ['ت,'د,'ض,'ط'], 2), ['س,' 'ص,'ز'], 3) ['س,'ث'], 4) ['ج,'ق'], 5) ['ق,'ك'], 6) ['ذ,' 'ز,'ظ'], and 7) ['ع,'ح'].

Step 2: Filter the Suffixes List

This step excludes some irrelevant suffixes according to: learner's answer and the set of error categories handled by the proposed system. For example, the previous list of 10 suffixes could be minimized to **five** solutions: 1, 4, 8, 9, and 10. There are two explanations behind this filtering. The system does not handle errors related to Arabic nouns which led to ignore the *second* and *seventh* solutions. Second, the other three eliminated solutions are discarded since their end case does not match the extra character و /w/.

Step 3: Extract a List of All Possible Prefixes

Extracting the prefixes list is the same as extracting the suffixes list except that the order of the match process begins at the *first* letter and proceeds *upwards*. Applying this step on Example 1 produces only null prefix solution:

1. [""]. NULL prefix.

Step 4: Filter the Prefixes List

As the prefixes list is null, the output of this step does not result in any filtered prefix.

Step 5: Construct All Possible Correct Stem Forms

To construct a possible correct stem, the system tries exhaustively to extract every possible stem (i.e., a substring that remains after removing prefixes and suffixes from the input word) such that either the compatibility conditions between affixes[8] is satisfied or the relaxed constraints are met. In Arabic, there are certain connected pronouns that can only be used with a certain verb tense. For example, the suffix pronoun 'نا' (Na) can only be used with the perfect tense while the prefix pronoun 'نـ'(Noon) can only be used with the imperfect tense. It is morphologically incorrect to use both pronouns at the same time (e.g. 'نذهبنا'*) as this will be considered as a severe contradiction in pronoun inflections which leads to a conflict in verb tense. Applying the constraint relaxation technique will split this erroneous word into: the prefix 'ن,' the stem 'ذهب,' and the suffix 'نا' even though the attachment constraint is not met.

The output of this step, using the results so far from Example 1, yields four solutions. Each solution consists of five elements constituting: *prefix, stem, suffix, feature structure (FS)*[9] that describes the analyzed word, and an initial *error indication*. The *error indication* is a list that denotes: the required operation (e.g., insert) to relax the affix, the actual character and the position where the operation should take place.

Solution (1):

*   *Null affixes*[10]: Null Prefix + "قالتو" + Null suffix
    Error indication: [];

Solution (2):

*   *Null prefix with first person singular perfect verb in active voice with extra Waw in the suffix*:
    Null Prefix "قال"+'ت'
    Error indication: [insert('و,'5)];

Solution (3):

*   *Null prefix with second person masculine plural imperative verb with deleted Alef in the suffix*: Null Prefix + "قالت" + 'وا'
    Error indication: [delete('ا,'6)];

Solution (4):

*   *Null prefix with third person masculine plural perfect verb in active voice with deleted Alef in the suffix*: Null Prefix + "قالت" + 'وا'
    Error indication: [delete('ا,'6)]

Notice that, in this example, the solution *"Null prefix with masculine plural imperfect verb with deleted Alef in the suffix"* is discarded as the combination between a null prefix with the imperfect

Figure 3. A finite-state automata for four Arabic verb patterns. The letter inside a square is generic.

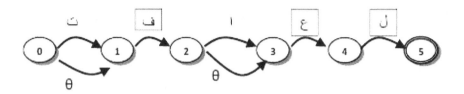

suffix 'وا' (Waw & Alef) (cf. the 9th suffix solution in *step 1*) is morphologically invalid (incompatible). This suffix can only be used together with either one of the following prefixes: 'ي' (Yeh) or 'ت' (Teh).

Step 6: Form Groups of Similar Stems

The current solution list may contain similar stem strings. So, in order to avoid redundancy, the list is organized into groups of lexicographically similar stems. The output of this step yields three groups in the solution stem list: {('قالتو', [1]), ('قال', [2]), ('قالت', [3, 4])}; where the number points to the corresponding five elements in the solution list.

Step 7: Get the Base Word Forms From Stem Strings

To get all possible base forms (normalized stems) from each string in the stem solution list, we need first to match with a list of Arabic verb patterns. These patterns are represented as deterministic FSA. Figure 3 illustrates a FSA of the relevant patterns فعل, فاعل, تفعل, تفاعل /tafAEala, tafoE~al, faEala, fAEala/. We differentiate between two types of characters in a pattern: *fixed* and *generic*. A generic character can represent any Arabic letter while a fixed character should represent an exact same character. For example, the pattern فعل / faEala/ has only three generic characters while

the pattern تفعل /tafoE~al/ has one fixed character ت /t/ and three generic characters.

The system matches characters of the stem string against characters of the verb pattern using the *three-way-match* technique but to relax only the missing and substituted letters that are similar in pronunciations. If a match succeeds, the resultant word is normalized to get the base form by deleting any weak or hamza letters and; then the obtained form is included in the base form solution list.

This step is applied to the current stem solution list {('قالتو', [1]), ('قال', [2]), ('قالت', [3, 4])}.

The first stem in this list is discarded as it does not match with any Arabic pattern. The processing of the second stem produces the base forms: {'قال' and 'قل'}; which after removing the middle weak letter (i.e. *Alef*) of the first one it becomes normalized to the second (i.e., 'قل'). The processing of the third solution produces the base forms {'قالت' and 'قلت' which is similarly normalized to 'قلت.'

Ultimately, the base form solution list consists of the base forms {('قل', [2]), ('قلت', [3, 4])} (cf. the 2nd, 3rd and 4th solutions in *step 5*).

Step 8: Match the Correct Answer Base Word Form with the Learner Answer Base Word Forms and Determine the Analyses of the Ill-Formed Learner Input

This step obtains first the base word forms of the roots stored with the question. Then, it matches each of these base forms with each base form in the learner's answer. This process is deterministic such that once a match is found all other forms from the solution list are discarded and the final word analysis is generated.

Applying this step on the base form solution list, the match succeeds with the first base word form[11] (i.e. 'قل'). This yields the final solution *"Null prefix with first person singular perfect verb in active voice with extra Waw in the suffix"* as the only possible word analysis for the erroneous word قالتو* / qAlo-tw / (told-I).

A comparison between the features of the correct word أقول />a-quwl/ (I-tell) and the features derived from the analysis of the incorrect word قالتو* /qAlo-tw/ (told-I) shows that the learner has made three errors:

1. **Verb tense** error since the correct tense is *imperfect* while the incorrect one is *perfect,*
2. **Short vowel substituted by long vowel** error since there is an extra *Waw* character in affix representation, and
3. **Verb conjugation** error since there is an extra character at position 2 of the stem قال /qAla/ and this character does not match the diacritic sign of the correct word which is ضمة /u/.

The system will provide an appropriate feedback describing these errors.

EXPERIMENT

We conducted an experiment that measures how successfully the proposed model generates *all* possible analyses of erroneous Arabic verbs that are used later to diagnose SLLs errors. The *quantitative* measures are used. These measures rely on collecting different test sets written by real SLLs in a typical teaching/learning environment. It was necessary that these learners have different backgrounds (i.e., differ in their first language) to test if the system is general enough and not aimed to a specific sort of learners. The different types of errors and the exact source of errors in the test set are *subjectively* identified by a human specialist to produce the reference set. The test set is then fed into the morphological analyzer and the detected and undetected errors are reported. These errors are based on analyses generated by the proposed model. The recall rate[12] for each error type is calculated. This measure has been used in evaluating similar research (cf. Wagner, Foster, and Genabith 2007; Sjöbergh and Knutsson 2005; Faltin 2003).

The above mentioned methodology is applied on a real test set that consists of 116 real Arabic sentences. The number of words per sentence varies from 3 to 15 words, with an average of 5.1 words per test sentence. The total number of words in all test sentences are 587 words, 118 of them have lexical verb errors. However, 60 of er-

Table 6. Evaluation results

Error Type	N	fully Diagnosed		General Error indication	
		N	%	N	%
CL	8	8	100	0	0
VL	24	19	79.2	5	20.8
VC	21	14	66.7	7	33.3
CP	7	6	85.7	1	14.3
Total	60	47	78.3	12	20

roneous verbs are *word formation* errors. Others are either errors in the word choice or errors at the interface between lexical and grammar which are irrelevant to this paper. Table 6 summarizes the evaluation results.

The last column in Table 6 shows the cases of general error indication (i.e. the system fails to detect the exact source of error the learner made). These cases arose because of ambiguity; the system does not have enough knowledge of what the student meant to express. For instance, consider the erroneous word أجوب. It is not clear whether the learner meant the word to be: 1) the imperfect verb أجيب />u-jiyb/ (I-answer), 2) or imperfect verb أجوب />a-juwb/ (I-explore).

CONCLUSION

Arabic is a highly derivational language that makes it a challenge to SLLs. Therefore, SLLs not only make errors done by native speakers but also others that arise due to competence issues. Consequently, using methods and tools designed for a native speaker spell checking is not a good way to proceed, especially for highly derivational and inflectional languages such as Arabic. Therefore, the nowadays methods and tools should be refined to meet the SLLs needs. In the absence of a complete computationally erroneous Arabic corpus that can be used to evaluate the proposed model, we have to manually collect the test set from the real teaching environment. The test set was relatively small but it was sufficient to show that the approach and techniques employed in this chapter have successfully generated all possible analyses of ill-formed verbs written by SLLs of Arabic, in particular, when it comes to difficult constructions such as Arabic weak verbs. From a pedagogical point of view, the achieved rich analyses enable feedback elaboration that helps learners to understand better their knowledge gab.

REFERENCES

Abd Alghaniy, K. E. (1998). *Arabic and Malaysian languages from phonological and morphological perspective: A contrastive analysis approach.* Master thesis, Cairo University, Egypt.

Ahmed, M. A. (2000). *A large-scale computational processor of the Arabic morphology, and applications.* Master thesis, Cairo University, Egypt.

Al-Sughaiyer, I. A., & Al-Kharashi, I. A. (2004). Arabic morphological analysis techniques: A comprehensive survey. *American Society for Information Science and Technology Journal, 55*(3), 189–213. doi:10.1002/asi.10368

Ali, M. B. (1998). *Linguistic analysis of mistakes by students at the University of Malaya: An error analysis approach.* Master thesis, Cairo University, Egypt.

Attia, M. A. (2006). An ambiguity-controlled morphological analyzer for modern standard Arabic modeling finite state networks. In *Proceedings of the Challenge of Arabic for NLP/MT Conference, 2006.* The British Computer Society, London.

Beesley, K. R. (2001). Finite-state morphological analysis and generation of Arabic at Xerox Research: Status and plans in 2001. In *Proceedings of the Arabic Language Processing: Status and Prospect,* (ACL 2001). Toulouse, France, (pp. 1-8).

Bowden, T., & Kiraz, G. A. (1995). A morphographemic model for error correction in non-concatenative strings. In *Proceedings of ACL 1995,* Boston, Massachusetts, (pp. 24-30).

Buckwalter, T. (2002). *Buckwalter Arabic morphological analyzer,* version 1.0. Linguistic Data Consortium, University of Pennsylvania, (LDC Catalog No. LDC2002L49). ISBN 1-58563-257-0.

Darwish, K. (2002). Building a shallow morphological analyzer in one day. In *Proceedings of the Workshop on Computational Approaches to Semitic Languages*, (ACL 2002), Philadelphia, PA, USA, (pp. 47-54).

El-Sadany, T. A., & Hashish, M. A. (1989). An Arabic morphological system. *IBM Systems Journal*, *28*(4), 600–612. doi:10.1147/sj.284.0600

Elmi, M. A., & Evens, M. (1998). Spelling correction using context. In *Proceedings of ACL 1998*, Montreal, Canada, (pp. 360-364).

Faltin, A. V. (2003). *Syntactic error diagnosis in the context of computer assisted language learning.* PhD thesis, University of Geneva, Switzerland.

Habash, N., & Rambow, O. (2006). MAGEAD: A morphological analyzer and generator for the Arabic dialects. In *Proceedings of the 21st International Conference on Computational Linguistics and 44th Annual Meeting of the Association for Computational Linguistics,* Sydney, Australia, (pp. 681–688).

Hsieh, C.-C., Tsai, T.-H., Wible, D., & Hsu, W.-L. (2002). Exploiting knowledge representation in an intelligent tutoring system for English lexical errors. In *Proceedings of the International Conference on Computers in Education ICCE 2002*, Auckland, New Zealand, (pp. 115-116).

Jassem, J. A. (2000). *Study on second language learners of Arabic: An error analysis approach.* Kuala Lumpur, Malaysia: A.S. Noordeen.

Jurafsky, D., & Martin, J. H. (2008). *Speech and language processing: An introduction to natural language processing, computational linguistic and speech processing.* Prentice Hall Series in Artificial Intelligence.

Sjöbergh, J., & Knutsson, O. (2005). Faking errors to avoid making errors: Machine learning for error detection in writing. In *Proceedings of RANLP 2005*, Borovets, Bulgaria, (pp. 506-512).

Soudi, A., Cavalli-Sforza, V., & Jamari, A. (2001). A Computational Lexeme-based Treatment of Arabic Morphology. In *Proceedings of the Workshop on Arabic Language Processing: Status and Prospects,* (ACL 2001), Toulouse, France, (pp. 155-162).

Tschichold, C. (2003). Lexically driven error detection and correction. *CALICO Journal*, *20*(3), 549–559.

Wagner, J., Foster, J., & Genabith, J. V. (2007). A comparative evaluation of deep and shallow approaches to the automatic detection of common grammatical errors. In *Proceedings of EMNLP-CoNLL 2007*, Prague, Czeck Republic, (pp. 112-121).

Wright, W. (1967). *A grammar of the Arabic language* (3rd ed.). Cambridge University Press.

ENDNOTES

[1] For transliteration, we refer the reader to Buckwalter (2002).

[2] The asterisk indicates an incorrect word or sentence.

[3] Faltin (2003) defines diagnosis term as "identification of the cause of error" while correction is "a thing substituted to what is wrong." In the following, we show an example that illustrates the difference between diagnosis and correction. (b) is a possible diagnosis of error of the example (a); while (c) is a correction of it.

(a) أريد أن أدرس لغة جديدة و لذلك * اخترت أن أدرس العربية (I want to learn a new language so I chose to learn Arabic)

(b) The Weak letter (ا) /A/ in the hollow (middle weak) verb اختار /{ixotAra/ (chose) cannot be used with the first person suffix pronoun ت /t/ because the last letter in verb ساكن /r/is (consonant) ر

(c) The correct sentence is:

; أريد أن أدرس لغة جديدة ولذلك اخترت أن أدرس العربية

where the hollow letter is curtailed.

4 The stem is a result of applying some roots into some patterns.

5 The first ninth forms are very common while the rest are very rare.

6 These examples are collected from different real materials which are committed by different Arabic SLLs.

7 A *base word* form is a, normalized, stem form after removing all weak and hamza letters to facilitate the matching of different verb conjugations of the same root without taking into consideration the lexicographic change (i.e. variants) that may happen to these irregular forms.

8 The compatibility table that encodes the relations between prefixes and suffixes is taken from the Buckwalter's Arabic morphological analyzer (Buckwalter 2002).

9 The FS includes the following features: *lexical category*, *pattern*, *tense*, *voice*, *mood*, *subject* and *object person*, *number*, *gender*, which is not shown due to space limitation.

10 This solution represents a perfect verb in the third person singular masculine active voice.

11 The base word form of the correct root ق-و-ل /q-w-l/ is قل after removing the weak letter و /w/.

12 The percentage of each error type in the test set that actually diagnosed by the system.

Chapter 23
Dynamic Effects of Repeating a Timed Writing Task in Two EFL University Courses:
Multi-Element Text Analysis with Coh-Metrix

Kyoko Baba
Kinjo Gakuin University, Japan

Ryo Nitta
Nagoya Gakuin University, Japan

ABSTRACT

The longitudinal effects of repeating a timed writing activity on English as a Foreign Language (EFL) students' second language (L2) writing development were investigated. Data for 46 students in two university classes (23 in each class), each with a different course objective, were collected 30 times in the same way over one year. The students' compositions were analyzed for fluency, grammatical complexity, and lexical complexity. Text analysis using Coh-Metrix showed that task repetition had an overall effect on L2 writing development. The text analysis was supplemented with a visual analysis using moving min-max graphs. Grammatical complexity developed more prominently than the other aspects of writing in both classes. This counter-predictive result points to the significance of the writers' reflective consciousness towards their own writing. This study also emphasizes that it is important to study the dynamics in L2 writing development with multi-wave data.

INTRODUCTION

This study investigated the longitudinal effects of repeating a timed writing activity on English as a Foreign Language (EFL) students' second language (L2) writing development. Studies on task repetition have shown that the quality of students' spoken language improves when the same task is repeated, because learners can pay focal attention to form the second time (Bygate & Samuda, 2005). However, it is unclear what effects repetition of a writing task brings about, assuming that learners are less pressured in writing.

DOI: 10.4018/978-1-60960-741-8.ch023

We have clarified a group of learners' developmental changes and focused on the non-linearity of writing development. We assessed which of the three principal aspects of L2 writing (fluency, grammaticalcomplexity, and lexical complexity) develop in one year. To analyze L2 writers' texts, we used the web-based computational tool *Coh-Metrix* (Graesser, McNamara, Louwerse, & Cai, 2004). The development of sophisticated computer programs such as Coh-Metrix coupled with a large corpus has made it possible to identify notable features of L2 texts (e.g., Crossley & McNamara, 2009a; McCarthy, Lehenbauer, Hall, Duran, Fujiwara, & McNamara, 2007). However, the corpora used in previous studies largely consisted of texts written by advanced L2 writers (e.g., high intermediate to advanced writers in Crossley & McNamara, 2009a and L2 scientists whose work had been published in academic journals in McCarthy et al., 2007). The students we focus on in this study are basic writers who had few chances to write in L2 outside the classroom. Their writing is usually short and contains many grammatical errors. Therefore, it is worth inquiring whether Coh-Metrix can capture the changes in such basic writers' performance. We assessed if any textual features in their writing changed significantly during one year. These changes are further examined with a graphical method.

The Dynamic Nature of L2 Writing Development

The significance of longitudinal research on L2 learning is often emphasized (Ortega & Iberri-Shea, 2005), but there is still a dearth of such research. Research on L2 writing development is no exception, although many studies have identified various characteristics of L2 writing at different developmental stages (Hinkel, 2002). However, scant attention has been paid to how these features change over time. Some longitudinal studies have looked at changes in L2 writing, but they were often either cross-sectional (Henry, 1996; Kern

& Schultz, 1992), did not look at a variety of text features (Bardovi-Harig, 2002), or focused on a small number of writers (Larsen-Freeman, 2006; Verspoor, Lowie, & van Dijk, 2008).

Moreover, two-wave research designs have often been used to investigate developments in learners' L2 writing skills. Usually, a pretest and a posttest are conducted, and a t-test or ANOVA assesses the difference between the two time points (e.g., Ishikawa, 1995; Shaw & Liu, 1998). However, while such an approach reveals *whether* L2 writers have developed or not, it is difficult to detect *how* they developed their writing. The two-wave research design assumes linear development, and rules out the possibility that writing may develop in a non-linear way.

To explore the *how* of L2 writing development, this study focuses on the non-linearity of language development (Larsen-Freeman & Cameron, 2008). The exploration of non-linear language development requires multiwave data (Willett, 1994). That is, data is collected from each participant multiple times, which enables us to plot growth trajectories. To analyze these trajectories, various (especially visual) tools have been proposed, such as a polynomial trendline, moving min-max graph, and detrended representation of L2 development (Verspoor, et al., 2008).

Larsen-Freeman (2006) studied the development of oral and written production by five Chinese adults living in an English-speaking country in terms of their fluency, accuracy, and complexity over six months. She collected data from these participants four times during the period. Each time, they engaged in the same task, writing a narrative about their life story and then talking about it. As a group, there was overall progress in all aspects of the participants' writing, and each aspect showed a rather linear progress. However, Larsen-Freeman also revealed that paths to development widely diverged from individual to individual in terms of the rate of developmental speed and the relationship among different features of writing. For example, one participant developed all the four features similarly in her writing while another participant developed lexical complexity, grammatical complexity, and fluency, but sacrificed accuracy.

While Larsen-Freeman (2006) collected data from participants only four times during half a year, Crossley and his colleagues collected spontaneous speech data more than 13 times from each participant over one year (Crossley, Salsbury, & McNamara, 2009b, 2010,2010). The participants in their studies were six ESL university students. The participants talked with English native speaking interviewers on a variety of topics every two weeks during one year. All the participants did not attend every data collection session, so data were collected from 13 to 18 times from each participant. Crossley et al. (2009b) investigated the development of hypernymic lexical knowledge and lexical diversity in the speech of the six learners. Results of a repeated-measures analysis of variance showed that the learners as a group significantly developed both aspects in their speech over one year. Moreover, results of another statistical analysis (a linear curve estimation) showed that five out of six participants showed a linear development in hypernymic lexical knowledge and lexical diversity.

Verspoor et al. (2008) collected 18 academic writing samples from a Dutch learner of English, JtB, over three years. Unlike Crossley et al. (2009b), they did not use statistical techniques to analyze the data but visually analyzed JtB's development with line graphs. For example, they plotted average-word-length development in his writing. If they had conducted a statistical analysis like Crossley et al., they might have found a statistically linear trend in JtB's development. However, their analysis of the line plot with the moving min-max graph (see the results section) provided more information about JtB's development than a mere statistical judgment of whether his development was linear or not. One of the key findings of their study was the observation that there were three stages in how he came to use

longer words. The first stage is stability at a low level (low performance with few fluctuations), the second is a major fluctuation period, where his performance went up and down (unstable performance with large fluctuations), and the third is stability at a high level (high performance with few fluctuations).

We extended the dynamic approach to the study of L2 writing development taken by Larsen-Freeman (2006) and Verspoor et al. (2008). Whereas the previous studies focused on a fairly small number of writers, our aim was to make a slightly broader generalization about developmental trajectories of a larger group of learners. We followed the development of L2 writing of two EFL university classes by considering each classroom as a system. Thus, the research questions of this study were as follows. First, we asked which textual features of students' writing change in two one-year EFL classes through repeating the same writing task. Second, if there are significant changes in their writing, how do the two classes develop each aspect of their writing?

METHODS

Participants

The study was conducted at two Japanese universities in two EFL classrooms (Classes A and B). Both courses (one-year course) were offered to first-year English major students and taught by the authors. One university was a women's university, so all the students in Class A were female. Class B involved about 60% of male students, and 40% of female students. Twenty-three students in each class were engaged in the project regularly until the end of the year. Thus, the compositions of a total of 46 students were used for the analysis. The two courses had different course objectives (Class A focused on English writing, while Class B was oriented more toward integrated skills of speaking, listening, and reading as well as writing).

All the students in both classes took the Test of English for International Communication (TOEIC) test at the beginning and end of the academic year. The average scores for Class A were 390.43 on the first, and 419.78 on the last TOEIC test. On the other hand, the average scores for Class B were 309.55 on the first, and 355.45 on the last test. There was a significant difference in the TOEIC scores between the two classes, both on the first test, $t(43) = 6.09$, $p <. 001$ (Cohen's $d = 1.86$), and on the last test, $t(44) = 3.76$, $p <. 01$ (Cohen's $d = 1.13$).

The students had little experience writing in English before entering university, and, even in university, they had little chance to write in English outside the classroom. Therefore, any progress in their writing is largely attributable to the classroom writing activities.

Data Collecting Schedule

The project was conducted over two academic terms consisting of thirty weeks in total (Class B canceled two classes in the first semester, so there were 28 weeks for Class B). The same procedures were followed in the two classes. In every class meeting, the students performed a timed writing task (Henry, 1996). Learners simply wrote about a topic for ten minutes without stopping. Each time they were given a topic list with three different topics in order to compensate for differences in their individual experiences and preferences. The topics were selected and adapted from the list of the essay topics for the Regents' Test (Weigle, 2006). We tried to devise such topics as would be easy for Japanese university students to write about and could be written on the basis of their personal experience. Examples of the topics are "What is your favorite source of entertainment? Explain why."; Take up some recent event (some news from the paper), and discuss what you think of it."; and "What do you hope to accomplish within the next ten years?"

Immediately after writing a composition, the students were requested to write reflective comments on their writing in Japanese (L1) about, for example, what they found difficult to write, what they thought during writing, etc. The collected writing was checked by the authors and returned with some feedback the next week. The aim of the feedback was to create a sense of audience and to maintain students' motivation for writing every week. Because the timed writing task focuses on meaning rather than form, linguistic correction was not offered. We told our students that grammatical accuracy was not so important for this task, and that they should focus more on fluency and contents in their writing. Despite this, few students wrote off-topic sentences, presumably because they knew that we would comment on what they had written.

A list of three topics was used two weeks in a row. The week after a new topic list was given, students were required to write about the same topic that they had chosen a week before (that is, they wrote about a topic twice). Then, the next week, another new topic list was given.

Text Measurements

In previous research, four main categories of measures have been used to study the development in the quality of texts by L2 writers: fluency, accuracy, lexical complexity, and grammatical complexity (Wolfe-Quintero, Inagaki, & Kim, 1998). Because we did not focus on accuracy (we neither told our students to pay attention to grammatical and lexical accuracy nor corrected errors in their writing), we looked at the other three aspects of text quality (i.e., fluency, lexical complexity, and grammatical complexity). In particular, we had expected that fluency would improve to some extent, as task repetition research has shown with spoken data (Bygate, 2001).

To analyze the approximately 1300 compositions that were written by the students over one year, we used *Coh-Metrix* (Graesser, McNamara, Louwerse, & Cai, 2004) available at http://cohmetrix.memphis.edu/cohmetrixpr/index.html (version 2.0). Spelling mistakes in the compositions were carefully corrected manually and also with a spelling checker. We selected the six most relevant measures of fluency, lexical complexity, and grammatical complexity as follows.

Fluency

"Fluency" in writing is an elusive concept, but it may usually mean either how fast or how coherently one writes. The present study used two text measurements to cover both meanings of fluency (speed and coherence). Speed is typically assessed with total number of words in a composition, for skilled writers tend to write longer (Wolf-Quintero et al., 1998). So, (1) text length (number of words per composition) was used as a measure of speed. Previous research has suggested that text length is a good indicator of L2 writing proficiency (Grant & Ginther, 2000), but that it is debatable how it may be improved by classroom teaching. For example, using the same 10-minute timed writing task, Henry's (1996) cross sectional study showed that text length was significantly prolonged between the first and second semesters in an EFL university course. On the other hand, Ishikawa (1996), whose participants were low-proficiency Japanese EFL university students, did not find such an effect of three-month instruction on text length.

To assess coherence, we used (2) Latent Semantic Analysis (LSALSALSA: Landauer, McNamara, Dennis, & Kintsch, 2007). LSA evaluates the similarity of meaning between words, sentences, and passages by analyzing large corpora. We used it as a measure of fluency because similarity of meaning across sentences and paragraphs is likely to contribute to coherence in text, which has been supported by Foltz, Kintsch, & Landauer (1998). There were three LSA measures on Coh-Metrix, and we chose LSA of all combinations of sentences. Crossley et al. (2010) found that the six participants in their study significantly developed higher LSA values for their speech over one year. However, since no study so far has examined the longitudinal change of LSA in written texts, little is known whether Crossley and colleagues' finding may be applicable to our written data.

Lexical Complexity

The operationalization of lexical complexity varies with the focus of study, but it generally denotes either lexical sophistication or lexical diversity in text. Therefore, we used two measures of lexical complexity: (3) word frequency values from the CELEX corpus (Baayen, Piepenbrock, & Bulikers, 1996), and (4) the Measure of Textual Lexical Diversity (MTLDMTLDMTLD: McCarthy & Jarvis, 2010). CELEX word frequency measure was the same index that Crossley et al. (2010) used in their longitudinal study. They found that the learners began to use more frequent words in their speech after four months. It is worth investigating if their finding is compatible with written data, because it is possible that writers may come to use lower frequency words as their writing skills develop. In order to compare our data with theirs, we used the mean logarithm of the word frequency (to the base of 10).

MTLD was chosen among other lexical diversity measures like type-token ratio and *vocd* (Malvern, Richards, Chipere, & Duran, 2004) because McCarthy and Jarvis (2010) have revealed that it is the only measure among the best established lexical diversity measures that is not affected by text length. We considered using *vocd* in addition to MTLD, but the correlation with the two measures was strong ($r = .76$). If any two pair of indices have a correlation higher than $r = .70$, it is likely to indicate colliniearity (McCarthy et al., 2007; Tabachnick & Fidell, 2001). Therefore, we dropped *vocd*. Crossley et al. (2009b) revealed that MTLD increased significantly in the speech of the six ESL learners over one year. So it is conceivable that the same tendency can be found in our study.

Grammatical Complexity

To measure grammatical complexity, we used (5) average sentence length and (6) STRUT (sentence syntax similarity, all sentences across paragraphs) (McCarthy, Cai, & McNamara, 2009). Average sentence length was used as a grammatical complexity measure because Ortega (2003), synthesizing studies on syntactic complexity in L2 writing, found that it largely differed according to L2 proficiency levels. STRUT gauges the degree of similarity in syntactic structures of sentences in a passage by comparing syntactic trees of each pair of sentences. A lower STRUT value possibly indicates greater grammatical complexity. Whereas Crossley, Greenfield, & McNamara (2008) did not analyze L2 writers' text, they revealed that STRUT was one of the three measures that contributed to readability judged by EFL learners.

Prior to the statistical analysis, data screening was conducted. The assumptions of multivariate normality, linearity, homogeneity of variance, and multicollinearity were satisfactory. However, there was one outlier for average sentence length (using Mahalanobis distance, $p < .001$, Tabachnick & Fidell, 2001). This outlier was the result of a student who wrote too long a sentence (probably he forgot to put a period somewhere). Therefore, we deleted this case.

RESULTS

A one-way multivariate analysis of variance (MANOVA) was separately conducted for Classes A and B to assess whether the six text measurements significantly changed over one year. The MANOVA compared the compositions that were written in the first and last weeks (Weeks 1 and 30 for Class A and Weeks 1 and 28 for Class B). It should be noted that on both weeks a new topic list was given to the students, so they wrote on a new topic. Table 1 displays the results for Class A. Significant differences were found among the first and last compositions on the dependent measures, Wilks's $\Lambda = .51$, $F(6,38) = 6.00$, $p < .001$. The multivariate partial η^2 based on Wilks's Λ was strong, .49. Thus, it was shown that there was a significant change in Class A students' writing over one year. Analyses of variances (ANOVAs) on each dependent variable were conducted as follow-up tests to the MANOVA. The means and standard deviations for the first and last week are displayed below each measure. To control for Type I error, we used the Holm method (Jaccard & Guilamo-Ramos, 2002). The family-wise error is set at $\alpha = .05$. When the significance probability for each follow-up ANOVA is sorted in ascending order, the smallest significance probability is considered significant if it is less than $p = .05 / 6$ (.008) (the MANOVA was followed by six follow-up ANOVAs). The second smallest significance probability is considered significant if it is less than $p = .05 / 5$ (.001). The same procedure is repeated until any significance probability turns out insignificant. The results of the ANOVAs for Class A showed that three measures changed significantly: MTLD, $F(1, 43) = 12.80$, $p = .001$, average sentence length, $F(1,43) = 13.47$, $p = .001$, and STRUT, $F(1, 43) = 7.73$, $p = .008$. However, the other three measures (text length, LSA, and CELEX word frequency) were insignificant.

The results for Class B are displayed in Table 2. Like Class A, significant differences were found among the first and last compositions on the dependent measures, Wilks's $\Lambda = .62$, $F(6, 36) = 3.70$, $p < .01$. The multivariate partial η^2 based on Wilks's Λ was weaker than that for Class A, but still fairly strong, .38. Thus, Class B also saw a significant change in the students' writing over one year. ANOVAs revealed that two measures were significant, average sentence length, $F(1, 41) = 9.53$, $p = .004$, and STRUT, $F(1,41) = 11.12$, $p = .002$. MTLD was not significant but was close to the significance level, $F(1, 41) = 8.22$, $p = .02$ (using the Holms method). Like Class A, the other three measures (text length, LSA, and CELEX word frequency) were insignificant.

Table 1. Multivariate and univariate analysis of variance F ratios for effects of task practice for text measures with means and standard deviations (Class A)

		ANOVA											
	MANOVA	TextL		LSA		MTLD		CELEX		ASL		STRUT	
Variable	$F(6, 38)$	$F(1, 43)$		$F(1, 43)$		$F(1, 43)$		$F(1, 43)$		$F(1, 43)$		$F(1, 43)$	
Time	6.00***	5.15*		.01		12.80***		.44		13.47***		7.73**	
		M	SD	M	SD	M	SD	M	SD	M	SD	M	SD
First		53.83	21.60	.20	.12	37.78	9.46	2.52	.22	7.66	1.92	.24	.08
Last		67.50	18.63	.19	.13	53.19	18.26	2.48	.20	10.30	2.84	.18	.08

Note. F ratios are Wilks's approximation of Fs. MANOVA = multivariate analysis of variance; ANOVA = univariate analysis of variance; TextL = text length; LSA = Latent Semantic Analysis; MTLD = the Measure of Textual Lexical Diversity; Wfreq = CELEX frequency of content words (the mean logarithm); ASL = average sentence length; STRUT = sentence syntax similarity.

*$p < .05$. ** $p < .01$. ***$p < .001$.

The results above suggest that the students in both classes improved grammatical complexity (average sentence length and STRUT) more markedly than the other text features. It is not surprising that both grammatical features changed concomitantly, because longer sentences tend to become more different. In fact, the two measures correlated with each other in both classes, $r = -.72, p < .01$ for Class A, and $r = -.52, p < .01$ for Class B. It was somewhat unexpected that fluency hardly improved in either class.

While the MANOVA and the ANOVAs were used to examine the general trends of these groups of students and to identify the differences of their compositions between the beginning and the end of the course, understanding the changes between the two points for the purpose of the present study is very important. Therefore, further analysis was done to illustrate in more detail how the fluency, grammatical complexity, and lexical complexity measures changed in each class. To do this, we used the moving min-max graph, which illustrates the width of changes in observed scores and highlights the score ranges in a longer span (van Greet & van Dijk, 2002, Verspoor et al. 2008). The moving min-max graph is drawn by calculating the minimum or maximum score within a certain period of time. For example, in the results for text lengths of weeks 1 through 5 are 51, 52, 50, 54, and 58, and the minimum score is 50 while the maximum score

Table 2. Multivariate and univariate analysis of variance F ratios for task practice effects for text measures with means and standard deviations (Class B)

		ANOVA											
	MANOVA	TextL		LSA		MTLD		CELEX		ASL		STRUT	
Variable	$F(6, 36)$	$F(1, 41)$		$F(1, 41)$		$F(1, 41)$		$F(1, 41)$		$F(1, 41)$		$F(1, 41)$	
Time	3.70**	1.19		2.30		6.22*		3.12		9.53**		11.12**	
		M	SD	M	SD	M	SD	M	SD	M	SD	M	SD
First		52.86	19.70	.22	.19	36.68	14.22	2.55	.24	7.72	1.28	.22	.08
Last		61.09	28.78	.15	.11	49.89	19.88	2.65	.16	9.73	2.72	.16	.04

Note. F ratios are Wilks's approximation of Fs. MANOVA = multivariate analysis of variance; ANOVA = univariate analysis of variance; TextL = text length; LSA = Latent Semantic Analysis; MTLD = the Measure of Textual Lexical Diversity; Wfreq = CELEX frequency of content words (the mean logarithm); ASL = average sentence length; STRUT = sentence syntax similarity.

*$p < .05$. ** $p < .01$.

is 58. In the same way, minimum and maximum scores were identified for weeks 2 through 6, and weeks 3 through 7, and so on (a moving window). These minimum and maximum scores are plotted as a line graph. The maximum and the minimum values were calculated by using a predetermined window of some time points. Following Verspoor et al. (2008), we used a moving window of five time points, which is mathematized;

- min (t1…t5), min (t2…t6), min (t3…t7), etc.
- max (t1…t5), max (t2…t6), max (t3…t7), etc.

The moving min-max graphs allow us to inspect whether there are any fluctuations and meaningful developmental paths over the period of investigation. In what follows, we present the moving min-max graphs for three measures, each one of which represents each aspect of L2 writing: STRUT for grammatical complexity (Figure 1), MTLD for lexical complexity (Figure 2), and text length for fluency (Figure 3). We used median instead of mean values to draw these graphs because the median seemed to better represent the performance of each class by minimizing the effects of idiosyncratic compositions.

A point worth noting from these figures is that the trajectories of the minimum line is not parallel to those of the maximum line. By inspecting the min-max graph of STRUT for Class A (Figure 1), we can see that the maximum line steadily goes down, while the minimum line goes up (between Weeks 4 and 17) and then returns to the initial level. (The downward trends in STRUT signifies "more different sentence structures"). In Class B, although the maximum line moves horizontally until Week 18, it then starts to go down for the rest of the year; on the other hand,

Figure 1. Min-max graphs of sentence syntax similarity (STRUT) for Classes A and B

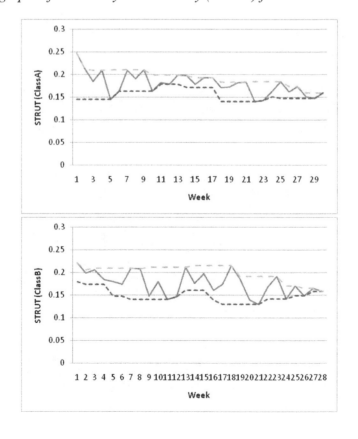

Figure 2. Min-max graphs of lexical diversity (MTLD) for Classes A and B

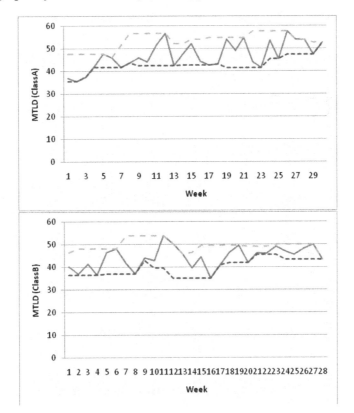

the minimum line moves up and down frequently until Week 17 but does not go down further after the week. It should also be noted that the width of band of fluctuations for Class A is narrower than that for Class B. This difference in the degree of fluctuations might be due to the effect of grammar instruction in Class A. Students in Class A might have steadily come to write more different sentences due to the grammar instruction while those in Class B might have exhibited more variability in their performance. The moving min-max graphs for MTLD show a similar tendency. There is a sharp rise from Week 1 to Week 4 and some development in the minimum lines after Week 24 in Class A and after Week 17 in Class B while the trajectories of the maximum lines fluctuate to a greater extent and does not show clear developmental trends on the whole in both classes (Figure 2). In contrast to the upward trends of the minimum lines for STRUT and MTLD,

both moving min-max graphs do not demonstrate a clear indication of development in text length. However, there is a sharp development of the minimum line from Week 5 to Week 6 for Class B due to a sudden drop of the median value in Week 5 (Figure 3). Otherwise, text length of each time point in both classes fluctuates within a certain width of band that does not move upward. With the exception of the difference in STRUT between the classes, the moving min-max graphs for each text measure look similar between Classes A and B despite different initial proficiency levels of the classes and teaching contents.

DISCUSSION

Our statistical analyses showed that the EFL students in two classes improved their writing over one year. The two classes were taught by a different

Figure 3. Min-max graphs of text length for Classes A and B

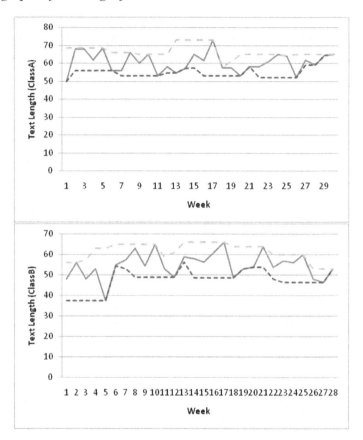

instructor, had a different course objective, and did not share any classroom activity except for the timed writing task. In addition, the English proficiency levels of the two classes were different throughout the whole academic year. Nevertheless, students in both classes significantly strengthened the same text features in their writing (MTLD, average sentence length, and STRUT).

The results of visual analysis of the moving min-max graphs have supported the development of STRUT and MTLD, and further provided new insights into the developmental trajectories. Because the students in the present study are beginning EFL writers, their L2 system is in the process of development and is largely unstable. This instability makes their writing performance highly variable and susceptible to various external (e.g., topic difficulty, classroom conditions) and internal

(e.g., physical and metal conditions) factors. As a result of this high variability and susceptibility, the gaps between their "good" and "poor" performance may range widely especially in the early period. However, as the more practiced and more skilled they became through repeating the present writing task, it seemed that the minimum quality of their compositions improved (for example, they came to write better even in difficult conditions such as when they were given a difficult writing topic). In other words, their minimum performance standards seemed to become more stabilized and less affected by learner and environmental factors. Another important finding is that the general trends of the moving min-max graphs for each measure are generally similar between Classes A and B despite different initial proficiency levels of the classes and different teaching contents.

The increase in lexical diversity (MTLD) supports Crossley et al.'s (2009b) finding that lexical diversity in ESL learners' spontaneous speech significantly developed over one year. Their results may not strictly be comparable with those of this study, because Crossley et al. did not employ the same oral task (the prompts that the interviewers used differed from time to time) and their participants were ESL learners and not EFL learners. Still, the results of this study have shown that repetition of a task over a certain period is likely to enhance lexical diversity not only in speaking but also in writing.

On the basis of the findings from previous research in task-repetition effects on speech production, we expected that at least writing fluency would improve among the three principal aspects of writing skills (fluency, lexical complexity, and grammatical complexity). However, there was not significant progress in fluency, in terms of either not only speed (text length) but also coherence (LSA). This finding may suggest that the development of fluency in L2 writing may take more than one year, especially when the learners write only once a week in EFL settings. This result may also points to another possibility, that the students had already hit a ceiling for text length at their English proficiency level. Unless English proficiency greatly improves, how much a learner can write within 10 minutes may remain largely the same.

A more important finding of this study is that grammatical complexity was the aspect of writing that changed most over one year in both classes. Both grammatical complexity measures (average sentence length and STRUT) significantly increased over one year. Because the course objectives of the two classes were different and the students had few chances to write in English outside classroom, it seems reasonable to suppose that these changes in grammatical complexity in writing are due to the repetition of the timed writing task.

It is debatable whether the increase in the grammatical complexity measures conclusively demonstrates that the students in this study became more competent in the use of grammatical structures in their writing. One may argue, for example, that the increase in STRUT does not necessarily lead to more skilled writing, for professional writers in a particular genre and in a particular culture tend to use a narrower range of grammatical structures than do native English writers (e.g., Japanese scientists in McCarthy et al.'s (2007) study preferred to use syntactically simple sentence structures). Or, longer sentences are apt to be avoided in a particular language. If the learner's L1 is such a language, they may avoid writing longer sentences even when they become advanced L2 writers. We do not dismiss these alternative explanations. What we can add here is, as mentioned above, that STRUT was useful to distinguish text difficulty for EFL readers (Crossley et al., 2008), and that average sentence length meaningfully differentiated learners at different proficiency levels in previous studies (Orgeta, 2003). These findings provide some support for the validity of the two indices of grammatical complexity.

Our qualitative data suggests that the students in our study consciously tried to develop their use of grammatical structures in their writing. The students who were interviewed after the one-year timed writing experience recalled that they had become more reflective about their own writing. Asuka, a student in Class A, said in the interview, "Consciousness towards my own writing changed. At first, I just tried to write longer. But gradually I came to think more about how to do so, such as giving examples" (all the protocols were spoken in Japanese, and translated by the authors). She also said, "At first, I just wrote something. But as I got used to this task, I tried to use grammatical structures that I had learned (in class)." She was then asked when she got used to the task, and she answered, "Probably in the middle of the academic year." Thus, it might have taken them some time (at least three or four months) to write more consciously. Other students also mentioned that they did this task rather aimlessly at first, but repeating the task gradually made them aware of the shortcomings (e.g., too short and with too many grammatical and lexical errors). They then aimed to improve their own writing. One of their attempts to achieve this aim was to apply newly learned grammatical structures to their compositions. Such attempts can be found in their writing. Composition (w1) below was written by Asuka on the first week.

Composition (W1)

I want to visit Korea. Because Korea has cheap variety goods. For example cosme. And if I go to Korea, I can experience Este. These days, Korea is popular in Japan. We know Fuyunosonata. Japan has "Kanryu-boom." Everyone knows Yon-sama and Che ziu. So I want to know about Korea, when I was a high school student. I studied about Korea's history. But I want know about it. So I decided to study Korean. (74 words)

Most sentences of Composition (w1) are short and simple. She wrote Composition (w21) about seven months after Composition (w1).

Composition (W21)

The advantage of marriage is that a couple enjoy life only two. And there is blessed with children. It is important that children is born. Because people grow frail under the weight of years, a couple is taken care by their son and their daughter. But the disadvantage of marriage is not doing what I want to do and increase what to do. That is to say, if I am a housewife, I must do household every day. So it is no time for myself. (85 words)

She made various grammatical errors here, as she did in Composition (w1). Moreover, the length of Composition (w21) is similar to Composition (w1). However, sentences in Composition (w21) are generally longer (average sentence length is 12.14) than those of Composition (w1) (average sentence length is 6.82), and their structures are more complex. Moreover, her instructor (one of us) could see that she was trying to use newly learned phrases ("That is to say") and structures (a relative clause, "what I want to do"). Immediately after writing this composition, she wrote a reflective comment on it, "I'm glad that I could use an emphatic sentence construction today though I'm not so sure if I'm using it in a correct way" (written in Japanese and translated by the authors). By "an emphatic sentence construction," she was referring to the third sentence, "It is important that children is born." This sentence does not have an emphatic sentence construction, but the point we wish to emphasize is that she intentionally tried to use a new grammatical structure in her writing.

Why did grammatical complexity significantly increase in spite of the facts that we did not give the students corrective feedback on their compositions and that we did not instruct them to heed grammatical structures for this timed writing task? The results of this study do not offer a decisive answer to this question. However, one plausible explanation is that grammatical complexity was easier to *consciously* improve than was fluency. For instance, it may be difficult for basic writers to consciously write longer compositions, but it may be possible for them to use a wider variety of grammatical structures by intention. In fact, Asuka said that she attempted to write longer compositions in the interview. However, her compositions did not become longer, or rather became shorter towards the end of the academic year. On the other hand, she came to write longer and more varied sentences over one year. Therefore, once basic writers become conscious of their own writing and set some goals for writing improvement, the initial step for them to try might have been to concentrate on their use of grammar in writing.

CONCLUSION

Our text analysis with Coh-Metrix has shown that one-year task-type practice had a general effect on the development of EFL learners' writing. This effect might have been even more noticeable because the students in the study were all basic L2 writers. Yet, it may be encouraging for EFL instructors and learners that the repetition of L2 writing only for 10 minutes over one year lead to the significant change in the basic writers' performance. The strength of the impact of the repetition seemed to vary with the aspect of writing. Contrary to our predictions, we found that grammatical complexity and lexical diversity (but not word frequency) grew more prominently than did fluency. This may imply that the development of fluency in EFL writing should be investigated over a longer span, or that it may be necessary to offer a more intensive pedagogical intervention to develop this aspect (e.g., the use of metacognitive strategies).

Because this study is only in its initial stages, it has some limitations. First, with regard to the analysis of text, it may be desirable to look at a wider variety of text measures. For example, we used STRUT as a grammatical complexity index, but Minimal Edit Distances (MED) could be used instead, because McCarthy et al. (2009) have shown that MED evaluated paraphrase quality better than STRUT. Second, this study has significant implications for L2 writing research in that it investigated the changes in writing with data that was collected with high frequency over a long period (30 times over one year). However, one year may not have been long enough to describe the changes in certain aspects of L2 writing, as the results above suggest. Third, the present study regarded a class of students as a system and examined its behavior, but it should be worthwhile to analyze individual student's performance and thinking.

To our knowledge, our study was the first to investigate the development in three main aspects of L2 writing with both a two-wave and a multi-wave research design. Therefore, it is far from describing the system in which learners learn and develop their L2 writing. In addition to overcoming the limitations mentioned above, future research should delve more into the writer's agency, such as their motivation to write, what the writers are attempting every time they write, and how their perceptions toward L2 writing change over time. As revealed in Asuka's interview, the writer's consciousness towards their own writing might play a crucial role in the development of L2 writing. The present study, although preliminary, has also revealed the significance of the use of multi-wave data. Our analysis of the moving min-max graphs has implied that learners' real L2 writing ability may lie in how well they can perform in a difficult situation. Such an insight may have more fruitful and meaningful implications towards the understanding of how L2 writers develop over a long period of time.

ACKNOWLEDGMENT

We are grateful that this research was supported by the Ministry of Education, Sports, Culture, Sports, Science, and Technology in Japan (Research Grant #21520643).

REFERENCES

Baayen, R. H., Piepenbrock, R., & Guilikers, L. (1996). *CELEX*. Philadelphia, PA: Linguistic Data Consortium.

Bardovi-Harlig, K. (2002). A new starting point? Investigating formulaic use and input in future expression. *Studies in Second Language Acquisition, 24*, 189–198.

Bygate, M. (2001). Effects of task repetition on the structure and control of oral language. In Bygate, M., Skehan, P., & Swain, M. (Eds.), *Researching pedagogic tasks: Second language learning, teaching and testing* (pp. 23–48). Harlow, England: Pearson Education.

Bygate, M., & Samuda, V. (2005). Integrative planning through the use of task repetition. In Ellis, R. (Ed.), *Planning and task performance in a second language* (pp. 37–74). Amsterdam, The Netherlands: John Benjamins.

Casanave, C. P. (1994). Language development in students' journals. *Journal of Second Language Writing, 3*(3), 179–201. doi:10.1016/1060-3743(94)90016-7

Crossley, S., Salsbury, T., & McNamara, D. (2009b). Measuring L2 lexical growth using hypernymic relationships. *Language Learning, 59*(2), 307–334. doi:10.1111/j.1467-9922.2009.00508.x

Crossley, S. A., Greenfield, J., & McNamara, D. S. (2008). Assessing text readability using cognitively based indices. *TESOL Quarterly, 42*(3), 475–493.

Crossley, S. A., & McNamara, D. S. (2009a). Computational assessment of lexical differences in L1 and L2 writing. *Journal of Second Language Writing, 18*, 119–135. doi:10.1016/j.jslw.2009.02.002

Crossley, S. A., Salsbury, T., & McNamara, D. S. (2010). The development of polysemy and frequency use in English second language speakers. *Language Learning, 60*(3). doi:10.1111/j.1467-9922.2010.00568.x

Crossley, S. A., Salsbury, T., & McNamara, D. S. (2010). The development of semantic relations in second language speakers: A case for latent semantic analysis. *Vigo International Journal of Applied Linguistics, 7*, 55–74.

Foltz, P. W., Kintsch, W., & Landauer, T. K. (1998). The measurement of textual coherence with latent semantic analysis. *Discourse Processes, 25*(2-3), 285–307. doi:10.1080/01638539809545029

Graesser, A. C., McNamara, D. S., Louwerse, M. M., & Cai, Z. (2004). Coh-Metrix: Analysis of text on cohesion and language. *Behavior Research Methods, Instruments, & Computers, 36*(2), 193–202. doi:10.3758/BF03195564

Grant, L., & Ginther, A. (2000). Using computer-tagged linguistic features to describe L2 writing differences. *Journal of Second Language Writing, 9*(2), 123–145. doi:10.1016/S1060-3743(00)00019-9

Henry, K. (1996). Early L2 writing development: A study of autobiographical essays by university-level students of Russian. *Modern Language Journal, 80*(3), 309–326.

Hinkel, E. (2002). *Second language writers' text.* Mahwah, NJ: Lawrence Erlbaum.

Ishikawa, S. (1995). Objective measurement of low-proficiency EFL narrative writing. *Journal of Second Language Writing, 4*(1), 51–69. doi:10.1016/1060-3743(95)90023-3

Jaccard, J., & Guilamo-Ramos, V. (2002). Analysis of variance frameworks in clinical child and adolescent psychology: Issues and recommendations. *Journal of Clinical Child and Adolescent Psychology, 31*(1), 130–146.

Jarvis, S., Grant, L., Bikowski, D., & Ferris, D. (2003). Exploring multiple profiles of highly rated learner compositions. *Journal of Second Language Writing, 12*, 377–403. doi:10.1016/j.jslw.2003.09.001

Kern, R. G., & Schultz, J. M. (1992). The effects of composition instruction on intermediate level French students' writing performance: Some preliminary findings. *Modern Language Journal, 76*(1), 1–13.

Landauer, T. K., McNamara, D. S., Dennis, S., & Kintsch, W. (Eds.). (2007). *Handbook of latent semantic analysis.* Mahwah, N.J.: Lawrence Erlbaum.

Larsen-Freeman, D. (2006). The emergence of complexity, fluency, and accuracy in the oral and written production of five Chinese learners of English. *Applied Linguistics, 27*(4), 590–619. doi:10.1093/applin/aml029

Larsen-Freeman, D., & Cameron, L. (2008). *Complex systems and applied linguistics.* Oxford, UK: Oxford University Press.

Malvern, D. D., Richards, B. J., Chipere, N., & Duran, P. (2004). *Lexical diversity and language development: Quantification and assessment.* New York, NY: Palgrave Macmillan. doi:10.1057/9780230511804

McCarthy, P. M. (2005). *An assessment of the range and usefulness of lexical diversity measures and the potential of the measure of textual, lexical diversity (MTLD).* Unpublished doctoral dissertation, The University of Memphis.

McCarthy, P. M., Cai, Z., & McNamara, D. S. (2009). Computational replication of human paraphrase assessment. In C. H. Lane & H. W. Guesgen (Eds.), *Proceedings of the 22nd International Florida Artificial Intelligence Research Society Conference* (pp. 266-271). Menlo Park, CA: The AAAI Press.

McCarthy, P. M., & Jarvis, S. (2010). MTLD, vocd-D, and HD-D: A validation study of sophisticated approaches to lexical diversity assessment. *Behavior Research Methods, 42*(2). doi:10.3758/BRM.42.2.381

McCarthy, P. M., Lehenbauer, B. M., Hall, C., Duran, N. D., Fujiwara, Y., & McNamara, D. S. (2007). A Coh-Metrix analysis of discourse variation in the texts of Japanese, American, and British Scientists. *Foreign Languages for Specific Purposes, 6*, 46–77.

Ortega, L. (2003). Syntactic complexity measures and theire relationship to L2 proficiency: A research synthesis of college-level L2 writing. *Applied Linguistics, 24*(4), 492–518. doi:10.1093/applin/24.4.492

Ortega, L., & Iberri-Shea, G. (2005). Longitudinal research in second language acquisition: Recent trends and future directions. *Annual Review of Applied Linguistics, 25*, 26–45. doi:10.1017/S0267190505000024

Shaw, P., & Liu, E. T.-K. (1998). What develops in the development of second-language writing? *Applied Linguistics, 19*(2), 225–254. doi:10.1093/applin/19.2.224

Tabachnick, B. G., & Fidell, L. S. (2001). *Using multivariate statistics* (4th ed.). Boston, MA: Allyn and Bacon.

van Geert, P., & van Dijk, M. (2002). Focus on variability: New tools to study intra-individual variability in developmental data. *Infant Behavior and Development, 25*, 340–374. doi:10.1016/S0163-6383(02)00140-6

Verspoor, M., Lowie, W., & van Dijk, M. (2008). Variability in second language development from a dynamic systems perspective. *Modern Language Journal, 92*(2), 214–231. doi:10.1111/j.1540-4781.2008.00715.x

Weigle, S. C. (2006). Investing in assessment: Designing tests to promote positive washback. In Matsuda, P. K., Ortmeier-Hooper, C., & You, X. (Eds.), *The politics of second language writing: In search of the promised land* (pp. 222–244). West Lafayette, IN: Parlor.

Willett, J. B. (1994). Measurement of change. In Husen, T., & Postlethwaite, T. N. (Eds.), *The international encyclopedia of education* (2nd ed., pp. 671–678). Oxford, UK: Pergamon.

Wolfe-Quintero, K., Inagaki, S., & Kim, H.-Y. (1998). *Second language development in writing: Measures of fluency, accuracy & complexity.* Honolulu, HI: Second Language Teaching & Curriculum Center, University of Hawaii at Manoa.

Chapter 24
A Comparative Study of an Unsupervised Word Sense Disambiguation Approach

Wei Xiong
New Jersey Institute of Technology, USA

Min Song
New Jersey Institute of Technology, USA

Lori Watrous deVersterre
New Jersey Institute of Technology, USA

ABSTRACT

Word sense disambiguation is the problem of selecting a sense for a word from a set of predefined possibilities. This is a significant problem in the biomedical domain where a single word may be used to describe a gene, protein, or abbreviation. In this paper, we evaluate SENSATIONAL, a novel unsupervised WSD technique, in comparison with two popular learning algorithms: support vector machines (SVM) and K-means. Based on the accuracy measure, our results show that SENSATIONAL outperforms SVM and K-means by 2% and 17%, respectively. In addition, we develop a polysemy-based search engine and an experimental visualization application that utilizes SENSATIONAL's clustering technique.

INTRODUCTION

Many English words have multiple meanings or senses. For example, the word *foot* in the sentence *The house is at the foot of the mountains* refers to the bottom part of the mountains, whereas in the sentence *One of his shoes felt too tight for his foot* it refers to the terminal part of the vertebrate leg upon which an individual stands. As we can see, the correct senses of the word *foot* can be inferred from its contextual words *house* and *mountains* in the first sentence and *shoes*, *felt*, and *tight* in the second sentence. The contextual words help in disambiguating and understanding the word that has multiple meanings. The ambiguity of an individual word or phrase that can be used in different contexts to express two or more different meanings is called polysemy.

DOI: 10.4018/978-1-60960-741-8.ch024

In general terms, Word Sense Disambiguation (WSD) involves the problem of determining the correct meaning an ambiguous word bears in a given context. This process relies to a great extent on the surrounding context of the word. It has been regarded as a crucial problem in many natural language processing (NLP) applications. For example, an information retrieval system could perform better if the ambiguities among queries were reduced. Other applied NLP applications that have benefited from WSD include information extraction (Stokoe, Oakes and Tait 2003), question answering (Pasca and Harabagiu 2001), and machine translation (Vickrey et al. 2005).

In the biomedical domain, WSD is a central problem. Many names of proteins and genes, abbreviations, and general biomedical terms have multiple meanings. For instance, *glucose* could be used to mean a biologically active substance which is a carbohydrate, or glucose measurement which is a laboratory procedure. These ambiguous words make it difficult for Natural Language Processing (NLP) applications and, in some cases, humans to correctly interpret the appropriate meaning.

SENSATIONAL is a novel unsupervised WSD technique proposed recently by (Duan, Song, and Yates 2009). Their original study presents impressive accuracy results. Our research contributes by benchmarking SENSEATIONAL against two well-received algorithms: Support Vector Machines (SVM) and K-means. Furthermore, we discuss SENSATIONAL's data preprocessing benefits related to reduced manual effort. These characteristics make SENSATIONAL's novel approach to WSD a very attractive application to a number of real-world problems in the area of search and data visualization that our research piloted for further exploration.

BACKGROUND

There are three types of WSD techniques (Ide and Veronis 1998): supervised learning, unsupervised learning and knowledge-based WSD. Supervised techniques need manually-labeled examples for each ambiguous term in the data set to predict the correct sense of the same word in a new context. This is referred to as training material which allows their corpus to build up a classification scheme based on the set of feature-encoded inputs and their appropriate sense label or category. The result of this training is a classifier that can be applied to future instances of the ambiguous word.

As a classification problem of machine learning, WSD has several characteristics that distinguish it from other traditional classification problems in NLP. Due to the difficulty of creating manually-labeled examples for the ambiguous terms, there is usually a small amount of training data available for WSD task. For example, the data set of ambiguous biomedical terms available from the National Library of Medicine (NLM) contains only 100 examples of each term being used in context. Also, the number of the senses of an ambiguous word for a WSD problem can be quite large. Take word *cold* as an example, there are more than 10 meanings of *cold* according to the Merriam-Webster Online Dictionary. Compared with WSD problem, for other classification problems in NLP, such as POS tagging (part-of-speech tagging which makes up the words in a text as corresponding to a particular part of speech), a word usually only has one or two POS's in a single language. Furthermore, the features, which are extracted from the context of a target word and used for classification, usually include lexical features. Without proper feature selection criteria, the amount of possible lexical features used by a machine learning algorithm can be very large, while the frequencies with which they occur in the data sets can be very low.

Knowledge-based WSD systems are similar to supervised learning because they use established, external knowledge, such as databases and dictionaries to disambiguate words. However, both of these approaches need extensive manual effort to create either training data or external resources. This can be time-consuming and expensive.

Unsupervised WSD techniques do not require the creation of these training sets or predefined knowledge bases. Instead, they are based on un-labeled corpora and use a training set of feature-encoded inputs but do not have these mapped to an appropriate sense label or category. While this technique reduces the manual, time-consuming effort, unsupervised WSD often generates less accurate results (Ide and Veronis 1998).

To respond to the costly manual effort while maintaining a high accuracy, (Duan, Song, and Yates 2009) proposed a novel unsupervised WSD technique, called SENSATIONAL. It uses a single threshold parameter that can be chosen by hand or set to a simple training procedure. It is not tied to the vocabulary thus making the resulting system extendable to new terms which allows for the analysis of multiple ambiguous terms simultaneously. A term that is ambiguous will hold the same meaning for a homogeneous document collection but because SENSATIONAL is not tied to a vocabulary, a term does not have to be retrained when ported to a new document collection. While the technique requires a small sample data set for initialization, the effort is smaller compared to supervised WSD techniques. SENSATIONAL is a relatively new technique with limited literature to compare it with other, more popular WSD techniques. Our objective is to compare SENSATIONAL with two well-received WSD techniques, one of which is SVM, and the second which is unsupervised, K-means.

The paper continues with a description of related work in Section 2. In Section 3 we introduce the SENSATIONAL algorithm for clustering word senses and provide a search engine and an experimental visualization application that utilizes this automatic clustering technique. Section 4 outlines our experimental setup and presents results. We discuss the future work for this ongoing research in Section 5.

RELATED WORK

In this section, we will review Word Sense Disambiguation techniques that are widely used in the biomedical domain.

Supervised Learning Techniques

Supervised learning is a set of machine learning techniques that use training data to create a generalized model which can be used to predict class labels for data. Training data consists of inputs that are tagged with the appropriate predefined class label. The accuracy of the techniques depends on the type of data that is selected for building the model. This training data must be representative of real-world conditions and contain sufficient variability to ensure nuances of the conditions are captured in the generalized prediction model. Not only must the corpus be large, but it must have the right inputs to provide the variables that can determine the correct class label. This makes supervised learning techniques dependent on a large labor intensive annotated corpus.

One of the most popular supervised learning techniques used for WSD is Support Vector Machines (SVMs). They are based on statistical learning theory (Vapnik 1995) which defines a decision boundary that separates one class from another. (Joshi, Pedersen, Maclin 2005) compare SVM with other four well-known supervised learning algorithms: Naïve Bayes, decision trees, decision lists and boosting approaches on a subset of the National Library of Medicine (NLM) WSD data set which consists of 50 highly frequently ambiguous words from 1998 MEDLINE (Medical Literature Analysis and Retrieval System Online). MEDLINE is a bibliographic database containing references to several journals related to life science. They converted the NLM formatted data into SENSEVAL-2 format data which is an XML format with certain pre-defined markup tags. The statistical significance test of the log likelihood measure was employed to identify bigrams (2 word collocation that has a tendency to express only one sense) that occur together more often than by chance. A frequency cut-off value was used to select the unigram features that are significant words occurring with an ambiguous term. Their evaluation results indicated that SVM obtained the best performance with unigram features selected using a frequency cut-off of four.

Naïve Bayes is another popular supervised learning technique widely used in biomedical domain. This simple probabilistic classifier is based on Bayes' theorem to predict class membership. It assumes the attributes of the data are independent of the class. (Leroy and Rindflesch 2005) use the Naïve Bayes classifier from the Weka data mining suite. Their experiments were performed with incremental feature sets, thus evaluating the contribution of new features over the previous ones. They achieved convincing improvements over the majority sense baseline in some cases, but observed degradation of performance in others. A comparative study conducted by (Pedersen and Bruce 1997) also shows that the Naïve Bayes classifier achieves a high level of accuracy using a model of low complexity.

Decision list learning is a rule-based approach. (Frank and Witten 1998) propose an approach for learning decision lists based on the repeated generation of partial decision trees in a 'separate-and-conquer' manner. They demonstrate rule sets can be learned one rule at a time without any need for global optimization. Decision Lists were one of the most successful systems on the 1st Senseval competition for WSD (Kilgarriff and Rosenzweig 2000).

The boosting approach is based on the observation that finding many rough rules of thumb can be much easier than finding a single, highly accurate predication rule (Schapire 2003). It combines many simple and moderately accurate hypotheses (called weak classifiers) into a single, highly accurate classifier for the task at hand (Es-

cudero, Marquez and Rigau 2000). They applied the boosting algorithm to WSD problem, and compared it with Naïve Bayes and Exemplar-based approaches with one goal of reducing the manual effort to develop and maintain a broad coverage, semantically annotated corpus. Their experiments on a set of 15 selected polysemous words show that the boosting algorithm out performs its rivals but when (Joshi, Pedersen, Maclin 2005) performed their comparisons, the Naïve Bayesian classifier out performed boosting. Other research has also indicated that boosting can improve performance for a Naïve Bayesian classifier (Elkan 1997).

Unsupervised Learning Techniques

Unsupervised learning (often called clustering) is a set of machine learning techniques which have no preconceived class labels. Therefore no training data can be created to derive a model. These techniques are well suited for problems which require labels to be discovered. The discovery technique attempts to find patterns between inputs. Most methods cluster "similar" items together and keep "dissimilar" items far apart. From these clusters, common labels can be selected. Algorithms for clustering are iterative and require the seeding of initial clusters. These can impact the end results. Therefore, the trade-off between unsupervised and supervised learning techniques is the accuracy of the resulting predictive model verses the labor intensive activity of developing and maintaining training data.

The K-means clustering (MacQueen 1967) is a common clustering algorithm used to automatically partition a data set into k groups. This clustering method will randomly select *k* data points as the initial seed clusters. It will then iteratively attempt to recenter the clusters until the grouping is stabilized or a predefined threshold is met. This technique is sensitive to the initial seed selections. (Schütze 1998) proposed an unsupervised technique for word sense disambiguation based on a vector representation of word senses that were induced from a corpus without labeled training instances or other external knowledge sources. The K-means vector model was used and demonstrated good performance of context-group discrimination for a sample of natural and artificial ambiguous words.

(Yarowsky 1995) propose an unsupervised learning algorithm to perform WSD, which is based on two powerful constraints: 1) that words tend to have one sense per discourse and 2) there is one sense per collocation. When trained on unannotated English text, the experimental results indicate that his algorithm is able to compete with supervised learning technique in accuracy.

An unsupervised approach for WSD which exploits translation correspondences in parallel corpora is presented by (Diab and Resnik 2002). The idea is that words having the same translation often share some dimension of meaning, leading to an algorithm in which the correct sense of a word is reinforced by the semantic similarity of other words with which it shares those dimensions of meaning. Based on fair comparison using community-wide test data, the performance of their algorithm has been evaluated. The results showed comparable or improved performance over other unsupervised systems even though the evaluation was based on cross-language analysis.

(Bhattacharya, Getoor and Bengio 2004) propose two unsupervised WSD systems that also use parallel corpora in two different languages. 'Sense Model' builds off of Diab and Resnik's work. It groups semantically related words from the two languages into senses. Translations are then generated by probabilistically choosing a sense and then words from that sense. The 'Concept Model' differs by analyzing each corpus individually to build a hierarchical model that uses a concept to relate the language specific sense labels. Their experimental results show that the concept model improved performance on the word sense disambiguation task over the previous approaches participated in 21 Senseval-2 English All Word competition.

Knowledge-Based WSD Systems

The availability of extensive knowledge sources such as Unified Medical Language System (UMLS) and WordNet are widely utilized to tackle WSD problems. These sources often contain linguistic, terminological, and semantic information specific to a domain or language. Augmenting machine learning techniques with these sources allows for the extraction of additional information that can be used to resolve ambiguity when mapping free-text to domain specific concepts.

(Widdows et al. 2003) propose their system for word sense disambiguation of English and German medical documents using UMLS. There results showed that lexical resources can be used for high quality disambiguation in another language. (Liu, Johnson and Friedman 2002) use UMLS as the ontology and identify UMLS concepts in abstracts. They then analyze the co-occurrence of these terms with the term to be disambiguated and built their word sense-tagged corpora automatically rather than by hand as in normal supervised techniques. The biggest challenge is ensuring there are enough instances for each sense. (Leroy and Rindflesch 2005) study the effect of different types of symbolic information for terms in medical text by mapping sentences to the UMLS. They use Naïve Bayes classifier to disambiguate medical terms and the UMLS for its symbolic knowledge.

(Mihalcea and Moldovan 1998) present a method for WSD that is based on measuring the conceptual density between words using WordNet. It takes advantage of sentence context in order to select the correct sense of an ambiguous word. (Inkpen and Hirst 2003) use WordNet to disambiguate near-synonyms in dictionary entries. Their approach is based on the overlap of words in the dictionary description and the WordNet glosses, synsets, antonyms, and polysemy information.

SENSATIONAL AND ITS APPLICATION

This section provides an overview of SENSA-TIONAL's clustering algorithm. It also suggests a polysemy-based search engine and an experimental visualization application that utilizes SENSATIONAL clustering technique.

SENSATIONAL Clustering

(Duan, Song, and Yates 2009) proposed a novel and efficient graph-based algorithm to cluster words into groups that have the same meaning. Their system, called SENSATIONAL, is built on the principle of margin-maximization. This principle finds a surface in the space of data points that separates the points in such a way that maximizes the smallest distance between points on opposite sides of the surface. Although it works accurately and effectively, max-margin clustering is computationally expensive.

To overcome this drawback, Duan et al. used a novel approximation algorithm for finding max-margin clusters in a document collection based on minimum spanning trees (MST). A MST is an undirected graph that can be computed efficiently and provides the smallest set of edges in the tree to connect all the data points together. A second characteristic of a MST is that for each data point, or node, there will be exactly one path to every other node. Therefore, we can divide a MST into sub-graphs by simply removing one edge.

To use MST in max-margin cluster, each word in a set of documents containing that word is stored in an *index*, which can be used to prune the set of edges that are added to a graph. After a weighted graph that represents the set of mentions of an ambiguous term is built, the MST for the graph is constructed, and the largest edge is removed from it. This splits the graph into two clusters which can then be further analyzed to determine if additional segmentation is needed. The largest edge of the MST provides a large margin between two clusters of the weighted graph. This insight forms the basis of the SENSATIONAL algorithm.

One weakness with this algorithm is the potential for outliers to skew the clusters. The SENSA-TIONAL system corrects this from happening by finding the roots of all the sub-trees and determines a path or backbone between these sub-trees. This Backbone-Finding algorithm identifies the core of the MST and helps prevent outliers skewing the clusters that are developed.

The beauty of SENSATIONAL is that the algorithm assumes essentially no input requiring significant manual input to construct, such as manually-labeled training examples for supervised learning algorithms or manually-constructed and manually-curated databases containing structured knowledge. It needs a single free parameter, which is essentially threshold that could be set by hand, but also could be trained with only a few hundred manually-labeled examples of one ambiguous term in context. This parameter is not tied to the vocabulary, and the system does not have to be retrained when ported to a new document collection. This means, after being trained, the system can be applied to any new term. We consider SENSATIONAL as an unsupervised system because it is common to refer to systems with a small number of free parameters as "unsupervised" (Davidov and Rappaport 2008).

Polysemy Extraction-Based Search Engine

SENSATIONAL's benchmarking results and data preprocessing features make it a very attractive technique for a number of real-world problems. The following describes a prototype of two novel approaches to search and data visualization.

In the case of search, it is well known that as our corpora continually grow, the current retrieval systems, modeled after card catalog systems, will become cumbersome and inefficient (Korfhage 1991). New ways to determine what end-users are searching for need to be developed that don't just present all possible query keyword matches, but also attempts to provide them with information to support iterative search requests that will isolate the documents relevant to their particular inquiry. This iterative 3-step process starts with a broad query which, in successive queries drills-down by either zooming in on wanted concepts or filtering out unwanted concepts. Finally details on specific content are examined and the process begins again (Koshman 2006).

Users search for different reasons. Two basic purposes are to find explicit information and to perform exploratory browsing. When searching for explicit information, we may or may not know the specific terms to use. Initial results returned must be examined and if inadequate summaries are provided, the user must open up documents and examine the content. This can be time consuming and frustrating. Exploratory browsing can be even worse. As a user moves from document to document, the "bigger picture" or reason for the browsing can soon be forgotten leading to wasted time and effort. Even worse, potential new discoveries can be hidden in the maze of lengthy lists of keyword matched content.

An exploratory polysemy extraction-based search engine was built to determine if SENSA-TIONAL could be used to identify clusters based on existing corpora. Preliminary results show we can identify the clusters via the Backbone-Finding algorithm and present topical terms.

The following example is a visual representation for the query "cold." A search was conducted on the PubMed collection using the query, "cold." A limit was placed on the search to retrieve up to 300 documents. The polysemy-based search engine identified 4 different senses. Figure 1 is a display of the results which shows the number of resources associated with each sense along with a machine generated meaning of the sense based on latent semantic indexing. For example, the first sense, labeled, "vitamin common cold revisited," includes 148 documents related to managing a common cold while the second sense

contains 11 documents describing an object used for pain relief.

This display can help a user focus their search which can reduce the amount of content an individual must examine. It may also help a user to determine if a repository contains the type of content they are interested in. Additionally, for users performing an explicit or exhaustive search, this format provides information on additional appropriate terms.

If a user decides they are interested in information about managing the common cold they can drill down to discover the Cluster Map shown in Figure 2. The Map shows 3 subtopics which are defined in the ovals beginning with the topic identifiers 1, 2, and 3. The identifiers are followed by a set of terms generated by latent semantic indexing and end with an overall count of the number of documents associated with the topic id. Since documents may have an overlap between these subtopics, the Cluster Map shows this by color coding the groupings and indicating an overlap by having the connecting pathways show the blending of the multiple colors. In the case of label 2, all six documents are also grouped within label 3 while label 1's document set has seven of its documents overlapping with subtopic 3 and a single outlier shown at the bottom of the display is not associated with any of the other subtopics.

This display not only identifies all the topical terms for a query but their inter-relationship within the collection being searched. This visual

Figure 1. Two-level search results display

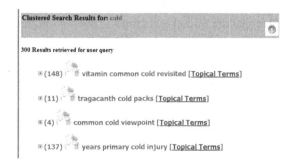

Figure 2. Visual representation of SENSATIONAL generated terms in existing corpora

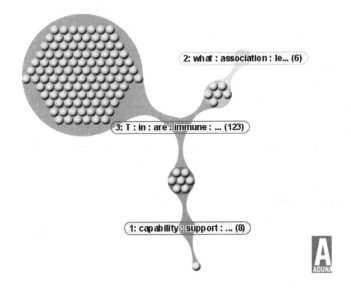

representation may help users understand the meanings and relationships of ambiguous terms. For users unfamiliar with the multiple meanings of a term or performing exploratory browsing, this high-level overview provides an organizational structure to help users focus on the intent of their search before opening any documents to determine if it meets their needs or not.

EXPERIMENT AND RESULTS

We performed an experiment to compare SENSATIONAL system against both SVM and K means.

Experimental Setup

We evaluated SENSATIONAL, SVM and K-means on the same data set that (Duan, Song, and Yates 2009) used to evaluate SENSATIONAL and we show their results below. The data set of keywords is from the National Library of Medicine (NLM) data set, plus a set of additional terms, including a number of acronyms. They collected a data set of PubMed abstracts for these terms. On average, 271 documents per keyword were col-

lected; no keyword had fewer than 125 documents, and the largest collection was 503 documents. They filtered out abstracts that were less than 15 words and manually labeled each occurrence of each term with an identifier indicating its sense in the given context. They collected data for a total of 21 keywords. Two of these were used for training, and the other 19 for tests.

We used LIBSVM by Chih-Chung Chang and Chih-Jen Lin (available for download at http://www.csie.ntu.edu.tw/~cjlin/libsvm). (Xu et al. 2006) applied SVM classifiers to perform WSD tasks on an automatically generated data set that contains ambiguous biomedical abbreviations. Their results indicated that there was no statistical difference between results when using a five-fold or ten-fold cross-validation method. In our case, for SVM we adopted the linear kernel and default parameter values, and ran a five-fold cross-validation.

Results

We evaluated SENSATIONAL against SVM and K-means based on the standard measure of accuracy, which is the percentage of the correctly classified instances.

Results for our comparison appear in Table 1. SENSATIONAL is able to outperform both SVM and K-means, by 2% and 17% on average across the keywords respectively. Considering that the size of our data set of keywords is smaller than 30, we performed K-S test for normality of distributions and the results (significance level > 0.05) suggest that the distributions are normal. The performance of SENSATIONAL compared to K-means and SVM is statistically significant at $p<0.05$ and $p=0.495$ respectively, using a paired t-test.

It is interesting to notice that some ambiguous words were more troublesome to the classifiers than others. Most words only had 2 senses in the data, with four exceptions: "BPD," "cold," "inflammation," and "nutrition" had 3 senses each. The WSD performance of these exceptions was generally poorer than others, which confirmed that the number of senses could be one of the determinants of the word ambiguity (Leroy and Rindflesch 2005). Unexpectedly, they found that ambiguous words that were troublesome to the human evaluators were generally also harder for the algorithms to correctly perform WSD.

DISCUSSION AND FUTURE WORK

We evaluated SENSATIONAL, a novel unsupervised WSD technique, in comparison with two popular learning algorithms, SVM and K-means. We manually curated the data set collected from National Library of Medicine (NLM). In addition, we develop a polysemy-based search engine and an experimental visualization application that utilizes SENSATIONAL clustering technique. These applications could help users understand the meaning and relationships of ambiguous terms, choose their next level of search and reduce the

Table 1. Comparison with SVM and K-means

Keyword	SVM	K-means	Sensational
ANA	0.82	0.72	1.0
BPD	0.97	0.42	0.53
BSA	0.99	1.0	0.95
CML	0.99	0.60	0.90
cold	0.68	0.45	0.67
culture	0.59	0.58	0.82
discharge	0.71	0.43	0.95
fat	0.51	0.53	0.53
fluid	0.92	0.60	0.99
glucose	0.51	0.58	0.51
inflammation	0.42	0.45	0.50
inhibition	0.50	0.67	0.54
MAS	1.0	0.51	1.0
mole	0.78	0.53	0.96
nutrition	0.53	0.44	0.55
pressure	0.82	0.68	0.86
single	0.95	0.84	0.99
transport	0.51	0.52	0.57
VCR	0.80	0.64	0.64
average	**0.74**	**0.59**	**0.76**

amount of content the individuals must wade through to find what is relevant to them.

The experiment that we have performed demonstrated that compared with K-means, SENSATIONAL is able to achieve a better accuracy. It outperforms K-means by 17%. However, compared with SVM, the performance of SENSATIONAL is not statistical significant, given that the significance level $p=0.495$. In addition, the performance of SVM could be improved by optimizing its parameter values and/or adopting different feature selections. In our experiments, we used the default parameter values and TF-IDF weight (term frequency-inverse document frequency) as our feature selection method.

So far the performance of SENSATIONAL is very encouraging, given that it assumes essentially no inputs that require significant manual input to construct. SENSATONAL's Max-margin technique combined with its Backbone-Finding algorithm is not only able to outperform the state-of-the-art unsupervised WSD technique, but also competitive against supervised learning algorithm. In future work, we plan to examine if the good performance of SENSATIONAL in medical domain will translate into general English word sense disambiguation, especially compared with other well-known machine learning algorithms.

REFERENCES

Bhattacharya, I., Getoor, L., & Bengio, Y. (2004). Unsupervised sense disambiguation using bilingual probabilistic models. *Proceedings of the Meeting of the Association for Computational Linguistics.*

Davidov, D., & Rappaport, A. (2008). Unsupervised discovery of generic relationships using pattern clusters and its evaluation by automatically generated SAT analogy questions. *Proceedings of the Annual Meeting of the Association of Computational Linguistics.*

Diab, M., & Resnik, P. (2002). An unsupervised method for word sense tagging using parallel corpora. *Proc. ACL.*

Duan, W., Song, M., & Yates, A. (2009). Fast max-margin clustering for unsupervised word sense disambiguation in biomedical texts. *BMC Bioinformatics, 10,* S4. doi:10.1186/1471-2105-10-S3-S4

Elkan, C. (1997). *Boosting and naive Bayesian learning. Technical report, Department of Computer Science and Engineering.* San Diego: University of California.

Escudero, G., Marquez, L., & Rigau, G. (2000). Boosting applied to word sense disambiguation. In *Proceedings of ECML-00, 11th European Conference on Machine Learning* (Barcelona, Spain, 2000), (pp. 129–141).

Frank, E., & Witten, I. H. (1998). Generating accurate rule sets without global optimization. In *Proceedings of the Fifteenth International Conference on Machine Learning,* (pp. 144–151).

Harley, A., & Glennon, D. (1997). Sense tagging in action. In *Proceedings of SIGLEX Workshop on Tagging Text with Lexical Semantics: Why, What and How.*

Humphrey, S. M., Rogers, W. J., Kilicoglu, H., Demner-Fushman, D., & Rindflesch, T. C. (2006). Word sense disambiguation by selecting the best semantic type based on Journal descriptor indexing: Preliminary experiment. *Journal of the American Society for Information Science American Society for Information Science, 57,* 96–113.

Ide, N., & Véronis, J. (1998). Introduction to the special issue on word sense disambiguation: The state of the art. *Computational Linguistics, 24,* 2–40.

Inkpen, D. Z., & Hirst, G. (2003). Automatic sense disambiguation of the near-synonyms in a dictionary entry. *Lecture Notes in Computer Science,* 258–267. doi:10.1007/3-540-36456-0_25

Joshi, M., Pedersen, T., & Maclin, R. (2005). A comparative study of support vector machines applied to the supervised word sense disambiguation problem in the medical domain. In *Proceedings of the 2nd Indian International Conference on Artificial Intelligence (IICAI'05),* (pp. 3449–3468).

Kilgarriff, A., & Rosenzweig, J. (2000). *English SENSEVAL: Report and results* (pp. 265–283). Athens: LREC.

Korfhage, R. R. (1991). To see, or not to see – Is that the query? *Proceedings of the 14th Annual International ACM SIGIR Conference on Research and Development in Information Retrieval,* (pp. 134-141). ACM.

Koshman, S. (2006). Visualization-based information retrieval on the Web. *Library & Information Science Research, 28*(2), 192–207. doi:10.1016/j.lisr.2006.03.017

Leroy, G., & Rindflesch, T. C. (2005). Effects of information and machine learning algorithms on word sense disambiguation with small datasets. *International Journal of Medical Informatics, 74*, 573–585. doi:10.1016/j.ijmedinf.2005.03.013

Liu, H., Johnson, S. B., & Friedman, C. (2002). Automatic resolution of ambiguous terms based on machine learning and conceptual relations in the UMLS. *Journal of the American Medical Informatics Association, 9*, 621. doi:10.1197/jamia.M1101

MacQueen, J. B. (1967). Some methods for classification and analysis of multivariate observations. In *Proceedings of 5ᵗʰ Berkeley Symposium on Mathematical Statistics and Probability*, (pp. 281-297).

Mihalcea, R., & Moldovan, D. (1998). Word sense disambiguation based on semantic density. In *Proceedings of COLING/ACL Workshop on Usage of WordNet in Natural Language Processing* (pp. 16–22).

Pasca, M., & Harabagiu, S. (2001). *The informative role of WordNet in open-domain question answering.* Workshop on WordNet and Other Lexical Resources at NAACL.

Pedersen, T., & Bruce, R. (1997). Knowledge lean word-sense disambiguation. In *Proceedings of the National Conference of Artificial Intelligence*, (pp. 814–814).

Schapire, R. E. (2003). *The boosting approach to machine learning: An overview. Lecture Notes in Statistics* (pp. 149–172). New York, NY: Springer Verlag.

Schütze, H. (1998). Automatic word sense discrimination. *Computational Linguistics, 24*, 97–123.

Stokoe, C., Oakes, M. P., & Tait, J. (2003). Word sense disambiguation in information retrieval revisited. In *Proceedings of the 26th Annual International ACM SIGIR Conference on Research and Development in Information Retrieval* (p. 166).

Vapnik, V. (1995). *The nature of statistical learning theory.* Spring, New York.

Vickrey, D., Biewald, L., Teyssier, M., & Koller, D. (2005). Word-sense disambiguation for machine translation. In *Proceedings of HLT/EMNLP,* vol. 5.

Widdows, D., Peters, S., Cederberg, S., Chan, C. K., & Steffen, D. (2003). Unsupervised monolingual and bilingual word-sense disambiguation of medical documents using UMLS. In *Proceedings of the ACL 2003 Workshop on Natural Language Processing in Biomedicine,* volume 13, (pp. 9–16).

Wilks, Y., Fass, D., Guo, C., MacDonald, J., Plate, T., & Slator, B. (1990). *Providing machine tractable dictionary tools.* MIT Press.

Xu, H., Markatou, M., Dimova, R., Liu, H., & Friedman, C. (2006). Machine learning and word sense disambiguation in the biomedical domain: Design and evaluation issues. *BMC Bioinformatics, 7*, 334. doi:10.1186/1471-2105-7-334

Yarowsky, D. (1995). Unsupervised word sense disambiguation rivaling supervised methods. In *Proceedings of the 33rd Annual Meeting on Association for Computational Linguistics* (pp. 189–196).

Chapter 25
Interlanguage Talk:
A Computational Analysis of Non-Native Speakers' Lexical Production and Exposure

Scott A. Crossley
Georgia State University, USA

Danielle S. McNamara
Arizona State University, USA

ABSTRACT

This study investigates the production of and exposure to lexical features when non-native speakers (NNS) converse with each other (NNS-NNS) engaging in interlanguage talk, as compared to when they engage in naturalistic speech with a native speaker (NS). The authors focus on lexical features that are associated with breadth of lexical knowledge including lexical diversity and lexical frequency. Spoken corpora from three types of dyads (NS-NNS, NNS-NS, NNS-NNS) are analyzed using the computational tool, Coh-Metrix. The results indicate that NNSs produce language with significantly greater lexical diversity and higher word frequency (i.e., more common words) when speaking to another NNS than when speaking to a NS. Hence, there is greater breadth of lexical knowledge apparent within interlanguage dyads (i.e., NNS-NNS) than within NNS-NS dyads in the variety of words produced, but not the frequency of the words. There were no significant differences in NNS exposure to breadth of lexical knowledge features as a function of whether the speaker was a NS or NNS. Hence, NNSs were exposed to similar levels of lexically comprehensible input regardless of interlocutor. These findings have important implications for the developmental role of interlanguage talk in reference to lexical production and exposure.

INTRODUCTION

When language learners are faced with learning a second language, they often must depend on other language learners in order to practice speaking and listening skills in that second language.

DOI: 10.4018/978-1-60960-741-8.ch025

These conversations between non-native speakers (NNS) are referred to as interlanguage talk (ILT; Long & Porter, 1985). Developing a better understanding of ILT has practical importance for second language instruction, particularly with regard to English as a foreign language (EFL) settings where NNSs may not have access to native speakers of English with whom they can practice their speaking skills and develop their linguistic competence in natural settings. Such instructional settings are likely the norm, with some researchers estimating that about 80% of verbal interactions in English that involve a NNS do not include a native speaker (NS; Beneke, 1991). Thus, the majority of NNS conversations occur with NNSs pushing NNSs to converse and a reliance on one another to practice and develop their language skills. ILT is also important instructionally with regard to English as a Second Language (ESL) settings where NNSs may have few opportunities to have natural conversations with native speaking English teachers. The scarcity of such opportunities can be partially attributed to the nature of classroom instruction, in which time is limited and teachers' attention is spread amongst the students in the classroom rather than any one particular student. ILT is thus a crucial element for providing NNSs with opportunities to practice their speaking skills and develop their second language (L2) in the absence of NSs.

The purpose of this study is to investigate the potential benefits of ILT by examining the use of lexical features in NNS dyadic speech, in particular those features that are reflective of NNSs breadth of lexical knowledge. Lexical features such as lexical diversity and lexical frequency are signals of a speaker's breadth of lexical knowledge because they indicate how many words the speaker knows. These features contrast with those features that are signals for a NNS's *depth* of linguistic knowledge (i.e., how well a learner knows a word). Our primary interest in this study is to examine differences in breadth of linguistic knowledge apparent in the NNS's English language production (i.e., output) when engaged in ILT (NNS-NNS) as compared to when they are engaged in naturalistic speech with a native speaker (NNS-NS). To compare the exposure to language (i.e., input) that NNSs receive, we are also interested in examining native speaker input to L2 learners (NS-NNS) to NNS-NNS dyads. We analyze the potential differences among the

dyads using the computational tool Coh-Metrix. Our goal is to examine if lexical production and exposure differs as a function of interlocutor and discuss the implications of the findings for second language acquisition with specific focus on the roles of input and output.

INTERLANGUAGE

Interlanguage refers to the systematic knowledge that comprises a NNS's second language. An interlanguage is a functional system that differs in accuracy and fluency when compared to the language system of a native language speaker. Unlike a native language, an interlanguage is fluid, demonstrates greater variation, and most likely will never reach a stage of fluency (Gass & Selinker, 2008). Crucial determinants in the development of an interlanguage are input and output.

Input refers to the language to which the NNS is exposed. Generally, NNSs receive modified input from NSs. This modified input is in the form of "foreigner talk" or "teacher talk." Both forms of input are similar and both are simplified at the lexical, phonological, and syntactic levels to allow for greater comprehension of linguistic features on the part of the NNS (Gaies 1983; Hatch 1983). It is argued that at the level of input, lexical recognition plays the greatest role in comprehension. As a result, comprehensible input is thought to lead to greater lexical acquisition. This contrasts with output, which refers to the production of language on the part of the NNS. Output is argued to force the NNS to move from lexical to syntactic processing and allow NNS the opportunity to experiment with new syntactic forms by testing hypotheses about language structure. When combined, input and output lead to interaction. Interactional theories of language learning hold that the conversational and linguistic modifications found in interactional conversation provide NNSs with the input needed to acquire language (Long, 1983a, 1983b, 1985). Interactional modifications that assist NNSs in recognizing and amending incomprehensible input have been termed negotiations (Gass & Varonis, 1989, 1994; Long, 1983a, 1983b, 1996; Pica, 1994). Negotiations occur when NNSs or NSs signal that they do not understand an utterance for lexical, phonological, morphosyntactic, or other reasons. This leads to an opportunity to negotiate for meaning and the resulting interaction allows participants to reconsider and restructure the language that caused the initial loss of meaning. The interaction that naturally occurs during the negotiation for meaning can lead to the introduction of new and varied linguistic input as well as new and varied output (Swain, 1985, 1995).

Interlanguage Talk

Key to the importance of interaction is the investigation of ILT. As noted earlier, ILT is communication between two non-native speakers of English. Communication between two non-native speakers of English has also been termed *English as an international language* (McKay, 2002), *English as a global language* (Crystal, 1997), *English as a world language* (Mair, 2003), and more recently as *English as a Lingua Franca* (ELF). ELF is likely the most common term found in the literature today. ELF is defined as a contact language (Firth, 1996) that generally involves interactions between speakers whose first language is not English, although it may include native speakers (House, 1999; Seidlhofer, 2004). ELF interactions, unlike ILT, are not classroom centered and generally occur in more professional settings such as business, politics, or science (Firth, 1990; 1996). Thus, ELF interactions are not measured against NS/NS and NS/NNS norms (House, 2009) and, in theory, may operate under different conditions such that ELF interlocutors use different communicative strategies than NSs (Pickering, 2006). Theoretical approaches to ELF also regard it as a legitimate language (i.e., a new and separate variety of English) that is shaped by its users and has unique similarities across users

(Firth, 2009; Seidlhofer, 2004). With this in mind, the purpose of EFL studies is to analyze the features of English that are important for international intelligibility in contrast to those features that do not cause misunderstandings, but may comprise the norms for idealized speakers such as NSs (Seidlhofer, 2005).

However, in many cases, ILT as compared to ELF is the primary source of input for NNSs (Flanigan, 1991). This is especially the case for learners who do not use English for professional purposes and instead depend upon instructional settings to provide them with the opportunity to practice their language skills. ILT in the L2 classroom is pedagogically important because pair work between NNSs increases opportunities for language practice and can lead to the development of increased interlanguage fluency (Long & Porter, 1985). For the purpose of this study, we are most interested in the latter (that ILT supports interlanguage development). This notion has been supported in various studies. For example, Porter (1983) investigated the linguistic features of speech between NNS-NNS and NNS-NS. Porter analyzed the speech of 12 NNSs and 6 NSs. The NNS participants ranged from intermediate to advanced learners of English. Porter found that NNS-NNS dyads produced more talk then NNS-NS dyads and that the NNS-NNS dyads showed no significant difference from the NNS-NS dyads in the number of grammatical and lexical errors observed. Porter's findings demonstrate that ILT has the potential to be more productive than NNS-NS talk while not resulting in an increase in errors. Additional studies have demonstrated that ILT rarely leads to the development of incorrect forms of language (Bruton & Samuda, 1980) and that ILT can facilitate lexical acquisition through hypothesis generation and testing (Swain & Lampkin, 1998).

Other studies supporting the strength of ILT have not so much focused on the linguistic features of ILT, but the use of negotiations in ILT. For instance, Varonis and Gass (1983) and Gass and Varonis (1989) found that there was a greater frequency of negotiation sequences in NNS-NNS dyads than in NNS-NS dyads, especially when the learners were of different language backgrounds and different proficiency levels. In a subsequent study, Doughty and Pica (1984) examined the language found in teacher centered lessons, pair work, and four person group work. Doughty and Pica found more negotiations in pair work than in teacher-centered lessons. Together, these studies support the notion that NNS-NNS conversations produce communicative contexts in which NNSs can develop their interlanguage skills through negotiation.

There is also a long history of ELF studies that have focused on describing the linguistic features found in NNS-NNS dialog. The majority of these studies have focused on phonology and pragmatics with little work devoted to the lexicon (Seidlhofer, 2004). The focus on phonology in ELF studies results from the notion that pronunciation difficulties are the most prominent indicators of comprehension problems in NNS-NNS dyads (Jenkins, 2000). Pragmatic studies of NNS-NNS discourse are less common than phonological studies because pragmatic studies are less structured and more difficult to analyze. From a pragmatic perspective, ELF researchers have focused on pauses, overlapping speech, and topic changes (Seidlhofer, 2004).

Word Frequency and Lexical Diversity

In this study, we are interested in lexical comprehensibility. We define comprehensibility as the ability of the listener to understand the meaning of a word or words (Smith & Nelson, 1985). The idea of comprehensibility can be condensed into the category of *form,* which refers to lexical decoding. Linguistically, we argue that both word frequency and lexical diversity are indicative of comprehensibility through form. Frequent words, for instance, are more accessible and more easily decodable and thus more comprehensible (Crossley, Greenfield, & McNamara, 2008; Perfetti, 1985; Rayner & Pollatsek, 1994). Lexical frequency also relates to the learning of categorizations from exemplars in that categorization acquisition is aided by the introduction of low variance samples that center on prototypical examples. From a lexical diversity perspective, the more tokens there are of an exemplar in the input, the greater the contribution of the exemplar will be to the development of the prototype (Ellis & Collins, 2009). Less lexical diversity also affords more overlap of ideas through simple word repetition and thus produces utterances that are more cohesive and more comprehensible (McCarthy & Jarvis, in press).

Both lexical diversity and word frequency are linguistic features associated with speakers' breadth of lexical knowledge because they are signals for the number of words that a speaker knows.[1] Breadth of lexical knowledge, which is a construct of lexical proficiency, is often contrasted with depth of lexical knowledge (i.e., the degree of organization of words in a learner's lexicon) and the accessibility of core lexical items (i.e., how accessible these words are to the learner). In this study, we focus solely on features related to breadth of lexical knowledge because they have been the most fruitful measures of lexical production, processing, and general proficiency. Lexical diversity is an important measure of lexical proficiency because it can be used to measure vocabulary knowledge and is also indicative of writing quality (Carrell & Monroe, 1993; Malvern, Richards, Chipere, & Duran, 2004; Ransdell & Wengelin, 2003). Lexical frequency is also an important feature of lexical proficiency because lexical proficiency is at least partially based on the distribution of frequent words. As a result, beginning L2 learners are more likely to comprehend, process, and produce higher frequency words (Ellis, 2002).

METHODS

This study examines differences in breadth of knowledge features between dyads (NS-NNS, NNS-NS, NNS-NNS) to investigate the potential benefits or disadvantages of ILT in L2 acquisition. We are primarily interested in potential NNS input (exposure) differences between NS-NNS and NNS-NNS dyads and potential NNS output (production) differences in NNS-NS and NNS-NNS dyads. Our hypothesis is that NS-NNS dyads will provide more comprehensible input to NNSs than NNS-NNS dyads because of NS's propensity to simplify language (i.e., foreigner talk). We also hypothesize that NNSs will produce more varied and more infrequent vocabulary when speaking with NSSs (NNS-NSS dyad) than with NNs (NNS-NN dyad) because in NNS-NNS dyads there would be less fear of making mistakes and thus greater linguistic risks would be taken. These risks might include testing new words leading both to more infrequent words and greater lexical diversity. To test these hypotheses, we analyze a corpus of spoken language texts using the computational tool Coh-Metrix.

Corpus

The corpus collected for this study comprised spoken conversations by NNSs and NSs. We selected a spoken corpus because spoken data allows us to examine reciprocal utterances that allow for the study of production and reception of language (Seidlhofer, 2004). All participants were students at a large university in the United Sates.

The NSs and many of the NNSs were students in a second language acquisition class. These students were asked to converse with an unknown NNS from a different language background who was studying English at the ESL center at the university as part of the class. The conversations were recorded and an excerpt from each recording was transcribed, thus comprising the texts in the corpus. All of the NNSs in the study were at the intermediate or advanced levels of language proficiency as classified by TOEFL tests (in the case of the NNS students in the SLA class) or internal classification assessments (in the case of the NNS students at the ESL center). The internal classification assessment used by the ESL center was a combination of the ACT Compass ESL reading and writing tests and internal tests of listening and speaking. The NSs in the study came from a variety of regions, but the majority were from the southern region of the United States. All NS were American except for one NS from Britain. The NNSs in this study came from a variety of first language (L1) backgrounds including Arabic, Japanese, Korean, Malay, Portuguese, Sri Lankan, Thai, French, Uzbek, and Spanish. The texts were collected over a five-year time span. Because of the instructional nature of the context, we categorize the collected speech transcripts as ILT and not ELF. Descriptive statistics from the total corpus are provided in Table 1.

Coh-Metrix

Coh-Metrix (Graesser et al., 2004) is a computational tool that provides hundreds of linguistic

Table 1. Descriptive statistics for interlanguage talk corpus

Condition	Number of Texts in the Corpus	Number of Words in the Corpus	Mean Number of Words per Text
NS-NNS	100	37509	375.090
NNS-NS	106	49046	462.698
NNS-NNS	200	82473	412.345

Notes: non-native speaker (NNS); native speaker (NS)

indices related to conceptual knowledge, cohesion, lexical difficulty, syntactic complexity, and simple incidence scores. Many of the measures reported by Coh-Metrix are related to lexical proficiency. This study focuses on lexical diversity and word frequency. These measures along with the respective indices reported by Coh-Metrix are discussed below.

Lexical Diversity

The premise behind lexical diversity indices is that more diverse vocabularies are indicative of more proficient and larger lexicons. From an input perspective, a lower lexical diversity score is thought to allow for more rapid acquisition of lexical prototypes. The majority of the indices related to lexical diversity concentrate on type token ratios (TTR), which are simple formulas that divide the number of different words (types) by the total number of words (tokens) in a given text. There are various deviations of simple TTR measures such as Corrected TTR (Carrol, 1964) and Log TTR (Herdan, 1960), and Advanced TTR (Daller, van Hout, & Treffers-Daller, 2003).

An important limitation of traditional LD indices is that while the number of tokens in a text will increase linearly, the relative number of types will steadily decrease. Thus, every new word is a new token at the beginning of a text, but, after relatively little text, tokens tend to be repeated. This relationship leads the number of types to asymptote. Thus, in general, TTR results correlate highly with text length. As a result, if a corpus of texts has token counts that distinctly differ, TTR results are not reliable (McCarthy & Jarvis, 2007). Traditional corrections of text length on measures of lexical diversity focused on using log values. Recent studies have demonstrated that one LD measure based on log values, Maas (*M*: 1972), shows little effect for text length across a wide range of text lengths (McCarthy & Jarvis, 2007). More sophisticated approaches to measuring lexical diversity have also been developed to correct

problems related to text length in traditional LD indices. Those reported by Coh-Metrix include the Measure of Textual, Lexical Diversity (MTLD; McCarthy & Jarvis, in press) and *D* (Malvern, Richards, Chipere, & Durán, 2004).

D, as reported by the vocd software, calculates lexical diversity based on random text samples of 35 tokens each. For each sample, vocd calculates the TTR. vocd then calculates the TTR for random samples of 36-50 tokens in length. From these samples, vocd creates an empirical TTR curve from the means of each of the samples. From this empirical TTR, a theoretical curve is produced that best fits the empirical curve. This calculation happens three times, with the average theoretical curve produced labeled *D*. However, as McCarthy and Jarvis (2007) have demonstrated, *D* actually calculates lexical diversity based on probabilities of word occurrences and thus approximates the hypergeometric distribution.

MTLD calculates lexical diversity by dividing a text into samples that have a TTR value of .71 starting from the beginning. The total samples in the text are then divided by the total number of words in the text (called the forward process). The same process is repeated, but starting at the end of the text instead of the beginning (called the reverse value). These two values are then summed and divided by 2 yielding the MTLD values for the text. In this manner, MTLD overcomes potential text length confounds (McCarthy & Jarvis, in press).

McCarthy and Jarvis (in press) demonstrated that all of the above lexical diversity indices (*M, D,* and MTLD) appear to control for text length to some degree. However, all of these indices seem to assess different latent traits of lexical diversity. In this manner, all of the indices capture unique aspects of lexical diversity suggesting that studies assessing lexical diversity should consider using a variety of lexical diversity indices instead of a single index. Thus, in our study, we follow the advice of McCarthy and Jarvis (in press) and use *M, D,* and MTLD to measure lexical diversity in NS-NNS, NNS-NS, and NNS-NNS dyads.

Lexical Frequency

The theoretical basis behind indices of word frequency is that they are able to measure lexical proficiency of learners with higher proficiency speakers using less frequent words. Most traditional frequency indices have depended on word frequency lists (Meara & Bell, 2001; Nation, 1988). These word frequency lists are placed in word frequency bands comprised of the first 1,000 most common words, the second 1,000 most common words, or the 1,000 most common words found in academic writing (e.g., Laufer & Nation, 1995; Nation & Heatley, 1996). As mentioned early, word frequency has traditionally been considered to be indicative of breadth of lexical knowledge. However, some researchers argue that the production and comprehension of words is a function of their frequency of occurrence in language (e.g., Ellis, 2002). This supports a distributional model of language learning in which word frequency helps determine lexical acquisition because each repetition of a word strengthens the connections between the word and its meaning categorization.

The lexical frequency indices reported by Coh-Metrix are different from traditional indices of word frequency used in lexical studies. The Coh-Metrix indices do not depend on lexical bands and instead take frequency counts from CELEX (Baayen, Piepenbrock, & Gulikers, 1995), a database provided by the Centre for Lexical Information, which consists of frequencies extracted from the 1991 version of the COBUILD corpus, a 17.9 million-word corpus.

When calculating word frequency, Coh-Metrix computes the mean logarithm of the word frequency for all of the words in the text that are also found in the COBUILD corpus. The logarithm values are to the base of 10. Coh-Metrix uses this data to report a variety of frequency indices. The common indices reported by Coh-Metrix calculate the frequency for content words in the text based on both spoken and written corpora. For this study, we selected two indices of word frequency: spoken content word frequency and written content word frequency. Supportive validation evidence for the word frequency measures reported by Coh-Metrix is available in past studies of lexical proficiency and lexical difficulty (Crossley, Salsbury, & McNamara, 2010). All indices of word frequency reported by Coh-Metrix control for text length by reporting normalized frequencies.

Statistical Analysis

To test differences between the dyads in their lexical diversity and frequency, we conducted a series of *t*-tests using the Coh-Metrix indices as the independent variables and the dyads as the dependent variables. More sophisticated analyses were not conducted because the goal of the study was to identify differences in mean scores between two independent samples.

RESULTS

Lexical Diversity Indices

Statistical results demonstrate that significant differences exist between the dyads for both indices of lexical diversity. The *t*-tests presented in the first row of Table 2 demonstrate that there were significant differences between the NNS-NS and NNS-NNS dyads for *D*, *M*, and *MTLD*. However, no significant differences were found between the NS-NNS and NNS-NNS dyad for *D*, *M*, or *MTLD* (see the second row of Table 2). Mean lexical diversity values from this analysis (see Table 3) indicate that NNS listeners receive input with statistically equivalent lexical diversity whether it comes from a NS or a NNS. However, when a NNS speaks to a NS, lexical diversity is significantly lower than when a NNS speaks to a NNS.

Table 2. Lexical diversity indices t-test results

Comparisons	D		M		MTLD	
	t value	*p* value	*t* value	*p* value	*t* value	*p* value
NNS-NS to NNS-NNS	2.673	<.010	3.355	<.001	4.394	<.001
NS-NNS to NNS-NNS	1.055	> .050	-1.009	> .050	0.662	> .050

Notes: (*D*); as reported by vocd, Maas (*M*); Measure of Textual, Lexical Diversity (MTLD); non-native speaker (NNS); native speaker (NS)

Table 3. Means (standard deviations) for lexical diversity indices

Dyad	D	M	MTLD
NS-NNS	48.690 (19.724)	265.00 (3.740)	40.532 (15.222)
NNS-NS	41.783 (16.014)	287.00 (4.780)	32.930 (13.054)
NNS-NNS	46.580 (14.333)	270.00 (3.830)	39.464 (12.002)

Notes: (*D*); as reported by vocd, Maas (*M*); Measure of Textual, Lexical Diversity (MTLD); non-native speaker (NNS); native speaker (NS)

Lexical Frequency Indices

Significant differences were found between the dyads for both indices of lexical frequency. The *t*-tests provided in the first row of Table 4 demonstrate that there were significant differences between the NNS-NS and NNS-NNS dyad for both spoken and written indices of lexical frequency. However, no significant differences were found between the NS-NNS and NNS-NNS dyad for either lexical frequency index (see the second row of Table 4). Mean lexical frequency values from this analysis (see Table 5) demonstrate that NNS listeners receive input with lexical items of the same frequency whether it comes from a NS or a NNS. However, when a NNS speaks to a NS, they use words of a lower frequency than when a NNS speaks to a NNS.

DISCUSSION

This study demonstrates that NNS speakers differ in lexical production in terms of both lexical diversity and lexical frequency depending on whether their interlocutor is a NS or a NNS. However, the lexical input that NNS listeners receive appears to be similar with no differences apparent between NNS-NNS and NS-NNS dyads. These findings have important implications for the benefits of ILT, comprehensible input, as well as theories of L2 output.

One important finding provided by this study is that the NNSs modified their output based on the native language of the interlocutor. If the interlocutor is a NS, the NNS uses language with significantly less lexical diversity than if the interlocutor is another NNS. This finding demonstrates that NNSs are more likely to produce a greater range of words when speaking with another NNS than with a NS. Knowing that word production is related to the development of a strengthening lexicon, this result further supports language pedagogy theories that emphasize the use of ILT inside and outside the L2 classroom. Additionally, the study shows that if the interlocutor is a NS, NNSs use significantly less frequent words than if the interlocutor is another NNS. This modification in language production likely indicates that NNSs at the intermediate and advanced levels simplify their speech to make it more comprehensible or understandable to NNSs. Together, the findings

Table 4. Lexical frequency indices t-test results

Comparisons	CELEX Written Frequency		CELEX Spoken Frequency	
	t value	*p* value	*t* value	*p* value
NNS-NS to NNS-NNS	4.267	<.001	3.525	<.001
NS-NNS to NNS-NNS	0.267	> .050	1.510	> .050

Notes: non-native speaker (NNS); native speaker (NS)

Table 5. Mean (standard deviations) for lexical frequency indices

Dyad	CELEX Written Frequency	CELEX Spoken Frequency
NS-NNS	2.059 (0.280)	2.027 (0.371)
NNS-NS	1.927 (0.336)	1.805 (0.479)
NNS-NNS	2.067 (0.238)	1.962 (0.479)

Notes: non-native speaker (NNS); native speaker (NS)

regarding language production in this study characterize the lexical features of NNS-NNS speech as more comprehensible and varied than that produced by NNSs when speaking to NSs. The findings also lend credence to the notion that language output does not simply afford NNSs the opportunity to move from lexical to syntactic processing, but allows NNSs to produce a variety of words at different levels of lexical sophistication.

From an input perspective, the study demonstrates that NNSs receive no specific lexical benefits related to lexical diversity and frequency from interacting with NSs. That is to say, the exposure to language that a NNS receives, whether from a NS or a NNS, is equally comprehensible in terms of breadth of lexical knowledge features. Such a finding goes a long way in supporting the notion that ILT is as beneficial as NS-NNS talk. Specifically, NNSs interacting with other NNSs are just as likely to receive important distributional elements of language such as more frequent words. The frequent words found in NNS input (whether from other NNSs or NSs) likely assist in developing patterns of occurrence that are important in acquiring language specific categories. In addition, the words that a NNS receives as input, whether

from NS or NNS are just as easily decodable (i.e., frequent). From a cohesion perspective, the input a NNS receives, whether from a NS or a NNI, contains similar lexical diversity values and thus similar word overlap. This finding suggests that both NNS and NS input are equally cohesive from a lexical repetition perspective.

Overall, the study illuminates salient features of ILT that appear irrespective of the NNS's first language or proficiency level (Seidlhofer, 2004). Interestingly, the findings from the study do not suggest that NNS-NNS speech is different from NS-NNS speech and, thus, our study does not support the notion that NNSs engage in communication strategies (i.e., lexical choice strategies) that are unique to NNS-NNS speech. While this may not directly confront an important underpinning of ELF theory because the participants in this study were not in a professional setting, it does suggest that NNS-NNS interactions do not significantly differ, at least lexically, from NS-NNS interactions. Such findings raise the possibility that communication strategies between NNSs and NSs in English may be similar in nature and call into question the notion that ELF is a new and separate variety of English.

CONCLUSION

Overall, this study presents strong, new evidence for the strength of ILT. This evidence is considered in light of new theories of input that regard the distributional properties of language. The evidence reported here supports the notion that NNSs receive similar lexical input from both NS and NNS interlocutors. The evidence also demonstrates that NNS output in ILT as compared to NNS-NS talk differs in the frequency of words used and the lexical diversity of those words, with ILT consisting of a greater variety of more frequent words.

This study also raises considerable research questions that our research design does not allow us to address. For instance, while our study supports the strength of ILT in naturalistic settings, an analysis of language collected from instructional settings would be crucial to extend the findings to a classroom environment. It would be especially important to collect data from NNS-NNS dyads where the learners were from the same first language. Such a study would do much to support the strength of ILT in EFL settings. The approaches reported in this paper should also be extended to ELF corpora and studies to assess claims that ELF is a separate variety of English. Additionally, we only consider measures associated with breadth of lexical knowledge. Expanding this approach to include measures of depth of knowledge (measures that examine how well a learner knows a word) could provide additional support for the benefits of ILT. Stronger links between interlanguage input and output and their effects on the frequency of negotiations should also be considered. Lastly, an analysis that includes a NS-NS dyad would provide important indications to the types of modifications that NSs make when partnering with a NNS as compared to another NS.

Explorations of the nature of language that emerges in second language learners will provide a richer and more complete understanding of the strengths of ILT from both an input and an output perspective. This initial study indicates that ILT is as beneficial as NS-NNS talk in terms of exposure to a wide range of words and familiar words. Further studies of these language dyads will benefit both language instruction practices as well as our theoretical understanding of second language acquisition.

ACKNOWLEDGMENT

The research reported here was supported by the Institute of Education Sciences, U.S. Department of Education, through Grant IES R3056020018-02 to the University of Memphis. The opinions expressed are those of the authors and do not represent views of the Institute or the U.S. Department of Education.

REFERENCES

Beneke, J. (1991). Englisch als lingua franca oder als Medium interkultureller Kommunikation. In R. *Grebing* (Ed.), *Grenzenloses Sprachenlernen* (pp. 54-66). Berlin, Germany: Cornelsen.

Bruton, A., & Samuda, V. (1980). Learner and research roles in the treatment of error in group work. *RELC Journal, 11*, 49–63. doi:10.1177/003368828001100204

Carrell, P. L., & Monroe, L. B. (1993). Learning styles and composition. *Modern Language Journal, 77*, 148–162.

Carrol, J. B. (1964). *Language and thought.* New Jersey: Prentice-Hall.

Crossley, S. A., Greenfield, J., & McNamara, D. S. (2008). Assessing text readability using cognitively based indices. *TESOL Quarterly, 42*(3), 475–493.

Crossley, S. A., Salsbury, T., & McNamara, D. S. (2009). Measuring L2 lexical growth using hypernymic relationships. *Language Learning, 59*(2), 307–334. doi:10.1111/j.1467-9922.2009.00508.x

Crossley, S. A., Salsbury, T., & McNamara, D. S. (2010). The development of polysemy and frequency use in English second language speakers. *Language Learning, 60*(3). doi:10.1111/j.1467-9922.2010.00568.x

Crossley, S. A., Salsbury, T., & McNamara, D. S. (2010). The development of semantic relations in second language speakers: A case for latent semantic analysis. *Vigo International Journal of Applied Linguistics, 7*, 55–74.

Crystal, D. (1997). *English as a global language.* Cambridge, UK: Cambridge University Press.

Daller, H., van Hout, R., & Treffers-Daller, J. (2003). Lexical richness in the spontaneous speech of bilinguals. *Applied Linguistics, 24*(2), 197–222. doi:10.1093/applin/24.2.197

Doughty, C., & Pica, T. (1984). *Information gap tasks: do they facilitate second language acquisition?* Paper presented at the 18th Annual TESOL Conference, Houston, March 1984.

Ellis, N. (2002). Frequency effects in language processing. *Studies in Second Language Acquisition, 24*(2), 143–188.

Ellis, N., & Collin, L. (2009). Input and second language acquisition: The roles of frequency, form, function. Introduction to the special issue. *Modern Language Journal, 93*(3), 329–335. doi:10.1111/j.1540-4781.2009.00893.x

Firth, A. (1990). Lingua franca negotiations: Towards an interactional approach. *World Englishes, 9*(3), 69–80. doi:10.1111/j.1467-971X.1990.tb00265.x

Firth, A. (1996). The discursive accomplishment of normality: On conversation analysis and Lingua Franca English. *Journal of Pragmatics, 26*, 237–259. doi:10.1016/0378-2166(96)00014-8

Firth, A. (2009). The lingua franca factor. *Intercultural Pragmatics, 6*(2), 147–170. doi:10.1515/IPRG.2009.009

Flanigan, B. O. (1991). Peer tutoring and second language acquisition in the elementary school. *Applied Linguistics, 12*(2), 141–157. doi:10.1093/applin/12.2.141

Gaies, S. J. (1983). The investigation of language classroom processes. *TESOL Quarterly, 17*(2), 205–217. doi:10.2307/3586650

Gass, S., & Varonis, E. (1985). Negotiation of meaning in nonnative speaker - nonnative speaker conversation. In Gass, S., & Madden, C. (Eds.), *Input and second language acquisition.* Rowley, MA: Newbury House Publishers, Inc.

Gass, S., & Varonis, E. (1989). Incorporating repairs in NNS discourse. In Eisenstein, M. (Ed.), *Variation and second language acquisition* (pp. 71–86). New York, NY: Plenum.

Hatch, E. (1983). *Psycholinguistics: A second language perspective.* Rowley, MA: Newbury House Publishers, Inc.

Herdan, G. (1960). *Type-token mathematics.* Gravenhage, The Netherlands: Mouton.

House, J. (1999). Misunderstanding in intercultural communication: Interactions in English as a lingua franca and the myth of mutual intelligibility. In Gnutzmann, C. (Ed.), *Teaching and learning English as a global language* (pp. 73–89). Tubingen, Germany: Stauffenburg.

House, J. (2009). Introduction: The pragmatics of English as a lingua franca. *Intercultural Pragmatics, 6*(2), 141–145. doi:10.1515/IPRG.2009.008

Jenkins, J. (2000). *The phonology of English as an international language.* Oxford, UK: Oxford University Press.

Laufer, B., & Nation, P. (1995). Vocabulary size and use: Lexical richness in L2 written production. *Applied Linguistics, 16*(3), 307–322. doi:10.1093/applin/16.3.307

Long, M. H. (1980). *Input, interaction and second language acquisition*. University of California at Los Angeles.

Long, M. H. (1983a). Linguistic and conversational adjustments to nonnative speakers. *Studies in Second Language Acquisition, 5,* 177–194. doi:10.1017/S0272263100004848

Long, M. H. (1983b). Native speaker/non-native speaker conversation and the negotiation of comprehensible input. *Applied Linguistics, 4,* 126–141. doi:10.1093/applin/4.2.126

Long, M. H. (1985). Input and second language acquisition theory. In Gass, S. M., & Madden, C. G. (Eds.), *Input in second language acquisition* (pp. 377–393). Rowley, MA: Newbury House.

Long, M. H. (1994). The role of the linguistic environment in second language acquisition. In Ritchie, W. C., & Bhatia, T. K. (Eds.), *Second language acquisition* (*Vol. 2*, pp. 413–468). New York, NY: Academic Press.

Long, M. H., & Porter, P. A. (1985). Group work, interlanguage talk, and second language acquisition. *TESOL Quarterly, 19*(2), 207–228. doi:10.2307/3586827

Maas, H. D. (1972). Zusammenhang zwischen Wortschatzumfang und Länge eines Textes. *Zeitschrift für Literaturwissenschaft und Linguistik, 8,* 73–79.

Mair, C. (2003). *The politics of English as a world language*. New York, NY: Amsterdam.

Malvern, D. D., Richards, B. J., Chipere, N., & Duran, P. (2004). *Lexical diversity and language development: Quantification and assessment*. Houndmills, UK: Palgrave Macmillan. doi:10.1057/9780230511804

McCarthy, P. M., & Jarvis, S. (2007). vocd: A theoretical and empirical evaluation. *Language Testing, 24*(4), 459–488. doi:10.1177/0265532207080767

McCarthy, P. M., & Jarvis, S. (in press). MTLD, vocd-D, and HD-D: A validation study of sophisticated approaches to lexical diversity assessment. *Behavior Research Methods*.

McKay, S. L. (2003). EIL curriculum development. *RELC Journal, 34*(1), 31–47. doi:10.1177/003368820303400103

Meara, P., & Bell, H. (2001). P_Lex: A simple and effective way of describing the lexical characteristics of short L2 texts. *Prospect, 16*(3), 5–19.

Nation, P. (1988). *Word lists*. Victoria, Canada: University of Wellington Press.

Nation, P., & Heatley, A. (1996). *VocabProfile, Word and Range: Programs for processing text*. LALS, Victoria University of Wellington.

Perfetti, C. A. (1985). *Reading ability*. Oxford, UK: Oxford University Press.

Pica, T. (1994). Research on negotiation: What does it reveal about second-language learning conditions, processes, and outcomes? *Language Learning, 44,* 493–527. doi:10.1111/j.1467-1770.1994.tb01115.x

Pickering, L. (2006). Current research on intelligibility in English as a lingua franca. *Annual Review of Applied Linguistics, 26,* 219–233. doi:10.1017/S0267190506000110

Porter, P. A. (1983). *Variations in the conversations of adult learners of English as a function of the proficiency level of the participants*. Ph.D. dissertation Stanford University.

Ransdell, S., & Wengelin, A (2003). Socioeconomic and sociolinguistic predictors of children's L2 and L1 writing quality. Arob@se, *1*(2), 22-29.

Rayner, K., & Pollatsek, A. (1994). *The psychology of reading*. Englewood Cliffs, NJ: Prentice Hall.

Seidlhofer, B. (2004). Research perspectives on teaching English as a lingua franca. *Annual Review of Applied Linguistics, 24,* 209–242. doi:10.1017/S0267190504000145

Smith, L., & Nelson, C. (1985). International intelligibility of English: Directions and resources. *World Englishes, 4,* 333–342. doi:10.1111/j.1467-971X.1985.tb00423.x

Swain, M. (1985). Communicative competence: Some roles of comprehensible input and comprehensible output in its development. In Gass, S., & Madden, C. (Eds.), *Input in second language acquisition* (pp. 235–253). Rowley, MA: Newbury House.

Swain, M. (1995). Three functions of output in second language learning. In Cook, G., & Seidlhofer, B. (Eds.), *Principle and practice in applied linguistics: Studies in honour of H. G. Widdowson* (pp. 125–144). Oxford, UK: Oxford University Press.

Swain, M., & Lampkin, S. (1998). Interaction and second language learning: Two adolescent French immersion students working together. *Modern Language Journal, 82,* 320–337.

Varonis, E., & Gass, S. (1983). *Target language input from non-native speakers.* Paper presented at the 17th Annual TESOL Convention, Toronto, March 1983.

ENDNOTE

[1] Word frequency measures also overlap with depth of knowledge measure in some models of lexical acquisition (e.g. Ellis, 2002). In such models, the repetition of high frequency words strengthens the connections between the word and its meaning. Therefore, word frequency effects can also be explained through connectionist models of lexical acquisition.

Chapter 26
Maximizing ANLP Evaluation:
Harmonizing Flawed Input

Adam M. Renner
The University of Memphis, USA

Philip M. McCarthy
The University of Memphis, USA

Chutima Boonthum-Denecke
Hampton University, USA

Danielle S. McNamara
Arizona State University, USA

ABSTRACT

A continuing problem for ANLP (compared with NLP) is that language tends to be more natural in ANLP than that examined in more controlled natural language processing (NLP) studies. Specifically, ineffective or misleading feedback can result from faulty assessment of misspelled words. This chapter describes the Harmonizer system for addressing the problem of user input irregularities (e.g., typos). The Harmonizer is specifically designed for Intelligence Tutoring Systems (ITSs) that use NLP to provide assessment and feedback based on the typed input of the user. Our approach is to "harmonize" similar words to the same form in the benchmark, rather than correcting them to dictionary entries. This chapter describes the Harmonizer, and evaluates its performance using various computational approaches on unedited input from high school students in the context of an ITS (i.e., iSTART). Our results indicate that various metric approaches to NLP (such as word-overlap cohesion scores) are moderately affected when student errors are filtered by the Harmonizer. Given the prevalence of typing errors in the sample, the study substantiates the need to "clean" typed input in comparable NLP-based learning systems. The Harmonizer provides such ability and is easy to implement with light processing requirements.

DOI: 10.4018/978-1-60960-741-8.ch026

INTRODUCTION

Technologies designed to provide interactive learning environments are a vital and growing aspect of research and development in Applied Natural Language Processing (ANLP). Computerized learning systems, in particular Intelligent Tutoring Systems (ITSs), offer the potential to substantially impact learning through student modeling, adaptive feedback, interactivity, and engaging learning environments. One means of providing adaptive tutoring within ITSs is through conversational dialogue between the computer interface and the student. In order for an ITS to successfully engage the student in meaningful conversational interactions, NLP algorithms can be used to evaluate students' natural language input into the system and direct responses to the student. In such systems, ITSs must rely on statistical and algebraic representations of human language to determine the most appropriate feedback to provide to the student. Successful and appropriate interactions between the student and an ITS are those in which the ITS accurately ascertains what the student *intended*. Such interactions are assumed to enhance both learning and motivation on the part of the student (Koedinger & Anderson, 1997). However, students do not always type or say what they mean. This aspect of natural dialogue renders accurate interpretations challenging because NLP techniques are not always designed to be used in naturalistic applications. As such, one major problem of ANLP within computerized educational programs such as ITSs is that many algorithms' accuracy can be compromised during interactions with real students, particularly less skilled students. As research progresses and more *intelligent* ITSs are developed to include increasingly sophisticated interactivity and adaptability, they must also utilize NLP techniques that are accurate and efficient, and thus applicable to students of all proficiencies.

The focus of this chapter is the optimization of a selection of established NLP techniques that have been applied within ITS environments. The growth of research in computational linguistics has led to major advances in development of NLP indices for evaluating edited, publishable texts (Foltz, Gilliam, & Kendall, 2000; Foltz & Wells, 1999). Although NLP techniques have been well-established for assessing *clean* texts, they have been less prevalent and less well developed for assessing *user-language* (i.e., typed input during interactions with an ITS; McCarthy & McNamara, 20011). This lack of progress is due, at least partially, to characteristics of user-language that complicate its evaluation. Consequently, the application of many NLP techniques (e.g., LSA, Entailer) may be less appropriate for assessing student language, which is often riddled with typographical and grammatical mistakes (McNamara, Boonthum, Levinstein, & Millis, 2007).

BACKGROUND

ITSs often assess user-language via *matching* principles. For instance, user input is compared to a pre-selected benchmark response (e.g., *ideal answer, solution to a problem, misconception, target sentence/text*) by measuring content word overlap or semantic similarity (McNamara et al., 2007). Systems that use this principle include AutoTutor (Graesser et al., 1999), Why2-Atlas (VanLehn et al., 2007), and iSTART (McNamara, Levenstein, & Boonthum, 2004). Although ITSs vary widely in their goals and composition, ultimately their feedback systems rely upon comparing one text against another and evaluating their degree of similarity. Similarity assessments may falter when dealing with user-language, which is usually unedited and abundant with typographical errors and poor grammar. For instance, a word in a target sentence that a user intended to type may not be matched properly if the user misspells the word. In order for traditional NLP tools to be robust to ITS user-language, the evident implication is that the input needs to be "cleaned" prior to assessment. In other words, editing is required.

The most common form of editing text is with spell-checkers, which were first developed in the 1960s along with the advent of the first mainframe computers (Kukich, 1992). Today, spell-check is a ubiquitous feature of word processors, web browsers, email applications, blogs, and social networking websites. The original method of correcting spelling mistakes involves the use of *minimum edit distance* (e.g., Wagner & Fischer, 1974; Levenshtein, 1965; Damerau, 1964). Edit distance refers to the number of character manipulations that are needed to transform a misspelled word into a correct one (i.e., by deleting, adding, transposing, or replacing a character). Thus, the procedure for most applications is to compare each word against the contents of a built-in lexicon, to flag the words not found in that lexicon, and to let the user select from a list of possible corrections that have the smallest edit distances from the original form (see Jurafsky & Martin, 2009). Recently, more sophisticated algorithms have focused on context-sensitive approaches in order to recognize misspelled words that are in the lexicon but do not fit co-occurrence measures (e.g., Golding & Roth, 1999). Additional statistical approaches to spelling correction include the use of word and letter n-gram models, Bayesian methods, POS tagging, and Markov models (Fossati & Di Eugenio, 2008). Although a variety of techniques have been developed, the majority of systems are not yet able to capture the entire range of mistakes that people make. Moreover, we submit that the traditional method of spell-checking is typically not viable to ITSs, as we will discuss further. These challenges continue to warrant further research on new correction techniques for specialized circumstances, in isolation or in combination with existing methods.

MAIN FOCUS OF THE CHAPTER

The practical limitations of implementing conventional correction tools into ITSs indicate a need to develop computationally light algorithms that can automatically proofread *and* make corrections to text prior to processing. In two preceding studies, we demonstrated that user errors pose a greater obstacle to successful learning interactions than is generally recognized (Renner, McCarthy, & McNamara, 2009; Renner, McCarthy, Boonthum, & McNamara, 2009). Because human judgments of user errors are often more accurate than computers (Chodorow & Leacock, 2000), we trained experts from our lab to identify, code, and correct a wide variety of typographical and grammatical errors found in the corpus, in accordance with validated models of grammaticality (e.g., Foster & Vogel, 2004). These exploratory studies showed that the chief component in misevaluations of ITS user-language was misspelled words contained within the benchmark responses (i.e., words that were elsewhere present, visible, and spelled correctly). The solution we propose is rather intuitive and puts a new spin on the traditional minimum edit distance approach. Additionally, the technique is easy to implement, light on processing requirements, and accounts for a large degree of variation of evaluations. The improved assessment of the NLP tools we tested might therefore optimize the similarity evaluation and feedback to the students, ensuring that the feedback algorithms operate as intended.

Issues, Controversies, Problems

Although spell-checking is pervasive in most computer applications, such support may actually be impractical or inappropriate for some ITSs. First, lexicons should be customized to fit the content or curriculum of the system, which may contain atypical words not found in common lexicons (e.g., technical terms). Maintaining these lexicons would be difficult for systems in the field, which are meant to be flexible in that they are intended to allow teachers to add their own texts (e.g., iSTARTSTARTSTART: Jackson, Guess, & McNamara, 2010). Second, standard spell-checkers may fail to detect or correct errors for relatively inexperienced users, such as younger students with poor reading or typing skills, or non-native speaking students (Heift & Rimrott, 2008). Such students produce errors that deviate from correct spellings to a greater number and degree (e.g., Heift & Nicholson, 2001). Therefore, ordinary spell-checkers may be more detrimental than beneficial for less proficient students because the intended word may not have a short edit distance to what was typed. Finally, students interacting with an ITS need to focus on the goal of the curriculum without being distracted by sub-tasks that they encounter along the way (Dalgarno, 1996), implying that corrections should be made *silently* so as not to divert the student's cognitive resources from the intended learning task.

As one would expect, several approaches have already been reported on techniques for correcting errors in ITS user-language. For instance, Why2-Atlas (VanLehn et al., 2002) and CIRCSIM-Tutor (Elmi & Evens, 1998) report considerable success in implementing lexicon-based and context-sensitive spell-checking, respectively. In addition, common spell-checking is not only useful for behind-the-scenes assessment, but is also a key training feature of ITSs that provide writing instruction to students (e.g., Summary Street: Wade-Stein & Kintsch, 2004; StoryStation: Robertson & Wiemer-Hastings, 2003). Nonetheless, a major drawback to these approaches has been that testing is limited to either artificial datasets (Fossati & Di Eugenio, 2008) or with students who are relatively proficient (Why2-Atlas, CIRCSIM). This is not to imply that relatively skilled students (e.g., introductory physics students or first year medical students) do not make many mistakes, but it is probable that there is a different distribution or profile of mistakes for more skilled students

as compared to those of less skilled students. The distinction is important because many ITS interventions have been shown to be of greatest benefit for low domain knowledge and low ability learners who make more of these types of errors (McNamara, O'Reilly, Best, & Ozuru, 2006; VanLehn et al., 2007). Although such techniques are undoubtedly valuable, further work is needed to develop spell-check methods that can generalize to the kinds of mistakes that less skilled students make and are suitable for appended systems.

Because current methods of spell-checking are often not viable to ITSs, many more systems may ignore correction tools altogether. For instance, many matching algorithms employ Latent Semantic Analysis (LSA), which assesses semantic similarity across units of texts (see Landauer, McNamara, Dennis, & Kintsch, 2007). Such indices are generally assumed to produce evaluations that are resistant to individual errors because the score is based on the similarity between the two "bags of words" (Landauer, Laham, Rehder, & Schreiner, 1997). As previously stated however, most NLP indices are trained on large bodies of texts or *corpora* that contain relatively few errors (e.g., Penn Treebank: Marcus, Santorini, & Marcinkiewicz, 1993). Similarity assessments only consider words that occur in the original training corpus. For this reason, LSA necessitates that words be spelled correctly in order to be matched within the LSA space. Consequently, student responses that contain typos may lead to lower values of similarity, which in turn may lead to erroneous or misleading feedback that reflects the misspelling rather than the student's grasp of the main concept (McCarthy et al., 2007). Augmenting this problem is the drawback that students' responses contain many instances of very short answers (Glass, 1997), giving the tool less to evaluate, meaning that errors can be weighted heavily on the final evaluation (Rus, McCarthy, Lintean, McNamara, & Graesser, 2008).

Solutions and Recommendations

The Harmonizer addresses the problem of misspellings not by "correcting" errors but, rather, by *harmonizing* them. That is, instead of using a maintenance-expensive lexicon of correctly spelled words, the Harmonizer simply preprocesses text using an array of matching algorithms (e.g., McCarthy, Cai, & McNamara, 2009). In an ITS environment, for which the Harmonizer was designed, this harmonizing typically takes the form of comparing a generated target sentence to a user input response. Thus, for example, a generated statement from our data was "Paraphrase the following text: *Over two thirds of heat generated by a resting human is created by organs of the thoracic and abdominal cavities and the brain.*" To which, one user input response was *a lot of heat made by a lazy person is made by systems of your stomack and thinking box.*

The Harmonizer functions as an automatic, internal spelling system. It is *automatic* in as much as spelling inconsistencies are addressed without user-intervention (or knowledge). The Harmonizer addresses *internal-spellings* in that it considers only those words that appear within the text that the user is attending to (i.e., it does not turn to a bag of words or external lexicon). Thus, any one word in the focus text is a potential match for any one word that the user inputs. The approach identifies the lowest edit distances between candidate matching words to determine matches. The system is not required to modify any word that does not have a near match in the other half of the sentence pair. The rational here is that matching (i.e., overlap evaluation) is the overarching goal. That is, if there is only one instance of a word, no overlap is possible and no computation is required.

The Harmonizer *harmonizes* textual inconsistencies (as opposed to correcting them). That is, the approach does not take one instance of a word as the *correct* form over the other; whether both are spelled correctly *or incorrectly* they are still matched. As such, the approach will harmonize one version of an incorrectly spelled word to another version of an incorrectly spelled word as readily as an incorrectly spelled word to the correct version. The key is simply to identify *matches* so that computational textual evaluation indices such as The Entailer (se Chapter X) and overlap measures (see Chapter X) can identify that the same word has been used in both sentences.

Most spell-checkers serve two main functions: first, to spot mistakes; and second, to suggest words that may replace the erroneous input. This second step typically involves calculating the minimum edit distance from an erroneous word to a potentially correct word. Although many variations on the minimum edit distance algorithm exist (including the aforementioned MED word position tool), to our knowledge this particular approach has not been applied within the context of an ITS. In other interactive systems such as word processors, minimum edit distance is used to produce a list of candidate words from which the user can choose. However, unlike word processors, an ITS that matches a user's input to a benchmark response (or in our case, a target sentence) can take advantage of making the correction automatically because there is a greatly reduced chance of having more than one candidate. In this sense, the Harmonizer is a contextual application of a method that has traditionally focused on correcting words in isolation.

METHOD

Corpus

To address the issue of computational similarity assessment in user-language, the present study focuses on evaluating the User-Language Paraphrase Corpus (McCarthy & McNamara, 2011: see Chapter X). The corpus comprises 1998 student paraphrases collected from interactions with iSTART, an ITS that provides students with self-explanation and reading strategy instruction (McNamara, Levinstein, & Boonthum, 2004; McNamara et al., 2006; see also Chapter X). The paraphrases were solicited from a total of 743 students (498 biology and 245 physical science students) at a Memphis public high school during the fall semester of 2007 and the spring semester of 2008. The ULPC corpus is unique because, as far as we know, it is the only sizeable, publically available collection of paraphrase data collected from an ITS. Unlike edited paraphrase corpora (e.g., Microsoft Research Paraphrase Corpus: Dolan, Quirk, & Brockett, 2005), the data in the ULPC comprises text that is characteristic of ITS input. Moreover, the students who provided the data were from a typical urban high school and therefore were able to supply a rich supply of diverse and challenging input.

Each paraphrase in the ULPC is evaluated by trained experts along 10 interrelated dimensions (e.g., semantic completeness, lexical similarity, syntactic similarity). In addition, each paraphrase is also evaluated by 10 computational indices (e.g., LSA, the Entailer, Minimum Edit Distance [MED]; for a detailed explanation of these indices, see Chapter X).

Frequency counts of the 1998 attempted paraphrases in the ULPC show that 83% of the student responses contained some form of linguistic error and 52% contained some forms of *spelling* error. Among those spelling errors, 63% were words the student could actually see in the target sentence that was displayed on the screen (i.e., they were *internal misspellings*). Altogether, internal misspellings were present in one-third of the attempted paraphrases. Consequently, we expected that this type of error would significantly influence the accuracy of the computational indices (for a more detailed description of the methodology, see Renner, McCarthy, & McNamara, 2009).

Indices

Latent Semantic Analysis (LSA)

LSA is a widely used statistical technique for assessing semantic similarity (Landauer, McNamara, Dennis, & Kintsch, 2007; Kintch & Kintch, this volume). It is based on occurrences of lexical items within a large corpus of text. LSA calculates a vector cosine value between adjacent pairs of texts to represent their degree of semantic overlap (values typically range from 0 to 1). LSA can measure similarity between sentences, paragraphs, or entire texts, but presently we are concerned with measuring similarity between adjacent sentences. Because this technique is based on a large corpus of well-formed texts and requires correct typographical form, but does not account for grammar and sentence structure, it was anticipated that spelling errors would have a large impact. Results of an exploratory study (Renner, McCarthy, & McNamara, 2009) provided confirmation for this rationale. A difference score was produced from two LSA evaluations: one comparing target text to original response, the other comparing target text to a human-corrected response. Correcting the original responses produced a significant difference in the LSA evaluations with a small effect size for the whole test set ($d = .194$). Results also showed that 35% of variance in the difference of LSA values was accounted for by misspelled words that were in the target text, and the effect size was much larger ($d = .522$) for only those cases that required a spelling correction.

The Entailer

Entailer indices are based on a lexico-syntactic approach to sentence similarity (Rus et al., 2008; Rus, McCarthy, McNamara, & Graesser, 2009). That is, the values generated for the indices are the weighted sum of one lexical and one syntactic component. Entailer indices are used to evaluate the degree to which one text is entailed by another text. Entailer assumes that the second sentence in any sentence pairing (e.g., student paraphrase of a target sentence) is shorter or the same length as the target, because that which is *entailed by a sentence* is likely to contain less information (and therefore, fewer words) than the sentence from which it is derived. However, when attempting a paraphrase (as in the current study) the opposite may be true. That is, the target sentence can be assumed to be an ideal version of a sentence. As such, attempting to rewrite it (especially given those who are asked to perform the task) is likely to bring about a sentence that is longer than the original (McCarthy, Cai, & McNamara, 2009). For this reason, the Entailment includes a *reverse* index. More specifically, the (standard) forward index is assumed to identify entailment; the *reverse* index is assumed to identify paraphrases from less-skilled users (e.g., high school students); and a combination of forward and reverse indices is assumed to assess ideal paraphrases (i.e., Sentence A entails Sentence B to the same degree that Sentence B entails Sentence A: For more details, see Rus, McCarthy, McNamara, & Graesser, 2009). The Entailer incorporates the Charniak probabilistic parser (2000), which is robust because it is trained on a large body of data for which no distinctions are made between the grammatical and the ungrammatical. Therefore, this approach could be expected to be more resistant to ill-formed input. However, an alternate hypothesis is that the range of mistakes in the ULPC would affect the accuracy of the Entailer because the parser component is trained on edited text (i.e., Penn Treebank: Marcus et al., 1993). As such, the Entailer indices could be expected to improve when misspelled target words were corrected. Results from prior research confirmed that differences were significant, again with small effect sizes for the entire test set ($d = .175, .225,$ and $.212$ for reverse, forward, and average entailment, respectively). Misspelled target words accounted for over 45% of variance in the

difference between evaluations of original and corrected paraphrase attempts (Renner, McCarthy, & McNamara, 2009). Effect sizes for the relevant cases (for which a misspelled target word was corrected) were unsurprisingly larger than for the entire test set ($d = .397, .534,$ and $.493$, for reverse, forward, and average entailment, respectively).

Minimal Edit Distances (MED)

MED indices assess *differences* between any two sentences in terms of the words in the sentences and the position of the words in the sentences (McCarthy, Guess, & McNamara, 2009). The MED assessment is a combination of Levenshtein distances (1965) and string theory matching (Dennis, 2007). This approach is useful for evaluating paraphrase and syntactic similarity because sentences with the same words do not necessarily have the same meaning if the position of those words is different. Final MED values fall in a range from 0 to 1, with 0 indicating maximum similarity and 1 indicating maximum difference. Thus, we expected that the values of MED indices would improve because they require words to match in the same order so as to assess their relative location. In other words, although MED is based on character position similarity, the final measure is used for word position similarity. Results of the exploratory analysis indicated that misspelled target words accounted for a maximum of 17% of variance in the difference score, with negligible effect sizes. The weaker result was caused by the human-made corrections encompassing not just spelling but also grammatical corrections (i.e., spacing, agreement, etc.), which likely played a significant role in the word position distancing and confounded the effect of the spelling corrections.

iSTART

iSTART (Interactive Strategy Training for Active Reading and Thinking, see Chapter X) is a web-based ITS that uses animated pedagogical agents to teach self-explanation and reading strategies to high school (grades 9-12) and college students (McNamara et al., 2004; McNamara et al., 2006). The goal of the program is to provide students with instruction and practice to use self-explanation in combination with reading strategies (i.e., comprehension monitoring, paraphrasing, elaboration, and making bridging inferences). After viewing introduction and practice phases of training, the final practice module has students apply the reading strategies by typing their own self-explanations of sentences in science texts. Texts vary on the level of difficulty (i.e., junior high, high school, freshman college) based on national educational standards. In the paraphrasing module, students are instructed to read a paragraph from a larger science text, and then to paraphrase a bolded sentence within that paragraph. For example, the following Target Sentence (TS) is from a science textbook and the student input, or paraphrase (P), is excerpted from the ULPC corpus.

- **TS:** *Over two thirds of heat generated by a resting human is created by organs of the thoracic and abdominal cavities and the brain.*
- **P:** *a lot of heat made by a lazy person is made by systems of your stomack and thinking box.*

The iSTART pedagogical agents instruct the student to self-explain certain sentences from a text, and the student's self-explanation (in this case an attempted paraphrase) is rated by the iSTART system so that the agents can provide feedback. The computational aspect of the system is based on a match between the student's paraphrase and the target sentence, which determines the feedback response. The same algorithm is used for paraphrases as for all other strategies in the iSTART system but with different thresholds. That is, the algorithm is designed to fit not only paraphrases, but the entire range of reading strategies covered in the iSTART curriculum.

The evaluation and feedback process comprises three stages. Initially, if the student's self-explanation contains more metacognitive or *FROZEN statements* (e.g. *I don't know*), the agent will respond to that content first (i.e., the student is asked to try again). Otherwise, that text is filtered from the remaining content of the user's input. Next, if the response has little in common with the target sentence (*i.e., IRRELEVANT*), the student is asked to add relevant information to the response. This procedure provides an important filter for the evaluation of paraphrases because the paraphrase must be suitably different from the target sentence yet still be relevant to it. Appropriateness of length is also assessed at this stage, such that if the self-explanation is *TOO SHORT*, more information is requested from the student. If it is not too short or irrelevant, then similarity to the target sentence is assessed. If the response is *TOO SIMILAR*, the student is asked to revise the response. Lastly, the response manager in the paraphrasing module evaluates self-explanations that are either adequate *PARAPHRASES* or responses that are *BETTER* than mere paraphrases (i.e., contains elaboration), resulting in positive feedback.

Evaluation Feedback Algorithm

The iSTART feedback system integrates word matching and LSA in its feedback algorithm. *Word matching* is a very simple and intuitive way to estimate the nature of a self-explanation. Words are matched against the benchmark in two ways: (1) literal matching – compare character by character, and (2) *Soundex* matching (Christian, 1998). Soundex is a phonological approach to compensate for misspellings by eliminating vowels and mapping similar sounding consonants or groups of consonants (e.g., *b, f, p, v*) to the same Soundex symbol. iSTART uses a simple version of Soundex that acts as a built-in phonetic spell-checker because it can provide a more proximal match for word overlap. However, Soundex can only be expected to overcome some of the spelling errors. According to Christian (1998), there are two fundamental principles of spelling that Soundex ignores. First, some sounds are not spelled with single letters but with letter combinations. For instance, *ch* and *tch* both correspond to the same sound, but are coded differently by Soundex. Second, clusters of consonants that are often not fully pronounced (e.g., *Christmas*) may not be coded appropriately. In this way, Soundex may not provide adequate corrections for some of the atypical vocabulary terms found in the iSTART curriculum. In other words, we expected that iSTART would not be able to compensate for *major* misspellings.

At the end of the matching process, the total matching word count is computed (literal match count plus Soundex match count) for each benchmark. Words that do not match to any of the benchmarks are counted as new words and are weighted against the matched words. LSA is used to provide a measure of semantic overlap between the student's response and the benchmarks and therefore represents the degree of conceptual overlap between the linguistic elements. LSA is often referred to as a "bag of words" approach (e.g., Kanejiya, Kumar, & Prasad, 2003; Wiemer-Hastings, 2000; Landauer, Laham, Rehder, & Schreiner, 1997) because semantic similarity is measured over the whole text while ignoring syntax and morphological variants. For any particular sentence pair, LSA creates a vector based on the bag of words in that sentence. This approach is assumed to render LSA more resistant to individual errors because it assesses the semantic similarity of the *whole* text. Evaluations of the iSTART algorithm can be found in (Jackson et al., 2010; McNamara et al., 2007; see also Chapter X, this volume).

In this study, we define a paraphrase on a sentential level as "the restating of a sentence such that the meaning of both sentences would generally be recognized as lexically and syntactically different while remaining semantically

equal" (McCarthy, Guess, & McNamara, 2009). Admittedly, definitions are debatable in this case, especially as it relates to the computational algorithm that is used to distinguish paraphrases from non-paraphrases. The evaluation algorithm is meant to allow students to use some words from the target text but discourages them from using all of the same words (i.e., it would be evaluated as too similar). The basis for determining a paraphrase is based on a threshold in the feedback system that is ultimately arbitrary. For instance, it can be argued that some paraphrases would retain a greater number of words from the original text than others. It may also be true that no paraphrase ever means exactly the same thing as the target text. However, we caution that the reader not fixate over this choice of measurement because at some point an operational definition must be made, and as such the selection of threshold was beneficial in providing students with training on how to generate paraphrases. Regardless of what is or is not a paraphrase, the overall system evaluation has been validated as comparable to trained human raters (see McNamara, Boothum, et al., 2007).

Procedure

The Harmonizer was trained on 50% of the ULPC (McCarthy & McNamara, this volume). As a result of analyses on the training data, the following major functions of the Harmonizer were developed:

1. Remove from consideration minimum length words and non-content words. Training revealed that only words of certain lengths needed to be considered for matching. That is, shorter words (fewer than 5 characters) were not misspelled, and were more likely to be mismatched if processed. Function words were also removed because overlap assessment is only relevant for content words.

2. Remove from consideration words in the user text (UT) that have a counterpart in

target text (TT). Words that already overlap do not require processing.

3. Remove vowels from remaining words. Like Soundex, vowels are found to be not necessary for matching.

4. Use minimum edit distancing to assess differences between TT and UT. The fewer the changes necessary to match two words, the higher the likelihood of a match.

5. Accept change if specified minimum distances are met and initial letter matches. The initial letter of a word is the least likely to be misspelled, and the most likely indicator of a matching word pair.

Initial evaluations from development and training of the Harmonizer were suggestive of high accuracy and precision. The approach is assumed to be applicable to both performance and competence-based errors (e.g., Veronis, 1988).

To evaluate whether the Harmonizer significantly affected the similarity assessments of the student paraphrases, two sets of analyses were conducted. The first goal was to assess the impact of correcting internal misspellings on three computational measures provided in the ULPC (LSA, Entailer, and MED). Because we are concerned with the effect of correcting misspelled words on computational assessment of paraphrases with errors (and not those that are error-free), cases in which the Harmonizer did not make a correction were filtered from the analyses. Paired-samples t-tests and effect sizes were calculated that compared the old and new values for each index, where the value of each index represents a potentially applicable evaluation of how similar the student's paraphrase attempt is to the target sentence. The second analysis was conducted in order to determine whether the iSTART paraphrase assessment and feedback algorithm was significantly affected by user errors. Both the original and corrected paraphrases were compared to the target sentence by iSTART. The categorical scores were then compared with a Marginal Homogeneity (MH) test, and crosstabs were generated.

RESULTS

Paired t-tests were conducted to compare the differences in the computational indices between the original and corrected versions of the student paraphrases (Table 1). Because of nonnormality and heteroscedasticity in the sample data (except for Entailer values), we also evaluated the results using arcsine-root transformations, which stabilizes the variances and makes the distribution of counts more closely normal when the data are proportional. Given that there were a large number of cases in the test set ($N = 358$), we expected the untransformed analyses to be robust to violating the typical assumptions. As expected, the results were unchanged by the transformations and thus we present only the results for the untransformed data.

As shown in Table 1, comparisons of the original to the corrected *harmonized* paraphrases indicated that the values of the computational indices changed significantly, in accordance with our predictions. For instance, the paired t-test for the LSA values showed a significant effect of the Harmonizer, $t(357) = 19.060$, $p < .001$, Cohen's $d = .577$, with harmonized paraphrases showing higher mean values than the originals. The results demonstrate increased similarity of student paraphrase to the target sentence when the input was filtered through the Harmonizer. These results replicated the results of our previous findings on manual corrections (see Renner, McCarthy, & McNamara, 2009; Renner, McCarthy, Boonthum, & McNamara, 2009). Because the indices indicated greater similarity between target sentence and student paraphrase, we can infer a significant *improvement* in the assessment indices. Moreover, the Harmonizer corrections were more beneficial than the manual corrections for LSA and MED indices, but not for Entailment indices (see Figure

Table 1. T-tests and effect sizes for differences in index value

	Mean (original)	**Mean (harmonizer)**	*t*	*Cohen's d*
LSA	.678 (.186)	.777 (.156)	19.060	0.577
Entailer-Reverse	.398 (.188)	.459 (.198)	17.246	0.316
Entailer-Forward	.497 (.195)	.577 (.203)	16.772	0.402
Entailer-Average	.447 (.183)	.518 (.188)	17.875	0.383
MED-all lemmas	.547 (.216)	.488 (.232)	-10.055	0.263
MED-all stems	.534 (.218)	.484 (.232)	-8.719	0.222
MED-all words	.592 (.224)	.495 (.233)	-12.867	0.424
MED-content lemmas	.450 (.229)	.530 (.212)	-12.390	0.363
MED-content stems	.511 (.217)	.444 (.229)	-10.783	0.300
MED-content words	.593 (.222)	.462 (.232)	-16.000	0.577
MED-all word tags	.415 (.179)	.383 (.190)	-6.826	0.173

Note: for all cases, N=358, p<.001

1). Note that the MED indices decreased in value whereas others increased. As a measure of textual similarity, MED emphasizes differences, and thus the *lower* MED values indicate greater similarity, whereas greater similarity is indicated by the *higher* value of the other measures. It is probable that the gambit of other types of manual corrections that were made (e.g., agreement, punctuation, word substitution, etc.) offset the effects of the spelling corrections, hence causing less change in MED word position similarity assessment for the manual condition. In contrast, harmonizing misspelled words alone would have only one type of effect on word position. Overall, changes in the indices show effect sizes ranging from small to moderately high, with changes in the LSA values displaying the largest effect size. We can thus conclude that misspelled target words can cause changes ranging from small to moderately high for any given similarity assessment. The Harmonizer made changes for at least one error in 74% of the total cases in which a change was made, further demonstrating that even a single misspelling can bear an adverse effect.

To assess the impact of the Harmonizer on iSTART, we assessed iSTART feedback system responses both *with* (Table 2) and *without* (Table

3) Soundex. The results of the Harmonizer-assisted analysis demonstrated a significant change in the iSTART feedback values. Generally, the shift in the categories indicated that the iSTART feedback system made more improved similarity assessments between the paraphrase and target sentence. For example, Table 3 shows that while 164 student paraphrases were initially rated as *better* than a paraphrase (i.e., contained new words/elaboration), 24 changed to just a paraphrase, while 16 of those were found to be *too similar* to the target sentence (i.e., the student only repeated the words). Likewise, 128 of the harmonized paraphrases were classified as *too similar* to the target sentence (and thus not an acceptable paraphrase), whereas only 99 were given that rating originally. A marginal homogeneity (MH) test was conducted to assess whether the two paired categorical measures (*original paraphrase* and *Harmonizer-assisted paraphrase*) differed significantly. Of the six response categories and 358 paraphrases from the test set, 36 (10%) cases changed as a result of the Harmonizer's spelling correction *with* Soundex (MH = 3.810, $p < .001$), compared to 64 (17%) *without* Soundex (MH = 4.351, $p < .001$). These changes amount to about half of the changes produced by manual correc-

Figure 1. Mean index values comparing student paraphrase attempts to a target sentence

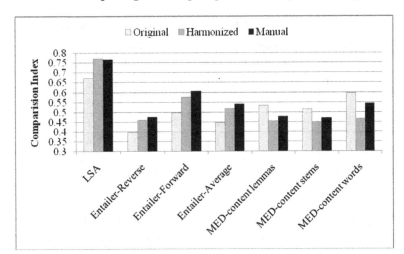

tions. In addition, comparison between the feedback responses of the Harmonizer-assisted evaluations *with* and *without* Soundex was *not* significant, indicating that Soundex makes no significant improvement in evaluation when the Harmonizer is used. This finding suggests that the Harmonizer outperforms Soundex, because the Harmonizer produced changes beyond Soundex when either was used in isolation. Altogether, the crosstab results indicate that although the iSTART feedback algorithm is reasonably robust, feedback was altered for a significant number of cases in which the Harmonizer made a correction. Because most of the changes indicate greater similarity of the harmonized paraphrase with the target sentence than the student's original

attempt, we can infer the Harmonizer assistance has *generally* led to a more accurate evaluation.

The cross-tabulation results reflect a general trend that the feedback categories indicated greater similarity once the paraphrases were corrected. This result indicates that the Harmonizer enables a more exacting evaluation of the student's attempt. Take the following example:

- **TS:** *During vigorous exercise, the heat generated by working muscles can increase total heat production in the body markedly.*
- **P:** *exercising vigorously icrease mucles total heat production markely in the body.* (good).

Table 2. Crosstabulation of iSTART feedback responses to user paraphrases (with soundex)

	iSTART response - harmonized paraphrases				
	Better	**Paraphrase**	**Too Similar**	**Too Short**	**Total**
Better	126	10	4	0	140
Paraphrase	2	59	17	0	78
Too Similar	2	0	107	0	109
Too Short	0	0	1	30	31
Total	130	69	129	30	358

Table 3. Crosstabulation of iSTART feedback responses to user paraphrases (no soundex)

	iSTART response - harmonized paraphrases				
	Better	**Paraphrase**	**Too Similar**	**Too Short**	**Total**
Better	124	24	16	0	164
Paraphrase	1	45	16	0	62
Too Similar	4	0	95	0	99
Too Short	0	0	1	30	31
Irrelevant	2	0	0	0	2
Total	131	69	128	30	358

- **P (harmonized):** *exercising vigorously increase muscles total heat production markedly in the body.* (too similar)

In the above instance, the harmonized corrections enabled the system to more accurately assess the response as *too similar* to the target sentence, whereas originally it assessed it as an acceptable paraphrase *good* because of the "new" words (i.e., misspelled words). The optimized evaluation is seen as even more essential in the following example:

- **TS:** *An increase in temperature of a substance is an indication that it has gained heat energy.*
- **P:** *tempature increses when a substance gains heat enery.* (better)
- **P (harmonized):** *temperature increase when a substance gained heat energy.* (too similar)

In this example, we see that iSTART originally misinterpreted the student's input. The original iSTART response would have evaluated this student's self-explanation as *better* than a mere paraphrase, when in fact the attempt was *too similar* to the target sentence to even be considered acceptable. By correcting the three misspelled words, the system was able to match those words to the target sentence as intended, resulting in

feedback that would have asked the student to revise their response. Thus, the Harmonizer allows the iSTART system to make a more accurate evaluation of paraphrases.

A secondary purpose of this research was to assess the degree to which the iSTART feedback system was predictive of human ratings of paraphrase quality. Analysis of variance (ANOVA) was conducted for each condition (i.e., original or harmonized input), including Paraphrase Quality as the dependent variable and the iSTART score as a fixed factor. We then conducted pairwise comparisons for each condition in order to obtain a more fine-grained analysis. Although the ANOVAs showed that the iSTART feedback system generally *can* differentiate between different values of Paraphrase Quality in both conditions, the pairwise comparisons of iSTART responses to the original paraphrases compared to the harmonized paraphrases showed *non-significant* improvement in iSTART's correspondence with human ratings of Paraphrase Quality. Although this analysis failed to support our hypotheses, the cross-tabulation did indicate a shift towards evaluations of greater similarity between target sentence and paraphrase. Thus, altogether our results suggest that the Harmonizer improves iSTART's assessment of student paraphrases (for more, see Renner, McCarthy, Boonthum, & McNamara, 2009).

FUTURE RESEARCH DIRECTIONS

Future research with the Harmonizer will endeavor to extend its application to word boundary errors. Generally, word boundary errors come in two forms: *joined* and *separated*, as in "musclescan" for "muscles can" and "ane mia" for "anemia" (Lee, Evens, Michael, & Rovick, 1990). The Harmonizer is calibrated to a certain size gap that can be adjusted depending on the desired weighting. For example, the difference between "musclescan" and "muscles can" is three characters in terms of length (i.e., a weighting of 3). Increasing the weighting would have signaled that "muscles" and "musclescan" share the same lexeme (i.e., they are different grammatical forms of the same word). Initial testing of the Harmonizer showed that increasing the weighting produced more errors than corrections, indicating that such adjustments would have been inaccurate. However, it would be possible to adjust the approach so that it would only recognize function words as part of word boundary errors. Thus, the Harmonizer could be fine-tuned to correct additional typographical errors.

The Harmonizer approach may also have applications outside the realm of ITS. The fact that the approach harmonizes (rather than corrects) implies that it can easily be applied with a content word overlap tool (e.g., Coh-Metrix: Graesser, McNamara, Louwerse, & Cai, 2004). For example, the Harmonizer could be applied to help assess cohesion. Moreover, because the approach is not to correct spelling, the correct form of the words is not at issue. Thus, the Harmonizer could be easily applied to many languages because the minimum edit distance technique is language-independent. The only requirement is that the language has an alphabet (or similar symbolization) and separates words by spaces (languages such as Japanese do not).

The practical implication from this study is to reaffirm the notion that ITSs can benefit from simple and inexpensive spell-checking programs. Although the need for such systems is certainly self-evident and well established in the literature (Rus, McCarthy, McNamara, & Graesser, 2008; Fossati & Di Eugenio, 2008; Elmi & Evens, 1998), our results provide further evidence that typos can significantly affect assessment in spite of assumptions that some indices may be robust to typos. In addition, many of the contemporary approaches within ITS settings were tested with artificial datasets or with datasets from more proficient populations. In contrast, the data on which the Harmonizer was developed corresponds to realistic errors made by actual students, addressing ecological validity concerns raised by comparable spell-check systems. Although more proficient populations (e.g., first-year medical students) certainly do make mistakes, the high school population represented in the ULPC may have produced a different distribution of errors compared to more skilled students. The distinction is important because a less skilled population is assumed to make typos more frequently and to a greater extent (i.e., they not only misspell words, they misspell them *badly*).

It is yet to be seen whether more erroneous data would prove problematic for existing correction techniques (e.g., Fossati & Di Eugenio, 2008; Elmi & Evens, 1998). Furthermore, we can only speculate as to how well our approach would compare with other methods. The literature on lexicon-based (Why2-Atlas: VanLehn et al., 2002) and lexicon-context hybrid methods (CIRCSIMCIRCSIMCIRCSIM: Elmi & Evens, 1998) only concern implementation, hence it is not viable to draw a straightforward comparison. Implicitly, our approach would not be as robust as systems that are intended to correct *all* words in the user's input, not just target words. On the other hand, our results are directly compared with Soundex, which is an equivalent system because it is a lightweight approach that requires no lexicon or extensive contextual cues in order to filter the input. As such, our results indicate that the Harmonizer significantly improves assessment beyond Soundex.

CONCLUSION

In this project, we tested the hypothesis that feedback in an ITS could be improved if the Harmonizer algorithm was applied to student paraphrases prior to assessment. Our results lend support to this notion because facilitating the overlap measurement significantly affects similarity indices compared to other types of errors (see Renner, McCarthy, & McNamara, 2009). Although the corrections produced NLP values that were indicative of greater similarity between the target sentence and user paraphrase, confirming our main hypothesis, the improved evaluations generally did not gain better correspondence to human ratings. Thus, although the Harmonizer approach does enhance similarity measures of NLP techniques, the improvements do not produce enough of an impact to make iSTART more comparable to a human tutor. The lack of improved association may be related to the notion that human ratings of paraphrases take on multiple dimensions of writing quality that spelling correction alone does not explain. Another possibility is that the raters themselves had to account for too many aspects when judging overall Paraphrase Quality. This possibility is supported by the indices' higher correlations with less complicated constructs (e.g., Lexical Similarity, Syntactic Similarity). Nonetheless, compared to the existing approach, we contend that the Harmonizer outperforms Soundex. Although the majority of feedback responses remained consistent, the preprocessing of student input yielded significantly improved feedback beyond that of Soundex alone. Thus, results of the final experiment are impressive, given the fact that the Harmonizer produced effects roughly equal to (or better than) manually correcting internal misspellings.

Our goal in this study was to assess the effect of a new autocorrection tool on the ability of an NLP feedback system to accurately evaluate paraphrases in iSTART. Overall, the results of this study demonstrate that when the Harmonizer is used

to filter high school students' user-language, the NLP indices comprising the feedback system can provide more accurate assessment and feedback to users. We can also reasonably deduce that ITSs that are unlike iSTART, not using any system of correction (e.g. AutoTutor: Graesser et al., 1999) will be more affected by internal misspellings. Although the majority of the iSTART evaluations did not change, it is evident that approximately 10-17% of the paraphrases in the test set were misclassified as a result of internal misspellings. Misclassifications can have both positive and negative repercussions. From a motivational standpoint, it may be better to evaluate a paraphrase too highly, so that the feedback generated to the user is more positive and encourages the user to continue. However, from an accuracy standpoint, the system misses something important, because user responses that are too similar (i.e., mere paraphrases) can pass as sufficiently different due to the errors. Thus, mere paraphrases may be misevaluated as more masterful self-explanations during other practice modules. In other words, while it may be motivationally beneficial to give more positive feedback, the effectiveness of the system may be compromised when the student's input does not merit the response. Although iSTART certainly performs well in its evaluations, the Harmonizer was successful in optimizing those evaluations and the subsequent feedback.

Results of this study indicated that traditional computational indices (LSA, the Entailer, MED) were significantly affected by misspelled words. The LSA component of the iSTART feedback system is a benchmark approach, requiring correct spelling to correctly match the input and the target concept in the LSA space. As previously mentioned, one reason that an ITS might not correct for spelling is because the statistical approaches such as LSA are expected to be more resistant to individual misspelled words. Our results suggest that LSA and other similarity indices are significantly affected by internal misspellings despite this assumption. As for the word matching component of the feedback system, the literal match undoubtedly gained from correcting misspelled words, as did the Soundex match. Contemporary computational approaches are trained on edited data sets and applied to ITS under the assumption that there is sufficient text for the approach to supply appropriate feedback. The results of this study suggest that those approaches are inadequate when applied to systems that typically expect short responses, especially when those responses are keyed in by users with relatively poor writing or typing skills. Thus, our results may also apply to other ITSs that use comparable matching techniques or are intended for similar populations. In sum, the results of this study suggest that established computational indices may require filtering prior to assessment of user input, and as a result, ITSs that use those indices can benefit by incorporating computationally lightweight and efficient tools such as the Harmonizer.

REFERENCES

Charniak, E. (2000). A maximum-entropy-inspired parser. In *Proceedings of the First Conference on North American Chapter of the Association for Computational Linguistics* (pp. 132-139). San Francisco, CA: Morgan Kaufmann Publishers.

Chodorow, M., & Leacock, C. (2000). An unsupervised method for detecting grammatical errors. In *Proceedings of the 1st Annual Meeting of the North American Chapter of the Association for Computational Linguistics*, (pp. 140-147).

Christian, P. (1998). Soundex – Can it be improved? *Computers in Genealogy, 6*(5).

Dalgarno, B. (1996). Constructivist computer assisted learning: Theory and techniques. *Making New Connections: Proceedings of ASCILITE '96*, University of Adelaide, (pp. 127-148).

Damerau, F. J. (1964). A technique for computer detection and correction of spelling errors. *Communications of the ACM, 7*(3), 171–176. doi:10.1145/363958.363994

Dennis, S. (2007). Introducing word order in an LSA framework. In Landauer, T., McNamara, D., Dennis, S., & Kintsch, W. (Eds.), *Handbook of latent semantic of analysis* (pp. 449–466). Mahwah, NJ: Lawrence Erlbaum.

Dolan, B., Quirk, C., & Brockett, C. (2005). Unsupervised construction of large paraphrase corpora: Exploiting massively parallel news sources. In *Proceedings of the 20th International Conference on Computational Linguistics* (pp. 350-356). Geneva, Switzerland: Coling.

Elmi, M. A., & Evens, M. (1998). Spelling correction using context. *Proceedings of the 17th International Conference on Computational Linguistics*, (pp. 360-364).

Foltz, P. W., Gilliam, S., & Kendall, S. (2000). Supporting content-based feedback in online writing evaluation with LSA. *Interactive Learning Environments, 8*, 111–129. doi:10.1076/1049-4820(200008)8:2;1-B;FT111

Foltz, P. W., & Wells, A. D. (1999). Automatically deriving readers' knowledge structures from texts. *Behavior Research Methods, Instruments, & Computers, 31*, 208–214. doi:10.3758/BF03207712

Fossati, D., & Di Eugenio, B. (2008). I saw TREE trees in the park: How to correct real-word spelling mistakes. In *Proceedings of the 6th International Conference on Language Resources and Evaluation*, (pp. 896-901).

Foster, J., & Vogel, C. (2004). Parsing ill-formed text using an error grammar. *Artificial Intelligence Review: Special AICS, 2003*(Issue, 21), 269–291. doi:10.1023/B:AIRE.0000036259.68818.1e

Glass, M. (1997). Some phenomena handled by the CIRCSIM-Tutor version 3 input understander. In *Proceedings of the Tenth Florida Artificial Intelligence Research Symposium*, Daytona Beach, FL. Menlo Park, CA: AAAI Press.

Golding, A. R., & Roth, D. (1999). A Winnow based approach to context-sensitive spelling correction. *Machine Learning, 34*, 107–130. doi:10.1023/A:1007545901558

Graesser, A. C., McNamara, D., Louwerse, M., & Cai, Z. (2004). Coh-Metrix: Analysis of text on cohesion and language. *Behavior Research Methods, Instruments, & Computers, 36*, 193–202. doi:10.3758/BF03195564

Graesser, A. C., Wiemer-Hastings, K., Wiemer-Hastings, P., & Kreuz, R. Tutoring Research Group. (1999). Auto Tutor: A simulation of a human tutor. *Journal of Cognitive Systems Research, 1*, 35–51. doi:10.1016/S1389-0417(99)00005-4

Heift, T., & Nicholson, D. (2001). Web delivery of adaptive and interactive language tutoring. *International Journal of Artificial Intelligence in Education, 12*(4), 310–324.

Heift, T., & Rimrott, A. (2008). Learner responses to corrective feedback for spelling errors in CALL. *System, 36*(2), 196–213. doi:10.1016/j.system.2007.09.007

Jackson, G. T., Guess, R. H., & McNamara, D. S. (2010). Assessing cognitively complex strategy use in an untrained domain. *Topics in Cognitive Science, 2*, 127–137. doi:10.1111/j.1756-8765.2009.01068.x

Jurafsky, D., & Martin, J. H. (2009). *Speech and language processing: An introduction to natural language processing, computational linguistics, and speech recognition* (2nd ed.). Upper Saddle River, NJ: Pearson Education.

Kanejiya, D., Kumar, A., & Prasad, S. (2003). Automatic evaluation of students' answers using syntactically-enhanced LSA. In *Proceedings of the Human Language Technology NAACL Workshop on Building Educational Applications Using Natural Language Processing* (vol. 2), (pp. 53-60).

Koedinger, K. R., & Anderson, J. R. (1997). Intelligent tutoring goes to school in the big city. *International Journal of Artificial Intelligence in Education, 8*, 30–43.

Kukich, K. (1992). Techniques for automatically correcting words in text. *ACM Computing Surveys, 24*(4), 377–440. doi:10.1145/146370.146380

Landauer, T. K., Laham, D., Rehder, B., & Schreiner, M. E. (1997). How well can passage meaning be derived without using word order? A comparison of latent semantic analysis and humans. In M. G. Shafto & P. Langley (Eds.), *Proceedings of the 19th Annual Conference of the Cognitive Science Society* (pp. 412-417). Mahwah, NJ: Erlbaum.

Landauer, T. K., McNamara, D. S., Dennis, S., & Kintsch, W. (Eds.). (2007). *Handbook of latent semantic analysis*. Mahwah, NJ: Lawrence Erlbaum.

Lee, Y. H., Evens, M., Michael, J. A., & Rovick, A. A. (1989). Spelling correction for an intelligent tutoring system. *Computing in the 90's: Proceedings of the First Great Lakes Computer Science Conference* (pp. 77-83). Kalamazoo, MI: Springer.

Levenshtein, V. I. (1965). Binary codes capable of correcting deletions, insertions, and reversals. *Soviet Physics, Doklady, 10*, 707–710.

Marcus, M., Santorini, B., & Marcinkiewicz, M. (1993). Building a large annotated corpus of English: The Penn Treebank. *Computational Linguistics, 19*(2), 313–330.

McCarthy, P. M., Cai, Z., & McNamara, D. S. (2009). Computational replication of human assessments of paraphrase. In C. H. Lane & H. W. Guesgen (Eds.), *Proceedings of the 22nd International Florida Artificial Intelligence Research Society Conference* (pp. 266-271). Menlo Park, CA: The AAAI Press.

McCarthy, P. M., Guess, R., & McNamara, D. S. (2009). The components of paraphrase evaluations. *Behavior Research Methods, 41*, 682–690. doi:10.3758/BRM.41.3.682

McCarthy, P. M., & McNamara, D. S. (2011). User language paraphrase corpus. In McCarthy, P. M., & Boonthum-Denecke, C. (Eds.), *Applied natural language processing: Identification, investigation, and resolution* (*Vol. 2*). Hershey, PA: IGI Global. doi:10.4018/978-1-60960-741-8

McCarthy, P. M., Rus, V., Crossley, S. A., Bigham, S. C., Graesser, A. C., & McNamara, D. S. (2007). Assessing entailer with a corpus of natural language. In *Proceedings of the 20th International Florida Artificial Intelligence Research Society Conference*, (pp. 247-252).

McCarthy, P. M., Rus, V., Crossley, S. A., Graesser, A. C., & McNamara, D. S. (2008). Assessing forward-, reverse-, and average-entailment indices on natural language input from the intelligent tutoring system, iSTART. In D. Wilson & G. Sutcliffe (Eds.), *Proceedings of the 21st International Florida Artificial Intelligence Research Society Conference* (pp. 165-170). Menlo Park, CA: The AAAI Press.

McNamara, D. S., Boonthum, C., Levinstein, I. B., & Millis, K. K. (2007). Evaluating self-explanation in iSTART: Comparing word-based and LSA systems. In Landauer, T., McNamara, D. S., Dennis, S., & Kintsch, W. (Eds.), *Handbook of latent semantic analysis* (pp. 227–241). Mahwah, NJ: Lawrence Erlbaum.

McNamara, D. S., Levinstein, I. B., & Boonthum, C. (2004). iSTART: Interactive strategy trainer for active reading and thinking. *Behavior Research Methods, Instruments, & Computers, 36*, 222–233. doi:10.3758/BF03195567

McNamara, D. S., O'Reilly, T., Best, R., & Ozuru, Y. (2006). Improving adolescent students' reading comprehension with iSTART. *Journal of Educational Computing Research, 34*, 147–171. doi:10.2190/1RU5-HDTJ-A5C8-JVWE

Renner, A. M., McCarthy, P. M., Boonthum, C., & McNamara, D. S. (2009). Spelling mistacks and typeos: Can your ITS handle them? *Proceedings of Workshop "Natural Language Processing in Support of Learning" at the 14th International Conference on Artificial Intelligence in Education* (pp. 26-33). Brighton, UK.

Renner, A. M., McCarthy, P. M., & McNamara, D. S. (2009). Computational considerations in correcting user-language in an ITS environment. In C. H. Lane & H. W. Guesgen (Eds.), *Proceedings of the 22nd International Florida Artificial Intelligence Research Society Conference* (pp. 278-283). Menlo Park, CA: The AAAI Press.

Robertson, J., & Wiemer-Hastings, P. (2003). Storystation: An intelligent tutoring system for story writing. In *Supplementary Proceedings of the 11th International Conference on Artificial Intelligence in Education*. Sydney, Australia.

Rus, V., McCarthy, P. M., Lintean, M. C., McNamara, D. S., & Graesser, A. C. (2008). Paraphrase identification with lexico-syntactic graph subsumption. In *Proceedings of the 21st International Florida Artificial Intelligence Research Society Conference*, (pp. 201-206).

Rus, V., McCarthy, P. M., McNamara, D. D., & Graesser, A. C. (2009). Identification of sentence-to-sentence relations using a textual entailer. *Research on Language and Computation, 7*, 1–21. doi:10.1007/s11168-009-9065-y

VanLehn, K., Graesser, A. C., Jackson, G. T., Jordan, P., Olney, A., & Rose, C. P. (2007). When are tutorial dialogues more effective than reading? *Cognitive Science, 31*, 3–62. doi:10.1080/03640210709336984

VanLehn, K., Jordan, P. W., Rosé, C. P., Bhembe, D., Böttner, M., & Gaydos, A. … Srivastava, R. (2002). The architecture of Why2-Atlas: A coach for qualitative physics essay writing. In *Proceedings of the 6th Intelligent Tutoring Systems Conference*, (pp. 158-167). Berlin, Germany: Springer.

Veronis, J. (1988). Morphosyntactic correction in natural language interfaces. In *Proceedings of the 12th International Conference in Computational Linguistics*, (pp. 708-713).

Wade-Stein, D., & Kintsch, E. (2004). Summary street: Interactive computer support for writing. *Cognition and Instruction, 22*, 333–362. doi:10.1207/s1532690xci2203_3

Wagner, R. A., & Fischer, M. J. (1974). The string to string correction problem. *Journal of the Association for Computing Machinery, 21*(1), 168–173.

Wiemer-Hastings, P. (2000). Adding syntactic information to LSA. In *Proceedings of the 22nd Annual Conference of the Cognitive Science Society*, (pp. 988-993). Mawhwah, NJ: Erlbaum.

ADDITIONAL READING

Damerau, F. J. (1964). A technique for computer detection and correction of spelling errors. *Communications of the ACM, 7*(3), 171–176. doi:10.1145/363958.363994

Graesser, A. C., McNamara, D., Louwerse, M., & Cai, Z. (2004). Coh-Metrix: Analysis of text on cohesion and language. *Behavior Research Methods, Instruments, & Computers, 36*, 193–202. doi:10.3758/BF03195564

Jurafsky, D., & Martin, J. H. (2009). *Speech and language processing: An introduction to natural language processing, computational linguistics, and speech recognition* (2nd ed.). Upper Saddle River, NJ: Pearson Education.

Kukich, K. (1992). Techniques for automatically correcting words in text. *ACM Computing Surveys, 24*(4), 377–440. doi:10.1145/146370.146380

Lee, Y. H., Evens, M., Michael, J. A., & Rovick, A. A. (1989). Spelling correction for an intelligent tutoring system. *Computing in the 90's: Proceedings of the First Great Lakes Computer Science Conference* (pp. 77-83). Kalamazoo, Michigan: Springer.

McNamara, D. S., Boonthum, C., Levinstein, I. B., & Millis, K. K. (2007). Evaluating self-explanation in iSTART: Comparing word-based and LSA systems. In Landauer, T., McNamara, D. S., Dennis, S., & Kintsch, W. (Eds.), *Handbook of Latent Semantic Analysis* (pp. 227–241). Mahwah, NJ: Lawrence Erlbaum.

KEY TERMS AND DEFINITIONS

Edit Distance: The number of operations required to transform one string of characters into another.

Feedback: A central component of intelligent tutoring systems; a response to the student's input that provides reinforcement and/or customized instruction based on that input.

Intelligent Tutoring System: A computer system that provides direct customized instruction to students.

Latent Semantic Analysis (LSA): A natural language processing technique for analyzing the semantic relationships between two texts.

Natural Language Processing: Systems or algorithms that convert human language into symbolic representations that can be processed and interpreted by computers.

Paraphrase: the restatement of a text that retains the original meaning but has variation of words and syntax.

Spell Checker: A program that flags misspelled words and/or automatically corrects them.

Chapter 27

Newness and Givenness of Information:
Automated Identification in Written Discourse

Philip M. McCarthy
The University of Memphis, USA

Zhiqiang Cai
The University of Memphis, USA

David Dufty
The Australian Bureau of Statistics, Australia

Danielle S. McNamara
Arizona State University, USA

Christian F. Hempelmann
Purdue University, USA

Arthur C. Graesser
The University of Memphis, USA

ABSTRACT

The identification of new versus given information within a text has been frequently investigated by researchers of language and discourse. Despite theoretical advances, an accurate computational method for assessing the degree to which a text contains new versus given information has not previously been implemented. This study discusses a variety of computational new/given systems and analyzes four typical expository and narrative texts against a widely accepted theory of new/given proposed by Prince (1981). Our findings suggest that a latent semantic analysis (LSA) based measure called span outperforms standard LSA in detecting both new and given information in text. Further, span outperforms standard LSA for distinguishing low versus high cohesion versions of text. Our results suggest that span may be a useful variable in a wide array of discourse analyses.

INTRODUCTION

One of the fundamental questions in discourse processing is how to differentiate new information from given information (Clark & Haviland, 1977; Haviland & Clark, 1974; Kennison &

Gordon, 1997; Poesio & Vieira, 1998; Prince, 1981). Given information matches antecedent information in the text, discourse space, or common ground between speaker and listener (Clark, 1996), whereas new information expands on the body of given information. Differentiating new versus given information applies to written text

DOI: 10.4018/978-1-60960-741-8.ch027

as well as oral conversation. To better understand the relationship between given text and new text, consider the following exchange in a conversation. *Person One* says "I haven't seen much of Jerry lately." *Person Two* replies "Jerry has a new job." In Person Two's reply, "Jerry" has already been introduced into the conversation. That part of Person Two's speech act is given rather than new information because it has already been introduced into the discourse space. In contrast, "has a new job" is new information. For written text, consider the following passage from the online edition of the *Wall Street Journal* (01-05-2008):

Time Warner Inc. Chief Executive Jeff Bewkes pulled the trigger on his first major move to shake up the company, unveiling plans to spin off Time Warner Cable Inc. But investors gave the widely-telegraphed move a lukewarm reception and shifted their attention to the fate of the AOL unit.

In this example, the second sentence refers to several ideas that are mentioned in the previous sentence but also introduces much new information. For example, the sentence refers to "investors," and "lukewarm reception," both new pieces of information. On the other hand, "the widely telegraphed move" clearly refers to the spin-off plans described earlier. This component of the sentence is not *new* because it has already been *given* to the reader. Interestingly, the content words do not overlap between the two constituents. This observation illustrates that the challenge of computing given information is much more complex than merely computing overlap words between an incoming sentence and the prior discourse context.

The importance of the new/given distinction is widely accepted, but there is not a uniform consensus on what counts as new versus given information. Does given information refer only to explicit antecedent information or can it refer to inferences suggested by the text? Does given information include shared knowledge of people in a community (e.g., the president of a country) or is it necessary to introduce given information in the verbal discourse or physical context of a particular spoken conversation? If we attempted to program a computer to compute new versus given information, what sort of algorithms would be adequate? Is it even possible to devise a complete and reliable algorithm? If not, then it will always be necessary for discourse processing researchers to annotate new versus given information by hand.

The present study examines some automated algorithms for computing new versus given information in printed text as well as conversational interaction. Some algorithms will be standard components developed in the field of computational linguistics (Jurafsky & Martin, 2008), whereas others will be statistical algorithms developed in cognitive science. Most notably, the primary statistical algorithm in this study, span, is a variant of Latent Semantic Analysis (LSA, Landauer & Dumais, 1997; Landauer, McNamara, Dennis, & Kintsch, 2007). LSA is the core component of a number of automated essay graders that can evaluate essays as reliably as expert human graders (Burstein, 2003; Landauer, Laham, & Foltz, 2003). LSA has also been used for a variety of other applications, such as information retrieval (Deerwester, Dumais, Furnas, Landauer, & Harshman 1990), automated tutoring systems (Graesser, Lu, et al. 2004; McNamara, Levinstein, & Boonthum, 2004), evaluation of text coherence (Foltz, Kintsch, & Landauer, 1998; Graesser, Jeon, Yang, & Cai, 2007; McNamara, Cai, & Louwerse, 2007), text type identification (McCarthy, Briner, Rus, & McNamara, 2007), and assessments of reading comprehension (Millis et al., 2004).

The LSA technique (see Chapter 9 for more details) requires a corpus analysis in which occurrences of all words in the corpus are recorded in a very large word-by-document matrix. This matrix is then reduced in size using a statistical compression technique called singular value decomposition. The resulting smaller matrix is referred to as the *LSA space*. The similarity of two words (or sentences, paragraphs, or entire texts) is computed by the similarity of their vectors in the LSA space. One virtue of LSA is that it can rate the meaning similarity of two constituents (phrases, sentences, paragraphs) even if they do not share any words, stems, morphemes, or lemmas. Because every word has a similarity score with every other word, these similarity scores can be used to compare the meaning similarity of any two constituents. This approach, of course, has direct relevance to computing new versus given information. A constituent in a sentence is given information to the extent that it matches any antecedent constituent in the text. LSA is one statistical method of computing such matches.

Alternative techniques of similarity matching between input sentences and antecedent information have had considerable success, but there are limitations to many of these approaches. In particular, the brute force LSA matching scheme and keyword matching schemes often result in classification errors when attempting to differentiate new versus given information. To this end, an alternative LSA-based algorithm, as implemented in the computer-based tutoring system, AutoTutor (Graesser, Penumatsa, Ventura, Cai, & Hu, 2007) is suggested. This algorithm estimates the amount of new versus given information in students' problem-solving or question-answering responses. That is, the algorithm estimates to what extent a single utterance or sentence in a tutoring session expresses new information versus information that was already given in the prior discourse context. This variant of LSA is an approach called span (Hu et al., 2003). The span approach, described in more detail below, involves statistically splitting the LSA representation of a constituent into *new* and *given* components. The span algorithm originated in the context of developing the conversational dialogue facilities of AutoTutor, but it can be applied to any class of discourse: monologue, dialogue, print, or oral discourse. In essence, the span algorithm computes the amount of new information in a sentence or utterance with respect to all previous sentences or utterances in the text or conversation.

The aim of this paper is to assess the effectiveness of several automated measures of newness and givenness (including the span technique) in assessing the amount of new information in sentences in printed texts. To conduct such an evaluation, the amount of new and given information in the text needed to be established independently of any automated measure. This evaluation was accomplished by having a Ph.D. student and a postdoctoral research fellow apply theoretical analyses of new/given to a corpus of texts. This paper identifies the theoretical bases for the proposed algorithms, articulates a set of alternative measures of newness/givenness, and presents empirical evaluations of these measures on a corpus of printed texts.

Theoretical Accounts of the New/Given Dimension

Textual constituents can be classified into three partitions: *given*, *partially given*, or *new* (Prince, 1981). To illustrate this distinction, consider the following excerpt from a news article.

1. Bush warns Iran in view of continued uranium suspicions. The American President is concerned about reports on Tehran preparing enrichment processes to produce weapon-grade nuclear material.

In this example, the word *Bush* is new when it is first mentioned, whereas *the American President* is scored as *co-referential* with it. Thus, at this stage of the text, *the American President* is given, regardless of the lexical differences. The compound noun *enrichment processes*, on the other hand, may be inferentially available from *uranium*. If so, it is neither fully new nor unexpected in view of the previous mention of *uranium*. Thus, *enrichment processes* is neither given nor new but considered to be somewhere in between.

There has been much discussion of what information in a text should be classified as given. Halliday (1967, p. 211) defines given information as "recoverable either anaphorically or situationally" from the preceding discourse, whereas new information, conversely, is not recoverable. Chafe (1975, 1987) defines given information more broadly than the immediate discourse context. For him, givenness is "knowledge which the speaker assumes to be in the consciousness of the addressee" (1975, p. 30). In Chafe's initial binary framework of given-new, given information is previously activated, whereas new information is activated only by the current segment of text. Chafe later introduced a distinction between new, given, and a third category, 'quasi-given' (1975, p. 34). This third category is related to the inferential availability of information, and has been a central concept in modern approaches. For example, Clark and Haviland (1977) extended the distinction using Gricean maxims, proposing a *given-new contract* on the inferential processes involved in meaning construction. They argue that a speaker will use speech acts linked by inferences to which the speaker believes the addressee has access.

Terminology

The terms *given* and *new* are often used to refer to *theme* and *rheme* and other similar dichotomies based on a functional sentence perspective. Issues like foregrounding, topicality, or saliency, are usually discussed in terms of theme/rheme, and interact with givenness, and for this reason the terms are often used synonymously. Steedman (2000) and Kruijff-Korbayová and Steedman (2003) provide a more extended discussion of relevant terminology and theoretical distinctions. In this paper, we are primarily interested in the contextual and semantic aspects of the given/new distinction. As a consequence, we define given/new as a separate dichotomy from theme/rheme and topic/comment. Such a distinction is not un-common. Indeed, Postolache, Kruijff-Korbayová, and Kruijff (2005) investigation of automated systems for classifying information structure in terms of "topic" and "focus" similarly argue that their analysis should be distinguished from "new and given." Thus, given-new, topic-focus, and theme-rheme are closely related but the investigation of their precise differentiation and interaction is beyond the scope of this paper.

Automated New/Given Systems

Hiyakumoto, Prevost, and Cassell's (1997) research on automating new/given detection culminated in the BEAT system (Cassell, Vilhjalmsson, & Bickmore 2001). The system of Hiyakumoto and colleagues classifies words as either given, equivalent, or new. This is accomplished by comparing lemmas (i.e., the root form of the words) with previous text, and using *WordNet* (Fellbaum, 1998; Miller, Beckwith, Fellbaum, Gross, & Miller, 1990) to find semantically similar words. Semantically similar words are defined as those close to each other in the WordNet category tree.

The identification of newness has received considerable attention in anaphoric reference research. Strube and Hahn (1999) investigated whether newness/givenness could be used in resolving anaphoric references instead of resolving references on the basis of grammatical relations, as is typically done in centering theory approaches (Grosz, Joshi, & Wienstein, 1995). Strube and Hahn hand-coded noun phrases on the given-new scale of Prince (1981, discussed below), and found substantial improvement over standard centering approaches.

Bunescu (2003) used word associations that were identified in an online search engine to determine the relationships between words and their potential antecedents. This approach has some similarities to the approach proposed in the present paper. Our approach differs in that we use LSA rather than related words derived from search engines. Moreover, we do not simply use the strength of association between pairs of words, but rather the association between the current sentence and all previous sentences in the text.

Vieira and Poesio (2000) used hand-crafted heuristics to identify discourse-new noun phrases. Specifically, they identified discourse-new words from the following properties: (1) restrictive modification (e.g., *the iniquities of the current land-ownership system*); (2) appositive constructions (*e.g., Glenn Cox, the president of Phillips Petroleum Co.*), and (3) copular constructions (e.g., *the man most likely to gain custody of all this is a career politician named David Dinkins*). Vieira and Poesio found only modest improvements to anaphoric resolution based on this method. However, recent developments that use a hybrid approach with machine learning techniques may be more promising (Poesio, Uryupina, Viera, Alexandrov-Kabadjov, & Goulart, 2004).

Prince's (1981) Systematic Taxonomy of New/Given

Prince (1981) developed a systematic taxonomy of given, inferable (or *evoked*), and new information that can be used to hand-code any text for givenness (van Donzel, 1994; Kruijff-Korbayová & Kruijff, 2004; Prince, 1988; Strube, 1998). We used the Prince taxonomy as a standard in our study for three reasons. First, in contrast to other approaches, Prince gives a sound theoretical rationale for the new/given scale based on the work of previous researchers (Chafe 1975, Clark & Haviland 1977, Halliday, 1967). In doing so, she avoids diluting givenness with other focusing and discourse structuring properties of text. Second, Prince provides sample analyses and thus a methodology to apply her model to real text. Third, Prince's taxonomy is a commonly used benchmark in computational linguistics (Strube & Hahn, 1999; Vieira & Poesio, 2000).

One disadvantage of the Prince scheme from our perspective is that her analyses are restricted to noun phrases (NPs). Our intention was to capture the newness of the entire discourse move, including all words, not just noun phrases. Despite this limitation, the Prince scheme provides a way of empirically evaluating the newness of any dialog move. Moreover, the vast majority of the predicate content, over and above the noun-phrases, constitutes new information.

Prince identifies three different sources of givenness of information in a text, all based on what the speaker believes about the hearer's knowledge state. It subsumes discourse familiarity because the speaker assumes that discourse-old items are old for the hearer/reader (for a further distinction, see Prince, 1992). The first source of givenness is *predictability/recoverability*. This type is based on the speaker's assumption that a reader/hearer would predict a particular word in that context. The second source is *saliency*, based on the speaker's assumption "that the hearer has or could appropriately have some particular thing/entity/... in his/her consciousness at the time of hearing the utterance" (1981, p. 228). The third source of givenness is *shared knowledge,* based on the speaker's assumption "that the hearer 'knows,' assumes, or can infer a particular thing (but is not necessarily thinking about it)" (1981, p. 230). On the basis of these three types and their interactions, Prince proposed a taxonomy for NPs that has an ordered list of categories from completely new information to completely given. The categories from new to given are as follows (explanations of each are given below)

1. **Brand New (BN).** The NP is neither previously mentioned in the text, inferable, nor shared knowledge. It is, as described, brand new information.

2. **Brand New Anchored (BNA).** These Brand New NPs are tied to an NP that is given. For example, a sentence from one of the texts

in our corpus is *Adding or taking away heat can change matter*. The NP *taking away heat* is Brand New Anchored because it is brand new, but is anchored to the NP "heat," which occurred previously in the discourse.

3. **Unused (U).** The NP is one that has not yet occurred in the discourse, but is shared, readily available information to members of a culture. For example, *the sun*, *the moon*, and *Barack Obama*, may not have been mentioned before in the text, but can be introduced at any time as familiar points of reference.

4. **Inferable (I).** The NP is not mentioned previously in the text and is not a common landmark referent in a culture, but it can be inferred from explicit ideas in the text. For example, if "lightning" has been mentioned, then "storm" can be inferred.

5. **Containing Inferable (Ic).** This is a second order inferable: an inference that can be made from other inferences. For example, in the text *Moving* (see Appendix), there is the following complex sentence.

   ○ And he knew he would miss his home: the nights in the den watching sports, the barbecue parties in the backyard, his hideout in the attic, and of course, his room.

During rater judgment evaluations, both annotators judged the NPs *the nights in the den watching sports, the barbecue parties in the backyard,* and *his hideout in the attic* as being Ic items. The head of the NP, *the nights in the den watching sports* is *the nights*, is not inferentially available from any item; however, from *his home* we can infer that he would (or could) have *a den*. And from *den* we can infer that he might *spend nights there watching sports*. Inferables are a debatable category, because the inference is based on the comprehender's world knowledge. In the analyses reported in this article, the annotators were not in unsolvable dispute over the items,

fortunately. However, it would be expected that disputes would arise among annotators in some contexts. Further discussions on these issues can be found in previous published reports (van Deemter & Kibble, 2000; Poesio & Vieira, 1998; Poesio et al., 2004).

6. **Evoked item (E).** This is one of the three Prince categories that are clearly *given* information. It is simply an NP that has been previously mentioned in the text. This type is the classic instance of given information.

7. **Situationally Evoked (Es).** The NP is given by virtue of the situation rather than the text. For example, the word *you* in a text is a given because you (the reader) are in fact reading the text and are therefore present.

8. **Stereotypic Assumption (SA).** Given the shared real world knowledge of members of a culture, the NP can be assumed. *Door* would be a stereotypical assumption when *house* is mentioned. Stereotypic assumptions are closer to an entailment (i.e., logical inference), whereas the category of inferable suggests an implicature (see Rus, McCarthy, McNamara, & Graesser, 2008 for a further discussion).

METHOD

Implementation of Prince

Four texts of approximately equal length were selected for the analysis. The texts comprised 195 sentences and were selected from textbooks of low grade levels (see Appendix). There were two narrative texts: Moving (McGraw-Hill Reading – TerraNova Test Preparation and Practice, Teacher's Edition, Grade 3) and Orlando (Addison Wesley Phonics Take-Home Reader, Grade 2). There were two expository texts: The Needs of Plants (McGraw-Hill Science) and Effects of Heat (SRA Real Science). These four texts were selected because they have been extensively analyzed in a project that investigates the impact of text cohesion on comprehension and memory (Best, Floyd, & McNamara, 2008; Ozuru, Best, Floyd, & McNamara, 2006). Scores were calculated for the amount of new information and the amount of given information for each sentence of each text, using each of the new/given measuring techniques under consideration. For example, for the sentence *The root is the part of the plant that grows underground*, the NP *the root* was classed as inferable, whereas *the part of the plant that grows underground* was classed as new.

All NPs in the sample corpus described in this section were hand-scored according to the Prince taxonomy. These raters studied and discussed Prince (1981) and then used the first of the sample texts presented by Prince for training. Category definitions used by the raters were taken *verbatim* from Prince (1981). These ratings were obtained through subjective judgments rather than using a Prince-inspired algorithm such as that used by Strube and Hahn (1999). Inter-rater agreement on our test corpus was computed by Cohen's kappa, which controls for base-rate guessing and the extent to which the distribution of scores is skewed. Following Landis and Kock (1977), the kappa scores varied from "moderate" (.551, Oralndo; .590, Needs of Plants) to "substantial" (.748, Moving; .765, Heat). Differences typically arose because NPs occasionally qualified for more than one category. For example, consider the sentence *When some of his friends came to say good bye, tears flowed down his face*. One rater viewed the NP *tears* as a BN whereas the other viewed it as Ic. Clearly there is a case for either. On the one hand, *tears* had not previously been mentioned (therefore *tears* is brand new); on the other hand, saying *goodbye* is often very sad, and sadness leads to *tears* (so *tears* could be a Containing Inferable).

Some categories in the evaluations had such low counts that analyses using these categories would be problematic. Specifically, because of the low counts for the categories of Unused, Containing Inferables, and Brand New Anchors, these were combined with other categories. Unused NPs were classed as Given, Containing Inferables were classed as Inferable, and Brand New Anchors were classed as Brand New. This conversion of categories resulted in five Prince categories in the final analysis.

Our goal was to evaluate sentences for their newness, as opposed to the newness of individual NPs *per se*. To do this, a Prince newness score was calculated for each sentence in the following way. Any NP that was Brand New (including the converted Brand New Anchors) was scored as 1, whereas all other classifications, including intermediate categories, were scored as 0. The average for each sentence was then computed. Thus, a sentence with two new NPs and one inferable NP would have a score of $(1 + 1 + 0)/3 = .67$ (scores were rounded to 2 decimal places). Conversely a score was also calculated for the Prince givenness of each sentence, such that NPs that are *given* were scored as 1, and all others, including intermediate categories, were scored as 0. It should be noted that givenness and newness need not add up to 1.0 because the intermediate category is not included in either the givenness or newness score.

The taxonomy provided by Prince (1981) allows quantifiable values for givenness to be calculated for any segment size of text. In our case, we adopted the sentence as a unit of analysis.

Measuring Givenness Automatically

Our underlying approach to automated computation of givenness was to use relatively shallow semantic features to predict deep semantic phenomena. A variety of shallow approaches could be applied, but of particular interest to us were techniques that use LSA (described earlier). For purposes of comparison, we tested a variety of simple overlap measures, including lexical overlap and constituent overlap. A more sophisticated method, ontological semantics, was also explored with the long-term objective of possible full-scale implementation in the future.

Similar work has been reported by Nissim (2006). Nissim's study consists of 147 dialogues of conversational English that were extracted from the Switchboard corpus (Godfrey, Holliman, & McDaniel, 1992). NPs from the selected dialogues were identified using syntactically parsed information provided in Carletta, Dingare, Nissim, and Nikitina. (2004). These NPs were in turn annotated by two raters into one of three information status groups: given, mediated, or new information. A decision tree model was then trained to classify the hand-coded NPs into one of the three groups. Nissim selected seven predictor variables, or features, for the model, each of which is provided from the markup of the switchboard corpus. These features include NP length, determiner type, and grammatical role.

The accuracy of the model was impressive for identifying old NPs (F1 = .928); good for identifying mediated NPs (F1 = .766, but note precision of .681); and poor for identifying new NPs (F1 = .320). The F1 index in this paper refers to an overall measure of accuracy that combines both precision and recall; F1 is an index that is routinely adopted in computational linguistics research (Jurafsky & Martin, 2008, p. 455). Nissim reports that grouping the categories of mediated NPs and new NPs together and comparing them to old NPs did not improve the results, although the results as a whole indicated that mediated NPs are more similar to new NPs than they are to old NPs.

While Nissim's work is valuable and interesting, it differs from ours in a number of ways. First, Nissim's research centers on dialogue, whereas ours focuses on written text passages. Second, Nissim's features are theoretically founded in their relation to NPs. Such an approach is reasonable, especially given the Prince (1992) framework. However, the span approach that we assess considers all parts of speech.

LSA-Based Measures

LSA might seem at first glance to be the ideal candidate for evaluating the newness/givenness of a segment of text. However, the concept of newness/givenness is related but distinct from the concept of difference/similarity. A sentence may be highly similar to a single previously occurring sentence, but have little similarity to *all* other previously occurring sentences. If all previous sentences are averaged to compute similarity, the strong overlap with a particular sentence can be diluted or lost. To solve this problem, the *span* method was developed (Hu et al., 2003; Olney & Cai, 2005a; Olney & Cai, 2005b). Two variants of LSA were therefore used to capture newness/givenness, as opposed to mere difference/similarity. To indicate how much of an improvement these span-based measures were over standard LSA, the standard LSA measure was computed using the conventional cosine match between the vector of sentence S and a prior text constituent or sentence.

The first LSA-based measure that we used was the *maximum LSA* value for a sentence when compared with each of the previous sentences (Graesser, Wiemer-Hastings, Wiemer-Hastings, & Kreuz, 1999; Graesser et al., 2007). We refer to this measure as *LSA (max)*. If a sentence is highly similar to a single previous sentence, then it is likely that the information in that sentence has already been presented and, therefore, *given*. If a sentence has an exact match with a previous sentence in the text (and is therefore totally given), the LSA(max) score would be 1. On the other hand, if a sentence is completely different from all previous sentences then its score would be close to 0 against all of them.

Span

Span captures newness in a more sophisticated way than a standard LSA cosine comparison. As discussed earlier, span has been incorporated into an artificial conversational agent, AutoTutor (Hu et al., 2003; Olney & Cai, 2005b), and has been applied to the problem of entailment (Olney & Cai, 2005a). The advantage of the span method is that the information contained in individual sentences is not diluted by aggregating them into a single vector. The span algorithm was developed specifically to detect new information. Span uses an LSA space to compute newness. The matches between an incoming sentence and previous sentences are not simply averaged when using the span technique to compare a sentence to all previous sentences. Instead, a high dimensional space is constructed, specifically a *hyperplane*, out of all previously occurring sentences. The vector for the incoming sentence is then split into two components: a component that lies within or parallel to the hyperplane, and the remainder, which lies perpendicular to the hyperplane. The sentence is compared to all previous sentences simultaneously in this analysis. The components that lie within or parallel with the hyperplane are considered to be given components of the sentence, whereas the components that are perpendicular are considered new components. To calculate the overall newness of the sentence, a proportion score is then taken: Span (new information) = New/(New+Given). Givenness is computed as 1- span (new information).

Other Measures

We wanted to evaluate the effectiveness of span as a measure of newness. To get a more complete picture of its value, we tested several other measures alongside it. For example, we included constituent overlap (as discussed below) and lexical overlap. Each of these measures had scores applied to each sentence as a unit of analysis in all statistical tests of reliability. However, the measures varied with respect to the particular words or constituents *within* the sentence that were involved in the computational algorithm, following the theoretical foundation that motivated

the measure. For example, some of the theories focus on the lexicon (but not syntax), others on noun-phrases, and yet others on other linguistic constituents. The algorithms were aligned with the relevant theoretical specification, but all yielded a single given/new score for each sentence.

Span should be theoretically superior to an LSA index that simply measures overall similarity with the preceding text. As such, we included standard LSA as a comparison index. We also included as a comparison a semantic similarity metric based on Ontological Semantics (Nirenburg & Raskin, 2004), which has been considered as a method for detecting the givenness of information and therefore may be effective either in combination with span or instead of it.

To obtain constituent overlap values, the text was syntactically parsed and then a constituent segmentation program arranged all sentences into constituents. For example, the sentence *the stem is the part that supports the plant* produces the following 10 constituents. The // signals junctures between constituents.

the stem is the part that supports the plant // the stem // is the part that supports the plant // is // the part that supports the plant // the part // that supports the plant // supports the plant // supports // the plant

The given score is the proportion of constituents that have occurred previously in the text. The new score is the proportion of constituents that have not occurred previously in the text. As can be seen from the example above, this is more inclusive than simply considering noun phrases.

Lexical overlap is another simple index of givenness. The given score is the proportion of words in the sentence that occurred previously in the text. The new score is the proportion of words that have not occurred previously in the text. Similarly, for lexical overlap of content words, the given score is the proportion of content words (open class words, such as nouns, main verbs, adjectives) in the sentence that have occurred previously in the text. The new score is the proportion of content words that have not occurred previously in the text.

For lemma overlap of content words, the given score is the proportion of content words in the sentence that have occurred previously in the text or that share the root with a word that has occurred previously (e.g., *housing* and *house*). The new score is the proportion of content words that have not occurred previously in the text and do not share a lemma with a previously occurring word. Similarly, for stem overlap of content words, the given score is the proportion of content words in the sentence that have occurred previously in the text or share a stem with a word that has occurred previously (e.g., *produce* and *production* [which share the same stem of *produc*]). The new score is the proportion of content words that have not occurred previously in the text and do not share a stem with a previously occurring word. All overlap scores were obtained using Coh-Metrix (Graesser, McNamara, Louwerse, & Cai, 2004), an online text analysis tool.

Another approach added a preprocessing step to the analysis of givenness. In this step the meaning of each sentence, in relation to the other sentences, was analyzed semantically and translated into propositional text-meaning representations (TMRs). The purpose of including these propositions is to represent the meaning of text in a conceptually rich and formal manner, with sufficient compositionality to be able to tag meaning-based units of the text rather than syntactic units. *Ontological Semantics* parses a text semantically with the help of a 100,000-entry English lexicon expressing word senses in terms of concepts from the ontology. It evokes all senses of words and matches those sense combinations that meet all ontological properties to disambiguate and represent text meaning automatically (see Nirenburg & Raskin, 2004, for additional details and Hempelmann & Raskin 2008).

The text meanings of the four sample texts were generated in a language-independent interlingua based on a very large ontology of concepts. The component concepts of these propositions were then tagged for newness. One advantage of analyzing newness at the level of units of meaning is to consider an alternative improved gold standard against which the less costly approaches described here can be evaluated in the future. We simplified the givenness hierarchy to a binary distinction of new vs. not-new. That is, if a concept was assumed to be related to a previously mentioned concept in the ontology, then it was scored as *not new*. This permitted us to correlate this method based on ontological semantics and the other measures under investigation. Our definition of coreference was based on Nirenburg and Raskin (2004, pp. 301-305), except that we restricted ourselves to nouns.

Each concept in the resulting text-meaning representation (TMR) was tagged according to the following criteria:

1. All instantiated concepts are candidates.
2. Concepts are new if
   a. they have not been instantiated before;
   b. they are not coreferential with a previously instantiated concept.
3. The implied speech-act events at the root node are not candidates.

Thus, concepts that had previously not been mentioned in the text can be assessed in terms of their inferential availability. Due to limitations in the software, there was no feature for automatically generating TMRs on request: At the time of our study, they had to be hand-crafted by viewing the relevant entries in the lexicon and ontology databases and matching their syntactic and semantic constraints. For this reason, the inclusion of this system is considered exploratory.

RESULTS

Correlations between Discourse Variables

Table 1 presents the full correlation matrix with all of the measures that were scaled. The first correlation of interest is that between Prince newness and Prince givenness ($r = .51$). Intuition suggests that newness and givenness should correlate negatively. However, the intermediate value of NPs in the Prince analysis was neither new nor given, so it does not follow that the two scores are in direct opposition. The positive correlation suggests that new information builds on the old. When something *very new* is to be presented, for example, a considerate writer would scaffold it to something *given*. And conversely, when something *not so new* is to be presented, there is less need for scaffolding. For example, the sentence *This gas is called water vapor* (see Appendix) introduces something very new (*water vapor*) by scaffolding it to something given (*this gas*).

The correlations between the three LSA-based measures suggest that each measure may be capturing different aspects of the text. The two measures introduced in this study, LSA(max) and

span, have significant moderate correlations with standard LSA scores: LSA (max) and LSA ($r = -.68$) and span and LSA ($r = .55$). The negative correlation between LSA (max) and LSA may appear counter-intuitive because both LSA (max) and LSA are essentially measures of overlap. However, recall that LSA (max) finds the highest value of overlap in previously occurring sentences, whereas the standard LSA index used here compares each sentence with the entire previous text. It follows mathematically that LSA (max) values will tend to be high, whereas standard LSA values will tend to decrease as the text develops. The positive correlation between span and standard LSA occurs for the reason already discussed, namely that new information builds on some edifice of given information. As would be theoretically expected, span and LSA (max) have a high negative correlation ($r = -.83$). Span is a strong measure of newness whereas as LSA (max) is a strong measure of givenness. The two measures are expected to be directly oppositional. This result also suggests that span may be capturing newness to a similar degree that LSA (max) captures givenness. Perhaps LSA (max) may be regarded as a pure measure of givenness.

Table 1. Bivariate correlation matrix for all variables

Variable	2	3	4	5	6	7	8	9	10	11
1. Prince NEW	0.51**	0.48**	-0.41**	0.21**	0.39**	0.40**	0.29**	0.27**	0.26**	0.22**
2. Prince GIVEN		0.43**	-0.31**	0.19**	0.29**	0.46**	0.20**	0.17*	0.17*	-0.03
3. Span			-0.83**	0.55**	0.48**	0.41**	0.40**	0.32**	0.33**	0.14
4. LSA (max)				-0.68**	-0.37**	-0.37**	-0.51**	-0.48**	-0.48**	-0.14*
5. Standard LSA					0.11	0.33**	0.74**	0.74**	0.74**	-0.05
6. Constituent overlap						0.13	0.33**	0.20**	0.19**	0.28**
7. Lexical overlap							0.35**	0.27**	0.26**	-0.11
8. Content Overlap								0.87**	0.87**	-0.01
9. Lemma Overlap									1.00**	0.04
10. Stem Overlap										-0.04
11. Ontological semantics										

Note: ** = $p < .001$; * = $p < .01$

When span and LSA(max) are compared, span results were somewhat more robust. Span correlated slightly more highly with Prince newness ($r = .48$) and Prince givenness ($r = .43$) than did LSA (max) with Prince newnness ($r = -.41$) and Prince givenness ($r = -.32$).

The overlap measures provide more explicit and shallow metrics of newness and givenness. Lexical overlap showed the highest correlations; Prince newness was $r = 40$ whereas Prince givenness was $r = .46$. The results for ontological semantics was comparatively weak.

Taken as a whole, the results suggest that span and LSA (max) may be the most useful indices for assessing newness and givenness in text, respectively. In contrast, the results also suggest that standard LSA, ontological semantics, and constituent overlap are considerably weaker indices.

Multiple Regression Analyses with Prince Newness and Givenness as Dependent Variables

The correlation analysis suggested that some variables performed better than others. However, the correlations among the variables varied from small to high, which opens the door to the possibility that particular variables capture underlying aspects of either newness or givenness. Multiple regression analyses were therefore conducted to assess whether span or LSA (max) is a better predictor of newness and givenness, and whether a combination of variables would be advantageous. The dependent variables for the analyses were the hand-coded Prince newness and Prince givenness indices. The independent variables were the computational indices described above. A forced entry regression was selected using SPSS software (Leech, Barrett, & Morgan, 2008). Because span and LSA (max) correlated highly ($r = -.83$), there was a strong collinearity effect and the two variables were assessed separately.

The first multiple regression analysis had Prince newness as the criterion variable and the set of computational variables as predictors, except for LSA(max). The combination of computational variables significantly predicted Prince newness, $F(8,186) = 15.87, p < .001$. Six of the variables significantly predicted Prince newness, whereas constituent overlap and content overlap were not significant. The model explained 38% of the variance, which is considered a strong effect according to Cohen (1988) and comparable to a .62 correlation. Of course, the correlation is not perfect, which could be attributed to an imperfection of the regression equation, the Prince analysis, or both. Tolerance values for most of the variables were low (i.e., less than 1, adjusted $R^2 = .620$, see Leech et al., 2008), meaning that multi-collinearity effects could make it difficult to tease apart the separate contribution of each predictor. The ontological semantics measure had the least amount of multi-collinearity with the other variables. Additionally, the standard LSA value was negative, whereas its correlation value was positive, a result that suggests a suppression effect. A follow-up multiple regression analysis was performed with two predictors, namely span and ontological semantics. Span had the highest bivariate correlation with Prince newness whereas ontological semantics had the least amount of multi-collinearity with the other variables. The combination of these two variables significantly predicted 25% of the variance of Prince newness, $F(2,192) = 33.37, p < .001$, as summarized in Table 2. Span clearly was the most robust predictor among the set of predictors. The other variables, in conjunction with ontological semantics, predicted a smaller percentage of the variance of Prince newness than did span.

The results were not as strong when the LSA (max) measure replaced span as the predictor of Prince newness. The combination of computational variables significantly predicted Prince newness, $F(8,186) = 13.92, p < .001$, explaining 35% of the variance. Six of the variables significantly contributing to the model, with standard LSA and content overlap being non-significant.

Table 2. Multiple regression analysis for the variables of span and ontological semantics predicting Prince newness

·	B	SE	**B**	t	P
Constant	-0.07	0.05		-1.35	0.18
Span	0.68	0.09	0.46	7.37	<0.01
Ontological semantics	0.02	0.01	0.16	2.50	0.01

As with the previous analysis, tolerance values for six of the variables were low (i.e., less than 1, adjusted R^2 = .65), meaning that multi-collinearity effects were once again an issue. Additionally, values for standard LSA, content word overlap, and stem-overlap suggested a suppression effect. A follow-up analysis included ontological semantics and LSA (max) as the predictor variables. The combination of these variables significantly predicted Prince newness, $F(2,192) = 23.13, p < .001$, with both variables significantly contributing to the model. The model explained 19% of the variance, which is lower than the variance explained by span.

Multiple regression analyses are next reported for Prince *givenness* as a criterion variable, following the same procedures as those for Prince newness. Ontological semantics was not included in this analysis as a predictor variable because the bivariate correlation was nonsignificant (r = -0.03). As before, LSA (max) was assessed separately from span because of the high collinearity between these two predictor variables.

The combination of variables significantly predicted Prince givenness, $F(7,187) = 11.875$, $p < .001$, explaining 28% of the variance. Lexical overlap and span were the only two significant predictors in the model. The standard LSA value, content word overlap, and lemma overlap produced reversed signs from their correlation analysis, suggesting a suppression effect. When we replaced span with LSA (max), the analyses did not change.

Taken together, the results suggest that a combination of span and ontological semantics best predicts givenness as well as newness in text. Ontological semantics contribution was significant, but small compared to that of span. LSA (max) values correlated highly with span as well as Prince newness and givenness, but the measure did not provide evidence that it out-performs span. We also note that the computationally less expensive variable of lexical overlap performed well. Indeed, lexical overlap was the only measure other than span or LSA(max) that contributed to Prince givenness. The performance of lexical overlap is not surprising because discourse repetition of a previously mentioned concept is likely to involve the same word or words to describe the concept. Lexical overlap is expected to capture the difference between ideas that have been explicitly mentioned and ideas that have not. In contrast, span is capturing other aspects of the distinction, in particular, the difference between ideas that have been directly inferred and those that have not. Standard LSA values in this analysis did not contribute to either of the final models.

A Second Analysis

The results from our primary study provide encouraging evidence for span's ability to assess newness/givenness in text. The results are also comparable with the research from AutoTutor that used span to analyze new versus given information of students during conversations with the computer system in natural language (Graesser et al., 2007; Olney & Cai, 2005b; van Lehn et al., 2007). This said, the requirement to meticulously hand-code the four texts in the primary study resulted in a corpus of limited size. Therefore, in order to provide greater confidence in the validation of span, we decided to conduct a second analysis.

One simple approach to further validation is to choose a second corpus and perform much the same task. Of course, even if the second corpus is larger and the values produced are similar to an initial analysis, such results are limited in their illumination because the task has just been lengthened rather than broadened. As such, for a second analysis, we chose a task that could assess span for a related but different assessment: *cohesion.*

Cohesion refers to the linking of lexical elements within a text. Cohesion may be marked in many ways, including causally (e.g., *because, so*), temporally, (e.g., *then, after that*), spatially (e.g. *on, under*), or of most interest to us in this study, referentially (i.e., the explicit or implicit repetition of content items). Cohesion has been shown in many studies to facilitate comprehension (Gernsbacher, 1990; Zwaan & Radvansky, 1998), particularly for low-knowledge readers (McNamara et al., 1996; McNamara, 2001) who may have more difficulty identifying the relationship between ideas and events in the text. That is, lower-knowledge readers find inferencing harder because they tend to lack the world knowledge necessary to make meaningful links between textual ideas.

Referential cohesion is of interest to us because conceptually it is similar to given/new (see Clark, 1996). That is, if one content element of a text references another element, then we can argue that one of these elements is given (or at least partially given), and the other is new (or, at least, partially new). As such, if span can be used as an assessment of newness, then span might also be valuable as an assessment of referential cohesion.

Recent studies, such as McNamara et al. (2010), have shown that LSA can assess referential cohesion in text. The finding is informative because it demonstrates that the readability of a text might be computed quickly and accurately. Such measurements facilitate both the designers of materials and teachers; the former can modify text prior to publication and optimize the readability of text; and the latter can better select materials that meet the needs of students. Given that the span approach outperformed standard LSA in our initial study, we hypothesized that it may also be competitive with standard LSA in an assessment of cohesion.

If so, the span approach would not only have been validated as a measure of textual givenness, but would also have provided evidence for its usefulness in wider areas of textual assessment.

To validate span as an assessment of referential cohesion, we used the same corpus as in McNamara et al. (2010). The corpus includes 19 original texts derived from a total of 13 independently published studies. Each of the 19 texts was manipulated by the original researchers so as to feature one low cohesion version and one high cohesion version. As such, there were 38 texts in total. Each study was manipulated differently, with co-reference changes described as *making clearer relations between reference and referent in the text, increasing the number of implicit connections between concepts,* and *increasing the number of links between subtopics and main topics.* Although the studies from which the texts were taken varied as to genre, manipulation methods, and target participants, each was consistent in demonstrating an effect of cohesion. More specifically, the studies collectively indicated that greater levels of cohesion tended to benefit readers.

To compare span to standard LSA, we used [1.0 - span (new)] to compute a givenness span value, consistent with our primary study. Following McNamara et al. (2010), we conducted a repeated measures analysis of variance (ANOVA) on the span givenness values that compared the low cohesion texts ($M = .36$, $SD = .07$) with the high cohesion texts ($M = .39$, $SD = .08$). The results supported our hypothesis that low cohesion texts would have significantly lower givenness values than high cohesion texts, ($F (1, 18) = 19.48$, $p < .001$, $\eta^2p = .52$). These higher values of givenness in the high cohesion version are largely the result of a greater frequency of co-reference (whether explicit as in *chair > chair*, or implicit as in *chair > furniture*). The standard LSA measure yielded similar results, although with a lower proportion of the variance explained (Low-cohesion: $M = .27$, $SD = .13$; High-cohesion: $M = .32$, $SD = .15$; $F (1, 18) = 9.64$, $p = .006$, $\eta^2p = .35$). We argue that this result further validates the span approach by showing that it can be generalized to a related task involving cohesion that is beyond the analysis of given-new in the 4-text sample and beyond the AutoTutor dialogue.

DISCUSSION

The span approach showed high bivariate correlations with both Prince newness and Prince givenness, demonstrating that span captures, at least to some degree, newness/givenness of text as defined by Prince (1981). LSA (max) was highly correlated with span ($r = -.83$) and also significantly correlated with the Prince values, although to a lesser degree. The high negative correlation between span and LSA(max) is due to the fact that LSA(max) robustly increases with increasing givenness, whereas span is the best of the alternative measures for detecting newness.

The other computational measures included in the analysis produced mixed results. Standard LSA performed relatively poorly, producing low correlations with the Prince levels of newness/givenness. Thus, we can argue that LSA, as well as the other computationally simpler unit overlap metrics, were inferior to span at detecting newness/givenness. Lexical overlap, a computationally simple metric, succeeded in detecting explicit givenness, which frequently involves words that actually occurred earlier in the text. This relationship was shown in the analysis of predictors of the Prince givenness variable, which represents purely given information. However, once the vagaries of inference are introduced, more complex constructs are needed, notably span and LSA(max).

The gold standard for assessing newness and givenness was the degree to which any particular noun phrase in text is "new" versus "given." We used a categorical scale from Prince (1981) to define the gold standard and a diverse range of metrics to attempt to capture it. The criterion measure at the center of our analysis was a con-

tinuous scale based on a plausible mapping of Prince's categories of semantic similarity and also the distribution of Prince categories in our corpus of texts. We assumed that the Prince categories can be viewed as points along this continuous scale, but a conceivable alternative is that the continuous scale is merely an approximation to a categorical ordering of states. Our position is that the fundamental property of interest is a psychological dimension that might be described as "density of new information" or novelty and that the Prince categories, span, lexical overlap, and other measures are attempts to quantify this property.

One possible concern with our study was the size of the corpus. The hand-coding of extensive texts did not allow for a very large corpus. Therefore, we further validated the span measure by assessing differences between pairs of texts that manipulated cohesion (high versus low). The high-cohesion texts were manipulated in published studies to include greater redundancy (i.e. given information) and thereby increase cohesion. The results of this analysis showed that the span measure outperformed the standard LSA measure. Thus, we have further supporting evidence that span offers a valuable indicator of the degree of new/given information in texts. Aside from these analyses of texts, there is evidence that span accounts for new versus given information in conversational turns of students who interact with AutoTutor, a computer tutor that helps students learn by holding a dialogue in natural language (Graesser et al., 2007; Olney & Cai, 2005b; VanLehn et al., 2007).

The way span is calculated creates a fundamental limitation in its generality, however. Specifically, it cannot be used for passages of more than a few hundred sentences. Briefly, span works by building a hyperplane out of the vector representations of all previous sentences. It follows mathematically that it cannot represent more sentences than there are dimensions in the LSA space. A typical LSA space has between 100 to

500 dimensions. The space used for this study had 200 dimensions. Therefore, there was an upper limit of 200 sentences on the calculation of span. In fact, this estimate is overly generous, because as the number of previous sentences approaches the limit, the allowable space for new information will become increasingly constrained and will introduce error into the results. This is not a limitation for an application such as AutoTutor, where conversations rarely, if ever, exceed 200 dialog moves. However, it may be a limitation for other applications of span, such as analyses of large textbooks. One suggestion to accommodate this limitation is to apply span to a smaller umbrella, such as paragraphs or sections in textbooks.

There are other possible solutions to this problem for large texts. Researchers could use a moving window of 10 to 50 previous sentences. Givenness would then be calculated in the local context. Such a method has the advantage of a standardized number of vectors as the reference for calculation, and would probably not result in givenness reaching an asymptote at 1. However, this solution raises additional issues to consider. For example, the third sentence of a text is compared to a hyperplane constructed from the two previous sentences, whereas a fourth sentence is compared to three previous sentences. These fluctuations in information size may differentially impact texts in different genres. Paragraphs tend to be short in novels and narratives, particularly when there are conversations between characters. Span metrics should no doubt be influenced by paragraph length and other dimensions of information packaging. Further research is needed to investigate span for different genres and text classifications.

Another solution to the limitation is to use LSA(max) as an estimate of span. LSA (max) showed two empirical advantages over standard LSA as an estimate of givenness. First, LSA(max) had bivariate correlations with both Prince newness and Prince givenness that were of a similar magnitude to span. Second, LSA(max) was highly correlated with span, even though LSA(max) did not predict newness/givenness to the degree that span did. However, LSA(max) has the mathematical advantage of being able to be used for an unlimited number of sentences, even though in practice this would produce combinatorial explosion and eventually asymptote at a givenness value of 1. For some purposes, LSA(max) may be an acceptable substitute for span as a measure of newness/givenness.

The LSA(max) measure provides us with a tool to capture the distance between a sentence and its predecessor that matches it to the highest degree. Researchers can compare the computational analyses to psychological data on bridging sentences and on reinstatement searchers, where old information from distant prior text is reintroduced to the current discourse space (Van Dijk & Kintsch, 1983). There is the psychological question of what distances can be bridged or reinstated.

Now that we have validated a fully automated mechanism for estimating new versus given information, we can explore a large landscape of research questions on language and discourse. This includes information load, information pacing, and other dimensions of information delivery. Is it best to have a constant stream of new information? Or is it best to oscillate back and forth between a high density of new information versus a high redundancy? Does the information management differ across genres or different populations of readers? We will explore these questions for large corpora of texts and conversations in the future.

ACKNOWLEDGMENT

This research was supported by the Institute for Education Sciences (IES R305G020018-02, R305H050169, R305B070349, R305A080589), the National Science Foundation (REC 0106965, REC 0126265, ITR 0325428, REESE 0633918),and the US Department of Defense Counterintelligence Field Activity (H9C104-07-

0014). Any opinions, findings, and conclusions or recommendations expressed in this material are those of the authors and do not necessarily reflect the views of NSF, IES, or DoD.

REFERENCES

Best, R. M., Floyd, R. G., & McNamara, D. S. (2008). Differential competencies contributing to children's comprehension of narrative and expository texts. *Reading Psychology, 29,* 137–164. doi:10.1080/02702710801963951

Bunescu, R. (2003). Associative anaphora resolution: A web-based approach. *Proceedings of the EACL 2003 Workshop on the Computational Treatment of Anaphora* (pp. 47-52). Budapest, Hungary: EACL.

Burstein, J. (2003). The E-rater scoring engine: Automated essay scoring with natural language processing. In Shermis, M. D., & Burstein, J. C. (Eds.), *Automated essay scoring: A cross-disciplinary perspective* (pp. 133–122). Mahwah, NJ: Lawrence Erlbaum Associates, Inc.

Carletta, J., Dingare, S., Nissim, M., & Nikitina, T. (2004). Using the NITE XML toolkit on the switchboard corpus to study syntactic choice: A case study. *Proceedings of the 4th International Conference on Language Resources and Evaluation* (pp. 1019-1022). Lisbon, Portugal: LREC.

Cassell, J., Vilhjálmsson, J., & Bickmore, T. (2001). BEAT: The behavior expression animation toolkit. *Proceedings of ACM SIGGRAPH 2001* (pp.477-486). Los Angeles, CA: ACM Press.

Chafe, W. L. (1975). Givenness, contrastiveness, definiteness, subjects, topics, and point of view. In Li, C. N. (Ed.), *Subject and topic* (pp. 26–55). New York, NY: Academic.

Chafe, W. L. (1987). Cognitive constraints of information flow. In Tomlin, R. S. (Ed.), *Coherence and grounding in discourse* (pp. 21–51). Amsterdam, The Netherlands: John Benjamins.

Clark, H. H. (1996). *Using language.* Cambridge, MA: Cambridge University Press.

Clark, H. H., & Haviland, S. E. (1977). Comprehension and the given-new contrast. In Freedle, R. O. (Ed.), *Discourse production and comprehension* (pp. 1–40). Norwood, NJ: Ablex.

Cohen, J. (1988). *Statistical power analysis for the behavioral sciences* (2nd ed.). Hillsdale, NJ: Erlbaum.

Deerwester, S., Dumais, S. T., Furnas, G. W., Landauer, T. K., & Harshman, R. (1990). Indexing by latent semantic analysis. *Journal of the American Society for Information Science American Society for Information Science, 41,* 391–407. doi:10.1002/(SICI)1097-4571(199009)41:6<391::AID-ASI1>3.0.CO;2-9

Fellbaum, C. (1998). Towards a representation of idioms in WordNet. *Proceedings of the COLING/ACL Workshop on Usage of WordNet in Natural Language Processing Systems* (pp. 52-57). Montréal, Canada: University of Montréal.

Foltz, P. W., Kintsch, W., & Landauer, T. K. (1998). The measurement of textual coherence with latent semantic analysis. *Discourse Processes, 25,* 285–307. doi:10.1080/01638539809545029

Gernsbacher, M. A. (1990). *Language comprehension as structure building.* Hillsdale, NJ: Lawrence Erlbaum.

Godfrey, J., Holliman, E., & McDaniel, J. (1992). SWITCHBOARD: Telephone speech corpus for research and development. *Proceedings of the IEEE Conference on Acoustics, Speech, and Signal Processing* (pp. 517-520). San Francisco, CA: IEEE.

Graesser, A. C., Jeon, M., Yang, Y., & Cai, Z. (2007). Discourse cohesion in text and tutorial dialogue. *Information Design Journal, 15,* 199–213.

Graesser, A. C., Lu, S., Jackson, G. T., Mitchell, H., Ventura, M., Olney, A., & Louwerse, M. M. (2004). AutoTutor: A tutor with dialogue in natural language. *Behavior Research Methods, Instruments, & Computers, 36*, 180–193. doi:10.3758/BF03195563

Graesser, A. C., McNamara, D. S., Louwerse, M. M., & Cai, Z. (2004). Coh-metrix: Analysis of text on cohesion and language. *Behavior Research Methods, Instruments, & Computers, 36*, 193–202. doi:10.3758/BF03195564

Graesser, A. C., Penumatsa, P., Ventura, M., Cai, Z., & Hu, X. (2007). Using LSA in AutoTutor: Learning through mixed initiative dialogue in natural language. In Landauer, T., McNamara, D. S., Dennis, S., & Kintsch, W. (Eds.), *Handbook of latent semantic analysis* (pp. 243–262). Mahwah, NJ: Lawrence Erlbaum Associates, Inc.

Graesser, A. C., Wiemer-Hastings, K., Wiemer-Hastings, P., & Kreuz, R. (1999). AutoTutor: A simulation of a human tutor. *Journal of Cognitive Systems Research, 1*, 35–51. doi:10.1016/S1389-0417(99)00005-4

Grosz, B. J., Joshi, A. K., & Weinstein, S. (1995). Centering: A framework for modeling the local coherence of discourse. *Computational Linguistics, 21*, 203–225.

Halliday, M. A. K. (1967). Notes on transitivity and theme in English. *Journal of Linguistics, 3*, 199–244. doi:10.1017/S0022226700016613

Haviland, S. E., & Clark, H. H. (1974). What's new? Acquiring new information as a process in comprehension. *Journal of Verbal Learning and Verbal Behavior, 13*, 512–521. doi:10.1016/S0022-5371(74)80003-4

Hempelmann, C. F., & Raskin, V. (2008). Semantic search: Content vs. formalism. *Proceedings of LangTech 2008*. Rome, Italy: Fondazione Ugo Bordoni.

Hiyakumoto, L., Prevost, S., & Cassell, J. (1997). Semantic and discourse information for text-to-speech intonation. *Proceedings of the 35th Annual Meeting of the ACL Workshop on Concept-to-Speech Generation Systems*. Madrid, Spain: ACL Press.

Hu, X., Cai, Z., Louwerse, M., Olney, A., Penumatsa, P., & Graesser, A. C., & the Tutoring Research Group. (2003). A revised algorithm for latent semantic analysis. In G. Gottlob & T. Walsh (Eds.), *Proceedings of the 2003 International Joint Conference on Artificial Intelligence* (pp. 1489–1491). San Francisco, CA: Morgan Kaufmann.

Jurafsky, D., & Martin, J. H. (2008). *Speech and language processing: An introduction to natural language processing, computational linguistics, and speech recognition*. Upper Saddle River, NJ: Pearson Prentice-Hall.

Kennison, S. M., & Gordon, P. C. (1997). Comprehending referential expressions during reading: Evidence from eye tracking. *Discourse Processes, 24*, 229–252. doi:10.1080/01638539709545014

Kruijff-Korbayová, I., & Kruijff, G. J. M. (2004). Discourse-level annotation for investigating information structure. *Proceedings of the ACL Workshop on Discourse Annotation* (pp. 41-48). Barcelona, Spain: Association for Computational Linguistics.

Kruijff-Korbayová, I., & Steedman, M. (2003). Discourse and information structure. *Journal of Logic. Language and Information: Special Issue on Discourse and Information Structure, 12*, 249–259.

Landauer, T., & Dumais, S. (1997). A solution to Plato's problem: The latent semantic analysis theory of acquisition, induction, and representation of knowledge. *Psychological Review, 104*, 211–240. doi:10.1037/0033-295X.104.2.211

Landauer, T., McNamara, D. S., Dennis, S., & Kintsch, W. (2007). *Handbook of latent semantic analysis*. Mahwah, NJ: Lawrence Erlbaum Associates, Inc.

Landauer, T. K., Laham, D., & Foltz, P. W. (2003). Automatic scoring and automation of essays with the intelligent essay assessor. In Shermis, M. D., & Burstein, J. (Eds.), *Automated essay scoring: A cross-disciplinary perspective* (pp. 87–112). Mahwah, NJ: Lawrence Erlbaum Associates, Inc.

Landis, J. R., & Koch, G. G. (1977). The measurement of observer agreement for categorical data. *Biometrics, 33*, 159–174. doi:10.2307/2529310

Leech, N. L., Barrett, K. C., & Morgan, G. A. (2008). *SPSS for intermediate statistics: Use and interpretation*. New York, NY: Lawrence Erlbaum Associates, Inc.

McCarthy, P. M., Briner, S. W., Rus, V., & McNamara, D. S. (2007). Textual signatures: Identifying text-types using latent semantic analysis to measure the cohesion of text structures. In Kao, A., & Poteet, S. (Eds.), *Natural language processing and text mining* (pp. 107–122). London, UK: Springer-Verlag. doi:10.1007/978-1-84628-754-1_7

McNamara, D. S. (2001). Reading both high-coherence and low-coherence texts: Effects of text sequence and prior knowledge. *Canadian Journal of Experimental Psychology, 55*, 51–62. doi:10.1037/h0087352

McNamara, D. S., Cai, Z., & Louwerse, M. M. (2007). Optimizing LSA measures of cohesion. In Landauer, T., McNamara, D. S., Dennis, S., & Kintsch, W. (Eds.), *Handbook of latent semantic analysis* (pp. 379–400). Mahwah, NJ: Erlbaum.

McNamara, D. S., Kintsch, E., Songer, N. B., & Kintsch, W. (1996). Are good texts always better? Interactions of text coherence, background knowledge, and levels of understanding in learning from text. *Cognition and Instruction, 14*, 1–43. doi:10.1207/s1532690xci1401_1

McNamara, D. S., Levinstein, I. B., & Boonthum, C. (2004). iSTART: Interactive strategy trainer for active reading and thinking. *Behavior Research Methods, Instruments, & Computers, 36*, 222–233. doi:10.3758/BF03195567

McNamara, D. S., Louwerse, M. M., McCarthy, P. M., & Graesser, A. C. (2010). Coh-Metrix: Capturing linguistic features of cohesion. *Discourse Processes, 47*, 292–330. doi:10.1080/01638530902959943

Miller, G. A., Beckwith, R., Fellbaum, C., Gross, D., & Miller, K. J. (1990). Introduction to WordNet: An on-line lexical database. *International Journal of Lexicography, 3*, 235–244. doi:10.1093/ijl/3.4.235

Millis, K., Kim, H. J., Todaro, S., Magliano, J. P., Wiemer-Hastings, K., & McNamara, D. S. (2004). Identifying reading strategies using latent semantic analysis: Comparing semantic benchmarks. *Behavior Research Methods, Instruments, & Computers, 36*, 213–221. doi:10.3758/BF03195566

Nirenburg, S., & Raskin, V. (2004). *Ontological semantics*. Cambridge, MA: MIT Press.

Nissim, M. (2006). Learning information status of discourse entities. *Proceedings of the 2006 Conference on Empirical Methods in Natural Language Processing* (pp. 94-102). Sydney, Australia: Association for Computational Linguistics.

Olney, A., & Cai, Z. (2005a). An orthonormal basis for entailment. *Proceedings of the 18th International Florida Artificial Intelligence Research Society Conference* (pp. 554-559). Menlo Park, CA: AAAI Press.

Olney, A., & Cai, Z. (2005b). An orthonormal basis for topic segmentation in tutorial dialogue. *Proceedings of the Human Language Technology Conference and Conference on Empirical Methods in Natural Language Processing* (pp. 971-978). Philadelphia, PA: Association for Computational Linguistics.

Ozuru, Y., Best, R., Floyd, R. G., & McNamara, D. S. (2006). Children's text comprehension: Effects of genre, knowledge, and text cohesion. In S. A. Barab, K. E. Hay, & D. T. Hickey (Eds.), *Proceedings of the 7th International Conference of the Learning Sciences* (pp. 37-42). Mahwah, NJ: Erlbaum.

Poesio, M., Uryupina, O., Viera, R., Alexandrov-Kabadjov, M., & Goulart, R. (2004). Discourse-new detectors for definite description resolution: A survey and a preliminary proposal. *Proceedings of the ACL Workshop on Reference Resolution.* Barcelona, Spain: ACL Press.

Poesio, M., & Vieira, R. (1998). A corpus-based investigation of definite description use. *Computational Linguistics, 24*, 183–216.

Postolache, O., Kruijff-Korbayovà, I., & Kruijff, G. (2005). Data-driven approaches for information structure identification. *Proceedings of HLT/EMNLP* (pp. 9-16). Vancouver, Canada.

Prince, E. (1981). Towards a taxonomy of given-new information. In Cole, P. (Ed.), *Radical pragmatics* (pp. 223–255). New York, NY: Academic.

Prince, E. (1988). Discourse analysis: A part of the study of linguistic competence. In Newmeyer, F. (Ed.), *Linguistics: The Cambridge survey* (pp. 164–182). Cambridge, MA: Cambridge University Press.

Prince, E. (1992). The ZPG letter: Subjects, definiteness, and information-status. In Thompson, S., & Mann, W. (Eds.), *Discourse description: Diverse analyses of a fundraising text* (pp. 295–325). Amsterdam, The Netherlands: John Benjamins.

Rus, V., McCarthy, P. M., McNamara, D. S., & Graesser, A. C. (2008). A study of textual entailment. *International Journal of Artificial Intelligence Tools, 17*, 659–685. doi:10.1142/S0218213008004096

Steedman, M. (2000). Information structure and the syntax-phonology interface. *Linguistic Inquiry, 34*, 649–689. doi:10.1162/002438900554505

Strube, M. (1998). Never look back: An alternative to centering. In C. Boitet & P. Whitelock (Eds.), *Proceedings of the 17ᵗʰ International Conference on Computational Linguistics* (pp. 1251-1257). Morristown, NJ: Association for Computational Linguistics.

Strube, M., & Hahn, U. (1999). Functional centering: Grounding referential coherence in information structure. *Computational Linguistics, 25*, 309–344.

van Deemter, K., & Kibble, R. (2000). On coreferring: Coreference in MUC and related annotation schemes. *Computational Linguistics, 26*, 629–637. doi:10.1162/089120100750105966

van Dijk, T. A., & Kintsch, W. (1983). *Strategies of discourse comprehension.* New York, NY: Academic Press.

van Donzel, M. E. (1994). How to specify focus without using acoustic features. *Proceedings of the Institute of Phonetic Sciences* (pp. 1-17). Amsterdam, The Netherlands: University of Amsterdam.

vanLehn, K., Graesser, A. C., Jackson, G. T., Jordan, P., Olney, A., & Rose, C. P. (2007). When are tutorial dialogues more effective than reading? *Cognitive Science, 31*, 3–62. doi:10.1080/03640210709336984

Vieira, R., & Poesio, M. (2000). An empirically based system for processing definite descriptions. *Computational Linguistics, 26*, 539–593. doi:10.1162/089120100750105948

Zwaan, R. A., & Radvansky, G. A. (1998). Situation models in language comprehension and memory. *Psychological Bulletin, 123*, 162–185. doi:10.1037/0033-2909.123.2.162

APPENDIX: SAMPLE TEXT

Effects of Heat

- Heat can move from one object or place to another.
- Heat moves from warm objects to cooler ones.
- You can warm your hands by holding a cup of warm soup.
- Heat moves from the soup through the cup to your hands.
- You can feel warm air rising above the cup.
- Heat moves through some materials more easily than others.
- Heat moves easily through conductors.
- Most metals are good conductors.
- Metal pots are used for cooking.
- Heat from the stove quickly moves through the metal.
- The heat warms the food.
- Other materials are not good conductors.
- But they may be good insulators.
- Insulators help keep heat from passing through.
- Most plastics are good insulators.
- So are clothes you wear, like sweaters and coats.
- You wear these clothes to keep warm when it is cold outside.
- Adding or taking away heat can change matter.
- Matter is something that takes up space.
- Matter can change from one state, or form, to another.
- An ice cube is solid water.
- Solid is one state of matter.
- Heat can melt an ice cube.
- The ice cube changes into liquid water.
- Liquid is another state of matter.
- When heat is taken away, the water can change back.
- Liquid water turns into solid water.
- Heat can make liquids boil.
- Water boils when it is heated.
- When the water boils, it turns into a gas.
- This gas is called water vapor.
- Solid, liquid and gas are three states of matter.
- Heat from the sun causes liquid water to turn into water vapor.
- Water vapor mixes with the air.
- This is called evaporation.
- Sometimes heat causes changes that cannot be changed back.
- Bread can change into toast when you heat it.
- Eggs change when you cook them in a pan.
- You cannot untoast a piece of toast.
- You cannot uncook an egg.

- Heat can warm air, too.
- A balloon is filled with air.
- When heat warms the air in the balloon, the air changes.
- The air takes up more space.
- Heat from the sun warms objects all around you, like rocks, streets, and buildings.
- These objects then warm the air.
- Warm air is lighter than cold air.
- Warm air goes up.
- Cold air takes its place.
- You can tell how hot or cold the air is.
- Temperature is a measure of how hot something is.
- People use thermometers to measure the temperature.

Chapter 28
Semantic Methods for Textual Entailment

Andrew J. Neel
The University of Memphis, USA

Max H. Garzon
The University of Memphis, USA

ABSTRACT

The problem of recognizing textual entailment (RTE) has been recently addressed using syntactic and lexical models with some success. Here, a new approach is taken to apply world knowledge in much the same way as humans, but captured in large semantic graphs such as WordNet. We show that semantic graphs made of synsets and selected relationships between them enable fairly simple methods that provide very competitive performance. First, assuming a solution to word sense disambiguation, we report on the performance of these methods in four basic areas: information retrieval (IR), information extraction (IE), question answering (QA), and multi-document summarization (SUM), as described using benchmark datasets designed to test the entailment problem in the 2006 Recognizing Textual Entailment (RTE-2) challenge. We then show how the same methods yield a solution to word sense disambiguation, which combined with the previous solution, yields a fully automated solution with about the same performance. We then evaluate this solution on two subsequent RTE Challenge datasets. Finally, we evaluate the contribution of WordNet to provide world knowledge. We conclude that the protocol itself works well at solving entailment given a quality source of world knowledge, but WordNet is not able to provide enough information to resolve entailment with this inclusion protocol.

INTRODUCTION

The task of recognizing textual entailment (RTE) as defined by (Dagan et al. 2005; Bar-Haim et al. 2006) is the task of determining whether the *meaning* of one *text* (the *hypothesis*) is entailed (or inferred) from another text (simply, the *text*) to humans. It differs from logical inferences because world knowledge is required to assess the hypothesis. While typical instances of RTE are easy for humans, it is conversely difficult for computers in most instances.

DOI: 10.4018/978-1-60960-741-8.ch028

The significance of finding a quality solution is high. Automatic solutions would have substantial impact on computers system's capability key textual entailment recognition tasks. Consider the task of automatic tutoring (Graesser et al. 2000; Graesser, Hu, and McNamara 2005), where a student provides answers to open ended questions asked by a tutoring system in natural language. Here, student answers must be evaluated against a number of known quality answers. Similarly, consider writing a program for a computer to automatically summarize textual knowledge of several documents (called the multi-document summarization problem). Here, it may be desirable to remove sentences from the text which could be inferred by another sentence. A third example is information retrieval (IR). Here, the goal is to find documents which are semantically similar in response to a query. Thus, the task for RTE is to evaluate the semantic closeness or relatedness of two documents and only provide a match when documents entail the query.

One related challenge to RTE is *Word Sense Disambiguation* (WSD). WSD literally applies knowledge of the world events to match words and phrases to meanings, herein called *synsets*. Similar to RTE, WSD is performed easily by humans but very poorly by computers. Thus, WSD also requires a protocol for disambiguating words and phrases into synsets *automatically* (i.e., without human assistance).

Humans implicitly disambiguate words by matching the word *in context* to *meanings* and *experiences* stored in memory. With humans, context and experience serve as world knowledge. Consider the following entailment instance: the text *"John Smith received a belt."* entails the hypothesis *"John Smith received a strip of leather to fasten around his waist."* In this example, "belt" may have the meaning of "a strip of leather to fasten around the waste," "a strip of leather with machine-gun ammo attached" or "a strong punch." The human may remember the full set of *potential meanings* but experience will quickly identify "a

strip of leather to fasten around the waste" as the specific and proper meaning. Resolving word/phrases to a list of synsets (i.e., a concept or meaning) is relatively easy. However, no automated solution has captured human experience sufficiently well to choose the appropriate meaning. Therefore, the crux of this issue is finding a representation of human world knowledge and experience in a model that will perform on computers the same function with a success comparable to humans.

Humans are very good at solving both entailment *and* WSD because we seem to be able to relate words and lexicon into what is meant by the speaker in the context of prior knowledge of the real world. This paper presents a solution for entailment that can be implemented easily by digital computer systems. Arguably, the closest digital equivalent to a human's experience with word relationships is WordNet (Kaplan and Shubert, 2001; Clark et Al., 2005). Here, the fundamental construct is not a word but an abstract semantic concept., called synset (synonymous set). Each synset may be expressed by different words, and, conversely, the same word may represent different synsets. As the name implies, the concepts of WordNet are inter-connected to provide a network relationships between synsets.

In this paper, we use semantic models of world knowledge as exemplified by WordNet to show that semantic graphs made of synsets and selected relationships between them enable fairly simple methods that provide very competitive performance to the problem of word sense disambiguation. Assuming a solution to WSD, we then show how these methods significantly improve the performance of entailment cases in the four basic areas of information retrieval (IR), information extraction (IE), question answering (QA), but mostly in multi-document summarization (SUM), as described using benchmark datasets designed to test the problems in the 2006 RTE challenge. These results are extended and improved based on the more recent RTE data sets. Finally, we explore whether the results would improve automatically by simply improving the WordNet database. The results presented in this paper were first presented in (Neel et Al., 2007) and (Neel and Garzon, 2010).

The paper is organized as follows. The next section provides the necessary background to explain the contribution of this work. First, a brief history of the RTE Challenge series is discussed. Next, the problem of Word Sense Disambiguation is clearly distinguished from RTE as a separate but related problem. Next, a brief look at conventional solutions is examined closely to better understand the nature of conventional RTE solutions. In the section "Entailment Assuming Word Disambiguation" solutions to RTE, protocols for solving RTE are introduced that assume that WSD has been performed as preprocessing (such as by a human). The next section, "Fully Automatic RTE Solution" introduces a method for automatic WSD using WordNet. The data is evaluated on RTE Challenge datasets from 2006-2008 (RTE-2, RTE-3, and RTE-4 (resp.)). Finally, the contribution of this protocol is fully discussed in the conclusion section.

BACKGROUND RESULTS

RTE Challenge

In 2005, a first challenge was put forth (Dagan et al. 2005) to researchers to find a method that resolves or approximately resolves entailment. The full problem is obviously hard, even for the average human. In order to be able to make objective comparisons between different solutions, a standard test data was published and has since been updated annually (Bar-Haim et al., 2006; Giampiccolo et al., 2007; Giampiccolo et al., 2008). Each challenge released datasets of 800 tuples across four domains or ontological categories. Each tuple consists of a "text" paragraph (T), at least one additional paragraph called "the hypothesis" (H), and the judgment about whether T entails H. The domains for each dataset include

Information Extraction (IE), Information Retrieval (IR), Question Answer (QA), and Summarization (SUM). For a description of the characteristics and challenges of each category, the reader is referred to (Bar-Haim et al., 2006).

The 2006 and 2007 RTE Challenge datasets provided 100 positive and 100 negative examples. In (Neel et al., 2007), the authors selected a subset of 80 tuples from the 2007 datasets (10 positive and 10 negative tuples for each of the four domains) as a training set. From the training set, the authors determined a threshold above which entailment was assumed.

The initial efforts for the RTE Challenge are credited to the professional network for Pattern Analysis, Statistical Modeling, and Computational Learning (PASCAL). In 2008, PASCAL partnered with the United States National Institute of Standards and Technologies to continue the recognizing textual entailment challenge series. The results of the challenge are now being distributed through the Text Analysis Conference (TAC) (Giampiccolo et al., 2008)

The TAC conference series (http://www.nist.gov/tac/) has held the challenge for two years and provided datasets with two important additional contributions. First, the length of tuple is provided. The intuition is that some solutions may be better suited for shorter problems than longer problems. Second, decision of entailment was shifted from a binary decision (yes/no answer) to a three-way decision (yes, no, or "undetermined" answer). For this paper, the "undetermined" answers are removed from the 2008 dataset in order to make proper comparisons with the 2006 and 2007 datasets. Thus, the protocols discussed herein only identify when entailment is clearly present. Therefore, the results are pessimistic in the sense that better figures might be obtained otherwise which may not be necessarily factual. In this paper, the accuracy of the protocol is evaluated against submissions to each challenge. The results are further analyzed within the four separate domains described above. In addition to the individual challenges of each category, any method faces the additional challenge of performance across all categories. Thus, we consider a fifth category consisting of the full set of 800 tuples.

Word Sense Disambiguation (WSD)

A chief problem in assessing entailment through automation is the complexity inherent in language. A critical example is that of determining the meaning (or sense) of a word or phrase used in the context of a given "text," such as a sentence or a paragraph. Most words, and phrases, are ambiguous in that they have more than one meaning. The task of WSD is that of determining which *meaning,* with respect to some glossary of meanings such as WordNet, a given word or phrase is intended where more than one interpretation is possible. For example, the word *kill* is ambiguous (without context) and can convey the concepts of "*murder,*" "*incidental death by accident*" or even "*intentional death through legal channels.*" In context of a particular example, "*She killed her husband.*" can only convey one of these meanings (*murder*). Most humans are excellent at WSD. The challenge is for intelligent systems to make that determination automatically.

A first step towards automated WSD is to construct a list of *all* possible meanings and their inter-relationship for *all* terms and for *all* languages. This challenge has been actively pursued at Princeton University under a project called WordNet (http://WordNet.princeton.edu) for over a quarter century.

WordNet is a large lexical database of English developed by George Miller (Beckwith and Miller 1990) to express nouns, verbs, adjectives and adverbs. They are grouped into sets of cognitive synonyms (*synsets*). Each synset expresses a distinct *concept.* Synsets are interlinked by means of lexico-semantic relations. The result can be thought of as a directed graph where the vertices are synsets and the edges/arcs are semantic re-

lationships between the synsets (not necessarily symmetric.)

Word relationships found in WordNet proved helpful in expanding queries for the task of Information Retrieval (Voorhees, 1994). Even without WordNet, WSD has been demonstrated experimentally to improve results for the tasks of Information Retrieval (Schütze and Pederson, 1995; Gonzalo et al. 1998) and Question Answering (Negri, 2004); though some have suggested the opposite that WSD is useless for Information Retrieval and possibly harmful in some cases (Salton, 1968; Salton and McGill, 1983; Krovetz and Croft, 1992; Voorhees, 1993). In (Schütze and Pederson, 1995), precision for the task of standard IR test collection (TREC-1B) improved by more than 4% using WSD. It is thus intriguing what advantages may exist in treating the entailment problem using a purely semantic approach rather than the more common syntactic and lexical approach.

Conventional Solutions

In the 1990s, semantic representations were approached by various methods, such as selecting and counting keywords. These solutions would typically assume that some meaning similarity existed between text fragments if *words* in one fragment overlapped a certain percentage of those in the other. More recent solutions have moved beyond mere lexicon and syntax into semantic models that attempt to dynamically resolve word meanings. Among the leaders of these semantic models is Latent Semantic Analysis, or LSA, (Deerwester et al., 1990) which captures the "synonym meanings" of words by the company each word keeps during a training phase. The ability of LSA to capture word meanings requires large quality input in the training phase. While this approach does not explicitly disambiguate words into a specific word meaning, it does improve meaning similarity results by correlating words that express the same concept in different ways.

Textual entailment differs from text similarity in that the relationship between the two fragments under consideration is unidirectional. One text T may entail another H, but H may not necessarily entail T. Recently, (Raina et al. 2005) attacked the problem on two fronts (lexical and semantic). The lexical approach used parse trees to capture syntactic dependencies and sentence structure. This structure was semantically annotated. The result protocol used logical formulas to achieve results that proved the highest confidence weighted score in the RTE Challenge of 2005.

In a similar vein, (Rus and Graesser, 2006) have addressed the issue of sentence structure. They proposed capturing sentence structure by mapping student answers and expectations (i.e., ideal answers) in AutoTutor, an intelligent tutoring system, into lexico-syntactic graphs. The degree of relatedness is measured by the degree of graph subsumption. This approach yields good results without an external knowledge source. However, this approach does not disambiguate terms before comparison and has not been demonstrated to address negation, although the authors indicate this might be possible.

By examination of the competitive submissions to the RTE challenge in 2006, we can gauge the approaches considered best by experts in the field. Although not a true scientific survey *per se*, the result is nevertheless telling of the current state of available solutions to entailment problems. Table 1 shows the result of an ontological sort of the more than 40 submissions to the RTE-2 2006 challenge. Results include semantic approaches (similar to LSA described above), lexical and syntactic (Rus and Graesser, 2006), and logical inference models (such as those proposed by (Raina et al., 2005)). Most submissions used a combination of techniques. The best scoring approaches used either inference models or included virtually every other model. The very best score of these submissions was accurate to about 0.75. The most frequent approach is "lexical relations," an approach that essentially infers meaning from

word-level relationships. The second most frequent approach uses syntax to match syntactic contributions (such as grammar and negation) to infer a semantic relationship if one were to exist. It is clear that the focus of conventional wisdom is to infer meaning from syntactic context and lexical comparisons.

As pointed out before, world knowledge is relevant, if not essential, to the RTE challenge. The critical issue appears to be disambiguation (assignment of meaning). Regardless of the approach, any general purpose solutions to the recognizing textual entailment problem will need to address, directly or indirectly, word-sense disambiguation (assignment of proper meaning to words), sentence structure (context, tense, etc.), and sentence negation. As can be seen with many of the approaches described in Table 1 and Figure 1, meaning is inferred without directly addressing the word-sense disambiguation problem. Any ideal solution would need to assume that *a priori* knowledge of the particular topic would not be provided. Once WSD is solved, the equally challenging issues of sentence structure and negation persist. An ideal solution may well require addressing all of the above.

Table 1. More than 40 submissions from over 20 experts are ranked by their approach to the entailment solution. The four most popular are highlighted in bold. Topping the list is "Lexical Relations."

Lexical Relations (32)
Subsequence overlap (11)
Syntactic Matching (28)
Semantic Role Labeling (4)
Logical Inference (2)
Web-Based Statistics (22)
Machine Learning Classification (25)
Paraphrase Template (5)
Acquisition of Entailment (1)

Figure 1. The entailment problem is addressed by partitioning the text and hypothesis into a bi-partite graph. Dots (dark spots) represent the set of synsets that could be represented by one word in either the text or hypothesis. Synsets with common meanings are connected by lines. The entailment is assessed by measuring the percentage of terms in the hypothesis included in the text or simply measuring the connections from hypothesis to the text.

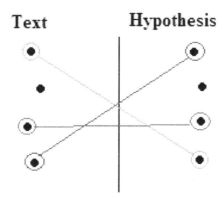

ENTAILMENT ASSUMING WORD DISAMBIGUATION

A natural question about entailment is thus to quantify precisely the benefit that word sense disambiguation (WSD) has to entailment problems. This approach essentially ignores negation, sentence structure and resolves entailment solely on the contribution of WSD. This section addresses this question by presenting a simple *inclusion* procedure to determine if a hypothesis (H) is entailed (or can be inferred) by a Text (T) assuming word disambiguation has already been resolved. This protocol assumes that meanings of terms have been assessed *a priori*. perhaps by humans. The algorithm determines the percentage of the overlap of synsets in the hypothesis with the synsets in the text.

Table 2 demonstrates the advantages of this approach. Key terms from two short paragraphs are disambiguated by human assessment using synsets provided by WordNet. In this example, *gunman* and *help* convey the same meaning as *shooters* and *aid* (respectively.) However, lexical term matching will not identify the terms as a match. Pure lexical comparison would only match four of the six words in the hypothesis. By using our protocol for WSD, all terms were matched despite very different words.

A more formal description of this entailment solution follows. A bi-partite graph is constructed for each tuple with one part corresponding to the text and the other to the hypothesis. The vertices are *synsets, not* words. Each part has an independent set of vertices where each represents one synset. The semantic relationships that would relate one word to another are represented by edges. Edges only connect vertices across regions. Both the semantic relationship and synsets associated with the text and hypothesis are determined by human assessment. Entailment is determined by how connected the synsets in part H are to the synsets in part T. The more H-vertices included in (connected to) T; the more likely it is that T entails H. Entailment is assumed to be false until enough of H connects to T. A threshold for how many connections are required to determine that an entailment is present was optimized experimentally. This threshold is optimized with a training dataset, as described above, so that the

Table 2. Two simple paragraphs (Text and Hypothesis) demonstrate the advantages of disambiguation to entailment. The words (first and third column) of the paragraphs are aligned in rows according to their semantic meaning (second column). The comparison of semantic meanings matches in two cases where lexical comparison fails.

Text: The shooters escaped as other soldiers tried to give aid to the wounded.				
Hypothesis: The gunmen escaped as the other soldiers tried to give help to the wounded.				
TEXT	**SYNSETS FROM WORDNET**	**HYPOTHESIS**	*Lexical*	*Semantic*
shooters	(n) gunman, gunslinger, hired gun, gun, gun for hire, triggerman, hit man, hitman, torpedo, shooter (a professional killer who uses a gun)	gunmen		X
escaped	(v) escape, get away, break loose (run away from confinement)	escaped	X	X
soldiers	(n) soldier (an enlisted man or woman who serves in an army)	soldiers	X	X
tried	(v) try, seek, attempt, essay, assay (make an effort or attempt)	tried	X	X
give	(v) give (transfer possession of something concrete or abstract to somebody)			
aid	(n) aid, assist, assistance, help (The activity of contributing to the fulfillment of a need or furtherance of an effort or purpose)	help		X
wounded	(n) wounded, maimed (people who are wounded)	wounded	X	X

solution would return the maximum number of correct answers. Later, the thresholds obtained from this optimization step (using the training dataset described above) were used to assess entailment with the full test set (Table 3).

As shown in Figure 2, a bi-partite graph is constructed for each tuple with one region corresponding to the text and the other to the hypothesis. The graph has two independent regions containing vertices. Each vertex is the synset that best disambiguates each corresponding word in the text and hypothesis. Edges connect vertices across regions that are the same semantically (i.e. has the same synsets). In this example, both the semantic relationships (edges) and synsets (vertices) associated with the text and hypotheses are determined by human assessment.

Entailment is assessed by measuring the connectedness of the two sets of synsets. The number of H-vertices connected to T-vertices indicates the number of concepts shared between the text and hypothesis. Entailment is scored by dividing the number of shared concepts by the number of H-vertices; entailment is assumed to be false and only change to true when the score crosses a threshold value. The threshold to determine entailment is optimized experimentally in order to return the maximum number of correct answers with the fewest false positives and false negatives. The range of thresholds tested was 30%-90%. Opti-

Table 3. Entailment by a simple semantic procedure is significantly better than other methods on the RTE challenge 2006 dataset, assuming a solution to disambiguation

	IE	IR	QA	SUM	Overall
(A) Total Correct	45%	70%	67%	80%	72.90%

Figure 2. Thresholds effectiveness around the optimal for IR (a), IE (b), QA (c), and SUM (d). The final thresholds were determined to be 0.8 for IE, 0.7 for IR, 0.82 for QA, and 0.7 for SUM.

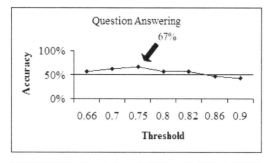
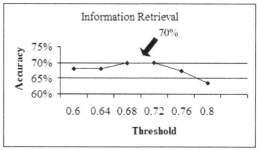
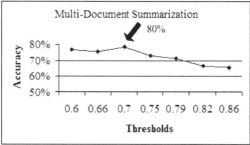
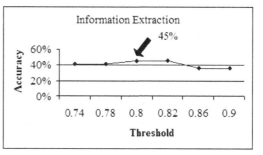

mization was performed for each of the four categories of the 2006 RTE Challenge dataset (IR, IE, QA, and SUM) as well as the overall score. Figure 2 shows the space of thresholds around the optimal for IR (Figure 2-a), IE (Figure 2-b), QA (Figure 2-c), and SUM (Figure 2-d). The final thresholds were determined to be 0.8 for IE, 0.7 for IR, 0.82 for QA, and 0.7 for SUM. Figure 2 shows the results of this algorithm perform by humans. This procedure answers correctly 7 out of 10 instances overall appears to work best for Information retrieval (IR) and Multi-document summarization (SUM). The success of this simple protocol clearly demonstrates the potential of solving entailment. The focus of this work is to test the effect of WD on entailment, so there has been no objective measure of the performance of manual disambiguation (e.g. agreement across subjects in a test using the kappa index).

This procedure depends heavily on WD to assess entailment. Table 3 suggests that some 70% of the RTE task for humans is matching concepts with other linguistic features such as negation and sentence structure accounting for the other 30%. If word disambiguation could be automated to approximate the human assessment of word meanings, this simple solution might be competitive with conventional solutions which scored about the same in the RTE 2006 challenge. In the next section, a procedure is actually introduced to perform WD *automatically*. Table 3 shows the result of this experiment for each category. This procedure answers correctly 3 times more frequently than incorrect. This procedure appears to work best for Information Retrieval (IR) and Multi-document summarization (SUM). Over all categories, this approach is correct 3 times more frequently than not.

Consequently, this procedure, hereafter referred to simply as the *inclusion protocol*, is a simple but clear demonstration that the human ability for assessing entailment depends importantly, if not critically, on the capability to disambiguate words. This inclusion protocol further shows that entailment could be assessed *automatically* by substituting the human assessment described in this section by a similar automatic WSD procedure. Though the next section will focus on one such word disambiguation solution, *any* word disambiguation method capable of assessing semantic meaning with limited context could be coupled with this inclusion procedure to produce a fully automated entailment solution.

RTE WITH FULLY AUTOMATED AUTOMATED WSD

This section is divided in three sections. The first section intoduces the protocol for automatic word-sense disambiguation. The next section evaluates RTE using the inclusion protocol with this automatic WSD solution using a 2007 edition of WordNet and the 2006 RTE Challenge Dataset. The third section then evaluates WordNet as the source of World Knowledge. The final section expands the evaluation of both WordNet and the inclusion protocol to include the RTE Challenge datasets of 2007 and 2008.

Automated Word Disambiguation

The first sense in WordNet for each word represents the most popular word meaning. The easiest algorithm for WSD is to simply assume every word in the tuple conveys the most popular meaning according to the language. This first algorithm was tested and shown not to help significantly. The result showed that assigning meanings in this way did not help entailment significantly since the *correct* synset was too often not the *most popular* synset. The general problem was that this approach did not capture enough of the context to discern when less frequent word meanings were used. This section presents a refinement of this procedure for disambiguating words automatically by combining *the context* of the text and hypothesis contained in the tuple with the word meanings and *relationships* captured in WordNet.

The simple protocol above fails probably because it does not incorporate *context* as humans do when assessing entailment. Therefore, a more advanced protocol was developed to disambiguated words automatically by combining *the context* of the text and hypothesis contained in the tuple with the word meanings and *relationships* captured in WordNet. This procedure for WD first extracts words and phrases from the 800 tuples. Articles, prepositions, and other common terms were sanitized from the word set. Hyphenated words were broken into their components. The spelling errors of the input set were preserved. The final word set contained about 5,500 unique words and phrases. All synsets for each word were then extracted from WordNet using a PERL script. Each synset was stored in a hash table and indexed by the word or phrase used to query WordNet. Each word that did not have any synset defined in WordNet was ignored and removed from the word set.

Word disambiguation is performed by the following protocol. The set of synsets associated with each word in the hypothesis are compared with each set of synsets associated with the words in the text. All synsets are represented by a single dot in Figure 3-A. Unlike the previous example, all synsets must be included because no human is available to select the correct synset. The resulting overlap (intersection) of synsets represents the meanings those words have in common (Figure 3-B). The most popular synset (according to Word-Net) *in the context of the paragraphs* is selected from the intersection (Figure 3-C). Thus, synsets that are more popular *according to WordNet* are ignored when there exists synsets which are more popular *according to the context of the paragraphs*.

The selected synset is assumed to be the intended meaning for words found in the text and hypothesis. This procedure is performed for each set of synsets in the hypothesis until all words have been disambiguated or the opportunities for disambiguation have been exhausted (Figure 3-D). At the close of the procedure, words that have exhausted all opportunities but remain ambiguous

Figure 3. Part (A) selects one word from the text and hypothesis and gathers all related synsets from WordNet. Part (B) compares the intersection of the synsets for each pair. Part (C) selects the strongest relationship from each pair according to WordNet and in context of the Text and Hypothesis. Part (D) shows the final result where all words have been disambiguated and related words from the text and hypothesis are connected.

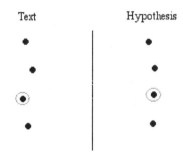

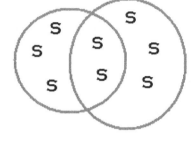

(A) Select the set of synsets that surround one word in text and one word in Hypothesis.

(B) Determine the intersection of synsets. If intersection, continue to (C). If not, return to (A).

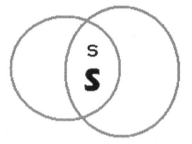

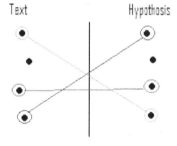

(C) The meaning of each word is the most popular (according to WordNet) shared synset.

(D) Repeat Procedure until disambiguation of all terms is complete.

are assigned the most popular meaning in Word-Net. The result of this procedure is a tuple that is fully disambiguated by the context of the text and hypothesis and in a ready state to assess entailment as described in the previous section.

This procedure for evaluating RTE with the inclusion protocol using the above automatic WSD solution follows. First, the words from the 800 tuples are extracted. Phrases were identified that express a single meaning with multiple words (e.g. *"au jus" or "hard disk"*). Articles, prepositions, and other common terms were sanitized from the word set. Hyphenated words were broken

into their components. In several cases, the input set contained spelling errors. These errors were preserved. The final word set contained about 5,500 unique words and phrases. Next, a simple PERL script extracted synsets from WordNet for each word. Each synset was stored in hash table and indexed by the word or phrase used to query WordNet. Each word that did not have any synset defined in WordNet was ignored and removed from the word set.

The set of synsets associated with each word in the hypothesis are compared with each set of synsets associated with the words in the text.

The resulting overlap (intersection) of synsets represents the meanings those words have in common. The most popular synset or meaning (according to WordNet) *in the context of the paragraphs* is selected from the intersection. Thus, synsets that are more popular *according to WordNet* are probably ignored when others are more popular *according to the context of the paragraphs*. The selected synset is assumed to be the intended meaning for words found in the text and hypothesis. This procedure was performed for each set of synsets in the hypothesis until all words have been disambiguated or the possibility for disambiguation has been exhausted after testing the full set of synets retrieved from WordNet. Words that exhaust all opportunities but remain ambiguous were assigned the most popular meaning in WordNet. The result of this procedure is an "optimistic" disambiguation based on the context provided in the tuple.

Semi-Automated Word Disambiguation

Next, it seemed prudent to perform a deep analysis of the failures of the automatic WSD protocol using WordNet as presented above. The clear intuition was that WordNet will fall short of humans performing the same task of WSD. Here, we explore why WordNet would fail in these cases. In particular, the results of the previous procedure were examined manually to determine any additional semantic relationships that could result in better disambiguation. The automated method for word disambiguation described above was performed first. Afterwards, human assessors reviewed the result by examining the subset of words whose resulting meaning was not correctly selected. Words that are clearly related but did not share a common synset were identified and paired together. The result of this procedure is an optimistic disambiguation based on the context provided in the tuple with additional experience from humans.

WordNet was then searched for semantic relationships (such as hypernym, synonym, antonym, etc.) that would express the semantic relationship of the pair. In less than 25% of the cases, the relationship was expressed through hypernym relationships. The majority of cases required information that was simply not available in WordNet. This fact highlights a potential limitation on WordNet's ability to capture and provide semantic meaning and relationships.

Automated WSD with Additional Semantic Relationships

This procedure automates word disambiguation with hypernymy relationships captured in Word-Net. Essentially, the automated WSD performed above is modified so that synsets related by hypernymy relationships are included. Hypernymy relationships express abstraction and generalization. Each relationship was exhaustively explored to extract related synsets. Hypernyms were stored in separate hash and indexed by the source word. Word disambiguation is performed using the same procedure as before but including hypernyms with the synsets. The result of this procedure is an optimistic disambiguation based on the context provided in the tuple and additional human experience captured in WordNet.

RTE using Automated WSD with WordNet

So far, entailment was determined by the degree of connectedness in a bipartite graph whose vertices are disambiguated synsets (words) and whose edges express "sameness" in meaning. In that instance, disambiguation was preprocessing performed by humans. Here, we replace the human judgment in the *inclusion protocol* with *automated WSD* procedures and compare the performance of the resulting procedures for entailment. In this test, we used the full set of 800 tuples. Here, edges express only the "equivalent" relationships between synsets (e.g. "kill" connects to "murder" only if both disambiguate to the same synset). The thresholds for determining whether entailment exists in this step had been assessed in the training phase and described in the section "Entailment assuming word disambiguation" above.

Table 4 row B (4.B) shows the performance of entailment using this procedure. Three of the four categories of data determined entailment better than just random guessing which is expected to be correct about 50% of the time. Information retrieval (IR) and summarization (SUM) were more than 15% above the simple guessing. Overall scores show a near 10% improvement over guessing. Only one case (IE) performed worse than guessing (> 5%). When compared to the same protocol using human disambiguation (Table 4.A), the scores for Information Extraction (IE) *improve by* 2%. The remaining three categories performed worse by 5-10% when compared with the protocol that assumes disambiguation. Overall scores are about 10% worse.

When this procedure was replaced with the semi-automated procedure (shown in Table 4.C), scores for Information Retrieval and Summarization improved while Question Answer and Information Extraction remained the same. When fully automated with hypernyms (Table 4.D), scores for Information Retrieval (IR) and Question Answering (QA) declined from the semi-automated procedure by 1%. Summarization (SUM) declined by 4% while Information Extraction (IE) remained static. Overall scores remained better

than simple guessing, but there is room for improvement when comparing to performance levels where disambiguation is performed by humans. This data was data was collected as part of the evaluation presented in (Neel et al., 2007). This simple automated WSD would have enabled the inclusion protocol to best 28 of 40 submissions to the RTE challenge of 2006.

Evaluating the Impact of WordNet

The results of the above experiment suggest that improving the quality of WordNet would improve WSD and consequently improve the inclusion protocols ability to recognize textual entailment. In essence, an evaluation of WordNet is required in order to assess the value of using WordNet to solving the problems of WSD and subsequently RTE. Consequently, the experiment above which disambiguated words to synsets only is revisited by substitution of WordNet-2007 used above with the November 2009 release of WordNet.

This edition of WordNet is essentially the same database but with 2+ years of additional world knowledge. The, same inclusion protocol for evaluation of entailment is used along with the same protocol for word-sense disambiguation. Only the source of world knowledge was updated. The first two sources included are human judgment of word-sense meaning and the 2007 edition of WordNet. Table 5 shows results of this evaluation. Row-1 (Human Evaluation) shows the performance of the protocol if the

Table 4. Scores are shown for three procedures B, C, & D in determining entailment automatically. These scores compare favorably to the scores of entailment assuming disambiguation (A) and are competitive with other solutions submitted to the 2006 RTE Challenge (Neel et al., 2007).

	IE	IR	QA	SUM	Overall
(A) Total Correct	45%	70%	67%	80%	72.90%
(B) Total Correct	47%	65%	56%	70%	59.10%
(C) Total Correct	47%	67%	56%	72%	60.10%
(D) Total Correct	47%	66%	55%	68%	58.80%

WSD is performed by humans. This portion of the data was data was collected as part of the evaluation presented in (Neel et al., 2007). The performance of the inclusion protocol improved across every category with WordNet-2009. Table 5 row-3 (WordNet-2009) shows the accuracy of the inclusion protocol with automatic WSD using WordNet-2009. IE improved by correctly evaluating 1 more tuple as an entailment. IR, QA, and SUM improved by 1, 5, and 9 tuples, respectively. Overall, WordNet-2009 enabled correct entailment in 17 more cases. As before, this result was compared with the scores of the RTE2 and found that simple inclusion protocol with our automatic WSD protocol using WordNet-2009 would have out-performed 35 of 40 submissions.

Further Evaluations

Here, the inclusion protocol is expanded from RTE2 in 2006 (Bar-Haim et Al. 2006) to the subsequent RTE Challenge datasets of RTE3 in 2007 (Giampiccolo et Al., 2007) and RTE4 in 2008 (Giampiccolo et Al., 2008). Table 6 compares the accuracy of the inclusion protocol using automatic WSD for RTE2, RTE3, and RTE4 (columns). The accuracy is reported for each domain of Information Extraction (IE), Information Retrieval (IR), question answering (QA), summarization (SUM), and overall performance (rows). (The

results of RTE2 are also presented in Table 3 and are simply quoted here.) The performance here would have outscored 35 of 40 submissions to the RTE2 challenge.

The protocol was performed without any modification on the RTE3 dataset (meaning that no modification was made at all to the WSD protocol or inclusion protocol for RTE.) Here, the protocol performed better with RTE3 (column-2 of table 6) in every domain except SUM. Further, the overall performance RTE3 was essentially identical to that of RTE2 (column-1 of Table 4). The only notable changes were in the domains of QA and SUM where the protocol's accuracy increased from 68.5% to 57.5% for QA and decreased from 74.5% to 57.5% for SUM. This result would have scored 27 of 45 submissions to the RTE3 challenge.

The protocol was once again performed without modification on the RTE4 dataset. Here, the protocol performed worse with RTE4 (column-3 of table 6) in every domain except IE. The overall performance decreased to slightly better than guessing. The full set of scores of submission to the RTE4 challenge was not available for comparison. Consequently, it was not possible to place our score in context with other submissions. However, the top eight scores were available for submissions making only a two-way decision (meaning they submission only assessed whether

Table 5. Accuracy of the inclusion protocol with automatic WSD using WordNet (Neel et al., 2007) increases with the quality of the world knowledge database. With the exception of IE, accuracy was significantly better than simply guessing. The overall accuracy of the 2007 evaluation outperformed 28 of 40 submissions to the 2006 RTE Challenge. The same procedure outperformed 35 of 40 using WordNet 2009.

	IE	IR	QA	SUM	Overall
Human WSD	45%	70%	67%	80%	72.90%
WordNet-2007	47%	65%	56%	70%	59.10%
WordNet-2009	47.5%	65.5%	57.5%	74.5%	61.25%
• *Improvement over 2007*	*+ 0.5% (2)*	*+ 0.5% (1)*	*+1.5% (5)*	*+4.5% (9)*	*+2.15% (17)*

entailment was present or not). In comparison to the eight reported scores, the protocol performed 8% worse than the lowest of the top eight scores. (Giampiccolo et Al., 2008) reported the average per domain as 52% for IE, 60% for SUM, 61% for IR, and 52% for QA. Here, our protocol beat the average for IE and tied with the average for QA.

An analysis of this result of RTE4 was performed focusing on WSD. It was found that the RTE2 and RTE3 datasets contained approximately 6,000 words. Of these words, WordNet matched all but 900 for RTE2 and all but 1000 for RTE3. The dataset of RTE4 contained no less than 8000 words (2000 additional words) additional words than either RTE2 or RTE3 datasets. Of the 8000 words, 1500 were not found in WordNet. Therefore it is reasonable to conclude that WordNet was not able to provide enough information to resolve entailment with the inclusion protocol.

Next, the inclusion protocol itself was examined. By examining each tuple closely and comparing it with the result of the entailment assessment from the inclusion protocol, it was determined that the number of false negatives substantially outnumbered the false-positives (the protocol returned a result of no-entailment when entailment was really present.) This result further emphasized that automatic WSD did not provide enough information to assess entailment.

To test this result, thresholds in the inclusion protocol were decreased by 10%. Consequently, the protocol would return entailment if the hypothesis contained 10% fewer matches than before. Column-5 of table 6 shows the result of this assessment. The performance improved in each domain to either tie or best the average. The overall performance was sufficient to move into 7th place in the two-way challenge.

Issues, Controversies, Problems

The inclusion protocol is an attempt to build into computers a process for recognizing textual entailment that is more similar to how humans perform textual entailment by matching word meanings. The chief problem here becomes word disambiguation. This WSD challenge requires quality structure for world knowledge. It remains unclear whether WordNet can be such a source of world knowledge. In fact, WordNet's ability to help and not hurt in capturing world knowledge has been argued (Kaplan and Shubert, 2001; Clark et Al., 2005) and remains an open issue. That said, WordNet remains the clear leader.

Solutions and Recommendations

The evidence presented here shows a protocol for assessing entailment that works well when substantial world knowledge is available for word sense disambiguation. The accuracy of the RTE protocol degrades as the quality or availability of world knowledge degrades. Still, the RTE protocol remains very competitive despite including only word-meanings (synsets).

FUTURE RESEARCH DIRECTIONS

The inclusion protocol essentially ignores the negation and sentence structure. Humans presumably apply both in performing entailment and word-sense disambiguation. Many conventional protocols include these features with great success. Despite poor performance with WordNet, it may be possible to improve the inclusion protocol with negation and sentence structure to further improve the results presented here. The experiments presented here also suggest that WordNet requires two or more years of development to capture enough world knowledge to disambiguate a word well enough to even approach the level of human evaluation. Tests which require very up to date world knowledge (such as the 2009 RTE Challenge) will perform poorly with WordNet. Even so, the next step of this research should be to compete openly with other conventional solution.

CONCLUSION

A novel semantic protocol for assessing entailment was introduced and shown to recognize textual entailment when humans are performing word-sense disambiguation. The same protocol performs competitively with conventional solutions to entailment when WSD is performed automatically instead of by human assessment. Additional information such as hypernnymic meanings are shown to confuse the inclusion protocol. As WordNet improves, the capability of the inclusion protocol to assess entailment improves. In the final analysis, however, WordNet still seems to be inadequate as a representation of world knowledge for the purpose of entailment and word disambiguation.

REFERENCES

Bar-Haim, R., Dagan, I., Dolan, B., Ferro, L., Giampiccolo, D., Magnini, B., & Szpektor, I. (2006). The second PASCAL RTE challenge. In *Proc of the 2nd PASCAL Challenge on RTE.*

Beckwith, R., & Miller, G. A. (1990). Implementing a lexical network. *International Journal of Lexicography*, 3(4), 302–312. doi:10.1093/ijl/3.4.302

Clark, P., Harrison, P., Jenkins, T., Thompson, J., & Wojcik, R. (2005). Acquiring and using world knowledge using a restricted subset of English. *In Proceedings of the Eighteenth International Florida AI Research Symposium.* FLAIRS, AAAI 2005, Clearwater Beach, Florida, USA, (pp. 506-511).

Dagan, I. Glickman. O., & Magnini, B. (2006). The PASCAL RTE challenge. *In Proceedings of the 1st PASCAL Challenge Workshop on RTE.*

Deerwester, S., Dumais, S., Furnas, G. W., Landauer, T. K., & Harshman, R. (1990). Indexing by latent semantic analysis. *Journal of the Society for Information Science*, 41(6), 391–407. doi:10.1002/(SICI)1097-4571(199009)41:6<391::AID-ASI1>3.0.CO;2-9

Giampiccolo, D., Dang, H. T., Magnini, B., Dagan, I., Cabrio, E., & Dolan, B. (2008). The fourth PASCAL recognizing textual entailment challenge. *In Proceedings of the Third PASCAL Challenges Workshop on RTE.*

Giampiccolo, D., Magnini, B., Dagan, I., & Dolan, B. (2007). The 3rd PASCAL recognizing textual entailment challenge. In *Proc. of the Third PASCAL Challenges Workshop on RTE.*

Gonzalo, J., Verdejo, F., Chugur, I., & Cigarran, J. (1998). Indexing with WordNet synsets can improve text retrieval. In *Proceedings of COLING-ACL '98 Workshop on Usage of Word. Net in Natural Language Processing Systems,* Montreal, Canada, August.

Graesser, A., Wiemer-Hastings, P., Wiemer-Hastings, K., Harter, D., & Person, N. Tutoring Research Group. (2000). Using latent semantic analysis to evaluate the contributions of students in AutoTutor. *Interactive Learning Environments*, 8, 149–169. doi:10.1076/1049-4820(200008)8:2;1-B;FT149

Kaplan, A. N., & Schubert, L. K. (2001). *Measuring and improving the quality of world knowledge extracted from WordNet.* (Tech. Rep. 751 14627-0226). Dept. of Computer Science, Univ. of Rochester, Rochester, NY, May.

Krovetz, R., & Croft, W. B. (1992). Lexical ambiguity and information retrieval. *ACM Transactions on Information Systems*, 10(2), 115–141. doi:10.1145/146802.146810

Neel, A., Garzon, M. H., & Rus, V. (2008). A semantic method for textual entailment. In *Proceedings of the Twenty-First International Florida AI Research Symposium*. FLAIRS, AAAI 2008, Coconut Grove, Florida, USA, (pp. 171-176).

Negri, M. (2004). Sense-based blind relevance feedback for question answering. In SIGIR-2004 *Workshop on Information Retrieval For Question Answering* (IR4QA), Sheffield, UK.

Raina, R., Ng, A., & Manning, C. D. (2005). Robust textual inference via learning and abductive reasoning. *Proc. of the 20th National Conf. on Artificial Intelligence*. AAAI Press.

Rus, V., & Graesser, A. (2006). Deeper natural language processing for evaluating student answers in intelligent tutoring systems. *Proceedings, The Twenty-First National Conference on Artificial Intelligence and the Eighteenth Innovative Applications of Artificial Intelligence Conference*, Boston, Massachusetts, USA.

Rus, V., Graesser, A., & Desai, K. (2005). Lexico-syntactic subsumption for textual entailment. *Proc. of Recent Advances in Natural Language Processing (RANLP 2005)*, Borovets, Bulgaria.

Salton, G. (1968). *Automatic information organization and retrieval*. New York, NY: McGraw-Hill.

Salton, G., & McGill, M. (1983). *Introduction to modern information retrieval*. New York, NY: McGraw-Hill.

Schütze, H., & Pederson, J. (1995). Information retrieval based on word senses. *Symposium on Document Analysis and Information Retrieval* (SDAIR), Las Vegas, Nevada, (pp. 161-175).

Voorhees, E. (1994). Query expansion using lexical-semantic elations. In *Proceedings of the 17th SIGIR Conference*, Dublin, Ireland, (June, 1994).

Voorhees, E. M. (1993) Using WordNet to disambiguate word senses for text retrieval. In *Proc. of the 16th Annual International ACM SIGIR Conference on Research and Development in Information Retrieval*, Pittsburgh, PA, USA, (pp. 171-180).

KEY TERMS AND DEFINITIONS

Hypernym: An abstract concept that conveys the meaning of several words or concepts.

Recognizing Textual Entailment: The process of determining whether one text (the "hypothesis") is entailed by another (the "text") in the context of current "world knowledge."

Synonym: A word whose meaning conveys an identical or similar meaning to another word.

Synset: The concept conveyed by a word when used in written or oral language.

Word-Sense Disambiguation: The process of determining the particular meaning of a word intended by the author of an oral or written statement (the "text").

Chapter 29
Mining and Visualizing the Narration Tree of Hadiths (Prophetic Traditions)

Aqil Azmi
King Saud University, Saudi Arabia

Nawaf Al Badia
General Organization for Social Insurance, Saudi Arabia

ABSTRACT

Hadiths are narrations originating from the words and deeds of Prophet Muhammad. Each hadith starts with a list of narrators involved in transmitting it. A hadith scholar judges a hadith based on the narration chain along with the individual narrators in the chain. In this chapter, we report on a method that automatically extracts the transmission chains from the hadith text and graphically displays it. Computationally, this is a challenging problem. Foremost each hadith has its own peculiar way of listing narrators; and the text of hadith is in Arabic, a language rich in morphology. Our proposed solution involves parsing and annotating the hadith text and recognizing the narrators' names. We use shallow parsing along with a domain specific grammar to parse the hadith content. Experiments on sample hadiths show our approach to have a very good success rate.

INTRODUCTION

Hadiths are oral traditions relating to the words and deeds of Prophet Muhammad. The traditional Muslim schools of jurisprudence regard hadith as an important tool for understanding the Qur'an

and in all matters relating to jurisprudence. The hadith consists of two parts: the actual text of the narrative, known as *matn* (المتن); and the chain of narrators through whom the narration has been transmitted, traditionally known as *isnad* (إسناد). The isnad consists of a chronological list of the narrators, each mentioning the one from whom they heard the hadith all the way to the prime

DOI: 10.4018/978-1-60960-741-8.ch029

narrator of the matn followed by the matn itself. The isnad system began during the lifetime of the Prophet and was used by the companions in transmitting the hadith. The political upheaval around 655 CE/35 AH[1] gave birth to the forgery of traditions in the political sphere, in order to credit or discredit certain parties. So, scholars became more cautious and began to scrutinize, criticize and search for the sources of information and that gave boost to the importance of isnad (Azami, 1978, pp. 246-7). And this gave birth to a new science, *'Ilm al-Jarh wa al-Ta'dil*. In the minds of hadith scholars there are several factors that contribute to the overall grading of a hadith: the individual narrators involved, the transmission chain itself, and the supporting statement from all available evidence. Typically a hadith scholar will end up consulting many volumes on narrator's biographic information for grading a single hadith. These books classify the narrators on their morality and their literary accuracy. Next, the chain of the transmission must not be broken, as a broken chain means a major defect in isnad. How does the hadith scholar decide this? By ensuring that there was an ample overlapping time between each pair of narrators in a chain to have met during their lifetime. Again this information is dug from narrator's biography. For more detail on the subject the reader is referred to the work of Azami (1977). In this paper we report on a software tool that will automatically generate the transmission chains of a given hadith, graphically rendering its complete isnad tree. Such a tool is useful for the students of hadith to study how a certain hadith has been propagated, while a hadith scholar will find it valuable for his work on grading the hadith. We tested our system on many sample hadiths and the outputs were verified by hadith scholars. Overall a success rate of slightly over 85% was achieved.

BACKGROUND

We will start by looking at what a hadith is. In the subsequent discussion we will be quoting Arabic text. For convenience it will be followed by transliteration and English translation as well. There are several Arabic text transliteration schemes; we for one will be using the Buckwalter Arabic transliteration ("Arabic Transliteration," 2002). Even though the Buckwalter transliteration is not intuitive and lacks readability, it has been used in many publications in natural language processing and in resources developed at the Linguistic Data Consortium (Habash, Soudi, & Buckwalter, 2007). The main advantages of the Buckwalter transliteration are that it is a strict one-to-one transliteration and that it is written in ASCII characters. The English translation will be based on (Al-Qushairy & Siddiqi, 1972). Before proceeding further, we feel it is necessary to write a few lines about Arabic for those who are not familiar with the language. The Arabic used in hadith is known as Classical Arabic, the Arabic of the Qur'an and early Islamic literature (7th – 9th century CE). However, this classical Arabic can be easily read and understood by anyone familiar with Modern Standard Arabic ("Modern Standard Arabic," n.d.).

In Depth Look at Hadith

Hadiths range in size from a few lines to a few hundred lines with the majority being five to six lines long. As an example of a hadith (the original Arabic followed by Buckwalter transliteration and English translation), see Figure 1.

This is a hadith with a single chain of narrators, however, not all hadiths have such a simple chain as we will later see.

The hadith corpus is quite huge. Early on, hadith scholars compiled it into six major collections; the bracketed numbers following the name of the collection refer to the number of hadiths in the compilation (from www.islamweb.net): Sahih

Figure 1.

حدثنا قتيبة بن سعيد حدثنا ليث عن هشام بن عروة عن أبيه عن عائشة رضي الله عنها أنها
قالت سأل حمزة بن عمرو الأسلمي رسول الله صلى الله عليه وسلم عن الصيام في السفر فقال
إن شئت فصم وإن شئت فأفطر [صحيح مسلم – كتاب الصيام/17]

Original Arabic

HdvnA qtybp bn sEyd HdvnA lyv En h$Am bn Erwp En >byh En EA}$p rDy Allh EnhA >nhA
qAlt s>l Hmzp bn Emrw Al>slmy rswl Allh SlY Allh Elyh wslm En AlSyAm fy Alsfr fqAl <n
$}t fSm w<n $}t f>fTr

Buckwalter Transliteration

"Narrated Qutaybah bin Sa'id narrated Laith from Hisham bin Urwah from his father from Aisha
(may Allah be pleased with her) who said, Hamzah bin 'Amr al-Aslami asked the Messenger of
Allah (may peace be upon him) about fasting while travelling, and he (the Prophet) replied: if you
wish to fast do so, and if you prefer to break your fast then you may do so."

English Translation

of Bukhari (7397); Sahih of Muslim (12000); Sunan of Abu Daud (5274); Sunan of Tirmizi (3956); Sunan of Nasa'i (5758) and Sunan of Ibn Majah (4341). There are other lesser known large collections (e.g. Muwatta' of Imam Malik and Musnad of Ibn Hanbal).

Significance of this Work

There is a huge literature that deals with hadith and hadith related subjects (e.g. narrators' biographies). And that literature is still growing. Many hadith scholars devoted their entire lives serving this literature. Their efforts have been purely manual. Of late scholars started to realize the importance of computers in this field. So now many of the hadith compilations exist in computer readable format, mainly as plain text, web contents or in proprietary locked databases. The only possible way to search these contents digitally is through the primitive search capability these tools provide or through traditional search engines, obviously both of which are incapable of analyzing and understanding the isnad context. Then, there exist some commercial products such as Hadith Encyclopedia by Sakhr. A software that was meant for the layman and hadith students. It

does offer a limited option to render the narration tree of a hadith. Nonetheless, these graphs have been manually pre-compiled and are hardwired into the hadith database. Our scheme will render the narration tree on the fly offering greater flexibility for future expansion.

Problems and Challenges

Processing natural languages has long been a hot topic of research. Regardless, today's programs are still not able to parse sentences and understand adequately the precise context as humans usually do. Basically, this is because natural languages tend to have substantial ambiguity in the way they are used, and consequently are very hard to process. Arabic, a morphologically rich language, poses some additional challenges. Here we list some of the peculiarities in the hadith text that pose a challenge.

1. **Anecdotal hadith verses deeds hadith:** The hadiths relating to the words of the prophet tend to have a simple structure: name → name → … → name → Prophet Muhammad (end of isnad) said: some saying of the prophet (end of matn). An example is shown in Figure 2.

Figure 2.

حدثني يحيى بن يحيى، قال: قرأت على مالك عن ابن شهاب، عن عطاء بن يزيد الليثي، عن أبي سعيد الخدري، أن رسول الله (ص) قال: إذا سمعتم النداء فقولوا مثل ما يقول المؤذن [صحيح مسلم – كتاب الصلاة/7].

Original Arabic

Hdvny yHyY bn yHyY, qAl: qr>t ElY mAlk En Abn $hAb, En ETA' bn yzyd Allyvy, En >by sEyd Alxdry, >n rswl Allh (S) qAl: <*A smEtm AlndA' fqwlwA mvl mA yqwl Alm&*n

Buckwalter Transliteration

"Narrated Yahya bin Yahya, said: I read to Malik from Ibn Shihaab, from 'Ata' bin Yazeed al-Laithy, from Abu Sa'id al-Khudary, that the Prophet said ..."

English Translation

On the other hand, hadiths involving the Prophet's deeds or customs are more involved (see Figure 3).

Here both Bilal and Ibn Umm-Maktoom are not part of the isnad even though they are both companions of the prophet.

2. **A network of narration chains:** When compiling hadith collections, some of the hadith scholars combined multiple isnad chains into a single hadith text provided they all shared the same matn, often marking the beginning of a new isnad chain by the Arabic letter (ح), for example, see Figure 4.

For brevity, the isnad part of the hadith in Figure 4 has been trimmed. The partial narration tree is shown in Figure 5. Anas, (narrator no. 5, 10 and 15) is the prime narrator (i.e. the one who reported this hadith directly from Prophet Muhammad).

3. **Identifying hadiths parts (isnad and matn):** Sometimes finding the border point of the isnad and matn is not a trivial task. There are hadith cases where the boundary is difficult to determine.

4. **Resolving ambiguity in the narrator's names:** In the hadith literature it is common

Figure 3.

حدثنا ابن نمير، حدثنا أبي، حدثنا عبيد الله، عن نافع، عن ابن عمر، قال كان لرسول الله (ص) مؤذنان بلال وابن أم مكتوم الأعمى [صحيح مسلم – كتاب الصلاة/4].

Original Arabic

HdvnA Abn nmyr, HdvnA >by, HdvnA Ebyd Allh, En nAfE, En Abn Emr, qAl kAn lrswl Allh (S) m&*nAn blAl wAbn >m mktwm Al>EmY

Buckwalter Transliteration

"Narrated Ibn Numayr, narrated from his father, narrated from Ubaydullah, from Nafi', from Ibn 'Umar, who said: that the Prophet of Allah had two Mu'azzins (those who call to prayer), Bilal and Ibn Umm-Maktoom the blind."

English Translation

Figure 4.

وحدثني أبو الربيع الزهراني، حدثنا حماد يعني ابن زيد عن ثابت، وعبد العزيز بن صهيب، عن
أنس؛ ح وحدثنا قتيبة بن سعيد، حدثنا حماد، عن ثابت، وشعيب بن حبحاب، عن أنس؛ ح وحدثني
قتيبة حدثنا أبو عوانة، عن قتادة، وعبد العزيز، عن أنس؛ ح وحدثنا ... [صحيح مسلم – كتاب
النكاح/ح/85].

Original Arabic

Hdvny >bw AlrbyE AlzhrAny, HdvnA HmAd yEny Abn zyd En vAbt, wEbd AlEzyz bn
Shyb, En >ns; H wHdvnA qtybp bn sEyd, HdvnA HmAd, En vAbt, w$Eyb bn HbHAb,
En >ns; H wHdvny qtybp HdvnA >bw EwAnp, En qtAdp, wEbd AlEzyz, En >ns; H
wHdvnA …

Buckwalter Transliteration

"Narrated Abu al-Rabi' al-Zahrani (1), narrated Hammad Ibn Zaid (2), from Thabit (3)
and Abdul-Aziz bin Suhayb (4), from Anas (5); ح and narrated Qutaiba bin Sa'id (6),
narrated Hammad (7), from Thabit (8) and Shu'ayb bin Habhab (9), from Anas (10); ح
and narrated Qutaiba (11), narrated Abu 'Awana (12), from Qatadah (13), and Abdul-
Aziz (14), from Anas (15); ح and narrated …"

English Translation

to refer to the same narrator with different names or alias. For example, see Figure 6.

Three different names for the same person. Sometimes we find that referencing terms (e.g. his father, his mother, his grandfather...) are used in the narration context, for example: "narrator

Figure 5. Partial isnad graph. The numbers refer to individual narrators in the hadith. Note that nodes no. 5, 10 and 15 all refer to the same prime narrator.

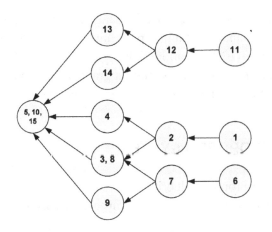

X who heard his uncle" without mentioning the latter's name (see Figure 7).

5. **Hadith referring to another:** Another common practice in the hadith literature is to list the isnad and perhaps a partial matn while referring to the matn of an earlier hadith. For example, see Figure 8.

The matn of this hadith refers to the matn of an earlier hadith (most likely with a different narration tree) that has Yunus and Malik as narrators.

Related Work

Though there are some commercial products that have computerized some aspects of hadith, nonetheless, as we noted earlier, these have been manually pre-compiled and locked into proprietary databases. And as such few research papers have been published in the area.

In Al Asaneed Tree (Al-Osaimi et al., 2008) the authors worked on an algorithm that draws

Figure 6.

ابن عمر ؛ عبد الله بن عمر ؛ عبد الله بن عمر ابن الخطاب **Arabic**
Abn Emr; Ebd Allh bn Emr; Ebd Allh bn Emr Abn AlxTAb **Buckwalter Transliteration**

Figure 7.

عن عبد بن تميم عن عمه ... **Arabic**
En Ebd bn tmym En Emh ... **Buckwalter Transliteration**

Figure 8.

حدثنا عبد بن حميد، أخبرنا عبد الرزاق، أخبرنا معمر، عن الزهري، أخبرني أنس، أن النبي (ص) سقط من فرسه فجحش شقه الأيمن، وساق الحديث وليس فيه زيادة يونس ومالك [صحيح مسلم – كتاب الصلاة/19]. **Original Arabic**
HdvnA Ebd bn Hmyd, >xbrnA Ebd AlrzAq, >xbrnA mEmr, En Alzhry, >xbrny >ns, >n Alnby (S) sqT mn frsh fjH$ $qh Al>ymn, wsAq AlHdyv wlys fyh zyAdp ywns wmAlk **Buckwalter Transliteration**
"Narrated Abd bin Humayd, told by Abdur-Razaq, told by Ma'mar, from al-Zuhry, told by Anas who reported that the Messenger of Allah fell down from his horse and his right side was grazed, and rest of the hadith is the same. In this hadith there are no additions (of words) as transmitted by Yunus and Malik." **English Translation**

the narration tree. Their system requires the user to enter individual narration chains which it will later draw into a tree form. It differs from our system where we semantically parse the hadith contents and draw the corresponding isnad tree.

An interesting and somewhat related work (Al-Salman, Al-Ohali, & Al-Rabiah, 2006) titled, "A Semantic Parse and Meaning Analyzer," attempts to reveal the word sense ambiguity by building a semantic parser supported by a statistical semantic analyzer. The authors of this paper have exerted great effort to build Arabic language grammar as rules and constraints represented in Backus-Naur Form (BNF) notation (Naur, 1960). This paper has inspired us to try to build a grammar for hadith and perform parsing to create a hadith parse tree.

PROPOSED SYSTEM

Our proposed algorithm is shown in Figure 9. It consists of a sequence of finite-state based processes, which constitute the procedure to analyze the hadith narration chain(s).

Our focus will be on natural language processing techniques to come up with a domain specific grammar for hadith. Next we go through each phase in more detail.

Preprocessing Phase

We need to lexically analyze the hadith text. This process is considered a preprocessing phase for the parser. Prior to passing the hadith to the lexical analyzer, we remove some of the unnecessary characters (parser noise characters). The stages of preprocessing phase are shown in Figure 10.

Sample Arabic input (text with full diacritical markings) and the output of the preprocessing phase is shown in Figure 11.

Note that we removed the diacritical marking since they are not used in this version of the system.

Grouping and Tagging Sets of Words into Categories

Shallow parsing is a natural language processing technique that attempts to provide some sort of machine understanding of the structure of a sentence but without parsing it fully into a parse tree form. Shallow parsing is also referred to as the task of chunking. The shallow parser produces and categorizes sentences into a series of words that have something in common. For instance, categorizing the sentences into noun, verb, preposition phrase, adjective, clause and other phrases (Stav, 2006). There is a noticeable difference between shallow parsing and full parsing in that the output of shallow parsing consists of a set of words that do not overlap and do not contain other chunks (non-recursive). We use shallow parsing to resolve two of the earlier mentioned challenges (see § Problems and challenges). For the deeds hadith it is used to remove unwanted sentences from the hadith that are not important to the full parsing process; it is also used to determine the border point of the isnad and matn.

Figure 9. Algorithm to analyze and visualize hadith narration tree

Input Hadith
Output Graphical display of all narration tree
Begin
   I. A preprocessor that identifies words and removes unnecessary characters
  II. A tagger that groups a set of words into categories, forming syntactic structure. Mainly, we are interested in Noun Phrases chunking, more specifically narrator names
 III. Use hadith grammar to build up the complete parse tree for the hadith isnad
 IV. Render the isnad chains graphically
End

Figure 10. Stages of preprocessing phase

Input Hadith
Output Preprocessed hadith
Begin
   I. Remove punctuations
  II. Remove diacritical markings (the tashkeel)
 III. Join lines (remove new lines)
 IV. Remove extra white spaces
  V. Replace the single white space that separates the words by the symbol ⊔
End

Figure 11.

حَدَّثَنَا مُحَمَّدُ بْنُ عَبْدِاللهِ بْنِ نُمَيْرٍ ، حَدَّثَنَا عَبْدَةُ عَنْ طَلْحَةَ بْنِ يَحْيَى ، عَنْ عَمِّهِ ، قَالَ : كُنْتُ عِنْدَ
مُعَاوِيَةَ بْنِ أَبِي سُفْيَانَ ، فَجَاءَهُ الْمُؤَذِّنُ يَدَعُوهُ إِلَى الصَّلاةِ فَقَالَ مُعَاوِيَةُ : سَمِعْتُ رَسُولَ اللهِ (ص)
يَقُولُ : الْمُؤَذِّنُونَ أَطْوَلُ النَّاسِ أَعْنَاقًا يَوْمَ الْقِيَامَةِ [صحيح مسلم – كتاب الصلاة/8]

Arabic (input)

Had~avanaA muHam~adu bonu EabodiAllhi boni numayorK , Had~avanaA Eabodapu
Eano TaloHapa boni yaHoyaY , Eano Eam~ihi , qaAla : kunotu Einoda muEaAwiyapa
boni >abiy sufoyaAna , fajaA'ahu Alomu&a*~inu yadaEuwhu <ilaY AlS~alApi faqaAla
muEaAwiyapu : samiEotu rasuwla Allhi (S) yaquwlu : Alomu&a*~inuwna >aTowalu
Aln~aAsi >aEonaAqFA yawoma AloqiyaAmapi

Buckwalter Transliteration

حدثنا ⎕ محمد ⎕ بن ⎕ بن ⎕ عبدالله ⎕ بن ⎕ نمير ⎕ حدثنا ⎕ عبدة ⎕ عن ⎕ طلحة ⎕ بن ⎕ يحيى ⎕ عن ⎕
عمه ⎕ قال ⎕ كنت ⎕ عند ⎕ معاوية ⎕ بن ⎕ أبي ⎕ سفيان ⎕ فجاءه ⎕ المؤذن ⎕ يدعوه ⎕ إلى ⎕
الصلاة ⎕ فقال ⎕ معاوية ⎕ سمعت ⎕ رسول ⎕ الله ⎕ ص ⎕ يقول ⎕ المؤذنون ⎕ أطول ⎕ الناس ⎕
أعناقا ⎕ يوم ⎕ القيامة

Preprocessed Arabic

There are few technical research studies on the Arabic language. Furthermore, Arabic is known for its variation and richness which makes building linguistic tools a challenging task. Thus, we will only focus on our research scope. We are interested in NP (Noun Phrases) chunking and more specifically, narrator's names. Therefore we will build a set of annotations to denote the chunks/categories that we intend to use as input for the full parser (hadith grammar). We devise the following notations to tag sentences: MT (sentence represents the matn); PM (sentence represents Prophet Muhammad); NN (sentence represents the Narrator's name); and CC (sentence represents closed class words). The closed class is the set of words used as transmission terms in hadith literature, e.g. حدثنا (haddathana), أخبرنا (akhbarana), قال (qaal) …etc.

Let us take an example to better illustrate the main concept of the shallow parser. Consider the hadith in Figure 12 and the corresponding output as produced by the shallow parser.

As demonstrated by the previous example shallow parsing can deal with contents that contain noise characters very well. Noise is often left outside chunks, and does no further damage; while in full parsing the parser will attempt to use it in deciding on higher-level parsed tree nodes. Next, we will see how to implement a shallow based parser. For the shallow parser we used a Memory-Based Learning model (Stanfill & Waltz, 1986). Memory-Based Learning (MBL) is a form of supervised, inductive learning from examples. The examples represent a vector of features assigned to a certain category. While training, the set of examples is streamed to the classifier and then added to the memory (knowledge base). During the test, a set of untrained data (new data) is presented to the classifier. For each test case, the distance is computed with all cases available in the memory. The nearest case category is used to predict the class of the test case.

There are many algorithms in AI that touch some aspects of MBL, such as example-base (Peirsman, 2006), similarity-based (Zavrel & Daelemans, 1997), lazy based (Daelemans, van den Bosch, & Weijters, 1997) … etc. We will be concentrating on the similarity based approach in this paper. The performance of MBL depends on the similarity metric (distance metric). According

Figure 12.

حدثنا محمد بن عبدالله بن نمير حدثنا عبدة عن طلحة بن يحيى عن عمه قال كنت عند معاوية بن
أبي سفيان فجاءه المؤذن يدعوه إلى الصلاة فقال معاوية سمعت رسول الله ص يقول المؤذنون
أطول الناس أعناقا يوم القيامة

Arabic (input)

HdvnA mHmd bn EbdAllh bn nmyr HdvnA Ebdp En TlHp bn yHyY En Emh qAl knt
End mEAwyp bn >by sfyAn fjA'h Alm&*n ydEwh <lY AlSlAp fqAl mEAwyp smEt
rswl Allh S yqwl Alm&*nwn >Twl AlnAs >EnAqA ywm AlqyAmp

Buckwalter Transliteration

([CC]حدثنا) (محمد بن عبدالله بن نمير[NN]) (حدثنا[CC]) (عبدة[NN]) (عن[CC]) (طلحة
بن يحيى[NN]) (عن[CC]) (عمه[NN]) (قال[CC]) كنت عند (معاوية بن أبي سفيان[NN])
فجاءه المؤذن يدعوه إلى الصلاة (فقال[CC]) (معاوية[NN]) (سمعت[CC]) (رسول الله[PM])
ص (يقول المؤذنون أطول الناس أعناقا يوم القيامة[MT])

Arabic (shallow parsed)

to (Veenstra & Buchholz, 1998) the most basic metric for patterns with symbolic features is the *overlap metric* given by:

$$\Delta(X, Y) = \sum_{i=1}^{n} \delta(x_i, y_i)$$

where $\Delta(X, Y)$ is the distance between patterns X and Y represented by n features, while δ is the distance per feature: $\delta(x_i, y_i) = 0$ if $x_i = y_i$ and 1 otherwise.

The above metric simply counts the number of mis/matching feature values in both patterns. The classifier will consider the features equally important. The features are weighted using Information Gain (IG), which measures how much information it contributes to our knowledge of the correct class label. The Information Gain of feature f is measured by computing the differences in uncertainty between the situation without and with knowledge of the value of that feature, and is given by the following equation (Daelemans, van den Bosch, & Weijters, 1997):

$$w_f = \frac{H(C) - \sum_{v \in V_f} P(v) \cdot H(C \mid v)}{si(f)}$$

where C is the set of class labels, $P(v)$ is the probability features vector, and Vf is the set of values for feature f The entropy of the class labels, $H(C)$ is given by:

$$H(C) = -\sum_{o \in C} P(c) \log P(c)$$

The split info $si(f)$ is included to avoid a bias in favor of features with more values. It is defined as:

$$si(f) = -\sum_{v \in V_f} P(v) \log P(v)$$

IB1-IG (Daelemans & van den Bosch, 1992) is a memory based learning algorithm that is used to build a data base of cases during the learning. The case is represented as a vector of features. The classification works by matching the test case (new) to all the test cases (training set) and calculating the distance between the new case and the case in the memory. In IB1-IG is a weighted sum of the distances per feature. The distance will be zero when the values of both cases for this feature are equal and one otherwise. The IB1-IG algorithm searches for the nearest neighbors which is an expensive operation. So to achieve a fast chunking we have selected the Information Gain Tree (IGTree) model. According to the study in (Veenstra & Buchholz, 1998), IGTree gives a high measure of precision and recall as well as good accuracy. The IGTree combines two algorithms; one for constructing decision trees, and one for retrieving classification information from these trees.

Hadith Grammar

The grammar is domain specific grammar in that it is only meant to parse hadith contents. This grammar requires a preprocessing phase which we refer to as "Lexical analysis" (Silberztein, 1997). The processing will remove the unneces-

sary characters such as punctuations, extra white spaces, newlines … etc.

As we stated earlier, full parsing is very sensitive to noise (typographical errors, repeated phrases, corrections etc). In comparison, chunking deals with noise very well; noise is often left outside chunks, and does no further damage, whereas in full parsing the parser will attempt to use it in deciding on higher-level parsed tree nodes.

In pursuing our effort to fully parse hadith contents we have created this domain specific grammar (Figure 13), setting rules and constraints to help prevent part of the context ambiguity. The grammar rules and constraints are described in extended Backus-Naur Form (EBNF) ("Extended Backus-Naur Form," n.d.). The EBNF is a

Figure 13.

```
Hadith = Isnad , ⊔ , Prophet_said , ⊔ , Matn;
Isnad = (Transmission_term , ⊔ , Narrator | Transmission_term , [⊔ ,
Transmission_term]) , { ⊔ , Transmission_term , ⊔ , Narrator | Transmission_term , ⊔ ,
Narrator , [⊔ , Transmission_term]};
Transmission_term = [Pre_transmission_term] , ⊔ , (”حدث“ | ”حدثناه“ | ”حدثني“ | ”حدثتني“
| ”سمعت“ | ”سمعنه“ | ”قال“ | ”قالا“ | ”قالوا“ | ”فقال“ | ”يقول“ | ”عن“ | ”أن“ | ”و“ | ”قرأت على“
| ”حدثناه“ | ”ثنه“ | ”يحدث“ | ”ثناه“ | ”أخبرنه“ | ”أخبرني“ | ”أخبرتني“ | ”أخبره“ | ”أخبر هه“ | ”نه“);
Pre_transmission_term = ”و“ | ”ف“ | ”وغيرهما“ | ”جميعا“ | ”أنه“ | ”كلاهما“ | ”كلهم“ | ”كل“
| ”هؤلاء“;
Narrator = [”يعني“ | ”أبي“ | ”ابن“) | [”أبي“] , ⊔ , ( ”ابن“ | ”أباه“ | ”أبو“ | ”أم“ , ⊔ , Name, [”أبي“|
”أبي“ | ”أمه“ | ”عمه“ | ”جده“ | ”جدي“ | ”الأخران“) , ⊔ , Name} (”أبيه“ | ”ابن“) | [”أبي“] , ⊔ , { ”أبي“ | ”و هو“) , ⊔ , [”أباه“ | ”أبو“
;
Name = Letter , {Letter};
Letter = ”ا“ | ”ب“ | ”ت“ | ”ث“ | ”ج“ | ”ح“ | ”خ“ | ”د“ | ”ذ“ | ”ر“ | ”ز“ | ”س“
| ”ش“ | ”ص“ | ”ض“ | ”ط“ | ”ظ“ | ”ع“ | ”غ“ | ”ف“ | ”ق“ | ”ك“ | ”ل“ | ”م“ | ”ن“ | ”و“ | ”هـ“
| ”ي“ | ”و“ | ”ء“;
Prophet_said = Precedence_term , ⊔ , (”رسول الله“ | ”النبي“ | ”نبي الله“ | ”رسول الله محمد“
| ”رسول الله محمد بن عبدالله“) , ⊔ , (”ص“) | ”صلى الله عليه وسلم“] , ⊔ , [ Post_term];
Precedence_term = ”سمعت“ | ”قال“ | ”عن“ | ”أن“;
Post_term = ”أنه قال“ | ”يقول“;
Matn = Word , ⊔ , {Word};
Word = Letter , {Letter};
```

meta-syntax notation used to express context-free grammars (CFG) (Chomsky, 1956). It is an extension to the regular Backus-Naur Form (BNF). In writing the grammar in EBNF we follow the ISO standard (International Standards Organization [ISO], 1996), in addition we use ⊔ to denote the white space.

Testing the Hadith Grammar

For testing purpose, we would like to apply our domain specific grammar on sample hadiths by drawing the derivation tree. For that we will rewrite the grammar in CFG notation which will simplify the task of drawing the derivation tree. This time however, the grammar will be written in Arabic. In fact the original hadith grammar was also written in EBNF form in Arabic. With hadith text in Arabic, the Arabic CFG will naturally flow with the text from right to left making it easier to trace (see Figure 14).

Figure 15 shows a successful derivation tree for the isnad and matn when the grammar is ap-

Figure 14. Hadith grammar in CFG notation

```
‹الحديث› → ‹السند›⊔‹قول رسول الله (ص)›⊔‹المتن›

‹السند› → ‹أداة إخبار›‹راوي›⊔‹السند› | ‹أداة إخبار›⊔‹راوي›⊔‹أداة إخبار›⊔
‹السند› | λ

‹أداة إخبار› → ‹سوابق أداة إخبار›⊔‹الأداة› | ‹سوابق أداة إخبار› ‹الأداة› | λ

‹الأداة› → حدث | حدثنا | حدثني | حدثتني | حدثناه | يحدث | ثنا | أخبرنا | أخبرني | أخبرتني |
أخبره | أخبرها | نا | سمع | سمعت | سمعنا | قال | قالا | قالوا | يقول | فقال | عن | أن | و | قرأت على

‹سوابق أداة إخبار› → و | ف | وغيرهما | جميعا | أنه | كلاهما | كلهم | كل هؤلاء | λ

‹راوي› → ‹اسم الراوي› | ‹استعاضة›

‹اسم الراوي› → ‹سوابق اسم الراوي›⊔‹اسم› | ‹سوابق اسم الراوي›⊔‹اسم›⊔‹توضيح›
⊔‹اسم الراوي›

‹توضيح› → يعني | هو | λ

‹سوابق اسم الراوي› → أبي | ابن | ابن أبي | بن | أباه | بن | أبا | أبو | أم | λ

‹استعاضة› → أبيه | الأخران | أبي | أمه | عمه | جده | جدي

‹اسم› → ‹كلمة›

‹كلمة› → ‹حرف› | ‹حرف›‹كلمة›

‹حرف› → ا | أ | إ | آ | ب | ت | ث | ج | ح | خ | د | ذ | ر | ز | س | ش | ص | ض | ط | ظ | ع |
غ | ف | ق | ك | ل | م | ن | و | ه | ي | ؤ | ئ | ء

‹قول رسول الله (ص)› → ‹سوابق اسم النبي›⊔‹اسم النبي›⊔ص | صلى الله عليه وسلم⊔
‹لواحق اسم النبي›

‹اسم النبي› → رسول الله | النبي | نبي الله | سول الله محمد | رسول الله محمد بن عبد الله

‹سوابق اسم النبي› → سمعت | سمع | قال | عن | أن

‹لواحق اسم النبي› → أنه قال | يقول | λ

‹المتن› → ‹كلمات›

‹كلمات› → ‹كلمة› | ‹كلمة›⊔‹كلمات›
```

Figure 15. A successful derivation tree. Only partial tree shown (full tree too big to fit)

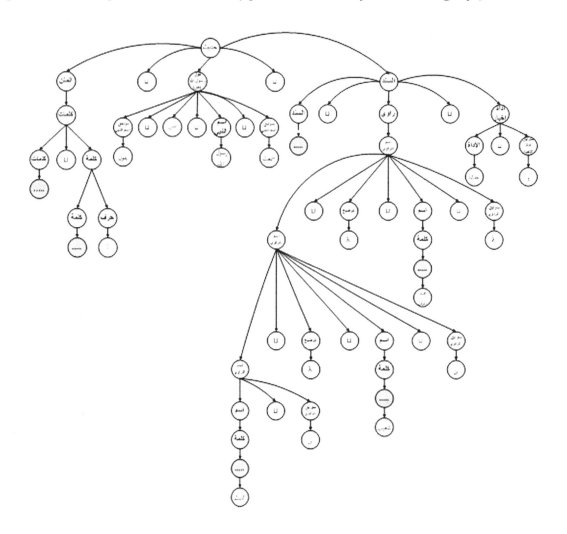

Figure 16.

وحدثنا عبدالملك بن شعيب بن الليث قال حدثني أبي عن جدي حدثني عقيل بن خالد قال قال ابن
شهاب أخبرني عبدالملك بن أبي بكر بن عبدالرحمن بن الحارث بن هشام أن خارجة بن زيد
الأنصاري أخبره أن أباه زيد بن ثابت قال سمعت رسول الله ص يقول الوضوء مما مست النار.

Arabic (preprocessed)

wHdvnA EbdAlmlk bn $Eyb bn Allyv qAl Hdvny >by En jdy Hdvny Eqyl bn xAld qAl
qAl Abn $hAb >xbrny EbdAlmlk bn >by bkr bn EbdAlrHmn bn AlHArv bn h$Am >n
xArjp bn zyd Al>nSAry >xbrh >n >bAh zyd bn vAbt qAl smEt rswl Allh S yqwl
AlwDw' mmA mst AlnAr

Buckwalter Transliteration

plied on the following preprocessed hadith shown in Figure 16.

Only part of the derivation tree is shown as the full derivation tree is too big to fit into a page.

Unfortunately, there were some cases where the text contains something we call "parser noise words." These are words that are not accurately parsed using the grammar. Figure 17 is one such example. I have grayed out the entire text leaving the offending part in black.

According to the hadith grammar, this portion of the hadith occurs in the Isnad part and so it is processed by it. But if we look closely, we see this portion of the hadith does not comply with the grammar rules and constraints set by the Isnad

part of the grammar. Detecting such noises in the preprocessing is not an easy task. In fact, there are some hadith cases where the context is very ambiguous even for the specialist readers. One possible solution is to deal with this kind of problems in post-processing phases.

Graphical Rendering of the Isnad Tree

One main objective of this work is to graphically represent the hadith narration flow diagram, a directed graph where nodes represent individual narrators. Going through different hadiths we noticed cases where a single narrator narrates to

Figure 17.

حدثنا محمد بن عبدالله بن نمير حدثنا عبدة عن طلحة بن يحيى عن عمه قال **كنت عند معاوية بن أبي سفيان فجاءه المؤذن يدعوه إلى الصلاة** فقال معاوية سمعت رسول الله ص يقول المؤذنون أطول الناس أعناقا يوم القيامة

Original Arabic

HdvnA mHmd bn EbdAllh bn nmyr HdvnA Ebdp En TlHp bn yHyY En Emh qAl **knt End mEAwyp bn >by sfyAn fjA'h Alm&*n ydEwh <lY AlSlAp** fqAl mEAwyp smEt rswl Allh S yqwl Alm&*nwn >Twl AlnAs >EnAqA ywm AlqyAmp

Buckwalter Transliteration

"... I was with Mu'awiya bin Abi Sufyan when a Mu'azzin came to him calling for the prayer ..."

English Translation (offending part only)

Figure 18.

حدثنا يحيى بن يحيى، وسعيد بن منصور، وأبو بكر بن أبي شيبة، وعمرو الناقد، وزهير بن حرب، **كلهم** عن ابن عيينة، ... [صحيح مسلم – كتاب الصلاة/9].

Original Arabic

HdvnA yHyY bn yHyY, wsEyd bn mnSwr, w>bw bkr bn >by $ybp, wEmrw AlnAqd, wzhyr bn Hrb, *klhm* En Abn Eyynp, ...

Buckwalter Transliteration

"Narrated Yahya bin Yahya, and Sa'id bin Mansur, and Abubakr bin Shaiba, and Amr al-Naqid, and Zuhair bin Harb *all* from Ibn 'Uyaynah ..."

English Translation

several others in the chain (one-to-many). As an example, note the term كلهم (meaning *all*) in the example of Figure 18.

Consequently there are also cases where a narrator hears the same hadith from two or more narrators in the hadith narration chain (many-to-one). So the result is too many narrators with complicated intersections that resemble a general tree. For the isnad to be readable on the display, the nodes need to be laid out perfectly with the minimum number of intersections and links crossing over. Although there are several techniques in graph theory that address the obstacles surrounding nodes representation, there is still a need to come up with new algorithms to better enhance the readability and usability of the represented graph. Figure 19 (the full version of the isnad chain shown in Figure 5) illustrates a non trivial narration tree of a hadith.

We will leave the detail of the isnad tree graphical display algorithm as it is outside the scope of this chapter. One thing we did not address in the current work is resolving the ambiguity in narrators' names (see § Problems and challenges). A list of equivalent names (different names or alias representing the same narrator) at best partly solves the problem. For a comprehensive solution we do need a huge database of student-teacher pairs.

EVALUATION AND RESULTS

For testing purposes we picked 32 hadiths from the simple cases and 55 from the hard cases, a total of 87 different hadiths. The hadiths were picked from Sahih of Bukhari and Sahih of Muslim since they are considered the most reliable of the collections. By simple cases we mean those hadiths that has a single narration chain, whereas the hard cases have more than one narration chain. The authors would like to thank Prof. Emeritus M.M. Al-Azami, a hadith scholar, for helping us verify the generated trees. The program successfully generated the narration chain of 28 hadiths from the simple cases and 48 hadiths from the hard cases. An overall success rate of 87%. Figure 20 is a screen shot of the narration tree of a hard case hadith.

Figures 21 and 22 show the narration trees of two hard case hadiths which were successfully generated and rendered. In fact Figure 21 is the full narration tree for the hadith whose partial isnad graph was featured in Figure 5.

Figure 19. A non trivial narration tree. The leftmost node is the prime narrator of the hadith.

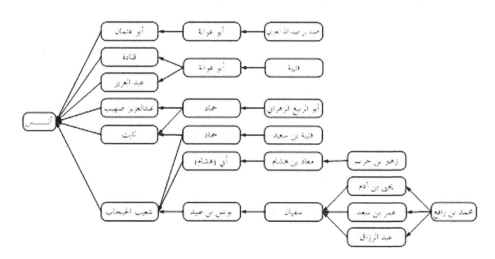

An example of a simple case hadith which our program failed to generate a correct narration chain was discussed as an example for inaccurate parsing (see § Testing the hadith grammar).

CONCLUSION AND FUTURE RESEARCH DIRECTIONS

Working on Arabic text processing is an abstruse topic, because of the Arabic language remarkable richness in derivations, vocabularies and grammatical structures. In this paper we tackled one

Figure 20. Screen shot of a successfully generated narration tree of the hadith (in upper left window). Prime narrator is the leftmost node.

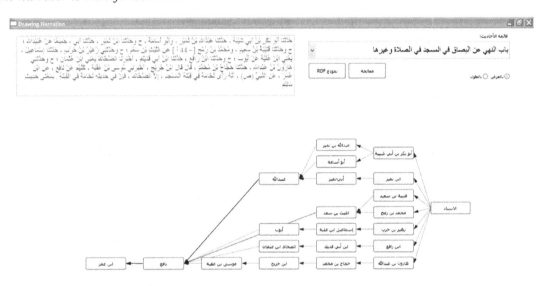

Figure 21. Successfully generated and rendered narration tree of a hard case hadith. This is the full isnad chain of the hadith featured in Figure 5. The prime narrator is the leftmost node in the figure.

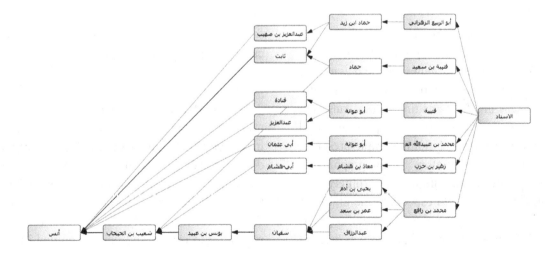

Figure 22. Another example of a successfully generated and rendered narration tree of a hard case hadith. The leftmost node is the prime narrator.

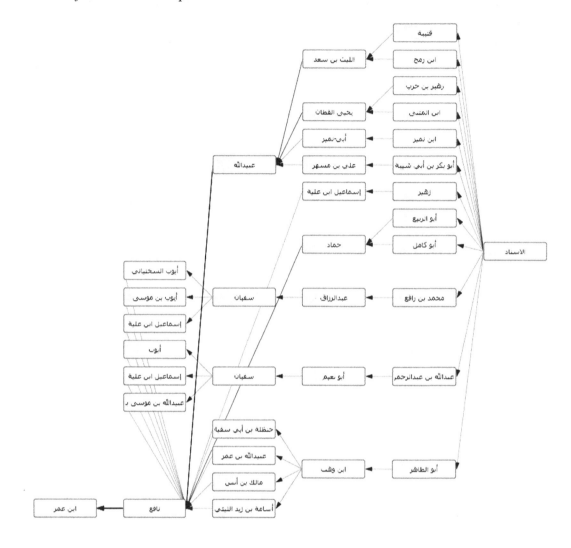

of the most celebrated classical Arabic literatures, the sayings and deeds of Prophet Muhammad. Our focus was on automatic generation and graphical visualization of the narration tree of the hadith. This process involved creating natural language lexer, perform shallow parsing, parsing, build syntactic analyzer and finally graph presenter that displays the narrators' chain graphically. We believe our contribution will definitely help researchers in this field especially the grammar to parse the isnad. Our domain specific grammar is built from the ground up and was derived from the many hadith samples that we studied carefully during this research. Experiments on sample hadiths show our approach to have a very good success rate.

The work is far from over and there is a lot of room for improvement. We need to refine the grammar to be able to handle cases which it currently does not. For future improvement, we suggest handling the equivalent names problem. This is necessary to properly render the narration chain. We also need to modify the graphical rendering algorithm to use curved lines or angled lines to link between different nodes. Of more practical improvement to the hadith scholars is to link the individual nodes in the graph with the narrator's biographic database. A defective link in the isnad can be displayed using dotted lines as opposed to solid lines for unbroken links (see § Introduction).

REFERENCES

Al-Osaimi, A., Al-Bassam, H., Al-Mazyad, K., Al-Yahya, K., Al-Ageel, M., Al-Rashed, R., & Al-Shalan, S. (2008). *Al Asaneed tree*. Retrieved November 15, 2009, from http://colleges.ksu.edu.sa/Arabic Colleges/ComputerScience/IT/DocLib/BSC projects/Al Asaneed Tree.pdf.

Al-Qushairy, M. H., & Siddiqi, A. H. (1972). *Sahih Muslim: Being traditions of the sayings and doings of the Prophet Muhammad as narrated by his companions and compiled under the title Al-Jami'-us-Sahih by Imam Muslim* (Siddiqi, A. H., Trans.). Lahore, Pakistan: Sh. Muhammad Ashraf.

Al-Salman, A. M., Al-Ohali, Y., & Al-Rabiah, M. (2006). An Arabic semantic parser and meaning analyzer. *Egyptian Computer Science Journal, 28*(3), 8–29.

Arabic Transliteration. (2002). *Qamus LLC website*. Retrieved November 10, 2009, from http://www.qamus.org/transliteration.htm.

Azami, M. M. (1977). *Studies in Hadith methodology and literature*. Indianapolis, IN: American Trust Publication.

Azami, M. M. (1978). *Studies in early Hadith literature* (2nd ed.). Indianapolis, IN: American Trust Publication.

Chomsky, N. (1956). Three models for the description of language. *Information Theory. IEEE Transactions, 2*(3), 113–124.

Daelemans, W., & van den Bosch, A. (1992). Generalization performance of backpropagation learning on a syllabification task. In M. Drossaers & A. Nijholt (Eds.), *Proc. 3rd Twente Workshop on Language Technology* (pp. 27-37). Enschede, The Netherlands: Universiteit Twente.

Daelemans, W., van den Bosch, A., & Weijters, T. (1997). IGTree: Using trees for compression and classification in lazy learning algorithms. In Aha, D. (Ed.), *Artificial Intelligence Review: Special Issue on Lazy Learning* (*Vol. 11*, pp. 1–5).

Extended Backus-Naur Form. (n.d.). In *Wikipedia*. Retrieved November 12, 2009, from http://en.wikipedia.org/wiki/Extended_Backus%E2%80%93Naur_Form.

Habash, N., Soudi, A., & Buckwalter, T. (2007). On Arabic transliteration. In A. Soudi, A. van den Bosch & G. Neumann (Eds.), *Text, Speech and Language Technology: Vol. 38. Arabic Computational Morphology: Knowledge-based and Empirical Methods* (pp. 15-22). The Netherlands: Springer.

International Standards Organization. (1996). *ISO/IEC 14977, Information technology – Syntactic metalanguage – Extended BNF*. Retrieved November 12, 2009, from http://standards.iso.org/ittf/PubliclyAvailableStandards/s026153_ISO_IEC_14977_1996(E).zip.

Modern Standard Arabic. (n.d.). In *Wikipedia*. Retrieved April 9, 2010, from http://en.wikipedia.org/wiki/Modern_Standard_Arabic.

Naur, P. (1960). Revised report on the algorithmic language ALGOL 60. *Communications of the ACM, 3*(5), 299–314. doi:10.1145/367236.367262

Peirsman, Y. (2006). Example-based metonymy recognition for proper nouns. *Proc. 11th Conf. of the European Chapter of the Assoc. for Computational Linguistics (EACL-2006): Student Research Workshop* (pp. 71-78). Trento, Italy.

Silberztein, M. D. (1997). The lexical analysis of natural languages. In Roche, E., & Schabes, Y. (Eds.), *Finite-state language processing* (pp. 175–204). MIT Press.

Stanfill, C., & Waltz, D. (1986). Toward memory-based reasoning. *Communications of the ACM, 29*(12), 1213–1228. doi:10.1145/7902.7906

Stav, A. (2006). Shallow parsing. In *Seminar in Natural Language Processing and Computational Linguistics*. Tel Aviv Univ. Retrieved December 10, 2008, from http://www.cs.tau.ac.il/~nachumd/NLP/shallow-parsing.pdf.

Veenstra, J., & Buchholz, S. (1998). Fast NP chunking using memory-based learning techniques. In F. Verdenius & van den Broek (Eds.), *Proc. of Benelearn '98* (pp. 71-78). Wageningen, The Netherlands.

Zavrel, J., & Daelemans, W. (1997). Memory-based learning: Using similarity for smoothing. *Proc. 35th Annual Meeting of the Assoc. for Computational Linguistics (ACL-97)* (pp. 436-43). Madrid, Spain.

ENDNOTE

[1]   Anno Hegirae (in the year of Hijra) is the Muslim lunar calendar. In reference to the Prophet's migration from Makka to Madina on 1 AH (corresponds to 621 CE).

Chapter 30
Using Event Semantics for Toponym Disambiguation

Kirk Roberts
University of Texas at Dallas, USA

Cosmin Adrian Bejan
University of Southern California, USA

Sanda Harabagiu
University of Texas at Dallas, USA

ABSTRACT

This chapter discusses a method for improving the disambiguation of location names using limited event semantics. Location names are often ambiguous, as the same name may refer to locations in different states, countries, or continents. Ambiguous location names, also known as toponyms, need to be disambiguated (or grounded) when resolving many spatial relations expressed in textual documents. Previous methods for disambiguating toponyms have utilized simple heuristics, statistical ranking, and ontological methods in order to resolve a location reference. However, since toponyms are used in documents that refer to events, semantic knowledge characterizing events can be used to ground location names. We propose an ontology-based method with a technique that considers the participants in events such as people, organizations, and other locations. Event semantics are integrated into an ontology that is used to distinguish geographical names through a probabilistic approach based on logistic regression. Our experimental results on the SpatialML corpus (Mani et al., 2008) indicate that using event structures improves the quality of disambiguated toponyms.

INTRODUCTION

Toponym disambiguation is the task of grounding ambiguous spatial locations in text (toponyms) by normalizing them to some structured representation (e.g., geo-coordinates, database entry,

or location within a geographic ontology). This task proves to be quite difficult for some highly ambiguous locations. For example, there are over one thousand places named Springfield. To be able to assess the level of location name ambiguity, we have performed a two-tiered study. In the study, we used two gazetteers to count the number of locations with ambiguous names:

DOI: 10.4018/978-1-60960-741-8.ch030

- Geographic Names Information System (GNIS)[1] provided by the U.S. Geological Survey (USGS), which contains over two million locations and facilities within the United States.
- GEOnet Names Server (GNS)[2] provided by the U.S. National Geospatial-Intelligence Agency (NGA), which contains over six million locations world-wide, excluding the United States.

We first determined that of more than two million unique location names in the two gazetteers, less than 20% are ambiguous. Then, to test the ambiguity of spatial locations in common use, we analyzed the SpatialML corpus (Mani et al., 2008), which contains 428 documents and 715 unique, manually-annotated location names. For these names, more than 80% are ambiguous. For example, our database contains 44 matches for "*America*," including América/Mexico, America/Guinea-Bissau, and the United States of America;

24 matches for "*Palestine*," including Palestine/Texas, and the Occupied Palestinian Territory; and 7 matches for "*Baghdad*," including both the Iraqi city of Baghdad and the Iraqi Governate of Baghdad that contains the city. For more details on this case study, see Table 1.

Since location name ambiguity is such a pervasive problem, we have developed a toponym disambiguation method that uses the hypothesis that locations are groundings of events. Therefore event semantics impacts the quality of toponym disambiguation. In our approach, toponyms are disambiguated by (1) taking into account all possible spatial relations induced from event structures in which they participate, and (2) scoring all paths in the ontology between toponyms and event participants. Scoring is performed by logistic regression.

Algorithm 1 illustrates a generalized method for toponym disambiguation used by many of the systems discussed later. First, the location mentions in the document are extracted (EXTRACT-

Table 1. Case study on ambiguous names. (a) Globally ambiguous names collected using USGS and NGA gazetteers. (b) Ambiguous names in corpus collected on 715 unique names in 428 documents from SpatialML (Mani et al., 2008).

Duplicates	Entries	Percent
(a)		
1	2,150,855	80.2%
2+	531,550	19.8%
5+	86,493	3.2%
10+	30,759	1.1%
50+	2,294	0.086%
100+	617	0.023%
1000+	5	0.0002%
(b)		
1	119	16.6%
2+	596	83.4%
5+	438	61.3%
10+	310	43.4%
50+	83	11.6%
100+	16	2.2%

Algorithm 1. Generalized method for toponym disambiguation. EXTRACTTOPONYMS, RETRIEVECANDIDATEsandScoreare *specific to the approach*

```
Input: A document dOutput: Array N[1..n], the best normalizations for each
toponym in dletT[1..n] = EXTRACTTOPONYMS(d)
letR[1..n] represent a list of retrieval candidate lists
fork = 1..nR[k] = RETRIEVECANDIDATES(T[k])
for each possible combination C[1..n] of candidates from RifSCORE(C, d) >
SCORE(N, d)
        N = C
```

TOPONYMS). These form the set of toponyms that require disambiguation. Then, the candidates for each toponym are retrieved from a knowledge resource, typically a gazetteer (RETRIEVECANDIDATES). Finally, those candidates are scored in a manner that takes the candidates for the other toponyms into account (SCORE).

In this chapter, we consider the results of EXTRACTTOPONYMS to be provided as the output of a named entity recognition (NER) system, and thus limit our scope to retrieval and scoring. Intuitively, the role of RETRIEVECANDIDATES is to return the correct resolution as often as possible, without too many extraneous candidates.

The central focus of most research in toponym disambiguation, however, is on the scoring/ranking of candidates (the SCORE function). We discuss our implementation in the disambiguation section. In our approach, we propose *event semantics,* specifically the interaction between an event and its participants, as a resource for enhancing the ranking. Because no known data set exists to evaluate ranking independent of retrieval, we must consider the retrieval step in our experiments as well.

Reasoning about the spatial aspects of events in documents has always required spatial locations to be grounded within the *event structure.* Yet, we believe that the reverse is true as well: the event structure contributes to the understanding of the spatial grounding. Consider the following sentence:

- Mikheil Saakashvili was elected President of Georgia in 2004.

Disambiguating the toponym "*Georgia*" requires the use of contextual cues we argue are best provided by the event structure. After identifying "*Mikheil Saakashvili*" and "*Georgia*" as participants in the "*elected*" event, it is likely that some spatial relationship exists between them. While there are numerous potential spatial relationships between participants in events, often defining the exact relationship requires the locations to already be spatially grounded. For the purpose of resolving toponyms, however, we only need to provide the disambiguation algorithm with enough information to choose the most likely candidate (i.e., "*Republic of Georgia*" over "*State of Georgia, USA*") using a shallow event structure.

In addition to our proposed approach, we present three baselines to judge the performance of our approach. The first is a simple linear classifier commonly employed in the literature. The second is an ontological approach that performs a document-wide classification. The final baseline is a simple combination of the two.

The rest of this chapter is organized as follows. We first discuss related work in toponym resolution and event detection. Second, we outline the structure for our ontology and how we incorporate events and their participants. Third, we outline our retrieval methods. Fourth, we propose four hypotheses (three baselines plus our primary approach) to show how events can contribute information to a disambiguation system. Fifth, we detail our experiments and discuss the results. Finally, we identify areas of future research and summarize our conclusions.

PREVIOUS WORK

Recognizing textual expressions as real-world geographic locations has a multitude of practical uses. This is especially true in an age where the Internet provides billions of pieces of text, many containing geographic information. One common use case is in Geographic Information Systems (GIS), which are used to capture, store, and analyze location data. A commonly used GIS is Google Maps, which links map data to web data. So-called "hyper-local" news sites such as EveryBlock.com are able to automatically analyze news articles, find and resolve geographic locations, and then use those locations to alert users to nearby events and items of interest. Additionally, location information may be utilized in a search capacity in Geographic Information Retrieval (GIR). This functionality is also coded into Google Maps. GIR systems allow for location-aware searches such as "hotels in London" that require a natural language search component backed by a more traditional GIS capable of proximity searches.

A major hurdle in the recognition of geographic locations is their ambiguity. Therefore, toponym disambiguation is similar to the problem of *word sense disambiguation* (WSD). The goal of WSD is to specify the particular meaning for polysemous words (e.g., recognizing that the string "chair" is a piece of furniture as opposed to the head of a committee). See Navigli (2009) for a survey of WSD methods. Most WSD methods use WordNet (Fellbaum, 1998) to specify the possible senses of a word. However, this is problematic for disambiguating locations because WordNet has poor coverage of proper names. For example, WordNet only contains 31 cities in Texas, a state with over

8,000 cities. Due to these limitations in coverage, conventional WSD methods are not very attractive.

An alternative approach is provided by *entity linking*, which deals with resolving named entities (such as proper names of people, organizations, as well as locations). Instead of using WordNet, the most common resource to use for resolution is Wikipedia. For instance, Cucerzan (2007) normalizes named entities to their proper Wikipedia page (e.g., "*UTD*" to "*University of Texas at Dallas*"). Wikipedia contains better coverage of locations than WordNet (at the time of this writing, almost 1,000 cities in Texas are listed in Wikipedia), but still lacks the coverage of a typical gazetteer database. Moreover, for many non-Western nations, coverage of locations in Wikipedia is far worse. For example, Wikipedia contains just over 100 cities in Uzbekistan, while our gazetteer contains over 3,700.

Real-world knowledge is an additional information source used in toponym disambiguation. To capture real-world knowledge, specialized heuristics are used. For example, Smith and Crane (2001) disambiguate toponyms for the purpose of visualizing information from a digital library. Their algorithm uses contextual heuristics derived using an expanding window technique. Leidner, Sinclair, and Webber (2003) utilized a "one sense per discourse" rule, "bounding box" distance, as well as other heuristics.

Ontological information encoded in gazetteers is the bread-and-butter for many toponym disambiguation approaches. Buscaldi and Rosso (2008) and Volz, Kleb, and Mueller (2007) employ ontologies to aid in the disambiguation process, but in much different ways. Buscaldi & Rosso (2008) use conceptual density (Agirre & Rigau, 1996) with an ontology built from WordNet holonyms. Volz, Kleb, and Mueller (2007), however, builds an ontology from gazetteers and sets class weights to rank candidates.

The most similar approach to our own was proposed by Hu and Ge (2007). They utilize a similar ontological structure, but cast learning as a linear optimization with features based on that structure. When classifying a given location mention, all locations within its context that have a potential resolution that is spatially related contribute to the given mention's score. The three spatial relation features they employ are identity (two locations are equal), similarity (two locations are siblings), and part (one location is a part of the other). They then learn the weights for each of these three features. This is similar to both the first baseline (in terms of learning) and the second baseline (in terms of the use of an ontology) we describe in the disambiguation section.

In order to evaluate toponym disambiguation systems, an annotated corpus of disambiguated spatial entities must be used. The SpatialML corpus (Mani et al., 2008) contains several types of spatial information such as distance normalization, spatial relations (e.g., in, near, equals), and toponyms disambiguated into publicly available databases such as the NGA and USGS gazetteers discussed earlier. They describe a statistical ranking method which we use as the first baseline for our approach. Unfortunately, the numbers in that paper are not easily comparable to our own, as we only intend to disambiguate a subset of the resolved toponyms in SpatialML, as described below in our Geo-Ontology.

THE GEO-ONTOLOGY

Incorporating event semantics into the task of toponym resolution requires a framework that can describe the relationship between the participants of an event. In traditional classification approaches, the set of possible outcomes is fixed to a relatively small number. However, for toponym disambiguation, the number of outcomes is equal to the total number of locations on the planet (or at least in our gazetteer), which creates a difficult task for a conventional learning system. Further, the training data only contains a small fraction of possible outcomes, yet we wish to classify

toponyms our system has never seen before. For these reasons our framework is not structured to learn which outcome to select in which situation, but rather what *spatial relationships* are the most important in choosing the correct normalized location.

Because the distribution of geographic entities in corpora skews toward well-known and often heavily populated places, simple linear classifiers with basic feature sets often perform remarkably well considering their lack of representational power. Heuristics such as "prefer more populous location," "prefer capitals over other cities," and "prefer countries over states over cities" can easily be encoded as real-valued features and weights may be learned by a linear classifier. But more advanced features that take advantage of the additional knowledge provided in the text are not so easily encoded into a linear classifier.

For this reason, we chose an ontological approach: a master graph is built containing geographic locations so that spatial relationships may be more easily represented. The challenge here is *learning*: while a linear approach makes learning easy and representation difficult, an ontological approach makes representation easier but learning a challenge. Training data indicates the correct location resolution, not the best ontology path-weighting scheme. In this chapter we show that without a proper learning approach, ontological approaches cannot overcome a simplistic linear classification technique.

To facilitate learning, we first simplify our geographic ontology to three levels: countries, states, and localities. Proper geo-ontologies that contain the exact hierarchical structure for every geo-political location are difficult for learning algorithms to generalize on as they vary heavily by local custom (e.g., New Zealand has no state/province structure, only counties; the Vatican is a city-state; while Russia has federal divisions, each of which may contain states (oblasts), semiautonomous Republics, federal cities, as well as other distinct types of administrative divisions each

Figure 1. Sample of our geo-ontology. The first tier of the ontology is composed of countries, the second tier is states/provinces, and the third is cities/counties/other localities. To see how an event fits into this ontology, see Figure 2.

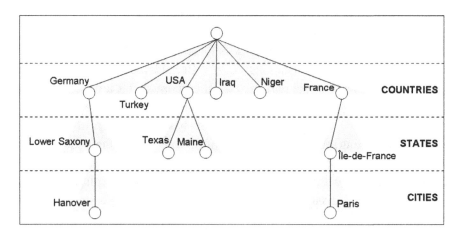

with different types of sub-divisions). Further, the structure we chose has strong consistency within countries, as cities rarely cross state lines, but regularly cross counties (e.g., each of New York City's five Boroughs is itself a county). We only allow geo-political entities (GPE) as specified by the ACE[3] guidelines, omitting continents and arbitrary regions like the Middle East. Examples of non-GPE locations are the Indian Ocean, the Nile River, and the Rocky Mountains. Figure 1 illustrates a small part of our ontological structure.

We have populated this ontology using the freely available Geonames[4] gazetteer. Geonames is actually a combination of the two most commonly used gazetteers (NGA's GNS and the USGS's GNIS, the most commonly used public gazetteers in SpatialML) as well as dozens of other resources. The version of Geonames we used contains 6,912,700 entries (2,720,984 of which we categorize as GPEs), each of which contain geo-coordinates, population data, and alternative names including acronyms ("*USA*" for "*United States*"), nicknames ("*Big Apple*" for "*New York City*"), and non-English spellings.

EVENT STRUCTURES

In a natural language context, an *event mention* is a text span that refers to a real-world event. The event may be a single action (e.g., "*the explosion*") or it may refer to some sequence of under-specified sub-events that form a coherent whole (e.g., "*the 2008 election*"). Often, various participants and properties of an event are communicated in the text. Take the following two sentence fragments as examples:

- a dissenting member of the UN panel, William Church, has now told the BBC that the Rwandan invasion was a false claim
- I have reviewed my analysis with the governments of the UK, US, EU, and the Netherlands[5]

The primary event in sentence (2) is "*told*," which contains three participants: (i) "*a dissenting member of the UN panel, William Church,*" (the SPEAKER), (ii) "*the BBC*" (the RECIPIENT), and (iii) "*the Rwandan invasion was a false claim*" (the MESSAGE). Further information about the event is embedded in participant (i). Specifically, we know that the head of the role, William Church, is part of a UN panel, which is itself part of the UN. Participant (iii) actually contains another event, "*the Rwandan invasion*," which is clearly connected to Rwanda, one of the geo-locations we seek to resolve. Additionally, "*dissenting*" may also be viewed as an event. Therefore, using the event structure, we have connected (a) the UN, an organization, (b) William Church, a person, (c) the BBC, an organization, and (d) Rwanda, a geo-location. We describe how these are extracted automatically later.

Sentence (3) is processed similarly. The primary event, "*reviewed*," contains participants (i) "*I*" (the REVIEWER), (ii) "*my analysis*" (the REVIEWED_ITEM), and (iii) "*the governments of the UK, US, EU, and the Netherlands*" (the REVIEW_PARTICIPANTS). Participant (i) is a pronoun that refers back to William Church. But more interesting in our case is participant (iii), which is a list of participants with the same role type. Thus we know (iii-a), the government of the UK, (iii-b), the government of the US, (iii-c), the government of the EU, and (iii-d), the government of the Netherlands, all participated in the same event.

For our purpose, the actual role type information (e.g., SPEAKER, MESSAGE, REVIEW_PARTICIPANT) is not as important as the participants themselves. The knowledge that the four participants in the event from (2) (UN, William Church, BBC, Rwanda) all participated in the same event suggests that there is perhaps a spatial relationship among them. The same applies for the participants of the event in (3). By spatial relationship, we do not intend to suggest that all participants were physically present at the event. Rather, we assert that some un-specified spatial relation exists (e.g., the UN has operations in Rwanda; William Church was in the same room as a BBC reporter; William Church has been to Rwanda). Again, we aren't as interested in *what* spatial relation there is, just the potential presence of one.

In all likelihood, the process for determining types of spatial relations requires the participants to already be grounded (i.e., the toponym disambiguation task that we are describing has already been performed). In the event from (3), we cannot determine the REVIEWER's spatial relation with the entity "*US*" until we resolve US to the country United States of America (as opposed to the Union State, a supranational entity consisting of Russia and Belarus). Therefore, depending on the participants in the event only and not the entire event structure makes sense when viewed as part of a pipelined system.

One resource for annotated events is the Time-Bank corpus (Pustejovsky et al., 2003). TimeBank encodes temporal relations between events and entities, but still annotates event mentions regardless of whether they take part in a temporal relation. TimeBank defines events using three syntactic classes:

1. Tensed verbs ("*has left*," "*was captured*," "*will resign*")
2. Stative adjectives ("*sunken*," "*stalled*," "*on board*")
3. Event nominals ("*merger*," "*Military Operation*," "*Gulf War*")

While an event itself might suggest how much spatial cohesion exists between the participants (e.g., "*met*" implies a tighter spatial relation than "*e-mailed*"), we leave that problem to future work. For now, our goal is merely to identify those entities that participate in common events. The event definition provided by TimeBank gives us a useful starting point, as we consider only the participants of an event that are syntactically dependent on the event mention.

To accomplish this, we have built a simple dependency parser that uses the syntactic parse of a full sentence to find NPs that are syntactically linked to the event mention extracted by a system trained on TimeBank. This dependency parse provides no information on the type of dependency, since again we only need to know the set of participants. Several heuristics are employed to select the correct level of the parse tree to set as the overall scope of the event. The scope depends on which of the three TimeBank event types previously described pertains to a given event mention. For tensed verbs, we include the verb's subject and objects. This sometimes includes dependent clauses like event (1) above. Clauses that contain another verbal event are not included, as this sometimes suggests a temporal and often spatial shift. In example (4) below, the participants "*British*" and "*Chamber of Commerce*" in the clause beginning with "*before*" would not be considered participants in the "*met*" event.

4.   Blair met Hong Kong leader Tung Chee-hwa Wednesday before addressing the British Chamber of Commerce at a luncheon.

For stative adjectives and event nominals, the scope is defined as the largest NP that does not contain a verb. Specifically we seek to include syntactically dependent PPs that often describe the participants. Consider the nominal event "*resolution*" in (5). While the lifting of economic sanctions forms part of the NP headed by "*resolution*," and certainly adds context, we would exclude Iraq as a participant in the event as this often leads to un-related entities.

5.   A US-British draft resolution to lift economic sanctions placed on Iraq in 1990

After the dependency scope is determined, the participants within that scope must be extracted. Our method is designed to maximize recall of the participants, so most entities within the scope will be selected. Rather than use heuristics to select participants, we use them to ignore participants based on observed tendencies from data. Take the following example sentence:

6.   Björn Ferry, of Norway, won the gold medal in the men's pursuit biathlon in Vancouver.

While there is certainly a spatial relationship between Björn Ferry and Norway, the event "*won*" does not contain "*Norway*" as a participant. Rather, the location Norway is present simply to add information about one of the participants in the event.

It should be noted that there are alternative strategies to acquiring these spatial relations. One method is to use a semantic parser based on PropBank (Palmer, Kingsbury, & Gildea, 2005) instead of TimeBank. PropBank encodes both verbal events and their arguments. However, we believe the non-verbal events in TimeBank provide greater event coverage while PropBank's argument identification is easily replaced by our dependency parser. Strategies that use less semantic information include considering all entities within a sentence as spatially related (analogous to one event per sentence where all entities are participants) and using token distance between entities. Results in Buscaldi and Rosso (2008) suggest that document context outperforms sentence context. Yet our results show that event context actually outperforms document context. This suggests semantically light methods fail to properly capture spatial relations, and in such conditions greater context is necessary for proper disambiguation.

Linking Event Participants

We consider three types of entity participants in events: people, organizations, and GPE locations. We start with the base ontology constructed using locations from Geonames. Our goal is to use Wikipedia to connect non-geographic entities to the geographic nodes in our ontology. First, we map both geographic ontology nodes and non-geographic entities to their respective Wikipedia articles. Then, we use the links from those articles to create edges in our ontology graph. Figure 2

Figure 2. Given the sentence fragment, the event "urging" is identified and its six participants are extracted with a dependency parser. Then, the non-location participants are linked into the ontology using Wikipedia. Finally, the subgraph containing all event participants is extracted (shaded).

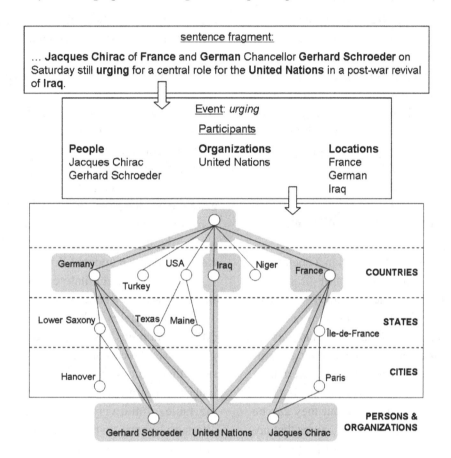

illustrates how one of these additional entities is connected to our ontology in an event. In the example, the *Jacques Chirac* is connected to *Paris* (where he was mayor) and *France* (where he was president). The shaded area around *Jacques Chirac, Gerhard Schroeder, United Nations, Germany, France,* and *Iraq* indicates an event involving all six as participants. The details behind selecting edges for an event are explained in the disambiguation section.

When mapping persons and organizations from text into Wikipedia, we assume disambiguation is not required. If Wikipedia indicates that the string "*Robert Burns*" predominately refers to the Scottish poet, our algorithm assumes that is what

the document is referring to. On the other hand, if Wikipedia uses a disambiguation page for entities such as "*William Knox*," we ignore the entity. Strategies for disambiguating individuals and organizations can be found in the entity linking literature referenced earlier. Additionally, no pronominal coreference is used to extend the number of events an entity participates in. Both these tasks are left to future work.

Locations in the ontology are mapped into Wikipedia using a simple heuristic. For countries and U.S. states, the name is assumed to be the exact Wikipedia article title. For cities in the U.S., the pattern [*city-name, state-name*] is used. For everything else, [*name, country-name*] is used.

Redirects are followed, so "*Paris, France*" would be redirected to the "*Paris*" page.

Once persons, organizations, and locations are mapped into Wikipedia, the links on their respective article pages can then be used to determine which entities are related. For instance, Jacques Chirac's page contains references to both the France and Paris pages, and since both of those pages were found to have corresponding nodes in the ontology, we can link the Jacques Chirac node to the geographic ontology nodes corresponding to the country France and its capital, Paris.

RETRIEVAL OF GEO-LOCATIONS

When disambiguating a toponym in a document, the first step is to determine a list of disambiguation candidates (from the RETRIEVECANDIDATES method from Algorithm 1). It involves querying a spatial database. Our database contains over 2.7 million geo-political locations with over 1.8 million alternative names. However, the alternative names do not cover every possible string that may be used to reference a location, but they can be automatically generated from the names that are present. In order to cover cases not provided by

the Geonames database, we must choose between one of two methods:

a. Generate all alternative names up front for every location in the database.
b. Generate alternative names on-the-fly for each unique location name discovered.

While both methods could theoretically achieve the same result in terms of retrieved database entries, the first method would prove infeasible on the 2.7 million locations, create an intractably large database, and severely over-generate needed alternations. Additionally, since some of our methods use Wikipedia, performing on-the-fly alternative name finding allows us to easily swap in an updated Wikipedia version.

Our on-the-fly alternative name finding algorithm is based on a series of alternation modules. The list of modules is shown in Table 2. Because different modules have a different impact on the precision and recall of the system, we have separated them into strategies, where each strategy inherits the strategies above it (as represented in the table). Intuitively, safer strategies produce alternative names that are more precise and lead to few misleading names. More aggressive strategies

Table 2. Gazetteer retrieval alternation modules and their respective strategies. All higher level strategies inherit alternation modules from lower level strategies (AGGRESSIVE is the highest level)

Method (with examples)	Strategy
None	Basic
Case: Alters capitalization. "*us*" to "*US*" and "*Us*"	Caseless
Type: Removes geo-type. "*New York City*" to "*New York*"	Safe
Direction: Removes direction. "*North Baghdad*" to "*Baghdad*"	
Abbreviation: Expands ISO-3166 abbreviations and normalizes. "*AF*" to "*Afghanistan,*" "*U.S.A.*" to "*USA*"	
Wikipedia Redirect: Uses Wikipedia redirect links, "*Myanmar*" to "*Burma*"	
Demonym: Maps gentilics to locations. "*Texan*" to "*Texas*"	
Wikipedia Suggest: Matches "For …, see XXX" pattern at top of Wikipedia pages. "*Washington*" to "*Washington, D.C.*"	Moderate
Comma Split: Takes first name in compounds. "*Atlanta, Georgia*" to "*Atlanta*"	
Wikipedia Disambiguation: Results from Wikipedia disambiguation pages. "*Lincoln*" to "*Lincoln, Nebraska*"	Aggressive

have greater recall but present the downstream disambiguator with more candidates to choose from, reducing the chances that the correct gazetteer entry will be chosen, if present. We now describe how these alternation modules are used.

Given a location mention and a set of alternation modules, our retrieval method works as follows. Alternation modules are split into two sets: A_1 and A_2. Then, given mention m, A_1 is run exhaustively on m. By this we mean that for every alternative name produced by an alternator in A_1, that alternative name is itself run through the alternators in A_1. This continues until no new alternative names are generated. Then each alternative name produced by A_1 is run through the alternators in A_2 once. Finally, the alternative names produced by A_2 are run though the exhaustive process using A_1.

Intuitively, A_2 is the set of alternation modules that have been observed in practice to work poorly in combination with other alternation modules. These modules may generate misleading alternative names which may lead to even more misleading alternative names. The only two alternation modules used in A_2 from Table 2 are the Wikipedia Suggest and Wikipedia Disambiguation modules.

As an example of how the modules work together in this exhaustive approach, consider the mention "*ny*" found in text and identified as a location by an NER system. First, "*ny*" is expanded to "*NY*" via the Case module. Then, "*NY*" is expanded to "*New York*" via the Wikipedia Redirect module. Finally, "*New York*" is expanded to "*New York City*" via the Wikipedia Suggest module. These four names would return two unique candidates from the gazetteer: the city and the state of New York (though likely several others as well). It is then the job of the disambiguation system to determine which fits best given the context.

DISAMBIGUATION OF TOPONYMS

Given a document with n toponyms, the retrieval step will generate n separate candidate sets. Next, we must have a method for scoring a given combination of candidates (the SCORE method from Algorithm 1) so that candidates may be ranked. Let C_i represent the set of candidates for the ith toponym mention in the document. The goal of the disambiguation step is then to rank all c in C_i such that the correct resolution, $\hat{c}$, is ranked in the top position. We propose four hypotheses: our main approach and three baselines. We refer to them as hypotheses as they each represent an approach similar to those proposed in previous work (in the case of Hypotheses 1 and 2), a logical combination of those systems (for Hypothesis 3), or the approach described in this chapter (Hypothesis 4).

Hypothesis 1: Use a Linear Approach

Similar to Mani et al. (2008) and Hu and Ge (2007), we propose a linear statistical ranking model that chooses the best toponym resolution. Specifically, given a set of target candidates C_i, we rank c in C_i by probability approximation function H_1:

$$H_1(c) = \frac{1}{1 + e^{-w^T x_c}}$$

where w is our learned weight vector and x_c is the feature vector that corresponds to candidate c. H_1 intentionally conforms with the classic sigmoid function in order to train a logistic regression classifier to maximize the probability that the candidate with the highest H_1 score is the correct resolution. We refer to this method as a bag-of-features disambiguator because it requires no ontological information.

Hypothesis 2: Use the Ontology Transition Probability

Similar to Volz, Kleb, and Mueller (2007) and Hu and Ge (2007), we propose an ontolgial ranking mechanism that determines the most likely paths through the ontology to disambiguate toponym candidates. Given n unique toponym mentions, there are $\Pi\ |C_i|\ (1 \leq i \leq n)$ possible combinations for resolving these mentions. Note that the unique toponym mention requirement structurally enforces a one sense per document requirement on the system. Let Ψ be our ontology graph containing both geo-locations and non-geographical entities. For each possible combination of candidates we create an *assignment tree A* that is the sub-graph of Ψ containing (i) one candidate node for each toponym mention from the document, and (ii) the minimum set of parent nodes and edges of Ψ such that the nodes in A form a complete tree. Both person and organization nodes may have more than one "parent" (i.e., geographic node they are attached to) in the ontology. When this happens, simple edge count distance is used to find the closest node in the assignment tree. Note that it is quite possible to have an intractable number of potential assignment trees. We discuss our handling of this problem in the next section.

We propose a statistical ranking model for finding the best assignment tree $\bar{A}$ that assigns every candidate to the correct entry in Ψ. Let the edge weight for an edge $e_{x,y}$ from parent x to child y in A represent the probability that a node within the sub-tree rooted by y contains a correct toponym resolution for an arbitrary toponym. Thus, the weight on $e_{x,y}$ can be seen as the transition probability from x to y. As in Hypothesis 1, we define the probability as a sigmoidal function of the weights and features:

$$P(e_{x,y}) = \frac{1}{1 + e^{-w^T x_e}}$$

where w, again, is the learned weights, but now x_e is the feature vector for edge $e_{x,y}$. We then define the probability approximation function H_2 to be the product of the probabilities of the edges in assignment tree A (following an independence assumption):

$$H_2(A) = \prod_{e \in A} P(e)$$

Note that our training method does not allow for direct training on the assignment trees. Rather we attempt to indirectly rank better assignment trees higher by adjusting edge weights based on pair-wise evaluations. The weight of an edge can then be thought of as the probability that the child (or a member of its sub-tree) is a correct toponym resolution. Since most sub-trees will not contain the correct resolution for a given training instance, this results in low probabilities for all edges.

Hypothesis 3: Use the Ontology Transition and Node Probability

Hypothesis 2 presents some severe theoretical limitations because it is limited to the product of edge probabilities. Most important among these is that no candidate will ever be selected if one of its ancestors is also a candidate (e.g., the state "*New York*" will always be selected over the city when both are candidates) because the assignment tree with the child node is guaranteed to have a lower probability. We therefore propose a statistical model that combines both node probabilities and edge probabilities. Since Hypothesis 1 attempts to estimate node probabilities, we can alter H_1 to work on assignment trees:

$$H_1(A) = \prod_{v \in A} H_1(v)$$

where v is both a vertex in A and a candidate for a mention. Now, H_3 is simply defined as the product of H_1 and H_2:

$$H_3(A) = H_1(A)H_2(A)$$

H_1 and H_2 are dependent probability estimators. However, H3 is simply the product of these models, ignoring the dependence. But this model does allow the disambiguator to overcome the *New York* problem from above if the H_1 probability of *New York City* is sufficiently high.

Hypothesis 4: Use the Ontology Event and Node Probability

We now describe an ontological model that accounts for the event structures found within a document. Instead of considering the complete document context, we only wish to consider event context. Toponyms not contained within an event are therefore ranked simply according to their H_1 score. Furthermore, we may have a toponym that participates in multiple events throughout the document and we wish its participation in each event to be measured. We therefore convert an assignment tree into an assignment forest by only considering the edge probabilities within events. Assignment tree A is then split into event assignment tree, A_e, for each event in the document. We then define H_4 similar to H_3:

$$H_4(A) = H_1(A)\prod_{A_e \in A} H_2(A_e)$$

Note that H_4 is capable of traversing the same edge probability multiple times if more than one event covers a node. The assignment forest is therefore not a graphical forest in the strictest sense, but we do wish to traverse the same edge multiple times when a toponym participates in more than one event. This occurrence is common in natural language documents and has a desirable

consequence: highly unlikely event assignment trees penalize H_4 multiple times.

Because H_4 makes no attempt to analyze the complete assignment tree, this model ignores document-wide context. Event context is assumed to be sufficient information to resolve mentions. Candidates that do not take part in an event are evaluated on their H_1 score alone.

Features

While there are numerous possible features for toponym resolution (see Leidner (2006) for an overview of such heuristics), experimental results identified just a few important features for both H_1 (5 feature types) and H_2 (6 feature types). In contrast to the complex heuristics mentioned in the section regarding previous work, our features are quite simple. Most of the more complicated features mentioned in those papers were largely ignored by the learning system in favor of features that provided a simple glimpse of the location's profile. In our experiments, we used the following features.

EXPERIMENTAL RESULTS

The SpatialML corpus (Mani et al., 2008) consists of 428 documents manually tagged with spatial information, including 6,337 PLACE (geo-location) annotations. Of these, 5,573 we consider to be GPEs. We have discarded 48 documents that contain no GPEs and 11 that contain only one, leaving 369 documents with 5,562 GPE annotations. Each PLACE annotation is then mapped to the Geonames ID for evaluation purposes.

Many SpatialML documents contain far too many ambiguous annotations to generate all potential assignment trees. For instance, using the MODERATE retrieval strategy we found 17 documents that would generate more than 2^{31} assignment trees. To provide a more computationally tractable dataset, we used the H_1 score

Table 3. Features used in our approach. Each feature is real-valued between 0 and 1. Furthermore, each feature had access to both the parent and child nodes, but primarily operated on the child.

Feature	Description/Purpose
Log(Population)	The population of the child node was the dominant indicator (a logarithmic function was used for scaling)
StringMatch	Exact string matches between the mention and gazetteer entry
SubstringMatch	Sub-string matches were used to help indicate spurious candidates
Admin	Assigns a value of 0.5 for state capitals and 1.0 for national capitals to give preference to administratively important locations
Type	Actually three boolean features to indicate the node is a country, state, or city
Edge	This feature has a constant value of 1, and its weight is determined by the logistic regression intercept. It is used to weight the default edge probability (and therefore not used in H_l), thus giving relative favor to assignment trees with fewer edges and accounting for how persons and organizations relate to the geographical nodes in the ontology

to limit each candidate set to 10 candidates. This alone would not be enough, for there would still be 10^n possible assignment trees for a document with n mentions. We therefore used the flat disambiguator again to choose the top 500 candidate combinations for each document. Evaluation on a small sub-set of documents indicates this actually improved results by a narrow margin.

For detecting people and organizations, we use the freely available BIOS named entity tagger[6]. It has an F-measure of 85.5 on person names and 92.2 on organization names on the CoNLL test set. For detecting events, we used the system described in Bejan (2007) based on the TimeBank 1.2 corpus (Pustejovsky et al., 2003). It achieves an F-measure of 82.94 using 5-fold cross validation.

Retrieval Experiments

For each of the 5,562 toponyms in SpatialML, we computed precision, recall, and F-measure for each of the five strategies listed in Table 2. The results are shown in Table 4. Precision is measured over all candidates, of which there can be at most one correct. This can be thought of as the precision of

a disambiguation system that chooses a candidate at random.

While the SAFE strategy achieved the highest F-measure, the retrieval module cannot be looked at as a complete system: the quality of the ranking system affects the choice of strategy. While higher precision certainly helps the downstream disambiguator, the retrieval recall fundamentally limits the final accuracy of the system. The MODERATE strategy performs best as input to the disambiguator. The additional incorrect locations are likely outliers that the disambiguator can easily ignore. The AGGRESSIVE strategy, however, is far too imprecise. It often returns common, populous locations as erroneous candidates, and thus heavily confuses the disambiguator. But to confirm

Table 4. Evaluation of gazetteer retrieval for all alternation strategies

Strategy	# Candidates	Precision	Recall	F
Basic	58,560	5.97	62.7	10.9
Caseless	67,154	5.71	68.8	10.5
Safe	83,800	6.31	94.8	11.8
Moderate	85,764	6.31	97.0	11.4
Aggressive	617,995	0.88	97.36	1.74

the point made above, the AGGRESSIVE strategy well outperforms both the BASIC and CASELESS strategies in limited end-to-end testing since many of the mentions do not use the official name for the location listed in the gazetteer.

Disambiguation Experiments

We evaluated all four hypotheses on the SpatialML data. Two metrics were used to evaluate the accuracy of our system. The first is simple accuracy, or the number of correct toponym resolutions ranked in the top position. The second is an ontology-inspired metric that assumes wrong answers that at least share a parent of the correct answer are better than ones that do not. For instance, if the correct resolution for the men-

Table 5. Accuracy scores for 5,562 mentions for our four hypotheses

Hypothesis	Accuracy	Ontology Score
H_1	92.0	93.3
H_2	87.9	92.1
H_3	92.4	94.7
H_4	93.6	94.8

tion *"Henry"* is *"Henry County, Virginia, USA,"* while both *"Henry, Georgia, USA"* and *"Henry, Zambia"* are incorrect, the location in Georgia is slightly more correct than the latter. We consider this is a valid approach for a secondary metric because many reasoning approaches might only need the state, country or distance between two locations. Therefore the "closer" location, while still wrong, is better.

Since our ontology has three levels of content, we award a full point for an exact match, 0.66 points for matching the correct state, and 0.33 points for matching the correct country. This metric gives us an idea of the type of errors each hypothesis makes by comparing the ontology score to the simple accuracy. The results on the four hypotheses using 5-fold cross validation are shown in Table 5.

The best performing hypothesis was H_4, which utilized event semantics as described in this chapter. It outperformed the three baseline hypotheses in both accuracy and ontology score. This suggests that event context provides a more reliable indicator of toponym disambiguation than document context despite the smaller number of locations available for comparison.

While H_2 (ontology only) was the worst performing system, it should be noted how close it

Table 6. Recall of best performing hypothesis when selecting the top N candidates ranked by the disambiguator

N	Recall	Ontology Recall
1	93.6	94.8
2	94.6	95.7
3	95.3	96.1
4	95.5	96.2
5	95.6	96.3
6	95.7	96.4
7	95.7	96.4
8	95.8	96.4
9	95.8	96.4
10	95.8	96.5

came to H_1's ontology score despite having an accuracy of 4% less. H_2 commonly selects small towns closer to the other nodes in the ontology instead of selecting large, well-known cities. This alone may validate the value of a geographic ontology: while H_2 has more difficulty selecting the best candidate, it usually selects candidates that are ontologically closer. Thus, using a simple un-weighted combination of H_1 and H_2 (i.e., H_3), we get the best of both systems: the precision of H_1 with the ontological closeness of H_2.

The lack of improvement of H_4 over H_3 in terms of ontology score is likely due to the fact that H_4 loses much of the ontological improvement we just discussed. Unfortunately, we were unable to create an approach incorporating document-level context that outperforms H_4, so we leave it to future work.

Additionally, we experimented with H_4 by measuring the recall in the top N positions. This evaluation is shown in Table 6. Only slight improvements are made by choosing more than one candidate in an attempt to maximize recall. Given our choice of the MODERATE retrieval strategy, the upper bound for recall is 97.0, suggesting that about 1% of the toponyms are extremely difficult to disambiguate, not even being selected in the top 10 ranked candidates.

Figure 3. Average error of disambiguated toponyms for hypothesis 1 and hypothesis 4

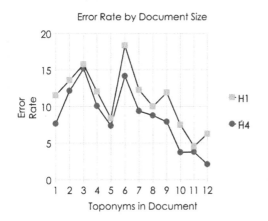

Furthermore, since ontological methods are designed to incorporate context, we experimented with disambiguator performance as a function of document size. Theoretically, an approach that uses more context would outperform one that does not on larger documents. Figure 3 illustrates the average error of H_4 as compared to H_1, our non-ontological model. Many of the larger documents proved easier for both hypotheses, though H_4 consistently performs better for $n > 6$. While documents with large numbers of toponyms do not necessarily contain large numbers of events, there is a correlation. The average document contains 1.2 events with more than one participant, while documents with at least 6 toponyms contain an average of 2.7 such events.

FUTURE RESEARCH DIRECTIONS

Integrating event semantics into toponym disambiguation is just the beginning of a process to incorporate more linguistic knowledge into the grounding of location names. One important next step is to identify the spatial commitment made by particular events. For instance, the event "*e-mailed*" contains almost no spatial commitment, while a literal use of the event "*embraced*" provides a significant spatial commitment. Our approach currently considers all events to have equal spatial commitment, yet we know this should not be the case. One resource for inducing commitment levels is FrameNet (Fillmore & Baker, 2001). FrameNet defines a large number of semantic frames, many of which describe classes of events such as motion, speaking, and purchasing. Additionally, FrameNet defines not only the events but the roles of participants in those events. This would allow discovery of which types of event participant are spatially related. For example, a FrameNet parse of the Björn Ferry sentence from the event structure section would identify "*Björn Ferry*" and "*Vancouver*" as participants in the WIN_PRIZE event, but not "*Norway*." This would then replace our syntactic dependency parse with a true semantic parse.

In this chapter, we only consider events at the sentence level, but events are often described over the course of a natural language discourse. Participants in these larger events may be determined through entity coreference (Grishman & Sundheim, 1996), extending semantic parsing beyond sentence boundaries (Ruppenhofer et al., 2009), or true event coreference (Humphreys, Gaizauskas, & Azzam, 1997). All these approaches could capture a greater context from which to disambiguate toponyms.

Finally, while our approach proved superior on the SpatialML dataset, this may not be true on all datasets. It should work reasonably well on unseen data since our features do not depend on specific locations in the training data. Nevertheless, we wish to evaluate our approach on new datasets. Of particular interest is web data from blogs and social media sites such as Twitter, as this often discusses locations rarely addressed in news articles. While SpatialML does contain such types of data, we hope to find more difficult datasets to further separate the capabilities of toponym disambiguation approaches.

CONCLUSION

In this chapter, we have shown how event semantics may be integrated into the task of toponym disambiguation. A large ontology consisting of millions of locations was created from a publicly available gazetteer. Spatial mentions in documents are mapped into this ontology using a series of alternation modules that seek to identify the proper name(s) that the location string might refer to. Three hypotheses using both linear and ontology based ranking were presented to compare our approach to. Then we discussed how to integrate event semantics into this ontology. Finally, our experiments give empirical evidence to the role event semantics play in how location names are disambiguated.

REFERENCES

Agirre, E., & Rigau, G. (1996). Word sense disambiguation using conceptual density. In *Proceedings of the 16th Conference on Computational Linguistics*, (pp. 16-22). Copenhagen, Denmark: Association for Computational Linguistics.

Bejan, C. A. (2007). Deriving chronological information from texts through a graph-based algorithm. In *Proceedings of the 20th Florida Artificial Intelligence Research Society International Conference* (pp. 259-260). American Association for Artificial Intelligence.

Buscaldi, D., & Rosso, P. (2008). A conceptual density-based approach for the disambiguation of toponyms. *International Journal of Geographical Information Science, 22*(3), 301–313. doi:10.1080/13658810701626251

Cucerzan, S. (2007). Large-scale named entity disambiguation based on Wikipedia data. In *Proceedings of the 2007 Joint Conference on Empirical Methods in Natural Language Processing and Computational Natural Language Learning*, (708-716). Prague, Czech Republic: Association for Computational Linguistics.

Fellbaum, C. (1998). *WordNet: An electronic lexical database*. Cambridge, MA: The MIT Press.

Fillmore, C., & Baker, C. (2001). Frame semantics for text understanding. In *Proceedings of the NAACL Workshop on WordNet and Other Lexical Resources*. Association for Computational Linguistics.

Grishman, R., & Sundheim, B. (1996). *Design of the MUC-6 evaluation*. Vienna, Austria: Association for Computation Linguistics.

Hu, Y., & Ge, L. (2007). A supervised machine learning approach to toponym disambiguation. In Scharl, A., & Tochtermann, K. (Eds.), *The Geospatial Web: How geobrowsers, social software and the Web 2.0 are shaping the network society* (pp. 117–128). Springer.

Humphreys, K., Gaizauskas, R., & Azzam, S. (1997). Event coreference for information extraction. In *Proceedings of the Workshop on Operational Factors in Practical, Robust Anaphora Resolution for Unrestricted Texts*, (pp. 75-81). Association for Computational Linguistics.

Leidner, J. (2006). *Toponym resolution: A first large- scale comparative evaluation*. Technical report.

Leidner, J., Sinclair, G., & Webber, B. (2003). Grounding spatial named entities for information extraction and question answering. In *Proceedings of the HLT-NAACL Workshop on Analysis of Geographic References*, (pp. 31-38). Association for Computational Linguistics.

Mani, I., Hitzeman, J., Richer, J., Harris, D., Quimby, R., & Wellner, B. (2008). SpatialML: Annotation scheme, corpora, and tools. In *Proceedings of the Sixth International Language Resources and Evaluation*.

McNamee, P., & Dang, H. T. (2009). Overview of the TAC 2009 knowledge base population track. In *Proceedings of the 2009 Text Analysis Conference*.

Navigli, R. (2009). Word sense disambiguation: A survey. *ACM Computing Surveys, 41,* 1–69. doi:10.1145/1459352.1459355

Palmer, M., Kingsbury, P., & Gildea, D. (2005). The proposition bank: An annotated corpus of semantic roles. *Computational Linguistics, 31*(1), 71–106. doi:10.1162/0891201053630264

Pustejovsky, J., Castano, J., Ingria, R., Saurí, R., Gaizauskas, R., & Setzer, A. ... Radev, D. (2003). *TimeML: Robust specification of event and temporal expressions in text*. In IWCS-5 Fifth International Workshop on Computational Semantics.

Ruppenhofer, J., Sporleder, C., Morante, R., Baker, C., & Palmer, M. (2009). SemEval-2010 Task 10: Linking events and their participants in discourse. In *Proceedings of the HLT-NAACL Workshop on Semantic Evaluations*, (pp. 106-111). Boulder, CO: Association for Computational Linguistics.

Smith, D. A., & Crane, G. (2001). Disambiguating geographic names in a historical digital library. In *Research and Advanced Technology for Digital Libraries. Lecture Notes in Computer Science, 2163,* 127–137. doi:10.1007/3-540-44796-2_12

Volz, R., Kleb, J., & Mueller, W. (2007). *Towards ontology-based disambiguation of geographical identifiers*. In The 16th International World Wide Web Conference, Banff, Alberta, Canada.

ADDITIONAL READING

Amitay, E. Har'El, N., Sivan, R., & Soffer, A. (2004). Web-a-Where: Geotagging Web Content. In *Proceedings of the Special Interest Group on Information Retrieval*. Sheffield, UK: Association for Computing Machinery.

Andogah, G., Bouma, G., Nerbonne, J., & Koster, E. (2008). Geographical Scope Resolution. In *Proceedings of the Sixth International Language Resources and Evaluation Conference Workshop on Methodologies and Resources for Processing Spatial Language*. Marrakech, Morocco: European Language Resources Association.

Bethard, S., & Martin, J. (2006). Identification of Event Mentions and their Semantic Class. In Proceedings of the 2006 Conference on Empirical Methods in Natural Language Processing. Sydney: Association for Computational Linguistics. Bloom, P. (ed.) (1996) *Language and Space*. MIT Press.

Boguraev, B., & Ando, R. (2005). TimeML-Compliant Text Analysis for Temporal Reasoning. In *Proceedings of the International Joint Conferences on Artificial Intelligence*. Edinburgh: IJCAI.

Buscaldi, D., & Rosso, P. (2008). Geo-WordNet: Automatic Georeferencing of WordNet. In *Proceedings of the Sixth International Language Resources and Evaluation Conference*. Marrakech, Morocco: European Language Resources Association.

Buscaldi, D., & Rosso, P. (2008). Map-based vs. Knowledge-based Toponym Disambiguation. In *Proceedings of the 17th Conference on Information and Knowledge Management Workshop on Geographic Information Retrieval*. Napa Valley: Association for Computing Machinery.

Csomai, A. & Mihalcea, R. (2008). Linking Documents to Encyclopedic Knowledge. *IEEE Intelligent Systems special issue on Natural Language Processing and the Web*, (34-41). IEEE Computer Society.

Fader, A., Soderland, S., & Etzioni, O. (2009). Scaling Wikipedia-based Named Entity Disambiguation to Arbitrary Web Text. In *Proceedings of IJCAI Workshop on User-Contributed Knowledge and Artificial Intelligence: An Evolving Synergy (WikiAI09)*. Pasadena: Association for the Advancement of Artificial Intelligence.

Garbin, E., & Mani, I. (2005). Disambiguating Toponyms in News. In *Proceedings of Human Language Technology Conference and Conference on Empirical Methods in Natural Language Processing* (363-370). Vancouver: Association for Computational Linguistics.

Hobbs, J., & Narayanan, S. (2002). *Spatial Representation and Reasoning. Encyclopedia of Cognitive Science*. MacMillan.

Jones, C. & Purves, R. (2008). Geographical information retrieval. *International Journal of Geographic Information Science*, 22:3, (219-228).

Leidner, J. (2005). An evaluation dataset for the toponym resolution task. In *Computers, Environment, and Urban Systems*.

Li, Y., Moffat, A., Stokes, N., & Cavedon, L. (2006). Exploring Probabilistic Toponym Resolution for Geographical Information Retrieval. In *Proceedings of the 3rd ACM Workshop on Geographic Information Retrieval*. Seattle: Association for Computing Machinery.

Mani, I., Hitzeman, J., & Clark, C. (2008). Annotating Natural Language Geographic References. In *Proceedings of the Sixth International Language Resources and Evaluation Conference Workshop on Methodologies and Resources for Processing Spatial Language*. Marrakech, Morocco: European Language Resources Association.

Meyers, A., Reeves, R., Macleod, C., Szekely, R., Zielinska, V., Young, B., & Grishman, R. (2004). The NomBank Project: An Interim Report. In *Proceedings of HLT-EACL Workshop: Frontiers in Corpus Annotation*. Association for Computational Linguistics.

Mihalcea, R. (2007). Using Wikipedia for Automatic Word Sense Disambiguation. In *Proceedings of the North American Association for Computational Linguistics*. Rochester, New York: Association for Computational Linguistics.

Overell, S., Magalhães, J., & Rüger, S. (2006). Place disambiguation with co-occurrence models. In *Proceedings of the Cross Language Evaluation Forum Workshop*. Alicante, Spain.

Pustejovsky, J., Knippen, B., Littman, J., & Saurí, R. (2005). Temporal and Event Information in Natural Language Text. *Language Resources and Evaluation*, 39. Springer Netherlands.

Saurí, R., Knippen, R., Verhagen, M., & Pustejovsky, J. (2005). Evita: A Robust Event Recognizer for QA Systems. In *Proceedings of the Conference on Human Language Technology and Empirical Methods in Natural Language Processing*. Vancouver: Association for Computational Linguistics.

Smith, D., & Mann, G. (2003). Bootstrapping toponym classifiers. In *Proceedings of the HLT-NAACL Workshop on Analysis of Geographic References*. Association for Computational Linguistics.

KEY TERMS AND DEFINITIONS

Event Mention: Span of text in a document that refers to some real-world event, such as an action.

Event Structure: The event mention combined with the participants in the event. The event structure describes how those participants are related in the event (e.g., a participant may be the agent that initiated the event, or the location at which the event is taking place).

Gazetteer: A geographical dictionary or database. May contain information such as a geographic place's name(s), latitude, longitude, population, administrative capacity, etc.

Logistic Regression: Method for predicting the probability of an event by fitting data to a logistic curve.

Named Entity Recognition: The process of recognizing names of entities/objects. Common examples are names of people, organization, and locations.

Ontology: A formal representation of knowledge using a set of concepts and a defined relationship between the concepts. A geographic ontology is one that describes how geographic concepts fit together (e.g., that states form part of a country).

Toponym: A place's name; the string used to identify a place in a natural language document.

ENDNOTES

[1] http://geonames.usgs.gov/domestic/download_data.htm

[2] http://earth-info.nga.mil/gns/html/

[3] http://www.itl.nist.gov/iad/mig/tests/ace/

[4] http://www.geonames.org/

[5] Both examples have been taken from the SpatialML (Mani 2008) corpus. The second example has been edited for grammar, for the purpose of clarity, but not in such a way that an automated system would fail to recognize the same participants.

[6] http://www.surdeanu.name/mihai/bios/

Chapter 31
Evaluation of Narrative and Expository Text Summaries Using Latent Semantic Analysis

René Venegas
Pontificia Universidad Católica de Valparaíso, Chile

ABSTRACT

In this chapter I approach three automatic methods for the evaluation of summaries from narrative and expository texts in Spanish. The task consisted of correlating the evaluation made by three raters for 373 summaries with results provided by latent semantic analysis. Scores assigned by latent semantic analysis were obtained by means of the following three methods: 1) Comparison of summaries with the source text, 2) Comparison of summaries with a summary approved by consensus, and 3) Comparison of summaries with three summaries constructed by three language teachers. The most relevant results are a) a high positive correlation between the evaluation made by the raters (r= 0.642); b) a high positive correlation between the computer methods (r= 0.810); and c) a moderate-high positive correlation between the evaluations of raters and the second and third LSA methods (r= 0.585 and 0,604), in summaries from narrative texts. Both methods did not differ significantly in statistical terms from the correlation among raters when the texts evaluated were predominantly narrative. These results allow us to assert that at least two holistic LSA-based methods are useful for assessing reading comprehension of narrative texts written in Spanish.

INTRODUCTION

In Latin America, comprehension skills associated with reading and writing are not effective enough for students to understand and produce texts that will allow them to perform well in today's society (Peronard, 1989; Peronard, Gómez,

Parodi & Núñez, 1998; PISA, 2007; Ibañez, 2008). There is general consensus between researchers studying reading comprehension as to the need of evaluating individuals psycholinguistic processes, highlighting several options for evaluation, such as answers to literal and inferential questions (both local and global), development of conceptual and/or mental maps, formulation of open-ended questions, paraphrasing, and summary writing.

DOI: 10.4018/978-1-60960-741-8.ch031

I am specifically interested in further inquiry regarding one of these options, which is the summary as an evaluation technique. The use of this technique is theoretically supported by the proposals of van Dijk (1978). From this psycholinguistic perspective, we attempt to formalize processes by the reader and subsequently incorporate them into memory. I first propose the so-called macrorules (van Dijk, 1978) for this purpose, followed by macrostrategies (van Dijk & Kintsch, 1983) to attempt an explanation as to why what person remembers and verbalizes after reading a relatively long text does not include all the ideas originally expressed in such texts. Good comprehenders apply rules and strategies, eliminating propositions they believe to be irrelevant, and reprocessing others in order to build their own version of the text. However, this evaluation technique features some problems, mainly regarding human variables such as the cognitive burden of the evaluator, parallel attention to formal elements of written production (spelling, handwriting), subjective aspects that may intervene, systemacity in the application of evaluation criteria, consensus between multiple evaluators, and the extensive amount of time required for evaluation.

These problems and readers interest in automatically capturing core text information have encouraged the study of summarizing and summary evaluation from a computational perspective. Automatic summary construction and automatic summary evaluation are problems that have been discussed since the mid-60s, although computer systems reliable enough to perform both tasks have not yet been found. However, advances based on computer linguistics, natural language processing, and the development of several information recovery techniques lead us to think that we are closer to improving the generation and evaluation of written summaries (Mani & Maybury, 2001).

Techniques for building and automatically evaluating text summaries are generally classified into two categories: linguistic and statistical. Linguistic techniques use knowledge regarding syntax, semantics or the use of language, while statistical techniques operate by computing values for words and phrases found in the text, using statistical techniques such as frequencies, n-grams, and co-occurrences.

There are several studies focusing on comprehension and the use of computer techniques in order to represent and evaluate the comprehension process. Kintsch (1998, 2000, 2001, and 2002) introduces the possibility of using latent semantic analysis (LSA) for extracting lexico-semantic similarities from the texts and accessing text propositions by means of statistical-mathematical training to simulate the comprehension process.

Theoretical and empirical studies concerning LSA have been extensively conducted in different languages, but most often in English (e.g., Landauer & Dumais, 1997; Landauer, Laham, Rehder & Schreiner, 1997; Rehder, Schreiner, Wolfe, Laham, Landauer, & Kintsch, 1998; Kintsch, Steinhart, Stahl, LSA Research Group, Matthews, & Lamb, 2000; Landauer & Psotka, 2000; Landauer, Laham, Foltz, 2003). These studies have focused on evidencing that vectorial models, and specifically LSA, can account for meaning processing conducted by human beings and are effective in the automated evaluation of essays and summaries. However, studies considering LSA in the field of summary evaluation in Spanish are still scarce (Pérez, Alfonseca, Rodríguez, Gliozzo, Strapparava & Magnini, 2005; León, Escudero, Cañas & Salmerón, 2005; Venegas 2007, 2009a, b). Therefore, this research aims to identify an automatic summary evaluation method for texts written in Spanish that are predominantly narrative and expository, using latent semantic analysis.

SUMMARY AS A TECHNIQUE FOR EVALUATING THE UNDERSTANDING OF WRITTEN DISCOURSE

Two types of semantic structures can be recognized in a text: microstructures and macrostructures

(Kintsch & van Dijk, 1978; van Dijk & Kintsch, 1983, Kintsch, 1988, 1998). Both semantic structures are conceptualized as relations established at different abstraction levels in the cognitive representation of the text (surface code, textbase, and situation model) proposed by van Dijk and Kintsch (1983). Those three levels are non-controversial components widely accepted by researchers in discourse processing (Graesser, Singer & Trabasso, 1994). According to van Dijk and Kintsch (1983), macrostructures are structures that organize texts globally, and microstructures organize texts locally. Given that texts are not just concatenations of sentences, texts need to be structured both locally (connections between clauses and sentences) and globally (larger fragments of discourse [e.g. paragraphs]). These microstructures organize sets of interrelated propositional representations of the phrases, clauses and sentences of the text. A proposition is understood as a unit of meaning that underlies phrases or clauses. Through macrorules and macrostrategies, the reader derives these sequences of propositions into a smaller set of more general propositions by deleting those that are less important for the overall meaning of the text, by generalizing propositions into supersets and by constructing new text units that replace the meaning of the old set. Macrostrategies and macrorules operate recursively, so that macrostructures that are formed may be subject to another cycle of macrorules, further generalizing the gist of the text. Macrostructures are therefore abstract semantic descriptions of the semantic content of the text, similar to the text's global meaning and theme and providing global coherence.

The macrostructure of a source text might be textualized in different forms; one of these can be a new text, which is called summary. In other words, a summary is the textualization of a meaning that abstractly represents the overall meaning of written or oral text contents.

From a pedagogical point of view, summarizing is a strategy that involves the ability of students to synthesize information from a text by explaining what the text is about using their own words. Improving students' ability to summarize text and their overall comprehension of text content are clearly important skills. Besides, it is the most common technique used to evaluate human comprehension on a given text (Zipitria, et al., 2004). Furthermore, summarization provides a more accurate view of student's understanding as compared to multiple choice or short answer exams (Steinhart, 2001) or even commonly used end-of-chapter questions (Wade-Stein & Kintsch, 2004). Thus, summary writing would be a more suitable technique for assessing students' macrostructure generation rather than other comprehension tests, because it is relatively easy to administer and state a difference between students who understood the gist of a text and those who did not (Peronard, 1997). However, some problems arise when using summary as an evaluation technique. Those problems arise because of factors related to raters, such as the lack of systemacity in the application of evaluation criteria and time required for evaluating the summaries.

LATENT SEMANTIC ANALYSIS (LSA)

LSA is a mathematical-statistical technique used for the extraction and representation of meaning relations between words and paragraphs from a large number of texts (Landauer, McNamara, Dennos & Kintsch, 2007). LSA extracts meaning representations from words and paragraphs exclusively based on mathematical-statistical analysis of the text. None of this knowledge comes from perceptual information about the physical world, from instinct, or from experience generated by bodily functions, feelings and/or intentions. Representation of meaning is therefore partial and limited, in that it does not make use of syntactic, logical or morphological relations. Notwithstanding, Landauer (2002) explains that, at least for English, 80% of a language's potential information lies in the choice of words, without considering the order in which these appear. This idea of meaning representation without resorting to syntax complemented the notion that there are weak semantic interrelations between words in these large amounts of corpora, which are empowered by the dimension reduction method known as Singular Value Decomposition (SVD) (Deerwester, Dumais, Furnas, Landauer & Harshman, 1990).

Singular value decomposition is used to construct a semantic space representative of the information required for one or several knowledge domains based on a text corpus. LSA thus enables the calculation of semantic similarities between words and paragraphs in texts, establishing measurements of vectorial representation by calculating the cosine of angles in a multivectorial space (Landauer, Foltz & Laham 1998; Landauer, McNamara, Dennos & Kintsch, 2007). The cosine values range from 1 for vectors running in the same direction (this means that what is measured is the same) to 0 for those orthogonal vectors (perpendicular in multivectorial space, meaning that what is measured is completely different). Values must be standardized in order to make more effective comparisons between these vectors, since longer vectors (corresponding to longer documents) could have an unfair advantage compared to shorter ones. In addition, the standardization of cosine values enables calculation as a simple product (vector multiplication) (Deerwester et al, 1990; Landauer et al, 1998, Manning & Schütze, 2003).

RELATED STUDIES

Different automatic summary evaluation studies have evidenced significant and positive correlations with evaluations made by humans.

Lin and Hovy (2003) and Lin (2004), for instance, developed an automatic summary evaluation system called "Recall-Oriented Understudy for Gisting Evaluation" (ROUGE). This program uses five measurements in order to automatically determine the quality of a summary compared to other summaries created by human beings. These measurements are based on counting the corresponding units such as n-grams and groups (and pairs) of words between the summary generated by the program and ideal summaries created by human beings. Therefore, in the case of values assigned by ROUGE to summaries and those assigned by human beings in the case of summaries of no more than 100 words, the correlation with three raters is r= 0.82 (Pearson). In the case of brief summaries (approximately 10 words) the correlation with four evaluators amounts to an average of 0.76 (Pearson). Finally, in the case of multidocument summaries, the average with 2 to 4 raters is 0.63 (Pearson). These correlations feature calculation of technique application considering the extraction of *stopwords* (i.e. words that are filtered out prior to or after processing of natural language data or texts). Finally, this type of evaluation considers correspondence between the words of both documents (automatic summary and human summary) and therefore the algorithms come to value zero in cases where different words with a similar meaning are used, which is potentially a problem in the automatized evaluation of human summaries (Lin, 2004).

Other studies in which LSA has been used report a high correlation between automatized evaluation and the judgment of human evaluators. For example, Kintsch et al. (2000) made two different comparisons between punctuation generated by LSA and evaluations made by raters of written summaries by 5th grade students (average length of 250-350 words). In the first comparison, the cosine between students' summaries and the source text read by these students is calculated. The correlation between the rater and LSA came to 0.64 in that study. In the second comparison, the authors investigated whether LSA could identify a given sentence in the source text with a summary sentence just as two human evaluators would do. The scores provided by LSA were 84.9% similar to the scores of first degree evaluators, and 83.2%

similar to second degree evaluators. Kintsch et al. (2000) concluded that LSA scores were highly comparable to evaluations that could be made by teachers with experience for these summaries and that LSA would work almost as well as human beings in order to determine the source of knowledge for a given sentence.

One of the most well-known programs that uses LSA for automatic essay evaluation and feedback is the IEA (Intelligent Essay Assessor) developed by Landauer, Laham and Foltz (2003). As opposed to other statistical methods, the authors used this program to suggest that LSA focuses on the semantic content of texts rather than the mechanical aspects of written production such as grammar, literal and punctual spelling, thus enabling more realistic evaluation of written discourse compression for subjects. (Landauer, Foltz, and Laham, 1998). This does not mean that IEA does not provide feedback regarding the formal aspects of essay evaluation. In fact, the program also evaluates aspects such as style, spelling and syntactic coherence.

LSA in IEA has been used to evaluate the quality and quantity of knowledge transmitted in an essay, applying three different methods in which the essay to be evaluated is compared with a) essays by other students that have been evaluated beforehand; b) model essays by experts and former publications regarding the issue; and c) internal comparison of a set of non-evaluated essays. These measurements indicate the degree to which a certain essay has the same meaning as the texts to which it is compared. According to the authors, this can be considered a quality measurement from a semantic perspective in the English language. In order to test the above, Landauer, Laham and Foltz (2003) report average correlations of 0.73 to 0.77 between IEA and the evaluators (at least 2) in several experiments (such as the production of brief essays, standardized tests and tests applied in classrooms on different issues) considering quantity and quality aspects of information included in the essays evaluated.

These results are in line with findings by Kintsch et al. (2000) and allow us to consider the convenience of using LSA in the automatized evaluation of summaries in other languages.

León et al. (2005) proposed the evaluation of very short summaries (50 words) for two types of text (narrative and expository) by means of LSA and comparing these results to evaluations by four human experts. The authors use LSA in order to estimate the semantic similarity between summaries by means of six different methods: four holistic and two componential methods. The evaluation is made for summaries written by 390 students between the ages of 14 and 16. Results obtained indicate the feasibility of developing a computer tool for automatic evaluation using human judgment and LSA. Results obtained are generally very similar to those obtained by Kintsch et al. (2000), with an average correlation between LSA methods and experts amounting to 0.58 (Pearson) for narrative summaries and a lower average correlation of 0.35 for expository summaries. In general terms, the ANOVA confirms that the holistic methods with LSA correlate better with the raters, especially in the case of brief summaries taken from narrative texts.

Pérez et al. (2005) propose a free text answer evaluation system for the automatic evaluation of texts called Atenea (Alfonseca & Pérez, 2004), which combines a modified version of the BLUE algorithm (BiLingual Evaluation Understudy algorithm) with LSA (Papineni, Roukos, Ward & Zhu 2001). This combination therefore considers the search for n-gram coincidences between student answers and reference documents. In addition, the semantic similarity is calculated for the same. This system is able to ask questions chosen at random or according to the student's profile and assign them a numerical score. Results of these experiments have shown that for all sets of data in which natural language processing techniques are used, the Pearson correlation between scores assigned by Atenea and scores assigned by raters for the same set of questions have been combined and reach an average correlation value of 0.55, improving prior evaluations that only considered the use of n-grams and other NLP techniques. A Spanish corpus translated automatically into English using Altavista Babelfish was used for LSA in Atenea and therefore tests were strictly applied in English (Perez et al. 2005).

Other research regarding summary evaluation using LSA in Spanish has been conducted by Venegas (2006b, 2009a, b). Venegas (2006b) compared the score assigned by LSA with the evaluation made by three language teachers who used a 30-point scale based on the presence and absence of main ideas. The current research presents evaluated summaries written by technical-professional high school students (14-16 years old) who produced summaries of expository and narrative texts (divided into summaries with high and low informational density). LSA analysis was conducted in terms of the cosine average obtained between each student summary and paragraphs from the source texts. Results obtained indicate a significant positive but low correlation between scores assigned by raters and by LSA (r =0.358). However, multiple comparison tests showed significant differences between the evaluation made using LSA and raters in all text types considered.

Venegas (2009a) considered some variations compared to prior research, including the following:

1. Summaries were divided into those with high and those with low achievement levels in the evaluation made by a team of comprehension researchers (Parodi, 2005). Segmentation was conducted using a 60% achievement threshold according to scores assigned by a 30-point criterion considering the presence and quality of ideas contained in the source texts. In contrast with the former research, scores assigned were approved by rater consensus.

2. Only segmentation between summaries of narrative and expository texts were considered (the linguistic density variable within the same text was not taken into consideration).

3. Three LSA scoring methods were used: a) summary-source text segmented into paragraphs; b) summary-complete text (without segmentation into paragraphs) and c) summary-summary approved by rater consensus. Just as summaries were segmented according to scores assigned by raters, a threshold was set for the values obtained using each method (60%) with relation to the highest cosine value by which the summaries were divided between those with a high achievement level (1) and those with a low achievement level (0). This classification was subsequently compared with results provided by researchers.

Precision, recall and F1 values were calculated in order to compare results obtained using the above three methods and results obtained by raters. General results demonstrate that method B, which calculated the semantic similarity between the summary made by each student and the complete text, is what best represents the summary evaluation made by raters (F1=0.64). In addition, this method is the most similar to human evaluation when these summaries are taken from expository texts (F1=0.55). As indicated in Table 1, in the case of summaries of narrative text, the method that considers the summary approved by consensus is the most similar to human evaluation (F1=0.79), although there is no major difference between this and the second method (F1=0.74).

Consequently, it was established that method B presents values highly similar to those provided by human evaluation, especially when these are considered with a high human achievement level. This confirms results obtained by León et al. (2000) as to the use of the holistic method and the greater correspondence between the evaluation made using LSA and by raters, especially for summaries of narrative texts. In the case of sum-

Table 1. Comparison between methods according to discourse organization mode (Exp: Expository; Narr: Narrative)

Comparison between methods	summary-source text segmented into paragraphs		summary-complete text		summary-summary approved by raters	
Discourse organization mode	Exp	Narr	Exp	Narr	Exp	Narr
Recall	0.22	0.82	0.90	0.77	0.88	0.93
Precision	0.43	0.63	0.40	0.71	0.40	0.69
F1-measure	0.29	0.71	0.55	0.74	0.55	0.79

maries written from expository text, all studies presented lower results when related to human and LSA scores.

THE STUDY

The Summaries

373 summaries were used for this research. These summaries were written by students between the ages of 15 and 16 attending technical-professional high schools (commercial, maritime, and industrial high schools) in the city of Valparaiso, Chile. As it was the case in Venegas (2006b and 2009a), these summaries were written from expository source texts and narrative source texts. The topics of expository texts were selected according to each specialized domain, while the topic from the narrative texts is the same for all students. These summaries were digitalized. Spelling mistakes were corrected in order to ensure that the LSA program could automatically calculate the lexico-semantic similarity between each summary and the source texts. Table 2 shows the descriptive values of the digitalized summaries according the amount of words.

These summaries are available on-line at www.elgrial.cl and correspond to the so-called DETP-2004 corpus (Technical-Professional Written Discourse).

Semantic Space and the Calculation of Lexico-Semantic Similarity

A 10,242,384-word corpus of diversified Spanish texts known as COTEGE (General Spanish Corpus) was considered for construction of semantic space. This corpus was put together based on five multiregister corpora:

1. **PUCV-2003 Corpus:** A corpus collected by the FONDECYT 1020786 research team. The PUCV-2003 Corpus is divided into 90 texts, equivalent to 1,466,744 words. In turn, this corpus is divided into three subcorpora (Technical-Scientific Corpus -CTC-, Written Latin American Literature Corpus -CLL-, and the Oral Interview Corpus -CEO-). This corpus is available on-line at www.elgrial.cl.

Table 2. Descriptive values according the text length (in terms of words of the summaries)

	Summaries	
	Expository	Narrative
N	244	129
Text length-min	8	16
Text length-max	141	124
Text length-average	60,0	72,2
Text length-median	59	75
Text length-stdev	25,7	22,6

2. **Oral Spanish Corpus:** A text corpus collected and transcribed by Universidad Autónoma de Madrid. The corpus contains a total 1,099,400 words and features 12 oral genres. This corpus is available at www.lllf. uam.es/corpus/corpus.html.

3. **Contemporary Spanish Reference Corpus**: A corpus collected by Universidad Autónoma de Madrid, which included the Reference Corpus for the Spanish Language in Chile and the Reference Corpus for the Spanish Language in Argentina. This corpus comprises a total 3,156,491 words with 10 different text genres. This corpus is available on-line at ftp://ftp.uba.ar/pub/misc/corpus/.

4. **Written Narrative Corpus:** A corpus collected in order to conduct the first computer system tests. This corpus contains 86, 3981 words and includes three written narratives (the Bible, Alice in Wonderland, and A Tale of Two Cities). It is available on-line at www. elgrial.cl.

5. **ARTICO Corpus**: The Corpus of Original Scientific Research Articles comprises 678 articles published in indexed Scientific Electronic Library Online (ScIELO) magazines between 2000 and 2003. The corpus comprises a total 3,655,768 words (available on-line at www.elgrial.cl).

This corpus, which was compiled to be subsequently transformed into a semantic space, is justified based on the findings of Olmos, León, Escudero and Botana (2009). These findings establish that dependency on the thematic domain affects automatized evaluation efficiency using LSA. Following the application of SVD, ES-COTEGE consisted of 297 dimensions and 99,966 unique words, with the assignment of their corresponding values and is available for use at www.elgrial.cl. (text comparison section or directly at: http://158.251.61.111/webapps/compareFiles/).

Semantic space was used to calculate the cosine value for each of the 373 summaries according to three different methods. The first method compared the summary and the complete source text. The second method compared the summary written by each student with a summary approved by consensus of a group of researchers for each source text. Finally, the third method compared each summary with three summaries written by the three raters. Two of the methods used in Venegas (2009a) were reimplemented without considering the method of segmenting a source text into paragraphs and including summaries written by raters (see Figure 1)

Raters and Evaluation Criteria

The raters were three Spanish language teachers, all students of the master in applied linguistics program at Pontificia Universidad Católica de Valparaíso, Chile. They were trained to evaluate these summaries. This training program was conducted between December 2008 and January 2009, for a total 60 hours. The training program reviewed theoretical aspects related to the evaluation of comprehension following Kintsch's (1988, 1998) perspective. Evaluation criteria were presented and explained and applied to a summary sample. Consensus was established from the application of criteria and grading, a new sample of summaries was re-evaluated and grading was calibrated. This was all conducted in order to prevent the impact of certain variables, such as inherent rater trends to evaluate certain aspects at the expense of others, or to evaluate aspects not considered in the criteria. Table 3 summarizes the results and indicates the Pearson correlations for the raters, and three kinds of inter-rater measures (correlation average, similarity correlations and the Cronbach's Alpha) according to the two organization mode of the source texts.

The inter-rater values indicate a consistent evaluation of narrative summaries by raters that is higher than the evaluation of expository text

Figure 1. A representation of the procedure to assess student's summaries using the three LSA-based methods

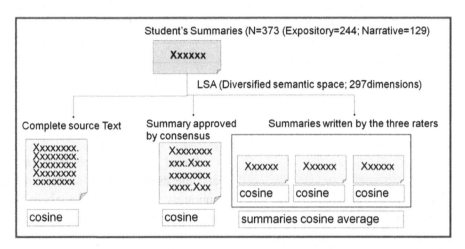

Table 3. Correlation and inter-rater measures according to text type

	Expository			Narrative	
	Rater2	**Rater3**		**Rater2**	**Rater3**
Rater1	0.670**	0.515**	Rater1	0.710**	0.743**
Rater2		0.564**	Rater2		0.651**
N		244	N		129
Average		0.583	Average		0.701
Similarity correlation		0.807	Similarity correlation		0.875
Cronbach's Alpha		0.807	Cronbach's Alpha		0.875

**all correlation values are significant at the level of 0.01

(sim r =0.807 and sim r= 0.875; Fisher Z-test p= 0.0273), which is consistent with data reported by León et al. (2005). The latter suggests that expository texts are more difficult to understand (see Otero, León & Graesser, 2002; Parodi, 2005) and show less consistency when it comes to evaluating between three trained raters.

In contrast to Venegas (2009a), summary evaluation criteria were drawn up for each of the original texts in this study. In order to draw up evaluation criteria in conformity with each source text, the following semantic-cognitive criteria were considered according to Kintsch's (1988, 1998) models: Presence of the main ideas, Integration of ideas, Generalization of ideas, Logical sequence, Macrosemantization. The criteria used are based on a six-point scale (McCarthy & McNamara, 2008). Scores were interpreted as follows: 1) If the criteria were fully respected; 2) If the criteria were generally respected; 3) If the criteria were satisfactorily respected, 4) If the criteria were not satisfactorily respected, 5) If the minimum requirements of the criteria were not respected 6) If the criteria were not respected at all. The criteria were validated (85% agreement) and improved according to the opinion of three expert judges.

Table 4. Correlation between the three LSA methods

	Method 1 summary-complete text	Method 2 summary-summary approved by consensus	Method 3 summary-rater summaries
Method 1	1	0.732**	0.820**
Method 2		1	0.880**
Method 3			1

**This correlation is significant at a level of 0.01 (N=373, bilateral).

RESULTS

A correlational study was conducted in order to compare between the different LSA methods used to score the summaries. Results of this study are indicated in Table 4.

This first result suggests that evaluating semantic similarity between student summaries using any of the three methods might be relatively similar. But according to the Fisher Z-test all correlations among the methods are different (M1-M2<M1-M3, p=0.00233; M1-M2<M2-M3, p=1.722914e-09; M1-M3<M2-M3, p=0.00290). These results suggest that the two most correlated methods involve summaries written by humans in computational terms that can be considered expensive for an algorithm to score summaries. The correlations used in Method 1 are lower, even when it is very easy to implement this computationally (it only requires the source text). If we consider the length of the text (in terms of words), it can be observed that the three methods correlate negatively with a moderate-low correlation magnitude (M3 r= -0.409; M1 r= -0.394; M2 r= -0.334) and that there is no difference between correlation scores (Fischer Z-test M3-M1 p=0.8459319; M3-M2 p= 0.2561375; M1-M2 p= 0.3465736). This result shows that the shorter the text, the higher the score provided by the three methods (1= the criteria were fully respected...6= the criteria were not respected at all), implying that the size of the texts should be taken into account when applying any of these methods.

Based on data taken from rater evaluation and the assignment of scores assigned to each summary, a correlational analysis between raters and the average score assigned by raters and each method has been conducted. This procedure reveals how similar scores given by the human raters and the three methods are to student summaries.

Table 5 shows correlational results obtained between raters and each of the methods, according to the type of source text. Word length is also included as a baseline.

As indicated in Table 5, all correlations between the methods and the raters are statistically significant and the magnitudes related to the Methods 2 and 3 are higher for narrative text summaries (Fischer Z-test M2 *p*=0.007; M3 *p*=0.010). Correlations between raters and Method 1 do not differ statistically (M1 p=0.1231536). Although the highest score is observed between raters and Method 3 (Summary-Rater Summaries) favouring summaries of narrative texts (r = 0.604), there is no difference when compared to the other two

Table 5. Comparison between LSA methods and the three raters

Correlational average	Expository	Narrative
Method1-Raters	0.328**	0.470**
Method2-Raters	0.359**	0.585**
Method3-Raters	0.393**	0.604**
Lenght-Raters	-0.491**	-0.337**
Methods-Lenght	-0.437**	-0.437**

**This correlation is significant at the level of 0.01 (Expository=244, Narrative=129).

methods (M1-M2 p=0.2042; M1-M3 *p*=0.133; M2-M3 *p*=0.816). As for length, a significant difference is observed comparing Methods 2 and 3 (M2 *p*=0.011; M3 *p*=0.006) when the summaries are from narrative texts and there is no difference between the correlation of raters and methods when the length is considered (p= 0.3497335). The latter implies that the effect of text size is similar to the methods and humans.

For the assessment of summaries written from expository text, the methods show lower correlation magnitudes and no difference between methods or between the methods and length. These results support the contention that Methods 2 and 3 enable assessment of student summaries of narrative texts in a similar manner compared to raters. However, given the fact that correlation average values between raters are higher according to magnitude (Expository r= 0.583; Narrative r= 0.701), we must confirm whether there is a significant difference between these correlation values and those obtained using each of the LSA methods and raters. Table 6 indicates the probability values obtained in the comparison of correlation coefficients, according to each method and text type.

The results of comparing correlation coefficients enabled us to establish that Method 1 (summary-complete source text) is different from the correlation obtained by raters in the evaluation of each type of summary and that Method 2 and 3 are different from human correlations when summaries are written from expository text. These differences allow us to assert that LSA-based methods are not suitable for the assessment of

summaries of expository texts in Spanish. On the other hand, Method 2 (summary-summary approved by consensus) and Method 3 (summary-rater summaries) are not different from the correlation jointly established by raters when evaluating summaries of narrative texts. The results confirm the idea that these LSA-based methods achieve results similar to human raters when scoring summaries of Spanish texts that are predominately narrative.

CONCLUSION

The results obtained allow us to conclude that automatized evaluation of summaries using LSA is very similar to that done by three raters trained to evaluate summaries taken from predominantly narrative Spanish texts. This holds true when considering both comparison between the summary to be evaluated and a summary approved by consensus (Method 2) or summaries written by teachers who would subsequently be raters (Method 3). It is noteworthy that the raters wrote their summaries before starting the training and evaluation process.

The fact that the summaries of narrative texts are more consistent than samples of expository texts in both assessments conducted by raters and those made using LSA-based methods is highly relevant, suggesting greater difficulty in both comprehending and assessing the texts. This situation confirms what was suggested in Kintsch et al. (2000), León et al. (2005), and Venegas (2009a).

Table 6. Comparison of correlation coefficients taken among raters and those taken among raters and each method

P Values in Fisher Z-Test	Raters & Method 1	Raters & Method 2	Raters & Method 3
Expository (n=244)	0.0003**	0.0013**	0.0057**
Narrative(n=129)	0.0043**	0.1137	0.1776

** This difference is significant at a level of 0.01.

Although Method 1 is less expensive and also positively and significantly correlated with rater assessments, it is significantly different in terms of correlation values, meaning that assessment using this method is not similar to the results reported by trained raters. This rather unexpected result moves away from what was observed in Venegas (2009a) and can be explained by the fact that both assessment criteria and rater training favour a stronger correlation between raters, which is different from the correlation between raters in this holistic method.

Finally, these results provide evidence that at least two of the three holistic methods can be used to evaluate relatively brief summaries, considering their semantic content. The results enables the projection of a computer system that considers both scoring the semantic content of summaries written by students based on the use of LSA and the provision of feedback for students. The implementation of an automatic summary assessment system also implies the consideration of semantic content and other aspects, such as rhetorical organization, spelling, style, cohesion. All of these aspects should be studied in greater depth for Spanish texts in order to develop a reliable automatic tool that will probably consider many other NLP techniques in order to achieve this task.

REFERENCES

Alfonseca, E., & Pérez, D. (2004). *Automatic assessment of short questions with a Bleu-inspired algorithm and shallow NLP.* Paper presented at the 4th International Conference, EsTAL 2004, Alicante, Spain.

Deerwester, S., Dumais, S. T., Furnas, G. W., Landauer, T. K., & Harshman, R. (1990). Indexing by latent semantic analysis. *Journal of the American Society for Information Science American Society for Information Science, 41*(6), 391–407. doi:10.1002/(SICI)1097-4571(199009)41:6<391::AID-ASI1>3.0.CO;2-9

Farr, R., & Carey, R. (1986). *Reading: What can be measured.* Newark, Delaware: IRA.

Graesser, A., Singer, M., & Trabasso, T. (1994). Constructing inferences during narrative text comprehension. *Psychological Review, 101*, 371–395. doi:10.1037/0033-295X.101.3.371

Ibañez, R. (2008). Comprensión de textos académicos en inglés: Relación entre nivel de logro y variables involucradas. *Revista Signos. Estudios de Lingüística, 41*(67), 203–229.

Kintsch, E., Steinhart, D., & Stahl, G.LSA Research Group, Matthews, C., & Lamb, R. (2000). Developing summarization skills through the use of LSA-based feedback. *Interactive Learning Environments, 8*(2), 87–109. doi:10.1076/1049-4820(200008)8:2;1-B;FT087

Kintsch, W. (1988). The role of knowledge in discourse comprehension construction-integration model. *Psychological Review, 95*, 163–182. doi:10.1037/0033-295X.95.2.163

Kintsch, W. (1998). *Comprehension: A paradigm for cognition.* New York, NY: Cambridge University Press.

Kintsch, W. (2000). Metaphor comprehension: A computational theory. *Psychonomic Bulletin & Review, 7*(2), 257–266. doi:10.3758/BF03212981

Kintsch, W. (2001). Predication. *Cognitive Science, 25*(2), 173–202. doi:10.1207/s15516709cog2502_1

Kintsch, W. (2002). On the notions of theme and topic in psychological process models of text comprehension. In Louwerse, M., & van Peer, W. (Eds.), *Thematics: Interdisciplinary studies* (pp. 151–170). Amsterdam, The Netherlands: Benjamins.

Landauer, T., McNamara, D., Dennos, S., & Kintsch, W. (Eds.). (2007). *Handbook of latent semantic analysis.* Mahwah, NJ: Erlbaum.

Landauer, T. K., & Dumais, S. T. (1997). A solution to Plato's problem: The latent semantic analysis theory of acquisition, induction and representation of knowledge. *Psychological Review, 104*, 211–240. doi:10.1037/0033-295X.104.2.211

Landauer, T. K., Laham, D., & Foltz, P. W. (2003). Automated essay scoring: A cross disciplinary perspective. In Shermis, M., & Burstein, J. (Eds.), *Automated essay scoring and annotation of essays with the intelligent essay assessor*. Mahwah, NJ: Lawrence Erlbaum Associates.

Landauer, T. K., Laham, D., Rehder, B., & Schreiner, M. E. (1997). How well can passage meaning be derived without using word order? A comparison of latent semantic analysis and humans. In M. G. Shafto & P. Langley (Eds.), *Minutes of The 19th Annual Meeting of the Cognitive Science Society* (pp. 412-417). Mahwah, NJ: Erlbaum.

Landauer, T. K., & Psotka, J. (2000). Simulating text understanding for educational applications with latent semantic analysis: Introduction to LSA. *Interactive Learning Environments, 8*(2), 73–86. doi:10.1076/1049-4820(200008)8:2;1-B;FT073

León, J., Olmos, R., Escudero, I., Cañas, J., & Salmerón, L. (2005). Assessing short summaries with human judgments procedure and latent semantic analysis in narrative and expository texts. *Behavior Research Methods, 38*(4), 616–627. doi:10.3758/BF03193894

Lin, C. (2004). ROUGE: A package for automatic evaluation of summaries. In *Proceedings of Workshop on Text Summarization Branches Out, Post-Conference Workshop of ACL 2004*, Barcelona, Spain.

Lin, C., & Hovy, E. (2003). Automatic evaluation of summaries using n-gram co-occurrence statistics. In *Proceedings of 2003 Language Technology Conference*, Edmonton, Canada.

Mani, I., & Maybury, M. (2001). *Advances in automatic text summarization*. Massachusetts: Massachusetts Institute of Technology.

Marinkovich, J., Peronard, M., & Parodi, G. (2006). *Programa de optimización de la competencia estratégica para comprender y producir textos escritos (LECTES)* [Online]. Retrieved from www.lectes.cl.

McCarthy, P., & McNamara, D. (2008). *The user-language paraphrase challenge* [Online]. Retrieved from https://umdrive.memphis.edu/pmmccrth/public/Phil%27s%20papers.htm?uniq=-xq6brv.

Olmos, R., León, J., & Escudero, I., & Botana. (2009). Efectos sobre el tamaño y especificidad de los corpus en la evaluación de resúmenes mediante el LSA y jueces expertos. *Revista Signos, 41*(69), 71–81.

Órdenes, A. (2009). *El resumen como instrumento de evaluación de la comprensión del discurso escrito: correlación entre evaluadores expertos*. Pregraduate thesis. Pontificia Universidad Católica de Valparaíso.

Otero, J., León, J., & Graesser, A. (2002). *The psychology of science text comprehension*. Mahwah, NJ: Erlbaum.

Parodi, G. (Ed.). (2005). *Discurso especializado e instituciones formadoras*. Valparaíso, Chile: EUVSA.

Parodi, G. (Ed.). (2007). *Lingüística de corpus y discursos especializados: Puntos de mira*. Valparaíso, Chile: EUVSA.

Pérez, D., Alfonseca, E., Rodríguez, P., Gliozzo, A., Strapparava, C., & Magnini, B. (2005). About the effects of combining latent semantic analysis with natural language processing techniques for free-text assessment. *Revista Signos, 38*(59), 325–343.

Peronard, M. (1989). Estrato social y estrategias de comprensión de lectura. *Lenguas Modernas, 16*, 19–32.

Peronard, M., Gómez, L., Parodi, G., & Núñez, P. (Eds.). (1998). *Comprensión de textos escritos: De la teoría a la sala de clases.* Santiago, Chile: Andrés Bello.

PISA. (2007). *PISA 2006: Science competencies for tomorrow's world.* Paris, France: OECD Publishing.

Rehder, B., Schreiner, M. E., Wolfe, M. B., Laham, D., Landauer, T. K., & Kintsch, W. (1998). Using latent semantic analysis to assess knowledge: Some technical considerations. *Discourse Processes, 25*, 337–354. doi:10.1080/01638539809545031

Shermis, M., & Burstein, J. (2003). *Automated essay scoring: A cross-disciplinary perspective.* Mahwah, NJ: Erlbaum.

Van Dijk, T. (1983). *La ciencia del texto. Un enfoque interdisciplinario.* Buenos Aires, Argentina: Paidos.

Van Dijk, T., & Kintsch, W. (1983). *Strategies of discourse comprehension.* New York, NY: Academic Press.

Venegas, R. (2005). *Las relaciones léxico-semánticas en artículos de investigación científica: Una aproximación desde el análisis semántico latente.* Ph.D. thesis, Pontificia Universidad Católica de Valparaíso, Valparaíso, Chile.

Venegas, R. (2006a). La similitud léxico-semántica en artículos de investigación científica en español: Una aproximación desde el Análisis Semántico Latente. *Revista Signos, 39*(60), 75–106.

Venegas, R. (2006b). *Comparación de la evaluación realizada por docentes y por el análisis semántico latente.* Research Report. Pontificia Universidad Católica de Valparaíso.

Venegas, R. (2007). Using latent semantic analysis in a Spanish research article corpus. In Parodi, G. (Ed.), *Working with Spanish corpora* (pp. 195–216). London, UK: Continuum.

Venegas, R. (2009a). Towards a method for assessing summaries in Spanish using LSA. In H. C. Lane & H. W. Guesgen (Eds.), *Proceedings of the Twenty-Second International Florida Artificial Intelligence Research Society Conference* (pp. 113-115). Washington, DC: AAAI.

Venegas, R. (2009b). Informe de Investigación Final Fondecyt N° 11070225. *Evaluación de resúmenes en español: Correspondencia entre profesores y el análisis semántico latente.*

Wade-Stein, D., & Kintsch, E. (2004). Summary Street: Interactive computer support for writing. *Cognition and Instruction, 22*, 333–362. doi:10.1207/s1532690xci2203_3

Zipitria, I., Elorriaga, J., Arruate, A., & de Ilarraza, A. (2004). *From human to automatic summary evaluation.* In Seventh International Conference on Intelligent Tutoring System. Maceió, Brazil.

Chapter 32
Using LIWC and Coh-Metrix to Investigate Gender Differences in Linguistic Styles

Courtney M. Bell
Northwest Community College, USA

Philip M. McCarthy
The University of Memphis, USA

Danielle S. McNamara
Arizona State University, USA

ABSTRACT

We use computational linguistic tools to investigate gender differences in language use within the context of marital conflict. Using the Language Inquiry and Word Count tool (LIWC), differences between genders were significant for the use of self references, but not for the use of social words and positive and negative emotion words. Using Coh-Metrix, differences were significant for the use of syntactic complexity, global argument overlap, and density of logical connectors but not for the use of word frequency, frequency of causal verbs and particles, global Latent Semantic Analysis (LSA), local argument overlap, and local LSA. These results confirmed some expectations but failed to confirm the majority of the expectations based on the biological theory of gender, which defines gender in terms of biological sex resulting in polarized and static language differences based on the speaker's gender.

INTRODUCTION

Men and women have long been in dispute over issues such as spending, emotions, division of labor, and male withdrawal during conflict. One of the factors that may contribute to the continuation of such disputes is language differences between the two genders. The *biological theory* and the *sociological theory* are the two competing theories that have evolved to explain linguistic differences between males and females. Language and gender research tend to provide little empirical evidence in support of the sociological theory (Eckert & McConnell-Ginet, 2003; Goodwin, 1990) because

DOI: 10.4018/978-1-60960-741-8.ch032

social psychologists have traditionally studied the decontextualized and mechanical features of language while isolating the individual from the social context (Coates & Johnson, 2001). Therefore, the biological theory is the most cited and accepted theory by default.

Currently, results from gender and language research are inconsistent. This is exemplified by the research on gender and interruptions. Evidence suggests that men are more likely to interrupt women (Aries, 1987; West & Zimmerman, 1983; Zimmerman & West, 1975) and overlap women's speech (Rosenblum, 1986) during conversations than the reverse. On the other hand, other research indicates either no gender differences in interruptions (Aries, 1996; James & Clarke, 1993) or insignificant differences (Anderson & Leaper, 1998). However, positing possible explanations for why these linguistic variations might exist is potentially more important than merely citing them. We approach that problem here by examining various expectations of language differences between genders based on the biological theory (Bergvall, 1999; Coates & Johnson, 2001; Leaper & Smith, 2004), the most dominant theory by which researchers define the construct of gender (see Sheldon, 1990, for a review). We do so using two computational tools, the Language Inquiry and Word Count (LIWC; Pennebaker, Francis, & Booth, 2001) and Coh-Metrix (Graesser, McNamara, Louwerse, & Cai, 2004), to perform corpus analyses of emotionally laden marital disputes.

Biological Theory of Gender

The biological theory defines gender in terms of biological sex. According to the theory, it is assumed that men outsize and outpower women (Bergvall, 1999; Tannen, 1993) and that gender polarities exist in language use. The theory gives little regard to language individualization (Coates & Johnson, 2001). The biological theory also assumes that gender roles are static and contextually independent.

Two examples illustrate the influence of researchers' theoretical orientation towards gender on their explanations of gender and language variation. Maltz and Borker's (1982) theory of gender-marked language use is based on the assumptions of the biological theory. Their model claims that male and female speech has different contents and serves different purposes. Male speech is characterized as competition oriented or adversarial while being used primarily to assert men's position of dominance, attract and maintain an audience, and to assert themselves when other speakers have the floor. In contrast, female speech is characterized as collaboration oriented or affiliative. Women use language more cooperatively than men, respond to and elaborate on what others have said, make more supportive comments, ask more questions, and work to keep conversations going. Finally, women use language to create and maintain relationships of closeness and equality, to criticize others in acceptable ways, and to accurately interpret other females' speech (Sheldon, 1990).

In addition to Maltz and Borker's model, Gilligan's (1982, 1987) theory of gender-marked conflict styles also provides an example of how researchers' theoretical orientation towards gender influences their explanations of gender and language variation. The theory is also based upon the assumptions of the biological theory of gender and suggests that males' conflict style has a justice orientation. The theory claims that during conflict, males maintain a universal point of view and use language to command respect while assuming separation between themselves and others. Finally, during conflict, males value logic and rationality while attempting to resolve differences through rules or reason.

Gilligan (1982, 1987) asserts that females' conflict style has a caring orientation, focuses on the relationship, and on maintaining connections between self and others. Her theory also claims that women use more collaborative speech acts, pay more attention to the needs of others, and frame resolutions in terms of the relationship. The theory suggests that contrary to males, females are less legalistic in their disputes and more willing to make exceptions to the rules. Both the Maltz and Borker (1982) and Gilligan (1982, 1987) theories are predicated on the assumptions from the biological theory of gender, which suggests that gender language differences are static and polarized. Consequently, both theories predict that males will always use a linguistic style that reflects their concern for themselves, rules, dominance, and competition, whereas females will always use a linguistic style reflecting their affiliative nature, concern for others rather than themselves, cooperation, nurturance, and submission (Sheldon, 1990).

Computational Linguistic Tools

One of the ways to investigate gender differences in language is through the use of computational linguistic tools. Two such tools are the Language Inquiry and Word Count (LIWC; Pennebaker, Francis, & Booth, 2001; see Chapter X) and Coh-Metrix (Graesser, McNamara, Louwerse, & Cai, 2004; see Chapter X). LIWC is an analysis tool that examines written text and classifies it along 70 dimensions such as self-references, social words, positive emotions, and negative emotions. Examples of self-references include personal pronouns such as *I, me,* and *my*. Social words are those used to make references to others and exemplified by *they, she, he, us, talk,* and *friends*. Examples of positive emotion words are *happy, love,* and *good*. Examples of negative emotion words include *sad, kill,* and *afraid*.

LIWC provides a word count for the text, calculates percentage of words matching up to 85 language dimensions, and records the data into one of 74 preset dictionary categories (Brownlow, Rosamond, & Parker, 2003). The LIWC dictionary comprises 2300 words and stems, and several sources such as natural language of conversing

adults, written diaries, speeches, a thesaurus, and an English dictionary.

Coh-Metrix is a text analysis tool that analyzes text using modules common to computational linguistics such as lexicons (Fellbaum, 1998), syntactic parsers (Charniak, 2000), Latent Semantic Analysis (LSA, Landauer, McNamara, Dennis, & Kintsch, 2007), corpora (Coltheart, 1981), and statistical representations of world knowledge (Burgess, Livesay, & Lund, 1998). Coh-Metrix produces over 400 indices of cohesion, language, and readability. These indices have been used to investigate texts in a number of studies. For example, using Coh-Metrix, Louwerse, McCarthy, McNamara, and Graesser (2004) found differences in spoken and written texts by comparing 236 language and cohesion features. McNamara, Ozuru, Graesser, and Louwerse (2006) compared high and low versions of texts and found that Coh-Metrix successfully detected levels of cohesion. McCarthy, Lewis, Dufty, and McNamara (2006) used Coh-Metrix to distinguish the writing styles of three authors, despite evidence suggesting that the writers' authorial styles shifted significantly during their careers. Of the 400 indices available in Coh-Metrix, nine were selected as possible indicators of gender linguistic styles: *syntactic complexity, frequency, global argument overlap, local argument overlap, global LSA, local LSA, density of logical connectors* and *clarifications,* and *causal verbs and particles.*

Syntactic Complexity

Syntactic complexity refers to sentences embedded with multiple clauses or phrases, and are structurally dense, syntactically ambiguous, or ungrammatical (Graesser, McNamara, Louwerse, & Cai, 2004). In Coh-Metrix, syntactic analyses are based on the Charniak parser (Charniak, 2000), which assigns tree structures to every sentence in the text (Graesser et al., 2004). Coh-Metrix measures syntactic complexity in three major ways. First, a noun-phrase density measure calculates the mean number of modifiers. Modifiers are optional elements used to describe the property of the head of a phrase and exemplified by adjectives that modify heads of noun phrases and adverbs that modify heads of verb phrases. *The lovely little girl* is an example of a noun phrase with three modifiers and a head. A second metric is the number of high-level constituents per word with high-level constituents being defined as sentence and embedded sentence constituents per word and per noun phrase. Higher constituent ratios indicate greater syntactic complexity. A third metric is the incidence of word classes that signal logical or analytical difficulty (i.e., *and, or, if-then,* conditionals, and negations).

Frequency

Word frequency refers to metrics of how frequently particular words occur in the English language (Graesser et al., 2004). In Coh-Metrix, the primary frequency counts come from *CELEX,* the database from the Dutch Centre for Lexical information, which consists of frequencies taken from the early 1991 version of the 17.9-million-word COBUILD corpus. The words come from both spoken and written sources.

Global and Local Argument Overlap

Argument overlap is a form of co-reference occurring when a noun, pronoun, or noun phrase in one sentence is a co-referent of a noun, pronoun, or noun phrase in another sentence. Global argument overlap refers to the proportion of all sentence pairs within a text that have co-referential connections within a text. Local argument overlap refers to the proportion of adjacent sentence pairs in the text that share a common noun argument.

Global and Local LSA

Latent semantic analysis (LSA) is a statistical representation of world knowledge used in Coh-

Metrix as a measure of semantic cohesion and coherence. Singular value decomposition (SVD) condenses a large corpus of text to 300-500 dimensions representing the frequency of a word's occurrence within a document (see Kintsch and Kintsch, Chapter X). The document can be defined as a sentence, paragraph, or larger portions of text. Each word, sentence, or text becomes a weighted vector. Cosines between two sets of vectors are compared in order to determine the semantic relationship between texts. Values theoretically range from -1 to 1 (although in practice the range is from 0 to 1 because, even after SVD, negative frequencies are rare). Higher scores indicate greater similarities between texts and greater text cohesion. The global LSA measure is the mean cosine value for all possible sentence pairs, whereas the local LSA measure is the mean cosine value between adjacent sentence pairs.

Density of Logical Connectors and Clarifications

Density scores measure the incidence, ratio, or proportion of particular word classes or constituents in the text (Graesser et al., 2004). The density of connectives and clarifications are two important metrics in Coh-Metrix for measuring text cohesion. Connectives play an important role in creating cohesive links between sentential ideas and refer to the proportion of words related to a text's abstractness. Examples of logical connectors include words such as *or, and, not,* and *if-then* combinations. Clarifying connectives are words use to explain relationships as exemplified by words such as *furthermore, next,* and *however.*

Causal Verbs and Particles

Causal cohesion refers to a texts ability to convey causal content and causal cohesion. Causality is relevant to texts that depend on actions or events that are causally related, but is not important for texts that describe static sense or express abstract logical arguments. In Coh-Metrix, causal cohesion is measured by calculating the ratio of causal verbs to causal particles. The number of causal verbs is based on the number of main causal verbs identified through WordNet (Fellbaum, 1998; Crossley, Louwerse, McCarthy, & McNamara, 2007) and includes words such as *kill, throw, drop,* and *pour.* The causal particle count is based on a pre-defined set of causal particles and include words such as *because, as a consequence, make, cause,* and *as a result.*

Purpose and Predictions

In light of Gilligan's (1982, 1987) and Maltz and Borker's (1982) theories of gender marked language and conflict styles in conjunction with the indices available in LIWC and Coh-Metrix, our goal in the current study is to use a computational linguistic approach to investigate certain predictions based on the biological theory of gender for gender styles of language use within one particular context: namely, marital conflict. Based on the model, we can expect males to use more *self-reference words* and linguistic styles marked by greater *syntactic complexity* than women. This expectation follows from the assumption that males use language to separate themselves from others and assert their dominance during conflict. Following the presupposition that women are more nurturing and concerned with others than themselves, we can also expect women to use more *social words* and linguistic styles marked by greater cohesion than males (i.e., higher word frequency, global argument overlap, local argument overlap, global LSA, local LSA, density of logical connectors and clarifications, and causal verbs and particles). Finally, to examine the assumption that women have a propensity towards caregiving, we explore whether women use more *positive emotions words* and men will use more *negative emotions words.* Negative emotion words convey a sense of separation between one's self and others while being thought of as showing less

cooperation and lack of interest in maintaining relationships.

METHOD

Materials

A corpus of 54 texts, 27 by males and 27 by females, was generated from counseling transcripts of the relationship column "Can This Marriage Be Saved?" from the *Ladies Home Journal* website at www.lhj.com. Texts covered a variety of issues, such as *sex, infidelity, jobs, illness, stepfamily, looks, children, addictions,* and *in-laws.* Appendix A provides examples of the transcripts. The corpus contained 41,081 words, 24,765 for females (*M*=917.22, SD=319.248) and 16,316 for males (*M*=604.30, SD=181.025). The texts were analyzed using LIWC and Coh-Metrix.

Procedure

Ladies Home Journal relationship column, "Can This Marriage Be Saved?" was selected because it contained texts divided according to gender and was representative of emotionally laden conflicts. Couples take turns talking to male or female counselors and therapists, who then offer resolutions ranging from small changes in the relationship to divorce. For our purposes, it was not necessary to include the counselors' speech. The first three episodes were selected from each relationship topic to have a consistent number across corpora. Clearly, the corpus is limited in terms of possible scenarios; however, the source appears to be a reasonable point of departure for such a project.

We analyzed the texts using LIWC and Coh-Metrix. We then recorded the percentages for self-references, social words, positive emotions, and negative emotions used within each text and the Coh-Metrix scores.

RESULTS

A series of one-way analysis of variance (ANOVA) were conducted to determine if there were differences in language use exhibited by the males and females within the transcripts. The between-subjects variable was the gender of the speaker and the dependent variables comprised the indices output from LIWC and Coh-Metrix.

We first examined the output from LIWC for differences in the number of self references, social words, and positive and negative emotion words for males and females. As shown in Table 1, there was a significant difference between males and females for self-reference words biased towards males. There was a marginally significant difference for social words biased towards females. There were no significant differences between males and females for positive and negative emotion words.

The second set of analyses focused on differences between males and females in terms of each of the nine Coh-Metrix indices. The results shown in Table 2 indicate that there were significant differences for syntactic complexity biased towards females, global argument overlap biased towards males, and density of logical connectors biased towards females. A marginally significant difference was found for global LSA biased towards males. There were no significant differences between males and females for word frequency, local argument overlap, density of

clarifications, density of logical connectors, and causal verbs and particles.

DISCUSSION

The purpose of this study was to use a computational linguistic approach to examine predictions emanating from the biological theory of gender. To do so, we capitalized on transcripts of men and women discussing their marital conflicts that were published on the Ladies Home Journal website.

A few of the predictions from the model were supported by the data, but most were not. The results indicated that women use more social words and logical connectors than men. In light of Maltz and Borker's (1982) and Gilligan's (1982, 1987) theories, women's greater use of social words may reflect their concern for others and for maintaining the relationship during conflict. In contrast, males are expected to be less likely than females to use social words because of their concern for self and their need to separate themselves from others during conflict.

The biological theory also led to the expectation that women would use fewer self-reference words because of their concern for maintaining the relationship. As predicted, the results also showed a significant difference between males' and females' use of self-reference words, with males using more self-references than females. This result was also consistent with Gilligan's (1982, 1987) claims that men use a linguistic style

Table 1. Means, standard deviations and effect size (partial eta squared) for the percentages of four types of words for males and females

Word Types	Male	Female	F(1,52)	MSE	p.η2
Self-reference	11.85 (1.42)	9.98 (1.56)	21.302*	47.358	0.291
Social	12.24 (2.49)	13.46 (2.45)	3.294	20.130	0.060
Positive emotions	2.54 (0.77)	*2.43 (0.67)	0.279	*0.146	0.005
Negative emotions	2.67 (0.84)	*2.40 (0.82)	1.377	0.949	0.026

Notes: *$p < .05$

Table 2. Means, standard deviations and effect size (partial eta squared) for the nine Coh-Metrix indices for males and females

Indices	Female	Male	F(1,52)	MSE	p.η2
Syntactic Complexity	2.833 (1.219)	1.757 (1.125)	11.364*	15.642	0.179
Global Argument Overlap	0.730 (0.091)	*0.789 (0.091)	*5.782*	*0.048	0.100
Global LSA	0.573 (0.088)	*0.532 (0.063)	*3.832	*0.023	0.056
Frequency	2.763 (0.049)	*2.788 (0.057)	*2.801	*0.008	0.051
Local Argument Overlap	0.812 (0.102)	*0.854 (0.100)	*2.279	*0.023	0.042
Local LSA	0.429 (0.108)	*0.364 (0.076)	*6.433	*0.056	0.110
Density of Clarifications	9.216 (4.018)	*9.066 (4.572)	*0.016	*0.303	0.000
Density of Logical Connectors	54.257 (8.772)	53.899 (8.386)	*0.024*	*1.732	0.000
Causal Verbs and Particles	29.395 (8.008)	29.118 (5.267)	*0.023	*1.038	0.000

Notes: *p < .05

during conflict revealing their concern for self and separation of self from others during conflict.

However, our results also showed no significant differences between males and females for both positive and negative emotion words. Similar uses of positive and negative emotion words can suggest that both males and females are equally likely to express their feelings during conflict or that both are unwilling to do so. Nonetheless, this result does not confirm expectations for females to use more positive emotions words and for males to use more negative emotions words.

In terms of the Coh-Metrix indices, Maltz and Borker's (1982) and Gilligan's (1982, 1987) theories led to the expectation that males would exhibit greater syntactic complexity than females. This expectation arises from the assumption that men use language to assert themselves over others, whereas women tend to use simple phrases to increase understanding. However, we found just the opposite: females' language showed greater syntactic complexity than did males' language. Thus, this expectation was not upheld.

The lack of differences in word frequency indicates that males and females used similar classes of words to express themselves. Similarities between men and women in terms of density of clarifications further indicate that the men and

women exhibited similar levels of expressing cause and effect relationships. This result is contrary to Maltz and Borker's (1982) and Gilligan's (1982, 1987) theories, which led to the prediction that the linguistic styles of women would include more clarification words.

Global argument overlap and global LSA scores, which indicate the cohesion across entire texts and serves as an indicator of theme continuity, also significantly distinguished the genders, with males' speech showing greater cohesion scores. However, the biological theory led to the expectation that women's speech would show higher global argument overlap and global LSA scores because females use language to explain, elaborate and comment on, and respond to the statements of others. High global argument overlap and global LSA scores indicate that the speaker remains on topic, and for current purposes, consistently discusses the conflict and not other matters. Thus, the results, contrary to expectations, indicated that the men were more likely to remain on topic than were the women.

The results further indicated that men used more logical connectors than did the women. This difference indicates that men were being more specific about their conflict than women, a fact that is contrary to predictions made by Maltz and Borker's (1982) and Gilligan's (1982,1987) theories. Nonetheless, it is notable that there was a difference between the average number of words per text for males and females, with the results indicating that females used more words. Although we did not predict this result, it is consistent with research suggesting that women are more verbose than men because of their tendency towards elaborating, question asking, and making supportive comments during conversations.

In sum, there were several expectations from the biological theory that were confirmed, but the majority were not, at least not within a context of marital conflict. Of the 13 indices examined, only 3 revealed patterns that were predicted from the biological theories of gender. Hence, these results provide some empirical evidence to suggest that men and women use a variety of linguistic styles, which is contrary to the biological theory's overarching prediction that male and female language use is static and polarized. These results in conjunction with those of Anderson and Leaper (2001) indicate that gender differences in language are not polarized, at least not as extensively as predicted by the biological theory.

Social Constructionist Theory

A strong possibility, not tested in the current study, is that context plays an important role in predicting who will use a particular language strategy and when. Unlike the generalizable differences assumptions that underlie the biological theory, Coates and Johnson (2001) suggested that language and communication are integrally tied to the context in which they occur. Several researchers have concluded that gender differences in language may be better described as gender preferential than gender exclusive because of the capabilities of both males and females to use various linguistic strategies and features within different contexts (Anderson & Leaper, 1998; Fitzpatrick, Mulac, & Dinidia, 1995; West & Zimmerman, 1983). Fitzpatrick and colleagues go a step further by

suggesting that the interaction context is a better predictor of interaction style than gender. Also, according to Hyde (2005), context can create, erase, or reverse gender differences.

For example, in a meta-analysis of gender differences in conversational interruption, researchers had the *a priori* belief that men interrupted more than women (Anderson & Leaper, 1998). However, averaged across all studies, only a small effect was found. The effect sizes for intrusive interruptions were larger, but the magnitude of gender differences varied depending on the social context (Anderson & Leaper, 1998). Anderson and Leaper's results suggest a smaller number of interruptions with dyads and a larger number with larger groups. The results also suggest there are more interruptions with friends than strangers. Considered in terms of overall results, the Anderson and Leaper study illustrates the importance that context plays in interpreting the results of gender differences and language.

Anderson and Leaper (1998) also found similar results in emotion talk between same and mixed-gender dyads. According to Coates and Johnson (2001), Anderson and Leaper's study of actual behavior revealed no significant differences between same and mixed dyads. Coates and Johnson also reported that emotion talk was best predicted by the topic of conversation such that when participants talked about an emotionally laden topic, more emotion talk occurred regardless of gender. Accordingly, a study reporting a lack of differences between males and females may be viewed by some as not contradicting the biological theory, but rather as providing evidence toward the social constructionist theory, which suggests that context plays an important role in the linguistic styles of males and females. Of course, strong evidence for the social constructionist theory will rely on varying the contexts of speech and having strong predictions for how and when speech patterns will vary.

From the outset, our current study has a number of limitations. First, it considers gender differences in only one context. Second, this study does not consider the context of the self reference, social, positive emotion, and negative emotion words. Finally, the use of the texts from the *Ladies Home Journal* may not be truly representative of natural speech acts for males and females because of the possibility that they were altered for publication purposes and audience appeal (although, we assume that they were not).

Future studies should further investigate the sustainability of the biological theory in light of varying factors such as contexts, time periods, education levels, religious ideologies, age, region, and years of marriage. Future research must also significantly broaden the corpus analyses into a variety of alternative registers, such as political speeches, newspaper editorials, blogs, and journals. Such research will offer empirical evidence as to where, when, and to what degree language differences can be associated with gender.

This study is important because it demonstrates how theories about male and female linguistic patterns can be empirically evaluated using computational technology such as LIWC and Coh-Metrix. Such empirical studies are expected to help to focus and direct gender theories by supplying data and analyses from a wide array of contexts. And, although neither LIWC nor Coh-Metrix were specifically designed for the purposes of evaluating gender differences, studies such as ours scaffold technology developers in designing and incorporating new indices so that researchers can more accurately assess the nature and use of language. Finally, supplying empirical data from a variety of computational approaches offers the possibility both of debunking gender stereotypes as well as illuminating-differences and similarities in language use as a function of gender.

ACKNOWLEDGMENT

The authors wish to thank Art Graesser, Max Louwerse, Zhiqiang Cai, and James W. Pennebaker for their contributions. This research was supported by an Institute for Education Sciences grant, IES #R305G020018-02 to Danielle McNamara.

REFERENCES

Anderson, K. J., & Leaper, C. (1998). Meta-analyses of gender effects in conversational interruption: Who, what, when, where, and how. *Sex Roles, 39,* 225–252. doi:10.1023/A:1018802521676

Aries, E. (1987). Gender and communication. In Shaver, P., & Hendrick, C. (Eds.), *Sex and gender.* Newbury Park, CA: Sage Publication.

Aries, E. (1996). *Men and women in interaction: Reconsidering the differences.* New York, NY: Oxford University Press.

Bergvall, V. L. (1999). Toward a comprehensive theory of language and gender. *Language in Society, 28,* 273–293. doi:10.1017/S0047404599002080

Brownlow, S., Rosamond, J. A., & Parker, J. A. (2003). Gender-linked linguistic behavior in television interviews. *Sex Roles, 49,* 121–132. doi:10.1023/A:1024404812972

Burgess, C., Livesay, K., & Lund, K. (1998). Explorations in context space: Words, sentences, and discourse. *Discourse Processes, 25,* 211–257. doi:10.1080/01638539809545027

Charniak, E. (2000). A maximum-entropy-inspired parser. *Proceedings of the First Conference on North American Chapter of the Association for Computational Linguistics* (pp. 132-139). San Francisco, CA: Morgan Kaufmann Publishers.

Coates, L., & Johnson, T. (2001). Towards a social theory of gender. In Robinson, W. P., & Giles, H. (Eds.), *The new handbook of language and social psychology.* New York, NY: Wiley.

Coltheart, M. (1981). The MRC psycholinguistic database. *Quarterly Journal of Experimental Psychology, 33A*, 497–505.

Crossley, S. A., Louwerse, M. M., McCarthy, P. M., & McNamara, D. S. (2007). A linguistic analysis of simplified and authentic texts. *Modern Language Journal, 91*(1), 15–30. doi:10.1111/j.1540-4781.2007.00507.x

Eckert, P., & McConnell-Ginet, S. (2003). *Language and gender*. Cambridge, UK: University Press. doi:10.1017/CBO9780511791147

Fellbaum, C. (Ed.). (1998). *WordNet: An electronic lexical database* [CD-ROM]. Cambridge, MA: MIT Press.

Fitzpatrick, M. A., Mulac, A., & Dindia, K. (1995). Gender-preferential language use in spouse and stranger interaction. *Journal of Language and Social Psychology, 14*, 18–39. doi:10.1177/0261927X95141002

Gilligan, C. (1982). *In a different voice: Psychological theory and women's development*. Cambridge, MA: Harvard University Press.

Gilligan, C. (1987). Moral orientation and moral development. In Kittay, E. F., & Meyers, D. T. (Eds.), *Women and moral theory*. Totowa, NJ: Rowman & Littlefield.

Goodwin, M. H. (1990). *He-said-she-said: Talk as social organization among black children*. Bloomington, IN Indiana: University Press.

Graesser, A. C., McNamara, D., Louwerse, M., & Cai, Z. (2004). Coh-Metrix: Analysis of text on cohesion and language. *Behavior Research Methods, Instruments, & Computers, 36*, 193–202. doi:10.3758/BF03195564

Hyde, J. S. (2005). The gender similarities hypothesis. *The American Psychologist, 60*, 581–592. doi:10.1037/0003-066X.60.6.581

James, D., & Clarke, S. (1993). Women, men, and interruptions: A critical review. In Tannen, D. (Ed.), *Gender and conversational interaction*. New York, NY: Oxford University Press.

Ladies Home Journal. (2005). *Can this marriage be saved?* Retrieved November 12, 2005, from www.lhj.com.

Landauer, T., McNamara, D. S., Dennis, S., & Kintsch, W. (Eds.). (2007). *Handbook of latent semantic analysis*. Mahwah, NJ: Erlbaum.

Leaper, C., & Smith, T. E. (2004). A meta-analytic review of gender variations in children's language use: Talkativeness, affiliative speech, and assertive speech. *Developmental Psychology, 40*, 993–1027. doi:10.1037/0012-1649.40.6.993

Louwerse, M. M., McCarthy, P. M., McNamara, D. S., & Graesser, A. C. (2004). Variation in language and cohesion across written and spoken registers. In K. Forbus, D. Gentner & T. Regier (Eds.), *Proceedings of the 26th Annual Cognitive Science Society* (pp. 843-848). Mahwah, NJ: Erlbaum.

Maltz, D., & Borker, R. (1982). A cultural approach to male-female communication. In Gumperz, J. (Ed.), *Language and social identity*. Cambridge, UK: Cambridge University Press.

McCarthy, P. M., Lewis, G. A., Dufty, D. F., & McNamara, D. S. (2006). Analyzing writing styles with Coh-Metrix. In *Proceedings of the Florida Artificial Intelligence Research Society International Conference (FLAIRS)* (pp. 764-769).

McNamara, D. S., Ozuru, Y., Graesser, A. C., & Louwerse, M. (2006). Validating Coh-Metrix. In R. Sun & N. Miyake (Eds.), *Proceedings of the 28th Annual Conference of the Cognitive Science Society* (p. 573). Mahwah, NJ: Erlbaum.

Pennebaker, J. W., Francis, M. E., & Booth, R. J. (2001). *The linguistic inquiry and word count*. Retrieved November 12, 2005, from http://liwc.net/liwcresarch.php.

Rosenblum, K. E. (1986). Revelatory or purposive? Making sense of a female register. *Semiotica, 59*, 157–170. doi:10.1515/semi.1986.59.1-2.157

Sekine, S., & Grishman, R. (199). A corpus-based probabilistic grammar with only two nonterminals. In *Fourth International Workshop on Parsing Technologies* (pp. 260-270). Prague, Czech Republic: Karlovy Vary.

Sheldon, A. (1990). Pickle fights: Gendered talk in preschool disputes. *Discourse Processes, 13*, 5–31. doi:10.1080/01638539009544745

Tannen, D. (1993). The relativity of linguistic strategies: Rethinking power and solidarity in gender and dominance. In Tannen, D. (Ed.), *Gender and conversational interaction*. New York, NY: Oxford University Press.

West, C., & Zimmerman, D. (1983). Small insults: A study of interruptions in cross-sex conversations between unacquainted persons. In Thorne, B., Kramarae, C., & Henley, N. (Eds.), *Language, gender and society*. Rowley, MA: Newbury House.

Zimmerman, D., & West, C. (1975). Sex roles, interruptions and silences in conversation. In Thorne, B., & Henly, N. (Eds.), *Language and sex: Difference and dominance*. Rowley, MA: Newbury House.

APPENDIX A

Female	Male
Why isn't Lane turned on by me? It's been 8 months since we last made love successfully that is. We've tried a few times but he loses his erection. Then he goes to sleep while I lie there confused and frustrated.	I can't make love anymore. Frankly I'm scared to initiate sex because I know I'll just fail again, and Angela doesn't hesitate to let me know how upset she is. She'll say things like I guess I don't turn you on anymore, and I don't know if I want to stay in a celibate marriage.
Soon we were fighting about sex. Naturally he was angry we weren't having it. When I'd say 'Let's try on Saturday' then back out because it hurt too much, he'd grow even more furious.	I don't want a divorce but I can't stay in an unconsummated marriage any longer said Brad 36 a creative director for an advertising agency. I've been patient over the past 11 years. I believed Natalie when she promised to solve her problem.
My husband never listens to me said Marcy 42 a marketing director and mother of two. Howard hears the little things like if I ask him to turn down the TV, but when it comes to major issues, he tunes me out. His indifference is why we are constantly at odds.	Marcy portrays me as the source of our problems, but she bears half the blame. One minute we're having a simple argument, the next she's calling me hateful names and dredging up my past sins. I've been hurt by Marcy's unfair and hostile criticisms, most of which center on her anger that I don't follow

Compilation of References

Abd Alghaniy, K. E. (1998). *Arabic and Malaysian languages from phonological and morphological perspective: A contrastive analysis approach*. Master thesis, Cairo University, Egypt.

Afantenos, S., Karkaletsis, V., & Stamatopoulos, P. (2005). Summarization from medical documents: A survey. *Artificial Intelligence in Medicine, 33*(2), 157–177. doi:10.1016/j.artmed.2004.07.017

Agirre, E., & Rigau, G. (1996). Word sense disambiguation using conceptual density. In *Proceedings of the 16th Conference on Computational Linguistics*, (pp. 16-22). Copenhagen, Denmark: Association for Computational Linguistics.

Ahmed, M. A. (2000). *A large-scale computational processor of the Arabic morphology, and applications*. Master thesis, Cairo University, Egypt.

Akers, A., Kaufer, D., Ishizaki, S., Seltman, H., & Greenhouse, J. (2009). *Computer-based methods for analyzing the language of medical focus groups. Technical report*. University of Pittsburgh Medical School.

Albertson, B. R. (2007). Organization and development features of grade 8 and grade 10 writers: A descriptive study of Delaware Student Testing Program (DSTP) essays. *Research in the Teaching of English, 41*, 435–464.

Alexandersson, J., & Reithinger, N. (1997). Learning dialogue structure from a corpus. In *Proceedings of Eurospeech '97 (5th European Conference on Speech Communication and Technology)*, Rhodes.

Alexandersson, J., Buschbeck-Wolf, B., Fujinami, T., Maier, E., Reithinger, N., Schmitz, B., & Siegel, M. (1997). *Dialogue acts in VERBMOBIL-2*, vol. 4, (pp. 2231-2235). Verbmobil Report 204, DFKI, University of Saarbruecken. Greece.

Alfonseca, E., & Pérez, D. (2004). *Automatic assessment of short questions with a Bleu-inspired algorithm and shallow NLP*. Paper presented at the 4th International Conference, EsTAL 2004, Alicante, Spain.

Ali, M. B. (1998). *Linguistic analysis of mistakes by students at the University of Malaya: An error analysis approach*. Master thesis, Cairo University, Egypt.

Allen, J. F., Schubert, L. K., Ferguson, G., Heeman, P., Hwang, C. H., & Kato, T. (1994). The TRAINS Project: A case study in building a conversational planning agent. *Journal of Experimental and Theoretical AI, 7*, 7–48. doi:10.1080/09528139508953799

Allen, J., Byron, D., Dzikovska, M., Ferguson, G., Galescu, L., & Stent, A. (2000). An architecture for a generic dialogue shell. *Journal of Natural Language Engineering, 6*(3), 1–16. doi:10.1017/S135132490000245X

Allen, J., Blaylock, N., & Ferguson, G. (2002). A problem solving model for collaborative agents. *Proceedings of the International Joint Conference on Autonomous Agents and Multi-Agent Systems*.

Al-Malki, A., Kaufer, D., Ishizaki, S., & Kira Dreher. (manuscript). *Old stereotypes in new media: Active/passive images of Arab women in translated news.*

Al-Osaimi, A., Al-Bassam, H., Al-Mazyad, K., Al-Yahya, K., Al-Ageel, M., Al-Rashed, R., & Al-Shalan, S. (2008). *Al Asaneed tree*. Retrieved November 15, 2009, from http://colleges.ksu.edu.sa/Arabic Colleges/ComputerScience/IT/DocLib/BSC projects/Al Asaneed Tree.pdf.

Al-Qushairy, M. H., & Siddiqi, A. H. (1972). *Sahih Muslim: Being traditions of the sayings and doings of the Prophet Muhammad as narrated by his companions and compiled under the title Al-Jami'-us-Sahih by Imam Muslim* (Siddiqi, A. H., Trans.). Lahore, Pakistan: Sh. Muhammad Ashraf.

Al-Salman, A. M., Al-Ohali, Y., & Al-Rabiah, M. (2006). An Arabic semantic parser and meaning analyzer. *Egyptian Computer Science Journal*, *28*(3), 8–29.

Al-Sughaiyer, I. A., & Al-Kharashi, I. A. (2004). Arabic morphological analysis techniques: A comprehensive survey. *American Society for Information Science and Technology Journal*, *55*(3), 189–213. doi:10.1002/asi.10368

Altenberg, B., & Granger, S. (2002). *Lexis in contrast: Corpus-based approaches*. Amsterdam, The Netherlands: Benjamins.

Anderson, D. P. (2009). An interview with Maurice Wilkes. *Communications of the ACM*, *52*(9), 39–42. doi:10.1145/1562164.1562180

Anderson, J. R., & Lebiere, C. (1998). *The atomic components of thought*. Mahwah, NJ: Erlbaum.

Anderson, K. J., & Leaper, C. (1998). Meta-analyses of gender effects in conversational interruption: Who, what, when, where, and how. *Sex Roles*, *39*, 225–252. doi:10.1023/A:1018802521676

Anderson, J. R., & Gluck, K. (2001). What role do cognitive architectures play in intelligent tutoring systems? In Klahr, D., & Carver, S. M. (Eds.), *Cognition & instruction: Twenty-five years of progress* (pp. 227–262). Hillsdale, NJ: Erlbaum.

Angros, R., Jr., Johnson, W. L., Rickel, J., & Scholer, A. (2002). Learning domain knowledge for teaching procedural skills. In *Proceedings of the International Joint Conference on Autonomous Agents and Multiagent Systems*.

Anthony, L., & Lashkia, G. (2003). Mover: A machine learning tool to assist in the reading and writing of technical papers. *IEEE Transactions on Professional Communication*, *46*, 185–193. doi:10.1109/TPC.2003.816789

Apte, C., & Weiss, S. M. (1997). Data mining with decision trees and decision rules. *Computer Systems*, *13*, 197–210.

Arabic Transliteration. (2002). *Qamus LLC website*. Retrieved November 10, 2009, from http://www.qamus.org/transliteration.htm.

Argamon, S., Koppel, M., Pennebaker, J. W., & Schler, J. (2007). Mining the Blogosphere: Age, gender and the varieties of self–expression. *First Monday*, 12.

Argamon, S., Whitelaw, C., Chase, P., & Hota, S. R. (2007). Stylistic text classification using functional lexical features. *Journal of the American Society for Information Science and Technology*, *58*(6). doi:10.1002/asi.20553

Argamon, S., Dawhle, S., Koppel, M., & Pennebaker, J. W. (2005). Lexical predictors of personality type. *Proceedings of Classification Society of North America*, St. Louis MI, June 2005.

Aries, E. (1996). *Men and women in interaction: Reconsidering the differences*. New York, NY: Oxford University Press.

Aries, E. (1987). Gender and communication. In Shaver, P., & Hendrick, C. (Eds.), *Sex and gender*. Newbury Park, CA: Sage Publication.

Atkinson, J. M., & Drew, P. (1979). *Order in court: Verbal interaction in judicial settings*. London, UK: Macmillan.

Atlas.Ti. (2007). *Computer program*, version 5.2. Berlin, Germany.

Attia, M. A. (2006). An ambiguity-controlled morphological analyzer for modern standard Arabic modeling finite state networks. In *Proceedings of the Challenge of Arabic for NLP/MT Conference*, 2006. The British Computer Society, London.

Atzmueller, M., & Puppe, F. (2006). SD-map - A fast algorithm for exhaustive subgroup discovery. In *Proceedings of the 10th European Conference on Principles and Practice of Knowledge Discovery in Databases (PKDD 2006)*, (pp. 6-17). Berlin, Germany: Springer.

Atzmueller, M., Kluegl, P., & Puppe, F. (2008). Rule-based information extraction for structured data acquisition using TextMarker. In *Proceedings LWA-2008, Special Track on Knowledge Discovery and Machine Learning*. Wuerzburg, Germany: University of Wuerzburg.

Atzuella, M. (in press). Data mining. In McCarthy, P. M., & Boonthum, C. (Eds.), *Applied natural language processing: Identification, investigation, and resolution*. Hershey, PA: IGI Global.

Austin, J. L. (1962). *How to do things with words*. Oxford, UK: Clarendon Press.

Azami, M. M. (1977). *Studies in Hadith methodology and literature*. Indianapolis, IN: American Trust Publication.

Azevedo, R. (2005). Computer environments as meta-cognitive tools for enhancing learning. *Educational Psychologist*, *40*, 193–197. doi:10.1207/s15326985ep4004_1

Azevedo, R., Cromley, J. G., & Seibert, D. (2004). Does adaptive scaffolding facilitate students' ability to regulate their learning with hypermedia? *Contemporary Educational Psychology*, *29*, 344–370. doi:10.1016/j.cedpsych.2003.09.002

Azevedo, R., & Witherspoon, A. M. (2009). Self-regulated use of hypermedia. In Hacker, D. J., Dunlosky, J., & Graesser, A. C. (Eds.), *Handbook of metacognition in education*. Mahwah, NJ: Erlbaum.

Azevedo, R. (in press). The role of self-regulation in learning about science with hypermedia. In Robinson, D., & Schraw, G. (Eds.), *Current perspectives on cognition, learning, and instruction*.

Azevedo, R., Witherspoon, A., Graesser, A. C., McNamara, D. S., Rus, V., Cai, Z., & Lintean, M. (2008). *MetaTutor: An adaptive hypermedia system for training and fostering self-regulated learning about complex science topics*. Annual Meeting of Society for Computers in Psychology, Chicago, IL.

Baayen, R. H. (2001). *Word frequency distributions*. Boston, MA: Kluwer Academic.

Baayen, R. H., Piepenbrock, R., & Gulikers, L. (1995). *The CELEX lexical database (Release 2)* [CDROM]. Philadelphia, PA: Linguistic Data Consortium, University of Pennsylvania.

Baayen, R. H., Piepenbrock, R., & Guilikers, L. (1996). *CELEX*. Philadelphia, PA: Linguistic Data Consortium.

Baba, K., & Nitta, R. (in press). Dynamic effects of task type practice on the Japanese EFL university student's writing: Text analysis with Coh-Metrix. In McCarthy, P. M., & Boonthum, C. (Eds.), *Applied natural language processing: Identification, investigation, and resolution*. Hershey, PA: IGI Global.

Bacchin, M., Ferro, N., & Melucci, M. (2002). The effectiveness of a graph-based algorithm for stemming. In *Proceedings of the 5th International Conference on Asian Digital Libraries* (pp. 117–128). London, UK: Springer-Verlag.

Baker, C. F., Fillmore, C. J., & Lowe, J. B. (1998). The Berkeley FrameNet project. In *Proceedings of the 17th International Conference on Computational Linguistics*, volume 1 (pp. 86-90). Morristown, NJ: Association for Computational Linguistics.

Balota, D., Black, D., & Cheney, M. (1992, May). Automatic and attentional priming in young and older adults: Reevaluation of the two-process model. *Journal of Experimental Psychology. Human Perception and Performance*, *18*(2), 485–502. doi:10.1037/0096-1523.18.2.485

Bandura, A. (1997). *Self-efficacy: The exercise of control*. New York, NY: Freeman.

Banerjee, S., & Pedersen, T. (2003). Extended gloss overlaps as a measure of semantic relatedness. In *Proceedings of the Eighteenth International Joint Conference on Artificial Intelligence*, (pp. 805-810).

Bangalore, S., & Stent, A. J. (2009). Incremental parsing models for dialog task structure. In *Proceedings of the 12th Conference of the European Chapter of the ACL*, (pp. 94–102). 30 March – 3 April. Athens, Greece.

Bard, E. G., Sotillo, C., Anderson, A. H., & Taylor, M. M. (1995). The DCIEM map task corpus: Spontaneous dialogues under sleep deprivation and drug treatment. In *Proc. of the ESCA-NATO Tutorial and Workshop on Speech under Stress*, Lisbon.

Bardovi-Harlig, K. (2002). A new starting point? Investigating formulaic use and input in future expression. *Studies in Second Language Acquisition*, *24*, 189–198.

Bar-Haim, R., Dagan, I., Dolan, B., Ferro, L., Giampiccolo, D., Magnini, B., & Szpektor, I. (2006). The second PASCAL RTE challenge. In *Proc of the 2nd PASCAL Challenge on RTE*.

Baylor, A. L., & Kim, Y. (2005). Simulating instructional roles through pedagogical agents. *International Journal of Artificial Intelligence in Education*, *15*, 5–115.

Bazerman, C. (1988). *Shaping written knowledge: The genre and activity of the experimental article in science*. Madison, WI: University of Wisconsin Press.

Beamer, B., Bhat, S., Chee, B., Fister, A., Rozovskaya, A., & Girju, R. (2007). UIUC: A knowledge-rich approach to identifying semantic relations between nominals. In *Proceedings of the 4th International Workshop on Semantic Evaluations* (pp. 386-389).

Beckwith, R., & Miller, G. A. (1990). Implementing a lexical network. *International Journal of Lexicography*, *3*(4), 302–312. doi:10.1093/ijl/3.4.302

Beeferman, D., Berger, A., & Lafferty, J. (1999, February). Statistical models of text segmentation. *Machine Learning*, *34*(1–3).

Beeferman, D., Berger, A., & Lafferty, J. (1997). Text segmentation using exponential models. In *Proceedings of the 2nd Conference on Empirical Methods in Natural Language Processing* (pp. 35–46). Providence, RI.

Beesley, K. R. (2001). Finite-state morphological analysis and generation of Arabic at Xerox Research: Status and plans in 2001. In *Proceedings of the Arabic Language Processing: Status and Prospect,* (ACL 2001). Toulouse, France, (pp. 1-8).

Bejan, C. A. (2007). Deriving chronological information from texts through a graph-based algorithm. In *Proceedings of the 20th Florida Artificial Intelligence Research Society International Conference* (pp. 259-260). American Association for Artificial Intelligence.

Bejan, C. A. (2008). Unsupervised discovery of event scenarios from texts. In *Proceedings of the Twenty-First International Florida Artificial Intelligence Research Society Conference* (pp. 124-129). Menlo Park, CA: AAAI Press.

Bejan, C. A., & Harabagiu, S. (2008a). A linguistic resource for discovering event structures and resolving event co-reference. In *Proceedings of the Sixth International Language Resources and Evaluation (LREC'08).* Marrakech, Morocco: European Language Resources Association (ELRA).

Bejan, C. A., & Harabagiu, S. (2008b). Using clustering methods for discovering event structures. In *Proceedings of the 23rd National Conference on Artificial Intelligence,* volume 3 (pp. 1776-1777). Chicago, IL: AAAI Press.

Bejan, C. A., & Hathaway, C. (2007). UTD-SRL: A pipeline architecture for extracting frame semantic structures. In *Proceedings of the 4th International Workshop on Semantic Evaluations,* (pp. 460–463).

Belanoff, P. (1991). Freewriting: An aid to rereading theorists. In Belanoff, P., Elbow, P., & Fontaine, S. I. (Eds.), *Nothing begins with N* (pp. 16–32). Carbondale, IL: Southern Illinois University Press.

Bell, C., Mccarthy, P. M., & Mcnamara, D. S. (in press). Gender and language. In McCarthy, P. M., & Boonthum, C. (Eds.), *Applied natural language processing: Identification, investigation, and resolution.* Hershey, PA: IGI Global.

Bellman, R. (1961). *Adaptive control processes: A guided tour.* Princeton, NJ: Princeton Univ. Press.

Beneke, J. (1991). Englisch als lingua franca oder als Medium interkultureller Kommunikation. In R. *Grebing* (Ed.), *Grenzenloses Sprachenlernen* (pp. 54-66). Berlin, Germany: Cornelsen.

Bergvall, V. L. (1999). Toward a comprehensive theory of language and gender. *Language in Society*, *28*, 273–293. doi:10.1017/S0047404599002080

Berkhin, P. (2002). Survey of clustering data mining techniques. In Kogan, J., Nicholas, C., & Teboulle, M. (Eds.), *Grouping multidimensional data* (pp. 25–72). Berlin, Germany: Springer.

Berners-Lee, T., Hendler, J., & Lassila, O. (2001). The Semantic Web: A new form of Web content that is meaningful to computers will unleash a revolution of new possibilities. *Scientific American*, *284*, 34–43. doi:10.1038/scientificamerican0501-34

Best, R. M., Floyd, R. G., & McNamara, D. S. (2008). Differential competencies contributing to children's comprehension of narrative and expository texts. *Reading Psychology*, *29*, 137–164. doi:10.1080/02702710801963951

Bethard, S., & Martin, J. H. (2008). Learning semantic links from a corpus of parallel temporal and causal relations. In *Proceedings of the 46th Annual Meeting of the Association for Computational Linguistics on Human Language Technologies: Short Papers* (pp. 662-678). Association for Computational Linguistics.

Bethard, S., Corvey, W., Klingenstein, S., & Martin, J. H. (2008). *Building a corpus of temporal-causal structure.* In Language Resources and Evaluation Conference (LREC).

Bhagat, R., Leuski, A., & Hovy, E. (2005). Statistical shallow semantic parsing despite little training data. In Association for Computational Linguistics (Ed.), *Proceedings of the Ninth International Workshop on Parsing Technology* (pp. 186-187). Vancouver, British Columbia, Canada.

Bhatia, V. (1997). Applied genre analysis and ESP. In Miller, T. (Ed.), *Functional approaches to written text: Classroom applications*. Washington, DC: USIA.

Bhattacharya, I., Getoor, L., & Bengio, Y. (2004). Unsupervised sense disambiguation using bilingual probabilistic models. *Proceedings of the Meeting of the Association for Computational Linguistics*.

Biber, D. (1989). A typology of English texts. *Linguistics, 27*, 3–43. doi:10.1515/ling.1989.27.1.3

Biber, D. (1993). Representativeness in corpus design. *Literary and Linguistic Computing, 8*(4), 243–257. doi:10.1093/llc/8.4.243

Bird, S., Klein, E., & Loper, E. (2009). *Natural language processing with Python*. O'Reilly Media.

Bird, S., Klein, E., Loper, E., & Baldridge, J. (2008). Multidisciplinary instruction with the natural language toolkit. In *Proceedings of the Third Workshop on Issues in Teaching Computational Linguistics*, Columbus, Ohio.

Bloom, B. S. (1956). *Taxonomy of educational objectives: The classification of educational goals. Handbook I: Cognitive Domain*. New York, NY: McKay.

Bond, G. D., & Lee, A. Y. (2005). Language of lies in prison: Linguistic classification of prisoners' truthful and deceptive natural language. *Applied Cognitive Psychology, 19*, 313–329. doi:10.1002/acp.1087

Bowden, T., & Kiraz, G. A. (1995). A morphographemic model for error correction in non-concatenative strings. In *Proceedings of ACL 1995*, Boston, Massachusetts, (pp. 24-30).

Bransford, J., Brown, A., & Cocking, R. (Eds.). (2000). *How people learn: Brain, mind, experience, and school*. Washington, DC: National Academy Press. Retrieved from http://www.nap.edu/html/howpeople1/.

Brill, E. (1995). Transformation-based error-driven learning and natural language processing: A case study in part of speech tagging. *Computational Linguistics, 21*(4), 543–565.

Brin, S., & Page, L. (1998). The anatomy of a large-scale hypertextual Web search engine. *Computer Networks and ISDN Systems, 30*, 107–117. doi:10.1016/S0169-7552(98)00110-X

Britton, B. K., & Gulgoz, S. (1991). Using Kintsch's computational model to improve instructional text: Effects of repairing inference calls on recall and cognitive structures. *Journal of Educational Psychology, 83*, 329–345. doi:10.1037/0022-0663.83.3.329

Brown, A. L., & Day, J. D. (1984). Macrorules for summarizing texts: The development of expertise. *Journal of Verbal Learning and Verbal Behavior, 22*, 1–14. doi:10.1016/S0022-5371(83)80002-4

Brownlow, S., Rosamond, J. A., & Parker, J. A. (2003). Gender-linked linguistic behavior in television interviews. *Sex Roles, 49*, 121–132. doi:10.1023/A:1024404812972

Brunelle, J. F., Jackson, G. T., Dempsey, K., Boonthum, C., Levenstein, I. B., & McNamara, D. S. (2010). Game-based iSTART practice: From MiBoard to self-explanation showdown. In H. W. Guesgen & C. Murray (Eds.), *Proceedings of the 23rd International Florida Artificial Intelligence Research Society (FLAIRS) Conference* (pp. 480-485). Menlo Park, CA: The AAAI Press. [PDF]

Bruner, J. (1986). *Actual minds, possible worlds*. New York, NY: Plenum Press.

Bruss, M., Albers, M. J., & Mcnamara, D. S. (2004). Changes in scientific articles over two hundred years: A Coh-Metrix analysis. In S. Tilley & S. Huang (Eds.), *Proceedings of the 22nd Annual International Conference on Design of Communication: the Engineering of Quality Documentation* (pp. 104-109). New York, NY: ACM Press.

Bruton, A., & Samuda, V. (1980). Learner and research roles in the treatment of error in group work. *RELC Journal, 11*, 49–63. doi:10.1177/003368828001100204

Bucci, W., & Maskit, B. (2007). Beneath the surface of the therapeutic interaction: The psychoanalytic method in modern dress. *Journal of the American Psychoanalytic Association, 44*, 1355–1397. doi:10.1177/000306510705500412

Bucci, W., & Maskit, B. (2005). Building a weighted dictionary for referential activity. In Qu, Y., Shanahan, J. G., & Wiebe, J. (Eds.), *Computing attitude and affect in text* (pp. 49–60). Dordrecht, The Netherlands: Springer.

Buchanan, L., Burgess, C., & Lund, K. (1996). Overcrowding in semantic neighborhoods: Modeling deep dyslexia. *Brain and Cognition, 32*, 111–114.

Buchanan, L., Westbury, C., & Burgess, C. (2001). Characterizing semantic space: Neighborhood effects in word recognition. *Psychonomic Bulletin & Review, 8*, 531–544. doi:10.3758/BF03196189

Buckwalter, T. (2002). *Buckwalter Arabic morphological analyzer,* version 1.0. Linguistic Data Consortium, University of Pennsylvania, (LDC Catalog No. LDC2002L49). ISBN 1-58563-257-0.

Bullinaria, J., & Levy, J. (2007). Extracting semantic representations from word co-occurrence statistics: A computational study. *Behavior Research Methods, 39*, 510–526. doi:10.3758/BF03193020

Bunescu, R. (2003). Associative anaphora resolution: A web-based approach. *Proceedings of the EACL 2003 Workshop on the Computational Treatment of Anaphora* (pp. 47-52). Budapest, Hungary: EACL.

Bunton, D. (1998). *Linguistic and textual problems in PhD and MPhil thesis: An analysis of genre moves and metatext.* Unpublished doctoral dissertation, The University of Hong Kong.

Burgess, C. (1998). From simple associations to the building blocks of language: Modeling meaning in memory with the HAL model. *Behavior Research Methods, Instruments, & Computers, 30*, 188–198. doi:10.3758/BF03200643

Burgess, C., & Livesay, K. (1998). The effect of corpus size in predicting reaction time in a basic word recognition task: Moving on from Kucera and Francis. *Behavior Research Methods, Instruments, & Computers, 30*, 272–277. doi:10.3758/BF03200655

Burgess, C., Livesay, K., & Lund, K. (1998). Explorations in context space: Words, sentences, discourse. *Discourse Processes, 25*, 211–257. doi:10.1080/01638539809545027

Burgess, C., & Lund, K. (1997). Modelling parsing constraints with high-dimensional context space. *Language and Cognitive Processes, 12*, 177–210. doi:10.1080/016909697386844

Burgess, C., & Lund, K. (2000). The dynamics of meaning in memory. In Dietrich, E., & Markman, A. B. (Eds.), *Cognitive dynamics: Conceptual and representational change in humans and machines* (pp. 117–156). Mahwah, NJ: Lawrence Erlbaum Associates.

Burstein, J., Marcu, D., & Knight, K. (2003). Finding the WRITE stuff: Automatic identification of discourse structure in student essays. *IEEE Intelligent Systems: Special Issue on Advances in Natural Language Processing, 18*(1), 32–39.

Burstein, J. (2003). The E-rater scoring engine: Automated essay scoring with natural language processing. In Shermis, M. D., & Burstein, J. C. (Eds.), *Automated essay scoring: A cross-disciplinary perspective* (pp. 133–122). Mahwah, NJ: Lawrence Erlbaum Associates, Inc.

Buscaldi, D., & Rosso, P. (2008). A conceptual density-based approach for the disambiguation of toponyms. *International Journal of Geographical Information Science, 22*(3), 301–313. doi:10.1080/13658810701626251

Bygate, M. (2001). Effects of task repetition on the structure and control of oral language. In Bygate, M., Skehan, P., & Swain, M. (Eds.), *Researching pedagogic tasks: Second language learning, teaching and testing* (pp. 23–48). Harlow, England: Pearson Education.

Bygate, M., & Samuda, V. (2005). Integrative planning through the use of task repetition. In Ellis, R. (Ed.), *Planning and task performance in a second language* (pp. 37–74). Amsterdam, The Netherlands: John Benjamins.

Caccamise, D. J., Snyder, L., Allen, C., Oliver, W., DeHart, M., Kintsch, E., & Kintsch, W. (in preparation). *Teaching comprehension via technology-driven tools: A large scale scale-up of Summary Street.*

Campbell, D. T. (1986). Relabeling internal and external validity for applied social scientists. In Trochim, W. M. K. (Ed.), *Advances in quasi-experimental design and analysis. New directions for program evaluation, no. 31.* San Francisco, CA: Jossey-Bass.

Carletta, J. (1996). Assessing agreement on classification tasks: The Kappa statistic. *Computational Linguistics, 22*(2), 249–254.

Carletta, J., Isard, A., Isard, S., Kowtko, J., Newlands, A., Doherty-Sneddon, G., & Anderson, A. (1997). The reliability of a dialogue structure coding scheme. *Computational Linguistics, 23*(1), 13–31.

Carletta, J., Dingare, S., Nissim, M., & Nikitina, T. (2004). Using the NITE XML toolkit on the switchboard corpus to study syntactic choice: A case study. *Proceedings of the 4th International Conference on Language Resources and Evaluation* (pp. 1019-1022). Lisbon, Portugal: LREC.

Carmody, A. (2009). *Vote May 19, 2009-2010 budget proposal*. Retrieved from http://www.websterschools.org/files/filesystem/200910%20Budget%20Newsletter.pdf.

Carrell, P. L., & Monroe, L. B. (1993). Learning styles and composition. *Modern Language Journal*, *77*, 148–162.

Carrol, J. B. (1964). *Language and thought*. New Jersey: Prentice-Hall.

Casanave, C. P. (1994). Language development in students' journals. *Journal of Second Language Writing*, *3*(3), 179–201. doi:10.1016/1060-3743(94)90016-7

Cassell, J., Vilhjálmsson, J., & Bickmore, T. (2001). BEAT: The behavior expression animation toolkit. *Proceedings of ACM SIGGRAPH 2001* (pp.477-486). Los Angeles, CA: ACM Press.

Chafe, W. L. (1975). Givenness, contrastiveness, definiteness, subjects, topics, and point of view. In Li, C. N. (Ed.), *Subject and topic* (pp. 26–55). New York, NY: Academic.

Chafe, W. L. (1987). Cognitive constraints of information flow. In Tomlin, R. S. (Ed.), *Coherence and grounding in discourse* (pp. 21–51). Amsterdam, The Netherlands: John Benjamins.

Chall, J. S., & Dale, E. (1995). *Readability revisited, the new Dale-Chall readability formula*. Cambridge, MA: Brookline Books.

Chall, J. S. (1983). *Stages of reading development*. New York, NY: McGraw-Hill.

Chambers, N., Allen, J., Galescu, L., Jung, H., & Taysom, W. (2006). Using semantics to identify web objects. In *Proceedings of the Twenty-First National Conference on Artificial Intelligence (AAAI-06)*.

Chang, D. S., & Choi, K. S. (2006). Incremental cue phrase learning and bootstrapping method for causality extraction using cue phrase and word pair probabilities. *Information Processing & Management*, *42*(3), 662–678. doi:10.1016/j.ipm.2005.04.004

Chapman, P., Clinton, J., Kerber, R., Khabaza, T., Reinartz, T., Shearer, C., & Wirth, R. (2000). *CRISP-DM 1.0 Step-by-step data mining guide*. Retrieved from http://www.crisp-dm.org/CRISPWP-0800.pdf.

Charniak, E. (1993). *Statistical language learning*. Cambridge, MA: MIT Press.

Charniak, E. (2000). A maximum-entropy-inspired parser. *Proceedings of the First Conference on North American Chapter of the Association for Computational Linguistics* (pp. 132-139). San Francisco, CA: Morgan Kaufmann Publishers.

Chi, M. T. H., Siler, S. A., & Jeong, H. (2004). Can tutors monitor students' understanding accurately? *Cognition and Instruction*, *22*(3), 363–387. doi:10.1207/s1532690xci2203_4

Chi, M. T. H., Siler, S. A., Jeong, H., Yamauchi, T., & Hausmann, R. G. (2001). Learning from human tutoring. *Cognitive Science*, *25*, 471–533. doi:10.1207/s15516709cog2504_1

Chklovski, T., & Pantel, P. (2004). Verbocean: Mining the web for fine-grained semantic verb relations. In. *Proceedings of EMNLP*, *4*, 33–40.

Chodorow, M., & Leacock, C. (2000). An unsupervised method for detecting grammatical errors. In *Proceedings of the 1st Annual Meeting of the North American Chapter of the Association for Computational Linguistics*, (pp. 140-147).

Choi, F. Y. Y., Wiemer-Hastings, P., & Moore, J. (2001). Latent semantic analysis for text segmentation. In *Proceedings of the 2001 Conference on Empirical Methods in Natural Language Processing*, (pp. 109–117).

Chomsky, N. (1965). *Aspects of the theory of syntax*. Cambridge, MA: MIT Press.

Chomsky, N. (1956). Three models for the description of language. *Information Theory. IEEE Transactions*, *2*(3), 113–124.

Christian, P. (1998). Soundex – Can it be improved? *Computers in Genealogy, 6*(5).

Chu-Carroll, J. (1998). A statistical model for discourse act recognition in dialogue interactions. In J. Chu-Carroll & N. Green (Eds.), *Working Notes of AAAI Spring Symposium on Applying Machine Learning to Discourse Processing*, (pp. 12–17). AAAI Press.

Chung, C. K., & Pennebaker, J. W. (2008). Revealing dimensions of thinking in open-ended self-descriptions: An automated meaning extraction method for natural language. *Journal of Research in Personality, 42*, 96–132. doi:10.1016/j.jrp.2007.04.006

Chung, C. K., & Pennebaker, J. W. (2007). The psychological function of function words. In Fiedler, K. (Ed.), *Social communication: Frontiers of social psychology* (pp. 343–359). New York, NY: Psychology Press.

Chung, C. K. (2009). *Predicting weight loss in blogs using computerized text analysis.* Unpublished dissertation. Austin, TX: The University of Texas at Austin.

Chung, C. K., Rentfrow, P. J., & Pennebaker, J. W. (2009). *This I believe: Validity of themes mapped across America using text analysis.* Unpublished data.

Clark, H. H., & Schaefer, E. F. (1989). Contributing to discourse. *Cognitive Science, 13*, 259–294. doi:10.1207/s15516709cog1302_7

Clark, H. H. (1996). *Using language.* Cambridge, UK: Cambridge University Press.

Clark, H. H., & Haviland, S. E. (1977). Comprehension and the given-new contrast. In Freedle, R. O. (Ed.), *Discourse production and comprehension* (pp. 1–40). Norwood, NJ: Ablex.

Clark, P., Harrison, P., Jenkins, T., Thompson, J., & Wojcik, R. (2005). Acquiring and using world knowledge using a restricted subset of English. *In Proceedings of the Eighteenth International Florida AI Research Symposium.* FLAIRS, AAAI 2005, Clearwater Beach, Florida, USA, (pp. 506-511).

Coates, L., & Johnson, T. (2001). Towards a social theory of gender. In Robinson, W. P., & Giles, H. (Eds.), *The new handbook of language and social psychology.* New York, NY: Wiley.

Cobb, T. 2003. Analyzing late interlanguage with learner corpora: Québec replications of three European studies. *The Canadian Modern Language Review/La Revue canadienne des langues vivantes, 59*(3), 393-423.

Cohen, P. A., Kulik, J. A., & Kulik, C. C. (1982). Educational outcomes of tutoring: A meta-analysis of findings. *American Educational Research Journal, 19*, 237–248.

Cohen, J. (1988). *Statistical power analysis for the behavioral sciences* (2nd ed.). Hillsdale, NJ: Erlbaum.

Cohen, W. (1996). Learning trees and rules with set-valued features. In *The 1996 13th National Conference on Artificial Intelligence, AAAI 96,* part 1(of 2) (pp. 709-716).

Cohn, M. A., Mehl, M. R., & Pennebaker, J. W. (2004). Linguistic markers of psychological change surrounding September 11, 2001. *Psychological Science, 15*, 687–693. doi:10.1111/j.0956-7976.2004.00741.x

Collins, J. L. (1998). *Strategies for struggling writers.* New York, NY: Guilford Publications.

Collins, A., Brown, J. S., & Newman, S. E. (1989). Cognitive apprenticeship: Teaching the craft of reading, writing, and mathematics. In Resnick, L. B. (Ed.), *Knowing, learning, and instruction: Essays in honor of Robert Glaser* (pp. 453–494). Hillsdale, NJ: Lawrence Erlbaum.

Collins, J. (2003). *Variations in written English: Characterizing the authors' rhetorical language choices across corpora of published texts.* PhD thesis, Carnegie Mellon University.

Coltheart, M. (1981). The MRC psycholinguistic database. *Quarterly Journal of Experimental Psychology, 33A*, 497–505.

Connor, U. (1987). Research frontiers in writing analysis. *TESOL Quarterly, 21*, 677–696. doi:10.2307/3586989

Connor, U. (1990). Linguistic/rhetorical measures for international student persuasive writing. *Research in the Teaching of English, 24*, 67–87.

Corbett, A. T. (2001). Cognitive computer tutors: Solving the two-sigma problem. *User Modeling: Proceedings of the Eighth International Conference, UM 2001,* (pp. 137-147).

Core, M., & Allen, J. (1997). Coding dialogs with the DAMSL annotation scheme. In *Working Notes of the AAAI Fall Symposium on Communicative Action in Humans and Machines,* (pp. 28–35). Cambridge, MA, November.

Corley, C., & Mihalcea, R. (2005). Measuring the semantic similarity of texts. In *Proceedings of the ACL Workshop on Empirical Modeling of Semantic Equivalence and Entailment,* Ann Arbor, MI.

Craig, S. D., Sullins, J., Witherspoon, A., & Gholson, B. (2006). Deep-level reasoning questions effect: The role of dialog and deep-level reasoning questions during vicarious learning. *Cognition and Instruction, 24*(4), 563–589. doi:10.1207/s1532690xci2404_4

Craig, S. D., Graesser, A. C., Sullins, J., & Gholson, B. (2004). Affect and learning: An exploratory look into the role of affect in learning with AutoTutor. *Journal of Educational Media, 29*, 241–250. doi:10.1080/1358165042000283101

Cremmins, E. T. (1996). *The art of abstracting* (2nd ed.). Arlington, VA: Information Resources Press.

Crismore, A., Markkanen, R., & Steffensen, M. S. (1993). Metadiscourse in persuasive writing: A study of texts written by American and Finnish university students. *Written Communication, 10*, 39–71. doi:10.1177/0741088393010001002

Croft, B., Metzler, D., & Strohman, T. (2010). *Search engines. Information retrieval in practice*. Boston, MA: Addison Wesley.

Crossley, S. A., Salsbury, T., & McNamara, D. S. (in press). The role of lexical cohesive devices in triggering negotiations for meaning. *Issues in Applied Linguistics.*

Crossley, S. A., Louwerse, M., McCarthy, P. M., & McNamara, D. S. (2007). A linguistic analysis of simplified and authentic texts. *Modern Language Journal, 91*, 15–30. doi:10.1111/j.1540-4781.2007.00507.x

Crossley, S. A., Dempsey, K. B., & McNamara, D. S. (Manuscript submitted for publication). Classifying paragraph types using linguistic features: Is paragraph positioning important? *Research in the Teaching of English.*

Crossley, S. A., & McNamara, D. S. (in press). Predicting second language writing proficiency: The role of cohesion, readability, and lexical difficulty. *Journal of Research in Reading.*

Crossley, S., Salsbury, T., & McNamara, D. (2009b). Measuring L2 lexical growth using hypernymic relationships. *Language Learning, 59*(2), 307–334. doi:10.1111/j.1467-9922.2009.00508.x

Crossley, S. A., Greenfield, J., & McNamara, D. S. (2008). Assessing text readability using cognitively based indices. *TESOL Quarterly, 42*(3), 475–493.

Crossley, S. A., Salsbury, T., & McNamara, D. S. (2010). The development of polysemy and frequency use in English second language speakers. *Language Learning, 60*(3). doi:10.1111/j.1467-9922.2010.00568.x

Crossley, S. A., Salsbury, T., & McNamara, D. S. (2010). The development of semantic relations in second language speakers: A case for latent semantic analysis. *Vigo International Journal of Applied Linguistics, 7*, 55–74.

Crossley, S., & McNamara, D. S. (in press). Interlanguage talk: What can breadth of knowledge features tell us about input and output differences? In McCarthy, P. M., & Boonthum, C. (Eds.), *Applied natural language processing: Identification, investigation, and resolution*. Hershey, PA: IGI Global.

Crossley, S. A., & McNamara, D. S. (2010). Cohesion, coherence, and expert evaluations of writing proficiency. In R. Catrambone & S. Ohlsson (Eds.), *Proceedings of the 32nd Annual Conference of the Cognitive Science Society.*

Crossley, S. A., McCarthy, P. M., & McNamara, D. S. (2007). Discriminating between second language learning text-types. In D. Wilson & G. Sutcliffe (Eds.), *Proceedings of the Twentieth International Florida Artificial Intelligence Research Society Conference* (pp. 205-210). Menlo Park, CA: The AAAI Press.

Crowhurst, M. (1990). Reading/writing relationships: An intervention study. *Canadian Journal of Education, 15*, 155–172. doi:10.2307/1495373

Crystal, D. (1987). *The Cambridge encyclopedia of language*. Cambridge University Press.

Crystal, D. (1997). *English as a global language*. Cambridge, UK: Cambridge University Press.

Csikszentmihalyi, M. (1990). *Flow: The psychology of optimal experience*. New York, NY: Harper and Row.

Cucerzan, S. (2007). Large-scale named entity disambiguation based on Wikipedia data. In *Proceedings of the 2007 Joint Conference on Empirical Methods in Natural Language Processing and Computational Natural Language Learning,* (708-716). Prague, Czech Republic: Association for Computational Linguistics.

D'Mello, S., & Graesser, A. C. (in press). Multimodal semi-automated affect detection from conversational cues, gross body language, and facial features. *User Modeling and User-Adapted Interaction.*

D'Mello, S., King, B., Chipman, P., & Graesser, A. C. (in press). Towards spoken human-computer tutorial dialogues. *Human-Computer Interaction.*

D'Mello, S. K., & Graesser, A. C. (in press). Automated detection of cognitive-affective states from text dialogues. In McCarthy, P. M., & Boonthum, C. (Eds.), *Applied natural language processing: Identification, investigation, and resolution.* Hershey, PA: IGI Global.

Daelemans, W., van den Bosch, A., & Weijters, T. (1997). IGTree: Using trees for compression and classification in lazy learning algorithms. In Aha, D. (Ed.), *Artificial Intelligence Review: Special Issue on Lazy Learning* (*Vol. 11*, pp. 1–5).

Daelemans, W., & van den Bosch, A. (1992). Generalization performance of backpropagation learning on a syllabification task. In M. Drossaers & A. Nijholt (Eds.), *Proc. 3rd Twente Workshop on Language Technology* (pp. 27-37). Enschede, The Netherlands: Universiteit Twente.

Dagan, I. Glickman. O., & Magnini, B. (2006). The PASCAL RTE challenge. *In Proceedings of the 1st PASCAL Challenge Workshop on RTE.*

Dalgarno, B. (1996). Constructivist computer assisted learning: Theory and techniques. *Making New Connections: Proceedings of ASCILITE '96,* University of Adelaide, (pp. 127-148).

Dalianis, H., Hassel, M., de Smedt, K., Liseth, A., Lech, T. C., & Wedekind, J. (2004). Porting and evaluation of automatic summarization. In Holmboe, H. (Ed.), *Nordisk Sprogteknologi 2003. Årbog for Nordisk Språkteknologisk Forskningsprogram 2000-2004* (pp. 107–121). Museum Tusculanums Forlag.

Dalianis, H. (2000). *SweSum - A text summarizer for Swedish.* Technical report TRITA-NA-P0015, IPLab-174, NADA, KTH, October 2000.

Daller, H., van Hout, R., & Treffers-Daller, J. (2003). Lexical richness in the spontaneous speech of bilinguals. *Applied Linguistics, 24*(2), 197–222. doi:10.1093/applin/24.2.197

Damerau, F. J. (1964). A technique for computer detection and correction of spelling errors. *Communications of the ACM, 7*(3), 171–176. doi:10.1145/363958.363994

Darwish, K. (2002). Building a shallow morphological analyzer in one day. In *Proceedings of the Workshop on Computational Approaches to Semitic Languages,* (ACL 2002), Philadelphia, PA, USA, (pp. 47-54).

Davidov, D., & Rappaport, A. (2008). Unsupervised discovery of generic relationships using pattern clusters and its evaluation by automatically generated SAT analogy questions. *Proceedings of the Annual Meeting of the Association of Computational Linguistics.*

de Saussure, F. (1916). *Course in general linguistics (trans. Roy Harris, 1983).* London: Duckworth.

Deerwester, S., Dumais, S., Furnas, G. W., Landauer, T. K., & Harshman, R. (1990). Indexing by latent semantic analysis. *Journal of the American Society for Information Science American Society for Information Science, 41,* 391–407. doi:10.1002/(SICI)1097-4571(199009)41:6<391::AID-ASI1>3.0.CO;2-9

Dempsey, K. B., McCarthy, P. M., Myers, J. C., Weston, J., & McNamara, D. S. (2009). Determining paragraph type from paragraph position. In C. H. Lane & H. W. Guesgen (Eds.), *Proceedings of the 22nd International Florida Artificial Intelligence Research Society (FLAIRS) Conference* (pp. 33-38). Menlo Park, CA: The AAAI Press.

Dennis, S. (2007). Introducing word order in an LSA framework. In Landauer, T., McNamara, D., Dennis, S., & Kintsch, W. (Eds.), *Handbook of latent semantic of analysis* (pp. 449–466). Mahwah, NJ: Lawrence Erlbaum.

Denzin, N. K., & Lincoln, Y. S. (Eds.). (2009). *The Sage handbook of qualitative research* (3rd ed.). Newbury Park, CA: Sage.

DeVillez, R. (2003). *Writing: Step by step.* Dubuque, IA: Kendall/Hunt Publishing Company.

Di Eugenio, B., & Glass, M. (2004). The Kappa statistic: A second look. *Computational Linguistics, 30*(1), 95–101. doi:10.1162/089120104773633402

Diab, M., & Resnik, P. (2002). An unsupervised method for word sense tagging using parallel corpora. *Proc. ACL.*

Dillon, J. (1988). *Questioning and teaching: A manual of practice.* New York, NY: Teachers College Press.

D'Mello, S., Olney, A. M., & Person, N. (in press). Mining collaborative patterns in tutorial dialogues. *Journal of Educational Data Mining.*

Doignon, J. P., & Falmagne, J. C. (1999). *Knowledge spaces.* Berlin, Germany: Springer. doi:10.1007/978-3-642-58625-5

Dolan, B., Quirk, C., & Brockett, C. (2004). Unsupervised construction of large paraphrase corpora: Exploiting massively parallel news sources. In *Proceedings of COLING*, Geneva, Switzerland.

Doughty, C., & Pica, T. (1984). *Information gap tasks: do they facilitate second language acquisition?* Paper presented at the 18th Annual TESOL Conference, Houston, March 1984.

Douglas, D. (1981). An exploratory study of bilingual reading proficiency. In Hudelson, S. (Ed.), *Learning to read in different languages* (pp. 33–102). Washington, DC: Center for Applied Linguistics.

Downs, W. (1998). *Language and society.* Cambridge University Press.

Drew, P., & Heritage, J. (1992). Analysing talk at work: An introduction. In Drew, P., & Heritage, J. (Eds.), *Talk at work* (pp. 3–65). Cambridge, UK: Cambridge University Press.

Duan, W., Song, M., & Yates, A. (2009). Fast max-margin clustering for unsupervised word sense disambiguation in biomedical texts. *BMC Bioinformatics*, *10*, S4. doi:10.1186/1471-2105-10-S3-S4

DuBay, W. (2004). *The principles of readability.* Costa Mesa, CA: Impact Information.

Dumais, S. T., Furnas, G. W., Landauer, T. K., & Deerwester, S. C. (1988). Using latent semantic analysis to improve information retrieval. In *Proceedings of CHI'88: Conference on Human Factors in Computing* (pp. 281–285), Washington DC, USA. May 15-19 1988.

Duran, N. D., Mccarthy, P. M., Graesser, A. C., & Mcnamara, D. S. (2007). Using temporal cohesion to predict temporal coherence in narrative and expository texts. *Behavior Research Methods*, *39*, 212–223. doi:10.3758/BF03193150

Duran, N. D., & McCarthy, P. M. (November, 2010). *Using statistically improbable n-gram features to reveal the thematic content of deception.* Paper presented at the Society for Computers in Psychology (SCiP), Houston, Texas.

Duran, N. D., Hall, C., McCarthy, P. M., & McNamara, D. S. (2010). The linguistic correlates of conversational deception: Comparing natural language processing technologies. *Applied Psycholinguistics.*

Duran, N., Bellissens, C., Taylor, R., & McNamara, D. (2007). Qualifying text difficulty with automated indices of cohesion and semantics. In D.S. McNamara & G. Trafton (Eds.), *Proceedings of the 29th Annual Meeting of the Cognitive Science Society* (pp. 233-238). Austin, TX: Cognitive Science Society.

Durda, K., & Buchanan, L. (2008). Windsors: Windsor improved norms of distance and similarity of representations of semantics. *Behavior Research Methods*, *40*(3), 705–712. doi:10.3758/BRM.40.3.705

Durda, K., Buchanan, L., & Caron, R. (2009). Grounding co-occurrence: Identifying features in a lexical co-occurrence model of semantic memory. *Behavior Research Methods*, *41*(4), 1210–1223. doi:10.3758/BRM.41.4.1210

Duval, S., & Wicklund, R. A. (1972). *A theory of objective self-awareness.* Oxford, UK: Academic Press.

Dyck, M. (2002). *The GNU version of the collaborative international dictionary of English, presented in the Extensible Markup Language.* Retrieved May 20, 2010, from http://www.ibiblio.org/webster/.

Dzikovska, M., Allen, J., & Swift, M. (2008). Linking semantic and knowledge representations in a multi-domain dialogue system. *Journal of Logic and Computation*, *18*(3), 405–430. doi:10.1093/logcom/exm067

Eckert, P., & McConnell-Ginet, S. (2003). *Language and gender.* Cambridge, UK: University Press. doi:10.1017/CBO9780511791147

Edwards, D. (1995). Two to tango: Script formulations, disposition, and rhetorical symmetry in relationship troubles talk. *Research on Language and Social Interaction*, *28*(4), 319–350. doi:10.1207/s15327973rlsi2804_1

Edwards, D. (1997). *Discourse and cognition.* London, UK: Sage.

Edwards, D. (2006a). Discourse, cognition and social practices: The rich surface of language and social interaction. *Discourse Studies, 8*, 41–49. doi:10.1177/1461445606059551

Edwards, D. (2006b). Facts, norms, and dispositions: Practical uses of the modal would in police interrogations. *Discourse Studies, 8*(4), 1–23. doi:10.1177/1461445606064830

Edwards, D. (2008). Intentionality and *mens rea* in police interrogations: The production of actions as crimes. *Intercultural Pragmatics, 5*(2), 177–199. doi:10.1515/IP.2008.010

Edwards, D., & Middleton, D. (1986). Joint remembering: Constructing and account of shared experience through conversational discourse. *Discourse Processes, 9*, 423–459. doi:10.1080/01638538609544651

Edwards, D., & Middleton, D. (1987). Conversation and remembering: Bartlett revisited. *Applied Cognitive Psychology, 1*, 77–92. doi:10.1002/acp.2350010202

Edwards, D., & Middleton, D. (1988). Conversational remembering and family relationships: How children learn to remember. *Journal of Social and Personal Relationships, 5*(3), 25.

Edwards, D., & Potter, J. (1992). *Discursive psychology.* London, UK: Sage.

Edwards, D., & Potter, J. (1993). Language and causation: A discursive action model of description and attribution. *Psychological Review, 100*(1), 23–41. doi:10.1037/0033-295X.100.1.23

Edwards, D. (2005). Discursive psychology. In Fitch, K. L., & Sanders, R. E. (Eds.), *Handbook of language and social interaction* (pp. 257–273). New Jersey: Lawrence Erlbaum.

Edwards, D., & Potter, J. (2005). Discursive psychology, mental states, and descriptions. In Molder, H. T. E., & Potter, J. (Eds.), *Conversation and cognition* (pp. 241–259). Cambridge, UK: Cambridge University Press. doi:10.1017/CBO9780511489990.012

Elbow, P. (1973). *Writing without teachers.* New York, NY: Oxford University Press.

Elkan, C. (1997). *Boosting and naive Bayesian learning. Technical report, Department of Computer Science and Engineering.* San Diego: University of California.

Elkner, J., Downey, A. B., & Meyers, C. (2009). *How to think like a computer scientist. Learning with Python* (2nd ed.). Retrieved December 27, 2009, from http://www.openbookproject.net/thinkCSpy.

Ellis, N. C., & Ferreira-Junior, F. (2009). Construction learning as a function of frequency, frequency distribution, and function. *Modern Language Journal, 93*, 370–385. doi:10.1111/j.1540-4781.2009.00896.x

Ellis, N. (2002). Frequency effects in language processing. *Studies in Second Language Acquisition, 24*(2), 143–188.

Ellis, N., & Collin, L. (2009). Input and second language acquisition: The roles of frequency, form, function. Introduction to the special issue. *Modern Language Journal, 93*(3), 329–335. doi:10.1111/j.1540-4781.2009.00893.x

Elmi, M. A., & Evens, M. (1998). Spelling correction using context. In *Proceedings of ACL 1998,* Montreal, Canada, (pp. 360-364).

El-Sadany, T. A., & Hashish, M. A. (1989). An Arabic morphological system. *IBM Systems Journal, 28*(4), 600–612. doi:10.1147/sj.284.0600

Emmison, M., & Danby, S. (2007). Troubles announcements and reasons for calling: Initial actions in opening sequences in calls to a national children's helpline. *Research on Language and Social Interaction, 40*(1), 63–87. doi:10.1080/08351810701331273

Endres-Niggemeyer, B., Maier, E., & Sigel, A. (1995). How to implement a naturalistic model of abstracting: Four core working steps of an expert abstractor. *Information Processing & Management, 31*(5), 631–674. doi:10.1016/0306-4573(95)00028-F

Ericsson, K. A., Charness, N., Hoffman, R. R., & Feltovich, P. J. (2006). *The Cambridge handbook of expertise and expert performance.* New York, NY: Cambridge University Press.

Ericsson, K. A., & Kintsch, W. (1995). Long-term working memory. *Psychological Review, 102*, 211–245. doi:10.1037/0033-295X.102.2.211

Ericsson, K. A. (2006). The influence of experience and deliberate practice on the development of superior expert performance. In Ericsson, K. A., Charness, N., Feltovich, P., & Hoffman, R. R. (Eds.), *Cambridge handbook of expertise and expert performance* (pp. 685–706). Cambridge, UK: Cambridge University Press.

Escudero, G., Marquez, L., & Rigau, G. (2000). Boosting applied to word sense disambiguation. In *Proceedings of ECML-00, 11th European Conference on Machine Learning* (Barcelona, Spain, 2000), (pp. 129–141).

Eui-Hong, S., Han, G., & Kumar, V. (2001). Text categorization using weight adjusted k-nearest neighbor classification. In *Proceedings 5th Pacific-Asia Conference on Knowledge Discovery and Data Mining* (PAKDD), (pp. 53-65). Springer.

Evens, M., & Michael, J. (2006). *One-on-one tutoring by humans and machines*. Mahwah, NJ: Erlbaum.

Extended Backus-Naur Form. (n.d.). In *Wikipedia*. Retrieved November 12, 2009, from http://en.wikipedia.org/wiki/Extended_Backus%E2%80%93Naur_Form.

Faaborg, A., & Lieberman, H. (2006). A goal-oriented web browser. In *Proceedings of the SIGCHI Conference on Human Factors in Computing Systems*.

Fairclough, N. (1989). *Language and power*. London, UK: Longman.

Faltin, A. V. (2003). *Syntactic error diagnosis in the context of computer assisted language learning*. PhD thesis, University of Geneva, Switzerland.

Farr, R., & Carey, R. (1986). *Reading: What can be measured*. Newark, Delaware: IRA.

Fast, L. A., & Funder, D. C. (2008). Personality as manifest in word use: Correlations with self-report, acquaintant report, and behavior. *Journal of Personality and Social Psychology*, *94*, 334–346. doi:10.1037/0022-3514.94.2.334

Fayyad, U. M., Piatetsky-Shapiro, G., Smyth, P., & Uthurusamy, R. (1996). From data mining to knowledge discovery: An overview. In Fayyad, U. M., Piatetsky-Shapiro, G., & Smyth, P. (Eds.), *Advances in Knowledge Discovery and Data Mining* (pp. 1–34). Cambridge, MA: AAAI Press.

Fazio, R. H., & Olson, M. A. (2003). Implicit measures in social cognition research: Their meaning and use. *Annual Review of Psychology*, *54*, 297–327. doi:10.1146/annurev.psych.54.101601.145225

Fellbaum, C. (1998). *WordNet. An electronic lexical database*. Cambridge, MA: MIT Press.

Fellbaum, C. (1998). Towards a representation of idioms in WordNet. *Proceedings of the COLING/ACL Workshop on Usage of WordNet in Natural Language Processing Systems* (pp. 52-57). Montréal, Canada: University of Montréal.

Ferguson, G., & Allen, J. (1998). TRIPS: An integrated intelligent problem-solving assistant. In *Proceedings of the National Conference on Artificial Intelligence (AAAI)*.

Fernando, S., & Stevenson, M. (2008). A semantic approach to paraphrase identification. In *Proceedings of the 11th Annual Research Colloquium of the UK Special-interest group for Computational Lingusitics*, Oxford, England, 2008.

Field, A. (2005). *Discovering statistics using SPSS* (2nd ed.). London, UK: Sage.

Fillmore, C., & Baker, C. (2001). Frame semantics for text understanding. In *Proceedings of the NAACL Workshop on WordNet and Other Lexical Resources*. Association for Computational Linguistics.

Firth, A. (1990). Lingua franca negotiations: Towards an interactional approach. *World Englishes*, *9*(3), 69–80. doi:10.1111/j.1467-971X.1990.tb00265.x

Firth, A. (1996). The discursive accomplishment of normality: On conversation analysis and Lingua Franca English. *Journal of Pragmatics*, *26*, 237–259. doi:10.1016/0378-2166(96)00014-8

Fitzpatrick, M. A., Mulac, A., & Dindia, K. (1995). Gender-preferential language use in spouse and stranger interaction. *Journal of Language and Social Psychology*, *14*, 18–39. doi:10.1177/0261927X95141002

Flanigan, B. O. (1991). Peer tutoring and second language acquisition in the elementary school. *Applied Linguistics*, *12*(2), 141–157. doi:10.1093/applin/12.2.141

Flowerdew, L. (2000). Using a genre-based framework to teach organizational structure in academic writing. *ELT Journal, 54*(4), 369–378. doi:10.1093/elt/54.4.369

Flowerdew, L. (2004in press). The argument for using English specialized corpora to understand academic and professional language. In Connor, U., & Upton, T. (Eds.), *Discourse in the professions: Perspectives from corpus linguistics.* Amsterdam, The Netherlands: John Benjamins.

Flowerdew, L. (1999). Corpus linguistics in ESP: A genre-based perspective. Penetrating discourse: Integrating theory with practice in second language teaching. *9th International Conference, Language Centre*, HKUST, Hong Kong (22-23 June, 1999), (pp. 21-35).

Foltz, P. W., Kintsch, W., & Landauer, T. K. (1998). The measurement of textual coherence with latent semantic analysis. *Discourse Processes, 25*(2-3), 285–307. doi:10.1080/01638539809545029

Foltz, P. W., Gilliam, S., & Kendall, S. (2000). Supporting content-based feedback in online writing evaluation with LSA. *Interactive Learning Environments, 8*, 111–129. doi:10.1076/1049-4820(200008)8:2;1-B;FT111

Foltz, P. W., & Wells, A. D. (1999). Automatically deriving readers' knowledge structures from texts. *Behavior Research Methods, Instruments, & Computers, 31*, 208–214. doi:10.3758/BF03207712

Fontaine, R. J., Scherer, K. R., Roesch, E. B., & Ellsworth, C. (2007). The world of emotions is not two-dimensional. *Psychological Science, 18*, 1050–1057. doi:10.1111/j.1467-9280.2007.02024.x

Fontaine, S. I. (1991). Recording and transforming: the mystery of the ten-minute freewrite. In Belanoff, P., Elbow, P., & Fontaine, S. I. (Eds.), *Nothing begins with N* (pp. 3–16). Carbondale, IL: Southern Illinois University Press.

Fossati, D., & Di Eugenio, B. (2008). I saw TREE trees in the park: How to correct real-word spelling mistakes. In *Proceedings of the 6th International Conference on Language Resources and Evaluation*, (pp. 896-901).

Foster, J., & Vogel, C. (2004). Parsing ill-formed text using an error grammar. *Artificial Intelligence Review: Special AICS, 2003*(Issue, 21), 269–291. doi:10.1023/B:AIRE.0000036259.68818.1e

Foucault, M. (1972). *The archaeology of knowledge.* London, UK: Routledge.

Frank, E., & Witten, I. H. (1998). Generating accurate rule sets without global optimization. In *Proceedings of the Fifteenth International Conference on Machine Learning*, (pp. 144–151).

Franzke, M., Kintsch, E., Caccamise, D., Johnson, N., & Dooley, S. (2005). Summary Street®: Computer support for comprehension and writing. *Journal of Educational Computing Research, 33*, 53–80. doi:10.2190/DH8F-QJWM-J457-FQVB

Fristrup, J. A. (1994). *USENET: Netnews for everyone.* Englewood Cliffs, NJ: Prentice Hall.

Gaies, S. J. (1983). The investigation of language classroom processes. *TESOL Quarterly, 17*(2), 205–217. doi:10.2307/3586650

Galley, M., McKeown, K., Fosler-Lussier, E., & Jing, H. (2003). Discourse segmentation of multi-party conversation. In *Proceedings of the 41st Annual Meeting of the Association for Computational Linguistics*, (pp. 562–569).

Garg, A. X., Adhikari, N. K., McDonald, H., Rosas-Arellano, M. P., Devereaux, P. J., & Beyene, J. (2005). Effects of computerized clinical decision support systems on practitioner performance and patient outcomes: A systematic review. *Journal of the American Medical Association, 293*, 1223–1238. doi:10.1001/jama.293.10.1223

Garland, A., Ryall, K., & Rich, C. (2001). *Learning hierarchical task models by defining and refining examples.* In International Conference on Knowledge Capture.

Gass, S., & Varonis, E. (1989). Incorporating repairs in NNS discourse. In Eisenstein, M. (Ed.), *Variation and second language acquisition* (pp. 71–86). New York, NY: Plenum.

Gass, S., & Varonis, E. (1985). Negotiation of meaning in nonnative speaker - nonnative speaker conversation. In Gass, S., & Madden, C. (Eds.), *Input and second language acquisition.* Rowley, MA: Newbury House Publishers, Inc.

Gee, J. P. (2005). *An introduction to discourse analysis* (2nd ed.). New York, NY: Routledge.

Geiser, S., & Studley, R. (2001, October). *UC and the SAT: Predictive validity and differential impact of the SAT I and SAT II at the University of California*. Paper presented at the Meeting of the Board of Admissions and Relations with Schools of the University of California.

Geisler, C. (2003). *Analyzing streams of language: Twelve steps to the systematic coding of text, talk, and other verbal data*. New York, NY: Longman.

Gernsbacher, M. A. (1990). *Language comprehension as structure building*. Hillsdale, NJ: Erlbaum.

Gholson, B., Witherspoon, A., Morgan, B., Brittingham, J. K., Coles, R., & Graesser, A. C. (2009). Exploring the deep-level reasoning questions effect during vicarious learning among eighth to eleventh graders in the domains of computer literacy and Newtonian physics. *Instructional Science, 37*, 487–493. doi:10.1007/s11251-008-9069-2

Giampiccolo, D., Dang, H. T., Magnini, B., Dagan, I., Cabrio, E., & Dolan, B. (2008). The fourth PASCAL recognizing textual entailment challenge. *In Proceedings of the Third PASCAL Challenges Workshop on RTE*.

Giampiccolo, D., Magnini, B., Dagan, I., & Dolan, B. (2007). The 3rd PASCAL recognizing textual entailment challenge. In *Proc. of the Third PASCAL Challenges Workshop on RTE*.

Gilbert, G. N., & Mulkay, M. J. (1984). *Opening Pandora's box: A sociological analysis of scientists' discourse*. Cambridge, UK: Cambridge University Press.

Gilhooly, K. J., & Logie, R. H. (1980). Age of acquisition, imagery, concreteness, familiarity and ambiguity measures for 1944 words. *Behavior Research Methods and Instrumentation, 12*, 395–427. doi:10.3758/BF03201693

Gill, R. (2000). Discourse analysis. In Bauer, M., & Gaskell, G. (Eds.), *Qualitative researching with text, image and sound* (pp. 172–190). London, UK: Sage.

Gilligan, C. (1982). *In a different voice: Psychological theory and women's development*. Cambridge, MA: Harvard University Press.

Gilligan, C. (1987). Moral orientation and moral development. In Kittay, E. F., & Meyers, D. T. (Eds.), *Women and moral theory*. Totowa, NJ: Rowman & Littlefield.

Girju, R. (2003). Automatic detection of causal relations for question answering. In *ACL 2003 Workshop on Multilingual Summarization and Question Answering - Machine Learning and Beyond (p. 83)*. Association for Computational Linguistics.

Girju, R., & Moldovan, D. (2002). Mining answers for causation questions. In *Proc. The AAAI Spring Symposium on Mining Answers from Texts and Knowledge Bases*.

Girju, R., Nakov, P., Nastase, V., Szpakowicz, S., Turney, P., & Yuret, D. (2007). SemEval-2007 task 04: Classification of semantic relations between nominals. In *Proceedings of the 4th International Workshop on Semantic Evaluations* (pp. 13-18). Association for Computational Linguistics.

Glass, M. (1997). Some phenomena handled by the CIRCSIM-Tutor version 3 input understander. In *Proceedings of the Tenth Florida Artificial Intelligence Research Symposium*, Daytona Beach, FL. Menlo Park, CA: AAAI Press.

Godfrey, J., Holliman, E., & McDaniel, J. (1992). SWITCHBOARD: Telephone speech corpus for research and development. *Proceedings of the IEEE Conference on Acoustics, Speech, and Signal Processing* (pp. 517-520). San Francisco, CA: IEEE.

Goethals, B. (2000). *Survey on frequent pattern mining*. Technical Report. Retrieved from http://www.cs.helsinki.fi/u/goethals/publications/survey.ps.

Goffman, E. (1959). *The presentation of self in everyday life*. New York, NY: Doubleday.

Golding, A. R., & Roth, D. (1999). A Winnow based approach to context-sensitive spelling correction. *Machine Learning, 34*, 107–130. doi:10.1023/A:1007545901558

Goldman, S., Graesser, A. C., & van den Broek, P. (1999). *Narrative comprehension, causality, and coherence*. Mahwah, NJ: Erlbaum.

Goldman, S. (2003). Learning in complex domains: When and why do multiple representations help? *Learning and Instruction, 13*, 239–244. doi:10.1016/S0959-4752(02)00023-3

Gonzales, A. L., Pennebaker, J. W., & Hancock, J. T. (2010). Linguistic indicators of social dynamics in small groups. *Communication Research*, *37*, 3–19. doi:10.1177/0093650209351468

Gonzalo, J., Verdejo, F., Chugur, I., & Cigarran, J. (1998). Indexing with WordNet synsets can improve text retrieval. In *Proceedings of COLING-ACL '98 Workshop on Usage of Word.Net in Natural Language Processing Systems*, Montreal, Canada, August.

Goodwin, C., & Heritage, J. (1990). Conversation analysis. *Annual Review of Anthropology*, *19*, 283–307. doi:10.1146/annurev.an.19.100190.001435

Goodwin, M. H. (1990). *He-said-she-said: Talk as social organization among black children*. Bloomington, IN Indiana: University Press.

Goodwin, C., & Goodwin, M. H. (2004). Participation. In Duranti, A. (Ed.), *A companion to linguistic anthropology* (pp. 222–243). Oxford, UK: Basil Blackwell.

Goodwin, M. H., & Goodwin, C. (2000). Emotion within situated activity. In Duranti, A. (Ed.), *Linguistic anthropology: A reader* (pp. 239–255). Oxford, UK: Blackwell.

Gottman, J. R., & Levenson, R. W. (2000). The timing of divorce: Predicting when a couple will divorce over a 14-year period. *Journal of Marriage and the Family*, *62*, 737–745. doi:10.1111/j.1741-3737.2000.00737.x

Gottschalk, L. A. (2000). The application of computerized content analysis of natural language in psychotherapy research now and in the future. *American Journal of Psychotherapy*, *54*, 305–311.

Grady, M. (1971). A conceptual rhetoric of the composition. *College Composition and Communication*, *22*, 348–354. doi:10.2307/356208

Graesser, A. C., & McMahen, C. L. (1993). Anomalous information triggers questions when adults solve problems and comprehend stories. *Journal of Educational Psychology*, *85*, 136–151. doi:10.1037/0022-0663.85.1.136

Graesser, A. C., & Olde, B. A. (2003). How does one know whether a person understands a device? The quality of the questions the person asks when the device breaks down. *Journal of Educational Psychology*, *95*, 524–536. doi:10.1037/0022-0663.95.3.524

Graesser, A. C., & Person, N. K. (1994). Question asking during tutoring. *American Educational Research Journal*, *31*, 104–137.

Graesser, A. C., McNamara, D. S., Louwerse, M. M., & Cai, Z. (2004). Coh-Metrix: Analysis of text on cohesion and language. *Behavior Research Methods, Instruments, & Computers*, *36*(2), 193–202. doi:10.3758/BF03195564

Graesser, A. C., & Person, N. K. (1994). Question asking during tutoring. *American Educational Research Journal*, *31*, 104–137.

Graesser, A. C., Chipman, P., Haynes, B. C., & Olney, A. (2005). AutoTutor: An intelligent tutoring system with mixed-initiative dialogue. *IEEE Transactions on Education*, *48*, 612–618. doi:10.1109/TE.2005.856149

Graesser, A. C., Jeon, M., & Dufty, D. (2008). Agent technologies designed to facilitate interactive knowledge construction. *Discourse Processes*, *45*, 298–322. doi:10.1080/01638530802145395

Graesser, A. C., McNamara, D. S., & VanLehn, K. (2005). Scaffolding deep comprehension strategies through Point&Query, AutoTutor, and iSTART. *Educational Psychologist*, *40*, 225–234. doi:10.1207/s15326985ep4004_4

Graesser, A. C., Person, N., & Harter, D. Tutoring Research Group. (2001). Teaching tactics and dialog in AutoTutor. *International Journal of Artificial Intelligence in Education*, *12*, 257–279.

Graesser, A. C., & Person, N. K. (1994). Question asking during tutoring. *American Educational Research Journal*, *31*, 104–137.

Graesser, A. C., Person, N. K., & Magliano, J. P. (1995). Collaborative dialogue patterns in naturalistic one-to-one tutoring. *Applied Cognitive Psychology*, *9*, 495–522. doi:10.1002/acp.2350090604

Graesser, A. C., Singer, M., & Trabasso, T. (1994). Constructing inferences during narrative text comprehension. *Psychological Review*, *101*, 371–395. doi:10.1037/0033-295X.101.3.371

Graesser, A. C., Jeon, M., Yang, Y., & Cai, Z. (2007). Discourse cohesion in text and tutorial dialogue. *Information Design Journal*, *15*, 199–213.

Graesser, A., Wiemer-Hastings, P., Wiemer-Hastings, K., Harter, D., & Person, N.Tutoring Research Group. (2000). Using latent semantic analysis to evaluate the contributions of students in AutoTutor. *Interactive Learning Environments*, *8*, 149–169. doi:10.1076/1049-4820(200008)8:2;1-B;FT149

Graesser, A. C., Jeon, M., Cai, Z., & McNamara, D. S. (2008). Automatic analyses of language, discourse, and situation models. In Auracher, J., & van Peer, W. (Eds.), *New beginnings in literary studies* (pp. 72–88). Cambridge, UK: Cambridge Scholars Publishing.

Graesser, A. C., Olde, B., & Klettke, B. (2002). How does the mind construct and represent stories? In Green, M. C., Strange, J. J., & Brock, T. C. (Eds.), *Narrative impact: Social and cognitive foundations* (pp. 231–263). Mahwah, NJ: Erlbaum.

Graesser, A. C., D'Mello, S., & Person, N. K. (2009). Metaknowledge in tutoring. In Hacker, D., Donlosky, J., & Graesser, A. C. (Eds.), *Handbook of metacognition in education* (pp. 361–382). New York, NY: Taylor & Francis.

Graesser, A. C., Hu, X., & McNamara, D. S. (2005). Computerized learning environments that incorporate research in discourse psychology, cognitive science, and computational linguistics. In Healy, A. (Ed.), *Experimental cognitive psychology and its applications* (pp. 59–72). Washington, DC: APA. doi:10.1037/10895-014

Graesser, A. C., Penumatsa, P., Ventura, M., Cai, Z., & Hu, X. (2007). Using LSA in AutoTutor: Learning through mixed initiative dialogue in natural language. In Landauer, T., McNamara, D., Dennis, S., & Kintsch, W. (Eds.), *Handbook of latent semantic analysis* (pp. 243–262). Mahwah, NJ: Erlbaum.

Graesser, A., Ozuru, Y., & Sullins, J. (2009). What is a good question? In McKeown, M. G., & Kucan, L. (Eds.), *Threads of coherence in research on the development of reading ability* (pp. 112–141). New York, NY: Guilford.

Graesser, A. C., Person, N., Lu, Z., Jeon, M. G., & McDaniel, B. (2005). Learning while holding a conversation with a computer. In Pytlik Zillig, L., Bodvarsson, M., & Bruning, R. (Eds.), *Technology-based education: Bringing researchers and practitioners together* (pp. 143–167). Greenwich, CT: Information Age Publishing.

Graesser, A. C., Hu, X., & Person, N. (2001). Teaching with the help of talking heads. In T. Okamoto, R. Hartley, Kinshuk, & J. P. Klus (Eds.), *Proceedings IEEE International Conference on Advanced Learning Technology: Issues, Achievements and Challenges* (pp. 460-461).

Graesser, A. C., McNamara, D. S., & Kulikowich, J. (in preparation). *Theoretical and automated dimensions of text difficulty: How easy are the texts we read?*

Granger, S. (Ed.). (1998). *Learner English on computer*. London, UK: Longman.

Granger, S., Hung, J., & Petch-Tyson, S. (Eds.). (2002). *Computer learner corpora, second language acquisition and foreign language teaching*. Amsterdam, The Netherlands: Benjamins.

Grant, L., & Ginther, A. (2000). Using computer-tagged linguistic features to describe L2 writing differences. *Journal of Second Language Writing*, *9*(2), 123–145. doi:10.1016/S1060-3743(00)00019-9

Graybeal, A., Seagal, J. D., & Pennebaker, J. W. (2002). The role of story-making in disclosure writing: The psychometrics of narrative. *Psychology & Health*, *17*, 571–581. doi:10.1080/08870440290025786

Greene, J. A., & Azevedo, R. (2009). A macro-level analysis of SRL processes and their relations to the acquisition of a sophisticated mental model of a complex system. *Contemporary Educational Psychology*, *34*, 18–29. doi:10.1016/j.cedpsych.2008.05.006

Grefenstette, G., & Tapanainen, P. (1994). What is a word, what is a sentence? Problems of tokenization. In *Proceedings of the 3rd International Conference on Computational Lexicography* (pp. 79–87), Budapest, Hungary.

Griffiths, T. L., Steyvers, M., & Tenenbaum, J. B. (2007). Topics in semantic representation. *Psychological Review*, *114*, 211–244. doi:10.1037/0033-295X.114.2.211

Griffiths, T. L., & Steyvers, M. (2002). A probabilistic approach to semantic representation. In W. D. Gray & C. D. Schunn (Eds.), *Proceedings of the Twenty-fourth Annual Meeting of the Cognitive Science Society* (pp. 244-249). Mawah, NJ: Erlbaum.

Grisham, R., & Sundheim, B. (1996). Message understanding conference-6: A brief history. In *Proceedings of the 16th Conference on Computational Linguistics, vol. 1.* (pp. 466-471). Morristown, NJ: ACM.

Grishman, R., & Sundheim, B. (1996). *Design of the MUC-6 evaluation.* Vienna, Austria: Association for Computation Linguistics.

Grosz, B. J., Joshi, A. K., & Weinstein, S. (1995). Centering: A framework for modeling the local coherence of discourse. *Computational Linguistics, 21,* 203–225.

Habash, N., & Rambow, O. (2006). MAGEAD: A morphological analyzer and generator for the Arabic dialects. In *Proceedings of the 21st International Conference on Computational Linguistics and 44th Annual Meeting of the Association for Computational Linguistics,* Sydney, Australia, (pp. 681–688).

Habash, N., Soudi, A., & Buckwalter, T. (2007). On Arabic transliteration. In A. Soudi, A. van den Bosch & G. Neumann (Eds.), *Text, Speech and Language Technology: Vol. 38. Arabic Computational Morphology: Knowledge-based and Empirical Methods* (pp. 15-22). The Netherlands: Springer.

Haberlandt, K. F., & Graesser, A. C. (1985). Component processes in text comprehension. *Journal of Experimental Psychology. General, 114,* 357–374. doi:10.1037/0096-3445.114.3.357

Haertl, B., & McCarthy, P. M. (in press). Differential linguistic features in U.S. immigration newspaper articles: A contrastive corpus analysis using the Gramulator. In C. Murray & P. M. McCarthy (Eds.), *Proceedings of the 24rd International Florida Artificial Intelligence Research Society Conference* (p. xx). Menlo Park, CA: The AAAI Press.

Haghighi, A., & Klein, D. (2006). Prototype-driven grammar induction. In *Proceedings of the 21st International Conference on Computational Linguistics and the 44th Annual Meeting of the Association for Computational Linguistics.* 17–21 July. Sydney, Australia.

Hall, M., Frank, E., Holmes, G., Pfahringer, B., Reutemann, P., & Witten, I. H. (2009). The WEKA data mining software: An update. *SIGKDD Explorations, 11*(1). doi:10.1145/1656274.1656278

Hall, C. (in press). Corpora and Concordancers. In McCarthy, P. M., & Boonthum, C. (Eds.), *Applied natural language processing: Identification, investigation, and resolution.* Hershey, PA: IGI Global.

Hall, S. (2001). Foucault: Power, Knowledge and Discourse. In Wetherell, M., Taylor, S., & Yates, S. J. (Eds.), *Discourse theory and practice: A reader* (pp. 72–81). London, UK: Sage.

Hall, C., McCarthy, P. M., Lewis, G. A., Lee, D. S., & McNamara, D. S. (2007). A Coh-Metrix assessment of American and English/Welsh Legal English. *Coyote Papers: Psycholinguistic and Computational Perspectives. University of Arizona Working Papers in Linguistics, 15,* 40-54.

Halliday, M. A. K., & Hasan, R. (1989). *Language, context, and text: Aspects of language in a social-semiotic perspective.* Oxford, UK: Oxford University Press.

Halliday, M. A. K. (1967). Notes on transitivity and theme in English. *Journal of Linguistics, 3,* 199–244. doi:10.1017/S0022226700016613

Halliday, M. A. K., & Hasan, R. (1976). *Cohesion in English.* London, UK: Longman.

Halliday, M. A. K. (1967). Notes on transitivity and theme in English. *Journal of Linguistics, 3,* 199–244. doi:10.1017/S0022226700016613

Han, J., Cheng, H., Xin, D., & Yan, X. (2007). Frequent pattern mining: Current status and future directions. *Data Mining and Knowledge Discovery, 15,* 55–86. doi:10.1007/s10618-006-0059-1

Han, J., & Kamber, M. (2006). *Data mining – Concepts and techniques* (2nd ed.). San Francisco, CA: Morgan Kaufman.

Hancock, J. T., Beaver, D. I., Chung, C. K., Frazee, J., Pennebaker, J. W., Graesser, A., & Cai, Z. (2010). Social language processing: A framework for analyzing the communication of terrorists and authoritarian regimes. *Behavioral Science of Terrorism and Political Aggression, 2,* 108–132. doi:10.1080/19434471003597415

Hancock, J. T., Beaver, D. I., Chung, C. K., Frazee, J., Pennebaker, J. W., Graesser, A. C., & Cai, Z. (2010). Social language processing: A framework for analyzing the communication of terrorists and authoritarian regimes. *Behavioral Sciences in Terrorism and Political Aggression. Special Issue: Memory and Terrorism, 2,* 108–132.

Hancock, J. T., Curry, L., Goorha, S., & Woodworth, M. T. (2008). On lying and being lied to: A linguistic analysis of deception. *Discourse Processes, 45*, 1–23. doi:10.1080/01638530701739181

Hancock, J. T., Bazarova, N. N., & Markowitz, D. (2009). *A linguistic analysis of Bush administration statements on Iraq*. Manuscript submitted for publication.

Harley, A., & Glennon, D. (1997). Sense tagging in action. In *Proceedings of SIGLEX Workshop on Tagging Text with Lexical Semantics: Why, What and How*.

Harris, Z. S. (1954). Distributional structure. *Word, 10*(23), 146–162.

Hart, R. P. (2000). *DICTION 5.0: The text analysis program*. Thousand Oaks, CA: Sage-Scolari.

Hassel, M. (2005). Word sense disambiguation using co-occurrence statistics on random labels. In *Proceedings of Recent Advances in Natural Language Processing 2005*. Borovets, Bulgaria.

Hassel, M. (2007). *Resource lean and portable automatic text summarization*. Doctoral thesis, School of Computer Science and Communication, Royal Institute of Technology. Stockholm, Sweden.

Hassel, M., & Sjöbergh, J. (2006). Towards holistic summarization: Selecting summaries, not sentences. In *Proceedings of Language Resources and Evaluation 2006*. Genoa, Italy.

Haswell, R. H. (1991). Bound forms in freewriting: The issue of organization. In Belanoff, P., Elbow, P., & Fontaine, S. I. (Eds.), *Nothing begins with N* (pp. 32–71). Carbondale, IL: Southern Illinois University Press.

Hatch, E. (1983). *Psycholinguistics: A second language perspective*. Rowley, MA: Newbury House Publishers, Inc.

Haviland, S. E., & Clark, H. H. (1974). What's new? Acquiring new information as a process in comprehension. *Journal of Verbal Learning and Verbal Behavior, 13*, 512–521. doi:10.1016/S0022-5371(74)80003-4

Haworth, K. (2006). The dynamics of power and resistance in police interview discourse. *Discourse & Society, 17*(6), 739–759. doi:10.1177/0957926506068430

Hayeri, N., Chung, C. K., & Pennebaker, J. W. (2009). *Arabic linguistic inquiry and word count: Viewing the world through English and Arabic eyes*. Manuscript in preparation.

Hearst, M. A. (1997). TextTiling: Segmenting text into multi-paragraph subtopic passages. *Computational Linguistics, 23*(1), 33–64.

Hearst, M. A. (1998). Automated discovery of wordnet relations. In Fellbaum, C. (Ed.), *WordNet: An electronic lexical database* (pp. 131–151).

Heift, T., & Nicholson, D. (2001). Web delivery of adaptive and interactive language tutoring. *International Journal of Artificial Intelligence in Education, 12*(4), 310–324.

Heift, T., & Rimrott, A. (2008). Learner responses to corrective feedback for spelling errors in CALL. *System, 36*(2), 196–213. doi:10.1016/j.system.2007.09.007

Hempelmann, C. F. (2007). Beyond proof-of-concept: Implementing ontological semantics as a commercial product. In V. Raskin & J. Spartz (Eds.), *Proceedings of the 4th Midwest Computational Linguistics Colloquium 2007*. Purdue University, West Lafayette, Indiana.

Hempelmann, C. F., & Raskin, V. (2008). Semantic search: Content vs. formalism. *Proceedings of LangTech 2008*. Rome, Italy: Fondazione Ugo Bordoni.

Hempelmann, C. F., Dufty, D., McCarthy, P. M., Graesser, A. C., Cai, Z., & McNamara, D. S. (2005). Using LSA to automatically identify givenness and newness of noun phrases in written discourse. In B. G. Bara, L. Barsalou, & M. Bucciarelli (Eds.), *Proceedings of the 27th Annual Conference of the Cognitive Science Society* (pp. 941-946). Mahwah, NJ: Erlbaum.

Hempelmann, C. F., Taylor, J. M., & Raskin, V. (2010). Application-guided ontological engineering. In H. A. Arabnia, D. de la Fuente, E. B. Kozerenko, & J. A. Olivas (Eds.), *Proceedings of International Conference on Artificial Intelligence*. Las Vegas, NE.

Hendersen, D. J. O., & Clark, H. (2007). Retelling narratives as fiction or nonfiction. In D. S. McNamara & G. Trafton (Eds.), *Proceedings of the 29th Annual Conference of the Cognitive Science Society* (pp. 353-358). Cognitive Science Society.

Henry, A., & Roseberry, R. (2001). A narrow-angled corpus analysis of moves and strategies of the genre: Letter of application. *English for Specific Purposes, 20*, 153–167. doi:10.1016/S0889-4906(99)00037-X

Henry, K. (1996). Early L2 writing development: A study of autobiographical essays by university-level students of Russian. *Modern Language Journal, 80*(3), 309–326.

Hepburn, A. (2005). "You're not takin me seriously": Ethics and asymmetry in calls to a child protection helpline. *Journal of Constructivist Psychology, 18*, 255–276. doi:10.1080/10720530590948836

Herdan, G. (1960). *Type-token mathematics.* Gravenhage, The Netherlands: Mouton.

Herder, E. (2007). *An analysis of user behavior on the web.* Saarbrücken, Germany: VDM Verlag.

Heritage, J. (1984). *Garfinkel and ethnomethodology.* Cambridge, UK: Polity Press.

Hestenes, D., Wells, M., & Swackhamer, G. (1992). Force concept inventory. *The Physics Teacher, 30*, 141–158. doi:10.1119/1.2343497

Hinkel, E. (2002). *Second language writers' text.* Mahwah, NJ: Lawrence Erlbaum.

Hinkle, S., & Hinkle, A. (1990). An experimental comparison of the effects of focused freewriting and other study strategies on lecture comprehension. *Teaching of Psychology, 17*, 31–35. doi:10.1207/s15328023top1701_7

Hipp, J., Güntzer, U., & Nakhaeizadeh, G. (2000). Algorithms for association rule mining-A general survey and comparison. *SIGKDD Explorations, 2*(1), 58–64. doi:10.1145/360402.360421

Hirschberg, J., & Litman, D. (1993). Empirical studies on the disambiguation of cue phrases. *Computational Linguistics, 19*(3), 501–530.

Hirschberg, J. (1998). *"Every time I fire a linguist, my performance goes up," and other myths of the statistical natural language processing revolution.* Paper presented at the Fifteenth National Conference on Artificial Intelligence (AAAI-98).

Hirst, G., & St-Onge, D. (1998). Lexical chains as representations of context for the detection and correction of malapropisms. In Fellbaum, C. (Ed.), *WordNet: An electronic lexical database.* MIT Press.

Hirst, G., DiMarco, C., Hovy, E., & Parsons, K. (1997). Authoring and generating health-education documents that are tailored to the needs of the individual patient. In *Proceedings of the Sixth International Conference on User Modeling* (pp. 107-118). New York, NY: Springer.

Hiyakumoto, L., Prevost, S., & Cassell, J. (1997). Semantic and discourse information for text-to-speech intonation. *Proceedings of the 35th Annual Meeting of the ACL Workshop on Concept-to-Speech Generation Systems.* Madrid, Spain: ACL Press.

Hobbs, J. R. (1993). The generic information extraction system. In *Proceeding of the 5th Message Understanding Conference (MUC)* (pp. 87-91). Morristown, NJ: ACM.

Hodges, A. (2000). *Alan Turing: The enigma.* Walker & Company.

Hoey, M. (2005). *Lexical priming: A new theory of words and language.* London, UK: Routledge.

Hopkins, A., & Dudley-Evans, T. (1988). A genre-based investigation of the discussion sections in articles and dissertations. *English for Specific Purposes, 7*, 113–121. doi:10.1016/0889-4906(88)90029-4

Hotho, A., Maedche, A., & Staab, S. (2002). Text clustering based on good aggregations. *Kuenstliche Intelligenz KI, 16*(4).

House, J. (2009). Introduction: The pragmatics of English as a lingua franca. *Intercultural Pragmatics, 6*(2), 141–145. doi:10.1515/IPRG.2009.008

House, J. (1999). Misunderstanding in intercultural communication: Interactions in English as a lingua franca and the myth of mutual intelligibility. In Gnutzmann, C. (Ed.), *Teaching and learning English as a global language* (pp. 73–89). Tubingen, Germany: Stauffenburg.

Howitt, D. (2010). *Introduction to qualitative methods in psychology.* Harlow, England: Prentice Hall.

Hsieh, C.-C., Tsai, T.-H., Wible, D., & Hsu, W.-L. (2002). Exploiting knowledge representation in an intelligent tutoring system for English lexical errors. In *Proceedings of the International Conference on Computers in Education ICCE 2002*, Auckland, New Zealand, (pp. 115-116).

Hsueh, P., Moore, J., & Renals, S. (2006). Automatic segmentation of multiparty dialogue. In *Proceedings of the EACL 2006*, (pp. 273–280).

Hu, X., & Graesser, A. C. (2004). Human use regulatory affairs advisor (HURAA): Learning about research ethics with intelligent learning modules. *Behavior Research Methods, Instruments, & Computers*, *36*, 241–249. doi:10.3758/BF03195569

Hu, Y., & Ge, L. (2007). A supervised machine learning approach to toponym disambiguation. In Scharl, A., & Tochtermann, K. (Eds.), *The Geospatial Web: How geo-browsers, social software and the Web 2.0 are shaping the network society* (pp. 117–128). Springer.

Hu, X., Cai, Z., Louwerse, M., Olney, A., Penumatsa, P., & Graesser, A. C., & the Tutoring Research Group. (2003). A revised algorithm for latent semantic analysis. In G. Gottlob & T. Walsh (Eds.), *Proceedings of the 2003 International Joint Conference on Artificial Intelligence* (pp. 1489–1491). San Francisco, CA: Morgan Kaufmann.

Hui, N. H. H., Tang, V. W. K., Wu, G. H. H., & Lam, B. C. P. (June, 2009). *ON-line to OFF-life? Linguistic comparison of suicide completer and attempter's online diaries.* Paper presented at the International Conference on Psychology in Modern Cities, Hong Kong.

Hullender, A., & McCarthy, P. M. (2011). *Analyses of modern art criticism and photography criticism as separate genres.* Paper presented at the South-eastern Conference on Linguistics (SECOL).

Humphrey, S. M., Rogers, W. J., Kilicoglu, H., Demner-Fushman, D., & Rindflesch, T. C. (2006). Word sense disambiguation by selecting the best semantic type based on Journal descriptor indexing: Preliminary experiment. *Journal of the American Society for Information Science American Society for Information Science*, *57*, 96–113.

Humphreys, K., Gaizauskas, R., & Azzam, S. (1997). Event coreference for information extraction. In *Proceedings of the Workshop on Operational Factors in Practical, Robust Anaphora Resolution for Unrestricted Texts*, (pp. 75-81). Association for Computational Linguistics.

Hyde, J. S. (2005). The gender similarities hypothesis. *The American Psychologist*, *60*, 581–592. doi:10.1037/0003-066X.60.6.581

Hymes, D. (1972). Models of interaction of language and social life. In Gumperz, J. J., & Hymes, D. (Eds.), *Directions of sociolinguistics: The ethnography of communication.* New York, NY: Holt, Rinehart and Winston.

Ibañez, R. (2008). Comprensión de textos académicos en inglés: Relación entre nivel de logro y variables involucradas. *Revista Signos. Estudios de Lingüística*, *41*(67), 203–229.

Ide, N., & Véronis, J. (1998). Introduction to the special issue on word sense disambiguation: The state of the art. *Computational Linguistics*, *24*, 2–40.

Inkpen, D. Z., & Hirst, G. (2003). Automatic sense disambiguation of the near-synonyms in a dictionary entry. *Lecture Notes in Computer Science*, 258–267. doi:10.1007/3-540-36456-0_25

Institute of Education Sciences. (2003). *The nation's report card: Writing 2002.* NCES 2003-529. Retrieved from http://nces.ed.gov/nationsreportcard/pubs/main2002/2003529.asp.

International Standards Organization. (1996). *ISO/IEC 14977, Information technology – Syntactic metalanguage – Extended BNF.* Retrieved November 12, 2009, from http://standards.iso.org/ittf/PubliclyAvailableStandards/s026153_ISO_IEC_14977_1996(E).zip.

Ireland, M. E., & Pennebaker, J. W. (2010). Language style matching in reading and writing: Synchrony in essays, correspondence, and poetry. *Journal of Personality and Social Psychology*, *99*, 549–571. doi:10.1037/a0020386

Ireland, M. E., & Henderson, M. D. (2009). *Verbal mimicry in negotiation: The language of the deal.* Manuscript submitted for publication.

Ishikawa, S. (1995). Objective measurement of low-proficiency EFL narrative writing. *Journal of Second Language Writing*, *4*(1), 51–69. doi:10.1016/1060-3743(95)90023-3

Ishizaki, S., & Kaufer, D. (in press). Computer-aided rhetorical analysis. In McCarthy, P. M., & Boonthum, C. (Eds.), *Applied natural language processing: Identification, investigation, and resolution*. Hershey, PA: IGI Global.

Ishizaki, S. (2009). *Toward a unified theory of verbal-visual strategies in communication design*. Best Paper. IEEE International Professional Communication Conference. Hawaii, July 19-22.

Ivanovic, E. (2005). Dialogue act tagging for instant messaging chat sessions. In *Proceedings of the ACL Student Research Workshop*, (pp. 79–84). 27 June, Ann Arbor, Michigan.

Jaccard, J., & Guilamo-Ramos, V. (2002). Analysis of variance frameworks in clinical child and adolescent psychology: Issues and recommendations. *Journal of Clinical Child and Adolescent Psychology, 31*(1), 130–146.

Jackendoff, R. (2002). *Foundations of language*. Oxford, UK: Oxford University Press. doi:10.1093/acprof:oso/9780198270126.001.0001

Jackson, G. T., & Graesser, A. C. (2006). Applications of human tutorial dialog in AutoTutor: An intelligent tutoring system. *Revista Signos, 39*, 31–48.

Jackson, G. T., Guess, R. H., & McNamara, D. S. (2010). Assessing cognitively complex strategy use in an untrained domain. *Topics in Cognitive Science, 2*, 127–137. doi:10.1111/j.1756-8765.2009.01068.x

Jackson, G. T., & Graesser, A. C. (2007). Content matters: An investigation of feedback categories within an ITS. In Luckin, R., Koedinger, K., & Greer, J. (Eds.), *Artificial intelligence in education: Building technology rich learning contexts that work* (pp. 127–134). Amsterdam, The Netherlands: IOS Press.

Jain, A. K., Murty, M. N., & Flynn, P. J. (1999). Data clustering: A review. [New York, NY, USA.]. *ACM Computing Surveys, 31*(3), 264–323. doi:10.1145/331499.331504

James, D., & Clarke, S. (1993). Women, men, and interruptions: A critical review. In Tannen, D. (Ed.), *Gender and conversational interaction*. New York, NY: Oxford University Press.

Jarvis, S., Grant, L., Bikowski, D., & Ferris, D. (2003). Exploring multiple profiles of highly rated learner compositions. *Journal of Second Language Writing, 12*, 377–403. doi:10.1016/j.jslw.2003.09.001

Jassem, J. A. (2000). *Study on second language learners of Arabic: An error analysis approach*. Kuala Lumpur, Malaysia: A.S. Noordeen.

Jenkins, J. (2000). *The phonology of English as an international language*. Oxford, UK: Oxford University Press.

Jeon, M. (2008). *Automated analyses of cohesion and coherence in tutorial dialogue*. Unpublished doctoral dissertation. University of Memphis.

Jing, H. (2000). Sentence reduction for automatic text summarization. In *Proceedings of the 6th Applied Natural Language Processing Conference* (pp. 310–315). Seattle, Washington. April 29–May 4, 2000.

Jing, H., & McKeown, K. R. (2000). Cut and paste-based text summarization. In *Proceedings of the 6th Applied Natural Language Processing Conference and the 1st Meeting of the North American Chapter of the Association for Computational Linguistics* (pp. 178–185), Seattle, Washington. April 29–May 4, 2000.

Joachims, T. (1998). Text categorization with support vector machines: Learning with many relevant features. In C. Nedellec & C. Rouveirol (Eds.), *In Proceedings of the 10th European Conference on Machine Learning*, (pp. 137-142). Berlin, Germany: Springer.

Joachims, T. (1999). Transductive inference for text classification using support vector machines. In *Proceedings of ICML-99, 16th International Conference on Machine Learning*, (pp. 143-151). San Francisco, CA: Morgan Kaufmann.

John, O. P., & Srivastava, S. (1999). The Big Five Trait taxonomy: History, measurement, and theoretical perspectives. In Pervin, L. A., & John, O. P. (Eds.), *Handbook of personality: Theory and research* (2nd ed., pp. 102–138). New York, NY: Guilford Press.

Johnson, W. L., & Valente, A. (2008). Tactical language and culture training systems: Using artificial intelligence to teach foreign languages and cultures. In *Proceedings of the 20th Innovative Applications of Artificial Intelligence (IAAI) Conference*.

Jones, M. N., & Mewhort, D. (2007). Representing word meaning and order information in a composite holographic lexicon. *Psychological Review*, *114*, 1–37. doi:10.1037/0033-295X.114.1.1

Jones, M. N., Kintsch, W., & Mewhort, D. J. K. (2006). High-dimensional semantic space accounts of priming. *Journal of Memory and Language*, *55*, 534–552. doi:10.1016/j.jml.2006.07.003

Jönsson, A. (1991). A dialogue manager using initiative-response units and distributed control. In *Proceedings of the Fifth Conference of the European Association for Computational Linguistics*, (pp. 233–238).

Joshi, M., Pedersen, T., & Maclin, R. (2005). A comparative study of support vector machines applied to the supervised word sense disambiguation problem in the medical domain. In *Proceedings of the 2nd Indian International Conference on Artificial Intelligence (IICAI'05)*, (pp. 3449–3468).

Jung, H., Allen, J., Galescu, L., Chambers, N., Swift, M., & Taysom, W. (2008). Using natural language for one-shot task learning. *Journal of Logic and Computation*, *18*(3), 475–493. doi:10.1093/logcom/exm071

Jung, H., Allen, J., de Beaumont, W., Blaylock, N., Ferguson, G., Galescu, L., & Swift, M. (2010To appear). Going beyond PBD: A play-by-play and mixed-initiative approach. In Cypher, A., Dontcheva, L. M., Lau, T., & Nichols, J. (Eds.), *No code required: Giving users tools to transform the Web*. Morgan Kaufmann Publishers.

Junghaenel, D. U., Smyth, J. M., & Santner, L. (2008). Linguistic dimensions of psychopathology: A quantitative analysis. *Journal of Social and Clinical Psychology*, *27*, 36–55. doi:10.1521/jscp.2008.27.1.36

Jurafsky, D., & Martin, J. H. (2008). *Speech and language processing: An introduction to natural language processing, computational linguistics, and speech recognition*. Upper Saddle River, NJ: Prentice-Hall.

Jurafsky, D. (2003). Pragmatics and computational linguistics. In Horn, L. R., & Ward, G. (Eds.), *Handbook of pragmatics*. Oxford, UK: Blackwell.

Jurafsky, D., Bates, R., Coccaro, N., Martin, R., Meteer, M., & Ries, K. ... Van Ess-Dykema, C. (1997). Automatic detection of discourse structure for speech recognition and understanding. In *Proceedings of the 1997 IEEE Workshop on Speech Recognition and Understanding*, (pp. 88–95). 14–17 December, Santa Barbara, CA.

Kacewicz, E., Pennebaker, J. W., Davis, D., Jeon, M., & Graesser, A. C. (2009). *Pronoun use reflects standings in social heirarchies*. Manuscript submitted for publication.

Kacewicz, E., Pennebaker, J. W., Davis, D., Jeon, M., & Graesser, A. C. (2009). *LSM as a function of status discrepancy*. Unpublished data.

Kanejiya, D., Kumar, A., & Prasad, S. (2003). Automatic evaluation of students' answers using syntactically-enhanced LSA. In *Proceedings of the Human Language Technology NAACL Workshop on Building Educational Applications Using Natural Language Processing* (vol. 2), (pp. 53-60).

Kanerva, P., Kristoferson, J., & Holst, A. (2000). Random Indexing of text samples for latent semantic analysis. In *Proceedings 22nd Annual Conference of the Cognitive Science Society*, Pennsylvania, USA.

Kantaardzic, M. (2002). *Data mining – Concepts, models, methods, and algorithms*. John Wiley & Sons. Kurgan, L., & Musilek, P. (2006). A survey of knowledge discovery and data mining process models. [Cambridge University Press.]. *The Knowledge Engineering Review*, *21*(1), 1–24.

Kaplan, A. N., & Schubert, L. K. (2001). *Measuring and improving the quality of world knowledge extracted from WordNet*. (Tech. Rep. 751 14627-0226). Dept. of Computer Science, Univ. of Rochester, Rochester, NY, May.

Kaufer, D. (2006). Genre variation and minority ethnic identity: Exploring the personal profile in Indian American community publications. *Discourse & Society*, *17*(6), 761–784. doi:10.1177/0957926506068432

Kaufer, D., & Al-Malki, A. (2009). A first for women in the kingdom: Arab/west representations of female trendsetters in Saudi Arabia. *Journal of Arab and Muslim Media Research*, *2*(2), 113–133. doi:10.1386/jammr.2.1and2.113/1

Kaufer, D., & Al-Malki, A. M. (2009). The war on terror through Arab-American eyes: The Arab-American press as a rhetorical counterpublic. *Rhetoric Review*, *28*(1), 47–65. doi:10.1080/07350190802540724

Kaufer, D., & Butler, B. (1996). *Rhetoric and the arts of design*. Mahwah, NJ: Lawrence Erlbaum and Associates.

Kaufer, D., & Butler, B. (2000). *Designing interactive worlds with words: Principles of writing as representational composition*. Mahwah, NJ: Lawrence Erlbaum and Associates.

Kaufer, D., & Hariman, R. (2008). A corpus analysis evaluating Hariman's theory of political style. *Text & Talk*, *28*(4), 475–500.

Kaufer, D., & Ishizaki, S. (2006). A corpus study of canned letters: Mining the latent rhetorical proficiencies marketed to writers in a hurry and non-writers. *IEEE Transactions on Professional Communication*, *40*(3), 254–266. doi:10.1109/TPC.2006.880743

Kaufer, D., Ishizaki, S., Butler, B., & Collins, J. (2004). *The power of words: Unveiling the speaker and writer's hidden craft*. Mahwah, NJ: Lawrence Erlbaum and Associates.

Kaufer, D., Ishizaki, S., Collins, J., & Vlachos, P. (2004). Teaching language awareness in rhetorical choice using IText and visualization in classroom genre assignments. *Journal for Business and Technical Communication*, *18*(3), 361–402. doi:10.1177/1050651904263980

Kaufer, D., Geisler, C., Ishizaki, S., & Vlachos, P. (2005). Computer-support for genre analysis and discovery in ambient intelligence for scientific discovery. In Cai, Y. (Ed.), *Ambient intelligence for scientific discovery* (pp. 129–151). New York, NY: Springer. doi:10.1007/978-3-540-32263-4_7

Kaufer, D. 2000. *Flaming: A white paper*. Retrieved from www.eudora.com.

KBAE. (2002). *Knowledge-based acquisition editor*, Purdue version 2.1. [Computer software]. W. Lafayette, IN: NLP Lab and CERIAS, Purdue University. Retrieved from http://kbae.cerias.purdue.edu:443/.

Keenan, J. M., Betjemann, R. B., & Olson, R. K. (2008). Reading comprehension tests vary in the skills they assess: Differential dependence on decoding and oral comprehension. *Scientific Studies of Reading*, *12*, 281–300. doi:10.1080/10888430802132279

Keizer, S., & op den Akker, R. (2005). Dialogue act recognition under uncertainty using Bayesian networks. *Natural Language Engineering*, *1*, 1–30.

Kelvin, W. T. (1889). *Popular lectures and addresses*. London, UK: Macmillan.

Kennison, S. M., & Gordon, P. C. (1997). Comprehending referential expressions during reading: Evidence from eye tracking. *Discourse Processes*, *24*, 229–252. doi:10.1080/01638539709545014

Kern, R. G., & Schultz, J. M. (1992). The effects of composition instruction on intermediate level French students' writing performance: Some preliminary findings. *Modern Language Journal*, *76*(1), 1–13.

Khoo, C. S. G., Chan, S., & Niu, Y. (2000). Extracting causal knowledge from a medical database using graphical patterns. In *Annual Meeting-Association for Computational Linguistics, 38*(1), 336–343.

Kilgarriff, A., & Rosenzweig, J. (2000). *English SENSEVAL: Report and results* (pp. 265–283). Athens: LREC.

Kingsbury, P., & Palmer, M. (2002). From treebank to propbank. In *Proceedings of the 3rd International Conference on Language Resources and Evaluation* (LREC-2002) (pp. 1989-1993).

Kintsch, E., Steinhart, D., Stahl, G., Matthews, C., Lamb, R., & Group, L. R. (2000). Developing summarization skills through the use of LSA-backed feedback. *Interactive Learning Environments*, *8*, 87–109. doi:10.1076/1049-4820(200008)8:2;1-B;FT087

Kintsch, W., & Mangalath, P. (2011). The construction of meaning. *TopiCS in Cognitive Science*, *3*, 346–370. doi:10.1111/j.1756-8765.2010.01107.x

Kintsch, W. (1998). *Comprehension: A paradigm for cognition*. Cambridge, MA: Cambridge University Press.

Kintsch, W., & van Dijk, T. A. (1978). Toward a model of text comprehension and production. *Psychological Review*, *85*, 363–394. doi:10.1037/0033-295X.85.5.363

Kintsch, E., Steinhart, D., & Stahl, G.LSA Research Group, Matthews, C., & Lamb, R. (2000). Developing summarization skills through the use of LSA-based feedback. *Interactive Learning Environments*, *8*(2), 87–109. doi:10.1076/1049-4820(200008)8:2;1-B;FT087

Kintsch, W. (1988). The role of knowledge in discourse comprehension construction-integration model. *Psychological Review*, *95*, 163–182. doi:10.1037/0033-295X.95.2.163

Kintsch, W. (2000). Metaphor comprehension: A computational theory. *Psychonomic Bulletin & Review*, *7*(2), 257–266. doi:10.3758/BF03212981

Kintsch, W. (2001). Predication. *Cognitive Science*, *25*(2), 173–202. doi:10.1207/s15516709cog2502_1

Kintsch, E., Caccamise, D., Franzke, M., Johnson, N., & Dooley, S. (2007). Summary Street: Computer-guided summary writing. In Landauer, T. K., McNamara, D., Dennis, S., & Kintsch, W. (Eds.), *Handbook of latent semantic analysis* (pp. 263–278). Mahwah, NJ: Erlbaum.

Kintsch, W. (2002). On the notions of theme and topic in psychological process models of text comprehension. In Louwerse, M., & van Peer, W. (Eds.), *Thematics: Interdisciplinary studies* (pp. 151–170). Amsterdam, The Netherlands: Benjamins.

Kintsch, W., & Kintsch, E. (in press). LSA in the classroom. In McCarthy, P. M., & Boonthum, C. (Eds.), *Applied natural language processing: Identification, investigation, and resolution*. Hershey, PA: IGI Global.

Kitzinger, C. (2007). Birth trauma: Talking with women and the value of conversation analysis. *British Journal of Midwifery*, *15*(5), 256–264.

Klare, G. R. (1974–1975). Assessing readability. *Reading Research Quarterly*, *10*, 62–102. doi:10.2307/747086

Klein, W. (1994). *Time in language*. London, UK: Routledge.

Klein, H. Klein H. (2009). *Text analysis info: Category systems*. Retrieved August 18, 2009, from http://www.textanalysis.info.

Klimt, B., & Yang, Y. (2004). Introducing the Enron corpus. In *Proceedings of the Conference on Email and Anti-Spam (CEAS)*. Mountain View, CA.

Knudson, R. E. (1989). Effect of instructional strategies on children's informational writing. *The Journal of Educational Research*, *83*, 91–96.

Koedinger, K. R., Anderson, J. R., Hadley, W. H., & Mark, M. (1997). Intelligent tutoring goes to school in the big city. *International Journal of Artificial Intelligence in Education*, *8*, 30–43.

Koedinger, K. R., & Anderson, J. R. (1997). Intelligent tutoring goes to school in the big city. *International Journal of Artificial Intelligence in Education*, *8*, 30–43.

Korfhage, R. R. (1991). To see, or not to see – Is that the query? *Proceedings of the 14th Annual International ACM SIGIR Conference on Research and Development in Information Retrieval*, (pp. 134-141). ACM.

Koshman, S. (2006). Visualization-based information retrieval on the Web. *Library & Information Science Research*, *28*(2), 192–207. doi:10.1016/j.lisr.2006.03.017

Koslin, B. L., Zeno, S., & Koslin, S. (1987). *The DRP: An effectiveness measure in reading*. New York, NY: College Entrance Examination Board.

Kowtko, J. (1994). On the function of intonation in wee utterances. In. *Proceedings of the Edinburgh Linguistics Department Conference*, *94*, 77–85.

Kozma, R. (2003). The material features of multiple representations and their cognitive and social affordances for science understanding. *Learning and Instruction*, *13*(2), 205–226. doi:10.1016/S0959-4752(02)00021-X

Kramer, A. D. I., Fussell, S. R., & Setlock, L. D. (2004). Text analysis as a tool for analyzing conversation in online support groups. *Extended Abstracts of the 2004 Conference on Human Factors and Computing Systems*, (pp. 1485-1488).

Krashen, S. D. (1988). *Second language acquisition and second language learning*. Prentice-Hall International.

Krovetz, R., & Croft, W. B. (1992). Lexical ambiguity and information retrieval. *ACM Transactions on Information Systems*, *10*(2), 115–141. doi:10.1145/146802.146810

Krovetz, R. (1993). Viewing morphology as an inference process. In R. Korfhage et al. (Eds.), *Proceedings of the 16th ACM SIGIR Conference* (pp. 191-202). New York, NY: ACM.

Kruijff-Korbayová, I., & Steedman, M. (2003). Discourse and information structure. *Journal of Logic. Language and Information: Special Issue on Discourse and Information Structure*, *12*, 249–259.

Kučera, H., & Nelson, F. (1967). *Computational analysis of present-day American English*. Brown University Press.

Kukich, K. (1992). Techniques for automatically correcting words in text. *ACM Computing Surveys, 24*(4), 377–440. doi:10.1145/146370.146380

Kumar, V., Sridhar, R., Narayanan, S., & Bangalore, S. (2008). Enriching spoken language translation with dialog acts. In *Proceedings of the 46th Annual Meeting of the Association for Computational Linguistics on Human Language Technologies*. June 19–20, Columbus, Ohio.

Kuramochi, M., & Karypis, G. (2001). Frequent subgraph discovery. In *Proceedings of the 2001 IEEE International Conference on Data Mining*, (pp. 313-320).

Ladies Home Journal. (2005). *Can this marriage be saved?* Retrieved November 12, 2005, from www.lhj.com.

Lamkin, T. A., & Mccarthy, P. M. (in press). The hierarchy of detective fiction. In C. Murray & P. M. McCarthy (Eds.), *Proceedings of the 24rd International Florida Artificial Intelligence Research Society Conference* (p. xx). Menlo Park, CA: The AAAI Press.

Lampert, A., Dale, R., & Paris, C. (2009). Segmenting email message text into zones, In *Proceedings of Empirical Methods in Natural Language Processing (EMNLP 2009)*, (pp. 919–928). August 6–7, Singapore.

Landauer, T. K., Foltz, P. W., & Laham, D. (1998). Introduction to latent semantic analysis. *Discourse Processes, 25*, 259–284. doi:10.1080/01638539809545028

Landauer, T., McNamara, D. S., Dennis, S., & Kintsch, W. (Eds.). (2007). *Latent semantic analysis: A road to meaning*. Mahwah, NJ: Erlbaum.

Landauer, T. K., & Dumais, S. T. (1997). A solution to Plato's problem: The latent semantic analysis theory of acquisition, induction and representation of knowledge. *Psychological Review, 104*, 211–240. doi:10.1037/0033-295X.104.2.211

Landauer, T. K., Laham, D., & Foltz, P. (2003). Automatic essay assessment. *Assessment in Education, 10*, 295–308. doi:10.1080/0969594032000148154

Landauer, T. K., Foltz, P. W., & Laham, D. (1998). Introduction to latent semantic analysis. *Discourse Processes, 25*, 259–284. doi:10.1080/01638539809545028

Landauer, T. K., Laham, D., Rehder, B., & Schreiner, M. E. (1997). How well can passage meaning be derived without using word order? A comparison of latent semantic analysis and humans. In M. G. Shafto & P. Langley (Eds.), *Minutes of The 19th Annual Meeting of the Cognitive Science Society* (pp. 412-417). Mahwah, NJ: Erlbaum.

Landis, J. R., & Koch, G. G. (1977). The measurement of observer agreement for categorical data. *Biometrics, 33*, 159–174. doi:10.2307/2529310

Larsen-Freeman, D. (2006). The emergence of complexity, fluency, and accuracy in the oral and written production of five Chinese learners of English. *Applied Linguistics, 27*(4), 590–619. doi:10.1093/applin/aml029

Larsen-Freeman, D., & Cameron, L. (2008). *Complex systems and applied linguistics*. Oxford, UK: Oxford University Press.

Lau, T., & Weld, D. (1999). *Programming by demonstration: An inductive learning formulation*. In International Conference on Intelligent User Interfaces.

Laufer, B., & Nation, P. (1995). Vocabulary size and use: Lexical richness in L2 written production. *Applied Linguistics, 16*(3), 307–322. doi:10.1093/applin/16.3.307

Leaper, C., & Smith, T. E. (2004). A meta-analytic review of gender variations in children's language use: Talkativeness, affiliative speech, and assertive speech. *Developmental Psychology, 40*, 993–1027. doi:10.1037/0012-1649.40.6.993

Lee, Y. H., Evens, M., Michael, J. A., & Rovick, A. A. (1989). Spelling correction for an intelligent tutoring system. *Computing in the 90's: Proceedings of the First Great Lakes Computer Science Conference* (pp. 77-83). Kalamazoo, MI: Springer.

Leech, N. L., Barrett, K. C., & Morgan, G. A. (2008). *SPSS for intermediate statistics: Use and interpretation*. New York, NY: Lawrence Erlbaum Associates, Inc.

Lehnert, W. G. (1978). *The process of question answering: A computer simulation of cognition*. Hillsdale, NJ: Erlbaum.

Leidner, J. (2006). *Toponym resolution: A first large-scale comparative evaluation*. Technical report.

Leidner, J., Sinclair, G., & Webber, B. (2003). Grounding spatial named entities for information extraction and question answering. In *Proceedings of the HLT-NAACL Workshop on Analysis of Geographic References*, (pp. 31-38). Association for Computational Linguistics.

León, J., Olmos, R., Escudero, I., Cañas, J., & Salmerón, L. (2005). Assessing short summaries with human judgments procedure and latent semantic analysis in narrative and expository texts. *Behavior Research Methods*, *38*(4), 616–627. doi:10.3758/BF03193894

Leroy, G., & Rindflesch, T. C. (2005). Effects of information and machine learning algorithms on word sense disambiguation with small datasets. *International Journal of Medical Informatics*, *74*, 573–585. doi:10.1016/j.ijmedinf.2005.03.013

Lesgold, A., Lajoie, S. P., Bunzo, M., & Eggan, G. (1992). SHERLOCK: A coached practice environment for an electronics trouble-shooting job. In Larkin, J. H., & Chabay, R. W. (Eds.), *Computer assisted instruction and intelligent tutoring systems: Shared goals and complementary approaches* (pp. 201–238). Hillsdale, NJ: Erlbaum.

Leshed, G., Haber, E., Matthews, T., & Lau, T. (2008). Coscripter: Automating and sharing how-to knowledge in the enterprise. In *Proceedings of the SIGCHI Conference on Human Factors in Computing Systems*.

Levenshtein, V. I. (1965). Binary codes capable of correcting deletions, insertions, and reversals. *Soviet Physics, Doklady*, *10*, 707–710.

Liddicoat, A. J. (2007). *An introduction to conversation analysis*. London, UK: Continuum.

Liddy, E. D. (1991). Discourse-level structure of empirical abstracts: An exploratory study. *Information Processing & Management*, *27*(1), 550–581. doi:10.1016/0306-4573(91)90031-G

Lifchitz, A., Jhean-Larose, S., & Denhière, G. (2009). Effect of tuned parameters on an LSA multiple choice questions answering model. *Behavior Research Methods*, *41*(4), 1201–1209. doi:10.3758/BRM.41.4.1201

Light, R. J. (2001). *Making the most of college: Students speaking their minds*. Cambridge, MA: Harvard University Press.

Lin, C. (2004). ROUGE: A package for automatic evaluation of summaries. In *Proceedings of Workshop on Text Summarization Branches Out, Post-Conference Workshop of ACL 2004*, Barcelona, Spain.

Lin, C., & Hovy, E. (2003). Automatic evaluation of summaries using n-gram co-occurrence statistics. In *Proceedings of 2003 Language Technology Conference*, Edmonton, Canada.

Lintean, M., & Rus, V. (2011). Dissimilarity kernels for paraphrase identification. *In Proceedings of the Twenty-Fourth International FLAIRS Conference*, Palm Beach, FL, May 2011.

Litman, D. J., Rose, C. P., Forbes-Riley, K., VanLehn, K., Bhembe, D., & Silliman, S. (2006). Spoken versus typed human and computer dialogue tutoring. *International Journal of Artificial Intelligence in Education*, *16*, 145–170.

Liu, H., Johnson, S. B., & Friedman, C. (2002). Automatic resolution of ambiguous terms based on machine learning and conceptual relations in the UMLS. *Journal of the American Medical Informatics Association*, *9*, 621. doi:10.1197/jamia.M1101

Liu, B. (2010). Sentiment analysis and subjectivity. In Indurkhya, N., & Damerau, F. J. (Eds.), *Handbook of natural language processing*. CRC Press. Taylor and Francis.

Long, M. H. (1980). *Input, interaction and second language acquisition*. University of California at Los Angeles.

Long, M. H. (1983a). Linguistic and conversational adjustments to nonnative speakers. *Studies in Second Language Acquisition*, *5*, 177–194. doi:10.1017/S0272263100004848

Long, M. H. (1983b). Native speaker/non-native speaker conversation and the negotiation of comprehensible input. *Applied Linguistics*, *4*, 126–141. doi:10.1093/applin/4.2.126

Long, M. H., & Porter, P. A. (1985). Group work, interlanguage talk, and second language acquisition. *TESOL Quarterly*, *19*(2), 207–228. doi:10.2307/3586827

Longo, B. (1994). Current research in technical communication: The role of metadiscourse in persuasion. *Technical Communication*, *41*, 348–352.

Louwerse, M. M. (2001). An analytic and cognitive parameterization of coherence relations. *Cognitive Linguistics, 12*, 291–315. doi:10.1515/cogl.2002.005

Louwerse, M. M. (2001). An analytic and cognitive parameterization of coherence relations. *Cognitive Linguistics, 12*, 291–315. doi:10.1515/cogl.2002.005

Louwerse, M. M., Graesser, A. C., & Olney, A., & the Tutoring Research Group. (2002). Good computational manners: Mixed-initiative dialog in conversational agents. In C. Miller (Ed.), *Etiquette for Human-Computer Work, Papers from the 2002 Fall Symposium, Technical Report FS-02-02*, (pp. 71-76).

Louwerse, M. M., McCarthy, P. M., McNamara, D. S., & Graesser, A. C. (2004). Variation in language and cohesion across written and spoken registers. In K. Forbus, D. Gentner, & T. Regier (Eds.), *Proceedings of the Twenty-Sixth Annual Conference of the Cognitive Science Society* (pp. 843–848). Mahwah, NJ: Erlbaum.

Luhn, H. P. (1959). The automatic creation of literature abstracts. *IBM Journal of Research and Development*, 159–165.

Luk, R. W. P. (1994). An IBM-PC environment for Chinese corpus analysis. In *Proceedings of the 15th Conference on Computational Linguistics* (pp. 584–587). Morristown, New Jersey, USA.

Lund, K., & Burgess, C. (1996). Producing high-dimensional semantic spaces from lexical co-occurrence. *Behavior Research Methods, Instruments, & Computers, 28*, 203–208. doi:10.3758/BF03204766

Lyons, J. (1963). *Structural semantics: An analysis of part of the vocabulary of Plato*. Oxford, UK: Blackwell.

Lyons, E. J., Mehl, M. R., & Pennebaker, J. W. (2006). Pro-anorexics and recovering anorexics differ in their linguistic Internet self-presentation. *Journal of Psychosomatic Research, 60*, 253–256. doi:10.1016/j.jpsychores.2005.07.017

Maas, H. D. (1972). Zusammenhang zwischen Wortschatzumfang und Länge eines Textes. *Zeitschrift für Literaturwissenschaft und Linguistik, 8*, 73–79.

MacQueen, J. B. (1967). Some methods for classification and analysis of multivariate observations. In *Proceedings of 5th Berkeley Symposium on Mathematical Statistics and Probability*, (pp. 281-297).

Magliano, J. P., Todaro, S., Millis, K. K., Wiemer-Hastings, K., Kim, H. J., & McNamara, D. S. (2004). Changes in reading strategies as a function of reading training: A comparison of live and computerized training. *Journal of Educational Computing Research, 32*, 185–208. doi:10.2190/1LN8-7BQE-8TN0-M91L

Mair, C. (2003). *The politics of English as a world language*. New York, NY: Amsterdam.

Mairesse, F., Walker, M. A., Mehl, M. R., & Moore, R. K. (2007). Using linguistic cues for the automatic recognition of personality in conversation and text. *Journal of Artificial Intelligence Research, 30*, 457–500.

Maltz, D., & Borker, R. (1982). A cultural approach to male-female communication. In Gumperz, J. (Ed.), *Language and social identity*. Cambridge, UK: Cambridge University Press.

Malvern, D. D., Richards, B. J., Chipere, N., & Durán, P. (2004). *Lexical diversity and language development: Quantification and assessment*. Houndmills, UK: Palgrave Macmillan. doi:10.1057/9780230511804

Mani, I., & Maybury, M. (2001). *Advances in automatic text summarization*. Massachusetts: Massachusetts Institute of Technology.

Mani, I., Hitzeman, J., Richer, J., Harris, D., Quimby, R., & Wellner, B. (2008). SpatialML: Annotation scheme, corpora, and tools. In *Proceedings of the Sixth International Language Resources and Evaluation*.

Manning, C. D., Raghavan, P., & Schütze, H. (2008). *Introduction to information retrieval*. Cambridge, UK: CUP.

Manning, C. D., & Schütze, H. (1999). *Foundations of statistical natural language processing*. Cambridge, MA: MIT Press.

Marcu, D., & Echihabi, A. (2002). An unsupervised approach to recognizing discourse relations. In *Proceedings of the 40th Annual Meeting on Association for Computational Linguistics* (pp. 368-375). Morristown, NJ: Association for Computational Linguistics.

Marcus, M. P., Santorini, B., & Marcinkiewicz, M. A. (1994). Building a large annotated corpus of English: The Penn Treebank. *Computational Linguistics, 19*(2), 313–330.

Marinkovich, J., Peronard, M., & Parodi, G. (2006). *Programa de optimización de la competencia estratégica para comprender y producir textos escritos (LECTES)* [Online]. Retrieved from www.lectes.cl.

Martindale, C. (1990). *The clockwork muse: The predictability of artistic change*. New York, NY: Basic Books.

Mayer, R. (2005). *The Cambridge handbook of multimedia learning*. New York, NY: Cambridge University Press.

Mccarthy, P. M., Hall, C., Duran, N. D., Doiuchi, M., Duncan, B., Fujiwara, Y., & Mcnamara, D. D. (2009). A computational analysis of journal abstracts written by Japanese, American, and British scientists. *The ESPecialist*, *30*, 141–173.

McCarthy, P. M., Myers, J. C., Briner, S. W., Graesser, A. C., & McNamara, D. S. (2009). A psychological and computational study of sub-sentential genre recognition. [PDF]. *Journal for Language Technology and Computational Linguistics*, *24*, 23–55.

McCarthy, P. M., Guess, R. H., & McNamara, D. S. (2009). The components of paraphrase evaluations. *Behavior Research Methods*, *41*, 682–690. doi:10.3758/BRM.41.3.682

McCarthy, P. M., & Jarvis, S. (2010). MTLD, vocd-D, and HD-D: A validation study of sophisticated approaches to lexical diversity assessment. *Behavior Research Methods*, *42*(2), 381–392. doi:10.3758/BRM.42.2.381

McCarthy, P. M., Renner, A. M., Duncan, M. G., Duran, N. D., Lightman, E. J., & McNamara, D. S. (2008). Identifying topic sentencehood. *Behavior Research Methods*, *40*, 647–664. doi:10.3758/BRM.40.3.647

McCarthy, P. M., & Jarvis, S. (2007). A theoretical and empirical evaluation of *vocd. Language Testing*, *24*, 459–488. doi:10.1177/0265532207080767

McCarthy, P. M., & Jarvis, S. (2010). MTLD, vocd-D, and HD-D: A validation study of sophisticated approaches to lexical diversity assessment. *Behavior Research Methods*, *42*, 381–392. doi:10.3758/BRM.42.2.381

McCarthy, P. M., Lehenbauer, B. M., Hall, C., Duran, N. D., Fujiwara, Y., & McNamara, D. S. (2007). A Coh-Metrix analysis of discourse variation in the texts of Japanese, American, and British Scientists. *Foreign Languages for Specific Purposes*, *6*, 46–77.

McCarthy, P. M., & Jarvis, S. (2007). vocd: A theoretical and empirical evaluation. *Language Testing*, *24*(4), 459–488. doi:10.1177/0265532207080767

McCarthy, P. M., Briner, S. W., Rus, V., & McNamara, D. S. (2007). Textual signatures: Identifying text-types using latent semantic analysis to measure the cohesion of text structures. In Kao, A., & Poteet, S. (Eds.), *Natural language processing and text mining* (pp. 107–122). London, UK: Springer-Verlag UK. doi:10.1007/978-1-84628-754-1_7

McCarthy, P. M., & McNamara, D. S. (in press). User language paraphrase corpus. In McCarthy, P. M., & Boonthum, C. (Eds.), *Applied natural language processing: Identification, investigation, and resolution*. Hershey, PA: IGI Global.

McCarthy, P. M. (2005). *An assessment of the range and usefulness of lexical diversity measures and the potential of the measure of textual, lexical diversity (MTLD)*. Unpublished doctoral dissertation, The University of Memphis.

McCarthy, P. M. (2010). GPAT paper: A genre purity assessment tool. In H. W. Guesgen & C. Murray (Eds.), *Proceedings of the 23rd International Florida Artificial Intelligence Research Society Conference* (pp. 241-246). Menlo Park, CA: The AAAI Press.

McCarthy, P. M. (April, 2010). *Special presentation of the Gramulator*. Presented at the South-eastern Conference on Linguistics (*SECOL*).

Mccarthy, P. M., Lewis, G. A., Dufty, D. F., & Mcnamara, D. S. (2006). Analyzing writing styles with Coh-Metrix. In *Proceedings of the Florida Artificial Intelligence Research Society International Conference (FLAIRS)* (pp. 764-770).

McCarthy, P. M., Rus, V., Crossley, S. A., Graesser, A. C., & McNamara, D. S. (2008). Assessing forward-, reverse-, and average-entailment indices on natural language input from the intelligent tutoring system, iSTART. In D. Wilson & G. Sutcliffe (Eds.), *Proceedings of the 21st International Florida Artificial Intelligence Research Society Conference* (pp. 165-170). Menlo Park, CA: The AAAI Press.

McCarthy, P., & McNamara, D. (2008). *The user-language paraphrase challenge* [On-line]. Retrieved from https://umdrive.memphis.edu/pmmccrth/public/Phil%27s%20papers.htm?uniq=-xq6brv.

McEnery, T., & Wilson, A. (1996). *Corpus linguistics.* Edinburgh, UK: Edinburgh University Press.

McEnery, T., Xiao, R., & Tono, Y. (2006). *Corpus-based language studies: An advanced resource book.* London, UK: Routledge.

McKay, S. L. (2003). EIL curriculum development. *RELC Journal, 34*(1), 31–47. doi:10.1177/003368820303400103

McKeown, K. R., & Radev, D. R. (1999). Generating summaries of multiple news articles. In Mani, I., & Maybury, M. T. (Eds.), *Advances in automatic text summarization* (pp. 381–389). Cambridge, MA: The MIT Press.

McKeown, K. R., Barzilay, R., Chen, J., Elson, D., Evans, D., & Klavans, J. … Sigelman, S. (2003). Columbia's Newsblaster: New features and future directions. In *Proceedings of the Human Language Technology Conference,* vol. II. Edmonton, Canada.

McKeown, K. R., Chang, S.-F., Cimino, J., Feiner, S. K., Friedman, C., & Gravano, L. … Teufel, S. (2001). PERSIVAL, a system for personalized search and summarization over multimedia healthcare information. In *Proceedings of the Joint ACM/IEEE Conference on Digital Libraries (JCDL-01),* (pp. 331–340). Roanoke, Virginia, June 2001.

Mckinlay, A., & McVittie, C. (2008). *Social psychology and discourse.* Chichester, UK: Wiley-Blackwell. doi:10.1002/9781444303094

McNamara, D. S. (2009). The importance of teaching reading strategies. [PDF]. *Perspectives on Language and Literacy, 35,* 34–40.

McNamara, D. S., Levinstein, I., & Boonthum, C. (2004). iSTART: Interactive strategy trainer for active reading and thinking. *Behavior Research Methods, Instruments, & Computers, 36*(2), 222–233. doi:10.3758/BF03195567

McNamara, D. S. (2001). Reading both high-coherence and low-coherence texts: Effects of text sequence and prior knowledge. *Canadian Journal of Experimental Psychology, 55,* 51–62. doi:10.1037/h0087352

McNamara, D. S., & Kintsch, W. (1996). Learning from text: Effects of prior knowledge and text coherence. *Discourse Processes, 22,* 247–287. doi:10.1080/01638539609544975

McNamara, D. S., Louwerse, M. M., McCarthy, P. M., & Graesser, A. C. (2010). Coh-Metrix: Capturing linguistic features of cohesion. *Discourse Processes, 47,* 292–330. doi:10.1080/01638530902959943

McNamara, D. S. (2004). SERT: Self-explanation reading training. *Discourse Processes, 38,* 1–30. doi:10.1207/s15326950dp3801_1

McNamara, D. S., Louwerse, M. M., & Graesser, A. C. (2002). *Coh-Metrix: Automated cohesion and coherence scores to predict text readability and facilitate comprehension. Technical report.* Memphis, TN: Institute for Intelligent Systems, University of Memphis.

McNamara, D. S. (2001). Reading both high and low coherence texts: Effects of text sequence and prior knowledge. *Canadian Journal of Experimental Psychology, 55,* 51–62. doi:10.1037/h0087352

McNamara, D. S., Crossley, S. A., & McCarthy, P. M. (2010). The linguistic features of quality writing. *Written Communication, 27,* 57–86. doi:10.1177/0741088309351547

McNamara, D. S., Louwerse, M. M., McCarthy, P. M., & Graesser, A. C. (2010). Coh-Metrix: Capturing linguistic features of cohesion. *Discourse Processes, 47,* 292–330. doi:10.1080/01638530902959943

McNamara, D. S., & Scott, J. L. (2001). Working memory capacity and strategy use. *Memory & Cognition, 29,* 10–17. doi:10.3758/BF03195736

McNamara, D. S., Levinstein, I. B., & Boonthum, C. (2004). iSTART: Interactive strategy trainer for active reading and thinking. *Behavior Research Methods, Instruments, & Computers, 36,* 222–233. doi:10.3758/BF03195567

McNamara, D. S., O'Reilly, T., Best, R., & Ozuru, Y. (2006). Improving adolescent students' reading comprehension with iSTART. *Journal of Educational Computing Research, 34,* 147–171. doi:10.2190/1RU5-HDTJ-A5C8-JVWE

McNamara, D. S., Kintsch, E., Songer, N. B., & Kintsch, W. (1996). Are good texts always better? Interactions of text coherence, background knowledge, and levels of understanding in learning from text. *Cognition and Instruction, 14,* 1–43. doi:10.1207/s1532690xci1401_1

McNamara, D. S., Jackson, G. T., & Graesser, A. C. (in press). Intelligent tutoring and games (ITaG). In Baek, Y. K. (Ed.), *Gaming for classroom-based learning: Digital role-playing as a motivator of study*. Hershey, PA: IGI Global.

McNamara, D. S., & O'Reilly, T. (2009). Theories of comprehension skill: Knowledge and strategies versus capacity and suppression. In Columbus, A. M. (Ed.), *Advances in Psychology Research, 62, (pp.)*. Hauppauge, NY: Nova Science Publishers, Inc.[PDF]

McNamara, D. S., Cai, Z., & Louwerse, M. M. (2007). Comparing latent and non-latent measures of cohesion. In Landauer, T., McNamara, D. S., Dennis, S., & Kintsch, W. (Eds.), *Handbook of latent semantic analysis* (pp. 379–400). Mahwah, NJ: Erlbaum.

McNamara, D. S., Boonthum, C., Levinstein, I. B., & Millis, K. (2007). Evaluating selfexplanations in iSTART: Comparing word-based and LSA algorithms. In Landauer, T., McNamara, D. S., Dennis, S., & Kintsch, W. (Eds.), *Handbook of LSA* (pp. 227–241). NJ: Erlbaum.

McNamara, D. S., Cai, Z., & Louwerse, M. M. (2007). Optimizing LSA measures of cohesion. In Landauer, T., McNamara, D. S., Dennis, S., & Kintsch, W. (Eds.), *Handbook of latent semantic analysis* (pp. 379–400). Mahwah, NJ: Erlbaum.

McNamara, D. S., Raine, R., Roscoe, R., Crossley, S., Jackson, G. T., & Dai, J. (in press). The Writing-Pal: Natural language algorithms to support intelligent tutoring on writing strategies. In McCarthy, P. M., & Boonthum, C. (Eds.), *Applied natural language processing: Identification, investigation, and resolution*. Hershey, PA: IGI Global.

McNamara, D. S., & Magliano, J. P. (2009). Towards a comprehensive model of comprehension. In Ross, B. (Ed.), *The psychology of learning and motivation*. New York, NY: Elsevier Science. [PDF]doi:10.1016/S0079-7421(09)51009-2

McNamara, D. S., Graesser, A. C., & Louwerse, M. M. (in press). Sources of text difficulty: Across the ages and genres. In Sabatini, J. P., & Albro, E. (Eds.), *Assessing reading in the 21ˢᵗ century: Aligning and applying advances in the reading and measurement sciences*. Lanham, MD: R&L Education.

McNamara, D. S. (2009). The importance of teaching reading strategies. *Perspectives on Language and Literacy, Spring,* 34-40.

McNamara, D. S., & Scott, J. L. (1999). Training reading strategies. In M. Hahn & S. C. Stoness (Eds.), *Proceedings of the Twenty-first Annual Meeting of the Cognitive Science Society* (pp. 387-392). Hillsdale, NJ: Erlbaum.

McNamara, D. S., Jackson, G. T., & Graesser, A. C. (2009). Intelligent tutoring and games (iTaG). In H.C. Lane, A. Ogan, & V. Shute (Eds.), *Proceedings of the Workshop on Intelligent Educational Games at the 14ᵗʰ Annual Conference on Artificial Intelligence in Education*(pp. 1-10). Brighton, UK: AIED. [PDF]

McNamara, D. S., Ozuru, Y., Graesser, A. C., & Louwerse, M. (2006). Validating Coh-Metrix. In R. Sun & N. Miyake (Eds.), *Proceedings of the 28th Annual Conference of the Cognitive Science Society* (p. 573). Mahwah, NJ: Erlbaum.

McNamee, P., & Dang, H. T. (2009). Overview of the TAC 2009 knowledge base population track. In *Proceedings of the 2009 Text Analysis Conference*.

Meara, P., & Bell, H. (2001). P_Lex: A simple and effective way of describing the lexical characteristics of short L2 texts. *Prospect, 16*(3), 5–19.

Mehl, M. R. (2006). The lay assessment of subclinical depression in daily life. *Psychological Assessment, 18,* 340–345. doi:10.1037/1040-3590.18.3.340

Mehl, M. R., Gosling, S. D., & Pennebaker, J. W. (2006). Personality in its natural habitat: Manifestations and implicit folk theories of personality in daily life. *Journal of Personality and Social Psychology, 90,* 862–877. doi:10.1037/0022-3514.90.5.862

Mehl, M. R., Vazire, S., Ramirez-Esparza, N., Slatcher, R. B., & Pennebaker, J. W. (2007). Are women really more talkative than men? *Science, 317,* 82. doi:10.1126/science.1139940

Mergenthaler, E. (1996). Emotion-abstraction patterns in verbatim protocols: A new way of describing psychotherapeutic processes. *Journal of Consulting and Clinical Psychology, 64,* 1306–1315. doi:10.1037/0022-006X.64.6.1306

Midgley, T. D. (2003). Discourse chunking: A tool in dialogue act tagging. In *Proceedings of the 41st Annual Meeting on Association for Computational Linguistics*, (pp. 58–63). 7–12 July, Sapporo, Japan.

Midgley, T. D. (2009). Dialogue segmentation with large numbers of volunteer Internet annotators. In *Proceedings of the 47th Annual Meeting of the ACL and the 4th IJCNLP of the AFNLP* (pp. 897–904). 2–7 August, Singapore.

Midgley, T. D., Harrison, S. P., & MacNish, C. (2006). Empirical verification of adjacency pairs using dialogue segmentation. In *Proceedings of the 7th SIGdial Workshop on Discourse and Dialogue* (pp. 104–108). 15–16 July, Sydney, Australia.

Mihalcea, R., & Csomai, A. (2005). SenseLearner: Word sense disambiguation for all words in unrestricted text. In *Proceedings of the ACL 2005 on Interactive Poster and Demonstration Sessions* (pp. 53-56). Morristown, NJ: Association for Computational Linguistics.

Mihalcea, R., & Moldovan, D. (1998). Word sense disambiguation based on semantic density. In *Proceedings of COLING/ACL Workshop on Usage of WordNet in Natural Language Processing* (pp. 16–22).

Mihalcea, R., Corley, C., & Strapparava, C. (2006). Corpus-based and knowledge-based measures of text semantic similarity. In *Proc. of the 21ˢᵗ Conference of American Association for Artificial Intelligence (AAAI-06)*, Boston, Massachusetts, July 16-20 2006.

Mill, J. S. (1843). *A system of logic, raciocinative and inductive*. London.

Miller, G. A., Beckwith, R., Fellbaum, C. D., Gross, D., & Miller, K. (1990). WordNet: An online lexical database. *International Journal of Lexicography, 3-4*, 235–244. doi:10.1093/ijl/3.4.235

Miller, G. A. (1995). WordNet: A lexical database for English. *Communications of the ACM, 38*(11), 39–41. doi:10.1145/219717.219748

Miller, G. A., Beckwith, R., Fellbaum, C., Gross, D., & Miller, K. (1990). *Five papers on WordNet*. Princeton, NJ: Princeton University Press.

Miller, G. A., Beckwith, R., Fellbaum, C., Gross, D., & Miller, K. J. (1990). Introduction to WordNet: An on-line lexical database. *International Journal of Lexicography, 3*, 235–244. doi:10.1093/ijl/3.4.235

Millis, K., Kim, H. J., Todaro, S., Magliano, J. P., Wiemer-Hastings, K., & McNamara, D. S. (2004). Identifying reading strategies using latent semantic analysis: Comparing semantic benchmarks. *Behavior Research Methods, Instruments, & Computers, 36*, 213–221. doi:10.3758/BF03195566

Millis, K., Cai, Z., Graesser, A., Halpern, D., & Wallace, P. (2009). Learning scientific inquiry by asking questions in an educational game. In T. Bastiaens, et al. (Eds.), *Proceedings of World Conference on E-Learning in Corporate, Government, Healthcare, and Higher Education* (pp. 2951-2956). Chesapeake, VA: AACE.

Min, H. C., & Mccarthy, P. M. (2010). Identifying varietals in the discourse of American and Korean scientists: A contrastive corpus analysis using the Gramulator. In H. W. Guesgen & C. Murray (Eds.), *Proceedings of the 23rd International Florida Artificial Intelligence Research Society Conference* (pp. 247-252). Menlo Park, CA: The AAAI Press.

Min, H. C., & McCarthy, P. M. (April, 2010). *Identifying variations in the discourse of American and Korean scientists. A contrastive corpus analysis using the Gramulator and Coh-Metrix*. Paper presented at the South-eastern Conference on Linguistics (*SECOL*).

Mitrovic, A., Martin, B., & Suraweera, P. (2007). Intelligent tutors for all: The constraint-based approach. *IEEE Intelligent Systems, 22*(4), 38–45. doi:10.1109/MIS.2007.74

Modern Standard Arabic. (n.d.). In *Wikipedia*. Retrieved April 9, 2010, from http://en.wikipedia.org/wiki/Modern_Standard_Arabic.

Moldovan, D., Harabagiu, S., Pasca, M., Mihalcea, R., Goodrum, R., Girju, R., & Rus, V. (1999). LASSO: A tool for surfing the answer net. In *Proceedings of the Text Retrieval Conference* (TREC-8), November, 1999.

Moreno, R., & Mayer, R. E. (2007). Interactive multimodal learning environments. *Educational Psychology Review, 19*, 309–326. doi:10.1007/s10648-007-9047-2

Mosenthal, P. (1996). Understanding the strategies of document literacy and their conditions of use. *Journal of Educational Psychology, 88,* 314–332. doi:10.1037/0022-0663.88.2.314

Mueller, E. T. (2007). Modelling space and time in narratives about restaurants. *Literary and Linguistic Computing, 22*(1), 67. doi:10.1093/llc/fql014

Mullen, B., Chapman, J. G., & Peaugh, S. (1989). Focus of attention in groups: A self-attention perspective. *The Journal of Social Psychology, 129,* 807–817. doi:10.1080/00224545.1989.9712089

Murdock, B. (1982). A theory for the storage and retrieval of item and associative information. *Psychological Review, 89,* 609–626. doi:10.1037/0033-295X.89.6.609

Murthy, S. (2004). Automatic construction of decision trees from data: A multi-disciplinary survey. [Berlin, Germany: Springer.]. *Data Mining and Knowledge Discovery, 2*(4), 345–389. doi:10.1023/A:1009744630224

Myers, J. C., McCarthy, P. M., Duran, N. D., & McNamara, D. S. (in press). The bit in the middle and why it's important: A computational analysis of the linguistic features of body paragraphs. *Behavior Research Methods.*

Nadeau, D., & Sekine, S. (2009). A survey of named entity recognition and classification. In Sekine, S., & Ranchhod, E. (Eds.), *Named entities: Recognition, classification and use* (pp. 3–25). Amsterdam, The Netherlands: John Benjamins.

Narayanan, S. (1997). *KARMA: Knowledge-based action representations for metaphor and aspect.* Ph.D. Dissertation, University of California, Berkeley.

Nation, P. (1988). *Word lists.* Victoria, Canada: University of Wellington Press.

Nation, P., & Heatley, A. (1996). *VocabProfile, Word and Range: Programs for processing text.* LALS, Victoria University of Wellington.

National Commission on Writing. (2004). *Writing: A ticket to work... Or a ticket out, a survey of business leaders.* Retrieved from http://www.host-collegeboard.com/advocacy/writing/publications.html.

National Reading Panel. (2000). *Teaching children to read: An evidence-based assessment of the scientific research literature on reading and its implications for reading instruction (NIH Pub. No. 00-4769)* (pp. 4-2–4-131). Jessup, MD: National Institute for Literacy.

Naur, P. (1960). Revised report on the algorithmic language ALGOL 60. *Communications of the ACM, 3*(5), 299–314. doi:10.1145/367236.367262

. Navigli, R. (2009). Word sense disambiguation: A survey. *ACM Computing Surveys, 41,* 1–69. doi:10.1145/1459352.1459355

Navigli, R., & Velardi, P. (2003). An analysis of ontology-based query expansion strategies. In *Proceedings of the Workshop on Adaptive Text Extraction and Mining (ATEM 2003) at the 14th European Conference on Machine Learning (ECML 2003)* (pp. 42-49). Cavtat-Dubrovnik, Croatia.

Navy Research Laboratory. (2001). *Speech in noisy environments.* Retrieved from http://www.ldc.upenn.edu/Catalog/CatalogEntry.jsp?catalogId=LDC2000S87.

Neel, A., Garzon, M. H., & Rus, V. (2008). A semantic method for textual entailment. In *Proceedings of the Twenty-First International Florida AI Research Symposium.* FLAIRS, AAAI 2008, Coconut Grove, Florida, USA, (pp. 171-176).

Negri, M. (2004). Sense-based blind relevance feedback for question answering. In SIGIR-2004 *Workshop on Information Retrieval For Question Answering* (IR4QA), Sheffield, UK.

Newell, A. (1994). *Unified theories of cognition.* Harvard University Press.

Newman, M. L., Groom, C. J., Handelman, L. D., & Pennebaker, J. W. (2008). Gender differences in language use: An analysis of 14,000 text samples. *Discourse Processes, 45,* 211–246. doi:10.1080/01638530802073712

Newman, M. L., Pennebaker, J. W., Berry, D. S., & Richards, J. M. (2003). Lying words: Predicting deception from linguistic style. *Personality and Social Psychology Bulletin, 29,* 665–675. doi:10.1177/0146167203029005010

Niederhoffer, K. G., & Pennebaker, J. W. (2002). Linguistic style matching in social interaction. *Journal of Language and Social Psychology, 21,* 337–360. doi:10.1177/026192702237953

Nietzsche, F. (1901). *Der Wille zur Macht* [Will to power]. Leipzig, Germany: Naumann.

Nijssen, S., & Kok, J. N. (2005). The Gaston tool for frequent subgraph mining. *Electronic Notes in Theoretical Computer Science*, *127*(1), 77–87. doi:10.1016/j.entcs.2004.12.039

Nirenburg, S., & Raskin, V. (2004). *Ontological semantics*. Cambridge, MA: MIT Press.

Nirenburg, S., Raskin, V., & Tucker, A. (1987). The structure of interlingua in TRANSLATOR. In Nirenburg, S. (Ed.), *Machine translation: Theoretical and methodological issues* (pp. 90–113). New York, NY: Cambridge University Press.

Nissim, M. (2006). Learning information status of discourse entities. *Proceedings of the 2006 Conference on Empirical Methods in Natural Language Processing* (pp. 94-102). Sydney, Australia: Association for Computational Linguistics.

O'Reilly, T., & McNamara, D. S. (2007). Reversing the reverse cohesion effect: Good texts can be better for strategic, high-knowledge readers. *Discourse Processes*, *43*, 121–152.

O'Reilly, T., Best, R., & McNamara, D. S. (2004). Self-Explanation reading training: Effects for low-knowledge readers. In K. Forbus, D. Gentner, T. Regier (Eds.), *Proceedings of the Twenty-Sixth Annual Meeting of the Cognitive Science Society* (pp. 1053-1058). Mahwah, NJ: Erlbaum.

Obrst, L. (2007). Ontology and ontologies: Why it and they matter to the intelligence community. In *ACM International Conference Proceeding Series; Vol. 171 archive. Proceedings of the Second International Ontology for the Intelligence Community Conference. OIC-2007*. Columbia, MD.

Odom, S. D. (2006). *A qualitative and linguistic analysis of an authority issues training group*. Unpublished doctoral dissertation, The University of Texas at Austin, Austin, TX.

Olmos, R., León, J., & Escudero, I., & Botana. (2009). Efectos sobre el tamaño y especificidad de los corpus en la evaluación de resúmenes mediante el LSA y jueces expertos. *Revista Signos*, *41*(69), 71–81.

Olney, A. M., Person, N. K., & Graesser, A. C. (2011). Guru: Designing a conversational expert intelligent tutoring system. In McCarthy, P. M., & Boonthum-Denecke, C. (Eds.), *Applied natural language processing and content analysis: Identification, investigation, and resolution*. Hershey, PA: IGI Global.

Olney, A. M., Graesser, A. C., & Person, N. K. (2010). Tutorial dialog in natural language. In Nkambou, R., Mizoguchi, R., & Bourdeau, J. (Eds.), *Advances in intelligent tutoring systems* (p. xx). New York, NY: Springer. doi:10.1007/978-3-642-14363-2_9

Olney, A. M. (2009). GnuTutor: An open source intelligent tutoring system based on AutoTutor. In *Proceedings of the 2009 AAAI Fall Symposium on Cognitive and Metacognitive Educational Systems* (pp. 70-75). Washington, DC: AAAI Press.

Olney, A., Louwerse, M., Mathews, E., Marineau, J., Hite-Mitchell, H., & Graesser, A. (2003). Utterance classification in AutoTutor. In J. Burstein & C. Leacock (Eds.), *Proceedings of the HLT-NAACL 03 Workshop on Building Educational Applications Using Natural Language Processing*. Philadelphia, PA: Association for Computational Linguistics.

Ong, W. (2004). *Ramus, method, and the decay of dialogue: From the art of discourse to the art of reason*. Chicago, IL: University of Chicago Press. (Original work published 1958)

Órdenes, A. (2009). *El resumen como instrumento de evaluación de la comprensión del discurso escrito: correlación entre evaluadores expertos*. Pregraduate thesis. Pontificia Universidad Católica de Valparaíso.

Ortega, L. (2003). Syntactic complexity measures and their relationship to L2 proficiency: A research synthesis of college-level L2 writing. *Applied Linguistics*, *24*(4), 492–518. doi:10.1093/applin/24.4.492

Ortega, L., & Iberri-Shea, G. (2005). Longitudinal research in second language acquisition: Recent trends and future directions. *Annual Review of Applied Linguistics*, *25*, 26–45. doi:10.1017/S0267190505000024

Ortuño, M., Carpena, P., Bernaola-Galvan, P., Munoz, E., & Somoza, A. (2002). Keyword detection in natural languages and DNA. *Europhysics Letters*, *57*, 759–764. doi:10.1209/epl/i2002-00528-3

Osborne, M. (2000). Shallow parsing as part-of-speech tagging. In *Proceedings of the 2nd Workshop on Learning Language in Logic and the 4th Conference on Computational Natural Language Learning.* September 13–14, Lisbon, Portugal.

Otero, J., & Graesser, A. C. (2001). PREG: Elements of a model of question asking. *Cognition and Instruction, 19,* 143–175. doi:10.1207/S1532690XCI1902_01

Otero, J., León, J., & Graesser, A. (2002). *The psychology of science text comprehension.* Mahwah, NJ: Erlbaum.

Otero, J. (2009). Question generation and anomaly detection in texts. In Hacker, D., Dunlosky, J., & Graesser, A. (Eds.), *Handbook of metacognition in education.* New York, NY: Routledge.

Over, P., & Yen, J. (2004). *An introduction to DUC 2004 intrinsic evaluation of generic new text summarization systems.* Retrieved from http://www-nlpir.nist.gov/projects/duc/pubs/2004slides/duc2004.intro.pdf.

Ozuru, Y., Dempsey, K., & McNamara, D. S. (2009). Prior knowledge, reading skill, and text cohesion in the comprehension of science texts. [PDF]. *Learning and Instruction, 19,* 228–242. doi:10.1016/j.learninstruc.2008.04.003

Ozuru, Y., Briner, S., Best, R., & McNamara, D. S. (2010). Contributions of self-explanation to comprehension of high and low cohesion texts. *Discourse Processes, 47,* 641–667. doi:10.1080/01638531003628809

Ozuru, Y., Best, R., Floyd, R. G., & McNamara, D. S. (2006). Children's text comprehension: Effects of genre, knowledge, and text cohesion. In S. A. Barab, K. E. Hay, & D. T. Hickey (Eds.), *Proceedings of the 7th International Conference of the Learning Sciences* (pp. 37-42). Mahwah, NJ: Erlbaum.

Paivio, A. (1965). Abstractness, imagery, and meaningfulness in paired-associate learning. *Journal of Verbal Learning and Verbal Behavior, 4,* 32–38. doi:10.1016/S0022-5371(65)80064-0

Palincsar, A. S., & Brown, A. L. (1984). Reciprocal teaching of comprehension-fostering and monitoring activities. *Cognition and Instruction, 12,* 117–175.

Palmer, M., Kingsbury, P., & Gildea, D. (2005). The proposition bank: An annotated corpus of semantic roles. *Computational Linguistics, 31*(1), 71–106. doi:10.1162/0891201053630264

Parks, R., Ray, J., & Bland, S. (1998). *Wordsmyth English dictionary – Thesaurus.* University of Chicago. [Online]. Retrieved from http://www.wordsmyth.net/.

Parodi, G. (Ed.). (2005). *Discurso especializado e instituciones formadoras.* Valparaíso, Chile: EUVSA.

Parodi, G. (Ed.). (2007). *Lingüística de corpus y discursos especializados: Puntos de mira.* Valparaíso, Chile: EUVSA.

Pasca, M., & Harabagiu, S. (2001). *The informative role of WordNet in open-domain question answering.* Workshop on WordNet and Other Lexical Resources at NAACL.

Patwardhan, S. (2003). *Incorporating dictionary and corpus information into a context vector measure of semantic relatedness.* Master's thesis, Univ. of Minnesota, Duluth.

Pedersen, T., & Bruce, R. (1997). Knowledge lean word-sense disambiguation. In *Proceedings of the National Conference of Artificial Intelligence,* (pp. 814–814).

Pedersen, T., Patwardhan, S., & Michelizzi, J. (2004). WordNet: Similarity - Measuring the relatedness of concepts. In the *Proceedings of the Nineteenth National Conference on Artificial Intelligence* (AAAI-04), (pp. 1024-1025). July 25-29, 2004, San Jose, CA (Intelligent Systems Demonstration) McCarthy, P. M., & McNamara, D. S. (2008). *User-language paraphrase corpus challenge.*

Peirsman, Y. (2006). Example-based metonymy recognition for proper nouns. *Proc. 11th Conf. of the European Chapter of the Assoc. for Computational Linguistics (EACL-2006): Student Research Workshop* (pp. 71-78). Trento, Italy.

Penev, A., & Wong, R. (2006). Shallow NLP techniques for internet search. In *Proceedings of the 29th Australasian Computer Science Conference,* vol. 48 (pp. 167–176). Hobart, Australia.

Pennebaker, J. W. (2011). *The secret life of pronouns: What our words say about us.* New York: Bloomsbury Press.

Pennebaker, J. W., & Beall, S. (1986). Confronting a traumatic event: Toward an understanding of inhibition and disease. *Journal of Abnormal Psychology, 95,* 274–281. doi:10.1037/0021-843X.95.3.274

Pennebaker, J. W., & Francis, M. E. (1996). Cognitive, emotional, and language processes in disclosure. *Cognition and Emotion, 10*, 601–626. doi:10.1080/026999396380079

Pennebaker, J. W., Francis, M. E., & Booth, R. J. (2001). *Linguistic inquiry and word count (LIWC) (Version LIWC2001)* [Computer software]. Mahwah, NJ: Erlbaum.

Pennebaker, J. W., Groom, C. J., Loew, D., & Dabbs, J. (2004). Testosterone as a social inhibitor: Two case studies of the effect of testosterone treatment on language. *Journal of Abnormal Psychology, 113*, 172–175. doi:10.1037/0021-843X.113.1.172

Pennebaker, J. W., & Harber, K. D. (1993). A social stage model of collective coping: The Loma Prieta Earthquake and the Persian Gulf War. *The Journal of Social Issues, 49*, 125–145. doi:10.1111/j.1540-4560.1993.tb01184.x

Pennebaker, J. W., & King, L. A. (1999). Linguistic styles: Language use as an individual difference. *Journal of Personality and Social Psychology, 77*, 1296–1312. doi:10.1037/0022-3514.77.6.1296

Pennebaker, J. W., & Stone, L. D. (2003). Words of wisdom: Language use over the lifespan. *Journal of Personality and Social Psychology, 85*, 291–301. doi:10.1037/0022-3514.85.2.291

Pennebaker, J. W., & Chung, C. K. (2008). Computerized text analysis of al-Qaeda statements. In Krippendorff, K., & Bock, M. (Eds.), *A content analysis reader* (pp. 453–466). Thousand Oaks, CA: Sage.

Pennebaker, J. W., & Huddle, D. (2009). *Detecting deception with courtroom transcripts*. Manuscript in preparation.

Pennebaker, J. W., Booth, R. J., & Francis, M. E. (2007). *Linguistic inquiry and word count (LIWC2007): A text analysis program*. Austin, TX: LIWC.net.

Pennebaker, J. W., Chung, C. K., Ireland, M. I., Gonzales, A. L., & Booth, R. J. (2007). *The development and psychometric properties of LIWC2007*. Austin, TX: LIWC.net.

Pennebaker, J. W., Slatcher, R. B., & Chung, C. K. (2005). Linguistic markers of psychological state through media interviews: John Kerry and John Edwards in 2004, Al Gore in 2000. *Analyses of Social Issues and Public Policy, Special Issue: The Social Psychology of the 2004 US Presidential Elections, 5*, 1-9.

Perelman, C., & Olbrechts-Tyteca, L. (1969). *The new rhetoric: A treatise on argumentation*. South Bend, IN: Notre Dame Press.

Pérez, D., Alfonseca, E., Rodríguez, P., Gliozzo, A., Strapparava, C., & Magnini, B. (2005). About the effects of combining latent semantic analysis with natural language processing techniques for free-text assessment. *Revista Signos, 38*(59), 325–343.

Perfetti, C. A. (1985). *Reading ability*. Oxford, UK: Oxford University Press.

Perfetti, C. A., Landi, N., & Oakhill, J. (2005). The acquisition of reading comprehension skill. In Snowling, M. J., & Hulme, C. (Eds.), *The science of reading: A handbook* (pp. 227–247). Oxford, UK: Blackwell. doi:10.1002/9780470757642.ch13

Peronard, M. (1989). Estrato social y estrategias de comprensión de lectura. *Lenguas Modernas, 16*, 19–32.

Peronard, M., Gómez, L., Parodi, G., & Núñez, P. (Eds.). (1998). *Comprensión de textos escritos: De la teoría a la sala de clases*. Santiago, Chile: Andrés Bello.

Person, N. K., & Graesser, A. C., & the Tutoring Research Group. (2002, June). *Human or computer? AutoTutor in a bystander Turing test*. Paper presented at the Intelligent Tutoring Systems 2002 Conference, Biarritz, France.

Petrie, K. J., Pennebaker, J. W., & Sivertsen, B. (2008). Things we said today: A linguistic analysis of the Beatles. *Psychology of Aesthetics, Creativity, and the Arts, 2*, 197–202. doi:10.1037/a0013117

Petzold, C. (2000). *Code: The hidden language of computer hardware and software*. Microsoft Press.

Pevzner, L., & Hearst, M. A. (2002). A critique and improvement of an evaluation metric for text segmentation. *Computational Linguistics, 28*(1), 19–36. doi:10.1162/089120102317341756

Philips, L. (1990). Hanging on the metaphone. *Computer Language, 7-12*, 39-43.

Phillips, L., & Jorgensen, M. W. (2002). *Discourse analysis as theory and method*. London, UK: Sage.

Phillips, N., & Hardy, C. (2002). *Discourse analysis: Investigating processing of social construction*. London, UK: Sage.

Pica, T. (1994). Research on negotiation: What does it reveal about second-language learning conditions, processes, and outcomes? *Language Learning, 44*, 493–527. doi:10.1111/j.1467-1770.1994.tb01115.x

Pickering, L. (2006). Current research on intelligibility in English as a lingua franca. *Annual Review of Applied Linguistics, 26*, 219–233. doi:10.1017/S0267190506000110

Pintrich, P. R. (2000). The role of goal orientation in self-regulated learning. In Boekaerts, M., Pintrich, P., & Zeidner, M. (Eds.), *Handbook of self-regulation* (pp. 451–502). San Diego, CA: Academic Press.

PISA. (2007). *PISA 2006: Science competencies for tomorrow's world*. Paris, France: OECD Publishing.

Poesio, M., & Vieira, R. (1998). A corpus-based investigation of definite description use. *Computational Linguistics, 24*, 183–216.

Poesio, M., & Mikheev, A. (1998). The predictive power of game structure in dialogue act recognition: Experimental results using maximum entropy estimation. In *Proceedings of ICSLP-98*, Sydney, 1998.

Poesio, M., Uryupina, O., Viera, R., Alexandrov-Kabadjov, M., & Goulart, R. (2004). Discourse-new detectors for definite description resolution: A survey and a preliminary proposal. *Proceedings of the ACL Workshop on Reference Resolution.* Barcelona, Spain: ACL Press.

Pon-Barry, H., Clark, B., Schultz, K., Bratt, E. O., Peters, S., & Haley, D. (2005). Contextualizing reflective dialogue in a spoken conversational tutor. *Journal of Educational Technology & Society, 8*, 42–51.

Popping, R. (2000). *Computer-assisted text analysis*. Thousand Oaks, CA: Sage.

Porter, M. F. (1980). An algorithm for suffix stripping. *Program, 14*, 130–137.

Porter, P. A. (1983). *Variations in the conversations of adult learners of English as a function of the proficiency level of the participants.* Ph.D. dissertation Stanford University.

Portet, F., Reiter, E., Gatt, A., Hunter, J., Sripada, S., Freer, Y., & Sykes, C. (2009). Automatic generation of textual summaries from neonatal intensive care data. [Essex, UK: Elsevier Science Publishers Ltd.]. *Artificial Intelligence, 173*(7-8), 789–816. doi:10.1016/j.artint.2008.12.002

Postolache, O., Kruijff-Korbayovà, I., & Kruijff, G. (2005). Data-driven approaches for information structure identification. *Proceedings of HLT/EMNLP* (pp. 9-16). Vancouver, Canada.

Potter, J. (1996). *Representing Reality: Discourse Rhetoric and Social Construction*. London: Sage.

Potter, J., & Edwards, D. (1990). Nigel Lawson's tent: discourse analysis, attribution theory and the social psychology of fact. *European Journal of Phycology, 20*, 405–424.

Potter, J., & Wetherell, M. (1987). *Discourse and social psychology: Beyond behaviour and attitudes*. London, UK: Sage.

Potter, J. (2009). Discourse analysis. In Bryman, A., & Hardy, M. A. (Eds.), *Handbook of data analysis* (pp. 607–624). London, UK: Sage.

Potter, J., & Hepburn, A. (2008). Discursive constructionism. In Holstein, J. A., & Gubrium, J. F. (Eds.), *Handbook of constructionist research* (pp. 275–293). New York, NY: Guildford.

Prince, E. (1981). Towards a taxonomy of given-new information. In Cole, P. (Ed.), *Radical pragmatics* (pp. 223–255). New York, NY: Academic.

Prince, E. (1988). Discourse analysis: A part of the study of linguistic competence. In Newmeyer, F. (Ed.), *Linguistics: The Cambridge survey* (pp. 164–182). Cambridge, MA: Cambridge University Press.

Prince, E. (1992). The ZPG letter: Subjects, definiteness, and information-status. In Thompson, S., & Mann, W. (Eds.), *Discourse description: Diverse analyses of a fundraising text* (pp. 295–325). Amsterdam, The Netherlands: John Benjamins.

Psathas, G. (1995). *Conversation analysis: The study of talk-in interaction*. London, UK: Sage.

Purver, M., Körding, K. P., Griffiths, T. L., & Tenenbaumm, J. B. (2006). Unsupervised topic modelling for multi-party spoken discourse. In *Proceedings of the 21st International Conference on Computational Linguistics and 44th Annual Meeting of the ACL*, (pp. 17–24).

Pustejovsky, J., Castano, J., Ingria, R., Saurí, R., Gaizauskas, R., & Setzer, A. … Radev, D. (2003). *TimeML: Robust specification of event and temporal expressions in text*. In IWCS-5 Fifth International Workshop on Computational Semantics.

Radvansky, G. A., Zwaan, R. A., Curiel, J. M., & Copeland, D. E. (2001). Situation models and aging. *Psychology and Aging*, *16*, 145–160. doi:10.1037/0882-7974.16.1.145

Rahati, A., & Kabanza, F. (2010). Persuasive dialogues in an intelligent tutoring system for medical diagnosis. In *Proceedings of the 10th Annual Intelligent Tutoring Systems International Conference* (pp. 51-61), Berlin, Germany: Springer.

Raina, R., Ng, A., & Manning, C. D. (2005). Robust textual inference via learning and abductive reasoning. *Proc. of the 20th National Conf. on Artificial Intelligence*. AAAI Press.

Ramirez-Esparza, N., Chung, C. K., Sierra-Otero, G., & Pennebaker, J. W. (in press). Cross-constructions of self-schemas: American and Mexican college students. *Journal of Cross-Cultural Psychology*.

Ramirez-Esparza, N., Pennebaker, J. W., Garcia, F. A., & Suria, R. (2007). La psicología del uso de las palabras: Un programa de comutadora que analiza textos en Español (The psychology of word use: A computer program that analyzes texts in Spanish). *Revista Mexicana de Psicología*, *24*, 85–99.

Ramirez-Esparza, N., Chung, C. K., Kacewicz, E., & Pennebaker, J. W. (2008). The psychology of word use in depression forums in English and in Spanish. Testing two text analytic approaches. *Proceedings of the 2008 International Conference on Weblogs and Social Media*, (pp. 102-108).

Ramshaw, L. A., & Marcus, M. P. (1995). Text chunking using transformation-based learning, In *Proceedings of the Third Workshop on Very Large Corpora*. Cambridge, MA, USA.

Ransdell, S., & Wengelin, A (2003). Socioeconomic and sociolinguistic predictors of children's L2 and L1 writing quality. Arob@se, *1*(2), 22-29.

Rashotte, C. A., & Torgesen, J. K. (1985). Repeated reading and reading fluency in learning disabled children. *Reading Research Quarterly*, *20*, 180–188. doi:10.1598/RRQ.20.2.4

Raskin, V. (1971). *K teorii yazykovykh podsistem* [Towards a theory of language subsystems]. Moscow, Russia: Moscow State University Press.

Raskin, V. (1986). Script-based semantic theory. In Ellis, D. G., & Donahue, W. A. (Eds.), *Contemporary issues in language and discourse processes* (pp. 23–61). Hillsdale, NJ: Erlbaum.

Raskin, V., Hempelmann, C. F., & Triezenberg, K. E. (2008). Ontological semantic forensics: Meaning-based deception detection. Paper presented at the *23rd International Information Security Conference (SEC 2008)*. Milan, Italy - September 8-10, 2008.

Ravichandran, D., & Hovy, E. (2002). Learning surface text patterns for a question answering system. In *Proceedings of ACL, 2*, 41-47.

Rayner, K., & Pollatsek, A. (1994). *The psychology of reading*. Englewood Cliffs, NJ: Prentice Hall.

Rehder, B., Schreiner, M. E., Wolfe, M. B., Laham, D., Landauer, T. K., & Kintsch, W. (1998). Using latent semantic analysis to assess knowledge: Some technical considerations. *Discourse Processes*, *25*, 337–354. doi:10.1080/01638539809545031

Reithinger, N., & Klesen, M. (1997). Dialogue act classification using language models. In G. Kokkinakis, N. Fakotakis, & E. Dermatas (Eds.), *Proceedings of the 5th European Conference on Speech Communication and Technology*, volume 4, (pp. 2235–2238). Rhodes, Greece, September.

Renner, A., McCarthy, P., Boonthum, C., & McNamara, D. S. (in press). Maximizing A NLP evaluation: Harmonizing flawed input. In McCarthy, P. M., & Boonthum, C. (Eds.), *Applied natural language processing: Identification, investigation, and resolution*. Hershey, PA: IGI Global.

Renner, A. M., McCarthy, P. M., Boonthum, C., & Mc-Namara, D. S. (2009). Speling mistacks and typeos: Can your ITS handle them? In P. Dessus, S. Trausan-Matu, P. van Rosmalen, & F. Wild (Eds.), *Proceedings of the Workshop on Natural Language Processing in Support of Learning; Metrics, Feedback, & Connectivity at the 14th International Conference on Artificial Intelligence in Education*(pp. 26-33). Brighton, UK: AIED. [PDF]

Renner, A. M., McCarthy, P. M., & McNamara, D. S. (2009). Computational considerations in correcting user-language. In C.H. Lane & H.W. Guesgen (Eds.), *Proceedings of the 22nd International Florida Artificial Intelligence Research Society (FLAIRS) Conference* (pp. 278-283). Menlo Park, CA: The AAAI Press. [PDF]

Renner, A. M., McCarthy, P. M., Boonthum, C., & Mc-Namara, D. S. (2009). Spelling mistacks and typeos: Can your ITS handle them? *Proceedings of Workshop "Natural Language Processing in Support of Learning" at the 14th International Conference on Artificial Intelligence in Education* (pp. 26-33). Brighton, UK.

Renner, A. M., McCarthy, P. M., & McNamara, D. S. (2009). Computational considerations in correcting user-language in an ITS environment. In C. H. Lane & H. W. Guesgen (Eds.), *Proceedings of the 22nd International Florida Artificial Intelligence Research Society Conference* (pp. 278-283). Menlo Park, CA: The AAAI Press.

Rennie, J., Shih, L., Teevan, J., & Karger, D. (2003). Tackling the poor assumptions of naive Bayes text classifiers. In *Proceedings of the Twentieth International Conference on Machine Learning*, (pp. 616-623). Menlo Park, CA: AAAI Press.

Renyolds, M. (1984). Freewritings origin. *English Journal*, *73*, 81–82. doi:10.2307/817229

Reutzel, D. R., & Cooter, R. B. Jr. (2007). *Strategies for reading assessment and instruction: Helping every child succeed* (3rd ed.). Upper Saddle River, NJ: Merrill Prentice Hall.

Richards, L. (1999). *Using NVivo in qualitative research*. London, UK: Sage.

Ritter, S., Anderson, J. R., Koedinger, K. R., & Corbett, A. (2007). Cognitive tutor: Applied research in mathematics education. *Psychonomic Bulletin & Review*, *14*, 249–255. doi:10.3758/BF03194060

Robertson, J., & Wiemer-Hastings, P. (2003). Storystation: An intelligent tutoring system for story writing. In *Supplementary Proceedings of the 11th International Conference on Artificial Intelligence in Education*. Sydney, Australia.

Rochon, E., Saffran, E. M., Berndt, R. S., & Schwartz, M. F. (2000). Quantitative analysis of aphasic sentence production: Further development and new data. *Brain and Language*, *72*, 193–218. doi:10.1006/brln.1999.2285

Rodd, J., Gaskell, G., & Marslen-Wilson, W. (2002). Making sense of semantic ambiguity: Semantic competition in lexical access. *Journal of Memory and Language*, *46*, 245–266. doi:10.1006/jmla.2001.2810

Rogoff, B. (1990). *Apprenticeship in thinking*. New York, NY: Oxford University Press.

Rohde, D. L. T., Gonnerman, L. M., & Plaut, D. C. (2007). *An improved method for deriving word meaning from lexical co-occurrence*. Unpublished manuscript. Cambridge, MA: Massachusetts Institute of Technology. Retrieved April 20th, 2007, from http://tedlab.mit.edu/~dr/.

Rohrbaugh, M. J., Mehl, M. R., Shoham, V., Reilly, E. S., & Ewy, G. A. (2008). Prognostic significance of spouse we talk in couples coping with heart failure. *Journal of Consulting and Clinical Psychology*, *76*, 781–789. doi:10.1037/a0013238

Rosenblum, K. E. (1986). Revelatory or purposive? Making sense of a female register. *Semiotica*, *59*, 157–170. doi:10.1515/semi.1986.59.1-2.157

Rosenshine, B., Meister, C., & Chapman, S. (1996). Teaching students to generate questions: A review of the intervention studies. *Review of Educational Research*, *66*, 181–221.

Rouet, J. F., Levonen, J., Dillon, A. P., & Spiro, R. J. (Eds.). (1996). *Hypertext and cognition*. Mahwah, NJ: Lawrence Erlbaum Associates.

Rude, S. S., Gortner, E. M., & Pennebaker, J. W. (2004). Language use of depressed and depression-vulnerable college students. *Cognition and Emotion*, *18*, 1121–1133. doi:10.1080/02699930441000030

Rufenacht, R. M., Mccarthy, P. M., & Lamkin, T. A. (in press). Fairy tales and ESL texts: An analysis of linguistic features using the Gramulator. In C. Murray & P. M. Mc-Carthy (Eds.), *Proceedings of the 24rd International Florida Artificial Intelligence Research Society Conference* (p. xx). Menlo Park, CA: The AAAI Press.

Ruppenhofer, J., Sporleder, C., Morante, R., Baker, C., & Palmer, M. (2009). SemEval-2010 Task 10: Linking events and their participants in discourse. In *Proceedings of the HLT-NAACL Workshop on Semantic Evaluations*, (pp. 106-111). Boulder, CO: Association for Computational Linguistics.

Rus, V., & Graesser, A. C. (Eds.). (2009a). *The question generation shared task and evaluation challenge.*

Rus, V., McCarthy, P. M., Graesser, A. C., & McNamara, D. S. (2009). Identification of sentence-to-sentence relations using a textual entailer. [PDF]. *Research on Language and Computation, 7*, 1–21. doi:10.1007/s11168-009-9065-y

Rus, V., Mccarthy, P. M., Mcnamara, D. S., & Graesser, A. C. (2008). A study of textual entailment. *International Journal of Artificial Intelligence Tools, 17*, 659–685. doi:10.1142/S0218213008004096

Rus, V., Lintean, M., Graesser, A. C., & McNamara, D. S. (2009). Assessing student paraphrases using lexical semantics and word weighting. In Dimitrova, V., Mizoguchi, R., du Boulay, B., & Graesser, A. C. (Eds.), *Artificial intelligence in education; Building learning systems that care; From knowledge representation to affective modeling* (pp. 165–172). Amsterdam, The Netherlands: IOS Press. [PDF]

Rus, V., Lintean, M., Graesser, A. C., & Mcnamara, D. S. (in press). Text-to-text similarity of sentences. In McCarthy, P. M., & Boonthum, C. (Eds.), *Applied natural language processing: Identification, investigation, and resolution.* Hershey, PA: IGI Global.

Rus, V. (2002). *Logic form for WordNet glosses and application to question answering.* Computer Science Department, School of Engineering, Southern Methodist University, PhD Thesis, May 2002, Dallas, Texas.

Rus, V., & Graesser, A. C. (2006). *Deeper Natural Language Processing for Evaluating Student Answers in Intelligent Tutoring Systems*, Proceedings of the Twenty-First National Conference on Artificial Intelligence (AAAI-06).

Rus, V., & Lester, J. (Eds.). (2009b). *Proceedings of the 2nd Workshop on Question Generation*, July 6, 2009, Brighton, UK.

Rus, V., Cai, Z., & Graesser, A. C. (2007). *Evaluation in natural language generation: The question generation task.* Workshop on Shared Tasks and Comparative Evaluation in Natural Language Generation, Arlington, VA, April 20-21, 2007.

Rus, V., Graesser, A., & Desai, K. (2005). Lexico-syntactic subsumption for textual entailment. *Proc. of Recent Advances in Natural Language Processing (RANLP 2005)*, Borovets, Bulgaria.

Rus, V., Lintean, M., Shiva, S., & Marinov, D. (submitted). *Automated identification of duplicate defect reports using word semantics.* Submitted to the Workshop on Mining Software Repositories.

Rus, V., McCarthy, P. M., Lintean, M. C., McNamara, D. S., & Graesser, A. C. (2008). Paraphrase identification with lexico-syntactic graph subsumption. In *Proceedings of the 21st International Florida Artificial Intelligence Research Society Conference*, (pp. 201-206).

Sacks, H., Schegloff, E. A., & Jefferson, G. (1974). A simplest systematics for the organisation of turn-taking for conversation. *Language, 50*(4), 696–735. doi:10.2307/412243

Sahlgren, M. (2006). *The word-space model: Using distributional analysis to represent syntagmatic and paradigmatic relations between words in high-dimensional vector spaces.* Doctoral thesis, Department of Linguistics, Stockholm University. Stockholm, Sweden.

Sahlgren, M., & Karlgren, J. (2005). Automatic bilingual lexicon acquisition using random indexing of parallel corpora. *Journal of Natural Language Engineering, Special Issue on Parallel Texts, 11*(3).

Salton, G. (1971). *The SMART retrieval system – Experiments in automatic document processing.* Upper Saddle River, NJ: Prentice-Hall, Inc.

Salton, G. (1968). *Automatic information organization and retrieval.* New York, NY: McGraw-Hill.

Salton, G., & McGill, M. (1983). *Introduction to modern information retrieval.* New York, NY: McGraw-Hill.

Salton, G., Allan, J., & Buckley, C. (1993). Approaches to passage retrieval in full text information systems. In *SIGIR-93* (pp 49-58). Pittsburgh, PA: ACM.

Samuel, K., Carberry, S., & Vijay-Shanker, K. (1998). Dialogue act tagging with transformation-based learning. In *Proceedings of COLING/ACL '98*, (pp. 1150–1156).

Sande, W., & Sande, C. (2009). *Hello world! Computer programming for kids and other beginners*. Manning Publications.

Sanders, T. J. M., & Noordman, L. G. M. (2000). The role of coherence relations and their linguistic markers in text processing. *Discourse Processes, 29*, 37–60. doi:10.1207/S15326950dp2901_3

Sarawagi, S. (2008). Information extraction. *Foundations and Trends in Databases, 1*(3), 261–377. doi:10.1561/1900000003

Schank, R. C. (1986). *Explanation patterns: Understanding mechanically and creatively*. Hillsdale, NJ: Erlbaum.

Schapire, R. E. (2003). *The boosting approach to machine learning: An overview. Lecture Notes in Statistics* (pp. 149–172). New York, NY: Springer Verlag.

Schegloff, E. A. (1968). Sequencing in conversational openings. *American Anthropologist, 70*(6), 1075–1095. doi:10.1525/aa.1968.70.6.02a00030

Schegloff, E. A. (1987). Analyzing single episodes of interaction: An exercise in conversation analysis. *Social Psychology Quarterly, 50*(2), 101–114. doi:10.2307/2786745

Schegloff, E. A., & Sacks, H. (1973). Opening up closings. *Semiotica, 7*(4), 289–327. doi:10.1515/semi.1973.8.4.289

Scholand, A. J., Tausczik, Y. R., & Pennebaker, J. W. (2010). Social language network analysis. *Proceedings of Computer Supported Cooperative Work, 2010*, 23–26.

Schütze, H. (1998). Automatic word sense discrimination. *Computational Linguistics, 24*, 97–123.

Schütze, H., & Pederson, J. (1995). Information retrieval based on word senses. *Symposium on Document Analysis and Information Retrieval* (SDAIR), Las Vegas, Nevada, (pp. 161-175).

Scott, M. (2004). *WordSmith tools 4.0*. Oxford, UK: Oxford University Press.

Scott, M., & Tribble, C. (2006). *Textual patterns: Key words and corpus analysis in language education*. Amsterdam, The Netherlands: John Benjamins.

Searle, J. R. (1969). *Speech acts: An essay in the philosophy of language*. Cambridge, UK: Cambridge University Press.

Searle, J. R. (1979). A taxonomy of illocutionary acts. In Searle, J. R. (Ed.), *Expression and meaning: Studies in the theory of speech acts* (pp. 1–29). Cambridge, MA: Cambridge University Press.

Sebastiani, F. (2002). Machine learning in automated text categorization. *ACM Computing Surveys, 34*(1), 1–47. doi:10.1145/505282.505283

Seidlhofer, B. (2004). Research perspectives on teaching English as a lingua franca. *Annual Review of Applied Linguistics, 24*, 209–242. doi:10.1017/S0267190504000145

Sekhon, J. (n.d.). *Bootstrap Kolmogorov-Smirnov*. Retrieved on March 28, 2010, from http://sekhon.berkeley.edu/matching/ks.boot.html.

Sekine, S., & Grishman, R. (199). A corpus-based probabilistic grammar with only two nonterminals. In *Fourth International Workshop on Parsing Technologies* (pp. 260-270). Prague, Czech Republic: Karlovy Vary.

Serafin, R., Di Eugenio, B., & Glass, M. (2003). Latent semantic analysis for dialogue act classification. In [May, Edmonton, Alberta, Canada.]. *Proceedings of the HLT-NAACL, 2003*, 28–30.

Sexton, J. B., & Helmreich, R. L. (2000). Analyzing cockpit communications: The links between language, performance, error, and workload. *Human Performance in Extreme Environments, 5*, 63–68.

Shanahan, T., Kamil, M. L., & Tobin, A. W. (1982). Cloze as a measure of intersentential comprehension. *Reading Research Quarterly, 17*, 229–255. doi:10.2307/747485

Shaoul, C., & Westbury, C. (2006). Word frequency effects in high-dimensional co-occurrence models: A new approach. *Behavior Research Methods, 38*, 190–195. doi:10.3758/BF03192768

Shaoul, C., & Westbury, C. (in press). Exploring lexical co-occurrence space using HiDEx. Accepted for publication in. *Behavior Research Methods*.

Shaoul, C., & Westbury, C. (in press). HiDEx: The high dimensional explorer. In McCarthy, P. M., & Boonthum, C. (Eds.), *Applied natural language processing: Identification, investigation, and resolution*. Hershey, PA: IGI Global.

Shaoul, C., & Westbury, C. (2007). *Usenet orthographic frequencies for the 40,481 words in the English lexicon project* (Tech. Rep.). Edmonton, Canada: University of Alberta. Retrieved from http://www.psych.ualberta.ca/~westburylab/downloads.html.

Shaoul, C., & Westbury, C. (2008). *HiDEx: The high dimensional explorer.* Edmonton, AB. Retrieved from http://www.psych.ualberta.ca/~westburylab/downloads.html.

Shaoul, C., & Westbury, C. (2009). *A Usenet corpus (2005-2009)* (Tech. Rep.). Edmonton, Canada: University of Alberta. Retrieved from http://www.psych.ualberta.ca/~westburylab/downloads.html.

Sharp, D. B. (2007). *Learn to write.* ISA Career website. Retrieved from http://www.isa.org/Template.cfm?Section=Careers&Template=/ContentManagement/ContentDisplay.cfm&ContentID=5328.

Shaughnessy, M. P. (1977). *Errors and expectations: A guide for the teacher of basic writing.* New York, NY: Oxford University Press.

Shaw, R., & Kitzinger, C. (2005). Calls to a home birth helpline: Empowerment in childbirth. *Social Science & Medicine, 61*(11), 2374–2383. doi:10.1016/j.socscimed.2005.04.029

Shaw, R., & Kitzinger, C. (2007). Problem presentation and advice-giving on a home birth helpline: A feminist conversation analytic study. *Feminism & Psychology, 17,* 203–213. doi:10.1177/0959353507076553

Shaw, P., & Liu, E. T.-K. (1998). What develops in the development of second-language writing? *Applied Linguistics, 19*(2), 225–254. doi:10.1093/applin/19.2.224

Sheldon, A. (1990). Pickle fights: Gendered talk in preschool disputes. *Discourse Processes, 13,* 5–31. doi:10.1080/01638539009544745

Shen, L., Satta, G., & Joshi, A. (2007). Guided learning for bidirectional sequence classification. In *Proceedings of the 45th Annual Meeting of the Association of Computational Linguistics (ACL 2007),* (pp. 760–767).

Shermis, M., & Burstein, J. (2003). *Automated essay scoring: A cross-disciplinary perspective.* Mahwah, NJ: Erlbaum.

Shiu, E., & Lenhart, A. (2004). How Americans use instant messaging. Retrieved October 14, 2005, from http://www.pewinternet.org/pdfs/PIP_Instantmessage_Report.pdf.

Shortliffe, E. H. (1987). Computer programs to support clinical decision making. *Journal of the American Medical Association, 258,* 61–66. doi:10.1001/jama.258.1.61

Shriberg, E., Dhillon, R., Bhagat, S., Ang, J., & Carvey, H. (2004). The ICSI Meeting Recorder Dialog Act (MRDA) corpus. In *Proceedings of the 5th SIGdial Workshop on Discourse and Dialogue at HLT-NAACL 2004* (pp. 97–100). April 30 – May 1, Cambridge, MA.

Siakaluk, P. D., Buchanan, L., & Westbury, C. (2003). The effect of semantic distance in yes/no and go/no-go semantic categorization tasks. *Memory & Cognition, 31,* 100–113. doi:10.3758/BF03196086

Silberztein, M. D. (1997). The lexical analysis of natural languages. In Roche, E., & Schabes, Y. (Eds.), *Finite-state language processing* (pp. 175–204). MIT Press.

Sillars, A., Shellen, W., McIntosh, A., & Pomegranate, M. (1997). Relational characteristics of language: Elaboration and differentiation in marital conversations. *Western Journal of Communication, 61,* 403–422. doi:10.1080/10570319709374587

Simmons, R. A., Gordon, P. C., & Chambless, D. L. (2005). Pronouns in marital interaction: What do you and I say about marital health? *Psychological Science, 16,* 932–936. doi:10.1111/j.1467-9280.2005.01639.x

Sinclair, J., & Coulthard, M. (1975). *Toward an analysis of discourse: The English used by teachers and pupils.* Oxford, UK: Oxford University Press.

Singer, M., & Leon, J. (2007). Psychological studies of higher language processes: Behavioral and empirical approaches. In Schmalhofer, F., & Perfetti, C. (Eds.), *Higher level language processes in the brain: Inference and comprehension processes.* Mahwah, NJ.

Sjöbergh, J., & Kann, V. (2004). Finding the correct interpretation of Swedish compounds a statistical approach. In [Lisbon, Portugal.]. *Proceedings of Language Resources and Evaluation, 2004,* 899–902.

Sjöbergh, J., & Knutsson, O. (2005). Faking errors to avoid making errors: Machine learning for error detection in writing. In *Proceedings of RANLP 2005*, Borovets, Bulgaria, (pp. 506-512).

Slatcher, R. B., Chung, C. K., Pennebaker, J. W., & Handelman, L. D. (2007). Winning words: Individual differences in linguistic style among U.S. presidential and vice presidential candidates. *Journal of Research in Personality, 41*, 63–75. doi:10.1016/j.jrp.2006.01.006

Slatcher, R. B., & Pennebaker, J. W. (2006). How do I love thee? Let me count the words: The social effects of expressive writing. *Psychological Science, 17*, 660–664. doi:10.1111/j.1467-9280.2006.01762.x

Sleeman, D., & Brown, J. S. (Eds.). (1982). *Intelligent tutoring systems*. Orlando, FL: Academic Press, Inc.

Smith, L., & Nelson, C. (1985). International intelligibility of English: Directions and resources. *World Englishes, 4*, 333–342. doi:10.1111/j.1467-971X.1985.tb00423.x

Smith, D. A., & Crane, G. (2001). Disambiguating geographic names in a historical digital library. In *Research and Advanced Technology for Digital Libraries. Lecture Notes in Computer Science, 2163*, 127–137. doi:10.1007/3-540-44796-2_12

Song, D., Bruza, P., Huang, Z., & Lau, R. Y. (2003). Classifying document titles based on information inference. In Carbonell, J. G., & Siekmann, J. (Eds.), *Foundations of intelligent systems* (pp. 297–306). Berlin, Germany: Springer. doi:10.1007/978-3-540-39592-8_41

Song, D., & Bruza, P. D. (2001). *Discovering information flow using a high dimensional conceptual space.* The 24th Annual International ACM SIGIR Conference on Research and Development in Information Retrieval (New Orleans, LO).

Song, D., Bruza, P., & Cole, R. (2004). *Concept learning and information inferencing on a high-dimensional semantic space.* ACM SIGIR 2004 Workshop on Mathematical/Formal Methods in Information Retrieval (MF/IR'2004), 30 July 2004, Sheffield UK.

Soudi, A., Cavalli-Sforza, V., & Jamari, A. (2001). A Computational Lexeme-based Treatment of Arabic Morphology. In *Proceedings of the Workshop on Arabic Language Processing: Status and Prospects,* (ACL 2001), Toulouse, France, (pp. 155-162).

Spärck-Jones, K. (1972). A statistical interpretation of term specificity and its application in retrieval. *The Journal of Documentation, 28*, 11–21. doi:10.1108/eb026526

Spärck-Jones, K. (1990). *Retrieving information or answering questions? British library annual research lecture.* London, UK: British Library.

Stallman, R. (2009). *GNU general public license.* Cambridge, MA. Retrieved from http://www.fsf.org/licensing/.

Stanfill, C., & Waltz, D. (1986). Toward memory-based reasoning. *Communications of the ACM, 29*(12), 1213–1228. doi:10.1145/7902.7906

Stav, A. (2006). Shallow parsing. In *Seminar in Natural Language Processing and Computational Linguistics.* Tel Aviv Univ. Retrieved December 10, 2008, from http://www.cs.tau.ac.il/~nachumd/NLP/shallow-parsing.pdf.

Steedman, M. (2000). Information structure and the syntax-phonology interface. *Linguistic Inquiry, 34*, 649–689. doi:10.1162/002438900554505

Stein, B., & Eissen, M. (2008). Retrieval models for genre classification. *Scandinavian Journal of Information Systems, 20*(1).

Stenner, A. J., Burdick, H., Sanford, E. E., & Burdick, D. S. (2006). How accurate are Lexile text measures? *Journal of Applied Measurement, 7*(3), 307–322.

Stirman, S. W., & Pennebaker, J. W. (2001). Word use in the poetry of suicidal and non-suicidal poets. *Psychosomatic Medicine, 63*, 517–522.

Stokoe, E., & Edwards, D. (2008). Did you have permission to smash your neighbour's door? Silly questions and their answers in police suspect interrogations. *Discourse Studies, 10*(1), 89–111. doi:10.1177/1461445607085592

Stokoe, C., Oakes, M. P., & Tait, J. (2003). Word sense disambiguation in information retrieval revisited. In *Proceedings of the 26th Annual International ACM SIGIR Conference on Research and Development in Information Retrieval* (p. 166).

Stolcke, A., Coccaro, N., Bates, R., Taylor, P., Ess-Dykema, C. V., & Ries, K. (2000). Dialogue act modeling for automatic tagging and recognition of conversational speech. *Computational Linguistics, 26*(3), 339–373. doi:10.1162/089120100561737

Stone, L. D., & Pennebaker, J. W. (2002). Trauma in real time: Talking and avoiding online conversations about the death of Princess Diana. *Basic and Applied Social Psychology*, *24*, 172–182.

Stone, P. J., Dunphy, D. C., Smith, M. S., & Ogilvie, D. M. (1966). *The general inquirer: A computer approach to content analysis*. Cambridge, MA: MIT Press.

Stone, L. D., & Pennebaker, J. W. (2004). What was she trying to say? A linguistic analysis of Katie's diaries. In Lester, D. (Ed.), *Katie's diary: Unlocking the mystery of a suicide*. London, UK: Taylor & Francis.

Strube, M., & Hahn, U. (1999). Functional centering: Grounding referential coherence in information structure. *Computational Linguistics*, *25*, 309–344.

Strube, M. (1998). Never look back: An alternative to centering. In C. Boitet & P. Whitelock (Eds.), *Proceedings of the 17th International Conference on Computational Linguistics* (pp. 1251-1257). Morristown, NJ: Association for Computational Linguistics.

Swade, D. (2002). *The difference engine: Charles Babbage and the quest to build the first computer*. Penguin.

Swain, M., & Lampkin, S. (1998). Interaction and second language learning: Two adolescent French immersion students working together. *Modern Language Journal*, *82*, 320–337.

Swain, M. (1995). Three functions of output in second language learning. In Cook, G., & Seidlhofer, B. (Eds.), *Principle and practice in applied linguistics: Studies in honour of H. G. Widdowson* (pp. 125–144). Oxford, UK: Oxford University Press.

Swain, M. (1985). Communicative competence: Some roles of comprehensible input and comprehensible output in its development. In Gass, S., & Madden, C. (Eds.), *Input in second language acquisition* (pp. 235–253). Rowley, MA: Newbury House.

Swales, J. M. (1990). *Genre analysis: English in academic and research settings*. Cambridge, UK: Cambridge University Press.

Tabachnick, B. G., & Fidell, L. S. (2001). *Using multivariate statistics* (4th ed.). Boston, MA: Allyn and Bacon.

Tannen, D. (1993). The relativity of linguistic strategies: Rethinking power and solidarity in gender and dominance. In Tannen, D. (Ed.), *Gender and conversational interaction*. New York, NY: Oxford University Press.

Tausczik, Y. R., Faase, K., Pennebaker, J. W., & Petrie, K. J. (in press). Public anxiety and information seeking following H1N1 outbreak: Weblogs, newspaper articles and Wikipedia visits. *Health Communication*.

Tausczik, Y. R., & Pennebaker, J. W. (2010). The psychological meaning of words: LIWC and computerized text analysis methods. *Journal of Language and Social Psychology*, *29*, 24–54. doi:10.1177/0261927X09351676

Tausczik, Y. R. (2009). *Linguistic analysis of workplace computer-mediated communication*. Unpublished Master's thesis. Austin, TX: The University of Texas at Austin.

Taylor, P., King, S., Isard, S., & Wright, H. (1998). Intonation and dialogue context as constraints for speech recognition. *Language and Speech*, *41*, 489–508.

Taylor, J. M., Hempelmann, C. F., & Raskin, V. (2010). On an automatic acquisition toolbox for ontologies and lexicons. In *Proceeding of ICAI'10*, Las Vegas, USA, July 2010.

Taylor, J. M., Raskin, V., Petrenko, M. S., & Hempelmann, C. F. (2010). *Multiple noun expression analysis. An implementation of ontological semantic theory*. Paper accepted at Computational Linguistics - Applications Workshop of the International Multiconference on Computer Science and Information Technology in Wisła, Poland, October 18-20, 2010.

Ten Have, P. (2007). *Doing conversation analysis: A practical guide* (2nd ed.). London, UK: Sage.

Ter Meulen, A. G. B. (1995). *Representing time in natural language: The dynamic interpretation of tense and aspect*. Cambridge, MA: MIT Press.

Terwilleger, B., & McCarthy, P. M. (in press). Bias in hard news articles from Fox News and MSNBC: An empirical assessment using the Gramulator. In C. Murray & P. M. McCarthy (Eds.), *Proceedings of the 24rd International Florida Artificial Intelligence Research Society Conference* (p. xx). Menlo Park, CA: The AAAI Press. Danby, S., & Emmison, M. (in press). Kids, counsellors and troubles-telling: morality-in-action in talk on an Australian children's helpline. In J. Cromdal & M. Tholander, Eds., *Children, morality and interaction*. New York, NY: Nova Science.

Thabtah, F. A. (2007). A review of association classification mining. *The Knowledge Engineering Review, 22*(1), 37–65. doi:10.1017/S0269888907001026

The College Board. (2005-2008). *SAT essay prompts.* Retrieved from http://www.onlinemathlearning.com/sat-test-prep.html.

Thoma, M., Cheng, H., Gretton, A., Han, J., Kriegel, H. P., & Smola, A. … Borgwardt, K. (2009). *Near-optimal supervised feature selection among frequent subgraphs.* In SIAM Intl Conf. on Data Mining.

Toglia, M. P., & Battig, W. F. (1978). *Handbook of semantic word norms.* New York, NY: Lawrence Erlbaum Associates.

Trabasso, T., & Bartolone, J. (2003). Story understanding and counterfactual reasoning. *Journal of Experimental Psychology. Learning, Memory, and Cognition, 29*, 904–923. doi:10.1037/0278-7393.29.5.904

Trappes-Lomax, H. (2004). Discourse analysis. In Davies & C. Elder (Eds.), *The handbook of applied linguistics,* (pp. 133–164). Oxford, UK: Blackwell.

Tschichold, C. (2003). Lexically driven error detection and correction. *CALICO Journal, 20*(3), 549–559.

Upton, T., & Connor, U. (2001). Using computerised corpus analysis to investigate the textlinguistic discourse moves of a genre. *English for Specific Purposes, 20*(4), 313–329. doi:10.1016/S0889-4906(00)00022-3

van Deemter, K., & Kibble, R. (2000). On coreferring: Coreference in MUC and related annotation schemes. *Computational Linguistics, 26*, 629–637. doi:10.1162/089120100750105966

Van der Meij, H. (1994). Student questioning: A componential analysis. *Learning and Individual Differences, 6*, 137–161. doi:10.1016/1041-6080(94)90007-8

van Dijk, T. A., & Kintsch, W. (1983). *Strategies of discourse comprehension.* New York, NY: Academic.

Van Dijk, T. (1983). *La ciencia del texto. Un enfoque interdisciplinario.* Buenos Aires, Argentina: Paidos.

Van Dijk, T. A. (2001). Critical discourse analysis. In Tannen, D., Schiffrin, D., & Hamilton, H. E. (Eds.), *The handbook of discourse analysis* (pp. 352–371). Oxford, UK: Blackwell.

van Donzel, M. E. (1994). How to specify focus without using acoustic features. *Proceedings of the Institute of Phonetic Sciences* (pp. 1-17). Amsterdam, The Netherlands: University of Amsterdam.

van Geert, P., & van Dijk, M. (2002). Focus on variability: New tools to study intra-individual variability in developmental data. *Infant Behavior and Development, 25*, 340–374. doi:10.1016/S0163-6383(02)00140-6

Van Kleek, M., André, P., Perttunen, M., Bernstein, M., Karger, D., Miller, R., & Schraefel, M. C. (2008). Personal reactive automation for the Web, In *Proceedings of the Annual ACM Symposium on User Interface Software and Technology.*

van Lent, M., & Laird, J. (2001). *Learning procedural knowledge through observation.* In International Conference on Knowledge Capture.

van Petten, C., & Kutas, M. (1991). Influences of semantic and syntactic context on open- and closed-class words. *Memory & Cognition, 19*, 95–112. doi:10.3758/BF03198500

vanLehn, K., Graesser, A. C., Jackson, G. T., Jordan, P., Olney, A., & Rose, C. P. (2007). When are tutorial dialogues more effective than reading? *Cognitive Science, 31*, 3–62. doi:10.1080/03640210709336984

VanLehn, K. (2006). The behavior of tutoring systems. *International Journal of Artificial Intelligence in Education, 16*(3), 227–265.

VanLehn, K., Graesser, A. C., Jackson, G. T., Jordan, P., Olney, A., & Rose, C. P. (2007). When are tutorial dialogues more effective than reading? *Cognitive Science, 31*, 3–62. doi:10.1080/03640210709336984

VanLehn, K., Jordan, P., Rosé, C. P., et al. (2002). The architecture of Why2-Atlas: A coach for qualitative physics essay writing. In S. A. Cerri, G. Gouarderes, & F. Paraguacu (Eds.), *Intelligent Tutoring Systems: 6th International Conference* (pp. 158-167). Berlin, Germany: Springer.

Vapnik, V. (1995). *The nature of statistical learning theory.* Spring, New York.

Varonis, E., & Gass, S. (1983). *Target language input from non-native speakers.* Paper presented at the 17th Annual TESOL Convention, Toronto, March 1983.

Veenstra, J., & Buchholz, S. (1998). Fast NP chunking using memory-based learning techniques. In F. Verdenius & van den Broek (Eds.), *Proc. of Benelearn '98* (pp. 71-78). Wageningen, The Netherlands.

Venegas, R. (2006a). La similitud léxico-semántica en artículos de investigación científica en español: Una aproximación desde el Análisis Semántico Latente. *Revista Signos, 39*(60), 75–106.

Venegas, R. (2006b). *Comparación de la evaluación realizada por docentes y por el análisis semántico latente.* Research Report. Pontificia Universidad Católica de Valparaíso.

Venegas, R. (2007). Using latent semantic analysis in a Spanish research article corpus. In Parodi, G. (Ed.), *Working with Spanish corpora* (pp. 195–216). London, UK: Continuum.

Venegas, R. (2005). *Las relaciones léxico-semánticas en artículos de investigación científica: Una aproximación desde el análisis semántico latente.* Ph.D. thesis, Pontificia Universidad Católica de Valparaíso, Valparaíso, Chile.

Venegas, R. (2009a). Towards a method for assessing summaries in Spanish using LSA. In H. C. Lane & H. W. Guesgen (Eds.), *Proceedings of the Twenty-Second International Florida Artificial Intelligence Research Society Conference* (pp. 113-115). Washington, DC: AAAI.

Venegas, R. (2009b). Informe de Investigación Final Fondecyt N° 11070225. *Evaluación de resúmenes en español: Correspondencia entre profesores y el análisis semántico latente.*

Venkataraman, A., Ferrer, L., Stolcke, A., & Shriberg, E. (2003). Training a prosody-based dialog act tagger from unlabeled data. In *Proceedings of the IEEE International Conference on Acoustics, Speech, and Signal Processing (ICASSP '03)*, vol. 1, (pp. 272–275).

Venkataraman, A., Stolcke, A., & Shriberg, E. (2002). Automatic dialog act labeling with minimal supervision. In *Proceedings of the 9th Australian International Conference on Speech Science & Technology.* 2–5 December, Melbourne, Australia.

Veronis, J. (1988). Morphosyntactic correction in natural language interfaces. In *Proceedings of the 12th International Conference in Computational Linguistics*, (pp. 708-713).

Verspoor, M., Lowie, W., & van Dijk, M. (2008). Variability in second language development from a dynamic systems perspective. *Modern Language Journal, 92*(2), 214–231. doi:10.1111/j.1540-4781.2008.00715.x

Vickrey, D., Biewald, L., Teyssier, M., & Koller, D. (2005). Word-sense disambiguation for machine translation. In *Proceedings of HLT/EMNLP,* vol. 5.

Vieira, R., & Poesio, M. (2000). An empirically based system for processing definite descriptions. *Computational Linguistics, 26,* 539–593. doi:10.1162/089120100750105948

Volz, R., Kleb, J., & Mueller, W. (2007). *Towards ontology-based disambiguation of geographical identifiers.* In The 16th International World Wide Web Conference, Banff, Alberta, Canada.

Voorhees, E. (1994). Query expansion using lexical-semantic elations. In *Proceedings of the 17th SIGIR Conference*, Dublin, Ireland, (June, 1994).

Voorhees, E. M. (1993) Using WordNet to disambiguate word senses for text retrieval. In *Proc. of the 16th Annual International ACM SIGIR Conference on Research and Development in Information Retrieval,* Pittsburgh, PA, USA, (pp. 171-180).

Voorhees, E. M., & Tice, D. M. (2000). The TREC-8 question answering track evaluation. In E.M. Voorhees & D. K. Harman, (Eds.), *Proceedings of the Eighth Text REtrieval Conference* (TREC-8). Retrieved from http://trec.nist.gov/pubs.htrul.

Vygotsky, L. S. (1978). Interaction between learning and development. In Cole, M., John-Steiner, V., Scribner, S., & Souberman, E. (Eds.), *Mind in society: The development of higher psychological processes* (pp. 79–91). (Lopez-Morillas, M., Trans.). Cambridge, MA: Harvard University Press.

Wade-Stein, D., & Kintsch, E. (2004). Summary Street: Computer support for writing. *Cognition and Instruction, 22*(3), 333–362. doi:10.1207/s1532690xci2203_3

Wade-Stein, D., & Kintsch, E. (2004). Summary street: Interactive computer support for writing. *Cognition and Instruction, 22,* 333–362. doi:10.1207/s1532690xci2203_3

Wagner, R. A., & Fischer, M. J. (1974). The string to string correction problem. *Journal of the Association for Computing Machinery, 21*(1), 168–173.

Wagner, J., Foster, J., & Genabith, J. V. (2007). A comparative evaluation of deep and shallow approaches to the automatic detection of common grammatical errors. In *Proceedings of EMNLP-CoNLL 2007*, Prague, Czeck Republic, (pp. 112-121).

Waltz, D. L. (1978). An English language question answering system for a large relational database. *Communications of the ACM*, *21*(7), 526–539. doi:10.1145/359545.359550

Warnke, V., Kompe, R., Niemann, H., & Nöth, E. (1997). Integrated dialog act segmentation and classification using prosodic features and language models. In G. Kokkinakis, N. Fakotakis, & E. Dermatas, (Eds.), *Proceedings of the 5th European Conference on Speech Communication and Technology*, volume 1, (pp. 207–210). Rhodes, Greece, September.

Webb, N., Hepple, M., & Wilks, Y. (2005). Dialogue act classification based on intra-utterance features. In *Proceedings of the AAAI Workshop on Spoken Language Understanding*, 9–10 July, Pittsburgh, PA.

Weigle, S. C. (2006). Investing in assessment: Designing tests to promote positive washback. In Matsuda, P. K., Ortmeier-Hooper, C., & You, X. (Eds.), *The politics of second language writing: In search of the promised land* (pp. 222–244). West Lafayette, IN: Parlor.

Weintraub, W. (1989). *Verbal behavior in everyday life.* New York, NY: Springer.

West, C., & Zimmerman, D. (1983). Small insults: A study of interruptions in cross-sex conversations between unacquainted persons. In Thorne, B., Kramarae, C., & Henley, N. (Eds.), *Language, gender and society*. Rowley, MA: Newbury House.

Weston, J., Crossley, S., & McNamara, D. S. (in press). Computationally assessing human judgments of freewriting quality. In McCarthy, P. M., & Boonthum, C. (Eds.), *Applied natural language processing: Identification, investigation, and resolution*. Hershey, PA: IGI Global.

Weston, J., Crossley, S. A., & McNamara, D. S. (in press). Differences in freewriting quality: Perspectives, approaches, and applications. In McCarthy, P. M., & Boonthum, C. (Eds.), *Applied natural language processing and content analysis: Identification, investigation, and resolution*. Hershey, PA: IGI Global.

Weston, J. L., Crossley, S. A., & McNamara, D. S. (2010). Towards a computational assessment of freewriting quality. In H. W. Guesgen & C. Murray (Eds.), *Proceedings of the 23rd International Florida Artificial Intelligence Research Society.* Menlo Park, CA: The AAAI Press.

Wetherell, M. (2001). Themes in discourse research: The case of Diana. In Wetherell, M., Taylor, S., & Yates, S. J. (Eds.), *Discourse theory and practice: A reader* (pp. 14–28). London, UK: Sage.

Whitten, I. A., & Frank, E. (2005). *Data mining*. San Francisco, CA: Elsevier.

Widdows, D., Peters, S., Cederberg, S., Chan, C. K., & Steffen, D. (2003). Unsupervised monolingual and bilingual word-sense disambiguation of medical documents using UMLS. In *Proceedings of the ACL 2003 Workshop on Natural Language Processing in Biomedicine*, volume 13, (pp. 9–16).

Wiemer-Hastings, P. (2000). Adding syntactic information to LSA. In *Proceedings of the 22nd Annual Conference of the Cognitive Science Society*, (pp. 988-993). Mawwhah, NJ: Erlbaum.

Wiggins, S. (2004a). Good for you: Generic and individual healthy eating advice in family mealtimes. *Journal of Health Psychology*, *9*(4), 535–548. doi:10.1177/1359105304044037

Wiggins, S. (2004b). Talking about taste: Using a discursive psychological approach to examine challenges to food evaluation. *Appetite*, *43*, 29–38. doi:10.1016/j.appet.2004.01.007

Wiggins, S., & Potter, J. (2003). Attitudes and evaluative practices: Category vs. item and subjective vs. objective construction in everyday food assessments. *The British Journal of Social Psychology*, *513*, 531.

Wilks, Y., & Brewster, C. (2006). Natural language processing as a foundation of the Semantic Web. *Foundations in Web Science*, *1*(3-4), 199–327.

Wilks, Y., Fass, D., Guo, C., MacDonald, J., Plate, T., & Slator, B. (1990). *Providing machine tractable dictionary tools*. MIT Press.

Wilks, Y. (2005). Unhappy bedfellows: The relationship of AI and IR. In Tait, J. I. (Ed.), *Charting a new course: Natural language processing and information retrieval. Essays in honour of Karen Spärck Jones* (pp. 255–282). Berlin, Germany: Springer. doi:10.1007/1-4020-3467-9_14

Wilks, Y. (1965). *The application of CRLU's method of semantic analysis to information retrieval.* Cambridge Research Unit Memo ML 173.

Willett, J. B. (1994). Measurement of change. In Husen, T., & Postlethwaite, T. N. (Eds.), *The international encyclopedia of education* (2nd ed., pp. 671–678). Oxford, UK: Pergamon.

Wilson, M. D. (1988). The MRC psycholinguistic database: Machine readable dictionary, version 2. *Behavior Research Methods, Instruments, & Computers, 201*, 6–11. doi:10.3758/BF03202594

Winne, P., & Hadwin, A. (2008). The weave of motivation and self-regulated learning. In Schunk, D., & Zimmerman, B. (Eds.), *Motivation and self-regulated learning: Theory, research, and applications* (pp. 297–314). Mahwah, NJ: Erlbaum.

Wirth, R., & Hipp, J. (2000). CRISP-DM: Towards a standard process model for data mining. In *Proceedings of the 4th International Conference on the Practical Application of Knowledge Discovery and Data Mining* (pp. 29–39). Morgan Kaufmann.

Witmore, M., & Hope, J. (2007). Shakespeare by the numbers: On the linguistic texture of the late plays. In Mukherji, S., & Lyne, R. (Eds.), *Early modern tragicomedy* (pp. 133–153). Cambridge, UK: D.S. Brewer.

Witte, S., & Faigley, L. (1981). Coherence, cohesion, and writing quality. *College Composition and Communication, 32*, 189–204. doi:10.2307/356693

Wodak, R. (2006). Mediation between discourse and society: Assessing cognitive approaches in CDA. *Discourse Studies, 8*, 179–190. doi:10.1177/1461445606059566

Wolf, M., Chung, C. K., & Kordy, H. (2010a). Inpatient treatment to online aftercare: E-mailing themes as a function of therapeutic outcomes. *Psychotherapy Research, 20*, 71–85. doi:10.1080/10503300903179799

Wolf, M., Chung, C. K., & Kordy, H. (2010b). MEM's search for meaning: A rejoinder. *Psychotherapy Research, 20*, 93–99. doi:10.1080/10503300903527393

Wolf, M., Horn, A. B., Mehl, M. R., Haug, S., Pennebaker, J. W., & Kordy, H. (2008). Computergestützte quantitative Textanalyse: Äquivalenz und Robustheit der deutschen Version des Linguistic Inquiry and Word Count [Computer-aided quantitative text analysis: Equivalence and robustness of the German adaption of the Linguistic Inquiry and Word Count]. *Diagnostica, 54*, 85–98. doi:10.1026/0012-1924.54.2.85

Wolfe-Quintero, K., Inagaki, S., & Kim, H.-Y. (1998). *Second language development in writing: Measures of fluency, accuracy & complexity.* Honolulu, HI: Second Language Teaching & Curriculum Center, University of Hawaii at Manoa.

Wood, L. A., & Kroger, R. O. (2000). *Doing discourse analysis: Methods for studying action in talk and text.* London, UK: Sage.

Woods, W. A., Kaplan, R. M., & Webber, B. N. (1972). *The lunar sciences natural language Information System: Final report. BBN Report 2378.* Cambridge, MA: Bolt Beranek and Newman, Inc.

Woofitt, R. (2005). *Conversation analysis and discourse analysis: A comparative and critical introduction.* London, UK: Sage.

Woolf, B. P. (2009). *Building intelligent interactive tutors.* Burlington, MA: Elsevier.

Woszczyna, M., & Waibel, A. (1994). Inferring linguistic structure in spoken language. In *Proceedings of the International Conference on Spoken Language Processing,* volume 2, (pp. 847–850). 18–22 September, Yokohama.

Wray, A., & Perkins, M. (2000). The functions of formulaic language: An integrated model. *Language & Communication, 20*, 1–28. doi:10.1016/S0271-5309(99)00015-4

Wright, W. (1967). *A grammar of the Arabic language* (3rd ed.). Cambridge University Press.

Xu, J., & Croft, B. (1998). Corpus-based stemming using co-occurrence of word variants. *ACM Transactions on Information Systems, 16*(1), 61–81. doi:10.1145/267954.267957

Xu, H., Markatou, M., Dimova, R., Liu, H., & Friedman, C. (2006). Machine learning and word sense disambiguation in the biomedical domain: Design and evaluation issues. *BMC Bioinformatics*, *7*, 334. doi:10.1186/1471-2105-7-334

Yan, X., & Han, J. (2002). gSpan: Graph-based substructure pattern mining. In *Proceedings of the 2002 IEEE International Conference on Data Mining (ICDM'02)*, (p. 721).

Yan, X., & Han, J. (2003). CloseGraph: Mining closed frequent graph patterns. In *Proceedings of the Ninth ACM SIGKDD International Conference on Knowledge Discovery and Data Mining*, (pp. 286–295).

Yarowsky, D. (1995). Unsupervised word sense disambiguation rivaling supervised methods. In *Proceedings of the 33rd Annual Meeting on Association for Computational Linguistics* (pp. 189–196).

Yates, M., Locker, L., & Simpson, G. B. (2003). Semantic and phonological influences on the processing of words and pseudohomophones. *Memory & Cognition*, *31*, 856–866. doi:10.3758/BF03196440

Zavrel, J., & Daelemans, W. (1997). Memory-based learning: Using similarity for smoothing. *Proc. 35th Annual Meeting of the Assoc. for Computational Linguistics (ACL-97)* (pp. 436-43). Madrid, Spain.

Zhang, Y., & Patrick, J. (2005). Paraphrase identification by text canonicalization. *In Proceedings of the Australasian Language Technology Workshop.*

Zhou, L., Burgoon, J. K., Twitchell, D., Qin, T., & Nunamaker, J. F. (2004). A comparison of classification methods for predicting deception in computer-mediated communication. *Journal of Management Information Systems*, *20*, 139–165.

Zimmerman, B. (2006). Development and adaptation of expertise: The role of self-regulatory processes and beliefs. In Ericsson, K., Charness, N., Feltovich, P., & Hoffman, R. (Eds.), *The Cambridge handbook of expertise and expert performance* (pp. 705–722). New York, NY: Cambridge University Press.

Zimmerman, B. J., & Risemberg, R. (1997). Self-regulatory dimensions of academic learning and motivation. In Phye, G. D. (Ed.), *Handbook of academic learning: Construction of knowledge* (pp. 105–125). New York, NY: Academic Press. doi:10.1016/B978-012554255-5/50005-3

Zimmerman, D., & West, C. (1975). Sex roles, interruptions and silences in conversation. In Thorne, B., & Henly, N. (Eds.), *Language and sex: Difference and dominance*. Rowley, MA: Newbury House.

Zipf, G. K. (1935). *The psychobiology of language*. New York, NY: Houghton-Mifflin.

Zipf, G. K. (1949). *Human behaviour and the principle of least-effort*. New York, NY: Addison-Wesley.

Zipitria, I., Elorriaga, J., Arruate, A., & de Ilarraza, A. (2004). *From human to automatic summary evaluation*. In Seventh International Conference on Intelligent Tutoring System. Maceió, Brazil.

Zwaan, R. A., & Radvansky, G. A. (1998). Situation models in language comprehension and memory. *Psychological Bulletin*, *123*, 162–185. doi:10.1037/0033-2909.123.2.162

Zwaan, R. A. (1993). *Aspects of literary comprehension*. Amsterdam, The Netherlands: John Benjamins.

Zwaan, R. A., Magliano, J. P., & Graesser, A. C. (1995). Dimensions of situations model construction in narrative comprehension. *Journal of Experimental Psychology. Learning, Memory, and Cognition*, *21*, 386–397. doi:10.1037/0278-7393.21.2.386

Zwaan, R. A., & Radvansky, G. A. (1998). Situation models in language comprehension and memory. *Psychological Bulletin*, *123*, 162–185. doi:10.1037/0033-2909.123.2.162

About the Contributors

Philip M. McCarthy is an Assistant Professor at The University of Memphis. He is also a member of the Institute for Intelligent Systems. His research is in the field of Applied Natural Language Processing (ANLP). His primary interest is devising algorithms for *contrastive corpus analyses*, particularly where such algorithms can be informative of the relationship between language, the mind, and the world.

Chutima Boonthum-Denecke is an Assistant Professor in the Department of Computer Science at Hampton University. Dr. Boonthum-Denecke earned her Ph.D. in Computer Science from Old Dominion in 2007; MS in Applied Computer Science from Illinois State University in 2000; and BS in Computer Science from Srinakharinwirot University in 1997. Dr. Boonthum-Denecke has been involved in several NSF-funded Broadening Participation in Computing (BPC) programs: ARTSI (Advancing Robotics Technology for Societal Impact) and STARS (Students and Technology in Academia, Research and Service) Alliances. She is also a faculty member of the Hampton University Information Assurance group. Dr. Boonthum-Denecke's research interests include artificial intelligence (natural language processing, computational linguistics), information retrieval, Web development technology, and cognitive robotics.

***

Nawaf Albadia works as a System Architect at General Organization for Social Insurance, Saudi Arabia. He is specialized in interoperability between heterogeneous systems, SOA design patterns, and enterprise systems development. He received his Master's Degree in Computer Science from King Saud. His research interests include data mining, text processing, and interoperability.

James Allen is Associate Director of the Institute for Human and Machine Cognition in Pensacola Florida. He also is the John H. Dessauer Professor of Computer Science at the University of Rochester. He received his PhD in Computer Science from the University of Toronto and was a recipient of the Presidential Young Investigator award from NSF in 1984. A Founding Fellow of the American Association for Artificial Intelligence (AAAI), he was editor-in-chief of the journal *Computational Linguistics* from 1983-1993. Over the past twenty-five years, he has been the principle investigator of research grants totaling over $30 million from agencies including DARPA, ONR, and NSF. He was general chair of the Second International Conference on Principles of Knowledge Representation held in Boston in 1991, and the Fourth Int'l. Conference on AI Planning Systems in Pittsburgh in 1999. He has authored numerous research papers in the areas natural language understanding, knowledge representation and reasoning, and spoken dialogue systems. His paper "Maintaining Knowledge About Temporal Intervals" (CACM, 1983) is regularly included in lists of the most-cited papers in Computer Science. He is the author of several books, including the influential textbook Natural Language Understanding (Benjamin

Cummings, 1987), with a second edition published in 1995. He has supervised 27 PhD dissertations and given over thirty keynote and invited plenary addresses at major conferences.

Martin Atzmueller is a Senior Researcher at the University of Kassel. He studied Computer Science at the University of Texas at Austin (USA) and at the University of Würzburg (Germany) where he completed his MSc (Diploma) in Computer Science. Martin earned his doctorate (PhD) from the University of Würzburg. He published more than 50 research papers in refereed international journals and conferences, and has been author, co-author, and co-editor of several books. His research areas include data mining, text mining, natural language processing, machine learning, web science, explanation, ubiquitous and collective intelligence, and the Social Semantic Web.

Roger Azevedo is a Professor in the Department of Educational and Counselling Psychology at McGill University. His main research area includes examining the role of cognitive, metacognitive, affective, and motivational self-regulatory processes during learning with computer-based learning environments. He is the director of the Laboratory for the Study of Metacognition and Advanced Learning Technologies (http://smartlaboratory.ca/). He has published over 100 peer-reviewed papers in the areas of educational, learning, and cognitive sciences. He serves of the editorial board of several top-tiered educational psychology and instructional science journals and is the current Associate Editor of the *Metacognition and Learning Journal*. He is a fellow of the American Psychological Association and the recipient of the prestigious Early Faculty Career Award from the National Science Foundation. Dr. Azevedo and his colleagues have designed, developed, and tested computer-based learning environments for the biological and medical sciences, including the RadTutor, CircSysWeb, and MetaTutor.

Aqil M. Azmi received his B.S.E degree from the University of Michigan, Ann Arbor in Electrical and Computer Engineering and the M.Sc and Ph.D from the University of Colorado, Boulder in EE and Computer Science respectively. Currently he is an Assistant Professor at the Dept. of Computer Science, King Saud University. His research interests include application of computers in religious studies, Arabic language processing, bioinformatics, and algorithms in general.

Kyoko Baba is Assistant Professor at Kinjo Gakuin University. She completed her Ph.D. at the Ontario Institute for Studies in Education of the University of Toronto. Her current research interests are in the learning of academic writing in a second language and complexity theory.

William de Beaumont graduated from the University of Rochester in 2006 with a B.S. in Computer Science, and clusters in Linguistics and Music Theory. Since then, he has been a Research Associate at IHMC working with James Allen on a number of projects involving natural language processing and artificial intelligence.

Cosmin Adrian Bejan is a postdoctoral researcher at the University of Southern California Institute of Creative Technologies. He received his Ph.D. degree with a specialization in natural language processing from the University of Texas at Dallas for his dissertation on "Learning Event Structures from Text." He received his M.S. and B.S. degrees in Computer Science from Alexandru Ioan Cuza University, Iasi, Romania. His research interests are in the areas of natural language processing, biomedical informatics, and machine learning with a focus on event semantics, commonsense knowledge extraction, and nonparametric Bayesian methods. Starting in June 2011, Cosmin will be working as a senior fellow in the Department of Medical Education and Biomedical Informatics at the University of Washington.

Courtney M. Bell is an instructor at Northwest Community College in Senatobia, MS, with research interests in areas that involve the application of cognitive principles to education, healthcare, and the development of expertise.

Nate Blaylock is a Research Scientist at the Florida Institute for Human and Machine Cognition (IHMC), where his is in the areas of natural language understanding, dialogue systems, and plan recognition. Before his appointment at IHMC, Nate managed two research projects as a research scientist at Cycorp, Inc., and managed the overall research efforts on a large, multi-university EU-funded research project (TALK) at Saarland University in Saarbrücken, Germany. While in Germany, Nate led a close research and system development collaboration between the university, DFKI, BMW, and Bosch, which resulted in the successful SAMMIE in-car dialogue system. Nate received a Ph.D. in Computer Science in 2005 from the University of Rochester, where his thesis dealt with modeling human-computer dialogue as collaborative problem solving, and fast machine learning algorithms to perform goal and intention recognition.

Zhiqiang Cai is a Research Assistant Professor in the Institute for Intelligent Systems at the University of Memphis. He has been a major software developer of software systems in tutoring and text analysis, including QUAID, AutoTutor, Coh-Metrix, MetaTutor, Operation ARIES!, and WPAL. He has been an author/co-author of 40 articles in journals, books, and conference proceedings.

Cindy K. Chung is a Postdoctoral Fellow in the Pennebaker Language and Health Psychology Lab in the Department of Psychology at the University of Texas at Austin. Her research examines how the words people use reflect their personality, psychological states, and social groups. Another line of research is focused on extracting patterns of word use to track topics over time, across cultures, and in multiple languages. All of her work involves the development and application of computerized text analysis tools for the social sciences.

Hercules Dalianis is an Associate Professor (docent) and Tenured Lecturer (universitetslektor) at the Department of Computer and Systems Sciences (DSV), Stockholm University. Dalianis held a three-year guest professorship at CST, University of Copenhagen during 2002-2005, founded by the Norfa, the Nordic council. Dalianis received his Ph.D in 1996. Dalianis was a Post Doc Researcher at University of Southern California/ISI in Los Angeles 1997-98. Dalianis works in the interface between industry and university and with the aim to make research results useful for society. Dalianis has specialized in the area of human language technology, to make computer to understand and process human language text, but also to make a computer to produce text automatically. Examples on applications are automatic text summarization and search engines with built in human language technology. Currently Dalianis works in the area of text mining and medical informatics focused on Electronic Patient Records.

Sidney D'Mello is presently a Research Assistant Professor in the Institute for Intelligent Systems at the University of Memphis. His primary research interests are in the affective, cognitive, and learning sciences. More specific interests include affective computing, artificial intelligence in education, human-computer interaction, speech recognition and natural language understanding, and computational models of human cognition. He has authored over 100 papers and presentations in these areas. D'Mello received his PhD. in Computer Science from the University of Memphis in 2009. He also holds a M.S. in Mathematical Sciences from the University of Memphis and a B.S. in Electrical Engineering from Christian Brothers University.

Aly Fahmy is the former Dean of the Faculty of Computers & Information (FCI), Cairo University and a Professor of Artificial Intelligence and Machine Learning. He was the Director of the first Center of Excellence in Egypt in the field of Data Mining and Computer Modeling (DMCM) in the period of 2005-2010. DMCM was a virtual research center with more than 40 researchers from universities and industry. He is currently involved in the implementation of Cairo University theses mining project to assist in the formulation of the University strategic research plan for the coming 2011 – 2015. Aly's main research areas are: data and text mining, computational linguistics, text understanding and automatic essay scoring and technologies of man- machine interface in Arabic. He authored in Arabic the book "Decision Support Systems and Intelligent Systems."

George Ferguson is a Research Scientist in the Computer Science Department at the University of Rochester in Rochester, New York. His research asks how people think about, talk about, learn about, and ultimately solve problems, and how can we build intelligent systems that work with them to help them solve those problems. Dr. Ferguson has a B.Sc. degree magna cum laude in Math and Computer Science from McGill University, an M.Sc. Degree from the University of Alberta, and M.Sc. and Ph.D. degrees in Computer Science from the University of Rochester. He has served on program committees and review panels for numerous conferences, journals, and agencies. He was Program Chair of the National Conference on Artificial Intelligence (AAAI-2004), founding chair of the AAAI Intelligent Systems Demonstrations Program, and a founding member of the University of Rochester's Center for Future Health.

Lucian Galescu has earned a PhD in Computer Science from University of Rochester and is currently a Research Scientist with the Florida Institute for Human and Machine Cognition (IHMC). His research expertise is primarily in the area of spoken language technology. Much of his work has been focused on studying language models for spoken language recognition, generation and synthesis, especially in dialogue systems. Dr. Galescu has developed techniques for rapid development of language models for new application domains, which have led to dramatic decreases in the turnaround time for dialogue systems in new application domains, as well as increases in their portability and adaptability. He has also worked on models for the recognition and pronunciation of new words and on language model adaptation to increase the accuracy of speech recognition in dialogue systems.

Max H. Garzon is a Professor of Computer Science and member of ACM, IEEE and Sigma Xi. His research interests focus on the area of interactive computation, particularly DNA computing and human-computer interaction. His main goal is to develop better understanding of the capabilities of ensembles of organic molecules (such as DNA, RNA and protein) to encode and process information. He is the co/author of over 150 books, research articles and publications in foundations of computing and biological information processing.

Art Graesser is a Professor in the Department of Psychology, an Adjunct Professor in Computer Science, and co-director of the Institute of Intelligent Systems at the University of Memphis. He and his colleagues have designed, developed, and tested software in learning, language, and discourse technologies, including AutoTutor, AutoTutor-lite, MetaTutor, GuruTutor, DeepTutor, HURA Advisor, SEEK Web Tutor, Operation ARIES!, iSTART, Writing-Pal, AutoCommunicator, Point & Query, Question Understanding Aid (QUAID), QUEST, & Coh-Metrix. In addition to publishing nearly 500 articles in journals, books, and conference proceedings, he has written two books and edited 11 books.

Martin Hassel is a Tenured Lecturer and Senior Researcher at the Department of Computer and Systems Sciences (DSV), Stockholm University, Sweden. Hassel's main expertise lies in efficient and flexible models of language use. These models have proven their mettle in an array of natural language processing and information extraction tasks. In 2007 this research resulted in the thesis "Resource Lean and Portable Automatic Text Summarization." Currently Hassel's main interest is in medical informatics, in particular modeling and mining of electronic health records from an information extraction perspective. Hassel continuously disseminates his research at international conferences and journals as well as in book chapters. Hassel also supervises Master and PhD students at Stockholm University, mainly in the field of language technology, and is as such affiliated with the Swedish National Graduate School of Language Technology (GSLT).

Christian F. Hempelmann is Director of Ontological Semantics at RiverGlass Inc. and Visiting Scholar at Purdue University, where he received his doctoral degree in 2003. Since then he was Assistant Professor at Georgia Southern University and CEO at the internet search engine hakia.com. His team at Riverglass has developed and implemented a unique natural language processing system based on ontological semantics and is currently expanding the range of its applications. In addition to his work in linguistic NLP, Christian has also published a book and numerous articles on the linguistics and psychology of humor.

Xiangen Hu is presently a Professor in the Department of Psychology at The University of Memphis. Dr. Hu received his Master (applied mathematics) from Huazhong University of Science and Technology in 1985, Master (Social Sciences) in 1991 and Ph.D. (Cognitive Sciences) in 1993 from the University of California, Irvine. He joined the University of Memphis in 1993. Dr. Hu's primary research areas include mathematical psychology, research design and statistics, and cognitive psychology. More specific research interests include General Processing Tree (GPT) models, categorical data analysis, knowledge representation, computerized tutoring, and advanced distributed learning. Dr. Hu has been a faculty member of the University of Memphis for over a decade. His research interests range from human learning and memory, computational linguistics, and artificial intelligence, to mathematical psychology, where he has published extensively. Dr. Hu has been active in the ADL Initiative from the beginning becoming one of the early advocates of SCORM (Sharable Content Object Reference Model), especially during his tenure as an R&D director at an e-Learning company in Memphis. He has developed several e-Learning applications and served as Computational Architect for several federal grants at the Institute for Intelligent Systems at The University of Memphis. In addition, Dr. Hu was (2008-2009) the President for the Society for Computers in Psychology (SCiP).

Suguru Ishizaki is an Associate Professor of Rhetoric and Communication Design in the Department of English at Carnegie Mellon University. His current research interests cover a broad range of questions surrounding the analysis of multimodal text. He also co-directs the joint Masters Program with the School of Design in Communication Planning and Information Design. Before this appointment, he worked at QUALCOMM on the research and development of mobile user interfaces. Prior to that, he was on the faculty of the School of Design at Carnegie Mellon. He is the author of *Improvisational Design: Continuous Responsive Digital Communication* (MIT Press, 2003), and a co-author of *The Power of words: Unveiling the Speaker and Writer's Hidden Craft* (Routledge 2004).

Tanner Jackson is a Postdoctoral Fellow at the University of Memphis and Institute for Intelligent Systems. His work involves the theoretical study of learning and motivation as well as the application of both pedagogical and motivational principles to educational practice. His current research focuses on the integration of game-based elements and intelligent tutoring techniques. This work combines a variety of topics including game design, natural language processing, tutorial pedagogy, and various feedback devices.

Patrick Jeuniaux is presently a Postdoctoral Researcher in the Department of Psychology at Université Laval (Québec, Canada). He received a B.A. in Psychology from Université Catholique de Louvain (Belgium) in 1999, a M.A. in Statistics from the same institution in 2000, a M.A. in artificial intelligence from Katholieke Universiteit Leuven (Belgium) in 2004 and a Ph.D. in Cognitive Psychology from University of Memphis (Tennessee, USA) in 2009. His primary research interests are the mechanisms of language processing and language learning in animals and machines.

Amy (Witherspoon) Johnson is a graduate student at the University of Memphis. She received her Bachelor's degree in 2004 and her Master of Psychology in General Psychology in 2008 from University of Memphis. She is currently working on the AutoMentor project, contributing to the development of a serious game aimed at advancing students' understanding of land sciences and systems thinking. She was also involved in the development of MetaTutor, an adaptive hypermedia system which scaffolds the use of self-regulated learning process during learning about complex science topics like the human circulatory system. Her individual research interests focus on facilitating comprehension of text and graphics through enabling the construction of co-referential connections between verbal and pictorial representations.

Hyuckchul Jung is a Research Scientist at the Florida Institute for Human and Machine Cognition (IHMC), a research institute of the Florida University System. He received his Ph.D. in Computer Science from the University of Southern California. His research interests include task learning, intelligent user interfaces, mixed-initiative interaction, decision theoretic reasoning, and human-machine teamwork. More information can be found at http://www.ihmc.us/~hjung.

David Kaufer is Professor of Rhetoric and Former Head of the Department of English. His research interests are rhetorical theory and textual analysis. He is the author of six books and over 100 articles on these topics. Among his most cited books are Communication at a Distance: The Influence of Print on Sociocultural Organization and Change (Routledge; with Kathleen Carley, 1993), and Rhetoric and the Arts of Design (Routledge, with Brian Butler, 1996). For much of the last decade he has been working on the DocuScope text analysis environment with Suguru Ishizaki (see The Power of Words: Unveiling the Speaker and Writer's Hidden Craft (Routledge, with Suguru Ishizaki, Brian Butler, Jeff Collins, 2004).

Eileen Kintsch is a Research Associate at the Institute of Cognitive Science whose interests have focused on text comprehension and learning, especially on the application of theories of comprehension to developing literacy interventions for struggling readers. Within this framework, her research has encompassed the design of computer assisted learning technology, studying how best to integrate such technology in classroom settings and how to assess learning from text.

Walter Kintsch received his PhD from the University of Kansas. He taught for most of his life at the University of Colorado in Boulder, Co, where he was professor of psychology and director of the Institute of Cognitive Science. He is now professor emeritus. He started out as a memory researcher, but specialized fairly soon in memory for text and learning from text. He was interested in modeling the psychological processes involved in text comprehension. Several decades of this work is summarized in his 1998 book "Comprehension: A paradigm for cognition." His work has had significant implications for classroom learning and teaching.

Travis A. Lamkin is a graduate student at The University of Memphis, in the Applied Linguistics program. His primary research area is Applied Natural Language Processing (ANLP). He is currently involved in the Gramulator Project. He is particularly interested in applying methods and tools, such as the Gramulator, to the studies of literary criticism and genre assessment.

Mihai Lintean is currently a Ph.D. Candidate in Computer Science at the University of Memphis and a graduate researcher in the Institute for Intelligent Systems (IIS) at the same university. He received his master and bachelor's degrees in Computer Science from Babes-Bolyai University of Cluj-Napoca, Romania. Mihai's primary research interests are in Natural Language Processing (NLP), with focused applicability on educational technologies such as intelligent tutoring systems. Particularly he is interested in measuring semantic similarity between texts, representing knowledge through relational diagrams of concepts, automatic generation of questions, and using various machine learning techniques to solve other complex NLP problems. Mihai has published numerous papers and articles in reputable, peer-reviewed conferences and journals. Currently, he serves as the co-chair of the Applied Natural Language Processing Special Track at the 24th International Conference of the Florida Artificial Intelligence Research Society (FLAIRS 2011).

Marwa Magdy is a Teaching Assistant at the Faculty of Computers & Information (FCI), Cairo University. Her master degree was in Arabic Intelligent Language Tutoring System. She is a PhD student at FCI. Marwa has worked as a research assistant at the first Center of Excellence in Egypt in the field of Data Mining and Computer Modeling (DMCM) in the period of 2009-2010. Her research interest includes Arabic Natural Language Processing and Computational Linguistic, in particular, intelligent language tutoring system, spelling checkers, named entities, opinion mining and information extraction.

Danielle McNamara is a Professor at the University of Memphis and Director of the Institute for Intelligent Systems, and the lead investigator on the Coh-Metrix project. Her work involves the theoretical study of cognitive processes as well as the application of cognitive principles to educational practice. Her current research ranges a variety of topics including text comprehension, writing strategies, building tutoring technologies, and developing natural language algorithms. She has published over 200 articles in journals, books, and conference proceedings and has edited two books.

T. Daniel Midgley is an Assistant Professor of Linguistics at the University of Western Australia, studying dialogue systems, speech act theory, and natural language processing. He is the presenter on the weekly language podcast "Talk the Talk" on RTRfm Perth.

Marie-Francine Moens is a Research Professor (BOF-ZAP) at the Katholieke Universiteit Leuven, Belgium. She received a PhD in Computer Science in 1999 from this university. She leads a research team specialized in information retrieval and text analysis. She is author of two monographs published by Springer and numerous articles in proceedings of international conferences and journals. She is involved in the organization or program committee of major conferences on computational linguistics and information retrieval (ACL, SIGIR, EACL, ECIR, CIKM). She is the current chair-elect of the European Chapter of the Association for Computational Linguistics.

Brent Morgan is a Graduate Researcher and doctoral student in Experimental Psychology at the University of Memphis, where he received a Master of Science degree in 2010. His research interests include cognitive adaptability and game-based Intelligent Tutoring Systems.

Andrew J. Neel is Adjunct Faculty at The University of Memphis and member of ACM and IEEE. He holds a doctorate in computer science for his research proving the viability of information storage and semantic retrieval in biological based memories. He is co/author of several research papers and publications in topics covering information storage and retrieval, biological based / inspired computing, and information security.

Ryo Nitta is an Assistant Professor at Nagoya Gakuin University. He holds an MA and a PhD from the University of Warwick. His research area includes task-based teaching, second language writing, and second language motivation.

Andrew Olney is presently an Assistant Professor in the Department of Psychology at the University of Memphis and Associate Director of the Institute for Intelligent Systems. Dr. Olney received a B.A. in Linguistics with Cognitive Science from University College London in 1998, an M.S. in Evolutionary and Adaptive Systems from the University of Sussex in 2001, and a Ph.D. in Computer Science from the University of Memphis in 2006. Dr. Olney's primary research interests are in natural language interfaces. Specific interests include vector space models, dialogue systems, unsupervised grammar induction, robotics, and intelligent tutoring systems.

James W. Pennebaker conducts research on the links between natural language use and social behavior. He also explores how expressive writing about emotional upheavals can influence people's physical and mental health. He has been at the University of Texas at Austin since 1997 and is the Liberal Arts Foundation Centennial Professor and Chair of the Department of Psychology.

Adam Renner is a Master's graduate of the Department of Psychology at the University of Memphis. His research interests cross multiple disciplines in cognitive science, including discourse analysis, natural language processing, multimedia learning and instructional design, and learning with pedogogical agents and games. His projects at Memphis include Coh-Metrix, Writing Pal, and iSTART. He currently resides in Atlanta, where he is job prospecting and cultivating an interest in politics and media discourse.

Vasile Rus is an Associate Professor of Computer Science with a joint appointment in the Institute for Intelligent Systems. His primary research area is natural language processing with an emphasis on knowledge representations for deep understanding of human languages. Dr. Rus' ongoing projects span topics such as automated question generation (www.questiongeneration.org; funded by NSF), intelligent tutoring systems with natural language interaction (www.deeptutor.org; funded by IES), and mining large software repositories (step.memphis.edu; funded by the University of Memphis' STEP program). Among other accomplishments, Dr. Rus has been recently named a Systems Testing Research Fellow of the Fedex Institute of Technology. Dr. Rus is currently Area Chair for the 49th Annual Meeting of the Association for Computational Linguistics, the leading conference on natural language processing/computational linguistics research.

Khaled Shaalan is a Professor of Computers Science at Faculty of Computers & Information, Cairo University. He is on secondment to The British University in Dubai (BUiD), Faculty of Engineering & IT, UAE. He is also an Honorary Fellow, University of Edinburgh, UK. He is a member of Association of Computational Linguistics (ACL). Khaled has a long standing expertise in Arabic natural language processing (ANLP) research area. Over the last two decades, he has been contributing to a wide range of topics in ANLP, including morphology, parsing, machine translation, named entity recognition, intelligent language tutoring, and diacritization. Khaled, led a diverse set of funded international and national research projects in machine translation, named entity recognition, intelligent language tutoring systems, and expert systems. Many of his research outcomes have been published in highly ranked and reputed journals and conferences.

Cyrus Shaoul is a doctoral candidate at the University of Alberta. Previous to entering graduate school, he worked in the Internet software industry where he became interested in vector space models of meaning and their application to search engine design. Previous to that, Cyrus got his undergraduate degree from the Massachusetts Institute of Technology. He is a past recipient of the Castellan Award (awarded to the outstanding student paper presented at a Society for Computers In Psychology conference) and an NSERC PGS-D scholarship. He currently lives in Edmonton, Alberta. To find out more about his latest activities, visit his website at http://www.ualberta.ca/~cshaoul/.

Min Song is an Assistant Professor of Department of Information Systems at NJIT. He received his M.S. in School of Information Science from Indiana University in 1996 and received Ph.D. degree in Information Systems from Drexel University in 2005. Min has a background in Text Mining, Bioinfomatics, Information Retrieval and Information Visualization. Prior to NJIT, Min worked at Thomson Scientific. At Thomson, the major responsibilities were to develop knowledge management tools, middleware components, and the search engine for citation database. His recent work in Text mining addresses automatic database selection, entity and relation extraction, high speed document filtering, algorithms that learn a person's information needs from experience, automatic analysis of gathered information. He is also involved in a variety of information visualization projects. Min is also interested in information and knowledge management in large organizations. Min is currently interested in applying text mining algorithms to bioinformatics.

Mary Swift is Research Scientist in the Department of Computer Science at the University of Rochester. She leads the design and development of broad-coverage lexical resources for deep language understanding and generation in intelligent systems. The focus of her research is on enhancing robustness for general purpose deep language understanding. She implemented a framework for augmenting deep semantic representations with large-scale computational resources such as WordNet to rapidly extend core lexical coverage while preserving semantic interpretation. She also led research on using statistical parsers to guide deep unification-based semantic parsing. She received her Ph.D. in linguistics and cognitive science in 2000 from the University of Texas at Austin. Her dissertation research in language acquisition was supported by a 3-year Ph.D. fellowship at the Max Planck Institute for Psycholinguistics in Nijmegen, The Netherlands. She held a NIH Postdoctoral Fellowship at the Center for Language Sciences at the University of Rochester from 2000 to 2003 where she conducted psycholinguistic research on speech processing. She has (co-)authored numerous publications in the fields of computational linguistics, psycholinguistics, and artificial intelligence, including one that received the AAAI Outstanding Paper Award.

René Venegas is Adjunct Professor at the Pontificia Universidad Católica de Valparaíso, Chile. He has a Ph.D. in Linguistics and teaches linguistics and semantics to undergraduate and postgraduate students. His primary research interests are academic discourse, the study of meaning with computer tools, and the development of computer tools for text analysis. Dr. Venegas is the Vicepresident of the Chilean Linguistic Society (SOCHIL). He has written several articles in journals, books, and conference proceedings. He serves as Editing Coordinator of the journal *Revista Signos. Estudios de Lingüística.*

Lori Watrous-de Versterre is a Ph.D. student at NJIT with over 25 years of industry experience in developing software components and leading high-tech commercial software projects. She also has 5 years of experience as an adjunct instructor and has taught sessions for NJIT's Technology for Teachers. As part of her dissertation, Lori is exploring the relationship between digital libraries and social collaboration techniques.

Shinobu Watanabe is a graduate student in the Applied Linguistic program at The University of Memphis. She is also a member of the Institute for Intelligent Systems Student Organization (IISSO). Her research interests include varied areas around language such as first and second language acquisition, language processing, and comprehension.

Chris Westbury is an Associate Professor in the Department of Psychology at the University of Alberta. His PhD is in Clinical Psychology, with an emphasis on neuropsychology, from McGill University in Montreal. He researches language processing in normal and aphasic populations, with a theoretical focus on statistical models of language processing that are consistent with neurobiological knowledge.

Wei Xiong is a Ph.D. student of Department of Information Systems at New Jersey Institute of Technology. He received his dual Bachelor's degree in Software Engineering and Marketing from Hubei University of Economics in 2007. His current research interests include large scale data mining, information retrieval, and machine learning. Wei's current projects focus on applying machine learning techniques to behavioral-targeting online advertising.

Index